T&T CLARK HANDBOOK OF POLITICAL THEOLOGY

T&T CLARK HANDBOOK OF POLITICAL THEOLOGY

Edited by Rubén Rosario Rodríguez

LONDON • NEW YORK • OXFORD • NEW DELHI • SYDNEY

T&T CLARK
Bloomsbury Publishing Plc
50 Bedford Square, London, WC1B 3DP, UK
1385 Broadway, New York, NY 10018, USA
29 Earlsfort Terrace, Dublin 2, Ireland

BLOOMSBURY, T&T CLARK and the T&T Clark logo are trademarks of
Bloomsbury Publishing Plc

First published in Great Britain 2020
This paperback edition published in 2022

Copyright © Rubén Rosario Rodríguez and contributors, 2020

Rubén Rosario Rodríguez has asserted his right under the Copyright,
Designs and Patents Act, 1988, to be identified as Editor of this work.

Cover photo by Omar Messinger/NurPhoto via Getty Images

All rights reserved. No part of this publication may be reproduced or transmitted
in any form or by any means, electronic or mechanical, including photocopying,
recording, or any information storage or retrieval system, without prior permission in
writing from the publishers.

Bloomsbury Publishing Plc does not have any control over, or responsibility for, any
third-party websites referred to or in this book. All internet addresses given in this
book were correct at the time of going to press. The author and publisher regret
any inconvenience caused if addresses have changed or sites have ceased to
exist, but can accept no responsibility for any such changes.

A catalogue record for this book is available from the British Library.

Library of Congress Cataloging-in-Publication Data
Names: Rosario Rodríguez, Rubén, 1970- editor.
Title: T&T Clark handbook of political theology / edited by Rubén Rosario Rodríguez.
Description: 1 [edition]. | New York : T&T Clark, 2019. | Includes bibliographical
references and index.
Identifiers: LCCN 2019007767 | ISBN 9780567670397 (hardback) |
ISBN 9780567670403 (epdf) | ISBN 9780567670410 (epub)
Subjects: LCSH: Political theology.
Classification: LCC BT83.59 .T27 2019 | DDC 201/.72—dc23
LC record available at https://lccn.loc.gov/2019007767

ISBN: HB: 978-0-5676-7039-7
PB: 978-1-3503-2037-6
ePDF: 978-0-5676-7040-3
ePUB: 978-0-5676-7041-0

Typeset by RefineCatch Limited, Bungay, Suffolk

To find out more about our authors and books visit www.bloomsbury.com
and sign up for our newsletters.

In memoriam

*James Hal Cone
(1938–2018)*

CONTENTS

Notes on Contributors x
Preface xix

Part One Where Was God? Jewish and Christian Theology in the Shadow of Auschwitz

1 From Holocaust Theology to a Jewish Theology of Liberation: On the Theo-Politics of Jewish Empowerment   3
   Marc H. Ellis

2 Christian Responses to the Holocaust: Political Theology in Europe   17
   Vincent Lloyd

3 Political Theology and the Theologies of Liberation   29
   Rubén Rosario Rodríguez

Part Two Scriptures and Traditions: Critical Retrieval of Historical Sources

4 The Cup Does Not Run Over: Political Theology in the Hebrew Bible   47
   Serge Frolov

5 Political Theology and the New Testament   61
   Neil Elliott

6 Qur'anic Political Theology: God's Law, Jews, and the Politics of Friendship   75
   Joshua A. Sabih

7 Augustine and Political Theory   89
   Michael Lamb

8 Thomas Becket: A Case Study in Medieval Church–State Relations   117
   Michael Staunton

9 The Political Praxis of Bartolomé de Las Casas   131
   Luis N. Rivera-Pagán

10 The Political and Legal Legacy of the Sixteenth-Century Reformations   145
    John Witte, Jr.

Part Three An Appraisal of Contemporary Political Theologies

11 Theology After the Death of God 161
    Brian D. Robinette

12 Karl Barth and the Barmen Declaration 177
    Amy Marga

13 Bonhoeffer in Latin American Liberationist Christianity and Theology 193
    Raimundo C. Barreto, Jr.

14 Jürgen Moltmann and the New Political Theology 211
    Scott Paeth

15 Social Ethics, Reinhold Niebuhr, and Political Theology 225
    Gary Dorrien

16 Gustavo Gutiérrez and Latin American Liberation Theology 241
    Michael E. Lee

17 James H. Cone and Black Liberation Theology 255
    Eboni Marshall Turman

18 Latina Feminist and *Mujerista* Theologies as Political Theologies? 271
    Neomi De Anda

19 Feminist Theologies 285
    Rachel Sophia Baard

20 The Exodus and Some Possibilities of Jewish Political Thought 301
    Geoffrey D. Claussen and Emily A. Filler

21 The Political Theology of Catholic Social Teaching 317
    María Teresa Dávila

22 Orthodox Christianity and Political Theology: Thinking Beyond Empire 337
    Nathaniel Wood and Aristotle Papanikolaou

Part Four Constructive Horizons in Political Theology

23 The Politics of the *Espíritu*: Ethic as Recognition–Assemblage–Decolonial Healing 355
    Oscar García-Johnson

24 Christian Humanism, *redivivus* 373
    Luke Bretherton

25 The Obstinate Legacy of Race and Colonialism 389
    Uzma Jamil

26 The Third City: Radical Orthodoxy's (Emphatically) Complex
   Political Theology 401
   Nicholas Krause and Jonathan Tran

27 Liberating Barth? From a Theological Critique of Idolatry to a Political
   Critique of Ideology 417
   Derek Alan Woodard-Lehman

28 New Directions in Protestant Social Ethics 433
   Emily J. Dumler-Winckler

29 *Lex Naturae*: A New Way into a Liturgical Political Theology 449
   Cláudio Carvalhaes

30 Slavoj Žižek: Christianity, the Death of God, and Enjoying Hopelessness 467
   Silas Morgan

31 State(s) of Exception: The United States, the State of Israel, and
   the Legacy of Chosenness 485
   Robert O. Smith

32 Praying to the O/other—Rethinking Ecclesiology in the Context of
   Increasing Islamophobia 495
   Gyrid Kristine Gunnes

33 Social Trinitarianism through Iconic Participation 513
   Jessica Wai-Fong Wong

Part Five The Future of Political Theologies

34 Toward an Islamic Theology of World Religions: From Polemics
   to a Critical Theology of Self and Other 527
   Vincent J. Cornell

35 Political Theologies in a Post-Christian World 547
   Hille Haker

36 Everybody Hates the Prophet: Failure and the Good Society in
   Jewish Political Theology 565
   Laurie Zoloth

INDEX 575

CONTRIBUTORS

Rachel Sophia Baard is assistant professor of Theology and Ethics at Union Presbyterian Seminary. She holds a PhD in Systematic Theology from Princeton Theological Seminary, and BA, BTh, and MTh degrees from the University of Stellenbosch in her native South Africa. Her research interests include feminist theologies, the theologies of Paul Tillich and Dietrich Bonhoeffer, and liberation and political theologies in general. Having recently completed a book manuscript titled *Sexism and Sin-Talk: Feminist Conversations on the Human Condition*, she is currently working on a book on Tillich and Bonhoeffer's responses to Nazism, tentatively titled *Tillich and Bonhoeffer: Responses to Nazism*.

Raimundo C. Barreto, Jr. is Assistant Professor of World Christianity at Princeton Theological Seminary. He earned degrees from the Seminário Teológico do Norte do Brasil, Escola Superior de Teologia, and McAfee School of Theology, and a PhD degree in Religion and Society from Princeton Theological Seminary. Having taught in Brazil for six years, he served as director of the Division of Freedom and Justice of the Baptist World Alliance (BWA) between 2010 and 2014. His publications include a number of journal articles, encyclopedia entries, and book chapters in English, Portuguese, and Spanish. He is the author of *Evangélicos e Pobreza no Brasil: Pistas para uma Ética Social Evangélica Brasileira* (Novos Dialogos, 2013), and the co-editor of *Engaging the Jubilee: Freedom and Justice Papers of the Baptist World Alliance* (Baptist World Alliance, 2015), and *World Christianity as Public Religion* (Fortress Press, 2017). He is also the editor of the Fortress Press series "World Christianity and Public Religion."

Luke Bretherton is Professor of Theological Ethics and Senior Fellow of the Kenan Institute for Ethics at Duke University. Before moving to Duke in 2012 he was Reader in Theology & Politics and Convener of the Faith & Public Policy Forum at King's College London. He has worked with faith-based NGOs and churches around the world and has been involved in various forms of grassroots democratic politics. His recent books include: *Christianity & Contemporary Politics: The Conditions and Possibilities of Faithful Witness* (Wiley-Blackwell, 2010), winner of the 2013 Michael Ramsey Prize for Theological Writing; *Resurrecting Democracy: Faith, Citizenship and the Politics of a Common Life* (Cambridge University Press, 2015), which was developed out a four-year ethnographic study of community organizing initiatives; and *Christ and the Common Life: Political Theology and the Cases for Democracy* (Eerdman, 2019). As well as academic articles, he writes in the media (including *The Guardian*, *The Times*, and the *Washington Post*) on topics related to religion and politics.

Cláudio Carvalhaes, theologian, liturgist, and artist, is native from Brazil. He currently teaches Worship at Union Theological Seminary in New York City. He is the editor of books in Portuguese celebrating Jaci C. Maraschin and Ivone Gebara. In English he published *Eucharist and Globalization: Redrawing the Borders of Eucharistic Hospitality* (Wipf & Stock, 2013) and *What's Worship Got to Do with It: Interpreting Life Liturgically*

(Cascade Books, 2018). He is the editor of *Liturgy in Postcolonial Perspectives—Only One is Holy* (Palgrave Macmillan: Postcolonialism and Religions Series, 2015). He also edited "Forms of Speech, Religion and Social Resistance," *CrossCurrents*, Vol. 66, No. 1 (Summer 2016) and "Black Religions in Brazil" (with Marcos Silva), *CrossCurrents*, Vol. 68, No. 1 (Winter 2017).

Geoffrey D. Claussen, Associate Professor of Religious Studies, Lori and Eric Sklut Scholar in Jewish Studies and Chair of the Department of Religious Studies at Elon University, is a scholar of Jewish ethics and theology. He has particular interests in questions of love and justice, war and violence, animal ethics, moral education, and the legacy of the nineteenth-century Musar movement. His book *Sharing the Burden: Rabbi Simhah Zissel Ziv and the Path of Musar* was published by SUNY Press in 2015, and he is presently completing a book titled *Modern Musar: Contested Virtues in Jewish Thought*.

Vincent J. Cornell is Asa Griggs Candler Professor of Middle East and Islamic Studies at Emory University in Atlanta, Georgia. His published works include over forty articles, three books, one book set, and a co-authored volume. These include *The Way of Abū Madyan* (The Islamic Texts Society, 1996), *Realm of the Saint: Power and Authority in Moroccan Sufism* (University of Texas Press, 1998), the five-volume set *Voices of Islam* (Praeger Publishers, 2007), and *Do Jews, Christians, and Muslims Worship the Same God?* (with Baruch Levine, Jacob Neusner, and Bruce Chilton, Abingdon Press, 2012). Since 2016 he has served as editor-in-chief of the *Journal of Islamic and Muslim Studies*, published by Indiana University Press. His academic interests cover the entire spectrum of Islamic thought from Sufism to theology and Islamic law. He is currently finishing *The Wiley-Blackwell Companion to Islamic Spirituality* with Bruce Lawrence of Duke University. His other current book projects include *Islam and Democracy: A Critical Analysis* and *The Shared Revelation: Ibn Sab'in (d. 669/1270) and Islamic Hermetism*. From 2002 to 2012 he was a key participant in the Building Bridges seminars of Christian and Muslim scholars organized by Archbishop of Canterbury Dr. Rowan Williams. Since 2001 he has also participated in theological projects organized by the Shalom Hartman Institute and the Elijah Interfaith Institute.

María Teresa Dávila, formerly Associate Professor of Christian Ethics at Andover Newton Theological School, is currently Lecturer in Theology and Religious Studies at Merrimack College. Her research focuses on reflections on the role of Christian ethics in the public square, specifically in the areas of racial and migrant justice, Catholic social teaching, the option for the poor, the ethics of the use of force, Latinx theology, and public theology. Her scholarship combines activism, especially dealing with immigration, homelessness, and racial justice, with scholarly work in these areas. Her current research examines the origin of the culture wars in the United States, while trying to address them through the optic of the option for the poor. She is a Roman Catholic lay woman.

Neomi De Anda, a Tejana scholar/activist and Catholic Lay Marianist, was raised between El Paso and Corpus Christi, Texas. She currently serves as Associate Professor at the University of Dayton in the Department of Religious Studies. She also teaches in the Women and Gender Studies Program. She holds a PhD in Constructive Theology. Her research interests include Latinas and Latin American women writers in religion 1600–1900; Christology; Latin@ Theology; theology and breast milk; the Intersection of race and migrations in conjunction with the Marianist Social Justice Collaborative Racial &

Immigrant Justice Team; and developing a border theology in partnership with the Hope Border Institute. She currently holds the position of President for the Academy of Catholic Hispanic Theologians of the United States. She has been awarded the Louisville Institute First Book for Minority Scholars grant and fellowships from the Hispanic Theological Initiative and the Wabash Center for Teaching and Learning in Religion and Theology. She gives much credit to her roots at St. Pius X Catholic Community in El Paso, Texas.

Gary Dorrien teaches at Union Theological Seminary and Columbia University. His eighteen books include *Kantian Reason and Hegelian Spirit: The Idealistic Logic of Modern Theology*, which won the Association of American Publishers PROSE Award in 2013, and *The New Abolition: W. E. B. Du Bois and the Black Social Gospel*, which won the Grawemeyer Award in 2017.

Emily J. Dumler-Winckler is Assistant Professor of Constructive Theology at Saint Louis University. Her research interests include premodern and modern virtue theory, the history of moral theology, and Protestant social ethics, particularly as these pertain to questions of race, class, gender, and sexuality, as well as personal and social transformation.

Neil Elliott is a New Testament scholar and Episcopal priest; he teaches biblical studies at Metropolitan State University. He is the author of *The Rhetoric of Romans: Argumentative Constraint and Strategy and Paul's Dialogue with Judaism* (JSOT, 1990), *Liberating Paul: The Justice of God and the Politics of the Apostle* (Orbis, 1994), and *The Arrogance of Nations: Reading Romans in the Shadow of Empire* (Fortress, 2008); co-author of *Documents for the Study of Paul* (Fortress, 2010); and co-editor of *Bridges in New Testament Interpretation* (Lexington/Fortress Academic, 2018).

Marc H. Ellis is Professor of History and Jewish Studies, formerly at the Maryknoll School of Theology and Baylor University, where he directed the Institute for Justice and Peace and the Center for Jewish Studies. Presently he directs the Center for the Study of the Global Prophetic. He has authored and edited twenty-seven books, including *Toward a Jewish Theology of Liberation* (Baylor University Press, 3rd edition, 2004), *Unholy Alliance: Religion and Atrocity in Our Time*, and *Finding Our Voice: Embodying the Prophetic and Other Misadventures* (Cascade Books, 2018). He has been a visiting fellow at Harvard University's Center for the Study of World Religions and the Center for Middle East Studies and has lectured around the world, including at Harvard University's John F. Kennedy School of Government, the Carter Presidential Center and the United Nations. He has been honored at the American Academy of Religion twice with full sessions devoted to his work and with a Festschrift Conference at the Perkins School of Theology.

Emily A. Filler, Assistant Professor of Jewish Studies, and Chair of the Jewish Studies Program at Earlham College, teaches and researches on the relationship between Judaism, philosophy, and classical Jewish textual interpretation. She is co-editor of the *Journal of Jewish Ethics*.

Serge Frolov, a native of St. Petersburg, Russia, has also lived in Jerusalem, Israel; Claremont, California; and Dallas, Texas. He holds PhDs in Modern History and Religious Studies. He has worked at the National Library of Russia, *Shorter Jewish*

Encyclopedia in Russian, and the Open University of Israel. Currently he is Professor of Religious Studies and Nate and Ann Levine Endowed Chair in Jewish Studies at Southern Methodist University. He is primarily a Hebrew Bible scholar, although his research interests also include religion and culture of the ancient Near East and Jewish history and thought. He has published more than 200 articles and two books, *The Turn of the Cycle: 1 Samuel 1–8 in Synchronic and Diachronic Perspectives* (De Gruyter, 2004) and *Judges* (Eerdmans, 2013).

Oscar García-Johnson, native from Honduras, is Associate Professor of Theology and Latino/a Studies and Assistant Provost for the Center for the Study of Hispanic Church and Community at Fuller Theological Seminary. He is a de/postcolonial theoretician, ecclesiologist, and practical theologian. His writings include *Spirit Outside the Gate: Decolonial Pneumatologies of the American Global South* (InterVarsity Press, 2019), *Conversaciones Teológicas del Sur Global Americano* (co-edited, Puertas Abiertas/Wipf & Stock, 2016), *Theology without Borders: Introduction to Global Conversations*, co-authored with William Dyrness (Baker Academic, 2015), and *¡Jesús, Hazme Como tú! 40 Maneras de Imitar a Cristo* (Wipf & Stock, 2014).

Gyrid Kristine Gunnes was born and raised in the Arctic part of Norway. She studied comparative religion, theology, criminology and sociology, and liberation theology in South Africa before becoming ordained as a priest in the Lutheran Church of Norway. She graduated from the University of Tromsø, Norway, and is, currently a PhD candidate at VID Specialized University, Oslo, Norway. When working as a parish priest in Arctic and rural Norway, Gunnes became publicly known for a strong commitment to gender inclusion at a time when this went against ecclesial order. She has published two non-academic books: a collection of theological poems *Hellig sårbar* (*Holy vulnerable*) (Portal, 2012) and the essay *Å forkynne Guds ord klart og urent—utkast til en feministisk prekenpraksis* (*to preach the word of God impurely—towards a feminist homiletics*) (Stemmer, 2013) before returning in 2013 to the academy to complete a PhD in *diakonia* (the social engagement of the church). In 2018, she was asked by the Norwegian National Broadcast (NRK) to give four homilies on their main channel but declined publically when NRK refused to accept one sermon on the Me Too movement, which explored the possible sexual nature of the torture of Jesus.

Hille Haker is the Richard McCormick, S.J., Chair of Moral Theology at Loyola University Chicago. Prior to joining the faculty at Loyola, she was Chair of Moral Theology and Social Ethics in the Catholic Theology Department of Frankfurt University (2005 to 2009), Associate Professor of Christian Ethics at Harvard Divinity School (2003 to 2005), and Heisenberg Research Scholar (2002–2003). In Frankfurt, she was a Colleague of the Institute of Social Research of the Frankfurt School and co-director of the Cornelia Goethe Center for Women's Studies. She has been a member of the European Group on Ethics in Sciences and New Technologies (EGE) of the European Commission from 2005 to 2015, and served on the Board of Editors of the International Journal of *Concilium* from 2001 to 2015, co-editing multiple issues. She was elected President of *Societas Ethica, European Society of Research in Ethics* in 2015, ending in 2018, after which she was elected to the Board of Societas Ethica. Her most recent book, *Going It Alone: Unaccompanied Minors and the Ethics of Child Migration* (co-edited with Molly Greening, Rowman & Littlefield, 2018), addresses ethical questions regarding unaccompanied migrant children (co-edited with Molly Greening, Lexington, 2018).

Uzma Jamil is a fellow in Muslim Studies in the InterReligious Institute at Chicago Theological Seminary. Her research expertise is in Critical Muslim Studies, Islamophobia, racism and whiteness, and Muslim minorities in Quebec. She is a founding member of the Editorial Board of *ReOrient: The Journal of Critical Muslim Studies*.

Nicholas Krause, PhD candidate in Theology and Ethics at Baylor University, works primarily in the fields of moral theology, social ethics, and political theology. His current dissertation research engages recent work in socialist and democratic theory concerning questions of ontology, pluralism, conflict, and difference in order to develop a political theology of radical democracy.

Michael Lamb is Assistant Professor of Politics, Ethics, and Interdisciplinary Humanities and Director of the Program for Leadership and Character at Wake Forest University. He is also a research fellow at the Oxford Character Project. He holds a PhD in Politics from Princeton University, a BA in Political Science from Rhodes College, and a second BA in Philosophy and Theology from the University of Oxford, where he studied as a Rhodes Scholar. His research focuses on the ethics of citizenship, the relationship between religion and politics, and the role of virtues in public life. He has published articles on Aristotle, Augustine, and Aquinas, and is currently finishing a book tentatively entitled *A Commonwealth of Hope: Reimagining Augustine's Political Thought*.

Michael E. Lee, is Professor of Theology at Fordham University, with affiliation in Fordham's Latin American and Latino Studies Institute. Born in Miami of Puerto Rican parents, he holds graduate degrees from the University of Chicago and the University of Notre Dame. He joined the Fordham faculty in 2004 and teaches courses in Roman Catholic theology, liberation theologies, Latin American and Latino/a theologies, Christology, and spirituality. He has served on the governing board of the Catholic Theological Society of America (CTSA) and as President of the Academy of Catholic Hispanic Theologians of the United States (ACHTUS). His published works include *Revolutionary Saint: The Theological Legacy of Óscar Romero* (Orbis Books, 2018), *Ignacio Ellacuría: Essays on History, Liberation, and Salvation* (Orbis Books, 2013), and *Bearing the Weight of Salvation: The Soteriology of Ignacio Ellacuría* (Herder & Herder, 2009).

Vincent Lloyd is Associate Professor of Theology and Religious Studies at Villanova University, where he is also affiliated with the Africana Studies Program. He has held fellowships from the American Council of Learned Societies, Emory University's James Weldon Johnson Institute, the Notre Dame Institute for Advanced Studies, and the University of Wisconsin's Institute for Research in the Humanities. His books include *Black Natural Law* (Oxford University Press, 2016), *In Defense of Charisma* (Columbia University Press, 2018), and the co-edited volume *Anti-Blackness and Christian Ethics* (Orbis, 2017). Lloyd co-edits the journal *Political Theology* and edits Reflection and Theory in the Study of Religion, a book series published by Oxford University Press in conjunction with the American Academy of Religion. His next book, *Break Every Yoke: Religion, Justice, and the Abolition of Prisons*, co-authored with Joshua Dubler, will be published by Oxford University Press.

Amy Marga is an associate professor of systematic theology at Luther Seminary. She is the translator of Karl Barth's *The Word of God and Theology* (T&T Clark, 2011). Her book *Karl Barth's Dialogue with Catholicism in Göttingen and Münster* was published by Mohr Siebeck in 2010. Other publications include "Jesus Christ and the Modern Sinner: Karl

Barth's Retrieval of Luther's Substantive Christology," in *Currents in Theology and Mission* (August 2007) and "Karl Barth's Second Dogmatic Cycle, Münster 1926–1928: A Progress Report," in *Zeitschrift für dialektische Theologie* (2005). Marga is a member of the American Academy of Religion, the North American Karl Barth Society, and the German-American Institute.

Silas Morgan lives in Minneapolis, Minnesota and works in trade acquisitions and marketing at Fortress Press. Formerly the managing editor at *Syndicate*, he holds a doctorate in theology from Loyola University Chicago and has taught theology and ethics at United Theological Seminary of the Twin Cities, Hamline University, and Loyola University Chicago among others. He is the co-editor of *Kierkegaard and Political Theology*, with Roberto Sirvent, published by Wipf & Stock (2018), and is the author of multiple articles and book chapters on theology and politics.

Scott Paeth is Professor of Religious Studies and Peace, Justice and Conflict Studies at DePaul University. Working in the fields of Christian Ethics and Public Theology, he is the author or editor of eight books and numerous articles. His books include *The Niebuhr Brothers for Armchair Theologians* (Westminster John Knox Press, 2013), *Public Theology for a Global Society: Essays in Honor of Max Stackhouse* (Eerdmans, 2010), and *Exodus Church and Civil Society: Public Theology and Social Theory in the Work of Jürgen Moltmann* (Ashgate, 2008). A prolific author and a popular speaker, he has written editorials for a number of newspapers, and was featured on PBS's *Religion and Ethics Newsweekly*. He is currently co-editor of the *Journal of the Society of Christian Ethics* while also working on a number of research projects, including a book, in progress, entitled *Christianity and the Economic Crisis*.

Aristotle Papanikolaou is Professor of Theology, Archbishop Demetrios Chair in Orthodox Theology and Culture, and Co-founding Director of the Orthodox Christian Studies Center of Fordham University. Among his publications, he is the author of *The Mystical as Political: Democracy and Non-Radical Orthodoxy* and co-editor of *Political Theologies in Orthodox Christianity*.

Luis N. Rivera-Pagán is the Henry Winters Luce Professor Emeritus of Ecumenics at Princeton Theological Seminary. Rivera-Pagán earned his MDiv at the Evangelical Seminary of Puerto Rico in 1966, STM (1967) and MA (1968) at Yale University and in 1970 his PhD, also at Yale with the dissertation *Unity and Truth: The Unity of God, Man, Jesus Christ, and the Church in Irenaeus*, under Jaroslav Pelikan. He is a prolific author, who has authored, co-authored, edited, and co-edited dozens of books, journal issues, chapters, articles, and reviews in books and journals. Presently he holds the chair of Humanities at the Faculty of General Studies of the University of Puerto Rico.

Brian D. Robinette is Associate Professor of Theology at Boston College. He researches and teaches in the areas of systematic, philosophical, and spiritual theology, with special interests in eschatology, anthropology, secularity, and contemplative theory/practice. He is the author of *Grammars of Resurrection: A Christian Theology of Presence and Absence* (Crossroad, 2009).

Rubén Rosario Rodríguez, a graduate of the College of William and Mary in Virginia, Union Theological Seminary in New York, and Princeton Theological Seminary, is

Professor of Systematic Theology in the Department of Theological Studies at Saint Louis University. An ordained Presbyterian minister, his first book, *Racism and God-Talk: A Latino/a Perspective* (NYU Press, 2008), won the 2011 Alpha Sigma Nu Book Award for Theology. His most recent publications include *Christian Martyrdom and Political Violence: A Conversation with Judaism and Islam* (Cambridge University Press, 2017) and *Dogmatics After Babel: Beyond the Theologies of Word and Culture* (Westminster John Knox Press, 2018).

Joshua A. Sabih is associate professor of Arabic, Hebrew, Jewish, and Islamic Studies in the Department of Cross Cultural and Regional Studies, University of Copenhagen. He is a cross-disciplinary scholar whose teaching and research cover different fields of inquiry: Bible, Qur'an, Judeao-Arabic cultures, Jewish and Islamic philosophy and theology, Karaite Studies, and Jewish–Muslim relations. He is the author of *Japheth ben Ali's Book of Jeremiah: A Critical Edition and Linguistic Analysis of the Judaeo-Arabic Translation* (Routledge, 2014). His two forthcoming monographs, *Zionism, Post-Zionism and the Palestinian Question: Arab Marxist Double Critique of Zionism and Arab Nationalism*, and *Islamic Bible Criticism: Polemics, Theology and Rationality: Ibn Hazm's Approach to the Jewish Scriptures*, will be published in 2019 and 2020 respectively.

Robert O. Smith (Citizen, Chickasaw Nation) serves as Director of Briarwood Leadership Center in northern Texas. Before that, he directed the University of Notre Dame's Jerusalem Global Gateway, while also holding concurrent faculty appointments in the Keough School of Global Affairs and the Department of Theology. He is an ordained minister in the Evangelical Lutheran Church in America who has served as Area Program Director for the Middle East & North Africa, and Special Adviser to the President of the Lutheran World Federation, Bishop Dr. Munib A. Younan. He earned his PhD in Religion, Politics & Society from Baylor University in 2010. With Charles Lutz, he is author of *Christians and a Land Called Holy: How We Can Foster Justice, Peace, and Hope* (Fortress, 2006). His second book, *More Desired than Our Owne Salvation: The Roots of Christian Zionism*, was published by Oxford University Press in 2013.

Michael Staunton is Associate Professor of History at University College Dublin. His most recent books are *The Historians of Angevin England* (Oxford University Press, 2017), and *Herbert of Bosham: A Medieval Polymath* (Boydell & Brewer, 2019). Previous books include *Thomas Becket and his Biographers* (Boydell & Brewer, 2006), *The Lives of Thomas Becket* (Manchester University Press, 2001), and *The Illustrated Story of Christian Ireland* (Emerald Press, 2001). He was awarded a Government of Ireland Senior Research Fellowship by the Irish Research Council, and has held visiting fellowships at the Center for Medieval Studies, Fordham University, New York, and a visiting professorship at Bard College, New York.

Jonathan Tran, George W. Baines Professor of Religion at Baylor University, is author of *The Vietnam War and Theologies of Memory: Time, Eternity, and Redemption in the Far Country* (Wiley-Blackwell, 2010) and *Foucault and Theology* (T&T Clark, 2011). His journal publications can be found in *Modern Theology*, *Journal of Religious Ethics*, *Journal of the Society of Christian Ethics*, and *Political Theology*. His research focuses on the theological, ethical, political, and social implications of the human life in words and he serves as Faculty Steward of Baylor's Honors Residential College.

Eboni Marshall Turman is Assistant Professor of Theology and African American religion at Yale University Divinity School in New Haven, CT. Her research interests span the varieties of twentieth-century US theological liberalisms, most especially black and womanist theological, social ethical, and theo-aesthetic traditions. She is the co-chair of the Women of Color Scholarship, Teaching, and Activism unit of the American Academy of Religion, and the co-convener of the African/African American Working and Interest groups of the Society of Christian Ethics. A first-career concert dancer and ordained National Baptist clergy, she holds degrees in philosophy, theology, and Christian ethics from Fordham University and Union Theological Seminary in the City of New York, respectively. In addition to several journal articles and book chapters, she is the author of *Toward a Womanist Ethic of Incarnation: Black Bodies, the Black Church, and the Council of Chalcedon* (Palgrave Macmillan, 2013). She is currently working on two monographs tentatively titled *Black Woman's Burden: Male Power, Gender Violence, and the Scandal of African American Social Christianity*, and *Loves the Spirit: The Womanist Theological Idea*.

John Witte, Jr. is Robert W. Woodruff University Professor of Law, McDonald Distinguished Professor, and Director of the Center for the Study of Law and Religion at Emory University. A leading specialist in legal history, family law, religious liberty, human rights, and law and Christianity, he has published 250 articles, 16 journal symposia, and 32 books. Recent titles include *The Western Case for Monogamy over Polygamy* (Cambridge University Press, 2015); *Religion and the American Constitutional Experiment* (Oxford University Press, 4th ed., 2016); *Christianity and Family Law: An Introduction* (Cambridge University Press, 2017); *Church, State, and Family: Reconciling Traditional Teachings and Modern Liberties* (Cambridge University Press, 2019).

Jessica Wai-Fong Wong is an Assistant Professor of Systematic Theology at Azusa Pacific University. Her work in Christian theology focuses on issues of visuality, race, and gender. She is an ordained elder in the Presbyterian Church (USA) and holds degrees in Christian theology and ethics from Duke Divinity School and Duke University. In addition to journal articles and chapter contributions, she is the author of *Anti-Iconicity of Blackness: A Visual Theology of Race in the Modern World* (Baylor University Press).

Nathaniel Wood is Associate Director of the Orthodox Christian Studies Center of Fordham University. His research interests lie primarily in Orthodox political theology, theologies of personhood, and the theology of human rights. His recent publications bring nineteenth- and twentieth-century Russian Orthodox political theologies into conversation with contemporary Anglo-American political theology, especially Radical Orthodoxy, and investigate the link between the doctrine of deification and liberal democracy.

Derek Alan Woodard-Lehman is a Lecturer in the Department of Theology and Religion at University of Otago (New Zealand) where he also serves as Wellington Programme Coordinator for the Centre for Theology and Public Issues. He works broadly in the moral and the theological traditions of Western Christianity, with an emphasis on Karl Barth's contributions to debates about the relationship between reason and revelation, the role of social practices in scriptural interpretation and ecclesial confession, and the nature of freedom in church and society. He is currently revising a manuscript entitled *Confessing Freedom: Karl Barth and the Spirit of Democracy*.

Laurie Zoloth, Margaret E. Burton Professor of Religion and Ethics Senior Advisor to the Provost for Programs on Social Ethics at the University of Chicago, is a leader in the field of religious studies with particular scholarly interest in bioethics and Jewish studies. Her research explores religion and ethics, drawing from sources ranging from biblical and Talmudic texts to postmodern Jewish philosophy, including the writings of Emmanuel Levinas, and she also researches the practices of interreligious dialogue, exploring how religion plays a role in public discussion and policy. She has been the president of the American Academy of Religion and the American Society for Bioethics and Humanities. She is the author of *Health Care and the Ethics of Encounter: A Jewish Discussion of Social Justice* (University of North Carolina Press, 1999) and co-editor of five books, including *Notes from a Narrow Ridge: Religion and Bioethics* (University Publishing Group, 1999) and *Jews and Genes: The Genetic Future in Contemporary Jewish Thought* (Jewish Publication Society, 2015).

PREFACE

Christian systematic theologian Shirley C. Guthrie begins his popular and widely read introduction to Christian doctrine with the following bit of conventional wisdom: "Sex, politics, and theology—these are the only things worth talking about."[1] That might be, but in my experience nothing shuts down polite dinner conversation faster than interjecting politics or religion—let alone both! I myself have ruined many a family Thanksgiving dinner by dropping what I assumed was a casual innocuous statement about this or that (one particular instance I remember commenting that not all the apostle Paul's letters were in fact written by Paul) only to be shocked by the passion and vehemence of the response. Consequently, another bit of conventional wisdom runs something like this: "When religion goes public, when theology gets mixed up with politics, things go terribly wrong."[2] No incident illustrates the controversial nature of mixing religion and politics better than when US Attorney General Jeff Sessions cited Romans 13 in defense of a border enforcement policy separating undocumented immigrants from their children. Regardless of where one stands on this administration's zero-tolerance border enforcement policy (full disclosure: this author finds current US immigration policy abhorrent, especially the practice of family separation), Sessions's choice of biblical texts is very troubling given the fact it was a favorite text of the pro-slavery antebellum South, most often cited in defense of the Fugitive Slave Act of 1850.[3] The fact remains, political candidates invoke God and cater to religious constituents all the time, and as messy as religion and politics in public conversation can get, theological (or pseudo-theological) arguments abound in the public discourse. Therefore, the need for political theology in our classrooms and informing our civic discourse; an open and respectful dialogue about the role of theological convictions in public life can only improve the quality of our life together in the polis.

Following the Second World War, theologians Jürgen Moltman, Dorothee Sölle, and Johann Baptist Metz articulated what became known as the New Political Theology, an explicitly Christian and European response to the horrors of the Holocaust—especially Christian complicity and culpability for the Holocaust—in critical conversation with the legal and political theorist Carl Schmitt, a controversial Nazi sympathizer who had given new life to the phrase "political theology." Yet it was Jewish thinkers like Richard Rubenstein and Elie Weisel with their existential cry "Where was God at Auschwitz?" who first articulated a Holocaust theology that challenged believers—Jewish and Christian alike—to reconcile the pervasiveness of radical evil with theistic belief. Rather than reconstruct traditional Jewish faith after Auschwitz, Holocaust theology reimagined theology as an argument with and about God, perhaps best conceived as a theology of protest. But it is shortsighted to presume that political theology began in reaction to Carl Schmitt, or that it is narrowly a Judeo-Christian concern, especially given the resurgence of political theology since the (ostensibly) religiously motivated terror attacks on US soil on September 11, 2001.

This handbook provides a more inclusive and expansive definition of "political theology" than other edited collections by looking at the rich historical resources within all three Abrahamic traditions in order to facilitate discussion on the interplay between *the theological* and *the political*. Since the 1960s the term political theology has been used almost exclusively to describe the New Political Theology, which in turn influenced—or so the dominant narrative goes—similar politicized theologies around the world that set about analyzing and critiquing inequalities of class, gender, and race in order to create more just social structures informed by traditional faith perspectives. However, the renewed interest in political theology is evidence of a greater diversity of perspectives now claiming the term, and calls into question the dominant narrative concerning the advent of modern political theology. Not only has the term political theology been used to describe the work of theologians who intentionally relate religious belief to larger societal issues, like the liberation theologies of Gustavo Gutiérrez and James H. Cone, but also to describe the work of earlier generations of theologians not explicitly engaged in doing political theology whose work has nonetheless had an impact on the broader civil society, like Augustine of Hippo and sixteenth-century reformer John Calvin.

Whatever genealogical narrative one chooses to embrace, the fact remains today there exists a great variety of political theologies that: (1) differ to the extent in which they employ the social sciences and other secular critical discourses, (2) differ in local flavor and context in relation to a particular people's cultural and historical experiences, (3) differ on how they adapt and employ the theological resources of their distinctive faith tradition, and (4) differ on their understanding of how faith communities relate and interact with the state as the locus of political life. Within this wide and varied mosaic, however, what distinguishes "political theology" from other types of theological discourse is conscious reflection on what constitutes the most appropriate relationship between the state and the communities of faith living under the authority of the state. In an effort to catalogue the multiplicity of contemporary perspectives, this handbook is conceived as both a reference resource and a collection of original constructive essays in the field of political theology. Unlike other such anthologies that focus almost exclusively on Christian political theology, this volume employs the theological resources of the three Abrahamic faiths in recognition of the long and complex history in the West of interfaith conflict, interaction, and cooperation between Judaism, Christianity, and Islam. To that end, I have procured a diverse group of scholars representing a broad base of perspectives, disciplines, and traditions in order to engender a lively discussion that provides a solid grounding in the contemporary state of the discipline of political theology without glossing over important differences.

If there is a guiding principle holding the volume together it is the simple idea that political theology—whatever *that* is—did not begin with Carl Schmitt's fetishizing of totalitarian power structures in the essay "Politische Theologie" (1922). The overall goal of the project is not to understand political theology as a single school of thought. Rather, the volume seeks to define political theology as a more inclusive category by looking at the rich historical resources within each of the Abrahamic religions that help each tradition unpack the complex relationship between the political and theological spheres. Perhaps a second guiding principle is the shared hope among the various contributors that through communal action we can make a radical break with the political status quo in order to bring about profound social transformation. Sadly, the pessimistic tone of contemporary political discourse threatens to undermine any hope of a common moral discourse.

Ethicist Alasdair MacIntyre, in his landmark book *After Virtue* (1981), described the political discourse today as "civil war carried on by other means"[4] leading him to conclude that our culture is entering a new Dark Ages. Consequently, the only hope for peaceful coexistence lies with a retreat into small intentional communities of shared belief "within which the moral life could be sustained so that both morality and civility and the intellectual moral life can be sustained."[5] In other words, "We are waiting not for a Godot, but for another—doubtless very different—St. Benedict."[6] Today this critical insight has been coopted by Christian evangelicalism, specifically Rod Dreher's impassioned plea for Christians to embrace the "Benedict Option," in which believers ought to follow the example of sixth-century monk Benedict of Nursia who established cloistered religious communities removed from the world while the Roman Empire collapsed all around them.[7] As a liberation theologian I am *fully aware* that I am engaged in a utopian project grounded on an eschatological promise *that might never be realized*. Nevertheless, hope for a common moral discourse remains because rather than expending energy in debating old and tired theological arguments, liberationists recognize that "Faith in God does not consist in asserting God's existence, but rather in acting on [God's] behalf."[8]

In many ways this collection is an experiment in academic writing. Each chapter is written by a different scholar (or scholars) on topics or subjects suggested by myself, though tailored and personalized in light of each author's research interests and areas of specialization. As editor I was not particularly troubled about attaining thematic and stylistic consistency among the contributions. Rather, the project was conceived as a snapshot of contemporary political theology through each scholar's distinctive work. Therefore, I encouraged individuality of approach and perspective. In other words, authors did not have to limit themselves to the title and subject I as editor had conceived, but were free to reconfigure the topic around their interests, specializations, and current writing. Furthermore, as editor I made a concerted effort to not only procure a diversity of cultural, religious, methodological, and disciplinary perspectives, but also intentionally recruited scholars at every stage of their professional development—from doctoral candidates to full professors, from first-time authors to long-established "stars"—in order to provide both a sense of history and a window into the future of the discipline. The resulting collection of essays represents a broad swathe of contemporary scholarship in theology, religion, philosophy, history, ethics, law, and political theory from leading scholars in their respective areas. These essays are representative of scholarship within a number of professional associations including the American Academy of Religion, the Society of Christian Ethics, the Society of Jewish Ethics, the American Society for Bioethics and Humanities, the Academy of Catholic Hispanic Theologians of the United States, the Society for the Study of Muslim Ethics, and Societas Ethica, reflecting ongoing dialogues from working groups and program units within these organizations on topics as diverse as race and gender, decolonialism, liberation theologies, political theology, Catholic moral theology, Protestant social ethics, and law and religion.

What unites the project, despite the diversity of theological perspectives, is a commitment from all the contributors to engage the political sphere (1) by locating himself or herself theologically within the interdisciplinary conversation, (2) by establishing clear methodological parameters for how she or he will participate in the conversation, and (3) by recognizing that this conversation takes place in a religiously and politically pluralist global setting. It is this third and final point that is crucial. Without denying that certain religious perspectives make exclusivist claims, as editor I have insisted these claims must be made and defended in the context of political pluralism, tolerance, and cooperation.

The book is organized in five parts. Part One, "Where Was God? Jewish and Christian Theology in the Shadow of Auschwitz," sets the stage by marking the birth of contemporary political theology with the work of Jewish thinkers to reconcile the Holocaust with theistic belief, followed by the Christian engagement of Holocaust theology in the First World, and then a chapter reflecting on the development of political theologies in the Third World. Part Two, "Scriptures and Traditions: Critical Retrieval of Historical Sources," provides historical resources, from sacred scriptures to customary legal precedent, from St. Augustine to Mohammed, for articulating a contemporary political theology through close study and analysis of classical texts and figures representative of the interaction between theology and politics within all three Abrahamic traditions. Part Three, "An Appraisal of Contemporary Political Theologies," then surveys the leading figures and movements that have had an impact on the discipline of political theology in the twentieth and twenty-first centuries. Though I have made every effort to have the volume reflect as broad a cultural representation as possible, the book goes to press with some glaring omissions. Though essays were procured in womanist theology and sub-Saharan African theology, due to a number of conflicting professional commitments these articles were not ready by the time the manuscript went to press and thus could not be included in the collection. Part Four, "Constructive Horizons in Political Theology," builds on the historical resources and methods presented earlier in the volume to constructively engage contemporary issues and challenges within the discipline of political theology, emphasizing interreligious dialogue and pursuit of common moral discourse, even while addressing concerns of relevance to a particular faith tradition (like Trinitarian theology or the racialization of Muslims). Finally, Part Five, "The Future of Political Theologies," concludes the volume with three essays that look at the future of political theology from the perspective of each of the three Abrahamic religions, cognizant of the fact that the future of political theology will of necessity—given global demographics shifts and changes—be framed as an interfaith dialogue.

In closing, I want to thank several individuals for their hard work and commitment to this project. First, I want to thank Marc Ellis for being the first author to contribute a chapter to the collection, and by doing so enticing others to join the project. Second, while he was unable to contribute a chapter to the handbook, I am deeply indebted to Jeffrey Stout, recently retired Professor of Religion at Princeton University, who supported the project by providing me with introductions to several contributors. Both these scholars exemplify the ideals of academic mentoring and have set standards the rest of us strive to embody. I want to thank my colleague at Saint Louis University, David Meconi, S.J., and Matthew Lundberg at Calvin College, for providing peer review of some of the essay submissions. Many thanks to my graduate assistant, Stephen Lawson, for his help with copyediting the typescript and in compiling the index. A second set of eyes is invaluable when editing such a large project. A huge word of thanks is due to Anna Turton, commissioning editor for Bloomsbury/T&T Clark, without whom this project would have never gotten off the ground. Finally, I want to thank all the contributors for their hard work, creativity, and patience.

Rubén Rosario Rodríguez

NOTES

1. Shirley C. Guthrie, *Christian Doctrine*, 50th anniversary edition (Louisville, KY: Westminster John Knox Press, 2018), 1.
2. Elizabeth Phillips, *Political Theology: A Guide for the Perplexed* (London: T&T Clark, 2012), 1–2.

3. See Lincoln Mullen, "The Fight to Define Romans 13," in *The Atlantic* (June 15, 2018). https://www.theatlantic.com/ideas/archive/2018/06/romans-13/562916/
4. Alasdair MacIntyre, *After Virtue: A Study in Moral Theory*, 2nd ed. (Notre Dame, IN: University of Notre Dame Press, 1984), 253.
5. Ibid., 263.
6. Ibid.
7. See Rod Dreher, *The Benedict Option: A Strategy for Christians in a Post-Christian Nation* (New York: Penguin Books, 2017), 14–19.
8. Gustavo Gutiérrez and Richard Shaull, *Liberation and Change* (Richmond, VA: John Knox Press, 1977), 89.

PART ONE

Where Was God? Jewish and Christian Theology in the Shadow of Auschwitz

CHAPTER ONE

From Holocaust Theology to a Jewish Theology of Liberation

On the Theo-Politics of Jewish Empowerment

MARC H. ELLIS

INTRODUCTION

With Elie Wiesel's death in 2016, fifty years after the publication of Richard Rubenstein's *After Auschwitz*, Holocaust theology effectively came to an end. The passing of Holocaust theology was as quiet as its beginning was earth shattering. What began as a subversive and disturbing theology that raised radical questions about God and the Jewish future had been brought low by its own success.[1]

As a subversive theology, Holocaust theology raised more questions than it answered. As an orthodoxy, Holocaust theology's answers became entangled in an unfolding history it could not control. Holocaust theology's success and failure happened in real time. Yet during the fifty years Holocaust theology held sway, the dream of Jewish life after the Holocaust, the state of Israel, turned into an apartheid nightmare.[2]

Theologies in traditions come and go over time, their arrival and decline numbered in generations and often centuries. In Jewish history, with many variations, a religious structure, Rabbinic Judaism, held sway for even longer. Depending on one's historical perspective, the rabbinic hold on Jewish life can be dated back a thousand years and more. Holocaust theology was the strongest challenge to the rabbis in known memory. At least in the eyes of Holocaust theologians, the Holocaust was an epochal event, where every known part of Jewish life was challenged to its core. That core was part theological, the question of God, and part political, the need for Jewish empowerment. Holocaust theologians fused the two into a dynamic combination, making them inseparable. In doing so, they redefined the sense of the sacred in Jewish life.

After the Holocaust, Jews lived in a state of existential crisis as the future of world Jewry seemed to be at stake. Without the fusion of the theological and the political, many Jews thought a Jewish future was in doubt. The old Rabbinic theology, with its distinctive Diaspora theo-political fusion, had reached an impasse, even a demise, in the Holocaust. Calling on God and negotiating as minorities with the powerful in the millennia-old Diaspora left Jews isolated, powerless, and unprepared for the Nazi onslaught. For

Holocaust theologians, the Jewish Diaspora as it had been defined and lived was a disaster. The development of a new post-Holocaust political theology was essential.

In the wake of the Holocaust, the Jewish world contracted numerically. One-third of the global Jewish population had been murdered, and geographically Europe, as the center of the Diaspora, was destroyed. The reconstruction of Jewish life would occur within a bipolar post-Holocaust world centered in the United States and the state of Israel. What this numerical and geographic displacement meant in the moment and could mean in the future was unclear. In the long history of Jews there have been momentous turnings in Jewish life, usually oriented around catastrophic events. The Holocaust was another such event.

For Holocaust theologians, the Holocaust was in continuity with other events of destruction experienced by Jews and, at the same time, was wholly Other. For Rubenstein and Wiesel, but also for other Holocaust theologians such as Emil Fackenheim and Irving Greenberg, the Holocaust was the end of that line and the beginning of a radically new era. In previous events of destruction, Jewry as a whole survived to begin again. Though Jews as a collective survived Hitler and the Nazis, the Nazi attempt to destroy Jews had no limits. Hitler sought to eliminate Jews from history, which, because of modern technology, was now within reach. It was the combination of traditional anti-Semitism and the modern technology of death that led Holocaust theologians to conclude that it was now or never for the Jewish people. The Jewish theo-political response to the Holocaust had to be as radical as Hitler's plan to eliminate Jews from the world.[3]

ON GOD, POLITICS, AND CHRISTIAN RENEWAL

On the question of God, Holocaust theologians are of one mind: the assertion of God's existence and activity in history is in doubt. At least, it cannot be asserted as a given. The plaintive cry "Where was God at Auschwitz?" is central to Holocaust literature and theology. That the theological response was, at best, agnostic is telling. Unlike most theologies, Holocaust theology did not take as its task a reconstruction of Jewish faith in God. Instead, and paradoxically, only by casting doubt on such faith could the question of God remain. Holocaust theologians saw the reliance on a pre-Holocaust faith, as if Auschwitz represented anything less than a shattering of faith, as unfaithful to the Holocaust experience. In a daring reversal, Holocaust theologians refused to overcome the shattering of the Jewish belief in God.

With this refusal, the Holocaust became a place of argumentation against, and sometimes with, God. By allowing, even encouraging, an argument about and with God, Holocaust theologians warned against resolving the God question. Their fear was that either/or in relation to God might further fracture the Jewish community. Divisions within the community in the post-Holocaust era were dangerous especially in the political arena. Jews could agree to disagree theologically. In order to survive, Jewish political unity was essential.[4]

Yet to base Jewish survival on political unity contained dangers of further divisions. After all, Jews are known to be fractious in politics as well as theology. To agree to disagree on God, to leave God as a place of argumentation, was a way of bracketing theological disputes as essential to Jewish identity during the post-Holocaust emergency years. Political divisions within the Jewish community often found along communist/socialist/liberal democracy lines were also rife before and after the Holocaust. Like theological divisions, they could signal disaster. Holocaust theology advised these divisions should be bracketed as well. By recasting and dividing the political into categories of lesser significance, Jews could agree to disagree about certain political viewpoints and agree on what all Jews had to affirm.

For Holocaust theologians, the essential affirmation for all Jews was Jewish empowerment, crystallized in support for the state of Israel. Support for Jewish empowerment in Israel thus transcended the political ordinary. In so doing, the empowerment of Israel became, as well, akin to a theological category. Rather than belief in God, Holocaust theology defined the authentic Jew of the post-Holocaust era as a supporter of Israel, almost without qualification. In turn, a Jew who affirmed God without supporting Israel had turned his back on the Jewish people. This mandated certain political stances within America as well. Left-leaning politics, so common among American Jewry, had to be tempered in light of support for Israel. By the mid-1970s, Irving Greenberg defined undermining Israel for Jews as the excommunicable sin in the post-Holocaust era.[5]

In order to transcend theological and political differences, unity around Israel had to be based in the Holocaust. In the view of Holocaust theologians, the Holocaust mandated Israel. Thus analysis of the Holocaust and Israel had to be restricted or, more to the point, elevated. The destruction of European Jewry could be studied within European history only when anchored in the broader history of Jews and the ravages of a perennial anti-Semitism; so too with Israel and the analysis of the formation and sustenance of the state of Israel. For Holocaust theologians, Israel was to be seen within the broader arc of Jewish history and the history of anti-Semitism. Holocaust theologians created a narrative arc around Holocaust/Israel that was so compelling it became the unifying theme of post-Holocaust Jewish life with a theo-political life of its own.

The most compelling narrative of the Holocaust/Israel axis assumed a liturgical sensibility, especially in the writing and speaking of Elie Wiesel. Yet, to make a theo-political statement was hardly enough. Though Holocaust theologians helped make the Holocaust and Israel essential to Jews and their future, the genius of Holocaust theologians was to take this version of Jewish history to the wider world. During the fifty years of Holocaust theology's ascendance, Holocaust theologians helped bring the Holocaust and Israel into the global political arena in a theo-political manner as well. Soon the Holocaust narrative, with Israel as its culmination, was central to European politics and the American political arena as well. Often dealings with Europe and America from those around the world were dependent on the affirmation of the Holocaust/Israel axis.

Crucial to the acceptance within the Jewish community of the Holocaust and Israel as central to Jewish identity in the post-Holocaust Jewish world was its insistence that Jews were innocent in suffering and in empowerment as well. Thus Jewish suffering allowed Israel to become a marker of Jewish history without inquiry into Israel's origins or sustenance. Kept at bay was the Palestinian issue. In Holocaust theology, Palestinians are virtually absent. If and when they appear, Palestinians appear as threats to the Jewish narrative, indeed drama, where Israel appears as innocent and in some ways redemptive in light of the Holocaust. Holocaust theologians were determined to keep the focus on the Holocaust with Israel as *the* appropriate response to the suffering of European Jewry. Thus those who opposed Israeli policies toward Palestinians, including Palestinians themselves, were faced with an impossible task of justifying their thoughts and actions. For who in their right mind wanted to thwart Israel as a response to Jewish suffering except those with untoward resentments toward Jewish life and perhaps justice and the norms of civilization itself?[6]

Holocaust theology appealed to Western Christians horrified at the history of Christian anti-Semitism. Struggling with the credibility of their Christian witness, Holocaust theology offered Christians an embrace of Jews in the present with Israel as the vehicle for their Christian repentance. Many Christians, especially those of the liberal persuasion, felt that because of their suffering at the hands of Christianity, Jews deserved a state of their own as recompense. As part of Christian renewal, the sign of authentic Christian witness was to embrace the needs of Jews for an empowered state. As with Holocaust theologians, the actual history of the state of Israel was largely beside the point. Like Jews, Israel became a dream response to unimaginable Jewish suffering inflicted by Christian anti-Semites. The innocence of Jews in suffering and empowerment became the hallmark of what might be called Christian Holocaust Theology.[7]

The Christian embrace of Holocaust and Israel, seemingly for their Jewish partners, was crucial to Christian renewal in the West after the Holocaust. Lacking resources for self-generation and suffering a huge credibility issue in relation to Jews and, to some extent, the wider world, Christians began to seek out their Jewish roots. Especially in their relation to the Hebrew Bible and the Jewishness of Jesus, Christians began to affirm their Jewish neighbors as the holder of the ancient and continuing covenant Christians were beholden to, indeed, following certain contemporary reinterpretations of Paul, grafted upon. The continuing witness of Jews was of extreme importance to the renewal of Christian faith. Israel played an important role here. If Jewish Holocaust theologians argued the centrality of Israel for Jewish survival and flourishing, Christians had to as well. This liberal variety of Christian renewal was in the forefront, theologically, to be complemented later by a resurgence of conservative Christian theology that emphasized the biblically based messianic prophecies surrounding the Jewish return to the land of Israel.[8]

The twin dynamic of Israel as the vehicle for Christian repentance and Israel as the flash point for the return of the messiah has had profound political effects on the European and American political process. Over the years, an authentic Christian came to be defined as being in support of an empowered Israel in the political realm. Those who question Israel and its policies are suspect politically, especially since the evolving sense of being Christian is equated with being civilized. Israel became a liberal beacon in an unwashed Middle East and turbulent world. Thus an attack on Israel became an attack on the Christian West and its values. Once defined as outside Christian civilization, in a curious twist of fate, Jews became the standard bearers of the Christian West.

THE GENIUS AND UNRAVELING OF HOLOCAUST THEOLOGY

All of this seems quite dated. The claims of Israel's innocence are muted now. Over time and with new global events of dislocation and death, the Holocaust has receded in importance. Yet the theo-political narrative of Holocaust theologians remains in its other, now more important, political dimension. Even under assault from dissident Jews and Christians for Israel's sins against the Palestinian people, especially seen today in the movement of Boycott, Divestment, Sanctions (BDS), Israel remains almost untouchable in European and American political discourse. Though the narrative of Israel as innocent and redemptive is more and more difficult to speak in public, the power of Israel continues to grow. Despite the traction gained by Palestinians in their critique of Israeli power, in the last decade Israel has solidified its hold within the Arab world as well. The main players in the Middle East now see Israel as part of their regional and national security shield.[9]

Looking back, Holocaust theology was hardly univocal. Early Holocaust theology contained a challenge within itself. Appealing to the ethical values of the Jewish tradition, Holocaust theologians laid the groundwork for a post-Holocaust Jewish life that was secure and life affirming. From the beginning, Israel was central to this vision; the Israel Holocaust theologians wrote of was dreamlike and depoliticized. Israel's victory in the 1967 War, the moment when Holocaust theology went from a subversive movement to the dominant understanding of contemporary Jewish life, was described to American Jews, at least, as a reluctant, necessary reaction to Arab intransigence. The idea that Israel would embark on a war of conquest to expand its borders was foreign to American Jews. Such statecraft, so common in the world, does not appear anywhere in Holocaust theology. It was only decades later, in 1988, in Irving Greenberg's response to the Palestinian Uprising, that the ethical question of Israel's use of force against Palestinians was seriously engaged.

Greenberg's 1988 essay carried the provocative and telling title "The Ethics of Jewish Power." Before Greenberg's essay, empowerment in Israel was mostly discussed as dreamlike, as in Wiesel's invocation of the Holocaust martyrs and all of Jewish history providing support for Israel's reluctant army in its 1967 victory over the Arab countries. Greenberg supports Israel's fight against the Palestinian Uprising in the late 1980s and early 1990s but only insofar as Palestinians endanger Israel's security. Though the Palestinian and Arab struggle against Israel has, in Greenberg's view, its irrational and anti-Semitic side, Israel should recognize the Palestinian desire for its own state. Israel can only use her power as a last resort to beat back a challenge to Israel's existence as a Jewish state.[10]

Greenberg's 1988 essay harkens back to an earlier lecture he gave at an important conference on the Holocaust in 1974. In "Cloud of Smoke, Pillar of Fire: Judaism, Christianity and Modernity After the Holocaust," Greenberg, while arguing for an empowered state of Israel as a response to the Holocaust and the sign of authentic Jewishness in the post-Holocaust era, was already concerned about Jews becoming self-righteous and using and supporting military force beyond what was needed to defend Israel. The specialness of Jews and Jewish destiny, so prominent in Holocaust theology, had to be maintained. The establishment of Israel as a Jewish state was mandated—Greenberg would countenance no argument about this. Nor was he willing to write about or hear objections about the establishment of Israel on Palestinian land or the ethnic cleansing of Palestinians that accompanied Israel's origins.[11]

The Israeli settlements in Jerusalem and the West Bank, already an emerging political issue in 1974, go unmentioned in Greenberg's lecture. Still the warnings are evident. Greenberg is concerned about Jews who refuse Israel as central to Jewish identity and Israel-identified Jews being consumed with Israel's newfound power. In his view, Jews could little afford to hold themselves above history and the culpability inherent in the use of power, but Jews would be remiss if they became like other nations lest Jews lose their raison d'etre for existing. In sum, Greenberg believed Israel and Jews in general had to adjust to the fact that wielding power opened Jews to its misuse. However, if the check and balances on that power, primarily the Jewish ethical tradition was abandoned, Israel and Jews would forfeit their destiny to be a light unto the nations.

This was the central dilemma Holocaust theology ultimately had to, but failed, to confront. In its first phase, the emergency years after the Holocaust, Holocaust theologians could hardly afford to think ethically outside the quest for Jewish survival. At least they thought this to be the case. Or was it just the tragic event of the Holocaust, followed so closely by the dramatic the emergence of the state of Israel, that forced Holocaust theologians to bury the issues raised by this unprecedented form of Jewish empowerment in a state? The struggle within the Jewish community was for acceptance of the Holocaust and Israel as central to Jewish identity. Until the 1967 War, the jury was still out about whether Holocaust theologians would succeed in their task. Before the 1967 War, the Holocaust and Israel, though known and supported, were far from central. Jewishness as liberal, enlightened, justice-oriented and interested in the universal values of human rights and freedom was, in the main, the order of the day. Holocaust theology represented an inward turning, a move away from the universal toward the particular, with ramifications that the Jewish establishment, with their enshrined institutional interests and their desire to assimilate into the mainstream of Jewish life, feared. The Jewish establishment was right to fear Holocaust theology. In the years following the 1967 War their power was largely eroded. They were left with little choice in the matter, either establishment Jews boarded the Holocaust/Israel train or they would be left behind.

Insurgent theologies stake out bold new territory. Yet to gain a broad constituency, theologians have to bring the faithful along. The genius of Holocaust theology was to argue and guide the Jewish ethical tradition into a particularistic sensibility that argued Jewishness and innocence at the same time. Since most Jews living outside of Israel had little knowledge of the formation of Israel beside the dramatic stories of besieged Jews fighting off marauding Arab armies, so current at the time, Holocaust theologians were able to gloss over the blood and guts of Israel's formation as a state. As well, Jewish propagandist sentiments were buoyed by a new and powerful Western orientation in favor of Jews, coupled with general Western sensibilities against the rising tides of resistance in what was known as the Third World. These convergences helped solidify and embolden Holocaust theologians: Jews were being celebrated in the West as repentance for the suffering they had endured and now in their glorious, almost miraculous, new found power. The unraveling of Holocaust theology is found in the details of history as they became available to be interpreted in Europe and America. Over the years, the ideological blinders concerning Israel began to change as well. In addition, as the continuing expansion of Israel, with its settlement policies in Jerusalem and the West Bank, as well as its escalating wars that could no longer be explained as defensive, Holocaust theology became increasingly challenged within the Jewish community in Israel and America. Something had gone terribly wrong, if not in Israel's origins, at least in its unfolding. From the time of the first Palestinian Uprising beginning in the late 1980s, Holocaust theology, now the orthodox theology of large parts of the Jewish world, was on the defensive. Its sense of Jews being innocent in suffering *and* in empowerment could no longer be argued. As well, the world outside the Jewish community, in the global political realm and in the Christian community in Europe and America, awakened to the suffering of the Palestinian people. While Holocaust theologians continued to hammer home Holocaust and Israel, their view of Jews and the world were becoming increasingly marginalized.[12]

From the beginning of Zionism, there had been Jewish dissent. Dissent increased as the prospect of the state of Israel loomed on the horizon, including from such Jewish luminaries as Albert Einstein, Hannah Arendt, Judah Magnes, and Martin Buber. Though each of these dissenters was a homeland or spiritual Zionist, they argued against a political Zionism that sought the establishment of a Jewish state. Their reasons are of interest historically and in the present. In general, as those who lived through the Holocaust, with three of the four mentioned becoming refugees from Nazi Germany, they worried that state Zionism enshrined in a Jewish state would encumber the Jewish witness to the world in a nationality that would displace the Arabs in Palestine and entangle Jews in a perpetual war in the Middle East. Perpetually defending Israel would become a rallying cry that diminished or eliminated critical thought within the Jewish community. As a modern-day Sparta, the Jewish state would force itself upon Jewish thought and life in a radical, perhaps irreversible, negative way.[13]

Magnes and Buber, especially, argued the religious and spiritual questions regarding Zionism and the Jewish state in a particularly forceful way. Both brought their concerns to the political table in Israel and the United States. Buber was known in Israel and beyond, so the Israeli political establishment knew his theo-political views. Buber met with David Ben-Gurion, Israel's first prime minister, on several occasions, discussing the policies of Israel with particular reference to Arab Palestinian refugees. Magnes, as Chancellor of Hebrew University, was also prominent in the pre-state Jewish intellectual and religious circles. However, Magnes took things a step further, spending his last years in Washington, DC, pressing his case in meetings with Secretary of State George Marshall and President Harry Truman. Magnes died soon after Israel became a state. He spent his last years pleading with the highest circles of the American government not to recognize the state of Israel but insure, instead, perhaps with military force, the unity of Palestine as a homeland for Jews and Arabs.[14]

The power of Holocaust theology was found in its ability for decades to override, indeed bury, this dissent, so much so that few Jews today know of the tradition of dissent regarding Zionism and the state of Israel. Though argued from a Jewish perspective and often tinged with colonial Western sensibilities vis-à-vis Arabs and the East, prominent Jewish dissidents were concerned about the harm a Jewish state would do to the Palestinian Arab population and the wider Middle East. For the most part, Holocaust theology is silent on these issues. Indeed, the positions of Einstein, Arendt, Magnes, and Buber, if taken today, would likely fall under Greenberg's definition of excommunicable sins, though it is difficult to know for certain since there are few references to these thinkers in Holocaust theology. When they are mentioned, their Jewishness and/or their political sensibilities are questioned as naive, if not derided.

A major fear of Holocaust theology can be found in how they treated Jewish dissidents, well known and unknown alike. Dissent on the question of God was fine; in fact, Holocaust theology sponsored and raised to a new level the Jewish tradition of arguing with God. The political side of dissent was different. Questioning was frowned upon and, if it continued, had to be disciplined. Greenberg is quite insistent here. In his seminal essays in 1974 and 1988, Greenberg is explicit in his warning: Jews, so used to being critical of the social, economic, and political arrangements of the societies where they live, have to realize that the new mandate for Jewish empowerment limits the application of that same critique to the internal workings of Jewish life. Such a critique, as forceful as it often was coming from Jewish thinkers, could undermine the state of Israel. Undermining the state of Israel intentionally or unintentionally would open Jews in Israel and perhaps beyond to a second Holocaust.

If Greenberg is wary of Jews becoming self-righteous and thus using Israel's power in other than self-defense, he is most afraid of the reemergence of the prophetic in Jewish life. From ancient Israel on the prophetic has shadowed Jewish life, essentially placing a political dichotomy at the center of Jewishness; on the one hand the pursuit of justice and community, on the other the pursuit of power and empire. Throughout the Bible and beyond, Jews have stood on both sides of the empire divide, as prophetic voices for justice and as the builders of empire. After the biblical period and as a defeated and dispersed national community, the rabbis placed textual interpretation and prayer at the center of Jewish life. Holocaust theology cautioned that the rabbis had adopted a pacific stance and negotiations with surrounding hostile powers in lieu of independent Jewish power. After the Holocaust, collective Jewish power was necessary and indeed assumed a kind of sacred transcendence. For Holocaust theologians, emerging Jewish power could deal with textual interpretations and prayer as long as both served or were subservient to that power. Aware of the prophetic in Jewish life as the only venue that could challenge Jewish power, Holocaust theology issued a direct and dire warning against the reemergence of the prophetic. For decades, that warning was Holocaust theology's strength. In the end, it was also Holocaust theology's weakness.

PROGRESSIVE JEWISH DISSENT AND THE EMERGENCE OF JEWS OF CONSCIENCE

By the 1980s, Holocaust theology had achieved its goal of establishing the Holocaust and Israel as central to Jewish identity. It also translated that centrality to the political process in the United States. The early critiques of Jewish statehood by homeland and spiritual Zionists faded, as did the early political debate about American interests in the Middle East residing with the more numerous Arab population and its vast oil resources. Holocaust theology had become the most widely shared orthodoxy in the Jewish community in America and beyond.

A political orthodoxy around Israel was fully in place. Perhaps the most potent symbol of Holocaust theology's achievement was the opening of the United States Holocaust Memorial Museum in Washington, DC. With authorization during the presidency of Jimmy Carter, the museum opened in 1993. Though the Holocaust occurred in Europe, rather than America, the museum's place in the most sacred American geography (near the monuments of America's founders) reinforces unquestioned US support for Israel. The Holocaust Museum preceded museums to Native Americans and African Americans by decades.[15]

Yet it was during the period of its ascendancy that the power of Holocaust theology was called into question. The Israeli invasion of Lebanon, the crushing of the Palestinian Uprising, and increasing sense that Jewish-only settlements in Jerusalem and the West Bank were permanent, events spanning the 1980s, alerted an increasingly vocal minority of Jews to think through the abuses of Jewish power. As predicted by previous Jewish dissidents, the abuse of Jewish power was two-fold: in Israel, regarding Palestinians, and in the United States, regarding attempts to censor Jewish dissent on the direction of the Jewish witness in the world. In the coming decades, Jewish voices of dissent grew louder and the policing of dissent stronger. By the 1990s, the Jewish world was engaged in a verbal civil war over the question of Israel and Palestine.[16]

In the beginning, Jewish dissenters used the Holocaust–Israel paradigm framed by Holocaust theologians. The added, subversive piece was Palestinians. In effect, Jewish dissent affirmed that Holocaust theologians had asked the next question after the Holocaust—the need for Jewish empowerment—but failed to address the issue that came within empowerment—the oppression of Palestinians. To these dissenting Jewish voices it was becoming clear that though Jews were innocent in suffering in the Holocaust, Jews were culpable in assuming power in Israel. Over the next decades, Palestinians, and ultimately Palestine, became the driving force of the next phase of Jewish life, as the Holocaust and Israel had been previously. And like Holocaust theology, the critique from Jewish dissenters carried a theo-political message.

As with much of contemporary Jewish life, critical thought that interrupted Holocaust theology was secular, though in a distinctively Jewish way. Holocaust theology had set the tone decades earlier by placing the political commitment to Israel as central to Jewish life, as almost a religious imperative. At the very least, support for Israel was determined to be the individual and collective sign of Jewish authenticity. Ironically, it was the context of Israel, for Holocaust theologians more or less a dream, and as a central part of Jewish destiny after the Holocaust, that provided the avenue for Jewish dissent. Often this dissent harkened back to the lessons of the Holocaust. If for Holocaust theologians the lesson of the Holocaust was Jewish empowerment in Israel, for Jewish dissenters the Holocaust lesson was never again to Jews, yes, but as well never again to others, including the Palestinians. Jewish dissenters asked how, if the Holocaust was the center of Jewish suffering, Jewish empowerment could cause suffering to others without demeaning the Holocaust itself. For these Jews, the Israeli bombing of Beirut, the crushing of the Palestinian Uprising, and the increasing number of settlements on Palestinian land was impossible to square with the insistence of Holocaust theologians regarding Jews as innocent in suffering and in power.

ADDRESSING HOLOCAUST THEOLOGY ON ITS OWN TURF

The first, found primarily in the writing and activism of Arthur Waskow and Michael Lerner and embodied most forcefully in Lerner's *Tikkun* magazine, featured a renewed rabbinic sensibility, infused with elements of New Age spirituality. The second, found primarily in the writing of Marc Ellis, especially in his books *Toward a Jewish Theology of Liberation* (1987) and *Beyond Innocence and Redemption: Confronting the Holocaust and Israeli Power* (1990), continued the arc of Holocaust theology and featured the Palestinians as the next and central challenge for the Jewish future.[17]

Though there were some similarities between the two streams of critical thought regarding Israel, the differences were important for the future. *Tikkun* came on to the scene with Elie Wiesel among its supporters, though he quickly resigned as a member of the editorial board when he understood *Tikkun*'s direction more fully. Though the notion of *tikkun*, to repair the world, was inviting to Wiesel, Lerner's broad critique of the direction of American society and his call for Israel to change direction and recognize a Palestinian state was too much for Wiesel. That being said, both the arc of Lerner's editorials and the overall direction of *Tikkun* were heavily oriented toward Jewish innocence and its recovery. For Lerner and *Tikkun*, the founding of Israel as a response to the Holocaust was unquestioned. After the 1967 War, again accepted as a defensive war on Israel's part, Lerner believed that the settlements in Jerusalem, the West Bank, and Gaza were carrying Israel's influence and power too far, thus undermining Israel's Jewish ethical foundations. For Lerner, as it was for Waskow, the treatment of Palestinian resistance during the Palestinian Uprising was brutal, wrong, and immoral.[18]

In general, *Tikkun* helped define what Jewish progressives felt to be legitimate criticisms of Israeli abuses of power. Criticizing Israel for its policies in East Jerusalem, the West

Bank and Gaza was legitimate as long as the critique started in the post-1967 era without stretching back to Israel's origins in 1948. For progressive Jews like Lerner and Waskow, the critique of Israel's policies toward Palestinians, Jewish history, and the need for a Jewish state remained in the forefront. Thus for Jewish progressives, Palestinians and Palestinian resistance could only be affirmed if Palestinians accepted the legitimacy of the state of Israel and accepted their own historic lack of affirmation of the Jewish state as wrong. As in Holocaust theology, the excommunicable sin for Jews was refusing to accept the Holocaust and Israel as central to Jewish identity. Jewish progressives extended that sin to Palestinians if they refused the same affirmation.

The theological side of *Tikkun* promised to reinvigorate the rabbinic aspect of Jewish spirituality, addressing the absence of God in Holocaust theology with a communal presence that came through the "politics of meaning." Jewish rituals were reinvigorated and reinterpreted and soon both Lerner and Waskow accepted non-traditional rabbinic ordinations. For progressive Jews, the bleakness of the Holocaust might sustain Jewish power, but without the values to guide that power toward justice Jewish history would be tainted and diminished. Compassion became a central theme among progressive Jews. Both justice and compassion became guiding lights to a broader renewal of Jewish life after the Holocaust and within a secure and flourishing Israel.

Though progressive Jews engaged Holocaust theology in a serious way, the struggle between the two strands of Jewish life issued into an internal, though quite public, feud. In the end the differences were less than advertised. In general, progressive Jews sought to assume leadership in the Jewish community, replacing the relatively new Holocaust/Israel-oriented Jewish establishment with more progressive leadership. The two sides bonded together on the issue of Jewish innocence, Jewish statehood and a paternalistic view of Palestinians and the Arab world. In the places they parted company there was struggle but when the chips were down progressive Jews retreated. Progressive Jews and the Jewish establishment expressly came together against Jewish dissidents to the left of them and Christians who, in the 1980s as well, began to mark out new territory of dissent that involved the origins of the state of Israel and what could be and not be said about Jewish power in public.

Though similarly concerned with the Holocaust and Israel, the development of a Jewish theology of liberation represented a different direction. Taking a more global perspective, Ellis placed the Holocaust and Israel in a broader frame. Along with more radical movements among Jews regarding the question of Palestine, Ellis featured Palestinian voices representing their own viewpoints independent of Jews inside and outside of Israel. Ellis also wrote of Israel's role on the world stage as a global arms dealer and as a surrogate for United States power in different parts of the world. In his Jewish theology of liberation and subsequent books on the subject, Ellis affirmed the importance of Holocaust theology's probing of God as well as it limitations regarding Israel's abuse of power. In the first edition of *Toward a Jewish Theology of Liberation*, written before the Palestinian Uprising, and in the second edition that featured an Epilogue written during the height of the Uprising outlining the relationship of the Palestinian Uprising to the future of the Jewish people, Ellis moved beyond the progressive Jewish positions on Israel. Included here was Ellis's argument for a full two state solution, as a free and unencumbered Palestine with East Jerusalem as its capital, a confession of the Jewish people to Palestinians for what Israel had done and was doing to them and Israeli reparations for the harm done to the Palestinian people since the formation of the Jewish state.[19]

After the failure of the Oslo Accords in the 1990s, the second Palestinian Uprising that began in 2000, and the subsequent building of Israel's Apartheid Wall, the dual trajectory of dissenting Jews crystallized. During this period, progressive Jews split, with some moving closer to the Jewish establishment and others, seeing the limitations and failure of progressive Jewish thought and action, embracing the liberationist stream. In effect, the Jewish community became defined by two constellations, a Constantinian Jewishness, that had assimilated to state power in the United States and Israel as the only way forward for post-Holocaust Jewry, and Jews of Conscience, who increasingly understood that only a radical break with the mainstream establishment and progressive Jewish community could anchor Jewish fidelity in history. Constantinian Jewishness promised its followers success, status and power; Jews of Conscience entered into a troubling, seemingly permanent exile.[20]

While the newly augmented Constantinian Jewishness continued on with parts of Holocaust theology, especially with regard to the centrality of Israel, the radical question of God diminished. Replacing it was an official, almost mandatory, praise of Israel and affiliation with politically well-placed synagogues as a public testimony to an empowered Jewishness. Jews of Conscience, as has often been the case in Jewish history, were renegades outside the establishment religious and political orthodoxies of the day. Years ago Jews of Conscience left behind the ritual pronouncements of the Jewish establishment but now this included the ritual pronouncements of what had become the progressive Jewish establishment: the New Age turn of *Tikkun* and its affiliates. Ellis defined what lay ahead as the embodiment of the "naked and unadorned prophetic."[21]

ON THE FIFTIETH ANNIVERSARY OF THE 1967 WAR/OCCUPATION

As the fiftieth anniversary of the 1967 War came and went in 2017, the mood among Jews in Israel and beyond was somber. With the passing of Elie Wiesel one year earlier, Holocaust theology had become an orphan. Existing without its most famous, honored, and politically connected spokesperson, the fifty-year occupation of Jerusalem and the West Bank was the headline news. Jewish empowerment had won out and, for most seasoned analysts, Israel's occupation had become permanent. Even the hopes of the Palestinian Authority comported with a permanent occupation of Palestine, though with military troops from international bodies complementing the Israeli soldiers that would be stationed within and on the borders of a diminished and fragmented Palestinian state.[22]

If the political hope of Holocaust theology had been accomplished, since Jews had achieved full empowerment in Israel and the United States, the ethical values of what would be left after empowerment were now uncertain. The Jewish civil war continued to escalate with Jews of all ages publically demonstrating against the continuing Israeli occupation of Palestine. Such groups as Open Hillel, IfNotNow, and Jewish Voice for Peace escalated their activity and rhetoric in a bold confrontation with the Constantinian and progressive Jewish establishments. As a sign of the time, anti-Zionist synagogue Tzedek Chicago was formed. Headed by Rabbi Brant Rosen, Tzedek Chicago sought to pioneer an intersectional Judaism for the future. At its opening, Jews of all stripes, especially those who found it difficult to find a home in established and progressive synagogues, were invited to join. Non-Jews who wanted to accompany Jews and contribute to a Jewish future were welcomed as well. Along with the poetic rendering of the Psalms, Rabbi Rosen also continued the evolving tradition of a Jewish liberation theology. Though the themes were similar to Ellis's, Rosen offered an updated version for Jews of Conscience. Both as a rabbi and political activist on the American front, Brant called for an interfaith assault against rampant militarism, endemic racism, and a deeply flawed capitalist system that divided Americans into the haves and have-nots. On Israel, decrying Jewish exceptionalism and white Jewish privilege, Brant called for a one-state solution in Israel–Palestine. Citing the origins of the Jewish state in the ethnic cleansing of Palestinians and the continuing oppression of Palestinians under occupation, Brant and his congregation argued for the end of Israel as a Jewish state and the inauguration of a democratic, secular state in Israel–Palestine.[23]

As the Jewish civil war escalated, divisions in the Jewish community hardened. Were they, like the Israeli occupation of Palestine, now permanent? On the one hand, the established Jewish community continued to enjoy unparalleled access to power in Israel and America. Conversely, the political reach of Jews of Conscience was severely limited. Though Israel's occupation of Palestinians had become an international issue of note, Israel was stronger and more entrenched than ever before in its history. As in other communities and issues, the Jewish politics of injustice was clearly triumphing over the Jewish politics of conscience. Theologically, too, the recognized norm of Jewish religiosity had become Constantinian, with its emphasis on Holocaust and Israel. Jews of Conscience were hardly known in the broader stream of Israeli and American politics. Where they were known, primarily through the BDS movement, Jews of Conscience with their Christian and Palestinian allies were often condemned as seeking the destruction of Israel, as self-hating Jews and anti-Semites.

Though without specific language, many Jewish and non-Jewish commentators alike saw the Jewish community as coming to a dead end. If there was a way forward, few could see it. The present situation of permanent occupation and internal civil war hardly augured a Jewish future worth bequeathing to the next generation of Jews. Some actually speculated that Jews had reached the end of Jewish history, at least to the ethical history contemporary Jews had known and inherited.

Holocaust theologians had noted an end—to a history of Jews without power. Only through empowerment could Jews survive and thrive in a hostile world. But the politics involved in that empowerment were "outed" by the revival of the Jewish prophetic, just as Holocaust theologians had feared. Once unleashed, the Jewish prophetic, returning inward where it began in biblical times, there was no going back. On the fiftieth anniversary of Israel's victory in the 1967 War and the permanent occupation Israel imposed, the question remained whether Jews of Conscience, as focused and active as they were, could create a distinctive Jewish future.

Was the Jewish future, at least for Jews of Conscience outside the mainstream Jewish community, with others, to be found in what has been called the New Diaspora? In the New Diaspora, exiles from all religions, political orders, and cultural norms gather, carrying the fragments of their previous backgrounds with them. In the New Diaspora, these fragments are shared, without attribution or destination. In the New Diaspora, no overarching political, religious, or cultural paradigm will emerge. As with all exiles, the question of what is handed down and what survives is real. For Jews, the matter of inheritance is crucial. If the future of Jews of Conscience is exile in the New Diaspora, what will survive of their Jewish inheritance, shattered as it is? What will become of the Jewish prophetic, the Jewish indigenous, and the root of the global prophetic in the future?

NOTES

1. Marc H. Ellis, "Elie Wiesel Is Dead," *Mondoweiss*, July 2, 2016. Also see Richard Rubenstein, *After Auschwitz: Radical Theology and Contemporary Judaism* (New York: Bobbs-Merril, 1966).

2. For an early and detailed analysis of Holocaust theology see Marc H. Ellis, *Toward a Jewish Theology of Liberation* (Maryknoll, NY: Orbis, 1987) and *Beyond Innocence and Redemption: Confronting the Holocaust and Israeli Power* (San Francisco: Harper & Row, 1990).

3. For an early example of these claims see Emil Fackenheim, *God's Presence in History: Jewish Affirmations and Philosophical Reflections* (New York: New York University Press, 1976).

4. See Irving Greenberg, "On the Third Era in Jewish History," National Jewish Resource Center, 1980.

5. On Emil Fackenheim's 614th Commandment that summarizes the position of empowerment as a sacred commandment after the Holocaust see Fackenheim, *God's Presence*.

6. On Israel as innocent and redemptive see Ellis, *Beyond Innocence and Redemption*. For my take in 1990 on the possible movement beyond both see pp. 156–190.

7. Examples of a Christian Holocaust Theology include, with a somewhat different emphasis, Paul M. Van Buren, *Discerning the Way: A Theology of the Jewish Christian Reality* (New York; Seabury, 1980) and Clark Williamson, *A Guest in the House of Israel: Post-Holocaust Church Theology* (Knoxville, TN: Westminster John Knox Press, 1993).

8. For a recent critical analysis of Christian Zionism see Robert O. Smith, *More Desired than Our Own Salvation: The Roots of Christian Zionism* (Oxford: Oxford University Press, 2013).

9. On BDS, see Omar Barghouti, *Boycott, Divestment, Sanctions: The Global Struggle for Palestinian Rights* (Chicago: Haymarket Books, 2011).

10. Irving Greenberg, "The Ethics of Jewish Power," in *Beyond Occupation: American Jewish, Christian and Palestinians for Peace*, eds. Rosemary Radford Ruether and Marc H. Ellis (Boston: Beacon Press, 1990): 22–74.

11. Irving Greenberg, "Cloud of Smoke, Pillar of Fire: Judaism, Christianity and Modernity After the Holocaust," in *Auschwitz: Beginning of a New Era: Reflections on the Holocaust*, ed. Eva Fleischner (New York: KTAV, 1974): 7–56.

12. The new Israeli historians, who began publishing their work critical of the founding of Israel in relation to the Palestinian people, were summed up later in Ilan Pappe, *The Ethnic Cleansing of Palestine* (London: Oneworld, 2007). My *Beyond Innocence and Redemption* was written in 1988–1989 as the Palestinian Uprising challenged directly the themes of Holocaust theology. For part of that challenge see pp. 73–133.

13. For my take on the history of Jewish dissent on Zionism see ibid., 56–72. Hannah Arendt is especially forceful in her "To Save the Jewish Homeland: There Is Still Time," in *The Jew as Pariah*, ed. Ron H. Feldman (New York: Grove Press, 1978): 181–222.

14. For a biography Magnes see Judah L. Magnes, *An American Jewish Non-conformist* (Syracuse: Syracuse University Press, 2010). For Buber's writing on Zionism, Israel, and Palestinians see Martin Buber, *A Land of Two Peoples: Martin Buber on Jews and Arabs*, ed. Paul Mendes-Flohr (Chicago: University of Chicago Press, 2005).

15. For a fascinating take on the development of the Holocaust Museum see Edward L. Linenthal, *Preserving Memory: The Struggle to Create America's Holocaust Museum* (New York: Columbia University Press, 2001).

16. On the Jewish civil war see Marc H. Ellis, "On the Jewish Civil War and the New Prophetic," *Tikkun* 16(July/August, 2001): 17–19.

17. For early essays by Michael Lerner and other progressive Jews see *The Tikkun Reader*, ed. Michael Lerner, Rachel Adler, and Zygmunt Bauman (Lanham, MD: Rowman & Littlefield, 2006). For early Waskow, see Arthur Waskow, *Godwrestling* (New York: Schocken, 1987).
18. See Lerner, "The Occupation: Immoral and Stupid," *Tikkun* 3 (March/April, 1988): 7–12.
19. Marc H. Ellis, *Toward a Jewish Theology of Liberation* (Maryknoll, NY: Orbis, 1987). Also see the 1989 edition also from Orbis with an epilogue. "The Palestinian Uprising and the Future of the Jewish People." The third edition brought together parts of the initial book and parts of *Beyond Innocence and Redemption* with updating. See Marc H. Ellis, *Toward a Jewish Theology of Liberation: The Challenge of the 21st Century* (Waco, TX: Baylor University Press, 2004).
20. I wrote about this shift in *Practicing Exile: The Religious Odyssey of an American Jew* (Minneapolis, MN: Fortress Press, 2002).
21. Marc H. Ellis, *Finding Our Voice: Embodying the Prophetic and Other Misadventures* (Eugene, OR: Wipf & Stock, 2018).
22. The fiftieth anniversary of the 1967 War evoked mixed emotions. See Jane Eisner, "Should We Celebrate the 50th Anniversary of the Six-Day War—Or Despair?" *Forward*, April 28, 2017; Sheren Khalel, "50 Years of Occupation: Palestinians Recall the 6 Days of the 1967 War," *Mondoweiss*, June 6, 2017.
23. For some of Brant Rosen's writing see Brant Rosen, *Wrestling in the Daylight: A Rabbi's Path to Palestinian Solidarity* (Chicago: Just World Books, 2012). Also see his second edition, 2017. For another and important take on contemporary Jewish life in a global perspective see Santiago Slabodsky, *Decolonial Judaism: Triumphal Failures of Barbaric Thinking* (New York: Palgrave, 2015).

SELECT BIBLIOGRAPHY

Buber, Martin (2005), *A Land of Two Peoples: Martin Buber on Jews and Arabs*, edited by Paul Mendes-Flohr, Chicago: University of Chicago Press.
Ellis, Marc H. (1987), *Toward a Jewish Theology of Liberation*, Maryknoll, NY: Orbis Books.
Ellis, Marc H. (1990), *Beyond Innocence and Redemption: Confronting the Holocaust and Israeli Power*, San Francisco: Harper & Row.
Fackenheim, Emil (1976), *God's Presence in History: Jewish Affirmations and Philosophical Reflections*, New York: New York University Press.
Rosen, Brant (2012), *Wrestling in the Daylight: A Rabbi's Path to Palestinian Solidarity*, Chicago: Just World Books.
Rubenstein, Richard (1966), *After Auschwitz: Radical Theology and Contemporary Judaism*, New York: Bobbs-Merril.
Ruether, Rosemary Radford and Marc H. Ellis (1990), *Beyond Occupation: American Jewish, Christian and Palestinians for Peace*, Boston: Beacon Press.
Slabodsky, Santiago (2015), *Decolonial Judaism: Triumphal Failures of Barbaric Thinking*, New York: Palgrave.
Smith, Robert O. (2013), *More Desired Than Our Own Salvation: The Roots of Christian Zionism*, Oxford: Oxford University Press.
Van Buren, Paul M. (1980), *Discerning the Way: A Theology of the Jewish Christian Reality*, New York: Seabury.
Williamson, Clark (1993), *A Guest in the House of Israel: Post-Holocaust Church Theology*, Knoxville, TN: Westminster John Knox Press.

CHAPTER TWO

Christian Responses to the Holocaust

Political Theology in Europe

VINCENT LLOYD

INTRODUCTION

The Second World War claimed the lives of at least sixty million people, including six million Jews killed by the Nazi regime. The war itself was devastating, but not unfamiliar; nearly twenty million had been killed in the First World War three decades earlier. But the targeted, systematic killing of a group of civilians struck many Europeans as novel, and utterly horrifying. For non-Europeans, there was less surprise. Aimé Césaire, writing from Martinique, meditates on "the very distinguished, very humanistic, very Christian bourgeois of the twentieth century" who "has a Hitler inside him." The great Caribbean poet and intellectual pointedly observes that Hitler "applied to Europe colonialist procedures which until then had been reserved exclusively for the Arabs of Algeria, the 'coolies' of India, and the 'niggers' of Africa."[1]

It was precisely this juxtaposition of European and global atrocities that motivated the most significant development in European theology in the second half of the twentieth century, the creation of political theology. Twenty years after the Jewish Holocaust, Europe was abuzz with talk and images of other holocausts, and other forms of violence against marginalized communities. In Vietnam, Africa, Latin America, and elsewhere, Europeans and Americans were committing mass murder. It was now clear that the Nazi era had not been anomalous: the distinguished, humanistic, Christian bourgeois of Europe apparently had a tendency toward complicity in bloodshed. While Auschwitz abbreviated this complicity—and also distanced a generation of Europeans from it—Auschwitz was named as a theological problem against the backdrop of the increasingly visible violence of the West on the global stage.[2]

Bourgeois European Christianity had a grisly problem, and bourgeois European Christians sought solutions. Frustration with the seemingly abstract, apolitical style of Christian thought gave rise to intellectual ferment under the label "political theology." While this term has been used in a wide variety of ways, this chapter is particularly concerned with a narrow sense of political theology, sometimes referred to as "new political theology," naming a cluster of Christian intellectual projects produced in Germany in the 1960s and 1970s. Even more narrowly, I will focus on the three leading figures in this cluster, the Protestants Jürgen Moltmann and Dorothee Sölle and the

Catholic Johann Baptist Metz. Initially, Sölle was the most widely known figure of this group, reaching a broad public audience in Germany, writing a book titled *Political Theology* (1971), and producing a steady stream of texts that were quickly translated into other languages. Moltmann's books from this period, *Theology of Hope* (1964) and *The Crucified God* (1972), have achieved canonical status and have contributed to the formation of Protestant ministers around the world. Metz represents the best of intellectually serious, progressive European Catholicism. For a few years, these three thinkers were in close conversation with each other, sharing a set of secular and Christian resources that they applied to shared concerns by means of a conceptual vocabulary that they developed together.

THREE LIVES

Moltmann was born in 1926, Metz in 1928, and Sölle in 1929. They each came of age when Germany was under National Socialist rule, their middle-class childhoods disrupted by the war. None of them report that their families were sympathetic to the Nazis. Nonetheless, the bourgeois lifestyle their families enjoyed entailed a general sense of patriotism and an aversion to activism that would too strongly oppose the political order. They were formed into a culture that valued the cultivation of the virtues, appreciation for the arts and the life of the mind, thoughtfulness, and moderation. Then they were confronted with twin catastrophes: first, war of a scale and severity Europe had never before seen; second, the fact that Germany had carried out genocide. In the traditional story about political theology's origins, the impetus of their theological work, and also its essential ambivalence, arises from this reckoning with the failures of formation, with a set of values and habits that had once seemed desirable but now were suspected of causing moral catastrophe. The solution, each concluded, was to sever Christianity from bourgeois culture and to recast it as motivating struggles for justice.

Moltmann grew up in a rural area outside of Hamburg.[3] His parents were part of a small community of sophisticates looking for a simpler life lived closer to the land. While there was a collectivist, free-wheeling spirit to the community, there was also classical education, with music, poetry, and Latin instruction. There was no church; indeed, Moltmann's grandfather had been a freethinker who wrote pamphlets against Christianity. Moltmann was required to participate in pre-military training in his youth and, in 1943, was conscripted into the air force auxiliary. He manned an anti-aircraft battery in Hamburg, and that was his occupation when the Allied firebombing began. Moltmann's position was hit, and a friend, standing next to him, was killed. It was that night, according to Moltmann, he first spoke to God—"My God, where are you?"—inaugurating a lifetime of theological questioning.[4] In his autobiography Moltmann connects his cry that night with his identity as a "survivor" of two Hamburg catastrophes: the 40,000 people, mainly women and children, killed by the Allied bombing of the city, and the 40,000 people who died at the Neuengamme concentration camp, a few miles from Hamburg. Moltmann seems entirely unaware of the tone deafness evidenced by the moral equivalence implied by this narrative—a sign of the unworked ambivalence characteristic of German political theology.

In the final days of the war the teenage Moltmann was assigned to the infantry and sent to the Western front. He was captured by the British and held as a prisoner of war until 1948. Detained in Scotland, Moltmann was given a Bible and found in the psalms and gospels expressions of anguish with which he could identify. As his religious interests developed, he was transferred to a camp where he could begin his theological education; the first book of theology he read was Reinhold Niebuhr's *The Nature and Destiny of Man* (1943). This theological education would continue when Moltmann returned to Germany, studying in Göttingen and writing a thesis on Moses Amyrant, the seventeenth-century Huguenot theologian. During the 1950s Moltmann was closely connected to church life, pastoring a rural congregation and teaching in a seminary. In 1964 he moved fully into academic theology, accepting a chair in Bonn, and in 1967 he moved to Tübingen, where he would be based for the rest of his career.

According to Moltmann, he first became aware of the Holocaust in 1944 when his father, who was an officer in the Ukraine, visited the young Moltmann at his training camp to alert him that Jews were being killed on a massive scale. Moltmann reports, "This completely put a stop to my willingness to serve in the war"—but it did not result in any action.[5] He felt helpless. Later, as a prisoner of war, Moltmann and his fellow German soldiers were shown pictures of the concentration camps, resulting in deep feelings of shame and disgrace. Moltmann does not suggest that there is a direct line from these experiences to the development of his theology. Rather, teaching a course on Dietrich Bonhoeffer, starting in 1959, and studying the work of Ernst Bloch, starting in 1960, gave Moltmann the intellectual resources he needed to write *Theology of Hope*, published in 1964. It was dialogue with Metz, and particularly Metz's reflections on Auschwitz, as well as his struggle to work through questions that remained unanswered in *Theology of Hope* that led to Moltmann's 1972 book *The Crucified God*. But the contemporaneous political context also mattered. Moltmann spent 1967–1968 based at Duke University in the United States, and his experience of the tumult of the civil rights era peaked when Martin Luther King, Jr. was assassinated during a conference on Moltmann's theology. (Moltmann would dedicate a collection of essays to King.[6]) He returned to Germany at the height of student protests over the Vietnam War, and he found his own work targeted by radical students for its perceived authoritarian tendencies. Moltmann identified himself as a proud liberal: in contrast to his conservative colleagues who disdained the students and used the threat of the police to maintain order in their classes, Moltmann realized that "most of those present [in his classes] wanted the lecture and not a political protest," so he simply took a vote, the students in favor of a traditional lecture won, and he proceeded as usual.[7]

In stark contrast to Moltmann, Sölle unequivocally placed herself on the side of protesters. Her theological writing, and her fame, grew out of a Christian theological-political protest she helped organize in Cologne, "Political Evensong." Starting in 1968, as anger about the Vietnam War mounted around the world, Sölle and her colleagues gathered an ecumenical group of Christians "who understood more and more plainly that theological reflection without political consequences was tantamount to blasphemy."[8] Mixing prayer, Bible readings, and religious reflections on political issues of the day, ranging from Vietnam to feminism, incarceration to the invasion of Czechoslovakia, these gatherings struck a chord. The very first Political Evensong attracted more than a thousand participants; they proceeded monthly through 1972. Starting in the late 1960s, Sölle published prolifically for a broad public audience, mixing political, mystical, poetic, and systematic-theological reflections in her texts—but never achieving a professorship at a German university. It was only in 1975 that she finally received a professorship, at Union Theological Seminary, in New York.

Where Moltmann has nary a harsh word to say about himself, Sölle vividly describes realizing her own cowardice when, as a girl, she witnesses police pursue another girl on a streetcar who was wearing a yellow star. She recalls an awareness of the concentration camps from the late 1930s (though not their murderous scale), and recalls that her family stood decisively against the Nazis. For a time they sheltered a Jewish acquaintance who revealed to the teenage Sölle that she carried poison with her to take in the event of her capture. While Sölle's family spoke out against the Nazi regime in private, they taught Sölle to keep such opinions to herself in public. For Sölle this cognitive dissonance was sustainable, even after she discovered she was herself one-eighth Jewish, and it was only in retrospect that she found her wartime experiences as worthy of guilt.

Sölle's comfortable childhood in Cologne was interrupted by the war; her house was destroyed in firebombing. Her family was short on food and needed to forage in the countryside. But after the war life returned to normal relatively quickly: she was back to admiring gardens and concerts, writing poems, reading Rilke and Goethe, and generally embracing the life of the apolitical bourgeoisie. To express her own existential angst, the angst of coming of age and of postwar bourgeois guilt, she turned first to existentialism. Eventually she read Kierkegaard, and she encountered a teacher who would combine the existentialism of Sartre and Heidegger with the Christianity of Bonhoeffer and Bultmann, opening the way for Sölle to study theology. After graduating in 1954 she taught at a girls' school in Cologne until 1960 while entering into a community of left-wing Christians. In the years after the war, she was astounded by how little the horror of the war, and especially the Holocaust, registered with her colleagues and neighbors. German Christian bourgeois habits and values in the 1950s looked frighteningly similar to the German Christian bourgeois habits and values before the war. And Sölle thought it was those habits and values that had made possible Hitler's rise to power.

Sölle's existential impulses were nurtured by reading Kierkegaard and Bultmann, but as she spent the two decades after the war trying to come to intellectual terms with the Holocaust, she realized that existential Christian thought focused too much on the individual. Even as it promised to radicalize the bourgeois European subject, pushing beyond liberal complacency, Sölle worried that existential Christianity was still working in terms organized around that bourgeois European subject. This worry was reinforced by Sölle's correspondence with Bultmann, who insisted that social structures are unrelated to sin; "sin is an offense of one person against another."[9] Bultmann went on to reveal the naiveté of such a position, writing "There is a difference, surely, between killing or robbing a banana worker and getting my bananas through the United Fruit Company. If the banana worker is paid a pittance for his labor, he always has the option of striking or going to court."[10] Sölle's immersion in leftist political circles made her realize immediately just how farcical such a statement was.[11]

What Bultmann had done for Sölle, Karl Rahner did for Metz. Rahner offered a way for intellectually serious Catholics to appreciate cutting-edge philosophical insights that spoke compellingly to a generation. For Rahner, Christian language must not simply be handed down from church authorities; it is felt in the soul. Metz agreed with this suspicion of calcified theological discourse, but urged that the soul must be understood in its social context, in the world—hence his first book, *Theology of the World* (1968), collecting essays he penned through the mid-1960s. Metz was not a system-builder, like Moltmann, nor did he write in a poetic, accessible style, like Sölle. Of the three, he was the most philosophically learned and rigorous, writing essay after essay that brought new resources and questions into the theological conversation.

Metz was born in Catholic Bavaria, from a village Metz describes as nearly medieval. Indeed, he suggests that this early personal experience outside of, or in opposition to, secular modernity disposed him to attend to the theological import of time out of synch later in his career.[12] He was not essentially urbane, like Moltmann and Sölle, and he reports a slow, difficult process of adjusting to the world of German high culture. When Metz was sixteen, he was conscripted into the German army. One evening he was sent to relay a message from his company to the battalion headquarters. When he returned to his company, he found everyone, more than a hundred men, dead. This, Metz reflects, was a world-shattering experience for him. "A great gap had been torn in my powerful Bavarian Catholic socialization with its well-knit trust."[13]

Like Moltmann, he was held as a prisoner of war; Metz was held in the United States. When he returned to Germany, he completed a dissertation on Heidegger, and a year later he was ordained a priest. In 1954 he began studies with Karl Rahner at Innsbruck, writing a dissertation on Thomas Aquinas and immersing himself in Rahner's own theological project. He took a professorship at Münster in 1963 and spent his career there. Metz co-founded the liberal Catholic journal *Concilium*; Moltmann would later serve on its editorial board. Metz was active in church life, consulting for the Vatican and for the West German bishops. While Metz may not have been on the front line of protests, like Sölle he was deeply involved in pastoral questions. Metz drafted "Our Hope: A Confession of Faith for Our Time" (1975), a reckoning with the Holocaust that grew out of four years of discussions among West German clergy and lay people.[14]

Metz describes confronting the Holocaust because of the volatile politics of 1968.[15] Students were seeking a revolution, a radical break with the status quo. Metz, it seems, felt that his theological vocabulary was impoverished—or, rather, too abstract, failing to respond to the real, acute suffering felt in the world. Reflecting on the Holocaust provided a way to grapple with the same failures of the bourgeoisie decried by the students in 1968, the same sense of moral atrocity, and the same sense of radical discontinuity in human history—real in the 1940s, potential in the 1960s. Where explicit reflection on the politics of the 1960s would have led to politicized reactions, reflection on the Holocaust offered distance and leverage, a way of explaining to an older generation why students might be acting as they were—and why the older generation might even want to consider joining them. For Metz to say theology can only be done in light of the Holocaust means that theology can only be done in light of the crises that are very real, right now, even though we (intellectuals) have difficulty seeing and feeling them. One suspects that Metz may be revealing what Moltmann and Sölle conceal: they, too, start writing about the Holocaust in the 1960s.

KEY THEMES

The label that grouped together Sölle, Moltmann, and Metz was "political theology." The three theologians were well aware that Carl Schmitt had used this term, and they constructed their project explicitly in opposition to his.[16] Schmitt was concerned with the homology between political sovereignty and theological sovereignty, and more generally between European politics and Christian theology. European states construct themselves as authoritative because they assume the role of divine government on earth, but the theological basis of secular authority has lately been repressed, or so Schmitt charges. When the connection is repressed, political authority can diminish, or misguided (e.g., pantheistic) theology can contaminate political concepts. This is the diagnosis Schmitt offered of Weimar Germany: parliamentary democracy did not acknowledge the proper relationship to proper theology and was therefore not up to the task of managing the social and economic crises of the day. The German leader should be re-imagined in the image of God, and this was what the National Socialists promised to do.

The German Protestant theologian Erik Peterson offered a historically grounded but politically pointed response to Schmitt in 1935.[17] In short, Peterson argued that the fundamental, distinguishing Christian commitment is to the Trinity. The analogy between political leader and God cannot be so straightforward if Christians believe in a God who is three-in-one. Indeed, the Christian theological tradition has spent much energy polemicizing against those who would turn the triune nature of God into a singular deity; if Schmitt's analogy is to hold, Christians ought to similarly attack the concentration of political sovereignty in a singular institution or individual. With Metz in the lead, a group of German theologians in the 1960s accepted the terms of the Schmitt–Peterson debate and sided with Peterson.[18] Over the centuries, Christianity has gone wrong when political power is aligned with God's power. Christianity is at its best when Christian doctrine is elaborated so as to challenge the finality of political authority. The doctrine of the Trinity is one way to do this (which Moltmann will develop in the 1980s), but there is a much wider vocabulary that could contribute to this project as well, including hope, memory, suffering, compassion, and dignity. In a sense, Metz, Moltmann, and Sölle thought Schmitt was right about political power modeling itself on religious ideas; they just diagnosed these religious ideas as heretical. Because of the very nature of Christianity, as Trinitarian, and the nature of the secular state, invested in consolidating power monolithically, the project of Christian theology is necessarily political, for every explication of Christian doctrine undercuts the authority of the secular state and motivates women and men to engage politically beyond the horizon set by the state. This project thus came to be known as a *new* political theology, in continuity with a certain problem posed by Schmitt but offering a quite different sort of response.

Another component of Schmitt's story, one that also was discussed in much wider intellectual and popular circles, concerned secularization. With religious authorities and languages losing their privileged position, what role should Christianity play in political life? For Schmitt, apparent secularity was actually a product of secularism, the repression of the continuing import of Christianity. For some Christian theologians, secularity was a cause for lament, or defensiveness. For others, it was a fact—God was dead in the contemporary world—that required Christians to speak in new ways, for example discarding antiquated doctrines and adopting secular, modern ways of expressing themselves.

The new political theologians accepted that the problem of secularization was pressing but portrayed it as an opportunity. Earlier, when Christian ideas and practices circulated more broadly, it was easier for those ideas and practices to be contaminated by their proximity to worldly power. With Christianity marginalized, it is easier to achieve clarity on the essentials of Christian faith. In other words, when Christianity mixes broadly with cultural and political realms, it becomes difficult to distinguish faith from idolatry; secularization involves the withering away of idols. Relatedly, secularization as an aspect of the social processes of modernization orients us toward the future.[19] It seems as if things are getting better, problems are being solved, and tomorrow will be better than yesterday. This is a mixed blessing. It can lead us to believe that human effort and rationality are sufficient to control the world and eliminate evil. On the other hand, it orients us to an important truth of Christianity: that hope is essential to Christianity, that God is essentially about the future. In the face of secularization, Christian theologians must refine the orientation toward the future to be found in the world, helping women and men distinguish hope from optimism, memory from nostalgia.

While Peterson responded to Schmitt by opposing a Triune God to a singular God, the new political theologians initially responded to Schmitt through an alternative account of time. The secular state attempted to concentrate in itself absolute control, and this extended not only to space but also to time, not only to territory but also to the past, present, and future. History is narrated by the state, molded to support the self-image of the state, and the future is to be determined by the state as it pursues projects steadily, rationally, continually improving upon itself. The new political theologians point out that this is not how Christians believe time works; indeed, it is idolatrous. Human time is subordinate to God's time; every attempt to collapse the difference between the two is an attempt to put humans in a place where only God ought to be. To demonstrate a commitment to Christian temporality, a sense of the past and future illegible from a secular perspective, is necessarily political, necessarily in opposition to the powers that be.

The Christian theological landscape the new political theologians entered in Germany promised to speak politically but did not deliver.[20] Theological liberalism saw evidence of God's work in the historical progress of humanity and commended Christians to participate in that forward motion. But such views, aligned with the middle class, were discredited by two world wars. Karl Barth famously responded to the first of those wars, and the theological liberalism he saw authorizing it, by developing a theology that emphasized God's existence as wholly other. This made Barth well positioned to condemn the National Socialists' efforts at directing Christian churches to support state ideology, culminating famously in the Barmen Declaration in 1934. Barth and fellow neo-orthodox theologians had powerful resources to say what Christians *ought not* to do politically, but they struggled to articulate a positive account of interventions Christians *ought* to make in politics. If God is wholly other, what criteria can be used to authorize this or that stance on an issue of justice today?

To move beyond this impasse, the new political theologians turned to Jewish and Marxist sources. One dimension of this retrieval was a turn to the Hebrew Bible, particularly to the promises and laments found there, and to the rich affective life of God suggested in those texts. Another dimension of this retrieval was a turn to Frankfurt School critical theory, specifically the thought of Walter Benjamin, Theodor Adorno, and Ernst Bloch. In these thinkers, the new political theologians found a suspicion of modernity's progress narratives that they fully shared, and they found sophisticated intellectual models for diagnosing the subtle ways in which such progress narratives make themselves seem natural and pervade our social worlds. But they also found an appreciation for theological temporality. Benjamin is fully committed to the reality of the messianic, interrupting secular history. Nevertheless, the more we work the negative, the more we critique the ideologies (or idolatries) that have a hold on us, the more receptive we will be to the interruptions of the messianic. Bloch makes another version of this argument, drawing explicitly on religious sources alongside the Marxist tradition. He charges that the more ideologies are challenged, the more we discern a basic, underlying human orientation toward the future.

For the new political theologians, the resurrection of Jesus Christ grounded the messianic orientation of Frankfurt School critical theory in historical specificity. While Benjamin, Adorno, and Bloch allow for a first step beyond neo-orthodoxy, adding a sense of interruption or future-orientation to the essentially negative implications of God as wholly other, reading the New Testament together with the Hebrew Bible narrative of messianic promise allows for a fulsome assurance that the negative moment will not have the last word. In the new political theologians' account, the New Testament is a story of the powers that be, specifically the Roman Empire, trying to quash the promise of redemption, specifically, God incarnated in a Jew. Just when it seems as though the powers that be have triumphed, putting Jesus to death, God reassures that it is God who has the final word, in the resurrection. Today, we can expect the powers that be, the ideological forces that accompany modernity, capitalism, empire, and much else, to try to crush us, to try to kill us, but we can be assured that God promises resurrection. Yet we have to recognize the crushing power of ideologies in order to be properly oriented toward the promise of resurrection. This is where bourgeois, liberal Christianity goes wrong. It does not recognize that the forces of the world are doing their best to crush us, so it necessarily misunderstands resurrection—and so misunderstands Christianity itself. Similarly, from the perspective of the new political theologians neo-orthodox theology appreciates the crucifixion but not the resurrection. We need to appreciate how the forces of the world render God illegible, but then we also need to be committed to the hope that God will be made legible in the world in God's own time.

These ideas were formulated in Moltmann's *Theology of Hope*, and that book was translated into English in 1967, attracting wide attention from an American audience. In 1966 the cover of *Time* magazine had asked if God was dead; two years later, the American media had found Moltmann leading a chorus of Christians answering decisively in the negative. "'God is Dead' Doctrine Losing Ground to 'Theology of Hope'," a front-page *New York Times* article proclaimed in an article that mentions Moltmann, Metz, Wolfhart Pannenberg, and Gerhard Sauter, but conspicuously omits Sölle.[21] This marked a high point in the public exposure of political theology, and its US reception was bolstered by Moltmann's lecture tour of the States in 1967–1968. But the views of the new political theologians were still developing, with the three protagonists pushing in different directions.

One of the criticisms faced by the early emphasis on hope was that it now focused too much on the resurrection, too little on the crucifixion. Moltmann sought to right this by taking seriously Jewish writers' reflections on the "pathos" of God. While it is common in the Christian tradition to identify God with love, a human emotion, Moltmann explored what it would mean to say that God suffers. This runs against a Greek-influenced philosophical-theological tradition that views God as incapable of suffering because of God's nature, but Polish-American Jewish thinker Abraham Joshua Heschel had suggested Israel's disobedience in the Hebrew Bible ought to properly be understood as causing God to suffer. Moltmann suggests that this allows us to take literally Elie Wiesel's observation, in his Holocaust memoir *Night*, that God is "hanging there on the gallows."[22] God is with those who suffer, and God suffers with them. This, Moltmann suggests, is the essential message of the New Testament, and of Christianity itself. Now Schmittean political theology is fully reversed. Instead of God's reign modeling the political sovereign's reign, it is now in the lowest places, in the gallows, among the victims of political regimes and ideologies, where God is to be found.

Moltmann's *The Crucified God* was published in 1972, and the next year Dorothee Sölle responded forcefully with her book *Suffering*. She opens with a vivid portrait of an acquaintance enduring an abusive marriage, harnessing readers' intuition that saying the woman ought to stay in this marriage, the "ought" of Christian piety, rejoicing in her suffering, is to endorse masochism. Then Sölle pivots to Moltmann: for him, God suffers and loves in Christ, but God as father is also the author of this suffering. Sölle opines that Moltmann "is fascinated by his God's brutality," with a sadomasochistic dynamic seemingly in play.[23] Sölle goes further, comparing Moltmann's theological argument with a speech by Nazi leader Heinrich Himmler where he commends SS leaders' ability to organize hundreds of corpses while still remaining "decent men." Moltmann may not be a Nazi, Sölle qualifies, but his style of theology "does school people in thought patterns that regard sadistic behavior as normal."[24]

Metz also held back from Moltmann's turn to divine suffering, though in less dramatic fashion than Sölle. Drawing on Rahner, he argues that speaking of the suffering God contributes to the "aestheticization of all suffering."[25] In doing so, the true horror of human suffering is concealed; it is stabilized, so to speak, when we think God shares in it. Suffering is so awful because it entails a sense of weakness, aloneness, and lovelessness. To imagine suffering without the risk of its meaninglessness is not to imagine suffering at all. This suspicion may be seen as part of Metz's wholehearted embrace of the negative, of ideology critique. Where Moltmann will go on to align himself with the politics of the European bourgeoisie, embracing human rights and the idioms of social democracy, Metz worries deeply about how all such aspirations are contaminated by the ideology of the wealthy, powerful, and white. The only place to turn, beyond the project of critique, is social praxis, which is Christian praxis. Praxis, according to Metz, includes a "pathic structure," it includes mourning, joyfulness, and solidarity, all forms of affect unauthorized by the powers that be in the world.[26] Rather than suffering always happening together with God, for Metz practices that mark suffering come from an affective palate that thwarts secular time. Naming suffering challenges worldly powers rather than participates in divine power.

In the late 1960s, Latin American liberation theologians, African American theologians, and others drew inspiration from German political theology, though sometimes the relationship between German academics and those in the global South was contentious. Moltmann and José Miguez Bonino critiqued each other, and the label "political theology" became toxic in some Latin American contexts, a sign of European intellectual imperialism.[27] In addition to vulgar Marxism, Moltmann worried that the focus on praxis and concrete historical projects distracted from the sense that God is identified with a future outside of human time, and he worried that when praxis becomes the criterion of theological truth it becomes impossible to judge better and worse praxis. Bonino worried that that the abstractness of Moltmann's hope and the systematizing impulse so evident in his writing spoke neither to nor from conditions of marginalization. Sölle sided with the liberation theologians, distancing herself from the project of political theology. Metz embraced the importance of de-centering European thought, an imperative he saw as following from the Second Vatican Council, but continued to insist on the label "political theology."

Moltmann visited a conference of liberation theologians in Mexico City in 1977 and felt attacked by those he felt were ideologues cut from the same cloth as East German apparatchiks. Finding himself labeled a European bourgeois, the precise identity he had spent his career attacking, he effectively conceded, deciding to turn his energy to more systematic rather than practical questions.[28] Despite these tensions with liberation theologians, the American-fueled dictatorships of Latin America attracted particular interest and provided inspiration for the new political theologians, including Moltmann. These issues were brought home to the German theological academy when Ernst Käsemann, a student of Bultmann and colleague of Moltmann at Tübingen, had a daughter abducted, tortured, and killed by the US-backed dictatorship in Argentina. Further, a translation of Moltmann's *The Crucified God* was found, bloodied, with the body of the assassinated theologian Ignacio Ellacuría in 1989.

These illustrate the salient political events for the new political theology. It was the political upheavals of the 1960s and 1970s, from the horrors of colonial violence in Vietnam to South African apartheid to the proliferation of nuclear weapons in Germany, rather than the Holocaust, that triggered theological innovation. Just as a story, now debunked, was once told about the Holocaust motivating the development of the international human rights regime, a story is told about the Holocaust standing at the origins of political theology.[29] Such a story merely reinforces the myth of the Holocaust's utter uniqueness and incommensurability, a myth that serves to justify the Israeli apartheid regime today, to diminish the moral horrors committed against indigenous, colonized, and enslaved people around the world, and, worst of all, to mystify the tragic suffering of those six million Jews who died in the camps. The new political theology was in fact motivated by the need to respond theologically to Césaire's insight: Hitler was doing in Europe what has been and will be done to black and brown people around the world, and a Hitler resides in each European bourgeois.

NOTES

1. *Discourse on Colonialism* (New York: Monthly Review Press, 2000), 36.
2. On this ambivalence in secular German culture, see Hans Kundnani, *Utopia or Auschwitz? Germany's 1968 Generation and the Holocaust* (New York: Columbia University Press, 2009).
3. Jürgen Moltmann, *A Broad Place: An Autobiography* (Minneapolis, MN: Fortress, 2008).
4. Ibid., 17.
5. Ibid., 20.
6. The conference proceedings were published as *The Future of Hope: Theology as Eschatology*, ed. Frederick Herzog (New York: Herder and Herder, 1970); Moltmann's collection of essays, delivered as lectures while in the United States, was published as *Religion, Revolution, and the Future* (New York: Scribner, 1969).
7. Moltmann, *A Broad Place*, 159.
8. Dorothee Sölle, *Against the Wind: Memoir of a Radical Christian* (Minneapolis, MN: Fortress, 1999), 38.
9. Ibid., 30.
10. Ibid., 30.
11. Her 1971 book *Political Theology* (Minneapolis, MN: Fortress, 1974) is subtitled (in the original, German edition) *Discussion with Rudolf Bultmann*, and it systematically re-interprets Bultmann's themes from the standpoint of the framework of the new political theology that she shared with Metz and Moltmann.
12. Johann Baptist Metz, "Productive Noncontemporaneity" in *Observations on "The Spiritual Situation of the Age,"* ed. Jürgen Habermas (Cambridge, MA: MIT Press, 1984), 171.
13. *How I Have Changed*, ed. Jürgen Moltmann (Harrisburg, PA: Trinity Press International, 1997), 31.
14. See Janice A. Thompson, "Renewing the Church as a Community of Hope: The German Catholic Church Confronts the *Shoah*," *Journal of Ecumenical Studies* 51:3 (Summer 2016), 337–364. Joseph Ratzinger, also a professor at Münster, who had recommended Metz's appointment there, initially participated in the discussions toward "Our Hope" as well, but moved away from the new political theology, worrying that it veered too close to Marxism. See Ratzinger's reflections on political theology in his *Milestones: Memoirs, 1927–1977* (San Francisco: Ignatius Press, 1998), 135–137.

15. Johann Baptist Metz, *A Passion for God: The Mystical-Political Dimension of Christianity* (New York: Paulist Press, 1998), 3.
16. *Political Theology: Four Chapters on the Concept of Sovereignty* (Cambridge, MA: MIT Press, 1985).
17. Erik Peterson, "Monotheism as a Political Problem" in *Theological Tractates*, ed. Michael J. Hollerich (Stanford, CA: Stanford University Press, 2011), 68–105.
18. Schmitt responded to Peterson, and also discussed Metz and Moltmann, in *Political Theology II: The Myth of the Closure of any Political Theology* (Cambridge: Polity, 2008).
19. On this point see also Edward Schillebeeckx, *God, the Future of Man* (London: Bloomsbury, 2014 [1968]).
20. For useful background see Werner G. Jeanrond, "From Resistance to Liberation Theology: German Theologians and the Non/Resistance to the National Socialist Regime," *Journal of Modern History* 64 (December 1992), S187–S203.
21. Edward B. Fiske in *The New York Times* (March 24, 1968), 1, 75. Moltmann suggests that the German media attention he received was prompted by the American media (*A Broad Place*, 99).
22. Jürgen Moltmann, *The Crucified God: The Cross of Christ as the Foundation and Criticism of Christian Theology* (New York: Harper & Row, 1974), 274.
23. Dorothee Soelle, *Suffering* (Philadelphia: Fortress, 1973), 27.
24. Ibid., 28.
25. Metz, *Passion for God*, 119. See also Metz, "Suffering Unto God," *Critical Inquiry* 20:4 (Summer 1994), 611–622.
26. Johann Baptist Metz, *Faith in History and Society: Toward a Practical Fundamental Theology* (New York: Crossroad, 2007), 67.
27. Moltmann, "An Open Letter to José Miguez Bonino," *Christianity and Crisis* (March 29, 1976), 57, 59–60; Bonino, *Doing Theology in a Revolutionary Situation* (Philadelphia: Fortress, 1975), Chapter 7; Bonino, "Reading Jürgen Moltmann from Latin America," *Asbury Theological Journal* 55:1 (Spring 2000), 105–114; Moltmann, *Experiences in Theology: Ways and Forms of Christian Theology* (Minneapolis: Fortress Press, 2000), Part III.
28. Moltmann, *A Broad Place*, 231. In Moltmann's autobiography, an unrelenting narrative of triumphs, he is pleased to discover that the Latin American liberation theologians love his new, systematic work, finding political applications for it in their context.
29. On human rights see Samuel Moyn, *The Last Utopia: Human Rights in History* (Cambridge, MA: Harvard University Press, 2010).

SELECT BIBLIOGRAPHY

Metz, Johann Baptist (1969), *Theology of the World*, New York: Herder and Herder.
Metz, Johann Baptist (1998), *A Passion for God: The Mystical-Political Dimension of Christianity*, New York: Paulist Press.
Metz, Johann Baptist (2007), *Faith in History and Society: Toward a Practical Fundamental Theology*, New York: Crossroad.
Moltmann, Jürgen (1967), *Theology of Hope: On the Ground and Implications of Christian Eschatology*, New York: Harper & Row.
Moltmann, Jürgen (1969), *Religion, Revolution, and the Future*, New York: Scribner.
Moltmann, Jürgen (1974), *The Crucified God: The Cross of Christ as the Foundation and Criticism of Christian Theology*, New York: Harper & Row.

Moltmann, Jürgen (1981), *The Trinity and the Kingdom: The Doctrine of God*, New York: Harper & Row.
Soelle, Dorothee (1967), *Christ the Representative: An Essay in Theology after the "Death of God"*, Philadelphia: Fortress Press.
Soelle, Dorothee (1973), *Suffering*, Philadelphia: Fortress Press.
Soelle, Dorothee (1974), *Political Theology*, Philadelphia: Fortress Press.
Soelle, Dorothee (2001), *The Silent Cry: Mysticism and Resistance*, Minneapolis, MN: Fortress Press.

CHAPTER THREE

Political Theology and the Theologies of Liberation

RUBÉN ROSARIO RODRÍGUEZ

INTRODUCTION

Without question, liberation theology is one of the most significant and influential theological movements of the last fifty years. Its impact has altered the canon of theological education in universities and seminaries,[1] changed the language of authoritative ecclesial statements,[2] and even crossed over into popular culture.[3] Yet, despite its global reach, it is difficult to pinpoint a single event as the genesis—or any one region as the birthplace—of liberation theology. One recurrent narrative is that liberation theology began in Latin America with similar developments throughout the Third World wherever the realities of absolute poverty[4] have sharply focused Christian theological reflection on the experiences of oppression, exploitation, and marginalization that give rise to poverty on such a large scale. However, this ignores the independent yet conceptually similar articulation of a black theology of liberation by James H. Cone in the First World context of white supremacy in the United States.[5] Still, the 1968 meeting of the Latin American Episcopal Council (CELAM) in Medellín, Colombia, stands as the first magisterial statements employing the language and analysis of liberation theology.[6] This narrative soon unravels for the simple reason that liberation theology did not proceed from official ecclesial statements, nor originate within academic theology, but existed as an organic, haphazard, and decentralized movement in a variety of different local contexts through primarily lay-led Christian base communities.[7] Not only were the seeds of liberation theology planted in the fertile soil of the ultimately doomed theology of revolution,[8] but the very concept of liberation within Latin America was being articulated in a variety of ways by both Catholic and Protestant thinkers.[9]

Nevertheless, many still view the Medellín council as the first concerted effort by the Latin American bishops to move the church toward a more progressive stance immediately following the epochal changes wrought by the Second Vatican Council (1962–65). The central themes of Medellín were the Latin American reality of absolute poverty, the struggle for peace and justice under regimes of institutionalized violence, and a renewed embracing of the political dimension of faith. Deeply influenced by the 1963 encyclical statement, *Pacem in terris* ("Peace on Earth"), from Pope John XXIII, the statements proceeding from Vatican II, and the 1967 encyclical statement, *Populorum progressio* ("On the development of peoples"), from Pope Paul VI, the documents from the second meeting of the Latin American Episcopal Council in 1968 serve as the first magisterial articulation of the new theology of liberation. Among the pastoral conclusions articulated by the bishops in the final documents was a commitment to work together to create conditions that make life "more human" for all by defending "the rights of the poor and oppressed according to the gospel commandment, urging our governments and upper classes to eliminate anything which might destroy social peace: injustice, inertia, venality, insensibility."[10] Consequently, in introducing the impact and scope of Latin American liberation theology on the broader theological conversation, and especially in light of the renewed interest in political theology after Auschwitz, it makes sense to narrow the discussion to the contributions of Catholic figures like Gustavo Gutiérrez (1928–), widely considered the "father" of liberation theology, while acknowledging the contributions of other voices. Furthermore, it will be argued that the greatest impact made by liberation theology came not from a theologian, but from a priest—Archbishop Óscar Romero of El Salvador—whose three years as archbishop not only elevated liberation theology onto the world stage, but whose four pastoral letters continue to serve as a roadmap for reimagining the church in a new key, no longer a church *for* the poor, but now a church *of* the poor.

SOME THEOLOGICAL THEMES AND HIGHLIGHTS

Gary Dorrien has opined that, "Political theology needs a better genealogy than the Carl Schmitt story it usually tells," while characterizing the New Political Theology (Moltmann, Metz, Sölle) as a burgeoning cottage industry attempting to reverse Schmitt's thesis that the concept of divine sovereignty has been replaced by "the sovereignty of the modern state."[11] Contained in Schmitt's reductionist, and ultimately fascist, theology is an unappealing conception of God (and state) as absolute tyrant: "There always exists the same inexplicable identity: lawgiver, executive power, police, pardoner, welfare institution."[12] Liberation theology, while born from the same troubled waters as the European political theologies, sought to articulate its own distinct genealogy on the assumption that the Christian tradition is broader and deeper, offering far richer resources than the "soulless subjectivity of Enlightenment rationality" for combating the "social ravages of unfettered . . . capitalism."[13] Gustavo Gutiérrez, upon returning from "The Theological Grand Tour" that included study in Belgium, France, and Rome—at the time common wisdom in Latin America viewed a European education as necessary for the formation of promising young candidates for ordination—found even the best of the *nouvelle théologie* ultimately lacking. To that end, he began to articulate an indigenous theology better suited to address the pastoral needs and social realities of the church in Latin America.

The introduction to the original edition of *Teología de la liberación* (1971)/*A Theology of Liberation* (1973) begins with this simple statement of intent: "This book is an attempt at reflection, based on the gospel and the experiences of men and women committed to the process of liberation in the oppressed and exploited land of Latin America."[14] More telling of the truly radical departure Gutiérrez was attempting, however, is his choice of epigraph at the beginning of the book, a passage from the novel *Todas las sangres* ("All the Bloods," 1964) by Peruvian novelist, poet, and anthropologist José María Arguedas (1911–1969).[15] Arguedas, the son of a circuit judge from the white Spanish ruling class, was raised by mestizo and Quecha Indian servants in his father's household, so he not only became fluent in Quecha, but from an early age was aware of the plight of the indigenous and mestizo populations in the rigidly stratified culture of Peru.

In this scene from the novel, a European (white) priest is preparing for mass with the aid of his mestizo church organist and sexton, while the priest complains about the folk religion and popular devotions of the Quecha Indians: "[They] repeat the words like parrots, without understanding; [they are] hardly not Christian. You are mestizo, organist, and you respond in Latin. The mass should have greater meaning for you." To which the sexton replies, "Dear father, you do not understand the soul of the Indians. La Gertrudis [St. Gertrude, an early devotee of the Sacred Heart of Jesus who was never formally canonized by the Church, became a popular devotion among the Quecha], without knowing [the Christian] God, is from God . . . She comforts the downtrodden, challenges the comfortable; she removes from the blood any and all impurities." After more back and forth conversation, during which it becomes obvious the mestizo sympathizes with the popular devotions of the Quechas, he proclaims, "The God of the masters is not the same [as Gertrudis]; he causes suffering without comfort." And the priest responds, "You are not a true Christian either. All those years as sexton of the church and still you think like a witch." The priest dismisses the religion of his indigenous parishioners as primitive idol worship, and offers in its stead a banal statement about Catholic sacramentality: "God is everywhere, God is everywhere . . ." Heartbroken about the exploitation of the poor in the silver mines, and the devastation of the land ("La Esmeralda") caused by mining, the sexton thinks to himself: "Was God in the hearts of those who beat and broke the innocent teacher Bellido? Is God in the bodies of the engineers that are killing 'La Esmeralda'? Is God in the overseer who stole the cornfields from their [original] owners, where the Virgin and her Son once played during the harvest?" To which the sexton can only shake his head as if to say, "No."

Arguedas and Gutiérrez met in 1968, becoming friends, and sharing a brief correspondence before the troubled author took his own life. Though from disparate backgrounds—Gutiérrez a mestizo priest born and raised in a poor barrio in Lima, Arguedas an agnostic intellectual of pure Spanish descent and the son of a judge—the two men came together on their commitment "to understand the poor and give voice to the voiceless."[16] This powerful scene from Arguedas's novel encapsulates the break liberation theology wanted to make with the theology of the colonizers. The sin under examination is idolatry, but the false idols in question belong to the Spanish landowners and the establishment church that had removed itself from the suffering of the poor, *not* the humble devotion of the mestizos and Quecha. As Gutiérrez notes, "I believe that José María was right . . . The God of the oppressors, of those who pillage and kill people, is not the God of the poor, not the same God at all."[17] Thus, liberation theology represents a paradigm shift in theology—every bit as radical as Karl Barth's break with Protestant liberalism on the publication of the second edition of his *Epistle to the Romans* (1922)— with Bartolomé de Las Casas (1474–1566), the Dominican priest who defended the indigenous people of the Americas from the ravages of the Spanish conquistadores, serving as both inspiration and guiding light.[18] From this perspective, the "dominant" theology of the church is implicated in the conquest, colonization, and exploitation of the indigenous and mestizo peoples of Latin America, and the new "liberation" theology seeks a way of becoming "church" that does not ignore the majority of its flock, the poor and disenfranchised. In the words of the Medellín council: "Peace is, above all, a work of justice . . . Where this social peace does not exist there will we find social, political, economic, and cultural inequalities, there will we find the rejection of the peace of the Lord, and a rejection of the Lord himself."[19]

In the 1960s the majority of Christians in Latin America were, for the most part, poor—struggling for basic subsistence—while Christians in the First World, even those considered "poor," had access to the basic necessities for sustaining life. The church in

Latin America operated under models developed in a First World context where churches, in general, were well established, financially endowed, resistant to change, and ministered to the needs of the middle and upper classes. Consequently, the church in Latin America became so integrated into the dominant socioeconomic system it rarely took stands against its own financial interests except when the rights of the church were threatened (the Catholic Church is one of the largest, if not the largest, nongovernmental landowner in Latin America).[20] This establishment church "moves within the world of the Enlightenment and is preoccupied with harmonizing faith and reason, proving the rationality of religious experience, and establishing rational foundations for their theological affirmations."[21] By contrast, the prophetic urgency among the poor churchgoers of Latin America reflects their daily struggle for survival, so that the need to articulate a theology of liberation is in fact—to paraphrase Gustavo Gutiérrez—the oldest, most persistent challenge to the ecumenical church: *How to tell the wretched of this world that God loves them.*

The church is confronted with an existential decision, and liberation theology insists it must choose sides. Though the phrase "preferential option for the poor" was not officially endorsed by any magisterial document until the third Latin American Episcopal Council, held in Puebla, Mexico in 1979, Gutiérrez is quick to point out that Medellín contained in its final documents a call for the church to give "preference to the poorest and most needy sectors and to those segregated for any cause whatsoever."[22] Medellín "made clear that poverty expresses solidarity with the oppressed and a protest against oppression," so much so that instead of "talking about the Church of the poor, we must be a poor Church."[23] Accordingly, the Latin America Church had to confront the historical reality of a deeply divided church in which fellow Christians were "among the oppressed and persecuted and others among the oppressors and persecutors, some among the tortured and others among the torturers or those who condone torture. This gives rise to a serious and radical confrontation between Christians who suffer from injustice and exploitation and those who benefit from the established order."[24] The consequent scandal breaches the very union in Christ that makes *ecclesia* ("assembly, gathering") possible in the first place: "Participation in the Eucharist, for example, as it is celebrated today, appears to many to be an action which ... *becomes an exercise in make-believe.*"[25] Such strong words are shocking coming from Gutiérrez, a Catholic priest guided by the communion ecclesiology articulated at Vatican II who views the sacrament as a universal invitation, "the efficacious revelation of the call to communion with God and to the unity of all humankind."[26] Yet, when confronted by the historical realities in Latin America, he is driven to conclude, "Without a real commitment against exploitation and alienation and for a society of solidarity and justice, the Eucharistic celebration is *an empty action*, lacking any genuine endorsement by those who participate in it."[27] Thus, the church has no choice but to divest itself from the centers of political and economic power and put its social weight behind the social transformation of Latin America on the side of the poor and oppressed. Inevitably, "The groups that control economic and political power will not forgive the Church for this."[28]

Gutiérrez's position is summarized as a clear choice *for* the poor over against the oppressors and exploiters of the poor, in effect making the judgment that those who unrepentantly continue to profit from this exploitation and keep the poor trapped in the certain death that is poverty are *not* genuine followers of Christ. For the church "must make the prophetic *denunciation* of every dehumanizing situation, which is contrary to fellowship, justice, and liberty. At the same time it must criticize every sacralization of oppressive structures to which the Church itself might have contributed. Its denunciation must be public, for its position in Latin American society is public."[29] The radical disjunction between the good news of salvation and the crushing political realities "in which the vast Latin American majorities are dispossessed and therefore compelled to live as strangers in their own land" has created a situation in which even "the men and women who try to side with the dispossessed and bear witness to God in Latin America must accept the bitter fact that they will be inevitably suspect."[30] Nevertheless, liberation theology calls the church to risk suspicion from the poor and oppressed and retribution from the rich and powerful, for "only a radical break from the status quo, that is, a profound transformation of the private property system, access to power of the exploited class, and a social revolution that would break this dependence would allow for the change to a new society."[31] In making a preferential option for the poor it is "to the oppressed that the Church should address itself and not so much to the oppressors; furthermore, this action will give true meaning to the Church's witness to poverty."[32] In the end, this non-neutral, activist commitment by the church generates a new spirituality of liberation grounded in "the blood-stained experience of the early Christian community," but characterized by a new generation of martyrs "who have devoted their lives, to the point of suffering death, in order to bear witness to the preference of the poor in the Latin American world and to the preferential love that God has for them."[33]

Not surprisingly, in writing the introduction to the revised fifteenth anniversary edition of *A Theology of Liberation*, Gutiérrez reflected on the cultural impact of liberation theology and came to focus on the assassination of Archbishop Óscar Romero in 1980 as a major turning point for the movement:

> This great bishop risked his life in his Sunday homilies . . . and in interventions that responded to First World pressures by continually calling for a peace founded on justice. He received several death threats . . . A month before his own death he said with reference to those in power in his country: "Let them not use violence to silence those of us who are trying to bring about a just distribution of power and wealth in our country." Calmly and courageously he continued: "I speak in the first person because this week I received a warning that I am on the list of those to be eliminated next week. But it is certain no one can kill the voice of justice."
>
> He died—they killed him—for bearing witness to the God of life and to his predilection for the poor and oppressed. It was because he believed in this God that he uttered an anguished, demanding cry to the Salvadoran army: "In the name of God and of this suffering people whose wailing mounts daily to heaven, I ask and beseech you, I order you: stop the repression!" The next evening his blood sealed the covenant he had made with God, with his people, and with his church.[34]

Romero's funeral drew a quarter of a million people to the capital of El Salvador, filling the cathedral and crowding the plaza, with Gutiérrez among those in attendance. As people were leaving the cathedral after Mass, members of the National Guard began firing on the crowd in the plaza, killing numerous civilians, and creating a panic that almost crushed the diminutive Fr. Gutiérrez, who "made it safely into the cathedral and administered the last rites of the church to a woman who had been shot and was bleeding to death."[35] Romero's death exemplified the political repression so commonplace in Latin America, but it brought the crisis into the international spotlight, causing Gutiérrez to comment (in an interview with Archbishop Romero's biographer, James Brockman, S.J.) that: "The most important event since the Puebla conference was the assassination of

Archbishop Óscar Romero of San Salvador. I think that his martyrdom . . . [illumines] something [that] has been happening in Latin America that some people refuse to recognize: the fact that many Christians are giving their lives, witnessing unto death to the gospel, to the God of love and the God of the poor."[36]

FROM LIBERATION TO MARTYRDOM?

Following the publication of Gutiérrez's seminal *A Theology of Liberation*, liberation theology experienced an eight-year period of expansion and growth. One of the most significant events for the global expansion of the liberation theology movement was the foundation of the Ecumenical Association of Third World Theologians (EATWOT) in 1976, bringing together theologians from Asia, Africa, and Latin America, as well as silenced and marginalized voices from Europe and North America, to reflect together on the challenges of poverty and oppression. In many ways, however, 1979 proved the high point for Latin American liberation theology with the convening of the Third General Conference of the Latin American Episcopate in Puebla de Los Angeles, Mexico.[37] Pope John Paul II, in his first papal visit, convened the Puebla conference on January 28, 1979, and in March 1979 approved its final documents, which employ the language of liberation and God's preferential option for the poor while providing a critical analysis of liberation theology under four major rubrics: (1) the church's commitment to undertake scientific analysis of social, economic, and political realities in Latin America; (2) the church's mission defined as liberative evangelization; (3) the church's commitment to a concrete program of liberation for the construction of a just society; and (4) doctrinal reflection on the church's preferential option for the poor. The bishops' final statement acknowledged the movement's progress and reaffirmed the church's commitment to historical liberation, even if tempered with some degree of compromise: "With its preferential but not exclusive love for the poor, the church present in Medellín was a summons to hope for more Christian and humane goals . . . This Third Episcopal Conference in Puebla wishes to keep this summons alive and to open up new horizons of hope."[38]

Nevertheless, the assassination of Archbishop Romero in March 1980, followed soon thereafter by the rape and murder of two Maryknoll Sisters, Maura Clarke, and Ita Ford, Ursuline Sister Dorothy Kazel, and lay missionary Jean Donovan by five members of the Salvadoran National Guard also marked a low point for the cause of liberation in Latin America. After three years of persistent, nonviolent resistance against the right-wing government of El Salvador that was running a covert assassination campaign against its political opponents, Romero pleaded with government forces from the pulpit. The day after commanding Christian soldiers serving in the Salvadoran Army to disobey orders and stop the repression of innocent Salvadorans, Romero was assassinated while celebrating mass by an off-duty army marksman acting under orders from Major Roberto D'Aubuisson, the acknowledged leader of the right-wing death squads that tortured and killed tens of thousands of civilians before and during the Salvadoran Civil War (1979–1992). Presciently, during Romero's last homily, mere moments before the assassin's bullet took his life, he remarked, "those who out of love for Christ give themselves to the service of others will live, like the grain of wheat that dies, but only apparently. If it did not die, it would remain alone. The harvest comes about because it dies, allowing itself to be sacrificed in the earth and destroyed. Only by undoing itself does it produce the harvest."[39] Immediately after his death, many faithful began visiting his grave, bringing prayers and supplications to their popular—though unofficial—saint: *San Romero the los*

Pobres ("St. Romero of the Poor"). Though the road to canonization has been strewn with political controversy and bureaucratic stalling, under the urging of Pope Francis I, the first Latin American pope and a long-time supporter of liberation theology, Romero was beatified on May 23, 2015, and canonized on October 14, 2018.[40]

The Latin American experience of persecution and martyrdom does not romanticize nor encourage martyrdom. When day-to-day survival is not taken for granted because one lacks adequate food, water, and shelter to live through another day, death is never good, never desired. As Gutiérrez reminds us, real poverty is evil, "something that God does not want,"[41] so given that material poverty leads to death, the church affirms death as contrary to the will of God who is the God of life. Still, Archbishop Romero often extolled the virtues of martyrdom from the pulpit, reminding us that "Christ invites us not to fear persecution because, believe me, brothers [and sisters], the one who is committed to the poor has to face the same fate as the poor. In El Salvador we know what it means to share the same fate as the poor: to be among the disappeared, tortured, imprisoned, to turn up as corpses."[42] The persecuted church of El Salvador became a martyr church, as can be gleaned from Romero's weekly descriptions of the atrocities endured by his flock: "It is my duty to collect the mutilated bodies, corpses, and everything else left behind by the persecution of the Church."[43] So their archbishop reminded them that, "Persecution is necessary for the Church. Do you know why? Because truth is always persecuted."[44] Jon Sobrino, Jesuit priest, theologian, and one-time colleague of Archbishop Romero, reflecting on the political realities of Latin America in which the struggle for human liberation has produced so many martyrs, affirms Romero's assertion that liberation and martyrdom walk hand-in-hand while questioning whether the persecution has made a "virtue of necessity: 'Since there is no liberation, let us praise martyrdom.'"[45] This emphasis in Romero's sermons—preparing the persecuted church for martyrdom—or Ignacio Ellacuría's plea on behalf of the "crucified people" of the Third World,[46] does not entail "abandoning liberation in favor of martyrdom"; rather, it speaks to the interconnectedness of both realities "because liberation is weakened if it is separated from the reality of martyrdom, and the reverse is also true."[47]

According to Sobrino, liberation and martyrdom are so intertwined that the very mission and death of Christ cannot be understood in isolation from the martyred people. Romero declared himself a voice for the voiceless by drawing attention to the thousands of anonymous victims of governmental repression that "disappeared" or were murdered each and every week during his three years as archbishop.[48] For Romero, the struggle of the Salvadoran Church had to be interpreted Christologically: "Had Christ realized his incarnation today, in 1978, he would be a man thirty years old, a peasant [campesino] from Nazareth, looking like any one of the peasants from our surrounding cantons so that the Son of God would be in the flesh and we would not recognize him, he would so resemble us!"[49] By emphasizing an incarnational Christology Romero is claiming that Jesus Christ is alive in the persecuted Church of El Salvador, that he is daily arrested, beaten, and killed:

> I am not saying that we postpone the liberation of the people until the afterlife. I am saying that the risen Christ belongs to the present and is the font of liberation and human dignity in history . . . Christ is Salvadoran for the Salvadorans. Christ is risen, here in El Salvador, for us, to help us realize through the power of the Holy Spirit our proper nature, our proper history, our proper liberty, our proper dignity as Salvadoran people.[50]

The church is able to endure persecution because it participates in the mystical body of Christ, something more than a mere moral *imitatio Christi* but a true communion of saints, which is why Romero remained adamant throughout his active struggle against the forces of dehumanization, exploitation, and death that the only truly Christian option is nonviolence. Romero's clarity on the necessity of nonviolence originates with the Christ encountered in the gospels: "The only violence permissible in the Gospel is that which one allows to be done to oneself. When Christ allowed himself to be killed is the only legitimate violence: to let oneself be killed ... It is easy to kill, especially when one is armed, but how hard it is to allow oneself to be killed for the love of humanity."[51] The majority of El Salvador's progressive Catholics who took part in El Salvador's struggle for human rights and democratic freedoms in the 1970s and 1980s committed themselves to resisting their corrupt government through nonviolence: "they have done so to the end, to death, and without making use of violence."[52]

ROMERO'S PASTORAL LETTERS: GUIDEPOSTS FOR THE CHURCH

Óscar Romero's all too brief tenure as Archbishop of San Salvador will always be remembered for his courageous stance for social justice and eventual martyrdom, but this does not overshadow the fact that Romero was also one of the most remarkable and successful pastoral leaders in recent memory. Archbishop Romero lived in an era of growing violence in El Salvador, which despite his efforts at nonviolent conflict resolution ultimately escalated into an all-out civil war that lasted until 1992. In the 1970s El Salvador's executive branch was controlled by the military and, after two fraudulent elections in 1972 and 1976, institutionalized violence became the government's primary means of maintaining power against the proliferation of popular revolutionary movements. Faced with this volatile political reality, in which Christians on both sides of the political spectrum were advocating violence, Romero proposed justice, dialogue, increased democratization, and the redistribution of wealth as the guiding virtues of a national conversation he hoped would result in genuine social transformation.

Through the use of timely pastoral letters, prophetic sermons from the pulpit, acts of direct intervention, and through pioneering legal advocacy, Romero utilized the office of archbishop to bring the church's resources—not to mention international attention—to bear on the crisis in El Salvador. He left behind a legacy of compassionate humanitarian aid focused on preserving the basic dignity of the victims of unjust social structures, while acting creatively to positively transform those very structures. Perhaps the most unheralded aspect of Romero's ministry was his establishment of the archdiocesan Office of Legal Aid, "made up of lawyers, law students, and consultants who considered that the legal system should be at the service of the very poorest" who stayed at Romero's side, supporting his vision of "legal help for the very poor" until his death.[53] The work of the Office of Legal Aid not only provided immediate legal help to those most in need, it developed a system of documenting human rights violations that has become the norm in truth commissions and nongovernmental human rights organizations around the world.

Romero was experienced with human rights work and had oriented his pastoral priorities as archbishop toward greater social justice through the defense of human rights. Therefore, he instructed the staff and volunteers of the Office of Legal Aid to carefully document the cases of torture, extrajudicial killings, and politically motivated disappearances through all available legal channels, carefully formulating "public accusations that could not be denied by the government nor the official justice system, as supported above all by formal testimonies from victims and vigorous as well as scrupulous investigations. In every case the archbishop would urge us to treat accusations within a legal framework—even though it was quite partial—but this would point out how meager and ineffective these "remedies" actually were."[54] Unquestionably, the legal system along with most other aspects of the government of El Salvador were ideologically compromised and far from impartial, but Romero was not documenting the government's crimes because he expected justice from an unjust regime. Rather, Romero lived with the hope that this regime would some day fall, and was thinking ahead to the rebuilding that would take place after the restoration of democratic governance:

> For Oscar Romero it was a very concrete way to place the value of human rights as essential to a life of democracy. "When all this violence is over, I want the poor to have better legal services and be able to count on our companionship in their lack of justice," he would say to us when he led and accompanied us in carrying out our itineraries to draw more lawyers to serve the Church as well as the help of specialized offices, since the problems were not only related to human rights but also to a variety of legal conflicts.[55]

Archbishop Romero promoted human rights for all persons without discrimination, worked tirelessly for increased democratization yet never bound himself to any single political party or agenda—he was always willing to speak with all sides in the conflict—and acted concretely out of a deep commitment to Christian nonviolence to condemn "any strategy or method based on violence."[56] So while he pioneered human rights legal activism, he did so out of a deep Christian conviction that sought to embody the simple yet challenging message of the Beatitudes and the Sermon on the Mount. Consequently, for a fuller understanding of Óscar Romero's theological argument for involving the church in social justice struggles, it is best to concentrate on his four pastoral letters as Archbishop of San Salvador. For Romero, the church post-Vatican II needs to think deeply about the church and its mission *in relationship to the world*, guided in great part by *Gaudium et spes* ("Joy and Hope"), the Pastoral Constitution on the Church in the Modern World (1965), which exhorted "Christians, as citizens of two cities, to strive to discharge their earthly duties conscientiously and in response to the Gospel spirit."[57] In that spirit, Romero focused his pastoral letters on two general themes confronting the nation: (1) the role of the church in politics, and (2) the escalation of violence in Salvadoran society.

From the beginning, following his strong stance after the assassination of his friend Fr. Rutilio Grande, when the archbishop refused to attend the inauguration of the newly elected president, General Carlos Humberto Romero, then insisted all Salvadorans attend the *misa única* ("single mass") as an act of solidarity uniting all the parishes of the archdiocese, its people, and its priests, Romero was accused of meddling in politics and dragging the church along with him. To this Romero replied with carefully worded pastoral letters outlining the relationship of the church to the political realm by arguing that the church is not meddling in politics but carrying out its prophetic mission. Thus, from the pulpit during the *misa única*, Romero declared, "Whoever touches one of my priests, touches me," to great applause from the cathedral congregation.[58] As he affirmed in his first pastoral letter, "The Easter Church" (April 10, 1977), "The church cannot be defined simply in political or socioeconomic terms. But neither can it be defined from a point of view which would make it indifferent to the temporal problems of the world."⁵⁹ He defends this position by appealing to *Evangelii nuntiandi* ("Evangelization in the Modern World"), the 1975 encyclical by Pope Paul VI, which states, "when preaching liberation and associating herself with those who are working and suffering for it, the Church is certainly not willing to restrict her mission only to the religious field and dissociate herself from man's temporal problems."⁶⁰ Acknowledging that the Church's mission is not political, Romero appeals to *Gaudium et spes* in order to argue that the Church's prophetic mission (rooted in God's act of historical liberation as narrated in the Exodus) nonetheless impacts the political realm:

> Christ, to be sure, gave His Church no proper mission in the political, economic or social order. The purpose which He set before her is a religious one. But out of this religious mission itself come a function, a light and an energy which can serve to structure and consolidate the human community according to the divine law. As a matter of fact, when circumstances of time and place produce the need, she can and indeed should initiate activities on behalf of all men, especially those designed for the needy, such as the works of mercy and similar undertakings.⁶¹

In other words, in carrying out the church's explicitly theological mission the church will have to engage the temporal political realm since "faith and politics ought to be united in a Christian who has a political vocation, but they are not to be identified . . . Faith ought to inspire political action but not be mistaken for it."⁶²

Sadly, Romero's fellow bishops wrote to Rome asking that he be removed as archbishop, necessitating he travel to Rome several times in order to defend himself, but he wisely and consistently acted under the guidance of official church doctrine as evidenced by his four pastoral letters. At a time when political tensions were on the rise in El Salvador, exacerbated by the proliferation of popular revolutionary movements organizing farmers, laborers, and students against the repressive government, Archbishop Romero published his third pastoral letter, "The Church and Popular Political Organizations" (with help from Jesuit theologian Jon Sobrino) on August 6, 1978, with a straightforward intent: "In this pastoral letter we . . . [want] to restate the right to organize and to denounce the violation of that right in our country."⁶³

What is an authentic Christian response to the anti-democratic repression by the state? In light of Catholic social teaching, what is the church's relationship to popular political movements advocating for more democratic freedoms for the majority of Salvadorans? As is always the case with Monseñor Romero, he answers with moral clarity, pastoral compassion, and unquestioned integrity: "It is here, faced with the absence of this real freedom, that we have to denounce this violation of this human right of association proclaimed by our Constitution and by an international declaration of human rights accepted by our country."⁶⁴ He then identifies three types of abuses perpetrated by the current regime: (1) discrimination among citizens, granting some the right of association while denying it to others; (2) these elite groups make up a minority of the population yet are granted more freedoms than the majority; and (3) the state has sown disorder and fostered conflict between different *campesino* groups in order to prevent them from uniting for social change. Throughout his pastoral letters, Romero never loses sight of the church's distinctive evangelical mission:

> However, on accepting the word of God, Christians find that it is a living word that brings with it awareness and demands. That is to say, it makes them aware of what sin

and grace are, and of what must be resisted and what must be built up on earth. It is a word that demands of our consciences and of our lives not only that we judge the world by the criteria of the kingdom of God, but that we act accordingly. It is a word that we must not only hear but put into practice.[65]

Theologically, Romero used his letters to name the false idols plaguing Salvadoran society—materialist greed, national security, and anti-democratic political organizations—and critiqued any group or agent who impeded democratic reforms that could bring about positive social change. In practical terms this meant the archbishop was making political enemies on both the right and the left, since not only were the right-wing government and its capitalist supporters responsible for the repression and dehumanization of the Salvadoran people, equally to blame were those political movements on the left that claimed to speak for the people yet refused to abandon violence in order to bring about a genuine national dialogue. Romero insisted that an "essential element of this dialogue is that an end be put to all kinds of violence," for "it is absurd to talk about dialogue" until all sides set aside political violence.[66]

CONCLUSION

Though Romero never advocated violence, he acknowledged the right of people to defend themselves in situations of political repression, when the state—ideally the guarantor of the people's freedoms—becomes the agent of tyranny and injustice. Therefore, in his fourth pastoral letter, Romero acknowledges the right of self-defense, but only under very unique circumstances, after "every other possible peaceful means has been tried," the Christian tradition allows for a just war in defense of others, insurrectional violence in the case of "prolonged tyranny," and a war of self-defense in response to unjust aggression.[67] However, to recognize the right of oppressed peoples to defend themselves is a far cry from arguing that political violence is a legitimate tool of social change. Though appealing to just war theory, Archbishop Romero is not trying to legitimate Christian political violence. Rather, he is advocating for the right of revolutionary political movements to take on the role of guardian of the people's interests in order to represent them in peaceful negotiations, but only *when* the government has become the people's persecutor. In other words, it is the breakdown of just governance that gives birth to violent revolutionary movements:

> The most reasonable and effective thing for a government to do, therefore, is to use its moral and coercive force not to defend the structural violence of an unjust order, but to guarantee a truly democratic state, one that defends the fundamental rights of all its citizens, based on a just economic order. Only in this way will it be possible to make those instances distant and unreal in which recourse to force, by groups or by individuals, can be justified by the existence of a tyrannical regime and an unjust social order.[68]

Governments do not exist to exercise the power of coercion—including the power of the sword; rather, governments exist to maintain a stable social order that preserves the basic human rights of its citizens.

Liberation theology arose as a movement within the Latin American church at a time when the global church was exploring the relationship between faith and politics, church and state, spiritual and temporal. Whether in the theology of Gutiérrez or the pastoral practice of Archbishop Romero, liberation theology offers an integral framework from which to address these concerns, grounded in the biblical narrative of God choosing sides with the poor and oppressed in order to bring about their liberation from slavery and death (Exodus). Furthermore, while in critical conversation with the dominant theological and philosophical traditions of the West, liberation theology articulates its own distinctive interpretation of the Western Christian tradition. So when Gutiérrez claims that God "is protector of the Israelite people to the extent that Yahweh is defender of the poor, for the defense of the poor is the ineradicable seal that permanently marks the covenant,"[69] he is making a dogmatic claim about the preferential option for the poor and oppressed. The hermeneutical perspective taken when the church identifies as the church *of* the poor, or more radically, the poor church, entails more than merely approaching the bible and the tradition from a new or different point of view ("the underside of history"). Rather, what Gutiérrez is suggesting is that God's preferential option is inextricable from who God *is* based on how God *acts* throughout the history of humanity's covenant with God: "We know the Lord from his works; these make it clear to us, as we have now been reminded, that God liberates because God is a liberator ... God is what God is."[70] Accordingly, belief in God demands liberation of the oppressed, justice for the victims, and most challenging of all love for the political enemy. This prophetic vision informs and guides a politics of nonviolent resistance that, when confronted with the realities of repressive violence, should be willing to "risk even martyrdom in defending the poorest of the poor and in resisting the oppressors with the testimony of their words and their lives."[71]

NOTES

1. See Carol Lakey Hess, "Religious Education," Emily Click, "Contextual Education," and Kathleen A. Cahalan, "Integration in Theological Education," in *The Wiley-Blackwell Companion to Practical Theology*, ed. Bonnie J. Miller-McLemore (Malden, MA: John Wiley & Sons, 2011). Also see Luis G. Pedraja, "Social Justice, Education, & the Future of Higher Education in America," in *Apuntes*, Vol. 33 No. 2 (Summer 2013), pp. 40–54.

2. Liberation theology has had its most direct impact on the official statements of the Roman Catholic Church, as evidenced by the conciliar statements of the Latin American (CELAM) and United States Bishops (USCCB), as well as more recent Vatican encyclicals like *Laudato Si'* (http://w2.vatican.va/content/francesco/en/encyclicals/documents/papa-francesco_20150524_enciclica-laudato-si.html). Within Protestant circles in the United States, the impact of liberation theology is most evident in the adoption by mainline denominations of the South African liberation confessional statement known as the Belhar Confession (http://oga.pcusa.org/site_media/media/uploads/oga/images/ga222/ga222-062316.pdf).

3. Liberation theologians figure prominently in *My Family/Mi familia* (1995, directed by Gregory Nava) and *Contact* (1997, directed by Robert Zemeckis, based on a novel of the same name by Carl Sagan). Many, however, first encounter Latin American liberation theology via the 1989 biopic of Archbishop Oscar Romero, *Romero* (1989, directed by John Duigan), starring popular Puerto Rican actor Raúl Juliá. More recently, the themes of black power and black liberation featured prominently in the immensely popular comic book movie *Black Panther* (2018, directed by Ryan Coogler). See Corey Patterson, "Liberation Theology in *Black Panther*," posted on *Popular Culture and Theology* (March 19, 2018). [https://popularcultureandtheology.com/2018/03/19/liberation-theology-in-black-panther/]

4. The United Nations defined absolute poverty as "a condition characterised by severe deprivation of basic human needs, including food, safe drinking water, sanitation facilities, health, shelter, education and information. It depends not only on income but also on

5. See James H. Cone, *Black Theology and Black Power* (New York: The Seabury Press, 1969) and *A Black Theology of Liberation* (Maryknoll, NY: Orbis Books, 1970).
6. See *Liberation Theology: A Documentary History*, edited with introductions, commentary, and translations by Alfred T. Hennelly (Maryknoll, NY: Orbis Books, 1990), 89–119.
7. See Leonardo Boff, *Ecclesiogenesis: The Base Communities Reinvent the Church*, trans. Robert R. Barr (Maryknoll, NY: Orbis Books, 1986); Andrew Dawson, "The Origins and Character of the Base Ecclesial Community: A Brazilian Perspective," in *The Cambridge Companion to Liberation Theology*, second edition, ed. Christopher Rowland (Cambridge: Cambridge University Press, 2007); Margaret Hebblethwaite, *Base Communities: An Introduction* (Geoffrey Chapman, 1993); and *The Church at the Grassroots in Latin America: Perspectives on Thirty Years of Activism*, eds. John Burdick and Warren Edward Hewitt (Greenwood Publishing Group, 2000).
8. A historic moment for what eventually became the theology of liberation took place at the third plenary session during the World Conference on Church and Society held in Geneva on July 14, 1966, when many in the global ecumenical church felt strongly that the "theology of revolution" seemed incommensurate with the nonviolent Christian Gospel. In Latin America, two key figures in this movement were Presbyterian theologian and missionary Richard Shaull, and Roman Catholic priest Camilo Torres. Richard Shaull (1919–2002), a long-time contributor to the journal *Iglesia y Sociedad en América Latina* ("Church and Society in Latin America"), was hugely influential in the early Christian Base Community movement, impacting both Protestants in Brazil and Catholics in Colombia, but is best known for articulating the Christian "theology of revolution" so hotly debated in Geneva. See M. Richard Shaull, *Encounter with Revolution* (New York: Association Press, 1955); Angel D. Santiago-Vendrell, *Contextual Theology and Revolutionary Transformation in Latin America: The Missiology of M. Richard Shaull* (Eugene, OR: Wipf & Stock, 2010); and J. M. Lochman, "Ecumenical Theology of Revolution," *Scottish Journal of Theology*, Vol. 21, No. 2 (June 1968), 170–186. Camilo Torres (1929–1966), a folk hero among Latin American revolutionaries, second only to Che Guevara in popular appeal, left the priesthood to become a guerrilla in the Colombian National Liberation Army. A few weeks into his life as a guerrilla, Torres was killed in his first military action. See Camilo Torres, *Revolutionary Priest: The Complete Writings & Messages of Camilo Torres*, ed. John Gerassi (New York: Vintage Books, 1971); and Joe Broderick, *Camilo Torres: A Biography of the Priest-guerrillero* (New York: Doubleday, 1975).
9. Among first-generation Latin American liberation theologians, Brazilian Presbyterian Rubem Alves is credited with first coining the term "theology of liberation" in his 1968 Ph.D. dissertation for Princeton Theological Seminary, "Toward a Theology of Liberation" two tears before Gutiérrez published his seminal *A Theology of Liberation*. However, that same year Gustavo Gutiérrez gave a talk (unpublished) to a gathering of priests in Chimbote, Peru (July 21–25, 1968) entitled, "Hacia una teología de la liberación" ("Toward a Theology of Liberation"), which greatly impacted what took place at the Medellín conference one month later. Other first-generation voices include Catholics Juan Luis Segundo, Leonardo Boff, and Jon Sobrino, and Protestants José Míguez Bonino and Jorge (George) Pixley.
10. Hennelly, *Liberation Theology: A Documentary History*, 112.
11. Gary Dorrien, *Imagining Democratic Socialism: Political Theology, Marxism, and Social Democracy* (New Haven, CT: Yale University Press, 2019), 2, 3.
12. Carl Schmitt, *Political Theology: Four Chapters on the Concept of Sovereignty*, trans. George Schwab, reprint (Chicago: University of Chicago Press, 2005), 38.

13. Dorrien, *Imagining Democratic Socialism*, 3.
14. Gustavo Gutiérrez, *A Theology of Liberation: History, Politics, and Salvation*, trans. and ed. by Sister Caridad Inda and John Eagleson, rev. (Maryknoll, NY: Orbis Books, 1988), xiii.
15. While the passage from *Todas las sangres* (1964) appears in the original Spanish edition of *Teología de la liberación* (1971), it did not appear in the English translation until the fifteenth anniversary edition of *A Theology of Liberation* (1988), and then left untranslated. Readers unable to read the original Spanish text cannot fully appreciate the fictionalized anticipation of what would become a "theology of liberation" a handful of years later. All translations of this passage are my own.
16. Curt Cadorette, *From the Heart of the People: The Theology of Gustavo Gutiérrez* (New York: Meyer Stone Books, 1988), 71.
17. Ibid., 75.
18. It is telling that Gutiérrez's largest single volume is his study and analysis of the life and work of Las Casas. See Gustavo Gutiérrez, *Las Casas: In Search of the Poor of Jesus Christ*, trans. Robert R. Barr (Maryknoll, NY: Orbis Books, 1993).
19. Hennelly, *Liberation Theology: A Documentary History*, 109–110.
20. Juan José Tamayo, *Presente y futuro de la teología de la liberación* (Madrid: San Pablo, 1994), 176.
21. Ibid., (my own translation).
22. Gutiérrez, *A Theology of Liberation*, xxv. Gutiérrez here cites paragraph 9 of the "Document on the Poverty of the Church" from the Medellín conference. See Hennelly, *Liberation Theology: A Documentary History*, 114–119.
23. Gutiérrez, *A Theology of Liberation*, 70.
24. Ibid., 75.
25. Ibid. (emphasis added).
26. Ibid., 146.
27. Ibid., 150 (emphasis added).
28. Ibid., 151.
29. Ibid., 153.
30. Gustavo Gutiérrez, *We Drink from Our Own Wells: The Spiritual Journey of a People*, 20th anniversary edition, trans. Matthew J. O'Connell (Maryknoll, NY: Orbis Books, 2003), 11, 12.
31. Gutiérrez, *A Theology of Liberation*, 17.
32. Ibid., 70.
33. Gutiérrez, *We Drink from Our Own Wells*, 23, 22.
34. Gutiérrez, *A Theology of Liberation*, xliii.
35. Robert McAfee Brown, *Gustavo Gutiérrez: An Introduction to Liberation Theology* (Maryknoll, NY: Orbis Books, 1990).
36. James Brockman, S.J., "The Prophetic Role of the Church in Latin America: A Conversation with Gustavo Gutiérrez," *Christian Century* (October 19, 1983), 931–935.
37. For the final documents of the Puebla conference see Hennelly, *Liberation Theology: A Documentary History*, 225–258.
38. Ibid., 258.
39. Óscar Romero, "Last Homily of Oscar Romero," in *Voice of the Voiceless: The Four Pastoral Letters and Other Statements*, trans. Michael J. Walsh (Maryknoll, NY: Orbis Books, 1985), 191–192.

40. Hannah Brockhaus, "Oscar Romero and Pope Paul VI to be canonized October 14," *Catholic News Agency* (May 19, 2018). https://www.catholicnewsagency.com/news/oscar-romero-and-pope-paul-vi-to-be-canonized-october-14-18991
41. Gutiérrez, *A Theology of Liberation*, xxv.
42. Monseñor Óscar Romero, *Su pensamiento*, 8 vols. (San Salvador: Publicaciones pastorales del Arzobispado, 1980–89), "Homily for February 10, 1980," 236 (all passages from Romero's homilies my own translation unless otherwise noted).
43. Romero, *Su pensamiento*, vol. 1–2 (June 19, 1977), 97.
44. Romero, *Su pensamiento*, vol. 1–2 (May 29, 1977), 73.
45. Jon Sobrino, "From a Theology of Liberation Alone to a Theology of Martyrdom," in *Witnesses to the Kingdom: The Martyrs of El Salvador and the Crucified Peoples* (Maryknoll, NY: Orbis Books, 2003), 102.
46. Ignacio Ellacuría, S.J., "The Crucified People," in *Mysterium Liberationis: Fundamental Concepts of Liberation Theology*, ed. Ignacio Ellacuría, S.J. and Jon Sobrino, S.J. (Maryknoll, NY: Orbis Books, 1993), 580–603.
47. Sobrino, "From a Theology of Liberation Alone to a Theology of Martyrdom," 103.
48. See Betanchur Belisario, Reinaldo Figueredo, and Thomas Buergenthal, "From Madness to Hope: The 12-year War in El Salvador: Report of the Commission on the Truth for El Salvador," published by the United Nations under the title El Salvador Agreements: The Path to Peace (DPI/1208, May 1992), United States Institute for Peace. According to the report the death squads were responsible for an estimated 35,000+ disappearances before the start of the war, and another 60,000+ during the 12 years of civil war. To this day, the mass graves are being uncovered and victims identified through forensic science and DNA fingerprinting. https://www.usip.org/sites/default/files/file/ElSalvador-Report.pdf
49. Romero, *Su pensamiento*, vol. 6 (December 17, 1978), 38.
50. Romero, *Su pensamiento*, vol. 8 (February 24, 1980), 263.
51. Romero, *Su pensamiento*, vol. 7 (August 12, 1979), 168.
52. Jon Sobrino, "Our World: Cruelty and Compassion," in *Concilium: Rethinking Martyrdom*, ed. Teresa Okure, Jon Sobrino, and Felix Wilfred (London: SCM Press, 2003), 18–19.
53. Roberto Cuéllar, "The Legal Aid Heritage of Oscar Romero," in *Archbishop Romero and Spiritual Leadership in the Modern World*, ed. Rev. Robert S. Pelton (Lanham, MD: Lexington Books, 2015), 147.
54. Ibid., 150.
55. Ibid., 153.
56. Ibid., 151.
57. Pastoral Constitution on the Church in the Modern World, *Gaudium et spes*, promulgated by His Holiness, Pope Paul VI (December 7, 1965), §43. http://www.vatican.va/archive/hist_councils/ii_vatican_council/documents/vat-ii_const_19651207_gaudium-et-spes_en.html
58. Romero, *Su pensamiento*, vol. 1 (March 20, 1977), 8.
59. Archbishop Oscar Romero, "First Pastoral Letter, The Easter Church," in *Voice of the Voiceless: The Four Pastoral Letters and Other Statements*, trans. Michael J. Walsh (Maryknoll, NY: Orbis Books, 1985), 59–60.
60. *Evangelii nuntiandi*, §34. Cited in "The Easter Church," 60.
61. *Gaudium et spes*, §42.

62. Archbishop Oscar Romero, "Third Pastoral Letter, The Church and Popular Political Organizations," in *Voice of the Voiceless: The Four Pastoral Letters and Other Statements*, trans. Michael J. Walsh (Maryknoll, NY: Orbis Books, 1985), 100.
63. Ibid., 89–90.
64. Ibid., 90.
65. Ibid., 95–96.
66. Archbishop Oscar Romero, "Fourth Pastoral Letter, The Church's Mission amid the National Crisis," in *Voice of the Voiceless: The Four Pastoral Letters and Other Statements*, trans. Michael J. Walsh (Maryknoll, NY: Orbis Books, 1985), 147.
67. Ibid., 144–145.
68. Ibid., 145.
69. Gustavo Gutiérrez, *The God of Life*, trans. Matthew J. O'Connell (Maryknoll, NY: Orbis Books, 1991), 22.
70. Ibid., 65.
71. Ignacio Ellacuría, "Trabajo no violento por la paz y violencia liberadora," in *Concilium* 215 (1988), 94 (my translation).

SELECT BIBLIOGRAPHY

Boff, Leonardo (1986), *Ecclesiogenesis: The Base Communities Reinvent the Church*, trans. Robert R. Barr, Maryknoll, NY: Orbis Books.
Brown, Robert MacAfee (1990), *Gustavo Gutiérrez: An Introduction to Liberation Theology*, Maryknoll, NY: Orbis Books.
Cone, James H. (1969), *Black Theology and Black Power*, New York: The Seabury Press.
Cone, James H. (1970), *A Black Theology of Liberation*, Maryknoll, NY: Orbis Books.
Ellacuría, S. J., Ignacio and Jon Sobrino, S.J., eds. (1993), *Mysterium Liberationis: Fundamental Concepts of Liberation Theology*, Maryknoll, NY: Orbis Books.
Gutiérrez, Gustavo (1988), *A Theology of Liberation: History, Politics, and Salvation*, trans. and ed. by Sister Caridad Inda and John Eagleson, rev. edition, Maryknoll, NY: Orbis Books.
Gutiérrez, Gustavo (1991), *The God of Life*, trans. Matthew J. O'Connell, Maryknoll, NY: Orbis Books.
Gutiérrez, Gustavo (2003), *We Drink from Our Own Wells: The Spiritual Journey of a People*, 20th anniversary edition, trans. Matthew J. O'Connell, Maryknoll, NY: Orbis Books.
Hennelly, Alfred T., ed. (1990), *Liberation Theology: A Documentary History*, Maryknoll, NY: Orbis Books.
Romero, Archbishop Oscar (1985), *Voice of the Voiceless: The Four Pastoral Letters and Other Statements*, trans. Michael J. Walsh, Maryknoll, NY: Orbis Books.
Romero, Monseñor Óscar (1980–1989), *Su pensamiento*, 8 vols., San Salvador: Publicaciones pastorales del Arzobispado.
Rowland, Christopher, ed. (2007), *The Cambridge Companion to Liberation Theology*, second edition, Cambridge: Cambridge University Press.
Sobrino, Jon (2003), *Witnesses to the Kingdom: The Martyrs of El Salvador and the Crucified Peoples*, Maryknoll, NY: Orbis Books.

PART TWO

Scriptures and Traditions: Critical Retrieval of Historical Sources

CHAPTER FOUR

The Cup Does Not Run Over

Political Theology in the Hebrew Bible

SERGE FROLOV

INTRODUCTION

The notion of political theology was born, for all we know, when Carl Schmitt pointed out, in a 1922 publication, that in modern times dominant political ideas in the West seem to mirror dominant theological concepts.[1] In Schmitt's original sense, the Hebrew Bible (henceforth HB) is a perfect showcase for political theology. As will be shown in the first, shorter part of the present chapter, the HB presents the divine and especially its relationship to worshippers, both individually and communally, in starkly political terms.

At the same time, it should be noted that Schmitt in no way associates the theological trajectories that he discusses with the scripture—including the HB and the New Testament—and its interpretation, the simple reason being that no such association can be traced. A normative theology may—but does not necessarily have to—use the HB as a proof text, but it is theology, not the Bible that holds primacy: it is the new doctrine that changes the way the scripture is read, not the other way round. The simultaneous paradigm shift that according to Schmitt took place in the nineteenth century in theology and political theory could have any number of causes—from the industrial revolution and explosion of scientific knowledge to the ennui that traditional religion produced in intellectual elites. But historical-critical study of the HB that emerged around that time was not one of these causes despite being instrumental in fleshing out the conceptuality of the corpus and especially the roots of this conceptuality in the Bible's ancient Near Eastern background. Likewise, theologies of the twenty-first century may be driven by anything from the lingering trauma of interlocked global-scale mass killings between 1914 and 1953 to accelerating globalization (and the backlash against it, often steeped in religion-based identitarianism), but not by concurrently flourishing postmodern approaches to the Bible, which at best may play the secondary role of providing scriptural justification.

Worse, even as a proof text the Bible is always a double-edged sword. Any text is open to interpretation and thoroughly, perhaps even infinitely, malleable through it; a corpus that is more than two millennia removed from its interpreters, with semantics of many lexemes difficult to ascertain (because comparative data are limited to non-existent), grammar and syntax often ambiguous, and underlying realia unintelligible, is malleable squared. Add to the mix the sheer length and diversity of the HB, creating a tangled web of contexts, and the net result is that the corpus can be co-opted, especially with a healthy mix of determination and ingenuity going into the effort, pro or contra any kind of political doctrine. And when an attempt is made to recover the overarching conceptuality operative in disparate pronouncements, regulations, characterizations, and plots twists, the result proves rather unexpected and not particularly promising as far as contemporary political theology is concerned. This is what I propose to demonstrate in the second, longer part of the chapter, using the topics of sovereignty and human rights as test cases.

POLITICS IN THEOLOGY

A deity known under a variety of appellations but most commonly referred to as YHWH, Elohim, or YHWH Elohim is the only supernatural character active throughout the HB. Existence of other gods is sometimes presupposed in a matter-of-fact fashion (most famously in Gen. 1:26; 3:22) but usually they are dismissed as "nothings" (e.g., 1 Sam. 12:21), "useless vanities" (Jon. 2:9; Ps. 31:7), "abominations" (e.g., Deut. 29:16; 1 Kgs. 11:5, 7; Ezek. 20:30; Dan. 12:11), and "non-divine spirits" (Deut. 32:17). Even when present on the scene, as seems to be the case in Psalm 82 ("God is erect in the divine assembly, in the midst of gods he would judge," v. 1), they are but passive recipients of denunciation that builds toward a death sentence ("Like humans you will die, like one of the princes you will fall," v. 7). They are also denied any kind of individuality: their names appear only in the context of (illegitimate and ultimately futile) worship, often in the plural, as though denoting a category rather than an individual entity (e.g., Ba'als = male deities, e.g., Judg 2:11; Ashtoreths = female deities, e.g., 1 Sam. 12:10).

By contrast, YHWH/Elohim is highly individualized and rarely out of the limelight. The entire Enneateuch (Genesis–Kings)[2] is, in a sense, an account of his relationship first with humanity as a whole (in Genesis 1–11) and then (in the rest of the corpus) with the community of Israel starting with its ancestors.[3] In prophetic books, YHWH/Elohim is the principal speaker whose discourse, as quoted by his emissaries, dwarfs and drowns out all other voices, including that of the narrator. The compositions that in the Masoretic canon are collected in the Writings section are more diverse, with the deity completely absent from two books (Esther and Song of Songs), at least at the surface level, and only desultorily present in three others (Proverbs, Ruth, and Ecclesiastes).[4] Yet, even here, several major texts are either dominated by human responses to YHWH/Elohim (Psalms, Job, and Lamentations) or represent variations on, and extensions of the Enneateuchal account (Chronicles, Ezra-Nehemiah, and Daniel).

The ubiquitous presence of YHWH/Elohim in the HB and the near-absence of other deities are two sides of the same coin. In polytheistic religions, certainly those of the Near East and the Mediterranean, chief gods are usually depicted, and often described as kings: this is true, in particular, of Enlil/Ellil in Mesopotamia, Ra in Egypt, El in Ugarit, and especially Zeus/Jupiter in the Greco-Roman world.[5] However, their standing is asserted and exercised primarily vis-à-vis other deities; it is the divine retinue that makes the divine king while humans rarely come into consideration and the chief god's interaction with them is neither continuous nor consistent.[6] Faint echoes of this mythological pattern can be found in Psalm 82 discussed above. However, overall the biblical framework does not allow much space for scenes of this kind, leaving the physical world in general and humankind in particular as the only loci for affirmation of the deity's kingship. The constant, one might even say relentless, involvement of YHWH/Elohim in human history as recounted by the HB consequently testifies to the importance of upholding the deity's royal status—and thus presenting the divine in political terms—for the biblical authors. Central in this respect is the notion of covenant and especially the formative role that it plays in the Enneateuch and elsewhere in the HB.

Making its first appearance in Genesis 9, the term *berit*, usually translated as "covenant," is used almost 300 times in the Masoretic canon. In more than 90 Enneateuchal instances and most of the time elsewhere in the HB, YHWH/Elohim is explicitly a party to the covenant. His counterparts are Noah's family and the entire creation (Gen. 9:9–17), Israel's ancestors (e.g., Gen. 17:4; Lev. 26:42), and—most frequently—the community as a whole (e.g., Exod. 19:5; Lev. 26:44; Deut. 5:2). Other sections of the HB corpus for the most part refer to the latter covenant (e.g., Josh. 7:15; Isa. 33:8; 2 Chron. 6:14).

A distinguishing feature of the covenant is that it is always initiated by the deity and never by humans. It may be (or at least seem) unconditional (as is the case in Genesis 9), in which case it can be categorized as the deity's unilateral promise.[7] Usually, however, it comes with conditions whose fulfillment by the second party signifies its acceptance of the covenant—as exemplified by circumcision as per Genesis 17 or by the commandments that the people of Israel promise to observe in Exodus 19:8; 24:3. Several studies have demonstrated that the latter pattern approximates that operative in ancient Near Eastern treaties between suzerains (kings of large territorial states, such as the Hittite empire or Assyria) and vassals (dependent rulers of smaller political entities).[8] Such treaties were invariably written as the suzerain's address to the vassal, presupposing a spontaneous and unilateral action of the former. They began with the suzerain's self-introduction and continued with a history of his relationship with the vassal often emphasizing the suzerain's unsolicited acts of grace towards the vassal. The body of the treaty consisted of the vassal's, but not suzerain's, obligations formulated apodictically and followed by blessings for carrying them out and curses for transgressing against them (Assyrian treaties contained only curses). Rounding off the document was a list of gods called upon as witnesses.

Both major legal collections in the HB, Exodus 20–Leviticus 26 and Deuteronomy 1–28, approximate this format. The former, formulated as the deity's speech, begins with YHWH/Elohim introducing himself and reminding the listeners that it was he who liberated them from Egyptian bondage (Exod. 20:2; cf. Exod. 19:4), continues with the people's (but not the deity's) obligations, mostly in apodictic form, and ends with blessings and curses (Lev. 26:3–45). The latter, couched as the last will and testament of Moses (although ultimately coming from YHWH/Elohim, Deut. 28:69), begins with a long historical preamble that stresses the deity's support of Israel during the people's march across the desert (Deut. 1:6–3:29, plus the flashback to the giving of the Decalogue in Deut. 5:1–30). It continues with the people's (but not the deity's) obligations, mostly in apodictic form, and ends with blessings and curses (Deut. 28:1–68; cf. Deut. 27:9–26). The notion of YHWH/Elohim as Israel's suzerain is thus embedded in the very generic fabric of the Enneateuch.

Furthermore, as I have argued elsewhere, the overall composition of the Enneateuch also broadly follows the suzerain–vassal treaty template.[9] The so-called primeval history (Genesis 1–11) introduces YHWH/Elohim as the creator of the world and Genesis 12–Exodus 19 traces the history of his relationship with Israel with an emphasis on the deity's spontaneous acts of grace, such as the promise to the ancestors and the liberation from Egyptian bondage. Exodus 20–Deuteronomy 28 lays out Israel's obligations while Joshua–Kings traces Israel's fortunes first under the blessing (Josh. 1:1–Judg. 1:26) and then under the curse (Judg. 1:27–2 Kgs 25:30). Since prophetic books constitute, in essence, the commentary of YHWH/Elohim on his relationship with Israel as laid out in the Enneateuch, especially in the "curse" section, and many of the Writings are interpretable as Israel's response, an important corollary of the above layout is that the idea of covenant, complete with the deity's political characterization inherent in it, reverberates throughout the HB. Although Walther Eichrodt may have gone too far in viewing covenant as the linchpin of biblical theology as a whole, the concept does play a major role in it.[10]

Pointing in the same direction are the references to Israel as the deity's *nahalah*, "hereditary estate" (e.g., Deut. 32:9; 1 Sam. 26:19; Jer. 10:16; Ps. 78:71 cf., e.g., 1 Kgs 21:3). On the one hand, these references suggest the deity's uncontested claim to both Israel's territory and its population, reducing even the largest—and therefore most powerful—human landowners not only to conditional and potentially temporary lessees but also to virtual serfs. On the other hand, the domain of YHWH/Elohim is thus circumscribed by highly specific geographical boundaries, such as those outlined in Numbers 34:2b–12 and elsewhere. Taken together, these two aspects yield a perfect image of a ruler in a premodern state.[11] The HB by no means shies away from demonstrating the deity's global control by portraying imperial potentates, such as Sennacherib of Assyria (2 Kgs 19:21–28 = Isa. 37:22–29), Nebuchadnezzar of Babylon (Jer. 25:8–9), and Cyrus of Persia (Isa. 44:28–45:6) as its puppets and claiming that peoples other than Israel also received their homelands from it (e.g., Amos 9:7). Nevertheless, the ultimate triumph of YHWH/Elohim predicted by the prophets is consistently presented as king's victory over his enemies, not as a pacification of an already existing empire (e.g., Mic. 4:8–14; Zeph. 3:8).

Finally, a few words need to be said about masculinity of the Bible's only divine actant. The nexus of virility and power, above all political power, is well established in a variety of cultures and throughout documented human history.[12] Accordingly, the chief gods of the ancient Near East and the Mediterranean are all unambiguously male, and so is YHWH/Elohim.[13] What is more, his male sex drive is much more apparent than that of Ra, Enlil/Ellil, and El (and, where this distinction exists, that of younger ruler deities, such as Osiris, Ba'al, and Horus). Only Zeus, with his multiple legitimate spouses and countless love affairs, is even more potent in this respect. At the same time, while Zeus's sex partners (and therefore by definition objects of his virile domination) are individual goddesses, demigoddesses, and women, with YHWH/Elohim it is for the most part the community of worshipers as a whole. Prophetic literature consistently represents the deity and Israel (under different guises—Jerusalem, Daughter Zion, the sisters Oholah and Oholibah, and the alleged prostitute named Gomer) as, respectively, husband and wife (Hos. 1:2–2:25; Isa. 1:8 and elsewhere; Jer. 3:1–13; Ezek. 16, 23); as already mentioned, traditional Jewish and Christian interpretations recognize the same couple in the anonymous lovers of the Song of Songs.[14] The representation goes beyond simply affirming the male potency of YHWH/Elohim and thereby his qualifications to rule (as is the case with Zeus). It not only further confirms that Israel is the deity's property (just as a woman in a patriarchal society is her husband's property), but also equates worshiper's lack of exclusive fidelity to the deity with betrayal—just as a subject's lack of exclusive fidelity to the king equals treason; hence the preoccupation of biblical authors with Lady Israel's alleged cheating.

YHWH/Elohim is thus clearly characterized in the HB primarily as the king of Israel. The corollaries of this characterization are, however, much less clear-cut, as will be demonstrated in the second part of the chapter.

THEOLOGY IN POLITICS

Sovereignty

It has been almost a truism of scholarship, especially in the last few decades, that the HB—or, at least, some of the sources or redactional layers behind it—is unfavorable towards the monarchic regime to the point of rejection.[15] This construal is, of course, attuned to—and, consciously or unconsciously, designed to bolster—the aversion of modern and especially postmodern Western society towards vesting sovereignty in a single individual. The political preference in question is especially strong in the United States whose founding narrative revolves around opposition and resistance to the "King of England."

In certain ways, the HB indeed stands much closer than any other work of ancient Near Eastern literature to the ideals of sovereignty that started gaining currency in the West in the late eighteenth and early nineteenth centuries. Most notably, it is relentlessly critical of many individual monarchs of Israel, to say nothing of foreign rulers—something that is nearly unheard of elsewhere in the region. In the Enneateuchal account, the first-ever Israelite kingdom, that of Abimelech in Judges 9, emerges out of mass fratricide (vv. 1–5) and collapses into a bloodbath (vv. 22–57). The narrator portrays the only three kings of Israel as a whole—Saul, David (by far the most paradigmatic of all), and Solomon—as highly flawed characters. Saul arbitrarily orders a mass execution (1 Sam. 22:6–19). David conspires to kill his own devoted soldier in order to cover up a rape (2 Sam. 11–12). Solomon mercilessly purges his opponents and rivals, including a half-brother (1 Kgs 2:13–46), not to mention his idolatry (1 Kgs 11:1–8) that causes YHWH/Elohim to split most of Israel's tribes away from his realm (1 Kgs 11:9–11, 29–39). Most of the subsequent rulers of two rival Israelite kingdoms are denounced for crimes against their subjects and/or the cult of YHWH/Elohim, and very few of those afforded at least some attention are pictured as blameless (Josiah in 2 Kgs 22–23 may be the only major exception). Israel's ultimate loss of the land that YHWH/Elohim promised to its ancestor as early as Genesis 12:7 is blamed upon the transgressions of King Manasseh of Judah (2 Kgs 21:1–16). Prophets specifically mention individual Israelite kings mostly to rebuke them (e.g., Isa. 7:10–13; Jer. 22:24–30), and apart from Cyrus (see above) they have nothing but destruction in stock for foreign potentates, even those previously serving as tools of YHWH/Elohim (e.g., Jer. 51:33–37 on Nebuchadnezzar). In Writings, profoundly satirical portraits of Babylonian and Persian kings in Esther and Daniel are of note.

More importantly, biblical opposition to the monarchy may seem to be focused on the institution as such rather than individuals representing it—in other words, it is a matter of principle rather than ad hoc concerns. The famous parable of Jotham in Judges 9:8–15 is commonly interpreted as claiming that no productive member of society would deign to be a king.[16] When Israel's elders ask Samuel in 1 Samuel 8:4–5 to set a monarch over them, not only the prophet (whom the petitioners seek to sideline), but also YHWH/Elohim, whom he consults, denounces the request (vv. 7–8); later, Samuel terms it "evil" (1 Sam. 12:20). Such a radical antagonism is, of course, by no means surprising in light of the concept discussed at length in the first part of the present chapter, that of the deity's kingship over Israel, and the HB would appear to confirm this in no uncertain terms. When Gideon, Abimelech's father, declines the crown that the people offer him, he states, "I will not rule over you, nor will my son rule over you; YHWH will rule over you" (Judg. 8:23). In his response to the elders' request for a king in 1 Samuel 8, YHWH/Elohim describes kingship as an abandonment of him and categorizes it as akin to foreign worship: "For it is not you [Samuel] that they have rejected, it is me that they have rejected from being their monarch—in line with everything that they have done from the day I brought them up from Egypt to this day, forsaking me and worshipping other gods" (vv. 7–8). Samuel voices similar concerns in 1 Samuel 10:19 ("And you today rejected your God who had saved you from all the evils and misfortunes that beset you, and told him, 'Just set a king over us'") and in 1 Samuel 12:12 ("You told me, 'No, just let a king rule over us,' whereas YHWH your God is your king!").

Yet, few things are clear-cut in the Bible, and the attitude towards human monarchy in Israel is not one of them. Instead of denouncing it, the normative part of the HB—the Torah, or Pentateuch—mandates it: "When you come to the land that YHWH your God gives you, and inherit it, and settle in it, and say, 'Let me set a king over me like all the peoples around me'—you should definitely set a king over you" (Deut. 17:14–15).[17] Certain conditions follow—the king must be chosen by YHWH/Elohim, he must not be a foreigner, etc.—betraying an assumption that the institution might work if these conditions are met. The next time the HB brings up the matter of the monarchy, it graphically demonstrates that human kingship indeed becomes a must once Israel feels the urge to have it. By denying the people's offer to enthrone him, Gideon paves the way to Abimelech's abortive but bloody reign (see above) and ultimately to the pandemonium of Judges 17–21, not so subtly punctuated by references to the absence of the monarchy that made it possible for "everyone to do what was right in their own eyes" (Judg. 17:6; 18:1; 19:1; 21:25).[18] Against this background, Judges 9, including Jotham's fable, reads as a denunciation of illegitimate rule, such as that of Abimelech, not of kingship as such.[19]

As though mindful of this, despite denouncing kingship as another kind of idolatry YHWH/Elohim commands Samuel in 1 Samuel 8 to grant the people's request for it (vv. 9, 22). Moreover, in the chapters that immediately follow, the king is celebrated, specifically as Israel's divinely commissioned savior from Philistine oppression (1 Sam. 9:16; cf. 10:24; 12:13), and those who do not recognize him are branded "worthless fellows" (10:27). Granted, this king, Saul, is quickly rejected (1 Sam. 13:13–14; 15:13–29) but a successor, David, is promptly appointed (16:1–13) with the possibility of not having a human monarch at all never coming up. Going much further than that, soon after David establishes his power over Israel as a whole YHWH/Elohim promises him that his dynasty would reign forever, regardless of transgressions its members might commit (2 Sam. 7:11b–16); human kingship in Israel is thus divinely sanctioned in perpetuity. That the promise does work becomes obvious already in the next generation, when David's son Solomon is punished for engaging in foreign worship (as a result of ignoring the conditions that Deuteronomy places on the monarch: compare Deut. 17:16–17 and 1 Kgs 10:14–11:8) with losing parts of his kingdom (1 Kgs 11:9–25) and his son Rehoboam losing even more (1 Kgs 12:1–24) but David's dynasty remains firmly on the throne. Moreover, after Assyrians destroy the political state created by the seceding tribes (2 Kgs 17) Davidides again find themselves in charge of all that is left of Israel. Even when this remnant loses its political independence and its land (2 Kgs 25:1–21), David's dynasty endures: in the last verses of the Enneateuch, there is no Israel left to speak of, but Jehoiachin, a Davidic scion, is back on the throne (2 Kgs 25:27–30).[20]

The trend outlined in the last two paragraphs is also traceable, albeit more remotely, in the prophetic corpus. Isaiah denounces King Hezekiah on at least one occasion (2 Kgs 20:12–19 = Isaiah 39) but also serves as his court diviner (2 Kgs 19:1–34 = Isa 37:1–35). Jeremiah, despite being unsparingly critical of individual Davidides, also cites YHWH as saying, "If you could undo my covenant of the day and my covenant of the night, so that day and night would not begin at their usual time, then my covenant with my servant David might be undone, denying him a son reigning on his throne" (33:20–21). Multiple prophets see re-establishment of the Davidic dynasty as indispensable to Israel post-exilic restoration (e.g., Jer. 30:9; Ezek. 37:24; Hos. 3:5; Amos 9:11–12; Hag. 2:20–23; Zech. 4) and not a single one explicitly objects. Moreover, in some books a future Davidide king is depicted as instrumental in attaining universal sovereignty of YHWH/Elohim and thus fundamentally transforming both human society and nature (especially Isa. 11; cf. also Mic. 5:1–3). This scenario, ultimately going back to 2 Samuel 7 (see above), lies at the root of the concept of *mashiah* (Messiah, literally "the anointed one" i.e. the king), highly influential in the Judeo-Christian tradition. In Writings, the concept is front and center in Psalm 2, where opposition to a king ruling from Zion—Davidic domicile (2 Sam 5:7–9)—is equated with that to YHWH/Elohim, Psalm 45, and parts of Daniel (7:13–14; 9:25–26). Likewise of note is the ascription of many texts in Writings (about half of the psalms, Ecclesiastes, and the Song of Songs) to David and Solomon (or another Davidide) as authoritative figures from the past, the Davidic culmination of Ruth (4:18–22), the centrality of Zerubbabel, a Davidic scion, in Ezra 1–5 (especially if Sheshbazzar in Ezra 1: 8, 11; 5:14, 16 is his alias), and the massive whitewashing of many Israelite kings, especially David and Solomon, in Chronicles (as compared to Samuel and Kings).

Several exegetes rightfully stress that although Deuteronomy 17 insists upon Israel having a king it also severely curtails the monarch's clout (vv. 16–17 bar him from hoarding precious metals, horses, and wives), fails to explicitly grant him any judicial, military, or cultic authority, and, even more importantly, subjects him to the commandments of the Torah, which he is required to copy and read continuously (vv. 18–20).[21] Indeed, the HB almost never shows actual kings legislating (one exception is David setting a precedent for division of spoils in 1 Sam. 30:21–25), on the reasonable assumption that YHWH/Elohim had promulgated all the provisions of any consequence long before the monarchy was even in the works. Neither does the HB bestow upon the king the right to cancel or suspend any part of the Torah; on the contrary, individual monarchs are denounced precisely for ignoring it. Under Schmitt's famous (or some would say, notorious) definition, "Sovereign is the one who decides on exception," the biblical king is not a sovereign.[22]

Perhaps unexpectedly but by no means illogically, neither is Israel's divine monarch. Just like ancient Near Eastern suzerain–vassal treaties, covenant does not have a cancellation or emendation clause, even implicit one, and nothing demonstrates this better than the deity's predicament when faced with the people's actual request for a human king. As noted above, in 1 Samuel 8 YHWH/Elohim apparently believes, perhaps under the influence of Gideon's misguided pronouncement in Judges 8:23, that on the part of his subjects such a request constitutes treason.[23] Yet, they do everything by the book—the Book of Deuteronomy (17:14–17): the land is under their control, they ask for a king because they want to have one, they leave it to a prophet to appoint him, and they do not insist on a foreigner. Indeed, they even quote from Deuteronomy (compare 1 Sam. 8:5b and Deut. 17:14b). This apparently leaves the deity no choice but to command Samuel to install a king.[24] In the three chapters that follow, sidelined Samuel grumbles (10:17–19; 12:8–12) and YHWH/Elohim rumbles (12:18) but neither makes any attempt to scuttle the newly minted institution. The deity's mind may change, but not its Torah.

The ideal political regime of the HB (as far as Israel is concerned) is thus neither a conventional monarchy nor theocracy (in the sense of direct rule by YHWH/Elohim). It should be properly called nomocracy, but since this term is already used in the broader sense of the "rule of law," I will dub it bibliocracy. Technically, under it no one would be a sovereign, at least not in Schmittian sense, because an exception to the Torah would be unthinkable. In practice, however, since any regulations need to be continuously adjusted based on the empirical experience of their workings and updated due to changed conditions actual sovereignty would belong in such case to those capable of making adjustments and updates without changing the letter of the Torah.[25] The authors of the HB thus reserved sovereignty to the intellectuals capable of creatively interpreting it, be they called scribes or rabbis, in other words, to themselves and their understudies.

Yet, crucially, they also needed a king, not as a subject of the law but as its enforcer, because, as most clearly demonstrated by Judges 19–21, when the people of Israel try to implement the law on their own the results are nothing short of disastrous.[26] Hence the harsh judgment that the Former and Latter Prophets pronounce on individual monarchs when they violate commandments instead of upholding them; even David is not spared such critique, precisely because he is the paradigmatic king. And hence the messianic longing for a monarch who can do no wrong, as expressed particularly in Isaiah 11:1–5.[27]

This regime is certainly very different from anything attested in antiquity but it is also unlike anything practiced or even seriously contemplated in today's world. It appears to stand closest to meritocracy, in requiring (actual) lawgivers whose authority stems from recognition of their supreme intellect and an executive whose authority stems from recognition of his supreme righteousness. It has never been tried in a full-fledged political state, and the only setting in which it has been historically practiced at least to some extent is that of autonomous and semi-autonomous Jewish communities. As will be shown in the next section, this is by no means a coincidence.

Human Rights

In a 1986 essay, Georg Braulik argued that many (indeed most) provisions of the 1948 Universal Declaration of Human Rights (UDHR) find parallels in the biblical Book of Deuteronomy.[28] To cite just a few examples, according to him Deuteronomy 25:3, by limiting corporal punishment to forty lashes, goes in the same direction as Article 2 of the UDHR that bans inhuman and degrading treatment. Deuteronomy 5:14, mandating cessation of work for Shabbat, safeguards the right to rest and leisure as per Article 24. And Deuteronomy 24:6, prohibiting expropriation of the upper millstone as a collateral, protects (among other stipulations) the right to own property enshrined in Article 17. Just two years earlier, Rabbi Meir Kahane used, among other sources, Deuteronomy 7:3 ("Do not intermarry with [the nations of Canaan], do not give your daughters to their sons and do not take their daughters for your sons") to justify a bill making sexual relations between Jews and non-Jews a criminal offense for the latter in the State of Israel.[29] And had he felt in need of further justification for his position, cognate Deuteronomic passages, such as 20:15–18, were at his disposal, not to mention multiple similarly minded texts from other biblical books.

Even very small fragments of the HB may simultaneously serve as proof texts for diametrically opposite stances with regard to human rights. Malachi 2:10a ("Do we not all have the same father? Did not the same deity create us?") has been used in multiple settings to make a case against racially, ethnically, or religiously based discrimination.[30] Yet in the very next verse, the speaker seems to endorse it by denouncing mixed marriages: "Judah committed treason, and a vile thing was done in Israel and Jerusalem, for Judah desecrated the sanctity of YHWH by loving and marrying a daughter of a strange god."[31]

In Genesis 9:5–6, shedding blood of fellow humans is prohibited with the justification that they alone were created in the divine image. This produces the impression that any killing is unacceptable, yet at the same breath the text mandates capital punishment for murderers, and, of course, other parts of the HB add a plethora of other capital offenses, to say nothing of the mandates to exterminate entire populations, such as Deuteronomy 20:15–18. Thus, there are valid reasons to translate the famous *lo' tirtsah* of the Decalogue (Exod. 20:13; Deut. 5:17) as both "thou shalt not kill" and "thou shalt not murder."

These examples already suggest that the HB can be easily cited to support both protection of human rights as they are commonly understood today and their gross violation. The pattern can be traced through all or almost all major issues. Both the Torah and prophetic books repeatedly and insistently urge acceptance and protection of resident aliens and other foreigners (e.g., Exod. 22:20; 23:9; Lev. 24:22; Deut. 24:14, 21), even of Israel's former oppressors, the Egyptians (Deut. 23:8–9). At the same time, biblical narrative cheerfully recounts wholesale slaughter of several groups, such as the Amalekites (1 Sam. 15:1–8; 30:17 cf. Deut. 25:17–19), Midianties (Num. 31), Canaanites (Josh. 6–8, 10–12; Judg. 1), and the subjects of Transjordanian kings Sihon and Og (Deut. 2:24–3:7), while others, such as Ammonites and Moabites, are specifically excluded from the community (Deut. 23:4–7). Rights of Israelite slaves are carefully spelled out, especially with regard to duration of the servitude (Exod. 21:2–11, 20–21, 26–27; Lev. 25:39–44; Deut. 15:12–18) but there are no such limitations with regard to bondage or forced labor for captive or conquered non-Israelites (Lev. 25:44–46; Deut. 20:10–15; Judg. 1:27–33; 1 Kgs 9:15–22).[32] Rape of an engaged or (by extension) married Israelite woman is punishable by stoning (Deut. 22:23–27) but the sentence for raping a virgin is lifelong marriage to her and a fixed payment to her father (Deut. 22:28–29), and rape of captive foreign women does not incur any legal consequences whatsoever (Deut. 21:10–14). Equity and impartiality in court are prescribed in strong terms (Exod. 23:1–3; Deut. 16:18–20; 19:15–20) but harsh—and in some cases seemingly extrajudicial—sentences are mandated for seemingly trivial offenses such as gathering firewood on Shabbat (Num. 15:32–36) or lack of respect and deference to one's parents (Exod. 21:17; Deut. 21:18–21). Care for living nature is urged (Deut. 20:19–20; 22:6–7) but destruction of all livestock belonging to the residents of the "idolatrous city" (Deut. 13:16) as well as to the Canaanites (e.g., Josh. 6:21) and Amalekites (1 Sam. 15:3) is required and so is killing of an animal involved in an act of bestiality (Lev. 20:15–16).

Of course, many, and perhaps all, "inconvenient" texts are open to reinterpretation. I have argued, for instance, that in the larger context of the Enneateuch the command to exterminate the "nations of Canaan" in Deuteronomy 20:15–18 can be plausibly construed as a warning against Israel's "Canaanization"—and, less directly, a means of discovering a measure of divine grace even in divine punishment—rather than a clarion call to eliminate all infidels.[33] But by the same token highly acceptable passages can be made less so. One example is the group of warnings against mistreating the *ger* (e.g., Exod. 22:20; 23:9; Lev. 24:22; Deut. 24:14). In the HB, the term most likely denotes a resident alien (from the verb *gur*, "to reside"), which is why these fragments have been quoted innumerable times on social media against the immigration policies of President Trump. Yet, in the post-biblical Jewish tradition the word came to denote a convert—in other words, a new and voluntary member of the community rather than a stranger living in its midst.

Moreover, in at least two areas—tolerance of dissent and gender and sexual orientation—the stance of the HB has few, if any, redeeming features to it. In the former regard, no cultic activity that the Torah does not authorize is allowed, be it worship of gods other than YHWH/Elohim (e.g., Exod. 22:19; Deut. 13:13–19; 17:2–7) or ill-defined "sorcery" and divination (e.g., Exod. 22:17; Deut. 18:10–14; cf. also 1 Sam. 28:3; 2 Kgs 9:22), with no meaningful distinction made between members of the community and outsiders. All these are considered capital offenses; even a mere suggestion to engage in foreign worship is punishable by (possibly extra-judicial) death (Deut. 13:2–12), as is blasphemy, even by a non-Israelite (Lev. 24:10–16, 23).[34] As far as gender is concerned, the HB is heavily skewed towards men, reserving to them the right to initiate divorce (Deut. 24:1–4) and implicitly allowing polygyny (e.g., Deut. 21:15–17) while making loss of virginity before marriage a capital offense for women only (Deut. 22:13–21). In addition, intercourse between two men is termed an "abomination" to be met with their execution (Lev. 18:22; 20:13), although the injunction is somewhat mitigated by the fact that the issue never explicitly comes up anywhere else in the HB and female homosexuality is not mentioned at all.

Along some lines, the conflict between the HB and the modern understanding of human rights is clearly a function of the former's historical milieu. In particular, patriarchy was common in the Near East and throughout the ancient world, and since the dawn of the political state it has been considered self-evident that non-citizens do not enjoy the same rights and privileges (and also do not bear the same obligations) as citizens.[35] However, some highly questionable trends discussed above, such as the obligations to violently suppress dissent and commit genocide, may stem directly from the bibliocratic character of the ideal Israelite polity as per the HB. Generally, violation of a law does not necessarily imply rejection of the sovereign that promulgated it; in particular, if a king issues a decree to worship one god and a subject worships another, that does not necessarily mean that the latter does not recognize the former. Yet, when the law is said to come directly from YHWH/Elohim heterodoxy becomes inherently antinomian. Hence the eliminationist attitude towards those who do not follow the prescribed ritual practices, starting within the community and ending with the populations claiming the same territory (such as the Canaanites and the subjects of Sihon and Og) or seen as encroaching on Israel in one way or another (Amalekites, Exod. 17:8–16; 1 Sam. 30:1–6; Midianites, Num. 22–25).[36] Contrariwise, resident aliens are apparently considered harmless because they neither belong to the Israelite community nor constitute one of their own (and may anyway be required to follow biblical commandments; see, e.g., with regard to keeping Shabbat, Exod. 20:10; Deut. 5:14).[37] Going in the same direction is, of course, the strict ban on intermarriage (Deut. 7:3–4), referenced alongside idolatry in Former Prophets (Josh. 23:12–13; Judg. 3:6; 1 Kgs 11:2) and prominent in Ezra (chs. 9–10) and Nehemiah (13:23–30).

Further, these provisions also reveal the ultimate purpose of the bibliocratic regime: to prevent Israel's assimilation by keeping it apart from other populations, if needs be by exterminating them or eliminating those who in one way or another contribute to cohesion with them. This objective is implicit already in Genesis 1 with its insistence that the process of creation was mostly that of differentiation (light from darkness, upper waters from lower waters, sea from dry land) and that the outcome is "good" primarily because the resultant entities never mix, transform into each other, or encroach on each other's niches. The pattern, reflected in biblical prohibitions to interbreed cattle and to combine different threads in the same fabric, different plants on the same field, and different animals in the same yoke (Lev. 19:19; Deut. 22:9–11), also explains prohibition of intercourse between two men (see above), which does not follow with necessity from either the overall patriarchal attitude of the corpus or the need to protect bibliocracy. Rather, it is the perception that in such intercourse one of the men in a sense becomes a woman that makes it intolerable (notably, both Lev. 18:22 and Lev. 20:13 compare it to "lying with a woman").[38]

CONCLUSION

The discussion in the present chapter suggests that political theology of the HB is narrowly tailored to a highly specific and in many respects idiosyncratic end: to preserve Israel as a distinctive community in a situation, such as that of the Babylonian exile or early post-exilic period, where written text was the mainstay of the Israelite identity. The concept of YHWH/Elohim as Israel's king but not its sovereign in the Schmittian sense, one who gave the community its law but cannot abrogate or change it, was designed first and foremost to circumscribe this identity and to prevent its dilution.

As vividly demonstrated by two and a half millennia of Israelite and then Jewish survival against unimaginable odds, the design, resulting in a bibliocratic regime, was nothing short of brilliant. But it also makes it impossible to employ the HB today as a valid source for constructive political theology—unless it pursues a similar purpose, and even then with substantial, likely crucial modifications adjusting for vastly changed global and local conditions, even as far as Jews are concerned. Of course, individual biblical fragments can still serve, the way they have for millennia, as proof texts. However, as amply demonstrated above, in this mode the HB can be made to underpin any theological or political system, which is an epistemological equivalent of actually supporting none of them. The Hebrew Bible is chock-full of political theology but its fullness does not run over.

NOTES

1. Carl Schmitt, *Political Theology: Four Chapters on the Concept of Sovereignty* (trans. George Schwab; Cambridge, MA: MIT Press, 1985), 36–52.
2. In the Jewish and (to a lesser extent) Christian traditions, the Torah or Pentateuch (Genesis–Deuteronomy) is seen as a corpus in its own right. However, in the biblical text proper the narrative that begins in Genesis runs without any formal or conceptual breaks all the way through Kings, forming (in the Masoretic text) a continuous and self-contained sequence of nine books, or the Enneateuch.
3. I use masculine pronouns of YHWH/Elohim for reasons explained below.
4. According to both Jewish and Christian traditions, the Song of Songs is an allegory or metaphor of the relationship between YHWH/Elohim as the male character and Israel as his inamorata. For an overview of this construal and competing premodern and early modern interpretations, see Marvin H. Pope, *Song of Songs: A New Translation with Introduction and Commentary* (AB 7C; New York: Doubleday, 1977), 89–132.
5. On Enlil/Ellil, see Stephanie Dalley (trans. and ed.), *Myths from Mesopotamia: Creation, The Flood, Gilgamesh, and Others* (Revised ed; Oxford World's Classics; Oxford: Oxford University Press, 2008), 9–35 (the text known as *Atrahasis*); on Ra, *ANET*, 10–11 (*Deliverance of Mankind from Destruction*); on El, Michael D. Coogan and Mark S. Smith (trans. and eds.), *Stories from Ancient Canaan* (2nd ed.; Louisville, KY: Westminster John Knox, 2012), 145 (*Ba'al* or *Ba'al and Anath*), on Zeus (and Kronos), Hesiod, *Theogony; Works and Days* (trans. M. L. West; Oxford World's Classics; Oxford: Oxford University Press, 1999), 17–18.

6. One major exception is *Deliverance of Mankind from Destruction* (see previous note) where Ra being a "king of men and gods all together" is indispensable for the plot.
7. Thus especially Moshe Weinfeld, "The Covenant of Grant in the Old Testament and in the Ancient Near East," *JAOS* 90 (1970): 184–203.
8. E.g., Dennis J. McCarthy, *Treaty and Covenant: A Study in Form in the Ancient Oriental Documents and in the Old Testament* (AB 21; Rome: Pontifical Biblical Institute, 1963); Klaus Baltzer, *The Covenant Formulary in Old Testament, Jewish, and Early Christian Writings* (trans. David E. Green; Philadelphia: Fortress, 1971), 1–93; Kenneth A. Kitchen and Paul J. N. Lawrence, *Treaty, Law, and Covenant in the Ancient Near East* (3 vols; Wiesbaden: Harrassowitz, 2012).
9. Serge Frolov, *Judges* (FOTL 6b; Grand Rapids: Eerdmans, 2013), 335–337; Frolov, "Structure, Genre, and Rhetoric of the Enneateuch," *Vestnik SPbSU: Philosophy and Conflict Studies* 33/3 (2017): 354–363.
10. Walther Eichrodt, *Theology of the Old Testament* (2 vols; trans. J. A. Baker; London: SCM Press, 1961).
11. This image is not without precedent in the ancient Near Eastern cultures that draw a distinction between the chief god (an older deity who reigns but for the most part does not rule) and the ruler god (a younger deity that is actually in charge). The latter seem to be depicted, more implicitly than explicitly, as sovereigns of specific locations—Babylon in Marduk's case, Ugarit and surrounding fertile areas in Ba'al's, Egypt in that of Osiris and Horus. Also notable is Ra's presentation as a Pharaoh in *Humankind's Deliverance from Destruction* (n. 4 above).
12. In the HB, this nexus can be seen in the multiple marriages of David (2 Sam. 3:2–5; 5:13–16) and especially Solomon (1 Kgs 11:1).
13. In a few HB texts, YHWH/Elohim seems to be portrayed as a mother, e.g., in Hosea 11 (see Helen Schüngel-Straumann, "God as Mother in Hosea 11," *A Feminist Companion to the Latter Prophets* [trans. L. M. Maloney; ed. Athalya Brenner; London: T&T Clark, 2004], 194–218), but these are the exceptions that confirm the rule.
14. Lady Israel is not necessarily the only girlfriend of YHWH/Elohim. Personified female wisdom (*hohmah*) seems to describe herself as such in Prov 8:22–31 (cf. Sir 9:9; Tikva Frymer-Kensky, *In the Wake of the Goddesses: Women, Culture and the Biblical Transformation of Pagan Myth* [New York: Fawcett Columbine, 1992], 179–183), and epigraphic evidence suggests that historically Asherah (the spouse of El in Ugaritic mythology) was seen as his consort (Raphael Patai, *The Hebrew Goddess* [3rd ed; Jewish Folklore and Anthropology; Detroit: Wayne State University Press, 1990], 34–53; Frymer-Kensky, *In the Wake of the Goddesses*, 153–161; William G. Dever, *Did God Have a Wife? Archaeology and Folk Religion in Ancient Israel* [Grand Rapids: Eerdmans, 2005], especially 176–251). However, these liaisons do not appear to have an immediate political import.
15. E.g., Martin Buber, *Kingship of God* (3rd ed; New York: Harper & Row, 1967); Frank Crüsemann, *Der Widerstand gegen das Königtum: Die antiköniglichen Texte des Alten Testamentes und der Kampf um den frühen israelitischen Staat* (WMANT 49; Neukirchen-Vluyn: Neukirchener Verlag, 1978); Ansgar Moenikes, *Die grundsätzliche Ablehnung des Königtums in der Hebräischen Bibel: Ein Beitrag zur Religionsgeschichte des Alten Israel* (BBB 99; Weinheim: Beltz Athenäum, 1995).
16. Buber, *Kingship of God*, 75, even called it "the strongest anti-monarchical poem of world literature."
17. English translations often tone down the stipulation along the lines of "you *may* set up a king over you" (e.g., JPS, RSV, and CEV). However, the absolute-infinitive-cum-finite-verb construction *som tasim* unambiguously signals an order rather than just permission.

18. See Frolov, *Judges*, 196–197.

19. Gordon K. Oeste, *Legitimacy, Illegitimacy, and the Right to Rule: Windows on Abimelech's Rise and Demise in Judges 9* (LHBOTS 546; New York: T&T Clark, 2011); Frolov, *Judges*, 193–197.

20. There is an ongoing scholarly debate whether 2 Kgs 25:27–30 should be understood as "the final nail into the coffin" of Israelite kingship (Richard D. Nelson, *The Double Redaction of the Deuteronomistic History* [JSOTSup 18; Sheffield: JSOT Press, 1981], 120) or an optimistic announcement "that a scion of David, king of Israel, is yet alive and well" (Jon D. Levenson, "The Last Four Verses in Kings," *JBL* 103 [1984], 353–361). That, of course, is another instance of the political stance of the HB being open to multiple interpretations.

21. Especially Bernard Levinson, "The Reconceptualization of Kingship in Deuteronomy and the Deuteronomistic History's Transformation of Torah," *VT* 51 (2001), 511–534.

22. Schmitt, *Political Theology*, 5.

23. On Gideon's profound cluelessness with regard to the relationship between Israel and its deity, see Frolov, *Judges*, 184–185.

24. More precisely, YHWH/Elohim tries the only loophole left to him by Deuteronomy: changing the people's minds about having a king by reminding them of the monarchy's high socioeconomic costs (1 Sam. 8:9–18). When they do not budge, the command to install a king is reiterated (vv. 19–22).

25. One showcase of such adjustment is the rabbinic treatment of the commandment to stone a stubborn and rebellious son (Deut. 21:18–21). Without actually abrogating it, the Mishnah (Sanh. 8:1–5) and the Talmud (b. Sanh. 68b–72a) render it entirely impossible to implement. For an argosy of further examples, see Aaron Panken, *The Rhetoric of Innovation: Self-Conscious Legal Change in Rabbinic Literature* (Lanham, MD: University Press of America, 2005).

26. See Frolov, *Judges*, 316–322.

27. Of course, the ultimate enforcer is YHWH/Elohim, in that he is the one who dispenses reward for observance and punishment for lack thereof. Yet, in the HB, the deity almost always does that through its agents, especially where entire communities are involved. The only major exception is the destruction of Sodom and surrounding cities in Genesis 19.

28. Georg Braulik, "Das Deuteronomium und die Menschenrechte," *Theologische Quartalschrift* 166 (1986): 8–24. English translation: Georg Braulik, *The Theology of Deuteronomy: Collected Essays* (trans. Ulrika Lindblad; North Richland Hills, TX: BIBAL Press, 1994), 131–150.

29. Yair Kotler, *Heil Kahane* (trans. Edward Levin; New York: Adama Books, 1986), 198–203.

30. For a concise review of such uses of the passage, see Ehud Ben Zvi, "'Have We Not All One Father? Has Not One God Created Us?' Revisiting Malachi 2:10a," in *Partners with God: Theological and Critical Readings of the Bible in Honor of Marvin A. Sweeney* (ed. Shelley L. Birdsong and Serge Frolov; Claremont Studies in Hebrew Bible and Septuagint 2; Claremont, CA: Claremont Press, 2017), 277–281.

31. Ben Zvi, "Revisiting Malachi 2:10a," 289–294, explains that in this larger context the reading would depend to a great extent on whether the father in v. 10 is identified as YHWH/Elohim, Adam, Abraham, Jacob, or yet another biblical figure.

32. However, according to 1 Kgs 5:27–30 Solomon imposed forced labor on "all Israel."

33. Frolov, "Diversity, Justice, and the Bible for Grown-Ups," in *God Loves Diversity and Justice: Progressive Scholars Speak about Faith, Politics, and the World* (ed. Susanne Scholz; Lanham, MD: Lexington, 2013), 147–159.

34. On blasphemy, see especially Julián Andrés González Holguín, "Leviticus 24:10–23: An Outsider Perspective," *HS* 56 (2015): 89–102.
35. Even the UDHR tacitly acknowledges this distinction when it states, "Everyone has the right to leave any country, including his own, and to return *to his country*" (article 13/2; emphasis added).
36. In Deut. 23:4–7, the charge of hiring Balaam to curse Israel is leveled against Ammonites and Moabites to justify, in part, their exclusion.
37. According to the Talmud (b. Ab. Zar. 64b–65a), *ger* should at the very least pledge acceptance of the so-called Noahide Laws, which include prohibition of idolatry.
38. Similar reasoning with regard to distinctions between humans and animals may underlie the treatment of male and female bestiality as a capital offense (Exod. 22:18; Lev. 18:23; 20:15–16). Female homosexuality is probably not prohibited because it is not seen as involving an intercourse that would render one of the participants male.

SELECT BIBLIOGRAPHY

Baltzer, Klaus (1971), *The Covenant Formulary in Old Testament, Jewish, and Early Christian Writings*, trans. David E. Green, Philadelphia: Fortress Press.

Birdsong, Shelley L. and Serge Frolov, eds. (2017), *Partners with God: Theological and Critical Readings of the Bible in Honor of Marvin A. Sweeney*, Claremont, CA: Claremont Press.

Buber, Martin (1967), *Kingship of God*, 3rd ed., New York: Harper & Row.

Eichrodt, Walther (1961), *Theology of the Old Testament*, 2 vols., trans. J. A. Baker, London: SCM Press.

Frolov, Serge (2013), *Judges* (Vol. 6, Part 2 of The Forms of the Old Testament Literature), Grand Rapids, MI: Eerdmans.

Kitchen, Kenneth A. and Paul J. N. Lawrence (2012), *Treaty, Law, and Covenant in the Ancient Near East*, 3 vols., Wiesbaden, DEU: Harrassowitz.

McCarthy, Dennis J. (1963), *Treaty and Covenant: A Study in Form in the Ancient Oriental Documents and in the Old Testament*, Analecta Biblica 21, Rome: Pontifical Biblical Institute.

Oeste, Gordon K. (2011), *Legitimacy, Illegitimacy, and the Right to Rule: Windows on Abimelech's Rise and Demise in Judges 9* (Library of Hebrew Bible/Old Testament Studies 546), New York: T&T Clark.

Schmitt, Carl (1985), *Political Theology: Four Chapters on the Concept of Sovereignty*, trans. George Schwab, Cambridge, MA: MIT Press.

Scholz, Susanne, ed. (2013), *God Loves Diversity and Justice: Progressive Scholars Speak about Faith, Politics, and the World*, Lanham, MD: Lexington Books.

CHAPTER FIVE

Political Theology and the New Testament

NEIL ELLIOTT

THE IDEOLOGICAL CONTEXT

The theology of liberation has arguably been the preeminent contemporary attempt to carry out a politically responsible theology since its beginnings in the late twentieth century. Its practitioners insist on beginning with "a solid knowledge of the real situation" in which "the gospel is proclaimed," including a "thorough analysis," social, political, and economic, "of the situation in which the church and today's humankind are living."[1]

In the early twenty-first century, an adequate attempt at that task must take account of the reigning neoliberal global order[2] and of the stark incompatibility of that order with any realistic prospects for the survival of many of the planet's species. Millions of human beings are already endangered, given the accelerating pace of anthropogenic climate change.[3] Indeed, material deprivation in the sprawling "zones of social abandonment" that seem inherently necessary to capitalism's continuation constitutes the primary context in which theology is carried out. The failure of liberation theology's proliferating progeny to sustain attention, let alone resistance, to such deprivation in the form of a meaningful socialist alternative marks the theological challenge of our era.[4]

We must also take account today of the rise of nationalist and quasi-fascist political movements throughout the developed Global North. These are often fueled, as in the United States, by long-lived cultural currents and institutional forms of misogyny and racism, the latter the enduring legacy of slavery. In the absence of a vibrant, coherent, and intersectional political Left, these movements serve to channel the frustrations of a proportionately declining demographic—white males who protest the loss of privileges previously afforded them by racist and kyriarchal cultural forms[5]—into resentment and violence toward ethnic and gender minorities and women, and especially against immigrants and refugees fleeing deteriorating prospects for life in the beleaguered Global South.

Finally, theology must describe and resist the rhetorical and ideological camouflage given to that resentment by ultraconservative forms of Christianity. So much was made clear by the course of the 2016 US presidential campaign and its eventual result. White evangelicals and white supremacists alike perceived in the incoming administration the promise of restoring some measure of white privilege[6] and normalizing an aggressively heterosexist patriarchy; that it also rolled back even modest limits on corporate, financial, military, and autocratic power was regarded as a rebuke to a secularist élite.[7] If today we are approaching the demographic "end of White Christian America,"⁸ that end apparently will not come without a fierce struggle. Yet as Jones shows, many white "mainline" churches are preoccupied with wresting the title away from white evangelicals, thus perpetuating in mutated form the fundamentalist-modernist controversies of the twentieth century, rather than addressing the urgent crises of the twenty-first.

To focus here on US society is not to indulge its imagined self-importance. It is to acknowledge the devastating effects of US corporate, governmental, and military support for the neoliberal order, as well as the worldwide reach of US material and electronic culture. Even as credentialed pundits in the US have puzzled over the naked ambition of self-styled evangelical leaders, observers elsewhere have readily enough identified their protégés as "the propagators of a new slave religion," "black and latinx . . . prosperity gospellers" bringing "a new Christian fundamentalism" in thrall to capitalist ideology, "with . . . devastating consequences for the peoples of the Global South."⁹

In this toxic ideological mix, the Bible continues to enjoy undimmed glory as "America's iconic book,"¹⁰ even as ever-greater majorities admit never to have read it.¹¹ If South Africa's anti-apartheid movement could calculate in the 1980s that the Bible remained its best resource among "very limited ideological options,"¹² a different calculus seems to apply in the US, where the Bible's prestige is often pressed into service to sustain a "counterrevolutionary situation."¹³ Unless political theology is grounded in an ideological-critical assessment of this situation, appeals to the New Testament as authorizing resource risk simply reinscribing unspoken, yet powerful assumptions about biblical authority that, in the current context, are normally retrograde.

THE NEOLIBERAL CAPTIVITY OF THE NEW TESTAMENT

In the US, a handful of New Testament phrases exert disproportionate power, in public discourse as well as ecclesiastical life, as condensed divine sanctions for kyriarchal relationships and social indifference to the poor and underprivileged. The "omnipresent" declaration that "The poor you always have with you" (Mt 26:11 par.) is wielded as axiomatic proof that poverty is inevitable, irreversible, and the fault of the poor themselves.¹⁴ The Pauline admonition that "the one who is unwilling to work should not eat" (2 Thess. 3:10) has become a watchword in Congressional debates to restrict funding for food supplements to the poor.¹⁵ The pseudo-Pauline household codes have been invoked so routinely in constraining women's aspirations to equality and preserving patriarchal privilege that their citation has been regarded as a practical measure of the likelihood of domestic violence¹⁶ and a buttress of anti-feminist policy alike.¹⁷ And, as almost quaint vestiges of a bygone past when conservatism was still yoked to meek conformity to government, the admonitions to "render unto Caesar" (Mt 22:15–22 par.) and "be subject to the governing authorities" (Rom. 13:1–7) are cited by prominent religious advisers to marshal Evangelical support whenever right-wing governmental policy faced popular dissent, though such invocations have been absent, for example, when more centrist administrations have proposed modest reforms, or when heavily armed right-wing militias have occupied federal property.

Whatever exegetical discussions have taken place among specialists regarding the "correct" interpretation of any of these passages, they have failed to dim their rhetorical power in public life. Outside of the US, similar patterns of the Bible's deployment in strategically selective ways prevail, as witnessed from the UK by James Crossley¹⁸ and from the Global South by the Kairos documents of 1988 (South Africa) and 1989 (Central

America, Africa, and Asia).[19] Evidently, in the present ideological context, key biblical texts serve less often as moral compass points than to provide "flak" for the dominant propaganda system.[20] Any approach to a responsible political theology must take this context, and the challenge of disarming a weaponized Bible, with utmost seriousness.

Instead, however, the New Testament is more regularly appropriated as a resource for preaching and theologizing from a posture of presumed ideological and even critical innocence. So, for example, even a renowned New Testament scholar has proclaimed that his own theological interpretation of the apostle Paul derives, not from a particular socioeconomic location, but from "[his] own acquaintance with Paul," and expressed approval of "the vast majority of Christians in the world today" who "read Paul with blissful ignorance" of critical interpretive issues.[21] Such homey disavowal of critical method, let alone of ideological awareness, perpetuates a popular understanding of the Bible as a text uniquely unconditioned by history and thus capable of mediating direct knowledge and experience of the divine will.

The claim to historical naiveté evades the ideological constraints evident in the production of texts and their subsequent reception alike.[22] In the case of the New Testament, that claim evades the historical intertwining of Christianity, colonialism, capitalism, and enslavement begun in the original theological displacement of one people, Israel, by another,[23] and threatens to render invisible to mainstream theology the continued crucifixion of peoples under racially inflected capitalism.[24] The constraints of capitalist thought are evident when "liberal" interpreters are satisfied to affirm social inclusiveness, the "social glue" of an inherently unjust order.[25]

Such constraints are not irresistible. Karl Kautsky already described the emergence of early Christianity against the horizon of the revolutionary potential of its origins and recognized that this potential was lost even as the movement spread ever outward from Judea. Eventually, "The destruction of Jerusalem meant that there was no longer any basis for an independent class movement of the Jewish proletariat."[26] Such plain language alarmed others, however, who are normally hailed today as scholarship's hallowed ancestors while Kautsky is banished from more decorous collective memory. "Absolute nonsense" was Max Weber's dismissal, for example. For the early Christians, "worldly aims were dangerous," and because of the expected "permanence of Roman rule until the end of time," they allegedly considered it "hopeless to strive for social reform." Such calculated despair led instead to "Christian love—purely ethical, charitable, and transcendental," and thus inherently apolitical.[27] Correspondingly, more recent interpreters have spoken of the "love patriarchalism" of Paul's communities in Asia Minor and Greece[28] or of the "mutualism" practiced by those communities as an urban "survival strategy."[29] Such observations implicitly corroborate Kautsky's description of Christianity in the environment of Greco-Roman cities, pointing to the material and ideological constraints on those communities. They fail, however, to emphasize (as Kautsky did) the distance from more emancipatory possibilities and the probable compromise of Paul's own purposes as well.[30]

Without such historical contextualization, an approach devoted to extrapolating patterns of political thought and action from the New Testament texts will inevitably be limited by the focus in those texts on individual piety, acts of charity, and affective bonds within the community, cast against an expectation of imminent divine intervention and reward for the virtuous. Such focus on deductive method, equating what was with all that could have been, restricts the horizon of the possible for political theology today. But the limitation to individual virtue, rather than collective political and planetary responsibility, is one we can no longer afford—if we ever could.[31]

Conversely, because of the ideological constraints of the first century—especially the presumption of kyriarchy in divine and human realms alike that informed messianic thought as well as imperial propaganda[32]—attempts to trace "nonconformist" impulses[33] through the New Testament writings might inevitably be partial and suggestive, at best, for serious contemplation of our own responsibilities. Such attempts are nevertheless valuable for counteracting, on one side, the popular understanding that conservative politics, Anglo-American exceptionalism, and unbridled capitalism simply *are* the politics and economics of the Bible, and, on the other, the insistence that the New Testament writings are primarily concerned with individual salvation and are thus on principle indifferent to politics and the political.

THE POLITICS OF READING THE POLITICS OF JESUS

It may prove useful to briefly survey what are still the dominant patterns of reading political themes and tropes from the New Testament writings.

The search for the "politics of Jesus" has proceeded in tandem with the search for the "historical Jesus." If late nineteenth-century European scholarship understood Jesus as a teacher of wise and congenially liberal ethics, Albert Schweitzer argued that he was driven instead by an intense expectation of divine intervention, more compatible with a modern world-mysticism than with a rationally developed ethics.[34] The subsequent effort to restore Jesus to his historical context as an eschatologically minded first-century Jew led S. G. F. Brandon[35] to the provocative thesis that Jesus and his family had shared the ardent and, ultimately, disastrous religious nationalism of the Zealots. The thesis was repudiated as misguided and speculative, or ignored by a majority of scholars, who instead relied on Gospel *logia*, regarded as authentic (an agenda established by Bultmann),[36] that depicted Jesus teaching renewal through the individual's transformation[37] and nonviolent resistance.[38]

In the last quarter of the twentieth century, however, scholars began to recognize the de-Judaizing effect of Bultmann's criterion of "double dissimilarity," and in the aftermath of the Vietnam War and counterinsurgency wars in Central America, some sought to restore Jesus to a context of material and political oppression and popular resistance to it.[39] The adoption of social-scientific perspectives promoted the thesis that Jesus' significance had less to do with his teaching of individual ethics than with his founding of (or participation in)[40] a social movement in Galilean villages, variously characterized as promoting egalitarian relationships; rejecting patronage and debt; repudiating purity laws, understood as inherently discriminatory toward the poor; restoring covenantal values at the level of agrarian village life; sharing meals openly across social statuses; and performing healings and exorcisms as the rejection of social stigma or colonial subjection.[41]

The academic, popular, and homiletic interpretation of Jesus' parables often betrays the influence of capitalist ideology. The parable of the talents (Mt. 25:14–30; Lk. 19:12–27) readily yields itself to being read as a "call to wise investment," indeed, as Jesus' "most direct teaching with respect to capital," a metaphor for "the necessity of risk-taking for the Kingdom of God."[42] There are other possible readings, informed by first-century agrarian values,[43] but these have been dismissed (when they have received attention at all) as the "unlikely" fantasy of "Marxist/liberationist hermeneutics."[44] The parable of the workers in the vineyard (Mt. 20:1–16) is almost universally read, and heard, as a repudiation of what Marx, or union members anywhere, might have called the labor theory of value; it is divine grace that all workers, regardless of their contribution, are paid the same "generous" amount as defined by an all-knowing owner who is disposing of his private property. William Herzog II[45] argued, to the contrary, that, freed from their artificial (and artificially allegorical) editorial framing in the Gospels, Jesus' parables constituted a "pedagogy of the oppressed," conscientizing peasants into the largely unseen but exploitive dynamics of the Roman economy. Here, the main character is not a God figure, but an abusive and expropriating landowner who deliberately humiliates the laborers he has hired in stages so as to maximize profit. (The NRSV's gloss of δηνάριον with "the usual daily wage" is questionable.)[46] But Herzog's important work has received scant attention; Luise Schottroff is a lonely exception.[47]

Despite impulses toward a more political reading of Jesus, however, important voices have insisted that the action most likely to have brought Jesus under Roman suspicion, then condemnation to be crucified—the attack on moneychangers' tables in the Temple (Mt. 21:12-17; Mk. 11:15-19; Lk. 19:45-48; John effectively removes the linkage, 2:13-16)—was not politically motivated, but was a symbolic gesture, at home in "Jewish restoration eschatology," predicting the divine destruction and eventual restoration of the Temple[48]—if, indeed, it happened at all.[49] Jesus may be hailed now as a *social* revolutionary, promoting communitarian values, but the hypothesis that his action might have been part of broader anti-Roman activity remains marginalized—though no less plausible for that.[50]

This sample cannot pretend to comprehend the breadth and variety of contemporary discussion. It may suffice to highlight the relevant questions for any attempt at interpreting Jesus for a political theology: How should we weigh our various sources (e.g., Mark, Q, Thomas, Josephus)? What role should we give different kinds of evidence (e.g., Jesus' actions vs. his words)? Which historical analogies are relevant (Greek symposia; itinerant philosophers; rabbinic schools; peasant insurrections)? And perhaps most important: Do we seek to read a coherent, practicable "politics of Jesus" from the Gospels, taking their narratives more or less at face value, or do we recognize the historical dimensions of his failure, that he "died in complete rupture with his own cause"?[51]

THE POLITICS OF READING THE POLITICS OF PAUL

The last question is only exacerbated when we move from the historical Jesus to the earliest written expressions of the conviction that God raised him from the dead. With the apostle Paul, we enter a dramatically different historical landscape, the urban environment of the Greek-speaking East (and the Jewish diaspora there). Here, references to the political contours of Jesus' own activity in Galilee and Judaea are nonexistent. The political character of his death is alluded to in quasi-numinous phrases that remain cryptically ambiguous for most scholars ("the rulers of this age," 1 Cor. 2:8; "dominion, authority, and power," 1 Cor. 15:24). Until the last decades of the twentieth century, the question of "Paul's politics" could be summarily answered by reference to the notorious admonition in Romans 13:1–7 to "be subject to the governing authorities," either inspiring contentment among better-situated readers or scorn among those agitating for social change. The effect of the household codes in the "deutero-Pauline" writings, even when these were recognized as pseudepigraphic, was to domesticate perceptions of Paul's own social views, e.g., in the interpretation of Philemon or the translation of 1 Corinthians 7:24.[52] Sympathetic readers excused Paul's relative indifference to social inequity and injustice by pointing to his conviction that Christ's return (and its presumed resolution of injustices) was near, and to his preoccupation with defending the inclusion of non-Jews in his assemblies—a theme that seems to limit appropriation of Paul to the liberal politics of inclusion.

Attempts to describe Paul as a more "liberative" figure have relied on reading some of his language as (not just "theological" but) a deliberate, though veiled, contestation of imperial ideological claims. He gathered "assemblies" (ἐκκλησίας) around the triumphant proclamation (εὐαγγέλιον) of a "lord" (κύριος), a "son of God" (υἱὸς τοῦ θεοῦ), who would bring about divine justice (δικαιοσύνη τοῦ θεοῦ) and "rule the nations" (ἀρχεῖν τὰ ἔθνη). His goal was to secure the "obedience" (ὑπακοή) and holy self-offering of the nations (προσφόρα τῶν ἐθνῶν), through the name of this lord, to God. That these phrases had political resonances within imperial propaganda and cult is now widely recognized, after decades of investigation of "Paul and politics" and "Paul and empire."[53] But whether Paul intended to evoke those resonances implicitly and challenge them in a partially "hidden transcript,"[54] or, whatever his intention, whether readers or hearers would have perceived such resonances, remains a matter of intense scholarly debate.[55]

Meanwhile, interrogations of the notions of "empire" and "imperialism" in terms of Hellenistic philosophical discourse about kingship[56] and rhetoric, popular among a provincial elite, about self-control[57] also bear on the interpretation of Paul's topoi. The more intimate negotiations of ethnic, gender, and social differences press for attention as well,[58] as do questions of Paul's engagement with slavery[59] and economic disparity.[60]

Where an earlier scholarship could lay Paul's allegedly accommodationist social ethic to the account of his anticipation of an imminent divine resolution of social ills,[61] in the latter half of the twentieth century, Paul could be understood as accommodating himself, inevitably, to a social order characterized by "ambiguous" social status and moderate upward mobility.[62] As Steven Friesen showed, a so-called "new consensus," hailed by Wayne A. Meeks and others, actually reprised the early twentieth-century repudiation of class struggle on the part of scholars (such as Adolf Deissmann and Adolf von Harnack) who were determined, in opposition to the inroads of socialism, "to deny a need for structural change in German society" and to insist "that the gospel could transform the lower classes without disrupting the status quo because the gospel brought inner enlightenment and peace to individuals."[63] The hypothesis of significant social stratification in Pauline assemblies (based on 1 Cor. 1:26: if "not many" were wise, powerful, nobly born, then presumably some were), with a rough "cross-section" of social statuses (advocates of the "new consensus" avoid the term *class*), serves similarly to deflect any implication that the Pauline mission had either a definite socioeconomic base or a sociopolitical agenda. Paul's assemblies necessarily met in the more capacious houses of wealthier members and thus inevitably yielded to the established social codes of patronage, even in the intimate space of domestic life, a compromise Paul himself promoted by insisting that the hungry "eat at home" (1 Cor. 11:17–34). But the patronage model has been challenged. Even in Corinth, members may have gathered in poorer—and more egalitarian—common spaces in *insulae*.[64] And in the context of scathing sarcasm throughout 1 Corinthians, Paul's terse "eat at home" might be read as rebuke, not advice.[65]

Remarkably, while professional New Testament scholars, steeped in historical method, have labored to establish the socioeconomic coordinates of Paul, his coworkers, and the members of his assemblies, Paul's alleged radicalism has been made a cause célèbre among Leftist Continental philosophers including Slavoj Žižek,[66] Alain Badiou,[67] and Giorgio Agamben.[68] Their various appeals to the apostle have at times relied more on rhetorical flamboyance than careful historical or exegetical analysis, but their insistence that Paul's thought is vitally relevant to contemporary political crises under neoliberal capitalism has made reconsideration of Paul's relevance for political theology not only salient, but urgent.[69] Even more urgent is the recognition, amply demonstrated in the works discussed, that the variety of characterizations of Paul and his audiences "are reflective more of the categories, inclinations, and desires of the proximate present than of the distant past."[70] The posture of hermeneutical naïveté, discussed above, is also one we can no longer afford.

THE POLITICS OF READING
THE POLITICS OF THE GOSPELS

Space does not allow a close reading of each of the canonical Gospels. Some interpretive issues have been discussed above vis-à-vis the politics of Jesus. Here it is relevant to observe that one important development in recent scholarship on the Gospels has been the resurgence within some academic circles of a popular, traditionalist view of the Gospels. That is, in reaction to the earlier form-critical and redactional-critical synthesis of Bultmann and his successors, according to which the Gospels were the products of anonymous communities both in the creation and transmission of oral tradition and in their eventual commitment to papyrus, we find the continuing insistence that the Gospels were intended primarily to preserve memories of Jesus after the death of the disciples;[71] indeed, that they were intended historiographically, to make the testimonies of eyewitnesses available as widely as possible to the broader church;[72] even in the increasingly variegated proliferation of gospels, every instance of "gospel writing" is "a movement forward that is also intended as a movement backward to Jesus himself."[73] Over against such "innocent" views of the Gospels we must pose characterizations of them as "identity-confirming narratives,"[74] "Christian propaganda."[75]

It bears note that the rise of a distinct discipline of "political theology" coincided with cultural, political, and theological efforts in post-Second World War Europe and the United States to come to terms with the catastrophic compatibility of some construals of Christianity with Nazism (e.g., the Deutsche Christen movement). Other postwar realities as well weighed heavily: an international Cold War between atomic superpowers, styled in the West as a mortal struggle between freedom and Communism; the hot wars of insurgency and counterinsurgency those superpowers delegated to their surrogates amid worldwide struggles for decolonization and self-government; and the "war against the poor" carried out through and beyond all these efforts.[76] The legacy of anti-Semitism weighed heavily enough that by the 1970s and 1980s, exposing and repudiating the "roots" of Christian supersessionism had become a fundamental agendum of New Testament studies.[77] Less so, however, the other concerns just named, which together constitute a pervasive supersessionism toward the poor and dispossessed that capitalist ideology has continued to represent as both natural and inevitable.

Against such supersessionism stand several historical judgments. Paula Fredriksen has observed, with typical concision, that "given Jesus' manner of death" on a Roman cross, "we can only assume that Pilate, and not the High Priest or the Sanhedrin, was responsible" for it.[78] But, she continues, "the task of the trial narratives [in the Gospels] is to reverse the burden of that responsibility in the face of the fact, too central to the tradition to be dropped or altered, that Jesus died on a cross."[79] The accounts of Jesus' trial before the Sanhedrin, "tendentious and artificial, do not inspire confidence"; their purpose is to emphasize that Jesus "died for religious reasons (hence at Jewish instigation), not political ones (hence not at Roman initiative)."[80] As for the trial before Pilate, the governor's "reported conduct as reluctant judge is scarcely credible as history, but it was very important theologically and politically" to the communities who produced the Gospels.[81] The scene, common to all four Gospels, where the Jews of Jerusalem cry out for the release of a rebel and a murderer at the cost of the life of an innocent man—indeed, of the messiah, a teacher of peace and righteousness, very son of God—is "absolutely unhistorical."[82] Jesus' crucifixion—the Roman punishment of the seditious—clearly indicates his status "as a political figure," yet the Gospels exert themselves to argue otherwise.[83] After the catastrophic war of 66–73 CE, Fredriksen summarizes, the church "had every reason to want to assure prospective Gentile audiences that the Christian movement neither threatened nor challenged imperial sovereignty the way the Jewish people had," and they sought to achieve that purpose through the Passion narratives.[84]

Scholars have exerted themselves to demonstrate the radical, egalitarian, socially revolutionary, or counter-imperial impulses not just of Jesus (see above) but of the Gospel writers as well.[85] But whatever exegetical acumen might be brought to bear on one or another Gospel passage, plot turn, or redactional feature, it is incumbent, especially on theologically minded *Christian* readers, to recognize that they were written to achieve simultaneously the inculpation of the Jews and Pilate's exculpation for Jesus' death,[86] which means the *depoliticization* of Jesus' life and death alike. It follows that any responsible political theology must approach the Gospels, and their portrayal of (for lack of a better phrase) Jesus' politics, with a thorough-going and well grounded suspicion of that agenda. Nor will it suffice to present hypotheses regarding one or another anonymous sectarian community to explain the perspective of an Evangelist. A politically sensitive theology must ask how the construal of each narrative served to shape the subsequent Christian imagination in its dread intertwining with colonialism, slavery, and capitalist dispossession.[87]

INTERROGATING THE LEGACY OF THE NEW TESTAMENT WRITINGS

It is now routine to describe the subsequent appropriation and re-interpretation of earlier New Testament writings in subsequent Christian generations: the Jesus tradition (or "movement") partly effaced by the Gospels; the Johannine community's devolution into intra-ecclesial contention and, eventually, Gnosticism; Paul's message extended (on one view) or subverted (on another) by the pseudo-Pauline epistles and beyond;[88] the eventual erasure of the very possibility of "Jewish Christianity" at the hands of Ignatius, the Epistle of Barnabas, and Melito of Sardis. The anti-Roman, "revolutionary" fury of the Revelation to John was clear enough to Friedrich Engels;[89] when its spirit emerged a century later as the "New Prophecy," it was swiftly condemned as a heresy, and still later, Augustine defended Christianity from its pagan despisers after the fall of Rome by allegorizing its two cities—smoldering "Babylon" and the heavenly Jerusalem—as the project of Roman civilization and the church as a loyal opposition within it (*The City of God*).

Professional biblical scholarship remains preoccupied with questions of historical origins and the original intent of texts. A political theology attuned to our historical situation must be equally preoccupied with the historical transmutations of meanings over the centuries and, not least, with the effects of the active ideological deployment of biblical tropes and phrases today. Seen from this perspective, some hermeneutical strategies will inevitably appear as tools of reactionary or revanchist cultural and political programs; others will declare their commitment to the enhancement of human striving and planetary sustainability in terms that properly sound revolutionary. Given the stakes, none of us should aspire to a broad "middle ground" in which the faithful might "just read the Bible." Such imagined innocence, however sincerely felt, is an abdication of responsibility.

NOTES

1. Peruvian Organizations, "The Role of the Laity" (1968), advisory paper to the episcopal conference at Medellín, prepared at Naña, Peru, June 1–2. Published in *Liberation Theology: A Documentary History*, ed. with Introductions, Commentary, and Translations by Alfred T. Hennelly, S.J. (Maryknoll, NY: Orbis, 1990), 84–88.
2. David Harvey, *A Brief History of Neoliberalism* (Oxford: Oxford University Press, 2006); Arundhati Roy, *Capitalism: A Ghost Story* (Boston: Haymarket, 2014).
3. Naomi Klein, *The Shock Doctrine: The Rise of Disaster Capitalism* (New York: Macmillan, 2007); Naomi Klein, *This Changes Everything: Capitalism vs. the Climate* (New York: Simon & Schuster, 2014).
4. Ivan Petrella, *Beyond Liberation Theology: A Polemic* (London: SCM, 2008).
5. On the term, Elisabeth Schüssler Fiorenza, *But She Said: Feminist Practices of Biblical Interpretation* (Boston: Beacon, 1992).
6. Ta-Nehisi Coates, "The First White President," *The Atlantic* (October 2017).
7. Naomi Klein, *No Is Not Enough: Resisting Trump's Shock Politics and Winning the World We Need* (Boston: Haymarket, 2017).
8. Robert Jones, *The End of White Christian America* (New York: Simon & Schuster, 2016).
9. Allan Aubrey Boesak, "Babblers to the Rabble, Prophets to the Powerful: Mission in the Context of Empire" (2016). Keynote address to the DARE Forum. Quoted with permission.
10. Martin Marty, "America's Iconic Book," in *Humanizing America's Iconic Book,* ed. Gene M. Tucker and Douglas A. Knight (BSNA 6; Chico: Scholars Press, 1982), 1–23.
11. Caleb Bell, "Poll: Americans Love the Bible But Don't Read It Much," *RNS* (April 23, 2013).
12. David Jobling, "Very Limited Ideological Options: Marxism and Biblical Studies in Postcolonial South Africa," in *Postcolonial Biblical Criticism: Interdisciplinary Intersections,* ed. Stephen D. Moore and Fernando F. Segovia (London: T&T Clark, 2005), 184–201.
13. Carter Heyward, "Doing Theology in a Counterrevolutionary Situation," in *The Future of Liberation Theology: Essays in Honor of Gustavo Gutierrez* (Maryknoll, NY: Orbis, 1989), 397–407; Neil Elliott, "A Famine of the Word: A Stringfellowian Reflection on the American Church Today," in *The Bible in the Public Square: Reading the Signs of the Times,* ed. Cynthia Briggs Kittredge, Ellen Bradshaw Aitken, and Jonathan A. Draper (Minneapolis, MN: Fortress Press, 2008), 185–196. On the term, Philip Berryman, "Doing Theology in a (Counter-) Revolutionary Situation," in *Theology in the Americas,* ed. Sergio Torres and John Eagleson (Maryknoll, NY: Orbis, 1976), 54–75.
14. Liz Theoharis, *Always with Us? What Jesus Really Said about the Poor* (Grand Rapids, MI: Eerdmans, 2017).
15. Michelle Goldberg, "Poverty Denialism," *The Nation* (Nov. 25, 2013), 6–8.
16. R. Emerson Dobash and Russell Dobash, *Violence against Wives* (New York: Free Press, 1979), chap. 3.
17. Susan Faludi, *Backlash: The Undeclared War against American Women* (New York: Crown, 1991), 233.
18. James G. Crossley, *Jesus in an Age of Terror: Scholarly Projects for a New American Century* (London: Equinox, 2008); James G. Crossley, *Jesus in an Age of Neoliberalism: Quests, Scholarship, and Ideology* (Durham: Acumen, 2012).

19. Robert McAfee Brown, ed. *Kairos: Three Prophetic Challenges to the Church* (Grand Rapids, MI: Eerdmans, 1990); Allan Aubrey Boesak, *Kairos, Crisis, and Global Apartheid* (New York: Palgrave Macmillan, 2015).
20. On the term, Noam Chomsky and Edward S. Herman, *Manufacturing Consent: The Political Economy of the Mass Media*, rev. ed. (New York: Random House, 1988).
21. N. T. Wright, *Paul in Fresh Perspective* (Minneapolis, MN: Fortress Press, 2005).
22. Fredric Jameson, *The Political Unconscious: Narrative as a Socially Symbolic Act* (Ithaca, NY: Cornell University Press, 1981).
23. Willie James Jenkins, *The Christian Imagination: Theology and the Origins of Race* (New Haven, CT: Yale University Press, 2011).
24. Ignácio Ellacuría, *El pueblo crucificado: Ensayo de soteriología histórica* (Mexico: CRT, 1978); Jon Sobrino, *No Salvation outside the Poor: Prophetic-Utopian Essays* (Maryknoll, NY: Orbis, 2008); James H. Cone, *The Cross and the Lynching Tree* (Maryknoll, NY: Orbis, 2013).
25. So Christopher Rowland, "Scripture: New Testament," in *The Blackwell Companion to Political Theology*, eds. Peter Scott and William T. Cavanaugh (Oxford: Blackwell, 2004), 23, referring to the fourth century CE; compare Petrella's indictment in Petrella, *Beyond Liberation Theology*, chap. 3, of a "theology of inclusion for the middle class" in the twenty-first.
26. Karl Kautsky, *Foundations of Christianity*, trans. Henry F. Mins (New York: Russell & Russell, 1953 [1908]), 334.
27. Max Weber, *The Agrarian Sociology of Ancient Civilizations* (London: Humanities Press, 1976). ET of German essays from 1896 and 1909; See Larry L. Welborn, "Marxism and Capitalism in Pauline Studies," in *Paul and Economics: A Handbook*, eds. Ray Pickett and Thomas V. Blanton IV (Minneapolis, MN: Fortress Press, 2017), 361–396.
28. Gerd Theissen, *The Social Setting of Pauline Christianity: Essays on Corinth*, trans. John H. Schutz (Philadelphia: Fortress Press, 1982).
29. Justin J. Meggitt, *Paul, Poverty, and Survival*. Studies of the New Testament and Its World (Edinburgh: T&T Clark, 1998).
30. So Larry L. Welborn, *That There May Be Equality: Pauline Economics in 2 Corinthians*, PCC n.s. (Lanham, MD: Lexington/Fortress Academic, forthcoming).
31. Bruce, Birch, Jacqueline Lapsley, Cynthia Moe Lobeda, and Larry Rasmussen, *Bible and Ethics in Christian Life: A New Conversation* (Minneapolis, MN: Fortress Press, 2018).
32. E.g. Neil Elliott, *The Arrogance of Nations: Reading Romans in the Shadow of Empire*. Paul in Critical Contexts. (Minneapolis, MN: Fortress Press, 2008), 152–166.
33. Rowland, "Scripture: New Testament."
34. Albert Schweitzer, *The Quest of the Historical Jesus: The First Complete Edition*, ed. John Bowden (Minneapolis, MN: Fortress Press, 2001). Translation of the second German edition, 1913; original publication 1906.
35. S. G. F. Brandon, *Jesus and the Zealots: A Study of the Political Factor in Primitive Christianity* (Manchester: Manchester University Press, 1967).
36. Rudolf Bultmann, *The History of the Synoptic Tradition* (New York: Harper & Row, 1927, German original 1921).
37. Martin Hengel, *Was Jesus a Revolutionist?* (Philadelphia: Fortress Press, 1971).
38. John Howard Yoder, *The Politics of Jesus: Vicit Agnus Noster* (Grand Rapids, MI: Eerdmans, 1983); see E. Bammel and C. F. D. Moule, eds. *Jesus and the Politics of His Day* (Cambridge: Cambridge University Press, 1984).
39. Richard A. Horsley, *Jesus and the Spiral of Violence: Popular Jewish Resistance in Roman Palestine* (San Francisco: Harper & Row, 1987).

40. Elisabeth Schüssler Fiorenza, *In Memory of Her: A Feminist Theological Reconstruction of Christian Origins* (New York: Crossroad, 1984).

41. Gerd Theissen, *Sociology of Palestinian Christianity* (Philadelphia: Fortress Press, 1978); Marcus Borg, *Conflict, Holiness, and Politics in the Teachings of Jesus* (New York: Mellen, 1984); John Dominic Crossan, *The Historical Jesus: The Life of a Mediterranean Jewish Peasant* (San Francisco: HarperSanFrancisco, 1991); Richard A. Horsley, *Sociology and the Jesus Movement* (New York: Continuum, 1994); Richard A. Horsley, *Jesus and the Politics of Roman Palestine* (Chapel Hill, SC: University of South Carolina Press, 2014).

42. Charles McDaniel, "Theology of the 'Real Economy': Christian Economic Ethics in an Age of Financialization," *Journal of Religion and Business Ethics* 2:2 (2014), Article 1; Charles McDaniel, "Financialization and the Changing Face of Poverty: Christian and Muslim Perspectives," In *The Bible, the Economy and the Poor*, ed. Ronald A. Simkins and Tom Kelly, *Journal of Religion and Society* Supplement Series 10 (2014), pp. 190–216.

43. Richard L. Rohrbaugh, "A Peasant Reading of the Parable of the Talents/Pounds: A Text of Terror?" *Biblical Theology Bulletin* 23 (1993), 32–39.

44. John L. Meier, *A Marginal Jew: Rethinking the Historical Jesus*, vol. 5: *Probing the Authenticity of the Parables* (New Haven, CT: Yale University Press, 2016), 356–358.

45. William Herzog II, *Parables as Subversive Speech: Jesus as Pedagogue of the Oppressed* (Louisville, KY: Westminster/John Knox, 1994).

46. Neil Elliott, "When Bridges Fail: Studying Economic Realities in New Testament Studies," in *Bridges in New Testament Interpretation*, ed. Neil Elliott and Werner Kelber (Minneapolis, MN: Fortress Press, 2018).

47. Luise Schottroff, *The Parables of Jesus* (Minneapolis, MN: Fortress Press, 2005).

48. E.P. Sanders, *Jesus and Judaism* (Philadelphia: Fortress Press, 1983), 73; Paula Fredriksen, *From Jesus to Christ: The Origins of the New Testament Images of Christ* (New Haven, CT: Yale University Press, 1988, 2nd ed. 2000).

49. Paula Fredriksen, *Jesus of Nazareth, King of the Jews: A Jewish Life and the Emergence of Christianity* (New York: Vintage, 1999), 251; Fredriksen, *From Jesus to Christ*, 2nd ed., xxi–xxiv.

50. Fernando Bermejo-Rubio, "(Why) Was Jesus the Galilean Crucified Alone? Solving a False Conundrum," *JSNT* 36(2) (2013), 127–154; Fernando Bermejo-Rubio, "Jesus and the Anti-Roman Resistance: A Reassessment of the Arguments," *JSHJ* 12 (2014), 1–105.

51. Jon Sobrino, *Christology at the Crossroads* (Maryknoll, NY: Orbis, 1978), 370.

52. Neil Elliott, *Liberating Paul: The Justice of God and the Politics of the Apostle* (Maryknoll, NY: Orbis, 1994).

53. See Klaus Wengst, *Pax Romana and the Peace of Jesus Christ*, trans. John Bowden (Philadelphia: Fortress Press, 1987); Dieter Georgi, *Theocracy in Paul's Praxis and Theology* (Philadelphia: Fortress Press, 1991; Ex libris publication 2009; German original 1987); Elliott, *Liberating Paul* (1994); Jacob Taubes, *The Political Theology of Paul*, trans. Dana Hollander, ed. Aleida Assmann, Jan Assmann, et al. (Stanford, CA: Stanford University Press, 2004; ET of *Die politische Theologie des Paulus*, Wilhelm Fink Verlag, 1993); the essays in Richard A. Horsley, ed., *Paul and Empire: Religion and Power in Roman Imperial Society* (Harrisburg: Trinity Press International, 1997): Richard A. Horsley, ed., *Paul and Politics: Ekklesia, Israel, Imperium, Interpretation: Essays in Honor of Krister Stendahl* (Harrisburg, PA: Trinity Press International, 2004); and Richard A. Horsley, ed., *Paul and the Roman Imperial Order* (Harrisburg, PA: Trinity Press International, 2004).

54. On the phrase, James C. Scott, *Domination and the Arts of Resistance: Hidden Transcripts* (New Haven, CT: Yale University Press, 1990).

55. Elliott, "A Famine of the Word"; Richard A. Horsley ed., *Hidden Transcripts and the Arts of Resistance: Applying the Work of James C. Scott to Jesus and Paul*, Semeia Studies 48 (Atlanta: SBL Studies, 2004); Davina A. Lopez, *Apostle to the Conquered: Reimagining Paul's Mission*, PCC (Minneapolis, MN: Fortress Press, 2008); James R. Harrison, *Paul and the Imperial Authorities at Thessalonica and Rome*. WUNT 273 (Tübingen: Mohr Siebeck, 2011); Contra: Seyoon Kim, *Christ and Caesar: The Gospel and the Roman Empire in the Writings of Paul and Luke* (Grand Rapids, MI: Eerdmans, 2008); John M. G. Barclay, "Why the Roman Empire Was Insignificant to Paul," *Pauline Churches and Diaspora Jews* (Tübingen and Grand Rapids, MI: Mohr Siebeck and Eerdmans, 2011), 363–388; see Scot McKnight and Joseph B. Modica, *Jesus Is Lord, Caesar Is Not: Evaluating Empire in New Testament Studies* (Downers Grove, IL: IVP Academic, 2013); Christoph Heilig, *Hidden Criticism? The Methodology and Plausibility of the Search for a Counter-Imperial Subtext in Paul*, WUNT 2.392 (Tübingen: Mohr Siebeck, 2015).

56. Bruno Blumenfeld, *The Political Paul: Democracy and Kingship in Paul's Thought*, JSNTSup 210 (Sheffield: Sheffield Academic Press, 2003).

57. Stanley K. Stowers, *A Rereading of Romans: Justice, Jews, and Gentiles* (New Haven, CT: Yale University Press, 1994).

58. Elizabeth A. Castelli, *Imitating Paul: A Discourse of Power* (Louisville, KY: Westminster/John Knox, 1991); Antoinette Clark Wire, *The Corinthian Women Prophets: A Reconstruction through Paul's Rhetoric* (Philadelphia: Fortress Press, 1994); Todd C. Penner and Caroline Vander Stichele, eds., *Her Master's Tools? Feminist and Postcolonial Engagements of Historical-Critical Discourse* (Atlanta: SBL, 2005); Joseph A. Marchal, *The Politics of Heaven: Women, Gender, and Empire in the Study of Paul*, PCC (Minneapolis, MN: Fortress Press, 2008); Joseph A. Marchal, *Studying Paul's Letters: Contemporary Perspectives and Methods* (Minneapolis, MN: Fortress Press, 2012); Matthew V. Johnson, James A. Noel, and Demetrius K. Williams, eds., *Onesimus Our Brother: Reading Religion, Race, and Culture in Philemon*, PCC (Minneapolis, MN: Fortress Press, 2012); Arminta M. Fox, *Paul Decentered: Reading 2 Corinthians with the Corinthian Women*, (Lanham, MD: Lexington/Fortress Academic, forthcoming).

59. Allen Dwight Callahan, et al., eds., *Slavery in Text and Interpretation*, Semeia 83/84 (Atlanta: Scholars Press, 2001); James Albert Harrill, *Slaves in the New Testament: Literary, Social, and Moral Dimensions* (Minneapolis, MN: Fortress Press, 2010).

60. Pickett and Blanton, *Paul and Economics*.

61. Albert Schweitzer, *The Mysticism of Paul the Apostle*, trans. William Montgomery (New York: Henry Holt, 1931).

62. Wayne A. Meeks, *The First Urban Christians: The Social World of the Apostle Paul* (New Haven, CT: Yale University Press, 1983).

63. Steven Friesen, "Poverty in Pauline Studies: Beyond the New Consensus," *JSNT* 26:3 (2004), 330–331.

64. David Horrell, "Domestic Space and Christian Meetings at Coirinth: Imagining New Contexts and the Buildings East of the Theatre," *NTS* 50:3 (2004), 349–369. Compare: Wire, *The Corinthian Women Prophets*, 1994; Robert Jewett, "Tenement Churches and Communal Meals in the Early Church: The Implications of a Form-Critical Analysis of 2 Thessalonians 3:10," *BR* 38 (1993), 23–43; Robert Jewett, *Romans*, Hermeneia (Minneapolis, MN: Fortress Press, 2008), 64–69; Peter Oakes, *Reading Romans in Pompeii: Paul's Letter at Ground Level* (Minneapolis, MN: Fortress Press, 2009).

65. Horsley, Richard A, *1 Corinthians*, ANTC (Nashville: Abingdon, 1998); Luise Schottroff, "Holiness and Justice: Exegetical Comments on 1 Corinthians 11:17–34," *JSNT* 79 (2000), 51–60; Neil Elliott, "Social Stratification and the Lord's Supper (1 Cor. 11:17–34)," in Pickett and Blanton, *Paul and Economics*, 245–275.

66. Slavoj Žižek, *The Fragile Absolute: Or, Why Is the Christian Legacy Worth Fighting For?* (London: Verso, 2011).

67. Alain Badiou, *Saint Paul: The Foundation of Universalism*, trans. Ray Brassier (Stanford, CA: Stanford University Press, 2003).

68. Giorgio Agamben, *The Time That Remains: A Commentary on the Letter to the Romans*, trans. Patricia Dailey (Stanford, CA: Stanford University Press, 2005).

69. See representative discussions in David Odell-Scott, *Reading Romans with Contemporary Philosophers and Theologians*. Romans through History and Culture (New York: T&T Clark, 2007); John D. Caputo and Linda Martín Alcoff, eds., *St. Paul among the Philosophers*. Indiana Series in the Philosophy of Religion (Bloomington, IN: Indiana University Press, 2009); Douglas Harink, ed., *Paul, Philosophy, and the Theopolitical Vision* (Eugene, OR: Cascade Books, 2010); John Milbank, Slavoj Žižek, and Creston Davis, *Paul's New Moment: Continental Philosophy and the Future of Christian Theology* (Grand Rapids, MI: Brazos, 2010); Christopher D. Stanley, ed., *The Colonized Apostle: Paul Through Postcolonial Eyes*, PCC (Minneapolis, MN: Fortress Press, 2011); Gordon Mark Zerbe, *Citizenship: Paul on Peace and Politics* (Winnipeg: CMU Press, 2012); Peter Frick, ed., *Paul in the Grip of the Philosophers*, PCC (Minneapolis, MN: Fortress Press, 2013); Ward Blanton, *A Materialism for the Masses: Saint Paul and the Philosophy of Undying Life*. Insurrections (New York: Columbia University Press, 2014); Larry L. Welborn, *Paul's Summons to Messianic Life* (New York: Columbia University Press, 2015).

70. Davina A. Lopez and Todd Penner, "Paul and Politics," *The Oxford Handbook of Pauline Studies*, ed. R. Barry Matlock (Oxford: Oxford University Press, 2017). Cited from Oxford Handbooks Online (www.oxfordhandbooks.com), 18.

71. K. F. Nickel, *The Synoptic Gospels: An Introduction* (Louisville, KY: Westminster/John Knox, 2001).

72. Richard J. Bauckham, *The Gospels for All Christians: Rethinking the Gospel Audiences* (Grand Rapids, MI: Eerdmans, 1998; 2nd ed., 2006).

73. Francis Watson, *Gospel Writing: A Canonical Perspective* (Grand Rapids, MI: Eerdmans, 2013), 605.

74. Fredriksen, *From Jesus to Christ*, 215.

75. John Dominic Crossan, *Jesus: A Revolutionary Biography* (San Francisco, CA: HarperSanFrancisco, 1994), 152.

76. On the last, Jack Nelson-Pallmeyer, *War against the Poor: Low-Intensity Conflict and Christian Faith* (Maryknoll, NY: Orbis, 1989).

77. See, among others, Rosemary Radford Ruether, *Faith and Fratricide: The Theological Roots of Anti-Semitism* (New York: Seabury Press, 1974).

78. Fredriksen, *From Jesus to Christ*, 121.

79. Ibid.

80. Ibid., 117.

81. Ibid., 120.

82. Crossan, *Jesus: A Revolutionary Biography*, 111.

83. Fredriksen, *From Jesus to Christ*, 124.

84. Ibid., 122.

85. Select examples include Warren Carter, *Matthew and Empire: Initial Explorations* (Harrisburg, PN: Trinity Press International, 2001), on Matthew; Ched Myers, *Binding the Strong Man: A Political Reading of Mark's Story of Jesus* (Maryknoll, NY: Orbis, 1988), on Mark; Halvor Moxnes, *The Economy of the Kingdom: Social Conflict and Economic*

Relations in Luke's Gospel (Minneapolis, MN: Fortress Press, 1988), on Luke; and Wes Howard-Brook, *Becoming Children of God: John's Radical Gospel and Radical Discipleship* (Maryknoll, NY: Orbis, 1994), on John.

86. Fredriksen, *From Jesus to Christ*, 121.
87. Jenkins, *The Christian Imagination*.
88. Richard I. Pervo, *The Making of Paul: Constructions of the Apostle in Early Christianity* (Minneapolis, MN: Fortress Press, 2010).
89. Frederick Engels, "The Book of Revelation," ET in *Marx and Engels on Religion* (1883; Progress Publishers, 1957).

SELECT BIBLIOGRAPHY

Briggs Kittredge, Cynthia, Ellen Bradshaw Aitken, and Jonathan A. Draper, eds. (2008), *The Bible in the Public Square: Reading the Signs of the Times,* Minneapolis, MN: Fortress Press.

Cone, James H. (2013), *The Cross and the Lynching Tree,* Maryknoll, NY: Orbis Books.

Crossan, John Dominic (1991), *The Historical Jesus: The Life of a Mediterranean Jewish Peasant,* San Francisco: HarperSanFrancisco.

Elliott, Neil (1994), *Liberating Paul: The Justice of God and the Politics of the Apostle,* Maryknoll, NY: Orbis Books.

Fredriksen, Paula (2000), *From Jesus to Christ: The Origins of the New Testament Images of Christ,* 2nd ed., New Haven, CT: Yale University Press.

Hennelly, S.J., Alfred T., ed. (1990), *Liberation Theology: A Documentary History,* with Introductions, Commentary, and Translations by Alfred T. Hennelly, Maryknoll, NY: Orbis Books.

Jenkins, Willie James (2011), *The Christian Imagination: Theology and the Origins of Race,* New Haven, CT: Yale University Press.

Jones, Robert (2016), *The End of White Christian America,* New York: Simon & Schuster.

Moore, Stephen D. and Fernando F. Segovia, eds. (2005), *Postcolonial Biblical Criticism: Interdisciplinary Intersections,* London: T&T Clark.

Petrella, Ivan (2008), *Beyond Liberation Theology: A Polemic,* London: SCM Press.

Schüssler Fiorenza, Elisabeth (1984), *In Memory of Her: A Feminist Theological Reconstruction of Christian Origins,* New York: Crossroad Publishing Company.

Schüssler Fiorenza, Elisabeth (1992), *But She Said: Feminist Practices of Biblical Interpretation,* Boston: Beacon Press.

Scott, Peter and William T. Cavanaugh, eds. (2004), *The Blackwell Companion to Political Theology,* Oxford: Blackwell Publishing.

Sobrino, Jon (2008), *No Salvation outside the Poor: Prophetic-Utopian Essays,* Maryknoll, NY: Orbis Books.

Torres, Sergio and John Eagleson, eds. (1976), *Theology in the Americas,* Maryknoll, NY: Orbis Books.

Žižek, Slavoj (2011), *The Fragile Absolute: Or, Why Is the Christian Legacy Worth Fighting For?* London: Verso.

CHAPTER SIX

Qur'anic Political Theology

God's Law, Jews, and the Politics of Friendship

JOSHUA A. SABIH

Do not ask me whether the Qur'an is created or eternal,
Ask me, instead,
Whether the *sultan* is a *thief*
Or a *half-prophet*.[1]

—Donqol 1987, 313

INTRODUCTION

In the aforementioned poetic verse, the Egyptian poet Amal Donqol (d. 1983) mentions two sets of hyphenations: the God-human nature of the Qur'an and the secular-theological portrayal of the ruler: *half-prophet*. One could say that it is impossible not to notice his criticism of the despotic political system that rules in the name of God through an ideology—false consciousness—of diversion and misplacement: rulers legitimizing their unjust politics. *Half-thief* (administration, law, economy, etc.) through a theological doctrine of divine rule, *half-prophet* (sovereignty), while their propaganda machine diverts people's attention from questioning and challenging the despotic nature of their ruler and the unfair distribution of wealth. Instead the despotic ruler occupies the masses with nonsensical issues—such as the nature of the Qur'an. In other words, the core of Donqol's ironic critique is that most rulers, in Egypt as well as in most Muslim countries, portray themselves and behave as semi-gods by means of a system of governance that is semi-theological and semi-secular; a hybrid system that seems to maintain the Muslim world in a "state of exception": neither theological nor secular, neither Western nor Muslim.

In traditional Islamic political theory, we find the following doctrine: Islam as a system of beliefs and code of behavior is considered as both *dīn* (often translated by the term religion) and *dawla* (often translated by the term state). It is believed that the formulation "Islam is religion and state" has replaced an earlier formulation: Islam is *dīn* and *dunyā* (this-world).[2] Interestingly, various explanations have been proposed as to what has caused this state of affairs. Here, we group them under two main perspectives: an intrinsic-essentializing perspective and a context-dynamic perspective. Religions such as Islam and Judaism are essentialized as being law-centric (nomos) religions, whereas Christianity, especially Pauline Christianity is considered anti-nomic religion. In other words, the unchangeable identity of Islam as being both *dīn* and *dawla*, the political and the theological are seen not only as having an intimate connection to the point of mutual identification, but also that this intimate relationship constitutes *the* intrinsic defining feature of the *true* Muslim; an identity that transcends history. Unlike the Christian West, Islamic countries have not been able to enter real modernity since they are not fully secular, i.e., there is no separation between religion and politics.

In the presence of what we today call "political Islam" and its violent forms, the intrinsic essentialist perspective has gained momentum. While it is true that the issue of the intimate relationship between the religious and the political in Islam in general, and in the Qur'an in particular, has never ceased to make its presence felt, with issues such as God's sovereignty and Mohammed's authority often construed as one and the same. But the question that everyone seeks an answer to is: How is this intimate relation between or hyphenation of the political and the religious been formed and articulated in the foundational texts of Islam, the Qur'an, and the prophetic experience of the prophet Mohammed? One should bear in mind that the experience of both the prophet Mohammed in both Mecca and Medina (610–632 CE), and the early community of believers in 632–661 CE, in which the emergence, construction, and articulation of these hyphenations have been later textually crystallized, represent today a reference, an ideal, and a legal argument still at work. For instance, the theological and the political in both so called "political Islam" and "moderate Islam" seem to stand out as inextricably mutually legitimizing in creating and maintaining a theo-political fallacy, a Janus-like situation that looks both secular and religious at the same time, and paradoxically creates the very conditions of a perpetual conflict: the political seeks to subjugate the religious, while the latter tries to replace the political. In his recent book, Benslama traces the invention of modern Islamism—or Jihadism—to the Hanbali scholar Ibn Taymiyya (1263–1328 CE) who tried to solve the dichotomy, religion/state or hyphenation, religion-politics, by stating that "*la religion est le-la politique*" (religion is the political/politics).[3]

In this chapter, the issue that I set out to investigate is not whether there is a link between the theological and the political, since for me this link is a given, but rather to look into these hyphenations and how they were structured in the early experience of the prophet and articulated textually in the Qur'an and in Mohammed's biography. In addition, along with the history of Islam and the Islamic societies, how these hyphenations have been perceived, ideologically interpreted, and politically-discursively deployed by the various schools of thought through a grid of a double link: the Qur'an/the prophet Mohammed's link with the doctrine that claims that Islam is both religion and state: *dīn* and *dawla*. As we know all political systems and regimes that have emerged in the Islamic world since the death of the prophet Mohammed in 632 have claimed to follow both approaches.

Concretely, I shall look into *how* the Qur'anic discourse reconstructs the intimate relation between the theological and the political through the narrative grids of Mohammed's biography. I postulate that discovering God's sovereignty through his revealed laws should be examined in the light of what the Qur'an says about the prophet's authority in matters relating to, *inter alia*, the question of alterity; in particular Jews as a people of the book. On the latter point, the fact that the Qur'anic discourse on friendship (*walāya*)—and non-friendship—is constructed in legal language does not exclude theologico-political understandings of the Qur'anic worldview. Rules that used to regulate forms of friendship—political, tribal, marriage, etc.—in addition to God's sovereignty and the prophet's authority, one of the two main features of Qur'anic political theology:

God's rule (ar. *al-hākimiyyah* : Q 5:41–53) and man's obligation to obey (ar. *al-tā'ah*: Q 4:59, 80). As mentioned earlier, this examination of political theology in Qur'anic discourse takes into consideration the historical reality as constructed by the textual body of Islamic historiography, Qur'an exegesis, and the literature of and about modern political Islam. The context-dynamic perspective, here, means that any discussion of Qur'anic political theology—God's sovereignty and Mohammed's authority—should take the immediate historical context of pre-Islam and early Islam into consideration, but also that every interpretive attempt since the prophetic experience bear the marks of its own historicity.

To the context-dynamic perspective, I add the transgressional reading of the Qur'anic text and Mohammed's biographical texts. Contrary to the traditional reading that simply adds to the core text other commentaries the sole task of which is to unveil the intrinsic meaning that is believed to be embedded in the text, transgressional reading's point of departure is that every signifying text is a literary symptom that brings the reader closer to the signified text. In other words, the texts that I am investigating in this chapter are studied through the network of inter- and intra-textuality.

> Yet if reading must not be content with doubling the text, it cannot legitimately *transgress* the text toward something other than it, toward a referent (a reality that is metaphysical, historical, psychobiographical, etc.) or toward a signified outside the text whose content could take place, could have taken place outside of language, that is to say, in the sense that we give here to that word, outside of writing in general.[4]

Muslims believe that the Qur'an—as text and discourse—is the word of God (ar. *kalāmu al-llāh*) and a revelation (ar. *wahy*) that began descending in Arabic upon Mohammed at the age of forty and lasted for a period of twenty-three years (610–623 CE). As the word of God, the Qur'an is also believed to be the word of the prophet Mohammed. The various perceptions of the prophet's status and function in both Qur'anic discourse and in Islamic tradition are not always stable. In post-Qur'anic Islam, the traditional picture of the prophet of Islam has been construed in terms of a dichotomy: a servant-messenger versus a prophet-king: the two bodies of the prophet or the two-bodied prophet. In order to dissect the anatomy—as it were—of this two-bodied prophet I have chosen three primary texts: Q. 5: 41–53, a hadith of the servant-messenger/king-prophet, and the narrative of the Jewess Zaynab b. al-Harith's attempt on the life of the prophet.[5]

THE TWO-BODIED PROPHET

I must confess that while the expression "two-bodied prophet"[6] and its application in Islamic Studies is a novelty, doctrines such as the pre-existence of the prophet, the light of Mohammed (ar. *nūr Mohammed*) and Mohammed as the perfect man (ar. *al-'insān al-kāmil*), however, are common in Sunni Islam.[7] The doctrine of the pre-existence of Mohammed is fundamentally enshrined in the theology of Sufism, in particular philosophical Sufism, by figures such as al-Hallaj (658–922 CE) and Ibn Arabi (1165v1240 CE).[8] In Shia Islam's political theology, the two-bodied quality of the Imam has been developed into its most political articulation in the doctrine of *wilayat al-faqih* after the establishment of the Islamic republic of Iran: the imam is also believed to be both divine and human.[9] Despite their variations, these doctrines share the same core idea, namely the indivisibility of the two bodies of the prophet (or of the Imams in Shia Islam), hence the two-bodied expression, which I prefer to Kantorowics's term "two bodies," in order to convey the idea of sacralisation of the body's hyphenation of God-prophet that paradoxically expresses God's absolute transcendence vis-à-vis his prophet as body natural and His immanence in him as body politic. I even dare to postulate that the *unthought of* in Islamic political theology is that both body natural and body politic of the prophet are politically *the same* but theologically *distinct*. My interpretation is supported by a number of primary texts that are gleaned from the hadith literature, Mohammed's biography and the Qur'anic text itself.

In the following hadith[10] quoted by Ibn Taymiyya (1263–1328 CE), the prophet of Islam, Mohammed, is given a choice to become either a *king-prophet* or a *servant-messenger*. A choice he made under the watchful guidance of the angel Gabriel, to whom Islamic tradition attributes the role of the intermediary agent between God and Mohammed; a friendly angel who used to descend with portions of the Qur'anic revelation to Mohammed from Allah. In addition to his choice to become a servant-messenger, Mohammed provides a reason for his choice. A reason that is very significant in terms of what the doctrine of the two-bodied prophet implies and in terms of this doctrine's theological affiliation to earlier theologies such as Judaism or Christianity in their pre-Islamic inter-Arabic contexts and in their global representations. The choice, we should remember, is a good gesture from God towards his Arab prophet and an expression of humility of the prophet. "Allah has made me choose between being a *king-prophet* or a *servant-messenger*. I have chosen to be a *servant messenger* . . . If I replied: I had chosen to be a king-prophet, the mountains would have become gold wherever I walked—if I so desired."[11] The way the hadith is formulated could be construed as if servant-*messenger* and a *king-prophet* were in opposition. The situation, however, is different: being *king-prophet* or servant-*messenger* are simply two categories within Islamic prophet-ology that refer to a difference of degree in the hierarchical relationship with the divine on the hand and the nature and burden of his mission as prophet/messenger on the other. Being a servant-messenger is nobler and higher in the eyes of Allah than being a king-prophet. Mohammed's choice to be a servant-messenger restores the order of things: the only king is God, whose law is expressed in nature and in his word, the Qur'an. In order to understand better the implications of this hadith and its theo-political content, I propose to examine another account in which a Jewess under the name of Zaynab, the daughter of al-Ḥārith, tries to murder Mohammed by poisoning him. In this account, which is gleaned from Mohammed's biography, Zaynab's motives are: (1) to avenge her husband, who has been killed in fighting Mohammed and his followers, and (2) to put Mohammed's prophethood to the test by poison. Mohammed's passing the test means that he is a prophet. The latter motive is more pertinent to the issue of the two-bodied prophet. It deals with the Jewish perspective that construes the dichotomy king/prophet as a mutually negating binary: Mohammed (d. 632) must either be king or a prophet in Zaynab's perspective, which seems to fit well with Mohammed's own. The premise that this account establishes, for both, Mohammed and Zaynab, the Jewess, is not that being a prophet excludes being a king, but Mohammed being a king excludes Mohammed being a prophet. He cannot be both at the time when Mohammed's prophethood is on trial by deadly poison:

> When the apostle had rested Zaynab d. of al-Ḥārith, the wife of Sallām b. Mishkam prepared for him a roast lamb, having first inquired what joint he preferred. When she learned that it was the shoulder she put a lot of poison in it and poisoned the whole

lamb. Then she brought it in and placed it before him. He took hold of the shoulder and chewed a morsel of it, but he did not swallow it. Bishr b. al-Barā' b. Ma'rūr who was with him took some of it as the apostle had done, but he swallowed it, while the apostle spat it out saying, 'This bone tells me that it is poisoned.' Then he called the woman and she confessed, and when he asked her what had induced her to do this she answered: 'You know what you have done to my people. I said to myself, *if he is a king I shall ease myself of him and if he is a prophet he will be informed* (of what I have done)'. *So, the apostle let her off.* Bishr died of what he had eaten.[12]

In the first tradition, the term "king" in the expression king-prophet seems to bear a tag with it, namely a king in the theological sense, i.e., a sovereign who decides on the state of exception and suspends the law of nature. Mohammed, if he wished, could have suspended laws of nature by making mountains turn into gold:[13] thus obtaining all the riches of the world. In the latter tradition, Mohammed survives but his companion Bishr dies. We have the crimes of murder and attempted murder. The law is clear in this case: capital punishment or blood money. Something else was on trial as well. Here, the pairing of king/prophet is held in absolute separation. A king is subject to natural law whereas a prophet has the power to suspend natural law through divine miracle: a proof by either suspending death or postponing it. In Zaynab's account, the issue is king versus prophet, not the hyphenation king-prophet.

Deciding on the murder committed by Zaynab, Mohammed's legal decision to let her go unpunished informs us a great deal about the prophet's authority. His decision seems to be taken as a divine decision, even though it goes counter to the expected judicial ruling on murder cases: capital punishment. In order words, Mohammed acts here as someone who has the divine right to suspend the law by divine decree. Here, Mohammed suspends God's law—capital punishment or compensation—by the divine authority invested in him as a prophet. The account does not say explicitly anything about whether Zaynab became Muslim as she witnessed Mohammed's miraculous escape from an inevitable death by poison; a proof of Mohammed being a prophet is that Mohammed's natural body will continue to bear the traces of that poison for the rest of his life. He succumbs to it at the age of sixty-three, in 632.[14] The decision by Mohammed to let Zaynab go unpunished is witness to the proof of Mohammed's prophethood—a common trope—and seems to contradict other decisions taken by the prophet of Islam vis-à-vis the Jews of Medina.[15]

Both accounts from the prophetic experience of Mohammed about the two-bodied prophet posit the theological and judicial grounds for the prophet's Sunna to be considered as a sort of an oral law in Islamic jurisprudence. So, in addition to the Qur'an, Mohammed's Sunna, as codified in Hadith corpus, are the two main sources of sacred law through which God's will is made known. This is why it is stated (in Q. 4: 59, 80) that it is incumbent upon Muslims to obey both God and his messenger. Failing to obey the prophet is understood as an outright rejection of God's right to rule:

> O you who believe! *Obey Allah* (ar. *'aṭī'ū llāha*) and *obey the Messenger* (ar. *wa-'aṭī'ū al-rasūla*), and those charged with authority among you (ar. *wa-'ūlī l-'amri minkum*). If you differ in anything among yourselves, refer it to Allah and His Messenger, if you believe in Allah and the Last Day: That is best, and most suitable for final determination ... Whoso obey the messenger has verily obeyed Allah, and whoso turns away [says no to the authority of the messenger]; [remember that] We have not sent you to them to be their keeper.
>
> —Q.4:59,80

In these verses, the verb that is used for "to obey" is in the fourth form with a causative/intensive meaning. It is derived from the first form *ṭāʿa*—which means to serve. Contrary to the first form *ṭāʿa*, the fourth form means "conscientiously, knowingly, and wilfully cause oneself to obey or comply wholeheartedly with"! Syntactically, the verb *'aṭāʿa* is used twice in Q.4:59: "obey God! and obey the messenger!" instead of being used once: "obey God and his messenger!" The clause "and those charged with authority among you" in verse 59 could be a specific kind or a group of addressees among the community of believers and means that they should also obey God and obey the prophet. The prevalent interpretation of this verse is that the addressees, all Muslims, in the verse should obey God, obey the messenger, and those charged with authority among them. The construction of the whole verse suggests that the first interpretation is the most plausible, since wholeheartedly complying with God's and Mohammed's rulings in matters of dispute means that those who are in charge are asked to settle matters of dispute that people come to them with according to God's and his prophet's Law. At the end of the day, both laws are the same. Differentiating between God and his messenger syntactically is a theological construction of God's transcendence. But it also means God's immanence in his prophet's authority: The latter is a manifestation of God's sovereignty. Q. 53:3–4 testifies to God-prophet hyphenation: transcendence in immanence: "And neither does he speak out of his own desire. What he conveys to you is but a revelation that he has received."

Islamic tradition extends the application of this verse to include Mohammed's utterings as well, i.e., Sunna. In Q.4: 80, obeying God is *de facto* complying with the authority of his messenger; there is no distinction between the two. The reception of the Qur'anic text during the historical experience of the prophetic mission of Mohammed by and through the immediate community(ies) meant that these communities—Muslim and non-Muslim—did not mean that what was asked of them was just accepting the theological content of the Qur'an: God is One God, but it meant also that people should comply wholeheartedly with the political authority of his messenger: Friends of God are those of whom his messenger approves. Since neither Mohammed nor his successors have succeeded in imposing his theological views, while Mohammed, however, managed to impose his political authority on even those who did not accept either him as God's prophet nor the Qur'an as the word of God. Whence Islamic monotheism's two-fold politico-theological doctrine: the Oneness of Divine Lordship (ar. *tawḥid al-rubūbiyya*) and the Oneness of Divinity or Worship (ar. *tawḥid al-ulūhiyya* or *tawḥid al-ʿibāba*). The first type of tawhid means the belief in Allah as One and Unique in terms of creation and sovereignty whereas the second type of tawhid means that Allah is the only One deserving of being worshiped, and whose commands deserving of being obeyed. In his polemics with the polytheists of Arabia, the prophet of Islam rejected their first type of tawhid as the only valid theological doctrine. He made clear to them that without the second type of tawhid their belief was not valid, and consequently they were considered as enemies of both Allah and his prophet:

> And if you ask them who created them, they will surely say: "Allah." How then are they turned away (from the worship of Allah Who created them)?
>
> —Q. 43:87

> And if you were to ask them: 'Who sends down water (rain) from the sky and gives life therewith to the earth after its death?' they will surely reply: "Allah." Say: "All the praises and thanks be to Allah!" Nay, most of them have no sense.
>
> —Q 29:63

The defining character of a Qur'anic tawhid's typology is inter-dependency of all its types. Any missing type would be considered heresy, if not outright kufr (unbelief): "And your Lord has decreed that you worship none but Him" (Q. 17:23). The act of worship here means that the Muslim is asked to perform it in the manner that God and his prophet have decreed. Submitting to God's rule as an act of worship has led some Muslim scholars to include *al-hākimiyya* verses in the second type of tawhid; a doctrine that has become foundational in the political theology of extremists, fundamentalists, and/or puritanical groups today. All those groups do claim a theologico-political genealogy of their own or to a doctrinal affiliation/filiation to the medieval Hanbali scholar Ibn Taymiyya.

TAWHID AL-HĀKIMMIYA AND POLITICS OF FRIENDSHIP

As a necessary step towards deconstructing the doctrine of the two-bodied prophet and its various hyphenations—as religion-politics, God-prophet, Muslims–non-Muslims—I consider Mohammed's politics of friendship a part and parcel of Qur'anic political theology, particularly Mohammed's politics towards Jews as a people of the book, i.e., people who have received a Divine revelation to which the Qur'an is indebted. For that purpose, I have chosen to focus on the politics of friendship since it has become a privileged site of hermeneutical contention within Islamic/Qur'anic exegesis and political theology. But first, I would like to bring to the reader's attention the following crucial political event.

On the first day of the Muslim holy month of Ramadan of the year 1435 AH (2014 CE), a former Iraqi sub-group of al-Qaeda—a territorialist transnational Islamist organization—officially declared the Islamic State of Iraq and Syria (ISIS; *dā'ish* in Arabic) as a global Islamic caliphate and its leader Abu Bakr al-Baghdadi a ruler "by order of God." He is now the "commander of the faithful," *de jure* and *de facto* caliph-at-large, and the "successor" of the Prophet Mohammed. To him all Muslims *should* swear allegiance and *perform* a hijra to the territories that now are *declared* a consecrated theo-political polis—*dār al-hijra* (home of migration)—wherein God's sovereignty is exercised according to his sacred law and through the agency of the *de facto* caliph. ISIS's conception of *hijra* shows structural and ideological differences from two prior models: the Egyptian model of the *al-takfīr wal-hijra* group of Mustapha Shukri (d. 1978) and *al-qaida-taliban* model in Afghanistan. ISIS's *hijra* is conceived as two inter-dependent acts: emigration–immigration. Emigration from the *outlawed* territories and political systems, and immigration to the now consecrated territories of ISIS. Building its legal legitimacy on the claim that it recreates a replica of the prophet's *state building experience* in Medina.

Noteworthy is the fact that ISIS's imagined genealogy in relation to the issue of God's sovereignty (the political) and Law (politics) is framed in terms of theory and practice as a theology of divine violence and a politics of friendship.[16] As a religious-political experience, ISIS claims to re-animate the two-bodied prophet's ideal. Labeling Islamic societies as non-Muslim, ISIS's theology of violence and politics of friendship subjects the world to a "management of savagery."[17] Not implementing God's sacred Law (ar. *sharī'a*), in this perspective, transcends the confines of jurisprudence proper, and becomes a theological matter. In other words, the question of who is Muslim and who is not is posed as a legal issue and decided by the sovereign who has the right to suspend the state of law by law—Divine Law. This issue, as we know, began as a political issue about who has the right to succeed Mohammed as the head of the Muslim community and state after his death in 632 and developed later into a theological/dogmatic issue; an issue that caused the first "civil wars" or religious-political wars among the various factions after the assassination of the third caliph, Uthman Ibn Affan (d. 656).

For the first time we see a hitherto minority opinion of an Islamic school of thought having great success in displacing stronger legal schools from the center by being able to mobilize various social classes across the borders of national states to its cause! The uniqueness of this school of thought is that while it portrays itself as an inheritor of an authentic and puritanical Muslim world view, it re-maps its political theology through a conceptual apparatus, the language of which is modern, digital, sophisticated, cynical, and most of all violent. The thing I would like to retain here is this minority's literal interpretation of *hākimiyya* verses, which has contributed to a political understating of the Oneness of Divinity and Worship and its politics of friendship: both the nominal Muslim and the non-Muslim are declared unbelievers, and as such his/her life and property are outlawed by Divine Law as interpreted by the rightly guided ruler.

The term *mawaddah*, which is translated into English as "affection" in Q. 60:1, is derived from the root *w,d,d*, and alludes to the sort of affection that the Greek word *philia* stands for. Together with the term *awliyyā'* (friends), which the verse sets in opposition to the term *'aduww* (enemy), specify the taxonomic feature and function of the Qur'an's politics of friendship within the theology of the Oneness of divinity and worship: no overt or covert affection or political friendship with God's enemy—those who "have rejected the truth (ar. *kafarū*) that has come to you"—and who, at the end of the day, are the enemy of both the prophet and the Muslim, i.e., "have driven out the Prophet and yourselves [from your homes] just because you believe in Allah your Lord!" (Q. 60:1).[18] Similarly, God warns the believers not to befriend either Jews or Christians lest they suffer the same curse.

The politics of friendship and its taxonomy in book five are embedded in and around the three *hākimiyya verses* of the same book (Q 5:44, 45, 47). In particular the Jewish figure is a *homo sacer* who is cursed, but God's law protects his life.[19] The Jew is considered a political enemy, not a theological one, and as such he is protected by the fact that he is subjected to God's law revealed to Moses and the prophets: the Jew, however, can be declared a non-believer by his own law also. In short, he is twice an unbeliever, though theologically and legally protected. In verse 42, the Qur'an presents a case in which Jews of Medina come to the prophet of Islam with a legal issue, asking him to be a judge. The Qur'an narrates this case in a scenario of condemnation: how could a Jew choose to be judged by a law that he does not believe is from God while forsaking the Torah that he believes is from God? The prophet of Islam is given the option by God to function as a judge or arbitrator for the Jews or decline. Legally speaking, Mohammed would be within his rights to decline. The question that should be asked here is: How could the prophet of Islam be a sitting judge for those whom he did not consider friends; political friends? The prophet's decision has actually come to function as a legal precedent in later Islamic legal systems dealing with religious minorities.

> They [Jews] are listeners of falsehood and greedy devourers of unlawful earnings. *If they come to you [Mohammed] you may either judge between them or turn away from them*. And were you to turn away from them they shall not be able to harm you; and were you to judge between them judge with justice. Surely Allah loves the just. How come they [these Jews] come to you [prophet] to be their judge (*yuḥakkimūka*) when they have the *Torah*, wherein Allah has delivered legal decisions? Yet even after that they turn away. Such people are not believers (*mu'minīn*). Lo! We did reveal the Torah,

wherein is guidance and a light, by which the prophets who surrendered (unto Allah) judged the Jews, and the rabbis and the priests (judged) by such of Allah's Scripture as they were bidden to observe, and thereunto were they witnesses. So, fear not mankind, but fear Me. And My revelations for a little gain. *Whoso judged not by that which Allah hath revealed: such are disbelievers.* And We ordained for them therein a life for a life, an eye for an eye, a nose for a nose, an ear for an ear, a tooth for a tooth, and for wounds is legal retribution. But whoever gives [up his right as] charity, it is an expiation for him. And *whoever does not judge by what Allah has revealed – then it is those who are the wrongdoers.*

—Q. 5: 42–45

The Tunisian Maliki scholar and Qur'an exegete quotes Malik and al-Bukhari as saying that the reason postulated by them for the revelation of these verses (ar. *asbāb al-nuzūl*) was the story of stoning: a case of adultery committed by two Jews of Medina who willingly came to Mohammed to be judged by him.[20] Now Muslim exegetes posit two different reasons for Jews soliciting to be judged by Mohammed instead of a rabbinic court: (1) hope for a more lenient verdict than the one found in the Torah, and (2) a test to see whether Mohammed was really a prophet: the proof here would be whether Mohammed knew of the biblical verdict (Deuteronomy 22:24): *death by stoning.*[21] As we know, death by stoning in cases of a married person committing adultery is a contentious issue in Islamic law since there is no Qur'anic verse containing such a verdict. The prophetic Sunna, however, shows that it used to be common practice at the time of Mohammed. Some Muslim scholars suggest that the stoning verse has been abrogated textually, but not legally.[22] The stoning story and the body-politics of Mohammed represent the immediate textual context of the *hākimiyya* issue. As we know, the first two *hākimiyya* verses (Q. 5: 44–45) apply to the Jews, whereas the third one Q. 5:46) applies to the Christians. The meaning of *hākimiyya* varies in modern Islamic thought. While Qur'an exegetes and jurists such as Ibn Ashur (d. 1973) maintains its legal content and that its application should be very specific: whether Islamic law is applicable to non-Muslims such as the Jews, the Egyptian Qur'an exegete and theoretician of so-called political Islam, Sayyed Qutb (d. 1966), claims that *hākimiyya* (Sovereign Will) is a theological principle (tawhid) that precedes and governs the sacred law.[23] I propose here that the *hākimiyya* stands for *the political*, whereas politics of friendship stands for (politics) in political Islam's political theology. The *hākimiyya* doctrine seems to replace symbolically in this the two-bodied prophet, maintaining God's transcendence and immanence operative in the hyphenation: religion-state. The Source of authority (the political) is God-prophet as articulated in tawhid typology, the model of the administration of authority (politics) is the two-bodied prophet doctrine, and politics of friendship is the domain in which "vivre-ensemble" becomes a challenging impossibility due to what Derrida calls opposition between laws of nature and laws of culture.[24]

In Q. 5: 50, the Qur'anic discourse calls the alternative to God's *hākimiyya* the rule of ignorance. This does not mean the rejection of Sharia as a judicial system, but a rejection of God's sovereignty, the premise of which the sacred law is built upon: "Is it then the judgment/governance (of al-*jāhiliyya*) that they desire? And who is better than Allah to judge/govern for a people who are sure)" (Q 5:50).

Today, political Islam and its Qur'anic exegesis of these verses consider the hākimiyya as the only authentic system of life in this world that has God's approval, which represents the true understanding of tawhid: God's sovereignty and man's submission to it. Any resistance to or rejection of God's sovereignty as exercised through his sacred Law is considered *jāhiliyya* (ignorance). Should the true believer find himself in this situation it becomes incumbent upon him to fight it, whence jihad. This is the case of Islamism.

This version of Islamism, which declares all Muslim countries juridically outlaws and theologically unbelievers, claims a dual genealogy: the prophetic ideal and eclectic-puritanical dogma. According to this dual genealogy the prophetic ideal is recast as a divine prototype that the true Muslim as both individual and community should both emulate and reproduce, whereas the eclectic-puritanical dogma is the very content of true faith in its relation to the other. The latter is construed and articulated in antonymic pair-concepts: *mu'min/kāfir* (believer/non-believer), *islām/jāhiliyya* (Islam/non-Islam), etc. Islamism's position in opposition to traditional Islamic political theory, claims that "there is no other politics than religion: *religion is the political*."[25] Paradoxically, this view that Islamism holds is considered by most Sunni scholars a militant religio-political ideology or an *antipolitical utopia in the face of the West* that *Muslims* themselves have invented from Islam. Islamists seek, through violence, to conquer power and establish a state that is exclusively "juridical-theological," in which the political should subordinate the religious. The latter, however, is construed as a theocracy or a prophetic-inspired system of governance, in which the political is subordinated to the theological. The different varieties of political Islam have engendered, inter alia, an unprecedented phenomenon: *le surmusulman* (the supermuslim) in the sense that its sociopolitical representations stand out as a violent phenomenon that seeks to subject the human polis to God's sovereignty (the political) through his law (politics).

CONCLUSION

If Sovereignty (the political) does belong to Allah alone, and no one else, in the logic of today's political Islam there is only one politic—including the politics of friendship—and it is religion. Contra Benslama's assumption that categories such as "theologico-politics" and "political theology" do not apply to modern Islamism, since they belong to Christianism and Aristotelian thought, I believe that Islamism's rejection of the doctrine that says that the "theological organizes and manages the affairs of the community of believers" remains a claim that my investigation in the Qur'anic text and Mohammed's biography has debunked. It appears that the doctrine of the two-bodied prophet has shown that hyphenations such as God-prophet and religion-state are but articulations of the theological tension between God's transcendence and immanence in the prophet's natural body and the prophet's divine/legal body respectively. Islamism's interpretation of tawhid's typology serves actually as an astute ideological observation to make the political (God's sovereignty) a theological principle that dictates Islam's politics of friendship.

NOTES

1. Amal Donqol, *Al-ʾaʿmāl Al-Shiʿriyya Al-Kāmila*. 3rd ed. (Cairo: Maktabat Madbūlī, 1987), 313.
2. The term *dunyā* corresponds to the two New Testament terms: *cosmos* (as in John 3:16 and 16:28) and *ainos* (as in 2 Cor. 4:4). In Islamic salvation doctrine, the term *dunyā* means the ephemeral world (Q 55:26–27) and is the antonym of *al-ʾākhira*, which means the real and lasting world, in which God's just rule will be inconstantly the sole rule.
3. Fethi Benslama, *Un Furieux Désir Du Sacrfice: Le Surmusulman* (Paris: Seuil, 2016), 74.

4. Jacques Derrida, *Of Grammatology*, trans. Gayatri Chakravorty Spivak (Baltimore, MD: Johns Hopkins University Press, 1998), 158.
5. Alfred Guillaume, *The Life of Muhammad: A Translation of Isḥāq's Sīrat Rasūl Allāh*, 13th ed. (Karachi: Oxford University Press, 1998), 515–516.
6. The expression and its applications take its cue from Ernest Kantorowics's work *The King's Two Bodies: A Study in Medieval Political Theology* (Princeton, NJ: Princeton University Press, 1997).
7. See Uri Rubin, *Muhammad the Prophet and Arabia* (Farnham: Ashgate, 2011).
8. See Saer El-Jaichi, *Early Philosophical Sufism: The Neoplatonic Thought of Ibn Al-Hallag* (Piscataway, NJ: Gorgias Press, 2018).
9. See Mohammad Ali Amir-Moezzi, *The Divine Guide in Early Shi'ism: The Sources of Esotericism in Islam* (New York: State University of New York Press, 1994).
10. The longer version of this hadith can be found in various Hadith sources as for instance the one quoted in Ibn Hanbal's *Musnad*: "on the authority of Abu Hurayra: Gabriel [the archangel] sat with the prophet, and he left his eyes up to the sky he saw an angel descending, and then he said: 'This angel has never descended to [earth] since he was created until this hour.' When he descended he said: 'O Muhmmad! Your Lord has sent me to ask you: do you want Him to make you a *king-prophet* or a *servant-messenger?*' Gabriel said: 'humble yourself before your Lord, O Mohammed!' Mohammed said: 'rather a servant-messenger'."
11. See Ahmed Ibn Taymiyyah, *Minhāj Al-Sunna Al-Nabawiyya Fī Naqḍ Kalām Al-Shī'a Wa-l-Qadariyya* (Cairo: Maktabat Dār al-ʿUrūb, 1962).
12. Alfred Guillaume, *The Life of Muhammad: A Translation of Isḥāq's Sīrat Rasūl Allāh*, 13th ed. (Karachi: Oxford University Press, 1998), 516.
13. This account is a milder version of the temptation account in the Gospel of Matthew 4:8–11. While the angel in account in Mohammed's tradition was meant to get the prophet of Islam to show humility, the spirit (devil) in the temptation account is out to get Jesus to worship him instead of the true God. The image of Jesus saying no to Satan's offer in the fourth chapter of the Gospel of Matthew is quite informative in this regard. Mohammed's narrative seems to stand out as a counter narrative to the arrogance of the Israelites when they asked Jahveh's prophet and judge Samuel to provide them with a human king (1 Sam 8:1–22).
14. It is equally interesting to notice that the fatal impact of poison was not totally eliminated but postponed. We have on record that Mohammed confessed to the sister of the other victim of Zaynab d. al-Harith's poison while on his deathbed: "The apostle had said in his illness of which he was to die when Umm Bishr d. al-Barāʾ came to visit him, 'O Umm Bishr, this is the time in which I feel a deadly pain from what I ate with your brother at Khaybar.' The Muslims considered that *the apostle died as a martyr in addition to the prophetic office with which God had honoured him*" (Guillaume, 5).
15. In Mohammed's biography and hadith literature, the story of the Jews of Banu Qurayza, their treachery and their execution inform us about the judicial character of Mohammed's decision to let the law of tribal-alliance—pre-Islamic tribal law—to take precedence over God's Law: "In the morning they [Jews of Banu Qurayza] submitted to the apostle's judgement and al-Aus [one of the two main Arab tribes who converted to Islam] leapt up and said: 'O, Apostle, they are our allies, not allies of Khazraj [the other Arab tribe]and you know how you recently treated the allies of our brethren.' . . . Thus the Apostle said: 'Will you be satisfied, O, Aus, if one of your own numbers pronounces judgment on them?' When they agreed he [the Apostle] said Saaʿd ibn Muʿād is the man . . . Saaʿd said: 'Then I give the judgement that the men should be killed, the property divided, and the women

and children taken as captives'" (Guillaume, 464–465). What is more informative to our doctrine of the two-bodied prophet is Mohammed's comment after hearing Saa'd's verdict: "You have given the judgment Allah above the seven heavens" (ibid., 465). In a hadith cited by al-Bukhari, the prophet is quoted saying: "You have judged amongst them with (or similar to) the judgment of the King Allah." https://www.call-to-monotheism.com/the_execution_of_the_jews_at_bani_quraydah

16. Fethi Benslama, *Un Furieux Désir Du Sacrfice: Le Surmusulman* (Paris: Seuil, 2016), 23.
17. See Abu Bakr Naji and William McCants, *The Management of Savagery: The Most Critical Stage Through which the Umma Will Pass* (Cambridge, MA: Harvard University Press, 2006).
18. The full verse of (Q. 60:1): "O you who believe! Take not *my enemy* (ar. *'aduwwi*) and *your enemy* (ar. *'aduwwakum*) as *political allied* (ar. *awliyyā* [friends]), wasting upon them affection (ar. *mawaddah*), when they have rejected the truth (ar. *kafarū*) that has come to you, and have driven out the Prophet and yourselves [from your homes] just because you believe in Allah your Lord! If you have come out to strive in My Way and to seek My Good Pleasure, (take them not as friends), holding secret converse of affection (and friendship) with them: for I know full well all that ye conceal and all that ye reveal. And any of you that does this has strayed from the Straight Path."
19. See Giorgio Agamben, *Cite Homo Sacer: Sovereign Power and Bare Life*, trans. Heller-Roazen (Redwood City, CA: Stanford University Press, 1998); and Colby Dickinson and Adam Kotsko, *Agamben's Coming Philosophy: Finding a New Use of Theology* (London: Rowman & Littlefield International, 2015).
20. Mohammed T. Ibn Ashur, *Tafsir of Liberation and Enlightenment*, Vol. 6 (Tunis: Dar al-Nashr al-Tunisia lil-Nashr, 1984), 224.
21. In addition to the legal implications of the story of stoning on Islamic jurisprudence, the trope presenting encounters between Mohammed and the Jews, for which we find some parallels in the Gospels, seem to consolidate why Jews were rejected by God and confirm the prophethood of Mohammed as it confirmed that Jesus was the Messiah in the Gospels.
22. See Joseph Schacht, *Introduction to Islamic Law* (Oxford: Clarendon Press, 1965).
23. S. Khatab, "Hakimiyyah and Jahiliyyah in the Thought of Sayyid Qutb," *Middle Eastern Studies* 38:3 (2002), 145–170.
24. Jacques Derrida, *Le Dernier Des Juifs* (Paris : Galilée, 2014), 34.
25. See Benslama, *Un Furieux Désir Du Sacrifice*.

SELECT BIBLIOGRAPHY

Agamben, Giorgio (1998), *Cite Homo Sacer: Sovereign Power and Bare Life*, trans. Heller-Roazen, Redwood City, CA: Stanford University Press.
Amir-Moezzi, Mohammad Ali (1994), *The Divine Guide in Early Shi'ism: The Sources of Esotericism in Islam*, New York: State University of New York Press.
Benslama, Fethi (2016), *Un Furieux Désir de Sacrifice: Le Surmusulman*, Paris: Seuil.
Derrida, Jacques (1998), *Of Grammatology*, trans. Gayatri Chakravorty Spivak, Baltimore, MD: Johns Hopkins University Press.
Derrida, Jacques (2014), *Le Dernier Des Juifs*, Paris: Galilée.
Dickinson, Colby, and Adam Kotsko (2015), *Agamben's Coming Philosophy: Finding a New Use of Theology*, London: Rowman & Littlefield International.
Donqol, Amal (1987), *Al-'a'māl Al-Shi'riyya Al-Kāmila*, 3rd ed., Cairo: Maktabat Madbūlī.

El-Jaichi, Saer (2018), *Early Philosophical Sufism: The Neoplatonic Thought of Ibn Al-Hallag*, Piscataway, NJ: Gorgias Press.
Guillaume, Alfred (1998), *The Life of Muhammad: A Translation of Isḥāq's Sīrat Rasūl Allāh*, 13th ed., Karachi: Oxford University Press.
Ibn Ashur, Mohammed T. (1984), *Tafsir of Liberation and Enlightenment*, Vol. 6 (30 vols.), Tunis: Dar al-Nashr al-Tunisia lil-Nashr.
Ibn Taymiyyah, Ahmed (1962), *Minhāj Al-Sunna Al-Nabawiyya Fī Naqḍ Kalām Al-Shī'a Wa-l-Qadariyya*, Cairo: Maktabat Dl-Naba'airo.
Kantorowicz, Ernest H. (1997), *The King's Two Bodies: A Study in Mediaeval Political Theology*, Princeton, NJ: Princeton University Press.
Khatab, S. (2002), "Hakimiyyah and Jahiliyyah in the Thought of Sayyid Qutb", *Middle Eastern Studies* 38 (3): 145–170.
Naji, Abu Bakr, and William McCants (2006), *The Management of Savagery: The Most Critical Stage Through which the Umma Will Pass*, Cambridge, MA: Harvard University Press.
Rubin, Uri (2011), *Muhammad the Prophet and Arabia*, Farnham: Ashgate.
Schacht, Joseph (1965), *Introduction to Islamic Law*, Oxford: Clarendon Press.

CHAPTER SEVEN

Augustine and Political Theory

MICHAEL LAMB

INTRODUCTION

While political theology has witnessed a revival in contemporary political theory, the discourse is far from new. A signature contribution of this volume is to elevate the history, diversity, and authority of a wide range of political theologians across multiple traditions. Within Christianity and Western political thought, Augustine of Hippo is arguably the most influential.[1]

AUGUSTINE'S LIFE AND LEADERSHIP

Augustine was born in 354 in Thagaste, a small town in North Africa on the edges of the Roman Empire.[2] Augustine's mother, Monica, was a Christian of Berber origin, and his father, Patricius, was a pagan of Roman descent who owned a small estate and served as a local imperial official.[3] Although Augustine was a bright and precocious student, his parents could not afford higher education, so when he was fifteen or sixteen, Augustine stayed in Thagaste for a year while his father tried to gather funds.[4] Luckily, the family found a patron in Romanianus, who supported Augustine's study in Carthage, where he became the top student in rhetoric.[5]

After teaching rhetoric in Carthage, Thagaste, and Rome, Augustine was appointed the imperial professor of rhetoric in Milan, a prestigious post within the Empire.[6] The thirty-year-old had an ambition to become a lawyer and serve in political office, potentially as governor of a local province,[7] but after two years in the rough and tumble of the imperial court, he became disillusioned with politics and accused rhetoricians of being more committed to flattery than telling the truth.[8] So, in the summer of 386, immersed in the philosophy of Cicero and the Neoplatonists and under the influence of Bishop Ambrose, his mother Monica, and the letters of St. Paul, Augustine abandoned his career as a rhetorician and retreated to a friend's villa in Cassiciacum, where he conducted philosophical conversations with family and friends, wrote a series of dialogues modeled on those of Cicero and the Platonists, and prayed the Psalms to prepare for Christian baptism.[9] Although Augustine had long resisted his mother's Catholic Christianity, he was baptized by Bishop Ambrose in Milan on Easter 387.[10] After a year in Rome, he then returned to North Africa to found a similar philosophical community on his family estate in Thagaste.[11] His mother, Monica, died during his journey home, and his son, Adeodatus, whom he had reared with his concubine of fifteen years, died two years later.[12]

Back in North Africa, Augustine continued to write dialogues and treatises against the Manicheans, a sect in which he had spent nine years as a follower or "hearer."[13] But in 391, on a visit to Hippo Regius, the Catholic congregation pressed him to become their priest, and he reluctantly agreed.[14] Four years later, he was appointed bishop, where he served until his death in 430 while Hippo was besieged by the "barbarian" Vandals.[15]

As Bishop of Hippo, Augustine was an active ecclesial and political leader. He preached regularly, ministered to his congregation, and founded a monastic community beside the basilica, developing the "Rule of St. Augustine" that still governs Augustinian orders today.[16] Frequently, he traveled to other cities to preach or participate in church councils.[17] Amidst these ecclesial duties, he also kept writing, producing over 100 books, thousands of sermons, and hundreds of letters, totaling more than five million words.[18] As he explains in *The Retractions*, a retrospective catalogue of his entire corpus, many of these works, including *City of God*, took over a decade to complete because of his practical involvement in the Catholic Church and Roman Empire.[19] During this time, he maintained an extensive correspondence with Christian bishops and Roman officials on matters of urgent concern, often advocating or interceding on behalf of the poor and vulnerable.[20] And on many mornings, he spent hours adjudicating minor legal cases as a member of the "bishop's tribunal."[21] As scholars have recently emphasized, Augustine's "political activism" shaped his thought in ways that many contemporary political interpreters neglect.[22]

AUGUSTINE AND THE HISTORY OF POLITICAL THOUGHT

While scholars are now attending to political themes in Augustine's sermons, letters, and theological treatises,[23] *City of God* remains the primary source for most accounts of Augustine's political thought.[24] Most interpreters focus narrowly on Book 19, which includes Augustine's most extensive reflections on politics. But as a whole, *City of God* is far from an abstract or systematic work of "political theory."[25] Its primary purposes are theological and apologetic, and its form is highly rhetorical, pastoral, and often polemical.[26] Throughout this "great and arduous" work, Augustine uses his rhetorical training, knowledge of Roman history, and theological imagination to refute pagan critics who blamed Christians for the sack of Rome and exhort readers to pursue the "everlasting felicity" of that "most glorious" City of God.[27]

With his extraordinary talents as an orator, writer, and thinker, his position of power in a church rising to prominence as paganism declined and various heresies and schisms threatened ecclesial unity, and his scrupulous efforts to catalogue and maintain copies of his written works, Augustine went on to exercise a significant influence on the history of Western thought, doing as much as anyone to transmit Greek and Roman ideas into Christian theology and Western political thought.[28] One prominent historian of political thought describes him as "the first and perhaps the greatest of Christian synthesizers,"[29] while another acknowledges that "Augustine's importance to the subsequent history of Europe is impossible to exaggerate."[30]

Much of Augustine's influence came through appropriations by medieval philosophers and theologians, often through collections that included extensive quotations from

Augustine's works.[31] The most influential was Peter Lombard's *Sentences*, a collection of passages that became the standard textbook on which those studying to become doctors of theology in the medieval university were required to lecture and write a commentary.[32] Four-fifths of Lombard's *Sentences* consists in quotations from Augustine.[33]

One of the students who wrote a commentary on Lombard's *Sentences* was Thomas Aquinas, who synthesized Aristotelian ethics with Augustinian Christianity.[34] Often scholars oppose Augustine to Aquinas, assuming that Augustine conceives politics negatively as a remedy for sin while Aquinas considers politics more positively as a natural good.[35] Recently, however, scholars have highlighted how much Aquinas's theology and political thought owe to Augustinian influences.[36] Eric Gregory and Joseph Clair even show how Aquinas sees his account of "natural" political order as compatible with Augustine's view.[37]

Augustine's influence was not limited to Catholics. In the early modern period, Protestant Reformers drew explicitly on Augustine to offer radically different views of sin, grace, and politics. Before posting his "95 Theses," Martin Luther was a friar and priest in the Order of St. Augustine and held a chair established by the Order at the University of Wittenberg, which identified Augustine as its patron saint.[38] Like Aquinas, Luther had studied Lombard's *Sentences,* noting on the first page of his copy that "Augustine can never be praised enough."[39] Influenced by his extensive study of Augustine's works and the Augustinian theology of the Order, Luther cited Augustine more than any other authority except Scripture, mining Augustine's anti-Pelagian writings to defend his views on sin and grace and invoking *City of God* to develop his account of the "two kingdoms" on the model of Augustine's "two cities."[40]

Similarly, John Calvin cited Augustine more than 1,700 times throughout his works and alluded to or paraphrased Augustine an additional 2,400 times.[41] "Augustine is so completely of our persuasion," Calvin wrote, "that if I should have to make written profession, it would be quite enough to present a composition made up entirely of excerpts from his writings."[42] This austere, sin-obsessed strand of Augustinian Protestantism found its way into Puritan America, particularly in fiery preachers like Jonathan Edwards, whom scholars have described as the "American Augustine."[43]

Influential political thinkers also engaged deeply, if critically, with Augustinian ideas.[44] In Italy, Dante drew on Augustine's *Confessions* to inform his spiritual autobiography in the *Convivio* and laced *The Divine Comedy* with themes of love, history, and politics drawn from Augustine's *City of God*, though with different emphases and implications.[45] In England, John Milton not only invoked Augustinian accounts of creation, free will, and the Fall in his "Augustinian epic," *Paradise Lost*, but the English republican also cited passages from *City of God* to challenge opponents who had used Augustine instead to defend the divine right of kings.[46] In France, another republican, Jean-Jacques Rousseau, challenged Augustinian ideas in debates with Jansenists and vigorously rejected Augustine's views on grace and original sin, but Rousseau's accounts of the "general will" and *amour-propre* bear distinct Augustinian imprints while his *Confessions* constitutes a direct reply to Augustine's.[47]

AUGUSTINE AND CONTEMPORARY POLITICAL THEORY

Augustine's complex legacy extends into contemporary political theory.[48] It is striking to see how many prominent political theorists—both religious and secular—critically engage

Augustine's work to advance their own. Among realists, for example, Reinhold Niebuhr and Judith Shklar have invoked Augustine's trenchant diagnosis of sin and self-interest to resist utopianism and emphasize the limits of politics,[49] while Jean Bethke Elshtain has cited Augustine to defend a "just war against terror."[50]

Among liberals, Martha Nussbaum has praised Augustine for restoring the emotions to "a place of centrality in the earthly life," even as she argues that his "otherworldly" account of love and exclusivist theology discourages "this-worldly striving" and the possibility of "pluralist politics."[51] John Rawls cites Augustine extensively throughout his senior thesis but presents his own account as an alternative to Augustine's "egoistic" account of love.[52] Later, Rawls identifies Augustine among thinkers whose "comprehensive doctrines" stand in opposition to his distinctly "political" liberalism.[53] More recently, however, liberals such as Robert Markus and Paul Weithman have defended a vision of Augustinian liberalism that aligns with Rawlsian accounts.[54]

Among traditionalists, Michael Oakeshott "read all that St. Augustine wrote," describing him, along with Montaigne, as "the two most remarkable men who have ever lived."[55] Alasdair MacIntyre begins his history of the Catholic philosophical tradition with a chapter on Augustine and has drawn explicitly on an "Augustinian alternative" to challenge liberal accounts of justice.[56]

Among continental philosophers and existentialists, Hannah Arendt wrote her dissertation on *Love and Saint Augustine* and parlayed Augustinian insights into her accounts of "natality" and the "banality of evil."[57] Albert Camus featured Augustine centrally in his dissertation on *Christian Metaphysics and Neoplatonism*, even suggesting that Augustinianism could be considered "a second revelation."[58]

Among radical democrats, Michael Hardt and Antonio Negri have enlisted Augustine's critique of empire to bolster their own,[59] while William Connolly and Romand Coles have argued instead that Augustine's "imperative" and "totalizing" vision embodies the dominating tendencies he otherwise resists.[60] The sheer variety of these accounts reveals the "Proteanism" of Augustine's authority.[61] Even if many of these political theorists engage Augustinian ideas primarily to contest them, the fact they take up his work at all highlights the extent of his influence.[62]

Augustine's political influence, moreover, is not confined to the academy. On various sides of ideological divides, pundits such as David Brooks, E. J. Dionne, and Jon Meacham, among others, have invoked Augustine to diagnose religion, politics, and culture,[63] while politicians and public intellectuals have occasionally trotted out Augustine to defend particular positions on public policy. After 9/11, Elshtain explicitly cited Augustine to provide intellectual support for the Bush Administration's decision to invade Iraq, while opponents invoked Augustine to challenge the decision.[64] In 2008, Speaker of the US House of Representatives, Nancy Pelosi, made national news when she recruited Augustine to defend her pro-choice stance on abortion in the first trimester, while Catholic critics cited Augustine's authority to contest Pelosi's claims.[65] More recently, US President Barack Obama enlisted Augustine's understanding of "just war" to defend his administration's use of drones, a statement that led one philosopher to wonder if the policy could be reduced to the question, "What Would Augustine Do?"[66]

Given the extent of Augustine's impact, an exhaustive analysis of his influence on political theory and practice is beyond the scope of this chapter. Instead, I will focus on the three most influential versions of Augustinianism within contemporary political theory—realism, liberalism, and communitarianism—and highlight a fourth—republicanism—that might offer new vistas on Augustine's relevance for political theory.

AUGUSTINIAN REALISM

One of the defining characteristics of Augustine's political thought is his emphasis on the depth of human sin. Against those who describe evil as an independent force in the world, Augustine locates the origin of sin in the will, in the privation or perversion of the human capacity to love.[67] Specifically, sin consists in disordered love, loving the wrong object or loving a good object in the wrong way.[68] Augustine's influential (and controversial) "order of love" is his attempt to redirect human love toward its ultimate object in God.[69]

For Augustine, the fundamental sin is pride, or excessive self-love. Citing the biblical claim that "pride is the beginning of sin" (Sirach 10:13), Augustine identifies pride as the cause of the Fall: Adam and Eve's original sin results from the "pride" manifest in their "appetite for a perverse kind of elevation."[70] Believing they could become gods, Adam and Eve presumed their own self-sufficiency rather than recognizing God as the "true ground of their being."[71]

Augustine suggests pride is the root of all sins, including those that afflict social and political life.[72] Because "pride hates a fellowship of equality under God, and wishes to impose its own dominion upon its equals, in place of God's rule," pride fuels a "lust for glory" that drives human beings to demonstrate their power and superiority.[73] In turn, this lust for glory feeds a "lust for domination" that seeks to attain glory by mastering others.[74] Augustine identifies the lust for domination as the chief characteristic of the "earthly city," which he finds manifest in the Roman Empire.[75]

In Book 19 of *City of God*, Augustine describes the political effects of sin and domination, highlighting the "great evils" that characterize the "miserable condition of this life," from "horror and cruelty" to "great wars" and "outpourings of human blood."[76] Frequent suspicions, injuries, and betrayals attest that even relationships with close friends and family are not immune from these "undoubted evils."[77] "If, therefore, there is no security even in the home from the common evils which befall the human race," Augustine asks, "what of the city? The larger the city, the more is its forum filled with civil law-suits and criminal trials. Even when the city is at peace and free from actual sedition and civil war, it is never free from the danger of such disturbance or, more often, bloodshed."[78] Augustine extends this litany of evils in Book 22.22–23, where he goes so far as to suggest that this "state of life" is "so miserable that it is like a hell on earth."[79]

Amidst the horrors of the twentieth century, many theologians and political theorists took these vivid descriptions of sin as proof-texts for Augustinian realism.[80] The most influential was Reinhold Niebuhr.[81] A vigorous critic of both communism and liberal idealism, Niebuhr challenged utopian and rationalist visions of politics that were blind to "the lust for power in the motives of men."[82] Niebuhr found a useful corrective in Augustine, whom he described as "the first great 'realist' in Western history."[83] Citing passages from *City of God*, especially Book 19, Niebuhr traces Augustine's realism to his "biblical rather than rationalistic conception of human selfhood," which recognizes how "pride" and "excessive love of self" can distort human reason and corrupt social relations.[84] Niebuhr was especially drawn to Augustine's "emphasis on the tensions, frictions, competitions of interest, and overt conflicts to which every human community is exposed."[85] For Niebuhr, such attention to self-interest rightly recognizes the vagaries and vicissitudes of power and thus chastens us from expecting too much from political leaders or institutions that remain susceptible to sin.

Niebuhr's Augustinian realism had a profound impact on American politics, religion, and culture. *TIME Magazine* put Niebuhr on its cover, while prominent public intellectuals embraced his cause.⁸⁶ Hans Morgenthau, a founder of realism in international relations, described Niebuhr as "the greatest living political philosopher in America," while Arthur Schlesinger praised him as "one of the great Americans of the century."⁸⁷ In the twenty-first century, Niebuhr's thought has witnessed a revival among a surprisingly diverse set of voices. US Senator John McCain included a chapter on Niebuhr in a recent book, while President Barack Obama described Niebuhr as one of his "favorite philosophers."⁸⁸ As *The Atlantic* put it, Niebuhr has become a "man for all reasons," with liberals, conservatives, Christians, Jews, and atheists claiming his Augustinian legacy as their own.⁸⁹

If Niebuhr's Augustinian realism has been most influential in contemporary politics, Herbert Deane's has been most prominent in academic political theory. In *The Political and Social Ideas of St. Augustine*, Deane provides an interpretation that emphasizes Augustine's "pessimistic realism."⁹⁰ Beginning with chapters on the theology and psychology of "fallen man" and comparing Augustine to Luther, Calvin, Machiavelli, and Hobbes,⁹¹ Deane emphasizes Augustine's "somber and pessimistic portrait" of human beings as "essentially selfish, avaricious, ambitious for power and glory, and lustful."⁹² For Deane, it is this "dark portrait of human life" that justifies Augustine's account of the "state."⁹³ Sinful human beings prone to pride, cruelty, and domination need a coercive political order to prevent violence and maintain an "external peace," which Deane defines negatively as the mere "absence of overt conflict and hostilities."⁹⁴ For Deane's Augustine, political institutions are simply a "remedy" and "punishment" for sin: "Their essential contribution is that they hold down the dark passions of sinful men and provide a measure of peace and stability."⁹⁵ Ultimately, politics serves no positive purpose.⁹⁶ Rather, it seeks to reduce violence and strife in a realm of sin, a lesson, Deane argues, that can be especially useful in an age when we are brutally aware of violence, terror, and domination.⁹⁷

Judith Shklar also invokes Augustine to support her political realism. A refugee from the Holocaust, Shklar experienced Nazism, racism, and fascism firsthand, which, along with her study of slavery and the wars of religion,⁹⁸ made her "mindful of the way ideologically inflamed people, possessed by a hope for a radically changed world, can make a hell on earth."⁹⁹ For Shklar, the best way to resist such evil is to recognize the human capacity for cruelty and develop political institutions to restrain it.¹⁰⁰ In this effort, she finds an ally in Augustine, who had "an unusually enlarged sense of the scope of injustice."¹⁰¹ Because finite human attempts to discover truth and do justice are always thwarted by pride and cruelty, we can never realize the City of God on earth. The best we can hope for is a government that seeks to "only prevent the worst."¹⁰² By "putting cruelty first" and "giving injustice its due," Shklar's "liberalism of fear" operationalizes these Augustinian insights.¹⁰³ For Shklar, like Deane, the purpose of government is primarily "negative," not positive: its aim is to prevent "ordinary vice" rather than foster extraordinary virtue.¹⁰⁴ This is why she does not "offer a *summum bonum* toward which all political agents should strive," but a *summum malum*—"cruelty and the fear it inspires"—which all of us should seek to avoid.¹⁰⁵ Fear, not hope, remains the orienting attitude of Shklar's Augustinian realism.¹⁰⁶

Among political theorists, such realism remains the prevailing interpretation of Augustine's political thought and helps to explain why the bishop is "usually numbered among the pessimists."¹⁰⁷ In recent years, however, a small but emerging group of scholars has contested this pessimism. In political theory, Jean Bethke Elshtain has challenged pessimistic interpretations that focus narrowly on selected passages of Augustine's corpus and ignore his celebration of temporal goods,¹⁰⁸ and John von Heyking has argued that Augustine's anti-political rhetoric veils a more positive view of politics as a form of "longing in the world," suggesting that Augustine sees politics as a natural good, not simply as a punishment for sin.[109] In theology and religious studies, Eric Gregory, Charles Mathewes, Sarah Stewart-Kroeker, and Joseph Clair, among others, have challenged common interpretations of Augustine's "order of love" and shown how Augustine encourages a love for temporal goods, including the goods of politics, as long as they are ordered ultimately to God.[110]

In my own work, I draw on Augustine's explicit order of love to reconstruct his implicit order of hope and explore its implications for politics. Against those who cite Augustine's account of social and political evils solely to justify their "pessimism," I show how the former professor uses rhetoric not to deny the value of politics or the world, but to reorder readers' hopes to God and chasten them from placing too much hope in politics to achieve salvation. Even Augustine's description of life as "hell on earth," I argue, functions not as an expression of pessimism but as a spiritual exercise meant to cultivate properly ordered hope.[111] Further, I show how this virtue of hope encourages hope for temporal goods, especially the good of civic peace, as long it avoids corresponding forms of disorder, namely the vices of "presumption" and "despair."[112] Against those who deem Augustine's hope to be exclusively otherworldly or anti-political, I suggest that Augustine encourages a hope for politics that finds a way between presumption and despair.[113]

AUGUSTINIAN LIBERALISM

Augustine's most enduring contribution to political thought is his account of the "two cities," the earthly and the heavenly.[114] In *City of God*, Augustine traces the history of these two cities from their heavenly origins in the angels and their human origins in Cain and Abel to their manifestations in the Roman Empire and ultimate eschatological consummation in heaven and hell.[115] While Augustine occasionally identifies the "earthly city" with the Roman Empire and the "heavenly city" with the Christian church, he insists that the two cities are distinguished not by membership in any earthly institution but by the ordering of their loves: "Two cities, then, have been created by two loves: that is, the earthly by love of self extending even to contempt of God, and the heavenly by love of God extending to contempt of self."[116] Given the limits of human knowledge and inscrutability of God's judgment, Augustine suggests that we cannot know who belongs to each city. Some members of the institutional church will not join God's kingdom, while some outside the church will become members of the heavenly city.[117] "In this world, the two cities are indeed entangled and mingled with one another; and they will remain so until the last judgment shall separate them."[118]

Unfortunately, Augustine's nuanced rendering of "two cities" has often been neglected by subsequent interpreters who assign institutional authority to the "two swords" or "powers" of church and state. Such institutional views, though with different aims and implications, were embraced by thinkers across the medieval and early modern period, from Pope Gelasius in the late 400s, Pope Gregory VII in the late 1000s, and Pope Boniface VIII and William of Ockham in the early 1300s to Martin Luther, John Calvin, and other Protestant Reformers in the 1500s whose "two kingdoms" theology echoed their Augustinian heritage.[119] As Henri-Xavier Arquillière's work demonstrates, identifying Augustine's two cities institutionally with "church" and "state" remained a distinctive feature of political Augustinianism through the early twentieth century.[120]

In the mid-twentieth century, however, scholars began to articulate a more complex vision that acknowledged a temporal overlap between the two cities during the *saeculum*, or "secular age," before the eschaton.[121] Although the French historian Henri-Irénée Marrou was the first to propose the possibility of a *tertium quid* that combines elements of both cities, Robert Markus's account of the *saeculum* has been the most influential.[122] His groundbreaking work remains the "scholarly lodestar for Augustinian liberalism."[123]

In *Saeculum*, Markus highlights how Augustine's "two cities" remain mixed and mingled during the "historical, empirical, perplexed and interwoven life of the two eschatological cities."[124] The *saeculum* thus refers to "the sphere of human living, history, society, and its institutions, characterised by the fact that in it the ultimate eschatological oppositions, though present, are not discernible."[125] In tracing the political implications of this secular age, however, Markus's interpretation takes on a distinctly liberal hue.[126] In particular, Markus argues that Augustine's "'secularisation' of the realm of politics implies a pluralistic, religiously neutral civil community."[127] Because we cannot discern who belongs to which city in the secular age, Markus concludes, politics must remain "neutral in respect of ultimate beliefs and values."[128]

Markus supports this emphasis on liberal neutrality by appealing to Augustine's alternative definition of a "commonwealth" (*res publica*) as the property of "an assembled multitude of rational creatures bound together by a common agreement as to the objects of their love."[129] In contrast to Cicero's s vision of a commonwealth united by a sense of justice and shared interest,[130] Markus notes that Augustine makes "no mention of justice or any other value" and casts his definition instead in "entirely neutral, positivistic terms."[131] For Markus, such neutrality seems necessary to allow members of both cities to share common objects of love during the secular age.

Restricting religious values to the private sphere and requiring public values to be neutral, Markus weds his vision of liberal neutrality with the realism advanced by other twentieth-century liberals. Noting that the "sphere of politics belongs irrevocably to the realm infected with sin," Markus suggests that remedial function of politics is the "safeguarding and fostering of a lowly form of 'peace': the public order and security which human sin has made unstable in society."[132] Rather than promoting "greater goods," political order simply aims to secure "a living space for society in the midst of strife and conflict."[133] Markus's emphasis on negative peace and the limited functions of politics echoes the Augustinian realism of Niebuhr, Deane, and Shklar.

While Markus's historical account of the *saeculum* marked a watershed in Augustinian studies, many critics resisted his liberal interpretation of the *saeculum*'s "autonomy" and "neutrality," arguing that it reflects his intellectual context more than Augustine's. Markus revises his views in *Christianity and the Secular*, where he acknowledges the influence of the "secularisation thesis" on his historical narrative and recasts his liberal interpretation as a "selective retrieval" and "reinterpretation" that goes beyond what Augustine could imagine.[134] But Markus maintains his ascription of "neutrality" and suggests that the "public" rather than "private" can be still "spoken of without reference to religion," concluding that "all that can be shared is a reduced, nonreligious, common ground."[135] Markus goes on to compare this "independent political ethic" of "consensus" to the "overlapping consensus" in Rawls's political liberalism, presenting an Augustinian liberalism that seeks common ground with the prevailing thought of his own age.[136]

Paul Weithman adduces similar Rawlsian insights to support his version of "Augustinian liberalism."[137] Like Augustinian realists, Weithman frames his account in terms of pride, which he conceives as an "undue desire for *preeminence* or *superiority*."[138] For Weithman, pride can manifest in the desire to win political arguments or impose one's own religious beliefs on fellow citizens.[139] Even "[a]dopting and adducing religious reasons for religiously inspired political positions can themselves be acts of pride," leading to political "contention," "discord," and "domination."[140] According to Weithman, liberalism resists such pride and domination because it restricts the reasons that can be offered to justify public policy or political power. By requiring citizens to engage in political advocacy based on "public" or "secular" reasons rather than religious reasons, liberalism provides an "effective check" on pride and fosters "habitual restraints on the desire to dominate others."[141] Ultimately, then, Weithman's Augustinian liberalism remains "a politics with limited ambitions": "It aims only at inculcating habits that hold pride and contempt in check," focusing "on the evils restrained rather than on the virtues elicited."[142] Weithman's Augustinian liberalism thus shares the more "pessimistic" view of realists who assume that "earthly peace" remains largely negative and limited.[143] While Weithman acknowledges that his version of political liberalism "departs significantly from Augustine's political thought in some respects," he concludes that "labeling this liberalism Augustinian is not without fidelity to Augustine's own views or to the tradition of their interpretation."[144]

In *Politics and the Order of Love*, Eric Gregory offers an alternative form of Augustinian liberalism—"civic liberalism"—that seeks to avoid the limitations of realist and proceduralist varieties.[145] Against liberal realists (such as Niebuhr and Markus) who overemphasize the effects of sin, Gregory argues that sin remains parasitic on love: without the capacity to love, humans would not have the capacity to sin.[146] For Gregory, this "dialectical relation between sin and love" funds a "virtue-oriented" politics that recognizes the realities of evil, the limits of politics, and dangers of political perfectionism while also acknowledging love as a basis for civic virtue, even if it is always threatened by vice.[147] Against liberal proceduralists (such as Weithman and Edmund Santurri[148]), Gregory contends that Augustine's emphasis on love acknowledges a role for "motivations, affections, and desires" that moves beyond the "Rawlsian preoccupation with epistemic virtue" and the liberal requirement of religious neutrality.[149] While Gregory affirms a proceduralist concern for justice, he argues that, for Augustine, justice remains dynamically dependent on love, which makes love a central civic virtue and provides a thicker political community than thin appeals to liberal neutrality afford. Finding expressions of this civic liberalism in the work of Timothy Jackson and the early work of Elshtain,[150] Gregory articulates a capacious account of his "Augustinian ethic of democratic citizenship" in conversation with feminist political theorists, ethicists of care, and Christian theologians.[151] Ultimately, Gregory elevates Gustavo Gutiérrez and Martin Luther King, Jr. as exemplars of Augustinian civic liberalism who recognize the dangers of domination yet nevertheless offer a more hopeful political theology of justice and love.[152]

Over the last decade, these varieties of Augustinian liberalism have generated significant debate within Augustinian studies and Christian ethics. While Augustinian liberals have attempted to forestall criticisms by describing their accounts as a "selective retrieval" or "rational reconstruction" of Augustine's views,[153] the most trenchant critiques have come from communitarians who contend that Augustinian liberalism fails to do justice to Augustine's concern for the community of the church. Ecclesiology has thus become a central focus of a third form of political Augustinianism—Augustinian communitarianism.

AUGUSTINIAN COMMUNITARIANISM

In *City of God*, Augustine frequently identifies the "heavenly city" with the church, the body of Christ.[154] The "'coming' of the Saviour," he writes, is "going on through this present age in His Church: that is, in His members."[155] Although Augustine insists that the two cities are entangled in the secular age and that the institutional church is not the same as "heavenly city," he nonetheless suggests that the institutional church—the "Church as she is now"—constitutes the City of God "in one sense" since it forms the community where members cultivate the virtues and order their loves.[156] Within the church, human beings can already begin participating in the City of God here and now, though in hope (*in spe*) if not in reality (*in re*).[157] In identifying the church as the heavenly city's earthen vessel, Augustine adopts an inaugurated or partially realized eschatology.[158]

As for the church's relation to politics, he rejects the idea that the church should rule politically over the temporal commonwealth.[159] Instead, following Paul in Romans 13, Augustine suggests that Christians should obey the laws and remain subject to the governing authorities, "provided only that they do not impede the religion by which we are taught that the one supreme and true God is to be worshipped."[160] But Augustine does suggest that there are times when the church should "dissent from the earthly city" and "become a burden to those who think differently."[161] In his most excessive moments, he even identifies the church as a "kingdom militant" in a battle with sin.[162] Thus, although the two cities are mixed and mingled in the secular age, the community of the church remains central to Augustine's vision of social and political life.

In *Theology and Social Theory,* John Milbank draws on Augustine's ecclesiology to elevate a "counter-kingdom" to modern liberalism, including its Augustinian varieties.[163] Challenging Markus's idea of an autonomous secular realm, Milbank criticizes Augustinian versions of liberalism for restricting politics to a neutral public sphere and "falsely attributing to Augustine an entirely privatized and spiritual notion of religion."[164] According to Milbank, by conceiving the state "merely as a compromise between individual wills for the satisfaction of material conveniences" and the church "as the collection of elect true believers, known only to God," Markus's liberal rendering of politics and purely eschatological rendering of the church assumes "an individualistic understanding of both Church and State" that downplays Augustine's emphasis on the institutional church as the corporate body of Christ.[165]

Against Markus's liberal interpretation, Milbank argues that, for Augustine, "[a]ll 'political' theory, in the antique sense, is relocated by Christianity as thought about the Church."[166] Radicalizing Alasdair MacIntyre's communitarian critique of liberalism, Milbank places the church at the center of his Augustinian communitarianism.[167] Because the church's ontology of peace "is firmly anchored in a narrative, a practice, and a dogmatic faith, not in an abstracted universal reason," Milbank argues that the church has a thick narrative unity that challenges the thin universality implicit in modern liberalism.[168] In particular, Milbank draws on Augustine to argue that the church embodies an "ontological priority of peace over conflict" that provides a stark contrast to the foundation of modern politics:

> The Church, for Augustine, is the society whose goal is peace, and whose means are non-coercive. This "city of God" exists in its full perfection in heaven, but nevertheless it is also a social reality here on earth where it is "on pilgrimage." The Church on earth is part of a *societas perfecta*, a properly self-sufficient society with its own means of establishing and maintaining norms, its own mode of social organization.[169]

Milbank's emphasis on the particular narratives, norms, and practices of the church—its "mode of social organization"—highlights his account of the church's distinctly political function.[170] For Milbank, Christians' primary political function is not to actively engage in secular politics, but to "be the Church," embodying a "peaceful community" that exposes secular politics and the world as dominating and destructive.[171]

Stanley Hauerwas draws on both MacIntyre and Milbank to advance a similar vision of ecclesial communitarianism.[172] Impugning the "false universalism of liberalism" that separates "public" from "private" and assumes "rationality" can provide a neutral source of political ethics, Hauerwas argues that liberalism denies the importance of the local and embodied "political community" of the church that unites Christians in the worship of God.[173] Moreover, by excluding religious citizens from public discourse or requiring Christians to give public reasons for their political positions, "liberal universalism" continues what Hauerwas sees as the "Constantinian" settlement, which accommodates the church to the state and thereby undercuts the church's political independence and theological integrity.[174]

Against such Constantinianism, Hauerwas asserts the theological and political primacy of the church. By joining Christians in a common narrative and shared practices of worship ordered to a common telos in God, the church provides a "community of character" that shapes Christians' virtues in ways that the liberal state precludes.[175] Rather than seeking to engage a world corrupted by sin, Hauerwas calls Christians to "be the church," creating a "contrast" society, a "peaceable kingdom," that cultivates the virtues and exposes the world's violence for what it is.[176] According to Hauerwas,

> Christians must again understand that their first task is not to make the world better or more just, but to recognize what the world is and why it is that it understands the political task as it does. The first social task of the church is to provide the space and time necessary for developing skills of interpretation and discrimination sufficient to help us recognize the possibilities and limits of our society. In developing such skills, the church and Christians must be uninvolved in the politics of our society and involved in the polity that is the church. . . . For the Christian, therefore, the church is always the primary polity through which we gain the experience to negotiate and make positive contributions to whatever society in which we may find ourselves.[177]

Like Milbank, Hauerwas defends this ecclesial communitarianism through direct appeal to Augustine, who "provides some hints of how to live in our awkward times."[178] In particular, "Augustine's very political account of salvation provides resources to help us call into question the church's accommodation to our world."[179] While Hauerwas acknowledges that Augustine's incisive diagnosis of sin "invites a Niebuhr-like interpretation," he suggests that realist and liberal interpretations ignore "Augustine's equally strong insistence that the church is the only true political society, because only in the church are we directed to worship the one true God. Only through the church do we have the resources necessary for our desires to be rightly ordered, for the virtues to be rightly formed."[180] For Hauerwas, liberalism is theologically and morally bankrupt because it denies a formative role for the church.[181]

Given their oppositional and often polemical rhetoric, Milbank and Hauerwas have been criticized for reducing Augustine's political theology to ecclesiology, denying sites and sources of virtue outside the church, and encouraging a sectarian retreat from the world.[182] In places, Milbank and Hauerwas resist such implications. Milbank occasionally acknowledges the blurry boundaries of the church and even concedes that the institutional church can sometimes "mimic the procedures of political sovereignty" through its "bureaucratic management of believers": "Better, then, that the bounds between Church and State be extremely hazy, so that a social existence of many complex and interlocking powers may emerge, and forestall either a sovereign state, or a statically hierarchical Church."[183] For his part, Hauerwas denies criticisms that he encourages exclusivism or sectarian withdrawal, claiming that he is "not asking the church to withdraw, but rather to give up the presumptions of Constantinian power, particularly when those take the form of liberal universalism."[184] Yet, at times, both Milbank and Hauerwas revert to excessive rhetoric that places the church in direct opposition to the world and the broader political society, with Milbank implicitly identifying Augustine's "earthly city" with the state and the "heavenly city" with the institutional church and Hauerwas calling for the "triumphant political community" of the church to stand "against the world" and "be uninvolved in the politics of our society."[185] As a result, their followers often assume their excessive rhetoric justifies opposition to the world and disengagement from practical politics, and strikingly, their followers are numerous. Far from being an isolated polemicist, Milbank is a founder of "Radical Orthodoxy," which continues to attract adherents in seminaries and sanctuaries across the world, and he has supplied the theological and philosophical foundations for the Red Tory and Blue Labour movements in British politics.[186] Meanwhile, *TIME Magazine* named Hauerwas "America's best theologian" in 2001, and a prominent scholar of religion has described him as "the most prolific and influential theologian" in the United States.[187] Given their influence, their communitarianism continues to fuel resentment among Christians who feel that political liberalism has diminished the role of the church and evicted religious citizens from the public square. This is one reason why debates about Augustine's legacy have practical relevance: competing interpretations of Augustine, whether liberal or communitarian, have become not merely matters of theoretical or theological interest but attempts to draw battle lines in a culture war between religion and secularism.

AUGUSTINIAN REPUBLICANISM

Within political theory, one prominent response to entrenched debates between liberals and communitarians has been to avoid both extremes by recovering an older tradition of political thought, *civic republicanism*, which weds a liberal concern with individual liberty and institutional checks and balances with a communitarian concern for civic virtue and the common good.[188] Historians of political thought such as Quentin Skinner have traced this republican tradition from ancient Rome through the early modern period, while philosophers such as Philip Pettit have drawn on this history to construct contemporary theories of republicanism.[189] In both historical and constructive accounts, however, political theorists often overlook republican themes in the thought of Augustine.

Recently, theologians and political theorists have begun to recognize Augustine's republican inheritance. Eric Gregory and Joseph Clair have challenged the common opposition between Augustine and Aquinas by highlighting how both thinkers distinguish "domination" from "political authority" and see political authority as a more "natural" good.[190] John von Heyking has identified ideas from Aristotle and Cicero in Augustine's use of rhetoric and "right-by-nature" form of politics, emphasizing that Augustine understood a "people" in a "republican mode."[191] And Charles Mathewes has defended a vision of "Augustinian Christian republican citizenship" that connects Augustinian concerns about sin, virtue, and the limits of politics with an analysis of "liberal-republican citizenship" in contemporary America.[192]

The most focused treatment is Paul Cornish's article "Augustine's Contribution to the Republican Tradition."[193] Noting Augustine's absence from traditional histories of republicanism, Cornish describes Augustine's "appraisal of the Roman republic" as "an important chapter in the historical development of the republican tradition."[194] In particular, Cornish draws three parallels between the thought of Augustine and Cicero. First, Augustine accepts Cicero's republican distinction between liberty and domination and recognizes that political rule is consistent with liberty in a way that slavery or domination is not.[195] Second, Augustine, like Cicero, views political order as "necessarily problematic and indeterminate," involving inevitable uncertainty given human finitude and fallenness.[196] Third, Augustine shares Cicero's views on the "tragic nature of political action" but, like Cicero, nonetheless encourages citizens to dutifully seek the peace of the city and serve the common good.[197] Cornish concludes that Augustine's recognition of the tragedy of politics itself marks "a major contribution to the history of republicanism."[198]

I endorse Cornish's emphasis on Augustine's republican inheritance. In a recent article, I argue that recognizing Augustine's republican commitments helps to contextualize his controversial defense of coercion, which remains one of the most contested issues in Augustine's political thought.[199] In particular, I show how political interpreters tend to read Augustine's defense of coercion through a liberal lens, assuming a modern conception of liberty as non-interference. By contrast, I argue that Augustine operates with the republican conception of liberty as non-domination, which opposes liberty not to coercion or interference, but to domination or arbitrary interference, the kind of rule a master wields over a slave.[200] In *On the Free Choice of the Will*, Augustine explicitly endorses a republican conception of liberty as the "'freedom' (*libertatem*) by which people who have no masters think of themselves as free."[201] With this conception in view, I show how Augustine defends coercion to preserve peace and curb domination but places moral and political constraints on its use to prevent it from constituting domination. He argues, for example, that coercion must be exercised by a legitimate public authority and according to a rule of law that constrains arbitrary power.[202] He requires coercion to be consistent with the interests of the coerced and moderated by the exercise of virtue, which offers internal constraints where external restraints are unenforceable or lacking.[203] And he defends his account of legitimate coercion through republican modes of dialogical reasoning, using publicity to encourage transparency and accountability and employing immanent critique to engage opponents on their own terms. By drawing on authorities that his opponents accept as legitimate, Augustine adduces justifications for coercion that are not arbitrary from his opponents' perspective, which aids his attempt to avoid the arbitrary interference that constitutes domination.[204]

While Augustine's republican mode of reasoning casts new light on his defense of coercion, it also highlights a mode of political dialogue that offers an alternative to the Rawlsian forms of public reason that Augustinian liberals such as Weithman recommend. Noting how invoking religious reasons in public debate can sometimes constitute domination, Weithman draws on Rawls's political liberalism to suggest that religious citizens should engage in political advocacy by appealing to neutral public reasons, which, he argues, is the best way to show respect to those with different conceptions of the good.[205] An Augustinian commitment to immanent critique, however, highlights a different way to show respect. On this account, religious citizens can show respect not by appealing to neutral public reasons that stand free of any comprehensive doctrine, but by engaging interlocutors on their own terms, justifying public policies with reference to reasons, doctrines, and authorities they accept as legitimate. Such dialogical exchange helps to prevent the domination that concerns Weithman without imposing one's beliefs on other citizens or requiring citizens to give neutral public reasons that may seem alien to their point of view. Thus, with communitarian critics of liberalism, an Augustinian republican account of political dialogue recognizes that politics and public debate are not neutral, but with Augustinian liberals, it affirms that civic peace requires resisting domination by any one group. In this way, an Augustinian practice of dialogical exchange and immanent critique fits with recommendations from contemporary critics of liberalism such as Jeffrey Stout who argues that neutralist forms of "public reason" place unfair burdens on religious citizens and proposes immanent critique as a more legitimate expression of respect.[206]

Recovering Augustine's republican commitments also highlights a different conception of "civic peace" that diverse citizens share in the commonwealth. Contrary to what Augustinian realists, liberals, and communitarians imply, civic peace is not merely a "negative" peace, the mere absence of hostility or violence.[207] Rather, Augustine explains the "well-ordered concord" of the city by invoking Cicero's two duties of justice: "the order of this concord is, first, that a man should harm no one, and, second, that he should do good to all, so far as he can."[208] While the first duty limits the effects of sin, the second, more positive duty highlights Augustine's republican conception of peace as a form of *concord* or *harmony* between citizens.[209] Moreover, in recognizing that "a man's fellow citizens are also his friends," Augustine follows Cicero and his republican predecessors in conceiving concord as a form of *civic friendship*, an ordered relationship between citizens.[210] By conceiving civic peace as a form of civic friendship, a republican reading thus affords a more capacious view of the civic peace that Christians and non-Christian citizens can share in the commonwealth and thus provides a more positive, relational view of politics than the negative,[211] institutional view common in realist, liberal, and communitarian interpretations.

Of course, more work needs to be done to examine Augustine's republican concepts in relation to his other commitments and to determine the extent to which "Augustinian republicanism" should be understood as either a "historical" or "rational reconstruction" of Augustine's thought.[212] However, regardless of whether we see Augustine as a republican or simply as someone who inherited and adapted republican concepts and commitments for his own context, a republican reading, I believe, can uncover valuable resources for contemporary republican theory. Elsewhere, I focus on four.[213] First, Augustinian republicanism recognizes a role for religion in republican theory, which is especially important given that many contemporary accounts downplay the traditional role of religion in republicanism.[214] Second, by engaging religious citizens on their own terms, Augustinian republicanism encourages religious citizens to participate in the public square without either requiring liberal neutrality or allowing one community to dominate. This republican posture helps to avert both liberal complaints against a totalizing communitarianism and communitarian complaints against a completely secularized liberalism. Third, like Gregory's civic liberalism, an Augustinian republicanism elevates love, virtue, and civic friendship in ways that are often downplayed in procedural forms of republicanism focused more on institutional design. Finally, an Augustinian emphasis on the "lust for domination" incorporates an element of political realism missing from more idealized and abstract forms of republican political theory. In these ways and others, an account of Augustinian republicanism opens promising new areas of inquiry for both Augustinian studies and contemporary political theory.[215]

CONCLUSION

Augustine's impact on political theory is varied and deep. From the fifth century onward, interpreters have adapted, appropriated, and contested Augustine's ideas in myriad and sometimes conflicting ways. Augustine would have expected no less. As he says in the

Confessions, imagining how he would want others to interpret Genesis had he written it, "I would hope to have written in such a way that if anyone else had in the light of truth seen some other valid meaning, that too should not be excluded, but present itself as a possible way of understanding in what I had said."[216] As we continue to consider and contest Augustine's legacy in political theory, we may yet discover valid but unexpected meaning in what he has said.[217]

NOTES

1. For a comprehensive account of Augustine's influence on important thinkers, doctrines, and ideas, see Karla Pollmann, ed., *The Oxford Guide to the Historical Reception of Augustine*, 3 vols. (Oxford: Oxford University Press, 2013), abbreviated as *OGHRA*; and Allan D. Fitzgerald, ed., *Augustine through the Ages: An Encyclopedia* (Grand Rapids, MI: Eerdmans, 1999), abbreviated as *ATA*. For a helpful overview of Augustine's contemporary reception, see Michael J. S. Bruno, *Political Augustinianism: Modern Interpretations of Augustine's Political Thought* (New York: Fortress Press, 2014).
2. For Augustine's narrative of his life, see Augustine, *The Confessions*, trans. Maria Boulding (New York: Vintage Books, 1998). For the first biography written by a fellow bishop and friend of Augustine, see Possidius, "The Life of Saint Augustine," in *Soldiers of Christ: Saints and Saints' Lives from Late Antiquity and the Early Middle Ages*, trans. F.R. Hoare, ed. Thomas F. X. Noble and Thomas Head (University Park, PA: The Pennsylvania State University Press, 1995), 31–73. For a masterful contemporary biography, see Peter Brown, *Augustine of Hippo: A Biography* (Berkeley, CA: University of California Press, 2000). For an alternative emphasis, see James J. O'Donnell, *Augustine: A New Biography* (New York: HarperPerennial, 2005). For more concise accounts, see Henri Marrou, *Saint Augustine and His Influence through the Ages*, trans. Patrick Hepburne-Scott and Edmund Hill (New York: Harper Torchbooks, 1957), and Garry Wills, *Saint Augustine* (New York: Viking, 1999).
3. Justo L. González argues that Augustine was a "mestizo" whose mixed backgrounds and ability to stand at the crossroads of cultures funded his "mestizo theology." See Justo L. González, *The Mestizo Augustine: A Theologian Between Two Cultures* (Downer's Grove, IL: InterVarsity Press, 2016), 9–10, 13–19, 171. Rosemary Radford Reuther suggests that "Augustine combined in his own biography all of the elements of the contradictory trends." See Rosemary Radford Reuther, "Augustine and Christian Political Theology," *Interpretation: A Journal of Bible and Theology* 29, no. 3 (1975): 252–265, at 257.
4. *Confessions*, 2.3.5–2.3.6; Brown, *Augustine of Hippo*, 9; O'Donnell, *Augustine*, 10.
5. *Confessions*, 3.3.6; Brown, *Augustine of Hippo*, 9–10, 26; O'Donnell, *Augustine*, 10, 89.
6. *Confessions*, 5.13.23; Brown, *Augustine of Hippo*, 54–61.
7. *Confessions*, 3.3.6, 4.11.20.
8. *Confessions*, 4.2.2, 6.6.9, 9.2.2, 9.5.13; Wills, *Saint Augustine*, 45.
9. *Confessions*, 9.4.7–9.5.13; Brown, *Augustine of Hippo*, 69–120.
10. *Confessions*, 9.6.14. On Augustine's baptism, see Garry Wills, *Font of Life: Ambrose, Augustine, and the Mystery of Baptism* (Oxford: Oxford University Press, 2012).
11. Possidius, "Life," §3; Brown, *Augustine of Hippo*, 124–130.
12. *Confessions*, 9.11.27; Brown, *Augustine of Hippo*, 122–123, 128.
13. *Confessions*, 4.1.1, 5.6.10; Brown, *Augustine of Hippo*, 35–49, 127.
14. See Augustine, Sermon 355.2, in *Sermons 341–400*, trans. Edmund Hill, ed. John E. Rotelle (New York: New City Press, 1995); Possidius, "Life," §4; Brown, *Augustine of Hippo*, 131–132.

15. Possidius, "Life," §8, §28–31; Brown, *Augustine of Hippo*, 133–138, 431–437.
16. See Possidius, "Life," §5–9, §19–20; Augustine, *The Monastic Rules*, trans. Agatha Mary and Gerald Bonner, ed. Boniface Ramsey (New York: New City Press, 2004).
17. Possidius, "Life," §7–9, §21; Robert Dodaro, "Between the Two Cities: Political Action in Augustine of Hippo," in *Augustine and Politics*, ed. John Doody, Kevin L. Hughes, and Kim Paffenroth (Lanham, MD: Lexington Books, 2005), 99–115, at 108–110.
18. Peter Brown, "Saint Augustine," in *Religion and Society in the Age of Saint Augustine* (New York: Harper & Row, 1972), 25–46, at 25; O'Donnell, *Augustine*, 135–136.
19. Augustine, *The Retractions*, trans. Mary Inez Bogan (Washington, DC: Catholic University Press, 1968), 2.69.1. See also Augustine, Letter 23A*.4, in *Letters 211–270, 1*–29**, trans. Roland Teske, ed. Boniface Ramsey (New York: New City Press, 2005).
20. See, e.g., Possidius, "Life," §19–20, §23–24; Dodaro, "Between the Two Cities"; Robert Dodaro, "Church and State," in *ATA*, 176–184.
21. Possidius, "Life," §19. Dodaro, "Between the Two Cities," 105–106; Dodaro, "Church and State," 174–178.
22. Dodaro, "Between the Two Cities," 99–100, 110–111.
23. See, for example, E. M. Atkins and Robert Dodaro, "Introduction," in Augustine, *Political Writings*, ed. E. M. Atkins and Robert Dodaro (Cambridge: Cambridge University Press, 2001), xi–xxvii; Dodaro, "Between the Two Cities"; Dodaro, "Church and State," and Joseph Clair, *Discerning the Good in the Letters and Sermons of Augustine* (Oxford: Oxford University Press, 2016).
24. Augustine, *The City of God against the Pagans*, ed. and trans. R. W. Dyson (Cambridge: Cambridge University Press, 1998). For a helpful overview, see Dyson, "Introduction," in *City of God*, x–xxix. For a comprehensive guide, see Gerard O'Daly, *Augustine's* City of God: *A Reader's Guide* (Oxford: Oxford University Press, 1999). For overviews of *City of God*'s reception and influence, see Michael C. Sloan, "*De civitate Dei*," in *OGHRA*, 255–261; and Bonnie Kent, "Reinventing Augustine's Ethics: The Afterlife of *City of God*," in *Augustine's* City of God: *A Critical Guide*, ed. James Wetzel (Cambridge: Cambridge University Press, 2012), 225–244.
25. See R. W. Dyson, "Introduction," xv, xxviii–xxix; Miles Hollingworth, *Pilgrim City: St Augustine of Hippo and His Innovation in Political Thought* (New York: T&T Clark, 2010), 6–7; Herbert A. Deane, *The Political and Social Ideas of St. Augustine* (New York: Columbia University Press, 1963), vii–ix; Dodaro, "Church and State," 181–182; Arjo Vanderjagt, "Political Thought," in *OGHRA*, 1562–1569, at 1562–1563.
26. See Deane, *Political and Social Ideas*, viii–ix, 13; Dyson, "Introduction," xv; Hollingworth, *Pilgrim City*, 64–65; John von Heyking, *Augustine and Politics as Longing in the World* (Columbia, MO: University of Missouri Press, 2001), 17–50; and Michael Lamb, "Beyond Pessimism: A Structure of Encouragement in Augustine's *City of God*," *Review of Politics* 80, no. 4 (2018): 591–624.
27. *City of God*, 1. Preface, 22.30. For Augustine's purposes in writing *City of God*, see *Retractions*, 2.69.1–2.
28. On the ways that Augustine established his authority, see James J. O'Donnell, "The Authority of Augustine," *Augustinian Studies* 22 (1991): 7–35. On Augustine as a "bridge" between ancient and medieval political thought, see Deane, *Political and Social Ideas*, 2–3. "Throughout history," Henri Marrou argues, "[Augustine's] influence is constantly present in the most widely different spheres of thought, education and religious life. It is hard to imagine, without actually verifying it, how much the example and teaching of St. Augustine have moulded the Latin tradition: with more justice even than Virgil he deserves the title of 'Father of the West'" (*Saint Augustine*, 151).

29. Sheldon S. Wolin, *Politics and Vision: Continuity and Innovation in Western Political Thought* (Princeton, NJ: Princeton University Press, 2004), 110.

30. Alan Ryan, *On Politics: A History of Political Thought from Herodotus to the Present*, Vol. 1 (New York: W.W. Norton, 2012), 149. Charles Taylor argues that the Western focus on interiority has its origin in Augustine (see Charles Taylor, *Sources of the Self: The Making of the Modern Identity* (Cambridge, MA: Harvard University Press, 1989), 127–142). Jennifer Herdt suggests that the rise of modern moral philosophy can be traced, in part, to the Augustinian "legacy of the splendid vices" (see Jennifer A. Herdt, *Putting on Virtue: The Legacy of the Splendid Vices* (Chicago: University of Chicago Press, 2008)), while Eric Gregory argues that "the continuing debate over modern liberalism has to a large extent consisted in variations on Augustinian themes and antiphonal responses to them" (see Eric Gregory, *Politics and the Order of Love: An Augustinian Ethic of Democratic Citizenship* (Chicago: University of Chicago Press, 2008), 1). John Rist traces Augustine's reception in the medieval and modern period with a particular focus on ideas of "freedom" and "will" (see John M. Rist, *Augustine Deformed: Love, Sin and Freedom in the Western Moral Tradition* (Cambridge: Cambridge University Press, 2014)).

31. See Kent, "Reinventing Augustine's Ethics," 228–229.

32. Nico den Bok, "Peter Lombard," in *OGHRA*, 1527–1530, at 1527; Joseph Wawrykow, "Peter Lombard," in *ATA*, 650–651; Kent, "Reinventing Augustine's Ethics," 231–234.

33. Alister McGrath, *Iustitia Dei: A History of the Christian Doctrine of Justification* (Cambridge: Cambridge University Press, 1972), 38, as cited by Bok, "Peter Lombard," 1527.

34. See Jean-Pierre Torrell, *Saint Thomas Aquinas, Vol. 1: The Person and His Work*, trans. Robert Royal, rev. ed. (Washington, DC: Catholic University of America Press, 2005), 39–45.

35. This contrast is especially common among Augustinian realists who emphasize a primarily negative and remedial account of Augustinian politics. See Markus, *Saeculum*, 197–230, and Deane, *Political and Social Ideas*, 233–234.

36. See, for example, Eric Gregory and Joseph Clair, "Augustinianism and Thomisms" in *The Cambridge Companion to Christian Political Theology*, ed. Craig Hovey and Elizabeth Phillips (Cambridge: Cambridge University Press, 2015), 176–195; Michael Dauphinais, Barry David, and Matthew Levering, eds., *Aquinas the Augustinian* (Washington, DC: Catholic University of America Press, 2007); Rudi te Velde, "Thomas Aquinas," in *OGHRA*, 1798–1803; and David Decosimo, *Ethics as a Work of Charity: Thomas Aquinas and Pagan Virtue* (Stanford, CA: Stanford University Press, 2014).

37. Gregory and Clair, "Augustinianisms and Thomisms," 186–190, citing Thomas Aquinas, *Summa Theologiae*, Ia.96.4.

38. Eric L. Saak, "Luther, Martin," in *OGHRA*, 1341–1345, at 1341; Philip D. Krey, "Luther, Martin," in *ATA*, 516–518.

39. *D. Martin Luthers Werke: kritische Gesammtausgabe* (Weimar: Hermann Böhlaus Nachfolger, 1883–2009), WA 9:29, ll. 5–6, as cited by Saak, "Luther, Martin," 1343.

40. For an overview of Luther's Augustinian influences and extensive citations of Augustine's works, see Saak, "Luther, Martin." On Luther's "two kingdoms," see Hollingworth, *Pilgrim City*, 111–127; George Klosko, *History of Political Theory: An Introduction, Volume 1: Ancient and Medieval*, 2nd ed. (Oxford: Oxford University Press, 2012), 326–352; and David vanDrunen, *Natural Law and the Two Kingdoms: A Study in the Development of Reformed Social Thought* (Grand Rapids, MI: Eerdmans, 2010), 55–62.

41. Luchesius Smits, *St. Augustin dans l'oeuvre de Jean Calvin* (Assen: Van Gorcum, Vol. 1, 1956, vol. 2, 1957), 6, as cited by David J. Marshall, "Calvin, John," in *ATA*, 116–120, at 117. See also Anthony N. S. Lane, "Calvin, John," in *OGHRA*, 739–743.

42. John Calvin, *Aeterna Dei praedestinatione* (1552), in *Ioannis Calvini opera quae supersunt omnia*, ed. Guilielmus Baum, Eduardus Cunitz, and Eduardus Reuss, Vol. 8 (Brunsvigae: C.A. Schwetschke, 1870), 266, as cited and translated by Marshall, "Calvin, John," 116.
43. George Marsden, "Jonathan Edwards, American Augustine," *Christianity Today*, Nov. 1, 1999, http://www.christianitytoday.com/bc/1999/novdec/9b6010.html?start=3.
44. For a broad thematic overview, see Vanderjagt, "Political Thought," in *OGHRA*, 1562–1569.
45. For an overview, see Winthrop Wetherbee, "Dante Alighieri," in *OGHRA*, 856–858.
46. See John Savoie, "Milton, John," in *OGHRA*, 1397–1399, at 1397, citing *Complete Prose Works of John Milton*, ed. D. Wolfe, 8 vols. (New Haven, CT: 1953–1982), 4.419. Savoie suggests that Augustine's "pervasive influence" on Milton "cannot be overstated" ("Milton," 1397, 1398). See also Sloan, *"De civitate Dei,"* 259.
47. For overviews of Rousseau's Augustinian influences, see Christopher Brooke, "Rousseau's Political Philosophy: Stoic and Augustinian Origins," in *The Cambridge Companion to Rousseau*, ed. Patrick Riley (Cambridge: Cambridge University Press, 2001), 94–123; and Matt Qvortrup, "Rousseau, Jean-Jacques," in *OGHRA*, 1675–1677. While Rousseau's thinking is "diametrically different" from Augustine's in many ways, Qvortrup argues, Rousseau "was at every level deeply influenced, inspired by, and indebted to the writings of Augustine" ("Rousseau," 1675). On Augustinian sources for the general will, see Patrick Riley, *The General Will before Rousseau: The Transformation of the Divine into the Civic* (Princeton, NJ: Princeton University Press, 1986), 3–26. On Augustinian sources for *amore-propre*, see Brooke, "Rousseau's Political Philosophy," and Qvortrup, "Rousseau," 1675–1676. On Rousseau's *Confessions*, see Qvortrup, "Rousseau," 1675–1676, and Ann Hartle, *The Modern Self in Rousseau's Confessions: A Reply to St. Augustine* (Notre Dame, IN: University of Notre Dame Press, 1983).
48. For summaries, see, for example, Joanna V. Scott, "Political Thought, Contemporary Influences of Augustine's," in *ATA*, 658–661, and Bruno, *Political Augustinianism*.
49. Reinhold Niebuhr, "Augustine's Political Realism," in *The Essential Reinhold Niebuhr: Selected Essays and Addresses*, ed. Robert McAfee Brown (New Haven, CT: Yale University Press, 1986), 123–141; Judith Shklar, "Giving Injustice Its Due," *Yale Law Journal* 98, no. 6 (1989): 1135–1151.
50. Jean Bethke Elshtain, *Just War Against Terror: The Burden of American Power in a Violent World* (New York: Basic Books, 2003), 46–58, 70, 101, 107–108, 125. For one insightful analysis and critique of Elshtain's appropriation of Augustine's account of just war, see James Turner Johnson, "Reading Augustine," *Providence Magazine*, Summer 2017, 48–56, available online at: http://providencemag.com/wp-content/uploads/James-Turner-Johnson-Reading-Augustine.pdf.
51. See Martha Nussbaum, *Upheavals of Thought: The Intelligence of Emotions* (New York: Cambridge University Press, 2001), 551, 552–553, 548–549.
52. John Rawls, *A Brief Inquiry into the Meaning of Sin and Faith*, ed. Thomas Nagel (Cambridge, MA: Harvard University Press, 2009), 209; cf. 161–162, 174–175, 182–183, 216–217, 220.
53. John Rawls, *Political Liberalism*, expanded ed. (New York: Columbia University Press, 2005), 134–135; John Rawls, "Justice as Fairness: Political not Metaphysical," *Philosophy & Public Affairs* 14, no. 3 (1985): 223–251, at 248.
54. Paul J. Weithman, "Toward an Augustinian Liberalism," in *The Augustinian Tradition*, ed. Gareth B. Matthews (Berkeley, CA: University of California Press, 1999), 304–322; R. A. Markus, *Christianity and the Secular* (Notre Dame, IN: University of Notre Dame Press, 2006), 49–69.

55. See Letter from Michael Oakeshott to Patrick Riley (1988), cited in Patrick Riley, "Michael Oakeshott, Philosopher of Individuality," *Review of Politics* 54, no. 4 (1992): 649–664, at 664. Oakeshott described Augustine's *Confessions* as "[p]erhaps the finest expression of what God means to the soul to be found in all of the literature of religion" in *What Is History? And Other Essays*, ed. Luke O'Sullivan (Exeter: Imprint Academic, 2004), 89n104. Oakeshott's undergraduate lecture on Augustine is included in Michael Oakeshott, *Lectures in the History of Political Thought*, ed. Terry Nardin and Luke O'Sullivan (Exeter: Imprint Academic, 2006), 323–340. On similarities between Augustine and Oakeshott, see Wendell John Coats, Jr., *Oakeshott and His Contemporaries: Montaigne, St. Augustine, Hegel, et al.* (Cranbury, NJ: Associated University Presses, 2000), 28–38; Glenn Worthington, "Michael Oakeshott and the City of God," *Political Theory* 28, no. 3 (2000): 377–398; Elizabeth Campbell Corey, *Michael Oakeshott on Religion, Aesthetics and Politics* (Columbia, MO: University of Missouri Press, 2006), 20–45; and Helen Banner, "Existential Failure and Success: Augustinianism in Oakeshott and Arendt," *Intellectual History Review* 21, no. 2 (2011): 171–194.

56. Alasdair MacIntyre, *God, Philosophy, Universities: A Selective History of the Catholic Philosophical Tradition* (Lanham, MD: Rowman & Littlefield, 2009), 21–32; Alasdair MacIntyre, "The Augustinian Alternative," in *Whose Justice? Which Rationality?* (Notre Dame, IN: University of Notre Dame Press, 1989), 147–163.

57. Hannah Arendt, *Love and Saint Augustine*, ed. and trans., Joanna Vecchiarelli Scott and Judith Chelius Stark (Chicago: University of Chicago Press, 1996). For an extensive analysis of Arendt's engagement with Augustine, see Gregory, *Politics and the Order of Love*, 197–240. On natality, see Hannah Arendt, *The Origins of Totalitarianism* (New York: Harcourt, 1968/1985), 479, citing *City of God*, 12.20; Hannah Arendt, *Between Past and Future: Eight Exercises in Political Thought* (New York: Penguin, 1968), 165–166; Joanna Vecchiarelli Scott and Judith Chelius Stark, "Rediscovering Hannah Arendt," in Arendt, *Love and Saint Augustine*, 113–211, at 132–133, 146–148; Joanna Vecchiarelli Scott, "Hannah Arendt's Secular Augustinianism," *Augustinian Studies* 30, no. 2 (1999): 293–310, at 298–302; and Jean Bethke Elshtain, *Augustine and the Limits of Politics* (Notre Dame, IN: University of Notre Dame Press, 1995), 72, 101. On "banality," see Hannah Arendt, *Eichmann in Jerusalem: A Report on the Banality of Evil* (New York: Penguin, 1964/1994); Scott and Stark, "Rediscovering Hannah Arendt," 120–121; Scott, "Hannah Arendt's Secular Augustinianism," 297, 309–310; Elshtain, *Augustine and the Limits of Politics*, 71–87; and Charles Mathewes, *Evil and the Augustinian Tradition* (New York: Cambridge University Press, 2001), 149–197.

58. Albert Camus, *Christian Metaphysics and Neoplatonism*, trans. Ronald D. Srigley (Columbia, MO: University of Missouri Press, 2007), 129.

59. Michael Hardt and Antoni Negri, *Empire* (Cambridge, MA: Harvard University Press, 2000), 205–208, 393.

60. William E. Connolly, *The Augustinian Imperative: A Reflection on the Politics of Morality* (New York: Rowman & Littlefield Publishers, 1993), xviii–xxxiv, 63–90, and Romand Coles, *Self/Power/Other: Political Theory and Dialogical Ethics* (Ithaca, NY: Cornell University Press, 1992), 51–52, 173–174, 179. For Augustinian responses to criticisms from radical democrats, see Kathleen Roberts Skerrett, "Sovereignty and Sadness: Tragic Vision and Wisdom's Grief," *Augustinian Studies* 41, no. 1 (2010): 301–314; K. Roberts Skerrett, "The Indispensable Rival: William Connolly's Engagement with Augustine of Hippo," *Journal of the American Academy of Religion* 72, no. 2 (2004): 487–506; Kristen Deede Johnson, *Theology, Political Theory, and Pluralism: Beyond Tolerance and Difference* (New York: Cambridge University Press, 2007), 82–260; Charles T. Mathewes, *A Theology of Public Life* (New York: Cambridge University Press, 2007), 105–142, 266–307; and Robert Dodaro, "Augustine's Secular City," in *Augustine and His Critics: Essays in Honour of Gerald Bonner*, ed. Robert Dodaro and George Lawless (New York: Routledge, 2000), 231–259.

61. Karla Pollman, "The Proteanism of Authority: The Reception of Augustine in Cultural History from his Death to the Present," in *OGHRA*, 3–14.

62. O'Donnell, "The Authority of Augustine," 7, 23; Lane, "Calvin, John," 739.

63. See, for example, David Brooks, "How Movements Recover," *New York Times*, March 14, 2013, https://www.nytimes.com/2013/03/15/opinion/brooks-how-movements-recover.html; David Brooks, *The Road to Character* (New York: Random House, 2015), 186–212; E. J. Dionne, Jr., *Souled Out: Reclaiming Faith and Politics after the Religious Right* (Princeton, NJ: Princeton University Press, 2008), 31, 185–186, 194; E. J. Dionne, Jr., "A Kinder Mix of Religion and Politics during Holy Week," *Washington Post*, April 4, 2012, https://www.washingtonpost.com/opinions/a-kinder-mix-of-religion-and-politics-during-holy-week/2012/04/04/gIQAuH26vS_story.html?utm_term=.7e57c70a01cb; Jon Meacham, "The End of Christian America," *Newsweek*, April 3, 2009, http://www.newsweek.com/meacham-end-christian-america-77125.

64. See Elshtain, *Just War Against Terror*, and Jean Bethke Elshtain, "But Was It Just? Reflections on the Iraq War," *NEXUS* 9 (2004): 69–77; Susan B. Thistlewaite, "'Just War,' or Is It Just a War?" *Chicago Tribune*, October 15, 2002, http://articles.chicagotribune.com/2002-10-15/news/0210150104_1_war-theory-cold-war-iraq; cf. Susan Brooks Thistlewaite, "The Iraq War: How Our Nation Lost Its Soul," *Washington Post*, March 18, 2013, https://www.washingtonpost.com/national/on-faith/the-iraq-war-how-our-nation-lost-its-soul/2013/03/18/259e6406-8fe5-11e2-9cfd-36d6c9b5d7ad_story.html?utm_term=.6d0c2405f4bb. For one academic analysis, see Peter Lee, "Selective Memory: Augustine and Contemporary Just War Discourse," *Scottish Journal of Theology* 65, no. 3 (2012), 309–322.

65. See, for example, Nancy Pelosi, Interview on *Meet the Press*, NBC News, August 24, 2008, http://www.nbcnews.com/id/26377338/ns/meet_the_press/t/meet-press-transcript-august/; Paul Kengor, "Pelosi vs. Augustine," *National Catholic Register*, September 9, 2008, http://www.ncregister.com/site/article/pelosi_v_augustine; and Julia Duin, "Catholics Rap Pelosi's Abortion Remarks," *Washington Times*, August 27, 2008, https://www.washingtontimes.com/news/2008/aug/27/catholic-bishops-assail-pelosi-over-her-remarks-on/. For one academic analysis, see D. A. Jones, "Thomas Aquinas, Augustine, and Aristotle on 'Delayed Animation'," *The Thomist* 76, no. 1 (2012): 1–36.

66. David Luban, "What Would Augustine Do? The President, Drones, and Just War Theory," *Boston Review*, June 6, 2012, http://bostonreview.net/david-luban-the-president-drones-augustine-just-war-theory.

67. *City of God*, 12.6–9, 14.6–7, 14.12, 15.22. For an Augustinian account of sin as perversion and privation, see Mathewes, *Evil and the Augustinian Tradition*, 75–81.

68. For illuminating accounts of Augustine's "order of love," see Gregory, *Politics and the Order of Love*, 197–362; Mathewes, *Theology of Public Life*, 74–104; and Sarah Stewart-Kroeker, "Resisting Idolatry and Instrumentalization in Loving the Neighbour: The Significance of the Pilgrimage Motif for Augustine's Usus-Fruitio Distinction," *Studies in Christian Ethics* 27, no. 2 (2014): 202–221.

69. See Augustine, *On Christian Teaching*, trans. R. P. H. Green (Oxford: Oxford University Press, 1997), Book 1; *City of God*, 15.22. For discussion of the "order of love" in relation to politics, see Gregory, *Politics and the Order of Love*, 197–362, and Michael Lamb, "Between Presumption and Despair: Augustine's Hope for the Commonwealth," *American Political Science Review* 112, no. 4 (2018): 1036–1049.

70. *City of God*, 14.13.

71. *City of God*, 14.13.

72. See *City of God*, 14.13, 19.12.

73. *City of God*, 19.12, 5.12–14, translation altered from "mastery" to "domination."
74. See *City of God*, 5.12, translation altered. See also *City of God*, 3.14, 5.19, 14.28, 15.5, and *On Christian Teaching*, 1.23.23.
75. *City of God*, 1.Preface, translation altered; cf. 14.28, 15.7.
76. *City of God*, 19.7.
77. *City of God*, 19.5.
78. *City of God*, 19.5.
79. *City of God*, 22.22–23.
80. For an overview of Augustinian realism, including Niebuhr and Deane, see Bruno, *Political Augustinianism*, 63–117.
81. "For many citizens, at least in American churches and universities," Gregory writes, "Niebuhr is the standard route into political Augustinianism" (*Politics and the Order of Love*, 82).
82. See Reinhold Niebuhr, *The Irony of American History* (Chicago: University of Chicago Press, 2008), 35.
83. Niebuhr, "Augustine's Political Realism," 124.
84. Niebuhr, "Augustine's Political Realism," 124–126.
85. Niebuhr, "Augustine's Political Realism," 127.
86. See *TIME Magazine* magazine, March 8, 1948.
87. Hans Morgenthau, "The Influence of Reinhold Niebuhr in American Political Life and Thought," in *Reinhold Niebuhr: A Prophetic Voice in Our Time: Essays in Tribute by Paul Tillich, John C. Bennett, Hans Morgenthau*, ed. Harold R. Landon (Greenwich, CT: Seabury Press, 1962), 97–109, at 109, as cited by Daniel Rice, "Reinhold Niebuhr and Hans Morgenthau: A Friendship with Contrasting Shades of Realism," *Journal of American Studies* 42, no. 2 (2008): 255–291, at 255; Arthur Schlesinger, Jr., "Reinhold Niebuhr's Long Shadow," *New York Times*, June 22, 1992, https://www.nytimes.com/1992/06/22/opinion/reinhold-niebuhr-s-long-shadow.html; cf. Arthur Schlesinger, Jr. "Forgetting Reinhold Niebuhr," *New York Times*, Sept. 18, 2005, https://www.nytimes.com/2005/09/18/books/review/forgetting-reinhold-niebuhr.html.
88. John McCain with Mark Salter, *Hard Call: The Art of Great Decisions* (New York: Twelve, 2007), 319–339; David Brooks, "Obama, Gospel and Verse," *New York Times*, April 26, 2007, https://www.nytimes.com/2007/04/26/opinion/26brooks.html.
89. Paul Elie, "A Man for All Reasons," *The Atlantic*, November 2007, https://www.theatlantic.com/magazine/archive/2007/11/a-man-for-all-reasons/306337/. See also Richard Crouter, *Reinhold Niebuhr: On Politics, Religion, and Christian Faith* (Oxford: Oxford University Press, 2010), 3–11.
90. Deane, *Political and Social Ideas*, xiii, 230, 241.
91. Deane, *Political and Social Ideas*, 13–77, 56, 234–236; cf. 46, 50, 59–60, 117, 144.
92. Deane, *Political and Social Ideas*, 56, 59.
93. See Deane, *Political and Social Ideas*, 66, 116–117, 143.
94. Deane, *Political and Social Ideas*, 117, 140–141, 102.
95. Deane, *Political and Social Ideas*, 117, 152.
96. Deane, *Political and Social Ideas*, 151–152, 240.
97. Deane, *Political and Social Ideas*, 221–223, 240–243.
98. Stanley Hoffman, "Editor's Preface," in Judith N. Shklar, *Political Thought and Political Thinkers*, ed. Stanley Hoffman (Chicago: University of Chicago Press, 1998), xxi–xxvi, at xxiii–xxiv.

99. George Kateb, "Foreword," in Shklar, *Political Thought*, vii–xix, at viii.
100. See Shklar, "Giving Injustice Its Due"; Judith N. Shklar, *Ordinary Vices* (Cambridge, MA: Harvard University Press, 1984), 1–44.
101. Shklar, "Giving Injustice Its Due," 1137–1138. Shklar is not totally uncritical of Augustine. She thinks his "assault" on Cicero is "entirely unfair," his hyper-spiritualized view of slavery fails to recognize the "victims" of physical cruelty, and his obsession with "cupidity" neglects the priority of "cruelty" ("Giving Injustice Its Due," 1140–1141, 1148; *Ordinary Vices*, 7, 240).
102. Shklar, "Giving Injustice Its Due," 1139.
103. Shklar, *Ordinary Vices*, 1–44, 237–242; Shklar, "Giving Injustice Its Due," and Judith N. Shklar, "Liberalism of Fear," in *Political Thought*, 3–20. See also Judith Shklar, "What Is the Use of Utopia?" in *Political Thought*, 189–190.
104. Shklar's *Ordinary Vices*, 1–9, 28–29, 37–44; cf. Kateb, "Foreword," xvi, and Michael Walzer, "On Negative Politics," in *Liberalism Without Illusions: Essays on Liberal Theory and the Political Vision of Judith Shklar*, ed. Bernard Yack (Chicago: University of Chicago Press, 1996), 17–24.
105. Shklar, "Liberalism of Fear," 10–11; cf. *Ordinary Vices*, 8.
106. Shklar, "Liberalism of Fear," 6–9; *Ordinary Vices*, 237–242. Kateb, "Foreword," viii–ix, notes Shklar's "unlurid pessimism."
107. Elshtain, *Augustine and the Limits of Politics*, 19. For a summary of these views, see Lamb, "Between Presumption and Despair," 1036–1037, and Lamb, "Beyond Pessimism.", 592–594.
108. Elshtain, *Augustine and the Limits of Politics*, esp. 19–47, 89–118; cf. Jean Bethke Elshtain, "Augustine," in *The Blackwell Companion to Political Theology*, ed. Peter Scott and William T. Cavanaugh (Malden, MA; Blackwell, 2007), 34–47. In later years, Elshtain's appropriation of Augustinian authority to justify war and some forms of "torture" gave her thought a more realist bent. See Elshtain, *Just War against Terrorism*, and Jean Bethke Elshtain, "Reflection on the Problem of 'Dirty Hands,'" in *Torture: A Collection*, ed. Sanford Levinson (Oxford: Oxford University Press, 2004), 77–90. For an illuminating collection of essays on Elshtain's thought by scholars from political theory, theology, and religious studies, see Debra Erickson and Michael Le Chevallier, eds., *Jean Bethke Elshtain: Politics, Ethics, and Society*, ed. (Notre Dame, IN: University of Notre Dame Press, 2018). In his essay in the collection, Nigel Biggar describes Elshtain as an "Augustinian realist" (see "Staggering Onward, Rejoicing: Jean Bethke Elshtain, Augustinian Realist," in *Jean Bethke Elshtain*, 150–161). Eric Gregory explicitly analyzes the Augustinian conception of love undergirding Elshtain's realism, along with her "applied Augustinianism" in relation to "torture" (see "Taking Love Seriously: Elshtain's Augustinian Voice and Modern Politics," in *Jean Bethke Elshtain*, 177–190). And Robin W. Lovin analyses the Augustinian commitments that support Elshtain's alternative vision of politics (see "The Limits of Politics and the Inevitability of Ethics," in *Jean Bethke Elshtain*, 367–379).
109. Von Heyking, *Augustine and Politics as Longing*, esp. 1–50.
110. Gregory, *Politics and the Order of Love*, 319–362; Mathewes, *Theology of Public Life*, 74–142; Stewart-Kroeker, "Resisting Idolatry and Instrumentalization"; Clair, *Discerning the Good*, 75–106. See also John Bowlin, "Augustine Counting Virtues," *Augustinian Studies* 41, no. 1 (2010): 277–300; and Luke Bretherton, *Christianity and Contemporary Politics: The Conditions and Possibilities of Faithful Witness* (Malden, MA: Wiley-Blackwell, 2010), 3–6, 71–125.
111. Lamb, "Beyond Pessimism."

112. Lamb, "Between Presumption and Despair." I am developing these ideas at greater length in an unpublished manuscript tentatively entitled, "A Commonwealth of Hope: Reimagining Augustine's Political Thought."
113. See Lamb, "Between Presumption and Despair," and "A Commonwealth of Hope." See also Johnson, *Theology, Political Theory, and Pluralism*, 169; Mathewes, *Theology of Public Life*, 214–260; Bretherton, *Christianity and Contemporary Politics*, 83; Richard Avramenko, "The Wound and Salve of Time: Augustine's Politics of Human Happiness," *Review of Metaphysics* 60, no. 4 (2007): 779–811.
114. *City of God*, 14.28.
115. See *City of God*, 15.1–9.
116. *City of God*, 14.28.
117. *City of God*, 1.35.
118. *City of God*, 1.35; cf. 15.22, 18.54.
119. For helpful overviews, see Klosko, *History of Political Theory*, 257–266, 339–354; and vanDrunen, *Natural Law and the Two Kingdoms*, 21–118.
120. Henri-Xavier Arquillière, *L'augustinisme politique: Essai sui la formation des théories politiques du Moyen Âge* (Paris: J. VRIN). For helpful analyses, see Douglas Kries, "Political Augustinianism," in *ATA*, 657–658; Bruno, *Political Augustinianism*, 35–42, and Gregory and Clair, "Augustinianisms and Thomisms," 179–180.
121. See Bruno, *Political Augustinianism*, 39–62, and Gregory and Clair, "Augustinianisms and Thomisms," 180–182.
122. Henri-Irénée Marrou, "Civitas Dei, civitas terrena: Num tertium quid?", *Studia Patristica* 2 (1957): 342–350; R. A. Markus, *Saeculum: History and Society in the Theology of St. Augustine* (Cambridge: Cambridge University Press, 1970), 45–71.
123. Gregory, *Politics and the Order of Love*, 77. For overviews of Markus's interpretation, see Gregory, *Politics and the Order of Love*, 83–95, and Bruno, *Political Augustinianism*, 127–134.
124. Markus, *Saeculum*, 101.
125. Markus, *Saeculum*, 133.
126. See Michael Hollerich, "John Milbank, Augustine, and the Secular," *Augustinian Studies* 30, no. 2 (1999): 311–326, at 320–322; Gregory, *Politics and the Order of Love*, 83–95. For a more schematic explanation of the liberal assumptions underwriting Markus's account, see Michael Lamb, "Augustinian Republicanism" (unpublished manuscript).
127. Markus, *Saeculum*, 173.
128. Markus, *Saeculum*, 151.
129. *City of God*, 19.24; Markus, *Saeculum*, 64–71.
130. *City of God*, 2.21, 19.21.
131. Markus, *Saeculum*, 65.
132. Markus, *Saeculum*, 173–174.
133. Markus, *Saeculum*, 174.
134. Markus, *Christianity and the Secular*, 2–3, 49.
135. Markus, *Christianity and the Secular*, 6–7.
136. See Markus, *Christianity and the Secular*, 7, 49–69, esp. 66–69.
137. Weithman, "Augustinian Liberalism."

138. Weithman, "Augustinian Liberalism," 308; cf. 309–313. Weithman prefers Aquinas's Augustinian analysis of pride to Augustine's "somewhat unsystematic" account (308).
139. Weithman, "Augustinian Liberalism," 313–314.
140. Weithman, "Augustinian Liberalism," 313–314.
141. Weithman, "Augustinian Liberalism," 313–316. Weithman (305, 314, 320n7–8) cites the work of liberals such as John Rawls, "The Idea of Public Reason Revisited," *University of Chicago Law Review* 64 (1997): 765–807, and Robert Audi, "The Separation of Church and State and the Obligations of Citizenship," *Philosophy and Public Affairs* 18 (1989): 259–96. Since both Christians and non-Christians can recognize pride and domination as dangers to democracy, Weithman suggests that they share overlapping justifications to accept this liberal restraint on political advocacy, though Augustinian Christians have further religious reasons to curb pride and domination since it "offends God" and harms the neighbor (314–317).
142. Weithman, "Augustinian Liberalism," 318–319.
143. Weithman cites Augustine's account of "earthly peace" in Book 19 of *City of God* to suggest that "[n]o one was more pessimistic than Augustine about reliance on political authority to do more than hold pride in check or to foster genuine moral improvement" ("Augustinian Liberalism," 318–319, 321–322n37).
144. Weithman, "Augustinian Liberalism," 307.
145. Gregory, *Politics and the Order of Love*, 10, 80–81, 107–125.
146. See Gregory, *Politics and the Order of Love*, 14–15, 19–22, 38–39, 68–69, 82–95.
147. See Gregory, *Politics and the Order of Love*, 14–15, 20–22, 35–47, 72–73, 77–81.
148. Edmund Santurri, "Rawlsian Liberalism, Moral Truth, and Augustinian Politics," *Journal of Peace and Justice Studies* 8, no. 2 (1997): 1–36.
149. Gregory, *Politics and the Order of Love*, 23, 58–74, 95–125.
150. Gregory, *Politics and the Order of Love*, 107–125.
151. See Gregory, *Politics and the Order of Love*, 149–196.
152. See Gregory, *Politics and the Order of Love*, 188–196; cf. 12, 18–19.
153. See, for example, Markus, *Christianity and the Secular*, 49, and Gregory, *Politics and the Order of Love*, 2.
154. See *City of God*, 20.5; *On Christian Teaching*, 1.15.14; Letter 199.45, in Augustine, *Letters 156–210*, trans. Roland Teske (New York: New City Press, 2004).
155. *City of God*, 20.5.
156. *City of God*, 20.9.
157. For an insightful analysis of hope (*spes*) and (*res*) in relation to Augustine's eschatology and ecclesiology, see David Vincent Meconi, "Heaven and the *Ecclesia Perfecta* in Augustine," in *The Cambridge Companion to Augustine*, ed. David Vincent Meconi and Eleonore Stump, 2nd ed. (Cambridge: Cambridge University Press, 2014), 251–272, at 268–270. For more on the relation between hope (*spes*) and reality (*res*) in Augustine's thought, see also Lamb, "A Commonwealth of Hope."
158. For more on Augustine's eschatology and its implications for politics, see Johnson, *Theology, Political Theory, and Pluralism*, 140–173, and Lamb, "A Commonwealth of Hope."
159. See *City of God*, 19.17.
160. See, for example, Letter 87.7–8, Letter 100.1, Letter 153.19, and Letter 220.4, in *Political Writings*, 141–142, 134–135, 82–83, 220; *City of God*, 19.17; and Dodaro, "Church and State," 181–182.

161. *City of God*, 19.17.
162. *City of God*, 20.9.
163. John Milbank, *Theology and Social Theory: Beyond Secular Reason*, 2nd ed. (Oxford: Blackwell, 2006), 382–442, at 383, 440. For overviews of Milbank, see Bruno, *Political Augustinianism*, 140–147; Gregory, *Politics and the Order of Love*, 125–148; and Hollerich, "John Milbank, Augustine, and the Secular."
164. Milbank, *Theology and Social Theory*, 392. For Milbank's critique of Niebuhr's Christian realism, see John Milbank, "The Poverty of Niebuhrianism," in *The Word Made Strange: Theology, Language, Culture* (Malden, MA: Blackwell: 1997), 233–254.
165. Milbank, *Theology and Social Theory*, 404; cf. 406.
166. Milbank, *Theology and Social Theory*, 410.
167. For Milbank's analysis of MacIntyre, see *Theology and Social Theory*, 327–381, esp. 327–333. On his preference for communitarian politics, see Nathan Schneider, "An Orthodox Paradox: An Interview with John Milbank," The Immanent Frame, March 17, 2010, http://blogs.ssrc.org/tif/2010/03/17/orthodox-paradox-an-interview-with-john-milbank/.
168. See Milbank, *Theology and Social Theory*, 392; cf. 382–383.
169. Milbank, *Theology and Social Theory*, 392; John Milbank, "An Essay against Secular Order," *Journal of Religious Ethics* 15, no. 2 (1987): 199–224, at 207, also cited by Bruno, *Political Augustinianism*, 143.
170. Milbank, "An Essay against Secular Order," 207; cf. Milbank, *Theology and Social Theory*, 392–394, 402–410, 428–429.
171. Milbank, *Theology and Social Theory*, 428–429, 440–442; John Milbank, "'Postmodern Critical Augustinianism': A Short *Summa* in Forty Two Responses to Unasked Questions," *Modern Theology* 7, no. 3 (1991): 225–237, at 229.
172. For his references to MacIntyre and Milbank, see Stanley Hauerwas, *After Christendom? How the Church Is to Behave If Freedom, Justice, and a Christian Nation Are Bad Ideas* (Nashville, TN: Abingdon Press, 1991), 8–9, 20–22.
173. Hauerwas, *After Christendom?*, 16, 26–31, 35.
174. Hauerwas, *After Christendom?*, 18; cf. 27–35; Stanley Hauerwas, *A Community of Character: Toward a Constructive Social Ethic* (Notre Dame, IN: University of Notre Dame Press, 1981), 72–86.
175. Hauerwas, *Community of Character*, 73–75, 83–86; *After Christendom?*, 26–31.
176. Stanley Hauerwas, *The Peaceable Kingdom: A Primer in Christian Ethics* (Notre Dame, IN: University of Notre Dame Press, 1983), 87–95, 96–115; Hauerwas, *Community of Character*, 83–86; cf. *After Christendom?*, 43–44.
177. Hauerwas, *Community of Character*, 74, cf. 83–86. See also *After Christendom?*, 44; *Peaceable Kingdom*, 96–115.
178. Hauerwas, *After Christendom?*, 39. Hauerwas also notes Augustine as an influence in *Peaceable Kingdom*, xix.
179. Hauerwas, *After Christendom?*, 19.
180. Hauerwas, *After Christendom?*, 40.
181. Hauerwas cites Augustine to suggest that "societies devoid of the church cannot have any authentic conceptions of virtue" (*After Christendom?*, 41).
182. For criticisms of Milbank and Hauerwas, see, for example, Gregory, *Politics and the Order of Love*, 125–148, and Jeffrey Stout, *Democracy and Tradition* (Princeton, NJ: Princeton University Press, 2004), 92–117, 140–161.

183. Milbank, *Theology and Social Theory*, 413.
184. Hauerwas, *After Christendom?*, 18; cf. *Community of Character*, 85.
185. See, for example, Milbank, *Theology and Social Theory*, 407–408, 411, 441–442; Hauerwas, *After Christendom?*, 36–38, citing Denny Weaver, "Atonement for the Nonconstantinian Church," *Modern Theology* 6 (1990): 307–323; and Hauerwas, *Community of Character*, 74. For analysis, see Stout, *Democracy and Tradition*, 100–107, 140–161; Gregory, *Politics and the Order of Love*, 125–148, esp. 135; Hans Boersma, "On the Rejection of Boundaries: Radical Orthodoxy's Appropriation of Augustine," *Pro Ecclesia* 15, no. 4 (2006): 418–448.
186. See Stout, *Democracy and Tradition*, 92; Schneider, "An Orthodox Paradox."
187. "Theologian: Christian Contrarian," *TIME Magazine* 158, no. 11, September 17, 2001; Stout, *Democracy and Tradition*, 140.
188. I develop the following analysis in more detail in Lamb, "Augustinian Republicanism."
189. See Quentin Skinner, *Liberty before Liberalism* (Cambridge: Cambridge University Press, 1998), and Philip Pettit, *Republicanism: A Theory of Freedom and Government* (Oxford: Oxford University Press, 1997).
190. Gregory and Clair, "Augustinianism and Thomisms," 186–190. In his virtue-oriented account of Augustinian "civic liberalism," Gregory also blends aspects of civic republicanism with liberalism (*Politics and the Order of Love*, 10).
191. John von Heyking, "Disarming, Simple, and Sweet: Augustine's Republican Rhetoric," in *Talking Democracy: Historical Perspectives on Rhetoric and Democracy,* ed. Benedetto Fontana, Cary J. Nederman, and Gary Remer (University Park, PA: Pennsylvania State University, 2004), 163–186; and von Heyking, *Augustine and Politics as Longing*, 1–109.
192. Charles Mathewes, "Augustinian Christian Republican Citizenship," in *Political Theology for a Plural Age*, ed. Michael Jon Kessler (Oxford: Oxford University Press, 2013), 218–249.
193. Paul Cornish, "Augustine's Contribution to the Republican Tradition," *European Journal of Political Theory* 9, no. 2 (2010), 133–148.
194. Cornish, "Augustine's Contribution," 133–134, 144.
195. Cornish, "Augustine's Contribution," 144. However, Cornish frequently equates "coercion" with "slavery" or "domination" in ways that obscure the fact that political rule can be coercive without be dominating ("Augustine's Contribution," 137–138, 143). For a distinction between coercion and domination in relation to Augustine's account of liberty as security against domination, see Michael Lamb, "Augustine and Republican Liberty: Contextualizing Coercion," *Augustinian Studies* 48, no. 1–2 (2017): 119–159, at 142–146.
196. Cornish, "Augustine's Contribution," 144–145; cf. 141–142.
197. Cornish, "Augustine's Contribution," 145; cf. 142–144.
198. Cornish, "Augustine's Contribution," 145.
199. Lamb, "Augustine and Republican Liberty."
200. Lamb, "Augustine and Republican Liberty," 142–146.
201. Augustine, *On the Free Choice of the Will*, ed. and trans. Peter King (New York: Cambridge University Press, 2010), 1.15.32.
202. Lamb, "Augustine and Republican Liberty," 147–149.
203. Lamb, "Augustine and Republican Liberty," 133–137, 149–151.
204. Lamb, "Augustine and Republican Liberty," 151–155.
205. Weithman, "Augustinian Liberalism," 317–318.

206. Stout, *Democracy and Tradition*, 63–91.
207. Lamb, "Between Presumption and Despair," 1044–1045.
208. *City of God*, 19.14, alluding to Cicero, *On Duties*, ed. M. T. Griffin and E. M. Atkins (Cambridge University Press, 1991), 1.31.
209. See Lamb, "Between Presumption and Despair," 1044–1045.
210. *City of God*, 19.3; cf. 19.13, 19.16. On concord, sociality, and civic friendship, see Elshtain, *Augustine and the Limits,* 38–39, 96–97; Elshtain, "Augustine," 38–44; von Heyking, *Augustine and Politics as Longing*, 77–89; von Heyking, "Disarming, Simple, and Sweet," 182–184; Gregory, *Politics and the Order of Love*, 350–362; Lamb, "Between Presumption and Despair," 1044–1045.
211. Lamb, "Between Presumption and Despair," 1044–1047.
212. I am currently working on a larger book project, tentatively entitled *Augustine and Republican Liberty*, to address such questions. On the distinction between "historical" and "rational reconstruction," see Richard Rorty, "The Historiography of Philosophy: Four Genres," in *Philosophy in History*, ed. Richard Rorty, J. B. Schneewind, and Quentin Skinner (Cambridge: Cambridge University Press, 1984), 49–75. For this distinction applied to interpretations of Augustine, see Gregory, *Politics and the Order of Love*, 2.
213. Lamb, "Augustinian Republicanism."
214. On the neglect of religion in contemporary republicanism, see Joseph Clair, "The New Republicanism without Religion?," *Political Theology* 79, no. 5 (2018): 397–420.
215. Lamb, "Augustinian Republicanism."
216. *Confessions*, 12.26.36.
217. I am grateful to Rubén Rosario Rodríguez for including me in this volume and offering helpful feedback on this chapter. I am also thankful for valuable feedback from Kendall Cox, Eric Gregory, David Meconi, and Cameron Silverglate and for research support from Wake Forest University.

SELECT BIBLIOGRAPHY

Augustine (1998), *The City of God against the Pagans*, ed. and trans. R. W. Dyson, Cambridge: Cambridge University Press.

Augustine (1998), *The Confessions*, trans. Maria Boulding, New York: Vintage Books.

Augustine (2001), *Political Writings*, ed. E. M. Atkins and Robert Dodaro, Cambridge: Cambridge University Press.

Bretherton, Luke (2010), *Christianity and Contemporary Politics: The Conditions and Possibilities of Faithful Witness*, Malden, MA: Wiley-Blackwell, 2010.

Brown, Peter (2000), *Augustine of Hippo: A Biography*, Berkeley, CA: University of California Press.

Bruno, Michael J. S. (2014), *Political Augustinianism: Modern Interpretations of Augustine's Political Thought*, Minneapolis, MN: Fortress Press.

Clair, Joseph (2016), *Discerning the Good in the Letters and Sermons of Augustine*, Oxford: Oxford University Press, 2016.

Deane, Herbert A. (2013), *The Political and Social Ideas of St. Augustine*, New York: Columbia University Press.

Doody, John, Kevin L. Hughes, and Kim Paffenroth, eds. (2005), *Augustine and Politics*, Lanham, MD: Lexington Books.

Elshtain, Jean Bethke (1995), *Augustine and the Limits of Politics*, Notre Dame, IN: University of Notre Dame Press.

Fitzgerald, Allan D., ed. (1999), *Augustine through the Ages: An Encyclopedia*, Grand Rapids, MI: Eerdmans.

González, Justo L. (2016), *The Mestizo Augustine: A Theologian Between Two Cultures*, Downers Grove, IL: IVP Academic.

Gregory, Eric (2008), *Politics and the Order of Love: An Augustinian Ethic of Democratic Citizenship*, Chicago: University of Chicago Press.

Hauerwas, Stanley (2011), *After Christendom: How the Church Is to Behave If Freedom, Justice, and a Christian Nation Are Bad Ideas*, Nashville, TN: Abingdon Press.

Hovey, Craig and Elizabeth Phillips, eds. (2015), *The Cambridge Companion to Political Theology*, Cambridge: Cambridge University Press.

Johnson, Kristen Deede (2007), *Theology, Political Theory, and Pluralism: Beyond Tolerance and Difference*, Cambridge: Cambridge University Press.

Klosko, George (2012), *History of Political Theory: An Introduction, Volume 1: Ancient and Medieval*, 2nd ed., Oxford: Oxford University Press.

MacIntyre, Alasdair (1989), *Whose Justice? Which Rationality?*, Notre Dame, IN: University of Notre Dame Press.

Markus, Robert A. (1970), *Saeculum: History and Society in the Theology of St. Augustine*, Cambridge: Cambridge University Press.

Markus, Robert A. (2006), *Christianity and the Secular*, Notre Dame, IN: Notre Dame University Press.

Mathewes, Charles (2007), *A Theology of Public Life*, Cambridge: Cambridge University Press.

Matthews, Gareth B., ed. (1999), *The Augustinian Tradition*, Berkeley, CA: University of California Press.

Milbank, John (2006), *Theology and Social Theory: Beyond Secular Reason*, 2nd ed., Oxford: Blackwell Publishing.

Nussbaum, Martha (2001), *Upheavals of Thought: The Intelligence of Emotions*, New York: Cambridge University Press.

Pollman, Karla, ed. (2013), *The Oxford Guide to the Historical Reception of Augustine*, 3 vols., Oxford: Oxford University Press, 2013.

von Heyking, John (2001), *Augustine and Politics as Longing in the World*, Columbia, MO: University of Missouri Press.

Wolin, Sheldon S. (2004), *Politics and Vision: Continuity and Innovation in Western Political Thought*, Princeton, NJ: Princeton University Press.

CHAPTER EIGHT

Thomas Becket

A Case Study in Medieval Church–State Relations

MICHAEL STAUNTON

INTRODUCTION

On December 29, 1170, Thomas Becket, Archbishop of Canterbury, was brutally murdered in the sanctuary of his own church by knights claiming to act on behalf of King Henry II of England. As the shock and outrage spread, pilgrims began to visit Becket's tomb, people throughout the Christian world claimed to have experienced his miraculous power, and within little over two years he was canonized as a martyr of the Church. Meanwhile, the murderous knights were banished to the Holy Land, and the king did penance, first before representatives of the pope, and then on his knees at Thomas's tomb. Thomas Becket's name remains well known today on account of the violence of his death and the scale of his posthumous acclaim, yet even before his death his quarrel with the king had made him famous. The "Becket dispute" was a personal clash between two headstrong individuals and former friends, but it was also the most dramatic confrontation between spiritual and secular power in England before the Reformation. It exposed tensions that had been building for some time, and brought into the open certain fundamental questions about the relationship between the two powers: What was the appropriate relationship between the priesthood and the crown? In what spheres were their respective rights and powers concentrated, and where was the dividing line? How ought relations between the English church, the king of England, and the papacy be conducted? This was most obviously a dispute between archbishop and king, but it was also a dispute within the Church that divided the English episcopate and the papal curia who asked further questions: In what circumstances was it legitimate for an ecclesiastic to resist the secular power? How best to balance principle against pragmatism?

The details of the dispute are easily summarized.[1] When Henry II came to the throne in 1154, he appointed Thomas Becket as royal chancellor and his most important adviser. In 1162 he installed Thomas as archbishop, trusting that he would work with him in reforming relations between the Church and the crown. To his surprise, Thomas became a vigorous defender of ecclesiastical rights. A series of public clashes between king and archbishop followed, the most contentious issue being criminal jurisdiction over churchmen. Henry demanded recognition for what he claimed were his customary rights as king in regard to the Church, but after some hesitation Thomas rejected them and was brought to trial. Refusing to hear sentence, he fled to France and remained in exile for nearly six years. The king confiscated his possessions and expelled his supporters, and

Becket retaliated with polemics and excommunications. A peace was patched up in 1170 and Thomas returned to his church, but continued to exacerbate his enemies. Henry's complaints about his unruly prelate prompted four knights to set out for Canterbury, where they entered the sanctuary of the cathedral, and killed the archbishop. This outrage shocked the Christian world, and precipitated St Thomas's speedy canonization as a martyr of the Church.

The dispute was driven by the actions of the two central protagonists, but it was also conducted in words. Though neither Henry nor Thomas were great political theorists, they liked to surround themselves with learned men. There is an imbalance here. In the twelfth century, literacy was largely the preserve of clerics, and whereas it often suited Becket's supporters to appeal to theology, canon law, and Christian history, Henry based his arguments primarily on unwritten custom. It was Becket's supporters and admirers who preserved the record of the dispute, in the massive collection of correspondence, and the numerous adulatory Lives of St Thomas. Even so, the scale of his posthumous acclaim made them confident enough to include many of the arguments of his opponents, both those associated with the king and those within the Church, allowing us to follow the debate in some detail. The Becket dispute, then, provides an insight into the practical points of conflict between spiritual and secular power, and also an illustration of how their relationship could be theorized in the central Middle Ages.[2]

THE CHURCH AND THE CROWN IN TWELFTH-CENTURY ENGLAND

In the twelfth century, people did not speak of "Church and State," but rather *sacerdotium* and *regnum*—priesthood and kingship. That does not mean that "Church and State" is an entirely anachronistic term when applied to twelfth-century England, as long as we do so with some qualification. Political theorists and participants in ecclesiastical and royal life were aware of the existence of two powerful spheres that were connected, but often distinct in their objectives, rights, and practices. Secular and spiritual rulers did not see their interests as necessarily opposed to each other. Kings acknowledged the grace of God in their exercise of power and promised to protect the Church and advance its interests, while churchmen looked to an ideal relationship of cooperation between the two powers, but they also recognized that the relationship could be difficult to balance.

Various images were invoked to capture the balance between the powers. In the late eleventh century, Anselm, Archbishop of Canterbury, described the English Church as a plough drawn by two oxen, the king and the archbishop of Canterbury, one ruling "by human justice and sovereignty, the other by divine doctrine and authority."[3] The plough is the contract between *regnum* and *sacerdotium*, and those who pull the plough are the individual kings and archbishops who determine how this contract is fulfilled. John of Salisbury in his *Policraticus*, written in 1159, adapted the ancient concept of the body politic to describe a political community with the king as the head, served by financial officers as the stomach, the soldiers and administrators as hands, the peasantry as feet, and the *sacerdotium* representing the soul. The king "is subject only to God and to those who exercise His office and represent Him on earth, just as in the human body the head is animated and ruled by the soul."[4] A more assertive image, popular among theologians in the Continental schools, was that of the two swords. In 494 Pope Gelasius I wrote to the emperor Anastasius: "There are two powers, august Emperor, by which this world is chiefly ruled, namely, the sacred authority of the priests and the royal power. Of these that of the priests is the more weighty, since they have to render an account for even the kings of men in the divine judgement."[5] In the twelfth century Gelasius's words were commonly interpreted as a commentary on Luke 22:38, where the disciples said to Jesus, "Look, Lord, here are two swords," and Jesus replied, "It is enough." Jesus's instruction to Peter to sheathe his sword (John 18:11) was interpreted to mean that the two powers had been granted to the Church, but churchmen were not allowed to exercise the temporal sword, i.e., physical coercion. Instead, the secular ruler exercised that sword on behalf of the Church, while the Church wielded the sword of the spirit, i.e., prayer and ecclesiastical censure.[6]

In the decades before the Becket conflict, changing circumstances within the universal Church and in England had made the potential for conflict greater. In the eleventh century a reform movement within the Church had sought to eliminate abuses among the clergy and to foster moral renewal, but also targeted lay control of church property and the appointment of ecclesiastics. Under Pope Gregory VII (reigned 1073–1085), it became a direct confrontation between the papacy and the German emperor. A dispute over "lay investiture"—the granting by laymen of the symbols of office to senior ecclesiastics—led Pope Gregory to excommunicate and depose the emperor, prompting civil war. Though the dispute ended in compromise, its most significant outcome was the enhanced status of the papacy. Gregory's vision was of a papal power that crossed national boundaries and governed not only the lives of the clergy but of all Christians. It gained expression in papal leadership of the Crusades, which began in the 1090s, and in the development of mechanisms of papal government: the college of cardinals, papal legates, and the systematization of canon law. In the schools of Continental Europe, masters disseminated "High Church" theories about the superiority of the spiritual sphere over the temporal, and many of their students came to populate the English Church.[7]

The other source of conflict lay in the changing status of royal power in England. The Anglo-Norman kings of England, the successors to William the Conqueror (reigned 1066–1087), had sought to impose firm rule on their subjects, using a combination of personal authority and sophisticated methods of administration and law. Strong royal government suffered a serious reversal in the middle of the twelfth century, however. When Henry I died in 1135, his daughter and chosen successor, Matilda, was passed over in favor of his nephew, Stephen of Blois. For nineteen years, King Stephen clung to power in the face of Matilda's challenge, but was unable to maintain control over the nobility or the Church. During his reign the English clergy gained greater freedom of action, for example in appealing to the jurisdiction of the pope. In 1154 Stephen died and was succeeded Matilda's twenty-one-year-old son, Henry. King Henry II came to the throne determined to restore and extend the power of the English crown in all spheres, including that of the Church.[8]

Henry II's succession was welcomed by the leaders of the English Church—indeed they had helped to broker the succession, hopeful that he would re-establish order in England. Among those prominent in arranging the succession were Archbishop Theobald of Canterbury, and his clerks John of Salisbury and Thomas Becket. The son of a London merchant, Thomas had briefly studied in Paris before returning to England and entering the archbishop's service. His main tasks were those of an administrator and advisor, and he showed little sign of a spiritual purpose beyond that required for a clerk in such an ecclesiastical environment, but much evidence of practical ability. It was apparently on Theobald's recommendation that he took up the position of royal chancellor to the new king. With Thomas at his side, the new king immediately reasserted royal authority in England, and insisted on strict law and order. He improved royal finances by re-establishing the Exchequer, and instituted legal reforms that made it easier for subjects to appeal to royal justice. The next step was to restore order to the relationship between royal and ecclesiastical power.

Henry's opportunity came with the death of Theobald in 1161. Now he was free to install his chancellor as archbishop of Canterbury, presumably to continue his reforms from within the Church. The only objections recorded to Thomas's appointment were from Becket himself, who protested that someone who had lived as secular a life as he might not be suitable for such a daunting spiritual role, and the Bishop of London, Gilbert Foliot, who murmured at such an obvious royal agent being chosen for the position. But when Thomas became archbishop, something changed. According to his posthumous biographers, he experienced a kind of "conversion" in which he turned to God, rejected his former life, and adopted a more spiritual purpose and a different attitude to the Church's rights. He secretly began to wear a hair-shirt to punish the flesh, and began a course of training in Scripture at the hands of his clerk and master of theology, Herbert of Bosham.[9] And he began to position himself in opposition to the king and as a defender of the Church's rights. He refused to continue as chancellor as the king had desired, and clashed with the king on a variety of matters that were relatively minor when taken individually, but soon went to the heart of the relationship between the two powers.

ROYAL CUSTOM AND CLERICAL LIBERTY

The two main issues of concern to Henry II were jurisdictional: the rights of royal justice versus those of ecclesiastical courts on the one hand, and the right of kings to limit papal jurisdiction on the other. A century earlier William the Conqueror had established separate ecclesiastical courts. They judged matters of morals and faith, and cases that directly concerned the clergy, such as disputes over church property and the misconduct of those in religious orders. The latter group included a wide range of people, not just bishops, priests, and monks but clerks. Clerks were set apart from the rest of society by their hair and dress, and might hold important positions in the Church. But they were not necessarily priests, they could even marry if they were in such minor orders as cantor, doorkeeper, or lector, and they constituted perhaps 5 percent of society.[10] From the king's point of view, the undue leniency of ecclesiastical courts—along with the growing practice of appealing ecclesiastical disputes to the papal court—undermined both his design to reassert order in the realm, and his authority as king.

It was the issue of "criminous clerks" (as it has become known to historians) that first brought king and archbishop to public confrontation.[11] Henry II summoned his senior churchmen to a council at Westminster in October 1163 and demanded from them that where clerks were convicted of serious crimes they be deprived of the Church's protection and handed over to the secular power. Thomas and his colleagues were unanimous in their rejection of the king's proposal, and Henry now took a different approach, demanding a general acknowledgment of the royal customs, that is, the rights he believed his predecessors had as regards the Church. Thomas, after consultation with the bishops, replied that he would only observe the king's customs "saving his order"—that is, where they did not conflict with the law of the Church. These matters were addressed again at a council of the realm at Clarendon in January 1164, where the king demanded a full public recognition of the royal customs, and they were put in writing. Not all of the "Constitutions of Clarendon" were contentious, but most were. Some of those in dispute addressed matters of royal and ecclesiastical jurisdiction, including the issue of "criminous clerks." Others concerned ecclesiastics' rights of excommunication, and appointments to vacant sees, and a further strand concerned relations with the pope.

Thomas's posthumous biographers present what they claim to be the arguments made by both sides at Westminster and Clarendon. Herbert of Bosham says that the king made his case on two grounds, both of them appeals to Church tradition. First, he pointed out that among the many canons addressing punishment of clerics, some sanctioned the handing over of the clergy to secular courts upon their deposition. Secondly, he noted that amongst the ancient Israelites, the Law of Moses did not exempt the priests or Levites.[12] Another account has Thomas's fellow bishops noting that since the Levites had a greater dignity on account of their order, their transgressions were judged and punished more severely than those of others.[13] William of Canterbury presents Thomas's counter-argument. First he cited a long list of canons to argue that in fact ecclesiastical law prohibited the handing over of clergy to secular judgment. Secondly, he appealed to Nahum 1:9 (in its Old Latin version): "God does not judge twice for the same thing." On this basis, he claimed, a clerk stripped of his office by a Church court ought not to sustain a subsequent punishment in a secular court for the same crime.[14] Some of these arguments were certainly made during Thomas's lifetime, and it is clear that they were informed by careful reading of canon law and commentaries upon it.

But as well as arguing in favor of clerical immunity from lay jurisdiction, Thomas can be found asserting ecclesiastical right more generally against royal custom. According to one report of the council of Westminster in 1163, Thomas told the king that since the Christian faith had first been established, it had its customs fully expressed in the canons and decrees of the apostles and the apostolic fathers, and it was not permitted to establish new institutions beyond these. King Henry protested that he sought to introduce nothing new, and only wished to have observed those customs that had been long established and observed in the time of his predecessors—and added that in those times there were better and more saintly archbishops who had no difficulties with their kings.[15] In another account, Thomas argues for the pre-eminence of God's law over any royal custom, reminding the king that the Lord said, "Keep my laws," and "Woe to those who decree iniquitous decrees"; God never said, "I am custom," but did say, "I am truth."[16] In a third account, Thomas is reported as saying:

> My lord king, sacrosanct Church, mother of all kings and priests, has two kings, two laws, two jurisdictions and two penalties. Two kings, Christ the heavenly king, and the worldly king; two laws, human and divine; two jurisdictions, priestly and legal; two penalties, spiritual and corporal. "Look, there are two swords." "It is enough," said the Lord. Neither is too much and these are sufficient.[17]

The clergy are set apart from the rest of society, and given over especially to the work of the Lord, and hence they are not subject to but superior to earthly kings. They appoint kings, and it is from them that the king receives the belt of knighthood and the power of the material sword. Therefore kings have no jurisdiction in these things, but rather the clergy are the judges of kings. In the words of Psalm 149, "They bind their kings with chains and their nobles with fetters of iron." Therefore, serving their own king, the King of heaven, not a worldly king, priests submit to their own law and their own punishment.[18]

Whether these arguments were made in such terms in 1163 and 1164, or whether they were projected back by Becket's learned men a few years later is unclear. Certainly,

Thomas did not stand unswervingly firm in defense of such principles. At Clarendon, after much pressure, Thomas was persuaded to give verbal recognition to the written constitutions, though he refused to affix his seal to the document as confirmation. In this way he managed to stoke the hostility of the king, while at the same time leaving himself open to the charge of failing to stand up for the Church.

Having failed to gain full recognition of his customs, King Henry escalated the dispute by bringing Thomas to trial at Northampton in November 1164. The charges related to Thomas's alleged failure to do justice to a tenant of the king's, and also financial irregularities during his time as chancellor, but the intention seems to have been to force him to resign his office. As it happened, the archbishop took it as an opportunity to raise the dispute to a higher level: as a battle between followers of Christ and his enemies, of good against evil. On the final day of the trial, Thomas celebrated, instead of the regular mass of that day, the mass of St. Stephen, with its introit, "Even though princes sit plotting against me, thy servant will meditate on thy statutes."[19] Then, as he was entering the court chamber, he took the cross, which was customarily carried before him, from the hands of his cross-bearer, and carried it into the chamber himself. In a society where ritual and visual symbolism were of great importance, this was as striking a statement of his position as any speech on the two swords. The trial ended with Thomas refusing to hear sentence, and that night he fled in disguise from the city, and made his way to the southern coast of England, from which he sailed to Flanders and made his way to the kingdom of France.

THE POLEMICS OF 1166

Thomas went first to Paris, where he met King Louis VII of France, who gave his enthusiastic support to the archbishop's cause. Louis was regarded as a pious king, but he also recognized the opportunity to undermine his rival, Henry II. Next Thomas visited the pope, who was then residing at Sens, a short journey south. One might expect the pope and his cardinals to have been even more enthusiastic supporters of Thomas. They too championed ecclesiastical liberties and sought to uphold the superiority of the spiritual power, and the pope had been known to wield "the sword of St. Peter" against enemies of the Church. But Pope Alexander was in a delicate position. When he was elected in 1159, a faction elected a rival pope, who gained the support of the German emperor, Frederick Barbarossa. Exiled from Rome, the pope and the cardinals relied on the support of King Louis of France and King Henry of England. When Thomas presented himself at Sens, then, Alexander condemned Henry's royal customs, but dispatched the archbishop to the Cistercian monastery of Pontigny in Burgundy to live simply and refrain from provoking the king for the time being.

There Thomas remained, reportedly studying biblical exegesis and practicing acts of asceticism. But after more than a year of seclusion, hearing of how the king had expelled his supporters and confiscated his property, Thomas roused himself to action. On June 12, 1166 he visited Vézelay Abbey, where he pronounced sentence of excommunication against several of the king's officials and supporters. This measure moved the dispute to a new level, not least because of what had not been done but remained a latent threat: the excommunication of the king. Around the same time, Thomas sent three letters to King Henry, reviewing the dispute, exhorting him to change his ways, and threatening reprisals should he not do so. The letters, filled as they are with allusions to the Bible, the Church Fathers, and canon law, are clearly indebted to the expertise of the learned advisors with whom Thomas surrounded himself. Nonetheless, they provide us with perhaps the clearest statement of Thomas's position—not just the substance of his quarrel with the king, but a rationale for his decision to take the dispute to such a level of crisis.

In the first letter,[20] Thomas announces his intention to speak freely to the king. He fears the king's wrath, but he is more fearful of being silent, recalling the Lord's word, "If you do not tell the wicked man his transgression and he dies in his sin, I shall require his blood from your hands."[21] In your land, he says, the Church is being held captive and oppressed. Reminding the king of the benefits he has received from God since the start of his reign, he urges him to free the Church, "so that God may bless you, your kingdom may begin at once to recover its strength, the shame be removed from your generation, and there may be the greatest peace in your times." The Lord is a patient requiter, but a most severe avenger.[22] If Henry does not do as Thomas says, he fears that "the Most Powerful will gird his sword upon his thigh"[23] and come with strong arms and a great army to free the Church from oppression. If he should listen to his advice, the Lord will add glory to his glory. Otherwise, Thomas fears that the sword will not depart from the king's house.[24] He reminds Henry that God established Solomon on the throne, but when that king turned to iniquity, He wrenched the kingdom away from him. Better, he says, to follow the example of David, who also offended the Lord, but then immediately humbled himself, corrected his fault, asked for mercy, and obtained pardon. Throughout this letter, Thomas draws a parallel between himself and Nathan who reminded King David of the favors God had done for him, and warned him to do penance for his sin.[25]

Thomas begins his second letter[26] by again setting out his duty to correct Henry. As his lord, he owes him counsel and service; as his king, he is bound to revere and warn him; as his spiritual son, he is bound to reprove and restrain him. Those kings who violated God's commands—Pharaoh, Saul, Nebuchadnezzar, and Solomon—had their glory taken away from them, but those who humbled themselves contritely before God—like David and Hezekiah—recovered God's favor all the more abundantly and perfectly. Then Thomas more directly addresses the relationship between the two powers:

> For God's Church consists of two orders, the clergy and the people. Among the clergy are the apostles, Popes, bishops, and other teachers of the Church, to whom is entrusted the care and rule of the Church itself, who have the ability to conduct ecclesiastical affairs so that they may direct the whole to the salvation of souls . . . Among the people are kings, princes, dukes, earls, and other men of power, who have the ability to conduct secular affairs that they may bring the whole to the peace and unity of the Church. And since it is certain that kings receive their power from the Church, and the Church receives hers not from them but from Christ, if you allow me to say so, you do not have the power to command bishops to absolve or excommunicate anyone, to draw clergy to secular judgments, to pass judgment concerning churches and tithes, to forbid bishops to hear cases concerning breach of faith or oaths, and many other things of this kind, which are written down among your customs, which you call "ancestral."[27]

For his part, Thomas says he is ready to serve his king loyally and devotedly in whatever way he can, saving the honor of God and the Church, but if the king does not do as he urges, "you may know for certain that you will suffer the divine severity and vengeance."[28]

In the third and longest letter,[29] Thomas says that he has waited patiently for the king to change his ways and do penance. As Henry rules the human affairs of the kingdom, he as archbishop has been given by God the responsibility to admonish, exhort, and correct the king's transgressions against the Church, and he who fails to correct what he should correct is judged to be a participant in that wrongdoing.[30] Thomas turns to the subject of clerical liberty. Christ's priests are the fathers and teachers of kings and princes, and it is folly for a son to attempt to subjugate his father or a pupil his master. A good and Catholic king acts as the son of the Church, not its director, and follows priests in ecclesiastical matters, rather than preceding them. The king enjoys privileges bestowed on him by God for the administration of public laws, and should not appropriate anything against the dispositions of heavenly ordinance. He reminds Henry, again in the manner of Nathan to David, how much God has exalted him, and he recalls the biblical examples of Saul, Uzziah, Ahaz, and Uzzah, rulers first favored by the Lord, but later struck down on account of their transgressions. God gave power of judgment over the clergy to bishops and priests, not to worldly powers. Indeed, he adds, there are many cases in history of priests judging kings, from Nathan onwards. Should Henry not follow the example of the penitent David, Thomas will have no option but to cry out, "Avenge, O Lord, the sufferings of your servants."[31]

In these lengthy and complex letters, packed with allusions to Christian tradition, Thomas sets out the various interlocking aspects of his position. First, he gives attention to defense of clerical liberty against the king's attempts to restrict it. Related to this are the statements of the relative merits and strengths of spiritual and secular power. These letters act as a formal three-part warning and call to penance to Henry in the manner of Nathan to David. At the same time, they provide a statement of and justification of Thomas's duty to correct the king. This is important, as some of the most heated debate during these years was not between the archbishop's side and the king's, but within the Church. It was Thomas's ecclesiastical colleagues who were most likely to have understood the erudite references in these letters, and it was they who needed to be encouraged or refuted.

THE DISPUTE WITHIN THE CHURCH

Becket's case was that Henry II's actions regarding the Church amounted to a persecution that fitted into a pattern of tyrannical behavior going back to Old Testament kings. The archbishop's duty was, then, to rebuke the king, as his saintly predecessors had, and stand as a wall of defense for the Church. Not everyone within the Church agreed. Though the bishops stood firm with the archbishop at the outset of the dispute, they soon splintered into a few vocal supporters of Thomas Becket, a few vocal opponents, and many in the middle who were more concerned to bring about a reconciliation between Henry and Thomas.[32] Thomas and his supporters often presented other members of England's senior clergy in hostile terms, as antithesis to Thomas, the champion of truth and justice. Thomas's biographer, Edward Grim, describes how, before the Council of Clarendon in January 1164, the unity of the episcopate began to fracture. The bishops of Chichester and London and the archbishop of York "were captured unarmed; rather, more truly, they threw down their arms on the ground and began to help the enemy . . . From these the error of the king gained, if not perhaps its beginning, at least its basis and increment."[33] While such a characterization is extreme, it reflects the fact that many of the English episcopate had, like Becket, risen through the royal service, and their interests were closely linked to the king's.

Thomas's most vocal and eloquent critic was Gilbert Foliot.[34] An austere Cluniac monk from a noble family, and a distinguished scholar, he was all that Thomas was not. Although his statements on Thomas were colored by his bitterness at being passed over for the archbishopric in 1162, they expressed concerns widely held. When Thomas fled to the pope at Sens, Gilbert followed, and made the king's case there. He is reported as saying:

> Recently, for a trivial and unimportant reason, a conflict has arisen in England between the crown and the priesthood which could have been avoided had a restrained approach been taken. But the lord of Canterbury, following his own individual counsel in this business, and not ours, took too vigorous a stand, not considering the evil of the time, or the danger that could result from such an impulse, and laid traps for himself and his brethren.[35]

Gilbert was not simply an apologist for the royalist cause: he shared Thomas's core principles but condemned his policies. For Gilbert, Thomas's strident actions were damaging above all to the Church's cause, which he claimed to espouse, and the crises that had beset relations between the Church and the crown were the direct result of Thomas's personal unsuitability for the job.

Writing to Thomas around September 1166, Gilbert set out his case against the archbishop. "It is difficult," says Gilbert, "for things begun with bad beginnings to be carried through to a good conclusion."[36] It was the election of a royal servant, so unsuitable a candidate for archbishop that made the current disastrous situation inevitable. Before Thomas's appointment, he says, peace reigned between the Church and the king. There was general contentment under the rule of a good king, the royal power gave devoted service to the priesthood, and the priesthood supported every command of the king. It was hoped that such cooperation would increase with Thomas's appointment, but instead, disagreements were multiplied, and hatred firmly entrenched. Speaking for the bishops, Gilbert insists that they had stood firm with their archbishop in defense of the Church. "Let the Lord judge between us,"[37] he writes, "let him judge for whom we stood, for whom we refused to give way before the threats of princes; let him judge who fled, who was a deserter in the battle."[38] It was Thomas who fled from righteousness by giving his assent to the king's customs, and then he literally took to flight, running away to France and leaving the Church bereft of its leader. From this distance, Thomas urges the ecclesiastics of England to suffer death for Christ, and not to fear to lay down their lives to free His Church: "Yet it is not the pain that makes the martyr, but the cause. To suffer hardships religiously is an honourable thing: to suffer hardships wrongly and obstinately is dishonourable."[39] Thomas has fled the sword that now threatens the Church in England, and if battle is joined with the king, Gilbert and his colleagues will not escape it. Gilbert goes on to reflect upon "the cause for which we should be persuaded to die."[40] There is no dispute about the faith among us, he says, none about the sacraments, none concerning morals. The whole dispute with the king merely concerns those customs that the king says his predecessors had enjoyed and he wishes to be observed too in his time. In the past, he says, wise men have succeeded in removing such customs, not by abuse or threats but by blessing and preaching. Had Thomas followed the advice of his brethren and the example of his prudent predecessors, and weighed the advantages and disadvantages to the Church, he might have achieved more, and averted destruction. Does anyone, he asks, reckon it among a doctor's skills to cure one wound by inflicting another, far greater and more dangerous?

Gilbert's is a clever rhetorical argument, turning on its head as it does Thomas's claim that he is the true defender of his Church. It is the most biting contemporary criticism that we have of the archbishop, but it reflects views found elsewhere. An account of the Council of Westminster in 1163, where the matter of the royal customs was first aired, has some bishops saying that it would be better that the Church's liberty perishes than that they all perish, adding, "We must make allowances for the evil of these times."[41]

We see similar opinions coming from the papal court. Herbert of Bosham says that when Thomas visited Sens in late 1164 he was confronted by various cardinals who expressed concern at the course he was taking. They put it to him that theirs was a time of darkness for the Church, a time of schism, "when Peter ought not to unsheathe his sword, but ought to replace it."[42] They supported their argument with scriptural readings: "Redeeming the time, because the days are evil" (Eph. 5:16), and "Therefore the prudent shall keep silence at that time, for it is an evil time" (Amos 5:13).[43] While it is doubtful that the cardinals spoke to Thomas in quite this way, it is likely that their words reflect accurately the views of many in the curia. Indeed they directly echo the words that Pope Alexander wrote to Thomas in the summer of 1165: "Since these are evil times, and much must be borne because of the temper of the times, we ask, advise, counsel and exhort your discretion to act with caution, prudence, and circumspection in everything concerning your own and the Church's affairs."[44] Alexander asks that he do nothing hurriedly or precipitately, but strive to recover the goodwill of the king by all means, while preserving the Church's freedom. A few years later, in 1169, the pope wrote to Thomas in similar terms, urging him to "carefully to bear in mind the difficulties and evils of the time, and remembering how our predecessors redeemed their times because of the evil of the day, to strive by every means possible to recover the grace and love of the king, as far as can be done, saving your order and your office."[45]

The debate within the Church was conducted between those who broadly shared the same principles. They upheld the superiority of spiritual over temporal power, and they sought the security and advancement of the Church, but they differed about how to achieve it. This came down to discordant interpretations of what was at stake: Was this a situation that placed the Church under insufferable danger, and required extreme action, or one that required more caution and tact? Was Thomas a successor to the saintly defenders of the Church, or one who postured as a martyr while shrinking from danger?

CONCLUSION

For many at the time, the events of December 1170 appeared to settle the matter, or at least to silence the debate. A few months earlier, papal envoys had pressured the king to abandon the customs, make peace with the archbishop, and allow him to return to his Church. Thomas landed in England in early December, but just before he did so, he sent ahead of him letters censuring three of his main adversaries within the Church, the bishops of London and Salisbury, and the archbishop of York. When the news reached King Henry, he spoke of his outrage at the ingratitude of one whom he had raised from nothing to such a position of power. Four knights who were present took this as their cue to set out for Canterbury to confront the archbishop. Although they may have intended to arrest Thomas when they entered the cathedral, soon the leader of the English Church lay dead on the floor of the mother church of England, murdered by the king's men.[46]

Thomas's posthumous biographers claimed that a knight's sword was shattered on the pavement of the cathedral at the force of the mortal blow to the archbishop, and they made much of its symbolism. But if Thomas the saint won a victory in death that does not necessarily mean that his cause triumphed. While disputes between archbishops and kings continued (notably that between Archbishop Langton and King John in the early thirteenth century), few people sought to revive the Becket conflict. Indeed some of Thomas's ageing supporters denounced his successors for failing to follow his path. The central issue in dispute—the royal customs—was removed, but deeper issues concerning the relationship between Church and crown remained unresolved, right up to the Reformation. When, in 1538 King Henry VIII suppressed Thomas's cult and destroyed his shrine, it showed how the Becket dispute continued to resonate, but it also showed that the dispute had done more to expose tensions between the two powers than to resolve them.

NOTES

1. For the main protagonists, see F. Barlow, *Thomas Becket*, 2nd ed. (Berkeley, CA: University of California Press, 1990), A. Duggan, *Thomas Becket* (London: Bloomsbury Academic, 2004), and W.L. Warren, *Henry II* (Berkeley, CA: University of California Press, 1973). The essential work on the intellectual background to the Becket dispute is B. Smalley, *The Becket Conflict and the Schools* (Oxford: Blackwell Publishing, 1973). See also M. Staunton, *Thomas Becket and His Biographers* (Woodbridge: Boydell & Brewer, 2006).

2. The Latin letters, Lives and miracles of Thomas Becket are collected in *Materials for the History of Thomas Becket, Archbishop of Canterbury*, 7 vols., ed. J.C. Robertson and J.B. Sheppard (London: Rolls Series, 1875–1885) [hereafter *MTB*]. Thomas's correspondence is edited and translated in *The Correspondence of Thomas Becket, Archbishop of Canterbury, 1162–1170*, ed. A. Duggan, 2 vols. (Oxford: Clarendon Press, 2000) [hereafter *CTB*]. Extracts from the Lives are translated in *The Lives of Thomas Becket*, ed. M. Staunton (Manchester: Manchester University Press, 2001).

3. *Eadmeri Historia Novorum in Anglia*, ed. M. Rule (London: Rolls Series, 1884), p. 35. Becket attempted to have Anselm canonized: see R.W. Southern, *St Anselm and his Biographer* (Cambridge: Cambridge University Press, 1966), pp. 339–344.

4. John of Salisbury, *Policraticus*, vol. 2 in *Ioannis Saresberiensis episcopi Carnotensis Policratici sive De nugis curialium et vestigiis philosophorum libri VIII*, ed. C.C.I. Webb, 2 vols. (Oxford: Clarendon Press, 1909), i, pp. 539–541. John dedicated the *Policraticus* to Thomas Becket.

5. *Epistolae Romanorum Pontificum Genuinae* I, ed. A. Thiel (Brunsberg: University of Brunsberg, 1868), no. 12, p. 350.

6. On the two swords theory see, for example, A. Stickler, "Concerning the Political Theories of the Medieval Canonists," *Traditio* 7 (1949–1951), pp. 450–463.

7. For the Investiture Contest and the debates it provoked, see I.S. Robinson, *Authority and Resistance in the Investiture Contest* (Manchester: Manchester University Press, 1978); U.-R. Blumenthal, *The Investiture Controversy: Church and Monarchy from the Ninth to the Twelfth Century* (Philadelphia: University of Pennsylvania Press, 1988); K.J. Leyser, "The Polemics of the Papal Revolution," in *Trends in Medieval Political Thought*, ed. B. Smalley (Oxford: Blackwell, 1965), pp. 42–65.

8. On the relationship between the Church and the crown in post-Conquest England, see Z. N. Brooke, *The English Church and the Papacy* (Cambridge: Cambridge University Press, 1931); F. Barlow, *The English Church, 1066–1154: A History of the Anglo-Norman Church* (London: Longman, 1979).

9. See D. Knowles, "Thomas Becket: A Character Study," in *The Historian and Character and Other Essays* (Cambridge: Cambridge University Press, 1963), pp. 98–128; M. Staunton, "Thomas Becket's Conversion," *Anglo-Norman Studies* 21 (1999), pp. 193–211.

10. See R. Bartlett, *England under the Norman and Angevin Kings, 1075–1225* (Oxford: Clarendon Press, 2000), pp. 377–378.

11. On this issue and the arguments advanced by both sides, see C. Duggan, *Canon Law in Medieval England: The Becket Dispute and Decretal Collections* (London: Variorum Reprints, 1982); Smalley, *Becket Conflict*, 123–133; *Councils and Synods with other Documents relating to the English Church, I, A.D. 871–1204. Part 2: 1066–1204*, ed. D. Whitelock, M. Brett, and C.N.L. Brooke (Oxford: Clarendon Press, 1981), pp. 855–877.
12. *MTB* iii, pp. 266–267; see Gratian, C. 11 qu. 1, cc. 18, 31, in *Corpus Iuris Canonici*, ed. E. Friedberg, 2 vols. (Leipzig: Bernhard Tauchnitz, 1879), i, pp. 631, 635.
13. *Summa Causae inter Thomam et Regem*: *MTB* iv, p. 203.
14. *MTB* i, pp. 25–29.
15. Anonymous I: *MTB* iv, p. 26.
16. William Fitzstephen: *MTB* iii, pp. 47–48; see Isa. 10:1; John 14:15–16; Gratian, D. 8 c. 5: i, p. 14.
17. Herbert of Bosham: *MTB* iii, p. 268.
18. Herbert of Bosham: *MTB* iii, p. 268; see Ps. 149:8.
19. Ps. 119 (118):23.
20. *CTB* no. 68, pp. 266–271.
21. Ezek. 3:18.
22. See Jer. 51:56–57.
23. See Ps. 44:4, 8 (45:3, 7).
24. See 2 Sam. 12:10.
25. 2 Sam. 7; 12; 1 Kings 1.
26. *CTB* no. 74, pp. 292–299.
27. *CTB* no. 74, pp. 296–297; see Isa. 10:1–12.
28. *CTB* no. 74, pp. 298–299.
29. *CTB* no. 82, pp. 328–343.
30. See Gratian, D. 86 c. 3: i, p. 298.
31. See Ps. 73 (74):22; Rev. 19:2.
32. See D. Knowles, *The Episcopal Colleagues of Thomas Becket* (Cambridge: Cambridge University Press, 1951).
33. *MTB* ii, p. 377.
34. See A. Morey and C.N.L. Brooke, *Gilbert Foliot and His Letters* (Cambridge: Cambridge University Press, 1965).
35. *MTB* ii, pp. 337–338.
36. *CTB* no. 109, pp. 498–537.
37. See 2 Cor. 1:17.
38. *CTB* no. 109, pp. 510–511.
39. See Augustine, *Epistulae*, ed. A. Goldbacher, *Corpus Scriptorum Ecclesiasticorum Latinorum*, lvii (Leipzig: G. Freytag, 1911, reprint edition New York/London, 1961), no. cciv, p. 319; *Epistulae*, ed. A. Goldbacher, *CSEL*, xxxiv/2 (Leipzig: G. Freytag, 1898), no. lxxxix, p. 419.
40. *CTB*, no. 109, pp. 526–567.
41. *MTB* iv, p. 203.
42. *MTB* iii, p. 343.
43. *MTB* iii, pp. 343–344.

44. *CTB* no. 54, pp. 224–225.
45. *CTB* no. 204, pp. 890–891.
46. On these events, see W. Urry, *Thomas Becket: His Last Days* (Stroud: Sutton Publishing, 1999).

SELECT BIBLIOGRAPHY

Barlow, Frank (1990), *Thomas Becket* (reprint), Berkeley, CA: University of California Press.

Duggan, Anne, ed. (2000), *The Correspondence of Thomas Becket, Archbishop of Canterbury, 1162–1170*, 2 vols., Oxford: Oxford University Press.

Duggan, Anne (2004), *Thomas Becket*, London: Bloomsbury Academic.

Knowles, David (1951), *The Episcopal Colleagues of Archbishop Thomas Becket*, Cambridge: Cambridge University Press.

Robertson, J. C. and J. B. Sheppard, ed. (1875–1885), *Materials for the History of Thomas Becket, Archbishop of Canterbury*, 7 vols., London: Longman & Co.

Smalley, B. (1973), *The Becket Conflict and the Schools*, Oxford: Blackwell Publishing.

Staunton, Michael, ed. (2001), *The Lives of Thomas Becket*, Manchester: Manchester University Press.

Staunton, Michael (2006), *Thomas Becket and His Biographers*, Woodbridge: Boydell & Brewer.

Urry, William (1999), *Thomas Becket: His Last Days*, Stroud: Sutton Publishing.

CHAPTER NINE

The Political Praxis of Bartolomé de Las Casas

LUIS N. RIVERA-PAGÁN

WHEN THINGS FALL APART

In 1566, after several decades of intense and exhausting endeavors to influence and shape the policy of the Spanish state and church regarding the Americas, years of drafting countless historical texts, theological treatises, colonization projects, prophetic homilies, juridical complaints, political utopias, and apocalyptic visions, Bartolomé de Las Casas knows very well that the end is at hand: the end of his life and the end of his illusions of crafting a just and Christian empire in the New World.[1] It is a moment of searching for the precise closure, the right culmination of a human existence that since 1502 had been intimately linked, as no other person of his time, to the drama of the conquest and Christianization of Latin America, a continent, as has been so aptly asserted, "born in blood and fire."[2]

He painfully knows that there will be no time to finish his *magnum opus*, the *History of the Indies*. Originally conceived as six volumes, each one intended to cover a decade between 1490 and 1550, it will be left partially written, with only the first three decades discussed. In his will, Las Casas makes provision for the preservation of that precious manuscript on which he has worked incessantly for almost forty years. It will survive as a clandestine subversive text for three centuries,[3] will not be published until the second half of the nineteenth century, only very recently has been the object of a truly scholar critical edition,[4] and still lacks a complete and adequate English translation.[5]

In the prologue to the *History of the Indies* Las Casas discloses the diverse objectives of the book: (1) To call the attention of the readers to the terrifying disparity between the missionary purpose of the encounter between Christians Europeans and Native Americans and the brutal exploitation of the second by the first. (2) To refute the, in his perspective, many mistakes and deceptions written by other Spanish historians, like Gonzalo Fernández de Oviedo y Valdés[6] and Francisco López de Gómara,[7] who, according to Las Casas, confuse and conflate historiography with sycophancy. (3) To proclaim the humanity of the indigenous peoples, their rationality, their personal and collective freedom. "All peoples are human," is the leitmotiv and guiding principle of the text. (4) To record a dissenting testimony with the hope that his *History* will one day be read, by future generations or even maybe at the eschatological moment of reckoning in which his nation, Spain, might hear, with fear and trembling, the fateful hymn—*dies irae, dies illa, solvet saeclum in favilla . . .* (5) To ease his profound agony of witnessing a tragic performance of human cruelty, to exorcise the stain of complicity in the atrocities performed.

The *History* contains the first recorded homily in the Americas, an earth shaking sermon preached by the Dominican friar Antonio de Montesinos, the fourth Sunday of Advent of 1511 in which this ardent priest, after reading the biblical passage of John the Baptist, *ego vox clamantis in deserto* (Mt. 3:3), preaches these scathing words to the leaders of the Spanish colonial establishment:

> You are in mortal sin ... for the cruelty and tyranny you use in dealing with these innocent people. Tell me, by what right or justice do you keep these Indians in such a cruel and horrible servitude? On what authority have you waged a detestable war against these people? ... Why do you keep them so oppressed? ... Are not these people also human beings? ... Be certain that in such a state as this you can be no more saved than a Moor or a Turk ...[8]

During his last year of existence, Las Casas fears that his life long struggle may have been fruitless. Since his first public intervention, a sermon preached the Day of the Assumption of Our Lady, August 15, 1514,[9] till his last writings more than five decades later, he would be possessed by one obsessive passion: to be the prophet of Spain, a man called by God to be the scourge of the conscience of his nation and to be the defender of the autochthonous communities, in whose misery he perceived "Jesus Christ ... not once, but thousand times whipped, insulted, beaten, and crucified ... by us the Spaniards, who destroy them."[10] If his first writings exude enthusiasm and optimism, the time is now at hand to contemplate the tragic fate of historical action. It is the time in which all things seem to fall apart.

It is the time, under the shadow of death, to look back at his life, a life of a man of letters and a man of action, a man of the church and of the people, a priest, a Dominican friar, a theologian, a prophet, and a bishop. The hour comes of final reckoning, in which the past overwhelms the mind with its fateful irreversibility, and the future with the certainty of dissolution. His was the bitter honor of having many public noisy detractors and many secret silent admirers, ever since that day, half a century earlier, in which he had the enigmatic intuition of been called to a prophetic vocation.[11] For Las Casas, that kairotic occasion was linked to a biblical text: *Ecclesiasticus* 34:20–21:

> To offer a sacrifice from the
> possessions of the poor
> is like killing a son
> before his father's eyes.
> Bread is life to the destitute,
> and to deprive them of it is murder.[12]

THE EPISTLE TO THE ROYAL COUNCIL OF INDIES: A CHALLENGE TO THE CROWN

Las Casas's intense prophetic self-awareness places him in the category of those who, when the final hour comes, go out fighting. Aware of the imminence of his death, he writes two epistles, short and sharp, restating the principles that had guided all his endeavors. These will constitute his last battle cry. One of the letters, written in 1565, is to the Royal Council of Indies, the other, drafted in 1566, to the recently elected Pope, Pius V. For a man accustomed to write compendious, copious, dense and labyrinthine texts, they are surprisingly, and refreshingly, brief, clear, and precise.

The tone of his farewell letter to the Council of Indies is sharp and blunt.[13] The old bishop, of more than eighty years of age, refuses to mellow. Las Casas becomes an Iberian Jeremiah confronting the unfaithful king of Judah. The epistle reiterates what he has been proclaiming during five decades. It emphasizes the missionary purpose of the Spanish dominion of the New World, excoriates the Spanish conquest and enslavement of the indigenous communities, calls for a radical change in the colonial policy, defends his ministry as protector of the Native Americans, proclaims the sacramental obligation of restitution as a requirement for the divine absolution of Spain's sins, and warns the authorities about an imminent eschatological divine condemnation.

The issues are not only political and economic. For the author, a bishop and theologian, the overarching theme is theological: the tragic history of God's grace and human sinfulness. The whole first book of the *History of the Indies* is guided by two conflicting ideas. First, the encounter between Christian Spaniards and Native Americans was a crucial act in the eschatological redemption of all nations, and as such it was a manifestation of divine grace. Second, Spain, the divinely chosen people, has proven to be as rebellious and sinful as the Old Testament Israel. It might thus be fated to share its same tragic destiny.

Always a man of letters, inclined to the process of dialogue and debate, he suggests that the Council convene a board of the best theologians and jurists to discuss the situation created by the violence, dispossession, and servitude suffered by the Native Americans. At the end of the letter, as a terrifying explosion of a volcano, comes the harsh enumeration of eight conclusions that such a theological and juridical board should discuss:

> First, all the wars usually called conquests were and are unjust and tyrannical.
> Second, we have illegally usurped all the kingdoms of the Indies.
> Third, all encomiendas are iniquitous and tyrannical.
> Fourth, those who posses them and those who distribute them are in mortal sin.
> Fifth, the king has no more right to justify the conquests and encomiendas than the Ottoman Turk to make war against Christians.
> Sixth, all fortunes made in the Indies are to be considered as stolen.
> Seventh, if the guilty of complicity in the conquests or encomiendas do not make restitution, they will not be saved.
> Eighth, the Indian nations have the right, which will be theirs till the Day of Judgment, to make just war against us and erase us from the face of the earth.[14]

There is in this missive a sense of urgency, an awareness of the proximity not only of his own individual death, but also something like the intuition, shared by several of his contemporaries,[15] that the end of all times, the consummation, both hoped and dreaded, of human history might be at hand. Las Casas fears that it might be a day of condemnation and punishment for his own nation, Spain. "A day," as he writes in his will, "in which God will pour his indignation and anger over Spain, for she has all, in greater or lesser degree, participated in the bloody riches stolen and illicitly acquired, and in the massacres and violence suffered by the Native Americans."[16]

The acts of the Council solemnly note that the letter was respectfully read, heard, and . . . filed.[17]

THE LETTER TO THE POPE: A CHALLENGE TO THE CHURCH

For a Roman Catholic bishop to write a letter to the pope seems initially neither surprising nor illicit. In sixteenth century Spain, it could be both. Early in that century, the crown had been able to exact from Rome extensive regulatory formal authority over the church in the Americas. The *Patronato Real* (Royal Patronage), based upon several papal decrees enacted under the relentless pressure of Ferdinand V, gave the crown ample powers over the demarcation, administration, and finances of the American dioceses, including the nomination of bishops.[18] Ferdinand V, Charles V and Philip II will consider those papal documents—Alexander VI's 1493 bulls *Inter caetera* and *Eximiae devotionis*, his 1501 bull *Eximiae devotionis*, and Julius II's 1508 bull *Universalis ecclesiae*—as the juridical foundation of their royal patronage over the American church.[19]

The royal patronage over the American church could even be said to function as sort of a royal vicariate, or at least such was the import of the legislative and juridical actions in ecclesiastical matters undertaken by the court.[20] According to a Spanish scholar, the Royal patronage "created a peculiar situation, extraordinary in canon law, characterized by a transfer to the state of powers and functions traditionally exercised exclusively by the supreme ecclesiastical authority."[21] As the sixteenth century evolved, this peculiar regime in which the crown had assumed, in the words of another scholar, a "quasi-pontifical character,"[22] began to acquire a precise juridical status in the emerging labyrinth of the Laws of Indies, a process that Rome observed with apprehension but also with relative powerlessness. The law required of all bishops and archbishops, before their entrance into office, to swear fealty to the crown and loyal obedience to the royal patronage. One of its consequences was that controversial matters between church and state, in the Americas, were usually submitted to the crown, rather than to Rome, for a normative resolution.

Even when the discursive rhetoric of many formal documents regarding church and state affairs, like the 1493 bulls[23] or the notorious *requerimiento*,[24] emphasized papal authority, it was eminently clear that the power for historical action was in the hands of the state.[25] The rhetoric might be ultramontane, but the political praxis was strongly royalist. The Burgos capitulations, signed in 1512 by the crown and the first three bishops named to the Americas, was one of the first expressions of that royal patrimony. It is a document with a strong juridical tenor, in which the crown establishes the boundaries of the functions and attributes of the American episcopacy.[26] For the royal court, the Burgos Capitulations became a paradigm of the jurisdiction it desired to exercise over ecclesiastical affairs.

This certainly does not mean that the relations between church and state were devoid of conflicts, or that the pope always agreed to remain a spectator at the margins of the exceptional historical drama unfolding in the Americas. In 1537, Pope Paul III enacted the bull *Sublimis Deus*, in which he used very strong language to call for the recognition and respect of the humanity and freedom of the autochthonous communities. The pope also sent a brief to the Archbishop of Toledo, *Pastorale officium*, urging the highest ecclesiastical hierarch of Spain to protect the liberties and rights of the Native Americans.[27] The reaction of the court of Charles V was swift and energetic, forcing the pope to retract, in 1538.[28] The traumatic events of the May 1527 sack of Rome, in which the imperial troops rampaged through the city, looted everything they could, and humbled ignominiously the *Vicarius Christi*, were still painfully fresh in the memory of the Roman authorities and prescribed supreme prudence before engaging in any possible confrontation with the Emperor.

One key dimension of the royal patronage was the *pase regio*, the royal *exequatur* or *placet*. According to it, all communications between Rome and the American church had to be sent first to the Council of Indies for its examination and approval. It was an important strategic resource for the centralizing politics of the Hapsburg monarchy. It was a strategy to impede the emergence, within the ranks of the church, of any serious challenge to the colonial metropolitan policies.

Las Casas's letter to Pope Pius V consciously disregards the *pase regio*.[29] The very act of writing to the pope without previously submitting the text to the Royal Council of Indies violates one of the main juridical premises of the church and state relations in the Americas. It is a transgression of the ecclesiastical policy so carefully crafted by the Spanish court.[30] True to form, even to his last breath, Las Casas would be the perennial dissenter. As bishop of Chiapas, he had imposed a set of norms that rigorously conditioned sacramental absolution of the Spaniards to the restitution of all goods and riches acquired on the basis of conquest or slavery of the Native Americans, a move that forced him to exile from his diocese; as a theologian, he printed and distributed, in 1552, a series of polemic treatises regarding the *status confessionis* in the New World, without requesting any official permission to do so; as a dying prophet he disregards the law of the state and appeals directly to the pope.

Las Casas begins in a rather professorial tone, devoid of the reverent language so frequent in communications to the successor of Saint Peter:

> What things are necessary for the correct way of preaching the Gospel to the infidels, and to render just and legitimate the wars against them, I have declared in the book that I sent to Your Beatitude . . . To Your Beatitude I beseech intensively, by the blood of our Redemption, to command that my book be examined and, if found right, that it be stamped . . .[31]

Las Casas holds onto the illusion that reason will, in the end, prevail over irrationality, goodness over evil, grace over sin, if only the main protagonists of the historical drama think things through adequately. He has the hope that, despite all the economic and political interests intertwined in the conquest of the Indies, despite the *conquistadores*'s quest for power, profit, and prestige, he might be able to convince the crown, the royal council, and the pope to follow the right path. Persuasion by means of the right arguments, the quotation of the proper authorities and texts, the coherence of logical reasoning: this is the illusion that has impelled him to write so many books, like his two apologies against Juan Ginés de Sepúlveda in which he buried his adversary, as well as the readers, under a deluge of references, authoritative quotations, and arguments.[32] If only the authorities, those who have the power to make decisions, would read his books and take the time to pay attention to his words!

There is no absolute certainty about the book he sent to the pope and whose official approval he is requesting. It might be *De unico vocationis modo omnium gentium ad veram religionem*, a text with a tortuous, and still somewhat obscure, manuscript history.[33] In it, one of the most important missiological books written in the sixteenth century, Las Casas vigorously insists that there is only one way to convert the innumerable that the Iberians were encountering in their global expeditions: the way of the apostles, through devout preaching, deeds of love, sacrifice, compassion, and confidence in the Holy Spirit. With extensive quotations from biblical, patristic, doctrinal, and canonical sources, this book is one of the most passionate and ardent defenses of the peaceful and nonmilitary missionary expansion of the Christian faith ever written.

It makes a powerful case for a peaceful nonmilitary extension of the Christian faith as well as a strong critique of the linkage between cross and sword that, in Las Casas's view, was corrupting the evangelizing of the Native Americans. He considers the Spanish wars against the Native Americans illegal, immoral, and sinful. They violate human, natural, and divine law. It was, indeed, a theme of ardent discussion among Spaniards theologians for the entire sixteenth century.[34] Las Casas asks that a board of theologians appointed by the pope examine his manuscript, and its suggested policy be declared official doctrine of the church.

Why is it so urgent for the Church to condemn the military conquests of the Native American nations? Here comes a shocking statement, an eschatological warning to the pope: "so that the truth be not hidden for the damnation and destruction of the Church, as the time may come (which might be already at hand) in which God unveils our blemishes and our nakedness is shown to the whole pagan world." Las Casas had warned the Royal Council of Indies that the final Day of Judgment might be near and that it might entail the eternal damnation of Spain. Now he admonishes the pope that unless the Church acts decisively on behalf of the oppressed Native Americans, it might also find itself condemned in that imminent fateful Doomsday. For a bishop to admonish a pope in this manner is, indeed, a dramatic expression of audacity.

But this is just the prologue to other daring requests to the pope. Veiled as petitions, they are indeed radical challenges to the Church. Las Casas demands from the pope an official normative declaration regarding the affairs of the Indies with its corresponding anathemas.

> Since so many are the flatterers who in secret, like dogs with rabies, bark against the truth, to Your Beatitude I humbly beseech that a decree be enacted in which are declared excommunicated and anathema, all those who affirm that wars against the infidels are just if waged to combat idolatry, or for the convenience of spreading the Gospel, specially in regard to those infidels who have never injured or are not injuring us.[35]

Idolatry was frequently used as a *casus belli* against the Native Americans. Columbus invoked idolatry as a justification to begin the American slave trade.[36] Hernán Cortés initiated the war against Tenochtitlán only after formally declaring it a crusade against idolatry.[37] Sepúlveda, among others, had emphasized idolatry as a legitimate reason to conquer the Native Americans through war, for idolatry is not only a grave blasphemy against divine and natural law in itself, but also the source of their alleged moral depravations: human sacrifice, cannibalism, and sodomy. Franciscan missionaries rationalized Cortés's conquest as a divine punishment against the idolatry of the natives, and tried to explain to the Mexican elders the demonic origin of their religious practices.[38] The condemnation of sacrilegious idolatry became a benchmark for the conquest and enslaving of native communities. The "extirpation of idolatry," so well studied regarding Perú by Pierre Duviols, was one of the ideological foundations of what Robert Ricard aptly named the spiritual conquest of the autochthonous communities.[39] Therefore, Las Casas's request to the pope that the invocation of idolatry for doing violence to the Native Americans be declared anathema goes to the heart of one of the main ideological resources behind the conquest of the Americas. The demand is grandiose, as will also be the silence of Rome.

The second principle that Las Casas requests to be included in the papal decree of anathemas is one very dear to his mind.

Or those who assert that the infidels are not true lords and owners of their properties; or those who affirm that they are unable to understand and receive the Gospel and eternal salvation, on the basis of their alleged lack of intelligence or acuity of mind, which in fact they do not lack, those Indians whose rights I have defended till my death, for the honor of God and the Church.[40]

Are the Native Americans equal to the Europeans in rationality and free will? This was, alas, a crucial question during the Christian expansion in early modernity. Aristotle's vision of the distinction between the Greeks, as a people of culture, and the "barbarians," and his discussion of just war and slavery in the first part of his *Politics*, were refurbished in the encounter between Christians Europeans and the indigenous American communities.[41] His arguments regarding the justice of warfare against the barbarians and their legitimate enslavement became relevant for the sixteenth-century theological discussions on war and slavery.[42] "Barbarian" became a frequent term of reference to the Native Americans. It is found in Francisco de Vitoria,[43] Sepúlveda,[44] and in many other sixteenth-century writers. Probably the best definition of what was meant by "barbarian" is provided by José de Acosta: "We call 'Indians' all the Barbarians that have been discovered in our time by the Spanish and the Portuguese . . . people who are not only deprived of the light of the Gospel but also unaware of civilization."[45] Barbarians are ignorant of both Christian faith and literary culture. They lack knowledge of Christ and of the alphabet.[46] They are, therefore, socially and culturally inferior.[47] Thus, according to the discourse of several court intellectuals, the Native Americans are unfit for self-government. They can be considered *natura servi*, fated by nature to servitude. For their own benefit, civilized Christians should rule them. If they resist, the war to subjugate them is, in principle, just and legitimate.

Las Casas devoted an extended section of his *Apology* against Sepúlveda to refute the vilification of the Native Americans implied by their categorization as barbarians. He also penned an ambitious and long manuscript on their cultural and cultic traditions, to prove the dignity of their culture and religiosity. That text—*Apologética historia sumaria*—is the longer and most passionate defense of the Native American cultures written in the sixteenth century.[48]

In this missive to the pope, Las Casas comes back to this crucial issue and requests a decree of anathema against any negation of the rationality of the Native Americans, their personal liberty, their right for public sovereignty or private ownership, or their ability to understand and accept the mysteries of the Christian faith. In all those essential dimensions of humanness, insists Las Casas, there is no fundamental ontological distinction between Europeans and Native Americans, and thus no legitimate justification for dispossessing them of their political sovereignty, their private goods, their personal freedom, or for abrogating their right to the ecclesiastical sacraments.[49] A much quoted text of the *Apologética* gives expression to the principle that underlies his lifelong exertions: "All the nations of the world are human and all share in the same definition: they are rational beings. All have intellect and will, as created in God's image and similitude."[50]

This has been the core of his struggles of more than five decades, for the sake of, as he writes to the pope, "those Indians whose rights I have defended till my death, for the honor of God and the Church."[51] Now, at the moment in which death is the only future for his flesh, he recapitulates that long dispute in a sharp challenge to the *Vicarius Christi* to rebuke and condemn all those who question the rationality, the political rights, the personal liberty, or the capability to the faith of the Native Americans. And then, always certain of his ability to persuade by means of logical argumentations and authoritative references, Las Casas concludes: "In my book I have clearly shown that all those assertions are against the sacred canons, as well as against natural law and the commandments of the Gospel, and I will confirm it even more, if that were possible, for I have exhaustively researched and corroborated this matter."[52]

The next three requests to the pope have to do with the church itself: the identity, vocation, and mission of the Christian Church in the New World. Mindful of the way in which the royal patronage has modeled a Church loyal to the State, Las Casas demands from the Roman Pontiff that he:

> Order the bishops of the Indies that, under holy obedience, they be concerned about those natives, who, with hard labors and tyrannies (more than what it could be believed), carry on their meager shoulders, against all natural and divine law, a heavy yoke and unbearable load, which makes it necessary that Your Holiness instruct those bishops to defend their cause, becoming a protecting wall for them, even to spill their own blood, as by divine law they are obliged, and that in no way they accept their appointment, if the King and his Council would not support them and uproot so many tyrannies and oppressions.[53]

The Church as the protector and defender of the Native Americans. That, in short, is his audacious request to the Pontiff, the vision of this obstinate and pugnacious dying bishop and prophet. Such conduct, according to Las Casas, is not optional. It is not a model of behavior that the Church might or might not assume. The bishops are obliged to follow this daring and perilous conduct "by natural and divine law," even if it entails the way of the cross, the tragic sufferings of martyrdom. Instead of the bishops pledging their fealty to the state policies, as done by the first American bishops in the Burgos capitulations, they should demand from the court an oath of support in the uprooting of "so many tyrannies and oppressions," before accepting their nominations to their dioceses.

The next request has to do with a sensitive issue in the evangelization of the Native Americans during the sixteenth century: language. Las Casas indicates the problem with his usual judgmental tone, but also with uncommon brevity: "Openly and unjustly the bishop ignores the language of his subjects, and does not attempt to learn it well." Therefore, the pope should order that the American prelates learn the native languages. "I humbly beseech Your Beatitude to order them to master the language of their sheep, showing that they are so commanded by divine and natural law, for at the moment many awful indignities occur ... caused by the negligence of the bishops in learning the language of their parishioners."[54]

One of the most impressive achievements of the contemporary Spanish missionary efforts had to do precisely with the alphabetization of the Native languages and the translation of homilies, liturgies, religious plays, prayers, and biblical texts into them. Yet, as Acosta would note two decades later, this was mainly the labor of friars within the religious orders. Most diocesan bishops and priests were reluctant to invest the time and energy required by the mastery of those languages. The debate whether to encourage the priesthood to learn the native languages or, on the contrary, to compel the natives to learn Spanish, frequently pitted the religious orders against the regular ecclesiastical ministry. This linguistic dilemma has to do with the proper communication of the Christian faith. But, as Las Casas is convinced, at a deeper level, it has also to do with the quality and character of its inculturation. Inculturation of the faith, in analogy to the Incarnation, begins with linguistic assimilation as an immersion in the culture of a community and its particular symbolic universe. The identification of the Church with the indigenous cultures has to traverse inevitably the complex path of linguistic identity.

If the previous requests are difficult to satisfy, the last one is even harder. The Church has not only to defend the Native Americans and to assimilate their language and culture; it should also share their poverty, their dispossession. The American Church is getting immensely rich in material goods thanks to the exploitation of the land and the work of the Native Americans. Several years later, Acosta will bewail the enrichment of priests and bishops, but will consider it a minor price in exchange for the preaching of the Christian faith.[55] For Las Casas, on the contrary, it constitutes a sinful scandal:

> Immense scandal and no less detriment to our most holy religion is that in such a new place bishops and friars and priests are getting rich and live sumptuously, while their recently converted subjects remain in so great and incredible poverty, that many of them die daily in profound misery, due to the tyranny, hunger and excessive work that they suffer.[56]

The contrast between ecclesiastical enrichment and the poverty of the Native Americans entails, for Las Casas, an intensely severe sentence: the Church is guilty of complicity in the dispossession, misery, and agony of the autochthonous communities. Now we discover the acuteness of his initial admonition that in the Day of Judgment the Church might be revealed to the Gentile nations as naked and blemished. The Church cannot reproach the conquistadores or encomenderos, if she does not deal with her own complicity in the oppression of the native peoples. Thus, the drastic and radical challenge of the dying bishop to the new pope:

> Therefore, to Your Holiness I humbly beseech to declare those ministers to be obliged by natural and divine law, as in fact they are, to restitute all the gold, silver, and precious stones they have acquired, for their wealth is taken from human beings who endure extreme need and who today live in misery, with whom, by divine and natural law, they are even beholden to share their own possessions.[57]

From his 1514 homily, when for the first time he denounced the enslavement of the Native Americans, till this last text, fifty-two years later, one theme is constantly repeated in the writings of Las Casas: the salvation of the Christians depends upon their disposition to restitute everything they have acquired by conquest and slavery. The duty of restitution is at the heart of the sacrament of penance and at the core of Las Casas's episcopal practice, prophetic message, and theological disquisition.

The surprising conclusion, therefore, of Las Casas's letter to the pope, is that in the history-making encounter between Christian Europeans and Native American infidels, what is mainly at stake and in doubt is the salvation of the first, the Christian Europeans. They—the Spanish state and the Roman Church—are called to do penance and to beg for divine forgiveness and absolution. This is indeed an extraordinary inversion of the usual understanding of the matter in the history of the global expansion of the Christian faith. Only now, after dispatching his farewell letters to the Royal Council of Indies and to the pope, can this bold and old bishop, theologian, and prophet rest in peace, eternally.

NOTES

1. There is a convenient edition of Las Casas's writings, *Obras completas*, in 14 volumes (Madrid: Alianza Editorial, 1988–1998), published under the supervision of the Spanish scholar Paulino Castañeda Delgado. The secondary bibliography is immense. Essential works are the following: Isacio Pérez Fernández, *Inventario documentado de los escritos de*

Fray Bartolomé de las Casas (Bayamón, Puerto Rico: CEDOC, 1981), Isacio Pérez Fernández, *Cronología documentada de los viajes, estancias y actuaciones de Fray Bartolomé de las Casas* (Bayamón, Puerto Rico: CEDOC, 1983), Gustavo Gutiérrez, *Las Casas: In Search of the Poor of Jesus Christ* (Maryknoll, NY: Orbis Books, 1993), and Marcel Bataillon (avec la collaboration de Raymond Marcus), *Études sur Bartolomé de las Casas* (Paris: Centre de Recherches de l'Institut d'Études Hispaniques, 1966).

2. John Charles Chasteen, *Born in Blood and Fire: A Concise History of Latin America* (New York: Norton, 2001).
3. Philip II ordered the confiscation of Las Casas's writings, after the bishop's death, according to Enrique Rosner, *Missionare und Musketen: 500 Jahre lateinamerikanische Passion* (Frankfurt am Main: Verlag Josef Knecht, 1992), 212.
4. *Historia de las Indias* (primera edición crítica), in Fray Bartolomé de las Casas, *Obras completas*, volumes 3–5.
5. There is an incomplete English translation: Bartolomé de las Casas, *History of the Indies*, ed. and trans. André Collard (New York: Harper & Row, 1971), a rather unsatisfactory rendering of this important work.
6. *Historia general y natural de las Indias, islas y tierra firme del mar Océano* (1535, 1547) (Madrid: Ediciones Atlas, 1959).
7. *Historia general de las indias* (1552) (Madrid: Espasa-Calpe, 1941).
8. *Historia de las Indias* [*HI*], l. 3, cs. 3–7, 1757–1774. Lewis Hanke baptised this sermon as "the first cry for justice in America," in his now classic book *The Spanish Struggle for Justice in the Conquest of America* (Philadelphia: University of Pennsylvania Press, 1949), 15–22.
9. *HI*, l. 3, c. 79, 2080–2085.
10. *HI*, l. 3, c. 138, 2366.
11. Demetrio Ramos Pérez, "La 'conversión' de Las Casas en Cuba: El clérigo y Diego Velázquez," in André Saint-Lu et al., *Estudios sobre Fray Bartolomé de Las Casas* (Sevilla: Universidad de Sevilla, 1974), 247–257.
12. *The Revised English Bible, with the Apocrypha* (Oxford University Press and Cambridge University Press, 1989,) section of the Apocrypha, 122. The Latin text used by La Casas is even stronger. "To offer a sacrifice from the possessions of the poor is like killing a son before his father's eyes" is rendered: *Qui offert sacrificium ex substantia pauperum, quasi qui victimat filium in conspectu patris sui.* The expression *ex substantia pauperum* ("from the substance of the poor") implies that what is taken from the dispossessed is decisive for their existence. The crux of the matter seems to be the life or death of the Native American peoples. Las Casas quotes this text in two slightly different ways in *HI*, l. 1, c. 24, 473, and *HI*, l. 3, c. 79, 2081.
13. Reproduced as appendix in Bartolomé de las Casas, *De regia potestate o derecho de autodeterminación*, ed. por Luciano Pereña et al (*Corpus Hispanorum de Pace*, Vol. VIII) (Madrid: Consejo Superior de Investigaciones Científicas, 1969), 279–283.
14. Ibid., 282–283.
15. John Leddy Phelan, *The Millennial Kingdom of the Franciscans in the New World* (Berkeley, CA: University of California Press, 1956). For a brief synopsis of the growth and ebb of apocalyptic urgency in the sixteenth-century Iberian missionary enterprise, see Marcel Bataillon, "Novo mundo e fim do mundo," *Revista de historia* (São Paulo), no. 18, 1954, 343–351.
16. *Obras escogidas de Fray Bartolomé de las Casas*, Vol. 5: *Opúsculos, cartas y memoriales*, 540.
17. Ibid., 538: "y a esto ninguna cosa proveyeron" ("regarding this petition, they did not take any action") is the austere testimony of Alonso de la Veracruz, an Augustinian friar who, accompanied by two Dominican friars, members of the small coterie of devout followers of Las Casas, read the letter to the Council, in representation of the ailing bishop.

18. See Pedro de Leturia, S I., *Relaciones entre la Santa Sede e Hispanoamérica*, Vol. 1: *Época del Real Patronato, 1493–1800* (Caracas: Sociedad Bolivariana de Venezuela, 1959) and William Eugene Shiels, S. J. *King and Church: The Rise and Fall of the Patronato Real* (Chicago: Loyola University Press, 1961).

19. Reproduced in Shiels, *King and Church*, 283–289, 294–295, and 310–313.

20. *Relaciones*, I, 101–152. See also Manuel Gutiérrez de Arce, "Regio patronato indiano (Ensayo de valoración histórico-canónica)," *Anuario de estudios americanos*, Vol. 11, 1954, 107–168, Alberto de la Hera, "El Patronato y el Vicariato Regio en Indias," in *Historia de la Iglesia en Hispanoamérica y Filipinas* (siglos xv–xix), obra dirigida por Pedro Borges (Madrid: Biblioteca de Autores Cristianos, 1992), Vol. I, 63–79.

21. Gutiérrez de Arce, "Regio patronato indiano, 109.

22. Shiels, *King and Church*, 184.

23. Manuel Giménez Fernández, *Nuevas consideraciones sobre la historia, sentido y valor de las bulas alejandrinas de 1493 referentes a las Indias* (Sevilla: Escuela de Estudios Hispano-Americanos de la Universidad de Sevilla, 1944) and, of the same author, "Algo más sobre las bulas alejandrinas de 1493 referentes a las Indias," *Anales de la Universidad Hispalense*, Sevilla, Año 8, Núm. 3, 1945, 37–86; Año 9, Núm. 1, 115–126.

24. For a concise analysis of the origin, evolution, and conflicting evaluations of the *requerimiento*, see Benno Biermann, O.P. "Das Requerimiento in der spanischen Conquista," *Neue Zeitschrift für Missionswissenschaft*, Vol. 6, Beckenried, Suiza, 1950, 94–114. Also Luis N. Rivera-Pagán, *A Violent Evangelism: The Political and Religious Conquest of the Americas* (Louisville, KY: Westminster–John Knox Press, 1992), 32–41.

25. Alberto de la Hera, "El regalismo indiano," in *Historia de la Iglesia en Hispanoamérica*, Vol. I, 81–97.

26. Reproduced in Shiels, *King and Church*, 319–325. The signing prelates were Fray García de Padilla, Pedro Suárez de Deza, and Alonso Manso, nominated bishops for the recently created dioceses of Santo Domingo, Concepción de la Vega, and San Juan, respectively.

27. Helen Rand Parish reproduces the Latin text of the bull and the brief, with a Spanish translation, in *Las Casas en México* (México, D.F. Fondo de Cultura Económica, 1992), 303–305, 310–312. There are English versions of both documents in Bartolomé de las Casas, *The Only Way*, edited by Helen Rand Parish and translated by Francis Patrick Sullivan, S.J. (New York: Paulist Press, 1992), 114–115, 156–157, and in Bartolomé de las Casas, *In Defense of the Indians*, translated by Stafford Poole, C.M. (DeKalb: Northern Illinois University Press, 1992), 100–103. In his anthology of ecclesiastical normative documents regarding the Spanish empire, Francisco Javier Hernáez reproduces *Pastorale officium*, but not *Sublimis Deus*, though he includes *Veritas ipsa*, a variant of *Sublimis Deus*. Francisco Javier Hernáez, *Colección de bulas, breves y otros documentos relativos a la iglesia de América y Filipinas* (1879) (Vaduz: Klaus Reprint, 1964), Vol. I, 101–104. *Pastorale officium* and *Veritas ipsa*, but not *Sublimis Deus*, are included in *America Pontificia. Primi saeculi evangelizationis, 1493–1592 documenta Pontificia ex registris et minutis praesertim in archivo secreto Vaticano existentibus*, collegit et edidit Josef Metzler (Città del Vaticano: Librería Editrice Vaticana, 1991), Vol. I, 359–361, 364–366. For a detailed analysis of these papal documents, see Alberto de la Hera, "El derecho de los indios a la libertad y a la fe: la bula *Sublimis Deus* y los problemas indianos que la motivaron," *Anuario de historia del derecho español*, Vol. 26, 1956, 89–182. Parish has given a closer look to the origin of these documents, including another 1537 papal bull, *Altitudo divini consilii*, regarding the perfomance of some sacramentos and liturgical ceremonies in the New World (*Las Casas en México*, 15–28, 82–90).

28. The abrogating papal brief, *Non indecens videtur*, is reproduced, in Latin with a Spanish translation, in Parish's *Las Casas en México*, 313–315. Francisco de Vitoria does not

mention *Sublimis Deus* in his 1539 lectures on the Native Americans (*De Indis*, I). Jeremy Lawrance suggests that the lecture might have been inspired by the controversy about the papal decrees. However, Vitoria deals mainly with matters regarding the justice of the wars against the Native Americans, not their slavery, which is the main theme of the Pope's bull. Francisco de Vitoria, *Political Writings*, edited by Anthony Pagden and Jeremy Lawrance (Cambridge: Cambridge University Press, 1996), 233, n. 3. José de Acosta barely alludes to it once in his 1588 important book on the the Christianization of the Americas. José de Acosta, *De procuranda indorum salute* (2 vols.), translated and edited by G. Stewart McIntosh, (Tayport: Mac Research, 1996), Vol. I, 114. Las Casas, for one, quoted both documents as valid and normative. Probably thanks to his influence many readers tend to disregard their revocation. Cf. Lewis U. Hanke, "Pope Paul III and the American Indians," *Harvard Theological Review*, Vol. 30, 1937, 56–102, Manuel María Martínez, "Las Casas-Vitoria y la bula *Sublimis Deus*," in André Saint-Lu et al., *Estudios sobre Fray Bartolomé de Las Casas* (Sevilla: Universidad de Sevilla, 1974), 25–51, and Gustavo Gutiérrez, "Las Casas y Paulo III," *Páginas* (Lima), Vol. 16, No. 107, febrero 1991, 33–42.

29. Manuscript in the National Library of Paris, ms. 325, fol. 312. Published for the first time in 1866 in the second volume of the *Colección de documentos para la historia de México*, edited by Joaquín García Icazbalceta (Nendeln, Liechtenstein: Kraus Reprint, 1971, 599–600). Reproduced in *Obras escogidas*, vol. V, 541–542 and in *Obras completas*, vol. 13, 370–371.

30. Juan Friede rightly stresses the importance of the letter as an act of legal disobedience. But, he does not perceive the originality of the challenges that the letter raises to the *Roman Church*, not to the *Spanish state*. Juan Friede, *Bartolomé de Las Casas: precursor del anticolonialismo* (México, D. F.: Siglo XXI, 1974), 214–216.

31. Bartolomé de Las Casas, *Obras completas*, vol. 13, 370.

32. One apology is written in Spanish, published for the first time in 1958 (reproduced in *Obras completas*, Vol. 10, 101–193) and the other in Latin, published for the first time in 1975 (reproduced in *Obras completas*, Vol. 9, 43–667). Regarding the dispute between Las Casas and Sepúlveda, the standard text is Lewis Hanke, *All Mankind is One: A Study of the Disputation between Bartolomé de Las Casas and Juan Ginés de Sepúlveda in 1550 on the Intellectual and Religious Capacity of the American Indians* (DeKalb, IL: Northern Illinois University Press, 1974).

33. It was first printed in the twentieth century in a Latin and Spanish edition with a fine introduction by Lewis Hanke. Fray Bartolomé de las Casas, *Del único modo de atraer a todos los pueblos a la verdadera religión* (México, D.F.: Fondo de Cultura Económica, 1942). It is reproduced in *Obras completas*, Vol. 2. There is an English version: Bartolomé de las Casas, *The Only Way*, edited by Helen Rand Parish and translated by Francis Patrick Sullivan, S.J. (New York: Paulist Press, 1992).

34. Vitoria deals will all possible pros and cons of the conquering first and converting afterwards approach in his *De Indis*, I. Sepúlveda was the most prestigious promoter of conversion *manu militari* in his book about the justice of the wars against the Native Americans. See his *Democrates secundus, sive de iustis belli causis*, edición crítica y traducción castellana por A. Coroleu Lletget, in Juan Ginés de Sepúlveda, *Obras completas*, (Pozoblanco: Excmo. Ayuntamiento de Pozoblanco, 1997), Vol. III, 38–134. Acosta, in his *De procuranda indorum salute*, defends the conjunction of military coercion and missionary persuasion, while, at the same time, trying to spell its limitations. Acosta argues that Las Casas's position does not take into account the ferocity and backwardness of the Native American "barbarians."

35. *Obras completas*, vol. 13, 370.

36. Christopher Columbus, *A New and Fresh English Translation of the Letter of Columbus Announcing the Discovery of America*, translated and edited by Samuel Eliot Morison

(Madrid: Gráficas Yagües, 1959), 14: "Their Highnesses can see that I shall give them . . . slaves, as many as they shall order, who will be idolaters."

37. Hernán Cortés, *Documentos cortesianos, 1518–1528*, ed. José Luis Martínez (México, D.F.: Universidad Nacional Autónoma de México/Fondo de Cultura Económica, 1990), 165: "In as much . . . the natives of these regions have a culture and veneration of idols, which is a great disservice to God Our Lord, and the devil blinds and deceives them . . . I propose to bring them to the knowledge of our Holy Catholic faith . . . Let us go to uproot the natives of these regions from those idolatries . . . so that they will come to the knowledge of God and of His Holy Catholic faith."

38. Christian Duverger, *La Conversion des Indiens de Nouvelle-Espagne avec le texte des "Colloques des douze" de Bernardino de Sahagún (1564)* (Paris: Éditions du Seuil, 1987).

39. Pierre Duviols, *La lutte contre les religions autochtones dans le Pérou colonial: l'extirpation de l'idolatrie entre 1532 et 1660* (París–Lima: Institut Français d'Études Andines, 1971). Robert Ricard, *The Spiritual Conquest of Mexico: An Essay on the Apostolate and the Evangelizing Methods of the Mendicant Orders in New Spain, 1523–1572*, translated by Lesley Byrd Simpson (Berkeley, CA: University of California Press, 1966).

40. *Obras completas*, vol. 13, 370.

41. *The Politics*, book I. Bruno Rech analyses the way Las Casas read Aristotle in his article "Bartolomé de las Casas und Aristoteles," *Jahrbuch für Geschichte von Staat, Wirtschaft und Gesellschaft Lateinamerikas*, Bd. 22, 1985, 39–68.

42. Lewis Ulysses Hanke, *Aristotle and the American Indians* (Bloomington, IN: Indiana University Press, 1970) and Anthony Pagden, *The Fall of Natural Man: The American Indian and the Origins of Comparative Ethnology* (Cambridge: Cambridge University Press, 1982).

43. *De Indis*, I, 233: "This whole dispute . . . has arisen again because of these barbarians in the New World, commonly called Indians, who came under the power of the Spaniards some forty years ago . . ." Nestor Capdevila points out a crucial semantic difference between Vitoria and Las Casas. While the first refers to the Native Americans as *barbaros . . . quos indos vulgo vocant* ("barbarians commonly called Indians"), Las Casas alludes to them as *Novi Orbi habitatores, quos vulgo Indos appelamus* ("inhabitants of the New World, which we commonly call Indians"). Capdevila (*Las Casas: une politique de l'humanité*, 270). For the literary context of the two quotations, see *Obras de Francisco de Vitoria: Relecciones teológicas. Edición crítica del texto latino, versión española, introducción general e introducciones con el estudio de su doctrina teológico-jurídica*, editadas por Teófilo Urdanoz, O.P. (Madrid: Biblioteca de Autores Cristianos, 1960), 642 and Las Casas, *Obras completas*, Vol. 9, 76.

44. *Democrates secundus*, 39: "If the war with which the monarchs of Spain have subjugated and attempt to subjugate under their dominion those barbarians . . . commonly called Indians . . . is just or not . . . is a very important issue."

45. *De procuranda indorum salute*, 4.

46. Regarding the ontological distinction between literary and oral peoples, see Walter D. Mignolo, *The Darker Side of the Renaissance: Literacy, Territoriality, & Colonization* (Ann Arbor, MI: University of Michigan Press, 1995).

47. See Luis N. Rivera-Pagán, "Qui est l'Indien? Humanité ou bestialité de l'indigène américain," *Alternatives Sud. L'avenir des peuples autochtones: Le sort des "premières nations"* (Centre Tricontinental, Louvain-laNeuve, Belgique), vol. vii, no. 2, 2000, 33–51.

48. *Apologética historia sumaria*. As many of Las Casas's writings, it was first published in its integrity only in the twentieth century. *Obras completas*, Vols. 6–8.

49. The Spanish theologians and missionaries debated the capability of the Native Americans to participate in the sacraments. Acosta defends their right to six of the seven sacraments but

opposes their priestly ordination, for it is wrong to consecrate to the ministry "the dregs of the people." *De procuranda indorum salute*, Vol. II, 146.
50. *Apologética historia sumaria*, c. 48; *Obras completas*, Vol. 7, 536.
51. *Obras completas*, vol. 13, 370.
52. Ibid.
53. Ibid., 371.
54. Ibid.
55. *De procuranda indorum salute*, Vol. I, 143: "For that is what the Spaniards are looking for after such a long ocean voyage, and it is through the metals [gold and silver] that commerce works, that the judges preside, and more often than not the priests preach the Gospel."
56. *Obras completas*, vol. 13, 371.
57. Ibid.

SELECT BIBLIOGRAPHY

Chasteen, John Charles (2001), *Born in Blood and Fire: A Concise History of Latin America*, New York: Norton.

de Las Casas, Bartolomé (1971), *History of the Indies*, ed. and trans. André Collard, New York: Harper & Row.

de Las Casas, Bartolomé (1988–1998), *Obras completas* (14 volumes), ed. Paulino Castañeda Delgado, Madrid: Alianza Editorial.

de Las Casas, Bartolomé (1992), *In Defense of the Indians*, trans. Stafford Poole, C.M., DeKalb, IL: Northern Illinois University Press.

Gutiérrez, Gustavo (1993), *Las Casas: In Search of the Poor of Jesus Christ*, trans. Robert R. Barr, Maryknoll, NY: Orbis Books.

Hanke, Lewis (1949), *The Spanish Struggle for Justice in the Conquest of America*, Philadelphia: University of Pennsylvania Press.

Hanke, Lewis (1970), *Aristotle and the American Indians*, Bloomington: IN: Indiana University Press.

Hanke, Lewis (1974), *All Mankind is One: A Study of the Disputation between Bartolomé de Las Casas and Juan Ginés de Sepúlveda in 1550 on the Intellectual and Religious Capacity of the American Indians*, DeKalb, IL: Northern Illinois University Press.

Mignolo, Walter D. (1995), *The Darker Side of the Renaissance: Literacy, Territoriality, & Colonization*, Ann Arbor, MI: University of Michigan Press.

Pagden, Anthony (1982), *The Fall of Natural Man: The American Indian and the Origins of Comparative Ethnology*, Cambridge: Cambridge University Press.

Ricard, Robert (1966), *The Spiritual Conquest of Mexico: An Essay on the Apostolate and the Evangelizing Methods of the Mendicant Orders in New Spain, 1523–1572*, trans. Lesley Byrd Simpson, Berkeley, CA: University of California Press.

Rivera-Pagán, Luis N. (1992), *A Violent Evangelism: The Political and Religious Conquest of the Americas*, Louisville, KY: Westminster-John Knox Press.

CHAPTER TEN

The Political and Legal Legacy of the Sixteenth-Century Reformations

JOHN WITTE, JR.

INTRODUCTION

The Protestant Reformation erupted in 1517 with Martin Luther's posting of the 95 Theses on the church door in Wittenberg, and his burning of the medieval canon law books at the city gates three years later. The Reformation soon split into four main branches—Lutheranism, Anabaptism, Anglicanism, and Calvinism—with ample regional and denominational variation within each branch. Lutheranism spread throughout the northern Holy Roman Empire, Prussia, and Scandinavia and their later colonies, consolidated by Luther's catechisms and the Augsburg Confession (1530), and by local liturgical books and Bible translations. Anabaptists fanned out in small communities throughout Western and Eastern Europe, Russia, and eventually North America, most of them devoted to the founding religious principles of the Schleitheim Confession (1527). Anglicanism was established in England by King Henry VIII and Parliament in the 1530s, and, once consolidated by the Great Bible (1539) and Book of Common Prayer (1559), spread throughout the vast British Empire in North America, Africa, the Middle East, and India. Calvinist or Reformed communities, modeled on John Calvin's Geneva and anchored by the Geneva Bible and Genevan Academy, spread into portions of the Swiss Confederation, France, the Palatinate, the Lowlands, Scotland, England, and North America. This checkerboard of Protestant communities, living tenuously alongside each other and their Catholic neighbors, was protected for a time by the Peace of Augsburg (1555), Union of Utrecht (1579), Edict of Nantes (1598), Peace of Westphalia (1648), and other peace treaties, though religious persecution and religious warfare were tragically regular events in early modern Europe.

While new confessions, creeds, and catechisms helped to inspire and integrate these Protestant movements, it was new law that usually set them in motion and consolidated them. Hundreds of local "church ordinances" (*Kirchenordnungen*), or "legal reformations" (*Rechtsreformationen*) were issued by Lutheran German cities, duchies, and principalities after 1520, and echoed in national church ordinances in Sweden, Denmark, Norway, Finland, and Iceland over the next half century. Local Anabaptist elders issued short "church orders" to establish and govern their small, self-sufficient Anabaptist communities, many of their rules drawn directly from biblical and early apostolic teachings. Parliament's Supremacy Act (1534) declared the English monarch to be "supreme head" and "defender of faith" in the free-standing Church of England (*Anglicana Ecclesiastica*). Geneva's "Reformation Edict" (1536), modeled on similar edicts passed the decade before in Zurich and other Swiss cities, was echoed in scores of European towns and provinces and later North American colonies that accepted Reformed Protestantism.

All these early Protestant legal declarations were, in part, firm rejections of the law and theology of Roman Catholicism. The Catholic Church had been the universal legal authority of the West since the twelfth century. Medieval church authorities claimed exclusive jurisdiction over doctrine, liturgy, clergy, polity, marriage, family, inheritance, trusts, education, charity, contracts, moral crimes, and more. They also claimed concurrent jurisdiction over many other legal subjects, sometimes filling gaps in local civil rules and procedures, but often rivalling local civil authorities in governing the local population. And the church had huge property holdings—more than a quarter of the land in some regions of Europe—all of which remained under exclusive church control and free from secular taxes and regulation. To exercise this power, the medieval church developed an intricate system of canon laws promulgated by the pope, bishops, and church councils, and enforced by a hierarchy of church courts and clerical officials under the final papal authority of Rome. A vast network of church officials, immune from secular legal control, presided over the medieval church's executive and administrative functions. The church registered its citizens through baptism. It taxed them through tithes. It conscripted them through crusades. It educated them in church schools. It nurtured them in cloisters, monasteries, chantries, hospitals, and guilds. It cared for them and their families even after death through perpetual obits, indulgences, and foundations. The medieval church was, in Harold Berman's apt phrase, "the first true state in the West."[1] Its canon law was the first international law in place since the fall of Rome and its Roman law in the fifth century.

Already in the fourteenth and fifteenth centuries, strong secular rulers started to rebel against the power, prerogatives, and privileges of the medieval church and put in place legal reforms. In fourteenth-century England, several statutes of "provisors" and "praemunire" limited papal control over local clerical appointments, church taxes, and local property disputes. Beginning in 1414, the Holy Roman Emperors called a series of great church councils that put limits on the operation of canon law and church courts in the Empire, and aimed to regularize papal succession and the appointments of bishops, abbots, and abbesses. In the Pragmatic Sanction of Bourges (1438) and again in the Concordat of Bologna (1516), French kings banned various papal taxes, limited appeals to Rome, required election of French bishops by local church councils called by the king, and subjected French clergy and church property to royal controls. Fifteenth-century Spanish monarchs subordinated church courts to civil courts on many legal subjects, and assumed political and legal control over the inquisition. Fifteenth-century German and Scandinavian princes and city councils passed numerous "legal reformations" that placed limits on church property and religious taxation, disciplined wayward clergy and monastics, and curtailed the jurisdiction of church courts over crime, family, inheritance, and contracts. Medieval reformers like Marsilius of Padua (c. 1280–c. 1343), John Wycliffe (c. 1330–1384), John Hus (c. 1370–1415), and several others pressed for attendant theological reforms, often at the cost of their lives.

The Protestant Reformers built on these late medieval reforms, but went beyond them. The Reformers now called for full freedom from the medieval Catholic legal regime—

freedom of the individual conscience from intrusive canon laws, freedom of political officials from clerical power and privilege, freedom of local clergy from centralized papal and conciliar rule. "Freedom of the Christian" was the rallying cry of the early Protestant Reformation. It led the Reformers to denounce canon law and clerical authority altogether and to urge radical legal and political reforms on the strength of the new Protestant theology. The church's canon law books were burned. Church courts and episcopal offices were forcibly closed. Clerical privileges and immunities were stripped. Mendicant begging was banned. Mandatory celibacy was suspended. Indulgence trafficking was condemned. Annates and tithe payments to Rome or to distant bishops were outlawed. Diplomatic and appellate ties to the pope and his curia were severed. Catholic bishops, priests, and monastics were banished from their homes, sometimes maimed or killed. The church's vast properties and institutions were seized, often with violence and bloodshed. Priceless church art, literature, statuary, and icons were looted, sometimes destroyed. And church sanctuaries, parsonages, and seminaries were confiscated and converted to Protestant control.

The Reformers defended this revolutionary purging of the church as a theological necessity. All the early Protestant leaders—Martin Luther (1483–1546), John Calvin (1509–1564), Thomas Cranmer (1489–1556), Menno Simons (1496–1561), and others—taught that salvation comes through faith in the Gospel, not by works of the Law. Each individual was to stand directly before God, to seek God's gracious forgiveness of sin and to conduct life in accordance with the Bible and Christian conscience. To the Reformers, the Catholic canon law administrated by the clergy obstructed the individual's direct relationship with God and obscured simple biblical norms for right living. All the early Reformers further taught that the church was at heart a community of saints, not a corporation of law. Its cardinal signs and callings were to preach the Word, to administer the sacraments, to catechize the young, and to care for the needy. The Catholic clergy's legal rule in Christendom obstructed the church's divine mission and usurped the state's role as God's vice-regent called to appropriate and apply divine and natural law in the earthly kingdom. Protestants did recognize that the church needed internal rules of order to govern its own polity, teaching, and discipline. Church officials and councils needed to oppose legal injustice and combat political tyranny. But, for most early Protestants, law was primarily the province of the state not of the church, of the magistrate not of the pastor.

These new Protestant teachings helped to transform Western law in the sixteenth and seventeenth centuries. The Protestant Reformation broke the international rule of the Catholic Church and the canon law, permanently splintering Western Christendom into competing nations and regions, each with its own religious and political rulers. The Protestant Reformation triggered a massive shift of power and property from the church to the state. State rulers now assumed jurisdiction over numerous subjects and persons previously governed by the church and its canon law.

These massive shifts in legal power and property from church to state in Protestant lands did not, however, signal the secularization of law or the cessation of traditional Christian influences on the law. For all of their early attacks on canon law, Protestant leaders eventually transplanted many Catholic canon law rules and procedures directly into the new Protestant state laws—some trimmed of theologically offensive provisions, others reformed in light of new teachings, but many retained largely in their medieval forms, but now administered by the state instead of the church. Moreover, in creating other new state laws, Protestant authorities drew anew on Christianized Roman law and medieval civilian jurisprudence, Christian republican political thought, and biblical and Talmudic law, all of which were staples in the new Protestant law faculties. And Protestant leaders worked hard to convert some of their own distinct new theological teachings, especially concerning family, charity, education, and crime, into new legal forms. What emerged from the Protestant Reformation were impressive new legal syntheses that skillfully blended classical and biblical, Catholic and Protestant, civilian and canonical teachings.

LUTHERANISM

The Lutheran Reformation of Germany and Scandinavia territorialized the Christian faith, and gave to the local Christian magistrate ample new political power over civil and spiritual affairs. Luther replaced medieval teachings with a new two kingdoms theory. The "invisible" church of the heavenly kingdom, he argued, was a perfect community of saints, where all stood equal in dignity before God, all enjoyed perfect Christian liberty, and all governed their affairs in accordance with the Gospel. The "visible" church of this earthly kingdom, however, embraced saints and sinners alike. Its members still stood directly before God and still enjoyed liberty of conscience, including the liberty to leave the visible church itself. But, unlike the invisible church, the visible church needed both the Gospel and human law to govern its members' relationships with God and with fellow believers. The clergy must administer the Gospel. The magistrate must administer the law.

Luther regarded the magistrate as God's vice-regent in the earthly kingdom, called to elaborate and enforce God's Word and will and to reflect God's justice and judgment for earthly citizens. "Law and earthly government are a great gift of God to mankind," Luther wrote. "Earthly authority is an image, shadow, and figure of the dominion of Christ," but magistrates also exercise God's judgment and wrath against human sin. "Princes and magistrates are the bows and arrows of God," equipped to hunt down God's enemies near and far, using military power and criminal punishment. The hand of the Christian magistrate, judge, or soldier "that wields the sword and slays is not man's hand, but God's."[2]

Luther further regarded the magistrate as the "father of the community" (*paterpoliticus*). He was called to care for his political subjects as if they were his children, and his political subjects were to "honor" and "obey" him as if he were their parent. Like a loving father, the magistrate was to keep the peace and to protect his subjects from threats or violations to their persons, properties, and reputations. He was to deter his subjects from abusing themselves through drunkenness, wastrel living, prostitution, gambling, and other vices. He was to nurture and sustain his subjects through the community chest, the public almshouse, and the state-run hospital. He was to educate them through the public school, library, and lectern. He was to see to their spiritual needs by supporting the ministry of the locally established church, and encouraging their attendance and participation through the laws of Sabbath observance, tithing, and holy days. He was to see to their material needs by reforming inheritance and property laws to ensure more even distribution of the parents' property among all children. He was to set a moral example of virtue, piety, love, and charity in his own home and private life for his faithful subjects to emulate and to respect.

Luther and his colleagues called on Christian magistrates to build their positive laws on the basis of the Ten Commandments, which they regarded as a universal statement of natural law. "The Decalogue is not the law of Moses," Luther wrote, "but the Decalogue of the whole world, inscribed and engraved in the minds of all men from the foundation of the world."³ The Christian magistrate is "a voice of the Ten Commandments" within the earthly kingdom, wrote Philip Melanchthon (1509–1560), a Wittenberg theologian and jurist with wide influence in Germany and Scandinavia. "When you think about *Obrigkeit*, about princes or lords, picture in your mind a man holding in one hand the tables of the Ten Commandments and holding in the other a sword."⁴

Melanchthon took this image directly into his theory of political authority and positive law, which he organized using the two tables of the Decalogue. The First Table of the Decalogue, he wrote, undergirded the state's positive laws that govern spiritual morality, the relationship between persons and God. The Second Table undergirded the state's positive laws that govern civil morality, the relationships between persons. As custodians of the First Table of the Decalogue, Melanchthon wrote, the magistrate must not only pass laws against idolatry, blasphemy, and violations of the Sabbath—offenses that the First Table prohibits on its face. He must also "establish pure doctrine" and right liturgy, "prohibit all wrong doctrine," "punish the obstinate," and root out the heathen and the heterodox.⁵ Melanchthon came to this position reluctantly in the 1530s and 1540s, knowing he was departing from Luther's early call for universal religious freedom. But Melanchthon lamented the perennial outbreaks of violent antinomianism, spiritual radicalism, "and "diabolical rages" by those who took too literally Luther's teaching of free grace. To allow such blasphemy and chaos to continue without firm rejoinder, Melanchthon believed, was ultimately to betray God and to belie the essence of the political office. Magistrates must "maintain external discipline according to *all* the commandments" and thus must "prohibit, abolish, and punish these depravities" and "compel them to accept the Holy Gospel."⁶

This was the theoretical basis for the welter of new religious establishment laws set out in the elaborate "church ordinances" promulgated in Lutheran and other Protestant lands in the sixteenth and seventeenth centuries. These church ordinances both reflected and directed the resystematization of dogma; truncation of the sacraments; reforms of liturgy, devotional life, and the religious calendar; vernacularization of the Bible, liturgy, and sermon; expansion of catechesis and religious instruction in schools and universities; revamping of corporate worship, congregational music, religious symbolism, church art and architecture; radical reforms of ecclesiastical discipline and local church administration; new practices of tithing, baptism, confirmation, weddings, burial; diaconal care, sanctuary, and much more. All these aspects of church and spiritual life had been governed in detail by the medieval church's canon laws and sacramental rules. They were now subject to the Protestant state's religious establishment laws. Particularly after the Peace of Augsburg (1555) and the Peace of Westphalia (1648) confirmed the constitutional principle that each civil ruler was free to establish the religion of his own local polity (*cuius regio eius religio*), these religious establishment laws became increasingly detailed, ornate, and routinized. Vestiges of these laws remain in place in Lutheran lands still today, though strong new policies of religious disestablishment are now afoot.

While the First Table of the Decalogue supported state positive laws governing relations between God and persons, the Second Table supported positive laws governing the relations between persons. Melanchthon and Lutheran jurists like Johan Oldendorp (c. 1486–1567) and Nicolaus Hemming (1513–1600) set out a whole series of positive laws under each Commandment of the Second Table. On the basis of the Commandment to "Honor thy father and mother," they argued, magistrates were obligated to prohibit and punish disobedience, disrespect, or disdain of authorities such as parents, political rulers, teachers, employers, masters, and others. They were also to build the positive laws of authority—constitutional law, administrative law, master–servant laws, and more. The Commandment, "Thou shalt not kill" undergirded laws against unlawful killing, violence, assault, battery, wrath, hatred, mercilessness, and other offenses against the bodies of one's neighbors. "Thou shalt not commit adultery" and "Thou shalt not covet thy neighbor's wife or maidservant" were the foundations of laws against sex crimes—adultery, fornication, incontinence, prostitution, pornography, obscenity, and similar offenses as well as positive laws of marital formation, maintenance and dissolution, child care, custody, and control, parental rights, roles, and responsibilities, and more. The Commandment "Thou shalt not steal" supported positive laws against theft, burglary, embezzlement, and similar offenses against another's property, as well as waste or noxious use or sumptuous use of one's own property. It also supported positive laws of real and personal property, its acquisition, use, maintenance, encumbrance, sale, alienation, and more. On the basis of the Commandment "Thou shalt not bear false witness," magistrates were to punish all forms of perjury, dishonesty, fraud, defamation, and other violations of a person's reputation or status in the community. And they were to build the positive laws of promises and contracts, of keeping one's word to one's neighbor, as well as the laws of procedure, evidence, and testimony in court proceedings. Finally, on the basis of the Commandment "Thou shalt not covet," magistrates were to punish all attempts to perform offensive acts against another's person, property, reputation, or relationships, and to establish the basic rules protecting the privacy of one's household from the covetous privations of neighbors.

Many of these aspects of social intercourse had been governed by the Catholic Church's canon law and organized in part by the church's seven sacraments. The sacrament of marriage, for example, supported the positive law of sex, marriage, and family life. The sacrament of penance supported the canon law of crimes against the persons, properties, and reputations of others. The sacraments of baptism and confirmation undergirded the constitutional law of natural rights and duties of Christian believers. The sacrament of holy orders supported the law of the clergy. The sacrament of extreme unction supported the positive laws of burial, inheritance, foundations, and trusts. Lutheran jurists used the Ten Commandments, instead of the seven sacraments, to organize the various systems of positive law. And they looked to the state, instead of the church, to promulgate and enforce these positive laws on the basis of the Ten Commandments and the biblical and extra-biblical sources of natural law and morality. This became a standard way of systematizing and teaching in many early modern Protestant state laws, eventually on both sides of the Atlantic.

ANABAPTISM

Early modern Anabaptists communalized the faith, by expounding a two-kingdoms theory that more fully separated the redeemed realm of religion and the church from the fallen realm of politics and the state. Emerging as a new form of Protestantism in the early 1520s, Anabaptists were scattered into various groups of Amish, Brethren, Hutterites, Mennonites, Baptists, and others. Some of the early splinter groups, like the followers of Thomas Müntzer (1489–1525) and Caspar Schweckenfeld (d. 1561), were politically radical or utopian spiritualists. Others, like the Anabaptist sect in Münster under John of Leiden (d. 1536), practiced polygamy for a short time, which they enforced ruthlessly against detractors. But most Anabaptist communities by the mid-sixteenth century were quiet Christian separatists, monogamists, and pacifists, taking their lead from such theologians as Menno Simons, Pilgrim Marpeck (d. 1556), Dirk Philips (1504–1568), and Peter Riedeman (1506–1556) who urged their followers to return to the simple teachings of the New Testament and apostolic church.

Anabaptist communities ascetically withdrew from civil and political life into small, self-sufficient, intensely democratic communities. These communities were governed internally by biblical principles of discipleship, simplicity, charity, and non-resistance. They set their own internal standards of worship, liturgy, diet, discipline, dress, and education. They handled their own internal affairs of property, contracts, commerce, marriage, and inheritance—so far as possible by appeal to biblical laws and practices, not those of the state. And they enforced these internal religious laws not by coercion, but by persuasion, and not for the sake of retribution, but for the redemption of the sinner and restoration of that person to community. Recalcitrant sinners and community members who grew violent, destructive, or persistently betrayed the community's ideals were shunned and if necessary banned from the community. Moreover, when Anabaptist communities grew too large or too internally divided, they deliberately colonized themselves, eventually spreading Anabaptists from Russia to Ireland to the furthest frontiers of North America.

The state and its law, most Anabaptists believed, was part of the fallen world, which was to be avoided so far as possible in accordance with biblical injunctions that Christians should not be "of the world" or "conformed" to it. Once the perfect creation of God, the world was now a fallen, sinful regime that lay beyond "the perfection of Christ" and beyond the daily concern of the Christian believer. God had built a "wall of separation" (*paries maceriae*) between the redeemed church and the fallen world, Menno Simons wrote, quoting Ephesians 2:14.[7] God had allowed the world to survive by ordaining magistrates and their positive laws who were empowered to use coercion and violence to maintain a modicum of order and peace. Christians should obey the laws of political authorities, so far as the Bible commanded—paying their taxes, registering their properties, avoiding theft and homicide, keeping their promises, and testifying truthfully. But Christians should avoid active participation in and unnecessary interaction with the world and the state—avoiding litigation, oath-swearing, state education, banking, large-scale commerce, trade fairs, public festivals, drinking houses, theaters, games, political office, policing, or military service. Most early modern Anabaptists were pacifists, preferring derision, exile, or death to active participation in war or violence. This aversion to common political and civic activities often earned Anabaptists scorn, reprisal, and repression by Catholics and Protestants alike—violent martyrdom in many instances.

While unpopular in its genesis, Anabaptism ultimately proved to be a vital source for Western legal arguments for the separation of church and state and for the protection of the civil and religious liberties of a plurality of all peaceable faiths. Equally important for later legal reforms was the Anabaptist doctrine of adult rather than infant baptism. This doctrine gave new emphasis to religious voluntarism as opposed to traditional theories of birthright or predestined faith, let alone traditional practices of coercing believers to accept the established religious faith or penalizing the wrong religious choices they made. In Anabaptist theology, each adult was called to make a free conscientious choice to accept the faith—metaphorically, to scale the wall of separation between the fallen world and the realm of religion to come within the perfect realm of Christ. And it was up to God, not to the state or to any other authority, to decide which forms of religions should flourish, and which should fade. In the seventeenth and eighteenth centuries, various Free

Church followers, both in Europe and North America, converted this cardinal image into a powerful platform of freedom of conscience and free exercise of religion. Particularly in America, diverse leaders like Roger Williams (c. 1604–1684), William Penn (1644–1718), Isaac Backus (1724–1806), and John Leland (1754–1841) grounded their religious freedom advocacy in these earlier Anabaptist arguments, and their views helped to shape new American constitutional laws that disestablished religion and protected freedom of conscience and free exercise of religion for all.

ANGLICANISM

Whereas Anabaptism communalized the Protestant faith, and Lutheranism territorialized it, Anglicanism nationalized the faith under the final spiritual and political rule of the Christian monarch. King Henry VIII resolved his bitter dispute with the papacy over dissolution of his marriage with Catherine of Aragon from 1527 to 1533 by cutting all legal and political ties with Rome, and declaring the Catholic Church in England to be the separate Anglican Church of England. Henry and early Anglican Reformers like Thomas Cranmer and Thomas Cromwell (1485–1540) pushed through Parliament a series of sweeping new laws that rapidly established the new Anglican order in top-down fashion, and with brutal executions of scores of dissenters and exile for thousands of others. The Supremacy Act (1534) declared the monarch to be the "Supreme Head" of the Church and Commonwealth of England. The Act for the Submission of Clergy and Restraint of Appeals (1534) gave the monarch final authority to appoint, discipline, and dismiss all clergy, to call church councils, to reform the church's doctrine, liturgy, and canon law, and to register church properties and personnel. The Act for First Fruits and Tenths (1534) required church tithes and taxes to be paid to the crown. The Act Dissolving the Greater Monasteries (1539) and later acts led to the massive seizure and dissolution of monasteries, cloisters, chapels, chantries, guilds, schools, colleges, hospitals, fraternities, almshouses, and other properties held by the church, cutting to the heart of the pre-Reformation church-based systems of welfare and education. Within a decade and a half of the break with Rome, the King and his retinue had replaced the pope and his curia as supreme rulers of the Church of England and its growing colonial empire.

Having seized the church's institutions and properties, the Anglican Reformers also moved rapidly to establish by law the new Anglican faith and worship, but this proved more difficult. Thomas Cranmer did issue, with royal approval, the Great Bible in 1539, an English translation based on the earlier masterwork of William Tyndale (1494–1536) and Miles Coverdale (1488–1569). This text was now to be used for Anglican worship and devotional life. Other Bible translations were censored, and would remain so until the King James Version (1611) became the authorized English Bible. Parliamentary Acts of Uniformity in 1549 and 1552 further mandated the use of Cranmer's Book of Common Prayer in Anglican worship, with escalating penalties for clergy and laity who deviated from its prayers, liturgy, and sacramental rites. The king also approved the Forty-Two Articles of the Faith, a new creed that, while consonant with medieval Catholic tradition on many matters, included a number of familiar Lutheran and Calvinist teachings about God, sin, salvation, and the sacraments and rejected Anabaptist teachings about adult baptism, biblical asceticism, and separation of church and state.

A more sweeping Reformation of Ecclesiastical Law, however, akin to the many legal reforms passed by Continental Protestants, floundered despite repeated efforts to enact it in 1552, 1559, and 1571. This proposed Reformation aimed to retain church courts in

England and to maintain their traditional jurisdiction over marriage, tithes, inheritance, defamation, and benefices. But the document also envisioned major new parliamentary reforms of each of these laws and stronger review of church courts by royal courts. It also proposed sweeping reforms of clerical and lay marriage, rights to fault-based divorce and remarriage, and annual conferences and regular democratic meetings between bishops, priests, and laity. None of these changes came to pass in the Reformation era. The structure of the church courts, and of the clerical hierarchy altogether, remained largely unchanged, though appeals from church court judgments now went not to the curia in Rome but to a new Court of Delegates in England, staffed by civilians and canonists. The law administered by these Anglican church courts remained largely the canon law of the medieval Catholic church, with only minor changes gradually introduced by Parliament and Convocation over the next three centuries.

This Anglican adherence to legal and religious tradition reflected not only inertia, but also ample resistance of the English clergy and laity to the crown's heavy-handed top-down reformation of church and state. Moreover, Queen Mary (r. 1553–1558) sought to return England forcibly to full communion with Rome. In twin acts of 1553 and 1555, Mary aimed to repeal all the Reformation laws and practices of her father Henry VIII and half-brother Edward VI, to repair England's relations with the papacy, and to restore to the Catholic Church and clergy their traditional power, property, and prerogatives. When church and state officials resisted these changes, too, more than 250 Protestant heretics were executed, and thousands more, called the Marian Exiles, fled to the Continent, leaving the English church, state, and society in turmoil.

During Queen Elizabeth's long reign from 1558 to 1603, England gradually settled on a via media between Roman Catholicism and Continental Protestantism, and this settlement, too, was legally prescribed and judicially enforced. Parliament issued an Act of Uniformity (1559) that reestablished clearly the Anglican doctrine, liturgy, and creed of the church and commonwealth. Communicant status in the Anglican Church was now made a condition for citizenship status in the English Commonwealth, for holding high political and religious office, acquiring professional licenses and charters, and for exercising many other basic rights. Parliamentary acts prohibited papal bulls and "traitorous" worship, publications, or teaching by Catholics and Protestant "sectaries," and these laws were enforced firmly in Star Chamber, High Commission, and other royal courts in Elizabeth's reign and even more firmly by her Stuart successors, Kings James I and Charles I. Elizabeth's Parliament further renewed the Act of Supremacy (1559), restoring to the crown final authority over the Anglican Church's clergy, polity, and property. The English church courts retained their jurisdiction, though new canons introduced piecemeal legal changes in 1571, 1575, 1585, 1597, and 1604. Parliament passed the Poor Relief Act (1598) and Charitable Uses Act (1601) that sought to restore some of the robust pre-Reformation welfare and educational system of England, now largely through Anglican parishes and crown-chartered private enterprises.

This Elizabethan settlement of church and state, and of law and religion, attracted new political and legal theories from such Anglican divines as John Jewel (1522–1571), Edmund Grindal (1519–1583), and Richard Bancroft (1544–1610). The most important defense came in the massive *Laws of Ecclesiastical Polity* by Richard Hooker (1553–1600), who defended the Anglican establishment against more radical Calvinist views of congregational and presbyterian forms of democratic church government. "The powers that be are ordained by God," Hooker quoted from Scripture, and reflect God's authority as supreme monarch over the entire universe, which he rules by his eternal law. The

Christian monarch on earth embodies God's monarchical government in heaven; indeed the monarch is a "god on earth" as Psalm 82:6 put it. And the monarch embraces God's law for all of religious and civil life.[8] As God's vice-regent, the monarch is called to promulgate positive laws to instruct humans on how to live together and to live well in Christian communion. While every individual has the rational capacity to ascertain the natural law for their private lives, Hooker wrote drawing on Thomas Aquinas (1225–1274), the monarch's positive laws of church and state must guide and govern their communal spiritual and temporal lives in accordance with the eternal laws of Christ. While different nations have formed their own voluntary compacts with God and their political rulers, England and its great common law tradition had formed a unique "covenant," with God's blessing, whereby the people had consented to this Christian monarchical reign of church, state, and society. Hooker's defense of Christian monarchy in a unitary church and commonwealth became more expansive in the theories of "the divine right of kings" and absolute monarchy offered by King James I, Sir Robert Filmer (1588–1653), and others in the seventeenth century—theories which John Locke (1632–1704) would later counter directly with his proto-democratic arguments in his *Two Treatises on Government* (1689).

CALVINISM

Calvinists charted a course between Lutherans and Anglicans who subordinated the church to the state, and Anabaptists who withdrew the church from the state and society. Like Anabaptists, Calvinists insisted on a basic separation of the offices and operations of church and state, leaving the church to govern its own doctrine and liturgy, polity and property, without interference from the state. Calvin set the foundation for this church-state division in the Ecclesiastical Ordinances (1541/1561) of Geneva, which were echoed in many later Calvinist cities. Like Lutherans, in turn, Calvinists insisted that each local polity be an overtly Christian commonwealth that adhered to the general principles of natural law and translated them into detailed new positive laws of religious worship, Sabbath observance, public morality, marriage and family, crime and tort, contract and business, charity and education. Calvin drafted many such laws for Geneva during his tenure from 1541 to 1564, drawing rules variously from the Bible and Talmud, classical Roman law and medieval canon law, and local customs and city ordinances. All these piecemeal laws were eventually integrated into the Civil Edict of Geneva (1568) drafted by Calvinist jurist Germain Colladon (1508–1594). Many other Calvinist cities, provinces, and colonies issued their own local Christian laws, too, often using Geneva as their model and source.

Unlike Lutherans, Anglicans, and Anabaptists, however, Calvinists stressed that both church and state officials were to play complementary roles in the creation of the local Christian commonwealth and in the cultivation of the Christian citizen. Calvinists emphasized more fully than other Protestants the educational use of the natural and positive law. Lutherans stressed the "civil" and "theological" uses of the law: the need for law to deter sinners from their sinful excesses and to drive them to repentance. Calvinists emphasized the educational use of the law as well: the need to teach persons both the letter and the spirit of the law, both the civic morality common to all persons and the spiritual morality that becomes the Christian life. It was the church's responsibility to teach aspirational spiritual norms, Calvinists argued. It was the state's responsibility to enforce mandatory civil norms. This division of responsibility was reflected in Geneva in the procedural divisions between the church consistory and the city council. For many nonviolent legal issues, the consistory was the court of first instance; it would call parties to their higher spiritual duties, backing their recommendations with (threats of) spiritual discipline. If such spiritual counsel failed, the parties were referred to the city council to compel them, using civil and criminal sanctions, to honor at least their basic civil duties.

In sixteenth-century Geneva and other Swiss cities, the consistory was an elected body of civil and religious officials, with original jurisdiction over cases of marriage and family life, charity and social welfare, worship and public morality. Among most later Calvinists, the Genevan-style consistory was transformed into the body of pastors, elders, deacons, and teachers that governed each local church congregation, but often played a less structured political and legal role in the broader Christian commonwealth. Yet local clergy still had a strong role in advising magistrates on the positive law of the local community, and local churches and their consistories also generally enjoyed autonomy in administering their own doctrine, liturgy, charity, polity, and property and in administering ecclesiastical discipline over their members without interference from the state courts.

In addition to reconstructing the law of church–state relations, Calvinists after 1560 also laid some of the foundations for Western theories of democracy and human rights, as they faced massive repression and genocide that were killing their coreligionists by the many thousands. One method, developed by Calvinist writers like Christopher Goodman (c. 1530–1603), Theodore Beza (1519–1605), and Johannes Althusius (1557–1638), was to ground fundamental rights in the duties of the Decalogue and other biblical moral teachings. Echoing earlier Protestants, these Calvinist writers argued that the two tables of the Decalogue prescribe duties of love owed to God and to neighbors respectively. But they now translated the person's First Table duties toward God as natural rights that others could not obstruct—the right to religious exercise: the right to honor God and God's name, the right to rest and worship on one's Sabbath, the right to be free from false gods and false oaths. They cast a person's Second Table duties towards a neighbor as the neighbor's right to have those duties discharged. One person's duties not to kill, to commit adultery, to steal, or to bear false witness thus gives rise to another person's rights to life, property, fidelity, and reputation. Goodman called all these "unalienable rights" rooted in the natural law of God. Later Calvinists like Beza, John Knox (c. 1514–1572), and Philippe Duplessis-Mornay (1549–1623) argued further that the persistent and pervasive breach of these "unalienable rights" by a tyrant triggered a further "fundamental right" to resistance, rebellion, revolution, even regicide.[9]

Another method, developed especially by Dutch and English Calvinists, was to draw out the legal and political implications of the signature Reformation teaching, coined by Luther, that a person is at once sinner and saint (*simul justus et peccatur*). On the one hand, they argued, every person is created in the image of God and justified by faith in God. Every person is called to a distinct vocation, which stands equal in dignity and sanctity to all others. Every person is a prophet, priest and king, and responsible to exhort, to minister, and to rule in the community. Every person thus stands equal before God and before his or her neighbor. Every person is vested with a natural liberty to live, to believe, to love and serve God and neighbor. Every person is entitled to the vernacular Scripture, to education, to work in a vocation. On the other hand, Protestants argued, every person is sinful and prone to evil and egoism. Every person needs the restraint of the law to deter him from evil, and to drive him to repentance. Every person needs the association of others to exhort, minister, and rule her with law and with love. Every person, therefore, is inherently a communal creature. Every person belongs to a family, a church, a political community.

By the later sixteenth century, Calvinists recast these theological doctrines into protodemocratic norms and forms. Protestant doctrines of the person and society were cast into democratic social forms. Since all persons stand equal before God, they must stand equal before God's political agents in the state. Since God has vested all persons with natural liberties of life and belief, the state must ensure them of similar civil liberties. Since God has called all persons to be prophets, priests, and kings, the state must protect their constitutional freedoms to speak, to preach, and to rule in the community. Since God has created persons as social creatures, the state must promote and protect a plurality of social institutions, particularly the church and the family.

Protestant doctrines of sin, in turn, were cast into democratic political forms. The political office must be protected against the sinfulness of the political official. Political power must be distributed among self-checking executive, legislative, and judicial branches. Officials must be elected to limited terms of office. Laws must be clearly codified, and discretion closely guarded. Officials must hold regular meetings to give account of themselves and to hear the people's petitions and grievances. If officials abuse their office, they must be disobeyed. If they persist in their abuse, they must be removed, even if by revolutionary force and regicide.

These Protestant teachings were among the driving forces behind the revolts of the French Huguenots, Dutch Pietists, Scottish Presbyterians, and English Puritans, against their monarchical oppressors in the later sixteenth and seventeenth centuries. They were also critical weapons in the eventual arsenal of the revolutionaries in eighteenth-century America and France. It is no small anecdote that, by 1650, almost every right listed 150 years later in the United States Bill of Rights (1791) and the French Declaration of the Rights of the Rights of Man and Citizen (1789) had already been defined, defended, and died for by Calvinists on both sides of the Atlantic.

NOTES

1. Quoted by Harold J. Berman, *Law and Revolution* (Cambridge: Harvard University Press, 1983), 276.
2. Quoted by John Witte, Jr., *Law and Protestantism: The Legal Teachings of the Lutheran Reformation* (Cambridge: Cambridge University Press, 2002), 87–117.
3. WA 39/1:478.
4. G. Bretschneider, ed., *Corpus Reformatorum* (Brunswick: H. Böhlau, 1864), 22: 615.
5. Ibid., 22: 617–618.
6. Philip Melanchthon, *Melanchthon on Christian Doctrine: Loci Communes 1555*, trans. and ed. Clyde L. Manschrek (Oxford: Oxford University Press, 1965), 324–336.
7. Quoted by Walter Klaassen, *Anabaptism in Outline* (Scottdale, PA: Herald Press, 1981), 245–257.
8. Richard Hooker, *The Laws of Ecclesiastical Polity*, ed. W. Speed Hill (Cambridge, MA: Harvard University Press, 1977), I.6–11; VIII.2–4.
9. Quoted by John Witte, Jr., *The Reformation of Rights: Law, Religion, and Human Rights in Early Modern Calvinism* (Cambridge: Cambridge University Press, 2007), 117–122, 137–138.

SELECT BIBLIOGRAPHY

Benedict, Philip (2002), *Christ's Church Purely Reformed: A Social History of Calvinism*, New Haven, CT: Yale University Press.
Berman, Harold J. (2003), *Law and Revolution II: The Impact of the Protestant Reformations on the Western Legal Tradition*, Cambridge, MA: Harvard University Press.
Ehler, Sidney Z. and John B. Morrall, eds. (1954), *Church and State through the Centuries: A Collection of Historic Documents with Commentaries*, London: Burns & Oates.
Haigh, Christopher (1993), *English Reformations: Religion, Society, and Politics Under the Tudors*, Oxford: Clarendon Press.
Heckel, Martin (2015), *Martin Luthers Reformation und das Recht*, Tübingen: Mohr Siebeck.
Klaassen, Walter (1981), *Anabaptism in Outline: Selected Primary Sources*, Scottdale, PA: Herald Press.
LeCler, Joseph (1960), *Toleration and the Reformation*, 4 vols., trans. T.L. Westow, New York: Association Press.
MacCulloch, Diarmaid (2016), *All Things Made New: The Reformation and its Legacy*, Oxford: Oxford University Press.
Mäkinen, Virpi, ed. (2006), *Lutheran Reformation and the Law*, Leiden: Brill.
Sichelschmidt, Karla (1995), *Recht aus christlicher Liebe oder obrigkeitlicher Gesetzesbefehl? Juristische Untersuchungen zu den evangelischen Kirchenordnungen des 16. Jahrhunderts*, Tübingen: J.C.B. Mohr.
Williams, George Huntston (2000), *The Radical Reformation*, 3rd rev. ed., Kirksville, MO: Truman State University Press.
Witte, John, Jr. (2002), *Law and Protestantism: The Legal Teachings of the Lutheran Reformation*, Cambridge: Cambridge University Press.
Witte, John, Jr. (2007), *The Reformation of Rights: Law, Religion, and Human Rights in Early Modern Calvinism*, Cambridge: Cambridge University Press.

PART THREE

An Appraisal of Contemporary Political Theologies

CHAPTER ELEVEN

Theology After the Death of God

BRIAN D. ROBINETTE

INTRODUCTION

The "death of God" has come to mean many things, and many things at once: the loss of transcendence, the weakening of the sacred, the upending of moral absolutes, the collapse of Christendom, the exhaustion of metaphysics, and the failure of theodicy in the midst of unspeakable evil. All of these meanings, and many more besides, can be stated more positively: the affirmation of immanence ("this-worldliness"), the ascendancy of the secular, the freedom to construct human values, the endless play of interpretation, and the honesty to face historical horrors without the false refuge of theodicies.

In its most radical formulation, perhaps the most logically consistent, the "death of God" implies the "death of humanity," in the sense that denying any underlying substance to "God" inescapably means the absence of any underlying essence to "humanity." Or so declared Friedrich Nietzsche, the philosopher most commonly associated with the announcement "God is dead." This interpretation immediately raises the question of nihilism, for to truly think the death of God all the way down is to recognize that even those seemingly stable foundations of human values we take for granted, and which we assume are "natural" or "self-evident," are in fact interpretations, historical accretions, and leftovers of a time when God was still thought credible. To recognize the foundationless character of inherited values, including those we deem scientific, is the only consistent atheism, and this requires us to face with courage, but also for Nietzsche exhilaration and unprecedented joy, our true situation.

Granted that there is no single meaning to the "death of God"—and this essay shall explore several of its meanings—in all cases its theological significance bears political significance. For some this political significance is explicit, while for others it is implicit. Likewise, for some this political significance yields proposals for how we ought to construe the polis, while for others such proposals are inchoate or rendered along negative lines, i.e., by unsettling all prevailing constructions of the polis, especially those tending towards sovereignty, heteronomy, or violent exclusion. Even this latter, more negative strategy presumes some qualitative distinction between kinds of political goods, which inevitably raises the question, "On what basis?" Is there or can there be any normative basis for determining relatively adequate constructions of the polis, of values, and how would we know it or possibly agree upon it? Such questions, and others like them, reflect the open wound of any thinking about the "death of God," and it is here where every theology *after* the death of God must begin.

FRIEDRICH NIETZSCHE AND THE DEATH OF GOD

In the second edition of *The Gay Science* (1887), Friedrich Nietzsche writes: "The greatest recent event—that 'God is dead'; that the belief in the Christian God has ceased to be believable—is already starting to cast its first shadow over Europe." This event has been suspected among those with strong enough vision, but on the whole "the event itself is much too great, too distant, too far from the comprehension of the many even for the tidings of it to be thought of as having *arrived* yet . . . and what must collapse now that this belief has been undermined—all that was built upon it, leaned on it, grew into it; for example, our whole European morality."[1]

Note here that while God is declared dead—a declaration memorably formulated by "the madman" in the first edition of *The Gay Science* ("'Whither is God' he cried. 'I shall tell you. *We have killed him*—you and I. All of us are his murderers'."[2])—God survives in European values. Even though the transcendent reality to which "God" refers is increasingly regarded as empty of substance, the cultural infrastructure by which its referential function was long propped up remains mostly intact, showing signs only here and there of cracking. The real event implied in the death of God is not the momentary recognition that what used to be regarded as transcendent is no longer present, or never having objective reality in the first place. Rather, the real event is the dawning awareness that everything grounded by the belief in God, including humanistic values and the ideology of scientific progress, is without an ultimate foundation and falling apart; that what we blithely take as facts and norms are a dense clustering of interpretations; that all absolutes amount to the clutching of air. This is not a passive recognition but one that requires courage, for the philosopher of God's death endeavors to diagnose and ferret out the survival of God in its myriad forms.

Nietzsche is hardly the first self-avowed atheist, and in fact the young Nietzsche took considerable inspiration from the likes of Ludwig Feuerbach, whose *The Essence of Christianity* (1841) he studied closely as a student of theology. The central thrust of Feuerbach's account of religion is that human beings transpose their subjective humanity into objective form, projecting onto an empty screen their own idealized humanity in the form of God or gods. "Religion is the dream of the human mind," writes Feuerbach, and to wake up from this dream is to reabsorb our projected humanity back into ourselves—to reduce theology to anthropology while exalting anthropology to theology.[3] Such human projection is ultimately alienating, for it reifies attributes of ourselves and renders us self-denigratingly dependent upon their displaced form. "God is the highest subjectivity of man abstracted from himself; hence man can do nothing of himself, all goodness comes from God."[4] Held out "above" in the form of a supreme God, such abstraction weakens human self-understanding and capacity.

Feuerbach's projection theory influenced such figures as Marx, Engels, Wagner, and Freud (the latter declaring Feuerbach the philosopher he admired the most), but Nietzsche turns out to be considerably less sanguine than Feuerbach about its further implications. Indeed, whereas Feuerbach heralds a number of the signature virtues of Christianity as worthy of recalibration in humanistic form, Nietzsche, although not entirely a despiser of Christianity—he expresses admiration for Jesus, if not many of his followers—was relentlessly critical of what he perceived as the largely self-denigrating shape of its moral vision. The doctrine of sacrificial atonement was particularly loathsome to Nietzsche for the way it casts God as "a being who is powerful, supremely powerful and yet enjoys revenge: his power is so great that no harm whatsoever can be done unto him except in matters of honour. Every sin is an injury of respect . . . Feeling spiritually crushed, degraded, wallowing in the dust—that is the first and last condition of his grace; in sum, restoration of his divine honour!"[5] The Christian suspicion of the body and the basic instincts of life is deeply woven into this sickly soteriological picture, Nietzsche insists, in that it despises as "impurity" and "sin" the vital forces contributing to human vigor.

Most scathing of all is Nietzsche's attack on the Judeo-Christian tradition's "transvaluation of values" leading to cultural decadence. By this Nietzsche means the idealization of weakness, humility, and pity. The "slave morality" originally fostered by the Jewish tradition is a form of revenge against the surrounding, dominant culture. Rooted in *ressentiment* towards the pagan virtues of vitality, nobility, and excellence, or what Nietzsche calls the virtues of a "master morality," the Hebrew scriptures record the process of subverting the dominant order by inventing the supreme moral authority of the victim. The value judgments of the master morality "presuppose a powerful physicality, a rich, burgeoning, even overflowing health, as well as all those things which help to preserve it—war, adventure, hunting, dancing, competitive games, and everything which involves strong, free, high-spirited activity."[6] Within this ethos there is only "good and bad," not "good versus evil." The "pathos of nobility and distance, the enduring, dominating, and fundamental overall feeling of a higher ruling kind in relation to a lower kind, to a 'below'— *that* is the origin of the opposition between 'good' and 'bad'." But those dominated by their masters undertake an "imaginary revenge" by transposing this opposition into "good" versus "evil," and thus endow their status as victims with supreme value.

> It has been the Jews who have, with terrifying consistency, dared to undertake the reversal of the aristocratic value equation (good = noble = powerful = beautiful = happy = blessed). . . . It is they who have declared: 'The miserable alone are the good; the poor, the powerless, and low alone are the good. The suffering, the deprived, the sick, the ugly are the only pious ones, the only blessed, for them alone is there salvation. You, on the other hand, the noble and powerful, you are for all eternity the evil, the cruel, the lascivious, the insatiable, the godless ones. You will be without salvation, accursed and damned to all eternity!' There is no doubt as to *who* inherited this Jewish transvaluation.[7]

Of course, it is Christians who have inherited this transvaluation of values and who have proliferated it throughout the world. Originally underwritten by theistic convictions, such values deeply shaped European culture, so much so that even when the God who revealed them is no longer believable, the values remain, but now under a humanistic guise. One of the chief ironies of secular humanism, claims Nietzsche, is that the God it claims to deny turns up again in the values it declares to be natural or self-evident. As Terry Eagleton puts it, "Modern secular societies . . . have effectively disposed of God but find it morally and politically convenient—even imperative—to behave as though they have not. They do not actually believe in him, but it is still necessary for them to imagine that they do."[8]

To fully think through the death of God is to flush out the survival of God in its covert forms and, more bracingly, to accept that what we take as our highest values are not only interpretations but reflective of the desire for power and advantage in the agonistic flux of life. Nietzsche therefore leaves us with a picture of "life itself as *essentially* appropriation, injury, overpowering of what is alien and weaker; suppression, hardness, imposition of one's own forms, incorporation and, at the least and mildest, exploitation," or what he expounds throughout his works as the "will to power."[9]

RADICAL THEOLOGY

We shall return to Nietzsche later regarding the question of ontological violence, and whether the "will to power" betrays a metaphysical commitment after all. Suffice to say that not all "death of God" theology—for that is what it is, *theology*—accepts Nietzsche's general agonistics. Whether any atheism can finally escape the conclusions Nietzsche draws out so uncompromisingly remains an unsettling question, but there are several theological movements that have taken heed of Nietzsche's declaration while advancing a self-descriptively Christian vision. For one such movement the death of God is the real "event" of Christianity itself—its inner dynamism and historical legacy.

Commonly referred to as "radical theology," and first making its mark in the 1960s, this movement exhibits two distinctive (though sometimes convergent) trends. The first and most speculative is tied to the work of Thomas Altizer, whose *The Gospel of Christian Atheism* (1966) and the co-edited *Radical Theology and the Death of God* (1966) constitute important landmarks in the attempt to theologize the death of God as the proper meaning of Christianity. According to Altizer, while the death of God is ultimately rooted in the event of Jesus' crucifixion ("My God, my God, why have you forsaken me?"), its abyssal depths are only now becoming apparent. Though Christians have long imagined God retaining transcendence throughout Jesus' ordeal—a point of view enshrined in the doctrine of Jesus' two natures (human and divine) and the doctrine of the Trinity—the shattering significance of Jesus' death is that the God whom Jesus called "Father" underwent total annihilation *in* Jesus' death. If Nietzsche claims, as do most atheists, that there never was any transcendent reality to which "God" referred in the first place, Altizer insists that the transcendent reality of God totally divested itself of all being on the cross. God *willed* God's own death in the apocalyptic event of Golgotha.

A fiercely dialectical reasoning is at work in this assessment, which Altizer traces through the works of Luther, Boehme, Hegel, Blake, Kierkegaard, Nietzsche, Heidegger, the early Barth, and the late Bonhoeffer, among others. This linkage may seem strained, not least because several of those named are theists, but Altizer identifies two key points in their tracing. The first is the Hegelian account of God "historicizing" God's self in the overcoming of separation from the world. History becomes that by which God realizes God's self as *Geist* (or Spirit), and thus history's meaning is no longer transcendently "beyond" but "within" it, i.e., in the overcoming of alienation and the realization of freedom in history. The distinction between God and world, as well as the "immanent" and "economic" Trinity, is thereby collapsed—or at least dialectically reconfigured as ongoing historical process. The second is the early Barth's radical view of revelation, which insists that we know nothing about God apart from God's self-revelation in Jesus. We never have access to God "behind" Jesus. Jesus *is* God's self-revelation; the rest is just empty projection, disguised anthropology. (Here we see Barth working to overcome Feuerbach with his dialectical understanding of revelation.) But Altizer claims that Barth didn't go quite far enough, or was inconsistent, and even began to backtrack later as he accommodated his earlier views in *The Epistle to the Romans* (1918) to a more creedal, ecclesiocentric, and creation-centered theology in the *Church Dogmatics* (1932–1967).[10] Taking Barth's early theology of revelation with absolute seriousness means that God finally willed to have no independent being apart from Jesus, so that when Jesus underwent suffering and death on the cross, so did God:

> For to know that God is dead is to know the God who died in Jesus Christ, the God who passed through what Blake symbolically named as 'Self-Annihilation!' ... The Christian alone knows the God who negates himself in his own revelatory and

redemptive acts. . . . The radical Christian proclaims that God has actually died in Christ, that this death is both a historical and cosmic event and as such, it is a final and irrevocable event, which cannot be reversed by a subsequent religious or cosmic movement.[11]

A famous *Time* magazine article featuring Altizer, among other radical theologians, put this audacious claim into public view. Entitled "Is God Dead?" (April 8, 1966), the article sparked considerable interest and controversy at the time, but also notoriety and professional hardship for some of those featured. One such person was William Hamilton, whose work represents the second, more ethically focused trajectory within radical theology. While sharing with Altizer the speculative claim that "only the Christian can celebrate an Incarnation in which God has actually become flesh, and radical theology must finally understand the Incarnation itself as effecting the death of God,"[12] Altizer regularly invokes apocalyptic, mysticism, and quasi-gnostic theologies to explore the dizzying significance of living in a godless world, whereas Hamilton looks more towards a Christological ethic as a way of "living in the time of the death of God."[13] There is, Hamilton observes, a negative dimension to this ethic insofar as it is learning to reject the false security that theism provides. Linking this negative dimension with the thrust of the Protestant Reformation's opting for the world over the cloister, and likewise the affirmation of secular existence over a sacralized cosmos, Hamilton takes his cue from the later Bonhoeffer, who in his posthumously published *Letters and Papers from Prison* gestures towards a "religionless Christianity." Though not an atheist, Bonhoeffer wrote of the need for humanity to "come of age," i.e., "to deal with himself in all quests of importance without recourse to the 'working hypothesis' called 'God'."[14] Christians must learn to live in a "religionless world," as if God did not exist.[15] Such cryptic remarks are all the more poignant when we recognize what occasioned them, namely, Bonhoeffer's imprisonment and eventual execution in 1945 for his failed attempt to assassinate Adolf Hitler. Hamilton aligns his own work as a radical theologian in this vein:

> My Protestant has no God, has no faith in God, and affirms both the death of God and the death of all the forms of theism. Even so, he is not primarily a man of negation, for if there is a movement away from God and religion, there is the more important movement into, for, toward the world, worldly life, and the neighbor as the bearer of the worldly Jesus.[16]

This focus on the "worldly Jesus" and the ethic of neighborly love is consistent with major trends in liberal Protestantism, in that they tend to deemphasize appeals to divine transcendence, dogmatic formulae, classical soteriology, and future eschatology in favor of immanence, moral instruction, solidaristic ethics, and accommodation to secular life. Such a statement is too sweeping to capture the internal diversity of radical theology, but it is an important observation to make. The reason is that while radical theology as a discrete movement may have been short lived—a *Time* magazine article entitled "Is God Coming Back To Life?" appeared just three years later (December 26, 1969)—its enduring significance becomes more intelligible when situated within the broader liberal Protestant project of seeking conciliation with the secular culture it helped to create.

This in part explains why more recent attempts to engage radical theology—or as one author puts it, "resurrect the death of God"[17]—have articulated a more explicitly political, rather than only moral or ethical, set of interests. For example, Jeffrey W. Robbins and Clayton Crockett, each in their own way, have heralded the contributions of radical theology while critiquing what they perceive as its insufficiently political character, especially as this concerns the threats of global capitalism to democracy.[18] They both worry that "God" survives in the presumed sovereignty of the nation-state, or hegemonic notions of the "will of the people," and, most pernicious of all, in the neoliberal ideology that views free-market capitalism as a numinous, self-generating force. The thrust of radical theology's critique is to dismantle every attempt to construct sovereignty, which is inescapably linked to the transcendence of God, or at least some nostalgia for it, and to advocate "for a more radical commitment to a genuine and thoroughgoing democracy, a commitment that goes beyond the modern liberal concept of popular sovereignty by appealing to the disparate and sometimes unruly voices of the multitude befitting a religiously diverse and politically mobilized world."[19]

WEAK THEOLOGY

Although radical theology may not loom large in the way contemporary theology is typically recounted, it nevertheless reflects and contributes to significant undercurrents in that history. One recent trend that cuts across philosophical and theological lines, namely, "weak theology," exhibits important continuities with radical theology. Frequently associated with Gianni Vattimo and John D. Caputo, weak theology represents the attempt to think theologically *after* the death of God.[20]

For Vattimo, one of Italy's foremost philosophers, the death of God means, as it did for Nietzsche, the end of absolutes. Values that appear "higher" or more authentic can no longer be regarded as metaphysically secured, whether by divine authority, nature, reason, or scientific objectivity. All human knowing is endlessly interpretable, and this implies that every attempt to rise above interpretation in order to adjudicate all truth-claims involves some kind of violence, some imposition or exclusion that gives false solidity to its own position at the expense of others. If "metaphysics" may be taken to mean the preoccupation with foundations for being and knowing—the assumption that behind all phenomena lies an ultimate, permanent, and intelligible basis for determining the true, good, and beautiful—then the "end of metaphysics" implies learning to live without foundations, without grasping at "being." This learning process is not merely a conversion undertaken by an elite few. It is the condition of our late-modern or postmodern age. The end of Modernity is an unfolding "event," a historical process at work in a great variety of domains, ranging from philosophy, religion, history, and science to culture, aesthetics, politics, economics, and technology.[21] Recognizing that this process gives rise to all manner of reactions to it, including fundamentalism, totalitarianism, and nativism, we are nevertheless witnessing the "weakening of being" in the sense that all values are increasingly recognized as endlessly interpretable, revisable, and without center or periphery. Structures that seemed to house human knowing and being within stable boundaries, including the most encompassing of them all, i.e., "God" or "the sacred," have become emptied of their self-subsistence and exposed to the endless flux of interpretation.

Vattimo explicitly links the weakening of being with the death of God, but instead of concluding this as inimical to Christianity, he interprets it as its fulfillment. The Christian identification of divine transcendence with the incarnation, with historicity and flesh, eventually drains transcendence of its objective character. Vattimo's reading of Western thought typically traces the struggle between the objectivist tendencies of classical metaphysics and the historicizing effects of the biblical traditions, especially Christianity, which by his account inaugurates the destabilizing of absolutes with its announcement that God became human. This hardly means that Christianity has not itself exhibited mixed forms, or tried to span the contradiction between "strong" and "weak" accounts of being, but internal to Christianity is the historical process of weakening absolutes, including the construction of the "sacred" as opposed to the "secular." Indeed, the emptying of the sacred is Christianity's greatest gift:

> Having recognized its family resemblance with the biblical message of the history of salvation and with God's incarnation, philosophy can call the weakening that it discovers as the characteristic feature of the history of Being secularization in its broadest sense, which comprises all the forms of dissolution of the sacred characteristic of the modern process of civilization. If it is the mode in which the weakening of Being realizes itself as the *kenosis* of God, which is the kernel of the history of salvation, secularization shall no longer be conceived of as the abandonment of religion but as the paradoxical realization of Being's religious vocation.[22]

Notice here the soteriological significance Vattimo gives to secularization. The weakening of being is liberative and creative, not a cause for despair. It does not result in a vapid relativism where "anything goes," and neither does it conclude with Nietzsche's embrace of the will to power as the essence of life—an assessment that only endows violence with some kind of metaphysical status, i.e., as an account of what the world is *really* like.[23] For Vattimo, the weakening of being implies the weakening of violence. As we let go of the compulsive need for absolutes, or as we empty ourselves of the need to secure identity through attachments to objective standards, including a substantialist God, we grow increasingly welcoming of others, hospitable to difference and ambiguity within the ceaseless play of interpretation. No longer must we acquire identity at the expense of others, whether through domination or expulsion. Rather, identity is discovered and continuously reborn in an open, fragile community of interpreters, in the constant exchange of "self" and "other." And so in this sense—and this sense only—there is a limit to secularization. That limit is charity. For Vattimo charity means hospitality to the other and "the possibility of community with a community of interpreters."[24] Put in theological terms:

> [T]hough the event of Christianity sets in motion the process of secularization, we may also find in Scripture a limit to secularization, hence a guide to desacralization— namely, that of charity. If you read the gospels or the fathers of the church carefully, at the end, the only virtue left is always that of charity. From Saint Paul we learn that the three greatest virtues are faith, hope, and love, "but the greatest of these is love." Even faith and hope will end at one point or another. As Saint Augustine instructs, "Love and do what you want."[25]

The difficulty of establishing this limit notwithstanding—a point to which we must return—the porosity between philosophical and theological language in this assessment is characteristic of John Caputo's work as well. Indeed, both Vattimo and Caputo exhibit passionate, if highly critical and often ambiguous, interests in Christian theology, and both have sought to complicate distinctions between theism and atheism. Vattimo, for instance, claims that the death of God means the death of "the moral God," of the "ultimate foundation," not the end of Christian faith or openness to the "event" of historical revelation.[26] The process of weakening means that just as there are no strong reasons for theism, neither are there strong reasons for atheism.[27] Caputo likewise maintains that God cannot be said to exist in any metaphysical sense. Adopting a more phenomenological style of reflection, along with a heavy dose of deconstruction, God is "otherwise than being," a "promise," a "call," an "event" that does not so much "exist" as "insist."[28] To substantialize God as *a* being, even the plenitude of being, is to encompass the unencompassable within an onto-theological horizon. To affirm or deny God as some being is to reify God and hence foreclose the "'holy undecidability' between theism and atheism."[29] It is *holy* because it is attitudinally hospitable to the God who *may* be, to the God "beyond being." Importantly, this hospitality to "the God who may be" allows us to grow welcoming of the irreducible strangeness of the other, the neighbor, whether religious or not.[30] Holy undecidability with respect to God does not imply lukewarmness or indifference. On the contrary, it is passionately interested in the question it cannot resolve in metaphysical terms, and this interest is not merely speculative. It is ethical (an "ethics of alterity") in that it concerns how we relate responsibly and compassionately to the other in our midst.[31]

Anyone familiar with postmodern discourses, especially those of Jacques Derrida and Emmanuel Levinas, will immediately recognize the above themes that pervade Caputo's work. These themes reach their most theologically explicit formulation to date in his *The Weakness of God: A Theology of the Event* (2003). Drawing inspiration from St. Paul's paradoxical formulation that God's strength is found in weakness, Caputo develops a wide-ranging project that opposes the metaphysical fixations of "strong theology" with the openness, undecidability, and hermeneutical playfulness of "weak theology." Subjecting to critique classical notions of divine transcendence and omnipotence, Caputo develops a more self-consciously subversive theology that highlights immanence and hopeful indeterminacy. Above all, Caputo maintains that we should abandon all metaphysical frameworks for thinking about God, especially God as "ultimate cause," and instead become open and freely disturbed by the "lure" of the *possible* God. In this sense, Caputo does not offer a death of God theology that presumes the bankruptcy of all God-talk. Rather, he wishes to free God-talk from metaphysics, to deconstruct it and redirect it towards "the event," by which he means "a summons, call, demand, claim or appeal, as well as a promise and a lure."[32] Practically speaking, this redirection looks to deconstruct all "strong" structures of identity and sovereignty that end up excluding or dominating others. This is a work of justice, claims Caputo, and it is a work that, like the Kingdom of God, is always "to come."[33]

DEATH OF GOD OR DEATH OF THE SACRED?

Having traced several lines of development from Nietzsche and Radical Theology to Weak Theology, we now turn to two (very) different responses that suggest further avenues for theologizing the death of God. Both avenues take Jesus' death with uncompromising seriousness, and both exhibit critical stances towards aspects of Weak Theology. But whereas the first avenue embraces the speculative ambitions of Altizer in pursuit of a dialectically robust atheism, the second remains just as robustly theistic by interpreting Golgotha as the death of "the sacred" that distorts true transcendence.

Slovenian philosopher Slavoj Žižek represents the first of these avenues. Appealing directly (if occasionally) to Altizer's work, Žižek weaves a dense fabric of interlocutors, including Hegel, Schelling, Marx, Kierkegaard, and Lacan, in order to account for the death of God as "the subversive core of Christianity."[34] Whereas Caputo represents a "'soft' postmodern theology" that treats the death of God non-apocalyptically, i.e., as an event that reduces it to mere deconstructive undecidability, Žižek urges us to take the likes of Altizer much more seriously: "For Altizer . . . what 'dies' on the Cross is not just the false (positive, ontic) envelope of Divinity, which was obfuscating its eventual core; what dies is God himself, the structuring principle of our entire universe, its life-giving force, the guarantee of its meaning."[35] There is something far more traumatic in Altizer's account: a shattering *apocalypsis* that refuses to smooth over Christ's death through vague appeals to a "possible" God or the "deferral" of meaning. Like Altizer, Žižek develops a dialectical approach that views Christianity as "the religion of the end of religion," to borrow a phrase from Marcel Gauchet.[36] As opposed to classical Christian theologies that attempt to hold God and humanity in paradoxical unity, Žižek contends that a dialectical understanding of the Incarnation, punctuated, as it is, by Jesus' cry of dereliction on the cross, reveals the abyssal truth—God *is not*. Christ is not the earthly manifestation of the absolute God who remains in self-subsistent reserve; rather—and here we see the Hegelian-cum-Lacanian stamp on Žižek's thought—the crucified Christ reveals the absolute *kenosis* of God by emptying the "Big Other" of its forbidding mystery and content. Žižek does not mean that once there was a transcendent God and now there is not, which is more properly Altizer's view. And yet, Žižek is no less insistent on the disorienting character of this kenotic event, since it means that there never was a transcendent God who might rescue this "miserable individual, this ridiculous and derided clown-king" from the horror of the cross.[37]

Drawing extensively from the psychoanalysis of Lacan, Žižek maintains that religions are prone to construing all things within a horizon of ultimate meaning. They construct enchanted worlds, harmonious wholes wherein the aching Void at the heart of human desire might be "domesticated."[38] Religion endows all things with "juicy sense," as Lacan puts it, with the promise that our aspirations for completeness are transcendently realizable. To posit God as the ultimate foundation or overarching goal of life, however, risks "drowning it in sense."[39] It only cures the symptom by repressing it. It only enfolds psychic discontinuity and historical rupture within a congruent whole, within an imagined One. But, Lacan asks, "is the *one* anterior to discontinuity? I do not think so, and everything I have taught in recent years has tended to exclude this need for a closed *one*. . . . Rupture, split, the stroke of the opening makes absence emerge—just as the cry does not stand out against a background of silence, but on the contrary makes silence emerge as silence."[40] What Žižek discerns at the heart of Christianity is the scandalous non-response of God to Jesus' cry of dereliction. If, prior to Christianity, God could be envisioned as enigmatically but perfectly Other—as the infinitely sublime Object transcending all limitations here below—then the Christian identification of God with the crucified humanity of Christ tears the veil between "us" and "God in himself," evacuating the latter of its exalted mystery:

> This total abandonment by God is the point at which Christ becomes FULLY human, the point at which *the radical gap that separates God from man is transposed into God Himself. Here, God the Father stumbles upon the limit of his omnipotence.* What this means is that the Christian notion of the link between man and God thus inverts the standard pagan notion according to which man approaches God through spiritual purification, through casting off the "low" material/sensual aspects of his being and thus elevating himself towards God. *When I, a human being, experience myself as cut off from God, at that very moment of the utmost abjection, I am absolutely close to God, since I find myself in the position of the abandoned Christ.*[41]

The dialectical framing of this view—God "is" where God "is not"—is operative in Žižek's account of Christian love: it is "always love for the Other insofar as he is lacking—

we love the Other BECAUSE of his limitation, helplessness, ordinariness even. In contrast to the pagan celebration of the Divine (or human) Perfection, the ultimate secret of the Christian love is, perhaps, the loving attachment to the Other's imperfection."[42] This framing also provides an important clue for understanding Žižek's insistence that the Christian love of imperfection, of the ordinary in all its misery and contradictoriness, is the decisive spark for a revolutionary politics that redirects attention away from the transcendental sublime to the historical and material conditions of human existence. Hence, the complicated (and eclectic) embrace of atheistic Christianity and dialectical materialism throughout his work.

If Žižek represents a Christian atheism in line with the speculative aims of Altizer, the work of René Girard represents a theistic alternative that nevertheless attributes to Christianity a decisive rupture of false transcendence. Girard's work comes close to Vattimo's in certain respects. Indeed, Vattimo cites his encounter with Girard as pivotal to his own understanding of secularization, stating: "Girard has persuasively demonstrated ... that if a 'divine' truth is given in Christianity, it is an unmasking of the violence that has given birth to the sacred of natural religion, that is, the sacred that is characteristic of the metaphysical God."[43] Vattimo refers here to Girard's central thesis that archaic religions long served the regulatory function of protecting human groups from the threat of contagious violence.[44] This threat constantly arises because human desire is so volatile. Due to our evolutionary heritage, which has equipped us with the capacity to imitate the desires of others, human relations can rapidly deteriorate into rivalry and extreme violence. Although leading to broad cooperation and deep belonging, our capacity to imitate the desires of others—to take on the *intentions* of others as our own—means that we are especially prone to conflict. The "mimetic desire" that draws us into intense proximity is the very desire that leads us into rivalry as we competitively pursue mutually desirable objects (toys, possessions, status, power, etc.). This mimetic attraction/repulsion is especially liable to reciprocal violence. Because we imitate one another so spontaneously, rivalry can quickly devolve into spiraling violence and threaten to consume all persons or groups involved. Obvious examples include fratricide, mob violence, genocide, terrorism, and war.

Based upon his wide-ranging study of comparative literature and cultural anthropology, Girard argues that archaic religions served to channel the volatility of human desire and its susceptibility to runaway violence. Although we may puzzle over the elaboration of sacrificial practices, interdictions, taboos, and social differentiations in archaic religions, we should discern in them the regulatory function of providing social order against the ever-present threat of violent disintegration. Central to this regulatory function is sacrifice. Girard points out the stereotypical patterns in ancient myths and cosmogonies that depict the sacrifice of a human (or a god) in the establishment of cosmic and social order. He concludes from their ubiquity that sacrificial practices in fact "worked," i.e., they had adaptive value in the early evolutionary history of our species. The mechanism by which this worked can be summarized as follows: as tensions within social groups rise and threaten dissolution, groups frequently (and quite spontaneously) redirect their hostilities towards some "outsider" or "other" as the cause of disorder. The discord threatening social harmony is canalized and directed outward towards some liminal figure (or group) regarded as monstrous, alien, or impure. Today we use the word "scapegoating" to refer to this phenomenon, by which we typically mean the expedient but ultimately self-deceptive unloading of blame upon an innocent victim.[45] Girard draws our attention to these more familiar forms of scapegoating, but he pushes further by arguing that ancient sacrificial practices, including their ritual memorialization, served this canalizing function by symbolically transferring group disorder onto a victim deemed responsible for it. The death of the victim, and the ritual remembrance of the death, cathartically resolves the tension of the group, restoring to it order and functional peace.

When Vattimo refers to the unmasking of the violent sacred, he is referring to Girard's contention that the Hebrew and Christian scriptures together show a strong tendency towards dismantling the structure of archaic sacred myths. They do this by privileging the perspective of the victim rather than the dominant group. On this point Girard agrees wholeheartedly with Nietzsche. From the story of Cain and Abel to the Exodus, from Joseph and his brothers to the Book of Job, from the psalmists' laments to the suffering servant motif in Isaiah, and, above all, the Gospel portrayals of an innocent victim crucified by the colluding powers of religious and imperial authorities: the Bible's most characteristic narratives assume the perspective of the victim, those rendered mute and marginalized by sacrificial violence, with the effect of demystifying and destabilizing its seductive power. The violent sacred is a canopy of transcendence, an encompassing milieu of mystery, awe, and order generated by a sacrificial logic, along with the narratives, symbols, proscriptions, and social differentiations that support it. The biblical traditions puncture this canopy of false transcendence and unleash in history the transvaluation of values of which Nietzsche spoke. In this sense we can speak of the "death of the sacred."

Earlier we saw that Nietzsche opposes the construction of a moral-spiritual world wherein the victim assumes a central focus. Girard, however, regards this key to divine revelation and the opening up of true transcendence—a God of unconditional love and peace. The identification of God with the crucified and risen Jesus does not imply the "death of God." Rather, it disrupts all constructions of transcendence premised upon violence. Girard makes his point by highlighting the dramatic conversions enshrined in the New Testament as Jesus' earliest followers encounter his risen presence. (Of all the authors considered here, Girard alone affirms Jesus' resurrection in the traditional sense.) Through the gratuitous offer of forgiveness and peace, the earliest followers came to see their implication in the dynamics of exclusionary violence leading to Jesus' death. The New Testament canon as a whole outlines a process in which the primitive Christian community is educated into a new way of desire founded upon mutual forgiveness and communion rather than mimetic rivalry and exclusionary violence.

Girard maintains that the Jewish and Christian traditions together unleashed a transformative historical process, however halting and subject to ironic mutations, that greatly weakens the violent sacred and establishes the inviolable dignity of the human person as core to its vision:

> [S]ince the High Middle Ages all the great human institutions have evolved in the same direction: more human private and public law, penal legislation, juridical practice, the rights of individuals. Everything changed very slowly at first, but the pace has been accelerating more and more. When viewed in terms of the large picture, this social and cultural revolution goes always in the same direction, toward the mitigation of punishment, greater protection for potential victims.[46]

Though not subscribing to a naïve view of historical progress, Girard insist that we are actors and witnesses to "a great anthropological first," in that our society "is the most preoccupied with victims of any that ever was."[47] Indeed, the status of the victim carries so much moral currency today that, notwithstanding the fact that there really are victims of injustice, virtually any person or group can lay claim to victimization in order to wield power. This insight was clearly seen by Nietzsche, and for this reason Girard regards him the most perspicacious thinker of the nineteenth century.

CONCLUSION

We have examined in this essay several meanings of the death of God in contemporary thought, noting important convergences and divergences along the way, as well some of their implications for political theology. While the focus of this essay has been largely schematic and descriptive, there are two brief points of evaluation worth articulating by way of conclusion.

The first is that while all of the authors surveyed take Nietzsche's announcement of God's death seriously—as entailing an "event" of epochal significance requiring ongoing interpretation—all reject Nietzsche's valorization of the will to power in the wake of this announcement. In one form or another, all of the above figures take with equal seriousness the significance of Jesus for shaping a spiritual and political vision that emphasizes solidarity with the marginalized and outcast. Even Vattimo's enthusiastic embrace of nihilism articulates a limit to the endless play of interpretation, namely, charity. Of course, we might ask Vattimo on what basis even this limit can be justified. If all is groundlessly interpretative, then it seems difficult to avoid the conclusion that the limit of charity amounts to an arbitrarily drawn boundary. For this reason, the sting of Nietzsche's announcement remains for all who interpret "God is dead" atheistically, or at least without reference to divine transcendence. This is why, as Girard puts it in his dialogue with Vattimo, that his own approach proceeds from the "fact" of revelation.[48] It is not the death of God, strictly speaking, that is of epochal significance but death of the sacred that obscures the true (one might say radical) transcendence of God. This God may appear "weak" in comparison to the worldly power of violence, but the nonviolent power of God dismantles violence from within by lovingly absorbing it on the cross and offering the gift of reconciliation. A political theology emphasizing divine transcendence in this way will therefore be just as motivated to articulate a political praxis of reconciliation as it will justice.

Second, it bears mentioning that all of the figures above, whether atheistic, theistic, or playfully "undecided," take the death of God as *theologically* significant. Compared to an atheism or agnosticism that does not take the question of God seriously enough to interpret Nietzsche's announcement as a matter of loss, tragedy, or even quandary, all those surveyed here share the view that the question of God, including God's absence, is fundamental to understanding our historical situation. Along these lines, each draws strong connections between Christianity and secularity. Rather than viewing secularity as a deviation from Christianity, they take the view that its seeds are found in Christianity itself. Of course, this hardly means that we should baptize all that is "secular" as covertly Christian, but we will not begin to understand the meaning and range of secularity, including its puzzling eventualities and ironic mutations, without seeing it, in part, as a particular kind of theological accomplishment. Secularity in the West has a Christian shape, however obliquely, including those iterations that are forgetful of or implacably opposed to the theological. It is for this reason that any political theory aspiring to a modicum of historical self-understanding will need to take the theological quite seriously; that even if it does not understand itself as a political theology, it cannot help but be a politics *after* the death of God.

NOTES

1. Friedrich Nietzsche, *The Gay Science*, trans. Josefine Nauckhoff (Cambridge: Cambridge University Press, 2001), 199.
2. Ibid., 119–120.
3. Ludwig Feuerbach, *The Essence of Christianity*, trans. George Elliot (Amherst, NY: Prometheus Books, 1989), xviii–xix.
4. Ibid., 31.
5. Nietzsche, *The Gay Science*, 124–125.
6. Friedrich Nietzsche, *On the Genealogy of Morals: A Polemic*, trans. Douglas Smith (Oxford: Oxford University Press, 1996), 19.
7. Ibid., 19–20.
8. Terry Eagleton, *Culture and the Death of God* (New Haven, CT: Yale University Press, 2014), 157.
9. Friedrich Nietzsche, *Beyond Good and Evil: Prelude to a Philosophy of the Future*, trans. R. J. Hollingdale (New York: Penguin, 1990), 194.
10. Thomas J.J. Altizer, "Theology and the Death of God," in *Radical Theology and the Death of God*, (New York: The Bobbs-Merrill Company, Inc., 1966), 105.
11. Thomas J.J. Altizer, *The Gospel of Christian Atheism* (Philadelphia, PA: The Westminster Press, 1966), 102, 111.
12. Thomas J.J. Altizer and William Hamilton, "Preface," in Thomas J.J. Altizer and William Hamilton, *Radical Theology and the Death of God* (New York: The Bobbs-Merrill Company, Inc., 1966), xii.
13. William Hamilton, "The Death of God Theologies Today," in *Radical Theology and the Death of God*, 35.
14. Dietrich Bonhoeffer, *Letters and Papers from Prison* (Minneapolis, MN: Fortress Press, 2015), 325.
15. Ibid., 280.
16. Hamilton, "The Death of God Theologies Today," 37.
17. Daniel J. Peterson, *Resurrecting the Death of God: The Origins, Influence, and Return of Radical Theology*, ed. Daniel J. Peterson and G. Michael Zbaraschuk (Albany, NY: State University of New York Press, 2014).
18. See Jeffrey W. Robbins, *Radical Democracy and Political Theology* (New York: Columbia University Press, 2001); Clayton Crockett, *Radical Political Theology: Religion and Politics After Liberalism* (New York: Columbia University Press, 2013).
19. Robbins, *Radical Democracy and Political Theology*, 127.
20. See John D. Caputo and Gianni Vattimo, *After the Death of God*, ed. Jeffrey W. Robbins (New York: Columbia University Press, 2007).
21. See Gianni Vattimo, *The End of Modernity: Nihilism and Hermeneutics in Postmodern Culture*, trans. Jon R. Snyder (Baltimore, MD: Johns Hopkins University Press, 1988).
22. Gianni Vattimo, *After Christianity*, trans. Luca D'Isanto (New York: Columbia University Press, 2002), 24.
23. Martin Heidegger developed this critique at length. See his *Nietzsche, Vol. 3: The Will to Power as Knowledge and as Metaphysics & Vol. 4: Nihilism*, trans. David Farrell Krell (New York: HarperCollins, 1982).
24. Vattimo, *After Christianity*, 67.

25. Gianni Vattimo, "Toward a Nonreligious Christianity," in *After the Death of God*, 41.
26. Vattimo, *After Christianity*, 3.
27. Ibid., 90.
28. John D. Caputo, *The Insistence of God: A Theology of Perhaps* (Bloomington, IN: Indiana University Press, 2013).
29. John D. Caputo, *The Weakness of God: A Theology of the Event* (Bloomington, IN: Indiana University Press, 2006), 269.
30. For similar themes see Richard Kearney, *The God Who May Be: A Hermeneutics of Religion* (Bloomington, IN: Indiana University Press, 2001) and *Anatheism: Returning to God After God* (New York: Columbia University Press, 2011).
31. Caputo, *The Weakness of God*, 136. For an earlier treatment of the theme, see John D. Caputo, *Against Ethics: Contributions to a Poetics of Obligation with Constant Reference to Deconstruction* (Bloomington, IN: Indiana University Press, 1993).
32. Caputo, *The Weakness of God*, 28–29.
33. Caputo develops a "messianic" approach to the Kingdom of God in dialogue with Derrida's "democracy to come" (ibid., 259–278). See also John D. Caputo, *What Would Jesus Deconstruct? The Good News of Post-modernism for the Church* (Grand Rapids, MI: Baker Academic, 2007).
34. Slavoj Žižek, "Dialectical Clarity Versus the Misty Conceit of Paradox," in Slavoj Žižek and John Milbank, *The Monstrosity of Christ: Paradox or Dialectic?* (Cambridge, MA: MIT Press, 2009), 260. See also Slavoj Žižek, *The Fragile Absolute: Or, Why is the Christian Legacy Worth Fighting For?* (London: Verso, 2000); *The Puppet and the Dwarf: The Perverse Core of Christianity* (Cambridge, MA: MIT Press, 2003).
35. Ibid.
36. Marcel Gauchet, *The Disenchantment of the World: A Political History of Religion*, trans. Oscar Burge (Princeton, NJ: Princeton University Press, 2003).
37. Slavoj Žižek, "The Fear of Four Words: A Modest Plea for the Hegelian Reading of Christianity," in *The Monstrosity of Christ*, 80.
38. Žižek, "Dialectical Clarity Versus the Misty Conceit of Paradox," 241.
39. Jacques Lacan, *Le triomphe de la religion* (Paris: Editions du Seuil, 2005), 80, 82, quoted in Žižek, "Dialectical Clarity Versus the Misty Conceit of Paradox," 241.
40. Jacques Lacan, *The Four Fundamental Concepts of Psycho-Analysis*, ed. Jacques-Alain Miller, trans. Alan Sheridan (New York: W.W. Norton & Company, 1981), 26.
41. Slavoj Žižek, *On Belief* (London: Routledge, 2001), 145–146.
42. Ibid., 147.
43. Vattimo, *After Christianity*, 38. See also the extended dialogue in Gianni Vattimo and René Girard, *Christianity, Truth, and Weakening Faith: A Dialogue*, ed. Pierpaolo Antonello, trans. William McCuaig (New York: Columbia University Press, 2006).
44. See René Girard, *Violence and the Sacred*, trans. Patrick Gregory (Baltimore, MD: Johns Hopkins University Press, 1977) and *Things Hidden Since the Foundation of the World*, trans. Stephen Bann and Michael Metteer (Stanford, CA: Stanford University Press, 1987).
45. See René Girard, *The Scapegoat*, trans. Yvonne Freccero (Baltimore, MD: Johns Hopkins University Press, 1986).
46. René Girard, *I See Satan Fall Like Lightning*, trans. James G. Williams (Maryknoll, NY: Orbis Books, 2001), 166.
47. Ibid., 161.

48. René Girard, "Not Just Interpretations, There are Facts, Too," in *Christianity, Truth, and Weakening Faith*, 88–108.

SELECT BIBLIOGRAPHY

Altizer, Thomas J. J. and William Hamilton (1966), *Radical Theology and the Death of God*, New York: The Bobbs-Merrill Company, Inc.
Bonhoeffer, Dietrich (2015), *Letters and Papers from Prison*, Minneapolis, MN: Fortress Press.
Caputo, John D. (2006), *The Weakness of God: A Theology of the Event*, Bloomington, IN: Indiana University Press.
Caputo, John D. (2013), *The Insistence of God: A Theology of Perhaps*, Bloomington, IN: Indiana University Press.
Caputo, John D. and Gianni Vattimo (2007), *After the Death of God*, ed. Jeffrey W. Robbins, New York: Columbia University Press.
Crockett, Clayton (2013), *Radical Political Theology: Religion and Politics After Liberalism*, New York: Columbia University Press.
Eagleton, Terry (2014), *Culture and the Death of God*, New Haven, CT: Yale University Press.
Feuerbach, Ludwig (1989), *The Essence of Christianity*, trans. George Elliot, Amherst, NY: Prometheus Books.
Heidegger, Martin (1982), *Nietzsche, Vol. 3: The Will to Power as Knowledge and as Metaphysics & Vol. 4: Nihilism*, trans. David Farrell Krell, New York: HarperCollins.
Nietzsche, Friedrich (1990), *Beyond Good and Evil: Prelude to a Philosophy of the Future*, trans. R.J. Hollingdale, New York: Penguin Books.
Nietzsche, Friedrich (1996), *On the Genealogy of Morals: A Polemic*, trans. Douglas Smith, Oxford: Oxford University Press.
Nietzsche, Friedrich (2001), *The Gay Science*, trans. Josefine Nauckhoff, Cambridge: Cambridge University Press.
Peterson, Daniel J. and G. Michael Zbaraschuk, eds. (2014), *Resurrecting the Death of God: The Origins, Influence, and Return of Radical Theology*, Albany, NY: State University of New York Press.
Robbins, Jeffrey W. (2001), *Radical Democracy and Political Theology*, New York: Columbia University Press.
Vattimo, Gianni (1988), *The End of Modernity: Nihilism and Hermeneutics in Postmodern Culture*, trans. Jon R. Snyder, Baltimore, MD: Johns Hopkins University Press.
Vattimo, Gianni (2002), *After Christianity*, trans. Luca D'Isanto, New York: Columbia University Press.
Žižek, Slavoj (2000), *The Fragile Absolute: Or, Why is the Christian Legacy Worth Fighting For?*, London: Verso.
Žižek, Slavoj (2003), *The Puppet and the Dwarf: The Perverse Core of Christianity*, Cambridge, MA: MIT Press.
Žižek, Slavoj and John Milbank (2009), *The Monstrosity of Christ: Paradox or Dialectic?* Cambridge, MA: MIT Press.

CHAPTER TWELVE

Karl Barth and the Barmen Declaration

AMY MARGA

INTRODUCTION

It is said that the long arc of history bends towards justice. For the adopters of the Barmen Declaration against the Nazi regime, there could be no justice without *freedom* first. As Nazi totalitarianism pushed its way into every corner of German Christianity, a group of Protestant congregations across the land adopted the Declaration in the city of Barmen, on May 31, 1934. This group, which came to be called the *Confessing Church*, declared that Jesus Christ was the sole and unequivocal authority of the Church above every and any other government or worldly authority.

The Barmen Declaration rejected the "natural" theology that fueled the political ideologies, social policies, and leaders of the time. None of these could function as channels of God's self-revelation. With this theological vision, the leaders of Evangelical German Christianity, consisting of the Lutheran, Reformed, and United Lutheran-Reformed churches, carved out a tiny space of freedom for the Church to operate in an increasingly tyrannical government. At its most fundamental level, the Barmen Declaration represents a pivotal moment in German Protestantism in which the Church turned away from being an institution of the State and reaffirmed itself as a *body of believers in Jesus Christ* over and against any other worldly authority. It had not thought of itself this way for a very long time.[1]

The accomplishment of Barmen Declaration is best understood in light of the bureaucratic structure of the German Evangelical Church. For centuries, Christianity had been intimately tied, politically and culturally, to local municipalities and local governments. This makes it somewhat difficult to translate it as a political-theological event in the twenty-first-century West, especially in the United States, when most faith communities enjoy relative freedom from governmental ties. Where there is political involvement today, many faith communities focus either on moral issues (such as abortion and sexuality) or on fighting for justice for the disenfranchised. Rarely does the church today struggle against local municipal interference or government encroachment. While the Confessing Church faced modern realities such as racism, sexism, and poverty, similar to today, it did not address them directly. It was in a fight for its own existence within a totalitarian regime.

Contrary to popular perception, the Barmen Declaration was also not an explicit movement of solidarity with the Jews. It did not directly protest the State-sponsored racism towards Jewish people, LGBT persons, the disabled, Gypsies, or other so-called non-Aryan people. Rather, it was born out of the Protestant Church's struggle with itself, by which the Confessing Church drew a line in the sand against factions in its own Christian body. It was out of this struggle, which came to be known as the German Church Struggle, that the Barmen Declaration arose.

This essay tells the story of both the internal and external politics of the German Church Struggle. It highlights the theology of the Barmen Declaration's main author, Karl Barth, and lays out the achievement and the limits of Barmen in the catastrophe of the Third Reich.

THE PAINFUL ROAD TO UNITY IN THE CHURCH STRUGGLE

The Crisis of the German Protestant Landeskirchen

In many ways, the German Church struggle began in 1918, as the First World War ended and the Weimar Republic began. Protestant regional churches and synods (*Landeskirchen*) had been in mutually reciprocal relationships with their local governments and the broader administration of the German Evangelical Church. As those local governments collapsed the *Landeskirchen* became unmoored; new church constitutions would have to be written, new laws enacted, and leadership shuffled. The vast network of localized Protestant *Landeskirchen* with their decentralized bureaucratic structure and their loyalties to local governments had no mechanism to develop a centralized voice or common political platform. The Nazi rise to power brought this fatal weakness into stark relief in the ways that it fueled confusion and disunity among congregations and synods. Strong factions such as the Deutsche Christen (the "German Christians") who supported Hitler's political policies were represented among all ranks of ecclesiastical offices and within most congregations. Indeed, many of the pastors and leaders who made up the Confessing Church itself came from all different political positions. Some supported the Nazi Party but not the Deutsche Christen, others were sympathetic to the Deutsche Christen while being against Hitler's anti-Semitic politics. Across the land, pastors were preaching sermons that ranged from nationalistic fervor to socialistic exhortations to an outright fear of godless Communism. From pulpits to the streets, no one was immune from political violence or rhetoric.

Out of all the Protestant groups, the German Lutherans seemed to be particularly receptive to Hitler's nationalistic and racist rhetoric. They had been hoping for national renewal, and they even employed their beloved Reformation father, Martin Luther, to that end.[2] They sought a unity of *Reich*, *Volk*, *Führer* and Lutheran church, and their message spread with fervor and speed throughout 1933. Many synods put out position documents and confessions[3] in which they proclaimed in one breath faith in Jesus Christ, German racial uniqueness, and support of the *Führer*. This flurry of confessional documents aimed at helping the Lutherans maintain their centrist message and preserve their power within the State government.[4] Actually, it served mostly to propel forward the agenda of the Deutsche Christen. Most other Protestant leaders maintained a wary distance to Hitler's rise; only a very small minority had the foresight to understand Hitler's totalitarian ambitions. Once Hitler came to power on January 30, 1933, he worked to exploit the weak structures of the independent *Landeskirchen*. The goal was a single German Reich Church which would be incorporated into the national government and run by someone loyal to himself.

The Dark Summer of 1933

As the Nazi State grew in power, the German Evangelical Church found itself in a profound internal struggle. With new constitutions being written and church elections held across the land, an intense vying for leadership prevailed. Synods eyed the gains that the Deutsche Christen were making in Hitler's government, and were wary of their leader, Ludwig Müller. Several synods and groups hastily moved together to name the first Reich Bishop in order to block Müller's rise. Their candidate, Friedrich von Bodelschwingh, was a stark opposite of the cunning and ambitious Müller. Von Bodelschwingh was a deeply pious and gentle leader of a center for orphans and epileptics. Reluctantly, he agreed go up against Müller and the Deutsche Christen and become the first elected Reich Bishop.

Von Bodelschwingh's election to Reich Bishop served as an early warning sign from the Protestant synods to the State that it would not bow to political pressure. It would continue to name its own leaders with the ethical mandate that they not be involved in violent social policies. In Von Bodelschwingh's words, the Church would be the "free helper of the state,"[5] with the emphasis on *free*. The Church insisted on its own *freedom* within the State. It alone would determine the kind of moral, spiritual program it would follow.

While well intentioned, von Bodelschwingh's tenure as Reich Bishop was by all accounts a disaster. He only lasted in office for about a month under immense pressure by the Deutsche Christen who furiously campaigned against him. They utilized the Nazi Party's propaganda machine and the feared Gestapo to push for new elections. Average Germans were encouraged to participate in Church politics for the good of the *Volk*. This inner-church power struggle caused such tensions that the State ended up appointing a lawyer to preside over all the business of one of the largest Protestant synods, the Evangelical Church of Prussia. At this point, von Bodelschwingh saw no option but to resign. The State was now in control of leading and reorganizing the Church. A month later, after more campaigning, as well as collaboration between Hitler and the Deutsche Christen, new church elections were held and the Deutsche Christen won. Ludwig Müller, originally appointed by Hitler to be his private chaplain, would now be Reich Bishop of the German Evangelical Church.

This development in church leadership shocked congregations and caught the German Evangelical Church off guard. It was not yet sure how to launch a resistance movement against the State at this fateful point in the summer of 1933. Leaders of what became known as the *Kirchenbund,* the Church Coalition, were still focused on jockeying for power within the State. They were caught up in political maneuvers and had not yet awakened to a *theological* vision that could give them the freedom they were seeking.

And the politics were growing dangerous indeed. Hitler's world view was based in a theology and white supremacy of the worst kind: he believed in a Manichean worldview in which a "good" race—the Aryan race—was to defeat an evil race, the Jews. Hitler had reason to believe that the Christian church would support his racism against the Jews because it too, had a long history of anti-Judaic sentiment. German Christianity also had, for centuries, nurtured a sentimental view of German culture and saw itself as the guardian of a peculiar and unique German "soul." Hitler exploited the entrenched Christian sentiment about Jews as the murderers of Christ, and he maximized a heroic notion of Jesus as the one who had to spill his own blood to save the world from "the Jewish poison."[6] But in truth, Hitler never had any intention of cooperating with the Church or letting it be free. In fact, he had plans to annihilate Christianity once he was done with the Jews.[7]

The Pastors' Emergency League

The dark summer of 1933 also saw the arrival of Aryan paragraphs into ecclesiastical laws. These clauses demanded that any person of Jewish descent or "non-Aryan extraction"—and those married to any non-Aryan person—could not hold any type of church or civil office. These laws also demanded that anyone holding church office must give complete support to the State. Not only did these laws result in fundamentally reorganizing the German Evangelical Church, it now made the Church legally complicit in State-sponsored racism.

Pastors across the land were highly alarmed by these political and social developments. In September, Martin Niemöller—an unsung hero of the Confessing Church—formed the Pastors' Emergency League. It protested the inclusion of Aryan paragraphs in church law and stood as best it could in solidarity with non-Aryan Christians and Jewish Church members. Niemöller boldly insisted that any pastor in the Emergency League must be committed only to Scripture and the Reformation Confessions. This was a small but bold step towards unifying Church leaders and pivoting them back to their own sources of authority. The Pastors' Emergency League clearly stated that Aryan clause was a "specific violation" of the Protestant Church's confessions,[8] and gave pastors four points of commitment[9] around which they could rally.

The response to the Pastors' Emergency League was overwhelming. A little over three months after it was formed, more than half of the pastors in Germany were already members of the League and it continued to grow in strength. It spoke for the first time in a unified voice about Jesus Christ as the one true authority—even over Hitler. It was the strongest and clearest political statement yet by the Protestants and a profoundly important step in the Confessing Church's expression of what it stood *for*. The leaders in the Emergency League stood in solidarity with the persecuted *because of* their commitment to the Church's historical confessions.

As the Pastors' Emergency League gained momentum, the Deutsche Christen began pushing their luck with an increasingly extremist message. At a large public rally at the Berlin Sports Palace on November 13, 1933, the Deutsche Christen put out a radical call to abolish the Old Testament, get rid of all Jewish elements in Paul's theology, and pledge allegiance to a heroic German-like Jesus. This radical call shocked and divided many sympathizers of the Deutsche Christen and precipitated its eventual demise. The Pastors' Emergency League seized upon this event and called for the resignation of the Reich Bishop Müller and other Deutsche Christen officials. It was their chance to finally force a split in the Evangelical German Church and ostracize the Deutsche Christen. Hitler was not pleased.

The Tide of Synodical Resistance

While the general realization of Hitler's totalitarian ambitions was a painfully slow process in German Evangelical synods and congregations, a tide of synodical resistance began to swell as congregations awakened to the dangers of the political moment.

Already in the weeks before Hitler's actual seizure of power on January 30, 1933, the Evangelical-Lutheran Church of Altona held a special worship service to denounce the violent agitations and street fights between Nazis and Communists that had been plaguing the surrounding communities. Pastor Hans Asmussen read out a bold statement—the Altona Confession—in which he asserted the Church's right to political resistance against dictatorial governments.[10] Even this most basic right had to be affirmed and argued for in light of the centuries-old cozy relationship that Christianity and the State had enjoyed. The Church was free to protest. In Hitler's Germany, this was another risky step. Asmussen would go on to lead the First Synod of Barmen.

Another risky confession came out from the pen of Dietrich Bonhoeffer and his colleagues, the Bethel Confession. More radical than the Altona Confession, the Bethel Confession drew in the voice of the highly respected Old Testament scholar Wilhelm Vischer to declare their solidarity with the Jews. Unfortunately, local synods were not ready to sign on to its clear and strong wording, and it never went forward.[11] As for Dietrich Bonhoeffer, he would continue his resistance against Hitler's tyranny, at the cost of his life.

By January 1934, after the debacle of von Bodelschwingh's tenure as Bishop and a year into Hitler's reign, a little-noticed Reformed community in Barmen-Germarke decided it was time that they pull out from the German Evangelical Church altogether. The racism and corruption in the larger Church had become too intense, and they formed the first "Free Synod"—that is, an evangelical synod that was free from the German Evangelical Church. This small step actually became the impetus for bringing numerous protest groups one giant step closer a unified Declaration. The Swiss-born theologian Karl Barth, at that time a professor in Bonn, and who by then had broken up with his comrades at the well-known Christian journal *Zwischen den Zeiten* over their sympathies to Nazi ideology, gave the keynote address at the first "Free Synod.'"

Unbeknownst to him at the time, Barth's lecture would become the rough draft of the Barmen Declaration. The paper, entitled the "Declaration on the Right Understanding of the Reformed Confessions in the German Evangelical Church of Today,"[12] clearly stated that the Church of Jesus Christ was never to be confined to culturally bound, State-bound, or race-bound conditions. Rather, the true Church exists and is found "in the various times, races, peoples, states, and cultures" across the globe.[13] With these words, Barth drew clear defining lines around what it means to for the Church to be a community of faith in Jesus Christ. Like the statements of Niemöller in the Pastors' Emergency League and of Hans Asmussen in the Altona Confession, Barth was laying down a positive foundation of Christian freedom and authority that Protestant leaders and congregations could get behind.

Other synod assemblies began putting out bolder and clearer statements of resistance in the months that followed. This wave produced more pamphlets and more conferences that called on Lutheran and Reformed churches to work together as *Christians* under *one Gospel message* rather than as historically distinct, locally bound communities. Such meetings, as well as strong individual leaders like the Erlangen pastor Herman Sasse, helped gather Lutheran, Reformed, and United congregations into a chorus against the Deutsche Christen and the Nazi government.

The winter meetings in 1934 gave way to more synod assemblies throughout the spring, not only in the Rhineland but in Berlin, Brandenburg, and Westphalia. The movement spread south to Barvaria and Württembürg as well. In each of these assemblies, congregations and synods in their own ways took back the authority of the Church away from Nazi-endorsed leaders like Reich Bishop Ludwig Müller. The message grew clearer by the day: the governing of the Church lies in the hands of *Jesus Christ* and never in the hands of the State. The Church has the authority to be *free from* State intervention.[14] This was the beginning of a new theological and political imagination for the German Evangelical Church.

One more momentous step towards Barmen occurred on April 3, 1934 at a worship service in the city of Ulm, where representatives of the Confessing groups met to worship and plan. Participants at the service acknowledged the break-away synods. For the first time, they declared that the Confessing Church too would break away from the historical bureaucracy of the German Evangelical Church. In fact, they named *Confessing Church itself* to be the "legitimate Evangelical Church of Germany."[15] Up until this point, much of the Church Struggle had been between individual synods and the Deutsche Christen. By the end of the worship service, Confessing Church leaders were finally at a point where they were ready to sign a statement approving the Confessing Church's new status. Hence the Ulm Declaration was brought forth.

The Ulm Declaration, and other declarations that followed, like the Kassel Declaration, asserted that the Evangelical German Church had a "constitutional" position as an institution. This meant that it had the power to excommunicate the Deutsche Christen. It also argued that it could reject the official Reich Church. Such assertions and boldness swelled in the tide of synodical resistance. But things were not perfect. The new confidence on the part of the Confessing Church provoked angst among some of its members. The idea of the myriad *Landeskirchen* rallying around a single confessional Gospel message felt strange. Many leaders remained uncertain.

The First Synod of Barmen, May 31, 1934

When the day had come, and representatives sat down on the day of the First Synod of Barmen, the majority of Confessing Church congregations were ready to stake their claim on the authority of Jesus Christ and the freedom of the Christian community from government interference. In early May, Karl Barth and two Lutheran delegates, Thomas Breit and Hans Asmussen, met in Frankfurt to compose a first draft of a Declaration that would be endorsed in Barmen. The six articles of Declaration itself, with the exception of one sentence, ended up being authored by Barth.[16] (Incidentally, he was almost left out of the synod itself because someone forgot to invite him.)

Led by Hans Asmussen, the First Synod of Barmen, held on May 31, 1934, was a momentous affair and a fateful day. After giving a commentary on the six articles of the Declaration, he led the group to a hearty endorsement of the Barmen Declaration. At last, the Confessing Church had finally achieved unity around its true authority, Jesus Christ, and demonstrated its power and critical mass over and against the many other German Evangelical Church factions still vying for power in the Nazi regime. The Confessing Church had staked its ground, had finally raised its *unified* voice of resistance—and discovered itself as community of Jesus Christ. The tide of synodical meetings and statements turned the multitude of congregations into one "*Confessing* Church." It oriented them finally to a *theological* vision of freedom, even while it remained deeply involved in politics. The Barmen Declaration indeed became a kind of north star for the Church and its freedom during the remaining years of Hitler's regime.

The glory and relief of the First Synod of Barmen must not overshadow the risky and unending work of average Protestant pastors. It would not have come about without the tireless, months-long, behind-the-scenes politicking and organization of numerous Protestant pastors and leaders. Along with Hans Asmussen's leadership at the Synod itself, two other men made the Barmen Declaration a reality: Martin Niemöller, who founded the Pastors' Emergency League and was a staunch supporter of a Christian stance against the Reich, and Karl Immer, who organized the different synodical meetings that led up to the Synod.[17] Immer was one of those rare pastors who had the acuity to see clearly that the power of Christian theology lay in the unified *diversity* of synods and the central role they had in their own local communities. It was his vision that encouraged the free synods to assert their power and their rights against the relentless consolidating movements of the Deutsche Christen and the Reich Bishop.

THE THEOLOGY OF BARMEN

The Barmen Declaration's first major accomplishment was to establish the Church's authority in Jesus Christ above any and every other earthly institution. Its first Thesis states:

> 1. Jesus Christ, as he is attested for us in Holy Scripture, is the one Word of God which we have to hear and which we have to trust and obey in life and in death. We reject the false doctrine, as though the church could and would have to acknowledge as a source of its proclamation, apart from and besides this one Word of God, still other events and powers, figures and truths, as God's revelation.[18]

This thesis anchors the entire Declaration because it pronounces a positive "Yes" to God's singular and unique revelation in Christ, apart from any kind of State or cultural interference. By orienting itself to Christ and his authority alone, it was also orienting itself to the First Commandment, "you shall have no other gods before me."[19] With this theological orientation, which was so slow in coming, the Declaration was able to carve out a tiny sphere of freedom within the Nazi totalitarian government. This was no small accomplishment. By insisting on its independence and its otherworldly ruler, the Confessing Church "denied the total claim of National Socialism on the whole of human life."[20] It put a tiny wrench in the crushing wheel of Hitler's totalitarian regime.

Thesis Five reasserts this as well:

> 5. 'Fear God, honor the King!' (1 Peter 2:17): Scripture tells us that by divine appointment the State, in this still unredeemed world in which also the Church is situated, has the task of maintaining justice and peace ... by means of the threat and use of force.... [The Church] trust and obeys the power of the Word, by which God upholds all things. We reject the false doctrine that beyond its special commission the State should and could become the sole and total order of human life and so fulfil the vocation of the Church as well. We reject the false doctrine that beyond its special commissions the Church should and could take on the nature, tasks and dignity which belong to the State and thus become itself an organ of the State.

According to this thesis, both Church *and* State are mere *relative* authorities under the authority of God. The government employs force to secure justice while the Church preaches grace, administers sacraments, and consoles humanity to secure peace and justice. In this thesis in particular, the Lutheran influence of the Confessing Church is felt because it relies heavily on the Lutheran doctrine of the Two Kingdoms where each sphere—State and Church—have different vocations. On many levels, this separation of powers harmed the Church because it allowed church leaders to hand the State its own Christian responsibility for human dignity, wellbeing, and protection. In its naive trust that the State would protect its citizens, the Church failed to address the racism and persecution it was witnessing. Only through the process of coming together at the First Synod of Barmen did Protestants begin to develop a modern theological imagination for the Church as an institution that would raise up a prophetic voice against the State in the name of justice.

It is not that the leaders of Barmen agreed with the racism of the State; quite the contrary. Barth himself held personal opinions that any acceptance of the Aryan paragraph by any Church synod was basically heretical.[21] Several months before the Barmen Declaration was drafted, Barth preached a sermon on Romans 15. In it he claimed that having faith in Christ who was Jewish meant that Christians had absolutely no reason to participate in the abuse of the Jews that was occurring. Such hate was not Christian but a sign of the "purest paganism."[22] Moreover, he preached, "Whoever turns against the Jews also turns against the God of free grace."[23] Several people walked out on him the day he preached this sermon.[24] (And later on he decided to send the sermon to Hitler!)

But when it came to including wording against Nazi-sanctioned racism in the Barmen Declaration itself, Barth, as its main author, sidestepped the issue. He did not include any clear statement of solidarity with Jewish people, and neither of his co-authors seemed to encourage him to do so. The Barmen Declaration contains no outright condemnation of the racism in German and Church culture, nor is there any call for the protection of Jewish German citizens.

This may have been Barmen's biggest mistake. As eminent church historian Klaus Scholder has asked, "Did 'theological existence' here become an end in itself?" He calls Barth's writing "almost prophetic"—with the emphasis on *almost*.[25] Barth's crucial weakness—and hence the weakness of Barmen—was that he did not find a way to unambiguously address the central problem for the Christian Church, namely Hitler's anti-Semitic, murderous policies that were crystalized in the Aryan Paragraph and acted out upon Jewish German citizens. Scholder remarks that Barmen's guilt of omission is "irrefutable."[26]

Barth's instinct was to *do theology* and not politics in the face of corruption, racism, and harmful social policies. Because Barth consistently refused to let theology have a direct political voice, he did not give any kind of Christian moral compass for average people. Indeed, he argued for a theological connection between Christianity and the Jews, but he did not show a way how to turn this Christian truth into political acts of faith. Looking back at history, there is little justification for this kind of tepid treatment of those who were being persecuted around him. But in many ways during this era in Germany, justice and protection were political issues, not theological ones. After all, justice was the job of the State, not the Church. Barth and his comrades did not have any kind of postcolonial view of Christianity in mind when they were writing the Barmen Declaration. They were worried about being colonized themselves by Nazi ideology, which had already colonized large parts of German Lutheranism.

In Barth's view at the time, political solidarity and social justice could easily distract the Church from its first task of speaking the Word of God. The falsehood of the distinction between theology and politics was a lesson that German theologians would only really comprehend in the decades after the German catastrophe and the Holocaust. Speaking the Word of God without solidarity, protection, and justice is not speaking the Word of God at all. Despite his own lack of clarity on the issue of a *Christian* call to justice, Barth's language in Thesis Two of the Barmen Declaration cracks open a door onto a theological vision for justice:

2. As Jesus Christ is God's comforting pronouncement of the forgiveness of all our sins, so and with equal seriousness, he is also God's vigorous announcement of his claim upon our whole life. Through him there comes to us joyful liberation from the godless ties of this world, for free, grateful service to his creatures.

Thesis Two speaks of the *liberating* authority and power of Jesus Christ. This affirmation of Christian liberation speaks straight into postcolonial and anti-racist theological projects of faith communities today. The liberating authority of Jesus Christ is a self-emptying, generous power. This kenotic vision of divine authority helps the Church understand its own power and can direct Christian energies at countering the effects of the imperialistic ways that European countries have exploited countries in Africa, Asia, and South America. It speaks to faith movements like feminist, womanist, and queer theology, as well as anti-racist, anti-capitalistic, and anti-colonial faith commitments.

While Thesis Two of the Barmen Declaration did not seem to inspire German Protestants in any obvious way to help their fellow Jewish citizens, it does point to the tasks and goals of political theologies today, for example the liberation and freedom of those who are exploited from economic systems, *in which the Christian Church itself has been complicit*. Just as parts of the German Christian Church were complicit in Hitler's rise to power and his destructive social policies, many parts of the Christian Church today are complicit with the oppressive economic strategies and policies of late-modern capitalism, militarism, and imperialism. Post-Holocaust, postcolonial political theologies are calling Christians to be liberated from the "godless ties of this world" in which the Christian Church itself has participated. Although Barmen did not live into this, it was a foreshadowing of postwar Christian priorities.

BARTH, BARMEN, AND GERMAN RACISM TOWARDS JEWISH PEOPLE

Barth's Commitment to Christ's Place in Society

In many ways, Karl Barth was the right person to be the main author of the Barmen Declaration. Not only had he been thinking about these issues for over a decade, but he also was a towering personality. Even though he had been deeply involved in politics since his earliest days as a pastor, he maintained an unwavering vision of theology above all else.

Barth was no stranger to religion and politics. In his days as a pastor in the Swiss village of Safenwil, he had been involved in socialist causes for better wages and working conditions for those in his congregation, and even became known as the "red pastor."[27] He was interested early on in the socialist philosophy of political thinkers like Leonard Ragaz, but he quickly learned that social justice movements could not be sustained if they are not grounded in a larger vision of reality and in an eschatological horizon for the future.

Barth's theological commitments that are seen in the Barmen Declaration can be traced back to 1919 and a public lecture that he gave on "The Christian's Place in Society." This lecture anticipated the kind of prophetic theology that would characterize Barmen. In it Barth argued that the Christian's place in society in not about the Christian *individual person* but rather about *Christ* himself. This was a move away from the centuries-long mistake that the Church had been making by focusing on pious sentimentality, individual morality, political involvement, or a romantic notion of history. Barth's early theology established that God is revealed only in Jesus Christ. No other pillar of human experience, such as the inner life, history, culture, or government could stand next to it as a source of God's revelation. God is truly an *Other Being* who breaks into world history, and who calls into question every human construction, institution, religion and imagination.

Against "Natural Theology"

Barth had a keen eye for how the German liberal Protestant tradition had gradually given up on the strange otherness of God's being. Theology had placed its faith in the progress of history and humanity and had forgotten what God's revelation means for the Church. Protestant theology gave in to the human tendency to turn humanly manufactured realities like governments, institutions, and even self-image into God's own revelation. It was this "natural" human tendency to domesticate the otherness of God that Barth referred to in his rhetoric against "natural theology." It had nothing to do with ecology, creation, or the environment, and everything to do with the natural human quest for power, resources, and identity. It is one of the reasons why liberal Protestantism fell under the spell of Hitler's nationalism and racism. And it also played a role in how slowly the Confessing Church progressed toward a unified theological vision: so many pastors were caught up the "natural theology" of German racial uniqueness as a part of God's revelation. Pastors were as entranced as anybody in 1933 with the magical historical moment of Hitler's seizure of power. His was not simply a crass political move, it was a revelation from God.

Once the Nazis took control of the Reichstag in January 1933, Barth became even fiercer in his criticism.[28] He expressed shock that the German churches agreed with the new Nazi regime's ideas. It was the ugliest manifestation of Protestantism's 200-year mistake of letting the State define authority rather than claiming some of that authority in the name of Jesus Christ. In the very first days of the Third Reich, Barth gave a lecture on "The First Commandment as a Theological Axiom." In it, he appealed to the first of the Ten Commandments to argue that the Church must serve God alone and no other "authorities." Authority about human dignity, ethics, and even political decisions needed to be based on God's revelation in Jesus Christ, not State priorities. Likewise, Christianity must not be employed to buoy political agendas. The Church must never give in to having "other gods" than God and it must turn away from every form of natural theology.[29]

This lecture inspired Barth to begin a new series of monographs, entitled *Theological Existence Today!* In it, he argued that the most important thing the Church could do in politically turbulent times was to *do theology* and *proclaim the Gospel* to the people. The Church has to "proclaim the Gospel even *in the* Third Reich, but not *under* it nor in *its* spirit." Belonging to a congregation must not be determined "by blood" or "by race." Precisely because the Church need not obey *humans*, it also then "does not have to serve the German people."[30] Under this logic, the Deutsche Christen faction of German Protestantism was heresy. This was a bold statement, but it did not stop Barth from sending a copy of this pamphlet to Hitler himself on July 1, 1933. Whether or not Hitler ever read it, it was banned seven days later, on July 28.[31] But unintended consequences followed: rather than preventing its circulation, the ban only made *Theological Existence Today!* even more sought after and it was widely circulated. Its reception among readers throughout Germany was so positive that Barth and his friend Eduard Thurneysen began publishing more monographs under the same title. To many readers, *Theological Existence Today!* became the "first trumpet blast of the 'Confessing Church.'"[32]

Barth's argument against natural theology was foundational for the Barmen Declaration. Next to the affirmation that Jesus Christ was the one Word and sole authority over the Church, the dispute against natural theology was Barth's highest priority. It is evidenced in the language of Barmen's rejection in Thesis One of "other events, power, historic figures, and truths" as part of God's revelation. It also shapes Thesis Three which states that the Church must not hand over its message of God's revelation in Christ to any "vicissitudes of the prevailing ideological and political convictions of the day."[33]

Barth carried his rejection of natural theology way beyond the Barmen Declaration. Months after the Barmen Declaration was adopted, he wrote an argument against his colleague Emil Brunner, with the highly polemical title of "No!" It seemed that Brunner wanted to affirm points of contact between humans and God's revelation.[34] But to Barth, any attempt to find a connection between earthly powers and the self-revelation of God was a fatal game to play. With the Church's life already hanging by a thread under the rule of Hitler and the ideology of the Deutsche Christen corrupting German Christianity, the only way it could preserve the freedom of the Gospel was to reject any and all theology that did not take a hard line against every creaturely attempt to connect the political or social conditions to God's revelation.

With all this political activity, Barth sensed that sooner or later he would be kicked out of his teaching post in Bonn. So, he used his time in Germany to call the church to resist State authorities who were trying to co-opt Christianity for the Nazi agenda. One notable instance was October 1933 when Barth spoke with the Pastors' Emergency League and asked them what the Church was going to do about the concentration camps and the treatment of the Jews. But at this point in time, the Confessing Church was not receptive to these pointed questions and several of its leaders ultimately played a part in his removal from his professorship in Bonn.[35] It did not help matters when Barth, in his commitment to the singular authority of the Word of God, refused to begin his class with an oath to Hitler. He was reported and fired. In March 1935 he was forbidden to speak in public. By May he had to leave the country and he returned to Basel.

Barth, the Jews, and Judaism

Although Barth's clarity about the freedom of the Gospel from the State and from all forms of natural theology was deeply consistent, his views on the Jews, Judaism, and the Jewish people were more complicated. Scholars to this day are divided in their interpretation of Barth on the Jews and Judaism. On the one hand, many scholars, from the well-known Kurt Scholder, F.W. Marquardt, and Katherine Sonderegger, have interpreted Barth's rhetoric and preaching during the Nazi regime as being *politically* against State racism toward the Jewish people, but *theologically* ambivalent about them as a group. However, Barth's former assistant and prolific interpreter of his theology, Eberhard Busch, sees it otherwise.

Common scholarly interpretation of Barth's theology of the 1930s focuses on the troubling dialectic in his theology of Israel and the Jews. Despite articulating a theology of shared covenant between Christians and Jews, Barth binds Israel and Judaism to the *rejection* and *judgment* of Jesus Christ because it has yet to see its own election in Christ. Barth equates Israel with God's taking on of perverse, resistant, and wayward flesh in order to show God's unbounded grace for sinners. His discussion of Judas, the disciple who betrayed Jesus, reveals this darker side of his view.[36] On the one hand, like Israel, Judas is the closest intimate to Jesus Christ. But on the other hand, Judas hands him over and is himself rejected. This view of Barth's theology focuses on how Barth disconnected a *Christianly defined* view of "Jewishness" from the living tradition of Judaism as it was practiced, self-defined, and handed down throughout time. He worked with an abstracted, formalized idea of Jewishness without considering rabbinic Judaism on its own terms. Barth awaited the day when Judaism would be converted to its own election in Christ.

Eberhard Busch, on the other hand, notes all the ways that Barth clearly and unequivocally stated his own support for the Jewish people. As early as his 1919 *Romans* commentary, he instinctually joined Christians and Jews together under one God. He developed this connection as a *covenantal* one and rooted it deeply in Christology. Jesus is not just Jewish flesh. As the eternal Son of God in the Jewish flesh, Barth states that Jesus is "eternally a Jew."[37] Salvation comes through Jesus the Jewish person, namely, through Israel and not without it. Any calls to tear the Old Testament away from the New were heretical.

In fact, Barth believed that there was enough evidence in Scripture to establish the indissoluble connection between Christians and Jews such that if Christians do not accept the Jews as the relatives and ancestors of Jesus, then they cannot accept Jesus himself. He was less concerned with how the Jews related to Jesus Christ and more concerned with how *Christ* is related to them through his unconditional and unbreakable "Yes" to his people. Both Jews who struggle with God and Gentiles who struggle with idolatry are all children of the one, unified, living God.[38] This community of Jews and Christians under the one covenant and Word of God could witness *together* to the lost German masses who were mesmerized by the ideology of the German tyrannical State.[39]

The fact that the Confessing Church remained ambivalent about the humanity and worth of their Jewish neighbors left Barth doubtful that it could even be a true Church. The existence of a true Church would have the capacity to stand in solidarity with Jews.[40] But the divisions, warring factions, and confusion about State and Church authority that prevailed among Confessing Church members left it with no capacity to help the Jews or condemn Hitler's destructive policies. In a letter to a colleague, in January of 1934, Barth called for the Church to resist, but he also admitted that such a church "as things are simply does not exist."[41] Unfortunately, Barth did not follow his instincts in the Barmen Declaration. A call for solidarity with the Jews did not make a clear and pronounced appearance in the Barmen Declaration. Barth's theology at the time was not able to energize Protestant individuals and communities to mobilize against the *racism* and the dehumanization that was happening right under the Confessing Church's nose. He would come to deeply regret this.[42]

A CONFESSION OF GUILT

Although the First Synod of Barmen was a moment when the Evangelical German Church refused to allow Hitler's totalitarianism to penetrate its own faith, and although it helped unite Protestants against the Third Reich, it did not speak clearly and boldly about the racism and genocidal tendencies that were present in German society, government, and even Christianity at the time. It was fighting for its own life; justice for others would have to wait. Barth himself admitted later that the Barmen Declaration was not enough in the face of the radical evil of the Third Reich.

For his part, Hitler knew from the beginning that both the Catholic and the Protestant churches in Germany had the potential to resist him. And yet they did not. They did not see the profound breach of justice and human dignity that occurred under his regime. Konrad Adenauer wrote to a pastor in Bonn before he became the first chancellor of the newly created West Germany, "I believe that if all the bishops had together made public statements from the pulpits on a particular day, they could have prevented a great deal. That did not happen . . . It would have been no bad thing if the bishops had all been put in prison or in a concentration camp as a result . . . But none of that happened and therefore it is best to keep quiet."[43]

The Evangelical Church in Germany also came to a similar conclusion as well. On October 19, 1945, the Evangelical Church in Germany (EKD) issued a church-wide statement that confessed its own complicity in the attempted extermination of the Jewish people. In what was titled the Stuttgart Declaration of Guilt, the church began a series of statements that explored and aired its special responsibility for the political catastrophe of Hitler's Germany.

Even though the Stuttgart Declaration of Guilt was not meant to be a political document, in many ways it had deep political consequences for the church. It put the Protestant church's theology on a very different footing when it came to engaging society and politics than it had previously been on. The Stuttgart Declaration of Guilt stated in the name of the Protestant German Church that "we accuse ourselves of not having confessed more boldly, prayed more faithfully, believed more joyfully and loved more ardently."[44] It opened up the German Church to more ecumenical possibilities and to its central role in social justice. Indeed, partly because of the Barmen Declaration and the Protestant willingness to examine itself, the churches themselves gained a profound influence on German individuals and German culture in the years after Germany's defeat.[45] The Church became a leader in the political discourse on human dignity, freedom, and justice. On many levels, the Stuttgart Declaration of Guilt, born out of the German Church Struggle and the Barmen Declaration, opened up a new era for the German Evangelical Church such that it now sees itself as a champion for issues of oppression, poverty, and injustices in the world.

CONCLUSION

The Barmen Declaration has emerged as one of the most important and heroic documents of twentieth-century Protestantism. Its heroism lies both in its success in carving out a sphere of freedom from tyranny for the Christian faith in the Nazi regime as well as in its nature as a document of the Church's own agonizing struggle in the face of a totalitarian ideology. To truly understand how difficult its birth was, and the significance it had for those who lived through Hitler's disastrous Third Reich, the stories of the men who worked to make it happen must be told and retold. They must be seen for what they were fighting for, namely freedom of the Church and the Christian imagination from totalitarian ideologies and government interference.

Even though Barmen fell short of energizing Christians en masse to take risks for their Jewish neighbors, and even though it did not give a clear signal about the Christian mandate to work towards justice, it did create a tiny pocket of power for the Evangelical German Church in the face of tremendous political pressure and a totalitarian regime. It put forth a theological vision that hopefully can still inspire faith communities today to fight for both freedom and justice.

NOTES

1. Eberhard Busch, Darrell L. Guder, and Judith J. Guder. *The Barmen Theses Then and Now: The 2004 Warfield Lectures at Princeton Theological Seminary*. English ed. (Grand Rapids, Mich.: W.B. Eerdmans Pub. 2010), 6.

2. The year 1933 was the 450th birthday of Martin Luther. All across Germany, festivals honoring the Reformer were used to rally Germans around nationalistic and racist sentiment. He was seen as a hero of the German people and was presented as a Christian figure in support of the Third Reich. The most-quoted text of his that year was "*Germanis meis natus sum, quibus et serviam*": "I was born for my beloved Germans; it is them I want to serve." See Klaus Scholder, *The Churches and the Third Reich*. Vol. 1 (Philadelphia: Fortress Press, 1988), 545.

3. Church historian Kurt Dietrich Schmidt collected seventy-five different texts from congregations and churches from the year 1933. Many of these represented racist views against the Jews and a priority for the German race. See Busch, *Barmen Then and Now*, 2.

4. As one Dr. Walther Grundmann stated, since the gospel had already been Hellenized without damage, it can now undergo a "'Germanizing' process" without damage. See Arthur C. Cochrane, *The Church's Confession Under Hitler* (Philadelphia: Westminster Press, 1962), 115.

5. Bodelschwingh quoted in Scholder, *The Churches in the Third Reich*, Vol. 1, 332.

6. Klaus Scholder and John Bowden, *A Requiem for Hitler: And Other New Perspectives on the German Church Struggle* (London: SCM Press, 1989), 173, quoting a speech Hitler gave in 1922 to a Roman Catholic audience. See the original source in E. Jäckel, ed., *Hitler: Sämtliche Aufzeichnungen 1905–1924* (Stuttgart: Deutsche Verlags-Anstatt, 1980), 623.

7. Scholder and Bowden, *Requiem*, 181. It is clear from monologues from 1941/42, found in the Führer's headquarters, that he planned on annihilating Christianity after he had exterminated the Jews.

8. Scholder and Bowden, *Requiem*, 101.

9. In summary, the four points were: 1) sole dedication to Holy Scripture and the Reformation confessional documents; 2) trusting von Bodelschwingh to lead in the vigilance of the confessions of the Church; 3) being responsible for anyone persecuted, as a sign of commitment to the confessions; and 4) rejecting the Aryan Paragraph.

10. See Rolf Ahlers, *The Barmen Theological Declaration of 1934, The Archeology of a Confessional Text*, Toronto Studies in Theology Volume 24, (Lewiston: The Edwin Mellen Press, 1986), 151ff.

11. Eberhard Bethge and Victoria Barnett, *Dietrich Bonhoeffer: Theologian, Christian, Man for His Times; a Biography*, rev. ed. (Minneapolis, MN: Fortress Press: 2000), 300–303.

12. Eberhard Busch, *Karl Barth: His Life from Letters and Autobiographical Texts* (Philadelphia: Fortress Press, 1976), 236.

13. Klaus Scholder, *The Churches and the Third Reich*, Vol. 1, 581.

14. For details of the many synodical meetings, see Klaus Scholder, *The Churches and the Third Reich*, Vol. 2, 53–62.

15. See Klaus Scholder, *The Churches and the Third Reich*, Vol. 2, 85–86.

16. As the seemingly true story goes, Barth drafted the text over a three-hour lunch break, fueled by "a strong coffee and one or two Brazilian cigars." See Eberhard Busch *Karl Barth*, 245.

17. Arthur Cochrane, *The Church's Confession*, 151. Karl Immer worked tirelessly to distribute the reports of the important synods of the Church. He was eventually seen as a danger by the Reich and arrested.

18. The translation used here is by Douglas Bax from 1984, from the *Journal of Theology for Southern Africa*, found in Eberhard Jüngel, D. Bruce Hamill, and Alan J. Torrance, *Christ, Justice and Peace: Toward a Theology of the State in Dialogue with the Barmen Declaration*. (Edinburgh: T&T Clark: 1992), xxi–xxix. The Scriptures that buttresses each of these theses are also omitted here. The full text of Barmen can be accessed online here: http://www.sacred-texts.com/chr/barmen.htm.
19. Barth expounded on this topic in a lecture entitled "The First Commandment as Theological Axiom," in Barth, *Theologische Fragen und Antworten: Gesämmelte Vorträge*, Vol. 3 (Zürich: Zollikon, 1957), 127–143.
20. Scholder and Bowden, *Requiem*, 104.
21. See Eberhard Busch, *Unter Dem Bogen Des Einen Bundes: Karl Barth Und Die Juden 1933–1945* (Neukirchen-Vluyn: Neukirchener, 1996), 60–64.
22. Busch, *Unter Dem Bogen Des Einen Bundes*, 173.
23. Busch, *Barmen Then and Now*, 33.
24. That sermon was preached on December 10, 1933. See Karl Barth, "Predigt über Römer 15:5–13," in Karl Barth, *Die Kirche Jesu Christi, Theologische Existenz heute*, 5 (München: Chr. Kaiser Verlag, 1933), 13–18.
25. Scholder, *The Churches and the Third Reich*, Vol. 1, 437.
26. Scholder and Bowden, *Requiem*, 104.
27. Busch, *Karl Barth*, 83.
28. Barth always thought that the teachings of the Deutsche Christen were only ever "a small collection of odds and ends from the great theological dusts-bins . . . of the despised eighteenth and nineteenth centuries." See Karl Barth, *Theological Existence To-Day!*, R. Birch Hoyle, trans. (Eugene, OR: Wipf & Stock, 2011), 53.
29. See Busch, *Karl Barth*, 224.
30. Barth, *Theological Existence To-Day!*, 51–52.
31. Busch, *Karl Barth*, 227.
32. Ibid., 226.
33. Jüngel, *Christ, Justice, and Peace*, xxvi.
34. For the full discussion between Barth and Brunner, see John Baillie, *Emil Brunner, and Karl Barth. Natural Theology: Comprising "Nature and Grace"* (London: Bles, 1946).
35. Common perceptions today place Barth's removal from Bonn squarely on the event of his refusal to take the Hitler oath. But as Busch points out, it was well known at the time that Barth's statements to the Pastors' Emergency League disturbed Protestant leaders and led to his removal. Eberhard Busch, *Reformationstag 1933: Dokumente der Begegnung Karl Barths mit dem Pfarrernotbund in Berlin* (Zürich: Theologischer Verlag, 1998), 69f., 106.
36. See Barth's discussion on Judas and the rejection of Christ in *Church Dogmatics* II/2, §§ 34, 35. See also Katherine Sonderegger, *That Jesus Christ was Born a Jew: Karl Barth's "Doctrine of Israel"* (University Park, PA: The Pennsylvania State University Press, 1992).
37. Richard E. Burnett, *The Westminster Handbook to Karl Barth*. First edition. The Westminster Handbooks to Christian Theology (Louisville, KY: Westminster John Knox Press, 2013), 119. See also Barth's preaching on the Jewishness of Jesus in his sermon for Advent 2, 1933, translated by John Michael Owen in *Karl Barth: Post-Holocaust Theologian?* George Hunsinger, ed. (New York: Bloomsbury T&T Clark, 2018), 15–32.
38. See Karl Barth, "Die Kirche Jesu Christi," in *Theologische Existenz Heute*, 5, Munich, 1933, p. 17.
39. Karl Barth, *Church Dogmatics*, II/2, 311ff.

40. When Barth published the second half of volume two of the *Church Dogmatics* in 1942, he makes clear arguments for Christian solidarity and fellowship with Jewish people. See *Church Dogmatics* II/2, 202, 289.
41. Barth wrote this in a letter to a Frau Schmidt on January 1, 1934 cited in Eberhard Busch, "The Covenant of Grace Fulfilled in Christ as the Foundation of the Indissoluble Solidarity of the Church with Israel: Barth's Position on the Jews During the Hitler Era," *Karl Barth: Post Holocaust Theologian?*, 33-54.
42. See Barth's letter to Eberhard Bethge from May 22, 1967 in Karl Barth, Jürgen Fangmeier, Hinrich Stoevesandt, and Geoffrey William Bromiley, *Letters, 1961-1968* (Grand Rapids, MI: Eerdmans, 1981).
43. See Konrad Adenauer, *Briefe 1945-1947*, Rhöndorf Edition (Berlin: Siedler, 1983), 172f.
44. Scholder and Bowden, *Requieum*, 122.
45. See Franklin Hamlin Littell, *The German Phoenix: Men and Movements in the Church in Germany* (New York: Doubleday, 1960), 3-16.

SELECT BIBLIOGRAPHY

Ahlers, Rolf (1986), *The Barmen Theological Declaration of 1934, The Archeology of a Confessional Text*, Toronto Studies in Theology Volume 24, Lewiston, NY: The Edwin Mellen Press.

Barth, Karl (1957), *Church Dogmatics: Volume II–The Doctrine of God Part 2–The Election of God; The Command of God*, trans. G.W. Bromiley, Edinburgh: Bloomsbury Publishing.

Barth, Karl (2011), *Theological Existence To-Day!* trans. R. Birch Hoyle, Eugene, OR: Wipf & Stock.

Barth, Karl, Jürgen Fangmeier, Hinrich Stoevesandt, and Geoffrey William Bromiley (1981), *Letters, 1961-1968*, Grand Rapids, MI: Wm. B. Eerdmans Pub. Co.

Bethge, Eberhard and Victoria Barnett (2000), *Dietrich Bonhoeffer: Theologian, Christian, Man for His Times; a Biography* (rev. ed.), Minneapolis, MN: Fortress Press.

Busch, Eberhard (1976), *Karl Barth: His Life from Letters and Autobiographical Texts*, Philadelphia: Fortress Press.

Busch, Eberhard, Darrell L. Guder, and Judith J. Guder (2010), *The Barmen Theses Then and Now: The 2004 Warfield Lectures at Princeton Theological Seminary*, Grand Rapids, MI: Wm. B. Eerdmans Pub. Co.

Cochrane, Arthur C. (1962), *The Church's Confession Under Hitler*, Philadelphia: Westminster Press.

Hunsinger, George ed. (2018), *Karl Barth: Post-Holocaust Theologian?* New York: Bloomsbury T&T Clark.

Jüngel, Eberhard, D. Bruce Hamill, and Alan J. Torrance (1992), *Christ, Justice and Peace: Toward a Theology of the State in Dialogue with the Barmen Declaration*, Edinburgh: T&T Clark.

Scholder, Klaus (1987), *The Churches and the Third Reich*, 2 volumes, London, SCM Press.

Scholder, Klaus and John Bowden (1989), *A Requiem for Hitler: And Other New Perspectives on the German Church Struggle*, London: SCM Press.

Sonderegger, Katherine (1992), *That Jesus Christ was Born a Jew: Karl Barth's "Doctrine of Israel"*, University Park, PA: Pennsylvania State University Press.

CHAPTER THIRTEEN

Bonhoeffer in Latin American Liberationist Christianity and Theology

RAIMUNDO C. BARRETO, JR.

INTRODUCTION

Dietrich Bonhoeffer was one of the most fascinating theologians of the twentieth century. According to Preston Parsons, "It is difficult to name another modern theologian who is claimed by as many different Christians."[1] At a time when many in Germany were flirting with the ideology of National Socialism, Bonhoeffer was one of the most significant prophetic voices refusing to blur the lines between the German identity and Christian faith. He lived his convictions and his journey ended dramatically as Hitler's regime imprisoned and executed him. Those who witnessed his farewell to his cellmates have stated that during his last hour his faith remained strong.[2] Several decades after his tragic death, many of Bonhoeffer's theological ideas continue to capture the imagination of Christians and theologians of all stripes and from all over the world.[3]

Bonhoeffer has contributed theological resources and has been an important partner in conversation for some of the Latin Americans involved in the development of liberationist and public theologies. The fact that Bonhoeffer's "theological theses are deeply imbued with the experiences of his life"[4] validates him even more as an important reference for those doing theology in the Latin American context. As Christiane Tietz highlights, "For many people, Bonhoeffer has become a memorial to what responsible action during the National Socialist era should have looked like. At the same time, he is also cherished as a model of credible Christian faith today."[5]

A group of young ecumenical Protestants were the first to express interest in Bonhoeffer in Latin America. These young people—many of whom were college and seminary students—were trying to live a faithful and authentic life under dire political and economic circumstances in the 1950s and 1960s. They promptly identified with him when they read his writings and learned about the circumstances of his life and death. For them, Bonhoeffer was not only an inspiration and a model of Christian faith, but he also offered theological insights that could help them develop their own theology of resistance and liberation.

English-speaking scholars have not yet noticed the extent to which Latin Americans have engaged Bonhoeffer's theological insights.[6] Likewise, in Latin America, only a limited number of publications in Spanish and Portuguese have addressed the impact of Bonhoeffer on Latin American theological thinking.[7] In spite of that, interest in Bonhoeffer in the region has been greater than one might expect. Writing on the reception of Bonhoeffer in Latin America, Luciana Soares Ramos concluded that a significant number of Latin American Protestant and Catholic authors have engaged Bonhoeffer's work over the years. For her, one can even find a Bonhoefferian "mark" in several of them.[8] That engagement, according to her, is a result of several shared themes between Bonhoeffer and Latin American theologians. Beyond that, she also highlights the perception of Bonhoeffer on a more popular level as an icon or symbol; Bonhoeffer is depicted as a pastor, prophet, martyr, or saint,[9] making his story particularly meaningful to those who have learned to see the world from the underside of history.

Rubem Alves, one of the founders of liberation theology, expresses the sensation that many young seminarians in his generation had when they began to read Bonhoeffer's *Letters and Papers from Prison*:

> The reading of the letters he wrote to some of his friends during this period gave us the singular impression of being one of them. As if his world was ours: same questions, same problems, same doubts. That is the reason why we cannot read him without becoming involved, even when we do not agree with his solutions. This happens because Bonhoeffer is one of those rare cases of a man who by living and articulating his personal experience, also lived and articulated the experience of an entire generation. Reading his texts, then, is almost like reading our own autobiography. The most important consequence of this fact is that his ideas are never simple curiosities to be examined, but tools that help us organize our own experience and our relationship with the world.[10]

Alves makes it clear that Latin American readings of Bonhoeffer are not simply an interpretation of his thought and life. They are instead inter-contextual readings, with one eye on Bonhoeffer and his context and the other eye carefully considering the Latin American reality. As such, Latin American readings of Bonhoeffer can both shed new light on the inexhaustible wealth of Bonhoeffer's theology (and its interpretations) and the Latin American context in which they have been read. Latin American theologians have dialogued with Bonhoeffer, in their search for meaningful theological language to help Latin American Christians to faithfully respond to a reality affected by political instability and enduring economic and social injustices.

This chapter traces some of these meaningful interactions with Bonhoeffer in Latin America, with particular attention to the Church and Society Movement, a Christian movement directly impacted by interactions with Bonhoeffer's writings. I discuss the context where such interactions have taken place, distinguishing the Protestant and Catholic contributions to the formation of Latin American liberation theology (LALT), while shedding light onto the relationship between that form of theologizing and Bonhoeffer's theological insights. In the process, the reader will be able to see the different points of contact between Bonhoeffer and Latin America, and the multiple and creative ways as Bonhoeffer has been interpreted in that context.

PAVING THE WAY FOR LATIN AMERICAN LIBERATION THEOLOGIES

There is no indication that Bonhoeffer's brief contact with Latin America made any lasting impact on his thinking.[11] At the time of his visit to Cuba and Mexico, there was no distinctly Latin American theology. Latin American theologies, both Catholic and

Protestant, began to emerge in their own right only around the mid-twentieth century, and a full-blown self-identified Latin American theology only rose in the early 1970s with the liberation theologies initially formulated by Rubem Alves and Gustavo Gutierrez.[12] Prior to the appearance of the now classic body of literature on Latin American liberation theology, a long period of incubation took place within Protestant and Catholic circles.[13] It was during such period of incubation that Bonhoeffer's ideas became an important resource, particularly for Protestant groups thinking about the social and political implications of their faith.

Michael Löwy coined the term "liberationist Christianity" to describe this incubation period: the social movement that anticipated the birth of liberation theology. At least a decade before there was an identifiable liberation theology, a liberationist socio-political-religious movement emerged whose praxis became the source for the incipient Latin American theological reflection.[14] What is very often overlooked, though, is that because of the polarization between Catholicism and Protestantism as antagonistic religious identities, there were two similar social movements—one Catholic and other Protestant—running side-by-side, with little communication between them. They had, however, similar ideals appealing to Christians on both sides of this divide.

Löwy does not take into full account the distinctive ways this movement took shape within Protestant circles. Although acknowledging the existence of the movement *Iglesia y Sociedad* (ISAL), which was the Protestant face of such liberationist Christianity, he does not pay much attention to how liberationist Christianity took shape among Protestants. Initiatives from the Protestant-based ISAL contributed to the formation of NGOs and civil society institutions, which like the Catholic movements studied by Löwy were key in the prophetic denunciation of the violation of human rights during the terrible years of Latin American national-security states. In order to do justice to Protestant and Catholic contributions to liberation theologies, one must acknowledge their distinct historical trajectories up to the point they began to cooperate. Bonhoeffer's life and theology first comes to play during the formation of a Protestant/ecumenical liberationist Christianity.

Describing Bonhoeffer as an influential figure in Latin American protestant liberation theology might be a controversial move, when one takes into account the Latin American criticism of Eurocentric modernity.[15] However, one can paradoxically claim that in Latin American Protestant theological circles this mindset began to change in the mid-twentieth century, exactly when some Latin American students, in conversation with Bonhoeffer's theology, started to take their own context and reality as the starting point for their theologizing. M. Richard Shaull, influenced by Paul Lehmann, one of the closest American friends of Dietrich Bonhoeffer's, played a key role in that process. Teaching at the Presbyterian Seminary in Campinas, he challenged a model of theological education that imposed Western ways of thinking upon Brazilian students.[16] The challenge for those students to think on their own, from a Latin American perspective, was a turning point in Latin American Protestant theological reflection, contributing to the birth of the Protestant stream of LALT. Introduced by Shaull, the reading of Bonhoeffer became decisive for the development of that movement. According to Julio de Santa Ana, no other Western theologian influenced the ISAL's discussions as deeply as Bonhoeffer. Santa Ana puts Bonhoeffer's influence even above Shaull's. He says that Shaull played a vital role, but the theological thinking of the movement "at that time was clearly oriented by Bonhoeffer."[17]

Latin America at the time was considered the religious domain of the Roman Catholic Church. At the end of the nineteenth century, Protestants represented an insignificant fraction of the Latin American population, and Protestantism was increasingly associated with the expansion of the political and economic influence of the United States.[18] In Latin America at that point in time, external missionary agendas still guided the Protestant project.

In the aftermath of the Congress of Panama (1916)—the first ecumenical meeting in Latin America, organized by the Committee on Cooperation in Latin America (CCLA)—a long awakening of a Latin American Protestant identity began to evolve. In the subsequent congresses of Montevideo (1925) and Havana (1929), when emerging Latin American Protestant thinkers played a more prominent role, the question about a Latin American Protestant identity came to the fore. Whereas the first Latin America leaders were still advancing a foreign missionary agenda, their voices became gradually distinct from the international agencies that sponsored their work.[19]

The idea of a come-of-age Latin American Protestantism received a renewed impulse in the beginning of the 1950s. The formation of national chapters of the Christian Student Movement (MEC) in the region singularly challenged Latin American Protestant students to reflect on and respond to the social, political, and economic problems in their societies. MEC students began to see themselves as part of a broader student movement, which became an important political force in Latin American universities, while seeking to discern what was their role and contribution as Christians in that scenario. Alan Neely stated that these student Christian groups "acted as ideological incubators for the production of young Protestant Christians sensitive to the social and political implications of the gospel and who subsequently became the main ambassadors of the ISAL movement in the 1960s."[20]

In 1955, Richard Shaull and Waldo Cesar created the Department of Social Responsibility of the Church in Brazil, which served as the ferment for the emergence of a broader Church and Society movement in the whole region. Formally created in 1961, ISAL interacted with workers' unions, secular student movements, the Catholic Left, and Marxist thinkers, offering a Protestant perspective to the struggle for the creation of a more just society in Latin America.[21] It laid the foundations for a new way of doing theology, which emphasized the presence and action of God in the world and called on Christians to take sides with the oppressed. Their interest in Bonhoeffer's life and thought was part of a process, which freed themselves to do theology in dialogue with life. Their effort to understand their social and political roles as Latin American Christians, led them to turn the revolutionary situation in Latin America into their *locus theologicus*. The need to theologize in that context would lead them towards the language of liberation. Some of the theologians that participated in the Protestant version of this proto-liberation theology effort were Sergio Arce Martinez, Adolf Ham Reyes, Richard Shaull, Beatriz Melano, Rubem Alves, José Miguez Bonino, and Julio de Santa Ana.

Many of the people involved in the work of ISAL and related ecumenical initiatives, would later become active members of broader ecumenical networks. Some of them were forced to leave their churches, and ended up joining non-religious social and political movements—including, in a few cases, armed revolutionary groups. In their struggle against the apparatus of the national security states that emerged in the region, beginning with the 1964 military coup d'état in Brazil, a number of them had to go into exile.

In the Catholic context, Löwy suggests that liberationist Christianity as a social movement within the Latin American Catholic Church resulted of "a combination or convergences of changes within and without the Church in the late 1950s," developing "from the periphery to the center of the institution."[22] This social movement was influenced by post-Second World War theological currents in Germany and France, including new forms of Christianity such as that expressed in the worker priests movement.[23] At the same time, significant political and social changes were underway in Latin America. Under those circumstances,

> Lay Catholic movements, such as Catholic University Youth, Catholic Workers Youth and Catholic Action, or popular educational movements (Brazil), committees for the promotion of land reform (Nicaragua), Federations of Christian Peasants (El Salvador), and above all, the base communities, were, during the early 1960s the social arena in which Christians actively committed themselves to people's struggles, reinterpreted the Gospel in light of their practice, and, in some cases, were drawn towards Marxism.[24]

Many of these movements became autonomous, as it was the case with the Brazilian Catholic Student Youth (JUC), which by 1962 founded a political organization of Marxist orientation called Popular Action.[25] With the direct participation of priests in revolutionary struggle, these movements began to impact the Church throughout the continent. The theological formulations that emerged in the context of this liberationist Christianity would later be known as liberation theology. As Löwy has put it, "liberation theology is the spiritual product . . . of this social movement."[26]

There is no indication that Bonhoeffer's theological insights had any impact on Catholic liberationist Christianity. However, several references to Bonhoeffer can be found in the writings of quite a few Catholic Latin American liberation theologians. In the following two sections, I offer an overview of theological interactions with Bonhoeffer in Latin America. I begin with three Catholic liberationist critical reflections on Bonhoeffer. Then I move to describe Bonhoeffer's important influence on the Protestant stream of LALT.

BONHOEFFER IN THE WRITINGS OF CATHOLIC LIBERATION THEOLOGIANS

Latin American Catholic theologians only interacted with Bonhoeffer after LALT was already a factor in Latin American theologizing. They were less impacted by his theology than their Protestant counterparts.[27] In his *A Theology of Liberation*, Gutierrez makes only a few references to Bonhoeffer, almost as footnotes to his theological reasoning. In his discussion of the theological meaning of liberation, Gutierrez brings the Apostle Paul to mind as someone who defined the core of Christian life in terms of "the passage from the old to the new person, from sin to grace, from slavery to freedom."[28] Gutierrez thus interprets the Pauline understanding of liberation as being an act of God in Christ to set us free from the sin of selfishness, turning us free to love.[29] The salvific gift not only promotes spiritual change, but also a social one. In his argument, Gutierrez cites a passage from Bonhoeffer's *Creation and Fall*: "In the language of the Bible, freedom is not something man has for himself but something he has for others . . . Being free means 'being free for the other.'"[30] Gutierrez refers to Bonhoeffer once again in his discussion of secularization as worldliness. Speaking of secularization as a process that allows human beings the possibility of being more fully human, Gutierrez suggests that worldliness is "a necessary condition for an authentic relationship between humankind and nature, among human beings themselves, and finally, between humankind and God."[31] Here he refers to Bonhoeffer's concept of a world come of age and his important question about how to speak of God in this adult world. Gutierrez uses Bonhoeffer to support his argument that religion needs to be redefined in relation to the profane, the worldly sphere, so the church's impact on "the process of transformation of social structures" can be of greater significance.[32]

Towards the end of the 1970s, Gutierrez addressed Bonhoeffer's work more directly in a critical essay called "The Limitations of Modern Theology: On a Letter to Bonhoeffer."[33] In this text, Gutierrez praises Bonhoeffer for the critical stance he took against the modern understandings of religion and theology by rejecting "the easy terms of peace that the world dictated."[34] Bonhoeffer's critique of modern theology is double-edged. On the one hand, modern theology has lost its capacity to play any critical or prophetic role, because it accepted to be defined in the terms dictated by the modern world, where God has been pushed away from life. Gutierrez agrees with Bonhoeffer's criticism of liberal theology, as having become "the theology of a self-assured middle-class Christianity."[35] Modern theology became captive to modern liberalism, therefore self-serving and irrelevant to the lives of most people. On the other hand, Bonhoeffer was equally harsh on his criticism of conservative apologetics, which he described as "pointless, ignoble and unchristian."[36] In Bonhoeffer's words, this kind of apologetics confuses Christ with a particular stage of human religiousness, namely, with human law."[37] Thus, it contributes to turn the secularized modern mind into an anti-Christian force, reinforcing the relocation of religion to the margins of the modern Western society.

For Gutierrez, Bonhoeffer liberated the Christian mind from these captivities when he acknowledged the historical dimension of faith, asking the important questions about the meaning of Christianity and of God for today's world. He thus avoided both the defensiveness of conservative theologies that sought protection under the cover of religion and the individualism of a liberal theology that makes religion irrelevant to the public matters of life. Gutierrez praises Bonhoeffer's commitment to life, the way his theology was tied to his ministry, and the political commitment of the later part of his life. Bonhoeffer's main concern is the proclamation of the gospel. But instead of trying to bring the world back to religion, Bonhoeffer chooses to speak of Christ in a world come of age.

What brings Bonhoeffer closer to Latin American liberation theology in Gutierrez's eyes is his emphasis on the weakness of God in Christ, of a God that is revealed in God's relation to human suffering. This is a theme that will be present particularly in the Christology of Latin American liberation theologians. This emphasis leads Bonhoeffer to take a further step, asking another important question: "Where is suffering taking place?" Bonhoeffer's response is found particularly in Bonhoeffer's famous passage challenging Christian theologians to stand in solidarity with those who suffer and to learn to see "the great events of world history *from below*, from the perspective of the outcast, the suspects, the maltreated, the powerless, the oppressed, the reviled—in short, from the perspective of those who suffer."[38]

Looking at that, Gutierrez concedes that Bonhoeffer moved in the direction of those "on the underside of history,"[39] deploring "the unjust suffering of the outcast of society," and proclaiming "the right to life in all its dimensions as an exigence of the Bible."[40] However, he believes that due to the lack of critical social analysis, Bonhoeffer overlooked the fact that the humanity's adulthood was "built upon a world of poverty and plunder."[41] According to Gutierrez' criticism, a deeper critique of the modern society that created the conditions for the rise of National Socialism was needed.[42]

Franz Hinkelammert came to a similar conclusion in a lecture originally delivered in Costa Rica, in 1988.[43] He describes Bonhoeffer as one of the most intriguing theologians of the twentieth century, affirming that, in contrast to the liberal theology of his professors, Bonhoeffer believed that the question about the role of the church in the contemporary world was central to theology.⁴⁴ According to Hinkelammert, in Bonhoeffer, the church is the Christ that exists in community. Since Christ is understood as the being-for-others, the church is then a community that exists for others. This locus of enunciation allows Bonhoeffer to radicalize his theological perspective, which Hinkelammert describes as a critique of religion in the name of Christianity.⁴⁵ Christ who, for Bonhoeffer, is the center of life, is present in human affairs through his weakness for the sake of others.

Hinkelammert also describes Bonhoeffer's theology as being, for the most part, "the theological reflection on his own life and the decisions he had to make."⁴⁶ His historicized theology stands in dialogue with the historical conditions and the contexts of life which it must address. That is the reason why, when Latin American theologians began to read Bonhoeffer, they had a profound sense of familiarity towards him.⁴⁷ However, while Bonhoeffer's theology addressed the problem of a church facing the inhuman regime of Nazism, he did not pay enough attention to the economic and social system within which such regime emerged. Latin American liberation theologians, on the other hand, cannot overlook those factors. They "face the destructiveness of this economic and social system which, by the human exploitation it creates, promotes the rise of the totalitarian despotisms of the National Security [State]."⁴⁸

Furthermore, Hinkelammert is interested in Bonhoeffer's concept of immanent transcendence. For him, that is crucial to understand what Bonhoeffer means by irreligious Christianity. Bonhoeffer sees Christianity as a religion of resurrection, not of redemption. Resurrection is something that is constitutive of the reality of the world and which invites God to its midst. Therefore, God's presence in the world reveals itself in the human relations with themselves and with the world.⁴⁹ Bonhoeffer proposes a revelation of God in a Christ who, as the being-for-others, is the realization of such immanent transcendence. Thus, human relation with God is defined in terms of our participation in Christ's being for others.⁵⁰ The church is no longer conceived as the religious community of worshippers, but as the Christ that embodies in human relations.⁵¹

Finally, Hinkelammert stands with Bonhoeffer in his contrasting of Christianity and religion as two poles. Bonhoeffer bases Christianity on God's commandment to live and live for others. Since God commands human freedom, obedience and freedom are two faces of the same coin. Religion, on the other hand, is defined in terms of law, as the negation of immanent transcendence.

> Christianity puts transcendence in the interior of the world. Religion, on the other hand, puts it outside the world to judge it. Religion is necessarily law and compliance, and fixes God on the transgressions of the law . . . The world, instead of submitting to inner transcendence to it, now determines the religion of the world. Christianity, by becoming religious Christianity, is determined by the laws of the world, seeking God from [the place of] the transgressions of those laws.⁵²

The God that is manifest in Christ as the being-for-others is not merely an extension *ad infinitum* of the world.⁵³ That is why transcendence is key for Bonhoeffer. However, like Gutierrez, Hinkelammert sees a problem in Bonhoeffer's confidence in this world-come-of-age, which he romantically pictures as a stage in human history where there are no idols. He criticizes Bonhoeffer's lack of a concept of idolatry as one of his shortcomings. Bonhoeffer's criticism of religion doesn't go far enough, because it does not go beyond Christianity. He ignores, for example, the fact that Nazism is in itself a religion, which pervades more than Christianity.⁵⁴ It is indeed "a religion without any Christianity, which uses marginally and eclectically some Christian elements."⁵⁵ Bonhoeffer's romanticized view of the world-come-of-age prevents him from discerning that idolatrous non-Christian religion for what it really was.

By contrast, Hinkelammert sees Latin American liberation theology as moving from the critique of religion to the critique of idolatry, particularly as it deals with the idolatry of modern capitalism. Contrary to the romantic expectations of Bonhoeffer, for Hinkelammert, when the world emancipates itself from God it does not become a place without idols. Instead, it builds its own idols. Speaking from the perspective of the impoverished, LALT is not as concerned about religion, but about the idolatry produced in the world.⁵⁶

A third important Catholic Latin American liberation theologian who engages Bonhoeffer is Jon Sobrino.⁵⁷ Walter Altmann identifies several topics in Sobrino's Christology which coincide with Bonhoeffer's Christological emphases. First both of them profoundly identify with the suffering God—in Sobrino's phraseology, "the God of the victims." Sobrino's Christology was shaped by his experiences in Central America, particularly El Salvador. That experience led Sobrino to deeply identify with Bonhoeffer's *dictum* that "only the suffering God can be of help."⁵⁸

Sobrino, whose own Christology revolves around the idea that, on the cross, Jesus Christ revealed himself as the God of the poor, addresses Bonhoeffer's widely known poem "Christians and Pagans,"⁵⁹ which pictures the cross as "the critique to any natural access of the human being to God."⁶⁰ Agreeing with Bonhoeffer, Sobrino affirms that the cross challenges common notions of transcendence, and helps us reformulate the whole question of God. On the cross, "God is to be recognized through what seems to be quite the opposite of divine; i.e., suffering."⁶¹ Thus, we are invited to adopt a new attitude toward God. Now, it is the oppressed person, the one who suffers, that mediates God by posing a radical question of what means to be a human being.⁶² Sobrino also welcomes Bonhoeffer's notion of discipleship, affirming that in order to understand Jesus, it is imperative to follow him in human history, alongside with those who suffer.⁶³ In short, Sobrino highlights the importance of Bonhoeffer's notions of Christ as "the man for others," and his insights on the centrality of the cross and on costly discipleship. However, he is also aware of the limits of Bonhoeffer's Christology. For him, Bonhoeffer pointed the way for further exploration,⁶⁴ which Latin American theologians have built upon.⁶⁵

On top of being a reference for critical reflection within Catholic LALT circles, occasionally Bonhoeffer's life has inspired comparisons with Latin American martyrs for justice, like Camilo Torres and D. Oscar Romero.⁶⁶ Others have found inspiration in Bonhoeffer's letters from the prison as they have themselves been incarcerated as a result of their resistance to authoritarian regimes in Latin America. Luciana Ramos mentions, for instance, the influence of Bonhoeffer's letters from prison on Frei Betto, a Brazilian Dominican who also wrote letters during his incarceration under the military dictatorship in Brazil.⁶⁷

As one can see, Catholic liberation theologians have interacted in different ways with Bonhoeffer's life and thought. Such interaction, though, was not as formative for the Catholic social movement that preceded liberation theology. First-generation liberation theologians engaged Bonhoeffer as a critical partner of conversation, drawing on some of his theological insights as they elaborated their own theologies. Yet, a number of others found in his popularized image as a prophet and a martyr inspiration that was helpful as they coped with the suffering they experienced in their efforts to resist injustice.

Theological engagement of Bonhoeffer among Catholic liberation theologians has been mostly based on the commonality of theological themes. The interactions with him, as shown above, were limited. Only in the case of Sobrino can one see a more prominent Bonhoefferian tone in his Christology. In spite of that limited formative influence, Catholic Latin American liberation theologians have welcomed some of Bonhoeffer's insights, while criticizing, and creatively interpreting them in the Latin American context. To that extent, he can be counted among the non-Latin American sources and partners of conversation for LALT. In contraposition, some of the criticism offered by Latin American liberation theologians can enrich South–North conversation about the meaning of Bonhoeffer's life and work for today's world.

BONHOEFFER IN THE PROTESTANT STREAM OF LALT

In the case of the Protestant theologians who contributed to the formation of LALT, the influence of Bonhoeffer was more direct and formative. Paradoxically, publications on Bonhoeffer from that end are also scarce. In a lecture on the influence of Bonhoeffer on liberation theology, delivered in Geneva on the occasion of the commemorations of Bonhoeffer's seventieth anniversary, Uruguayan theologian Julio de Santa Ana categorically affirmed that in the case of the Protestants who contributed to the development of a LALT, "It could even be said that the German theologian's influence was decisive in the development of their present positions. This does not necessarily mean that Bonhoeffer was the forerunner of the theology of liberation, but simply that the Protestant contribution to it cannot be explained without his influence.[68] As mentioned earlier, information about Bonhoeffer's life and thought reached Latin American Protestants at a time when progressive Protestant sectors in Latin America were gaining greater awareness of their Latin American-ness. The Church and Society Movement (ISAL) was at the epicenter of Bonhoeffer's initial reception. Some of the participants in this movement, including Beatriz Melano, Richard Shaull, and Rubem Alves, studied at Princeton Theological Seminary and were directly or indirectly influenced by Paul Lehmann, who, in turn, had in Bonhoeffer one of his important references, and in Barth an influence shared with Bonhoeffer.

Richard Shaull first introduced Bonhoeffer to Latin American students during a seminar sponsored by the World Student Christian Federation in Sitio das Figueiras, Brazil, in 1952.[69] At that point they only discussed *The Cost of Discipleship*. In 1953, however, when he started teaching at the Presbyterian Seminary of Campinas, he also used *Life in Communion* and *The Letters and Papers from Prison* in his classes.[70]

Bonhoeffer soon became a common point of reference for an entire generation of Protestant students who would a few years down the road contribute to the creation of the first homegrown Latin American theology. Santa Ana uses the adjective *maieutic* to describe the nature of Bonhoeffer's influence on the development of this Protestant stream of LALT, since it happened in the context of sustained dialogue with his work, which enabled those young Latin American theologians to work on their own solutions to the problems they faced in their context. Santa Ana highlights three main questions they were dealing with: (a) the overcoming of the church/world dualism and the awareness of the deep implications of the process of secularization; (b) the relationship between faith and ideologies; and (c) the question of discipleship, i.e., how to follow Christ in a context where there seems to be no room for that.[71]

Around the time ISAL began to be articulated as a movement, Shaull and a group of Brazilian students were expelled from the Presbyterian Seminary in Campinas. ISAL became not only an alternative space for coordinated action, but also a think tank for an emerging progressive movement.[72] The many texts that were published by ISAL exhaled a theology filled with Bonhoeffer's themes and concerns.

ISAL's study guide published in 1964—the year of the US-backed military coup d'état in Brazil—as a reflection on Christian social responsibility in Latin America, has numerous references to Bonhoeffer's life and thought. In his contribution to that study guide, the Rev. Richard Couch addressed the need to overcome the dualism that seems to render the Protestant faith confined to individual concerns, referring to Bonhoeffer's views on the essential worldliness of the Gospel. "Dietrich Bonhoeffer, in his insistence on reality as the truth about the world and about God as it is united in Jesus Christ, has probably painted with more strength than any other modern theologian this dimension of 'worldliness'."[73] He then quotes from Bonhoeffer's *Ethics:*

> In Jesus Christ, the reality (*Wirklichkeit*) of God entered into the reality of this world ... God and the world consist of this name. In Him all things subsist (Col. 1:17) (Bonhoeffer, *Ethik*, 60). This double reality of God and the world is so deeply forged in one, according to Bonhoeffer, that in practice one cannot take God seriously without taking seriously the world in which he puts us, and vice versa.[74]

In his conclusion, he states that in the moment when this truth begins to inform our way of being and of walking in this world, "We will understand the deeply social nature of the purposes of God for man and the deep and intimate relationship between what the Church is and what men long for in society."[75] References to Bonhoeffer are found basically in the writings of all ISAL thinkers. The influence of Bonhoeffer on Richard Shaull, the mentor of the young theologians who founded that movement, partially explains that. Among other things, in his attempt to move towards a non-religious Christianity, Shaull boldly advanced a diasporic ecclesiology; i.e., a secularized and radical ecclesiology, leading to new forms of ecclesial life that identified with the reality of a continent undergoing profound social transformations.[76] Moved by this view of diasporic ecclesial communities living in the modern world, Shaull encouraged his students to form small communities in blue-collar industrial areas, where they would develop meaningful relationships with workers and college students. The most famous of these communities, which anticipated the Christian Base Communities that would emerge later in Catholic settings, was the one in Vila Anastacio, São Paulo. With some support from a local Presbyterian Church and the Union of Christian Students in Brazil (UCEB), a community of six people—including a pastor and a seminarian—worked in the steel industry and lived together as a Christian commune whose members intentionally engaged the concrete needs of the workers whom they related to. This small commune existed only for two years. In the process, a congregation was formed, which continued to exist for another ten years. That experiment, although limited in scope, served as a model for similar communities formed later in Brazil and in other countries.[77]

In contrast to what we saw in our overview of the interaction with Bonhoeffer's work in Latin American Catholic theologians, in the Protestant context, Bonhoeffer's influence was integral to the formation and development of the Church and Society Movement and to the liberation theology that sprang from it. It is worth noting that there was a significant theological production within that movement, which preceded the appearance of the body of literature known as LALT. Few of the ISAL Protestant theologians engaged Bonhoeffer more thoroughly and critically. But this entire generation of young thinkers read Bonhoeffer and found in him inspiration and a language that helped them formulate their Christian identity as responsible members of their societies in a very troubling time.

Some participants of this movement, such as Jose Miguez Bonino, Emilio Castro, Rubem Alves, and Julio de Santa Ana, became prolific writers. Their work is infused with references to Bonhoeffer and to his theology. Alves is credited with the prominent title of being the first to write a book-length treatise on liberation theology. His case, then, is worth some attention. Bonhoeffer and Lehmann are a visible influence in Alves' book *A Theology of Human Hope* (1969). His indebtedness to Lehmann is noted even in his suggestion of the expression "humanistic messianism," which became a key concept in Alves' discussion of political humanism.[78] Alves distinguished between humanistic messianism and messianic humanism. The latter is dependent on transcendent human power. The former, although firmly grounded in the historical experience, affirms the humanizing determination of the transcendent. That enables him to offer a theological account born out of the historical experience of liberation in Latin America, in spite of the collapse of all human resources. Alves evokes Bonhoeffer a number of times, making it clear very early in his argument that his messianic humanism is in the spirit of Bonhoeffer's description of the demand for an immanent transcendence that can address all the important issues of life "without recourse to God as a working hypothesis."[79] Later, he states that his hope for liberation is based on God's participation in the weakness and sufferings of the oppressed. "The sufferings of God are thus the ground of hope for those who are without hope."[80] Finally, he makes recourse to Bonhoeffer's image of the polyphony of life to bring freedom and life together "in such a way that the 'flesh' of God's freedom for man is man's freedom for life."[81]

Bonhoeffer's theological insights help Alves frame his language and argument in a way that is not so evident in the Catholic liberation theologians we examined earlier. On the other hand, there is less critical engagement of Bonhoeffer in this book. Bonhoeffer is not taken on simply as a partner for critical conversation, being instead a background influence impacting Alves' argument.

After the 1964 coup in Brazil, a number of the Brazilians participating in ISAL opted for a political engagement in their attempt to change a situation that became increasingly grimmer as they approached the 1970s. The military coup in Brazil was followed by similar take overs in other Latin American countries. Those totalitarian and repressive regimes caused the death of thousands, and turned the cruel practice of torture into a routine in militarized states. Many participants of ISAL experienced imprisonment, physical and/or psychological torture, and forced exile, with a few being counted among the "disappeared"—murdered by the military regimes. In Brazil, that was the case with Ivan Mota Dias and Paulo Wright—one of the six participants of the commune in Vila Anastacio. Wright's case is telling. The son of US missionary parents, born in Brazil, he was an ordained pastor in the Brazilian Presbyterian Church, who, influenced by Shaull and reading Bonhoeffer, took part in the Vila Anastacia experiment, where he worked in a steel factory, and later joined a political movement called Popular Action. He was elected state representative in Santa Catarina, but his mandate was revoked by the military and he was forced to leave the country, becoming a clandestine leader of Popular Action for nine years. In 1973 he was detained, tortured, and killed by the Department of Investigation (DOI-COI).[82] Several other liberation theologians and priests, in Brazil and in other Latin American countries, faced similar situations. The case of Wright has been documented in a book written by his niece, which contains some of the letters he wrote when he ran for office and later, when he lived in exile, and then returned to Brazil to participate in the armed resistance.[83] As he took each step, he reflected on his actions, reaffirming his commitment to witness his Christian faith in those complex circumstances. Having been prevented from contributing to the future of his country through political means, he came to the conclusion that the only option left was insurrection. His process of trying to discern the work of God in the world during a very complex time when it seemed that there was no way for one to profess one's faith safely indicates the indelible influence of Bonhoeffer, Lehmman, and Shaull on his life. To the end of his life he continued to affirm his faith and persisted reflecting on the distinction between faith and religion. He never regretted the options made for action. The only thing he regretted was not having been able to do more to change the situation of those facing the scandalous injustices, which pervaded Brazilian society. Nevertheless, he reaffirmed with confidence that, regardless how dire circumstances, in the end God's justice would prevail over all injustice. In one of his letters, he said:

> Our commitment is to discern the work God is doing, testifying God's redemptive action, experiencing complete freedom to take sides, suffering with those who are suffering, crying with those who are crying . . . feeding those who are hungry . . . Our attitude for sure cannot conserve the enormous and scary imbalances that exist in our society. Our missionary and political witness is to be always on the side of the disinherited, spiritually or materially so, because God loved the world to the point of sending God's son, who became the most impoverished of all human beings so that we could find in him the meaning of life, which is abundance.[84]

Paulo has never been forgotten. He was not the only one who changed the course of his life to participate in the political struggle to resist an oppressive regime and promote liberation. As I mentioned earlier, Frei Betto, a Dominican friar, also encountered in Bonhoeffer's letters an inspiration during his own incarceration. However, Wright, like Alves, found in him a language to frame his theological reflection, which moved away from the institutional church into the sphere of politics and subversive action.

BY WAY OF CONCLUSION . . .

The reception of Bonhoeffer by most of the thinkers and practitioners mentioned in this chapter was not meant to generate expertise in his theology.[85] At a time when Latin American Christians were still discerning what it meant to be a Christian in Latin America, and what theological language they could use to articulate their own faith, they were introduced to Bonhoeffer and became fascinated by his life story and theological insights, which proved helpful in constructing a distinctly Latin American theological language.

Different streams of liberation theologians have related differently to Bonhoeffer. Catholic liberation theologians found him later, and engaged him as a partner for critical conversation. Although they learned something from Bonhoeffer, and adopted some of his insights into their own theology, they also criticized him, showing the limits of his arguments. Protestant theologians, on the other hand, encountered Bonhoeffer earlier, and, fascinated by him, adopted some of his theological insights as they worked to frame their nascent liberationist theology. Their lives, more broadly, were impacted by many of Bonhoeffer's ideas, which can be identified in their writings and actions even when they do not explicitly identify where they came from.

LALT was preceded by Latin American Liberationist Christianity. It sought to provide language that could speak to a reality, which in many ways persist with us. Although the world has significantly changed since the late 1960s, some of the problems LALT addressed are even more pressing today, particularly the problems related to the increasing accumulation of capital in the hands of few, and the power of corporate capitalism to negatively impact the environment and the wellbeing of so many, near and far. On the other hand, there are many issues not addressed either by Bonhoeffer or by the first generation of liberation theologians. *Mujerista*, womanist, black, LGBTQ, and postcolonial/decolonial theologies have raised new questions and offered fresh language to address the challenges of the day. Both Bonhoeffer's theology and LALT are contextual theologies, which by definition are open to learn from changes and dynamically respond to them. As Lehmann suggests, the ethical mandate to discern the humanizing actions of God in the world opens theologians and ethicists to learn anew what God is doing and consequently continuously adjust their theological agendas.

Bonhoeffer's polyphonic understanding of reality on the cross, his view of Christ as being formed in community, and his insights on the weakness of a God whose means for salvation is the deep identification with human suffering, remain important for Latin America theologizing. Likewise, Bonhoeffer's critique of religion and LALT's critique of idolatry are still important conceptual tools these days, when renewed harmful forms of nationalism, white supremacy, neocolonialism, and predatory globalization seem to be aggressively provoking significant disenfranchisement of vulnerable populations across the globe.

NOTES

1. Preston D. S. Parsons, "Who Is Dietrich Bonhoeffer, for Us, Today? A Survey of Recent Studies of Bonhoeffer," *Anglican Theological Review* 97/4 (2015): 671–684 (672).

2. His last words said to Payne Best before he left his cell to face the SS tribunal, according to Eberhard, were, "This is the end—for me the beginning of life." Eberhard Bethge, *Dietrich Bonhoeffer: A Biography*, Revised Edition (Minneapolis, MN: Fortress Press, 1999), 927.

3. See, for instance, G. Clarke Chapman Jr., "Bonhoeffer: Resource for Liberation Theology," *Union Seminary Quarterly Review* 36/4 (1981): 225–242; Paul S. Chung, "Engaging Dietrich Bonhoeffer in Comparative Theological Study:Political Minjung and Confucian Ethics of Rectification," *Ching Feng* 11/2 (2012): 123–144; David Thang Moe, "What Has Dietrich Bonhoeffer to Do with Asian Theology," *Asia Journal of Theology* 28/2 (2014): 175–202; Carlos Caldas, "70 Years Later: What Do We Have to Learn from Bonhoeffer in Latin America Today?" *Stellenbosch Theological Journal* 2/1 (2016): 27–42; John W. de Gruchy, "Bonhoeffer's Legacy and Kairos-Palestine," *Journal of Theology for Southern Africa* 143 (2012): 67–80; Dirk J. Smit, "On the Reception of Bonhoeffer—A Case Study of South–South Dialogue," *Stellenbosch Theological Journal* 2/1 (2016): 89–107; and Maurice Schild, "Dietrich Bonhoeffer and the Burden of Discipleship in Contemporary Australia," *Lutheran Theological Journal* 39/2–3 (2005): 169–180.

4. Christiane Tietz, *Theologian of Resistance: The Life and Thought of Dietrich Bonhoeffer* (Minneapolis, MN: Fortress Press, 2016), vii.

5. Ibid., 111.

6. The resources available in English on Bonhoeffer in Latin America are very limited. See, for instance, Julio de Santa Ana, "The Influence of Bonhoeffer on the Theology of Liberation," *The Ecumenical Review* 27/2 (1976): 188–197; Beatriz Melano, "The Influence of Dietrich Bonhoeffer, Paul Lehmann, and Richard Shaull in Latin America," *Princeton Seminary Bulletin* 22/1 (2001): 64–84; Walter Altmann, "Bonhoeffer in Latin American Perceptions: An Inspiration to Overcome Structures of Injustice?" *Stellenbosch Theological Journal* 2/1

(2016): 13–26; Rudolf von Sinner, "The Ethics of the Penultimate in a Situation of Ambiguity: A Possible and Relevant Interpretation of Bonhoeffer in Brazil today," *Stellenbosch Theological Journal* 2/2 (2016): 77–91; and Carlos Caldas, "70 Years Later— What Do We Have to Learn from Dietrich Bonhoeffer in Latin America Today?" *Stellenbosch Theological Journal* 21/ (2016): 27–42.

7. See Altmann, "Bonhoeffer in Latin American Perceptions," for a list of the most important publications. In her master's thesis at the Universidade Metodista de São Paulo (UMESP), Luciana Ramos provides a more complete list and discussion of published and resources. Luciana Soares Ramos, *A Recepção da Teologia de Dietrich Bonhoeffer na América Latina*. Master's Thesis (São Bernardo do Campo: UMESP, 2007). For a more recent source on the reception of Bonhoeffer with a focus on Brasil, see Carlos Caldas, *Dietrich Bonhoeffer e a Teologia Pública no Brasil* (São Paulo, SP: Garimpo Editorial, 2016), particularly 116–128.

8. Ramos, *A Recepção da Teologia de Dietrich Bonhoeffer na América Latina*, 132.

9. Ibid., 138ff.

10. Rubem Alves, "Dietrich Bonhoeffer: Teólogo da Vida," *CEI Suplemento* 22 (1970): 1–4 (1). Translation is mine.

11. By contrast, Reggie Williams has persuasively argued for the influence of the Harlem renaissance on Bonhoeffer's mature theological thought. His encounter with the Black Jesus, according to Williams, would have informed his prophetic legacy of resistance against the Nazi, led him to reassess his theology of the cross, and taken him to a deeper identification with the wretched of the world. See Reggie L. Williams, *Bonhoeffer's Black Jesus: Harlem's Renaissance Theology and an Ethic of Resistance* (Waco, TX: Baylor University Press, 2014).

12. Rubem Alves (1969) and Gustavo Gutierrez (1971) wrote respectively the two first book-length treatises published on Latin American theologies. They worked independently, and met for the first time during a conference in Cartigny, Switzerland, in 1969. See David Tombs, *Latin American Liberation Theology* (Boston: Brill, 2002), 112. In July 1968, Gutierrez delivered a paper at the *Encuentro Nacional del Movimiento Sacerdotal ONIS*, in Chimbote, Peru, which he titled *Hacia una Teologia de la Liberacion*. That paper was presented again at the Consultation of Theology and Development organized by SODEPAX in Cartigny, in 1969, and published as "Notes on a Theology of Liberation," in *In Search of a Theology of Development: A Sodepax Report* (Lausanne, 1970). See Gustavo Gutierrez, *A Theology of Liberation*, 15th Anniversary Edition (Maryknoll, NY: Orbis Books, 1988), xiii. That paper was the basis for Gutierrez's book, originally published in Spanish in 1971. On the Protestant camp, also in 1968, Rubem Alves wrote his doctoral dissertation at Princeton Theological Seminary. Alves' dissertation was titled *Towards a Theology of Liberation: An Exploration of the Encounter between Humanistic Messianism and Messianic Humanism* (Princeton, NJ: 1968). A year later, it was published as *A Theology of Human Hope* (Washington, DC: Corpus Books, 1969).

13. In this chapter, I follow Löwy's understanding of liberation theology as the "body of writings produced since 1970 by figures like Gustavo Gutierrez (Peru), Rubem Alves, Hugo Assmann, Carlos Mesters, Leonardo and Clodovis Boff, Frei Betto (Brazil), Jon Sobrino, Ignacio Ellacuría (El Salvador), Segundo Galiea, Ronaldo Muñoz (Chile), Pablo Richard (Chile-Costa Rica), José Míguez Bonino, Juan Carlos Scannone, Ruben Dri (Argentina), Enrique Dussel (Argentina-Mexico), Juan Luis Segundo (Uruguay), Samuel Silva Gotay (Puerto Rico), to name only some of the best known." Michael Löwy, *The War of Gods: Religion and Politics in Latin America* (London: Verso, 1996), 32.

14. This movement included priests, religious orders, and bishops, along with lay religious movements such as Catholic Action, Christian University Youth, Young Christian Workers, and popularly based pastoral workers, and ecclesiastic base communities (CEBs). On top of

those, popular organizations created by CEB activists such as neighborhood associations and peasant or workers' unions were also part of it. This social movement played an important role in the emergence of the new workers' movement in Brazil and the rise of revolution in Central America and Chiapas. Ibid.

15. See, for instance, Enrique Dussel. *The Invention of the Americas: Eclipse of "the Other" and the Myth of Modernity*, translated by Michael D. Barber (New York: Continuum, 1995), 12.

16. Jovelino Ramos, "Você Não Conhece o Shaull," in *De Dentro do Furacão: Richard Shaull e os Primórdios da Teologia da Libertação*, Richard Shaull (São Paulo: Ed. Saragana, 1985), 25–32 (27). Inspired by Bonhoeffer, Richard Shaull taught a "mundane" theology, concerned with the Brazilian people and the reality in which they lived.

17. See Santa Ana, "The Influence of Bonhoeffer on the Theology of Liberation," 189. See also Clarke Chapman, "Bonhoeffer and Liberation Theology," in *Ethical Responsibility: Bonhoeffer's Legacy to the Churches*, eds. John Godsey et al. (Toronto: Edwin Mellen Press, 1981), 147–95 (160).

18. Virginia Garrard-Burnett, "'Like a Mighty Rushing Wind': The Growth of Protestantism in Contemporary Latin America," in *Religion and Society in Latin America: Interpretive Essays from Conquest to Present*, eds. Lee M. Penyak and Walter J. Petry (Maryknoll, NY: Orbis Books, 2009), 190–206 (192).

19. Jean-Pierre Bastian, *Breve História do Protestantismo en America Latina* (Mexico City: Casa Unida de Publicaciones, 1986), 11.

20. Alan Neely, "Protestant Antecedents of the Latin American Liberation Theology" (PhD diss., The American University, 1977), 185.

21. For more information on the Church and Society movement in Brazil, see Raimundo C. Barreto Jr., "The Church and Society Movement and the Roots of Public Theology in Brazilian Protestantism," *International Journal of Public Theology* 6 (2012), 70–98.

22. Löwy, *The War of Gods*, 40.

23. Ibid.

24. Ibid., 41.

25. Ibid., 42.

26. Ibid., 34.

27. Altmann, "Bonhoeffer in Latin American Perceptions," 18.

28. Gutierrez, *A Theology of Liberation*, 23.

29. Ibid., 24.

30. Dietrich Bonhoeffer, *Creation and Fall, Temptation* (New York: Macmillan Publishing, Co., 1966), 37. Cited in Gutierrez, *A Theology of Liberation*, 24.

31. Gutierrez, *A Theology of Liberation*, 42.

32. Ibid.

33. Gustavo Gutierrez, *Essential Writings*, edited with an introduction by James B. Nickoloff (New York: Orbis Books, 1996), 35–42. This article first appeared in a May 1979 Spanish issue of *Concilium* as "Los límites de la teología moderna: un texto de Bonhoeffer."

34. Ibid., 36. See Dietrich Bonhoeffer, *Letters and Papers from Prison*, New Greatly Enlarged Edition (New York: Touchstone Books, 1997), 324–329 (327).

35. Gutierrez, *A Theology of Liberation*, 36.

36. Bonhoeffer, *Letters and Papers from Prison*, 327.

37. Ibid.

38. Dietrich Bonhoeffer, "After Ten Years," in *Dietrich Bonhoeffer: Writings Selected with an Introduction*, ed. Robert Coles (New York: Orbis Books, 1998), 114. This passage is quoted in Gutierrez, *A Theology of Liberation*, 40.
39. Ibid., 40.
40. Ibid., 41.
41. Gutierrez, *A Theology of Liberation*, 38.
42. See James Nickholoff's brief introduction to Gutierrez's text. Ibid., 35. See also Robert McAfee Brown, *Theology in a New Key: Responding to Liberation Themes* (Philadelphia, PA: The Westminster Press, 1978), 50.
43. Franz J. Hinkelammert, "La Critica de la Religion en Nombre del Cristianismo: Dietrich Bonhoeffer," in *Teología Alemana y Teología Latinoamericana de la Liberación: Un Esfuerzo de Diálogo*, ed. Franz J. Hinkelammert, et al. (San Jose, Costa Rica: Editorial DEI, 1990), 45–66.
44. Ibid., 45.
45. Ibid.
46. Ibid., 47.
47. Ibid., 48.
48. Ibid. Translation is mine.
49. Ibid., 49.
50. Ibid., 51.
51. Ibid., 52.
52. Ibid., 55.
53. Ibid., 57.
54. Ibid., 63.
55. Ibid., 64.
56. Ibid.
57. Jon Sobrino refers to Bonhoeffer in a number of his works. See, for instance, *Christology at the Crossroads: A Latin American* Approach (Maryknoll, NY: Orbis Books, 1978), *Jesus the Liberator: A Historical-Theological Reading of Jesus of Nazareth* (Maryknoll, NY: Orbis, 1993), and *Christ the Liberator: A View from the Victims* (Maryknoll, NY: Orbis, 2001).
58. Altmann, "Bonhoeffer in Latin American Perceptions," 24. Bonhoeffer, *Letters and Papers from Prison*, 361. The way that statement is translated in Sobrino's book slightly differs from the English version of Bonhoeffer's statement: "Only a God Who Suffers Can Save Us." Sobrino, *Christology at the Crossroads*, 197.
59. Bonhoeffer, *Letters and Papers from Prison*, 348ff.
60. Altmann, "Bonhoeffer in Latin American Perceptions," 24.
61. Sobrino, *Christology at the Crossroads*, 222.
62. Ibid., 223.
63. Altmann, "Bonhoeffer in Latin American Perceptions," 24.
64. Sobrino, *Christology at the Crossroads*, 274.
65. Other Latin American liberation theologians, like Juan Luis Segundo, Leonardo Boff, and Jose Miguez Bonino, also mention Bonhoeffer in their work.
66. See Jeffrey B. Kelly, "Bonhoeffer and Romero: Prophets of Justice for the Oppressed," *Union Seminary Quarterly Review*, 46/1 (1992): 85–105.

67. Ramos, *A Recepção da Teologia de Dietrich Bonhoeffer na América Latina*, 100. His letters were published as Frei Betto, *Cartas da Prisão*. 2ed (Rio de Janeiro: Civilização Brasileira, 1977) 170, 177.
68. Santa Ana, "The Influence of Bonhoeffer on the Theology of Liberation," 188.
69. Ibid.
70. Melano, "The Influence of Dietrich Bonhoeffer, Paul Lehmann, and Richard Shaull in Latin America," 77. Portions of *Letters and Papers from Prison* were translated into Spanish in 1954, and a couple of years later into Portuguese.
71. Santa Ana, "The Influence of Bonhoeffer on the Theology of Liberation," 189.
72. ISAL held important consultations, and for several years published the journal called *Cristianismo y Sociedad*, a kind of incubator for an incipient Protestant liberation theology.
73. Richard A. Couch, "La Comunicación del Evangelio en Medio de los Rapidos Cambios Sociales," in *La Responsabilidad Social del Cristiano: Guia de Estudios* (Montevideo: Iglesia y Sociedad en America Latina. Junta de Estudios, 1964), 113–121 (117). Translation is mine.
74. Ibid.
75. Ibid.
76. Eduardo Galasso Faria, *Fe e Compromisso: Richard Shaull e a Teologia No Brasil* (São Paulo: ASTE, 2002), 156.
77. Ibid., 115ff.
78. Rubem Alves, *A Theology of Human Hope* (Washington, DC: Corpus Books, 1969), 171.
79. Ibid., 29.
80. Ibid., 117.
81. Ibid., 152.
82. Faria, *Fe e Compromisso*, 117.
83. Jan Wright, *O Coronel Tem um Segredo: Paulo Wright Não Está em Cuba* (Petrópolis, Brazil: Vozes, 1993).
84. Ibid., 22–23. Translation is mine.
85. Only in the 1990s a chapter of the International Bonhoeffer Society was created in Brazil. That initiative has promoted greater scholarly interest in Bonhoeffer's work in recent years.

SELECT BIBLIOGRAPHY

Altmann, Walter (2016), "Bonhoeffer in Latin American perceptions: An inspiration to overcome structures of injustice?" *Stellenbosch Theological Journal* 2/1: 13–26.
Alves, Rubem (1969), *A Theology of Human Hope*, Washington, DC: Corpus Books.
Alves, Rubem (1970), "Dietrich Bonhoeffer: Teólogo da Vida," *CEI Suplemento* 22: 1–4.
Barreto Jr., Raimundo C. (2012), "The Church and Society Movement and the Roots of Public Theology in Brazilian Protestantism," *International Journal of Public Theology* 6, 70-98.
Bastian, Jean-Pierre (1986), *Breve História do Protestantismo en America Latina*, Mexico City: Casa Unida de Publicaciones.
Bethge, Eberhard (1999), *Dietrich Bonhoeffer: A Biography*, rev. ed., Minneapolis, MN: Fortress Press.
Bonhoeffer, Dietrich (1966), *Creation and Fall, Temptation*, New York: Macmillan Publishing, Co.
Bonhoeffer, Dietrich (1997), *Letters and Papers from Prison*, New Greatly Enlarged Edition, New York: Touchstone Books.

Caldas, Carlos (2016), "70 Years Later—What Do We Have to Learn from Dietrich Bonhoeffer in Latin America Today?" *Stellenbosch Theological Journal* 21: 27–42.
Caldas, Carlos (2016), *Dietrich Bonhoeffer e a Teologia Pública no Brasil*, São Paulo: Garimpo Editorial.
Dussel, Enrique (1995), *The Invention of the Americas: Eclipse of "the Other" and the Myth of Modernity*, trans. Michael D. Barber, New York: Continuum.
Gutierrez, Gustavo (1988), *A Theology of Liberation*, 15th Anniversary Edition, Maryknoll, NY: Orbis Books.
Löwy, Michael (1996), *The War of Gods: Religion and Politics in Latin America*, London: Verso.
Melano, Beatriz (2001), "The Influence of Dietrich Bonhoeffer, Paul Lehmann, and Richard Shaull in Latin America," *Princeton Seminary Bulletin* 22/1: 64–84.
Parsons, Preston D. S. (2015), "Who Is Dietrich Bonhoeffer, for Us, Today? A Survey of Recent Studies of Bonhoeffer," *Anglican Theological Review* 97/4: 671–684.
Ramos, Luciana Soares (2007), *A Recepção da Teologia de Dietrich Bonhoeffer na América Latina*, Master's Thesis, São Bernardo do Campo: UMESP.
Santa Ana, Julio de (1976), "The Influence of Bonhoeffer on the Theology of Liberation," *The Ecumenical Review* 27/2: 188–197.
Sobrino, Jon (1978), *Christology at the Crossroads: A Latin American Approah*, Maryknoll, NY: Orbis Books.
Sobrino, Jon (1993), *Jesus the Liberator: A Historical-Theological Reading of Jesus of Nazareth*, Maryknoll, NY: Orbis Books.
Sobrino, Jon (2001), *Christ the Liberator: A View from the Victims,* Maryknoll, NY: Orbis Books.
Tietz, Christiane (2016), *Theologian of Resistance: The Life and Thought of Dietrich Bonhoeffer*, Minneapolis, MN: Fortress Press.
Williams, Reggie L. (2014), *Bonhoeffer's Black Jesus: Harlem's Renaissance Theology and an Ethic of Resistance*, Waco, TX: Baylor University Press.

CHAPTER FOURTEEN

Jürgen Moltmann and the New Political Theology

SCOTT PAETH

INTRODUCTION

"Political Theology seeks to awaken the political consciousness of any Christian theology."[1] This statement summarizes the intent and approach to the project of political theology as developed by Jürgen Moltmann. In the second half of the twentieth century, there are few figures who have been as central to the development of a new and relevant form of Christian political theology as has Moltmann. Rooting his conception of Christian social engagement in the dialectical relationship between the Cross and Resurrection of Jesus Christ, he fashioned an approach that took seriously the pressing social questions confronting Europe and North America in the decades after the Second World War, while providing an important, though often contested, perspective informing the developing approaches to liberation theology throughout the world.

My goal in this chapter is to present an account of the development of Moltmann's approach to political theology in his own context, as well as to examine how that theology was received and critiqued by those who, while often appreciative of Moltmann's contributions, were also cognizant of the degree to which his context rendered him unable to speak authoritatively to those settings which diverged substantially from his own.

Ultimately, I propose, Moltmann's theology has offered an important impetus to the development of a socially engaged and astute theological program that recognizes the need for Christian theology to enter into the complexities and ambiguities of its public setting, while remaining rooted in the life of Jesus Christ, and the expectation of his coming Kingdom.

THE "OLD POLITICAL THEOLOGY" OF CARL SCHMITT

In the years following the Second World War, the term "political theology" was problematic within the German context. Associated as it was with the prewar development of a conservative, pro-Nazi form of "political theology" by Carl Schmitt, it was associated with National Socialist ideology and authoritarian political action.

Schmitt's political theology was not, contrary to the name, a theological conception of the role of Christianity in the political realm. It was not theological in any sense. Rather, as laid out in the book of that name, it was a purely political account of the nature of sovereignty in politics. That is to say, what Schmitt was primarily concerned with was the question of what the political character of leadership consisted in. "Sovereign," he writes, "is he who decides the state of exception."[2] In other words, the chief character of the political sovereign is their capacity to act outside of the rule and limitations of the law. Thus he writes:

> In a more familiar vein it was asked, Who is supposed to have unlimited power? Hence the discussion about the exception, the *Extremus necessitatis casus*. This is repeated with the same legal-logical structure in the discussions on the so-called monarchical principle. Here too, it is always asked who is entitled to decide those actions for which the constitution makes no provision; that is, who is competent to act when the legal system fails to answer the question of competence.[3]

The sovereign thus possesses a freedom vis-à-vis the limitations of the law. He has "unlimited power" and is thus able to act when and where the rule of law cannot.

Schmitt's argument in *Political Theology* builds on his earlier work *On Dictatorship*, where he initially defended the concept of the "state of exception" in the context of the Weimar Constitution.[4] His disposition to authoritarian political action led him to argue that the leader had the power to suspend the constitution indefinitely under the conditions of emergency.[5] In *The Concept of the Political* he argues that the most extreme conflict is that between "friend" and "enemy."[6] In particular, it is the authority of the sovereign to distinguish friend from enemy. He writes:

> The enemy is not merely any competitor or just any partner of a conflict in general. He is also not the private adversary whom one hates. An enemy exists only when, at least potentially, one fighting collectivity of people confronts a similar collectivity. The enemy is solely the public enemy, because everything that has a relationship to such a collectivity of men, particularly to a whole nation, becomes public by virtue of such a relationship.[7]

In the words of Leo Strauss, Schmitt's philosophy could be summarized in the following way: "men can be unified only in a unity against . . . other men. Every association of men is necessarily a separation from other men."[8] Schmitt's writing was highly influential on the governing legal philosophy of the Nazi Party. The inherent weakness of democracy is its incapacity to distinguish between friend and enemy. In particular his arguments on behalf of the role of the sovereign were used to justify the suspension of the Weimar Constitution, repeatedly, under Hitler (in the role of the sovereign), and his description of the political as having to do with the distinction of friend from enemy was deployed in the service of Nazi anti-Semitism.

Schmitt's political theology was deeply skeptical with regard to the prospects of democracy. Politics is defined not in terms of the larger public good or the need for the constructive governance of society, but solely in terms of violence. The sovereign is granted political power in a Hobbesian sense, in the name of the protection of the people from the threat represented by the "enemy." Schmitt's desire for a "qualitatively total state" was rooted in the authoritarian goal of privatizing all elements of human life that cannot be brought under the direct role of the state.[9] Only through the power of the dictator can stability be established in human life and society.[10]

Schmitt was a political thinker rather than a theologian, and his concept of political theology, as noted above, was not rooted in any more general theological concerns. That said, a God-concept does emerge from his conception of power, violence, and the nature of the state. As God is toward the world, so the dictator is toward the nation. God's unalterable omnipotence is the model for the dictator's rule. The idea of a crucified God, embedded in the heart of the Christian tradition, is alien to any idea of God compatible with Schmitt's program.

Moltmann, Metz, and the other advocates of the "new" form of political theology were at pains to distinguish their own project from that of Schmitt. Moltmann's development of his own form of political theology was informed far more by the work of Ernst Bloch than by Schmitt, although he did engage Schmitt at a number of points. Nevertheless, he recognized that the themes of Schmitt's political theology completely contradicted a political theology emerging from the Christian Gospel. He distinguished his thought from Schmitt's in two ways: first by making his approach explicitly and confessionally theological, and second by disregarding the Schmittian arguments in favor of authoritarianism and separation of friend from enemy, and instead embracing principles of democratic equality and universal human rights.

THE BIOGRAPHICAL CONTEXT OF MOLTMANN'S THEOLOGICAL DEVELOPMENT

In order to understand how Moltmann's approach to political theology developed, it is necessary to situate it in the context of Moltmann's formative experiences as a theologian, which means understanding his experiences as a soldier and prisoner of war during the Second World War. These experiences contributed to his understanding of Christian moral responsibility and the need for political engagement by the church within society. While his theology cannot be reduced to those biographical experiences, they do offer important context for the subsequent development of his thought.

Moltmann's experiences as a young soldier, as described in *A Broad Place*, gave shape to the themes that would underlie his later theology. Raised in a secular household, Moltmann did not have a religious framework into which to place his experiences of the horror of war—in particular, his experiences as an anti-aircraft gunner during "Operation Gomorrah" in 1943. He describes it vividly:

> I can remember every detail of the first night. Bomber squadrons approaching over the North Sea set off air raid sirens. . . . There were more than 1,000 aircraft in the attack. Round about us explosive and incendiary bombs rained down, most of them falling in the water. Helplessly we looked on as St. George's began to burn, and then city hall, and finally Hamburg's churches, which flared up like torches. The RAF's tactics were simple: First explosives, then incendiaries. What had been chosen as a target was the densely built-up working class area of East Hamburg. The bombs set off a firestorm with a temperature of about 1000°C, which burnt up everything, even the people in the air raid shelters. . . . It was on the last night, or the last but one, that an explosive bomb hit the platform where we were standing with our useless firing device. The mass of splinters destroyed the firing platform and tore apart my friend Gerhard Schopper, who was standing next to me. . . . During that night I cried out to God for the first time in my life and put my life in his hands. I was as if dead, and ever after received life every day as a new gift. My question was not, "Why does God allow this to happen?: but "My God, where are you?" And there was the other question, the answer to which I am still looking for today: Why am I alive and not dead too, like the friend at my side.

I felt the guilt of survival and searched for the meaning of continued life. I knew that there had to be some reason why I was still alive. During that night I became a seeker after God.[11]

Shortly after these events, Moltmann was taken captive by the British and sent to a prisoner of war camp in Scotland. It was here that he continued to deepen and explore his newfound thirst for God, reading the psalms and taking comfort in the sense of companionship with the suffering of Christ. "I began to understand the assailed, forsaken Christ because I knew that he understood me. The divine brother in need, the companion on the way, who goes with you through this 'valley of the shadow of death,' the fellow-sufferer who carries you, with your suffering."[12] Here he first encountered Bonhoeffer's *Nachfolge* and Niebuhr's *The Nature and Destiny of Man*. What he learned in the "monastic" world of the camp became his first theological education.[13] "I have never again lived so intensive an intellectual life as I did in Norton Camp. We received what we had not deserved, and lived from a spiritual abundance we had not expected."[14]

It was also during this period that he was confronted with images from the concentration camps in Belsen and Buchenwald, which had a profound effect on his understanding of just how horrifically Germany had behaved, and how monstrous were the consequences:

> For me, every patriotic feeling for Germany—"holy Fatherland"—collapsed and died. . . . Depression over the wartime destruction and a captivity with no end in sight was compounded by a feeling of profound shame at having to share in shouldering the disgrace of one's own people. That really choked one, and the weight of it has never left me to the present day.[15]

As Geiko Müller-Fahrenholz notes, "in this basic experience lies the nucleus of the decision for a politically conscious theology . . . the political dimension of Christian faith was already forming in the British prisoner-of-war camp."[16]

In the years after his return to Germany and the beginnings of his own theological work, Germany was in a period of cautious conservatism with respect to most things, including theology. The German ethos, as Moltmann described it, was *kein experimenten*—"no experiments!" The reality of the Holocaust was pressed into the background of German self-consciousness and seldom remarked upon. However, the 1960s began a period of often-radical change within German society generally and in theology in particular. Moltmann was one of the key participants in that process of change, particularly in his use of the philosophical tools provided by Ernst Bloch and the Frankfurt School as lenses through which to examine the perennial questions of Christian theology.

FROM THE THEOLOGY OF HOPE TO THE CRUCIFIED GOD

As Moltmann describes it in *Theology of Hope*, his encounter with Bloch's *Das Prinzip Hoffnung* was a transformative experience for his approach to theology. The key insight that he derived from Bloch was the need for Christian faith to rediscover the concept of active hope for the coming Kingdom of God. He writes:

> So engrossed was I in the book that the beauty of the Swiss mountains passed me by unnoticed. Why has Christian theology allowed hope to escape it, when this is its very own, special theme? That was my first impression. And then: What has happened to

the early Christian spirit of active hope today? That was my first question. I did not imitate Bloch's philosophy of hope. Nor did I "baptize" it, as Karl Barth suspiciously conjectured. I simply built a theology of hope on the foundation of what I saw as the presupposition of the theology of Christianity and Judaism. For Ernst Bloch, atheism was the presupposition of active hope; for Jean-Paul Sartre, atheism was the presupposition of human freedom. But for me, the God of promise and exodus, the God who has raised Christ and who lets the power of the resurrection dwell in us, is the ground for active and for passive hope. The atheism that wants to free men and women from superstition and idolatry and the Christianity that wants to lead them out of inward and outward slavery into the liberty of the coming kingdom of God—these two do not have to be antagonists. They can also work together.[17]

A Christian theology that takes the promise of the resurrection seriously as the heart of its faith must, Moltmann concluded, take seriously the need for political engagement with the world. Christian hope is not a call to quietism, but to action. Against the objection that Christian hope deprives us of present happiness, he writes:

Does this hope cheat man of the happiness of the present? How could it do so! For it is itself the happiness of the present. It pronounces the poor blessed, receives the weary and heavy laden, the humbled and wronged, the hungry and the dying, because it perceives the parousia of the kingdom for them. Expectation makes life good, for in expectation man can accept his whole present and find joy not only in its joy but also in its sorry, happiness is not only in its happiness but also in its pain. Thus hope goes on its way through the midst of happiness and pain, because in the promises of God it can see a future also for the transient, the dying and the dead. That is why it can be said that living without hope is no longer living. Hell is hopelessness, and it is not for nothing that at the entrance to Dante's hell there stand the words: "Abandon hope, all ye who enter here."[18]

For this hope to become operative in the world, it must embody the anticipation of God's coming Kingdom through the action of the Christians and their communities. Thus the Church becomes an "exodus church," through which individuals enact their hope for the Kingdom of God in the midst of their earthly vocations, participating fully in the world and its obligations toward justice and righteousness, while belonging to the church through which that justice and righteousness is given its fullest form in the hope for God's reign.[19]

Theology of Hope was very much a book of its time: A time of tremendous optimism in both the United States and Europe. But this spirit of hope was quickly replaced by a pessimism about the possibility of any genuine social transformation. As Moltmann reflects:

In 1968 the tanks of the Warsaw Pact mowed down socialism with a human face in Czechoslovakia. The Vietnam War brought the United States into a tragic conflict with itself. The world-wide economic crisis of 1972 made it clear to all of us that we are not after all living in a world of boundless opportunities, but that we have to content ourselves with this earth and its limited resources. Hope in the world of unrestricted future possibilities was replaced by resistance against the real destructions of our earth.[20]

Into this environment Moltmann introduced his second major treatise on political theology, *The Crucified God*. Whereas *Theology of Hope* was deeply immersed in the philosophy of Bloch, *The Crucified God* is influenced by the work of Horkheimer and particularly Adorno. One can see in the argument Moltmann presents in this volume, echoes of Adorno's *Negative Dialectics*, particularly in his assertion that "unless it apprehends the pain of the negative, Christian hope cannot be realistic and liberating."[21]

In *The Crucified God*, Moltmann presents the cross of Jesus Christ as critical theory. Building on the work of the Frankfurt School philosophers, he examines the way in which the cross stands in contradiction to all present reality. In this way, it becomes a form of judgment against a Christianity for which the cross has become a symbol of triumph and the success of the *status quo* and those forms of smug atheism that view Christianity as a mere superstition. Using Luther's theology of the cross as a referent, he distinguishes between the *theologia crucis* and the *theologia gloriae*, arguing not only against complacent Christianity but also rationalist forms of atheism. The theology of the cross raises far deeper existential questions than either of these viewpoints is willing to contemplate. If Christ died in a state of God-abandonment, then this raises troubling questions about God's existence and goodness that are far beyond either of these outlooks to answer.

While the *theologia gloriae* and rationalist atheism take refuge in abstraction, the *theologia crucis* makes common cause with *protest* atheism. Unlike its rationalist cousin, protest atheism recognizes that the existence of evil and suffering in the world are the chief objections to either the goodness or the existence of God. A good God would not allow such evil to exist, so either God exists but is not good, or does not exist at all. The cross, from the position of atheism, represents the ultimate refutation of God's existence. It represents on one viewpoint "a *rebellion* against God at the very beginning of Christianity."[22]

Yet Moltmann's response to this challenge is to reaffirm the centrality of the incarnation in our understanding of the crucifixion. Christ is not *merely* the man dying God abandoned on the cross. Rather, as the second Person of the Trinity, Christ is also the incarnation of God in the midst of the human experience. Rather than a rebellion against a distant and uncaring God, the cross is—on the contrary—the ultimate expression of God's *solidarity* with the reality of human suffering. God stands with God's creatures in the midst of their suffering, and takes that suffering into the divine being through the sacrifice of Christ on the cross. In this way it declares along with protest atheism that human suffering is an abomination against God's intentions for human life, and that in Jesus Christ God is seeking to share that suffering, to overcome it, and to transform it. This is why he views Horkheimer's approach to critical theory as a form of apophatic theology, writing:

> In his critical theory [Horkheimer] challenges both traditional theism and its brother, traditional atheism. There is no theistic answer to the question of human suffering and injustice, but far less is there any atheistic possibility of avoiding this question and being content with the world. It is impossible to be content with one's own possibilities, which are always limited. So Horkheimer uses the formula of "longing for the wholly other," which hovers between theism and atheism.[23]

This is not a "solution" to the problem of human suffering, in the sense that it offers a satisfactory explanation as to why suffering exists. Rationalistic attempts to offer such an explanation are doomed to failure. But atheism fails to take seriously the dying cry of Christ on the cross—"My God why have you forsaken me!" Thus Christianity "takes the 'metaphysical rebellion' up into itself because it recognizes in the cross of Christ a rebellion in metaphysics, or better, a rebellion in God himself: God himself loves and suffers the death of Christ in his love."[24]

The development of Moltmann's theological hermeneutic does not reflect a change in Moltmann's underlying political theology. Rather, the movement of thought that takes place between *Theology of Hope* and *The Crucified God* reflects the underlying dialectical structure to Moltmann's entire theological project: One cannot talk about Christian hope except in the shadow of the cross, and one cannot fully understand the implications of the cross except in the light of Christian hope.

THE DIALECTIC OF TRANSFORMATION AND CRITIQUE

At the heart of Moltmann's political theology is a dialectical relationship between the cross and the resurrection—between a moment of critique, through which the real existence of human suffering and evil are subjected to the reality of Christ's co-suffering with humanity through the crucifixion, and a moment of transformation, through which the hope for future redemption creates the imperative toward social change in the name of the coming kingdom of God. As Moltmann writes: "hope without remembrance leads to illusion, just as conversely, remembrance without hope can result in resignation."[25]

Moltmann understands the political dimension of Christian eschatology through the concept of *anticipation*. The kingdom of God is the anticipatory horizon against which our current context is judged and found to be wanting. Human society is relativized to the values of the kingdom, and the anticipation of that kingdom becomes the norm for human moral action. It impels us toward an ideal society that we cannot fully embody within history, but toward which we can strive to approximate. The resurrection of Jesus Christ is a testimony to the triumph of God's grace over the power of death. As Moltmann writes, Christ's resurrection was "recognized and proclaimed within a horizon of apocalyptic expectation: resurrection as an eschatological event—Jesus as the first fruits of the resurrection."[26] The kingdom of God overturns the existing order and inaugurates the *kairos* of God's peace and justice.

However, in the present context the coming kingdom dwells under the sign of the cross. It is coming, but it is not yet in existence. And so we continue to grapple with evil, suffering, and death in the midst of our experience, even as we anticipate the coming transformation:

> Thus the kingdom of God is present here as promise and hope for the future horizon of all things, which are then seen in their historical character because they do not yet contain their truth in themselves If it is present as promise and hope, then this its presence is determined by the contradiction in which the future, the possible and the promised, stands to a corrupt reality. In the Reformers it was said that the kingdom of God is a *tectum sub cruce et sub contrario*. This was intended to mean that the kingdom of God is here hidden beneath its opposite: Its freedom is hidden under trial, its happiness under suffering, its right under rightlessness, its omnipotence under weakness, its glory under unrecognizability. Here the kingdom of God was seen in the form of the lordship of the crucified one. This is a true insight, and one that cannot be relinquished. Only, the kingdom of God does not end in the paradoxical form of a presence of this kind. Its paradoxical hiddenness "under the contrary" is not its eternal form.[27]

Because we know Christ "*sub contrario*" we are empowered to strive toward the eschatological horizon of God's promise. Our willingness to move toward that anticipatory horizon of which Moltmann speaks is a demonstration of the faith we have in the promise of God's coming kingdom. And thus our desire to act on behalf of peace and justice in the midst of the ambiguities of the present moment is an expression of that hope in a world that is not yet arrived and often not detectable. Yet the naive optimism of much liberal theology is avoided precisely because the cross looms over all of our action.

Crucial to Moltmann's understanding of the political dimension of the cross is the recognition that Christ died as a rebel against systems of political and religious power. Because crucifixion was a punishment reserved for political crimes, Christ's death is inescapably political. His teaching stood in direct contradiction to the tyranny of the Roman Empire, and his proclamation of a kingdom "not of this world" unveiled the corruption of the kingdoms which are of this world. Thus he was condemned precisely because he was dangerous to the political order of the dominant society to which he was subject.

Furthermore, in his crucifixion Christ died as one who was "Godforsaken"—his cry of abandonment on the cross was not for show, but was rather a sincere declaration of anguish in the face of God's absence. Yet even so, in the midst of Christ's experience of Godforsakenness, God is nevertheless present. In identifying with suffering humanity on the cross in the form of his Son, God identifies not only with the suffering of physical pain and death, not only with the reality of injustice oppression, but also with the fundamental suffering of alienation from God.

This dialectical motion between cross and resurrection provides the dynamic that motivates Christianity toward political action and away from passivity and quiescence. It provides the theological structure that offers an interpretive framework through which Christianity understands its identity as at one time in the world and yet belonging to a world that is coming to be midst of our present circumstances. It provides the resources of political critique as well as the spiritual core of political transformation and commits Christianity to a moral imperative toward action that embodies a concern for peace, justice, and human rights against systems of dehumanization, hatred, and violence.

MOLTMANN'S POLITICAL HERMENEUTIC

The dialectic of transformation and critique that Moltmann develops in *Theology of Hope* and *The Crucified God* stands at the heart of the political hermeneutic he develops, a hermeneutic rooted in Christian expectation and praxis. Out of this dialectic emerges a Christian ethic of concrete social responsibility in and for the world. Thus he writes:

> Political hermeneutics links up with the eschatological hermeneutic. Earlier hermeneutic usually remained at one level: from text to text, from understanding to understanding, from faith to faith. When hermeneutic, however, involves a promissory history, when the way of interpretation goes from promise to fulfillment, when it involves a history of hope, then interpretation goes from expectation to realization. When it involves the remembrance of liberation, then the way goes from oppression to freedom, that is, hermeneutic does not remain on the intellectual theoretical level, but wants to lead, by way of the experience of understanding hope, to a new praxis of hope.[28]

In opposition to both individualistic forms of existential hermeneutics and Marxist materialist atheism, Moltmann posits a form of revolutionary Christianity that embraces radical social engagement.

This radical engagement is rooted in a number of core concepts. First, God's reign is from and for the poor and outcast. *"Those who labor and are heavily laden"* and *"the humiliated and abused."*[29] Thus from the socially marginalized comes the call to overcome the conditions of their marginalization and oppression in the name God's coming kingdom. This hope is founded on the innate and created dignity of every human being. "Poverty, hunger, and sickness rob a man of all dignity."[30]

Second, it is in and through Jesus Christ as the incarnate Son of God that the kingdom is inaugurated among and on behalf of the poor. As the incarnation of the divine *Logos*, Christ brings the divine presence into solidarity with the concrete socioeconomic as well as psychological and spiritual suffering of the human community. War, poverty, and injustice, in stripping dignity from humanity, are a violation of the mandate of respect toward all persons, and thus those who seek to identify themselves with God-in-Christ are called to stand against that which stands against God.

Third, a Christian political hermeneutic must be realized in the concrete action of Christians in the world. It is not sufficient to take refuge in abstraction. Rather, "this hermeneutic must bind reflection and action together, thus requiring reflection in action as well as action in the reflection."[31] It is the work of the entire Christian community to make God's kingdom manifest in the midst of the world. Thus the key interpretive task of a political hermeneutic is to "discover the unconditioned within the conditioned, the last in the next to last, and the eschatological in the ethical just as we believe that the blood and the body of Christ are present in the bread and wine of the Eucharist."[32] Christian political action thus has a sacramental as well as a moral character to it. It is an outward and visible sign of the grace of God, acting in the world for the sake of its transformation because it cannot rest content with the world as it stands. What this means in a concrete sense is conveyed by Moltmann in a powerful passage from *The Crucified God*:

> Only when, with all the understanding and consistency he possesses, a man follows Christ along the way of self-emptying into non-identity, does he encounter contradiction, resistance and opposition. Only when he leaves behind the circle of those who share and reinforce his opinions in the church, to go out into the anonymity of slums and peace movements, in a society "where the absence of peace is organized," is he tempted and tested, inwardly and outwardly. Then the crisis inevitably comes, in which the identity of that for which he involves and commits himself comes into question, and a decision has to be made about it. It is these active trials and temptations which at the present day teach us to pay attention to the word of the cross.[33]

Critics of Moltmann have noted that there are "tensions" within Moltmann's thought which call into question the viability of this political hermeneutic. Of particular note, Arne Rasmusson sees Moltmann's "positive Christian reception of modernity," including such concepts as "freedom," and "human rights" as inescapably placing Moltmann at the mercy of precisely the enlightenment individualism that he is seeking to reject.[34] Rasmusson argues in a Milbankian fashion that the Christian church must reject modernity and form alternative communities that are capable of standing in contrast to the ideologies of violence inherent to modernity. Ultimately he views Moltmann's theology as too thoroughly compromised by his reliance on modernity, as illustrated by his reliance on Bloch, Horkheimer, and Adorno, to be capable of embodying such an alternative community.

In a similar vein, critics of Moltmann's theology from within the tradition of Liberation Theology, while recognizing the debt that Liberation Theology owes to the Theology of

Hope, argue that Moltmann's theology is too beholden to bourgeois European categories of analysis to be of much use for the concrete task of liberation in the rest of the world, particularly in light of the dynamics of the "savage capitalism" manifested by economic globalization. In discussing the larger problems confronted by Latin American theology in light of the social transformations of the past several decades Jose Miguez-Boniño discusses Moltmann in the context of the need for European theology to take the concrete social and economic realities faced by the majority world more seriously:

> In other words, we may still have much to talk about and discuss in relation to the specific face of oppression and struggles for liberation in our respective conditions, but it seems that we can share an increasing awareness of the "global" nature of our problematics and of the challenge of a theology concerned with liberation." This is a particularly acute problem because it is precisely in this area where we miss in our European friends—Moltmann included—a more direct engagement with the global economic processes which are shaping—although in different forms and with diverse intensity—the nature and future of all our societies. While we have felt that theology cannot avoid, without betraying our responsibility, examining the economic and social nature and consequences of the so called "new international economic order" and to discuss its quasi-religious language and its theological legitimation, it seems that our North Atlantic colleagues (with some exceptions, to be sure) have concentrated too exclusively in the psychological, cultural, or ecological side-effects.[35]

Moltmann himself has recognized the limitations of his own Eurocentric perspective on theology. On the one hand, he has sought to define the task of political theology differently from that of liberation theology, stating that "political theology is the *internal* criticism of the modern world. Liberation theology is the *external* criticism of the modern world."[36] At the same time, he has criticized Boniño and others for focusing too exclusively on the socioeconomic dimensions of liberation while neglecting how those elements are intertwined with the psychological and ecological dimensions of human life.

As regards Rasmusson's critique, Moltmann's project actually envisions a "contrast society" in many ways similar to that embraced by Rasmusson. However, while Rasmusson thinks that such a society is only possible through the rejection of modernity, Moltmann believes that those categories are not in contradiction to the need for a distinctive Christian community to act in the world. Rather, he sees the nature of the community in ways that are distinct from Rasmusson's approach, and which offers a more provocative model for Christian political engagement in the midst of the world.

THE POLITICS OF THE EXODUS CHURCH

The form of "contrast society" envisioned by Moltmann is described in some detail in the final chapter of *Theology of Hope*, under the category of the "exodus church." By this he means that the church's identity within society is primary a *missionary* identity, in the sense that the Christian community is not called together in order to separate it self from society, preserving its purity from contamination. Rather, the church is gathered in order to be *sent* out into the world, to act as a leaven within the social settings and institutions within which Christians inescapably function within society. In a sense, Moltmann's understanding of the church is more mendicant than monastic: Christians are called to preach the gospel in the midst of the world.

In describing the church as an "exodus" community, what he means is that it is a church "on the move" in the midst of its social setting. Rather than simply being a bulwark for the preservation of an unchanging and unchangeable tradition—a "Benedict community" in the contemporary sense—the church as Moltmann envisions it is never to rest content with either the world as it finds it, or its own place within society. As an ever-expectant community it is always moving toward the coming kingdom of God. The church thus embodies what Ernst Bloch called the "not-yet-conscious" nature of expectation.[37] The role of the church is to become the conduit for the realization of that not-yet-conscious expectation in the present time and place through the proclamation of Christ's resurrection.

The Church, in Moltmann's view, has an obligation to resist the tendency to reduce religion to a matter of private expression, and to insist on its public role and responsibility in making the public character of the kingdom of God manifest. Yet in doing this, it also contradicts society precisely at those points and in those ways that it fails to embody the reign of God. Thus the church in society does not affirm the status quo but always challenges and engages it directly through the witness and action of the Christian community. It is called to break out of its socially designated role and become something more than society wants or needs it to be:

> If Christianity, according to the will of him in whom it believes and in whom it hopes, is to be different and to serve a different purpose, then it must address itself to no less a task than that of breaking out of these its socially fixed roles. It must then display a kind of conduct which is not in accordance with these. That is the conflict which is imposed on every Christian and every Christian minister. If the God who called them to life should expect of them something other than what modern industrial society expects and requires of them, then Christians must venture an exodus and regard their social roles as a new Babylonian exile. Only where they appear in society as a group which is not wholly adaptable and in the case of which the modern integration of everything with everything fails to succeed, do they enter into a conflict-laden, but fruitful partnership with this society.[38]

The church must then insist on being unassimilated and unassimilable within the society through which it moves upon its exodus, and yet at the same time be active and involved in the anticipation of the kingdom in the midst of that setting. The proper role of the church is not to exist as "resident aliens" within society, but to act as a partner, drawing society along toward its destination, and calling it to accompany the church on its exodus: "Here the task of Christianity today is not so much to oppose the ideological glorification of things, but rather to resist the institutional stabilizing of things, and by 'raising the question of meaning' to make things uncertain and keep them moving and elastic in the process of history."[39]

The church that rests content with its place in society fails to fully be the church. Unless it embodies in its preaching and action that dialectic of transformation and critique in the midst of its common life, and brings those poles of political hermeneutic out of the pews and into the world, it fails in its mission. Unless all Christian moral action is oriented toward the anticipation of the kingdom of the midst of the present moment, it fails to be faithful to the life and teaching of Jesus Christ. And unless Christian proclamation is always in critical tension with the givenness of its political setting, standing on the side of the poor, the outcast, and the dispossessed, it will fail to function as a theologically rich form of political theology.

CONCLUSION

Over five decades, Moltmann's political theology has developed to encompass the wide array of institutional forms through which human society is organized. He has sought to understand the way in which Christ's proclamation of God's kingdom brings the Christian community into contact with the political necessities of the world in all of its contextual particularity. The dialectic of the cross and resurrection gives form to the way in which the narrative of God's salvation in history motivates the Christian community to action within the world. This extends not only to concern for those pushed to the margins of society by poverty, racism, and sexism, but also to the natural environment in which we dwell. The recognition that the Coming of God that stands as the promise toward which Christians look as the culmination of their hope is a coming to and for the whole cosmos, and not only for human beings.

Moltmann's political theology was able to provide inspiration and impetus for the development of theologies of liberation throughout the Christian world—in Africa, Latin America, and Asia as well as Europe and North America. But Moltmann was also able to recognize that he was but one voice in a larger conversation, and that it was not for him to develop a comprehensive theology capable of addressing every context and every situation. Thus he has been as willing to listen to and learn from other theologies as to offer his own critical voice to the conversation.

In more recent years, Moltmann has increasingly taken to referring to his political theology by the moniker of "public theology," a concept with less currency in the German context, but which has been an increasingly important category of theological interpretation in North America. The fundamental intention of this theology has nevertheless remained the same, which is to proclaim a theology rooted in the anticipation of the coming kingdom of God:

> If the church takes theology seriously, it must like the church, become a function of the kingdom of God in the world. As a function of the kingdom of God, theology belongs within all the different sectors of a society's life too—political, cultural, economic and ecological. This is demonstrated in political theology and the theology of culture, in the theology of education, in ecological theology and the theology of nature. In all these sectors, kingdom-of-God theology is *public theology*, which participates in the *res publica* of society, and 'interferes' critically and prophetically, because it sees public affairs from the perspective of God's coming kingdom.[40]

The question of whether political theology can be subsumed within the category of public theology is an ongoing and much controverted subject. Moltmann has come to identify his theology in that way, but at the same time he insists that the political character of Christian theology remains an inescapable aspect of its identity. As long as the identity of the Christian community is tied to the life and teaching of Jesus Christ, it will be kingdom of God theology, grounded in eschatological expectation and hope, and thus open to the political horizon of the not yet within that which is. And as long as the identity of the Christian community is tied to Christ's crucifixion, it will be grounded in the radical critique of what is on the grounds of God's solidarity with the outcast and marginalized.

As political theology continues to be a significant category of Christian reflection in a new generation, Moltmann's theology will continue to serve as a resource and inspiration to the continuing development of a theology that holds the hope of a better future at the core of its identity, and the commitment to solidarity with the poor and oppressed as the maxim of its social action.

NOTES

1. Jürgen Moltmann, *Politische Theologie Politische Ethik* (München: Chr. Kaiser Verlag, 1984), 39.
2. Carl Schmitt, *Political Theology: Four Chapters on the Concept of Sovereignty* (Chicago: University of Chicago Press, 1985), 5.
3. Ibid., 10–11.
4. Carl Schmitt, *Dictatorship* (Cambridge: Polity Press, 2014).
5. Ibid.
6. Schmitt, *The Concept of the Political* (Chicago: University of Chicago Press, 1996).
7. Ibid., 28.
8. Heinrich Meier, *Carl Schmitt and Leo Strauss: The Hidden Dialogue* (Chicago: University of Chicago Press, 1995), 125.
9. Meier, *Carl Schmitt and Leo Strauss*, 22.
10. It should be noted that Schmitt's conception of the dictator in his writing was not specifically intended as an endorsement of Hitler in particular. However, his participation in the Nazi Party, his insistence that politics is inherently rooted in violence on the one hand and the friend/enemy distinction on the other, and his general anti-Semitism associate his thought irretrievably with Nazi ideology.
11. Jürgen Moltmann, *A Broad Place* (Minneapolis, MN: Fortress Press, 2008), 16–17.
12. Ibid., 30.
13. Ibid., 32.
14. Ibid., 33.
15. Ibid., 29.
16. Geiko Müller-Fahrenholz, *The Kingdom and the Power: The Theology of Jürgen Moltmann* (Minneapolis, MN: Fortress Press, 2001), 23–24.
17. Moltmann, *Theology of Hope* (New York: HarperCollins, 1991), 9.
18. Ibid., 32.
19. Ibid., 304ff.
20. Ibid., 10.
21. Jürgen Moltmann, *The Crucified God* (New York: HarperCollins, 1991), 5.
22. Richard Bauckham, *The Theology of Jürgen Moltmann* (Edinburgh: T&T Clark, 1995), 81.
23. Moltmann, *The Crucified God*, 224.
24. Ibid., 227.
25. Ibid., ix.
26. Moltmann, *Theology of Hope*, 218.
27. Ibid., 223.
28. Jürgen Moltmann *On Human Dignity: Political Theology and Ethics* (Philadelphia: Fortress Press, 1984), 106–107.
29. Jürgen Moltmann, *Religion, Revolution, and the Future* (New York: Charles Scribner's Sons, 1969), 104. (Italics in original.)

30. Ibid., 103.
31. Moltmann, *On Human Dignity*, 107.
32. Ibid., 109.
33. Moltmann, *The Crucified God*, 18.
34. Arne Rasmusson, *The Church as Polis: From Political Theology to Theological Politics as Exemplfied by Jürgen Moltmann and Stanley Hauerwas* (Notre Dame, IN: Univeristy of Notre Dame Press, 1995), 89ff.
35. Jose Miguez-Boniño, "Reading Jürgen Moltmann from Latin America," *Asbury Theological Journal*, vol. 55, no. 1 (2000), 111.
36. Jürgen Moltmann, *God for a Secular Society* (Minneapolis, MN: Fortress Press, 1999), 62.
37. Ernst Bloch, *The Principle of Hope* (Cambridge, MA: MIT Press, 1986), 114.
38. Moltmann, *Theology of Hope*, 231.
39. Ibid., 324.
40. Moltmann, *God for a Secular Society*, 252.

SELECT BIBLIOGRAPHY

Bauckham, Richard (1995), *The Theology of Jürgen Moltmann*, Edinburgh: T&T Clark.
Bloch, Ernst (1986), *The Principle of Hope*, Cambridge, MA: MIT Press.
Meier, Heinrich (1995), *Carl Schmitt and Leo Strauss: The Hidden Dialogue*, Chicago: University of Chicago Press.
Miguez-Boniño, Jose, "Reading Jürgen Moltmann From Latin America," in *Asbury Theological Journal*, vol. 55, no. 1 (2000), 105–114.
Moltmann, Jürgen (1969), *Religion, Revolution, and the Future*, New York: Charles Scribner's Sons.
Moltmann, Jürgen (1984), *On Human Dignity: Political Theology and Ethics*, Philadelphia: Fortress Press.
Moltmann, Jürgen (1984), *Politische Theologie Politische Ethik*, München: Chr. Kaiser Verlag.
Moltmann, Jürgen (1991), *Theology of Hope*, New York: HarperCollins.
Moltmann, Jürgen (1991), *The Crucified God*, New York: HarperCollins.
Moltmann, Jürgen (1999), *God for a Secular Society*, Minneapolis, MN: Fortress Press.
Moltmann, Jürgen (2008), *A Broad Place*, Minneapolis, MN: Fortress Press.
Müller-Fahrenholz, Geiko (2001), *The Kingdom and the Power: The Theology of Jürgen Moltmann*, Minneapolis, MN: Fortress Press.
Rasmusson, Arne (1995), *The Church as Polis: From Political Theology to Theological Politics as Exemplfied by Jürgen Moltmann and Stanley Hauerwas*, Notre Dame, IN: University of Notre Dame Press.
Schmitt, Carl (1985), *Political Theology: Four Chapters on the Concept of Sovereignty*, Chicago: University of Chicago Press.
Schmitt, Carl (1996), *The Concept of the Political*, Chicago: University of Chicago Press.

CHAPTER FIFTEEN

Social Ethics, Reinhold Niebuhr, and Political Theology

GARY DORRIEN

INTRODUCTION

Reinhold Niebuhr stands at the center of the overlap between Christian social ethics and political theology. He was emphatically a social ethicist, plus famously devoted to a realist version of it, drawing from Augustine, Martin Luther, Thomas Hobbes, and Karl Marx an imperative about separating politics from morality. Niebuhr was averse to political theology for the same reason that he attacked the social gospel: politicizing theology is bad, something very different from being impelled by good theology to enter the political arena. But Niebuhr took for granted the social gospel basis of the field he taught, social ethics, *and* the necessity of dancing perilously with Augustine and Hobbes. He never relinquished the activist orientation of social gospel ethics; in fact, Niebuhr epitomized it. Christian realism, in his conception, was a realistic brake on the idealistic and rationalistic illusions of the social gospel, a tradition that expounded explicitly political theologies decades before Carl Schmitt. As such, and because he was the towering Christian social ethicist of the twentieth century, Niebuhr is the most significant social ethicist for political theology.

He became the most influential social ethicist and American theologian of the twentieth century by vigorously addressing every social and political crisis of his time. Niebuhr began his career as a social gospel interventionist during the First World War, converted to a pacifist version of the social gospel in 1923, embraced Norman Thomas socialism in 1928, dropped pacifism for Marxist reasons in the early 1930s, implored Americans to fight fascism and resigned from the Socialist Party in 1940, dropped socialism and joined the Democratic Party establishment in 1947, mythologized the Cold War in the late 1940s and early 1950s, reconsidered Cold War containment in 1958, and shocked many Niebuhrians in 1966 by turning against the Vietnam War. The driving force of his theological career was his concern about what the federal government should do about major national and international issues. Niebuhr's theology did not change as many times as his politics, but the kind of theological career that he had was inconceivable before the social gospel.

Niebuhr was born in Wright City, Missouri, in 1892, to Gustav Niebuhr, a pastor in the German Evangelical Synod of North America who immigrated to the USA in 1881, and Lydia Hosto Niebuhr, the daughter of an Evangelical Synod missionary based in

Northern California. Gustav Niebuhr grew up on a German family farm dating to the thirteenth century and fled to America at the age of eighteen. He dreaded his father's autocratic bearing, usually not mentioning that he also fled from Germany's required military service. Gustav and Lydia Niebuhr were married in 1887, two years after he graduated from Eden Seminary, and their first three children were born in San Francisco—Hulda, Walter, and Herbert. In 1892 they moved to Wright City, where Karl Paul Reinhold was born the same year, and Helmut Richard in 1894.

Reinhold and Richard did not see much of their father during their ten years in Missouri, as Gustav Niebuhr planted churches for the Evangelical Synod across the state. Gustav was more Americanized than most Synod pastors, and loved to run things. He was vigorous, opinionated, and high-minded, blasting fundamentalists and modernists alike in liberal evangelical fashion. He studied the Bible in Hebrew and Greek, read modernist theologians, and defended the biblical miracles. He opined about politics with equal vigor, supporting Teddy Roosevelt. Socialism, alcohol, and feminism were anathema to him for destroying the family. Gustav defied German American contentions that temperance was a plot against German culture, and told his daughter Hulda that higher education was wasted on girls. She should be like her mother, a pastor's wife and helper whose life was a seamless web of domestic and parish tasks. Gustav preached that the church had a mission to promote a good society and the federal government was morally obligated to restrain the excesses of capitalism. In 1902 he wearied of the road, accepting a pastoral call to Saint John's Church in Lincoln, Illinois, where Reinhold was the chief beneficiary.[1]

Gustav Niebuhr decidedly favored his child who was most like him, the second youngest. Hulda was a girl, Walter was rebellious, Herbert died in infancy, and Richard was introverted. Reinhold, alone, was all the right things: male, extroverted, ebullient, disciplined, cooperative, and fascinated by his father's work and opinions. To Reinhold, Gustav Niebuhr was by far the most interesting person in town, and a model. Lincoln, a county seat of 9,000 residents walled with corn, was mostly German American. By the age of twelve, Reinhold knew that he wanted to be a minister like his father. To shy, introspective Richard, on the other hand, Gustav was a cold and disapproving tyrant. When the brother theologians, in later life, discussed their father, they remembered contrasting figures—although Richard Niebuhr characteristically waited until the 1930s to inform his brother.

In 1907 Niebuhr moved from the ninth grade to Elmhurst College, an unaccredited "pro-seminary" fifteen miles west of Chicago that prepared Evangelical Synod boys for Eden Seminary, near St. Louis. Later he regretted having missed high school math, science, and modern history. Elmhurst was a pre-seminary boarding school offering a lowly version of a German *Gymnasium* curriculum of classics and ancient history. Eden was slightly better because Niebuhr found the first of his surrogate fathers there, English professor Samuel Press, the first Eden scholar to teach courses in English. Gustav Niebuhr realized that his favorite son needed the training of an elite American institution. Union Theological Seminary would have been ideal, but Niebuhr had no chance of being admitted to Union. Yale School of Religion, reeling from twenty years of stagnation and decline, became a possibility by lowering its admission requirements. Niebuhr was admitted to Yale in 1913 as a third-year Bachelor of Divinity student, planning to enroll in September, when his father fell ill and died unexpectedly in April.

Gustav Niebuhr was fifty years old and had been diagnosed with diabetes. Insulin was not yet available and he was ordered to rest, but that seemed ridiculous to him, so he kept working until he passed out. Reinhold and Richard were summoned from Eden, Reinhold filled Gustav's pulpit on April 20 as his father lay in a comatose state, and the next day Gustav died. The funeral lasted all afternoon, with memorial addresses by fifteen ministers. For five months Niebuhr took over for his father as interim pastor. For many years afterward he felt called to complete his father's life and work.

From the beginning he preached sermons marked by an emphasis on the sin of selfishness and the paradoxical character of Christianity and life. Niebuhr preached that Matthew 10:39 expressed "the paradox of all life: that self-preservation means self-destruction and self-destruction means self-preservation." Only the person who gives up one's life can be saved, he said. The problem of every human life is every person's captivity to selfishness, and the solution to it is love and self-sacrifice: "The image of God that is still within us will never be satisfied until it is satisfied by the principle that made it—love." Socialism was no better than capitalism, because socialism merely substituted the selfishness of the working class for that of the upper class. Love divine was far better than both. Niebuhr confessed that he did not understand the doctrines of the divinity of Christ, the two natures of Christ, the divine Trinity, and the communion of the Spirit, "and maybe you don't either." But everyone could understand "the moral and social program of Christ."[2]

Gustav Niebuhr, though a preacher of love divine with a version of the social gospel, would not have shoved aside orthodox doctrines, or claimed that love is the answer to all problems of individuals and society, or ended by laying everything on Christ's "moral and social program." Reinhold had arrived at social gospel progressivism before he got to Yale. At Yale his rough manners and Midwest accent marked him as a rube among classmates whose middle and last names reeked of New England elitism. Niebuhr told Press that his English was inadequate for Yale, he was forgetting how to speak German, and his grossly deficient education left him feeling humiliated and frustrated: "I feel all the time like a mongrel among thoroughbreds and that's what I am."[3]

Young Canadian theologian D.C. Macintosh, recently graduated from the University of Chicago Divinity School, facilitated the best parts of Niebuhr's two years of study at Yale. Under Macintosh's guidance, Niebuhr embraced the pragmatism of William James, writing a thesis on James. Niebuhr aspired to a doctorate in theology, but earned mediocre grades in too many courses to qualify for a doctoral program. Macintosh's abstract theorizing about epistemology finished off Niebuhr's dreams of a doctorate, although in later years he said he was bored, not defeated. In June 1915 the school surprised Niebuhr by awarding him a Master of Arts degree, apparently on Macintosh's urging.

Niebuhr's brother Walter had supported the Niebuhr family for two years. A few weeks after Niebuhr graduated from Yale, he discovered that Walter was ruined financially. The family breadwinner role fell to Niebuhr, just before synod President-General John Baltzer assigned him to Bethel Evangelical Church on the northwest edge of Detroit. Niebuhr was deflated. He had never dated, and now his life was a web of responsibilities. He asked for a progressive, Americanized, reasonably well-paying church, only to get a German-speaking mission church long on pro-German nationalists. Niebuhr lamented to Press that this group would never abide his liberal theology and pro-Americanism. He wrote pro-Americanizing articles while his mother ran the congregation's daily business, Sunday school program, and choir. Niebuhr's first article for a national magazine, "The Failure of German-Americanism," was published in July 1916. He said German culture at its best was liberal, cosmopolitan, and forward looking, but German American Protestantism usually conveyed German culture at its worst—conservative, provincial, and stodgy. German Americans, he admonished, needed very much to become better Americans; moreover, Americans were not wrong in disliking German militarism.[4]

Niebuhr's fixations with the USA, being American, and relating Christian ethics to political problems were abiding. His entire career was a love affair with America that diagnosed its neuroses and pretensions, defended its interests, and assumed that Christians have a social responsibility to work for a reasonably just order. After the US intervened in the First World War, Niebuhr wanted desperately to enlist as a military chaplain, but had to settle for running the synod's War Welfare Commission, touring military training camps. Niebuhr preached Wilsonian sermons about creating a new world order based on reconciliation, democracy, free trade, and the League of Nations. Then the Paris Peace Conference vengefully demonstrated, to him, the literal weakness of liberal idealism. Niebuhr judged that Woodrow Wilson was a "typical son of the manse," believing too much in words and ideals: "We need something less circumspect than liberalism to save the world."[5]

This sentiment eventually made Niebuhr famous. Bethel Church grew tremendously in the early 1920s, feeding off the skyrocketing growth of Henry Ford's Detroit, despite Niebuhr's frequent absence. Americanization was the wave of the future in the Evangelical Synod and Niebuhr was its apostle, winning a following on the social gospel lecture circuit. In 1922 he caught the attention of Charles Clayton Morrison, editor of the liberal Protestant flagship the *Christian Century*. Morrison concentrated on defending prohibition and committing the churches to antiwar activism. He encouraged Niebuhr to write about these issues and everything else related to the social gospel. Sherwood Eddy, a wealthy social gospel missionary, hosted Niebuhr's tour in 1923 of occupied postwar zones and trade unions in Europe, where Niebuhr crossed a fateful line. France's abuse of Germans in the occupied Ruhr valley repelled him. Like many liberal clergy of the time, Niebuhr vowed to never preach another pro-war sermon: "This is as good a time as any to make up my mind that I am done with the war business . . . I am done with this business. I hope I can make that resolution stick."[6] He no longer felt pressed to prove his Americanism, and he had lost his other reasons for not being a pacifist; thus he vowed to be a Christian pacifist disciple.

For nearly ten years he struggled to keep this resolution, all the while objecting that his colleagues in the pacifist Fellowship of Reconciliation (FOR) were sentimental and idealistic. Niebuhr chafed at social gospel idealism while calling for more of it, not knowing what else to say. Always he aspired to be realistic, which led him into the Socialist Party of Norman Thomas in 1928, the same year that Niebuhr moved to New York. Eddy paid Niebuhr's entire salary to teach half-time at Union Theological Seminary and edit the socialist-pacifist magazine *World Tomorrow*. This one-year proposal squeaked through the Union faculty by one vote, as they considered him unqualified to teach at Union. Niebuhr won them over by teaching overflow classes and connecting Union students to his socialist-pacifist network. He taught that the capitalist lust for profit was the chief cause of the First World War. Then it caused the collapse of capitalism itself. The Great Depression drove Niebuhr to Marx's verdict that capitalism depended on profits it could not sustain. In 1930 Niebuhr cofounded, with Eddy, Kirby Page, and John C. Bennett, the Fellowship of Socialist Christians, not yet acknowledging that his increasingly radical socialism conflicted with pacifism.[7]

Niebuhr believed that his socialist turn took him beyond the boundary of social gospel progressivism. It did not matter that the social gospel had an explicitly socialist flank founded by W.D.P. Bliss and George Herron, championed by Walter Rauschenbusch and

Vida Scudder, and carried on by Eddy, Mordecai Johnson, and Niebuhr's colleague at Union, social ethicist Harry Ward. In Niebuhr's experience, the social gospel was primarily a pacifist phenomenon. It preached about responding to evil with love, following Jesus to the cross, loving enemies, and following the example of Mohandas Gandhi. In 1932 Niebuhr ran for Congress on the Socialist Party ticket and told New Yorkers that only socialism could save Western civilization: "It will be practically impossible to secure social change in America without the use of very considerable violence." Niebuhr was done with imploring that socialism and pacifism had to go together. He expounded this message in his greatest book, published in December 1932, *Moral Man and Immoral Society*.[8]

Social ethics had no history or basis apart from the social gospel. What did it mean to be a social ethicist if one did not believe in redeemed institutions, the progressive character of history, or an idealistic theology of social salvation? Niebuhr's icy, aggressive, sarcastic book offered an answer that launched a new era in American theology and ethics. Politics is about struggling for power. Human groups never willingly subordinate their interests to the interests of others. Liberal denials of this truism are stupid. Morality belongs to the sphere of individual action. On occasion, individuals rise above self-interest, motivated by compassion or love, but groups never overcome the power of self-interest and collective egotism that sustains their existence. Niebuhr said the capitalist ruling class blighted the lives of everyone else by wielding organized power. The Marxian idea of proletarian revolution was "a very valuable illusion for the moment," for it would take "a sublime madness in the soul" to defeat "malignant power and 'spiritual wickedness in high places.'"[9]

With this book, "stupid" became Niebuhr's favorite epithet, followed closely by "naïve." Liberal idealists failed to recognize the brutal character of human groups and the resistance of all groups to moral suasion. Secular liberals like philosopher John Dewey appealed to reason; Christian liberals appealed to reason and love; Niebuhr said both were maddeningly stupid. Christianity needed to regain a sense of the tragedy of life. The historical sweep of human life always reflects the predatory world of nature. Resigning from FOR, Niebuhr declared that liberal Christianity was too consumed with its pretense of virtue to attain justice: "Recognizing, as liberal Christianity does not, that the world of politics is full of demonic forces, we have chosen on the whole to support the devil of vengeance against the devil of hypocrisy." He chose to support Marxist vengeance, knowing there was a devil in it, rather then allow the devil of hypocrisy to avoid conflict and preserve the status quo. To avoid trafficking with devils was to make oneself an accomplice to injustice and tyranny.[10]

Niebuhr's signature work, *An Interpretation of Christian Ethics* (1935), said that Jesus taught an ethic of love perfectionism, which is not socially relevant. He put it starkly:

> The ethic of Jesus does not deal at all with the immediate moral problem of every human life—the problem of attempting some kind of armistice between various contending factions and forces. It has nothing to say about the relativities of politics and economics, nor of the necessary balances of power which exist and must exist in even the most intimate social relationships.

The teachings of Jesus are counsels of moral perfection. Jesus lacked any horizontal point of reference and had nothing to say about how a good society should be organized. His points of reference were vertical, defining the moral ideal for individuals in their relationship to God. Jesus called his followers to forgive because God forgives; he called them to love their enemies because God's love is impartial. He did not teach that hatred could be disarmed by returning evil with love. This Gandhian sentiment was commonplace in liberal sermons, but Jesus-style love perfectionism was not a social ethic.[11]

In Niebuhr's telling, the teaching of Jesus had social relevance in only one sense: it affirmed that a moral ideal exists, which judged all forms of social order. Jesus is no help with the problem of justice because justice is about gaining and defending a relative balance of power. The highest good in the political sphere is to establish justice, which cannot dispense with violence. Even Gandhian nonviolent resistance is a form of coercive violence, although Gandhians advisedly never put it that way.

Niebuhr contended through the 1930s that history would either move forward to revolutionary socialism or backward to fascist barbarism. There was no third way. Capitalism was finished and Franklin Roosevelt was kidding himself, as were the social gospel liberals who supported the New Deal. Niebuhr implored liberal Protestants to turn to the left politically and to the right theologically. He was clear that radical state socialism was the only cure, waving off Marx's anti-statism, and vague about his theological shift. Niebuhr wanted the federal government to nationalize the commanding heights of the economy, replicate the pricing decisions of markets, and organize an economy not linked by markets. When he began delivering the Gifford Lectures in Edinburgh in the spring of 1939, Niebuhr was still a state socialist, but pulling back from his polemics against the New Deal, belatedly acknowledging that it enacted most of the Socialist Party platform. Then Germany invaded Poland, German planes bombed an Edinburgh naval base a few miles from Niebuhr's October Gifford lecture on human destiny, and the Socialist Party stuck to its anti-war position, causing Niebuhr to resign from the party in 1940.[12]

To Niebuhr, it was desperately important that the USA come to Britain's aid before Hitler conquered Europe. He had to battle against US American isolationism *and* the revulsion for war that he helped to cultivate in liberal Protestantism. Niebuhr railed powerfully against permitting "the triumph of an intolerable tyranny," imploring that only a "very, very sick" liberal Protestantism believed that fighting the Nazis was worse than capitulating to them. He blasted the *Christian Century* for somehow ignoring that the Nazi regime "is seeking to extinguish the Christian religion, debases its subjects to robots who have no opinion or judgment of their own, threatens the Jews of Europe with complete annihilation and all the nations of Europe with subordination under the imperial dominion of a 'master race.'"[13]

In Edinburgh he stuck to theological high ground while fretting that the war made his lectures irrelevant. Niebuhr's Gifford Lectures, published in 1941 and 1943 as *The Nature and Destiny of Man*, unveiled the theological position on which he finally settled after absorbing Richard Niebuhr's critique that he conceived Christianity in modern progressive terms, not the Reformation categories of Luther and Calvin. Niebuhr said his theology was a form of biblical realism in the tradition of Augustine. He contrasted the "biblical" view of human nature and destiny with the classical Platonist, Aristotelian, and Stoic concept that human beings are spiritual beings gifted with self-reflective reason and thus unique within nature. In the biblical view, Niebuhr argued, the self is a created finite unity of body and spirit. Augustine caught the significance of the biblical idea, conceiving the self as a mysterious integral identity transcending its mind and yet able to use mind and will for its purposes. To Augustine and Niebuhr, God was beyond society and history, yet also intimately related to the world. The human spirit finds a home and catches a glimpse of its freedom in God's transcendence, but also finds in divine transcendence the limit of the self's freedom, a divine judgment against human pride, and divine mercy for sin. God's redeeming grace enables sinful egotists to surrender their prideful attempts to master their existence. Niebuhr presumed to describe all human beings in this account, not asking whether pride and will-to-power were the characteristic sins of the women he knew—a question pressed by feminist theologians in the 1970s.[14]

The second volume of *Nature and Destiny* was better than volume one because Niebuhr enlisted his wife, Barnard College religion professor Ursula Niebuhr, to smoothen his prose and restrain his shooting gallery polemics. In chapter nine he developed a vintage Niebuhr dialectic on "The Kingdom of God and the Struggle for Justice." Niebuhr argued that the struggle for justice is more revealing of the possibilities and limits of human powers than the quest for truth. The relationship of the kingdom of God to history is inescapably paradoxical. History moves toward the realization of the kingdom, yet every occasion of its realization falls under divine judgment. This argument was the seed of Niebuhr's mature political philosophy, which he developed in November 1943 while FDR, Winston Churchill, and Joseph Stalin met in Tehran to plan the Allied invasion of Europe. In January 1944, Niebuhr gave the Raymond F. West Lectures at Stanford. The following summer, while Allied forces launched D-Day, Niebuhr expanded his Stanford lectures into a book, *The Children of Light and the Children of Darkness*.[15]

Liberals applied the old Wilsonian arguments to the Second World War as soon as they faced up to being in it. That evoked a bad memory for Niebuhr. *Children* derided modern liberals as spiritual cousins of John Locke, Adam Smith, Jean-Jacques Rousseau, Thomas Jefferson, and G.W.F. Hegel. All were children of light who believed that the conflict between self-interest and the general interest could be resolved. All were unbearably stupid on this account. Locke's social contract, Smith's harmonizing invisible hand, and Rousseau's general will needed only minimal restraints on human egotism, because Locke, Smith, and Rousseau had overweening confidence in reason and/or nature. Jefferson and Hegel were equally besotted with their enlightenment, and Niebuhr lumped Marxists and Catholics with "other stupid children of light." Marxists believed the state would be unnecessary after the proletarian revolution, and Catholics described feudalism as a Christian civilization: "The blindness of Catholicism to its own ideological taint is typical of the blindness of the children of light." In six blistering pages, Niebuhr used the word "stupid" six times to characterize the children of light. He enjoyed the irony of charging that the icons of modern culture, besides being naïve, were not very smart either.[16]

All manner of modern liberals, democrats, Marxists, and Catholics defended democracy badly against children of darkness, who were wise and strong in their cynicism. Niebuhr said the children of darkness understood self-interest terribly well and were not constrained by a moral law. Hobbes and Machiavelli provided theory for them, exemplifying the toxic corruption of realism lacking a moral dimension. Luther was a child of darkness for railing against reason and morality, providing Lutheran cover for state absolutists and anti-democrats. The epitome of toxic darkness, Nazi barbarism, plunged Europe into total war, shredding the classic liberal picture of a benign, individualistic society. Niebuhr derided the liberal idea that democracy fulfilled an ideal that people deserved on account of their moral worth. The children of darkness understood that will-to-power drives politics and history. This dialectic yielded Niebuhr's most famous epigram: "Man's capacity for justice makes democracy possible, but man's inclination to injustice makes democracy necessary." Liberal democracy is worth defending because it is the best way to restrain human egotism and will-to-power, not because it fulfills an ideal.[17]

In 1944, Niebuhr still believed that political democracy needed to grow into economic democracy to attain social justice and protect democracy itself. Political democracy lacking economic democracy led to the capitalist class owning the political system. Economic democracy was needed to break the greed and will-to-power of the capitalist class: "Since economic power, as every other form of social power, is a defensive force when possessed in moderation and a temptation to injustice when it is great enough to give the agent power over others, it would seem that its widest and most equitable distribution would make for the highest degree of justice."[18]

"It would seem" was a retreat, however. Niebuhr still believed in economic democracy as an ideal, even that it was essential to social justice. But he no longer believed it was possible in his country, unlike what his Labour Party friends in England were about to do. Sticking with socialism on ethical grounds made no sense to Niebuhr because Marx was right about ethical socialism—it was useless idealism. In the 1930s Niebuhr was consumed with one principle of justice, equality. Now he believed that freedom and order are equally important. In the past he took for granted that believing in a common humanity compelled him to work for a just world order. Now he was chastened by Augustine's caution that language and ethnicity, which bind communities on one level, are divisive at higher levels. Augustine's realism was "excessive," Niebuhr allowed. Augustine had no basis for distinguishing between government and slavery, or between a commonwealth and a band of robbers. All were forms of rule over human beings by human beings. Modern Christian realism had to do better, defending liberal democracy without enshrining any ideology as an object of faith.[19]

These arguments pulled Niebuhr into the mainstream of the Democratic Party. After leaving the Socialist Party in 1940 he spearheaded a pro-interventionist coalition of politicians, trade unionists, and intellectuals, the Union for Democratic Action (UDA). Niebuhr worked hard for the UDA, undertaking fundraising tours for it. This group was his last-ditch attempt to build a party of labor leaders and intellectuals outside the Democratic Party. In 1947 the UDA merged with a new organization, Americans for Democratic Action (ADA), an advocacy group in the center-left of the Democratic Party. Other ADA founders included Eleanor Roosevelt, Hubert Humphrey, and Arthur Schlesinger Jr. Niebuhr repented of blasting the New Deal, aligning with establishment liberals who treasured it. The Old Leftists that came with Niebuhr into the ADA were valuable to it because they were veterans of the battles to expel Communists from the trade unions and Socialist Party. The best anti-Communists were Socialists or former Socialists, because they hated Communism for ruining something they prized, and they knew how Communists subverted democratic organizations. They boasted that they were the experts on thwarting Communism.

Niebuhr provided this group's signature version of anti-Communist ideology, an argument he developed in tandem with State Department guru George Kennan. Fascism, Niebuhr reasoned, could be smashed by direct force because it lacked an inspiring ideal that transcended national boundaries. But Communism had the moral power of a utopian creed that appealed to deluded leftists and to millions in the Third World. Thus it had to be fought differently. Communism, though tactically flexible, was inherently fanatical, resting on a "simple" distinction between oppressors and oppressed, and simplistic concepts of class and exploitation. Old-style realists viewed Soviet Communism as a new form of Russian imperialism; Niebuhr countered that traditional *realpolitik* failed to grasp the "noxious demonry" of Communism. At the same time, he counseled against a crusading hot war. America's battle against Communism needed to walk a fine, patient, vigilant line between treating the Soviet regime as a geopolitical Great Power rival and a Nazi-like enemy.[20]

In power politics, Niebuhr cautioned, a perverted moralism is always more dangerous than explicit evil. For this reason, Communism was capable of creating greater and longer-lasting evils in the world than fascism. Niebuhr argued that the best analogy for the Communist threat to the West was the rise of militant Islam in the high Middle Ages, not the Third Reich. Just as Islam brandished a quasi-universal ideology that transcended nationalism while being rooted in the Arab world, the Communist movement wielded a pseudo-universal creed that served Russian imperial ambitions. Niebuhr believed that equating Soviet tyranny with Islam validated his conception of Soviet Communism as an evil religion. He took for granted that his audience did not object to his slur that Islam was similarly demonic, and he was not called on it. Usually he added that the Islamic concept of a holy war against infidels was analogous to the Communist concept of an inevitable war against capitalism.[21]

Niebuhr hung a vast ideological scaffolding on this argument, teaching that Communism was an evil religion devoted to the establishment of a new universal order, not merely the supremacy of a race or nation, and thus had to be contained through diplomatic pressure and military force. In 1952 Niebuhr clarified what he didn't mean in *The Irony of American History*. His brand of anti-Communism did not rest on America's typical conceits about its innocence. Niebuhr said America's innocent self-image inoculated Americans from recognizing their nation's imperialism. This innocence was functional for America's imperial role, except when it wasn't. *Irony* made a case for a bit of modesty, countering the fearfully self-righteous mood of the time. But the point was to help America do a better job of running its empire. Niebuhrian realism was geared to the worldview and problems of Cold War diplomats, a fact appreciated by Niebuhr's friends in the US State Department. He continued to castigate all Communist regimes as evil, describing Communism in 1953 as "an organized evil which spreads terror and cruelty throughout the world and confronts us everywhere with faceless men who are immune to every form of moral and political suasion."[22]

At the time, FBI agents scoured Union Seminary and a flock of Old Left organizations for incriminating details about Niebuhr's past. It was an ugly, demeaning, mendacious period. Like his ADA allies, Niebuhr detested Senator Joseph McCarthy's wild charges that vast numbers of government officials were Communists. Niebuhr and the ADA were determined not to allow McCarthy to monopolize the anti-Communist issue, which was too important to be left to reactionaries, especially because the McCarthy version demonized the entire political Left. Niebuhr spurned McCarthy, demonized Communists in Old Left sectarian fashion, and implicitly condoned parts of McCarthy's campaign to smoke out Communists from government, education, and religion. In 1953 Niebuhr wrongly claimed that McCarthy's assistant, J.B. Matthews, accurately identified more than a dozen pro-Communist church leaders, and he strongly supported the government's execution of Julius and Ethel Rosenberg for stealing atomic secrets. Niebuhr stayed in this mode until 1954, when McCarthy self-destructed. Years later, he apologized for giving ballast to the smear tactics of McCarthy and Matthews. Niebuhr's vulnerability was a factor; his FBI file swelled in the 1950s on the FBI's premise that he was "still" a Communist.[23]

Niebuhr subscribed to Kennan's contention that the Soviet regime was unsustainable. Sooner or later, Soviet Communism would implode from the contradictions and failures of its unworkable system. The purpose of containment strategy was to keep enough diplomatic and military pressure on the Soviets to accelerate the implosion. Kennan's historic "Mr. X" blueprint for containment, published in *Foreign Affairs* in 1947, was eerily prescient, though off by thirty years, contending that ten to fifteen years of patient containment would undermine the discipline of the Soviet party. If it happened, Kennan said, "the chaos and weakness of Russian society would be revealed in forms beyond description. Soviet Russia might be changed overnight from one of the strongest to one of the weakest and most pitiable of national societies."[24]

Niebuhr endorsed this idea of what containment was designed to do, until 1958—two years after Soviet premier Nikita Khrushchev denounced Stalin's purges and instituted de-Stalinizing reforms. Niebuhr began to question the two pillars of containment: Communism would not survive and it was incapable of internal reforms. The Soviets were advancing in science and technology, and Khrushchev had a reform agenda. Niebuhr's intellectual partner, Bennett, proposed that the US relinquish its "perpetual official moral diatribe" against Communism, aiming for some kind of coexistence. Niebuhr stunned many by moving to the same view. He no longer believed that Soviet Communism was an immutable monolith, a global conspiracy, or an implacable enemy with which the USA could not coexist. In 1959 Niebuhr made a case for coexistence, contending that realism demanded "a less rigid and self-righteous attitude toward the power realities of the world and a more hopeful attitude toward the possibilities of internal development in the Russian despotism."[25]

Christian realists sharply debated Niebuhr's surprising turn, which Kennan influenced, although Kennan still believed the Soviet system was inherently unstable. Kennan and Niebuhr argued that containment acquired an overly militarized meaning in American policy, and American policymakers overestimated Soviet political, economic, and military strength. Secretary of State John Foster Dulles epitomized policymaker arrogance with quotes from Niebuhr, offending Niebuhr. Dulles described the Cold War as a struggle between good and evil, and brandished America's nuclear arsenal as a threat. Niebuhr countered that Dulles over-moralized the Cold War and over-relied on the threat of nuclear force. He told friends that Dulles and President Eisenhower were too stupid to be entrusted with America's fate.

Otherwise the Eisenhower years were short on divisive issues for the Niebuhrians, because they prized America's bipartisan consensus on foreign policy, including fateful overthrows in Iran and Guatemala, and waging war in Korea. Kennan, Bennett, Schlesinger, Hans Morgenthau, Kenneth W. Thompson, and Paul Ramsey were leading Niebuhrian realists in foreign policy, combining global anti-Communism and American nationalism. In 1956 the Soviet invasion of Hungary confirmed Niebuhr's belief that the USA had to preserve its nuclear dominance to sustain its dominance in Europe. Very few American Christian ethicists disputed this "consensus" position in the 1950s.[26]

Then came the exotic turbulence of the 1960s and the end of consensus. President Kennedy appointed several Niebuhrians to high positions, notably Schlesinger and Paul Nitze. Niebuhr supported Kennedy while fretting that he was shallow and sexually promiscuous. Kennedy's disastrous attempt to overthrow the Castro government in Cuba deepened Niebuhr's misgivings, and the Berlin crisis of 1961 convinced Niebuhr that America should adopt a policy of no-first-use of nuclear weapons, although he put it with clueless amnesia, contending that American democracy could not survive the "monstrous guilt" of a nuclear triumph. Remarkably, though typically for the time, Niebuhr ignored that American democracy had survived Hiroshima and Nagasaki.[27]

The Niebuhr/Bennett shift on nuclear policy sparked a fractious debate among Niebuhrians, a prelude to implosion. Niebuhr continued to support nuclear deterrence, while admitting he had undermined his argument for it. Then the Vietnam War shattered the consensus. For two decades after the Chinese revolution, Niebuhr opposed US intervention in Asian civil wars. He did not consider Korea an exception, because the Korean War was launched by a Soviet-backed invasion. But Vietnam was a postcolonial civil war *and* a Soviet proxy war. Niebuhr accepted the domino theory that Communists would conquer Southeast Asia if the US withdrew from Vietnam, but the American-backed Diem regime in South Vietnam was a repressive dictatorship, so both options looked bad to him. In 1965 President Lyndon Johnson massively escalated in Vietnam and Niebuhr yearned for a third way. Winning the war seemed unlikely, but losing the region to Communism seemed intolerable. Niebuhr implored Johnson to persuade Thailand to offer asylum to the region's anti-Communist warriors "and then defend this asylum with massive military power." This absurd proposal had nothing to recommend it except, to Niebuhr, one terribly important thing: America needed to stand tall, reminding other nations of its superior might and will.[28]

In January 1966 Niebuhr was still exhorting Johnson to take a stand in Thailand, but by the end of the month he felt acutely embarrassed for his friend, Vice President Humphrey, who gamely defended the war. Niebuhr turned the other way, contradicting Humphrey: no important security interest was at stake in Vietnam, and the war was a futile enterprise. Above all, the carnage of the war sickened Niebuhr. He denounced America's use of chemical weapons and added that bombing North Vietnam was pointless. The following year Niebuhr urged Johnson to withdraw from Vietnam, calling for an outcry "against these horrendous policies." He told friends that his lack of patriotic feeling frightened him: "For the first time I fear I am ashamed of our beloved nation."[29]

That reaction appalled many Niebuhrians. Ramsey protested that Niebuhr carried on as though Niebuhr had never existed. The real Niebuhr would not have stumped for disarmament or cutting out of Vietnam, Ramsey suggested. To Ramsey and what became the neoconservative reaction, it was all very sad.[30]

Two contrasting reactions to the 1960s symbolized the fate of Niebuhrian theology: liberation theology and neoconservatism. Liberationists charged that Niebuhrian realism was an ideology of the hegemonic American order, and feminist liberationists criticized Niebuhr's lack of an ethical critique of sexism. Many feminist theologians described Niebuhr as a leading purveyor of sexist dualism in theology, while Cornel West described Niebuhrian realism as a "form of Europeanist ideology that promoted and legitimated U.S. hegemony in the world." West explained that Western Europe and the USA comprised a superior civilization to Niebuhr, a prejudice that underwrote Niebuhr's support of US domination of Latin America, European colonialism in Africa, and an Israeli state led by European Jews that oppressed the Palestinians. West said there were two streams of Niebuhrian realism. One sought to shore up a declining liberal Democratic Party establishment; West called them "desperate" defenders of a "discredited" perspective. The other group turned Niebuhr's Euro-American supremacism and Cold War militarism into an ideology of American empire.[31]

The second stream was the neoconservative movement. Many of the original neocons had backgrounds in the Old Left, some came straight from Niebuhr's circle, notably Ramsey and Ernest Lefever, and others lionized Niebuhr after they became neoconservatives, notably Michael Novak and Richard Neuhaus. Novak said that America in 1972 desperately needed the Niebuhr of 1952, who would not have tolerated the feminists, Black Power radicals, and progressive idealists who took over theology and the Democratic Party between Niebuhr's retirement in 1960 and death in 1971.[32]

Meanwhile the field of social ethics retained many liberal centrist Niebuhrians who reminded critics that Niebuhr spent his entire career in the liberal Left and never lost his passion for social justice. Bennett, Ronald Stone, Charles West, and a bit later, Robin Lovin, were prominent in this school. They contended that Niebuhrian realism at its best was an antidote to America-the-Greatest imperialism, not a species of it. In their reading, the neocon Niebuhrians had never taken Niebuhr seriously when he criticized America's fantasies of omnipotence and righteousness. Thus the neocons were too surprised when he applied this critique to America's disaster in Vietnam.

The Niebuhr who criticized American arrogance got recycled in 2003 after the US invaded Iraq in the hope of remaking the entire Middle East. Niebuhr had less of a legacy on racial justice, although he wrote nearly a dozen articles on this subject, more than any white theologian of his generation. He described racism as a form of self-worship that ignores the conditioned character of one's life and culture. Racism feeds on the pretense that one's race or culture represents a final good. Ultimately it is a spiritual issue, for the sin of racism is an especially toxic form of evil as egotism.

But Niebuhr never featured this subject in his major works, and he never gave it the high priority that he gave to pacifism in the 1920s, Marxian socialism in the 1930s, anti-fascism and Vital Center liberalism in the 1940s, and anti-Communism in the 1950s. He was inordinately impressed with Gunnar Myrdal's seminal work *An American Dilemma* (1944), which recycled stereotypes about the supposed backwardness and pathology of black American culture, even as Myrdal opposed racial discrimination. Niebuhr did the same thing, asserting that black American culture was backward and distorted on account of discrimination.[33]

In 1956, Niebuhr advised Democratic presidential candidate Adlai Stevenson to say as little as possible about civil rights, and the following year Martin Luther King, Jr. asked Niebuhr to support a petition asking Eisenhower to enforce the *Brown* decision in the South. Niebuhr turned him down, explaining that he opposed anything smacking of Yankee interference or moral presumption. Elsewhere he said that when white liberal Christians apologized to African Americans or Jews for the sins of white America, they won moral points for humility and contrition, but wrongly. Confessions of this sort were dictated by pride; thus they carried a whiff of hypocrisy. Instead of expressing a real confession, the penitent communicated his or her moral superiority. Northern white liberals needed to go slow on this account, like him. Niebuhr's zeal for the interests of the Democratic Party and his Lutheran aversion to false righteousness thus stifled his voice on civil rights, when it mattered.[34]

White liberals of the 1950s took pride in having no racial biases, which made them liberals. The goal was to open opportunities for people of color and abolish discriminatory laws and policies. Niebuhr took for granted that the problem for whites was to eliminate racial bias, not to dismantle an entire culture of white supremacism. But US American racism was and is a white problem, a gaping evil in the culture of whiteness. It is a structure of power based on privilege that presumes to define what is normal.

The closest that Niebuhr ever came to acknowledging it was in the essay referenced above about African American culture. As usual, he argued that the human capacity for free and responsible agency is the highest expression of humanity's spiritual nature and destiny. Only individuals can do that, for groups have no capacity for self-transcendence. Groups cannot organize for ethical ends; they merely seek to preserve themselves. But Niebuhr argued that backward cultures do not recognize there is such a thing as an individual. This idea existed only in advanced societies and cultures. The dominant white culture of the USA nurtured and prized individuality, but African Americans could achieve moral agency only by being allowed to by the dominant society *and* by overcoming the backward pathologies of their own culture. Thus Niebuhr sprinkled his writings with references to "talented exceptions" that succeeded.[35]

The way that Niebuhr developed this line of argument—which has a long history on both sides of the color line—violated his own maxim against treating any social scheme as ethically normative or inscribed with divine favor. Black Americans were told, in effect, that to become actualized moral agents, they had to become culturally white. Niebuhr did not recognize that white supremacism was a deeper evil than racist moral bias because he took for granted the superiority of Euro-American culture and democracy.

The social gospel tried to moralize the public square, but Niebuhr countered that politics is a struggle for power driven by interest and will-to-power. The social gospel said that a cooperative commonwealth is achievable, but Niebuhr countered that the very idea of a good society must be given up. He got the first thing right and the second thing wrong, which has compelled social ethicists ever since to struggle with both sides of his legacy. Niebuhr's polemic against the idea of a good society was costly for social ethics. This idea is always in process of revision and debate, but to discard it is to undercut the struggle for attainable gains toward justice, negating the elusive but formative vision of what is worth struggling for. Without a vision of a better society than the existing one, ethics and politics remain captive to the dominant order, restricted to marginal reforms. The borders of possibility remain untested.

The later Niebuhr who wrote new prefaces to his early books realized what was missing in the severe dualism of *Moral Man and Immoral Society* and *An Interpretation of Christian Ethics*. Justice cannot be defined abstractly, because justice is a relational term that depends on the motive force of love. It emerges in the interaction of love and situation, through the principles of equality, freedom, and order. The upshot is paradoxical, as the later Niebuhr perceived. Love is uncalculating concern for the dignity of persons; as such it asserts no interests. But because love motivates concern for the dignity of persons, it motivates a passion for justice overflowing with interests and requiring principles of justice. To Niebuhr, the love ethic was always the point, the motive, and the end, even when it had no concrete social meaning, and even when he said otherwise.

NOTES

1. Gary Dorrien, *The Making of American Liberal Theology: Idealism, Realism, and Modernity*, 1900–1950 (Louisville, KY: Westminster John Knox Press, 2003), 434–437. This article summarizes arguments that I have made in many books and articles on Niebuhr.
2. Reinhold Niebuhr, Union Service Sermon, August 17, 1913, Reinhold Niebuhr Papers, Library of Congress, Washington, DC.
3. Reinhold Niebuhr to Samuel D. Press, March 3, 1914, Niebuhr Papers.
4. Reinhold Niebuhr, "The Failure of German-Americanism," *Atlantic* (July 1916), 16–18.
5. Reinhold Niebuhr, *Leaves from the Notebook of a Tamed Cynic* (1st ed., 1929; New York: Meridian Books, 1966), "typical," 40; Niebuhr, Letter to the Editor, *The New Republic* (June 14, 1919), "we need," 218.
6. Niebuhr, *Leaves from the Notebook of a Tamed Cynic*, quotes 68, 69.
7. Reinhold Niebuhr, *Does Civilization Need Religion?* (New York: Macmillan, 1928), 1–28.
8. Reinhold Niebuhr, "Catastrophe or Social Control?" *Harper's* 165 (June 1932), 118.

9. Reinhold Niebuhr, *Moral Man and Immoral Society: A Study in Ethics and Politics* (New York: Scribner's 1932), quotes 277.
10. Reinhold Niebuhr, "Why I Leave the F.O.R.," *Christian Century* (January 3, 1934), reprinted in Niebuhr, *Love and Justice*, ed. D. B. Robertson (Philadelphia: Westminster Press, 1957), quote 259.
11. Reinhold Niebuhr, *An Interpretation of Christian Ethics* (New York: Harper & Row, 1935), quote 23.
12. Reinhold Niebuhr, "Religion and Marxism," *Modern Monthly* 8 (February 1935), 714; Niebuhr, "The Blindness of Liberalism," *Radical Religion* 1 (Autumn 1936), 4; Niebuhr, "The Idea of Progress and Socialism," *Radical Religion* 1 (Spring 1936), 28; Niebuhr, "Roosevelt's Merry-Go-Round," *Radical Religion* 3 (Spring 1938), 4.
13. Reinhold Niebuhr, "To Prevent the Triumph of an Intolerable Tyranny," *Christian Century* 57 (December 18, 1940), "very," 1579; Niebuhr, *Christianity and Power Politics* (New York: Scribner's, 1940), "is seeking," 44.
14. Reinhold Niebuhr, *The Nature and Destiny of Man*, 2 vols. (New York: Scribner's, 1941, 1943).
15. Niebuhr, *The Nature and Destiny of Man*, II: 244–286.
16. Reinhold Niebuhr, *The Children of Light and the Children of Darkness* (New York: Scribner's, 1944), "other stupid," 32, "the blindness," 13.
17. Niebuhr, *The Children of Light and the Children of Darkness*, quote xi.
18. Niebuhr, *The Children of Light and the Children of Darkness*, quote 113–114.
19. Reinhold Niebuhr, *Christian Realism and Political Problems* (New York: Scribner's, 1953), quote, 127.
20. Reinhold Niebuhr, "The Change in Russia," *The New Leader* 38 (October 3, 1955), "simple," 1819; Niebuhr, *Christian Realism and Political Problems*, "noxious," 34; Niebuhr, *Christian Realism and Political Problems*, 33–42.
21. Niebuhr, "The Change in Russia," 18–19; Reinhold Niebuhr, "The Peril of Complacency in Our Nation," *Christianity and Crisis* 14 (February 8, 1954), 1.
22. Reinhold Niebuhr, *The Irony of American History* (New York: Scribner's, 1952); Niebuhr, *Christian Realism and Political Problems* (New York, Scribner's, 1953), "an organized," 34.
23. Reinhold Niebuhr, "Communism and the Protestant Clergy," *Look* (November 17, 1953), 37.
24. "X," (George F. Kennan), "The Sources of Soviet Conduct," *Foreign Affairs* 25 (July 1947), 579–580; Niebuhr, *The Irony of American History*, 129.
25. John C. Bennett, "A Condition for Coexistence," *Christianity and Crisis*, 18 (April 28, 1958), "perpetual," 53; Reinhold Niebuhr, "Uneasy Peace or Catastrophe," *Christianity and Crisis* 18 (April 28, 1958), 54–55; Niebuhr, *The Structure of Nations and Empires* (New York: Charles Scribner's Sons, 1959), "a less," 282.
26. Reinhold Niebuhr, "Our Moral Dilemma," *The Messenger* (November 5, 1957), 5; George F. Kennan, *The Nuclear Delusion: Soviet–American Relations in the Atomic Age* (New York: Pantheon Books, 1982), ix–xxx; author's interview with Bennett, January 2, 1993.
27. John C. Bennett and Reinhold Niebuhr, "The Nuclear Dilemma: A Discussion," *Christianity & Crisis* 21 (November 13, 1961), quote, 201; Niebuhr, "Logical Consistency and the Nuclear Dilemma," *Christianity & Crisis* 22 (April 2, 1962), 48.
28. Reinhold Niebuhr, "Consensus at the Price of Flexibility," *The New Leader* (September 27, 1965), "and then," 20.

29. Reinhold Niebuhr, "The Peace Offensive," *Christianity and Crisis* 25 (January 24, 1966), 301; Niebuhr, "Escalation Objective," *The New York Times* (March 14, 1967), "against"; Richard W. Fox, *Reinhold Niebuhr* (Ithaca, NY: Cornell University Press, 1996), "for the," 285; Niebuhr, Foreword to *Martin Luther King, Jr., John C. Bennett, Henry Steele Commager, Abraham Heschel Speak on the War in Vietnam* (New York: Clergy and Laymen Concerned About Vietnam, 1967), 3.
30. Paul Ramsey, *The Just War: Force and Political Responsibility* (1968; repr., Lanham, MD: University Press of America, 1983), 458.
31. Cornel West, *Prophetic Fragments: Illuminations of the Crisis in American Religion and Culture* (Grand Rapids, MI: Eerdmans, 1988), quotes 148, 152.
32. Michael Novak, "Needing Niebuhr Again," *Commentary* 54 (September 1972), 52.
33. Gunnar Myrdal, *An American Dilemma: The Negro Problem and Modern Democracy* (New York: Harper, 1944), 928–930; Reinhold Niebuhr, *The Godly and the Ungodly; Essays on the Religious and Secular Dimensions of Modern Life* (London: Faber & Faber, 1958), 80–99.
34. Reinhold Niebuhr to Adlai Stevenson, February 28, 1956, Niebuhr Papers; Niebuhr, "A Theologian's Comments on the Negro in America," *Reporter* (November 29, 1956), 24; Carol Polsgrove, *Divided Minds: Intellectuals and the Civil Rights Movement* (New York: Norton, 2001), 42–48.
35. Niebuhr, *The Godly and the Ungodly*, 80–99.

SELECT BIBLIOGRAPHY

Dorrien, Gary (2003), *The Making of American Liberal Theology: Idealism, Realism, and Modernity, 1900–1950*, Louisville, KY: Westminster John Knox Press.

Niebuhr, Reinhold (1932), *Moral Man and Immoral Society: A Study in Ethics and Politics*, New York: Scribner's.

Niebuhr, Reinhold (1935), *An Interpretation of Christian Ethics*, New York: Harper & Row.

Niebuhr, Reinhold (1941, 1943), *The Nature and Destiny of Man*, 2 vols., New York: Scribner's.

Niebuhr, Reinhold (1944), *The Children of Light and the Children of Darkness*, New York: Scribner's.

Niebuhr, Reinhold (1952), *The Irony of American History*, New York: Scribner's.

Niebuhr, Reinhold (1958), *The Godly and the Ungodly; Essays on the Religious and Secular Dimensions of Modern Life*, London: Faber & Faber.

Niebuhr, Reinhold (1966), *Leaves from the Notebook of a Tamed Cynic*, New York: Meridian Books.

Polsgrove, Carol (2001), *Divided Minds: Intellectuals and the Civil Rights Movement*, New York: Norton.

Ramsey, Paul (1983), *The Just War: Force and Political Responsibility*, reprint, Lanham, MD: University Press of America.

West, Cornel (1988), *Prophetic Fragments: Illuminations of the Crisis in American Religion and Culture*, Grand Rapids, MI: Eerdmans.

CHAPTER SIXTEEN

Gustavo Gutiérrez and Latin American Liberation Theology

MICHAEL E. LEE

INTRODUCTION

If the twentieth century is remembered as the period in which Christianity took on an authentically global, and not just colonial, character, then the liberation theologies that emerged from Latin America in the 1950s and 1960s must be seen as a primary catalyst of this transformation. Just as Paris, Bologna, and other early university centers transformed medieval theology away from the monasteries, so Lima, Rio de Janeiro, and San Salvador have harkened a new locus for theology in the modern world. Without a doubt, that theology is political at its core. It makes the scandalous reality of global poverty and violence the starting point for Christian reflection. However, despite the claims of some critics, liberation theology is also profoundly theological, bringing the wealth of the Christian tradition to address these contemporary issues, while also ushering in deeper insights to the meaning of the tradition itself. As a political theology, therefore, liberation theology must be assessed not only in how it inspires Christian attempts at transforming the world, but how it does so while illuminating new riches of the gospel.

Though liberation theologies—and one must really speak of the plural—have come from various contexts and have articulated distinct understandings of the Christian faith, perhaps no other figure and text has made as deep an impact as Gustavo Gutiérrez and his *Teología de la liberación—Perspectivas*.[1] Since its 1971 publication, the book has endured as a classic text of the movement sketching out its principal themes and approach. Moreover, Gutiérrez himself, while his reflection has deepened and matured over the years, has remained at the forefront of liberation theological thinking, influencing others around the globe.[2] Indeed, without homogenizing what has become a truly global phenomenon, it would be difficult to identify a liberation theology that has not either dialogued or been inspired by his work.[3]

Thus, while respecting the variety of liberation theologies that exist today, and acknowledging the impossibility of being comprehensive in scope, this chapter will survey the development and content of Gutiérrez's liberation theology as a way to understand the basic underpinnings and trajectories of one of the most important political theologies practiced today. Without a doubt, the particularity of this choice, to study the work of a male Roman Catholic priest, can be seen as overshadowing or erasing the contributions of others, particularly women. However, because of his historical importance and the way that his fundamental ideas have been adopted, reinterpreted, and even challenged by others, it is hoped that this analysis will encourage readers to go beyond this iconic figure, investigate those other works, and appreciate the richness and ongoing contributions of liberation theologians around the globe.

Though many lenses could be used, this chapter examines Gustavo Gutiérrez's liberation theology specifically as a political theology. It conducts this examination in three steps. First, it explores the origins of liberation theology in terms of its theological and political roots. The former lies in the turn away from neo-scholastic theology characteristic of mid-twentieth-century Catholic theology to a more historically oriented engagement with the world. This theological shift occurs in conjunction with a set of socioeconomic and political factors in Latin America that put the notion of liberation at the forefront of intellectual debate and popular movements. Though interdisciplinary by its very nature, a liberation theology is still a theology with its own important disciplinary contributions. Therefore, the second section of this chapter identifies central theological topics in the Christian tradition that liberation theologies have reconfigured.

Finally, the chapter will conclude by delving into the most important developments and controversies concerning liberation theology in the decades since its development. In particular, Gustavo Gutiérrez has responded to the European political theology developed by figures such as Johannes Metz, and he has responded to accusations regarding the use of Marxism in his own thought. In recent years, Gutiérrez's liberation theology has demonstrated a deeply mystical-political character. In his reflections on language, prayer, the limits (and seeming failure) of human praxis, and humanity's utter dependence on God, he has forged a liberation spirituality that nurtures political commitments and a theological politics deeply rooted in the search for God and the preferential option for the poor.

UNCOVERING FAITH AS POLITICAL

In a general sense, of course, all theologies are political. That is, they make normative claims that influence believers' actions in the polis. Yet, that kind of political character can operate at a level unacknowledged or even explicitly denied by a particular theological discourse.[4] What made liberation theology so distinctive and, on many levels, revolutionary was that it emerged in contrast to a reigning mode of theology that treated its content as ahistorical. So as a first step, understanding liberation theology involves viewing it contextually as confronting the theology that had dominated Roman Catholicism from the late nineteenth century to the middle of the twentieth: neo-scholasticism.

Like many Latin American seminarians of the 1950s, Gustavo Gutiérrez encountered neo-scholastic theology as he pursued his studies for priestly formation in Europe. From 1951 to 1955, he studied psychology and philosophy in Louvain, Belgium. He then went on to do graduate work in theology in Lyon, France (1955–1959) and Rome, Italy (1959–1960) before returning to Peru.[5] The so-called "manual" theology that structured priestly formation in this era—and it must be remembered that Catholic theology at this time was an exclusively clerical task and privilege—functioned as a deductive method. Truths of the "deposit of faith" were clearly defined and ordered along the principal themes of the creed (e.g., God as Trinity, God as Creator, Christ as Redeemer, Church, Sacraments). They were justified with reference to the Scriptures, sources from the tradition (such as church councils), and great theologians such as Augustine of Hippo and preeminently

Thomas Aquinas.[6] This style of theology did not consider the doctrines nor the sources in their historical contexts, rather it presented them as unchanging truths to be memorized and passed on. Furthermore, the future priests were expected to apply these theological truths in a one-way fashion with no expectation that human experience might move them to a new or modified understanding of faith.

Though the neo-scholastic manual tradition presented itself as a collection of timeless truths unperturbed by history or politics, in reality, it emerged from, and responded to, a particular historical and political situation. It was a defensive Catholic response to modernity's significant challenges, including: Enlightenment thought, the Protestant Reformation, the developing scientific methods, and the rise of secular nation-states.[7] All of these elements contested the Church's authority, and thus, the manuals were meant to equip Catholic priests with a clear sense of doctrinal authority to defend the Church. Methodologically, the truths of the faith were already formulated and were not subject to the vicissitudes of changing times. History and politics were not relevant to the eternal truths of faith, and this assumption grounded a spirituality that also turned its back on the world.

Though much more could be said about the theological formation in neo-scholasticism, for the purposes of this study, it is more important to note how the first generation of liberation theologians responded to it. In the case of Gutiérrez, the encounter with the *"nouvelle theologie"* and the French ecclesial-political milieu represented a decisive turn, in method and content, away from the neo-scholasticism and a move toward a theology of liberation for a pair of important reasons.

These new theologies represented a departure from the neo-scholastic manuals because of their historical character. Pioneering figures such as Marie-Dominique Chenu, Yves Congar, Henri de Lubac and Jean Daniélou, who were associated with the Jesuit school of Fourvière and the Dominican Le Saulchoir, were conducting historical and theological research that would pave the way for new theological methods and a different approach of the Catholic Church to the world around it.[8] Their work was "historical" in a dual sense. It was a *ressourcement*, a return to the ancient and medieval sources of Christian thought that illuminated the development of Christianity and nuanced the contexts in which figures like Augustine or Aquinas wrote. Yet, it was also historical in that it focused on how the church and Christian life should make an impact on (present) history, and on this point, there were many pastoral lessons that made France a pivotal influence on Gutiérrez and other liberation theologians.

Along with this intellectual influence, Gutiérrez was impacted by the French church's history of dealing with modernity's challenges. From the anti-clericalism after the French Revolution to grappling with urban industrialization and the trauma of the world wars, the challenges to Catholicism spurred the development of different pastoral models than those traditionally utilized in Europe and in Latin America.[9] In particular, Gutiérrez's exposure to movements such as the worker-priests, the *Jeunesse ouvrière chrétienne*, and a range of others under the umbrella of *Action Catholique* would spur new paths regarding how Christians engage the social questions of their day. Indeed, upon his return to Lima, Gutiérrez would be appointed national ecclesiastical assistant to UNEC (the National Union of Catholic Students), which would adopt the methodology of Catholic Action. During this period (1960–1968), Gutiérrez formally develops a theology of liberation utilizing this method.[10]

The methodology of Catholic Action, popularly known as "see–judge–act," was an inductive approach that began with analysis of the current reality (see), that would then be understood in light of biblical and church teaching (judge), and finally carried out in creative pastoral plans (act).[11] Importantly, the method is circular such that after action a new situation presents itself for a new "seeing" and thus a renewal of the process. The method is also correlative—not only was the situation to be judged utilizing Christian teaching, but that teaching itself could be understood and articulated in new ways because of human experience.[12] Thus, the deductive method of neo-scholasticism was turned completely on its head to spur a Christian theology and praxis that embraced the world and history.

Certainly, the journey from neo-scholastic theology to a theology of liberation cannot be told without including developments in European thought. However, it would be erroneous to treat the Latin American theologies as merely derivative of their European influences.[13] These important historical and theological insights, along with the pastoral attempts to respond more directly to the problems of the modern world, influence Gutiérrez a great deal during his time in Europe, but his theology sharpens as he returns to Peru. Theoretically and experientially, it is the challenge faced by the Latin American church that represents the decisive impetus to develop a theology of liberation.

As early as 1964, Gutiérrez grapples with the historical and political implications of theology by analyzing how the church had conceived its relationship to the world over time. Crucial to this analysis is the conviction that theoretical/theological ideas develop in conjunction with practical/pastoral models of the church. Therefore, he identifies distinct models by which the church understood itself and the world. The models that Gutiérrez lays out make clear both that the teaching and practice of the Catholic Church had always, despite the ostensible claims of neo-scholastic theology, been historical and political in nature.[14] Beginning with the model he calls "Christendom," Gutiérrez demonstrates both the political implications in how the Catholic Church responds to the question of faith and history, and how a doctrine like salvation informs an ecclesiology and pastoral approach.

Considering the arrival of Christianity in the Americas, Gutiérrez identifies the model of "Christendom" as operative in the Spanish and Portuguese conquest. In what he terms a "political Augustinianism," the conviction that the Church is the sole vehicle of salvation drives its direct intervention directly in the affairs of the world.[15] For their part, laypeople in this model see their task as simply "to work for the direct and immediate benefit of the Church."[16] Though obviously the historical and social context where Christian faith and Western European society were so closely linked had faded by the twentieth century, it does not mean the worldview had disappeared altogether. Indeed, Gutiérrez sees a contemporary mindset of Christendom active in Latin America. In institutions and powerful figures, too often it engenders pastoral attitudes that are "dysfunctional" and "out of touch with reality," and manifests in radically conservative political positions that wish to restore or shore up an obsolete social order.

If the Christendom model characterized the Christianity that arrived in Latin America through to the twentieth century, another model emerged as the autonomy of secular rulers and the secular sphere (characteristic of post-Bolivarian Latin America) took hold. Taking its name from the subtitle of Jacques Maritain's important book *Humanisme intégral: Problèmes temporels et spirituels d'une nouvelle chrétienté* (1936), Gutiérrez sees in the "New Christendom" model a modification in the Church's self-understanding and its conception of how it relates to the wider society. Based more on a Thomist model than Augustinian, the New Christendom encouraged the creation of Christian institutions that try to transform society using Christian principles. In Latin America, this model was evident in the Christian political parties and unions, such as the Christian Democrats, that emerged in the 1930s and 1940s. While this effort to incarnate Christian principles in society was admirable in some ways, New Christendom still relied on an ecclesiology that saw the Church as the exclusive vehicle of God's saving work. Its efforts at social transformation were thus tempted to equate one's political ideology and platform with Christianity itself.

In contrast to the exclusivity latent in the first two models, the third model, one that Gutiérrez calls the "Distinction of Planes," acknowledged the relative autonomy of the world while retaining the theological and salvific priority of the Church's mission.[17] While the former models subordinated the work of lay people simply as assisting the hierarchy in their mission, this model presented a more robust role for them in political life.[18] Rather than encouraging explicitly Christian institutions, however, such as political parties, this model saw the role of the Church as empowering lay people to participate in secular institutions that they influenced as leaven. They engaged the world while "the Church," understood as the ordained ministers and hierarchy, remained in the sphere of the "spiritual."

This differentiation and separation of spheres reflected the ongoing influence of neo-scholastic theology even as its dominance began to wane. The retrieval of Aquinas and his distinction between "natural" and "supernatural" planes undergirded the vision of this third model. Positively, it guarded against the abuses and temptations present when priests, bishops, or the pope were seen as possessing political-military power, and it opened the door for lay Christians to appropriate a faith lived out in meaningful praxis. However, practically speaking, this opening was accessible only to an elite group of Christians who could be formed, rather than the poor masses or anyone outside of the institutional Church. Moreover, while theologically it represented an opening of salvation from the *nulla salus extra ecclesiam* ("outside the church there is no salvation") assumption in the first two models, it did so in a post-historical manner that relativized political activity. The gain of autonomy for the world in this model was still tempered by subordination to the spiritual. Still, Gutiérrez saw it as a positive development in relation to the two prior models, and it seems that he himself began his work in Peru (and specifically with the Catholic Action inspired UNEC) with this model as operative.

Liberation theology would emerge out of the inadequacy of the "Distinction of Planes" model to address the reality of Latin America. Pastorally speaking, as lay movements and conscientious Christians got involved in social movements and the work for justice, they found a calling to deepen their commitments stunted by the notion of a Church that remained in the spiritual sphere. With such a strong separation between the material and spiritual, how much energy should one expend on transforming a world that essentially does not matter? Moreover, as they learned more about the socioeconomic and political realities of their countries, they became aware of how the Church was often linked with the very persons and institutions that wielded power and influence unjustly. Politically and pastorally, the distinction of planes mentality faced a crisis that it did not have the resources to address.

Theologically, the strict distinction of planes also proved inadequate. Theologians such as Henri de Lubac and Karl Rahner had demonstrated how neo-scholasticism's rigid natural–supernatural distinction ignored the already-graced character of creation and humanity.[19] In light of advancing biblical studies, theologians also explored the theme of salvation history.[20] By the time Gutiérrez writes *A Theology of Liberation*, he speaks about the unity of history rather than a distinction of planes.[21] Thus, by the time he is formulating a theology of liberation in the mid- to late 1960s, Gutiérrez advocated for a fourth model, a prophetic-pastoral one, that could more adequately meet the challenges of the Latin American reality faced by the church. This model envisioned the role of the church, institutionally and as a people, as participating in the struggles for liberation faced by the poor and oppressed.

We have seen how Latin American liberation theologians, particularly the Roman Catholics, were deeply influenced by the opening to the world and history characteristic of the mid-twentieth-century European theologians pivotal in the Second Vatican Council. Like their European counterparts, Latin Americans like Gustavo Gutiérrez, Juan Luis Segundo, Ignacio Ellacuría, and others, sought to overturn the dualisms inherent in neo-scholastic theology, and gave voice to notions of grace that accounted more adequately for the various challenges of the modern world such as secularism and religious pluralism. Certainly, the Council made great advances in its ecclesiological identification of the church as the People of God and in addressing a secular world and recognizing other religious traditions. Yet, despite acknowledging powerful moments in documents such as the Pastoral Constitution on the Church in the Modern World (*Gaudium et spes*), the Latin Americans came away from the Council identifying a significant lacuna.

While it did much to address the "non-believer," the Council did not fully engage the question of the "non-person." That is, for figures like Gutiérrez, the Council did not adequately address the global reality that the majority of its population lived in conditions of poverty.[22] This insight, born from the immediate experience in his own country, would drive Gutiérrez to forge a theology of liberation. He has often said that at the heart of liberation theology lies a simple question that came from his pastoral experience in Lima: "How can I say to the poor, 'God loves you'?"[23] The response to this question would not only mean the profound political engagement of liberation theologies, but a way for that political engagement to reread the Christian tradition and reach new depths of meaning in its core teachings.

A THEOLOGICAL POLITICS OF SALVATION

The political dimension of liberation theology comes precisely from the term "liberation." In its economic and political connotations, the term liberation became ubiquitous in Latin America in the post-Second World War period. Everyone from political parties, social scientists, and even guerrilla forces intoned the term liberation as an aspiration for the people of Latin America. Economically, the failure of the 1950s "decade of development" meant enormous debts for many Latin American nations. In turn, the diagnosis of the continent's economic problem shifted from one of simple underdevelopment to one of dependence.[24] With this shift of diagnosis came a corresponding shift in the solution. When Latin America's problems were thought to be underdevelopment, then logically it was development that was seen as the cure. However, as the debt crisis showed, the attempts at development were part of a different problem. Latin America's problem was not one of underdevelopment, but dependence on and exploitation by the wealthy countries of the North. In this scenario, the proper solution to Latin America's problems was liberation from the economic exploitation carried out by the economically powerful nations of the North and their multinational corporations.

Similarly, the political connotation of liberation came as a response to the military national security states that emerged in the unrest of the 1950s. Hand in hand with the economics of development, a wave of populist governments inspired nationalism and promised general prosperity as the fruit of development. However, the benefits accrued only to the elites and business classes, while the majority of citizens remained mired in either rural poverty or urban shantytowns.[25] As unrest grew among the poorer classes, military dictators and strongmen, garnering the support of the United States with their anti-Communist rhetoric, denied political freedom and enforced their regimes with military and paramilitary repression.[26]

Vatican II's *Gaudium et spes* begins with the famous stirring words, "The joys and the hopes, the griefs and the anxieties of the people of this age, especially those who are poor or in any way afflicted, these too are the joys and hopes, the griefs and anxieties of the followers of Christ."[27] In this light, one can say that liberation theology was precisely that response to the joys, hopes, griefs, and anxieties bound up with the meaning of and struggle for liberation. Yet, as Rossino Gibellini has pointed out, the theology of liberation cannot be seen simply as another "theology of" a particular theme, such as hope or the body.[28] No, the theology of liberation represents a new way of doing theology that has implications across the entire discipline, and indeed for the understanding of the Christian faith as a whole.

At its core, Christian theology addresses the aspirations tied to the term liberation through the language of salvation. It can be argued that at the heart of liberation theology is a soteriology—a Christian description of salvation that views the element of human liberation as necessary and constitutive. Salvation is not an individualized fate in a post-historical setting; rather, the "political" thrust of liberation theology is rooted in a vision of salvation that is historical (at least incipiently), corporate, and inclusive. Frequently Gutiérrez describes salvation as the "communion with God and others."[29] This differentiates it from many theologies that ignore or subordinate human community, since for liberation theologies communion with God is impossible unless there is communion with others. This notion also differentiates liberation theologies from secularist activism by viewing the communion with others within the context of full communion with God. Again, one cannot speak of a full human communion without talking about communion with God.

Liberation theologies not only posit salvation as communion with God and others but also make an important claim about how that communion is attained (or at least striven for); namely, it is in the commitment to justice where human communion is found and how humans in turn find intimacy with God. Commitment and solidarity are not pleasant byproducts of an already-achieved or established faith/communion with God, but provide a path, a primary means by which God self-reveals and invites humans into communion. Participating in the struggle for justice is a participatory foretaste of the full communion that is ultimately an eschatological hope.

For Gutiérrez, a theological response to the aspiration for liberation had a troubling obstacle. As a continent that suffered under massive-scale poverty groaned, Christian theology often spoke glowingly about poverty. How could these two facts be reconciled? Pastoral experience showed poverty to be dehumanizing, but there was no denying a long tradition in the scriptures ("blessed are the poor") and spirituality (e.g., religious vows of poverty) that esteemed poverty. Clearly, a more nuanced approach to poverty was needed. In the course of the 1960s, Gutiérrez's articulated three distinct meanings to poverty to clarify this obstacle to Christian engagement in the pressing reality of the modern world.[30]

In Gutiérrez's schema, the most basic idea that needs asserting is the fact that material poverty, the deprivation of basic human rights, must be considered evil. As a violation of God's loving will to see human flourishing, material poverty can be evaluated in no other way than as sin. Obviously, poverty is a complex phenomenon, and the notion of being a "non-person" often involves other factors than solely economic ones. However, what is most important is that Christians must view material poverty as sin and use their energies to eradicate it (and thus participate in the process of human liberation/communion). Having established the evil of material poverty, Gutiérrez notes the biblical language of poverty in relation to God. This "spiritual poverty" is the disposition of utter dependence on God. From the Hebrew Bible's covenant between God and the people to the New Testament's beatitudes, spiritual poverty is that humble recognition that everything comes from God and that all creaturely existence is dependent on God. Thus, the poetic language of (spiritual) poverty's beauty must be differentiated from the ugly reality that is material poverty. Yet, that distinction is still not enough.

In addition to material and spiritual poverty, Gutiérrez sees in the scriptures and in the vast history of Christianity another form of poverty: poverty as solidarity or commitment to those who suffer from material poverty. This notion has been explicated as the "preferential option for the poor." While generations had been inculcated into a spirituality of fatalism in regard to poverty, the notion of poverty as solidarity means that the reality of material poverty demands resistance—including those who suffer under its power. As an option, this solidarity is not a matter of volition ("optional"), but rather underscores the need for commitment ("opting") by individuals and institutions.[31] This opting can take many forms. For the Latin American Bishops, it was the call to live more simply.[32] The US Catholic Bishops described the preferential option for the poor as "to speak for the voiceless, to defend the defenseless, to assess lifestyles, policies and social institutions in terms of their impact on the poor."[33]

The new understanding of poverty stemmed from pastoral work among those who were poor. It came from the practical and political process of encountering marginalized human beings not as lazy and indigent creators of their own problems, but as victims of a situation with deep historical and structural causes. To be sure, liberation theologies do not romantically declare all poor persons to be virtuous. However, because of their material reality, these people demand primacy of attention. Indeed, the reality of the poor is an epistemological key both politically and theology. Politically, the reality of the poor reveals the way economic and political structures truly work. Theologically, it is in the reality of the poor that God self-reveals, and in the struggle for human liberation that the incipient participation in God's saving will is made available to humanity. For Gutiérrez, the process of liberation, "leads history to its fulfillment in the definitive encounter with God."[34]

From the 1960s through the 1970s, Gutiérrez and others flesh out the central insights of liberation theology. Among them: the view of history's unity, where creation and salvation are moments of one history in which the human striving for justice participates in the self-revelation of God. The view of Jesus as a liberator who proclaims and manifests the Reign of God characterized by the integral liberation of human beings. Gutiérrez asserts that Jesus' life and teaching "touch the very heart of political behavior, giving it its true dimension and depth. Misery and social injustice reveal 'a sinful situation,' a disintegration of fellowship and communion; by freeing us from sin, Jesus attacks the roots of an unjust order."[35] The view of the church as that body called to read the signs of the times, to announce a salvation that is good news to the poor, and to act in a praxis of solidarity in the struggle for justice. It enacts a preferential option for the poor that is not simply an ethical directive, but a theocentric option—an option through which God self-reveals a love beyond human calculus or cold rationality. This latter point demonstrates that, from its inception, Gutiérrez's liberation theology had a mystical seed that coexisted with its political thrust, and it is this mystical-political content that has characterized his most profound development in recent years.

THE MYSTICAL-PROPHETIC TURN

After its initial elaboration in the 1960s and 1970s, liberation theology entered a new phase in the 1980s. These were difficult years politically and ecclesially. The revolutionary fervor of the previous decade began to diminish, either crushed by repressive forces or disillusioned by corrupt changes in power. In either case, it was a time of martyrdom as many in the base communities paid the price for their struggles for justice. Meanwhile, ecclesial authorities had taken notice of liberation theology and implemented steps to curb its influence. In the Roman Catholic Church, the change in perspective came in the papacy of John Paul II. Under his predecessor, Paul VI, the Vatican's International Theological Commission issued a 1977 report that was cautiously supportive of liberation theology. Indeed, many liberation theologians drew from his encyclicals as a theological support.[36] The 1980s would see a much different approach.

In 1984, Cardinal Josef Ratzinger, Prefect of the Congregation for the Defense of the Faith, released the "Instruction on Certain Aspects of Liberation Theology." Though not explicitly condemning liberation theology, its negative tone and various criticisms came to be seen by many as a rejection of liberation theology. The document cited no particular work or author, but it warned of the influence of Marxism in the work of liberation theologians and a consequent reductionism in the mysteries of the faith. As for Gutiérrez himself, Cardinal Ratzinger and the CDF had written "Ten Observations on the Theology of Gustavo Gutierrez" the previous year that accused him of uncritically accepting Marxism, giving "an exclusively political meaning" to biblical texts such as Exodus or the Magnificat, and reducing sin to "political alienation."[37] Cardinal Ratzinger met with the Peruvian bishops' conference in the hope of eliciting a condemnation of Gutiérrez, but there were not enough votes. The Vatican would continue to keep a file open on Gutiérrez's works for the next couple of decades, but unlike other liberation theologians, he would never be censured nor his works officially identified as containing theological errors.

During this difficult period, and perhaps in part because of it, Gutiérrez turns his attention to language and spirituality and deepens the insights of liberation theology. Shortly after the release of the CDF's Instruction, Gutiérrez wrote "Theology and the Social Sciences," an essay that explores the stated interdisciplinary question and addresses the relationship of liberation theology to Marxist analysis.[38] Theologically, the essay does not stray from the ideas he elaborated in *A Theology of Liberation*, but he does more than simply restate them. For example, since the 1960s, he had always adverted to theology as a "second" moment to praxis. More formally, it is a "critical reflection on praxis in light of the word of God."[39] While he does not reject this notion, Gutiérrez clarifies that the first moment of practice is both the contemplation of God in faith and the praxis of loving one's neighbor, particularly the poor. "Contemplation and commitment make up what liberation theology calls practice, 'the first act' . . . only then can this life inspire 'second act,' a process of reasoning."[40]

In addition, Gutiérrez insists that theology generates two kinds of language, prophetic and mystical. Considering the former, liberation theology had drawn upon the social sciences to examine the reality of the poor in all of its complexity. Yet, it is only an overly simplistic view that would identify these sources as exclusively Marxist. To take one prominent example, the dependency theory that influenced so many liberation theologians was not espoused exclusively by Marxist theorists, nor was it universally accepted by Marxists. Furthermore, Gutiérrez emphasizes that while Marxist theories may be employed to some value, this critical use does not mean a blind acceptance of a unified, "Marxist" ideological worldview.[41] Making this accusation of liberation theology means carrying out the very reduction of theology to politics of the accusation itself. Liberation theology employs the social sciences to better understand the "situation" and more effectively proclaim the gospel as truly good news to the poor, but not to derive a partisan political platform. "It is not possible, however, to deduce political programs or actions from the gospel or from reflection on the gospel. It is not possible, nor should we attempt it; the political sphere is something entirely different."[42]

The defense of liberation theology and its relationship to Marxism flows from the prophetic language that had been developed by Gutiérrez and the first generation of liberation theologians. Gutiérrez had always linked this prophetic call to spirituality. However, he deepens his thought by reflecting on the nature of mystical language develops his thought in this later period. In 1985, he published *On Job*, a reflection on the biblical book that came out of weekly gatherings with parishioners in Lima. In this profound work, Gutiérrez links the ethical-prophetic thrust of liberation theology to a mystical-contemplative dimension. While not lessening the insistence on radical solidarity with the poor, Gutiérrez realizes that this prophetic commitment must ultimately lead to the recognition of utter dependence on the gratuitousness of God. In this period, Job's relentless pursuit of God in the midst of suffering provides a mystical complement to the earlier use of the Exodus paradigm for human liberation. As Gaspar Martinez has demonstrated, Gutiérrez's Christology shifts from the "Christ of *actio*" to a "Christ of *passio*" who in radical solidarity with the poor remains utterly hopeful in the promise of the gratuitous God. Gutiérrez's theology retains its prophetic commitment to denounce injustice and to struggle for the integral liberation of all persons.

LIBERATION THEOLOGY AND POLITICAL THEOLOGY

In Roman Catholic circles, liberation theology developed alongside of European political theology, primarily that of Johannes Metz.[43] Though there are many affinities between the two, there are also significant differences. Gutiérrez has always held an admiration for the work of J.B. Metz, particularly as the latter served as a pivotal figure in moving Roman Catholic theology away from its neo-scholastic dualisms and for fighting against the privatization of religion characteristic of much post-Enlightenment theology. However, in *A Theology of Liberation*, he expresses two reservations.

First, Gutiérrez believes that though it marks an important break from the individualistic tendencies in the transcendental thought of his mentor Karl Rahner, Metz's work at the time remained highly abstract. Though Metz is keenly aware of oppression, it is from a distance, a lens primarily from the perspective of the oppressor. Liberation theology stresses the experience and perspective of those who are marginalized. Knowledge of that experience and perspective can come only through participation in the struggle for justice.[44] In addition, there was a totalizing assumption in Metz's work that does not apply to the reality of Latin America, and by extension, much of the developing world. For though Metz, through the influence of the Frankfurt school, aptly diagnoses the effect of the Enlightenment privatization of religion in Western Europe, the case of Latin America is radically different. There, religion remains a very public and symbolic presence that cannot be ignored. The distortion of religion in Latin America is not solely in a "bürgerliche religion" that worships at the altar of the market, but a continuing Christendom that substitutes idols of power and repression for the true God.

Though Metz himself has developed his theology to address these critiques, the latter remain an important reminder of the difference between these two strands of thought. As we have seen, liberation theology, as a political theology, follows from the recognition of the world's value. No longer simply a "vale of tears" to be endured until heavenly bliss, the twentieth-century recognition of the world and the church's role in it, placed the task of discerning the "signs of the times" at the forefront of the Christian mission. In this, Latin American liberation theology shares much with European and North American progressive theologies. However, it is precisely in the reading of the signs of the times that we find their essential differences.

In the two-thirds world, the primary signs of our times are relentless poverty and injustice. The hope for liberation is the aspiration that liberation theology has spoken to, and in turn, has been that which has clarified what theological terms like salvation and sin mean today. Gustavo Gutiérrez articulated his theology as a "second moment" of critical reflection on the praxis by many Christians to make the world look more like the Reign of God about which Jesus of Nazareth spoke. This theology, derived from the reality of "non-persons," has demanded a conversion of the mighty down from their thrones. As so-called revolutions and saviors have come and gone, liberation theology has remained as both a prophetic word for justice and a mystical longing for communion with God.

NOTES

1. All citations here come from the English translation of the revised edition: *A Theology of Liberation*, 15th anniv. ed. (Maryknoll, NY: Orbis Books, 1973, 1988). [Henceforth, *TL*.].

2. See Marc H. Ellis and Otto Maduro, eds., *Expanding the View: Gustavo Gutiérrez and the Future of Liberation Theology* (Maryknoll, NY: Orbis Books, 1990).

3. The landmark 1975 encounter between Latin American and US liberation theologians is documented in Sergio Torres and John Eagleson, eds., *Theology in the Americas* (Maryknoll, NY: Orbis Books, 1976). It is interesting to note that James Cone's *A Black Theology of Liberation* was published at the same time as Gutiérrez's book. Though not an initial influence, Cone and Gutiérrez would become friends and dialogue partners, particularly after Gutiérrez taught courses at Cone's Union Theological Seminary.

4. Consider how recent scholarship has unearthed the role that Christian theology played in the discursive support of racism in the Atlantic slave trade and founding of the United States. See, J. Cameron Carter, *Race: A Theological Account* (New York: Oxford University Press, 2008) and Jeannine Hill-Fletcher, *The Sin of White Supremacy: Christianity, Racism, and Religious Diversity in America* (Maryknoll, NY: Orbis Books, 2017).

5. On this period in Gutiérrez's life, see Robert McAfee Brown, *Gustavo Gutiérrez: An Introduction to Liberation Theology* (Maryknoll, NY: Orbis Books, 1990), 22–49.

6. For a classic English-language example, see Ludwig Ott, *Fundamentals of Catholic Dogma* (St. Louis, MO: B. Herder Book Co., 1952, 1955).

7. Recall that it was not until 1870 that we see the cessation of the Papal States as a sovereign nation with its own standing army.

8. Jürgen Mettepenningen, *Nouvelle Théologie–New Theology: Inheritor of Modernism, Precursor of Vatican II* (New York: T&T Clark, 2010).

9. As Mark Schoof attests, "Since Loisy, the relationship between faith and history... has been seen by the French as the basic theological problem." *A Survey of Catholic Theology 1800–1970* (New York: Paulist, 1970), 100–101.
10. Cecilia Tovar, "UNEC: Cincuenta años de camino," *Páginas* 111 (Oct. 1991): 92–94.
11. For a useful explanation of this method in a Latin American context, see Clodovis Boff, "Epistemology and Method of the Theology of Liberation," in Jon Sobrino and Ignacio Ellacuría, eds., *Mysterium Liberationis* (Maryknoll, NY: Orbis Books, 1993), 57–85.
12. For more on the correlational method, particularly as "mutually-critical" process, see David Tracy, *The Analogical Imagination* (New York: Crossroad, 1981), 24–26, 405–421.
13. In Protestant circles, see the well-known debate between Miguez Bonino and Jürgen Moltmann. See José Miguez Bonino, "Reading Jürgen Moltmann from Latin America," in *The Asbury Theological Journal* (Spring 2000), vol. 55, no. 1, 105–114; also see Jürgen Moltmann, *Experiences in Theology: Ways and Forms of Christian Theology*, trans. Margaret Kohl (Minneapolis, MN: Fortress Press, 2000), 217–248.
14. While the text cited here will be *A Theology of Liberation* chapters 4 and 5, they are adapted from Gutiérrez's 1968 publication, *Líneas pastorales de la Iglesia en América Latina* (Lima, Peru: Centro de Estudios y Publicaciones, 1988). See Gaspar Martínez, *Confronting the Mystery of God: Political, Liberation, and Public Theologies*, (New York: Bloomsbury Publishing, 2002), 113ff. on the history of this text.
15. The influence of Henri de Lubac's *Augustinianism and Modern Theology* (New York: Geoffrey Chapman, Ltd., 1969) is clear here.
16. *TL*, 34.
17. As Dean Brackley points out, a mistranslation of *TL*, 39 makes it seem as if New Christendom and The Distinction of Planes are the same model. It reads "The acceptance of the New Christendom position entails of course a rejection of previous approaches; it in turn, however is criticized because of its position on the distinction of planes." The last phrase should read, "it in turn, however *is criticized by the position of* the distinction of planes." (translation and italics mine). Brackley, 168, n. 10.
18. In earlier lectures, Gutiérrez calls this model "mature faith." Cf. Líneas pastorales.
19. See Henri de Lubac, *The Mystery of the Supernatural* (New York: Geoffrey Chapman, Ltd., 1967); and Karl Rahner, *Spirit in the World* (New York: Bloomsbury Academic, 1994) and *Hearer of the Word: Laying the Foundation for a Philosophy of Religion* (New York: Bloomsbury Academic, 1994).
20. Many theologians of this period were influenced by Gerhard von Rad, *Old Testament Theology* (New York: Harper & Row, 1957, 1962).
21. See *TL*, 86ff.
22. This was true despite John XXIII's calling for a "church of the poor" and Cardinal Giacomo Lercaro's intervention during the Council's first session. For Gutiérrez's reflections on these, see *The Truth Shall Make You Free* (Maryknoll, NY: Orbis Books, 1990), 167–168.
23. See Gustavo Gutiérrez, "Saying and Showing to the Poor: 'God Loves You'" in Jennie Weiss Block and Michael Griffin, eds., *In the Company of the Poor* (Maryknoll, NY: Orbis Books, 2013), 27.
24. Influential theorists of the so-called "dependency theory" include: Gunder Frank, Theotonio dos Santos, and Fernando Cardoso. On the relationship between liberation theology and dependency theory see, Arthur McGovern, *Liberation Theology and Its Critics* (Maryknoll, NY: Orbis Books, 1989).
25. For a good survey of examples across Latin America, see Jeffrey Klaiber, *The Church, Dictatorships, and Democracy in Latin America* (Maryknoll, NY: Orbis Books, 1998).

26. Military dictatorships in the period include: Guatemala (1954), Peru (1963), Brazil (1954), Mexico (1968), Bolivia (1971), Chile (1973), Paraguay (1975), and Argentina (1976).
27. *Gaudium et spes*, par. 1, in Walter M. Abbott, ed., *The Documents of Vatican II* (New York: The America Press, 1966), 199.
28. Rosino Gibellini, *La teologia del xx secolo* (Brescia: Editrice Queriniana, 1993).
29. See, for example, *TL*, 85, or *The Power of the Poor in History* (Maryknoll, NY: Orbis Books, 1983), 31.
30. Gutiérrez synthesizes this material in "Option for the Poor," in Jon Sobrino & Ignacio Ellacuría, eds., *Mysterium Liberationis* (Maryknoll, NY: Orbis Books, 1989), 235–250. However, he was an instrumental contributor to the CELAM document, "The Poverty of the Church," that first makes these distinctions.
31. Gutiérrez notes that "the poor themselves must make this decision." See "Option for the Poor," in Jon Sobrino and Ignacio Ellacuría, eds., *Mysterium Liberationis* (Maryknoll, NY: Orbis Books, 1993), 240.
32. Second General Conference of Latin American Bishops, "The Church in the Present-Day Transformation of Latin America in the Light of the Council," in Alfred Hennelly, ed., *Liberation Theology: A Documentary History* (Maryknoll, NY: Orbis Books), 115–118.
33. USCCB, Economic Justice for All, #16.
34. *TL*, 160.
35. *TL*, 134.
36. In particular, his *Populorum progressio* (called "watered-down Marxism" in a *Wall Street Journal* review) and *Evangelii nuntiandi* were influential.
37. See Alfred Hennelly, *Liberation Theology: A Documentary History* (Maryknoll, NY: Orbis Books, 1990).
38. The essay may be found in Gustavo Gutiérrez, *The Truth Shall Make You Free* (Maryknoll, NY: Orbis Books, 1986, 1990). This important volume also contains the "discussion" with the Lyon theological faculty that would grant him his doctorate based on the corpus of his writings, and an essay responding to points in the CDF's second instruction on the theme of liberation.
39. *TL*, xxix, 5, 9–12.
40. Gutiérrez, "Theology and the Social Sciences," in *The Truth Shall Make You Free*, 56.
41. In this nuanced reading of Marxism, Gutiérrez shows great affinities with the great Peruvian intellectual, José Carlos Mariátegui. On this point and the relationship between the two men, see Gaspar Martinez, *Confronting the Mystery of God*, 128–129, 32–34.
42. "Theology and the Social Sciences," 64.
43. In Protestant circles, the famous exchange between José Miguez Bonino and Jürgen Moltmann shows a much more contentious atmosphere. See note 13 above.
44. Gutiérrez remarks, "Because the climate in which his reflections develop is far from the revolutionary ferment of the Third World countries, [Metz] cannot penetrate the situation of dependency, injustice, and exploitation in which most of humankind finds itself." *TL*, 129.

SELECT BIBLIOGRAPHY

Abbott, Walter M., ed. (1966), *The Documents of Vatican II*, New York: The America Press.
Carter, J. Kameron (2008), *Race: A Theological Account*, New York: Oxford University Press.
Cone, James H. (1970, 1990), *A Black Theology of Liberation*, Maryknoll, NY: Orbis Books.

Ellis, Marc H. and Otto Maduro, eds. (1990), *Expanding the View: Gustavo Gutiérrez and the Future of Liberation Theology*, Maryknoll, NY: Orbis Books.

Gutiérrez, Gustavo (1973, 1988), *A Theology of Liberation: History, Politics, and Salvation*, trans. Sister Caridad Inda and John Eagleson, 15th anniversary edition, Maryknoll, NY: Orbis Books.

Gutiérrez, Gustavo (1983), *The Power of the Poor in History*, trans. Robert R. Barr, Maryknoll, NY: Orbis Books.

Gutiérrez, Gustavo (1986, 1990), *The Truth Shall Make You Free: Confrontations*, trans. Matthew J. O'Connell, Maryknoll, NY: Orbis Books.

Gutiérrez, Gustavo (1987), *On Job: God-talk and the Suffering of the Innocent*, trans. Matthew O'Connell, Maryknoll, NY: Orbis Books.

Hennelly, Alfred (1990), *Liberation Theology: A Documentary History*, Maryknoll, NY: Orbis Books.

Martínez, Gaspar (2002), *Confronting the Mystery of God: Political, Liberation, and Public Theologies*, New York: Bloomsbury Publishing.

Mettepenningen, Jürgen (2010), *Nouvelle Théologie–New Theology: Inheritor of Modernism, Precursor of Vatican II*, New York: Bloomsbury T&T Clark.

Sobrino, Jon and Ignacio Ellacuría, eds. (1989), *Mysterium Liberationis: Fundamental Concepts of Liberation Theology*, Maryknoll, NY: Orbis Books.

CHAPTER SEVENTEEN

James H. Cone and Black Liberation Theology

EBONI MARSHALL TURMAN

ORIGINS

> From the time of my childhood to the present, the problem of white racism has been my primary concern, emotionally and intellectually.[1]

James Hal Cone (1936–2018), the progenitor of twentieth-century black liberation theology, was born to Charlie and Lucy Cone on August 5, 1936 in Fordyce, AK, nearly "sixty miles southwest of Little Rock."[2] Prior to his second birthday, the Cone family relocated to Bearden, AK, a small, rural community of approximately twelve hundred persons, where his humble beginnings in the American South would come to seemingly defy his unremitting ascendance in the theological academy, that ultimately led to his appointment as the Bill and Judith Moyers Distinguished Professor of Systematic Theology at Union Theological Seminary, New York City. During his long and storied tenure at Union, Cone wrote and edited more than a dozen books and trained three generations of black and black womanist theologians, pastors, and religious leaders. He prepared and propelled more black theologians into the theological academy than any other theological educator to date, and offered intellectual license to the expansion of liberation theological inquiry across minoritized social distinctions.

In the beginning, though, following his brief interval as a student at Shorter College, a small then-unaccredited African Methodist Episcopal (AME) school in North Little Rock, Cone completed his undergraduate studies at Philander Smith College, a slightly larger historically black Methodist institution in the capitol city of Little Rock, where he earned the Bachelor of Arts degree (1958). Compelled in large part by the ways in which his undergraduate major in religion and philosophy stimulated his "search for a reasoned faith in a complex and ever changing world," as well as his thinking about making a better future for black people, Cone pursued formal training in systematic theology at Garrett Biblical Institute (now Garrett-Evangelical Theological Seminary) and Northwestern University in Evanston, IL, where he would earn the degrees of Bachelor of Divinity (1961), Master of Arts (1963), and Doctor of Philosophy (1965), respectively.[3] Cone's formation as a systematic theologian under the direction of William Hordern and Philip S. Watson granted him expertise in Barthian anthropology, broad fluency in European theological discourses, and directed his attention to faithful study of "philosophy and theology—from the pre-Socratics to modern existentialism and linguistic analysis, from Justin Martyr, Irenaeus, and Origen to Karl Barth, Bultmann, and Tillich."[4] Nevertheless,

Cone unambiguously concedes that his early theological reflection, and the vision and dexterity that would come to characterize his theological contributions over his lifetime are inseparable from their roots in his experience of being raised black in Bearden, and his Christian formation at the Macedonia AME Church where "the Black Spirit of God . . . descended" such that Cone could discover himself "as *black* and *Christian*."[5]

The centrality of the Black Church[6] for the development of black theology cannot be overstated. It is precisely at the intersection of Cone's social location as a young black man/child in the Jim Crow South and his Christian faith that was nurtured within the Black Church as the institutional descendant of slave religion that the question, namely, "what does it mean to be black and Christian?" would emerge. This decisive question would eventually compel what black theologian and pastor Raphael G. Warnock characterizes as "the fourth moment in the history of black religious resistance to racism," and thus the twentieth-century systematization of "a radical and independent" black theology with a "mission of liberation . . . that defines the true church" in the US.[7] Throughout his corpus, Cone identifies the unremitting white racism that induced black suffering, as well as resolute black faith in the face of "the harsh realities of white injustice that was inflicted daily upon the black community" as the dual realities that prompted his theological quest to understand why, if God is good and all powerful, "blacks get treated so badly."[8] The Black Church was where black people were "given a faith that sustained [their] personhood and dignity in spite of" the dehumanizing ethos of "white people's brutality."[9] To be sure, Cone credits his parents, especially his father, for emphasizing and embodying resistance to injustice. In one particularly memorable account, Cone recalls how "Bearden whites began to talk about lynching Charlie Cone" for his refusal to remove his name from a lawsuit against the Bearden School Board in the early 1950s. Cone remembers his family's fear and his father's courage:

> We were all afraid for my father's life and urged him to leave for his own safety. My father responded: No white person is going to make me leave my own house. Let the sons of bitches come. They may lynch me; but with this double-barrel shotgun and my pistol, some of them will die with me.[10]

At the literal risk of life and limb, Cone acknowledges his father as his first image of black dignity; dignity that demanded resistance against the oppressive "climate of . . . black–white social arrangements."[11] Yet it was in the church of his mother, Mrs. Lucy Cone, who he recollects as "one of the pillars of Macedonia and a firm believer in God's justice," where the social significance of black resistance against racism that had been regularly demonstrated by his father was contextualized in relation to God's righteousness.[12] It was also in his mother's church where he witnessed those who had been "treated as things for six days of the week" affirming and experiencing "another definition of their humanity . . . as children of God whose future was not defined by the white structures that humiliated them."[13] In contradistinction to compensatory patterns of religious experience that assert black Christian faith as cathartic escape from the harsh realities of everyday life, for Cone the Black Church and its religion of Jesus was a primary source of identity, survival, and empowerment. Amidst the struggle for freedom, the church was where Cone first encountered blacks who believed that God was on the side of the oppressed and "against the satanic force of white supremacy."[14]

Cone's theological formation at the interstices of the Jim Crow South, the Black Church, and the white theological academy cannot be overemphasized. As noted above, the Black Church asserted the sacred value, potential, and significance of black life in the sight of God.

The theological academy, however, typically aligned with the racist ethos of the nation. Accordingly, some of Cone's graduate school professors regularly intimated his embodied incongruity with his academic pursuits. At least one of his professors went so far as to tell him that he would never be accepted into a doctoral program, and even refused to shake his hand upon his successful completion of his PhD.[15] This incoherent theological and social landscape squarely positioned Cone to interrogate the glaring contradictions "between theology as [an academic] discipline and the struggle for black freedom in the streets."[16]

As noted in his autobiographical writings, Cone consistently challenged racism throughout his early life and formal academic training. It was not, however, until his mid-1960s return to Philander Smith College as a professor during the apex of the twentieth-century Civil Rights Movement that he began to think critically about what he would later come to identify as the irrelevance of theology. While the value of experiential reflection had been disregarded by the European navel gazing of his academic interlocutors during his time as a student, Cone's blackness in the US context—the spiritual strivings of which W.E.B. Dubois had characterized more than a half-century prior as "an American, a Negro; two souls, two thoughts, two unreconciled strivings; two warring ideals in one dark body, whose dogged strength alone keeps it from being torn asunder"—would not be silenced.[17] Cone's experience of being a black man in America provoked his intellectual consideration of the necessary correlation of God-talk and black life. To be sure, such deliberation began with his critical interrogation of the discontinuity between his object of study in Barth, Tillich, Brunner, and Niebuhr, and the flesh and blood realities of "young black girls and boys coming from the cotton fields of Arkansas, Tennessee, and Mississippi."[18] It was, however, the 1964 publication of African American religious scholar Joseph R. Washington, Jr.'s *Black Religion: The Negro and Christianity in the United States*, "which many blacks regarded as combining poor scholarship and bad taste," that, for Cone, first articulated the stark distinctions between white faith and the Black Church with uncompromising lucidity that would further compel him concerning the development of his theology of black liberation. Washington essentially argued that the Black Church was unchristian *because* "it identified the gospel with the struggle for social justice in society."[19] Moreover, Washington contended

> that black churches and denominations lacked ... "a dynamic theology" capable of explicating for black Christians the meaning of the faith and serving as a corrective for theological error regarding the church's reason for being. Theology is faith's critical and questioning side, and without it, Washington reasoned, there could be no guard against heresy and no guarantee of an authentic connection to Christian Tradition.[20]

Echoing many white churches and the majority of their theologians, Washington further and most strikingly maintained that, "the gospel ... has to do with faith and the creeds of the church, and not with justice and the civil rights movement."[21] Accordingly, the theological error of the Black Church was located in its confusion of "the Christological essence of the faith with the ethics of the faith."[22]

As whites praised the book, Cone admits that he existentially rejected Washington's thesis. The problem for Cone, though, was that the fundaments of his graduate-level theological training actually supported Washington's argument. In other words, the presumption of black theological deformity, namely, the disfigured incongruity of blackness and Christian faith, was sustained and promoted by the theological academy. Having been trained in white theology, Cone supposed that he did not have the intellectual breadth at the time to publicly refute Washington. He admits that:

If I accepted the definition of Christianity as taught in graduate school, then Washington had a strong case. Although I did not like his conclusions anymore [sic] than any black person, they seemed logical, given his premises. In order for me to challenge Washington, I had to challenge the entire white theological establishment, and I was not ready to do that. But the problems he raised stayed on my mind constantly . . .[23]

Washington's identification of Christian faith with the faith and practice of white churches could not be left unchallenged. Yet, at the time, the theory and development of black theology as such eluded Cone, mostly because he "was so involved in the politics of [Philander Smith] and the various adjustments of being a new teacher," there was "no time left for independent thinking."[24] Still, amidst the *zeitgeist* of black freedom as expressed in the twentieth-century Civil Rights and Black Power movements, Cone continued to wrestle with Washington's scathing condemnation of the Black Church as unchristian. In 1966, when the administration of Philander Smith College made it clear to him that his departure would be welcome, Cone transitioned to teach at Adrian College in rural Michigan. Although physically isolated from the black community that had defined his entire existence, Cone was thrust into communion with black music and literature—gospel, jazz, the spirituals, and the blues, as well as "the writings of Baldwin, Wright, Fanon, Camus, Sartre, and Ellison . . . and Leroi Jones." Amidst an obstinate white world, the fruit of the opaque synthesis Cone found between enduring black faith, black history, and black culture propelled his deep thinking about the "theological meaning of black people's commitment to political and social justice," which induced the beginnings of his intellectual structure of black theology.[25]

BLACK LIBERATION THEOLOGY: PRETEXT

If Christ was not to be found in black people's struggle for freedom, if he were not found in the ghettos with rat-bitten black children, if he were in rich white churches and their seminaries, then I wanted no part of him.

—MSLB, 44

Recent black theological scholarship has broadly emphasized three interlocking, though "salient moments of African American Christian resistance" that preceded the twentieth-century "forging of a self-conscious" black liberationist theology; namely, the "formation of a liberationist faith" in the context of the invisible institution, the "founding of a liberationist church" as the substance of the independent black church movement, and the "fomenting of a church led liberationist movement" that manifested in the twentieth-century struggle for civil rights.[26] Such framing situates the beginnings of the expansive tradition of black resistance to white racism in the context of the transatlantic slave trade and its concomitant formation of race and religion in US culture in ways that make legal chattel enslavement and its legacies essential to the origin narrative of black theology.[27] Echoing first-generation black theologian Gayraud S. Wilmore's earlier assertion of a three-stage development of black theology, Cone likewise negotiates a long historical purview of black theological origins while also underscoring the critical role of black clergy.[28] In particular, he stresses the significance of the National Committee of Negro Churchmen, that is, the NCNC (which would later become the National Conference of Black Churchmen, the NCBC), that, with the scholarly support of black religious clergy-intellectuals like Wilmore, Vincent Harding, Preston Williams, and Henry Mitchell, insisted that, "the black power revolution . . . demanded a relevant theology."[29] In fact, Wilmore's fall 1968 NCBC theological commission project report is the first recorded use of the term "black theology," not only as a disavowal of racist white churches but also as a new theological starting point for black people:

> The term 'black theology' . . . did not emerge from the ivory tower of black university and seminary professors. It emerged as the black clergy was compelled by the urgency of the time to make theological sense out of the struggle for black freedom. To advocate a *black* theology meant that the black clergy wanted the whole world to know that it . . . would clearly distinguish its perspectives from the alternatives provided by whites and adopted by conservative blacks.[30]

Accordingly, the academic development of James H. Cone's black liberation theology cannot be fully understood apart from its practical origins in the radical ministry and activisms of black clergy. Morally anchored in the Black Church, its gospel of Jesus Christ, and the varied traditions of integrationism and nationalism that propelled the Civil Rights and Black Power movements, respectively, the revolutionary commitments of black clergy were largely guided by the witness of Martin Luther King, Jr. and Malcolm X: "two great African-American leaders" struggling against the evil of racism and demanding freedom for black people in America.[31]

Despite the contrasting images, and the incompatibility of the social and theological perspectives of Martin Luther King, Jr. and Malcolm X in the US imaginary, Cone's black liberation theology presumes that "both are needed for a critical understanding of the meaning of America" for black people. Cone contends that: "Martin and Malcolm together embodied both aspects of the African American struggle for identity. If we choose one and reject the other, it is like splitting ourselves in half, leading to our certain death. We cannot choose between them and still survive."[32] Malcolm provoked unity, self-knowledge, self-love, self-defense, and separation (not segregation) as the inherent right of black people to be claimed, "by any means necessary."[33] In contradistinction, King was guided by his understanding of the universality of humanity and "neighborly love for the enemy" as "the means by which justice is established" in the struggle for freedom.[34] Nevertheless, Cone is careful to highlight the profound theological and philosophical similarities between these two sons of Baptist preachers: likenesses that were grounded in the singular goal of freedom for African Americans.

To be sure, the life and legacy of Martin Luther King, Jr. has been sanitized by dominant and distorted accounts of his philosophy of love, nonviolence, and integration that endeavor to suppress King's radical anti-war and anti-poverty perspectives and activisms. Cone asserts that the radicality of King's political revolution can be found in his deep conviction that the eradication of segregation is consonant with the biblical notion of God's justice. Compelled by the divine mandate of freedom that is central to the traditions of the Black Church, as well as the American democratic tradition, King maintained that justice could not only be approximated through love but, even more, that the deepest significance of justice was found in love. This love ethic undergirded the nonviolent direct action that became the key aspect of King's philosophy of social change. Accordingly, King's exhortation to "love our white brothers" was demonstrated through nonviolent direct action that confounded and disarmed the oppressor, with aim of transforming the enemy into a friend.

The Black Church and its distinct politics of respectability that appealed to middle-class blacks played a pivotal role in the Civil Rights efforts to dismantle *de jure* segregation in the South.³⁵ The church's politics of respectability and its emphasis on self-respect, high moral standards, wholehearted work, leadership, and nonviolent direct action as the means to approximate full integration into white society framed King's struggle for racial justice. At a time when black people were legally barred from voting, King endeavored to speak in a language that would appeal to the arbiters of the law toward the dissolution of legal segregation. His rhetoric and direct action consistently inferred the distinction of "high moral ground," and applied the tactic of moral suasion in order to entice the democratic sensibilities of the white liberal middle class. Nevertheless, white racists, whose pseudo-theological claims, "did not recognize that the truth of the gospel meant that all persons were created equal," regularly targeted black churches, neighborhoods, and leaders.³⁶ Compelled by faith, black Christians who dared to gather outside of the gaze of white control to worship a God of justice and strategize for freedom were commonly caricatured as dangerous as they strove to undermine Jim Crow law and practices through a variety of acts of civil disobedience.

In the North, on the other hand, the overwhelming majority of blacks were not "middle class"; moreover, *de jure* segregation was not their primary social concern. Northern blacks were desperately impoverished and confined to urban ghettos where unemployment, underemployment, overcrowding, drugs, violence, police brutality, and other social inequities were consistent realities. Malcolm X identified the impoverishment of black life in the North as an insurmountable nightmare. In contrast to King, who admittedly did not fully appreciate the distinctions and challenges of black life in the North when he took leadership of the Montgomery Improvement Association in 1955, Malcolm X contended that the high moral standards and democratic principles that were paraded by the Black Church and its elevation of wholehearted work, leadership, and nonviolence were irrelevant to a community that had been cut down by rampant unemployment, ghettoization, and police brutality. Malcolm perceived that "a white man's heaven is a black man's hell"; therefore, he

> rejected Martin's idea that blacks should love whites and insisted instead that they should separate from them so that they could avoid the coming destruction of Western civilization. He interpreted justice, love, and hope in the light of the all-important symbol of blackness. In Malcolm's theology, God, Jesus, the Prophets, and the 'Original Man' [sic] were portrayed as black, and the devil and all evil things were pictured as white . . .³⁷

While King's theology of justice was grounded in divine love and democratic principle, Malcolm X asserted a theology of justice rooted in blackness. He primarily positioned the project of black freedom and justice in the North, where *de facto* segregation was the rule of the day, as a matter of personhood rather than of legislation. Said differently, in the North blacks could, relatively, shop and/or eat wherever they wanted. Yet, they were still subject to the problem of the non-human and acknowledged as inferior to whites. On the side of the black poor—the unchurched, the uneducated, the unemployed, and the disrespected—Malcolm confronted an elusive black death in the North and indicted white America for it. His straightforward and scathing critiques visibilized an "invisible" black community that lived beyond the respectability of the "high moral standard" of the black middle class and its oft-desired adjacency to white middle-class values. Wholly dismissing the validity of white liberal democratic principles and the presumed moral episteme of white virtue, Malcolm X called whites out for their blatant hypocrisies and asserted blackness as beautiful, godly, and worthy of justice.

Beyond his philosophical appeal, Cone emphasizes Malcolm X's life and legacy as a critical theological conversation partner for the Black Church. To be sure, Malcolm rejected Christianity. He unreservedly characterized it as "the white man's religion" and contended that it served as the root cause of the "physical, mental, and spiritual oppression of black people."[38] Nevertheless, Cone admits that Malcolm was a deeply religious man whose Muslim faith was a product of black religious experience in America.[39] As a disciplined student of the Bible, history, and the Qur'an, Malcolm did not oppose the way of Jesus per se, but opposed the practices of white racists who self-identified as Christians.[40] Given the overwhelming physical, social, economic, and psychological violence visited upon black people, what Cone would go on to assert as "the killing of so many blacks in the cities," he argues that Malcolm's God-talk was "not only theologically defensible, but . . . a necessary corrective against the powers of domination."[41] His "theological statement about God" defiantly proclaimed, "God is black," amidst a social context wherein "blacks [had] been enslaved and segregated for nearly four centuries by whites because of their color and where evil [had] been portrayed as 'black' and good as 'white' in religious and cultural values."[42] Consequently, blackness functioned as the dominant symbol of Malcolm's theological idea. Love and justice were always interpreted in light of blackness, which, for Malcolm, rested on "God's love of black people and his judgement of white America."[43] The critical confluence of Malcolm's justice imperative that was built on the theological claim that God is black "black is beautiful" that exhorted suffering blacks to love themselves, and King's love imperative rooted in the cross of Jesus Christ that urged suffering blacks to love the enemy as God loves all humanity, served as the definitive precursor to black liberation theology's late-twentieth-century emergence.

Following the February 1966 assassination of Malcolm X, the physical and moral exhaustion of young black Student Nonviolent Coordinating Committee (SNCC) activists in the face of black impoverishment, the hypocrisy of white liberalism, black disenfranchisement, and the surge of white terrorism in the South collided with the differing philosophical and theological perspectives of the Civil Rights Movement and the Black Power sentiments of black nationalism. In June 1966, Stokely Carmichael who was then chair of SNCC, proclaimed "Black Power" at a Civil Rights march headed by King in Greenwood, MS, in order to call attention to the glaring contradiction of preaching love of white brethren, while simultaneously preaching the funerals of black freedom fighters who had been killed by them. One month later, the Black Church represented by an ad hoc committee of black preachers, pastors, and scholars, known as the National Committee of Negro Churchmen,[44] publicly affirmed Black Power by publishing a full-page advertisement in *The New York Times*. Its three primary claims, namely, that there is a disjunction between white power and black conscience, that white conscience is corrupt because it meets little resistance and black conscience is corrupt because it is powerless, and that black intracommunal reconciliation, that is, self-love, is a primary task, prompted Cone to write his very first essay, titled "Christianity and Black Power." A "decisive departure from the pristine . . . and dispassionate theoretical analysis of the theological anthropology" of normative white theology, "Christianity and Black Power" dared to identify black power with the gospel of Jesus, this manifesto wrestled with the intersection of Christian and black identities and endeavored to explore "whether the biblical Christ is . . . limited to the prejudiced interpretations of white scholars."[45]

The assassination of Martin Luther King, Jr. on April 4, 1968 marked the turning point in the political and theological consciousness of many black Christians. By that time, Cone had already embraced Black Power; however, King's murder intensified his conviction that there is no choice to be made between one's blackness and one's Christian faith. In fact, blackness is the prerequisite of Christian faith.[46] Moreover, Cone was convinced now more than ever that the Black Church did, indeed, have a theology—a black theology. Warnock further explains that in the aftermath of King's death, Cone, "incited by the pain of the black poor exploding in riot-torn cities," went in dogged pursuit of "a theological word that would ring true for his own people" who "were being shot in the streets of American cities by white policemen."[47] His first book, *Black Theology & Black Power*, initially released in March 1969, was the first publication to use the expression "black theology" toward the development of a constructive theological posture which not only argued "that black power [is] the gospel of Jesus Christ" but, further and more provocatively, that, given its "support of slavery and segregation," the white church, not black power, is the Antichrist.[48] Said differently, "white Christianity in America . . . was born in heresy" and the white church is precisely what Christ is not.[49] Immediately following the publication of *Black Theology & Black Power*, Cone was invited to join the Theological Commission of the National Conference of Black Churchmen (NCBC). Thinking alongside other black theologians and preachers for the first time, Cone would figure prominently in the drafting of the NCBC's preeminent "Statement on Black Theology" which, foretelling Cone's second monograph published the following year, *A Black Theology of Liberation* (1970), decisively asserted that:

> Black theology is a theology of liberation. It seeks to plumb the black condition in the light of God's revelation in Jesus Christ, so that the black community can see that the gospel is commensurate with the achievement of black humanity. Black theology is a theology of "blackness." It is the affirmation of black humanity that emancipates black people from white racism . . . The message of liberation is the revelation of God as revealed in the incarnation of Jesus Christ. Freedom IS the gospel. Jesus is the Liberator! "He has sent me to preach deliverance to the captive".
>
> —Luke 4:18[50]

THE CONTEXT OF BLACK LIBERATION THEOLOGY

Theology is never neutral. Black liberation theology emerges from identification with oppressed blacks in the US and seeks to interpret the gospel of Jesus in light of the black condition.[51] It begins with the provocative claim that "Christian theology is a theology of liberation," and further asserts that the only reason for its "existence as a discipline" is to "assist the oppressed" in the work of liberation that aims for the total destruction of white racism.[52] For Cone, there is no other task of Christian theology beside its explicating "the meaning of God's liberating activity so that those who labor under enslaving powers will see that the forces of liberation are the very activity of God" in the world.[53] It affirms black humanity and liberates the black poor from the hegemony of white racism and its far-reaching consequences. Above all, black liberation theology proclaims that freedom is the "good news" and, as revealed in the ministry of Jesus as gospel, the message of liberation is the intention of God:

> The Spirit of the Lord is upon me,
> Because he has anointed me to bring good news to the poor.
> He has sent me to proclaim release to the captives and recovery of sight to the blind,
> To let the oppressed go free, to proclaim the year of the Lord's favor.[54]

Liberation is the fulcrum, that is, "the controlling key," of political black theology.[55] Its thematic emergence is found in and through the historical trajectory of revolutionary black Christian thought as it first formed in the invisible institution of slave religion, and was later propelled by the antebellum Black Church. Cone's historiographical method interprets liberation/freedom as the radical center of black Christian faith since its origins in the hush arbors of the American South. It positions liberation not only as the "theological mark of the true church," but as "the criterion by which the faithfulness of US churches ought to be measured at all times."[56]

Identifying Cone as chief among the black political theologians, distinct from the black cultural theologians, second-generation black theologian Dwight N. Hopkins contends that divine freedom is the fundament of black liberation theology that seeks to interpret the political movement for black freedom through "the systematic doctrines of classical theology."[57] Echoing Paul in Galatians 5:1, Cone argues that, "God became man . . . so that man might become what he is."[58] God created humanity in freedom. The problem of the non-human that characterizes black life as bestial, and thus wholly subordinate to white humanity, however, plagues black people through various mechanisms of structural racism that dispossess blacks, such that "he [sic] is not free to become what he [sic] is—human."[59] Freedom, nevertheless, is God's creative intention and God participates with humankind in the realization of liberation in history as an act of divine justice. A black theology of liberation presumes that through God in Christ, who is "the man for others," the black poor are free to rebel against anything that opposes their humanity, assured that the resurrected Christ is alive and active in the struggles of the oppressed.[60]

The radicality of Cone's effort cannot be overstated given that no black systematic theologies existed when he initiated his project, and especially given that the very few black theologians and religious scholars, like George Kelsey and Nathan Scott, Jr., "were not interested in associating the Christian gospel with the black experience":

> Their views were similar to those of their white teachers . . . who maintained that the universal character of the Christian faith precluded the very idea of black theology: it would reduce Christian theology to the particularity of one people . . . In the absence of substantial theological texts on black theology and with most major established black scholars remaining cool or openly rejecting such an idea, white Christians and almost all white theologians dismissed black theology as insubstantial . . . Many blacks had the impression that only Europeans and persons who think like them could define what theology is . . . In order to challenge the white monopoly on the definition of theology, [I] realized that [I] had to carry the fight to the seminaries where theology was being written.[61]

To that end, Cone's life work and scholarly corpus endeavored "to develop a systematic and comprehensive exposition of the Christian faith using the black experience of struggle as the chief source"; that is, as the primary determinant of the character of black theology.[62] Building directly upon Tillichian and Barthian emphases, respectively, Cone posits six primary sources for black theology *in this order*, while noting their interdependence and thus the challenge of determining the order of import: black experience, black history, black culture, revelation, scripture, and tradition.[63] Attention to the experience of black suffering and humiliation as a result of white racism, the history of what whites did to blacks and black resistance to white racism, as well as the creative forms of expression that emerge as social and political reflections of this experience, i.e., Negro spirituals and the blues, reveal the historical "struggle for black survival" born from the black community's acceptance of itself as "people of the Spirit" who knew that by the power of God "no chains can hold the Spirit of black humanity in bondage."[64]

Such acceptance is affirmed through revelation, which for Cone is always a black event. Careful to emphasize the significance of God's self-revelation to humankind throughout the entire history of Israel, most specifically in the event of the Exodus, as well as "God's revelatory event that takes place in the person of Jesus . . . who tells us who God is by what God does for the oppressed," Cone asserts that there is no revelation of God apart from history.[65] Black liberation theology never cedes revelation to a past event. Revelation must mean something in history; that is, *now* for the black community who are the oppressed. It is what blacks are doing to participate in what God is doing on the side of the oppressed. The biblical witness of scripture affirms a God of liberation who is active in history. Alongside an evaluation of the history of the Western church since the fourth century, tradition as a primary source for black theology similarly focuses on the history of the pre-Civil War black church in America and its emphasis on the political, economic, and social liberation of blacks as the key to interpreting the gospel.

The sources of black liberation theology are always subject to this theological norm, "the interpretive principle that specifies how sources are to be used." Because for Cone black theology is Christian theology, black liberation, its aim, is grounded in Jesus Christ—not, however, as espoused by white Christians and white churches. Their white Jesus has corrupted the cross in its historical efforts to oppress black people. White theology is the antichrist insofar as it arises from identification with the white community and places God's approval of white oppression on non-white existence. White Jesus has nothing to do with black theology and has no place in the black community. In fact, Cone goes as far to contend that if God [in Christ] "is white and not black, he [sic] is an oppressor, and we must kill him [sic];" asserting that it is the duty of the black community "to kill gods" that belong to white oppressors.[66] Jesus Christ as the norm of black theology takes the black condition seriously and is accountable to biblical revelation; thus, black theology cannot speak of Jesus without concurrently speaking of black liberation and vice versa. Black theology that cannot separate the revelation of Christ and the liberation of blacks situates the black Christ as its norm.

GOD IS BLACK

> When the master and the slave spoke of God, they could not possibly be referring to the same reality.[67]

The doctrine of God in black liberation theology begins with the claim that to accept a white God—the God of white Christianity that builds churches over slave dungeons and decimates indigenous nations—is to accept the reality of good in evil. To be sure, Cone's assertion of the blackness of God was not fashioned *ex nihilo*. Long before the late-twentieth-century systematization of black theology, black clergy freedom fighters articulated the impossibility of the oppressed and oppressors meaning the same thing when they spoke of God. In 1898, Henry McNeal Turner, the first southern bishop of the African Methodist Episcopal Church (AME) publicly declared that, "God is a Negro."[68] Approximately seventy years later, black Christian nationalist pastor Albert Cleage (Jaramogi Abebe Agyeman) of Detroit's Shrine of the Black Madonna, similarly wrestling with the revelation of God in light of black experience, asserted Jesus as the revolutionary "Black Messiah" whose "tribal love ethic" exhorted the black Nation Israel to love themselves.[69] Cone's unique contribution here is not the claim of God's blackness itself;

rather, it is found in his distinct employment of the two hermeneutic principles of black theology; namely, God's active participation in history in the Exodus that liberates Israel from the hand of Pharaoh (Ex. 3:6–11), and the life of Jesus Christ who, as gospeled, is the Oppressed One (Matt. 25:34–36, 40). These hermeneutical principles drive black liberation theology's central claim that God is black and that the blackness of God is the heart of God's identity, such that "God has made the oppressed condition God's own condition" and thereby makes the black experience God's own.[70] Consequently, this black God is the Creator who brings all things into being and explicitly *identifies* with oppressed Israel; the Redeemer who *becomes* oppressed in Jesus so that all may be liberated; and the Holy Spirit who *continues* the work of liberation in the world.[71]

Cone readily admits that:

> It is the black theology emphasis on the blackness of God that distinguishes it sharply from contemporary white views of God. White religionists are not capable of perceiving the blackness of God, because their satanic whiteness is a denial of the very essence of divinity . . . White theologians would prefer to do theology without reference to color, but this only reveals how deeply racism is embedded in . . . their culture.[72]

Surely, the historical Jesus was not white, but the blackness of God does not refer to a biological condition. In much the same way that blackness functions as a Christological title that will be discussed more below, in black liberation theology blackness functions as an attribute of God that signifies God's revelatory presence where people experience humiliation and suffering. God's blackness is symbolic. Resisting the white charge that God's blackness "is an ideological distortion of the New Testament for political purposes," Cone asserts God's blackness as a symbol that best describes oppression in America.[73] Wherever the oppressed are, God is there. Suffering in the black experience in relationship with biblical revelation compels black theology's assertion: God is black; for not only is God on the side of the oppressed, but in Christ, God becomes them—the poor, the criminal, the marginalized—such that it is written, "can there any good thing come out of Nazareth?" (John 1:46).

THE BLACK CHRIST

Cone emphatically claims that if Jesus is to hold any significance for black people, "he must leave the security of the suburbs and join blacks in their condition."[74] This hermeneutics contends that for black people, Jesus must be black Jesus because encountering Jesus in one's historical experience is of primary significance to black theology. He affirms Jesus' Jewishness and, "on the basis of the soteriological meaning of the particularity of his Jewishness" in relation to theological content, argues for the "Christological significance of Jesus' present blackness."[75] Asking the critical question for the church, "Who is Jesus Christ for us today?" Cone contends that Jesus *is* black precisely because he *was* a Jew.[76] While this literally means that Jesus becomes "One with the oppressed blacks, taking their suffering as his suffering," it does not mean that only blacks experience pain in a white racist society. Symbolically, the particularity of the blackness of God in Christ gestures toward the universal affirmation that God has never left the poor and the helpless alone.[77]

In opposition to the theological claims of Søren Kierkegaard, Emil Brunner, Rudolf Bultmann, Ernst Kasemann, and early Barth who argued in various ways that history is irrelevant to the Christian Gospel, Cone's black liberation theology asserts that it is precisely the historical Jesus that must be taken seriously in christological inquiry.[78] It is precisely in the historical record where one finds Jesus' identification with the poor as his sole reason for existence. Cone presses this critical point by emphasizing four characteristics of the New Testament Jesus that are central for the development of black liberation theology: his birth, baptism and temptation, public ministry, and death and resurrection. In the first place, his birth in the poverty of a barn as one of the humiliated and abused not only reveals God's "concern for the lonely and downtrodden," but also his oppressed condition as "an expression of the very being of God."[79] Further, Jesus' embrace of a sinner's baptism defines his existence and coming kingdom as one with and for the outcast, in much the same way that his temptation demonstrates his refusal to be diverted from his mission to the poor with self-glorifying power. His public ministry announces and clarifies God's decision for the oppressed and reveals Jesus as the Oppressed One whose work is liberation.

Most critically for Cone, however, is Jesus' death on a cross, "as a public spectacle accompanied by torture and shame," the consummation of his earthly ministry with the poor.[80] Crucifixion was a most humiliating and painful death; a form of execution reserved for those deemed rebels and insurrectionists by the Roman Empire. For Cone, the cross, which is the universal symbol at the heart of the Christian story, stands as the ultimate demonstration of Jesus' identification with the poor and the oppressed. Jesus was not just a good man who liked the poor but he is the suffering servant who, as recorded in Isaiah 53:4–5,

> Hath borne our griefs, and carried our sorrows: yet we did esteem him stricken, smitten of God, and afflicted. But he was wounded for our transgressions, he was bruised for our iniquities: the chastisement of our peace was upon him; and with his stripes we are healed.

Victimized by mob hysteria and state-sanctioned violence, in death Jesus becomes one with crucified people; those like Emmett Till, Addie Mae Collins, Cynthia Wesley, Carole Robertson, Carol Denise McNair, Trayvon Martin, Eric Garner, and Nia Wilson—"those who are hung, shot, burned, and tortured."[81] He takes on the totality of human oppression through the facts of history. But in a remarkable transvaluation of value and power, Jesus inverts the cross in his resurrection, disclosing a God who is not defeated by oppression, but who transforms it into freedom.[82] The historical Jesus whose "crucifixion was . . . a first-century lynching" that mirrors the experience of African Americans as "innocent victims of white mobs thirsting for blood," reveals that violence and death do not have the last word: "O death where is thy sting? O grave where is thy victory . . . but thanks be to God who giveth us the victory through our Lord Jesus Christ" (I Cor 15:55–57). Cone concedes that Christ has conquered the death of "the lowest of the low in society," for cursed is the one who hangs from a tree (Deut. 21:23), despite the threat of death, the oppressed are free to say no to the oppressor "because God has said yes to them, thereby placing them in a state of freedom. They can now deny any values that separate them from the reality of their new being."[83] Cone contends that descendants of enslaved blacks now sing "before I'll be a slave, I'll be buried in my grave and go home to my Lord and be free," precisely because black Christian faith grasps how the lynched Christ who is risen sets the oppressed free from death.[84] The dialectical meaning of Jesus Christ for black liberation theology is found in the confluence of who Jesus was, who Jesus is, and who Jesus will be. Jesus—who *was* born in the poverty of a barn, baptized by a wild man in a country river, who ministered to the outcast, died a slave on a cross, and was buried in a borrowed tomb—stands with oppressed blacks *now* amidst the rope and faggot of the new Jim Crow and its disproportionate state-sanctioned physical, social, economic, and environmental violence. This Black Christ is *emanu-el* as blacks continue in the struggle of inaugurating futures, in the present, where black lives matter beyond the brutalities of white power, its racist god, and its demonic god-talk.

NOTES

1. James H. Cone, *My Soul Looks Back* (Nashville: Abingdon, 1982), 114.
2. James H. Cone, *God of the Oppressed* (New York: Orbis, 1997), 1.
3. James H. Cone, *Risks of Faith: The Emergence of a Black Theology of Liberation* (Boston: Beacon Press, 1999), xiii; Cone completed his dissertation in 1964 but participated in commencement exercises in the spring of 1965.
4. Cone, *God of the Oppressed*, 5, 3.
5. Cone, *Risks of Faith*, 9.
6. Black churches are not homogeneous. The "Black Church" is a rhetorical device that signifies the historical expression of black Christian faith that is no greater than the sum of its varied parts. The "Black Church" refers to the seven primary historically black Christian denominations—African Methodist Episcopal (AME), African Methodist Episcopal Zion (AMEZ), Christian Methodist Episcopal (CME), Church of God in Christ (COGIC), National Baptist Convention of America (NBCA), National Baptist Convention, USA, Inc. (NBC), and the Progressive National Baptist Convention, Inc., (PNBC). In addition, it also includes primarily black congregations in historically white denominations, multicultural non-denominational churches whose liturgy is informed by African American traditions; as well as black Christian communities throughout the African diaspora, including Europe, South America, and the Caribbean. For further treatment, see Stacey Floyd-Thomas, et al., *Black Church Studies: An Introduction* (Nashville, TN: Abingdon Press, 2007).
7. Raphael G. Warnock, *The Divided Mind of the Black Church: Theology, Piety, and Public Witness* (New York: New York University Press, 2014), 33–34.
8. Cone, *My Soul Looks Back* (Nashville, TN: Abingdon, 1982), 18
9. Ibid.
10. Ibid., 21–22.
11. Ibid., 19.
12. Ibid., 22.
13. Ibid., 23.
14. Ibid., 23, 25. For further treatment, see also James H. Cone, *Risks of Faith*, x.
15. Cone, *My Soul Looks Back*, 38.
16. Ibid.
17. Henry Louis Gates Jr. and Terri Hume Oliver, eds., *The Souls of Black Folk* (New York: W.W. Norton & Company, 1999), 11.
18. Cone, *My Soul Looks Back*, 38–39.
19. Ibid., 39.
20. Warnock, *The Divided Mind of the Black Church*, 53–54.
21. Cone, *My Soul Looks Back*, 39.
22. Warnock, *The Divided Mind of the Black Church*, 54.
23. Cone, *My Soul Looks Back*, 39.

24. Ibid., 41.
25. Ibid., 39–42.
26. Warnock, *The Divided Mind of the Black Church*, 20.
27. Ibid. For further treatment of the origins of Black liberation theology, see Dwight N. Hopkins, *Shoes that Fit Our Feet: Sources for a Constructive Black Theology* (New York: Orbis, 1993); Dwight N. Hopkins, *Down Up and Over: Slave Religion and Black Theology* (Minneapolis: Fortress, 2000); and Dwight N. Hopkins, *Introducing Black Theology of Liberation* (New York: Orbis, 1999).
28. For more on Gayraud S. Wilmore's emphasis on the development of black theology, see James H. Cone, *For My People: Black Theology and the Black Church* (New York: Orbis, 2002), 24–27.
29. Cone, *For My People*, 23.
30. Ibid., 24 (original italics).
31. Cone, *Martin & Malcolm & America: A Dream or a Nightmare* (New York: Orbis, 2000), 2.
32. Cone, *Risks of Faith*, 100.
33. Ibid., 104.
34. Cone, *Martin & Malcolm & America*, 126.
35. See Evelyn Brooks Higginbotham, *Righteous Discontent: The Women's Movement in the Black Baptist Church, 1880–1920* (Cambridge, MA: Harvard University Press, 1993), 186–188. The phrase "politics of respectability" refers to the idea that if black people act a certain way—that is, if they assimilate into white standards of normalcy and morality—they will inherit or achieve equal status.
36. Cone, *Martin & Malcolm & America*, 145.
37. Ibid., 160.
38. Ibid., 166.
39. Ibid., 122.
40. Ibid., 167. Malcolm X dismissed the case for Jesus' divinity and considered him as a great prophet, on par with Moses and Mohammed.
41. Ibid., 160.
42. Ibid.
43. Ibid., 165
44. The NCNC would later change its name to the National Committee of Black Churchmen (NCBC). It would finally settle on the National Conference of Black Churches (NCBC). For further treatment, see Dwight N. Hopkins, *Introducing Black Theology of Liberation* (New York: Orbis, 1999), 40.
45. Cone, My Soul Looks Back, 44.
46. NCBC, "Statement on Black Theology."
47. Warnock, *The Divided Mind of the Black Church*, 89. See also Cone, *My Soul Looks Back*, 82.
48. Hopkins, *Introducing Black Liberation Theology*, 40. See also, Warnock, *The Divided Mind*, 90–91.
49. Warnock, *The Divided Mind*, 93.
50. National Conference of Black Churchmen, "Black Theology," Cone, et al., *Black Theology: A Doc Hist, V. 1* (New York: Orbis, 1993), 101.

51. James H. Cone, *A Black Theology of Liberation* (New York: Orbis, 2001), 5.
52. Ibid., 1, 4. See also Hopkins, *Introducing*, 56.
53. Cone, *A Black Theology of Liberation*, 3.
54. Luke 4:18–19, *The Holy Bible*, NRSV.
55. Hopkins, *Introducing*, 54.
56. Warnock, *The Divided Mind*, 53.
57. Hopkins, *Introducing*, 54; Hopkins is careful to distinguish between black political theology and black cultural theology. He contends that black political theologians have historically emphasized "opposing racism in the white American political system, church, and theology," resisting "inhuman practices of white political power." Black cultural theologians ask, "how can the black political theologian attack racism in . . . theology . . . while using the intellectual categories of white theology?" Black cultural theologians therefore condemn the cultural structure of white supremacist religion and theology, calling for "a fundamental shift in the development of religion" and God-talk. For further treatment, see Hopkins, *Introducing*, 52–84. Raphael G. Warnock identifies Cone as the most prolific contributor to shaping of content and meaning of black liberation theology across forms in *The Divided Mind*, 88.
58. James H. Cone, *Black Theology & Black Power* (New York: Orbis, 1999), 39.
59. Ibid.
60. Warnock, *The Divided Mind*, 92.
61. Cone, *For My People*, 53–54.
62. Ibid., 53. See also Cone, *A Black Theology of Liberation*, 21.
63. Cone, *A Black Theology of Liberation*, 23–35.
64. James H. Cone, *The Spirituals and the Blues* (New York: Orbis, 1992), 1, 4.
65. Cone, *A Black Theology of Liberation*, 30.
66. Ibid., 111, 27.
67. Cone, *God of the Oppressed*, 10.
68. Henry McNeal Turner, "God is a Negro." https://comebyyuh.wordpress.com/2013/01/22/bishop-henry-mcneal-turners-god-is-a-negro/
69. Warnock, *The Divided Mind of the Black Church*, 105–106. See also JoAnne M. Terrell, *Power in the Blood? The Cross in the African American Experience* (Eugene, OR: Wipf & Stock, 2005), 71–98.
70. Cone, *A Black Theology of Liberation*, 63.
71. Ibid., 64.
72. Ibid.
73. Cone, *God of the Oppressed*, 122–123.
74. Ibid., 111.
75. Cone, *God of the Oppressed*, 123.
76. Ibid.
77. Ibid., 126.
78. Cone, *A Black Theology of Liberation*, 111–113.
79. Ibid., 114–115.
80. James H. Cone, *The Cross & Lynching Tree* (New York: Orbis, 2011), 1.
81. Ibid., 26.

82. Cone discusses Reinhold Niebuhr's repeated us of the phrase "transvaluation of values" in his discussion of the cross and what it means for God's revelation in Jesus' suffering to contradict "historical values and expectations (35)." For further treatment, see Cone, *The Cross & the Lynching Tree*, 34–38. See also Cone, *A Black Theology of Liberation*, 118.
83. Cone, *A Black Theology of Liberation*, 118.
84. Cone, *The Spirituals and the Blues*, 29.

SELECT BIBLIOGRAPHY

Cone, James H. (1984), *For My People: Black Theology and the Black Church*, Maryknoll, NY: Orbis Books.
Cone, James H. (1986), *My Soul Looks Back,* Maryknoll, NY: Orbis Books.
Cone, James H. (1990), *A Black Theology of Liberation*, Maryknoll, NY: Orbis Books.
Cone, James H. (1992), *The Spirituals and the Blues*, Maryknoll, NY: Orbis Books.
Cone, James H. (1997), *Black Theology and Black Power*, Maryknoll, NY: Orbis Books.
Cone, James H. (1997), *God of the Oppressed*, Maryknoll, NY: Orbis Books.
Cone, James H. (1999), *Risks of Faith: The Emergence of a Black Theology of Liberation*, Boston: Beacon Press.
Cone, James H. (2000), *Martin & Malcolm & and America: A Dream or a Nightmare*, Maryknoll, NY: Orbis Books.
Cone, James H. (2011), *The Cross & Lynching Tree*, Maryknoll, NY: Orbis Books.
Cone, James H. (2018), *Said I Wasn't Gonna Tell Nobody: The Making of a Black Theologian*, Maryknoll, NY: Orbis Books.
Cone, James H., et. al. (1993), *Black Theology: A Documentary History 1966–1979, Vol. One*, Maryknoll, NY: Orbis Books.
Cone, James H., et. al. (1993), *Black Theology: A Documentary History 1980–1992, Vol. Two*, Maryknoll, NY: Orbis Books.
Douglas, Kelly Brown (1993), *The Black Christ*, Maryknoll, NY: Orbis Books,
Higginbotham, Evelyn Brooks (1993), *Righteous Discontent: The Women's Movement in the Black Baptist Church, 1880–1920*, Cambridge, MA: Harvard University Press.
Hopkins, Dwight N. (1993), *Shoes that Fit Our Feet: Sources for a Constructive Black Theology*, Maryknoll, NY: Orbis Books.
Hopkins, Dwight N. (1999), *Introducing Black Theology of Liberation*, Maryknoll, NY: Orbis Books.
Hopkins, Dwight N. (2000), *Down, Up, and Over: Slave Religion and Black Theology*, Minneapolis, MN: Fortress Press.
Hopkins, Dwight N. (2003), *Cut Loose Your Stammering Tongue: Black Theology in the Slave Narratives*, Louisville, KY: Westminster John Knox Press.
Terrell, JoAnne M. (2005), *Power in the Blood? The Cross in the African American Experience*, Eugene, OR: Wipf & Stock.
Warnock, Raphael G. (2014), *The Divided Mind of the Black Church: Theology, Piety, and Public Witness*, New York: New York University Press.

CHAPTER EIGHTEEN

Latina Feminist and *Mujerista* Theologies as Political Theologies?

NEOMI DE ANDA

INTRODUCTION

Latina feminist and *mujerista* theologies are broad umbrella terms that help those of us who are from these various backgrounds come together in solidarity. Yet, there are many particularities and specificities within these umbrellas. For example, I am a Tejana, I come from a place where the histories of the USA and Mexico intertwine, mostly by conflict and domination.[1] María Teresa Davila writes from a Puerto Rican perspective. Jacqueline Hidalgo develops scripturalizing as a method of interlacing social injustices with marginalized people dreaming about alternate ways. While these few examples represent a contextualized way of theorizing and theologizing, many more points of view are needed.

Because I theologize from this particular location, I find contextual situatedness to be among the most important pieces for developing theological reflection. Therefore, much of this chapter will draw upon my particular context and my daily life as a Tejana who grew up between El Paso and Corpus Christi in Texas. Because my communities make sure I am held accountable as a theologian I tend to focus on specific social issues that have become part of my life. It is because of my communities' emphasis on theology's impetus for social change from *lo cotidiano*[2] ("the day to day") as *locus theologicus* that I have been named by other academics as a political theologian. It is because my communities continue to pray for me and support my work that I give them the credit for making me the theologian I am today. Yet, I do not consider myself a political theologian.

I do question if Latina feminist and *mujerista* theologies can be considered political theologies and whether political theology has space for Latina feminist and *mujerista* theologies. Because of their social location, embodiment, contextualization, *mujerista* and Latina feminist theologies fundamentally stand outside of the realm of political theology while also challenging it. Latina feminist and *mujerista* theology have always been theologies with political perspectives. Yet, these theologies have not always been taken as contributions central to theological discussions, even those which consider themselves political theologies. Furthermore, because of Latinas' second-class treatment in the USA context,[3] Latina feminist and *mujerista* theologies also challenge the entire project of political theology when one takes the political as coming from Roman and Greek notions of living together as community and as citizens with rights which are afforded to all.[4] Because of the embodied lived reality of Latinas and the reality of our cultures being suppressed and annihilated, the Latina reality exists as something entirely different from a Western Euro-American and/or white framework. *Mujerista* and Latina feminist theologies challenge the white supremacist biases found in many Western Euro-American/white/Anglo theologies. In fact, the all-Latina presidential leadership of the Academy of Catholic Hispanic Theologians of the United States (ACHTUS) worked with the Black Catholic Theological Symposium to overtly speak out against actions happening in the USA at the time in a statement entitled "ACHTUS/BCTS Statement Regarding the Most Recent Surge in Racist Hate Crimes in the United States,"[5] which drew upon both communities' shared experience as second-class citizens in the USA.

No one theology can handle dealing with all of the injustices of the world. Therefore, to think beyond categorical umbrellas remains necessary for the purposes of dreaming of alternative possibilities and working toward justice. *Mujerista* and Latina feminist theologies fundamentally challenge political theology by their existence and embodiment. As Teresa Delgado states, "the very act of writing is an act of rebellion, evidence of a revolutionary spirit and impulse in a repressive environment where the silence of those numbed by the weight of colonialism is preferred."[6] For those who have written as *mujerista* and Latina feminist theologians and scholars, the struggle is not only against social injustices and second-class treatment. A daily struggle within academia also exists. The strictures of the academy do not allow for a fuller flourishing of Latina feminist and *mujerista* theologies in order to both engage and build upon the intricacies of *mujerista* and Latina feminist theologies, this chapter will be divided into two major parts. First, I will discuss some of the pieces of the fabric that constitute Latina feminist and *mujerista* theologies. This discussion will engage some of the categories flowing through these works but will not be exhaustive. These pieces will help to understand how *mujerista* and Latina feminist theologies engage with what other theologies call the political or public spectrums. Second, I will weave my own constructive theological contribution to Latina feminist and *mujerista* theology shaped by these pieces of fabric.

FABRICS OF *MUJERISTA* AND LATINA FEMINIST THEOLOGIES

Clamor and Struggle for Life

The most important piece of Latina feminist and *mujerista* theologies is the work of life. María Pilar Aquino uses *Nuestro clamor por la vida* ("our cry for life") as the central title for her book describing theology from this perspective and Ada María Isasi-Díaz elaborates her *mujerista* theology *En la Lucha* ("in the struggle"). Aquino, a Latina-Latin American woman broadly construed, stands as a strong feminist thinker. Aquino's title has been translated into English as *Our Cry for Life*.[7] Yet, the word "clamor" has a much stronger sense. In Spanish, a "clamor" is raucous and demanding. It inherently carries a sense of agency for those clamoring; those demanding to be heard; those fighting against the oppressive injustices of social systems created to use, abuse, and even annihilate these lives.

Isasi-Díaz discusses a theological anthropology from a *mujerista* perspective. She rightly claims, "An anthropology developed out of the lived-experience of Latinas centers on a subject who struggles to survive and who understands herself as one who struggles.

A small but common indication of this is how, to the casual question 'How are you?' grassroot Latinas commonly respond just as casually, 'Ahí, en la lucha.'"[8] Both of these women demonstrate agency in struggling for life against oppression and historical injustices as central to Latina theological reflection.

Highlight Space Pried Open by Latinas

"How come nobody told me an aria, a piece of stained glass, a painting, a sunset can be God too?"[9] *Mujerista* and Latina feminist theologies reflect the theological engagement of women. They serve to answer this very question as posed by Cisneros. These theologies highlight space pried open by Latinas against limiting, oppressive, and even annihilating social constructs and systems, especially those found in theological discourse.

Self-Naming

Self-naming is extremely important for Latina feminist and *mujerista* theologians.[10] A large part of the historical oppression and marginalization experienced by these women has come because others have named us and our reality. In the worst of cases, Latinas have not been named at all, e.g., the US Constitution and the early (Anglo) feminist movement. The ability to name oneself and claim that space breaks the barriers of oppression and allows for the struggle against marginalization to move forward.

In theologies and other studies of religion, those working in these areas may or may not choose one title—Latina feminist or *mujerista*—over the other. Some may use Latina, Chicana, queer, lesbian, trans, Tejana, gurl, boi, *tica*, *boriqua* instead of or in addition to Latina feminist and *mujerista*. Again these titles are but broad umbrellas to unify the struggle and clamor for life from women's daily living. Another part of self-naming includes language preference. Language matters. For Latinas, functioning among various languages constitutes daily life. Therefore, the writings of Latina feminist and *mujerista* theologians flow among these languages seamlessly. Sometimes this language is written in a way that is purposefully disruptive for those from another perspective.

The Particular

Congruent with self-naming, Latina feminist and *mujerista* theologies engage the particular and highlight the importance of difference. Latinas have long been treated as second-class persons within what are now the boundaries of the USA. The British occupation of Florida, the treaty of Guadalupe Hidalgo, the USA occupation of Puerto Rico, as well as the bloody and fraught US history with Central American nations, from the first implementation of Manifest Destiny until today, name some of the many histories which laid the groundwork for the treatment of Latinas as second-class persons. In some cases, Latinas have been completely dehumanized by the system all together. Therefore, those of us who are citizens may have had it a little better than those whose documents are not recognized by the USA government. Because of the Cuban Adjustment Act, the USA government has better served Cubans than other Latina groups in the second half the twentieth century (at least until the writing of this chapter), but even this act does not alleviate the trauma caused by dangerous and/or lonely migrations. The importance of the particular for *mujerista* and Latina feminist theologies has also taken into account notions of intermixing and different types of intermixing, e.g., *mestizaje, mulatez,* Afro-Latina, etc.[11] Although, this area remains a growth point for Latina feminist and *mujerista* theologies to expand their engagement.

Justice

Because Latina feminist and *mujerista* theologies take *lo cotidiano* and *lo popular* ("the popular," often referring to the people's religious practices) as their theologically rooted places and because women from these places have cried out against injustices suffered, these theologies struggle for justice by demanding better social relationships and fuller flourishing of life. The starting point of justice-seeking as a construct for these theologies comes from political moves made against Latina bodies and identities. In so doing, they can be considered political projects. Justice is not measured in huge outcomes or massive amounts of social and structural change. For *mujerista* theologies, justice is measured in small bits gleaned in our daily existence. For this reason, the theological category is *"un poquito de justicia"*[12] because just a little bit of justice continues the momentum in the cry and struggle for life.

Lo Popular

As part of LatinoXa[13] theologies, *mujerista* and Latina feminist theologies use *lo popular* as central to their work. *Lo popular* may be understood as

> The term is applied to practices, worldviews, epistemologies, beliefs, political options, and so forth, whose source and author are "the people" (frequently interpreting the latter to be the culturally and/or socially marginalized Latino/a majority). Consequently, that which is widespread is not necessarily popular in this sense. Furthermore, something may be said to be "popular" when it truly reflects *latinidad* (literally means "Latina/o-ness") as its core and source.[14]

Some of the themes covered by Latina feminist and *mujerista* theologies regarding *lo popular* include social media, sexuality, breast milk, murals, poetry, and fiction as sources and locations for theologizing.

Lo Cotidiano

Also, as part of LatinoXa theologies, *lo cotidiano* is central as *locus theologicus* for Latina feminist and *mujerista* theologies. The focus upon daily-lived experience takes into account the real lives of real women. The use of *lo cotidiano* allows for the messiness of life to be central to theological engagement. In connection with living toward justice, Latina feminist and *mujerista* theologies operate in a liberationist mode working toward structural change. Yet this structural change must be rooted in the daily lives of people.[15]

Conjunto

LatinoXa theologies also use the term *"conjunto"* as a central theological category. The intentional use of this term breaks open a number of possibilities for these living theologies. The term focuses on the sociocentric notion familiar to the majority of our communities. *Conjunto* has two further designations in LatinoXa theologies: *"en y de."* *"En conjunto"* encompasses theologies done together. While a single author may eventually write these theologies, the reflections come from *lo cotidiano*, *lo popular*, and many times have engaged other Latino/a ministers and scholars of religion. They come from the community. Carmen Nanko-Fernández utilizes Juan Flores' work to explain additional dimensions of *"en conjunto."* She says, "Flores observes that the term accentuates the two constitutive parts, común, i.e., what we share in common, and unidad, i.e., what binds us beyond our 'diverse particular commonalities.'"[16] *"De conjunto"* signifies that the theologies belong to our communities. They are also gifts for the broader world to understand Latino/a theological perspectives. As has been previously stated, "We affirm a multiplicity of understandings of processes and outcomes in *teología en y de conjunto.*"[17] *Mujerista* and Latina feminist theologies, in the spirit of *"en y de conjunto,"* also make a commitment to cite women of color and queer scholars.

The second part of this chapter attempts to give language to how Latina feminist and *mujerista* theologians function as *tejedoras* ("weavers"). For over thirty years, Latinas in the academy have been fighting for a broadening of sources for doing theology. The majority of Latina theologies are not grounded in the reading of Aquinas, Augustine, and Justin Martyr. They are done in and through *lo cotidiano*.

LAS TEJEDORAS OF THE FABRICS

Mujerista and Latina feminist theologians work as *Tejedoras* in that we interweave many different aspects of life. These theologies take *lo cotidiano en conjunto* with a clamor for *un poquito de justicia* and tell stories/*cuentitos* to highlight the spaces where Latinas bring forward new life. These theologies are not only interdisciplinary but interspacial. They take intersectionality and weave the messiness and complications of life. *En y de conjunto*, they lift-up solutions and dreams from *lo cotidiano* of women. They move beyond the confines of the academy, although these theologians have been formed mostly to remain within the confines of the ivory tower. Latina feminist and *Mujerista* theologies are done with others and by writing and watching telenovelas; by creating art; by playing music and dancing with it; by composing short stories, poetry and novels; by working as chefs and community organizers; by dancing as part of Matachines celebrating *Nuestra Señora de Guadalupe* and by playing Bomba; by fighting for the cultural traditions of their communities while breaking open doors and shattering glass ceilings. The next two sections illustrate how these theologies interweave what many call the political or the public. Specifically, *Mujerista* and Latina feminist theologians engage the familiar and bring out *la chingona* (a Mexican slang term used to refer to a particularly "badass" woman, which some might consider profane).

Lo/the Familiar

Mujerista and Latina feminist theologies are/*son familiar*. I envelop this word to break it open in both English and Spanish. It is a Spanglish conceptualization. These theologies are familiar (English) in the sense of knowing well the lives about which they write. The authors write about that which they often encounter and have good knowledge through the experiences of others as well as their own experiences. These theologies are also familiar (*español*) in the sense of relating in intimate ways, like family, with that about which they write. It also draws on the notion of *conjunto* in that what is familiar can be used to described something with shared ownership like a car. These theologies also use vocabulary and language which comes from within communities; from women in faith sharing groups; from women organizing for justice; from women who care for children.

Because of the familiar of Latina feminist and *mujerista* theologies, they expose the mirage of created national borders and see these lands as one interconnected piece called "América."[18] Therefore, to be "*de* América" is to claim an identity as part of the entire land masses and in relationship with the many people on this side of the earth. The exposure of this mirage allows for reimagination of the flourishing of life beyond some very oppressive national and international structures.

To highlight this point, I turn to *cuentitos* ("intimate/familial stories") and grassroots examples. As a scholar who has lived most of her life between the Mexico/US border and a variety of other contexts in the USA, I find it extremely important to highlight some current issues and practices guided and informed by religion, mostly Catholicism at the Mexico/USA border, marked by Pope Francis' visit to Juárez in February 2016 as well as the ongoing work of the Hope Border Institute. Hope Border Institute (HBI) is an independent grassroots community organization working in the El Paso-Ciudad Juárez-Las Cruces region that seeks to bring the perspective of Catholic social teaching to bear on the social realities unique to our region.

As a way to enter into more specific understanding from *lo cotidiano* in the *clamor* and struggle for justice, I am highlighting two interconnections of social issues: (1) labor and trade and (2) detention and the prison industrial complex. I share *cuentitos* because it is in the little stories where we find many complexities which theory can only begin to unpack. Sharing these stories allows for just *un poquito de justicia*. *Acompañamiento* ("accompaniment") is the starting point of justice. Latina feminist and *mujerista* theologies do not separate the political from *lo cotidiano*; they do not need a different label to continue to struggle for justice; they use stories and life experience to embody the sorrow caused by "the love-child of conquest, colonization, and empire."[19] So, I begin with stories on labor. There are a number of issues facing the Mexico/US border region regarding labor and trade. Concerning the crossroads of labor and religion, I focus on two women.

First, Daisy Flores Gámez spoke during Pope Francis' visit to Juárez and his meeting with the world of labor. Her husband, Jesús Gurrola Varela, and their two children accompanied her on the stage during her speech. Ms. Flores Gámez, as one of two women speaking during a pope's visit to Juárez, is significant in a number of ways. She spoke to 3,000 people present at this meeting as the representative of the world of work in factories that are little more than sweatshops—*maquilas*—in this Mexico/US border metroplex. These factories have been known for maintaining low wages and long hours for workers on both sides of the Mexico/US border both in the *maquilas* and more broadly to other parts of society. Beyond the sexist issues faced by women through both church and society, Juárez has also been known as a city of feminicide where women have been brutally abused, raped, and killed. Daisy's speech shed a glimpse of hope for a better future for her own children as well as forthcoming generations as she named very specific areas which need attention toward systemic change. She says addressing Pope Francis,

> We ask for your Holiness to pray for us—as Juárez intercedes for you—families who are subjected to unjust networks of the market, as well as systems which are too pragmatic and bureaucratic. We live in terrible working conditions in which we disproportionally spend effort, time, and energy ... Every home and every family should be a school of humanity where essential things are learned: solidarity, appreciation, care for one another, respect, and human dignity. Nevertheless, at least in this city, and we believe many others as well, our homes have become merely places to sleep.[20]

The second labor *cuento* points to issues of international trade partnerships such as NAFTA and CAFTA. Maria Guadalupe Ortega Gonzalez is a Raramuri woman who lives 33 kilometers outside of Juarez. She is one of 250,000 people employed by the *maquilas* in Juárez. She was hired after NAFTA passed and many jobs from El Paso were moved overnight to Juárez. Originally when hired, she and other workers were under the impression that they would be provided a reliable shuttle and lunch. Such was not the case. She does not have transportation to get to her place of work because she lives in a rural community and does not own a car. She asks how bringing jobs to a region is a good idea when one must wake at 3:30 am to make it to work. The average *maquila* worker in Juárez earns $7 per day. Maria knows that she and the other workers are taken advantage of because they are illiterate. According to the Hope Border Institute and various labor organizations organizing to raise salaries to a living wage, trade agreements such as "The Trans Pacific Partnership would destroy hopes of living wages and worker protections. The twelve nations that make up this trade deal represent 40% of the world economy."[21]

The issues surrounding trade and labor affect all of the Américas. The way labor has been constructed as an expense to be minimized by the greed of globalized capitalism oppresses and ruins many lives. International treaties break people from every country involved. NAFTA took jobs from the US side and plopped them into the Mexican side without a question. Entire families lost livelihoods in El Paso and the systems have been set to highly exploit in Juárez.

The second issue, the Prison Industrial Complex, is pressing on both the US and Mexican sides of the border. During Pope Francis' visit to Juárez, the world heard from Evelia Quintana. She had me in tears discussing the struggles people face while in prison in Juárez and how some people spend years incarcerated before being sentenced. Evelia Quintana Molina has been an inmate of the Juárez prison system for over five years. She is a single mother of a daughter. She asked the pope to bless her daughter, and Francis granted her this wish. Ms. Quintana Molina, as one of two women speaking during a pope's visit to Juárez, is significant in a number of ways. The violence in Juárez and response by local authorities has led to an overwhelming increase in those who are considered criminals. The prison system has become a place of backlog, abandonment, and hopelessness for many of the inmates. Evelia's speech shed a glimpse of hope for a better future for her own daughter as well as forthcoming generations. She states:

> Not all has ended here. It is just a pause in our lives, a time to reflect about how one wants to live and how you wish your children to live. Let us work so that our children do not repeat our story. On a personal note, the great blessing of seeing my daughter grow and become a young lady with long hair and huge eyes which I triumphantly see from the moment the visitors' door opens in the prison and allow her to enter. Her smile and seeing her run to my arms give me a little life. An "I love you mom!" from her beautiful lips will give me the strength with which to survive the following days in prison. If life and our acts placed us in darkness, maybe it is not so we die in it; rather that we brighten it with our faith and our desire to change . . . The day I was given my sentence, someone told me, "No longer ask yourself why you are here. Better, ask yourself for what reason are you here?" One day I found myself sad to be far away from my home without my daughter and family. In my interior I thought, God I accept your will. And I said, "God, I only ask that you help me see that your plans are better than mine." And it was at that moment that I received the response of the reason why I am here.[22]

Ms. Quintana Molina's speech sheds just a glimmer of light on the complexities of the prison industrial complex and the criminalization of so very many populations. Connections must always be made between the US prison industrial complex and immigration. The same mentality that is keeping people in prison, especially in for-profit prisons, holds people, even children, in detention.

In the USA, the Hope Border Institute held a baby shower as a form of protest against the prison industrial complex, specifically migrants being held in detention many times in for-profit facilities. The event was called "No Diapers in Detention." The invitation read:

> Please join Hope Border Institute, Detained Migrant Solidarity Committee, CAFe New Mexico, Border Peace Presence, Pax Christi, and faith-based advocates and community members at a "baby shower" for ICE El Paso. [The event was held on Friday, 2 September 2016.] This action is part of a larger movement to deliver these baby showers to U.S. Immigration and Customs Enforcement (ICE) Field Offices, local jails and detention centers across the country to draw attention to the scandalous practice by ICE of incarcerating children and mothers fleeing violence in their home countries. In El Paso, children are not detained, but rather, women and men are held at the El Paso Processing Center, and thus systematically separated from their children. We call to put an end to this cruel separation and hope this event is an opportunity to educate the public about family detention processes and touch the hearts of families in El Paso who have never had to be separated because of the United States' immigration detention practices.

This nonviolent direct action called for an end to family detention and family separation in immigrant detention centers across the USA nearly two years before the creation of the Tornillo tent city that created so much national outrage in June 2018. Systems by governments on both sides have forced the separation of close relations, especially blood relatives. The election of the new US administration in 2016 brought panic to many who live between these and other international borders. Within three days after the forty-fifth President of the USA was elected, at least eight immigrants committed suicide in Chicago. Many have highlighted the connection between the prison industrial complex and unjust immigrant detention. As just one example, the South Texas Family Residential Center in Dilley, Texas has a capacity of 2400. The business owners of this detention center have a US government contract through 2021. In 2015, it was estimated that the cost for this facility was $233 to $300 per person per day. In the company's 2016 10–K Report, this detention facility was listed under "Development and Expansion Opportunities" and, just a few pages later, the report states that strong government regulation of these facilities keeps profit margins lower.[23] This company also owns a number of for-profit prisons, so a direct connection exists between asylum seekers, immigrants, and prisoners. The greed of these systems and the mistreatment of the lives involved continues to lead to extreme oppression, trauma, and death.

In response to the heightening of family separations and immigrant criminalization at the Mexico/US border BCTS and ACHTUS issued a bilingual joint statement on the treatment of families at the US/Mexico Border lifting up biblical traditions which "measure justice according to society's care for the most vulnerable" and supporting legislation and policies "that sustain union between all loved ones crossing any of our international borders."[24] Because of *lo/the familiar*, *mujerista* and Latina feminist theologies will continue to clamor and struggle against these systems. The clamor and struggle comes because we are the scholars who have lived these migratory struggles; have lost livelihood from closed factories; have loved ones in prison or may have served time in prison even before a conviction or sentence; live with corporate executives who make the hardest decisions of who will lose a job due to new tariff codes; worship with foster parents helping their foster children to find parents who have been deported; teach those who fear daily because their documents are not recognized by the USA government.

La Chingona

Popular culture has picked-up the term *"chingona"* to mean "a mujer who is intelligent, fearless, and can get these things done. Also see 'Boss' or 'Badass'."[25] One can purchase buttons, tote bags, t-shirts downing the word. With this specific definition, one even finds and small business entrepreneurial venture.[26] Latina feminist and *mujerista* theologies highlight *la chingona* of Latinas.

As Sandra Cisneros articulates:

> It takes a long time for women to feel it's alright to be chingona. To aspire to be a chingona! We outta give lessons on how to be a Chingona in ten easy steps, right? You are saying, "This is my camino, this is my path and I'm gonna follow it, regardless of what culture says." I don't think the church likes chingonas. I don't think the state likes chingonas! And fathers definitely do not like chingonas. And boyfriends don't like chingonas.[27]

A scholar could add to this quote—the academy does not like *chingonas*.[28]

To be a *chingona* connotes large levels of power over one's own life. The theological perspectives of women clamoring for life and living in *la lucha* both possess the agency of Latinas in their own lives. The term *"chingona"* may also be understood as a crude way for describing a woman engaging in the sexual act. For a woman to claim this for herself means that she has taken agency for her body and that which she does with her body as well as what she allows others to do with her body. Engaging in these sexual acts is theological and doing theology from the perspectives of Latina feminist theologies means engaging our sexuality.[29] *Mujerista* and Latina feminist theologies feature agency, determination, and power over and against oppression and domination.

As examples from *lo cotidiano* about being *chingonas*, I share mas *cuentitos* from labor. I checked into a hotel room very early at 9:30 am to continue working on this chapter. Staying at this hotel probably violated most of my moral codes, but this hotel offered a number of amenities I needed to get this chapter finished, including an extremely early check-in. I checked into my room at 9:30 am As I arrived on the ninth floor, two women were cleaning rooms. When I went to key-in to my room, one of the women, Berta, walked over to me. Berta is about sixty years old. She held a tea bag. She struggled to tell me in English why she was holding this tea bag. Once we both confirmed that we spoke Spanish, Berta explained that she had forgotten to place the green tea bag in my room because each room takes a purple tea bag and a green tea bag. Such minimal details from my perspective because I just check-in to hotel rooms and take whatever is placed there. I do it often and sadly, with little reflection. Until that moment, I had never thought that an important detail to someone's job was to place one green and one purple tea bag next to the coffee pot.

Later that morning, I went down the hall to the ice machine. Berta saw me in the hallway and started talking with me about the difficulty of the work and the extremely high expectations of the job. Some might see this action as someone just complaining, but

I took it as Berta speaking up for herself and for the rest of the housekeeping staff to someone who both understood her and might actually do something about it. She assessed the moment and knew she could speak out against what was unjust about the treatment in this particular hotel. If I had complained about the missing tea bag, she would have been reprimanded or, even worse, lost her job. Instead, I could comment to the hotel management and owners about the positives of the work the housekeepers are doing as well as how they should be treated regarding fair labor practices. Berta took the opportunity to make me see the importance of the finest of details and how these details become so important for so many lives. She took hold of the entire moment to speak out against injustice. She exemplifies being a *chingona*.

On another occasion, I was at a restaurant and was being served by a young woman whose nametag read "Yesenia." She took great pride in her job. She made sure the restaurant was very clean and that the customers' needs were all met. She began speaking with me because few people in the restaurant spoke Spanish. She told me she was seventeen and working this job to help her mom and younger siblings financially. She told me about how she wanted to go to culinary school and own her own restaurant one day. Then she told me that when she owns her own restaurant, she will listen to her employees. Which quickly led me to ask if she was being mistreated. She said that she was not being mistreated but that she had repeatedly asked the restaurant manager to change her nametag because her name was misspelled. Her name was actually "Jesenia" not "Yesenia." She explained to me that her own name is very important and that the misspelling was a real disrespect to her. Jesenia also told me that her mother had given her that name with that spelling, so she would stand out in a crowd. She understood the power and importance of claiming a name for oneself. Then, she asked me to go to the website of the restaurant's website and Yelp and write a review asking for her nametag to be changed. Jesenia had thought through this entire system for how to get her proper nametag. She was just waiting for her accomplice! Jesenia is constructing her path. She finds ways to get past the obstacles, the limitations, the oppressions. She challenged me to be a *chingona* in her life path.

CONCLUSION

Latina feminist and *mujerista* theologies function as *tejedoras* who interweave many aspects of life. We bring out *la chingona* to clamor and struggle against oppression. Through the naming and engagement of our own categories, we walk with the daily pain, suffering, joys, anxieties, melancholy, elations of members of our own communities. We work toward systemic change in church, society, and academy because of *lo/the familiar*. Some may call these moves political or public theology. In the end what stands out is that *en conjunto* through self-naming, the particular, *lo popular*, *lo cotidiano*, *mujerista*, and Latina feminist theologians seek "*un poquito de justicia*" in opening paths for new life. Many more scholars are needed to engage these ways of theologizing from their own various perspectives for both the academy and society and to continue these underserved and under-sourced possibilities for the expansion of life.

NOTES

1. For more on framings of domination, see Gloria Anzaldua, *Borderlands La Frontera: The New Mestiza, 25th Anniversary* (San Francisco, CA: Aunt Lute Books, 2007), 53.

2. I do not italicize Spanish or Spanglish. I do not differentiate Spanish or Spanglish as foreign or unknown languages. Spanish was the first language used for publication in what is now the USA. In many places found within the borders and territories of the USA, Spanish is used as much as, if not more than, English still today. Spanglish is a creation of ~~LatinoXas~~ (see note 13 on this term) and is commonly used as a way to go between English and Spanish for those who live these realities. Finally, I was raised fully bilingual in the USA. I do not understand Spanish as a foreign language. To italicize Spanish, therefore, perpetuates the sins of English colonization on ~~LatinoXas~~. However, in keeping with stylistic guidelines employed in this published collection, the editor has chosen to italicize Spanish and Spanglish terms in order to have stylistic consistency throughout the volume.

3. At best, Latinas receive second-class citizenship in the USA due to a variety of factors stemming from racism, sexism, and heterosexism. At worst, the systems of the USA treat Latinas as less than human and disposable.

4. See Daniel S. Richter, *Cosmopolis: Imagining Community in Late Classical Athens and the Early Roman Empire* (Oxford: Oxford University Press, 2011).

5. "ACHTUS/BCTS Statement Regarding the Most Recent Surge in Racist Hate Crimes in the United States" promulgated September 4, 2017, http://www.achtus.us/news/ (accessed August 10, 2018)

6. Teresa Delgado, "Prophesy Freedom: Puerto Rican Women's Literature as a Source for Latina Feminist Theology," in *A Reader in Latina Feminist Theology: Religion and Justice*, eds. María Pilar Aquino, Daisy L. Machado, and Jeanette Rodriguez (Austin, TX: University of Texas Press, 2002), 25.

7. María Pilar Aquino, *Our Cry for Life: Feminist Theology from Latin America* (Maryknoll, NY: Orbis Books, 1993).

8. Ada María Isasi-Díaz, *En la Lucha/In the Struggle: Elaborating a* Mujerista *Theology*, Second Edition (New York: Fortress Press, 2004), 178.

9. Sandra Cisneros, "Tenemos Layaway, or, How I Became an Art Collector," in *A House of My Own: Stories from My Life* (New York: Vintage, 2015).

10. Ada María Isasi-Díaz, "Mujeristas: A Name of Our Own!!" *Christian Century*, 107, no. 11 (May 1989): 560. María Pilar Aquino, Daisy L. Machado, and Jeanette Rodriguez, *A Reader in Latina Feminist Theology: Religion and Justice* (Austin, TX: University of Austin Press, 2002), xiv.

11. See Ada María Isasi-Díaz, *Mujerista Theology: A Theology for the Twenty-First Century* (Maryknoll, NY: Orbis Books, 1996); Ada María Isasi-Díaz, "A New Mestizaje/Mulatez: Reconceptualizing Difference," in *A Dream Unfinished: Theological Reflection on America from the Margins*, eds. Eleazar S. Fernández and Fernando F. Segovia (Eugene, OR: Wipf & Stock, 2001), 203–219; Michelle Gonzalez, *Afro-Cuban Theology: Religion, Race, Culture, and Identity* (Gainsville, FL: University Press of Florida, 2006). For an expanded analysis on conceptualizations and uses of mestizaje, see Néstor Medina, *Mestizaje: Remapping Race, Culture, and Faith in Latina/o Catholicism.* (Maryknoll, NY: Orbis Books, 2009).

12. Ada María Isasi-Díaz, *Mujerista Theology* (Maryknoll, NY: Orbis Books, 1996), 105–108.

13. As stated in Jeremy Cruz, Neomi De Anda, and Néstor Medina, "Respondiendo a las Demandas Históricas: Analysis of the Transformative Legacy of Samuel Ruiz García of Chiapas, México," *Journal of Hispanic/Latino Theology* 19, no. 1 (November 2013): 5; "We have chosen to use this format to signify the naming of our complex realities for the following reasons. The inclusive "a" and "o" point to the need to omit an often created gender binary and allows for more fluidity as the "X" can also be seen as briding the "o" and "a" together . . . The think horizontal line symbolizes that no matter which descriptor is used for identifying our communities, none fully engage/reveal the complexity of realities.

We understand the aforementioned list to be descriptive and limited not prescriptive and all encompassing." The online publication of this term allowed for multiple colors which signify "the diversity of our communities with particular attention to race, ethnicity and sexuality." I now add that the "X" can also be seen as annihilating the need for a gender binary or gendering all together.

14. "Glossary," in *From the Heart of Our People*, eds. Orlando O. Espín and Miguel H. Díaz (Maryknoll, NY: Orbis Books, 1999), 263.
15. Ada María Isasi-Díaz, "Lo Cotidiano: A Key Element of Mujerista Theology," *Journal of Hispanic/Latino Theology* 10, no. 1 (August 2002): 5–17.
16. Carmen M. Nanko-Fernández, "Lo Cotidiano as Locus Theologicus" in *The Wiley Blackwell Companion to Latino/a Theology*, ed. Orlando O. Espín (Hoboken, NJ: Wiley Blackwell, 2015), 17.
17. Neomi De Anda and Néstor Medina, "Convivencias: What Have We Learned? Toward a Latino/a Ecumenical Theology" in *Building Bridges, Doing Justice: Constructing A Latino/a Ecumenical Theology*, ed. Orlando O. Espín (Maryknoll, NY: Orbis Books, 2009), 185.
18. For an extended discussion on this notion see Daisy L. Machado, "History and Latino/a Identity: Mapping a Past That Leads to Our Future" in *The Wiley Blackwell Companion to Latino/a Theology*, ed. Orlando O. Espín (Hoboken, NJ: Wiley Blackwell, 2015), 35–52. Also, Los Tigres del Norte's song "De América Yo Soy" describes this reality well.
19. María Teresa Davila. "Introduction," at Panel on Puerto Rico at AAR/SBL 2017, November 19, 2017.
20. Daisy Flores Gámez, "Pope Francis in Mexico: Meeting with the World of Labour," https://www.youtube.com/watch?v=FXeUU_ZoJ-A&list=PLC9tK3J1RlaYEG9DdLtKljIcPvPq1-mQx&index=92+eRemarks&t=720 (accessed August 10, 2018). Written translation, https://politicaltheology.com/speeches-of-two-women-frame-pope-francis-visit-to-the-us-mexico-border-neomi-deanda-and-nestor-medina/ (accessed August 13, 2018).
21. Hope Border Institute, "Faces of Trade: María Guadalupe Ortega Gonzalez: Worked at various Juárez maquilas for 11 years," https://www.hopeborder.org/stop-the-trans-pacific-partnership (accessed August 13, 2018).
22. Evelia Quintana Molina speech at "Pope Francis in Mexico: Visit to the Penitentiary of Ciudad Juárez," https://www.youtube.com/watch?v=-oXaW2H0m5Q&list=PLC9tK3J1RlaYEG9DdLtKljIcPvPq1-mQx&index=93Remarks&t=1800 (accessed August 10, 2018). Written translation, https://politicaltheology.com/speeches-of-two-women-frame-pope-francis-visit-to-the-us-mexico-border-neomi-deanda-and-nestor-medina/ (accessed August 13, 2018).
23. CoreCivic 2016, "Report form 10-K" pp. 24, 34–35.
24. "ACHTUS/BCTS Statement on the Treatment of Families at the USA/Mexico Border" promulgated June 21, 2018, http://www.achtus.us/news/ (accessed August 13, 2018).
25. @ChingonaDefinition, https://medium.com/@CoachellaUninc/chingona-definition-reclaiming-what-it-means-to-be-a-fearless-latina-ce904efa4be2 (accessed August 8, 2018).
26. https://chingonadefinition.com (accessed July 21, 2018).
27. Sandra Cisneros, "The Latino List," released September 29, 2011 at HBO Latino, Falls Church, VA. Video, 38:50–39:25.
28. Néstor Medina, Facebook message to author, August 10, 2018.
29. For a longer analysis on the complexities of sexuality, especially the violence against women, see María Pilar Aquino, *Our Cry for Life: Feminist Theology from Latin America* (Maryknoll, NY: Orbis Books, 1993), 97–101.

SELECT BIBLIOGRAPHY

Anzaldúa, Gloria (1987), *Borderlands/La Frontera: The New Mestiza*, San Francisco, CA: Aunt Lute Books.

Aquino, María Pilar (1993), *Our Cry for Life: Feminist Theology from Latin America*, Maryknoll, NY: Orbis Books.

Aquino, María Pilar, Daisy L. Machado, and Jeanette Rodríguez (2002), *A Reader in Latina Feminist Theology: Religion and Justice*, Austin, TX: University of Texas Press.

Brazal, Agnes M. and María Teresa Dávila (2016), *Living With(out) Borders: Catholic Theological Ethics on the Migrations of Peoples*, Maryknoll, NY: Orbis Books.

Delgado, Teresa (2017), *A Puerto Rican Decolonial Theology: Prophesy and Freedom*, New York: Palgrave Macmillan.

Espín, Orlando O. (2015), *The Wiley Blackwell Companion to Latino/a Theology*, Oxford: Wiley-Blackwell, 2015.

Gonzalez, Michelle A. (2009), *Embracing Latina Spirituality: A Woman's Perspective*, Cincinnati, OH: St. Anthony Messenger Press.

Hidalgo, Jacqueline M. (2016), *Revelation in Aztlán: Scriptures, Utopias, and the Chicano Movement*, New York: Palgrave Macmillan.

Isasi-Díaz, Ada María (1996), *Mujerista Theology*, Maryknoll, NY: Orbis Books.

Isasi-Díaz, Ada María (2004), *En la Lucha/In the Struggle: Elaborating a Mujerista Theology*, Minneapolis, MN: Fortress Press.

Martell-Otero, Loida I., Zaida Maldonado Perez, and Elizabeth Conde-Frazier (2013), *Latina Evengélicas: A Theological Survey from the Margins*, Eugene, OR: Cascade Books.

Nanko-Fernández, Carmen (2010), *Theologizing en Espanglish: Context, Community, and Ministry*, Maryknoll, NY: Orbis Books.

Pineda, Ana María and Roberto Schreiter (1995), *Dialogue Rejoined: Theology and Ministry in the United States Hispanic Reality,* Collegeville, MN: Liturgical Press.

Pineda-Madrid, Nancy (2012), *Suffering and Salvation in Cuidad Juárez*, Minneapolis, MN: Fortress Press.

Rivera, Mayra (2015), *Poetics of the Flesh*, Durham, NC: Duke University Press.

CHAPTER NINETEEN

Feminist Theologies

RACHEL SOPHIA BAARD

INTRODUCTION

The well-known feminist expression "the personal is political" is rooted in the recognition that issues such as reproductive rights, the "second shift," and violence against women are not merely personal or family issues, and that the feminist movement's political agenda needed to go beyond earlier feminist concerns such as voting rights. It is, as such, the recognition that feminism, no matter which issues it focuses on, is always political. Consequently, a reflection on feminist theology as political theology will go beyond the work of feminist theologians whose work can be seen as part of an explicitly named "political theology" category, such as Dorothee Sölle, whose theology is often associated with the post-Holocaust New Political Theology of Jürgen Moltmann and Johann Baptist Metz.[1] Like post-Holocaust theology and other prophetic forms of political theology that arose in the second half of the twentieth century out of a variety of liberation struggles, feminist theology is prophetic in tone, focused on justice and human flourishing, and critical of the oppressive elements in religious traditions. Feminist theology, well defined by Maria José Rosado-Nunes as the "radical critique of patriarchal reasoning in the field of theology," is characterized by great ideological, theological, ethnic, cultural, religious, and contextual diversity, so much so that one should in fact speak of "feminist theologies."[2] In what follows, I will first provide an overview of that diversity, then suggest a helpful way to map feminist theologies as political theologies, and end with a general perspective on the political concerns of feminist theologies.

MANY SHADES OF PURPLE

In 1895, a committee led by Elizabeth Cady Stanton published *The Woman's Bible*, which contained a strong feminist critique of traditional (Christian) religion, but it was rejected by both traditionalists (for its "scandalous" content), and feminists, who thought it might harm the cause of female suffrage. So the birth of feminist theology as a scholarly field had to wait for the Second Wave feminism of the mid-to-late twentieth century. One of the original feminist theological texts in this period was Valerie Saiving's 1960 essay "The Human Situation: A Feminine View," in which she argued that the classical Christian emphasis on the sin of pride inadequately reflects the realities of women.[3] This started a theological conversation that is still ongoing, in which religious texts, symbols, structures, and practices are critically examined from the perspective of women's experiences, and in which social concerns are addressed from a feminist religious perspective. In the decades since then, feminist theologians such as Judith Plaskow and Susan Nelson Dunfee took

Saiving's critique of classical Christian sin-talk further.[4] Feminist theologians like Sallie McFague and Elizabeth A. Johnson sought new language for God in order to move beyond the traditional patriarchal image of God, while others focused on the figure of Christ, even going as far as asking whether a male Savior can save women (Rosemary Radford Ruether), while yet others moved "beyond God the Father" (Mary Daly) and embraced a Goddess spirituality (Carol Christ).[5] Other classical Christian symbols such as the doctrine of the *imago Dei*, Mariology, and ecclesiology have also been examined critically.[6] The Christian Scriptures, too, have been subjected to a feminist critical hermeneutic, as can be attested by the work of scholars such as Elizabeth Schüssler Fiorenza and Phyllis Trible.[7] A further feminist theological task has been to retrieve silenced voices in the church's tradition.[8] Feminist theologians have also been concerned with public concerns such as the environment and violence against women.[9]

The essentialist assumptions of some of the earlier feminist texts were eventually challenged by new perspectives on the constructed nature of gender. One theologian who has been critical of essentialist assumptions in feminist theology is Marcella Althaus-Reed, whose *Indecent Theology* makes use of poststructuralist, postcolonial, queer, and gender theory to both continue and disrupt feminist and liberation theologies, and to resist heterosexism.[10] Mary McClintock Fulkerson likewise adopts a poststructuralist perspective to argue for a discursive view of the subject of feminism.[11] Serene Jones, while accepting the insights of poststructuralism, nevertheless opts for what she calls "strategic essentialism" that can both avoid the risk of erasing the subject of feminism, and enable broad-based feminist political critique.[12]

By the 1980s the dominance of white women in the feminist movement was challenged by authors such as Audrey Lorde, Alice Walker, Gloria Anzaldúa, and Cherrie Moraga.[13] Alice Walker coined the new term "womanist" to define a "black feminist or feminist of color," who is "[c]ommitted to survival and wholeness of entire people, male *and* female."[14] The term therefore arose out of the need to address the specific gender and racial experiences of African American women. A decade later, the term *mujerista* was coined by Ada María Isasi-Diaz to speak of the specific cultural experiences of Latina women in the United States. Isasi-Diaz argues that feminism has come to be associated with the concerns of white women, and that it is therefore an inadequate concept for the struggles of Latinas. She writes that a *mujerista* "is a Latina who makes a preferential option for herself and her Hispanic sisters, understanding that our struggle for liberation has to take into consideration how racism/ethnic prejudice, economic oppression, and sexism work together and reinforce each other."[15] By making race and class explicit parts of feminist reflection, womanist and *mujerista* theologies offer a broader perspective than some of the earlier (white) feminist theologies, and in fact challenge feminist theologies to be more mindful of the intersections between gender and other identity markers such as race. Womanist and *mujerista* theologians have also made valuable contributions to the process of rethinking religious symbols, often emphasizing community experience as an essential part of reflection on God and Christ.[16]

As important as it is to recognize the distinctiveness of womanist and *mujerista* voices, it is also important to emphasize that feminism does not in fact belong to white women. As we shift our perspective beyond the US context, I suggest that we extend Alice Walker's lovely metaphor that "womanist is to feminist as purple is to lavender" in order to describe the global feminist theological conversation. One might imagine an intricate quilt made up of various shades of purple, lavender, lilac, mauve, periwinkle, violet, and more, constructed by women of different racial/ethnic, national, or religious backgrounds.

Much like the various shapes and colors in a quilt come together to become a thing of beauty and utility, so the political and theological power of the feminist theological conversation lies in its pluriformity.

Latin American feminist theologian María Pilar Aquino argues that the response to the marginalization of Latina feminists by white feminists must not be to give up the term "feminist," but rather to counter the idea that feminism is a white endeavor in the first place.[17] Latin American feminist theologies are moving toward a theological paradigm that is intercultural. In fact, a sense of the intercultural has been present in Latina theologies since the publication of Gloria Anzaldúa's *Borderlands/La Frontera* in 1987, in which she developed the concept of *mestizaje* to express the experience of people living in in-between physical and psychic spaces.[18] Anzaldúa's influence can be seen in Maricel Mena-López and María Pilar Aquino's introductory remarks in the volume *Feminist Intercultural Theology*, that "we ourselves are 'frontier bodies,' because we move among different places." For that reason, they continue, "we proclaim and we celebrate the diversity of the faces of feminism: African American, Amerindian, Latina, Latin American—and every other frontier feminism that is open to the intermingling of wisdoms in the metaphorical space of *Nepantla*."[19] *Nepantla* is the Mexican Nahuatl term for "land in the middle," which once again expresses the idea of hybridity.[20] The hybrid identity of Latina feminist theologies continues in its relationship to postcolonial theology, which, as Michelle Gonzales notes, is a complicated one due to the *mestiza* identity that carries within it the genetic heritage of both colonized and colonizer.[21] Some Latinx theologians have instead embraced a "decolonizing" epistemology, which seeks to decenter Western ways of knowing.[22]

Asian feminist theologies seem to be more comfortable with a postcolonial perspective, although its focus is also in part on decentering Western epistemology.[23] For example, in her book *Postcolonial Imagination and Feminist Theology*, Hong Kong-born theologian Kwok Pui-lan seeks to deconstruct the universalizing of white women's experiences.[24] When speaking of Asian feminist theologies, some care should be taken to avoid cultural essentialism that generates a "generalized, monolithic and ahistorical" image of Asian women.[25] The reality, as Naga/Indian theologian Atola Longkumer notes, is that "there is not one homogenous contextual reality that represents the conventional continent of Asia."[26] Nevertheless, she suggests four common issues that require interrogation from the gender margins within the varied Asian contexts: gender inequality in the church and ecclesial organizations; economic concerns (including issues such as human trafficking); peace building (which would include a focus on gender violence); and inter-religious dialogue.[27] These concerns obviously overlap with feminist concerns in other contexts as well, but given the religious pluralism in Asian contexts, the latter is particularly significant. Indonesian feminist theologian Marianne Katoppo, for example, in one of the first major books in Asian feminist theology, *Compassionate and Free*, expresses her sense of being the other as a Christian woman living in a predominantly Muslim society.[28] Korean theologian Chung Hyun Kyung shifts the focus to poverty as the lived reality of many Asian women, thus highlighting a further central theme in Asian feminist theologies. Chung appropriates the Korean shamanistic term *han-pu-ri* to develop a feminist theological approach which includes listening to women's stories (what she calls the ghost stories that expresses the *han* or suffering of people) for the sake of healing, critical thinking, and change.[29] When it comes to examining doctrine, Asian and Asian-American feminist theologies are often characterized by a focus on Christology, although Mariology and other doctrinal symbols are also examined. Examples would include Grace Ji-Sun Kim's *The Grace of Sophia* and Wonhee Anne Joh's *Heart of the Cross*.[30]

African feminist theologians share many of the concerns of Latina and Asian feminists, and like US womanists, they include race, class, and culture in their analysis. However, as Cameroon-born US theologian Alice Yafeh points out, while the term "womanist" transcends the United States context due to a collective consciousness of race, it is rooted in the distinctive history of slavery in the United States, and as such does not address the specific concerns of African women. Yafeh therefore opts to describe her work as "Afro-Womanist-Feminist," affirming both the key feminist principle of the full humanity of women, and the womanist broadening of that principle to include race and class, but also moving beyond both in order to speak from the colonial experience of women in Africa.[31] South African feminist theologian Roxanne Jordaan makes a similar move to a specific context when she speaks of a distinct black feminist theology that "is lived in the streets of downtrodden Soweto."[32] The mother of African feminist theologians is without a doubt Mercy Amba Oduyoye from Ghana, who has done groundbreaking work in developing an indigenous African feminist theology, and in leading other women theologians in the Circle of Concerned African Feminist Theologians in addressing issues of sexism, racism, gender violence, education, poverty, and the impact of HIV/AIDS on African women.[33] African feminist theologians such as Musa Dube have also been interested in developing African perspectives on the Bible, while others like Elizabeth Amoah have examined doctrinal symbols in light of the specific cultural contexts in Africa.[34]

Christian feminist theologies have so far been fairly dominant in scholarly discourse, in part due to the dominance of American and European scholarship in the field, and in part due to the fact that theology, as opposed to ritual, meditation, or law, has been a major religious expression in Christianity. But feminist theologies are also constructed in other religions, offering valuable insights to the global feminist theological conversation. In what follows, I aim to provide an admittedly limited perspective on the feminist theological conversations within Judaism, Islam, Hinduism, and Buddhism.

Jewish feminist theologians have explored questions regarding women's status in Jewish law, sexuality, the male focus of the Torah, names of God, and the Holocaust, among others. One of the earliest expressions of Jewish feminist theology is a 1982 volume titled *On Being a Jewish Feminist*, in which feminist theologians contributed essays on topics as wide-ranging as "Reactions to a Woman Rabbi" (Laura Geller), "Scenes from the Life of a Jewish Lesbian" (Alice Bloch), and "Steps Toward Feminine Imagery of Deity in Jewish Theology" (Rita Gross), etc.[35] Judith Plaskow's 1990 book *Standing Again at Sinai*, perhaps the first systematic reflection on Judaism from a feminist perspective, focuses on "the absence of women's history and experiences as shaping forces in the Jewish tradition."[36] Recognizing the deeply patriarchal language in which even the justice-oriented prophetic tradition is cloaked, she proposes a re-examination of various themes such as Torah, community, God-images, sexuality, and the Jewish emphasis on repairing the world (*tikkun olam*). Writing nearly a decade later, Rachel Adler, in *Engendering Judaism*, argues that Judaism recognizes that it is affected by social conditions, and as such it can be developed to be more inclusive of women's experiences and concerns. She therefore proposes a "Judaism that men and women recreate and renew together as equals."[37] Jewish feminist theology has also started to make its mark in post-Holocaust theology. In *The Female Face of God in Auschwitz*, Melissa Raphael argues that post-Holocaust theology has largely ignored the specific experiences of women in the death camps. She traces the roots of the Holocaust back to toxic masculinity, and argues that the God concept that died in the camps was that of the omnipotent patriarchal God. In their reliance on each other amidst the horrors of the camps, she says, women experienced the immanent presence of God, the *Shekinah*.[38] Feminist theology is also done within Orthodox Judaism: for example, Tamar Ross' *Expanding the Palace of Torah* examines the implications of women's changed social status for Jewish Orthodoxy, recognizing and embracing both the importance of halachic law in preserving Jewish identity, and the theological challenges posed by feminism.[39] While these five examples are by no means exhaustive, they illustrate some of the themes in Jewish feminist theology, as well as differences and commonalities between Jewish feminists and their Christian and Muslim counterparts.

Muslim feminist theology has to find a way between defending Islam against stereotypes of it as a woman-hating religion, on the one hand, and battling its internal patriarchy, on the other hand. The language of feminism has often (and ironically) been used to justify Western colonial domination of Muslim societies or to oppress Muslim minorities in Western societies, resulting in a reluctance among female Muslims scholars to embrace the terminology of feminism. Nevertheless, as Aysha Hidayatullah notes, there are "powerful connections and synergy between Muslim and non-Muslim efforts to reclaim our various religious traditions as expressions of the full human and moral dignity to women by God."[40] Muslim feminist theologies often attempt to retrieve liberating elements in the tradition. For example, Moroccan sociologist Fatima Mernissi, widely hailed as one of the founders of Islamic feminism, re-examined the position of women in Muslim societies in her 1975 book *The Veil and the Male Elite*, and pointed to evidence in the Sunna that women were influential in the early Muslim community.[41] Similarly, in *Women and Gender in Islam*, Leila Ahmed argues that the gender oppression that is often associated with Muslim societies are not in fact historically rooted in Islam or the Qur'an, but are due to cultural influences.[42] Kecia Ali, in her book *Sexual Ethics and Islam*, while not suggesting that there was ever a pure feminist-friendly Islamic tradition, pleads for the recognition of the complexity within Muslim interpretative traditions, and for responsible interpretative practices.[43] A further important focus in Muslim feminist theology is reinterpreting the Qur'an by doing close analysis of specific terms that have been used against women. An example of this can be found in the work of Amina Wadud, who argues that the controversial verse in Sura 4:34, which apparently advises husbands to beat rebellious wives, is in fact merely descriptive of the context of the time.[44] Azizah al-Hibri takes a more theological route by focusing on the Islamic principle of the oneness of God (*tawḥīd*), to argue that all God's creatures are placed on the same level of subservience to God, therefore implying that the claim that men are superior to women is a form of idolatry.[45]

Unlike the Abrahamic religions, the traditional religions of Asia do not have a single male divinity. In their introduction to *Is the Goddess a Feminist?*, editors Alf Hiltebeitel and Kathleen Erndl note that "[o]f all the world's religions, Hinduism has the most elaborate living Goddess traditions."[46] For Western feminists this could appear to be very attractive, but Tracy Pintchman cautions against Western feminist appropriation of Indian Goddesses in the absence of sufficient cultural understanding.[47] Moreover, it is not clear that the presence of powerful Goddesses is necessarily empowering to women. One example of that ambivalence can be found in the warrior goddess Durga, who is often associated with Indian nationalism as *Bharat Mata* (Mother India). Durga "reverses the normal role for females," as David Kinsley notes, but Cynthis Humes points out that she does not necessarily function as a role model for ordinary women.[48] Moreover, Sunder Rajan reminds us that there are a variety of goddesses in Hinduism (some fierce, some submissive), and warns about the limits of religious symbols for both cross-cultural feminist projects and national politics.[49] A case can be made that the real feminist theology currently taking place within Hinduism is not necessarily explicitly theological, but rather resides in broader feminist work for women's rights.[50] But perhaps the most significant feminist theological development within the sphere of Hinduism has been the rise of Dalit feminism. Dalit women have criticized feminism for focusing on the interests of upper-caste Hindu women and ignoring those of Dalit women. This has led to the formation of organizations such All India Dalit Women's Forum, the National Federation of Dalit Women, and Dalit Solidarity, which focus on the gendered implications of caste based oppression.[51]

There is a significant body of formal feminist scholarship in Buddhism, although much of it is from the West. Rita Gross describes Buddhist feminism as "the radical practice of the co-humanity of women and men."[52] As an essentially non-theistic religion, Buddhism does not have the dominant male divinity that plagues feminists from the Abrahamic traditions, which is one of the reasons why Buddhism is often attractive to Western feminists. But Jean Byrne points to deep and rampant sexism in Buddhism, expressed in its "negative portrayal of women, treatment of women as second class citizens and questioning of women's spiritual capabilities," leading her to conclude that "[i]t is clear that the teachings of Buddhism are not inherently emancipatory."[53] The issue that Byrne sees is that, despite the teaching of non-duality, Buddhism in fact operates with gender dualism. While Byrne's critique suggests that (Western) feminist assumptions about Buddhism's easy affinity with feminism are not quite warranted, that does not preclude the possibility of Buddhist feminist theology, as attested by Sandy Boucher in her essay "Appreciating the Lineage of Buddhist Feminist Scholars."[54]

This is obviously a very brief overview that leaves out more than it includes. Feminist theologies are done, often in less formal ways, in a variety of contexts and spiritual movements that do not necessarily fall under the heading of stereotypical geographical or cultural contexts, or within the major world religions (many of which I have not examined here). But it should be clear that feminist theologies are a form of prophetic political theology aimed at the full inclusion and recognition of women within their religions and societies, however varied. In the next two sections I want to suggest a new way of looking at the prophetic, political task of feminist theologies, and then provide a framework for understanding the political concerns of feminist theologies.

FEMINIST THEOLOGIES AS RHETORICAL THEOLOGIES

It is common (at least when speaking of Christian feminist theologies) to distinguish among more "radical" feminist theologians who leave their tradition behind to embrace a Goddess spirituality, more conservative/reformist feminists who focus primarily on internal religious matters, and more revisionist/reconstructionist feminists who adopt a critically loyal position to their tradition while also focusing more on social concerns. Within such a schema, the first group would seem to withdraw from the world into a subculture, while the second focuses only on religious matters, leaving only the third group to be political. This is not a very helpful distinction for our purposes, since, if the personal is political, then all feminist theologies, no matter their specific focus, are in fact political. Moreover, those distinctions do not necessarily operate within a global and multi-religious feminist theological conversation. It is more helpful to map feminist theologies as political theologies via a rhetorical approach. Political theology is inherently rhetorical, i.e., interested in the praxis that follows upon the creation of theology. This implies a twofold task for prophetic political theologies: criticizing oppressive religious rhetoric and praxis, as well as deliberately aiming at certain praxis outcomes in the construction of religious symbols. Feminist theorist M.E. Hawkesworth identifies four different feminist rhetorical strategies, which can be helpful in mapping the contours of feminist theology as political theology.[55]

First, the tactic of the feminist *rhetoric of oppression* interprets history as a record of atrocities, aiming to break through denial by "providing a pitiless description that forces its own acceptance."[56] One sees this rhetorical strategy in the work of Mary Daly, who speaks of patriarchy as the prevailing "religion" of the entire planet, and calls all religions "parts of the male's shelter against anomie," i.e., women as the projected personifications of "The Enemy."[57] Daly also refers to violence against women as "the various manifestations of Goddess-Murder on this patriarchal planet," the "deep and universal intent to destroy the divine spark in women."[58]

Quite different in tone is the second strategy, that of the feminist *rhetoric of difference*, which is rooted in claims of women's specific moral endowments and the value of women's traditional activities. The rhetoric of difference often operates with the French feminist concept of *différence*, which states that "the sexed embodiedness of women repressed by the phallic order must be reclaimed by the creation of a place for the feminine in language."[59] Another version of this kind of rhetoric can be seen in the work of scholars such as Carol Gilligan, whose landmark book *In a Different Voice* argues that the relationality traditionally associated with women should form the basis of ethics.[60] In its positive valuation of women's traditional activities and bodies, the rhetoric of difference promises wholeness through the recovery of the repressed. A reversed version of this strategy can be seen when feminist theologians (e.g., Valerie Saiving) emphasize the particular sins to which women are prone, in order to construct theology that reflects and can address the whole human experience.

Perhaps the most commonly used feminist rhetorical strategy is that of the *rhetoric of reason*, which focuses on exposing and correcting misinformation about women contained in classic texts, and often emphasizes the principle of equality.[61] An example of this rhetorical strategy would be Rosemary Radford Ruether's focus on the underlying dualistic thought patterns in Western thought, which contributes to the devaluing of the body and as such to the oppression of women, but also to anti-Semitism, racism, and ecological irresponsibility.[62] Likewise, feminist theologians aiming at exposing patriarchal rhetoric or androcentric assumptions in scriptures or scriptural interpretation, such as Elizabeth Schüssler Fiorenza or Amina Wadud, utilize a version of this strategy.

Hawkesworth favors a fourth feminist rhetorical strategy, which she calls the *rhetoric of vision*. This strategy combines many aspects of the other feminist rhetorical strategies, such as the recognition of language as a powerful ideological weapon, and the simultaneous recognition of both women's unique traits and contributions, and their equality to men in worth and human dignity. This strategy combines the more critical strategies with a constructive aim, targeting the imagination as the primary site of ideological struggle. Because it sees the recoding of dominant cultural symbols as the key to social transformation, the rhetoric of vision is consciously engaging in the literary production of reality. The strength of this approach is that it creates some space in our conceptual and perceptual worlds "within which women can expand their subversive activities."[63] In targeting the imagination as the site of struggle, the rhetoric of vision recognizes that misogyny is rooted in more than ignorance. In viewing language as a powerful force, it recognizes the political nature of discourse. Various forms of such a visionary strategy can be discerned in most feminist theologies, particularly in constructive theological work.

Examples would include Elizabeth A. Johnson's reimagining of God-language in terms of the concept of divine Sophia (wisdom), or Rachel Adler's vision of an engendered Judaism in which women are full participants.

Hawkesworth's analysis of different feminist rhetorical strategies is helpful insofar as it enables us to analyze the mechanisms and ends of seemingly opposing types of feminist discourse. It also supports a reading of feminist theology as political theology, since rhetoric places emphasis on the practical outcomes of language—both critically examining the practical effects of sexist rhetoric, and rhetorically proposing better practical outcomes. That raises the question, which practical outcomes are feminists concerned with?

FEMINIST CONCERNS

One handy way of looking at the political concerns of feminist theologies is via Iris Marion Young's "five faces of oppression": exploitation, marginalization, powerlessness, cultural imperialism, and violence.[64] Exploitation occurs when the people who produce social goods do not share fully in the accumulated benefits of labor. Things such as the wage gap, the "second shift," or the fact that traditionally "female" jobs are usually deemed less worthy of compensation are all indicative of this face of oppression in the lives of women. The most extreme forms of exploitation of women usually occurs when gender constructs intersect with racial or class constructs, resulting in practices such as the exploitation of poor women of color in slavery, underpaid domestic service, or sweatshops. This "ideology of exploitation," argues Rosemary Radford Ruether, is linked to dualistic thought patterns that denigrate women.[65]

Young's second "face" of oppression, marginalization, refers to a permanent underclass of the despised underemployed or unemployed. Marginalization frequently occurs along racial lines, and often hits the elderly, persons with disabilities, single mothers, or members of the LGBTQ community. Although Young identifies marginalization primarily in economic terms, it also has cultural and religious aspects. For example, Stephen Ray singles out marginalization as one of the primary results of a skewed understanding of sin, since "the cultural discourse about sin has increasingly focused . . . on the actions of persons and groups within society who have the least social power."[66] Conversely, the language of sin can create a social underclass as those who are associated with moral irresponsibility are pushed to the margins. An example of this is the scapegoating of persons with AIDS, which associates those who have contracted the HIV virus with particular sinfulness, thus creating and justifying their marginalization.[67] Another obvious example of religious marginalization can be seen in the Hindu caste system's creation of an entire human category of "untouchables."

Thirdly, women of all economic and racial groups also experience powerlessness to a lesser or greater degree. This face of oppression has to do with who has a voice and who does not, who makes decisions, and who follows orders. Powerlessness is made up of both structural elements (economic disparities, lack of access to education, slavery, etc.), and cultural elements (the creation of a culture of silence even to the point where the oppressed believe that they have no right to control their fate or to speak up). In most of the world's religions, men hold the power, and in many cases, women are directly admonished to be submissive and silent. As a result, one of the central concerns of the feminist movement, and of feminist theologies, is the empowerment of women, both by seeking structural change and by forming supportive communities that can help women overcome internalized powerlessness.

Young identifies the fourth face of oppression as cultural imperialism, i.e., the universalization of the dominant group's experience and the stereotyping and othering of non-dominant groups. A form of this oppression occurs in religions when men are taken to be the norm (androcentrism), which not only reinforces a sense of powerlessness in women, but also depicts women as the "other," often to the point of justifying violence against women (e.g., the witch hunts).[68]

Young defines the fifth face of oppression, *violence*, in terms of the vulnerability of some social groups to the constant and systematic social practice of violence. Those in targeted groups live with the constant fear of seemingly random, unprovoked attacks on their persons or property. Police shootings of black men, violence against LGBTQ individuals or groups, and violence against women are all examples of this kind of violence. Such violence is employed as an enforcement of the exploitation, marginalization, powerlessness, and cultural imperialism faced by these groups—it is, in other words, violence done for the purpose of social control. This can take the form of state-sanctioned violence in the name of the law (e.g., the enforcement of segregation laws in the United States until the 1960s, or strict interpretations of sharia law in Saudi Arabia), but it can also occur outside of the law while expressing and effecting control of subjugated groups by dominant groups.[69] In fact, violence against women should be seen as a patriarchal control mechanism, since it is systemic and rooted in sexist cultural practices and perspectives, and it leads women to adjust behavior in order to avoid violence.

Although Young's analysis has its limits, it does provide a handy way to point to the different types of oppression that women experience, which shape the political concerns of feminist theologies. The details will differ from context to context, but the reality is that violence against women, the relative powerlessness of women in their specific contexts, the way women's voices are often silenced in their religions and societies, the economic exploitation of women, and the marginalization of women to various degrees in religion and society are issues of concern for feminist theologians across contexts. When doctrinal symbols, holy writ, or religious practices and structures are critically examined, it is with these concerns in mind: how can these symbols, scriptures, rituals, and religious structures be changed in order to address the oppression of women and create religions and societies in which women are recognized as fully human, fully entitled to respect and equal treatment, and in which traditionally female traits can be recognized as valuable (but without thereby stereotyping women either)? At the same time feminist theologies have also brought specific feminist insights to issues of social concern, such as the ecological crisis, and it has added valuable insights to the different religions' self-understanding. Feminist theology is still a relatively young scholarly field. The feminist theological conversation is expanding at a rapid rate as the voices of women all over the world join the conversation. Together, these voices, rooted in the wisdom of the ancients but also critical of the exclusions in that ancient wisdom, and speaking with the voice of the prophets, speak up for justice for themselves, for their communities, and for the world.

NOTES

1. Dorothee Sölle, *Political Theology* (Minneapolis, MN: Fortress Press, 1974).
2. Maria José Rosado-Nunes, "New Paradigms in Feminist Theological Thought: The Longing for a Just World," in *Feminist Intercultural Theology: Latina Explorations for a Just World*, eds. María Pilar Aquino and Maria José Rosado-Nunes (Maryknoll, NY: Orbis, 2007), 1.

3. Valerie Saiving, "The Human Situation: A Feminine View," *The Journal of Religion* 40:2 (1960): 100–112.
4. Judith Plaskow, *Sex, Sin, and Grace: Women's Experience and the Theologies of Reinhold Niebuhr and Paul Tillich* (New York: University Press of America, 1980); Susan Nelson Dunfee, "The Sin of Hiding: A Feminist Critique of Reinhold Niebuhr's Account of the Sin of Pride," *Soundings* 65 (Fall 1982), 316–327. (Although Plaskow is a prominent Jewish feminist theologian, she has also made her mark in conversation with Christian theology.)
5. Sallie McFague, *Models of God: Theology for an Ecological, Nuclear Age* (Minneapolis, MN: Fortress, 1987); Elizabeth A. Johnson, *She Who Is: The Mystery of God in Feminist Theological Discourse* (New York: Crossroad, 1995); Rosemary Radford Ruether, *Sexism and God-Talk: Toward a Feminist Theology* (Boston: Beacon, 1983); Mary Daly, *Beyond God the Father: Toward a Philosophy of Women's Liberation* (Boston: Beacon, 1973); Carol P. Christ, *Rebirth of the Goddess: Finding Meaning in Feminist Spirituality* (New York: Routledge, 1997).
6. See, for example, Mary Catherine Hilkert, "Cry the Beloved Image: Rethinking the Image of God," in *In the Embrace of God: Feminist Approaches to Theological Anthropology*, ed. Ann O'Hara Graff (Maryknoll, NY: Orbis, 1995), 190–205; Elizabeth A. Johnson, *Truly Our Sister: A Theology of Mary in the Communion of Saints* (New York: Continuum, 2004); and Letty M. Russell, *Church in the Round: Feminist Interpretation of the Church* (Louisville, KY: Westminster John Knox, 1993).
7. Elizabeth Schüssler Fiorenza, *In Memory of Her: A Feminist Theological Reconstruction of Christian Origins* (New York: Crossroad, 1998), and *But She Said: Feminist Practices of Biblical Interpretation* (Boston: Beacon, 1992), among others; Phyllis Trible, *Texts of Terror: Literary-Feminist Readings of Biblical Narratives* (Minneapolis, MN: Fortress, 1984).
8. E.g., Rosemary Radford Ruther, *Visionary Women: Three Medieval Mystics* (Minneapolis, MN: Fortress, 2001).
9. Rosemary Radford Ruther, *Gaia and God: An Ecofeminist Theology of Earth Healing* (San Francisco, CA: Harper, 1994); Marie M. Fortune, *Sexual Violence: The Unmentionable Sin* (Cleveland, OH: Pilgrim Press, 1983).
10. Marcella Althaus-Reed, *Indecent Theology: Theological Perversions in Sex, Gender and Politics* (New York: Routledge, 2000).
11. Mary McClintock Fulkerson, *Changing the Subject: Women's Discourses and Feminist Theology* (Eugene, OR: Wipf & Stock, 2001).
12. Serene Jones, *Feminist Theory and Christian Theology: Cartographies of Grace* (Minneapolis, MN: Fortress, 2000), 45. On the two problems mentioned, see Nancy Hartsock, "Rethinking Modernism: Minority vs. Majority Theories," *Cultural Critique* 7 (Fall 1987): 196, and Nancy Fraser and Linda Nicholson, "Social Criticism without Philosophy: An Encounter between Feminism and Postmodernism," in *Feminism/Postmodernism*, ed. Linda J. Nicholson (New York: Routledge, 1990), 23.
13. Cherríe Moraga and Gloria Anzaldúa, eds., *This Bridge Called My Back: Writings by Radical Women of Color* (Watertown, MA, 1981); Audrey Lorde, *Sister Outsider: Essays and Speeches* (Trumansburg, NY: Crossing Press, 1984); Alice Walker, *In Search of Our Mothers' Gardens: Womanist Prose* (New York: Harcourt, 1983).
14. Walker, *In Search of Our Mothers' Gardens*, xi (italics original).
15. Ada María Isasi-Díaz, *En La Lucha/In the Struggle: Elaborating a Mujerista Theology* (Minneapolis, MN: Fortress Press, 2004), 23. The first edition, published in 1993, was titled *En La Lucha/In the Struggle: A Hispanic Women's Liberation Theology*.
16. See, e.g.: Delores S. Williams, *Sisters in the Wilderness: The Challenge of Womanist God-Talk* (Maryknoll, NY: Orbis, 1993); Jacquelyn Grant, *White Women's Christ and*

Black Women's Jesus: Feminist Christology and Womanist Response (Atlanta, GA: Scholars Press, 1989); Ada María Isasi-Díaz, "Identifícate con Nosotras: A Mujerista Christological Understanding," in *La Lucha Continues: Mujerista Theology* (Maryknoll, NY: Orbis, 2004).

17. María Pilar Aquino, Daisy L. Machado, and Jeanette Rodriguez, eds., *A Reader in Latina Feminist Theology: Religion and Justice* (Austin, TX: University of Texas Press, 2002), 135.
18. Gloria Anzaldúa, *Borderlands/La Frontera: The New Mestiza* (San Francisco, CA: Aunt Lute Books, 1987).
19. Maricel Mena-López and María Pilar Aquino, "Feminist Intercultural Theology: Religion, Culture, Feminism, and Power (Symposium Abstract)," in *Feminist Intercultural Theology*, xv.
20. Daisy L. Machado, "Voices from *Nepantla*: Latinas in U.S. Religious History," in *Feminist Intercultural Theology*, 96.
21. Michelle A. Gonzales, "Who is Americana/o: Theological Anthropology, Postcoloniality, and the Spanish-Speaking Americas," in *Postcolonial Theologies: Divinity and Empire*, eds. Catherine Keller, Michael Nausner, and Mayra Rivera (St. Louis, MO: Chalice Press, 2004), 64.
22. Ada María Isasi-Díaz and Eduardo Mednieta, eds., *Decolonizing Epistemologies: Latina/o Theology and Philosophy* (New York: Fordham University Press, 2012).
23. With regards to the term "feminist," it is worth noting that while it is often used in Asian women's theologies, it is not without hesitation. Kwok Pui-lan notes that she continues to use the term "feminist" because she does not think that any group should have a monopoly on it, and that "[f]emale theologians in Asia have not conjured up another name for the kind of theology they are doing because there is no common language we can use together," although the term "feminist" is not without its problems for Asian women theologians due to "connotations of a militant, man-hating, and separatist stance of some women in the West (Kwok Pui-lan, "The Future of Feminist Theology: An Asian Perspective," in *Feminist Theology from the Third World: A Reader*, ed. Ursula King (Maryknoll, NY: Orbis, 1994), 65).
24. Kwok Pui-lan, *Postcolonial Imagination and Feminist Theology* (Louisville, KY: Westminster John Knox, 2005).
25. Kwok Pui-lan, *Introducing Asian Feminist Theology* (Cleveland, OH: Pilgrim Press, 2000). See also Namsoon Kang, "Re-constructing Asian Feminist Theology: Toward a Global Feminist Theology in an Era of Neo-Empire(s)," in *Christian Theology in Asia*, ed. Sebastian C.H. Kim (Cambridge: Cambridge University Press, 2008), 205–226.
26. Atola Longkumer, "Doing Asian Women's Theology," in *The Ecumenical Review* 66:1 (2014): 84. Atola Longkumer hails from Nagaland, which is part of India, but culturally and ethnically distinct—as such, her own ethnicity and location illustrate her point well.
27. Ibid., 88–92.
28. Marianna Katoppo, *Compassionate and Free: An Asian Woman's Theology* (Maryknoll, NY: Orbis, 1980), 1–6.
29. Chung Hyun Kyung, "'Han-pu-ri': Doing Theology from Korean Women's Perspective," in *Ecumenical Review*, 40 (January 1988): 27–36. See also her *Struggle to be the Sun Again* (Maryknoll, NY: Orbis, 1990).
30. Grace Ji-Sun Kim, *The Grace of Sophia: A Korean North American Women's Christology* (Eugene, OR: Wipf & Stock, 2010); Wonhee Anne Joh, *Heart of the Cross: A Postcolonial Christology* (Louisville, KY: Westminster John Knox, 2006).
31. Alice Yafeh, *Paul's Sexual and Marital Ethics in 1 Corinthians 7: An African-Cameroonian Perspective* (New York: Peter Lang, 2015), 154–155.

32. Roxanne Jordaan and Thoko Mpumlwana, "Two Voices on Women's Oppression and Struggle in South Africa," in *Feminist Theology from the Third World*, 154.
33. For an introduction to Oduyoye's work and to African feminist theologies in general, see Mercy Amba Odyoye, *Introducing African Women's Theology* (Sheffield: Sheffield University Press, 2001).
34. Musa W. Dube, *Postcolonial Feminist Interpretation of the Bible* (St. Louis, MO: Chalice, 2000); Thérèse Souga and Louise Tappa, "The Christ-Event from the Viewpoint of African Women," and Elizabeth Amoah and Mercy Amba Oduyoye, "The Christ for African Women," in *With Passion and Compassion: Third World Women Doing Theology*, eds. Virginia Fabella and Mercy Amba Oduyoye (Maryknoll, NY: Orbis, 1989), 22–34, 35–46.
35. Susannah Heschel, ed., *On Being a Jewish Feminist: A Reader* (New York: Schocken Books, 1982). (Rita Gross is better known as a Buddhist feminist theologian, but at the time of this publication, Gross was practicing Judaism.)
36. Judith Plaskow, *Standing Again at Sinai: Judaism from a Feminist Perspective* (San Francisco, CA: Harper, 1990), 1.
37. Rachel Adler, *Engendering Judaism: An Inclusive Theology and Ethics* (Boston: Beacon, 1999), xiv.
38. Melissa Raphael, *The Female Face of God in Auschwitz: A Jewish Feminist Theology of the Holocaust* (New York: Routledge, 2003).
39. Tamar Ross, *Expanding the Palace of Torah: Orthodoxy and Feminism* (Waltham, MA: Brandeis University Press, 2004).
40. Aysha Hidayatullah, "Inspiration and Struggle: Muslim Feminist Theology and the Work of Elisabeth Schüssler Fiorenza," *Journal of Feminist Studies in Religion* 25:1 (2009), 163.
41. Fatima Mernissi, *The Veil and the Male Elite: A Feminist Interpretation of Women's Rights in Islam*, trans. Mary Jo Lakeland (Cambridge, MA: Perseus Books, [1975], 1991).
42. Leila Ahmed, *Women and Gender in Islam: Historical Roots of a Modern Debate* (New Haven, CT: Yale University Press, 1993).
43. Kecia Ali, *Sexual Ethics and Islam: Feminist Reflections on Qur'an, Hadith and Jurisprudence* (Oxford: OneWorld, 2006).
44. Amina Wadud, *Qur'an and Woman: Rereading the Sacred Text from a Woman's Perspective* (New York: Oxford University Press, 1999), 77.
45. Azizah al-Hibri, "An Introduction to Muslim Women's Rights," in *Windows of Faith: Muslim Scholar-Activists in North America*, ed. Gisela Wenn (Syracuse, NY: Syracuse University Press, 2000), 51–52.
46. Alf Hiltebeitel and Katlheen Erndl, eds., *Is the Goddess a Feminist? The Politics of South Asian Goddesses* (Sheffield: Sheffield Academic Press, 2000).
47. Tracy Pintchman, "Is the Hindu Goddess Tradition a Good Resource for Western Feminism," in *Is the Goddess a Feminist?*, 191–192.
48. David Kinsley, *Hindu Goddesses: Visions of the Divine Feminine in the Hindu Religious Tradition* (Oakland, CA: University of California Press, 1988), 97; Cynthia Humes, "Is the Devi Mahatmya a Feminist Scripture?," in *Is the Goddess a Feminist?*, 144–146.
49. Sunder Rajan, "Real and Imagined Goddesses," in *Is the Goddess a Feminist?*, 281–282.
50. For an overview, see Maitrayee Chaudhuri, *Feminism in India* (London: Zed Books, 2005).
51. Geetanjali Gangoli, *Indian Feminisms: Law, Patriarchies and Violence in India* (New York: Routledge, 2016), 10–12.
52. Rita M. Gross, *Buddhism After Patriarchy: A Feminist History, Analysis, and Reconstruction of Buddhism* (New York: State University of New York Press, 1992), 127.

53. Jean Byrne, "Why I am Not a Buddhist Feminist: A Critical Examination of 'Buddhist Feminism'," *Feminist Theology* 21:2 (2012), 188.
54. Sandy Boucher, "Appreciating the Lineage of Buddhist Feminist Scholars," in *Feminist Theologies: Legacy and Prospect*, ed. Rosemary Radford Ruether (Minneapolis, MN: Fortress, 2007), 117–128.
55. M.E. Hawkesworth, *Beyond Oppression: Feminist Theory and Political Strategy* (New York: Continuum, 1990), 111–129.
56. Ibid., 113.
57. Mary Daly, *Gyn/Ecology: The Metaethics of Radical Feminism* (Boston: Beacon, 1978), 39.
58. Ibid., 315.
59. Ibid., 116.
60. Carol Gilligan, *In a Different Voice: Psychological Theory and Women's Development* (Cambridge, MA: Harvard University Press, [1982], 2016).
61. Hawkesworth, *Beyond Oppression*, 121.
62. See, for example, Rosemary Radford Ruether, *Faith and Fratricide: The Theological Roots of Anti-Semitism* (New York: Seabury Press, 1974), *Sexism and God-Talk: Toward a Feminist Theology* (Boston: Beacon, 1983), and *Gaia and God: An Ecofeminist Theology of Earth Healing* (San Francisco, CA: HarperCollins, 1994).
63. Hawkesworth, *Beyond Oppression* 125.
64. Iris Marion Young, *Justice and the Politics of Difference* (Princeton, NJ: Princeton University Press, 1990).
65. Rosemary Radford Ruther, "Dualism and the Nature of Evil in Feminist Theology," *Studies in Christian Ethics* 5:1 (1992), 26–39.
66. Stephen G. Ray, Jr., *Do No Harm: Social Sin and Christian Responsibility* (Minneapolis, MN: Fortress 2003), 3.
67. See, inter alia, Sarojini Nadar, "'Barak God and Die!' Women, HIV, and a Theology of Suffering," and Malebogo Kgalemang, "John 9: Deconstructing the HIV/AIDS Stigma," in *Grant Me Justice! HIV/AIDS & Gender Readings of the Bible*, eds. Musa W. Dube and Musimbi Kanyoro (Maryknoll, NY: Orbis, 2004), 60–79, 141–168.
68. Stephen Harold Riggins, "The Rhetoric of Othering," in *The Language and Politics of Exclusion: Others in Discourse*, ed. Stephen Harold Riggins (Thousand Oaks, CA: Sage Publications, 19–97), 1–30.
69. Ann E. Cudd, *Analyzing Oppression* (New York: Oxford University Press, 2006), 107.

SELECT BIBLIOGRAPHY

Ahmed, Leila (1993), *Women and Gender in Islam: Historical Roots of a Modern Debate*, New Haven, CT: Yale University Press.

Ali, Kecia (2006), *Sexual Ethics and Islam: Feminist Reflections on Qur'an, Hadith and Jurisprudence*, Oxford: OneWorld.

Althaus-Reed, Marcella (2000), *Indecent Theology: Theological Perversions in Sex, Gender and Politics*, New York: Routledge.

Anzaldúa, Gloria (1987), *Borderlands/La Frontera: The New Mestiza*, San Francisco, CA: Aunt Lute Books.

Aquino, María Pilar and Maria José Rosado-Nunes, eds. (2007), *Feminist Intercultural Theology: Latina Explorations for a Just World*, Maryknoll, NY: Orbis Books.

Aquino, María Pilar, Daisy L. Machado, and Jeanette Rodriguez, eds. (2002), *A Reader in Latina Feminist Theology: Religion and Justice*, Austin, TX: University of Texas Press.
Chaudhuri, Maitrayee (2005), *Feminism in India*, London: Zed Books.
Christ, Carol P. (1997), *Rebirth of the Goddess: Finding Meaning in Feminist Spirituality*, New York: Routledge.
Chung, Hyun Kyung (1990), *Struggle to be the Sun Again*, Maryknoll, NY: Orbis Books.
Daly, Mary (1973), *Beyond God the Father: Toward a Philosophy of Women's Liberation*, Boston: Beacon Press.
Daly, Mary (1978), *Gyn/Ecology: The Metaethics of Radical Feminism*, New York: Continuum.
Dube, Musa W. (2000), *Postcolonial Feminist Interpretation of the Bible*, St. Louis, MO: Chalice Press.
Fabella, Virginia and Mercy Amba Oduyoye, eds. (1989), *With Passion and Compassion: Third World Women Doing Theology*, Maryknoll, NY: Orbis Books.
Fortune, Marie M. (1983), *Sexual Violence: The Unmentionable Sin*, Cleveland, OH: Pilgrim Press.
Fulkerson, Mary McClintock (2001), *Changing the Subject: Women's Discourses and Feminist Theology*, Eugene, OR: Wipf & Stock.
Gilligan, Carol (2016), *In a Different Voice: Psychological Theory and Women's Development*, Cambridge, MA: Harvard University Press.
Grant, Jacquelyn (1989), *White Women's Christ and Black Women's Jesus: Feminist Christology and Womanist Response*, Atlanta, GA: Scholars Press.
Gross, Rita M. (1992), *Buddhism After Patriarchy: A Feminist History, Analysis, and Reconstruction of Buddhism*, New York: State University of New York Press.
Hawkesworth, M.E. (1990), *Beyond Oppression: Feminist Theory and Political Strategy*, New York: Continuum.
Heschel, Susannah, ed. (1982), *On Being a Jewish Feminist: A Reader*, New York: Schocken Books.
Hiltebeitel, Alf and Kathleen Ernd, eds. (2000), *Is the Goddess a Feminist? The Politics of South Asian Goddesses*, Sheffield: Sheffield Academic Press.
Isasi-Díaz, Ada María (2004), *En La Lucha/In the Struggle: Elaborating a Mujerista Theology*, rev. ed., Minneapolis, MN: Fortress Press.
Isasi-Díaz, Ada María and Eduardo Mednieta, eds. (2012), *Decolonizing Epistemologies: Latina/o Theology and Philosophy*, New York: Fordham University Press.
Joh, Wonhee Anne (2006), *Heart of the Cross: A Postcolonial Christology*, Louisville, KY: Westminster John Knox.
Johnson, Elizabeth A. (1995), *She Who Is: The Mystery of God in Feminist Theological Discourse*, New York: Crossroad.
Johnson, Elizabeth A. (2004), *Truly Our Sister: A Theology of Mary in the Communion of Saints*, New York: Continuum.
Jones, Serene (2000), *Feminist Theory and Christian Theology: Cartographies of Grace*, Minneapolis, MN: Fortress Press.
Katoppo, Marianna (1980), *Compassionate and Free: An Asian Woman's Theology*, Maryknoll, NY: Orbis Books.
Kim, Grace Ji-Sun (2010), *The Grace of Sophia: A Korean North American Women's Christology*, Eugene, OR: Wipf & Stock.
King, Ursula, ed. (1994), *Feminist Theology from the Third World: A Reader*, Maryknoll, NY: Orbis Books.
Kwok, Pui-lan (2000), *Introducing Asian Feminist Theology*, Cleveland, OH: Pilgrim Press.

Kwok, Pui-lan (2005), *Postcolonial Imagination and Feminist Theology*, Louisville, KY: Westminster John Knox Press.

Lorde, Audrey (1984), *Sister Outsider: Essays and Speeches*, Trumansburg, NY: Crossing Press.

McFague, Sallie (1987), *Models of God: Theology for an Ecological, Nuclear Age*, Minneapolis, MN: Fortress Press.

Mernissi Fatima (1991), *The Veil and the Male Elite: A Feminist Interpretation of Women's Rights in Islam*, trans. Mary Jo Lakeland, Cambridge, MA: Perseus Books.

Moraga, Cherríe and Gloria Anzaldúa, eds. (1981), *This Bridge Called My Back: Writings by Radical Women of Color*, Watertown, MA: Kitchen Table/Women of Color Press.

Odyoye, Mercy Amba (2001), *Introducing African Women's Theology*, Sheffield: Sheffield University Press.

Plaskow, Judith (1980), *Sex, Sin, and Grace: Women's Experience and the Theologies of Reinhold Niebuhr and Paul Tillich*, New York: University Press of America.

Plaskow, Judith (1990), *Standing Again at Sinai: Judaism from a Feminist Perspective*, San Francisco, CA: Harper.

Raphael, Melissa (2003), *The Female Face of God in Auschwitz: A Jewish Feminist Theology of the Holocaust*, New York: Routledge.

Ross, Tamar (2004), *Expanding the Palace of Torah: Orthodoxy and Feminism*, Waltham, MA: Brandeis University Press.

Ruether, Rosemary Radford (1983), *Sexism and God-Talk: Toward a Feminist Theology*, Boston: Beacon Press.

Ruether, Rosemary Radford (1994), *Gaia and God: An Ecofeminist Theology of Earth Healing*, San Francisco, CA: Harper.

Ruether, Rosemary Radford (2001), *Visionary Women: Three Medieval Mystics*, Minneapolis, MN: Fortress Press.

Russell, Letty M. (1993), *Church in the Round: Feminist Interpretation of the Church*, Louisville, KY: Westminster John Knox.

Schüssler Fiorenza, Elizabeth (1992), *But She Said: Feminist Practices of Biblical Interpretation*, Boston: Beacon Press.

Schüssler Fiorenza, Elizabeth (1998), *In Memory of Her: A Feminist Theological Reconstruction of Christian Origins*, New York: Crossroad.

Sölle, Dorothee (1974), *Political Theology*, Minneapolis, MN: Fortress Press.

Trible, Phyllis (1984), *Texts of Terror: Literary-Feminist Readings of Biblical Narratives*, Minneapolis, MN: Fortress Press.

Wadud, Amina (1999), *Qur'an and Woman: Rereading the Sacred Text from a Woman's Perspective*, New York: Oxford University Press.

Walker, Alice (1983), *In Search of Our Mothers' Gardens: Womanist Prose*, New York: Harcourt.

Williams, Delores S. (1993), *Sisters in the Wilderness: The Challenge of Womanist God-Talk*, Maryknoll, NY: Orbis Books.

Yafeh, Alice (2015), *Paul's Sexual and Marital Ethics in 1 Corinthians 7: An African-Cameroonian Perspective*, New York: Peter Lang.

Young, Iris Marion (1990), *Justice and the Politics of Difference*, Princeton, NJ: Princeton University Press.

CHAPTER TWENTY

The Exodus and Some Possibilities of Jewish Political Thought

GEOFFREY D. CLAUSSEN
AND EMILY A. FILLER

INTRODUCTION

The biblical Book of Exodus, the second book of the Hebrew Bible, opens in Egypt with a description of a small people, the Israelites, becoming a large, oppressed, and enslaved one. When the book closes forty chapters later, the Israelites dwell in the desert: led by Moses, liberated from slavery, and accountable only to the God who has given them the vast body of commandments that will now regulate their communal life. From the wilderness, the Israelites then enter into the land that God has promised, through divinely commanded violence that establishes the people's sovereignty in the land.

Among other things, then, the narrative of the Exodus is a story of the development of the people Israel as a distinctive and defined people, with an exclusive relationship to the God who has brought them into the wilderness and is leading them toward the land this God has promised them. It is surely not surprising, therefore, that among the many biblical narratives, the Exodus stands out as a narrative understood to have broad and enduring political implications: among its chief themes are the constitution of a community, questions of leadership and agency, the striving for land, and the presence of divine and human violence in the achievement of this goal. As contemporary political theorist Michael Walzer observes in *Exodus and Revolution* (1985), his important study of the narrative's political implications, "The Exodus is an event cut to a human scale, and so it echoes not only in the literature of the millennium but also in historical and political literature. If we listen closely to the echoes, we can 'hear' the Exodus as a story of radical hope and this-worldly endeavor."[1]

But while Walzer offers one interpretation of the Exodus, grounded in a particular set of theological and political assumptions, the Jewish tradition has no consensus on the specific political or ethical significance of the narrative's details. This chapter, therefore, seeks to illustrate the breadth of modern Jewish political theology (from the late eighteenth century to the present day) by attending to the diversity of Jewish approaches to the Exodus narrative. By focusing our attention on this foundational narrative of the Jewish tradition, we can concretely illustrate the vastly different meanings that generations of readers have found in this narrative, even when addressing precisely the same passages from the biblical text. This "close reading" approach can serve to illuminate some of the chief challenges and disagreements of modern Judaism's political thought.

Importantly, this study is not intended as a comprehensive account of Jewish interpretations of the Exodus and its political implications. In addition to our focus on modern interpretation in particular, we have also chiefly drawn from theorists in the United States, Europe, and Israel. This chapter does intend, however, to facilitate a more expansive "conversation" between modern interpreters of the Exodus than has previously been done. To this end, the chapter draws upon the work of Jewish philosophers, ethicists, rabbis, political leaders, and theorists in order to bring many more voices into the interpretive endeavor and more fully showcase the diversity of Jewish understandings of the Exodus and its potential political implications and uses.

As an introductory example, consider the opening chapter of the Book of Exodus, which establishes the Israelites' new circumstances and setting. Having journeyed to Egypt in the last chapters of Genesis to join their brother Joseph, who has risen to political power there, the conclusion of Genesis suggests a prosperous future for this growing family of Abraham's descendants. But just eight verses into Exodus, there is an ominous shift: "A new king arose over Egypt who did not know Joseph." Devoid of their connection to the seat of power, the Israelites' circumstances are rapidly and dramatically reduced, as the new Egyptian leadership fears the Israelites' growing numbers: "And he said to his people, 'Look, the Israelite people are much too numerous for us. Let us deal shrewdly with them, so that they may not increase; otherwise in the event of war they may join our enemies in fighting against us and rise from the ground'" (Exodus 1:9–10). In response, the Egyptians seek to limit the Israelites' power and ability to reproduce, both by pressing them into arduous forced labor and by charging the Hebrew midwives to kill boy babies as they are being born (Exodus 1:11–15).

Modern Jewish interpreters have disputed the political significance and normative potential of the text's dramatic opening episode. Some modern readers have argued that this violent opening scene should serve as a dire warning to Jews not to enter into the kind of fear-based demographic battle sparked by Egypt's pharaoh. A contemporary modern Orthodox rabbi in Israel, Avidan Freedman, raises the question of asylum seekers to the State of Israel and the demographic concerns raised by some opponents of asylum, and finds troubling resonance between the two, saying, "The ancient texts are speaking to us. But what are they saying? That we are Pharaoh?"[2] While Freedman hastens to nuance his claim, his invocation of Pharaoh's decree to wrestle with this contemporary political and ethical challenge is instructive. A contemporary Reconstructionist rabbi in the United States, Brant Rosen, asks a similar question, invoking both the colonial American displacement of indigenous peoples and the ongoing Israeli occupation in his reflection on the significance of Pharaoh's fearful attempt to minimize the Israelite threat.[3] For both writers, the narrative of Exodus 1 serves as a fundamental reminder of how modern Jews ought not to think about the lives and needs of others in their midst.

But for other contemporary interpreters, the meaning and significance of this opening text lies in its emphasis on the Israelites' refusal to stop having children, a refusal famously aided, the passage tells us, by the Hebrew midwives' fear of God, as a result of which they "did not do as the king of Egypt had told them; they let the boys live" (Exodus 1:17). In a short essay on the importance of fertility for Jewish national identity, the Israeli scholars Yedidia Stern and Karen Friedman-Stern invoke these opening verses of Exodus in order to argue, controversially, for the importance of maintaining Jewish birthrates, particularly in the modern Israeli state; the writers suggest that this early biblical text has helped to create a Jewish communal commitment to the propagation of children. For Stern and Friedman-Stern, the midwives' legacy is directly inherited by the state when it advances policies that will promote Jewish fertility and ensure a Jewish majority in Israel. In sharp contrast to the authors discussed above, Stern and Friedman-Stern see entering into a "demographic battle" as essential for the state.[4]

From the first verses of the Book of Exodus, therefore, we see the text's distinctive ability to serve as the basis of much modern Jewish political reasoning—and also the consistently and deeply contested nature of this interpretive work. In what follows, we consider at greater length a series of disputed questions in Jewish political thought: What is good leadership? How should we judge violence? May the Exodus be a universal paradigm for liberation? Who is the community of Israel that experienced the Exodus? What is the significance of the covenant between God and the community? What was the purpose of the Exodus? For each of these questions, we seek to showcase some of the debates that have led to divergent approaches to modern Jewish political theology.

WHAT IS GOOD LEADERSHIP?

Among the basic political questions that have been fiercely contested by modern Jews are questions of authority: who should lead political communities, and what are their responsibilities as leaders?[5] While a number of Jewish thinkers have drawn on models of leadership found in the Exodus narrative, especially the model of Moses' leadership, they have understood the implications of the Exodus in very different ways.

For example, the Hasidic rabbi Naḥman of Bratslav, Ukraine (1772–1810) built on traditional kabbalistic sources as he taught how the people of Israel were tasked with purifying Egypt, a task which they could only perform by relying on a *tzaddik*—a figure linking God with God's people and deserving tremendous authority. The first of the Israelites to descend into Egypt, Joseph, had been a *tzaddik* who deserved to rule in Egypt on account of his divine characteristics of sexual restraint; God then sent Moses, a *tzaddik* who even more fully embodied the core aspects of the divine and who completed the process of purifying Egypt.[6] Moses' efforts began with killing an Egyptian taskmaster (Exodus 2:12), whom Naḥman understands as an incarnation of the demonic figure of Cain;[7] they culminated with the passage of the people of Israel through the Sea of Reeds, where the people put aside their pursuit of foreign wisdom and "had faith in the Lord and in His servant Moses" (Exodus 14:31)—and so, in Naḥman's interpretation, unquestioningly accepted Moses's total authority as God's prophet. Naḥman justifies his Hasidic model of political leadership with reference to this moment: Jews today should, likewise, accept the total authority of the rare "tzaddik of the generation," "accepting whatever he says . . . and never sidestepping from what he tells you, neither to right nor to left," purging one's mind of all philosophical thinking and foreign wisdom and instead filling it, "as if you had no mind of your own, only with the knowledge you receive from the tzaddik, the true rabbi."[8]

Other modern Jews who have also seen Moses as a figure who deserves great power have drawn on his story for very different political purposes. Consider an interpretation by Vladimir (Ze'ev) Jabotinsky (1880–1940), the secular Revisionist Zionist leader often regarded as "the father of modern Jewish militarism" and deeply invested in the project of establishing a Jewish-majority nation-state discussed above.[9] Jabotinsky depicts Moses as accused by his fellow Jews of "adventurism" when he impulsively—and rightly—killed the Egyptian taskmaster; Jabotinsky thereby defends Zionist youth who were accused of reckless "adventurism" as they engaged in illegal and sometimes violent acts.[10] Jabotinsky's Moses is not, like Naḥman's Moses, expressing divine attributes and bringing God's purifying flow into the world; God is not a part of Jabotinsky's story, and Jabotinsky's Moses is taking power into his own human hands rather than channeling divine intervention. But just as Naḥman may invoke Moses in seeking to justify his own power as a Hasidic leader, so too Jabotinsky may be asserting his own power as he asserts that, like Moses, he is uniquely able to determine when "adventurism" is appropriate and when it is not.[11]

Others have invoked Moses's leadership not because of its authoritarianism but precisely because of its acceptance of limits. The American political scientist Aaron Wildavsky (1930–1993), a popular theorist among contemporary Israeli neoconservative intellectuals,[12] argues that Moses is deeply concerned with limiting power and warning against its abuses. For Wildavsky, Moses's killing of the taskmaster is a well-considered action that offers a warning against those who would abuse power; and so too Moses ultimately decides to limit his own power as a monarch in line with the best traditions of liberalism, realizing that "ambition must be controlled."[13] Whereas Naḥman of Bratslav had seen God as using Moses to complete the work begun by Joseph, Wildavsky sees Moses as the "anti-Joseph," rejecting the model of dictatorship that Joseph had favored as Pharaoh's deputy in Egypt.[14] Wildavsky's Moses also seeks to learn from non-Israelites (e.g., Jethro), realizing (in sharp contrast to the teaching of Naḥman) that "wisdom is not confined to the chosen people."[15]

Other modern Jews have been more critical of Moses' leadership style, sometimes on feminist grounds. Thus, for example, the American historian Judith Rosenbaum has pointed to the weakness of Moses' leadership style in comparison to that of his sister Miriam. At the Sea of Reeds, Rosenbaum notes, whereas Moses calls out that "I will sing to the Lord" (Exodus 15:1), Miriam leads with more inclusive language, inviting the entire community to "sing to the Lord" (Exodus 15:21). Whereas "Moses celebrates by himself, Miriam brings the entire Jewish community into her celebration," Rosenbaum writes, teaching us "that the best leaders place community at the center of their work."[16] The focus on the solitary Moses who kills the taskmaster, who stands above his people at the Sea, or even who serves as a limited constitutional monarch, is here challenged by finding a more democratic model in verses that are often ignored by the men who have defined traditional Jewish discourse.

HOW SHOULD WE JUDGE VIOLENCE?

In a similar vein, seeking to create new interpretive traditions about Israelite women during the Exodus, the American feminist scholar Rabbi Margaret Moers Wenig (b. 1957) has imagined that Miriam objected to Moses' model of fighting the Egyptians through violent plagues. In Wenig's telling of the Exodus narrative, Miriam refuses to believe that God wants all of the Egyptians to suffer. She asks Moses to challenge the plan to kill all Egyptian firstborns, just as Abraham challenged God at Sodom, and rather than embracing violence she helps to lead a coalition of Israelite and Egyptian women in a campaign of nonviolent resistance against Pharaoh. But her efforts fail, due to Pharaoh's obstinacy. And while Moses is able to lead his people to freedom and celebrate God as "a man of war" in his song at the sea (15:1–18), Wenig explains why the Torah records so little of Miriam's own song at the sea (15:21): she is saddened by the violence and the death of beloved Egyptian friends, and she cannot continue as Moses does.[17]

Wenig resists the idea that God truly wanted the violence described in the Exodus narrative. An alternative modern Jewish effort to develop a nonviolent politics, formulated by the Eastern European rabbi Aharon Shmuel Tamaret (Tamares, 1869–1931), has imagined that God did willingly inflict the plagues on Egypt but did so without allowing the Israelites to participate in the violence, precisely in order to teach the Israelites that they were forbidden to use such violence themselves. In Tamaret's understanding, God emphasizes that God "and not an intermediary" will act upon Egypt in order to emphasize that violence is God's prerogative alone; human beings should not emulate this divine action.[18] Tamaret's commitment to human nonviolence underscored his opposition to state Zionism and all other forms of political nationalism.[19]

One can find the opposite understanding of how human beings should relate to divine violence among modern Jews who have most forcefully advocated Jewish nationalism—leaders of messianic Religious Zionism, the Orthodox movement that attributes messianic significance to the Zionist enterprise. For example, the French-born Israeli rabbi Shlomo Aviner (b. 1943) has explained that fighting for the state of Israel is one of the ways of cleaving to God's attributes and thereby coming to know God: "Just as the Holy Blessed One is a 'man of war,' so we enlist in the Israel Defense Forces."[20] For Tamaret, this was precisely the divine quality to which human beings could not "cleave"; for Aviner, it is a central divine attribute for modern Jews to emulate. While Aviner acknowledges that God acted directly against the Egyptians without asking for humans to participate in the violence, he explains that this was necessary given the helplessness of the Israelites. Building on the teachings of the founder of messianic religious Zionism, Rabbi Abraham Isaac Kook (1865–1935), Aviner notes that, at the time of the Exodus, "we were like babies for which everything was done." But "now, we are no longer babies," such that the Israel Defense Forces can emulate God directly rather than seeking God's supernatural intervention. In this way, the messianic redemption being brought about by the establishment and defense of Israel is on a higher level than the redemption from Egypt. As Kook had argued, Zionism continues the process of redemption that began with the Exodus from Egypt, but moves the world far closer to messianic redemption.[21]

As we saw above, however, Jewish support for political violence need not be grounded in messianism or in ideas of emulating God. Aaron Wildavsky, for example, saw Moses' violence against the taskmaster as a reasonable act of justice; so too, he appreciates the necessity for Moses' violence against Israelites who, immediately following the Exodus, worship the idol of the Golden Calf. "The good leader uses force when necessary," Wildavsky writes, even as "the great leader seeks to make force unnecessary."[22] In a similar vein, Michael Walzer seeks to develop an understanding of the Exodus narrative that is non-messianic and secular while also avoiding the extreme secular violence of Leninism. Still, as Bonnie Honig has noted, Walzer accepts that the violence authorized by Moses after leaving Egypt may be necessary: "at some point I suppose the counter-revolution must be defeated if Egyptian bondage is ever to be left behind," Walzer admits.[23] In Honig's analysis, Walzer thus shows "his realist acceptance of the violence" as a necessary means to an end, and he criticizes idealists who would decry the violence.[24] While the Exodus narrative has sometimes inspired modern Jewish "idealists" (such as Wenig and Tamaret) to reject its violence as a model for human politics, it has often helped others to justify political violence, including those who claim to be secular, moderate, reasonable theorists.

MAY THE EXODUS BE A UNIVERSAL PARADIGM FOR LIBERATION?

Whom is the Exodus narrative for? Walzer's Exodus-inspired theorization demonstrates the ability of the narrative to serve as a more general paradigm for political reasoning. But as we will see, this approach is certainly not self-evident. Among Jewish thinkers, there is significant divergence in their understanding of how, or if, the Exodus may provide a "blueprint" for other political aspirations. Given the myriad and evocative theo-political themes of the Exodus, to whom may these themes apply, and who may employ them for modern ends? May the Exodus story serve as a universal paradigm for liberation, or should it be understood only as a liberatory narrative of one particular people, the chosen Israelites?

The foundational work of Moses Mendelssohn (1729–1786), eminent philosopher and architect of the Jewish Enlightenment, provides one early and important response to this question. In his most famous work, *Jerusalem* (1783), Mendelssohn takes up the question of Jewish citizenship in the burgeoning European nation-states. Against thinkers claiming that Jews' adherence to a set of traditional and exclusive commandments rendered them unable to participate in the ostensibly rational and universalist Enlightenment political project, Mendelssohn claims, perhaps counterintuitively, that the particularist nature of the Exodus narrative was precisely what would make Jews such good modern citizens. In fact, Mendelssohn subtly argues, not only should Jews be able to participate in the nation-state project, they are necessary to its success.

For Mendelssohn, the fact that the Exodus—as a historical event described in the Bible—occurred only to one people is sufficient indication that it was not meant to apply to all peoples; for the rationalist philosopher, anything required of all people must be equally accessible to all people by reason, whereas the Exodus was a singular event witnessed and testified to by one people alone.[25] But while this insistence on the exclusivity of the event might seem to undermine Mendelssohn's argument regarding Jewish participation in the nation-state, Mendelssohn sees its significance elsewhere: having accepted the particularity of the Exodus experience and God's subsequent commands exclusively to the Israelites, modern Jews would be able to understand that not all religious experiences are the basis for universal claims. Unlike Christians, who (Mendelssohn argues) understand the revelation of Christ to apply to all, the historical contingency of the Exodus can imbue Jews with insight as to the essential limitations of the state to compel religious belief or practice to a diverse citizenry. Such insight, which Mendelssohn argues is embedded in the particularism of the Exodus narrative, is necessary to create a truly rational and liberal state.

Though Mendelssohn's appeal to the Exodus remains a controversial claim, his broader political vision is, of course, shared by the vast majority of modern and contemporary Jews. But for many later thinkers, the Exodus may provide a more inclusive model for liberation. In a powerful 1917 Passover sermon by Rabbi J. Leonard Levy (1865–1917), an American Reform rabbi, we see an appeal to the Exodus narrative that, while certainly claiming it as the particular heritage of the Jewish people, asserts its profound ability to anticipate a more just world for all. Levy had been a committed pacifist, but once the United States entered into the First World War, he lent his support to the war effort, hoping that the intervention of America—"the champion of universal democracy"—would help bring about liberty and democracy throughout the entire world, a transformation which seemed to be already beginning with the recent Bolshevik revolution.[26]

All of this, Levy declares, is prefigured by the Exodus:

> The Rabbis taught that the Passover of Egypt prefigured the *Pesah L'athid*, 'The Passover that is to Be', that the downfall of the one Pharaoh was a forecast of the final overthrow of every Pharaoh, that the emancipation of a handful of slaves on the banks of the Nile was a sign and token of the ultimate emancipation of the human race.

For Levy, the Passover in itself was a relatively small event, involving only "a handful of slaves on the banks of the Nile." But it may nevertheless prefigure the ultimate liberation of the world; as he concludes, "small nations and large nations alike will enjoy the blessings of liberty, democracy, and fraternity; and peace will crown the earth with joy, as a result of a struggle which now engages the representatives of the world's democracies."[27] Levy, taking his cue from a classical rabbinic conception of the Exodus' significance, unapologetically asserts that the "original" Exodus is only a foretaste of the universal event that is surely to come—and as such, all peoples may take ownership of the narrative.

Levy's fiery rhetoric is dependent on his assertion that the Exodus narrative may be understood to "apply" to all peoples, at least in its final form. The biblical account, while assuredly important for Jews, is but a small and hopeful expression of what is yet to come. For the contemporary feminist rabbi Lynn Gottlieb (b. 1950), however, it is an error to universalize the meaning of the narrative without first carefully considering how Jewish readers have deployed the text for exclusive political ends. Gottlieb argues that the liberative potential of the Exodus narrative takes on a disturbing tinge when the text, understood as a specifically Jewish account of liberation, is encountered by others—in particular, by Palestinians. As she reflects, "We have always seen ourselves [as Jews] as the victims in the story, seeking relief from those who oppress us. Are we able to reverse our identification with the weak and see ourselves as wielders of state power over a stateless and exploited people? . . . [Are we able] to let another people go?"[28]

Gottlieb's questions do affirm the historical and theological significance of the Exodus narrative for Jews in particular, reflecting the famous assertion of the *hagaddah*—the ritual text of Passover, wherein the Exodus narrative takes center stage—that every generation of Jews should regard themselves as having gone forth from Egypt. But it is that same particular communal identification that Gottlieb now experiences as a political burden; the uncompromising biblical language should not allow contemporary Jewish readers to consider the ancient Exodus text without also reflecting on the broader question of modern Jewish political power—particularly when, as she says, many Jews must now understand themselves as "wielders of state power over a stateless and exploited people," the Palestinians.

For Gottlieb, the ways in which contemporary Jews identify themselves in the text must shift—lest the biblical narrative come to serve not as a spur to Jewish political action, but as a means of deceptively reassuring modern Jews that their political status should be defined largely by the perpetual call for Jewish liberation alone. Jews must re-read the Exodus narrative in a way that reminds Jews of the value of the lives of the Egyptians, embracing the classical midrash that states that God prevented the angels from singing in joy while the Egyptians were drowning in the Sea of Reeds; traditions like this can help Jews to affirm the value of the lives of Palestinians while allowing the particularism of the Exodus narrative to challenge modern Jews' self-understandings of their relationships to power.[29]

In Mendelssohn, Levy, and Gottlieb, we see three approaches to the question of particularity or inclusivity: who may appeal to the narrative and to what ends? All three thinkers, however, affirm the Exodus as a narrative that affirms broad human rights claims, even as they differ significantly in their understanding of how the narrative advances those ends. But not all Jews are willing to allow the Exodus to play this role. We can find a counterpoint to these political assumptions, for example, in the writings of the militant Orthodox rabbi and Israeli politician Meir Kahane (1932–1990). Kahane denounced Jews who could not accept what he saw as the clear message of the Exodus narrative, affirmed in biblical and rabbinic texts: that God took the people of Israel out of Egypt so that they could conquer the Canaanites and live "in a single, distinctive land of their own, isolated—yes, isolated, not integrated—from gentile and foreign influences which can and must corrupt the pure totality and distinctiveness of G-d's society."[30]

Contrary to Mendelssohn, Kahane emphasizes that as God's chosen people, superior to other peoples, Jews are uniquely susceptible to the impurity of other nations, and he lambasts the idea that Jews should integrate into other nation-states. In contrast to Levy, he ridicules the idea that the Exodus narrative would support world democracy and the equality of all peoples, citing midrashic texts that affirm that God separates the chosen from the unchosen and drowns those Egyptians who fail to acknowledge God's chosen people. And whereas Gottlieb affirms that Jews must move beyond seeing themselves as victims, Kahane emphasizes how Jews are always threatened by non-Jews (or assimilated Jews) who challenge their purity and rightful power.[31] He particularly mocks Jews like Gottlieb who celebrate Passover while emphasizing the rights of Palestinians, since he understands the Exodus narrative as culminating precisely with the destruction of those non-Jews in Israel ("the 'Palestinians' of that time") who fail to accept Jewish sovereignty and supremacy.[32] While Kahane acknowledges the midrashic tradition favored by Gottlieb affirming that God silenced the angels, he also points to midrashic traditions that emphasize that God certainly wanted the people of Israel to sing the song recorded in Exodus 15:1–21 and thereby to affirm that "when the wicked perish, there is rejoicing" (Proverbs 11:10).[33]

WHO IS THE COMMUNITY OF ISRAEL?

Kahane also condemned secular Zionism, which he saw as corrupting Jewish identity by adopting "gentilized" values (including the aspiration to be like other nations).[34] He did not see secular Zionists as embodying profound holiness, as did messianic religious Zionists such as Rabbi Abraham Isaac Kook, mentioned earlier in this chapter; but neither did he exclude secular Zionists from membership in the community of Israel. Kahane's views on this subject may be contrasted with Kook's more inclusivist position regarding secular Zionists, on the one hand, as well as more exclusivist ultra-Orthodox positions, on the other. This question of community extends well beyond the politics of modern Zionism, encompassing feminist arguments about the place of women in the Jewish community, and even the degree to which communal membership is determined not on the basis of background or particular theological conviction but on the strength of one's attention to universal ethical demands.

Kook stressed in his writings that the ultimate messianic redemption being made possible by secular Zionism was part of the same process that began with the Exodus from Egypt; God's "mighty hand and outstretched arm" (Deut. 7:19) which brought Israel out of Egypt and to rule the land of Israel will make possible the ultimate redemption marked by their rule in the land today.[35] Kook insisted that even secular Zionists, whom he viewed as evil and insolent in many ways, could contribute to the process of messianic redemption, as he believed that God's inspiration had been with all members of the people of Israel (at least those committed to their nation) since the Exodus from Egypt.[36] Kook claimed that slavery in Egypt had forged the entire people of Israel into a superior nation endowed with holiness and divinity, and that their holiness remained even when many of their ideas and practices were corrupted.[37] He emphasized that Moses was right to accept even the "mixed multitude" who left Egypt along with Israel (Ex. 12:38)—a group depicted in kabbalistic literature as the source of great evil but a group viewed by Kook as ultimately bringing benefit to the world.[38] Similarly, Kook himself sought to see secular Zionists and all other Jews as an important component of the political community of Israel and, ultimately, the redemptive process.[39]

Anti-Zionist Orthodox Jews, though working with many of the same Kabbalistic sources as Kook, disagreed vociferously, and used the Exodus narrative to explain how Zionists were not part of the people of Israel. For example, the Hungarian-born Jerusalem rabbi Yeshaya Margaliot (Margolis, 1894–1968) argued that secular Zionists were clearly a part of the "mixed multitude," which he saw as a Satanic force, "the offspring of Pharaoh," and clearly not part of the people of Israel.[40] Whereas Kook saw Moses as accepting the mixed multitude as part of the Exodus, Margaliot saw Moses as firmly rejecting them from the community of Israel, and so too he insisted that present-day rabbis should follow Moses' example in hating and excluding present-day Zionist heretics.[41]

Though Kook and Margaliot were arch-enemies and defined the people of Israel in very different ways, they were united not only by their conviction that Israel is superior to other peoples but also by their conviction that men are superior to women and that Israel should be conceptualized in primarily male terms. Among those who have argued against these sorts of hierarchical constructions of Jewish identity is the American feminist theologian Judith Plaskow, who has done so in part with reference to the Exodus from Egypt. Plaskow rejects the concept of chosenness, which can too easily "justify any sort of abuse of the non-Jewish other"; she instead urges a politics that is grounded in "the injunction of memory: 'You shall not wrong or oppress a stranger, for you were strangers in the land of Egypt.'"[42] Furthermore, Plaskow sees "the memory of slavery in Egypt" as properly leading to a political theology that demands justice for women—including rectifying the injustice of traditional Exodus narratives that fail to include women as full members of the community of Israel.[43] As Plaskow notes, even when the biblical text does include women in its narrative, the traditional text used to retell the story (the Passover *haggadah*) systematically excludes them.[44] And the biblical text dramatically excludes women when it describes God as addressing only men when, after leaving Egypt, they arrive at Mount Sinai (Exodus 19:15).[45]

Inspired by the philosopher Emmanuel Levinas and the Musar movement theorist Rabbi Simhah Zissel Ziv, the American Conservative movement theologian Rabbi Ira Stone broadens the meaning of Israelite identity in a different way, teaching that Israel is only chosen to the degree that they take responsibility for others. Moses was chosen when he saw the suffering of others and took responsibility for them, beginning with the moment that he asked an Israelite acting unjustly, "why do you strike your fellow?" (Ex. 2:13). Other Israelites were chosen when they, similarly, took responsibility; but so too, those who are not Israelites are equally chosen when they, like Moses, seek to prevent injustice. Unlike Plaskow, Stone embraces the language of chosenness, but he sees non-Jews as able to be "equally elected" to Jews.[46] In fact, in sharp contrast to Kook or Margaliot, for whom the Exodus narrative strictly defines Jewish identity, Stone sees the narrative pushing its readers to see that "at the horizon of our religious imagination, the distinction between 'Jew' and 'non-Jew' loses its importance."[47]

WHAT IS THE SIGNIFICANCE OF THE COVENANT?

Above we see a series of attempts to circumscribe or expand the boundaries of who is counted as "Israel"—attempts that find their basis in the Exodus narrative and its account of group of people bound together by their shared experiences both in Egypt and after their liberation from slavery. We can further consider the stakes of this boundary question by considering the covenant between these people and God—a new covenant forged at the base of Mount Sinai, and defined by the Israelites' acceptance of an extensive set of commandments from the God who has claimed them as his people.

The meaning of this covenant, both in its existence and in its content, has inspired a diverse array of theo-political conclusions among modern Jews. As discussed previously, Moses Mendelssohn's famous argument regarding the possibilities of Jewish citizenship was based in his insistence that the Exodus was an event witnessed only by the Israelites, and therefore inaccessible by reason to others who had not been witnesses. In response to the challenges of his contemporaries, Mendelssohn appealed particularly to Exodus 20, which opens with God's famous words to the Israelites: "I the Lord am your God who brought you out of the land of Egypt, the house of bondage" (Ex 20:2). In this verse, after which begins the long litany of commandments that will be the basis of the covenant, Mendelssohn locates the foundation for this major theo-political claim.

For Mendelssohn, when God speaks in Exodus 20, he speaks as one claiming his people; God's famous assertion should be understood, therefore, as God reminding the Israelites that he is the "Lord *your* God"—and that the "divine legislation," as Mendelssohn terms it, is therefore only applicable to the Israelites and their descendants; no other people shall be responsible for the particularities of the commandments. In Mendelssohn's characterization, the establishment of this covenant both forms the Israelites as a distinct people with a distinct relationship to God—and creates the conditions under which this people may live alongside others without compelling them to adhere to the legislation revealed only to the Israelites.

Michael Walzer, further reflecting on the implications of the narrative, also identifies the covenant given to the Israelites after their liberation from Egypt as politically foundational, though his understanding of its meaning diverges from Mendelssohn's own. Walzer views the establishment of the new covenant as first and foremost an act of political creation: in the establishment of this new relationship, the Israelites exist as a meaningful political unit for the first time. Prior to the covenantal relationship described in Exodus, Walzer argues that the Israelites' political identity, "like that of all men and women before liberation, is something that has happened to them."[48] But with the establishment of the new covenant, they become a self-determined people: "capable of sustaining a moral and political history, capable of obedience and also of stiff-necked resistance, or marching forward and of sliding back."[49] In the people's agreement to the demands of the covenant, they shift from a fragmented group united largely by their shared history of enslavement to a people defined by a shared purpose and future. In short, having made a communal decision to enter into the covenant, the people are now able to become political actors.

This reading is enabled by Walzer's emphasis, far more than what can be found in Mendelssohn, on the communal decision-making of the body of Israelites at Sinai. For

Mendelssohn, the salient point for his theo-political vision is that God acted upon the people; in Mendelssohn's emphasis on God's definitive language, the Israelites remain defined by their relationship to the God who has called them in particular. Walzer, however, locates the Israelites' acceptance of the covenant as the central act of the narrative; the performance of this collective act serves to constitute them as a political community for the first time. Of course, there is no covenant without God—but for Walzer, it is in the human will necessary to accept the covenant and step forward as a covenanted people that we see the political significance of the new relationship between the Israelites and their God. So too this act serves to define the Israelites' acceptance as a paradigmatic act, representative not only of itself but of the political will necessary for any oppressed people to re-define themselves and begin to forge a new political destiny.

Though Mendelssohn's understanding of the covenantal relationship is more robustly "theological" than Walzer's, both assume the God–Israel covenant as described in the biblical narrative as the basis of their theorization. By contrast, we might consider sources that eschew the divine basis of the covenant, asserting instead the necessity of human action in lieu of misplaced hopes in divine salvation or election. In the creative Passover haggadahs of secular Jewish leftist groups in Europe and the United States, the notion of the relationship between a human community and their God is unapologetically replaced by an emphasis on, and critique of, unjust human institutions.

For example, the Passover Haggadah of the Jewish Labor Bund, published in 1900, reflects the radical anti-capitalist and anti-religious convictions of its eastern European creators. This haggadah does not do away with invocations of God altogether, though the register is decidedly different from traditional haggadot. In response to a traditional question attributed to a "wise son" and posed during the seder regarding the meaning of God's laws and commandments, the Haggadah responds skeptically:

> What are the laws to discuss that God has given you? How can a God give such laws, that all of humankind shall trudge toward toil and barely have enough to keep their souls, and that a small part of them shall take all of what the rest have and waste and squander and live in a sea of pleasure?

The haggadah thus responds not by praising or explicating the divine commandments referenced in the wise son's traditional question, but by calling attention to a quite worldly phenomenon: the presence of a gross disparity between the masses who suffer under exploitative labor practices and the "small part of them" who maintain and benefit from this exploitation. When the haggadah asks, "how can a God give such laws," it does not seem that the precise question is why God has ordained labor exploitation—this is a human phenomenon—but rather how it is that God has not seen fit to intervene to address this perpetual human misery. In these circumstances, there can be no meaningful covenant between God and workers, whether ancient Israelites or modern Europeans, for the laws governing these workers' lives have been ordained by humans. If there is a covenant, it is between "all of humankind," and it has been broken.

Thus the Bundist haggadah insists on the awareness that the only trustworthy covenant is the one that people must now make among themselves, refusing to defer to the claims of capitalists, rabbis, or others who claim authority. The haggadah goes on to instruct its readers in the correct response to he who is in the traditional haggadah the "wicked son" and in this modern haggadah an unjust overseer: "You shall but show your teeth and say, 'Remember, once upon a time we freed ourselves from the slave-houses, from Egypt, and we will surely free ourselves from our current yoke.'"[50] This will happen "with arm outstretched"—not with God's "mighty hand and outstretched arm," but following what "our heroic fighters have exhorted: Hold high with outstretched hands our red flag of socialism!"[51]

WHAT WAS THE PURPOSE OF THE EXODUS?

The very different political approaches discussed in this essay reflect very different conceptions of the purpose of the Exodus. For some modern Jewish thinkers, the Exodus does not point to any radical remaking of the world. For Walzer, for example, the Exodus "does not require the miraculous transformation of the material world"[52] but should ideally inspire this-worldly movements for social democracy. For Aaron Wildavsky, the Exodus might more generally inspire this-worldly regimes that effectively mix hierarchy and equity, with wise and appropriately constrained leaders.

Other thinkers have seen the Exodus as inspiring human beings to work for a more radical transformation of the world, often conceived in messianic terms. J. Leonard Levy sees the Exodus as prefiguring the American-led warfare that will ultimately bring about a messianic peace characterized by universal democracy. Abraham Isaac Kook similarly sees the Exodus as leading to world peace, though that peace will ultimately be made possible by the achievement of Jewish state power in the land of Israel and a universal recognition of the Jews' preeminence. Lynn Gottlieb, on the other hand, sees the Exodus as inspiring the overthrow of all oppressive state powers, as well as the end of myths of national exceptionalism that are so important to figures like Levy and Kook. The authors of the Bundist Haggadah see the Exodus as inspiring a liberation of the masses through the overthrow of capitalism (as well as an overthrow of rabbis who claim authority, such as Levy, Kook, and Gottlieb).

For still others, the Exodus may be framed not as inspiring human political agency but as prefiguring a transformation of the world that will come about through direct, supernatural divine intervention. For Naḥman of Bratslav or for Yeshaya Margaliot, for example, God will bring about the messianic era by destroying the "mixed multitude" and by restoring the people of Israel to sovereignty in their land, ruled by the ultimate *tzaddik*—the messiah, who is prefigured by Moses. But for all that Naḥman and Margaliot reject (or would reject) human involvement in modern political movements such as liberalism, Zionism, or Bundism, they join the other figures discussed in this essay in demanding that humans take the initiative to create certain kind of polities. For Naḥman and Margaliot, God demands that human beings establish certain kinds of communities in the pre-messianic era, submitting to "the tzaddik of the generation" (as we saw Naḥman emphasize) and, as Margaliot emphasized in a later era, battling against Zionism.

CONCLUSION: EXPANDING THE CONVERSATION

This chapter opened with the observation that the prominence of the Exodus narrative in Jewish political thought is not surprising. Rather, the distinctiveness of the Exodus is precisely in its compelling and complex account of an enslaved and fragmented people, the Israelites, becoming a liberated and covenanted people—a process that, as this chapter demonstrates, has served as the basis for myriad and dramatically divergent points of view in modern Jewish political theology. We have chosen to ground our discussion in this narrative not only as a means of bringing specificity to the vast category of Jewish political reasoning, but also in hopes of demonstrating the value of the analysis of classical Jewish texts as a generative basis for modern political theology.

Though our method obviously excludes those who do not engage with the Exodus narrative, it allows us to facilitate a strikingly diverse conversation between thinkers working in vastly different time periods, cultural contexts, and philosophical idioms. While other accounts of Jewish political theology might limit themselves to a more conventional set of contemporary Jewish political theorists, this chapter's basis in the Exodus has allowed us to draw upon a much wider array of thinkers, brought together by their shared appeal to this narrative as the basis of Jewish political reasoning. Thus the ostensibly limiting factor of the text actually allows for a more diverse presentation of political theology.

Of course, while this approach may help to curate a more expansive conversation about the questions of Jewish political theology, we are not offering a comprehensive account. Rather, we aim to showcase a distinctive method of taking up these questions—one that may serve as a model for future accounts of Jewish political reasoning that extend well beyond the narrative of the Exodus.

NOTES

1. Michael Walzer, *Exodus and Revolution* (New York: Basic Books, 1985), 17.
2. Avidan Freedman, "Are We the Modern Pharaoh?," *The Times of Israel*, December 18, 2013, http://blogs.timesofisrael.com/are-we-the-modern-pharaoh.
3. Brant Rosen, "On Passover, Israel and 'Demographic Threats,'" *Truthout*, April 28, 2016, http://www.truth-out.org/opinion/item/35811-on-passover-israel-and-demographic-threats.
4. Yedidia Stern and Karen Friedman-Stern, "Ma'aseh Imahot Siman Le-Banot," *Musaf Shabbat (Makor Rishon)*, January 20, 2017, https://musaf-shabbat.com/2017/01/22/מעשה-אמהות-סימן-לבנות-ידידיה-צ-שטר.
5. See Michael Walzer et al., eds., *The Jewish Political Tradition*, vol. 1 (New Haven, CT: Yale University Press, 2000).
6. On Joseph, see Naḥman of Bratslav, *Mo'adei Hashem* 107 (#186) (Jerusalem: n.d.); on Moses, see Naḥman of Bratslav, *Likutey Moharan*, trans. Moshe Mykoff, vol. 3 (Lessons 17–22) (Jerusalem: Breslov Research Institute, 1990), 226–227 (1.20:10). The idea of Joseph as an exemplar of sexual self-restraint emerges from Genesis 39, wherein Joseph rejects the advances of the wife of his patron, Potiphar.
7. Naḥman of Bratslav, *Mo'adei Hashem* 107 (#185). See Genesis 4 for the famous story of Cain, who murdered his brother Abel.
8. Naḥman of Bratslav, *Likutey Moharan*, trans. Moshe Mykoff, vol. 10 (Lessons 109–194) (Jerusalem: Breslov Research Institute, 1992), 80–83 (#123). Translation from Joseph Dan, ed., *The Teachings of Hasidism* (New York: Behrman House, 1983), 78.
9. Ehud Luz, *Wrestling with an Angel: Power, Morality, and Jewish Identity*, trans. Michael Swirsky (New Haven, CT: Yale University Press, 2003), 178.
10. Zeev Jabotinsky, *Ba-Derekh La-Medinah* (Jerusalem: Arei Jabotinsky, 1959), 21–23.
11. Glenn Dynner, *Men of Silk: The Hasidic Conquest of Polish Jewish Society* (New York, NY: Oxford University Press, 2006), 10; Daniel Kupfert Heller, *Jabotinsky's Children: Polish Jews and the Rise of Right-Wing Zionism* (Princeton, NJ: Princeton University Press, 2017), 120–121.
12. As evidenced by its recent republication by the Shalem Center.

13. Aaron Wildavsky, *Moses as Political Leader*, 2nd ed. (Jerusalem: Shalem Press, 2008), 193–196.
14. Aaron Wildavsky, *Assimilation Versus Separation: Joseph the Administrator and the Politics of Religion in Biblical Israel* (New Brunswick, NJ: Transaction Publishers, 1993), 193–200. On Joseph as a leader in Egypt, see Gen. 41–47.
15. Wildavsky, *Moses*, 163.
16. Sharon Cohen Anisfeld, Tara Mohr, and Catherine Spector, eds., *The Women's Passover Companion: Women's Reflections on the Festival of Freedom* (Woodstock, VT: Jewish Lights, 2003), 111.
17. Ibid., 121–125.
18. Abraham Samuel Tamaret, "Passover and Nonviolence," in *Roots of Jewish Nonviolence*, ed. Allan Solomonow, trans. Everett Gendler (Nyack: Jewish Peace Fellowship, 1981), 50–61.
19. See Aryeh Cohen, "'The Foremost Amongst the Divine Attributes Is to Hate the Vulgar Power of Violence': Aharon Shmuel Tamares and Recovering Nonviolence for Jewish Ethics," *Journal of Jewish Ethics* 1, no. 2 (2015): 233–252.
20. Shlomo Aviner, "Mahi Yerushalayim?," *Bisdei Ḥemed* 9–10 (1995), http://www.daat.ac.il/he-il/kitveyet/bisde_hemed/aviner-yerushalayim.htm.
21. Shlomo Aviner, "The Redemption from Egypt and Today's Redemption," posted by Mordechai Tzion, *Torat HaRav Aviner*, April 12, 2009, http://www.ravaviner.com/2009/04/redemption-from-egypt-and-todays.html; see Shlomo Aviner, *Nifgashim Ba-Parashah: Siḥot Al Parashat Ha-Shavua*, ed. Nehemia Lavi (Bet El: Hava, 2015), 130.
22. Wildavsky, *Moses*, 137.
23. Walzer, *Exodus and Revolution*, 69.
24. Bonnie Honig, "Between Sacred and Secular? Michael Walzer's Exodus Story," in *Race and Political Theology*, ed. Vincent W. Lloyd (Stanford, CA: Stanford University Press, 2012), 196–197, 207.
25. Mendelssohn expounds upon these distinctions in *Jerusalem: Or on Religious Power and Judaism* (Hanover: Brandeis University Press, 1983), 91–92.
26. Marc Saperstein, *Jewish Preaching in Times of War, 1800–2001* (Oxford: Littman Library of Jewish Civilization, 2008), 344–345.
27. Ibid., 345.
28. Anisfeld, Mohr, and Spector, *Women's Passover Companion*, 253.
29. Ibid., 252.
30. Meir Kahane, *Beyond Words: Selected Writings of Rabbi Meir Kahane, 1960–1990*, ed. David Fein (Brooklyn: Institute for Publication of the Writings of Rabbi Meir Kahane, 2010), 6: 274.
31. See Geoffrey Claussen, "Two Orthodox Approaches to Vulnerability and the Exodus Narrative: The Stranger in the Writings of Irving Greenberg and Meir Kahane," *Studies in Judaism, Humanities, and the Social Sciences* 2, no. 1 (2018), 46–60.
32. Kahane, *Beyond Words*, 7: 116–117.
33. Ibid., 7: 119–120.
34. See Meir Kahane, *Uncomfortable Questions for Comfortable Jews* (Secaucus, NJ: Lyle Stuart, 1987), ch. 11.
35. Abraham Isaac Kook, *Orot* (Jerusalem: Mossad Ha-Rav Kook, 2005), 44 (#28).
36. Kook, *Orot*, 88 (#53).

37. Ibid., 156; Abraham Isaac Kook, *Seder Tefillah Im Peirush Olat Re'ayah* (Jerusalem: Mossad Ha-Rav Kook, 1985), 2: 287.
38. Abraham Isaac Kook, *Ein Ayah*, vol. 3 (Jerusalem, 1994), 105–106.
39. See Abraham Isaac Kook, *Rav A.Y. Kook: Selected Letters*, trans. Tzvi Feldman (Ma'aleh Adumim: Ma'aliot Publications, 1986), 66–74.
40. Aviezer Ravitzky, *Messianism, Zionism, and Jewish Religious Radicalism*, trans. Michael Swirsky and Jonathan Chipman (Chicago: University of Chicago Press, 1996), 56; Motti Inbari, *Jewish Radical Ultra-Orthodoxy Confronts Modernity, Zionism and Women's Equality*, trans. Shaul Vardi (New York: Cambridge University Press, 2016), 185.
41. Yeshaya Asher Zelig Margaliot, *Ashrei Ha-Ish* (Jerusalem: Breslov Press, 1921), 43b; Inbari, *Jewish Radical Ultra-Orthodoxy*, 189.
42. Judith Plaskow, *Standing Again at Sinai: Judaism from a Feminist Perspective* (New York: HarperSanFrancisco, 1991), 118, quoting an altered translation of Exodus 22:20.
43. Ibid., 30.
44. Anisfeld, Mohr, and Spector, *Women's Passover Companion*, 11.
45. Plaskow, *Standing Again at Sinai*, 25–26.
46. Ira F. Stone, *A Responsible Life: The Spiritual Path of Mussar* (New York: Aviv Press, 2006), 188. See also the comments on chosenness in Stone, xx, 15–16, 100.
47. Ibid., 187.
48. Walzer, *Exodus and Revolution*, 76.
49. Ibid., 76.
50. David Philip Shuldiner, *Of Moses and Marx: Folk Ideology and Folk History in the Jewish Labor Movement* (Westport, CT: Bergin & Garvey, 1999), 157.
51. Ibid., 159.
52. Walzer, *Exodus and Revolution*, 17.

SELECT BIBLIOGRAPHY

Anisfeld, Sharon Cohen, Tara Mohr, and Catherine Spector, eds. (2003), *The Women's Passover Companion: Women's Reflections on the Festival of Freedom*, Woodstock, VT: Jewish Lights.
Heller, Daniel Kupfert (2017), *Jabotinsky's Children: Polish Jews and the Rise of Right-Wing Zionism*, Princeton, NJ: Princeton University Press.
Inbari, Motti (2016), *Jewish Radical Ultra-Orthodoxy Confronts Modernity, Zionism and Women's Equality*, trans. Shaul Vardi, New York: Cambridge University Press.
Kahane, Meir (1987), *Uncomfortable Questions for Comfortable Jews*, Secaucus, NJ: Lyle Stuart.
Luz, Ehud (2003), *Wrestling with an Angel: Power, Morality, and Jewish Identity*, trans. Michael Swirsky, New Haven, CT: Yale University Press.
Plaskow, Judith (1991), *Standing Again at Sinai: Judaism from a Feminist Perspective*, New York: HarperSanFrancisco.
Ravitzky, Aviezer (1996), *Messianism, Zionism, and Jewish Religious Radicalism*, trans. Michael Swirsky and Jonathan Chipman, Chicago: University of Chicago Press.
Saperstein, Marc (2008), *Jewish Preaching in Times of War, 1800–2001*, Oxford: Littman Library of Jewish Civilization.
Walzer, Michael (1985), *Exodus and Revolution*, New York: Basic Books.

Walzer, Michael et al., eds. (2000), *The Jewish Political Tradition*, vol. 1, New Haven, CT: Yale University Press.
Wildavsky, Aaron (1993), *Assimilation Versus Separation: Joseph the Administrator and the Politics of Religion in Biblical Israel*, New Brunswick, NJ: Transaction Publishers.
Wildavsky, Aaron (2008), *Moses as Political Leader*, 2nd ed., Jerusalem: Shalem Press.

CHAPTER TWENTY-ONE

The Political Theology of Catholic Social Teaching

MARÍA TERESA DÁVILA

INTRODUCTION

Two recent moments in the Catholic social teaching tradition help frame this discussion. They point to complexities with respect to the reception, adoption, and implementation within Catholic circles and in society at large of the principles embodied within its documents and teaching. In 1991, while the world was still catching its breath from the whirlwind of the geopolitical transformations that marked the previous three years, Pope John Paul II released the encyclical *Centessimus Annus—On the Hundredth Anniversary of Rerum Novarum*.[1] This official document of Roman Catholic teaching marked one hundred years from the publication of *Rerum Novarum—The Condition of Labor*, in 1891.[2] John Paul II struggled with the meaning of the fall of Soviet communism and the transformation of former Soviet states into emerging capitalist democracies for the global human family and the future of economic and political relations across the world. This echoed the ways in which a hundred years earlier Pope Leo XIII struggled with the evolving conditions of labor during the industrial explosion of the second half of the nineteenth century. *Rerum Novarum* described and pronounced judgment on the ways in which industrialization was affecting family life, urban development, and the conditions of labor, all the while observing how the shifting political and ideological grounds in Europe at the time impacted the viability of the Church as a public institution with power and influence over its faithful beyond the confines of the sanctuary. Both documents sought to apply elements and principles of the Christian tradition to new circumstances facing the human family in society, politics, and economics, the task at the heart of the body of documents known as Catholic social teaching.[3]

But John Paul II's efforts were not necessarily received with broad support. The encyclical appreciated how capitalist markets offered more opportunities for the flourishing of human freedom than socialist economies as experienced,[4] but also recognized the materialist anthropology under which it operates.[5] Commenters within Catholic neoliberal circles, for example, appreciated the strong condemnation of socialist economies and the welfare state in favor of capitalism, while ignoring the stern warnings issued by the pope in the document against the dehumanizing tendencies of capitalist markets.[6] The biased interpretation of this landmark document secured unwavering support for market capitalism from US business elites, with little or no concern for its totalizing and dehumanizing practices, or the ways deep inequality worsens under neoliberal policies, as John Paul II and subsequent popes have warned.[7]

Prior to this, in 1986, the United States Catholic bishops attempted to speak to the economic challenges of the US market economy through the pastoral letter *Economic Justice for All*.[8] Though not possessing the same authoritative weight as a papal encyclical, the letter represented three years of study and consultation by the US bishops on economic matters. Their recommendations spanned from labor laws, wages, and practices, to the right to form unions and their role in contributing to a just society, inequality, and poverty in the US, and the changing landscape of the agricultural economy and how these elements contributed to or impacted the common good and human dignity, especially the wellbeing of the most vulnerable members of the US economy. In addition, the bishops raised questions regarding labor justice within Church-related institutions such as hospitals, schools, and parishes.[9] But the document was met with resistance and harsh criticism.[10] Central to this criticism was questioning the wisdom of the bishops in matters of economic policy, highlighting ways in which much economic thinking at the time could not support their recommendations for the labor and agricultural markets, and outright condemning their words as dangerous for the prosperity of the US economy.[11]

These two episodes are witness to the complex contributions of Catholic social teaching to the life of the Church and the larger discussion of religious contributions to the development and protection of the common good through the social, economic, and political life of the human family. This body of work from the Catholic Church, which it presents as a contribution for "all people of goodwill,"[12] is considered authoritative as to the principles it uses and develops over time through which it interprets new situations facing the human family. And yet its specific observations are perceived more as recommendations for human flourishing rather than hard and fast rules for economic and political life. It is a developing and evolving body of work, struggling to bring increasingly complicated human interrelationships toward a vision of the good life that holds human dignity and integral human and, more recently, ecological development as its highest ideals. This essay entertains a political theology for Catholic social thought by looking at what it intends to be (and some perspective on what it most definitely is not) in the life of the Church and the larger public square, discussing its vision and guiding principles for life in community, and examining emerging themes and objectives of the first five years of Pope Francis' leadership.

My discussion of the political theology of this body of work is read through the lens of *the preferential option for the poor*, which I consider to be the key principle at the core of this teaching. From this perspective Catholic social teaching can be said to include inherent biases and contradictions that get addressed more adequately when read through that particular lens, such as its partiality toward private industry (for example, corporations and free markets), its lack of acknowledgment of how gender plays a role in local and global economic and political conditions for human flourishing, and its apparent allergy to confronting conflict in history as a direct challenge to the common good of the poor and vulnerable.

CHALLENGES TO CATHOLIC SOCIAL THOUGHT AS POLITICAL THEOLOGY

Catholic social thought seeks to bring the resources of the Christian tradition to bear on life in community for the human family. As such, it draws most heavily from the Bible and the tradition of theological reflection and doctrinal developments within the Church, less so from the witness of history and human experience, and, more recently, the social sciences.[13] The tradition spans the entire history of Christianity, but as a body of work defined by the writings of popes and others in the hierarchy of the Church, the 1891 publication of *Rerum Novarum* is considered the beginning of the systematic analysis of "the sign of the times" through the lens of the Christian tradition. Key moments in history and human experience since then—the Great Depression,[14] the rise of fascism and communism,[15] decolonization,[16] war,[17] nuclear militarization,[18] human rights,[19] poverty and global inequality,[20] the sexual revolution and reproductive rights,[21] immigration,[22] environmental degradation and climate change[23]—have all been directly addressed.

This documentary tradition is shaped by the rubric "see–judge–act," developed in the 1920s and 1930s in the Catholic youth movements in Europe,[24] with the intention of "seeing" a situation, particularly how certain conditions, events, or circumstances impact the person and life in community, make a judgment using the resources of the tradition, and promote particular avenues for action at different levels of power and influence to transform the situation toward greater humanization.[25] This process gives rise to a set of principles (discussed below) that come to stand for compact expressions of key ethical norms arising from the Christian tradition but understood as having universal validity.

The goals of Catholic social teaching are to promote human dignity and offer both judgment and opportunity for conversion and action wherever human dignity is challenged, but it is difficult to consider how this works out as political theology. Catholic social thought is not a political or economic program. It offers no specific plan for democratization, though it lauds accountability and political participation of all members of society as important values for the promotion of human dignity. It does not have a set level of immigration that conforms to biblical ideals, though it recognizes the rights of people to migrate in search for a better life, and points out their privileged place in the Bible as a category of persons close to God's mercy. It does not have any set of labor laws or minimum wage prescriptions, though it promotes the rights of workers to collectively bargain for their salaries and benefits.

Articulating a political theology from Catholic social teaching is further complicated by its role within the structures of official Church teaching. While many documents within the tradition are recognized as magisterial teaching,[26] there is a range of authority and classification for different contributions to the body of documents. Added to the absence of specific prescriptions, many have interpreted this dimension of Catholic doctrine as recommendations or observations rather than hard and fast rules, or even criteria against which to measure our best efforts for life in community. This is increasingly the case the more specific the documents get with respect to prescriptive instructions, when the authority of the authors' observations and wisdom on a topic, whether popes or bishops—even in consultation with experts—is questioned. In contemporary discussions on climate change, for example, Pope Francis' reading of the science of climate change, and his recommendations with respect to alternative energy sources, and reparations to the areas around the globe most impacted by resource extraction and rising sea levels, are challenged on the grounds that he is not a trained expert in economic, environmental, or climate sciences.[27]

Given these challenges, what resources ought one to draw from in articulating a political theology of Catholic social teaching? First, the tradition of Catholic social teaching offers alternative visions for addressing the needs of life in community from the perspective of the suffering of so many in the human family. It also offers cohesive and systematic observations of the human condition. In particular, it offers assessment of the immediate and distant impacts of corporations and institutions in a changing global economy, and the ways ideological extremes taint our best efforts at democratic reforms. Second, it offers the development of a set of principles that, though not presenting prescriptions to specific situations, provide significantly robust criteria for enriching the social, economic, and political arenas. Third, and related to the second, it does this within an evolutionary framework. While it claims to stand on universal principles present in scripture and throughout the Christian tradition, their expression and affirmation arise at particular times in human history, responsive to transformations from one era to the next, suggesting an evolving tradition able to adapt to the most critical challenges of the time. Finally, it does this within the framework of the struggle between the vagaries of human existence and belief in a God that has a plan for creation, where providence affirms God's active and redemptive role in history.

Within Catholic social teaching this activity is affirmed as having directionality and an eschatological endpoint. Although Catholic social thought does not venture to read this endpoint with 100 percent certainty, it attempts to interpret this telos for each era, and, perhaps more importantly, for our time. This it does in light of God's most definitive act in history through the cross and resurrection, where the suffering of the world is reconciled to God's self, inviting the faithful to live and transform communities as if the Kindom is already here.[28] In discussing the political theology of Augustine, Catholic theologian Francis Fiorenza describes it thus: "Augustine presents a vision of transcendence and of a transcendent city that alone can be the source and locus of that well-being that is not mere temporal, but eternal. In short, utilitarian argument is presented in favor of political theology and it is criticized by a metaphysical analysis and an appeal to a higher transcendental goal."[29] This "transcendental goal" is the horizon of Catholic social teaching. It attempts to balance "universal truths" with "social utility,"[30] presenting a faithful response to some of the most pressing challenges facing the human family.

TEN PRINCIPLES FOR LIFE IN COMMUNITY

Catholic social teaching has developed a set of principles that, though not specific prescriptive statements, provide significantly robust criteria for life in community. Using tradition and scripture, Catholic social teaching attends to "the signs of the times" in order to develop these principles.[31] While it ultimately does not yield authority to human experience, these experiences have shaped the principles of Catholic social teaching in concrete ways. Its attention to the "see" dimension of the pastoral cycle see–judge–act, means that it implicitly takes into account human experience and context, especially political, cultural, and economic experiences, in developing faithful responses to ongoing threats to human dignity.[32]

Thomas Massaro, SJ, presents what I believe to be a thorough as well as complex articulation of the principles of Catholic social teaching.[33] This articulation combines the theological/ethical vision of each principle with its concomitant political function. Alternately, this somewhat belies a partiality toward liberal political democracy in his formulation of the principles themselves that I would argue is embedded in the Catholic social tradition itself. These principles represent the space where doctrine and human experience interact, sometimes in flexible and evolving ways. As principles distilled from the tradition engaging human experience, they in turn shape the further development of Catholic social teaching, echoing the pastoral cycle of "see–judge–act" in dialectical engagement. For these reasons even conclusively naming, numbering, or ordering these principles becomes a jarring challenge, sometimes prone to ideological manipulation intended to privilege certain principles, or elements within principles, over others. While there are variations in the numbering and naming of these principles among various analysts of the tradition, the essential doctrines and values these represent are not in question.

1. *Human dignity and human rights*[34]—This first principle represents the centrality of the human dignity of every person as bearer of the image of God (Gen. 1:26) in tandem with human rights. This foundational principle in Catholic ethics shapes all aspects of life in community, demanding that our economic, cultural, political, and social systems affirm and protect the inviolable dignity of every person. This norm aligns with human rights, among these the right to life, the right to freedom, and the right to determine the political future of one's community and country. But further elucidation of the kinds of rights this principle translates into has been the topic of much confusion. The right to migrate, for example, is explicitly mentioned in key document of the tradition such as *Rerum Novarum* (1891) and *Pacem in Terris* (1963).[35] But how to balance this with the rights of nation-states to regulate borders and the passage of migrants, refugees, and asylum seekers? Other rights mentioned, such as the right to an education, the right to healthcare, and the right to potable water[36] raise difficult questions as to the limits of ever expanding lists of positive rights required for human survival, development, and thriving, versus the ability of states, regional bodies, and international agencies to properly provide for them. The subsequent principles help discern the hierarchy of norms that further nuance to this question, definitively clarifying how human rights ought to promote human dignity in every case and for every person.[37]

2. *The preferential option for the poor*—Developed as a phrase in the work of the Latin American bishops and theologians during the 1950s through the 1980s, it encapsulates centuries of Christian thought about the particular place of the poor, excluded, oppressed, and suffering in the eyes of a God who chooses to be active in history. This same God also chooses to *identify* with the poor in history as evidenced by the narratives of Exodus, the Psalms, the Prophets, and in Jesus' ministry, parables, and his own arrest and execution. In Matthew 25:31–46 Christians get the definitive declaration of Christ's identification with the poor, sharing in their destiny, and in turn impacting the destiny of those who choose to be indifferent or cruel to the hungry, the sick, the imprisoned, the migrant, and the naked. As a principle of Catholic social thought, this preferential option orients policy considerations to advocate for the most vulnerable, and judges their effectiveness according to how they impact the prospects for survival and flourishing of the most vulnerable as integral members of the community.

3. *Solidarity, common good, and participation*[38]—Where God has placed the utmost importance (the dignity of every human being made in Divine image and likeness), and where the Christian experience proclaims this experience in history (the mystery of the incarnation and the God who becomes one with us), becomes the principle that unifies both. Through solidarity we are able to share in the suffering of another through the practice of mercy and compassion in imitation of Christ as we acknowledge the moments, systems, experiences, ideologies, and everyday practices that betray and harm human dignity. As a virtue it demands that our

attention go to those who most need our advocacy, support, and transformative action. The common good and participation are ways in which we institutionalize the call to safeguard human dignity, and practice solidarity with the most vulnerable. They demand that political and economic systems be organized for the benefit of all, and pay particular attention to the places where systems act against the human dignity of particular groups for the benefit of a few. The common good institutionalizes solidarity by insuring that all are able to participate in the goods, rights, and benefits therein. Participation is the political and social practice by which all members of society engage and impact the structures that determine their destinies, guarding against systemic exclusions. This ensures that solidarity is not interpreted as charity alone, but as robust walking with marginalized, excluded, and oppressed groups for the transformation of the political, economic, and social structures that impact their lives.

These first three principles hinge on biblical notions of who God is, how God relates to the human family within history, and the most immediate demands of human beings toward each other. The following six principles describe with more specificity the kinds of relations we ought to have politically and economically with each other. Rather than being ordered according to degree of importance or authority, these ought to be considered as a web of interrelationships.

4. *Family life*[39]—Catholic social teaching considers protection of the family one of the primary responsibilities of the state and civil and civic organizations while acknowledging the rights of parents to exercise prudence in the raising of children extends to many areas of life including education, and the right to migrate. Policies regarding education, healthcare, housing and aid to the homeless and housing insecure, the regulation of the number of births, food security, environmental concerns, urban planning, economic development, and immigration, just to name a few, impact the integrity and safety of the family, and are therefore the concern of Catholic social thought.

5. *Dignity of work, rights of workers and support of labor unions*[40]—These principles on human labor and work were articulated from the beginning of the modern Catholic social teaching tradition. In *Rerum Novarum* (1891) Pope Leo XIII affirmed the rights of workers to just wages, a safe environment, rest, and collective bargaining following the biblical appeals for justice for workers whose labor often contributes to the riches of a few, while unjust wages keep them in economically desperate conditions that cry out to God.[41] Through work persons and communities build up the necessary elements of family and community life. Work makes us co-creators with God, in the exercise of our physical, intellectual, and artistic capacities.[42] Therefore, working conditions and remuneration ought to reflect the dignity of labor as a share in God's creative work, as well as be sufficient to sustain and promote the common good. Catholic social teaching is attentive to the ways in which the dignity of workers is violated, including unjust wages, unsafe conditions, benefits such as healthcare, and terms of employment. At times, these circumstances warrant the intervention of subsidiary agencies such as collective laborer organizations. In this way Catholic social teaching acknowledges the power differential that can leave workers at a significant disadvantage in protecting their rights and dignity. It also recognizes the tendency

in most systems for employers to take advantage of laborers for the benefit of the unjust accumulation of profit. Government intervention and regulation in the labor market become necessary tools to establish minimum standard for labor and wage conditions, especially where vast inequalities, or political and economic conditions of marginalized groups make workers particularly vulnerable. Local and international agencies are tasked with the responsibility to prevent, pursue, and prosecute slavery and human trafficking networks, which today impact the lives of over 20 million persons.[43]

6. *Subsidiarity and the proper role of government*[44]—One of the longest-standing questions facing the Church is the proper role of government. Primarily responsible for protecting the common good, the government ought to be an institution that protects these rights according to the dictates of communities seeking to uphold the dignity of all its members in particular ways. At the center of Catholic social teaching's understanding of the role of government is the construction of bodies that responsibly, reliably, and transparently guarantee that the basic necessities for life in community are safeguarded. Alternately, different communities ought to be able to build their own immediate structures for addressing the needs closest to them, unimpeded by cumbersome government processes or excessive regulations. Catholic social teaching strongly promotes a notion of human agency that empowers local bodies to build community grounded on bonds of proximity and solidarity, with care that tight identity boundaries not leave particular sectors unaided or vulnerable. Communities are at freedom to determine the best forms of participatory and representative government that uphold the rights of all its members, including material rights, which leads to broad and often problematic disagreement among those who would narrowly interpret Catholic social teaching as supporting certain neoliberal practices. For example, those who employ Catholic social teaching to argue that governments ought to be as small as possible while leaving the guarantee of rights and the protection of human dignity to subsidiary institutions. Others propose that Catholic social teaching, with its primary emphasis on human dignity for all, is partial to forms of government that more robustly intervene to insure that a basic floor of material and political conditions are met for the population, rather than leave it to the whim and limited resources of subsidiary institutions.

7. *Private property, the universal destination of material goods, and rights and responsibilities*[45]—The right to private property has always been recognized in Christian ethics, maintaining that no authority has the right to illegally or forcefully take possession of the fruits of one's labors. Systems that overlook or reject this principle place the fruit of one's labor at the whim of oppressive or illegitimate taxation, the taking of lands, homes, or other capital, by government authorities or economic elites. However, this right is balanced with the acknowledgment that creation is a gift from God, and sufficient to sustain human life. Therefore, the principle of human dignity stipulates all persons ought to have access to the goods necessary for life without which this quality of life diminishes and human dignity is threatened. These two seemingly opposing concepts find a kind of balance through their expression in rights and responsibilities. While one has the right to private property as the product of one's labor, this has the ultimate purpose of serving the larger community, especially when a deep need is

present, such as during a drought or other natural disaster, or during deep economic downturns. Through the balance of rights and responsibilities Catholic social teaching acknowledges that often material and economic goods that become the private property of some are not gained directly from one's work, but through unjust labor relations. It also acknowledges that social and political conditions may lead to deep inequalities, and the exclusion of entire groups from just compensation for their labor, as well as unemployment and underemployment.

8. *Colonialism and economic development*[46]—With the post-Second World War decolonization of most nations that had been integral to the military and economic expansion efforts of European nations, the need for ongoing development efforts became more apparent. However, this development ought not to depend on new forms of colonialism—political, economic, or ideological.[47] This principle points to the right of nations to seek avenues regionally and globally to develop their economies for the benefit of their population without having to yield their sovereignty. This does not point to an uncritical appreciation of international financial bodies whose function is to provide nations with access to capital, such as the World Bank, since these international bodies can also impose regulations and conditions on their development aid that seriously impinge on a nation's sovereignty and self-determination that may result in new forms of colonialism.

9. *Peace and disarmament*[48]—The ultimate goal of Christian ethics with respect to the use of force is peace. It is stated as a principle because in a fallen world this cannot be taken as assumed by the community of nations and even within nations, where taking up arms to resolve conflict has become the initial avenue rather than the last resort. Even while Catholic social teaching upholds the criteria from just war theory as a way to limit the evil of war, it continues to promote an understanding of the human being made for peace, with each other, with creation, and with God. Promotion of nonviolence as the political stance that ought to guide our encounter with others, from our personal engagements to the international community, has gained new ground in a body of work that up until recently was partial to just war theory as a sufficient tool to contain, reduce, or eliminate the need for the use of force.[49] As Pope Francis declared in his visit to the United States, disarmament, eliminating the sale of weapons to other states, to groups or factions within a state, and to individuals must be a priority of all governments, but especially the United States.[50] Disarmament as a principle of Catholic social teaching developed at a time when the nuclear arms race and their potential use threatened the entirety of human existence. It supported the work of international and regional bodies whose efforts attempted to curve and reduce this nihilistic quest for nuclear superiority. After the end of the Cold War it continues to see the reduction in weapons production, sales, and acquisition as an important goal for the construction of peace.

10. *Care of creation*[51]—This most recent principle responds to a world clamoring for its natural environment. While critiques of excessive consumerism, misuse of natural resources, and a throwaway culture were already present in Catholic social teaching, the overwhelming scientific evidence of the environmental crisis caused by climate change brings to the surface elements from the Bible and the early Christian tradition that speak to the beauty and blessedness of creation.

The biblical heritage keeps us in touch with the ways in which creation is one of the most evident ways in which God shows us care. Creation, and all that is part of it, is good in and of itself, and worthy to be protected. But today, the projections of the various peoples who will be most directly impacted by climate change—small island nations, and low-lying communities, women who are responsible for gathering food and water for their household, children who will not get the adequate nutrition for brain and bodily development, masses of people led to migrate because of drought, fires, floods, and other forms of impact from climate change[52]—led Pope Francis to unequivocally declare climate justice and care of creation one of the primary responsibilities and challenges for the human family, causing a ripple effect on all dimensions of life, from personal consumption habits to governmental oversight, to international agreements that seek to stem the tide of climate change.[53]

This brief overview of the key principles of Catholic social teaching also highlights some of the difficulties of articulating a comprehensive political theology grounded in Catholic social teaching. First, while the understanding on authoritative teaching is that it does not change in the life of the Church, clearly there is development in Catholic teaching. Its methodology demands attention to historical events, which often prompt the articulation of new or more detailed principles. Colonialism and development of newly independent and poorer countries was not on the radar of Pope Leo XIII when he wrote *Rerum Novarum* (1891), nor was climate change a dominant feature of *Pacem in Terris* (1963). The preferential option for the poor is the historically bound articulation of the consistent teaching of God's solidarity with the suffering and the excluded as it was first expressed in the oppressive conditions of economic and political inequality in Latin America of the 1960s.[54] However, there are those who view the notion of a developing tradition to discount the prescriptive statements of Catholic social teaching as mere recommendations for prudential judgment, rather than direct authoritative teaching.

Critics also argue that these principles present seemingly inherent contradictions, such as balancing human dignity and participation in the common good with the primacy of the family as the essential social unit. Or supporting economic development for impoverished countries while also caring for the environment. Interpreting and applying these principles cannot be a process of arranging them in an intransigent hierarchy of values. Rather, they require balance and overlay, applying multiple principles to a particular social challenge. Used in concert, they help correct the over-application of any one of them, which might lead to isolationist policies, on the one hand, or a strictly materialistic understanding of the person and communities, on the other. Questions also arise as to the feasibility of these guiding principles in a world where deepening inequality, ongoing civil and political strife, exclusion, and persecution impact the life of millions on a daily basis. How effective are principles grounded on the *ideal* human community in the face of so much brokenness? Inherent to the formulation of these principles are the various historical circumstances in which they developed. These moments are far from ideal, and marked by social and structural conflict and sin. Ultimately, they attempt to represent the love of God becoming incarnate in the most challenging of circumstances. Catholic social teaching does not uphold these principles as unrealistic ideals, but as maps toward establishing the Beloved Community.

Finally, the principles seem to be focused on the social dimensions of human experience. Are they translatable to the personal life of the faithful? The documents from which these principles are distilled all conclude with a call to personal conversion, highlighting the notion that individuals make up social structures and are able to create change when informed and motivated to do so. All Christians are called to be agents shaping the destinies of their communities, and to play a role in establishing more just conditions locally and globally, to promote human dignity for all, and to work in solidarity with the suffering and the poor. But these principles for justice in political and economic communities also ought to guide life in the family—the most basic social unit—by promoting acts of solidarity, privileging care for the suffering, eliminating boundaries of exclusion and marginalization, and encouraging subsidiary agency.

PRIMACY OF OPTION FOR THE POOR

By placing solidarity among the top three principles I stress what Christians ought to hold most deeply in social matters: the immediate suffering of others. While the inviolable human dignity of every person is the foundational principle of Catholic social teaching, I suggest that tensions among the principles stated above can be arbitrated by privileging the option for the poor as an organizing principle. Its development in the second half of the twentieth century represents a history of deep conflict, one where the Church had to come to terms with the ways it was capitulating the Bible's emphasis on love and justice for the poor as key to the story of salvation. When after Vatican II the bishops were asked to return home and more deeply "see" the (local) context in which they were called to be church, Latin American bishops and theologians saw that they lived in a continent that was majority Christian, but also majority poor. This reality, combined with the specter of political persecution and repression by military and economic elites, challenged the Latin American Church to rethink its apparent impartiality that was effectively providing support to political regimes and economic systems heavily dependent on an oppressed and extremely poor peasant class. The preferential option for the poor, though not directly articulated at the bishops' meeting in Medellín (1968), develops as the theological and ethical response to "a deafening cry [that] pours from the throats of millions of men [sic], asking their pastors for a liberation that reaches them from nowhere else."[55]

Though the work of Latin American and other liberation theologians received extensive criticism and correction from the Magisterium,[56] it was integrated into Magisterial expressions of Catholic social teaching by 1991, in John Paul II's *Centesimus Annus*, ensconcing it definitively in the tradition.[57] It represents a Christic value, that is, one which at its heart is fully about becoming incarnate in the suffering of another for the task of solidarity and transformation, akin to Christ's solidary bridging of divine life with the suffering of human death.

The common good, subsidiarity, human rights, the dignity of labor, care for the family—all of these principles of Catholic social teaching must follow the compass of the option for the poor, which asks that our best efforts at building political and economic systems bear in mind the destiny of the poor and oppressed first and foremost. The very logic embedded in Catholic social teaching of recognizing that most states, businesses, economic systems, and communities do not operate under ideal conditions, but, rather, often help establish and perpetuate violent inequalities that attack the dignity of whole groups of people, provides the justification for the primacy of the option for the poor. This principle becomes the orienting and organizing compass providing directionality and immediate measures for applying all the other principles to a situation. However, this is not necessarily a shared understanding of how to organize the principles of Catholic social teaching. For many, privileging the option for the poor is not a recipe for building and protecting the common good, but, rather, a recipe for fanning the fires of class warfare, emphasizing inequalities that might very well be a natural state for various healthy economic systems. In my estimation such assessments hide a partiality against challenging privilege and unjust economic gain, just as neoliberal commentators read *Centessimus Annus* as judging free-market capitalism as the economic system that most favored a Christian understanding of human freedom. The pastoral cycle "see–judge–act" cannot be applied indiscriminately, but must employ the option for the poor as a way to orient the gaze toward the crucified peoples, those with whom Jesus most closely identified: the migrant, the poor, the sick, and the marginalized other.

CRITIQUES AND FAILURES

It is important to briefly note not just complications arising from Catholic social teaching, but outright failures that up until now plague the tradition. Historically this is a body of work that represents a reactionary rather than a proactive stance, even in Pope Francis' time. In its effort to not appear partial toward any one system, or to seem to be proposing the elusive "third way," the documentary history reflects in large part a church struggling to make sense of the current moment, even as any particular challenge slips away in a rapidly changing sociopolitical global landscape. The strength of Catholic social teaching is its keen ability to describe human suffering in personal and systemic ways while preserving the principle of human dignity, but until recently this commitment to human dignity was not able to overcome the teaching's partiality toward liberal democratic capitalist societies as the model of political and economic community most amenable to encourage human freedom and flourishing. In my estimation, appreciation for this system gets in the way of the radical and necessary critiques that must be engaged against such systems for the way its practices impact the poor and vulnerable globally.[58]

According to some, Catholic social teaching is difficult to implement. Many Catholic faithful question whether its principles are mere theory or cause for direct action. Until recently dissemination of these documents was limited to bullet-point information cards shared with local churches after the release of a document. Only the more committed adult study groups along with learned theologians and seminary students took the time to read and analyze a document in its entirety, while pastors in many parts of the world, most certainly in the US, were hesitant to preach from the content of these documents. Advances in communications media and widespread accessibility to the Internet have significantly transformed dissemination of these documents to the point that news of the release of an encyclical is publicized well in advance of the actual release, prompting analyses and discussions from multiple perspectives across a wide array of fora. Still, there remains widespread confusion as to *how* these documents and principles are to be lived in community. Their indicting words against the status quo make it difficult to approach in middle-class or other privileged communities, while their insistence that they do not represent a "third way" leave many without proper recourse for its practical application. Ethicist Paul Lakeland notes the common critique that Catholic social teaching is understood to be more a theory of praxis rather than a theory *for* praxis.[59]

Traditionally Catholic social teaching has avoided reading history from the perspective of the conflicts that mark the everyday lives of so many. While it recognizes the suffering of wars, and institutionalized forms of violence, it fails to label these as conflict; with the consequence that Catholic social teaching doesn't always adequately acknowledge the challenges facing entire communities struggling for justice and peace for their people and their nations. Again, Lakeland points out that Catholic social teaching maintains a significant distance from the grassroots of history, "undermin[ing] those things of undoubted value which it proclaims."[60]

It is also important to note the failure of Catholic social teaching to properly address the way in which social and political conditions particularly impact the dignity of women beyond the privileged spaces of motherhood and family.[61] Kristin Heyer argues, "a generic construal of justice issues without attention to gendered elements is likewise dangerously inadequate."[62] It has been a long road for Catholic social teaching to acknowledge, for example, the particular effects and consequences of sexual violence, especially when used as a weapon of war and conflict; the mounting challenges on women who migrate; the vulnerabilities of women in low wage work; the unique challenges facing women in the areas of labor justice; political, religious, and social representation; and health and education outcomes. Finally, I note the perennial tension between Catholic social teaching and other liberationist perspectives in Christian political thought. In the end, Catholic social teaching places conversion of heart as the primary tool for transformation of social and political structures. Its central conviction is that without love of God and love of neighbor we will rarely effect the true change needed to establish just structures that uphold the human dignity of all persons and the environment, even as it makes recommendations at the level of policies and systemic change. Liberationists, however, acknowledging both the role of conflict in history and the urgent need for transformation and liberation will highlight the ways principles of justice, human dignity, and the option for the poor come across as profound challenges to entrenched systems of privilege and exclusion. Though they do not advocate further conflict as foundational to the path of justice and peace, it realizes that power will hardly ever yield its privilege unless it is wrested from the powerful, a process that may result in conflict and even violence, even as the ultimate goal is still love of neighbor and the creation of a more just society.

CONCLUSION: THE POPE FRANCIS MOMENT

The election of Pope Francis in 2013 welcomed the first Latin American pope, and with this a greater opening to the liberationist thought that had marked many strands of Catholicism in the continent. As the first pope to take full advantage of the Internet and social media, Francis' initial interviews, prayers, and addresses signaled significant developments in the trajectory of Catholic social teaching.

In the apostolic exhortation *Evangelii Gaudium* (2013) Francis clearly linked the message of the gospel and encountering Christ to the lives of the poor. Specifically, he urges the Church to move out of its sanctuary and beyond its doors, to encounter the poor and recognize the ways we participate in the structures that oppress them, and do grave damage to the environment. Perhaps most innovative is his acknowledgment that greed and pursuit of money is the cause of much suffering and grief personally and socially, a direct consequence of systems that revolve around the production of the most profit possible.[63] Unequivocally, Francis places the poor at the heart of the mission of the Church, and therefore at the core of the work of evangelizing, a task that is demanded of every faithful. The option for the poor becomes the privileged lens through which Francis officially inaugurates his papacy, hopefully transforming how Catholic social teaching ought to be read and implemented henceforth.

While Benedict XVI had placed climate change and care of creation as key concerns of Catholic social teaching,[64] Francis determinedly brings the principle of care of creation to the fore in *Laudato Si* (2015). This encyclical, above any other before, innovatively integrates two unique sources into the tradition: the witness of the natural sciences and the social teaching coming from regional and local bishops' conferences struggling with the issue of climate change in their immediate context. Here the voice of the poor—who are the first to experience the violence of climate change—receives a privileged space, while business leaders and policymakers are encouraged to move out of their centers of power and decision making in the great capital cities of the world in order to pay attention to what the poor are saying about climate change. Francis also lifts up the role of popular movements in shaping how we "see–judge–act" with respect to the climate crisis.[65]

In *Gaudete et Exsultate* (2018), Francis affirms the call for every faithful to be holy, and to humbly and actively walk the path of holiness that is the call of every Christian community.[66] Again affirming the primacy of the option for the poor, Francis lifts up "The Great Criterion" by which holiness is measured in the gospels, and by which others will know of our love and conviction in Christ: the mandate to care for the poor in Matthew 25:31–46.[67] More specifically, Francis warns against ideologies that are contrary to the gospel that are suspicious of the social concern of the Church as if it were materialist ideology or socialist or populist.[68] Rather, Francis wants the faithful to realize the intimate link between social concerns and the journey of holiness, our spiritual destinies tied up with the real destinies of the poor and oppressed.

Most recently, on August 2, 2018, Francis released a restatement of Catholic teaching on the death penalty as written in the Catholic Catechism.[69] This restatement represents decades of development and ongoing teaching from the Church on the topic of human dignity and the various arenas in which this is threatened by political and economic systems. The teaching, which originally permitted the death penalty as a last resort to prevent the criminal from committing further crimes and therefore fall further into sin, now states that the capital punishment is inadmissible in all cases. Much as with John XXIII, John Paul II, and the release of *Laudato Si*, critics coming mainly from the US privileged class have pointed out that Francis has no authority to shift centuries-old Catholic teaching on capital punishment. The severity of the moment cannot be overstated. At stake is clarification on the understanding of the teaching tradition of the Church as an adaptive and developing tool for understanding universal principles at different stages of human history. Alternately, we may begin to acknowledge that the Magisterium of the Church ought always be receptive to learning new things, especially as it concerns the needs of local church communities and other social and political bodies.

Clearly, the rich heritage of Catholic social teaching, with its flaws and failures, provides a robust yet flexible and developing political theology for life in community, grounded on human dignity as oriented by the option for the poor. Over its modern documentary history it moves toward further and deeper solidarity with the poor and oppressed as well as establishing clearer commitments to ways to alleviate suffering, even as it tiptoes around the issue of promoting a "third way." With respect to the flaws mentioned before, there is hope in its adaptability and evolution. By *Laudato Si* we come to a document that speaks clearly to how climate change impacts the life of the poor first,[70] recognizing that the natural sciences point to severe conflicts arising from competition for precious resources such as water and arable land.[71] In its jostling with reality Catholic social teaching struggles with the question of God's plan and providence as active in history. In Christian doctrine these elements have always implied directionality and an eschatological endpoint that, although we cannot augur with 100 percent certainty, we can venture to interpret it for our times. We do this in light of what the cross means for transforming the suffering of the world, witnessing to a God who, in the deepest act of solidarity, takes on the tragic finality of human death. For this very reason, if anything is said to be "evolving" in Catholic teaching it is the tradition of its social thought. This it does from the radically incarnational stance embedded in the praxis of the pastoral cycle of see–judge–act, letting the option for the poor orient its gaze to where incarnational transforming love is needed most.

NOTES

1. John Paul II, *Centesimus Annus—On the Hundreth Anniversary of* Rerum Novarum (May 1, 1991), http://w2.vatican.va/content/john-paul-ii/en/encyclicals/documents/hf_jp-ii_enc_01051991_centesimus-annus.html.
2. Leo XIII, *Rerum Novarum—On Capital and Labor* (May 15, 1895), http://w2.vatican.va/content/leo-xiii/en/encyclicals/documents/hf_l-xiii_enc_15051891_rerum-novarum.html.
3. The exact label used to name this body of work has been occasion for some confusion. Currently the Catholic Church identifies this body of work as doctrine. Its recent summary of the heritage of this tradition of teachings is titled *Compendium of the Social Doctrine of the Church* (2004), http://www.vatican.va/roman_curia/pontifical_councils/justpeace/documents/rc_pc_justpeace_doc_20060526_compendio-dott-soc_en.html. As such, it constitutes teaching considered official for the faithful of the Roman Catholic tradition. However, many other documents and works are considered part of the social teaching of the church. This would include documents from national and regional bodies of bishops, and non-Magisterial documents (key addresses and sermons) from the popes that also deal with the essentials of political and economic life. I refrain here from using the most expansive term, Catholic social thought, which moves beyond the material just listed in order to include secondary literature that interprets Catholic social teaching or doctrine in broader terms, and by authors without an authoritative mandate to do so.
4. John Paul II, *Centesimus Annus*, 32, 34, 35, 43, 48.
5. Ibid., 33–37.
6. John Pawlikowski, "The Three Recent Papacies: Continuity or Discontinuity on Economic Issues," Unpublished presentation (Manila, Philippines, 2015).
7. See, for example, Benedict XVI, *Caritas in Veritate—On Integral Human Development in Charity and Truth* (July 7, 2009), http://w2.vatican.va/content/benedict-xvi/en/encyclicals/documents/hf_ben-xvi_enc_20090629_caritas-in-veritate.html; and Francis, *Evangelii Gaudium—Apostolic Exhortation On the Proclamation of the Gospel in Today's World* (November 24, 2013), http://w2.vatican.va/content/francesco/en/apost_exhortations/documents/papa-francesco_esortazione-ap_20131124_evangelii-gaudium.html.
8. United States Catholic Bishops, *Economic Justice for All: Pastoral Letter on Catholic Social Teaching and the U.S. Economy* (November 1986), http://www.usccb.org/upload/economic_justice_for_all.pdf.
9. Ibid., Section 3: "The Church as Economic Actor."
10. Ari L. Goldman, "American Bishops Criticized on the Poor," *The New York Times* (November 5, 1986), https://www.nytimes.com/1986/11/05/us/catholic-bishops-criticized-on-poor.html.
11. Ibid. See also John Langan, "The Pastoral on the Economy: From Drafts to Policy (Notes on Moral Theology)," *Theological Studies*, 48 (March 1987), 144–147.

12. With the papacy of John XXIII, 1958–1963, a shift occurred in the addressee of most papal encyclicals. While previously the audience was often stated as the Catholic faithful, the hierarchy of the Church, and sometimes extended to the faithful of other Christian traditions in communion with the Roman Catholicism, John XXIII's *Pacem in Terris—On Establishing Universal Peace in Truth, Justice, Charity, and Liberty* (April 11, 1963) began the custom of including "all men [sic] of goodwill." The importance of this for a discussion on the political theology of Catholic social teaching lies in the assumption that after the *aggiornamento* of Vatican II the Church made a conscious decision to address a broader, more plural audience.

13. María Teresa Dávila, "The Role of the Social Sciences in Catholic Social Thought: the Incarnational Nature of the Option for the Poor and Being Able to 'See' in the Rubric 'See, Judge, Act'," *Journal of Catholic Social Thought*, vol.9, no. 2 (Summer 2012), 229–244.

14. Pope Pius XI, *Quadragesimo Anno—On Reconstruction of the Social Order* (May 15, 1931), http://w2.vatican.va/content/pius-xi/en/encyclicals/documents/hf_p-xi_enc_19310515_quadragesimo-anno.html.

15. Ibid.

16. Pope Pius XII, *Fidei Donum—On the Present Condition of the Catholic Missions, Especially in Africa* (April 21, 1957), http://w2.vatican.va/content/pius-xii/en/encyclicals/documents/hf_p-xii_enc_21041957_fidei-donum.html; and Second Vatican Council, *Gaudium et Spes—Pastoral Constitution of the Church in the Modern World* (December 7, 1967), http://www.vatican.va/archive/hist_councils/ii_vatican_council/documents/vat-ii_const_19651207_gaudium-et-spes_en.html. It is important to note that the Church's treatment of the topic of decolonization—as with other topics listed above—leaves much to be desired. As the essay will explain, in its attentiveness not to appear as taking sides on political issues which they determined as fraught with complex dynamics that could lead to conflict, and where, in their estimation, overall political and economic conditions could worsen, the Church either remained silent, made observations from a distance without committing to any one possible outcome, or made pronouncements after the fact. In the case of decolonization, its support for the project of expansion of Western civilization, a key element for the global spread of Christianity, prevented it from proposing possibilities for the liberation and emancipation of former colonies as central to the quest for human liberation and dignity. See Donald Dorr, "Pius XII: Anticommunism and Decolonization," in *Option for the Poor and for the Earth: from Leo XIII to Pope Francis*, revised edition (Maryknoll, NY: Orbis Books, 2016, Kindle edition).

17. John XXIII, *Pacem in Terris—On Establishing Universal Peace in Truth, Justice, Charity and Liberty* (April 11, 1963), http://w2.vatican.va/content/john-xxiii/en/encyclicals/documents/hf_j-xxiii_enc_11041963_pacem.html; *Gauidum et Spes* (1967); Pontifical Council for Justice and Peace, *The International Arms Race: An Ethical Reflection* (Libreria Editrice Vaticana: Vatican City, 1994).

18. United States Conference of Catholic Bishops, *The Challenge of Peace: God's Promise and Our Response* (May 3, 1983), http://www.usccb.org/upload/challenge-peace-gods-promise-our-response-1983.pdf; and the ten-year anniversary reflection, *The Harvest of Justice is Sown in Peace* (November 17, 1993), http://www.usccb.org/beliefs-and-teachings/what-we-believe/catholic-social-teaching/the-harvest-of-justice-is-sown-in-peace.cfm.

19. *Pacem in Terris* (1963); Pope John Paul II, *Centessimus Annus* (1991).

20. Pope Paul VI, *Populorum Progressio—On the Development of Peoples* (March 26, 1967), http://w2.vatican.va/content/paul-vi/en/encyclicals/documents/hf_p-vi_enc_26031967_populorum.html.

21. Pope Paul VI, *Humanae Vitae—On the Regulation of Birth* (July 25, 1968), http://w2.vatican.va/content/paul-vi/en/encyclicals/documents/hf_p-vi_enc_25071968_humanae-vitae.html.

22. *Pacem in Terris* (1963); Pontifical Council for the Pastoral Care of Migrants, *Refugees: A Challenge to Solidarity* (Vatican City: Libreria Editrice Vaticana, 1992); United States Conference of Catholic Bishops, *Welcoming the Stranger Among Us: Unity in Diversity* (November 15, 2000), http://www.usccb.org/issues-and-action/cultural-diversity/pastoral-care-of-migrants-refugees-and-travelers/resources/welcoming-the-stranger-among-us-unity-in-diversity.cfm.

23. Pope Francis, *Laudato Si—Care for our Common Home* (May 24, 2015), http://w2.vatican.va/content/francesco/en/encyclicals/documents/papa-francesco_20150524_enciclica-laudato-si.html.

24. Mary Irene Zotti, "The Young Christian Workers," *U.S. Catholic Historian*, vol. 9, no. 4 (Labor and Lay Movements, Part II) (Fall 1990), 387.

25. Pope John XIII, *Matter et Magistra—On Christianity and Social Progress* (May 15, 1965), http://w2.vatican.va/content/john-xxiii/en/encyclicals/documents/hf_j-xxiii_enc_15051961_mater.html, 236.

26. When pronounced as an encyclical or other papal document, or from a Synod of Bishops. Even within this nomenclature there are different levels of authority.

27. R.R. Reno, "The Weakness of Laudato Si," *First Things* (July 1, 2015), https://www.firstthings.com/web-exclusives/2015/07/the-weakness-of-laudato-si.

28. Among liberationist, womanist, *mujerista*, and other feminist theologians the use of the term "kindom" has replaced the use of the term "kingdom" to refer to the reality that is and will be God's reign. Briefly, two considerations come into play here. First, by replacing the term "kin" for "king" the emphasis shifts from a top-down, monarchical rule to a more horizontal vision of the Beloved Community in which Jesus Christ's fraternizing function (making us all sisters and brothers to each other) has been fulfilled. Second, it wrests sovereignty from the masculine vision of the Divine, helping to dismantle patriarchal theological imagery. Both are steps toward engaging a theological imaginary that more aptly reflects the experience of salvation for all by an all loving, all merciful God.

29. Francis Schüssler Fiorenza, "Political Theology as Foundational Theology," *Proceedings of the CTSA - Thirty-Second Annual Convention* (1977), 153, https://ejournals.bc.edu/ojs/index.php/ctsa/issue/view/269.

30. Fiorenza, 156: "The principles of natural religion are based on a universal truth, whereas the principles of civil religion are based on social utility."

31. Edward P. DeBerri and James Hug, et al., *Catholic Social Teaching: Our Best Kept Secret*, Fourth Revised and Expanded Edition (Maryknoll, NY: Orbis Books, 2004), 16; Paul Lakeland, "The Politics of Catholic Social Teaching," *Cross Currents*, vol. 35, no. 4 (Winter 1985–1986), XX.

32. Dávila, "The Role of the Social Sciences in Catholic Social Thought."

33. Thomas Massaro, SJ, *Living Justice: Catholic Social Teaching in Action* (Lanham, MD: Sheed and Ward, 2000), 115–164. Subsequent Classroom Editions of this volume have expanded the material to include the social teaching of Popes Benedict XVI and Francis. This also impacts his numeration of key principles, adding care for creation as the most recent articulation of these perennial Christian values.

34. Ibid., 115.

35. For a thorough review of the topic in official Catholic social teaching, see Michael A. Blume, S.V.D., "Migration and the Social Doctrine of the Church," *People on the Move*, No. 88–89 (April–December 2002), http://www.vatican.va/roman_curia/pontifical_councils/migrants/pom2002_88_90/rc_pc_migrants_pom88-89_blume.htm, a publication of the Pontifical Council for Migrants and Refugees.

36. See John XXIII, *Matter et Magistra*, 3, 94–96; Pontifical Council for Justice and Peace, *Compendium of the Social Doctrine of the Church* (April 2, 2004), http://www.vatican.va/roman_curia/pontifical_councils/justpeace/documents/rc_pc_justpeace_doc_20060526_compendio-dott-soc_en.html, 166, 182, 245, 222, 293, 447, 478; and Francis, *Laudato Si*, 27–31, respectively on these three topics.

37. Every attempt at clarity as to this point will inevitably run into complex and legitimate discussions regarding hard decisions made at multiple levels with regard to upholding human dignity within the confines of limited resources. To these quite real limits we must add conflicting sets of values that often coexist in pluralist societies with respect to shared or conflicting visions of the good life. Space does not permit a proper acknowledgment of this challenge, which surfaces as soon as one tries to negotiate these principles in the realm of public policy, governance, finance, and the markets. An excellent primer on this challenge is David Hollenbach, *Claims in Conflict: Retrieving and Renewing the Catholic Human Rights Tradition* (New York: Paulist Press, 1979).

38. Massaro, *Living Justice*, 119.

39. Ibid., 124.

40. Ibid., 138.

41. United States Conference of Catholic Bishops, "The Dignity of Work and the Rights of Workers," http://www.usccb.org/beliefs-and-teachings/what-we-believe/catholic-social-teaching/the-dignity-of-work-and-the-rights-of-workers.cfm.

42. John Paul II, *Laborem Exercens—on Human Work* (September 14, 1981), http://w2.vatican.va/content/john-paul-ii/en/encyclicals/documents/hf_jp-ii_enc_14091981_laborem-exercens.html.

43. International Labor Organization, "New ILO Global Estimate of forced Labor: 20.9 Million Victims" (June 1, 2012), http://www.ilo.org/global/about-the-ilo/newsroom/news/WCMS_182109/lang--en/index.htm.

44. Massaro, *Living Justice*, 128.

45. Ibid., 132. The iteration of this set of principles in Massaro's volume does not include "the universal destination of material goods."

46. Ibid., 142.

47. John XXIII, *Populorum Progressio*, 7, 52, 63.

48. Massaro, *Living Justice*, 150.

49. Joshua McElwee, "Landmark Vatican Conference Rejects Just War Theory, Asks for Encyclical on Nonviolence," *National Catholic Reporter* (April 14, 2016), https://www.ncronline.org/news/vatican/landmark-vatican-conference-rejects-just-war-theory-asks-encyclical-nonviolence.

50. Francis, "Transcript: Pope Francis' Speech to Congress," *The Washington Post* (September 25, 2015), https://www.washingtonpost.com/local/social-issues/transcript-pope-franciss-speech-to-congress/2015/09/24/6d7d7ac8-62bf-11e5-8e9e-dce8a2a2a679_story.html?utm_term=.0a2295e5ceab.

51. Francis, *Laudato Si*.

52. An excellent survey of current scientific evidence on climate change, political challenges, impact to different groups of people, and discussion of various dimensions of the encyclical *Laudato Si* is found in *The Theological and Ecological Vision of Laudato Si: Everything is Connected*, edited by Vincent Miller (London: Bloomsbury T&T Clark, 2016).

53. Francis, *Laudato Si*, Chapters 5 and 6.

54. María Teresa Dávila, "A Liberation Ethic for the One-third World: the Preferential Option for the Poor and Challenges to Middle-class Christianity in the United States," PhD diss. (Boston College, 2007), 246–250.

55. Consejo Episcopal Latinoamericano (CELAM), *Medellín: Poverty of the Church* (September 6, 1968), http://www.povertystudies.org/TeachingPages/EDS_PDFs4WEB/Medellin%20Document-%20Poverty%20of%20the%20Church.pdf, 1.2.

56. See the two instructions from the Sacred Congregation for the Doctrine of the Faith, *Instruction on Certain Aspects of Theologies of Liberation* (June 1984), http://www.povertystudies.org/TeachingPages/EDS_PDFs4WEB/Medellin%20Document-%20Poverty%20of%20the%20Church.pdf; and *Instruction on Christian Freedom and Liberation* (March 22, 1986), http://www.vatican.va/roman_curia/congregations/cfaith/documents/rc_con_cfaith_doc_19860322_freedom-liberation_en.html.

57. John Paul II, *Centesimus Annus*, 11, 57.

58. An example of this is the lack of a thorough critique of the ways racism seems to permeate most liberal democracies, especially since many participated in one way or another in the global slave trade. While much has been made within Catholic social teaching about contemporary networks of slave labor, racism remains a hidden crisis, included in lists that enumerate grave social sins, but rarely tackled directly by the tradition. On this topic see Bryan Massingale, *Racial Justice and the Catholic Church* (Maryknoll, NY: Orbis Books, 2010); and María Teresa Dávila, "Racialization and Racism in Theological Ethics," in *Catholic Theological Ethics Past, Present, and Future*, edited by James Keenan (Maryknoll, NY: Orbis Books, 2011), 307–321.

59. Paul Lakeland, "The Politics of Catholic Social Teaching," *Cross Currents*, vol. 35, no. 4 (Winter 1985–1986), 395.

60. Ibid.

61. Kristin Heyer, "A Feminist Appraisal of Catholic Social Thought," Lane Center for Catholic Studies and Catholic Social Thought Fall Lecture Series, University of San Francisco (November 9, 2007), 2.

62. Ibid.

63. Francis, *Evangelii Gaudium*, 53–60, 197–208.

64. Benedict XVI, *Caritas in Veritate*, 27, 48–67.

65. Space does not permit a deeper analysis of the importance of popular movements for Francis' papacy and understanding of how Catholic social teaching is put into action on the ground. Helpful in understanding this influence in his thought are his addresses to the World Gathering of Popular Movements in Bolivia on July 2015, http://w2.vatican.va/content/francesco/en/speeches/2015/july/documents/papa-francesco_20150709_bolivia-movimenti-popolari.html; Rome on November 2016, http://w2.vatican.va/content/francesco/en/speeches/2016/november/documents/papa-francesco_20161105_movimenti-popolari.html, and during the first regional meeting of popular movements in the US, in California on February 2017, http://w2.vatican.va/content/francesco/en/messages/pont-messages/2017/documents/papa-francesco_20170210_movimenti-popolari-modesto.html.

66. Francis, *Gaudete et Exsultate—Apostolic Exhortation on the Call to Holiness in Today's World* (March 19, 2018), http://w2.vatican.va/content/francesco/en/apost_exhortations/documents/papa-francesco_esortazione-ap_20180319_gaudete-et-exsultate.html.

67. Ibid., 96–99.

68. Ibid., 101.

69. Elizabeth Povoledo and Laurie Goodstein, "Pope Francis Declares Death Penalty Unacceptable in All Cases," *The New York Times* (August 2, 2018), https://www.nytimes.com/2018/08/02/world/europe/pope-death-penalty.html.

70. Francis, *Laudato Si*, 13, 16, 20. The poor and poverty receives preferential treatment in this encyclical. See María Teresa Dávila, "The Option for the Poor in *Laudato Si*: Connecting Care of Creation with Care for the Poor," *The Theological and Ecological Vision of* Laudato Si: *Everything is Connected*, edited by Vincent Miller (London: Bloomsbury T&T Clark, 2017), 145–159.
71. Ibid., 31, 48.

SELECT BIBLIOGRAPHY

Blanco, Pablo Alberto (2012), "La Convertibilidad y la Crisis del 2001 en Argentina: Crónicay Revisión de un Final Anunciado a la Luz de la Doctrina Social de la Iglesia," Buenos Aires, Argentina: Pontificia Universidad Católica de Argentina.

Brazal, Agnes and María Teresa Dávila, eds. (2016), *Living With(out) Borders: Catholic Theological Ethics on the Migrations of Peoples*, Maryknoll, NY: Orbis Books.

Clark, Charles (October 2012) "From the 'Wealth of Nations' to '*Populorum Progressio*' (On the Development of Peoples): Wealth and Development from the Perspective of the Catholic Social Thought Tradition," *American Journal of Economics and Sociology*, vol. 71, no. 4: 1047–1072.

Clark, Meghan (2014), *The Vision of Catholic Social Thought: The Virtue of Solidarity and the Praxis of Human Rights*, Minneapolis, MN: Fortress Press.

Dorr, Donald (2016), *Option for the Poor and For the Earth: From Leo XIII to Pope Francis*, rev. ed., Maryknoll, NY: Orbis Books.

Himes, Kenneth, et al. (2018), *Modern Catholic Social Teaching: Commentaries and Interpretations*, 2nd ed., Washington, DC: Georgetown University Press.

Hinga, Teresia (2008), "Women, Religion, and HIV/AIDS in Africa: Responding to Ethical and Theological Challenges," Pietermaritzburg, Cluster Publications.

Miller, Vincent (2017), *The Theological and Ecological Vision of Laudato Si: Everything is Connected*, London: Bloomsbury T&T Clark.

O'Brien, David and Thomas Shannon, eds. (2010), *Catholic Social Thought: A Documentary Heritage*, expanded edition, Maryknoll, NY: Orbis Books.

Orobator, Agbonkhianmeghe (2011), *Reconciliation, Justice, and Peace: The Second African Synod*, Maryknoll, NY: Orbis Books.

Peppard, Christiana Z. (2014), *Just Water: Ethics and the Global Water Crisis*, Maryknoll, NY: Orbis Books.

Pontifical Council for Justice and Peace, "Compendium of the Social Teaching of the Catholic Church," April 2005. http://www.vatican.va/roman_curia/pontifical_councils/justpeace/documents/rc_pc_justpeace_doc_20060526_compendio-dott-soc_en.html.

Rajendra, Tisha (2017), *Migrants and Citizens: Justice and Responsibility in the Ethics of Immigration*, Grand Rapids, MI: Wm. B. Eerdmans Publishing Co.

Schlag, Martin (2017), *Handbook of Catholic Social Thought: A Guide for Christians in the World Today*, Washington, DC: Catholic University of America Press.

CHAPTER TWENTY-TWO

Orthodox Christianity and Political Theology

Thinking Beyond Empire

NATHANIEL WOOD
AND ARISTOTLE PAPANIKOLAOU

INTRODUCTION

Scholarly engagement with Orthodox Christian theology has become increasingly common in recent years, but Orthodox political theology has attracted relatively little attention.[1] In fact, Orthodoxy is not really known for having much of a political theology, or at least none that speaks to the concerns of contemporary scholars in the field. Nor do the popular images associated with Orthodoxy—the mystical and apophatic character of its theology, its focus on patristic exegesis, its emphasis on asceticism and hesychastic prayer, its seemingly private and otherworldly understanding of salvation as personal union with God—intuitively suggest much relevance for current sociopolitical challenges. Even while Orthodox theology is gaining a more prominent place in Western scholarship, political theology remains overwhelmingly Catholic and Protestant.[2]

There are good reasons for this. To start with, the Orthodox were almost entirely absent from the development of modern political theology in the latter half of the twentieth century. It is not that non-Orthodox theologians ignored Orthodox voices; the Orthodox simply did not produce anything like the body of political theological scholarship that Catholics and Protestants did. The dominant Orthodox theological paradigm since the 1940s, the so-called "neopatristic synthesis" pioneered by the Russian émigrés Georges Florovsky (1893–1979) and Vladimir Lossky (1903–1958), did not have much to say about politics, and the major works of the movement offer little substantial engagement with contemporary political questions.[3] Part of the reason for this lack of engagement is what the Greek theologian Pantelis Kalaitzidis describes as the introverted turn of Orthodox theology during the period.[4] In response to what was perceived as the captivity of the previous generation of Orthodox theology to modern Western philosophy, neopatristic theology prioritized the articulation of a "de-Westernized" Orthodox theological identity through a perpetual return to the Greek Fathers. One result of this "return to the Fathers" is that patristic exegesis, especially that which highlights the distinctiveness of Orthodoxy's mystical theology vis-à-vis the supposed reductive rationalism of the West, tended to overshadow productive encounter with modernity, including modern politics. Therefore, while this neopatristic revival has led to important work on topics like the Trinity, eucharistic ecclesiology, and theologies of personhood and communion, Orthodox theologians usually have not extended their work in these areas into the domain of political theology.

However, it would be wrong to suppose that Orthodox theology is inherently indifferent to politics. Eastern Christians have been reflecting on Christianity's relationship to politics since the time of the Church Fathers, and they have produced numerous political theologies throughout the centuries. The mystical orientation of Orthodox faith and practice has never precluded concern for the political. The spiritual heart of the Orthodox tradition—the doctrine of *theosis*, or "deification," the principle of divine–human communion—can evoke images of Manichean withdrawal from history and world-denying struggle toward mystical union with the divine. Such images might suggest that detachment from the affairs of this world is fundamental to the Orthodox ethos. In reality, however, there has always been recognition within the tradition that deification includes the transformation of the social order, along with the whole of creation, in conformity to God's own likeness. After all, it is the *whole* human person who is called to be deified, body as well as soul, including the social, political, and economic dimensions of his or her life. There is no question that Orthodox theology should have some bearing on politics. The question is *how* Orthodoxy should relate to the political.

This essay will examine some of the ways in which modern Orthodox theologians have responded to this question, particularly in relation to liberal democracy. The question has always been an important one, but it has become especially urgent now that the Orthodox, for the first time, are being forced to come to terms culturally and theologically with the rise of modern democracy, human rights theory, and the secularization of the political sphere. Compared to Catholics and Protestants, the Orthodox do not have much experience thinking through these issues. For most of its history, Orthodox reflection on politics was carried out in relation to imperial power structures. Orthodox political theology developed almost entirely within the context of Christian empires such as Byzantium and Russia, only to have its evolution cut short by nearly four centuries of Ottoman Muslim rule and the militant atheism of the Soviet Union. Except for a brief period leading up to the Russian Revolution of 1917, Orthodoxy has mostly been shielded from the intellectual currents that gave rise to political liberalism. Now, however, following the collapse of communism in the traditionally Orthodox countries of Eastern Europe, Orthodox Christians have been given an unprecedented opportunity—as well as the responsibility—to consider new approaches to Christian politics.

The rehashing of patristic and Byzantine models will not be sufficient to address the challenges of pluralist democratic societies. The current situation requires the renewal of truly *constructive* Orthodox political theology, political theology that puts Orthodoxy's core theological principles into mutual dialogue with modern political thought, including the liberal tradition. Currently, in response to the post-communist situation, Orthodox political theology is experiencing such a renewal, even if, in many cases, the most visible reactions to liberal democracy do not make that clear. In light of reactionary stances towards liberal democracy coming out of traditionally Orthodox countries, it is especially important to elevate Orthodox political theologies that highlight the political-theological creativity and versatility of which the Orthodox tradition is capable.[5]

SYMPHONIA AND BEYOND

Orthodox responses to liberal democracy have often been hampered by nostalgia for lost Christian empires, which still holds sway over Orthodox political imagination. Many of the responses have been uncritically reactionary and theologically superficial, relying on "fundamentalist" readings of the tradition that treat the latter as a fixed artifact, something already perfected in the past and closed off to further development. One of the crucial tasks for a constructive Orthodox political theology is to challenge such readings. According to the nineteenth-century Russian philosopher Vladimir Soloviev, the first systematic modern Orthodox political theologian, "Sacred tradition must be a perpetual buttress of contemporaneity, a token and rudiment of what is approaching."[6] What is approaching, of course, is the Kingdom of God, which cannot be confused with any earthly kingdoms past or present. Byzantine political theology was an attempt to negotiate the Church's political role in relation to existing imperial structures in light of Orthodox Christianity's foundational belief that the world was created for communion with God.[7] Contemporary Orthodox theologians must engage the present situation in a similar fashion by reflecting on the political implications of central Orthodox doctrines in relation to new political realities. While always maintaining the distinction between divine and earthly rule, it must seek signs of advancement towards the Kingdom within the flow of political history, including, in our time, within the global rise of liberal democracy.

Does liberal democracy present new opportunities for a Christian politics faithful to the Gospel that imperial theocracy did not allow for? To address this question, Orthodox political theology must learn to think beyond its imperial heritage. But what is that heritage?

Although the Orthodox have understood their relationship to political power in various ways, the dominant trend throughout its imperial history was to sacralize imperial power by granting it an ontological foundation within the divine rule. The classical expression of this trend is the Byzantine model usually known as *symphonia*, the ideal of a complementary "harmony" between the Church and the emperor, two ministries of the divine government that work together for the sake of human salvation and the perfection of the social order. The model is sometimes mistakenly described as "caesaropapism" on the belief that the emperor rules over the Church, but this characterization misses the fact that "imperial power is a form of ecclesiastical service" that exists *"within the Church."*[8] *Symphonia* maintains an official distinction between the ecclesiastical and imperial authorities, granting each its own sphere of competence, while their respective "sacred" and "secular" ends are harmonized into a divine–human whole, like the two natures in Christ—a testament to the promised deification of the world. The *symphonia* doctrine received its most famous articulation in the sixth century in Emperor Justinian's *Sixth Novella*, but its underlying logic—the fusion of imperial and ecclesiastical interests—has dominated Eastern Christian political thought since the conversion of Constantine and provided the foundation for the political theologies of post-Byzantine Orthodox states. It relied on a mystical correspondence between imperial power and divine rule, treating the empire as the earthly image of the heavenly Kingdom, with the emperor as God's viceroy enacting God's rule on earth.[9] As Eusebius of Caesarea said of Constantine, the emperor is an icon of the "heavenly sovereignty" who "frames his earthly government according to the pattern of the divine original" in "conformity to the monarchy of God."[10]

The *symphonia* doctrine has had many lasting consequences for Orthodox political thought. Historically, one of its functions was to provide a theological justification for autocracy against alternatives, including democracy. It has imbued Orthodox political thought with a predominantly "royalist" orientation, enshrining the ideal of Christian monarchy as the only *true* Orthodox politics. Furthermore, it has tended to bind the very idea of Orthodox Christianity to the idea of Christian empire, suggesting that there could be no church without empire. This sentiment was famously expressed in a 1395 letter from Ecumenical Patriarch Anthony of Constantinople to Grand Prince Vasily I of Moscow when Vasily had refused to pay homage to the Byzantine Emperor: "You are wrong to affirm that we have the church without an emperor, for it is impossible for Christians to have a church and no empire. The *Basileia* [empire] and the church have a great unity and community—indeed they cannot be separated."[11] Of course, in 1453, barely half a century after the Patriarch sent his letter, Constantinople would fall to the Ottomans, and the imperial political theology would be transferred to Russia with the adoption of tsarist autocracy and the doctrine of Moscow as the "Third Rome."

One of the merits of imperial political theology is that it recognized the deep "harmony" between the mystical and the political: deification is not complete apart from the redemption of the social order, without the establishment of the Kingdom of God. In principle, and many times in practice, the close link between the Church and imperial power could mean holding imperial power accountable to the norms of divine justice, bending it towards a greater reflection of the Kingdom. However, as Kalaitzidis notes, one of Orthodoxy's perennial temptations is to confuse the current political order with the Kingdom's eschatological realization, allowing the Church's social mission to become entangled with the preservation of political power and allowing a conservative defense of the present order to take precedence over prophetic social criticism and proper attention to the demands of human freedom and social justice. For Kalaitzidis, the imperial legacy has given Orthodox politics a generally conservative and authoritarian bent, which helps to explain why, with rare exceptions, Orthodoxy has not developed political theologies in the "liberating and radical sense" one finds in the work of leading Catholic and Protestant theologians such as Johann Baptist Metz, Jürgen Moltmann, and the Latin American liberation theologians.[12]

Today, there are no more Christian empires, but the continued influence of imperial theology still complicates responses to liberal democracy in the post-communist Orthodox world. Even if most Orthodox recognize that a literal return of *symphonia* is impossible, many Church leaders hope to enact a kind of "cultural *symphonia*" through the restoration of a "Christian society" under ecclesiastical influence and officially backed up by the state. To this end, there have been attempts at restoring special cooperative relationships between the national Orthodox churches and state power, which too often brings the churches into alliances with nationalist and anti-liberal political forces, as is the case in Vladimir Putin's Russia.

Complicating matters is the fact that Orthodox responses to liberal democracy are usually entangled with Orthodox suspicion towards Western culture. There has been a longstanding tendency within Orthodoxy to define Orthodox identity over against "the West."[13] At least since the time of the nineteenth-century Russian Slavophiles, this polemical construction of "the West" has indicated not only the alleged heresies of Catholic and Protestant Christianity, but also their supposed conclusion: secular modernity, along with its political expressions, including liberal individualism. We find the first gestures toward a modern Orthodox political theology in this nineteenth-century context, where they were bound up with nationalism and anti-Westernism that spilled over into anti-liberalism and a critique of human rights.[14] Nowhere are the effects of this attitude more visible than in post-communist Russia. As post-Soviet Orthodox struggle to reconstruct their religious and cultural identities following decades of communist oppression, many have embraced some version of this anti-Western stance, showing suspicion toward liberal democracy and liberal conceptions of individual rights as godless

Western imports alien to the traditional Orthodox ethos. For example, the head of the Russian Orthodox Church (ROC), Patriarch Kirill of Moscow, has remarked on some Western notions of individual rights being "heresy."[15] Resistance to liberal rights language also appears in official ROC documents, such as a major 2008 statement outlining the Church's *Basic Teaching on Human Dignity, Freedom, and Rights*. While not rejecting human rights language wholesale, the 2008 document divorces human rights from a liberal individualist framework and refashions it along what it considers to be distinctively Eastern and Orthodox lines, with some troubling results—by subordinating, for instance, individual rights to the community's "traditional values."[16] The ROC's rejection of a liberal democratic understanding of human rights has come to serve Russian national interests, as it has since been appropriated by Vladimir Putin to forge a new geopolitical East–West divide, with Russia taking the lead as the defender of "traditional values" against the godless, immoral liberalism of the West, in alliance with, ironically, American Evangelical Christians.[17]

One of the important tasks for Orthodox political theology is to consider whether such skepticism toward liberalism and human rights reflects something fundamental about the Orthodox faith, or whether it is only a product of historical circumstances that can be corrected by fresh engagement with Christian doctrine. Does Orthodox theology *essentially* lead to monarchic and theocratic political conclusions, with other types of government being, at best, a compromise of Orthodox principles? Or, instead, might the core principles of Orthodox theology lead to a Christian politics that is compatible with liberal democracy, or even a politics that *favors* certain features of liberal democracy over the Byzantine model and its offshoots?

Such questions have been central in the current revival of Orthodox political theology. Orthodox theological engagement with liberal democracy is not monolithic, but one thing the literature makes clear is that simplistic narratives of a "clash of civilizations" between the Orthodox East and the liberal democratic West endorsed by some Western observers do not tell the whole story.[18] Orthodox responses to liberal democracy are much more complex and varied than what the news headlines might suggest. Recognizing the general irrelevance of Byzantine political theology for the modern world, several Orthodox theologians have recognized the need for "something less like a debate and more like a creative dialogue" between Orthodoxy and the liberal democratic tradition[19] and have argued that the central themes of Orthodox theology point toward the possibility of productive encounter between the two. Notable in this regard are two major recent monographs, Kalaitzidis's *Orthodoxy and Political Theology* and Aristotle Papanikolaou's *The Mystical as Political*. Kalaitzidis argues that a better understanding of eschatology can overcome Orthodox fascination with the imperial past as well as all "far-right" temptations to confuse political power with the Kingdom of God, providing the basis for an Orthodox "liberation theology" and justification for Orthodox support for democracy, human rights, and church–state separation. Papanikolaou similarly makes a theological case against the confusion of the ecclesial and the political and in favor of liberal democracy and the secularization of the political sphere, principally on the basis of the doctrine of deification.

This current constructive work has been accompanied by the rediscovery of certain "minority" Orthodox voices from the past. There has been a great renewal of interest, both within and outside Orthodoxy, in the work of nineteenth- and early-twentieth-century Russian philosopher-theologians such as Vladimir Soloviev (1853–1900), Nikolai Berdyaev (1874–1948), and especially Sergei Bulgakov (1871–1944), key pioneers of modern Orthodox political theology whose writings have become increasingly available in translation.[20] Unfortunately, these thinkers mostly fell out of favor in the Orthodox world following the critiques of figures like Lossky and Florovsky,[21] but their work is significant as a record of Orthodoxy' first, albeit brief and inconclusive, encounter with liberalism in the twilight of the Russian Empire. Faced with the decline of the Russian theocracy and the rise of militant Marxism, these thinkers sought to forge a distinctively Christian alternative to both in dialogue with liberal and socialist thought. What is especially noteworthy is their recognition that the Russian theocracy had failed to meet the demands of human freedom and social justice that were entailed by the Gospel's promise of deification and its acknowledgment of the divine dignity of the person. While the resulting political theologies were not exactly liberal in the standard sense, their concern for the dignity of the person and their willingness to engage the liberal tradition moved Orthodox political theology in a liberal direction: affirming, for instance, religious toleration, human rights, free speech, and other hallmarks of liberal politics.[22]

The remainder of this essay will illustrate a small part of the variety of modern Orthodox political theology by looking at two sorts of examples of how Orthodox encounter with liberal democracy has sparked creative theological reflection on the meaning of Christian politics. The examples are different in key ways—one mostly critical toward liberalism, the other consciously attempting to integrate liberal principles into Orthodox politics—but they both show that Orthodoxy is not captive to traditional understandings of *symphonia* but is capable of constructive political theology rooted in the tradition's core doctrines. In both examples, the doctrine in question is *theosis*, along with its implications for the nature of human personhood.

DEIFICATION AND LIBERAL DEMOCRACY

The guiding doctrinal principle of the "liberalizing" Russian political theology was that of deification or divine–human communion. However, there are certain ambiguities surrounding the political implications of deification in relation to liberal democracy. Some of the most famous twentieth-century Orthodox theologians, such as Lossky, John Zizioulas, and Dumitru Staniloae, popularized the perception of *theosis* as central to modern Orthodox theology, but they did not develop political theologies based on the doctrine. For Soloviev and Bulgakov, on the other hand, a theology of deification could not be anything but a political theology, since it is at heart a theology of the dignity and freedom, the "absolute, divine significance," of the human person,[23] and thus entails a politics centered on "the creation of the conditions for the free development of human personhood."[24] In fact, thinkers such as Soloviev and Bulgakov were instrumental in the modern revival of constructive Orthodox theologies of deification, and they turned to deification in part to ground a philosophical and political defense of the free human person against both the mass poverty and political repression of the Russian Empire and the fanaticism of Russian Marxism, which subordinated particular persons to the pseudo-religious idol of "social progress."[25]

Deification is linked to human dignity in neopatristic theology as well. Here, however, the relationship between human dignity and liberal democracy is less clear, not only because it usually is not explored, but also because also because deification usually undergirds certain conceptions of personhood and communion that appear to be at odds with the supposed anthropological presuppositions of liberalism. Zizioulas's classic study *Being as Communion*[26] is the most recognizable in this regard, but books such as *Person and Eros* by Christos Yannaras,[27] who is less well known outside Greece, advance a similar link between deification and a theological personalism centered on communion. These works develop approaches to personhood that highlight the difference between an Orthodox theocentric view of the person-in-communion and secular Western individualism. A fundamental distinction between *person* and *individual* has become closely associated with theologies of deification, where personhood is inherently relational: to be a person is to exist as irreducibly unique and in *ecstatic* freedom from the necessity of sinful nature in communion with and for other persons. Deification is fundamentally about *becoming a person,* which is to say that deification is about the building up of communion; whereas individualism, on the other hand, is associated with sin, disintegration, and death. Therefore, if liberalism is presumed to be founded on the assumption that human beings are basically self-enclosed individuals who form social contracts on the basis of their private self-interest, then it seems as if the promise of deification is a promise for salvation from the very sort of individualism upon which liberal democracy is founded.

Zizioulas does not draw out an explicit politics from his theology of personhood, though Papanikolaou does argue for liberal democratic understandings of human rights on the basis of Zizioulas's theology of personhood.[28] Papanikolaou claims that although human rights language does not point to all that is possible for humans, it functions to structure relationships within a political community toward the embodied experience of irreducible uniqueness analogous to that experienced within the Eucharist.

In contrast, Yannaras treats his theocentric view of the person as the basis for a critique of Western liberal and human rights traditions. Yannaras's political theology rests on a contrasting of the "apotheosis of egoism and individualism in the West that births modern liberal democracy, modernity, secularization, and the culture of human rights to the event of communion, which he sees in the democracy of ancient Greece," whose "direct heir" is the Orthodox *ecclesia*, "which meets to constitute and reveal itself in the Eucharist according to the truth and after the image of the Trinity where many are one."[29] For Yannaras, an Orthodox theology of personhood entails what he calls a "communo-centric politics" as opposed to a liberal politics founded on individual rights.[30] A communo-centric politics is needed because "the Western politics of individual right is fundamentally incompatible" with the Orthodox view of the person,[31] since according to Orthodoxy, "The autonomous, independent, self-referential human unit posited by the concept of individual right does not exist."[32] The problem with Western democracy, moreover, is that by adopting this false anthropology, it is rendered "fundamentally anti-community," because democratic society presupposes the fundamental reality of ineradicable conflict and exists only to mitigate the most destructive effects of that conflict by channeling it into a contractual agreement. "People with common *individual* interests make common cause in order to protect and advance *their* interests against the other interests that threaten them."[33] But such superficial, self-serving unity is certainly not real community. Hence the necessity of the Church as a political reality: only the Church, with its foundation in the Trinity and the Eucharist, can "reorient Western political culture away from individual right and towards a politics of relationship."[34]

Despite several differences, Yannaras's contemporary Greek political theology resonates with the general mood of Russian Slavophile political theology from the 1840s and 1850s. Key members of this movement include Alexei Khomiakov (1804–1860), Ivan Kireevsky (1806–1856), and Konstantin Aksakov (1817–1860). While none of the Slavophiles were systematic theologians, they were among the first modern Orthodox

Christians to engage in something like a constructive political theology, albeit primarily in service to an anti-Western polemic. The Slavophiles formulated their vision of politics by drawing an explicit contrast between Western democratic society and an Orthodox theology of communion. Against the position of the Russian "Westernizers" that social progress in Russia required turning to the Western intellectual tradition, the Slavophiles searched for a foundation for progress in Russia's own cultural heritage, whose center was the Orthodox Church. Their most recognizable contribution to Orthodox theology was Khomiakov's ecclesiological concept of *sobornost'*, an approach to the Church's "conciliarity" or "all-togetherness" derived from the Slavonic translation of the Nicene Creed.[35] The main idea of Khomiakov's ecclesiology is that divine grace can never be the possession of the isolated individual but resides within the communion of the Church, circulating, like blood through an organism, throughout the Church's members through their mutual service and self-sacrificial love for each other. What this means is that self-perfection requires the kenotic renunciation of self-sufficiency, in which individuals trade their natural individuality (here again associated with humanity's fallenness) for a higher "choral" personality that is realized within communion, within "a concord of equally self-sacrificing persons."[36]

For the Slavophiles, *sobornost'* was not just an ecclesiological doctrine, but like Yannaras's eucharistic community, is also the basis of the social order. Ecclesial communion is the "highest social principle" upon which Orthodox societies must be based.[37] In the polemical context of their dispute with the Westernizers, the Slavophiles formulated this principle in direct opposition to what they saw as one the founding principles of the Western social order: a "feudal" conception of personhood based in the absolute right of individual self-ownership, which births an interpersonal conflict (Hobbes's universal war) which is resolved only through the "external" and "artificial" unity of social contract.[38] Like Yannaras, the Slavophiles reject individual rights as the basis of society because it is based on the assumption of primordial conflict and is incapable of enacting genuine community rather than the mere coordination of private self-interest.

Sobornost' thus had direct political implications, including the rejection of democracy in favor of autocracy. The Slavophiles imagined a kind of *symphonia* between the Church and the Russian state, but one radically altered from the Byzantine model of the politically strong ecclesiastical hierarchy. For the Slavophiles, the goal of *symphonia* was to *remove the Church from the sphere of the political*, since politics is inherently conflictual and thus antithetical to communion. The problem with democracy is that, by admitting Christians into the sphere of political conflict, it competes with the educative influence of the Church, and risks forming people into the sort of atomistic, self-serving individuals from which the Church promises salvation. In other words, as a politics of self-interest, democracy interferes with Christians' progress towards deification by hindering the cultivation of communion. The role of autocracy, therefore, was to serve as a buffer against democracy for the people's own spiritual wellbeing: by handing over the minimal but necessary work of coercive state politics to the autocrat, the Church is free to get on with its real social mission of learning to *be* the Church, a communion of lovers.[39]

Largely, then, the critique of democracy is also a critique of the ways in which distorted forms of Russian *symphonia* had subordinated the Church to the interests of imperial power, as it had done under the Western-facing reforms of Peter the Great, robbing the Church of its independent voice to speak out (in an ironically "liberal" fashion) against such social sins as serfdom, censorship, and capital punishment.[40] As such, their thought reveals something of the *complexity* of modern Orthodox political theology; even in criticizing liberal democratic West, it does not always fit simplistic caricatures of uncritical "conservatism." The Slavophiles offered a creative, if unfeasibly romantic, attempt at rethinking Orthodoxy's political heritage in response to modernization.[41] Yannaras's critique of individual rights, too, is more nuanced than often presented: individual rights are not *inherently* incompatible with a politics of communion, but "can productively serve a politics that prioritizes relationships and community" as long as private self-interest is not treated as the end goal of politics, as he thinks is the case with liberal democracy.[42]

Nevertheless, if Yannaras and the Slavophiles represent a generally negative way of relating Orthodox theology to liberal democracy, thinkers like Soloviev and Bulgakov represent a generally more positive alternative. Soloviev's was the first truly systematic modern Orthodox political theology, and, taking shape within the Russian imperial context, it still takes for granted the reality of autocracy and the ideal of *symphonia*. However, Soloviev's idea of theocracy was what he called "free theocracy," which introduced elements of liberal church–state separation into the theocratic framework. Soloviev's free theocracy found positive significance in the freedom of the state, civil society, and the economy from ecclesiastical control: "The Church must have no power of compulsion, and the power of compulsion exercised by the state must have nothing to do with the domain of religion."[43] For Soloviev, such freedom followed directly from the Christian doctrine of deification and its affirmation of the absolute significance of the human person. Even if the Church can have no power over the different spheres of society, Soloviev's position remains "theocratic" insofar as the promise of deification gives those spheres "a higher purpose and absolute norm for their activities."[44] In keeping with *symphonia*, the role of political power is to assist in the world's deification, but since deification is fundamentally about "the free development of human personhood," this assistance is incompatible with all forms of coercion in moral and religious matters. The state's "theocratic" function is thus the primarily "secular" function of protecting individual freedom and social justice: "The state should interfere as little as possible with the inner moral life of man, and at the same time should as securely and widely as possible ensure the external conditions of his worthy existence and moral development."[45] This is the basis of Soloviev's willingness to engage constructively with the liberal tradition, since liberalism, more than any political system, has created conditions in which human freedom and dignity can flourish, thus establishing the material and social conditions in which human persons can best pursue their deification.

In similar fashion, Bulgakov advanced a Christian politics centered on "the freedom of the individual" as "the program of all programs,"[46] again on the basis of deification and its implications for human personhood. For Bulgakov, the political problems of freedom and justice were also *dogmatic* problems, since they are inseparable from the theology of deification, and thus needed to become a focus of Orthodoxy's dogmatic development in the twentieth century. To address these problems, Bulgakov thought, Orthodox theology would have to "become the teaching of liberation."[47] In his 1905 pamphlet *An Urgent Task*, which proposed a "Union of Christian Politics" to take advantage of the opportunities presented by the newly formed Russian Duma (parliament), Bulgakov insisted that "the external—that is, political and economic—liberation of the person" would be the Union's "fundamental and general task"[48] and should in general be "the guiding norm of Christian politics."[49] The pamphlet criticizes the "centralist, autocratic despotism" that characterized Orthodox politics and hopes for its eventual replacement with "a federative union of democratic republics, a worldwide United States."[50] Statements such as this one display an unprecedented level of openness to liberal democracy, and although Bulgakov became disillusioned with the prospects of liberal politics in Russia, he continued to show admiration for liberal democracy throughout his career. Thirty years after *An Urgent Task*, writing in diaspora, Bulgakov argued that the liberty of American democracy is "the regime most favorable to the Church," not only because it frees the Church from state domination, but because it liberates the Church to "exercise its influence on souls by way of liberty, which alone corresponds to Christian dignity."[51]

CONCLUSION

The above summaries are but a small sampling of the ways that modern Orthodox theologians have thought constructively about politics following an encounter with liberal democracy. Although they do not offer any definitive conclusions about Orthodoxy's compatibility with liberalism, they do make it clear that Orthodox responses to liberalism, even critical ones, need not rely on "fundamentalist" allegiance to Byzantine theology but can instead involve reading the tradition in fresh ways. Furthermore, despite the general absence of Orthodox voices from mainstream political theology in the twentieth century and the silence on political matters in the major works of neopatristic theology, Orthodoxy is not lacking in political-theological reflection, nor do its core doctrines entail a disinterest in the political. The context of Orthodox political theology is different from that of Western political theology and gives a distinctive shape to its concrete proposals, but Orthodox attempts to do political theology beyond the legacy of Christian empire merit the attention of Catholic and Protestant scholars and deserve a place in the mainstream of Christian political theology in the twenty-first century.

NOTES

1. One exception are theologians associated with the Radical Orthodoxy movement, especially John Milbank. The most significant Radical Orthodox engagement with Orthodox political theology is found in *Encounter Between Eastern Orthodoxy and Radical Orthodoxy: Transfiguring the World Through the Word*, eds. Adrian Pabst and Christoph Schneider (Farnham: Ashgate, 2009). However, the engagement tends to be rather indirect, especially in Milbank's case. Although Milbank identifies the "Sophiology" of Russian Orthodox thinkers like Vladimir Soloviev and Sergei Bulgakov as an important resource for contemporary Christian responses to secular politics, he says almost nothing about those thinkers' own extensive bodies of writing specifically on *political* theology, perhaps because, in many ways, the Russian thinkers contradict Milbank's own political agenda. See Milbank's essay in Pabst and Schneider, "Sophiology and Theurgy: The New Theological Horizon." For critical analyses of Milbank's use of Orthodox theology, see David J. Dunn, "Radical Sophiology: Fr. Sergej Bulgakov and John Milbank on Augustine," *Studies in Eastern European Thought* 64 (2012); Aristotle Papanikolaou, *The Mystical as Political: Democracy and Non-Radical Orthodoxy* (Notre Dame, IN: University of Notre Dame Press, 2012); and Nathaniel Wood, "Deifying Democracy: Liberalism and the Politics of Theosis," PhD. diss., Fordham University (May 2017).
2. Consider, for example, *The Blackwell Companion to Political Theology*, eds. Peter Scott and William T. Cavanaugh (Malden, MA: Wiley-Blackwell, 2004), which contains only one brief essay on the Orthodox tradition. By contrast, *The Cambridge Companion to Christian Political Theology*, eds. Craig Hovey and Elizabeth Phillips (Cambridge: Cambridge University Press, 2015), includes no survey of Orthodox political theology alongside its treatments of Catholic and Protestant political theologies.

3. For an overview of the development of neopatristic theology, see Paul Gavrilyuk, *Georges Florovsky and the Russian Religious Renaissance* (Oxford: Oxford University Press, 2014).

4. Pantelis Kalaitzidis, *Orthodoxy and Political Theology*, trans. Fr. Gregory Edwards (Geneva: World Council of Churches Publications, 2012).

5. Attention to the variety of Orthodox political theologies also makes possible serious Orthodox intervention into mainstream Christian political theology in the West. At the same time that some Orthodox in Eastern Europe are heightening the tension between Orthodoxy and liberal democracy, some Western Christian theologians have begun looking to Orthodox theology to find support for their own critiques of liberalism. The most significant of these is John Milbank, who has appropriated Orthodox theological concepts like *theosis* and *sobornost'* for anti-liberal ends, and who has defended a model of Christian monarchy that draws inspiration from Byzantine imperial theology. Thus, by examining points of compatibility between Orthodox theology and liberalism, Orthodox theologians can respond to such anti-liberal trends in Western theology. See Papanikolaou, *The Mystical as Political*; Wood, "Deifying Democracy"; and David Dunn, "*Symphonia* in the Secular: An Ecclesiology for the Narthex," PhD diss., Vanderbilt University (August 2011).

6. Vladimir Soloviev, "Byzantinism and Russia," In *Freedom, Faith, and Dogma: Essays by V.S. Soloviev on Christianity and Judaism*, trans. and ed. Vladimir Wozniuk (Albany, NY: SUNY Press, 2008), 218.

7. For more on how deification factored into imperial theology, see Papanikolaou, *The Mystical as Political*, 14–28.

8. V.V. Zenkovsky, *A History of Russian Philosophy*, vol. 1, trans. George L. Kline (New York: Columbia University Press, 1953), 37. Zenkovsky notes that the Church's obligation to the emperor is to assist the emperor in carrying out his ecclesiastical service, which includes criticism and resistance when the emperor abandons his holy mission.

9. Steven Runciman, *The Byzantine Theocracy* (Cambridge: Cambridge University Press, 1977).

10. Eusebius of Caesarea, "A Speech for the Thirtieth Anniversary of Constantine's Accession," trans. E.C. Richardson, in Oliver O'Donovan and Joan Lockwood O'Donovan, eds., *From Irenaeus to Grotius: A Sourcebook in Christian Political Thought* (Grand Rapids, MI: William B. Eerdmans, 1999), 60.

11. "Letter of Patriarch Anthony," in *Byzantium: Church, Society, and Civilization Seen Through Contemporary Eyes*, ed. Deno John Geanokopolos (Chicago: University of Chicago Press, 1984), 143.

12. Kalaitzidis, *Orthodoxy and Political Theology*, 9.

13. George E. Demacopoulos and Aristotle Papanikolaou, eds., *Orthodox Constructions of the West* (New York: Fordham University Press, 2013).

14. Vasilios N. Makrides, "Political Theology in Orthodox Christian Contexts: Specificities and Particularities in Comparison with Western Christianity," in *Political Theologies in Orthodox Christianity: Common Challenges—Divergent Positions*, eds. Kristina Stoeckl, Ingeborg Gabriel, and Aristotle Papanikolaou (London: Bloomsbury T&T Clark, 2017), 42–43.

15. Anna Dolgov, "Russia's Patriarch Kirill: Some Human Rights Are 'Heresy.'" *The Moscow Times*, March 21, 2016, https://themoscowtimes.com/articles/russias-patriarch-kirill-some-human-rights-are-heresy-52213 (accessed November 9, 2017).

16. The English translation of *The Russian Orthodox Church's Basic Teaching on Human Dignity, Freedom, and Rights* is available online at the website of the Russian Orthodox Church's Department for External Church Relations: https://mospat.ru/en/documents/dignity-freedom-rights/ (accessed November 9, 2017). For a discussion of the document's

treatment of individual rights in relation to "traditional values," see Kristina Stoeckl, "Moral Arguments in the Human Rights Debate of the Russian Orthodox Church," in *Christianity, Democracy, and the Shadow of Constantine*, eds. George E. Demacopoulos and Aristotle Papanikolaou (New York: Fordham University Press, 2017), 11–30; or for a longer treatment, Kristina Stoeckl, *The Russian Orthodox Church and Human Rights* (New York: Routledge, 2014).

17. Kristina Stoeckl. "The Russian Orthodox Church as Moral Norm Entrepreneur," *Religion, State and Society* 44/2, 132–151.

18. The classic version of this thesis was advanced by Samuel Huntington, "The Clash of Civilizations," *Foreign Affairs* 72, no. 3 (1993): 22–50. For a competing perspective on Orthodox culture's compatibility with democracy, see Nikolas K. Gvosdev, *Emperors and Elections: Reconciling the Orthodox Tradition with Modern Politics* (Huntington, NY: Troitsa Books, 2000).

19. Dunn, "Radical Sophiology," 228.

20. For an excellent introduction to Soloviev and Bulgakov, see Paul Valliere, *Modern Russian Theology: Bukharev, Soloviev, Bulgakov: Orthodox Theology in a New Key* (Grand Rapids, MI: Wm. B. Eerdmans, 2001). There has been significantly less interest among theologians in the work of S.L. Frank (1877–1950), who wrote political theology in the same vein as Soloviev and further developed some of Soloviev's key insights, even though his major political writings being available in English since the 1980s. Frank's two major political monographs are *The Light Shineth in Darkness: An Essay in Christian Ethics and Social Philosophy*, trans. Boris Jakim (Athens, OH: Ohio University Press, 1989) and *The Spiritual Foundations of Society: An Introduction to Social Philosophy*, trans. Boris Jakim (Athens, OH: Ohio University Press, 1987).

21. The neopatristic synthesis took shape in response to the "Russian religious philosophy" of thinkers like Soloviev and Bulgakov. See Gavrilyuk, *Georges Florovsky and the Russian Religious Renaissance*.

22. Also noteworthy is the fact that the work of thinkers like Soloviev and Bulgakov responds to the earlier nineteenth-century upsurge of anti-Western and anti-liberal Orthodox theology found in the Slavophile movement and thus is instructive for contemporary Orthodox theologians attempting to respond to similar attitudes in the Orthodox world today.

23. Vladimir Soloviev, *Lectures on Divine-Humanity*, trans. Peter Zouboff, revised by Boris Jakim (Hudson, NY: Lindisfarne Press, 1995), 17.

24. Sergei Bulgakov, "Basic Problems of the Theory of Progress," in *Problems of Idealism*, ed. Pavel Novgorodtsev, English edition trans. and ed. by Randall A. Poole (New Haven, CT: Yale University Press, 2003), 104.

25. Bulgakov, himself a former Marxist economist, became a harsh critic of Russian Marxism's assault on the person. In addition to "Basic Problems of the Theory of Progress," he critiques Marxist anti-personalism in *Karl Marx as a Religious Type: His Relation to the Religion of Anthropotheism of L. Feuerbach*, trans. Luba Barna, ed. Virgil R. Lang (Belmont, MA: Nordland Publishing, 1979).

26. John Zizioulas, *Being as Communion: Studies in Personhood and the Church* (Crestwood, NY: St. Vladimir's Seminary Press, 1985). Zizioulas further develops his theology of personhood in *Communion and Otherness: Further Studies in Personhood and the Church* (London: T&T Clark, 2006).

27. Christos Yannaras, *Person and Eros*, trans. Norman Russell (Brookline, MA: Holy Cross Orthodox Press, 2008).

28. Papanikolaou, *The Mystical as Political*, chapter 3.

29. Brandon Gallaher, "Eschatological Anarchism: Eschatology and Politics in Contemporary Greek Theologhy," in *Political Theologies in Orthodox Christianity: Common Challenges—Divergent Positions*, eds. Kristina Stoeckl, Ingeborg Gabriel, and Aristotle Papanikolaou (London: Bloomsbury T&T Clark, 2017), 138.

30. Yannaras develops this "communo-centric politics" in book *The Inhumanity of Right*, which has not yet been translated from the Greek. A summary of the book's contents is found in Jonathan Cole, "Personhood, Relational Ontology, and the Trinitarian Politics of Eastern Orthodox Thinker Christos Yannaras," *Political Theology* 34 (2017): 1–14, http://dx.doi.org/10.1080/1462317X.2017.1291127 (accessed December 10, 2017); and in Jonathan Cole, "The Communo-Centric Political Theology of Christos Yannaras in Conversation with Oliver O'Donovan," in *Mustard Seeds in the Public Square: Between and Beyond Theology, Philosophy, and Society,"* ed. Sotiris Mitralexis (Wilmington, DE: Vernon Press, 2017), 61–93.

31. Cole, "Personhood," 7.

32. Ibid., 8.

33. Ibid., 9.

34. Ibid., 11.

35. For the classic formulation of *sobornost'* ecclesiology, see Alexis Khomiakov, "The Church is One," in *On Spiritual Unity: A Slavophile Reader*, trans. and eds. Boris Jakim and Robert Bird (Hudson, NY: Lindisfarne Books, 1998).

36. The phrasing is Konstantin Aksakov's. Quoted in Sergey Horujy, "Slavophiles, Westernizers, and the Birth of Russian Philosophical Humanism," trans. Patrick Lally Michelson, in *A History of Russian Philosophy 1830–1930: Faith, Reason, and the Defense of Human Dignity*, eds. G.M. Hamburg and Randall A. Poole (Cambridge: Cambridge University Press, 2010), 42.

37. Aleksei Khomiakov, *To the Serbs: An Epistle from Moscow*, in *A Documentary History of Russian Thought from Enlightenment to Marxism*, trans. and eds. W.J. Leatherbarrow and D.C. Offord, (Ann Arbor, MI: Ardis Publishers, 1987), 93–94.

38. A clear summary of this view of the West is found in Ivan Kireevsky, "On the Nature of European Culture and Its Relation to the Culture of Russia: A Letter to Count E. E. Komorovskii," in *Russian Intellectual History: An Anthology*, ed. by Marc Raeff (Atlantic Highlands, NJ: Humanities Press, 1978).

39. In their desire to shift the focus of Christian politics towards "being the Church," the Slavophiles have certain resonances with contemporary "Church-as-polis" political theology as advanced by theologians such as Stanley Hauerwas and William Cavanaugh. For a detailed comparison between the Slavophiles and Cavanaugh, see Nathaniel Wood, "*Sobornost'*, State Authority, and Christian Society in Slavophile Political Theology," in *Religion, Authority, and the State: From Constantine to the Contemporary World*, ed. Leo D. Lefebure (New York: Palgrave Macmillan, 2016), 179–199.

40. Susanna Rabow-Edling, *Slavophile Thought and the Politics of Cultural Nationalism* (New York: SUNY Press, 2006), 127–128.

41. This is not to overlook the very real dangers of the Slavophile perspective, especially their insistence that community must be founded on *consensus* rather than contract. Community requires unanimity on "a single idea, a single way of looking at things, one conviction and one way of life" (Ivan Kireevsky, "A Reply to Khomiakov," in *A Documentary History of Russian Thought from Enlightenment to Marxism*, trans. and eds. W.J. Leatherbarrow and D.C. Offord, (Ann Arbor, MI: Ardis Publishers, 1987), 84). Whatever the merits of consensus as an ecclesiological principle, when transposed into politics, it not only runs up against liberal ideals of pluralism, but also can be used as a theological justification for the subordination of individual freedom to "traditional values."

42. Cole, "Personhood," 9. In this sense, Yannaras is more moderate than the Slavophiles, whose rejection of liberal democracy entailed what Andrzej Walicki calls "legal nihilism," the complete rejection of legal and political rights. See Andrzej Walicki, *Legal Philosophies of Russian Liberalism* (New York: Oxford University Press, 1987).
43. Vladimir Soloviev, *The Justification of the Good: An Essay in Moral Philosophy*, trans. Nathalie A. Duddington and ed. Boris Jakim (Grand Rapids, MI: Wm. B. Eerdmans, 2005), 394.
44. Vladimir Solovyov, *The Philosophical Principles of Integral Knowledge*, trans. Valeria Z. Nollan (Grand Rapids, MI: Eerdmans, 2008), 54.
45. Soloviev, *Justification*, 394.
46. Quoted in Catherine Evtuhov, *The Cross and the Sickle: Sergei Bulgakov and the Fate of Russian Religious Philosophy* (Ithaca, NY: Cornell University Press, 1997), 76.
47. Ibid., 106.
48. Sergei Bulgakov, "An Urgent Task," in *A Revolution of the Spirit: Crisis of Value in Russia, 1890–1924*, eds. Bernice Glatzer Rosenthal and Martha Bohachevsky-Chomiak (New York: Fordham University Press, 1990), 158.
49. Ibid., 143.
50. Ibid., 144.
51. Sergius Bulgakov, *The Orthodox Church*, trans. Lydia Kesich (Crestwood, NY: St. Vladimir's Seminary Press, 1988), 163.

SELECT BIBLIOGRAPHY

Bulgakov, Sergius (1988), *The Orthodox Church*, trans. Lydia Kesich, Crestwood, NY: St. Vladimir's Seminary Press.
Bulgakov, Sergius (2000), *Philosophy of Economy: The World as Household*, trans. and ed. Catherine Evtuhov, New Haven, CT: Yale University Press.
Demacopoulos, George E. and Aristotle Papanikolaou, eds. (2013), *Orthodox Constructions of the West*, New York: Fordham University Press.
Demacopoulos, George E. and Aristotle Papanikolaou, eds. (2016), *Christianity, Democracy, and the Shadow of Constantine*, New York: Fordham University Press.
Dunn, David J. (2011) "*Symphonia* in the Secular: An Ecclesiology for the Narthex," PhD dissertation, Vanderbilt University.
Evtuhov, Catherine (1997), *The Cross and the Sickle: Sergei Bulgakov and the Fate of Russian Religious Philosophy*, Ithaca, NY: Cornell University Press.
Frank, S. L. (1989), *The Light Shineth in Darkness: An Essay in Christian Ethics and Social Philosophy*, trans. Boris Jakim, Athens, OH: Ohio University Press.
Gavrilyuk, Paul (2014), *Georges Florovsky and the Russian Religious Renaissance*, Oxford: Oxford University Press.
Gvosdev, Nikolas K. (2000), *Emperors and Elections: Reconciling the Orthodox Tradition with Modern Politics*, Huntington, NY: Troitsa Books.
Jakim, Boris and Robert Bird, trans. and eds. (1998), *On Spiritual Unity: A Slavophile Reader*, Hudson, NY: Lindisfarne Books.
Kalaitzidis, Pantelis (2012), *Orthodoxy and Political Theology*, trans. Fr. Gregory Edwards, Geneva: World Council of Churches Publications.
Leatherbarrow, W.J. and D.C. Offord, trans. and eds. (1987), *A Documentary History of Russian Thought from Enlightenment to Marxism*, Ann Arbor, MI: Ardis Publishers.

O'Donovan, Oliver and Joan Lockwood O'Donovan, eds. (1999), *From Irenaeus to Grotius: A Sourcebook in Christian Political Thought,* Grand Rapids, MI: William B. Eerdmans.
Pabst, Adrian and Christoph Schneider, eds. (2009), *Encounter between Eastern Orthodoxy and Radical Orthodoxy: Transfiguring the World Through the Word,* Farnham: Ashgate.
Papanikolaou, Aristotle (2012), *The Mystical as Political: Democracy and Non-Radical Orthodoxy,* Notre Dame, IN: University of Notre Dame Press.
Soloviev, Vladimir (1995), *Lectures on Divine-Humanity,* trans. Peter Zouboff, revised by Boris Jakim, Hudson, NY: Lindisfarne Press.
Solovyov, Vladimir (2005), *The Justification of the Good: An Essay in Moral Philosophy,* trans. Nathalie A. Duddington, ed. Boris Jakim, Grand Rapids, MI: Wm. B. Eerdmans.
Solovyov, Vladimir (2008), *Freedom, Faith, and Dogma: Essays by V. S. Soloviev on Christianity and Judaism,* trans. and ed. Vladimir Wozniuk, Albany, NY: SUNY Press.
Solovyov, Vladimir (2008), *The Philosophical Principles of Integral Knowledge,* trans. Valeria Z. Nollan, Grand Rapids, MI: Eerdmans.
Stoeckl, Kristina (2014), *The Russian Orthodox Church and Human Rights,* New York: Routledge.
Stoeckl, Kristina, Ingeborg Gabriel, and Aristotle Papanikolaou, eds. (2017), *Political Theologies in Orthodox Christianity: Common Challenges—Divergent Positions,* London: Bloomsbury T&T Clark.
Valliere, Paul (2001), *Modern Russian Theology: Bukharev, Soloviev, Bulgakov: Orthodox Theology in a New Key,* Grand Rapids, MI: Wm. B. Eerdmans.
Williams, Rowan, ed. (1999) *Sergiii Bulgakov: Towards a Russian Political Theology,* Edinburgh: T&T Clark.
Wood, Nathaniel (2016), "*Sobornost'*, State Authority, and Christian Society in Slavophile Political Theology," in *Religion, Authority, and the State: From Constantine to the Contemporary World,* ed. Leo D. Lefebure, New York: Palgrave Macmillan, 179–199.
Wood, Nathaniel (2017), "Deifying Democracy: Liberalism and the Politics of *Theosis*," PhD dissertation, Fordham University.
Yannaras, Christos (2008), *Person and Eros,* trans. Norman Russell, Brookline, MA: Holy Cross Orthodox Press.
Zenkovsky, V.V. (1953), *A History of Russian Philosophy,* vol. 1, trans. George L. Kline, New York: Columbia University Press.
Zizioulas, John (1985), *Being as Communion: Studies in Personhood and the Church,* Crestwood, NY: St. Vladimir's Seminary Press.
Zizioulas, John (2006), *Communion and Otherness: Further Studies in Personhood and the Church,* London: T&T Clark.

PART FOUR

Constructive Horizons in Political Theology

CHAPTER TWENTY-THREE

The Politics of the *Espíritu*

Ethic as Recognition–Assemblage–Decolonial Healing

OSCAR GARCÍA-JOHNSON

INTRODUCTION

Numerous theologians in the traditions of the West have suggested different ways to articulate an ethical discourse about how Christians relate to the world around us. Generally, these approaches use a common binary that recurs throughout history: *The City of God and the City of Man* (Augustine); *The Kingdom of God and the Kingdom[s] of the World* (Luther); *The Church and Society* (Troeltsch); *Christ and Culture* (Niebuhr).

My goal in this essay is threefold. First, I will briefly review the binary and its theological implications in the ethic of John Howard Yoder against the backdrop of the dominant ethics of the Niebuhr brothers. Arguably the herald of an ethical alternative in his time, Yoder became a significant influence in the development of Latino Protestant ethical discourse across the Americas (the US included), and very particularly among the Latin American Theological Fellowship. Second, I will examine several ethical approaches that have emerged from within the context of US Latina[1] Protestant diaspora, many of which were influenced also by liberation theology. Here we will notice yet another alterity differentiated from that of Yoder that problematizes the Niebuhr–Yoder Western ethical tension. Finally, I will introduce the concept of *the politics of the Espíritu* as an outline proposal for a decolonial ethics of the South. The politics of the *Espíritu* continues De La Torre's ethical project pursued in *The Politics of Jesús* by shifting from Christology to pneumatology of the South. In short, it reroutes ethics by challenging the place where thinking and praxis have happened for centuries in Westernized ethical discourses, which have generally overlooked both the agency of the Spirit and the non-Westernized ethical traditioning communities of the Americas.

I intend to show that political resistance of the *Espíritu* has happened for centuries across the American continents. However, this political resistance of the *Espíritu* has been exerted by marginalized (unaccounted) communities and through heterodox forms of sociopolitical resistance that escape the reach of Westernized ethics, that is, those discourses trapped within the logics of colonial modernity. While Niebuhr–Yoder presents us with an important ethical tension within the West, and De La Torre and other Latinx theologians add original ethical tissue from the margins of the US context (politics of *Jesús*), still, the agency and ethical embodiment of the *Espíritu* remains unattended, and it is precisely through such pneumatological agency that we may be able to identify a *communal ethic in transit* as a way of resisting systemic deicides, ethnocides, genocides, matricides, ecocides, and epistemicides inflicted by colonial modernity world-systems. My outline proposal is for a social ethic of human *recognition*, social *assemblage*, and decolonial *healing* of the peoples of the South.

DOMINANT ETHICS AND THE POLITICS OF JESUS

John Howard Yoder developed his theological discourse against the ethical discourse that was dominant in his time.[2] In his magnum opus, the widely recognized *The Politics of Jesus* (1972), Yoder traces the fundamental bases of this dominant ethical discourse, highlighting how it promoted the idea that any ethics of "imitating Jesus" was irrelevant.

To make his case, Yoder first shows how the ethical irrelevance of the historical Jesus is a clear conclusion arrived at by the lines of argumentation of the dominant ethics. The argument can be summed up briefly: (a) The ethics of Jesus were only concerned with one's internal character; (b) Jesus was a simple rural figure—he did not provide solutions for the problems found in complex cities; (c) Jesus and his followers lived in an uncontrollable world—due to their context they did not yet believe it was possible to possess social power or to meaningfully transform society; (d) Jesus' message was, by nature, ahistorical—he struggled against spiritual or existential realities rather than social or concrete ones; (e) Jesus was a radical monotheist—he intensified the "ethical chasm" between God and humanity by completely relativizing human values; and (f) Jesus only came to give his life for the sins of humanity, nothing else.[3] Those who lead this school of ethical thought, Yoder summarizes, arrive at the tacit conclusion that the *imitatio Christi*, ethically speaking, is simply irrelevant: "His [Jesus'] apocalypticism and radical monotheism may teach us to be modest, his personalism may teach us to cherish the values of face-to-face relationships, but as to the stuff of our decision-making, we shall have to have other sources of help."[4] Second, Yoder shows how the dominant ethic of his time built upon the idea that "there must be some kind of bridge or transition . . . into another mode of thought when we begin to think about ethics . . . [and] the substance of ethics must be reconstructed on our side of the bridge."[5] Starting from this claim, the modality of the dominant ethic, according to Yoder, presumes that "the reconstruction of a social ethic on this side of the transition will derive its guidance from common sense and the nature of things."[6]

Arguably, the dominant ethic to which Yoder is responding was mainly articulated by the so-called Christian historical-realism[7] of the Niebuhr brothers in the decades following the Second World War.[8] Yoder gives particular attention to the influence of Helmut Richard Niebuhr, who, with his literary and political contributions, "taught more than a generation of mainstream American ethical thinkers . . . [and whose] pupils have led the Christian social ethics guild in North America ever since."[9] It is necessary, then, to introduce some of H. Richard Niebuhr's basic ideas in order to flesh out the ethical framework that eventually gave birth to Yoder's theological alternative.

H. Richard Niebuhr maintained that "human beings are creatures of faith in the sense that we center our lives around objects of devotion."[10] This implies the possibility of creating lives that revolve around false "objects" or "idols," such as a nation, a political structure, an economic system, a race, etc. Niebuhr emphasized the ease with which people give these sociocultural realities the same devotion they might give to "true" objects of Christian faith, causing confusion about which loyalties should take precedence. Niebuhr wanted to prophetically call Christians to true devotion to God, "a genuine faith . . . that displaces the inappropriate centers and leads us to critique and rebuild our daily lives."[11] This is made possible when we recognize that God, in Christ Jesus, is not just the "transcendent friend" of the sociocultural, economic, and political structures that govern our community, but rather that he is the "immanent enemy" of everything that rises to the status of "false idol."[12] This recognition, therefore, should lead us to a "permanent conversion and revolution of our human religion through Jesus Christ."[13]

Following this framework for socio-theological reflection, H. Richard Niebuhr ventures into a socio-ethical project focusing on practical application with his influential book *Christ and Culture*.[14] The "enduring problem," according to Niebuhr, is precisely the struggle between loyalties that saturate the gestalt of contemporary Christianity. This problem means different things for different communities; for the Christian community it represents a battle between loyalties that must be resolved favorably in a Christocentric way, while for the secular world it suggests, rather, a possible answer to the question: how relevant is Jesus today?

Niebuhr proposes a general typology for how historic Christianity has expressed its allegiance to God and wrestled with understanding Jesus' relevance to society. The first type (or category) is "Christ against culture," which asserts that loyalty to Christ demands antagonism toward or retreat from "secular space." The second type is the "Christ of culture," or the belief that divinity embodies itself within culture and all of its noblest ideals, which means that to be loyal to Christ is to be loyal to those ideals. The other three types—"Christ over culture," "Christ and culture in paradox," "Christ transforming culture"—exhibit a clear distinction between Christ and the world while maintaining some form of Christian responsibility to the world.[15] These last three types differ from an approach that would subsume one culture's values under another in order to change them. Although the five options described above can be found in various Christian communities today and come with their own advantages and disadvantages, it is Niebuhr's category of "cultural conversion"—Christ transforming culture—that really stands out.

Richard Niebuhr's social ethics points toward a *transforming faith*[16] that evolves to produce *cultural conversion*.[17] This raises a few questions: What criteria should we follow to achieve this transformation? Do we have any models or case studies of cultural conversion occurring so that we might know what a "converted" culture, community, or world would actually look like? And if we call ourselves followers of Christ, what role do Jesus and the New Testament play in this process of cultural conversion? For theologians like Yoder, these questions demand the concrete and historical, the specific and local, with the Bible as the ethical referent. For Yoder, it might seem like the only adequate response is a different form of radicalism (Yoder's neo-Anabaptism), which prioritizes *difference* and *alterity*. This having been said, there are some influential ethicists who argue that H. Richard Niebuhr's ethics did offer a more concrete way forward than Yoder credited to him.[18]

Thus far I have introduced the ethical frameworks that were dominant when John Yoder began writing. Yoder would go on to critique these frameworks, arguing that they were biblically, ecclesiologically, and sociologically inadequate. In the process of making these critiques, Yoder would propose his own influential ethical alternative with unique ethical accents, which merit further elaboration.

Many scholars have attempted to summarize John Yoder's central thesis. Some understand the ethicist to be primarily concerned with demonstrating that "the moral character of God is revealed in Jesus; in his vulnerable love for his enemies and his renunciation of domination."[19] Others believe *The Politics of Jesus* contains Yoder's seminal idea that "Christian ethics is necessarily the ethic of Jesus lived out by the

Christian community in the world."[20] Still others—without disregarding the above—prefer a more scriptural approach to Yoder's theological reflection, emphasizing that it is the *biblical* Jesus that is the source of Yoder's ethics. The following lines will most closely resemble this last group, presupposing that, for Yoder, "the New Testament portrayal of Jesus must be maintained as the fundamental norm for all Christian ethics."[21]

Through careful theological scholarship in *The Politics of Jesus*, Yoder was able to push back against a prevailing ethic that was indifferent to Jesus' normative reality and that privileged theological reflection over meaningful action. The book contains three central arguments, which Richard Hays helpfully summarizes: (1) The New Testament consistently bears witness to a Jesus who renounces violence and coercive power. (2) The example of Jesus remains relevant, obligatory, and normative for the Christian community. (3) Our commitment to imitating the example of Jesus is a deeply political decision, not a withdrawal from the political arena.[22] Yoder, using the narrative of the Gospel of Luke as a frame of reference, highlights the political shape of Jesus' life—a life that offered an alternative to the existing political, social, and religious structures. Through a campaign of "radical discipleship" Jesus began to build a new social reality and a new political order characterized not by the usual systems of domination but by an ethos of "serving and sharing."[23] In the words of Yoder himself, "Jesus . . . calls [us] to be part of a community of voluntary commitment, willing to bear the hostility of society on behalf of the call. . . . To be a disciple is to share in a lifestyle that culminates in the cross."[24]

With this claim, Yoder brings us closer to the reality of the cross and its ethical implications. For Yoder, the reality of the cross is the reality of the present kingdom on earth.[25] Hays argues that the dominant "focal image" or hermeneutical metaphor in Yoderian ethics is "the cross . . . through which the whole canonical story should be read."[26] But Yoder is clear that the reality of the cross will take us far beyond mere acts of interpretation; it will enable us to embody a prophetic social ethic: "Only at one point, only on one subject—but then consistently, universally—is Jesus our example: in his cross."[27]

For Yoder, the cross embodies normative reality because, even though he sees some salvific dimensions in the historical life of Jesus, it is the cross that demands a universal ethical praxis that defines, in part, what constitutes authentic discipleship. This ethical praxis has sociopolitical implications for the Christian community. Yoder's ethic of the cross gives form and content to Christian praxis in the world because "the believer's cross must be, like that of his Lord, the price of social non-conformity . . . it is the social reality that characterizes a world indisposed to the Order Yet to Come."[28]

The cross as a norm of ethical praxis also denotes an alternative revolution that challenges the methodologies of violence and domination and creates nonviolent initiatives capable of achieving social change. But where are we to see Jesus' praxis concretely embodied and his politics reflected? The Christian community is the community of Jesus, and, according to Yoder, "the call of the church is to live in a way that reflects 'the politics of Jesus,' continuing the task of unmasking and disarming the powers"[29] that violently challenge the lordship of Jesus. That the church is the moral agent of the kingdom with the task of modeling and incarnating the political reality of Jesus in the world is without a doubt the core concept of John H. Yoder's alternative ethic. While the dominant ethical discourse perceived the church to be "a cultural product of a different kingdom,"[30] Yoder saw it as "the conscience and the servant of human society."[31] In this sociocultural role, the church is not a mere sample of the spiritual kingdom here on earth; it is the "alternative community," the "culture of Christ,"[32] that prophetically coexists with secular society.

True transformation occurs, according to Yoder, "in and through" the Christian community. In its transformative mission, this new "social order," instituted and sustained by Jesus, is called to "find . . . the interworld transformational grammar to help us to discern what will need to happen if the collision of the message of Jesus with our pluralist/relativist world is to lead to a reconception of the shape of the world."[33]

In summary, with the New Testament's portrait of Jesus—a fully cultural, social, and political character—Yoder attempts to show us a Christ who, in Friesen's words, "represents a cultural vision" rather than a cultural tension.[34] Yoder's imposing alternative social ethic, with its emphasis on the "otherness of the church," serves as a prophetic voice that illuminates a Western ethical and Christological tension (Niebuhr–Yoder) too often overlooked. Conversely, Yoder's ethical alterity comes as a dialogical ethical discourse with other voices or "cultural visions" evoked in the context of the American Global South (Latin America and the US Latina diaspora). To these voices we turn next, anticipating that Niebuhr's historical realism and Yoder's alternative communalism will be further problematized due to their inability to escape the gatekeeping epistemology of colonial modernity.

THE POLITICS OF JESUS AND BEYOND IN THE AMERICAN GLOBAL SOUTH

It can be maintained that three self-determined and generative theological narratives have shaped Latinx theological discourses in the Americas (the US included): Latin American liberation theologies, Integral Mission, and US Latina diaspora theologies. While none of these narratives can be said to claim either Niebuhr's historical realism or Yoder's alternative communalism as their "core" ethics, clearly Integral Mission and its main theological forum, Latin American Fellowship, would explicitly identify with John H. Yoder's ethical legacy, due to both its biblico-theological premises and Yoder's personal influence on them. Likewise, I venture to suggest that different US Latina diaspora ethical voices have incorporated historical realism or Yoder's alternative ethics in their discourses as they have deemed appropriate. We will check these affirmations out as we move from Yoder's "politics of Jesus" to De La Torre's "Politics of *Jesús*."

THE POLITICS OF JESUS IN LATIN AMERICA

In a collaborative work by John H. Yoder, Lilia Solano, and C. René Padilla entitled *Iglesia, Ética y Poder*, the main proponent of Integral Mission, C. René Padilla, acknowledges that at least six seminal Yoderian ideas have shaped the Latin American Fellowship: (1) the prophetic denunciation of the church's Constantinian alliance with the state; (2) the separation of the church and the state and the challenge to any type of religious establishment; (3) the need for faith to extend to the political realm on the basis of the *Politics of Jesus*; (4) a gospel-rooted social ethic that includes the life, death, resurrection, and exaltation of Jesus Christ; (5) the normative character of the New Testament teachings of Jesus for Christian life, centered on love and marked by the renunciation to any form of violence; (6) the church as a visible community, radically distinct from the surrounding world: a creative minority that is a faith community that makes love, forgiveness, and communion concrete to the point that the community itself embodies the concreteness of the message proclaimed.[35] Highlighting the influence of these ideas, Padilla simply claims that one can see them appear with greater frequency and centrality "by various authors that self-identify as members of the Latin American Fellowship."[36]

Padilla laments that the rapid growth of *evangélicos* and neo-Pentecostals/Charismatics has led many Latin American Protestants to desire governmental political power that had previously been monopolized by Roman Catholic or secular figures, with many countries forming evangelical political parties.[37] The plan to replace political Roman Catholicism with political evangelicalism will only be a disaster, Padilla says, and already many *evangélico* pastors have fallen prey to the "Constantinian temptation" and become corrupt opportunists, authoritarians, and the like.[38] Echoing Yoder, Padilla wishes these pastors would remember that there is no such thing as a "Christian politics" only "Christians in politics that serve God and their neighbors in the political realm."[39] Padilla's vision for the future of the Latin American church is one "modeled by the politics of the crucified Messiah."[40] In short, Yoder's work offered a guiding corrective that the Latin American Fellowship saw as important for preventing *evagélicos* and neo-Pentecostals/Charismatics from falling into the trap of Constantinian co-option. Now we move to the context of US Latinx Protestant discourses.

TOWARD THE *POLITICS OF JESÚS* IN THE US LATINA DIASPORA

Marginalization, oppression, and interstitial living are sociocultural narratives of alterity inescapably informing the Latinx condition. On the one hand, peripheral and interstitial living (third spaces) reflects the worldwide effects of the modern "epistemic machine."[41] Such an epistemic machine has functioned for centuries as a mode of *unrecognizing* the human value, *disassembling* the social self, and reproducing the colonial *wound* of subaltern communities sharing modern-colonial-imperial subjugations. On the other hand, when the subaltern reads the Christian Bible, identifies with the experiences of Jesus of Nazareth, and participates in the polyphonic/hybrid community of the Spirit, an epistemic realization dawns that brings hermeneutical and decolonial consequences. Said differently, Latinx Christian scholars concur on the perception that the incarnate God chose the peripheral and interstitial human geography—the oppressed/impoverished (Isasi-Díaz) who live, believe, think, and act in the colonial difference (García-Johnson)— to be a locus of revelation and divine action.[42] Thus, living in the periphery, liminality, in-between-ness, interstitiality, and as a hybrid discloses not only the barbaric civilizing ethos of a conquering ethics of the West but also a distinct and advantageous geopolitics of knowledge recognized as a privileged hermeneutical space for border thinking and political resistance.

I suggest that Latinx experiences of sociocultural alterity and the socially emancipating "cultural vision" of Jesus of Nazareth's own experience at the margin are two key components of Latina social ethics constituting what De La Torre would call *the politics of Jesús*. However, these components take on unique shapes and hues depending on the traditions, interests, and social locations of each social ethicist. To illustrate this, I will examine three Protestant Latinx ethical voices.

Eldin Villafañe, in *The Liberating Spirit: Toward an Hispanic American Pentecostal Social Ethic* (1992), certainly takes the two key components into account, although he proposes his own variation. Instead of a "cultural vision of Jesus" he offers a "cultural vision of the

Spirit" (i.e., the risen Jesus). In his effort to construct a Pentecostal social ethic, Villafañe discerns a pneumatological ethical paradigm based on his reading of Galatians 5:25. He argues that "living by the Spirit" implies *theological* discernment and "walking in the Spirit" implies *ethical* discernment. Regretfully, this is mostly treated as a US Latinx Pentecostal construct.[43] Although the Hispanic Pentecostal ethic has historically exhibited a rather individualistic character, Villafañe hopes to extend the ethic to include sociocultural responsibility as well. Thus, the "community of the Spirit" is called to "participate in the Reign of God," which results in "the challenge to confront structural sin and evil" and the "challenge to fulfill the prophetic and vocational role of 'baptism in the Spirit.'"[44] Suffice it to say that Villafañe combines the experience of the Spirit as a basis for ethical reflection with the experience of sociocultural alterity to propose a socio-ethical missiology that calls the church to live as the corporeal presence of the Spirit in and for the world.[45]

The Hispanic ethicist Ismael García constructs a helpful ethical framework in his book *Dignidad: Ethics through Hispanic Eyes*, where he highlights "the moral practices shared by Hispanics" and how they are related to and in tension with the surrounding political community.[46] García examines three "Hispanic styles of moral reasoning" or ethical characteristics: "a commitment to moral principles, a concern with character formation, and a question for group recognition and care"[47] and recognizes that the latter takes precedence for most of the "militant" Latinx theologians. García argues that this "ethics of recognition and care" is an alternative approach to moral reasoning. Hispanic ethics, García says, is a

> care for the powerless and poor; it is an ethics of love within a loveless society that is significantly less able to allow those culturally different members within it to realize their hopes. . . . It is a mode of ethical reflection that has as one of its primary concerns the transforming of the conditions of oppression and discrimination experienced by our people. . . . it is a politics of compassion and love.[48]

In his review of the main themes of the Christian faith, García presents an ethical vision of a Jesus who is, for Hispanics, "the prototype of what humanity means . . . and much more."[49] In Jesus, García sees the ethical standard for what it means to "love and serve."[50] These central themes provide a vision of God's kingdom and embody hope and affirmation for the Latinx population. These themes of practical morality are instruments of social transformation capable of "freeing us to become creative agents within the divine design of justice and love."[51]

The church, as a "community of resistance and source of dignity," plays an essential role in García's ethical vision. In his own words, "The church is called to resist, within every sphere of life, that which violates God's will and purpose for creation."[52] García, like Yoder, expresses a certain kind of radicalism regarding the role of the church and its ethical allegiances:

> In this vision of the church, a commitment to justice for the poor and oppressed, those seen as lacking in dignity, has priority over mutual beliefs and orthodoxy. The assumption is made that the church's mission for life—inclusiveness, care, and mutuality—is better served if it keeps its distance from centers of power and focuses directly on the imperative of realizing God's kingdom by serving those who are presently deprived of their human dignity.[53]

Finally, De La Torre's *The Politics of Jesús* (2015) represents the most distinct articulation of social ethics to date from the Hispanic/Latinx *evangélica* perspective.

Responding *latinamente* to the Euroamerican Christological constructs informing the normative ethical discourses in America, De La Torre's transgressive interrogation and ethical construct the *politics of Jesús* begins by recognizing that Christology in the West has been inescapably a cultural articulation of Jesus, done from particular social locations and yet communicated as universal perspectives for all other cultures and communities to use as normative ethical devices. This goes not only for the Niebuhr brothers, but also for ethicists such as John H. Yoder and Stanley Hauerwas.[54] To be sure, De La Torre values the methodological insights in Yoder's *The Politics of Jesus* (biblical realism) and considers Yoder a dialogical partner, but he takes issue with the fact that Yoder's construct of Jesus results in a pacifist (white) Mennonite figure that resonates much more with many Euroamericans than the marginalized minorities. In De La Torre's words,

> In all honesty, we should not be surprised, for we all create Jesus in our own image. Christology at times tells us more about the culture from which the Jesus narrative is interpreted than anything specific about who historically or theologically was Jesus. If this is true, then all the Jesuses constructed serve the important function of uniting people into communities that share a similar Christian-based worldview.[55]

Throughout his work, De La Torre consistently exposes the geopolitics of Western knowledge as applied to Christology and the elaboration of Christian ethics, arguing that "there is no true Jesus that can be objectively known; there only exists subjective interpretations of Jesus."[56] Using Christological suspicion first employed by liberation theology and then by postmodern and subsequently postcolonial critical theories, De La Torre builds a methodological pathway for his *Politics of Jesús*:

> What if we radically employ a hermeneutical suspicion to Christology—not simply to debunk the normative Eurocentric understanding of Jesus but to construct a new Jesus? If Yoder could give us a pacifist Mennonite Jesus created in his own image, why then can I not provide us with a liberative Hispanic Jesús created in my and my community's image? The difference is that while Yoder made his subjective Jesus objective for all people, I recognize that my Jesus, or better yet, my Jesús, is definitively subjective. While I may hope that some of the traits of my Jesús might resonate with other disenfranchised communities, I lack the hubris to claim that my constructed Jesús is universal for all.[57]

There is a danger, acknowledges De La Torres, in a "quest for a Jesús created in the image of Latino/as" that needs to be constantly recognized and dealt with by attending to the biblical narrative as faithfully as possible, exercising a hermeneutics of suspicion on historical methodologies, and embedding ourselves in our communities as much as possible.

So what is De La Torre's ethical proposal in *The Politics of Jesús*? I suggest there are at least three ethical propositions with many ramifications, all of which further problematize the Niebuhr–Yoder Western ethical tension: (1) To recognize our epistemic positionality when doing social ethics, which involves the acknowledgment of our epistemic ignorance, incompleteness, the need of the other, and the temptation to exercise epistemic violence by totalizing our discourse for the sake of cultural entitlement (the West) or emancipation (the Rest). (2) To embrace hopelessness as our unavoidable ethical hermeneutics for the praxis of sociopolitical solidarity with the disfranchised, oppressed, marginalized who "occupy the Holy Saturday, the day after Friday's crucifixion" and who should not be deceived by an ethics that hurries on to Easter Sunday through the rhetoric of hope at the expense of accompanying them as they deal with their immanent desperation. (3) To resist with Jesús, who is construed as a troublemaker and trickster whose task is to disrupt colonial modernity world-systems and their legitimizing ideologies, dogmas, structures, and global designs operating as gatekeepers for the privileged political economy (the so-called 1 percent).

In many ways like Yoder—except very different in its being *De La Torrean*—*The Politics of Jesús* is a social ethic that calls the church to be a prophetic witness not merely to the state (Yoder) but to the matrix of colonial power of the world-systems in place that for centuries have built a racialized political economy at the expense of subaltern communities sharing modern-colonial-imperial subjugations. In short, De La Torre's ethic is a call to be a church as an alternative community whose radical disciples follow *Jesús* in the way to the cross but, ultimately, stay with *Jesús* in Holy Saturday when the only tactic that seems available to survive oppression is *j*der* (f**k) the modern colonial world-system.

CRITICAL OBSERVATIONS

Some critical observations with respect to the ethical voices presented so far are appropriate before transitioning into the final section. First, Yoder's cultural vision, as he advocates for rigorous New Testament exegesis and mission praxis, is more fluid and complex than Niebuhr's. Yoder finds allies in Latinx ethicists in rejecting both, (a) the concept of culture as fundamentally monolithic, as well as (b) personal ethics being more fundamental than social ethics. Two, Yoder's ambitious project is successful in finding a social ethics in the historic person of Jesus of Nazareth as he sees him reflected in the New Testament narratives. Nevertheless, his prototype for Jesus and social ethics suffered an inescapable racial-religious accommodation he seemed unaware of and yet detectable by the self-aware cultural other, namely, a pacifist (white) Mennonite Jesus (De La Torre). For the same reason, Latinx ethicists look for a Jesus of Nazareth who functions as their contemporary, that is, a *Jesús* of the marginalized, oppressed, and excluded of society. Third, the cultural *telos* of Yoder revolves around a concept of the church as a community that lives under the lordship of Jesus with the mission of embracing the surrounding communities and transforming them into a "culture of Christ." On the other hand, Latino ethicists conceived of the cultural *telos* as a communal geography (zip code) yet to be freed, dignified, fully embraced, and ultimately healed—a place where the sense of peoplehood can be realized, the cultural self re-assembled, and social emancipation pursued. De La Torre's *The Politics of Jesús* is an ethical articulation in this direction that acknowledges the fact that the zip code of oppression is not going to be freed or transformed by traditionally Western means—Christian or otherwise (a rhetoric of hope)—and hence requires the radical embrace of hopelessness as a rerouting subversion for liberative praxis.

THE POLITICS OF THE *ESPÍRITU*

> "Christ is with you. Do not abandon Him and He will not abandon you. You will see great sorrow, and in that sorrow you will be happy."[58]

In this final section I want to make the case for a decolonial ethics of the *Espíritu*, one that takes into account the agency of the Spirit and the storied contributions of the peoples of the American Global South. While Niebuhr–Yoder presents us with an important ethical tension within the West, and De La Torre and other Latinx theologians add original ethical tissue from the context of US Latinx diaspora (the politics of *Jesús*), still, the agency and ethical embodiment of the *Espíritu* in the stories of the disfranchised and oppressed remain unattended. And it is precisely through such agency and embodiment that we may be able to identify a *communal ethics in decolonial transit* as a way of resisting systemic deicides, ethnocides, genocides, matricides, ecocides, and epistemicides inflicted by colonial modernity world-systems. In other words, we want to move beyond the theology of the cross/glory binary so far encrypting Christological ethics. But where do we start?

In *Spirit Outside the Gate: Decolonial Pneumatologies of the American Global South* (InterVarsity Press, 2019) I argue that Christology has been so implicated in the colonizing and neocolonizing processes of the Americas that any attempt to begin with Christology (as such) is going to carry within itself colonial diseases—distinctly Western and hegemonic theological frameworks (gates) that inhibit the development of a truly liberating discourse. Christology requires a pneumatological turn for it to be healed. Unless we understand the wounding dialectics (coloniality/modernity/Occidentalism) operating at the core of Iberian Christology and stop reacting to it with modern christological attempts, we will not be able to overcome the epistemic gates limiting the Christian imagination in the Americas. This claim applies straightforwardly to ethics.

What I called *the problem of Iberian Christologies* speaks to a dialectical colonial construct, succinctly articulated by José de Acosta in the sixteenth century and later recovered by Gustavo Gutiérrez in the twentieth century: "if there is no gold, there is no God in the [West] Indies."[59] This constitutes a hermeneutical key that unlocks the problem of Christology since the beginnings of the Americas, and by extension the problem of ethics from the perspective of the peoples of the South. This ethical problem points to the lack of self-understanding and self-determination of the people of the Americas and to its eclipsed *imago Dei* as the effect of the Conquest and colonial modernity world-systems that developed later on. I discern three narratives expressing the Christological colonial effects on the peoples of the Americas, all of which disclosed not only the conquering ethics of the West but also the resisting ethics of the people of the South.

The first construct, *orphanhood*, sought to demonstrate how Christology was used to justify and spiritualize the pillaging and commodification of a land and people. Since Christ was wed to Christendom and the spread of the empire, the indigenous population were to understand the European matrix of domination of the Americas as both divinely ordained and a "blessing" for their salvation, and if the indigenous population resisted this form of colonialism (Conquest), their access to salvation, to Jesus, would be jeopardized. In Gutiérrez's words: if there is no gold, there is no God. The second construct, *subhuman poverty*, by way of being subjects of the crown and civilizing evangelization, sought to demonstrate that to be saved by this Christ of Christendom required that one "convert" into a particular kind of subject of the empire. That is, as long as Christology was modeled after the European colonizer, Indians' "conversion" (Christoformity) would always be incomplete, leaving them in a state of perpetual childhood and impoverishment, in need of constant oversight by the more mature Christians/magistrates. The third construct, *vicarious aesthetics*, by way of indigenous embodiment of historical tragedy and resistance through the arts (*Indianianized* Jesuses), sought to document the way many indigenous people developed aesthetic and theological syntheses that enabled them to participate in Christian rituals and symbols in ways that were culturally meaningful and empowering as well as constitutive pathways for resisting epistemically and sociopolitically.

The politics of the *Espíritu* is proposed then as an ethic of recognition–assemblage–decolonial healing in correspondence to resisting performances of the people of the South. As a consequence, such an ethic is only possible if placed in the Transoccidental-pneumatological difference, not in the Western/modern/christological ethical imaginary. The Transoccidental-pneumatological difference is a hermeneutical space (horizon) for epistemic resistance by re-classification, transmission, and sociopolitical embodiment—in other words, a new geopolitics of the American ethical self in response to five centuries of modernity/coloniality/Occidentalism. This new geography of the American Self points to healing the *imago Dei* of subaltern communities sharing colonial-modern-imperial subjugations "in the erasures of coloniality."[60] The politics of the *Espíritu* is, ultimately, an ethic of life, for life is the very ground of pneumatology and ethics in the American Global South. This ethics is built on the basis of a decolonial shift currently underway in the Americas:

- from monocultural Occidentalism to multicultural Transoccidentality;
- from Western christocentrism to border (decolonial) pneumatology;
- from general ecclesiology to *glocal* ecclesiality;
- from ethics of Western morality to ethics of world sustainability.

With this multidimensional theological shift in mind, I proceed to outline an ethical proposal that finds resonance with a selected group of traditioning communities of the American Global South located in the colonial difference: Original Americans (Indians), Afro-Latinxs, and immigrant Latina women. I consider these groups to exemplify the most ethically mistreated people of faith (Fanon's *Damnés de la Terre*) in our American Christian traditions, in part because there has been no *locus theologicus* able to host them without converting them into an object of study. The politics of the *Espíritu*, therefore, speaks to a social ethics of border people of faith engaged with and enabled by the Spirit Outside the Gate at the border of life and death, oppression and justice, Orthodoxy and heterodoxy, poverty and affluence, the West and the non-West, hopelessness and utopia, Holy Saturday and Easter Sunday.

ETHICS AS RECOGNITION–ASSEMBLAGE–DECOLONIAL HEALING

Recognition as I intend it here conveys the ethical task of mapping the multiple "spatialities, views of the self, and epistemologies that contribute" (Nelson Maldonado-Torres) to decolonizing the world of subaltern communities sharing modern-colonial-imperial subjugations in the American Global South.[61] But recognition as stated is only possible from within an "incarnational imagination" (Mayra Rivera Rivera) or, better, a "reconfiguring corporeal imaginary," where the physical and cognitive are not separate as in Western colonial modernity. This corporeal assemblage of the self, without pretention of pristine wholeness, functions to "theorize-in-the-flesh" (Cherríe Moraga) as part of the ethical performing task.[62] Since the American Selves are wounded by coloniality/modernity/Occidentalism, the *Espíritu* plays the theological role of a cognitive, corporeal, sociopolitical healer. The politics of the *Espíritu* results in decolonial ethics, one that is not compartmentalized or sectionalized but functions intersectionally and rhizomatically seeking knowledge, corporeal reconfiguration, and sociopolitical healing at the erasures of coloniality/modernity/Occidentalism.

The Osage–Christian American Indian theologian George Tinker illustrates this ethical effort as he elaborates a Native American theology of liberation through the *Spirit of resistance*, where he clearly states, "What we call spirituality is for us, as it is for most indigenous peoples, a way of life, not a mere singular category of life called 'religion.' Indeed, it encompasses the whole of life."[63] The Spirit is engaged in every step of the experience, reflection, and praxis of liberation and indigenous reimagination: epistemic, spatial, relational, and historic. Tinker further elaborates what I am calling an ethic of recognition–assemblage–decolonial healing as follows:

> a question that precedes reclaiming our rightful cultural and spiritual heritage has to do with why the particulars of that heritage have been suppressed, repressed, and even lost in so many cases across the continent. More to the point, any attempt to write a Native American theology must speak to Indian peoples about the present context of the peoples' oppression and alienation. Thus, an Indian theology must begin with the present-day social disintegration experienced by every Indian community, and begin to name the causes for the disintegration . . . It is not even enough to recognize the loss of ancestral spiritual traditions, because we have lost much more than stories and ceremonies. The very social fabric that once held our communities together has been shredded by the continuing events of the European conquest.[64]

As Tinker accentuates, the ethical task in the context of subaltern communities sharing modern-colonial-imperial subjugations is not sectional, lineal, or even progressive but involves intersectionality, simultaneousness, multi-chronic logics (dealing with the multiple historical layers of reality embodied in the communities). Thus, as one deals ethically with the current conditions of cultural disintegration, one must also map "spatialities, views of the self, and epistemologies" that contribute to a delinking from wounding colonial narratives, and simultaneously provide an "incarnational imagination" of corporeal assemblage, while exercising decolonial sociopolitical practices or tactics as a counternarrative to the hegemonic colonial modernity world-systems. I argue that this matrix of sociopolitical resistance of the *Espíritu* has been present in various ways since day one of the European conquest and is identifiable in communities such as Original (Indian) Americans, Afro-Latinxs, and, more recently, immigrants of the South.

In *Spirit Outside the Gate* I demonstrated that the theological imagination of the Original American communities has dealt with civilizing missions and Occidentalization by both resisting and reconstructing Christian meaning. This goes for their ethics as well, which is ethics of life (survival) and good living (communal emancipation). The *Espíritu* has been present in the land and communities of Original Americans, whether in *indigenous cultural forms* as illustrated by the Andean *Corpus Procession* in Cusco since the 1600s; whether through *indigenous religious content* vested in theological languages that enable us to call God in our own native languages with names like *Pachacamac* (el Inca Garcilazo de la Vega) or as the American Indian duality *wakon'da* Above and *wakon'da* Below and Grandfather (*itsi'ko*) and Grandmother (*i'ko*), as Sky and Earth;[65] whether through Quechua *indigenous rites* such as the *apachetas* (offerings to Pachacamac) or *wakas* (holy spirits in sacred places and objects), which were made in reverence to the omnipresent God *Illa Tecce Viracocha* (Mestizo Blas Varela); whether in *Original Christian indigenous religiosities* such as the one illustrated in *Neo-Inca Christianity* or *Neo-Mexica Christianity* in early colonial times.[66]

De La Torre's ethical discovery of tricking the colonial modernity world-system when it comes to the marginalized and disenfranchised is seconded by my research on indigenous resistance in the American Global South. However, instead of focusing on a reconstructed *Jesús*, it is the *Santo Espíritu*, in the Yoruba-Christian sense, who functions as a "guide for life representing the Jesus who died, [as] . . . the ancestors in traditional Yoruba religion guide the living relatives after death."[67] Across America, broadly speaking, *disguise* has been a mechanism used by subaltern communities sharing colonial-modern-imperial subjugations to survive and resist culturally, religiously, politically, and epistemically. In order to escape death, the subaltern has systematically recurred to disguise as an ethics of survival and communal emancipation. In the context of the Afro-Latinxs, again I suggest the *Espíritu* may be understood as a "guide for life representing the Jesus who died, [as] . . . the ancestors in traditional Yoruba religion guide the living relatives after death."[68] Likewise, the politics of the *Espíritu* corresponds to an ethic of recognition–assemblage–colonial healing that fills subaltern Afro-Latinxs with holy knowledge, with purpose, prophecy, cultural and racial worth, and makes them dance, sing, shout, and move up the ladder of social, economic, and educational advancement against the systemic assault on their social mobility by world-systems designed to keep them at the bottom of the social order.

Finally, the politics of the *Espíritu* through the voice of *la mujer latina* (Latina woman) is cunning. This has been captured in the work of Loida Martell-Otero, Zaida Maldonado Peréz, and Elizabeth Conde-Frazier, *Latina Evangélicas: A Theological Survey from the Margins* (2013). This work notices an insubordinate and decolonizing pattern when it comes to how ethics is articulated as the *politics of the Espíritu* against the conquering christological ethics of the West. In their words,

> At the heart of the project is a powerful image: the Holy Spirit as the wild child of the Trinity. As Martell-Otero describes her, she is creative, uncontrolled, and musical. She moves between people, making connections, bringing life to the party, inspiring fresh vision and grand stories. She also brings her wild comfort to places of pain and despair, and she is honest. Sometimes she dances in line with others, finding good partners in her Trinitarian trot. More often than not, though, she breaks with tradition and improvises, impishly, wisely, delightedly. When she breaks into such an improvisational dance, the world around her is suddenly made light with creative, unimagined possibility. . . . Read the book carefully but with a light and open heart. . . . There is much to be learned here, especially, about the Holy Spirit.[69]

The politics of the *Espíritu* through the Latina *evangélica* voice is rooted in *abuelitas-madres-comadres-tias*[70] wisdom and ethics: "they nurtured us with a keen sense of the Spirit's ability to create anew."[71] This ethical voice sees *Espíritu* as she who (a) legitimizes women suppressed by patriarchal, racist, ecclesial structures, (b) is the subversive One pouring out charisms and enabling women as *personas llamadas* (called persons), (c) is the wild child of the Trinity who saves, heals, affirms, calls, empowers, and transforms persons and communities, (d) is one who goes native, (e) is the communal healer (*katartismos*), and (f) is a (decolonial) healer of the Latina woman commonly treated as *sata* (mongrel, mutt) and *sobraja* (leftover) by the oppressive and patriarchal world designs surrounding her, but is redeemed as *santa* (holy woman) by the *Espíritu* who pulls her away from the *habitus* of death on a personal and interpersonal level.

De La Torre suggests that most Western Christian ethics have been done illusively from the Sunday Easter account of history, hence neglecting the unaltered reality of the disenfranchised and the oppressed. This Western ethical positionality ends up favoring those who have been historically privileged by racial, political, and economic constructs. The oppressed and disenfranchised Latinxs live, insists De La Torre, in Holy Saturday when and where everything seems lost, hence the politics of *Jesús* is (has been) our most obvious option. We take it from here and suggest that the *Espíritu* (Spirit Outside the Gate) is not circumscribed to Holy Saturday or Easter Sunday. Rather, she is (has been) present in Holy Saturday, not romanticizing a colonial *wound*, but providing a sociocultural *womb*, building tunnels of life in the midst of death for subaltern communities sharing colonial-modern-imperial subjugations to survive, resist, and persist by means of the politics of the *Espíritu*. Ultimately, it is the narrative of Pentecost—not the binary Cross/Resurrection—that should orient the politics of the *Espíritu*. The *Espíritu* knows the language of lament of Holy Saturday, but she is also a dancing spirit, a singing spirit, who alongside the Indians and Africans and immigrants of the South has been dancing together with the subaltern under the decolonizing beats of the drums of indigenous resistance announcing the ending of terminal knowledges and wounding world designs, time after time. So far, oppressive world-systems have been able to cut our tongues but never to stop our music.

NOTES

1. Throughout this essay I use the terms "Latino, Latina, Latino/a, and Latinx" interchangeably to show the intention of inclusivity when addressing the US diaspora of the peoples of the American Global South. It goes without saying that any attempt to totalize representations of the US Latina community will fail. It is clear for me that while "Latino/a" points to gender inclusivity and epistemologies from the perspective of many voices from the previous generations of scholars, "Latinx" points to gender fluidity and epistemologies from the perspective of many emerging voices. Gladly, I do not have to choose one over the other.
2. John Howard Yoder, *The Politics of Jesus* (Grand Rapids, MI: Eerdmans, 1994), 4–8.
3. It is important to mention that in the epilogue of the first chapter in the revised edition (*Politics of Jesus*, 1994), Yoder goes into more detail about the claims made by those who think it is impossible to imitate Jesus in the socio-ethical realm or who label Jesus as an apolitical character. These additional details, in my opinion, do not substantially affect the author's original presentation (1972), which is why I do not include them. See Yoder, *Politics of Jesus*, 8.
4. Ibid.
5. Ibid.
6. Ibid.
7. Richard Hays, in his analysis of the biblical ethic of Reinhold Niebuhr, defines Christian realism as "a prophetically and biblically informed criticism of ideologies of the left and the right." See Richard B. Hays, *The Moral Vision of the New Testament: Community, Cross, New Creation* (San Francisco, CA: Harper, 1996), 215. Glen Stassen proposes the term "historical realism" when referring to the approach of Richard Niebuhr, which "points to what we know and can know." See Glen Harold Stassen, D. M. Yeager, and John Howard Yoder, *Authentic Transformation: A New Vision of Christ and Culture* (Nashville, TN: Abingdon, 1996), 151. It is understood that despite being brothers and having both influenced the sphere of American Christian ethics, Reinhold and Richard were not theologically symmetrical. For example, Yeager recognizes that there were points of tension

between Reinhold and Richard with respect to the normative and concrete nature of Richard's conversionist concept (Stassen, Yeager, and Yoder, *Authentic Transformation*, 100). In addition, Roger Shinn observes that "Reinhold was called to reform the culture while Richard was called to reform the church," which naturally caused Reinhold to gain greater public visibility. See Roger L. Shinn, "Reinhold and Richard Niebuhr (1892–1971 and 1894–1962)," in *The Oxford Companion to Christian Thought: Intellectual, Spiritual, and Moral Horizons of Christianity*, ed. Adrian Hastings, Alistair Máson, and Hugh Pyper (Oxford: Oxford University Press, 2000), 481–486.

8. Hays, *Moral Vision*, 240.
9. Stassen, Yeager, and Yoder, *Authentic Transformation*, 31.
10. Douglas F. Ottani, "H. Richard Niebuhr 1894–1962," in *A New Handbook of Christian Theologians*, ed. Donald W. Musser and Joseph L. Price (Nashville, TN: Abingdon, 1996), 325.
11. Ibid. This is an interpretation of *Church Against the World*.
12. Ibid., 326.
13. H. Richard Niebuhr, *Meaning of Revelation* (New York: Macmillan, 1941), 139.
14. H. Richard Niebuhr, *Christ and Culture* (New York: Harper Torchbooks, 1951).
15. Ibid., 40.
16. Faith plays a definitive role for Niebuhr because it is faith that, by grace, reaches us and draws us into Christ, and it is faith "for which we have been chosen" and by which we reason and make decisions (Niebuhr, *Christ and Culture*, 225, 252). This is a faith that exists uniquely in a "community of selves in the presence of a greater cause" (253).
17. This is the argument Diane M. Yeager makes in defense of the Niebuhrian ethic. See Stassen, Yeager, and Yoder, *Authentic Transformation*, 126.
18. Diane M. Yeager argues, responding to claims made by critics that perceive Niebuhr's "ethical offer" as inadequate and abstract, that the very idea of a "Christian social ethic" is incoherent (Stassen, Yeager, and Yoder, *Authentic Transformation*, 92–95). Christian ethics pursues, according to Yeager, "personal conversion, not social reform." Following this logic, Niebuhr understands ethics as "a personal system that recognizes the structural and social contours of our lives, but treats them as a backdrop" (Stassen, Yeager, and Yoder, *Authentic Transformation*, 96) and thus refuses to prescribe "norms" or criteria that might offer "the correct Christian response" for questions of economics, education, politics, etc. In *Christ and Culture*, Yeager continues, Richard Niebuhr suggested the "material content" (motif) of social transformation but not the "form" that such transformation should take. Glen H. Stassen chooses a more inclusive and creative route when dealing with the aforementioned questions. Stassen recognizes the historical deficiencies and overly abstract nature of the "conversion model" Niebuhr presents in *Christ and Culture*, but argues that there are philosophical and theological reasons for it. Stassen goes beyond a mere "apology" and argues that Niebuhr was, in fact, interested in "the concrete," and that this was made very clear in his treatises on ecclesiology (127–142). In short, Stassen maintains that "as long as Niebuhr remained consistent with his rejection of Kantian universal rationality and Kantian agnosticism, he developed a strong basis for theocentric ethical norms that can be historically concrete" (161).
19. See Nancey C. Murphy, "John Howard Yoder's Systematic Defense of Christian Pacifism," in *The Wisdom of the Cross: Essays in Honor of John Howard Yoder*, ed. Stanley Hauerwas et al., Reissue edition. (Eugene, OR: Wipf & Stock Pub, 2005), 48.
20. See Mark Thiessen Nation, "John H. Yoder, Ecumenical Neo-Anabaptist: A Biographical Sketch," in *The Wisdom of the Cross: Essays in Honor of John Howard Yoder*, ed. Stanley Hauerwas et al., Reissue edition. (Eugene, OR: Wipf & Stock Pub, 2005), 20.

21. Hays, *Moral Vision*, 252.
22. Ibid., 240–241.
23. Ibid., 241.
24. Cited in ibid., 241.
25. Yoder, *The Politics of Jesus*, 51.
26. Hays, *Moral Vision*, 241.
27. Yoder, *The Politics of Jesus*, 95.
28. Cited in Hays, *Moral Vision*, 243.
29. Ibid., 244.
30. Stassen, Yeager, and Yoder, *Authentic Transformation*, 103.
31. Yoder, *The Politics of Jesus*, 155.
32. Duane K. Friesen, *Artists, Citizens, Philosophers: Seeking the Peace of the City* (Scottsdale, PA: Herald Press, 2000), 53.
33. John Howard Yoder, *The Priestly Kingdom: Social Ethics as Gospel* (Notre Dame, IN: University of Notre Dame Press, 1985), 11.
34. Friesen, *Artists, Citizens, Philosophers*, 53.
35. John Howard Yoder, Lilia Solano, C. René Padilla, *Iglesia, ética y poder* (Buenos Aires : Kairós, 1998), 5.
36. Ibid., 6.
37. Ibid., 76.
38. Ibid., 78.
39. Ibid.
40. Ibid., 84.
41. See Eduardo Mendieta, "The Ethics of (Not) Knowing: Take Care of Ethics and Knowledge Will Come of Its Own Accord," in *Decolonizing Epistemologies: Latina/o Theology and Philosophy*, ed. Ada María Isasi-Díaz and Eduardo Mendieta (New York: Fordham University Press, 2012), 247–264.
42. See Ada María Isasi-Díaz, "Mujerista Discourse: A Platform for Latinas' Subjugated Knowledge," in *Decolonizing Epistemologies: Latina/o Theology and Philosophy*, ed. Ada María Isasi-Díaz and Eduardo Mendieta (New York: Fordham University Press, 2012), 44–67; and Oscar Garcia-Johnson, *Spirit Outside the Gate: Decolonial Pneumatologies of the South* (Downers Grove, IL: InterVarsity Press, forthcoming, 2019), chaps. 1–6. In addition, this is a subject carefully addressed at the beginnings of US Latina theology by Virgilio Elizondo (*The Galilean Journey*), and also Orlando Costas (*Christ Outside the Gate*).
43. Eldin Villafañe, *The Liberating Spirit: Toward an Hispanic American Pentecostal Ethics* (Lanham, MD: University Press of America, 1992), 193–195.
44. Ibid., 195.
45. Ibid.
46. Ismael García, *Dignidad: Ethics through Hispanic Eyes* (Nashville, TN: Abingdon, 1997), 16.
47. Ibid., 28.
48. Ibid., 53–54.
49. Ibid., 142.
50. Ibid., 143.

51. Ibid.
52. Ibid., 151.
53. Ibid., 152.
54. In the case of Niebuhr, De La Torre offers strong critiques while still agreeing with Niebuhr that "any claim concerning justice is both contextual and historical." For De La Torre, Niebuhr's "realism" accepted US imperialism as something that needed to be operated within (in fact, as something divinely ordained to prevent communist or Nazi imperialism), rather than something to be overthrown. By the 1950s Niebuhr was an apologist for US colonialism and imperialism, justifying the negative aspects of colonialism in light of the advancements it bestowed upon the communities that experienced what he called the "tutelage of colonialism." See Miguel De La Torre, *Latina/o Social Ethics: Moving Beyond Eurocentric Moral Thinking* (Waco, TX: Baylor University Press, 2010), 14, 15, 18–19.
55. Miguel A. De La Torre, *The Politics of Jesús: A Hispanic Political Theology*, Religion in the Modern World (Lanham, MD: Rowman & Littlefield, 2015), Kindle ed.
56. Ibid., 7.
57. Ibid., 7–8.
58. Fyodor Dostoyevsky, *Karamazov Brothers* (Wordsworth Editions, 2007), 80.
59. Gustavo Gutiérrez, *Dios O el Oro en las Indias: Siglo XVI* (San Salvador: UCA Editores, 1991), 113.
60. Walter D. Mignolo, *The Idea of Latin America* (Malden, MA: Blackwell, 2005), 48.
61. Nelson Maldonado-Torres, "Epistemology, Ethics, and the Time/Space of Decolonization: Perspectives from the Caribbean and Latina/o Americas," in *Decolonizing Epistemologies: Latina/o Theology and Philosophy*, ed. Ada María Isasi-Díaz and Eduardo Mendieta (New York: Fordham University Press, 2012), 195.
62. Mayra Rivera Rivera, "Thinking Bodies: The Spirit of a Latina Incarnational Imagination," in *Decolonizing Epistemologies: Latina/o Theology and Philosophy*, ed. Ada María Isasi-Díaz and Eduardo Mendieta (New York: Fordham University Press, 2012), 207.
63. George E. Tinker, *Spirit and Resistance: Political Theology and American Indian Liberation* (Minneapolis, MN: Fortress, 2004), Kindle loc. 1565–1568.
64. Ibid., Kindle loc. 79–84.
65. Ibid., Kindle loc. 1505.
66. Garcia-Johnson, *Spirit Outside the Gate,* chaps. 7, 10.
67. Samuel Cruz, *Masked Africanisms: Puerto Rican Pentecostalism* (Dubuque: Kendall/Hunt Publishing, 2005), 64.
68. Ibid.
69. Martell-Otero, Maldonado Pérez, and Conde-Frazier, *Latina Evangélicas*, Kindle loc. 107–137.
70. That is, grandmas-moms-midwives-aunts.
71. Martell-Otero, Maldonado Pérez, and Conde-Frazier, *Latina Evangélicas*, Kindle loc. 162.

SELECT BIBLIOGRAPHY

Cruz, Samuel (2005), *Masked Africanisms: Puerto Rican Pentecostalism*, Dubuque, IA: Kendall/Hunt Publishing.

De La Torre, Miguel (2010), *Latina/o Social Ethics: Moving Beyond Eurocentric Moral Thinking*, Waco, TX: Baylor University Press.

De La Torre, Miguel (2015), *The Politics of Jesús: A Hispanic Political Theology*, Religion in the Modern World, Lanham, MD: Rowman & Littlefield.

Dostoyevsky, Fyodor (2007), *Karamazov Brothers*, Wordsworth Editions.

García, Ismael (1997), *Dignidad: Ethics through Hispanic Eyes*, Nashville, TN: Abingdon Press.

Garcia-Johnson, Oscar (forthcoming 2019), *Spirit Outside the Gate: Decolonial Pneumatologies of the American Global South*, Downers Grove, IL: InterVarsity Press.

Gutiérrez, Gustavo (1991), *Dios O el Oro en las Indias: Siglo XVI*, San Salvador, El Salvador: UCA Editores.

Hays, Richard B. (1996), *The Moral Vision of the New Testament: Community, Cross, New Creation*, San Francisco, CA: HarperCollins.

Isasi-Díaz, Ada María and Eduardo Mendieta, eds. (2012), *Decolonizing Epistemologies: Latina/o Theology and Philosophy*, New York: Fordham University Press.

Martell-Otero, Loida, Zaida Maldonado Peréz, and Elizabeth Conde-Frazier (2013), *Latina Evangélicas: A Theological Survey from the Margins*, Eugene, OR: Cascade Books.

Mignolo, Walter D. (2005), *The Idea of Latin America*, Malden, MA: Blackwell Publishing.

Niebuhr, H. Richard (1941), *Meaning of Revelation*, New York: Macmillan.

Niebuhr, H. Richard (1951), *Christ and Culture*, New York: Harper Torchbooks.

Stassen, Glen Harold, D. M. Yeager, and John Howard Yoder (1996), *Authentic Transformation: A New Vision of Christ and Culture*, Nashville, TN: Abingdon Press.

Tinker, George E. (2004), *Spirit and Resistance: Political Theology and American Indian Liberation*, Minneapolis, MN: Fortress Press.

Villafañe, Eldin (1992), *The Liberating Spirit: Toward an Hispanic American Pentecostal Ethics*, Lanham, MD: University Press of America.

Yoder, John Howard (1985), *The Priestly Kingdom: Social Ethics as Gospel*, Notre Dame, IN: University of Notre Dame Press.

Yoder, John Howard (1994), *The Politics of Jesus*, Grand Rapids, MI: Wm. B. Eerdmans Publishing Co.

Yoder, John Howard, Lilia Solano, C. René Padilla (1998), *Iglesia, ética y poder*, Buenos Aires: Kairós.

CHAPTER TWENTY-FOUR

Christian Humanism, *redivivus*

LUKE BRETHERTON

INTRODUCTION

Some notion of a shared humanity is central to any conception of a common life that extends beyond parochial boundaries of kinship or locality. However, the boundaries of who counts as human, and thence whose moral and political agency deserves recognition, along with the question of how to distinguish humans from other kinds of being, is always vehemently contested. However, in the contemporary context, the concept of humanity itself is in question even as the need for it grows more acute. The ability to edit human DNA, the capacity to merge humans and machines at a cellular level, and the prospect of artificial intelligence that shares characteristics of human consciousness lead some to ask whether there will emerge different kinds of humans or even post-humans. Conversely, attention to how humans are not self-sufficient as a species, but biologically symbiotic with other forms of life, particularly the microbiome, and how the quality of these symbiotic relations directly effects what are taken to be specifically human capacities, notably higher level reasoning, blurs the sense of humanity as a singular phenomenon.

If on the one hand, there are moves towards the dissolution of humanity as a thinkable entity, there is, on the other hand, an ever-greater impetus to use humanity as a category for delineating moral and political responsibilities. One speculative example of this dynamic is how space exploration and the possibilities of relations with life on other planets asks questions about the moral and political responsibilities of humanity as a species. A more pressing example is the concept of the anthropocene, whereby humans are seen to impact the geological formation of the planet, and its negative manifestations in such things as climate change and mass-level extinctions. Folded within ethical and political reflections on anthropogenic climate change are concerns about how economic globalization unequally distributes costs and benefits and produces structural inequalities at a global level, even as globalization connects humans more intricately and enables a consciousness of all humans as participants in a shared time and space. These interplanetary, planetary, and global concerns connect to more established foci in which humanity is the primary locus of moral and political concern; namely, the legitimacy and efficacy of human rights, and aligned notions such as crimes against humanity, global citizenship, and humanitarianism.

This chapter reviews recurrent ways in which humanity as a moral and political concept is understood and how humanity can be imagined and narrated theologically.

First, I distinguish humanity as a biological claim from humanity as a moral and political one. Second, I identify two basic moves through which a notion of a shared humanity can be arrived at, namely, either beginning with what humans share or beginning with how humans are different. Third, I compare the way these starting points generate anthropocentric approaches to conceptualizing humanity with a theocentric way of grounding a moral and political commitment to a shared humanity. Lastly, I reflect on how humanity can function as a moral and political category in a way that attends to the tensions and paradoxes explored over the course of the chapter.

NATALITY, MORTALITY, AND THE TELEOLOGICAL NATURE OF BEING HUMAN

There are claims about humanity as a biological species that are proper to science. But it is not the mere fact of shared biology that is salient morally and politically. To meet another *homo sapien* is not to encounter one who necessarily makes a claim on me or "us." It is in encountering someone with a need that a moral and potentially political claim is made upon me or "us." But, conversely, the sense that this other human is in need depends on a sense that they are indeed another human. It is their humanity rather than their need that I must deny if I am to ignore or discount the moral claim this human in need makes upon me (i.e., this is not a human, or at least, not the same kind of human as me, and so their need for food, water, comfort, liberation, etc., makes no claim upon me). Political and religious identities can function to discount the needs of whole classes of humans. Conversely, humanitarianism is a paradigmatic example of how a shared sense of humanity and a sense that this person or group is in need, is the basis of moral and political claims. The enduring and widespread appeal of the Good Samaritan parable turns on the recognition of a fellow human as the basis of recognizing one in need of help.

The use of humanity as both a biological and moral term obscures what prior conceptual frameworks separated. The ancient Greeks distinguished between *zoe*—the biological or physical life that plants, animals, and humans share (and which can be a divine gift)—and *bios*—the manner, form, and means of life (which is a moral and political construct). There is a parallel distinction in Scripture, although it operates with a different cosmology and anthropology. To be human/*adam* is to be made of the soil/*adamah*: that is, the ground all animate life and inanimate things share. But to be this kind of creature is also to be Spirit breathed soil (*nephesh ḥayyah*), a condition shared with all animate life (Genesis 2:17, 19; Psalm 104:27–30; Ecclesiastes 3:18–21). But the pneumatological, biological, and material conditions of life do not exhaust and define what it means to be human. When alone with other forms of animate life, Adam cannot realize the plenitude of human being. It is only in and through communion with another human that what it means to be *human* can be named and lived out. And ultimately, human personhood can only be fulfilled in and through communion with Christ.

The specific ways in which humans are animate creatures needs attention. Any account of human being as an assemblage of life entails moral claims about the distinction between animate life and being a person, between being alive and being someone situated within a meaningful and purposeful moral and political community that is open to and always already called into a specific kind of relationship with God. To be human, on this account, is to be goal directed—the question is what goals or visions of the good life we desire and pursue and the quality and kind of relationships needed to fulfill such an end. The further implication of this interpersonal and covenantal delineation of what constitutes a human being is that to become human is to be embedded in relations of care. This pushes against individualistic and competitive conceptions of humanity. It is not our essential condition but a failure of humanity when, as per Hobbes, we are "wolves" to each other. As in the story of Cain and Abel, to deny how we are constituted through mutually responsible, cooperative fellowship with others that must be ordered in relationship to God is to deny and diminish our humanity. Love of God and love of neighbor (which includes non-human creation) are the ground and fulfillment of what it means to be human.

On a Christian theological reading, to be human is to exist within a shared realm of human and divine meaning and agency. Such a realm comes to be through divine action—paradigmatically, through the incarnation of Jesus Christ—and is always already a cultural, political formation in which we live and move and have our being. Claims about humanity, theological or otherwise, cannot be separated from determinate forms of life and their ecological-cultural-historical practices. In evolutionary terms, humans are what are called "ultra-social" animals, with no clear boundary between humans and other-than-human-animals. What is specifically human is not that we are rational, or use tools, or have language or culture and animals do not. Rather, it is the practices through which we become human that mark humanity as a distinctive kind of animal. It is the specific ways humans care for and cooperate with each other that accounts for what differences there are between humans and, for example, our primate cousins.[1] The first of these practices is that humans cook and need to cook their food and animals do not. I contend that beginning with cooking, the specific ways in which humans are precarious and thereby dependent on the care of others to live, means it is constellations of practices of care that constitute humanity as a moral and political entity. By beginning with cooking I am emphasizing that practices of care mark our natality—that which creates life, energy, joy, and intimacy—and thereby marks the beginning of identifiably human forms of life together. But practices of care also mark our mortality—that is, our finitude, frailty, and suffering.

Arguably, something else uniquely human is an awareness of mortality and the sense of finitude. Again, this generates practices of care. As Judith Butler notes: "Precisely because a living being may die, it is necessary to care for that being so that it may live. Only under conditions in which the loss would matter does the value of the life appear. Thus, grievability is a presupposition of the life that matters."[2] Mythopoetically, humans mark lives that matter through mortuary and funerary practices that locate us as neither gods (who as immortal do not need burial) nor beasts (who do not bury).[3] Theologically, humans are those who live in-between heaven and earth, this world and the next, animals and angels, biological kinship and a communion of saints. Phenomenologically, marking death and the dead gives birth to community as existing through time. The remembrance and marking of the dead is, paradoxically, a stake in a future and ongoing life together, a life together in which the dead can be remembered as a past to our future. This is taken up in the birth of philosophy and axial religions like Confucianism, Judaism, Buddhism, Hinduism, Zoroastrianism, and classical Greek philosophy and theater, which posit a duality between transcendent and mundane orders of space and time. The premise of this duality is the ability to both reach back and reach beyond what is seen and heard to posit a relationship between bodily life and a deeper/transcendent horizon of meaning and action.

As a practice that situates humans in relations of proximity and natality, cooking points to how a notion of humanity must include all those who currently exist at this moment (i.e., be synchronic). While care for the dead, which situates humans as having a past and a future and as finite, points to how conceptions of humanity must incorporate not just those humans who are currently alive but also the dead and the unborn, ancestors and generations to come (i.e., be diachronic). Thus, as a moral claim, humanity carries tacit commitments to the honoring of those who came before us as well as a commitment to the tending and handing on of what we have received, which is to say, it incorporates relations of reception and trans-generational transmission. Inhumanity is the refusal to engage in or intentionally destroy and violate the kinds of practices that receive, tend, and pass on the ability to participate in the work of becoming human. There are the obvious brutal forms of this such as enslavement, conquest, and genocide, but there are also more subtle forms, such as the debasement and distortion of language itself through propaganda and systematic lying. As evidenced in totalitarian regimes and dictatorships, this latter form of inhumanity deprives humans of the ability to trust each other, thereby dissolving the capacity to generate shared meaning and action.[4]

To recognize another as human and to claim there is a humanity all share is not just to claim that there is a common realm of meaning and action, it is also to make a teleological claim. Humanity presumes a movement from biological life to personhood. But as a teleological notion, humanity entails some normative measure of what it means to be human. It is at this point that problems arise: who or what constitutes that normative measure? Babylonian elites? The gnostic elect? White, European men? The proletariat? Those made in the image of God? In which case who and what determines what that image consists of? Or is there a necessary apophaticism when it comes to defining what it means to be human—its grasp eluding any final, normative conceptualization? Given the inherent cultural and historical dimensions of humanity as a moral and political claim, there is a paradox at the heart of it. It is a claim that is diachronically and synchronically universal in scope, but which can only be understood and realized through determinate forms of life. We come to what is common through the specific. The knowledge and realization of humanity only comes by means of historically mediated particularity. As I shall argue in due course, acquisition of this knowledge necessarily entails politics.

Knowledge of another as human is always personal and cultural.[5] It is not speculative knowledge but knowledge that connects our affective response and self-reflexive sense of self to a concrete other or group of others. The paradox of humanity is that we need modes of attending to particularity to establish what is shared by all and modes of attending to what is common to safeguard our particularity. Linguistically and conceptually, we must name people within bounded categories or as types so that they might be intelligible, but our classificatory systems are inherently exclusionary frameworks: they exclude recognition of those who don't fit the categories and types we use to apprehend another as human.

The way invocations of humanity are always particular points to a problem that humanity as a moral category seeks to address, namely, how to respond to the other, the one not like me, the stranger. This is a problem that is central to the formation of all social and political orders. Determinations of who is a friend and who is a stranger, who is "inside" and who is "outside" the boundaries of the community shape and form the identity and practices of a polity. The word *humanity* is a place-holder for the commitment to discover a shared way of being alive with outsiders. Talk of humanity is an invitation to extend the reach of who to include in the common life rather than limit who is judged to be human to one group. Talk of humanity is thereby also a refusal to absolutize friend–enemy relations. It is a way to keep open the possibility of discovering with strangers a shared realm of meaning and action rather than either killing or coercing them. But contrary to what many humanists have argued, talk of humanity is not thereby pre-, post-, or anti-political. It is inherently political talk.[6] In short, there is no knowledge of humanity beyond or beneath politics.[7]

As political talk, talk of humanity contests the boundaries of citizenship. In doing so, it functions first and foremost as a form of dissent, contesting definitions of what it means to be human derived solely from what is inherited and familiar. This has been a central theme of cosmopolitan thought in the West from Diogenes the Cynic onwards, whose claim to be a "citizen of the cosmos" was a way to question the institutions and conventions of his polity. In the contemporary context claims to humanity have often functioned to agitate those reasonably secure in their status as equals to recognize those still struggling to achieve such equality.[8] Talk of humanity thereby pushes against closed or totalizing systems of thought, insisting on the open-ended nature of who or what defines humanity. As will be seen, talk of humanity must account for and work with the grain of finitude (the temporal and spatial limits of human being), but in doing so pushes against the deformation of particularity into parochialism, communalism, and the sacralization of contingent and unjust hierarchies.

Babylonians, Egyptians, and Sumerians—to name but a few of our antecedents—all envisaged themselves as civilized in contrast to various "barbarian" others. Their creation myths inscribed this distinction into the cosmos. The civilized were children of the gods—and so masters by divine inheritance whose social and political order was an analog of the cosmic divine order—while those outside its boundaries were savages who were either natural slaves or who existed in a realm of chaos. Such a framework is completely uninterested either in understanding the other as the same as me or how the other is not like me. The other is *not* a focus of moral and political concern. This contrasts with axial religions and philosophies and their canonical texts. In these traditions, we see two moves for framing those not like us, both of which generate problems, but which also need understanding as moral gestures of concern for those we find strange.

The first move is to posit that all humans are the same (the common humanity frame), the second is to begin moral and political reflection on humanity from how humans are different (the ethnographic frame).[9] Both moves are born out of concern for justice, that is, how to give strangers what is due to them. Common humanity frames are generally aspirational and based on theoretical reason. They seek to establish normative conditions for the recognition of a shared world of meaning and action. Ethnographic frameworks presume interaction and knowledge of others. They are attempts to name the stranger in dialogue with the stranger's own terms of reference based on inductive, practical reason, seeking to aid prudential judgments about how to act fittingly in relationship with a stranger. Scripturally these two moves are marked, and to a certain extent coordinated, by two distinct but related covenants. The first is the Noahide covenant that calls all humans to be a specific kind of creature. The second is the Abrahamic covenant that calls the people of God to bear witness to who God is amidst the nations through a distinctive pattern of life.

In what follows I examine variations of the common humanity and ethnographic frames as ways of coming to make judgments about who or what is human. However, as will be seen, problems arise when one aspect of how humanity constitutes a moral and political category is emphasized to the exclusion of others.

COMMON HUMANITY OR BEGINNING WITH HOW HUMANS ARE THE SAME

Common humanity frameworks are philosophical or theological moves that speculate how, despite different forms of life, the other is like us. Often involving a high level of abstraction, such frameworks appeal to what are presumed to be universal sets of values and human commonalities while bracketing cultural differences. As a moral discourse, frameworks that focus on our common humanity transform a stranger into a fellow human being yet emerge from within the intellectual resources of a particular tradition.[10] Versions of this move in the contemporary context include human rights and humanitarianism. Within Christianity, Judaism, and Islam some version of natural law is a primary instantiation of such a framework.[11]

Epistemically, common humanity frames too easily slip into positing a false transparency that obfuscates how others are different. A primary way this manifests itself is through the creation of categories that predetermine how to interpret others. In doing so moral concern, combined with an asymmetry of power, becomes a colonial imposition that forces others to conform to an account of what it means to be human that is not just alien to them but often destructive of their own way of life.[12] Immanuel Kant represents an example of liberal cosmopolitanism displaying this problem. Kant critiqued colonialism, but he was an early proponent of scientific racism.[13] However, alongside his justifications of white supremacy and his pointed silence regarding chattel slavery, even his conception of cosmopolitanism, which might be presumed to contradict the racial hierarchy he advocated, reveals a decided Eurocentrism that imposes itself as a universal standard of adjudication. For Kant, "Since the earth's surface is not unlimited but closed, the concepts of the right of a state and of a right of nations lead inevitably to the idea of a right for all nations (*ius gentium*) or cosmopolitan right (*ius cosmopoliticium*)."[14] There is a difference, however, between a concept of *ius gentium* in which each people is recognized as having their own law and Kant's cosmopolitan vision in which the laws of European peoples become the law of all peoples. Kant follows a trajectory of thought away from explicitly theological formulations of natural law towards the extension of a Westphalian model of cooperation between nation-states as *the* model for "perpetual peace" in all places. As embodied in the United Nations, such an order is arrived at through the negotiation of relations between nation-states in which a monistic European standard of what a nation-state looks like determines what constitutes a legitimate sovereign power. While such a liberal cosmopolitan vision proposes that all nations are free and equal, it hides how some nation-states, by dint of access to resources, setting legal norms, military power, and historical precedent are more equal than others.

If Kant represents the attempt to conceptualize humanity in terms of a shared territory, that nevertheless places Europeans as the ideal of that nature most fitted to rule over all other "races," Hegel represents the attempt to conceptualize common humanity as derived from humans existing within a shared history. For Hegel, there is a single history and this history has a teleologically ordered purpose, which is to unfold the spirit of freedom and authentic humanity. Hegel envisages European modernity as the zenith and crowning achievement of this history. His *Lectures on the Philosophy of World History* portray humanity as finding its center and fulfillment in Europe (specifically, Germany, France, and Britain) such that all other times and spaces are judged in relation to Europe understood as the *telos* of world history. Hegel's philosophy of history does not simply sacralize history and humanity, it sacralizes *European* humanity as the true end toward which history progresses.[15]

Karl Marx turned Hegel on his head but continues to work with the same logic. In place of Western European man, Marx substitutes the proletariat as the subject of history. Only the experience and consciousness of the proletariat is the authentically human consciousness (i.e., their experience, structural location, and material conditions means only they can rightly interpret reality). Anything else is false consciousness. After Marx, in the wake of Gramsci, and the shift from economic to cultural production as the primary generator of an authentically human and emancipated way of experiencing and understanding the world, numerous other subjects of history replace the proletariat. Maoism posits the Chinese peasant; some strands of feminism, women's consciousness; and certain strands of Black Power, black consciousness. Each of these represents a different subject of history who possesses the key to understanding reality and living out a truly emancipated, authentically human form of life. The problem with such approaches is twofold. First, like Hegel, they absolutize the friend–enemy distinction through dividing up the world between those who are on the right and wrong side of history (the friend–enemy distinction thereby operating on a temporal rather than spatial division). Second, they totalize one set of experiences (this time of the oppressed rather than the privileged) as all-determinative of what it means to be human.

The challenge is to recognize the reality of friend–enemy relations without absolutizing or ontologizing them. In the same breath, experiences of oppression must be recognized as epistemologically prior (they give a better read on what is really going on) without slipping into a view that says the oppressed are ontologically privileged and their experience is infallible (i.e., they can do no wrong because their structural location makes them a better kind of human and their experience is all determinative). I argue, here and elsewhere, that the way to thread this needle is through democratic politics—the difficult and risk-laden negotiation of a common life through a dance of conflict and conciliation in pursuit of goods in common on which the flourishing of all depends.

Kant, Hegel, and humanitarianism are instances of using the common humanity frame from a position of strength and their alignment with colonialist projects of one kind or another. But a common humanity frame can also be used to resist domination "from below." Human rights discourses are one obvious example. Another is what Vincent Lloyd calls the black natural law (BNL) tradition. Lloyd's account also represents an example of threading the needle through politics that I outline above. For Lloyd, black natural law emerges from reflection on human nature as experienced within conditions of systemic oppression and the work of organizing done to end this oppression. He argues that the oppressed, of which, in the context of the United States, African Americans are the paradigmatic instance, have an epistemic priority in determinations of human nature.[16] Failure to grant this epistemic priority leads to false constructions of human nature that re-inscribe unjust systems and oppressive forms of life. As a form of natural law thinking, BNL has a normative conception of what it means to be human, one grounded in theistic conceptions of all humans as made in the image of God. This conception can be appealed to as part of challenging idolatrous, hegemonic constructions of what it means to be human that privilege some and exclude others (notably, white supremacy, and its manifestation in such systemic injustices as mass incarceration).

ETHNOGRAPHY OR BEGINNING WITH DIFFERENCE NOT SAMENESS

Ethnographic frameworks presume the other is not like us, but "we" must try to understand "them" in relation to their own customs and language. In contrast to the common humanity frame, epistemically, an ethnographic starting point begins with the recognition of a certain opacity to the lives of others. However, rather than viewing the other as alien or incomprehensible, their form of life has an intelligible order that must be understood in its own terms of reference if we are to understand the other and how they see us. An ethnographic framework entails an act of moral imagination rather than speculative reasoning. This most often emerges at close quarters, when negotiating a common life amid a sense of difference and thus the need to make sense of others is existentially pressing. Siep Stuurman notes that whereas common humanity is expressed mainly in the languages of theology and philosophy, the primary discourses of ethnographic frameworks are history, geography, and anthropology.[17] Stuurman gives the examples of Herodotus's analysis of the Scythians in his *Histories*, Sima Qian's discussion of the Xiongnu in his *Records of the Historian*, and Ibn Khaldun's treatment of the nomadic Berbers in his *Muqaddimah*. To these, we might add the travelogues of Muhammad Ibn Battuta and Marco Polo, and the ethnographic reports of numerous missionaries.

Still, ethnography is not automatically the panacea for overcoming abstract and alien categories in the interpretation of others. Ethnographies can exoticize strangers, rendering them objects rather than those with whom we might share a reciprocal common life. Edward Said names one example of this dynamic "Orientalism."[18] The other becomes simultaneously a source of fear and fascination by being portrayed as both a source of vitality, authenticity, and strength, and, in contrast to the decadent and corrupt ways of "our" civilization, they represent a way to reconnect to what is real and true. At the same time, the other represents a form of life that is less than or a potential threat to "our" civilized way of life. As with common humanity frames, there are ways ethnographic frames can be deployed "from below."

If Orientalism represents an ethnographic frame "from above," then black nationalism, and its subsequent iteration in Black Power, represents an ethnographic claim "from below." The claim to be a nation within a nation is a claim to be all that being a nation invokes as a "social imaginary": belonging, sense of place, a history, a future, self-determination, citizenship, and a distinctive culture. It is a claim to possess a way of being in the world that lives an alternative to racialized constructions of blackness as a form of non-being and an anti-type of the good citizen. Rather than "integration," black nationalism seeks to radically reconfigure a polity so that those of African descent (whether in the US, UK, or Brazil) can be at home where they live while at the same time forging anti-racist forms of "intercommunal" life with others.[19] That said, some strands of black nationalism, for example the Nation of Islam, can absolutize friend–enemy relations and thereby refuse the possibility of a shared humanity, at least between blacks and whites. If either a common humanity or ethnographic framework is to generate change through enabling wisdom and insight about others, it must be orientated toward discovering ways of interpreting and experiencing reality that decenter one's own experience and history and open up the terms and conditions of life together.

THEOLOGICAL ANTHROPOLOGY OR BEGINNING WITH GOD

As already indicated, Christianity has sponsored variations on both the common humanity and the ethnographic frames and their characteristic pathologies. I turn now to examine theological ways of conceptualizing humanity. A (political) theology of humanity is necessary as any talk of humanity builds on a metaphysical conception of human being, so Christian usages of the term humanity need to be consonant with theological understandings of who God is and who humans are in relation to God. Theologically, knowledge of what it means to be human and what kind of thing humanity is comes through reflection on the relationship God cultivates with creation and with humans as creatures. In other words, the discovery of who, how, and what a human being is comes through participating in and reflecting on how God relates to human beings and calls them to relate to one another and to other than human life. And this cannot be done apart from reflection on the self-revelation of God in Israel and in Jesus Christ. It is this starting point that generates Paul's conception of redeemed humanity in terms of a differentiated unity of Jews and Gentiles in Christ rather an abstract humanity that supersedes the particular histories of each.[20]

On a theological account, the status of being a human is not something other humans can grant or remove. The intrinsic value of every human is determined through how each human is always already situated in and open to relation with God. By implication, one's humanity is not owned like a piece of property and so it cannot be revoked or alienated. Nor can it be reduced to some inherent essence or substance. Rather, our humanity resides in a set of dependent and interdependent relations. Sin is the shattering of the finite and historically contingent meshwork of relations on which the flourishing of human and other than human life depends. It occurs when humans either over-determine or fail to cultivate the kinds and character of relations that enable this meshwork to be fruitful and humans to fulfill their vocation to be a specific kind of creature that is blessed by and blesses other than human life. Christ's work of redemption is both the healing of this meshwork and bringing it to fulfillment so that all creation may fruitfully participate in communion with God. The paradox for humanity is that to fulfil what it means to be human, to bring to blossom the vocation given to us as creatures, we must grow into and become like that which we are not, namely, God.[21] To become like the God whose paradigmatic way of relating to us as creatures are incarnation, crucifixion, and Pentecost renders contingent and relativizes any attempt to identify a single class, gender, or ethnos as defining and fulfilling what it means to be human.

A central Christian confession is that each person has an inviolable dignity born out of an equality of status in relation to God and all other humans. Often missed, however, is the threefold structure to creaturely personhood necessary to realizing human dignity. While we are the same as all other persons, we are more like some persons than others, and we are also like no other person; each person is unique. This basic structure of human being is at once assumed and affirmed in the incarnation of Jesus Christ. Jesus is human; Jesus is unique; and Jesus, as a historical person, is more like some than others and enmeshed in a particular ecology. Encounter with and reception of strangers, if it is to be fruitful and respect the dignity of each, must attend to this three-fold pattern of interpersonal and intra-creational relationships. To welcome the other is to recognize one who is the same as me (common humanity frame). Yet to welcome the other is to be in a place of welcome, to be at home, and thus in a relationship with others who are more like me than the stranger welcomed, and thereby recognize that the stranger comes from a different form of life than me (ethnographic frame). However, to truly welcome another is to welcome one who is like nobody else, affording them the attention and respect that communicates recognition of their uniqueness.

Contrasting humans with the status of animals and plants is frequently a way of formulating human dignity. A central feature of such contrasts is the mistaken account of humans having dominion over/ownership of the rest of creation. The character of this dominion is then said to mirror God's rule understood in sovereign or patriarchal terms: God as king, master, or paterfamilias. But when God's relationship to God's *oikonomos* is properly understood as a gardener cultivating life or an artisan crafting creation who calls humans to participate in this cultivation, then the analogies and metaphorical frameworks change. Humans are gardeners or artisans of life who are not just psychosomatic, cultural-political persons but also biospiritual creatures, whose own cultivation and flourishing are interconnected with the cultivation and flourishing of other ways of being alive.[22] Humans participate in transcendence by becoming fully alive; that is, attuned to, resonating with, and fulfilling the relations within which we are enmeshed and through which we live and breathe and have our being. As Irenaeus puts it: "The Glory of God is a human fully alive."[23] Being fully alive entails the flourishing of the microbiome in our gut with which we have a symbiotic relation through to the flourishing of the wider eco-systems on which all animate life depends. Right relations with God are the condition and possibility of loving and just (i.e., fruitful) inter-subjective human relations and loving and just relations with non-human ways of being alive. Thus, we must ask how "nature" should participate in human society, how human society should participate in other than human forms life, and how both, symbiotically, may participate in the Triune life.

Human activity understood as the cultivation of a garden should seek to fructify creation, and so enable the wonder and goodness of what God has created to shine forth as part of fostering reciprocal relations of praise and thanksgiving with creation. As exemplified in the preparation of food and wine, such priestly activity enables opportunities for human fellowship. This priestly activity is affirmed and fulfilled in the Eucharist: Christ did not take grain and grape, but the products of human labor and creativity, and used them as an anticipation of the coming eschatological fulfilment of all creation.[24] What is received is freely and joyously offered back as thanksgiving and praise within an ecology of blessing. East of Eden, however, the groaning of creation and the blood of Abel that cries out from the soil are one and the same cry for justice and liberation. All interpersonal and political problems are also ecological problems and vice versa. "Am I my brother's keeper?" we ask as we extract and exploit what we can from land, sea, and air and in that process, enslave our brothers and sisters for material gain. We cannot separate the conversion of the soul from the cultivation of the soil and the cure of the city. They are intertwined. What and how we eat is shaped by what and how we produce and consume and both shape how we relate to God, other humans, and the rest of creation. A political economy is always already a political ecology, a culture a form of cultivation.

The picture of the fulfilment of all things in Christ is one of cosmic eschatology where there is not a separation out of human and non-human creation but their perichoresis as the presence of God transfigures them. The people of God are to bear witness to a messianic banquet (i.e., the priesting of creation in feasting and fellowship) and the New Jerusalem (i.e., a garden-city that signifies the healed and harmonious interrelationship between human political economy and non-human life).[25] Irrespective of whether one agrees with the data on anthropogenic climate change, it is always incumbent upon Christians to forge just and loving relations with other than human life. Theologically, any account of human flourishing must entail concern for the flourishing of all creation and conversely, no conception of what a flourishing environment might entail can be a true account if it excludes an account of human flourishing.

"HUMANITY" AS MORAL AND POLITICAL JUDGMENT

Talk of humanity is political talk because it is talk about the conditions and possibilities of a shared world of meaning and action with those we find strange. It is a recognition that to be human we need others, and this entails negotiating some form of common life with the other, either though positing a common humanity or through bringing alterity into fruitful relationship, which entails a political process of conflict and conciliation through which a just and compassionate common life might be discovered. War, alongside forms of domination, are refusals of politics and represent the absolutizing of friend–enemy relations. Avoiding war or domination has, historically, depended on a relative symmetry of power. Too great an asymmetry and the frequent move is to determine the other as subject to "our" categories.

The account of humanity developed here pushes against sacralizing local, regional, or national identities that overvalue a sense of place *and* cosmopolitanisms that value no place because humanity is understood as existing in an undifferentiated time and space. Rather, I have tried to situate humanity as a claim that values intimate and proximate communities while at the same time locating human being within a broader set of relations that need coordinating fruitfully in recognition of what it means to always already be in a relationship with near and distant neighbors.

Confronted with the rise of fascism and a bourgeois cosmopolitanism, Karl Barth reflected on the question of how to order our love of near and distant neighbors. He concluded that:

> To unite loyalty towards those who are historically near with openness towards those who are historically distant will always involve the enduring of a tension and overcoming of an antithesis within which the individual practical decisions may be very different. The man who is obedient to the command of God will always be summoned and ready to endure this tension and to seek to overcome this antithesis.[26]

He goes on to say: "And so the command of God does not see and meet him either at the one point or the other, as a member of his own people and then perhaps as a participant in its relationships with other peoples, but always as one who is on the way from the one to the other."[27] He understands cultural-political communities as a necessary condition for human flourishing but as always in a state of flux and convergent with other communities. To fulfill what it means to be human is to live in cultural-political communities, but such communities are only ever a beginning point for a movement beyond the inherent boundaries of intimacy and proximity, leading relentlessly from a narrower to a wider sphere, from our own people to other human peoples. Barth's position reflects a deep theo-logic within the Christian tradition that orders the good of a particular community as being fulfilled in the good of humanity as a whole, which is itself fulfilled in communion with God. We live in concentric circles, so rather than proclaiming a love of humanity at the expense of any regard for local relationships, or a love of the local, regional or national leading to disregard, fear and hatred of outsiders, we are, as Barth puts it "always on the way from one point to another."

One way of moving beyond myopic, self-limiting spatial and temporal frames of the kind Kant and Hegel exemplify is through a theological imaginary in which the local is not absolutized or made an end in itself; instead, it is the necessary beginning point for the pilgrim's journey that culminates in communion with God. Within a Christian, dialogical, *and* agonistic cosmopolitan vision, a sense of place—that is, our social, economic, political, and historical location in creation—helps constitute human particularity. But our humanity is also partly constituted by how our sense of place is related to other places. Politics within a Christian, dialogical, and agonistic cosmopolitan vision involves the formation of a common world of meaning and action within and between different places. It also requires situating one's own sense of place within concentric circles of human sociality that culminate, via historical relations of conflict and conciliation, in an eschatological, Christologically shaped horizon of fulfillment. This horizon of fulfillment both draws in and constantly interrupts all attempts to make any place or scale of human interaction idolatrously self-sufficient or totally encompassing in terms of economic, political, and social relationships. On this account, various forms of localism, nationalism, and identity politics radically overvalue the particularity of a place or culture or history, while many cosmopolitan and global conceptions of citizenship and a neoliberal vision of economic globalization radically undervalue it.

The Latino/a *theological* use of the term *mestizaje* points toward a dialogical and agonistic cosmopolitanism, both pushing back on and opening a way toward the constructive development of Barth's account of near and distant neighbors. It draws on the experience of peoples living in the Americas as those whose identity and history is a confluence of multiple ethnicities.[28] That said, *mestizaje* has proven problematic. Its non-theological uses include being deployed to support racist constructions of national identities that direct attention away from histories of slavery, and render invisible African and indigenous contributions to Central American and Caribbean history.[29] However, as a theo-political and intercultural category, *mestizaje* (or *mestizaje-mulatez* and *mezcolanza*) refuses any attempt to create binary or essentialist identities: black/white; Hispanic/non-hispanic, etc.[30] As Ada Maria Isasi-Diaz puts it, *mestizaje* and *mulatez* refer not only to ethnic and racial diversity but also to the "ability to sustain a sense of community in spite of religious and political differences, to identify and maintain similarities without ignoring specificities and particularities, to insist on a continuum of differences that not only permits diversity but actually welcomes it."[31] It is also suggestive of what it might mean to have a sense of shared humanity while recognizing that any sense of a shared humanity is born out of tragic and brutal histories of domination.[32]

It is not the case that humanity only entails a sense of being on our way from and to some place. The formation of a sense of humanity is also and always an intermixture, containing seeds of hope amidst grotesque exploitation and misery. In this respect, the specific Nahautl term *nepantla,* meaning "to be between" or "torn between ways," draws this out even more sharply and is used by some as an alternative to *mestizaje*.[33] It denotes a middle ground that is made up of bits and pieces of various traditions and recognizes that people have multiple loyalties. As a category, it calls for attention to different histories, geographical situations, and ongoing conflicts through which a sense of shared humanity emerges. In Gloria Anzaldua's use of the term, it suggests that we cannot simply react to what is oppressive but must forge a habitable way of life out of what is there by passing on what is valuable from our histories amid the contradictions of what is cruel and coercive.[34] She calls this "the great alchemical work" of "morphogenesis" that unfolds a new way of being in the world.[35] Unlike the concepts of hybridity, nomadism, or fugitivity—which suggest we can live anywhere, come from nowhere, and have no duty of care to tend and pass on the means of generating some kind of common life with others—*mestizaje-mulatez* and *nepantla* recognize the possibilities of a common life or *convivencia* while contending that no single voice or culture can determine it, and any form of shared life must attend to the brutal histories that inevitably form its backdrop.

Such conceptualizations, while helpful, are still anthropocentric in focus. The Southern African term *ubuntu* has an analogous emphasis on relationality and in-betweenness that more clearly situates humanity within a cosmic and ecological framework. As a term it has been taken up in political theology, most notably by Desmond Tutu. Michael Onyebechi Eze contends that *ubuntu* is a modern term that draws on multiple southern African traditions to generate a conception of humanity as a single moral community. On one maxim, it means *umuntu ngumuntu ngabantu*—a person is a person through other people.³⁶ According to another take *ubuntu* means, a human being is a human being through the otherness of other human beings.³⁷ Eze calls *ubuntu* a "bold conjecture" that, despite its often romanticized and reified use, provides a basis to move beyond particularism through "creative dialogue."³⁸ As a conceptuality, it emphasizes how humanity is a creative convergence that emerges through a process that can involve conflict but also cross-pollination (rather than mere intersection) and reconciliation (rather than sublation):

> *A person is a person through other people* strikes an affirmation of one's humanity through recognition of an 'other' in his or her uniqueness and difference. . . . This idealism suggests to us that humanity is not embedded in my person solely as an individual; my humanity is co-substantively bestowed upon the other and me. Humanity is a quality we owe to each other. We create each other and need to sustain this *otherness* creation. And if we belong to each other, we participate in our creations: *we are because you are, and since you are, definitely I am.*³⁹

The dialogical and agonistic constitution of humanity across generations and between places is not just between humans, it also entails the encounter with the divine and non-human forms of life.⁴⁰ As Leonard Chuwa puts it: "In Ubuntu the physical and the spiritual, the living and the non-living, the human and the non-human are perceived as necessary in sustenance of human life. Human life comes from, and is sustained by both organic and inorganic cosmos."⁴¹

CONCLUSION

The use of the terms *mestizaje-mulatez*, *nepantla*, and *ubuntu* point to possibilities for re-framing how we imagine humanity within non-Eurocentric conceptualities that can encompass a sense of humanity as simultaneously shared (community humanity frame) while emerging from distinctive patterns of life (ethnographic frame). Western European conceptions of humanity have been tested and found gravely wanting due to how they buttressed colonialist projects. This does not necessarily mean that notions such as human rights or natural law should be dismissed since they may prove to be, as Dipesh Chakrabarty puts it, indispensable but inadequate.⁴² Their inadequacy points to the need for other kinds of conceptual frameworks, which both provincialize European ways of understanding humanity and provide non-anthropocentric, dialogical, and agonistic conceptualizations of humanity. Reaching beyond Western conceptual frameworks is itself a performance of humanity and the need for others in the realization of a shared humanity. At the same time, no language that connects humans beyond small-scale kinship structures is innocent of inhumanity. I write this in a Latin alphabet with words inflected with the blood of conquest by Romans, Vikings, and Normans and those cut from peoples the English conquered in turn. To think humanity is to draw on words and concepts torn and shredded by brutality. Seeking out words such as *neplanta* and *ubuntu* could be just another case of the West, yet again, cannibalizing other cultures for its own benefit. But while the conditions of conceptualizing and speaking about humanity are never innocent, the challenge of imagining and narrating humanity as a moral and political category is as urgent now as it ever was, if not more so.

NOTES

1. There are obvious resonances with a feminist "ethics of care" and contemporary restatements of virtue ethics. For a synthesis of the two see, for example, Raja Halwani, "Care Ethics and Virtue Ethics," *Hypatia* 18 no. 3 (2003): 161–192.
2. Judith Butler, *Frames of War: When is Life Grievable?* (London: Verso, 2010), 14.
3. The ur-text in this "mortalist" conception of what it means to be human is Sophocles' play, *Antigone*. On this see Bonnie Honig, *Antigone, Interrupted* (Cambridge: Cambridge University Press, 2013), 1–35. Honig critiques a mortalist conception, not to dismiss it, but to extend it to what she calls an "agonistic humanism."
4. George Orwell's *1984* is a study in this latter form of inhumanity.
5. Raimond Gaita, *A Common Humanity: Thinking about Love and Truth and Justice* (London: Routledge, 2000), 259–285.
6. Anne Phillips, *The Politics of the Human* (Cambridge: Cambridge University Press, 2015), 44.
7. I am echoing here Bonnie Honig's conception of "agonistic humanism" (*Antigone, Interrupted*, 19).
8. Phillips, *Politics of the Human*, 133–135.
9. This distinction draws on Siep Stuurman, "Common Humanity and Cultural Difference on the Sedentary-Nomadic Frontier: Herodotus, Sima Qian, and Ibn Khaldun," in *Global Intellectual History*, ed. Samuel Moyn and Andrew Sartori (New York: Columbia University Press, 2013), 33–58.
10. Stuurman, "Common Humanity," 36–37.
11. The most obvious historical exemplars are Maimonides, Ibn Sina, and Thomas Aquinas. But, within Christianity, more significant for the purposes of this essay, are Bartolome de las Casas's response to the indigenous peoples of the Americas and Matteo Ricci's response to Confucianism, both of which drew on natural law to argue for the shared humanity of non-European others.
12. An example of this problem within an Aristotelian-Thomistic conception of natural law thinking is José de Acosta Porres. See Willie Jennings, *The Christian Imagination: Theology and the Origins of Race* (New Haven, CT: Yale University Press, 2010), 65–116.
13. Robert Bernasconi, "Kant as an Unfamiliar Source of Racism," *Philosophers on Race: Critical Essays*, ed. Julie Ward and Tommy Lott (Oxford: Blackwell Publishers, 2002), 145–166.
14. Immanuel Kant, *The Metaphysics of Morals*, trans. Mary Gregor (Cambridge: Cambridge University Press, 1996), 89.
15. Matthew Jantzen, "Hermeneutics of Providence: Theology, Race, and Divine Action in History" (ThD thesis, Duke University, 2017), and Robert Bernasconi, "'The Ruling Categories of the World': The Trinity in Hegel's Philosophy of History and the Rise and Fall of Peoples," in *A Companion to Hegel*, ed. Stephen Houlgate and Michael Baur (Oxford: Wiley-Blackwell, 2016), 315–331.
16. Vincent Lloyd, *Black Natural Law* (Oxford: Oxford University Press, 2016), ix.
17. Stuurman, "Common Humanity," and "Herodotus and Sima Qian: History and the Anthropological Turn in Ancient Greece and Han China," *Journal of World History* 19, no. 1 (2008): 1–40.
18. Edward Said, *Orientalism* (New York: Vintage Books, 1979).

19. The term "intercommunal" draws on Huey Newton's work. For an account of the development of his thought, see Judson Jeffries, *Huey P. Newton: The Radical Theorist* (Jackson, MS: University Press of Mississippi, 2002).
20. Eugene Rogers, *After the Spirit: A Constructive Pneumatology from the Resources outside the Modern West* (Grand Rapids, MI: Eerdmans, 2005), 86–88.
21. Kathryn Tanner, *Christ the Key* (Cambridge: Cambridge University Press, 2010), 28–57.
22. Stewardship within this framework is not about dominion understood as mastership or management. Rather, the steward is one who receives an endowment or role in trust, primarily related to the provision of food, which is to be tended so as to ensure the flourishing of all.
23. *Against Heresy* IV, 20, 7.
24. Luke 22:16, 19.
25. Jürgen Moltmann, *The Coming of God: Christian Eschatology*, trans. Margaret Kohl (Minneapolis, MN: Fortress Press, 1996), 313–315.
26. Karl Barth, *Church Dogmatics: The Doctrine of Creation* III/ 4, trans. A. T. Mackay et al. (Edinburgh: T&T Clark, 1961), 297–298.
27. Ibid., 298.
28. Virgil Elizondo, "*Mestizaje* as a Locus of Theological Reflection," *Mestizo Christianity: Theology from the Latino Perspective*, ed. Arturo J. Bañuelas (Maryknoll, NY: Orbis, 1995), 7–27, and Benjamín Valentín, "Mestizaje," in *Hispanic American Religious Cultures*, ed. Miguel de la Torre (Santa Barbara, CA: ABC-CLIO, 2009), 351–356.
29. Nestor Medina, *Mestizaje: (Re)Mapping Race, Culture, and Faith in Latino/a Catholicism* (Maryknoll, NY: Orbis, 2009), 48–49. It is also a term that is posed negatively as a contrast to notions of indigeneity.
30. For an overview of different uses and formulations of *mestizaje* as a constructive theological and ethical category, see Ruben Rosario-Rodriguez, *Racism and God-Talk: A Latino/a Perspective* (New York: NYU Press, 2008), 69–110.
31. Ada Maria Isasi-Diaz, "Strangers No Longer," in *Hispanic/Latino Theology: Challenge and Promise*, ed. Ada María Isasi-Díaz and Fernando F. Segovia (Minneapolis, MN: Fortress Press, 1996), 370.
32. Rosario-Rodriguez, *Racism and God-Talk*, 108–110.
33. Lara Medina, "Nepantla," in *Hispanic American Religious Cultures*, ed. Miguel de la Torre (Santa Barbara, CA: ABC-CLIO, 2009), 403–408.
34. Gloria Anzaldúa, *Borderlands: The New Mestiza = La frontera* (San Francisco, CA: Aunt Lute Books, 1987), 77–82.
35. Ibid., 81.
36. Michael Onyebechi Eze, *Intellectual History in Contemporary South Africa* (New York: Palgrave Macmillan, 2010), 155. See also Leonard Chuwa, *African Indigenous Ethics in Global Bioethics: Interpreting Ubuntu* (New York: Springer, 2014), 12.
37. Chuwa, *African Indigenous Ethics*, 15.
38. Eze, *Intellectual History in Contemporary South Africa*, 154.
39. Ibid., 190–191.
40. Chuwa, *African Indigenous Ethics*, 13–17.
41. Ibid., 14.
42. Dipesh Chakrabarty, *Provincializing Europe: Postcolonial Thought and Historical Difference* (Princeton, NJ: Princeton University Press, 2007), 16.

SELECT BIBLIOGRAPHY

Scriptures: Genesis 1–2; 8–9:1–17; 11:1–9; and 15; Isaiah 25:6–10; Luke 10:25–37; Acts 2; Revelation 5.

Barth, Karl (1961), "Near and Distant Neighbors," in *Church Dogmatics: The Doctrine of Creation*, vol. III, part 4, trans. A. T. Mackay et al, Edinburgh: T&T Clark, 285–305.

Bretherton, Luke (2019), *Christ and the Common Life: Political Theology and the Case for Democracy*, Grand Rapids, MI: Eerdmans.

Equino, Olaudah (1789), *The Interesting Narrative of the Life of Olaudah Equino, or Gustavus Vassa, the African. Written by Himself*. Various editions.

Gaita, Raimond, (2000), *A Common Humanity: Thinking about Love and Truth and Justice*, London: Routledge.

Isasi-Diaz, Ada Maria (1996), *Hispanic/Latino Theology: Challenge and Promise*, ed. Ada María Isasi-Díaz and Fernando F. Segovia, Minneapolis: Fortress.

Kant, Immanuel, (1970) "Perpetual Peace: A Philosophical Sketch," in *Kant: Political Writings*, Cambridge: Cambridge University Press, 93–130.

Lloyd, Vincent (2016), *Black Natural Law*, Oxford: Oxford University Press.

MacIntyre, Alasdair (1999), *Dependent Rational Animals: Why Human Beings Need the Virtues*, London: Duckworth, 1999.

Nyssa, Gregory of (1993), "Fourth Homily on Ecclesiastes," in *Homilies on Ecclesiastes: An English Version with Supporting Studies*, ed. Stuart George Hall, New York: Walter de Gruyter, 73–75.

Sophocles, *Antigone*.

Sullivan-Dunbar, Sandra (2017), *Human Dependency and Christian Ethics*, Cambridge: Cambridge University Press.

Universal Declaration of Human Rights (1948).

de Vitoria, Francisco (1991), "On the American Indians (*De Indis*)," in *Vitoria: Political Writings*, ed. Anthony Pagden and Jeremy Lawrance, Cambridge: Cambridge University Press, 231–292.

Walker, David (1829), *Appeal to the Colored Citizens of the World*. Various editions.

CHAPTER TWENTY-FIVE

The Obstinate Legacy of Race and Colonialism

UZMA JAMIL

INTRODUCTION

We are living in a political context where far-right nationalists have mobilized politically across Western countries, calling for a "return" to a "white nation."[1] In Charlottesville, Virginia in August 2017, a rally by Unite the Right brought together far-right white nationalists, chanting "White Lives Matter," "You will not replace us," and "Blood and soil."[2] The rally turned violent that weekend, leading to the death of one woman hit by the car of a far-right supporter. Across the Atlantic, on November 11, 2017, Poland's independence day, about 60,000 demonstrators reflecting far-right white nationalist and fascist groups marched in Warsaw. They carried banners with slogans such as "white Europe of brotherly nations," "pure Poland, white Poland," "we want God," and "pray for Islamic holocaust."[3] Earlier in the year, in January 2017, Alexandre Bissonnette shot and killed eight Muslim men who were worshipers at a mosque in Quebec City. Bissonnette had expressed sympathies with the far-right populist movement in France and views against immigrants and refugees on social media.[4]

None of these events were unique or isolated. Instead, they are linked together by political views that center a racialized view of a "white nation" and exclude racialized minorities, immigrants, and refugees as threats to this imagined national homogeneity. But, perhaps surprisingly, these political events also highlight the role of religion, and specifically a pro-Christian and anti-Muslim sentiment.

These incidents, and the rise of the far right and white nationalists, raise important questions for the role of politics, religion, and racialization today. How do we understand these calls for national purity and "Islamic holocaust" in the collective global consciousness? How do we make sense of this political moment, where religion and race appear to be recuperated as integral to a white nationalist agenda across Western countries? In particular, how do we understand these political events in relation to Muslims in the West, who have been singled out as non-white and non-Christian others?

THE PROBLEM OF MUSLIMS

This chapter focuses on the "problem" of Muslims, who are perceived as such because of both their religion—Islam—and their categorization as a racialized minority. Muslims are disruptive to the dominant white Christian narrative of national belonging in the West.

The conceptualization of this "problem" takes many different forms: Muslims as a problem of "too many immigrants"; Muslims as a problem of "too many refugees"; Muslims as a problem of "national values"; Muslims as a problem of multiculturalism; Muslims as a problem of secularism; Muslims as a problem of patriarchy and the oppression of women; Muslims as a problem of hijabs and niqabs; Muslims as a problem of national security.

While post 9/11, the "war on terror" as a global political context has heightened the visibility of Muslims, this issue has existed for many decades in Europe and North America. The framing of Muslims as a problem at best, and an existential threat at worst, is an enduring expression of coloniality.[5] Coloniality refers to the hierarchical relationship between the West and the non-West, and all that each of these categories represents, as a continuation of the political systems and relationships that existed under former European colonial empires. The "problem" of Muslims is not an outcome of religious differences alone, though that remains a factor, but the ongoing outcome of politics and history, including a history of racism and colonialism.

In this chapter I discuss how this "problem" of Muslims in the West is framed as solely a "problem" of religion. I critique the assumptions that sustain this view and discuss the role of religion and race in defining the racialized non-Christian other in the West, arguing that Muslims have long been part of the arc of Western history culminating today in their marginalization within white, Western nations. In the second part of this chapter, I critique the framing of Muslims as "religious" in relation to the West as "secular." Drawing on the work of Talal Asad, I analyze how the construction of these categories makes possible the positioning of Muslims as perpetually alien to the idea of white, Christian nation. In the conclusion, I return to the question of coloniality and its implications.

A CRITICAL MUSLIM STUDIES FRAMEWORK

I develop my argument within the field of Critical Muslim Studies, which addresses the "Muslim question" through an interrogation of its ontological premises, including a critique of Eurocentrism.[6] Related to this point is a critique of positivist approaches that seek to produce "neutral" and "objective" knowledge about Muslims.[7]

The best-known work in this regard is by Edward Said, who critiques the production of knowledge about Muslims through the lens of Orientalism. Orientalism is a discursive formation sustained through the logic of an ontological difference and hierarchy between the Orient and the West. These ontological distinctions are framed as binaries of civilized/violent and barbaric, secular/religious, and gender equality/patriarchal, among others, as enduring characteristics of the West in contrast to the Orient.[8] This framing limits the ways in which Muslims are "intellectually knowable," such that they can only be represented through a Western gaze which normalizes the idea of Muslims as a particular kind of homogeneously "religious" minority in the Western context. This is what we see happening in the world today, such that Muslims are reduced to being only a religious other within a predominantly Christian, Western nation.

Through a critique of Orientalism and coloniality, I am ultimately making an argument for a more complex understanding of their subjectivity as Muslims in the contemporary political context. Muslims are "known" as homogeneous and singularly religious minorities, without sufficient interrogation of how this religiousness is constructed in relation to a historical and political context of colonialism and racialization in the West. I am also proposing that the Muslim question, which is often framed in religious terms, be reframed as a political question.[9]

MUSLIMS AS MINORITIES IN THE WEST

Muslims are a global religious community constituted of many different racial and ethnic communities. Muslims constitute almost two billion people on this planet and live primarily in countries outside of Europe and North America. Despite recognition of this demographic reality, the focus in this discussion is on how Muslims are constructed as minorities, as a category of people in the Western context. In other words, this is not an empirical question, but an ontological one.

The global Western discourse about Muslims situates them primarily as post-Second World War immigrants, and in more recent decades as refugees from political conflicts in the Middle East and other parts of the world. They are identified primarily through their countries of origin, i.e., as Syrians, Somalis, Turkish, Pakistanis, etc. This national origin has overlapped with ethnic markers of identity, and/or with cultural markers in the multicultural contexts of Canada and the UK, for example.[10]

Yet, there are earlier histories of Muslim arrival and settlement in North America and Europe that are erased through these discourses. The transatlantic slave trade brought to the Americas many West African Muslims, whose religious identities were erased along with their personhood as slaves.[11] The exact numbers of Muslims among the millions of enslaved Africans transported between 1500 and the mid-1800s is unknown.[12] However, the first enslaved Muslims arrived in Hispaniola in 1502 from Spain, where they had escaped the Spanish Inquisition. Enslaved African Muslims from Morocco were also present in the areas that are now known as Arizona and New Mexico.[13]

Also overlooked in the discourses about Muslim settlement as immigrants has been the presence of itinerant salesmen, or peddlers, in the US and Canada at the turn of the twentieth century. These early migrants came from what was then the Ottoman Empire in the late 1800s and early 1900s. In a political context of "white" immigration policies severely restricting the arrival of non-European migrants, they were identified as Syrians, Turks, or Arabs, depending on the immigration officer who marked their names and records. In Canada, these itinerant salesmen plied their wares in Quebec, Ontario and in western Canada. In the US, at the turn of the twentieth century, Bengalis settled in New York,[14] while Syrians worked in other parts of the country.[15]

Lastly, Muslims were part of the colonized peoples in many of the areas of the world controlled by European colonial powers, from the eighteenth century onwards. Many served in the armies of the British during both world wars.[16] This colonial history is often erased and divorced from the post-Second World War, postcolonial migrations that led to the settlement of large numbers of the formerly colonized in the European metropoles. For example, a large portion of the South Asian population in the UK, most of whom are Muslims from Pakistan and Bangladesh, settled there after 1947, and today are still seen as immigrants, even into the second generation.[17]

In brief, Muslims have been historically present in Western countries in different ways, but they have not been visible as a politically enfranchised people. I use "political" in the line of Schmitt, following Mouffe's description of the political. She refers to it as a distinction between "us" and "them" which is the antagonistic dimension of all social relations, but can take many different forms.[18] The us/them relation can become the distinction between "friends" and "enemies" in the constitution of political identities, when "the others who up to now were considered as simply different, start to be perceived as putting into question *our* identity and threatening *our* existence."[19]

The significance of Muslims is thus not a question of numbers, but about the political. This political distinction is made possible through the erasure of the long history of Muslim settlement in the West, and its reduction to the contemporary period. Today, Muslims are racialized and viewed almost exclusively as religious minorities in a political context that valorizes national identity as white and Christian and demarcates the boundaries of the nation through the exclusion of the Other. But this outcome is the result of a historical and political process, which is why this chapter has situated the discussion of the "Muslim problem" within this long history.

The next two sections describe how Muslims have come to be viewed as racialized, religious others in the West, but not *of* the West. The first traces the historical process of racial formation of religious others in the West, dating back to the Iberian Moors during the Spanish Inquisition. Muslims are part of this long history through which Europe and later the West came to define its white, Christian identity through practices of exclusion. The second section is about the problematization of Muslims as "religious" in a West that proclaims itself "modern" and "secular." Drawing on the work of Talal Asad, I analyze how the construction of these categories makes possible the positioning of Muslims as perpetually alien to the idea of white, Christian nation. I use political events in Quebec, which proclaims itself a "secular" society, to illustrate this point. In the Conclusion, I return to the issue of coloniality and discuss its implications.

THE HISTORICAL PROCESS OF RACIALIZATION

Muslims are a racialized category within a global racial system as well as within national political contexts. Linking together pre-colonial and national racial hierarchies is important to understand the position of Muslims as minorities today in the US, Canada, and Europe.[20] These histories identify political contexts that gave rise to the racialized religious other. Muslims are part of this long line of figures of racialized religious others that shape the dominant idea of the West and Europe.[21] I focus here on two, the Moor and the indigenous, which highlight the links between religion, racialization, and colonialism.

The contemporary racialization of Islam and Muslims emerges from a long history of global racial formation in which racialized and religious others are defined in relation to and within a European history of colonialism and whiteness. Rana and Majid trace this history back further to a pre-colonial, premodern (before 1492) time period: "The racialization of Islam emerged in the Old World, was transposed on indigenous peoples of the New World, and subsequently took significance in relation to black America and the Muslim immigrants."[22] Rana's statement expands the frame of how to understand Muslims as political subjects in the West. Though he focuses on the United States, which has a very specific history of transatlantic slavery that shapes racial relations, his broader point is relevant in many contexts.

Rana traces the intertwining of race and religion in Europe, beginning with Catholic Spain in the fifteenth and sixteenth centuries, where the figure of the Moor became the repository of difference that made him distinct from European Christian whiteness. The primary marker of difference was based on religion, as the Moor symbolized the non-Christian other, which in fact included Jews and Muslims. But this became mixed together with other characteristics denoting the Moor as a non-white *and* non-Christian other.[23] The Moor was also the antecedent of the "barbaric" and "uncivilized" Muslim colonial subject of later centuries. As a racialized religious other, the Moor served as a connection between the Spanish desire for religious-racial purity in the fifteenth and sixteenth centuries and the importance of national homogeneity in the modern Western nation. The Moor is "a figure that stands for anyone who is not considered to be part of the social mainstream. It is in this *symbolic* or *metaphorical* sense that minorities living in the west after 1492 are the descendants of the Moors."[24]

In 1492, a year that is commonly cited as the "discovery" of the Americas by Columbus, was an important year in Spain as well. Catholic Spanish King Ferdinand and Queen Isabella conquered Islamic Spain, leading to the surrender of the ruling dynasty in Granada. It set in motion a series of events, with increasingly stricter and exclusionary laws that connected racialization to exclusion based on religion, leading to the Spanish Inquisition and the expulsion of Jews and Muslims.[25] Their conversions were seen as suspect and therefore "tainting" the religious-political community of the newly unified Catholic nation.

The *limpieza de sangre*, purity of blood requirement, a statute passed in 1449, created a genealogical element to faith and membership in the political community. Race was not yet formalized as a biological difference, a meaning that would become more prominent in the nineteenth century. However, the purity of blood requirement indicated a "proto racist process."[26] It essentialized religious difference, and made it fixed and unchanging.[27] This meant that converts, known as Moriscos, were suspect because they "had no genealogical claims to Catholicism."[28] Thus, "racialization became an issue of religious passing."[29] To be accepted, to be able to pass as Christian meant that converts had to be visibly different, through "adopting different styles of dress, appearance, bodily comportment and religious ritual."[30]

The terms "Moro" and "Morisco" came to be associated with darker skin, with blackness although this was not a phenotypic difference but an amalgamation of markers. "Phenotype ... represented a number of discursive logics that connected culture to appearance, skin color, and all of the features that normally were presumed to stand in for race."[31] Though Muslims were known collectively as "Moors," they included a variety of people, including Arabs, Berbers, and Africans. It was not meant to be a specifically and exclusively racial category, but a combination of racial and cultural characteristics that distinguished white, Christian, Europeans from "Moors."[32] "Renaissance representations of the Moor were vague, varied, inconsistent and contradictory ... The term 'Moor' was used interchangeably with such similarly ambiguous terms as 'African', 'Ethiopian', 'Negro' and even 'Indian' to designate a figure from different parts or the whole of Africa (or beyond) who was either black or Moslem, neither or both."[33]

As the Moors were being expelled from Spain, and as European explorers ventured overseas on colonial expeditions, the need to differentiate European identity also emerged. The term Europe was rarely used before the fifteenth century. European identity needed to be named; Europe needed to be able to define itself as white. While Moors became the racialized other of Europe internally, indigenous people served the same purpose outside of Europe.[34]

The Spanish described the indigenous peoples with the same categories that they used with the Moors.[35] The figure of the Moor represented how religious difference became part of a spectrum that included racial and cultural differences, but when applied to the indigenous people of the New World, it took on other nuances. Religion also became a code for categories of civilization and barbarity placed along a racial hierarchy.[36] Europeans arriving in the Americas saw the difference of the indigenous peoples as both racialized and religious:

Religion was defined not only in broad ideologies of belief but also as states of being in relation to cultural notions of civilization and barbarity—as the terms of inclusion and exclusion within the "family of man." . . . Religion was thought of as a universal category of natural being in a hierarchy of civilizations—hence, the fervor to convert non-believers.[37]

Ideas about difference embodied in the figure of the Moor contributed to the construction of the indigenous in the New World. Both were linked through their religious difference from white European Christians. Jews and Arabs were considered to be "people with the wrong religion" in relation to Christianity. In contrast, indigenous peoples were deemed to be "people without a religion" and therefore "subhuman" to Europeans.[38] It is this inferiorization below the "human," to the level of animals, which turned indigenous peoples in the Americas into racialized subjects.[39] The violence against "uncivilized" and "primitive" indigenous peoples was justifiable in the eyes of Spanish rulers precisely because of this division of humanity. The racialized and religious difference of the Moor served to mark the difference of the indigenous in the New World, who became the first racialized subject of the modern/colonial period after 1492.[40]

The indigenous as racialized subjects were linked to colonial subjects in other parts of the world, as a "people without religion" easily became "people who were not human," "uncivilized," and "primitive."[41] The civilizing mission of European colonialism in Africa, Asia and the Middle East, encapsulated in Kipling's "White Man's Burden," is indicative of this transformation and global expansion of racial hierarchies in the seventeenth, eighteenth, and nineteenth centuries. Alongside colonialism came the emergence of a biological understanding of race in the eighteenth and nineteenth centuries. This "scientific racism" supported the ideology of white supremacy and colonialism.

SECULARISM, RELIGION AND MUSLIMS

Having traced the history of racialization of religion in Europe and in the Americas, I focus on the question of how the religiousness of Muslims is framed in relation to the idea of a secular West that also emerges from a Christian context.

Charles Taylor associates secularism with Western liberal democracies and the modern nation-state.[42] Although he recognizes that secularism emerges in the political context of early modern Western Christian society, he considers it a universal category, which can be applied to non-Christian, non-Western societies as a measure of their "modernity."[43] According to Taylor, the "imagined community"[44] of the modern nation-state allows for a transcendental form of secular citizenship, which brings together citizens and allows them to overcome the differences of religion, among other markers of identity. "Secularism is an enactment by which a political medium (representation of citizenship) redefines and transcends particular and differentiating practices of the self that are articulated through class, gender and religion."[45] This understanding of secularism is based on a distinction between the private and the public spheres, where religion is confined to the private and secularism functions as a principle for regulating the political community of citizens in the public sphere.[46]

Talal Asad argues that both the concepts of the secular and religious have genealogies in Europe. Both emerge as part of Christian arrangement of ideas and practices, which is connected to modernity. Asad questions the assumptions that link secularism with Western modernity as a hegemonic project, what Taylor takes for granted as a starting point. Asad asks why modernity "has become hegemonic as a political goal, what practical consequences follow from that hegemony and what social conditions maintain it."[47] Modernity is a project, though it may not be a "totally coherent" nor a "clearly bounded" one. It aims to institutionalize a number of, at times conflicting, principles, including democracy and secularism.[48] The constructions of the categories of the secular and religion/religious are thus related to this hegemonic project of modernity. "Representations of the 'secular' and the 'religious' in modern and modernizing states mediate people's identities, help shape their sensibilities and guarantee their experiences."[49]

More importantly, "the process by which conceptual binaries are established or subverted tells us how people live the secular—how they vindicate the essential freedom and responsibility of the sovereign self in opposition to the constraints of the self by religious discourses."[50] This statement raises key elements that define the secularism question as a variation of the Muslim question in Western contexts. This idea of the modern, secular individual who is unfettered by the constraints of religion is integral to the naming of Muslims as religious. Their attachment to their religion is seen as antithetical to this conceptualization of individual choice as a marker of the modern secular. As a result, public expressions of Muslim religiosity, such as the consumption of halal meat, the wearing of hijabs or niqabs by Muslim women, or the building of mosques, all represent challenges to the assumptions of the modern, secular, Western nation. Simply put, the difference of Muslims is highlighted in the way in which they are situated as part of the non-West, defined by their "un-modern" attachment to their religion. Through this construction of categories, Muslims are asked to choose. If they want to "become modern," they must give up their visible attachment to their religion, on the terms defined by the "secular" majority.[51]

Secularism is used to regulate Muslim populations within democratic Western societies. On the one hand, there is the idea that Muslims can never quite make it, that they remain excluded more or less permanently from attaining "full" citizenship status. On the other hand, there is also the argument that if they "assimilate" and "integrate," they can become "one of us." These two lines of argument seem contradictory but they are both present in the secularism vs. Muslims issue. Secularism is meant to underline the religiousness of Muslims as an inherent and fixed negative characteristic, and therefore to indirectly legitimize the progressive and modern nature of the West. But by presenting secularism as a choice, a set of behaviors that can be changed, i.e., by removing the hijab or niqab, secularism also shifts the blame onto Muslims as unwilling citizen-subjects. They are considered to be unwilling to be secularized, Westernized, assimilated, or integrated, as different ways of saying the same thing. In effect, they are seen as unwilling to accept the West and its modernity as the natural and superior form of progress. And yet, as many Muslim women in Europe and elsewhere can attest, not wearing visible religious symbols does not give them any protection from discrimination, nor does it serve as the final legitimation of their presence as citizens in Western countries. Muslims highlight the contingency of secularism. "Muslims come to represent anti-secularism simply by virtue of the fact that the designation 'Muslim' is interpreted as being religious, and their appearance within public spaces of Western plutocracies therefore seems to erode the divide that secularism seeks to institutionalize."[52]

To go one step further with this argument, it means that the presence of Muslims as religious minorities in Western democracies also highlights the contingency of democracy as a "natural" progression and a "universally" beneficial way of ordering political relations between different groups. This support for democracy is also gendered, such that "saving

Muslim women" from "patriarchal and oppressive Muslim men" is part of the process of ensuring the maintenance of Western democracy, both within the West and outside its boundaries.[53] This claim to universal progress is based on a de facto separation between religion and politics, which is meant to underscore the exclusion of all claims to religious authority from the public sphere. It is based on the idea that the authority of God is not as legitimate as the authority of human beings as a way of understanding politics.[54]

This brings us, then, to secularism as the relationship between the government and the people, which varies across Western countries, even if they share ontological basis. Secularism is a way to demonstrate the power of the state to define the relationship to religion as a category.[55] It is also an illustration of how the majority defines itself and its relationship to its minorities through the distinction drawn between secularism and religion.[56] What is implicit in this distinction is that secularism "belongs" to the majority, and is defined by them, while minority religions, particularly their religious expression in public life, are seen as a challenge to both majority power and to secularism. Thus, the preoccupation with the regulation of religious symbols by the state has particular significance in the desire to articulate a secular identity.

Although secularism is a political doctrine that arose in modern Europe and North America, it takes different forms in different countries. While it is sometimes understood as the removal of religion from public life, in other places it is understood as the state not favoring any one religion over another. For example, France and Quebec share similarities in their cultural attachment to national identity as a secular identity, when it comes to Muslims. However, Quebec occupies a unique position because although it leans toward the secular cultural orientation of France, it is also part of Canada, which explicitly recognizes religious discrimination as a legal issue. For example, the banning of the niqab and the banning of burkinis in France are both framed as issues that reflect the secular character of the nation as well as the structure of the French state. In Quebec, the discourse is similar, claiming that covering the face is antithetical to national identity as secular. This political discourse has a long history of at least one decade, if not longer. Bill 62, passed in the Quebec National Assembly in October 2017, prevents Muslim women who wear the niqab from receiving public services. However, a portion of it was stayed as a result of a legal challenge based on religious discrimination.

CONCLUSION

Returning to the issue of coloniality raised in the introduction, how is it relevant for understanding contemporary politics? I have shown that the contemporary political context comes out of long histories of European imperialism and colonialism, which shape the racialization of Muslims as religious minorities in the West today. Muslims are also postcolonial subjects within an ongoing system of coloniality. They continue to be seen as cultural outsiders and threats to the white, Western nation, the "uncivilized" to Western civilization.

Rather than seeing contemporary far-right and white nationalist protests as a confirmation of white and Western privilege, in fact, it demonstrates the waning of Western hegemony. Unlike colonialism, which had a particular institutional structure that ensured that the colonizer and the colonized stayed in their "proper" places, in the contemporary Western nation, there is no such structure. The formerly colonized are living in the metropole, and as citizens, no less. Thus, these political protests are perhaps more readily understood as protests against the loss of power and white privilege, the ability to determine the terms under which non-white, non-Christian others belong and the ability to preserve the imagined purity of the white, Christian West. This is a gendered view, given the predominantly white male members of the far-right and nationalist groups. Their perceived masculinity is tied to their white privilege and embodiment of national dominance, all of which are seen as being at risk. The "problem" of Muslims is ultimately about the fear that their idea of the West and their place within it is no longer the center of the world.

NOTES

1. Ghassan Hage, *White Nation: Fantasies of White Supremacy in a Multicultural Society* (Sydney: Pluto Press, 1998).

2. Joe Heim, "Recounting a Day of Rage, Hate, Violence and Death," *The Washington Post* (August 14, 2017). https://www.washingtonpost.com/graphics/2017/local/charlottesville-timeline/?utm_term=.845471ce6c8d (accessed November 22, 2107).

3. Mark Taylor, "'White Europe': 60,000 Nationalists March on Poland's Independence Day," *Guardian* (November 12, 2017). https://www.theguardian.com/world/2017/nov/12/white-europe-60000-nationalists-march-on-polands-independence-day

4. Les Perrauex and Eric Andrew-McGill, "Quebec City Mosque Attack Suspect Known as Online Troll Inspired by French Far-Right," *The Globe and Mail* (January 30, 2017). https://www.theglobeandmail.com/news/national/quebec-city-mosque-attack-suspect-known-for-right-wing-online-posts/article33833044/ (accessed November 29, 2017).

5. See S. Sayyid, *Recalling the Caliphate: Decolonization and World Order* (London: Hurst and Company, 2014); and Walter Mignolo, *The Darker Side of Western Modernity: Global Futures, Decolonial Options* (Durham, NC: Duke University Press, 2011).

6. Sayyid, *Recalling the Caliphate: Decolonization and World Order*, 12–13.

7. ReOrient Editorial Board (2015), "ReOrient: A Forum for Critical Muslim Studies," *ReOrient: The Journal of Critical Muslim Studies* 1(1): 6.

8. Edward Said, *Orientalism* (New York: Vintage Books, 1978), 300–301.

9. Sayyid, *Recalling the Caliphate: Decolonization and World Order*, 3.

10. See S. Thobani, *Exalted Subjects: Studies in the Making of Race and Nation in Canada* (Toronto: University of Toronto Press, 2008); and *Islamophobia: Still a Challenge for Us All*, eds. F. Elahi and O. Khan (London: Runnymede Trust, 2017).

11. See Sylviane A. Diouf, *Servants of Allah: Africans Enslaved in the Americas* (New York: New York University Press, 1998).

12. Richard Brent Turner, "African Muslim Slaves and Islam in Antebellum America," in *The Cambridge Companion to American Islam*, eds. J. Hammer and O. Safi (Cambridge: Cambridge University Press, 2013), 28–44.

13. Ibid., 29.

14. See Vivek Bald, *Bengali Harlem and the Lost Histories of South Asian America* (Cambridge, MA: Harvard University Press, 2015).

15. Sarah Gualtieri, *Between Arab and White: Race and Ethnicity in the Early Syrian American Diaspora* (Berkeley, CA: University of California Press, 2009).

16. See Ben Quinn, "The Muslims Who Fought for Britain in the First World War," *Guardian* (August 1, 2014). https://www.theguardian.com/world/2014/aug/02/muslim-soldiers-first-world-war (accessed November 26, 2017).

17. See N. Ali, V.S. Kalra, and S. Sayyid, *A Postcolonial People: South Asians in Britain* (London: Hurst Publishers, 2006).

18. C. Mouffe, *Agonistics: Thinking the World Politically* (London: Verso Books, 2013), 2.
19. Ibid., 5 (italics in the original).
20. See A. Majid, *We Are All Moors: Ending Centuries of Crusades Against Muslims and Other Minorities* (Minneapolis, MN: University of Minnesota Press, 2009); and J. Rana, *Terrifying Muslims: Race and Labor in the South Asian Diaspora* (Durham, NC: Duke University Press, 2011).
21. See I. Kalmar, and D.J. Penslar, eds., *Orientalism and the Jews* (Hannover, NH: University Press of New England, 2005); also Rana, *Terrifying Muslims*.
22. Rana, *Terrifying Muslims*, 31.
23. See Majid, *We Are All Moors*; and S.R. Arjana, *Muslims in the Western Imagination* (New York: Oxford University Press, 2015).
24. Majid, *We Are All Moors*, 5 (emphasis in the original).
25. Ibid., 31.
26. R. Grosfoguel, "The Multiple Faces of Islamophobia," *Islamophobia Studies Journal* 1:1 (2012), 12.
27. Majid, *We Are All Moors*, 53.
28. Ibid., 34.
29. Rana, *Terrifying Muslims*, 34.
30. Ibid.
31. Ibid., 36.
32. Ibid., 37.
33. Majid, *We Are All Moors*, 63.
34. Grosfoguel, "The Multiple Faces of Islamophobia," 11.
35. N.I. Matar, *Turks, Moors and Englishmen in the Age of Discovery* (New York: Columbia University Press, 1999), 98.
36. Rana, *Terrifying Muslims*, 32.
37. Ibid.
38. Grosfoguel, "The Multiple Faces of Islamophobia," 13.
39. Ibid., 12.
40. Ibid.
41. Grosfoguel, "The Multiple Faces of Islamophobia," 13.
42. See Charles Taylor, "Modes of Secularism," in *Secularism and its Critics*, ed. Rajeev Bhargava (New Delhi: Oxford University Press, 1998).
43. T. Asad, *Formations of the Secular: Christianity, Islam, Modernity* (Stanford, CA: Stanford University Press 2003), 2.
44. See B. Anderson, *Imagined Communities: Reflections on the Origin and Spread of Nationalism* (New York: Verso Books, 2006).
45. Asad, *Formations of the Secular*, 5.
46. Ibid., 8.
47. Ibid., 13.
48. Ibid., 14.
49. Ibid.
50. Ibid., 15–16.

51. See Sayyid, *Recalling the Caliphate*.
52. Ibid., 34.
53. See Saba Mahmood, "Secularism, Hermeneutics, and Empire: The Politics of Islamic Reformation." *Public Culture* 18, no. 2 (2006), 323–347.
54. Sayyid, *Recalling the Caliphate*, 33–34.
55. T. Asad, "French Secularism and the 'Islamic Veil Affair,'" *The Hedgehog Review* Spring/Summer 2006: 95.
56. Asad, *Formations of the Secular*, 5.

SELECT BIBLIOGRAPHY

Ali, N., Kalra, V.S., and S. Sayyid (2006), *A Postcolonial People: South Asians in Britain*, London: Hurst Publishers.

Anderson, B. (2006), *Imagined Communities: Reflections on the Origin and Spread of Nationalism*, New York: Verso Books.

Arjana, S.R. (2015), *Muslims in the Western Imagination*, New York: Oxford University Press.

Asad, T. (2003), *Formations of the Secular: Christianity, Islam, Modernity*, Stanford, CA: Stanford University Press.

Asad, T. (2006), "French Secularism and the 'Islamic Veil Affair,'" *The Hedgehog Review* Spring/Summer: 93–106.

Bald, V. (2015), *Bengali Harlem and the Lost Histories of South Asian America*, Cambridge, MA: Harvard University Press.

Bayoumi, M. (2015), *This Muslim American Life: Dispatches from the War on Terror*, New York: New York University Press.

Diouf, S.A. (1998), *Servants of Allah: Africans Enslaved in the Americas*, New York: New York University Press.

Grosfoguel, R. (2012), "The Multiple Faces of Islamophobia," *Islamophobia Studies Journal* 1(1): 9–33.

Gualtieri, S. (2009), *Between Arab and White: Race and Ethnicity in the Early Syrian American Diaspora*, Berkeley, CA: University of California Press.

Hage, G. (1998), *White Nation: Fantasies of White Supremacy in a Multicultural Society*, Sydney: Pluto Press.

Heim, J. (2017), "Recounting a Day of Rage, Hate, Violence and Death," *Washington Post*, August 14. https://www.washingtonpost.com/graphics/2017/local/charlottesville-timeline/?utm_term=.845471ce6c8d (accessed November 22, 2107).

Kalmar, I and D.J. Penslar, eds. (2005), *Orientalism and the Jews*, Hannover, NH: University Press of New England.

Mahmood, S. (2006), "Secularism, Hermeneutics, and Empire: The Politics of Islamic Reformation," *Public Culture* 18(2): 323–347.

Majid, A. (2009), *We Are All Moors: Ending Centuries of Crusades Against Muslims and Other Minorities*, Minneapolis, MN: University of Minnesota Press.

Matar, N.I. (1999), *Turks, Moors and Englishmen in the Age of Discovery*, New York: Columbia University Press.

Mignolo, W. (2011) *The Darker Side of Western Modernity: Global Futures, Decolonial Options*, Durham, NC: Duke University Press.

Mouffe, C. (2013), *Agonistics: Thinking the World Politically*, London: Verso Books.

Perreaux, L. and E. Andrew-McGill (2017), "Quebec City Mosque Attack Suspect Known as Online Troll Inspired by French Far-Right." *The Globe and Mail*, January. 30. https://www.theglobeandmail.com/news/national/quebec-city-mosque-attack-suspect-known-for-right-wing-online-posts/article33833044/ (accessed November 29, 2017).

Quinn, B. (2014), "The Muslims Who Fought for Britain in the First World War." *Guardian*, August 1. https://www.theguardian.com/world/2014/aug/02/muslim-soldiers-first-world-war (accessed November 26, 2017).

Rana, J. (2011), *Terrifying Muslims: Race and Labor in the South Asian Diaspora*, Durham, NC: Duke University Press.

ReOrient Editorial Board (2015), "ReOrient: A Forum for Critical Muslim Studies," *ReOrient: The Journal of Critical Muslim Studies* 1(1): 5–0.

Runnymede Trust (2017), *Islamophobia: Still a Challenge for Us All*, eds. F. Elahi and O. Khan. London, UK.

Said, E. (1978), *Orientalism*, New York: Vintage Books.

Sayyid, S. (2014), *Recalling the Caliphate: Decolonization and World Order*, London: Hurst and Company.

Taylor, Charles (1998), "Modes of Secularism," *Secularism and its Critics*, ed. Rajeev Bhargava, New Delhi: Oxford University Press.

Taylor, Mark (2017), "'White Europe': 60,000 Nationalists March on Poland's Independence Day," *Guardian*, November 12. https://www.theguardian.com/world/2017/nov/12/white-europe-60000-nationalists-march-on-polands-independence-day

Thobani, S. (2008), *Exalted Subjects: Studies in the Making of Race and Nation in Canada*, Toronto: University of Toronto Press.

Turner, Richard Brent (2013), "African Muslim Slaves and Islam in Antebellum America," *The Cambridge Companion to American Islam*, eds. J. Hammer and O. Safi, Cambridge: Cambridge University Press, 28–44.

CHAPTER TWENTY-SIX

The Third City

Radical Orthodoxy's (Emphatically) Complex Political Theology

NICHOLAS KRAUSE
AND JONATHAN TRAN

INTRODUCTION

Radical Orthodoxy addresses its political vision to "the human future."[1] That vision contains within it a picture of one such future and a warning about where the present will take us should we fail to achieve it.[2] It might be audacious to pair the former with the latter but this kind of ambition is the usual stuff of political theory, promises and warnings of what might be, investigations at the intersection of hope and despair. Radical Orthodoxy's particular vision comes readymade with an account of political space complex enough, it believes, to capture the full array of creaturely possibility: a spiraling circulation of exchange that unfolds within the eternal gratuity of the Triune life. In Radical Orthodoxy (RO) one encounters a daring theoretical resumption of Christendom that ascends to the heights of divine economy, an aesthetic of such bold expectation that all other political theories are left looking like mere things of the world.

Observers troubled by RO's pretentions usually explain away its extravagant claims, especially its overt espousal of Christendom, in one of two ways, both of which make RO more palatable by taking it less seriously. The first is to associate its vision of Christianity with historical Christendom, suggesting that the racist colonialism that materialized during the expansion of Western Christendom is constitutive of all attempts at Christendom, RO's included. Observers worry that RO's complicated relationship with difference already portends the kinds of eventualities that could befall its theoretical program: updated versions of imperialism, patriarchy, slavery, genocide, and so on.[3] In this case it is exactly the presumption to aesthetic symmetry (tying practical judgments to a fundamental ontology, what RO calls a "politicized metaphysics") that makes observers nervous.[4] This dismissive strategy leaves undefended two premises: first, the idea that the ethos driving RO's Christendom is operationally the same as that which drove historical Christendom; second, that "colonization" names exclusively one kind of project, a project which is unavoidably and inherently violent. If RO can show these premises to be false then the dismissal will be taken off the table and observers will be forced to address RO's case for Christendom on its own terms. The second, reductive strategy takes a different route. Rather than emphasizing RO's potential dangers, it reduces RO's ambitions to certain real world political measures in order to suggest that RO is ultimately only after the regular old stuff of politics as usual. By reading Red Toryism or Blue Labour, respective movements within Britain's Conservative and Labour parties, as political expressions of RO without remainder, these observers can conceptually relegate RO to the familiar parochial world of contemporary politics. But this strategy comes with its own unproven premises: that no fundamental tensions exist between RO's aspirations to full Christendom and a pluralist and truly participatory democracy.

This chapter examines RO's political vision, what we have so far described as its aesthetical divine economy, and evaluates whether the two dismissive strategies have done anything to diminish its promise. Our conclusion about the first, related to Christendom and colonization, will be that RO turns those concerns on their head and makes Christendom's colonization, of a sort, strangely logical. It is precisely this coherence that makes RO's vision both inspiringly bold and consistently worrisome. We will conclude that the second question remains open, specifically as it relates to Blue Labour, with the connections with RO still developing, and instructively so. The promise here is that Blue Labour will press into service RO's aesthetics and make it do work it has yet to do, and that, in turn, RO will offer to Blue Labour conceptual resources for construing its politics as a theological aesthetics, and reasons for why such a move matters. While we will leave untreated RO's relationship to Red Toryism, we do think it rather remarkable that some within both major UK political parties have found common cause with RO's extravagant political vision.[5] Our conclusion about these matters will be that the unfinished business of determining RO's practical relationship to politics, itself an endlessly provisional affair, leaves troubling the air of finality looming over its theological narrative.

One final note before starting: we will identify Radical Orthodoxy with the work of John Milbank. In the late 1990s when RO was getting off the ground, it could count among its company a host of theologians, some of whom have stayed (e.g., Conor Cunningham, Phillip Blond, and others) and others who have for whatever reason departed its company (e.g., Mary-Jane Rubenstein, William Cavanaugh, Peter Candler, and others). At RO's core was Milbank, along with Catherine Pickstock and Graham Ward, the primary progenitors of its vision and brand. With Pickstock's and Ward's allegiance to RO now less obvious, we are left, in the end, with Milbank as its chief defender. As the most ambitious of RO's founding members, Milbank should be seen as articulating RO's vision in its most characteristic, formidable, and comprehensive form.

PERPETUAL EUCHARIST

In popular rendering RO is seen as a religious critique of secular accounts of "pure" difference, or what can be called differential ontologies. This rendering envisages RO's project as primarily reactionary and regressive, a menacing vision of social harmony predicated on a return to premodern notions of hierarchy and complementarity, wherein Christendom institutionalizes Christianity's rejection of postmodern difference. When observers identify in RO a nostalgia for medieval Christendom, they point to its seeming desire to turn back the clock on freedoms gained during and since the Enlightenment—freedoms from the various hierarchies and social organizations of an oppressive Christendom. This perception is somewhat deserved since RO offers a direct and often pugnacious challenge to secular modernity in both its intellectual and political forms. In Milbank's hands, Kant and Hegel and Deleuze and Derrida are all made to look simultaneously noxious and silly, as is the entire enterprise of cultural despising that ended the West's long-held religious enchantment.[6] If postmodernity has made its name by accusing Christians of oppressing difference then Milbank, in attacking postmodernity, seems suspiciously to be attacking difference. His counterintuitive claim that postmodernity, not Christianity, endangers difference, and that Christianity is the best chance difference will ever have, strikes many as philosophically bizarre and empirically ridiculous. RO goes so far as to locate the origins of postmodernity within Christianity itself, insisting on a declension narrative where the distorted desire to be like God, predicating a human concurrence separate from God (amounting to a type of equality with God), resulted in the collapse of the very conceptual infrastructure by which humans rightly could be like God.[7] RO counters postmodernity's genealogies with one of its own, asserting that the Triune God has everything to do with difference and only by properly regarding God can one properly regard difference. The only response one can and should have to postmodern "ontologies of violence," RO claims, is a counter-mythos of "ontological peace" whereby difference gets theologically placed as expressive of the divine insofar as it enters into a fundamental social harmony. This strategy will sound to many as all too familiar, especially to postmodern ears already weary of theological arrogance. Is not RO's vision just another iteration of Christianity's dreadful relationship with difference?

Yet RO's criticisms of postmodernity and its counter-ontology of difference are meant to serve a positive vision that has ended up getting lost in arguments about the accuracy and fairness of RO's critiques and RO's appetite for entertaining them. Unable to convince its detractors that its rejection of secularism's account of difference did not amount to a rejection of difference as such, RO became mired in endless metaphysical debates about difference and various intellectual-historical arguments, ultimately obscuring the force of its constructive vision. This positive overarching vision, within which RO makes its case against postmodern secularism, is a distinctly political-theological one: a Christian socialism which RO believes to be liturgically and philosophically basic to Christian orthodoxy. Thus, Milbank writes in the preface to the second edition of *Theology and Social Theory* that the aim of the book's argument is decidedly political and progressive: "[to] supply again a new ontological and eschatological basis for socialist hope."[8] Such an ontology of mutuality and cooperation is precisely what postmodern differential ontologies lack, RO contends.[9] According to what RO considers Christianity's Trinitarian metaphysics and participatory ontology of peace, sacramentally present everywhere in creation (creation as sacramental presence) is a dynamic gift-structure that exhibits God by gifting (*ad intra*) the natural with a share of the supernatural—creation as gift.[10] A politics responsive to these claims is what RO is after.

RO's positive political vision starts from a baseline orthodoxy. The distinct persons of the Trinity are identified by the gifts each gives and reciprocates. For RO, the oneness of the Triune God consists in an eternal exchange of charity amidst difference. The divine Trinity is "transcendental peace through differential relation"[11] and the Triune life is a sociality of harmonious difference.[12] Divine simplicity and eternality logically require that this exchange be elegant, where God's giving does not issue in distinct parts (say, something outside of God) or distinct moments (say, gaps arising between divine longing and divine satisfaction). For Milbank, the possibility of creaturely difference comes by analogical participation and consists in elegant relations of gift-exchange—creaturely economies participating in, and derivative of, the divine economy.[13] God's life of difference images itself in every aspect (*vestigium trinitatis*) of creaturely life, though, as temporal and not eternal, creaturely life is complex inversely to how divine life is elegant.[14] Creation is possessed of the integrity of its own exchange but in a manner befitting its temporal status, hence Milbank speaks of creaturely gift-exchange in terms of "prophetic delay," "non-identical repetition," and "asymmetrical reciprocity."[15] The complexity of creaturely life matches its contingent constitution, comprised as it is by time and its distinctions between actuality and possibility, as well as the distensions constitutive of life under sin.[16] Creaturely existence is complex, utterly dependent on God, and as composite, capable of coming undone when distanced from God.[17] Creatures are capable of harmony—indeed, they are created in and for it—but harmony, while necessary *for* their existence, is not necessary *of* their existence. Genuine and genuinely social human gift-giving becomes the occasion of creaturely harmony, where gift-giving assumes an ascending spiral, each gift reciprocated by something new as creatures journey into God as creation rises in divinizing harmony.[18]

According to Milbank, the constitutive human activities of language and making—the creative activities fundamental to politics—reveal the *verbum* that is the Son and the *donum* that is the Spirit, God the Father grounding divine gift-giving and exchange.[19] Structured this way, language and making each gesture beyond themselves, inclining toward God for the completion of their activity in what Milbank calls a "supernatural pragmatism."[20] Because satisfaction in God entails satisfaction in God's creation, because God has structured creation this way, human desire in language and making requires others with whom to speak and make. Christian *social*ism expresses in political form the inexhaustibly social nature of creation, "the echo of divine creation and divine grace," with sin evinced as those instances when creatures privatize that which is meant to be shared.[21] Just as socialism is the economic form of human mimesis, so is neoliberal capitalism, especially in its post-Keynesian modality, the form of its human distortion, made possible by the interstices of time and realized in the creature's unwillingness to gracefully bear time's complexities. RO's case for Christian socialism then is its espousal for an expressed and harmonious complexity that inclines creation toward God, an entirely plausible social form given creation's "supernaturalized" constitution.[22] Such a politics of mutuality, reciprocity, cooperation, and solidarity is "more realist than mere realism," for it reflects creation's most basic ontological composition.[23] At the heart of RO is thus a series of liturgical conventions natural to all that exists in God insofar as it exists at all. Milbank terms this "perpetual Eucharist," wherein "gifts collected, offered by all, as all, to the all who is One," are then "received back by all from the One, who are all thereby received into these same different gifts which are his Word."[24] Socialism simply names the politics of this Eucharistic exchange.

CHRISTENDOM AS THE THIRD CITY

Within Augustine's well-known earthly/eternal cities schematic, Milbank imagines a "third city."[25] But contrary to other Augustinians who thematize this third space between the earthly and eternal cities in terms of a mixed *tertium quid* (Henri Irénée Marrou) or a neutral *saeculum* (R.A. Markus) which divides the world into sacred and secular spheres, for Milbank this city is the *social* form Christian pilgrimage assumes in the world. The third city is an aspiring cosmopolis that fuses the natural goodness and desire of the earthly city to its completion and consummation in the eternal. This follows RO's conviction that there is not, and cannot be, some autonomous secular space outside of God, a natural order not always already "supernaturalized." Given the social nature of creation this fusion must, RO believes, emanate in actual political arrangements. The third city is Christendom, the church's "extending the sphere" of its "socially aesthetic harmony"[26] into political life, infusing the natural goodness of political society with divine governance. This step marks an important conceptual development (or at minimum, explication) for RO, moving from an earlier polemicized political theory that pitted Christianity and secularity against one another, to a via media between them, allowing RO to critique political concepts and practices when they fail to embody the politics of the third city and to endorse them when they do. One witnesses here a theoretical benefit to RO's insistently participatory ontology, which should never have been allowed to permit of polemics but instead highlights a common humanity and possibilities of genuine political cooperation across difference.

According to Milbank, the politics of the third city includes two primary loci, initially a positive function that relationally operationalizes human language and making, institutionalization as artistic endeavor. There is also a negative function, and here readers of *De Civitate Dei* will recognize the Augustinian imperative to restrain evil and its effects. Milbank interprets the imperative's internal logic as pushing toward the more primary positive goal, pressing beyond the innately dissatisfying work of restraint toward the positive pursuit of goodness, to action as such, wherein human artifice participates in God, as already evidenced in the third city's first function.[27] Milbank pushes these considerations to their logical, but still stunning, conclusion: "Without this bending, justice cannot itself remain just and law cannot itself remain legitimate. And yet exactly this bending of the necessary but imperfect towards the unnecessary but perfect, exactly this Christian politics, actually belongs to the primary task of Christian conversion. This is one reason why the idea of Christianity without Christendom is a self-deluding and superficial illusion."[28] According to RO, just as Christians should, without controversy, believe that being Christian is better than not being Christian, so Christians should believe that a Christian society is better suited for human flourishing than a society ruled otherwise. Thus, Milbank believes that for every morally important action, no matter how quotidian (e.g., *Beyond Secular Order* uses the example of driving), there are properly moral ways things should go (i.e., one should drive locally and globally conscious of others), and Christians are best positioned to know as much. Some will take this to be culturally invasive, but Milbank sees it as the logical conclusion of the following sequence: (1) The world is designed by God for creaturely flourishing; (2) Christians are those who attempt to live in accord with God's design for creaturely flourishing; therefore, (3) Christians will best manage creaturely affairs for flourishing. RO thinks it programmatically absurd for Christians (likely suffering from false humility and/or a failure of nerve) to claim 1 and 2 without 3. RO's argument about difference—that Christianity is most able to appropriately relate to difference—simply falls within this logical sequence, and it is *principally* for that reason, in RO's vision, the church should be in charge of managing society. The church alone is the paradigmatic social community, called to love neighbors, pray for enemies, serve the poor and sick, and otherwise live peaceably and encourage others to do so. Only in this arrangement, RO contends, will human society be able to properly receive difference, including the difference that is the non-Christian. The third city is thus the political manifestation of Christian hospitality.

Much of the conceptual payoff of RO's fundamental ontology comes from its recognition of creaturely complexity and the need to politically account for that complexity.[29] If one does not understand this complexity and the need to organize for it, one will not understand the point of RO's ambitions, including its criticisms of neoliberalism, which RO sees as reductive exactly where complexity is needed. Similarly, if one does not recognize that creaturely complexity participates in divine elegance, where God's eternality funds, through the Son's *verbum* and in the Spirit's *donum*, the perpetual circulation of charity, then one misses the elegant cosmic foundation of that complexity, its impetus and possibility. Understanding RO as primarily oriented toward a constructive political project, where a Christian socialist ontology occasions and enables practical political entailments, contextualizes RO's considerable attention to secular critical theory (i.e., Nietzsche and his inheritors—Deleuze, Derrida, and Foucault). Within this context one comes to see RO's critical moves as but conceptual ground clearing for that which RO understands to be its more immediate deconstructive goal: unmasking late capitalism's disastrously possessive commodification of creation.[30] RO views secularism's differential ontologies as incapable of grounding the kinds of social solidarity, commonness, and unity necessary for resisting neoliberal capitalism and realizing a politics of the common good. Discourses that prioritize alterity to the exclusion of community end up casting the social in terms of Darwinian tragedy, where only the "fittest" survive and thus *should* rule.[31] Differential ontologies, RO believes, in their rejection of the possibility of unity or commonness across difference, substantiate neoliberalism's essential logic.[32] As much as these discourses would like to think they honor difference, RO contends they end up establishing the conditions for its erasure. Difference without harmonious relation—what Milbank terms an "ontology of violence"—either disintegrates into atomization or gives rise to domination. Milbank challenges postmodern theorists of difference to supply a better ontology for their likely own espousals of socialism. He refers to socialism as "the joker in the pack of left-wing options," insofar as "its account of society as the upshot of visionary work requires a certain appeal to the 'sacrality of the many' or the 'mystique of the collective.'" In other words, secular socialisms lack the necessary theological and ontological grounds for socialist community, and therefore must appeal to theological, metaphysical, and almost mystical notions of utopian community.[33]

In contrast to political economies that presume Darwinian tragedy and its suppositions of scarcity and competition, RO's socialism presupposes charity as the most basic law of creation, God's plenitude coursing through all of creaturely life and enabling a politics of mutuality, solidarity, and equity.[34] RO turns the tables on concerns about RO's latent colonialism by arguing that it is indeed a neoliberal ontology with its espousal of an originary and originating agonistic violence that inaugurates a dark age of imperial conquest. Therefore, RO rhetorically asks: Why wouldn't the church see as its mission the constraint of *that* violence? How else can that be pursued except by political rulership? If RO's project is finally deemed a colonizing censure of difference, it must be acknowledged to be a *socialist* one, unrelenting in its denunciation of capitalism's anti-social operations and effects. RO believes the human future is worth fighting for, and (obviously) does not dither from advocating for (over against neoliberal exploitation) "the international spread of the charitable *politeia* which was the *ecclesia*."[35]

The complexity of creaturely life, with its horizontal and vertical investments, requires, according to RO, a complex mixed governance, comprised of a democratic populace apprenticed by a *morally* elite aristocracy charged with forming citizens' democratic sensibilities and habits, and finally a monarchical cultural reservoir of institutional memory—and all of this as uniquely and constitutively Christian achievements.[36] Only by first being formed in character, which requires mnemonic anchoring, can citizens be trusted to act in their own best interest, where their best interests naturally includes, insofar as it supernaturally inclines to God, the best interest of communities. Citizens grow in virtue by first mimicking the practices of "the virtuous few" who are liturgically formed in kenosis, and then carry political traditions forward toward new ways of seeing (through natural conventions) and being (through creative activity) in the world.[37] RO speaks of a republican hierarchy that is both authoritative and self-cancelling; the more the elite succeeds in forming a new generation, the less it will need to exercise authority, eventuating in perpetual replacement.[38] Not only might citizens transform the discourses they inherit, they are expected to, and, given creation's deep gift-structure, enabled to—such is RO's conception of democracy as a *supernaturally* pragmatic tradition. Its account of formation is hierarchical precisely in this way, masters training apprentices until those apprentices assume mastery. Without apprenticeship (whether through wise individuals or seasoned associational communities), the citizenry will not realize its democratic power; without apprentices adapting traditions to new contexts, democracy will turn up empty.[39] Such political formation and education occurs, RO maintains, within the manifold associations and intermediary institutions that comprise the "complex space" between the individual and state, and which shields individuals, families and communities from the sheer power of the state and market.[40] Such a complex and plural space contests the unilateral sovereignty of the neoliberal market-state which threatens to reduce citizens to passive consumers of ever new goods.

RO's hierarchical account of democratic citizenship can be described in the terms of gift-giving, with masters gifting their students by teaching them and students reciprocating those gifts with ones of their own, moving the tradition forward.[41] If teachers do not raise up new generations of citizens to exercise political judgment, the community will die; if students fail to provide a new generation of judgments, the community will die. Human civilization is entirely dependent on the gift-structure of its existence. To be sure, RO's account of mixed governance presumes distinctions between relative faculties of and maturations in goodness, truth, and beauty, but it is hard to imagine any account of diversified political life—what Milbank variously describes as "Baroque", "poetic," and "gothic"—that does not. This is the thrust of Milbank's critique of differential ontologies: they imagine difference as anarchic and chaotic, manifesting in various competitive relations and agonistic struggles.[42] It is only within ontologically structured processional hierarchy, an ordered and peaceful unfolding of difference, that difference thrives.[43] Therein, not only relative virtues, but also roles, distinguish between the specific features that comprise a society: passions and skills and callings and dispositions and personalities and gifts and histories, so on and so forth.[44] It is within a hierarchically ordered politics that difference can be accommodated, not by atomizing and thereby sequestering difference but by properly identifying it so that it can be positioned to flourish. RO's political vision includes then both a requirement to creatively accommodate difference and an account of how that accommodation will grow a society by pragmatically adopting it to the local conditions of difference. Human existence is not only ontologically ecstatic, forever growing into God, but also pragmatically so, forever growing into creation, the latter participating in the former, the former growing out of the latter. Local conditions of speaking and making bespeak and fashion a politics; hence, there is no one form of governance sufficient for every situation. Rather, each hierarchy will need to accommodate to "particular geographical, social and historical circumstances"; political community is "not a utopia to be imposed, but something only achievable in certain historical circumstances."[45] In this regard, Milbank positions his Christian socialism—shaped as it is by traditions of guild socialism, syndicalism, and Anglican Christian socialism—against the idealistic orientations of certain Marxian varieties.[46] Socialist community must come "by grace," which means it cannot be rationally planned or anticipated by utopian visions. These latter strategies enforce an artificial unity upon difference, whereas Milbank insists genuine socialism must come organically from within local cultures and traditions.[47] Such socialist communities are premised on the right ordering of differences in charitable relation, which, according to RO, manifests in a hierarchical ordering.[48]

It is, from RO's perspective, hierarchy then that makes flourishing democracy possible, hierarchy not only *of* difference but *for* difference.[49] "Thus, paradoxically, the real rationale for democracy is *extra*-democratic": the legitimacy of popular assent lies in its eventual conversion, through education and training in virtue, to the common good.[50] Once again, the plane of immanent life is seen as unfolding within and expressing a higher life, the creature's ascent to the divine, which cannot be had except within the structures of creation.[51] Milbank is especially subtle here, as one would need him to be, suggesting that hierarchy does not undermine the integrity of each station of being, but rather affirms its absolute necessity in the order of things.[52]

The full flowering of RO's political vision comes in the rich complexity of its political economy, what Milbank calls a "gift economy" and develops as a "civil economy socialism."[53] For Milbank, economy is necessarily political, wherein economic exchange is a form of gift-sharing. Milbank's civil economy then focuses on the "family, guild, fraternity, commune, corporation"—those relational networks necessary for the cultivation of economic virtue, the temporal basis of all other virtues.[54] Such social forms also entail hierarchical relations, both within groups and between them, as each serves different roles and raises up initiates to take up their roles in ever new ways. But within RO's account of hierarchy superiority is always being given up, given away, capitulated, and gifted—that is, shared.[55]

Fusing elements of Catholic Social Teaching and Italian civil economy,[56] RO advances a vision of a forthrightly socialized economy. It calls for re-embedding markets within social relations by directing the free activities of work and trade to the common good, ordering legitimate profit-making activities to human flourishing and social benefit, and encouraging and rewarding virtuous behavior in the marketplace through tax incentives and the bestowing of public honor.[57] Practically, this means encouraging greater sharing of profits and risks between capital and labor, lenders and borrowers; strengthening professional vocational associations and guilds and their roles within industry; and providing more robust legal frameworks within which negotiations of wages, prices, and share-values are jointly determined by owners, consumers, workers, and other stakeholders.[58] In short, RO's civil economy seeks to integrate aspects of the market economy (legitimate profit-seeking, competition, trade) with a concern for social welfare and genuine human flourishing. Markets, RO holds, are most truly free not when they are subjected to capitalist logics and neoliberal policies, but rather when they are socialized and ordered to the common good.

Unlike doctrinaire socialisms, then, with their Manichean attitudes toward capitalism, RO is not opposed to eventualities like money, contracts, property, ownership, and the like.[59] Nor is it so naive as to believe that state possession of these eventualities makes them immune from corruption. RO is opposed to their distortion, including their state-sponsored distortions, further demonstrating its Augustinian *uti/frui* approach to worldly affairs. It worries that the privatizing of capital benefits some to the exclusion of the commons, gifts now ripped out of their structure of exchange and manipulated for artificial gain; money becomes vicious when it is sought for its own sake, as in the case of usury; ownership becomes deadly when instead of gathering community, it breaks down and divides community. RO thus proposes the fusion of contract with gift, the democratization and wide distribution of property, and the recovery of cooperative and "associationist" modes of labor.[60] In short, RO seeks a truly social economy. Its socialism should be thought of less in terms of the standard tenets of an economic doctrine—the overcoming of class, just distribution of goods, and public control of the means of production—and more as a mode of *social*-ism where those tenets organically take root.

RADICAL ORTHODOXY'S ENDURING SERIOUSNESS

Milbank asks, "Does all this sound fantastic? No, the fantastic is what we have: an economy that destroys life, babies, childhood, adventure, locality, beauty, the exotic, the erotic, people and the planet itself."[61] It is precisely this kind of rhetorical confidence that raises worries of an extravagance that too easily lends itself to colonialism. Milbank's response to these charges is to question received notions of colonization by: first, distinguishing between kinds of colonization and their respective ends; second, suggesting colonization's unavoidability; in order that, third, historical colonization and some possible colonization be more hopefully interpreted as aspiring toward certain kinds of futures.[62] Aside from the question of whether Milbank arrives at his point through revisionist history, a more important question is whether Milbank can actually avoid the pitfalls he believes he anticipates.

At the end of *Beyond Secular Order*, Milbank calls for a new politics that "fuses Christian socialism with a new sense of what is valid in the 'conservative' critique of modernity ... a (genuinely) 'third way' beyond modern left and right."[63] Considering how seriously RO takes the applicability of its theories, one senses that Milbank has specifics in mind. As it turns out, RO has found common cause with some advancing a new Blue Labour politics, blending traditions of economic radicalism within Britain's Labour Party with a "blue" conservative appreciation of local cultures, mediatory institutions, religious traditions, and the family.[64] Yet the relationship between RO and Blue Labour is more complicated than some, including Milbank, might suppose, possessing certain tensions still to be resolved. Reading Blue Labour as an instantiation of RO's political vision is wishful thinking, far ahead of a number of practical and theoretical considerations to be determined. While much of Blue Labour's platform, especially its economic vision, embodies the gift economy RO speaks of, Blue Labour's grassroots, radically democratic orientation complicates RO's "mixed polity" comprised as it is of elite "philosopher-rulers," and Blue Labour's vital emphasis on pluralism clearly pushes against RO's case for Christendom.

The principal merits Milbank finds in Blue Labour are twofold. First, Blue Labour's economic vision, chiefly developed by Jewish theorist Maurice Glasman, is consonant with much of RO's proposals for civil economy socialism. No wonder the majority of Milbank's engagement with Blue Labour has been specifically on matters of political economy. Second, Blue Labour's re-centering of virtue, the common good, and a moral "ethos" to politics echoes much of RO's "politics of virtue." Milbank understands this virtuous politics to entail a renewed appreciation for a virtuous aristocracy, public honor and democracy's dependency on hierarchies of virtue.[65] Indeed, relating it to RO's stridently theological vision highlights the ingenuity of Blue Labour's political offerings, the possibility of holding together an account of virtue substantial enough to resist the corrosive effects of neoliberalism and a practice of politics capacious enough to generously receive radical difference. As mentioned earlier, it is somewhat remarkable that RO, with its self-consciously audacious claims and aspirations, has found a place for itself within Britain's political future. But it is not entirely surprising, especially if one imagines those aspirations arising within the same context (historical, economic, social, ecclesiastical, etc.) that animates much of British politics.

Yet it must be remembered that RO's politics of the "third city" is a vision of Christendom that cannot simply be reduced to a democratic political platform. To do so is to soften and mitigate the radicalism of RO's divine politics. RO aspires to see the political instantiation of its Christian ontology and so approaches politics as the enterprise of realigning political society in light of these philosophical commitments. It is on this point that one notices the greatest tensions between RO's political philosophy and Blue Labour's radically democratic sensibilities, embodied in figures like Glasman, Arnie Graf, and Luke Bretherton, for whom Blue Labour arose out of the experiences of grassroots organizing.[66] Bretherton writes that Blue Labour is not a "political philosophy" at all, but a mode of political *practice*—one which prioritizes "practice before theory," "people before programme," and "politics before procedure."[67] Politics belongs properly to the realm of practical reason, rather than ideology or speculative philosophy, and thus Blue Labour understands the work of politics to be not the instantiation of any particular conceptualization of the good life or version of the common good, but rather the formation of a common life amidst difference. Blue Labour as a mode of political *praxis* thus entails practices of listening, collective deliberation and judgment-making amidst communities of great difference, so as to conciliate various interests and discern and pursue goods in common.

Blue Labour, then, would complicate RO's insistence that democracy be disciplined by hierarchies of virtue and constrained by the wisdom of elites. Whereas RO worries about democracy's tendency to become untethered from the metaphysically true and so seeks to ground political order in a philosophically derived vision of the common good, Blue Labour suggests politics is primarily "the negotiation of a shared life among diverse and competing interests," which "does not demand that those with different interests, loyalties or views leave the room before the negotiations begin."[68] Because Blue Labour presumes a radically pluralist set of political actors and seeks to forge a common life amidst their differences, it is not clear that RO can rest content with such a politics, insofar as RO aspires to the construction of a "third city" whose constitution reflects the divine life, in which difference is always reconciled in unity.[69] Blue Labour's *praxis* seeks not the conversion of difference to a shared, singular conception of the good life and the common good, but rather the negotiation of difference and the establishment of relations of neighborliness and friendship across such difference. Whether or not RO can come to appreciate this kind of radical democracy and politics of difference is dependent on how it comes to see the relation between its ontology and that ontology's practical entailments. Must difference be managed and ordered to a vision of political community known in advance of democratic negotiation, or can politics become, for RO, a site of genuine encounter with difference, wherein the "third city" is perpetually co-created with others in new and unexpected ways?

Interestingly it is at the point of just this set of concerns that Milbank reasserts his case for imperial over secular order, and here we return to the two strategies of dismissal with which this essay began. Discussing RO's possible consilience with Blue Labour, Milbank invokes a "more benign, plural and inclusive" empire that can be more determined by "indigenous modes of political control, while also fostering a certain cross-cultural and international modulation" than that which comprised historical British imperialism. Milbank assays a Christendom that has learned from its mistakes: "That this destiny has often been pursued with brutality and was abandoned so recklessly and irresponsibly—with dire consequences in the Near East—only precludes us trying to pursue it in the future more charitably and cooperatively if we act out of guilt, which is always to act in bad faith."[70] Notice Milbank's aforementioned move to complexify the historical legacy of European colonization, intimating its irresponsibly premature conclusion, as part of the rationale for a new colonization. How is one to take this emblem of RO, seemingly guileless in its pretentions and possibly deadly for that reason? If we have successfully provided reasons to take RO seriously, to not dismiss out of hand its pro-Christendom stance, then we are faced with an importantly interesting puzzlement. One might look at RO and its emphasis on ontological peace and its practical urgings for socialism and decide, given the seeming goodwill and the desired beneficial outcomes, its proposal does not amount to what was pernicious about historical colonization—say, its motivations and impulses and seminal expressions. Or, one might, upon examining its case, decide that its emphases and practical urges, especially its seeming goodwill and benevolences, just *is* what colonization has always amounted to. One is left with either a very provocative way of talking about Christian social engagement, mission, and conversion (the bitter pill of recognizing that *all* social and political programs are "colonizing" insofar as they prescribe what they take to be true), or a very polite and elegant way of dressing up the same old colonial impulse.

In an essay early in RO's history, Gerard Loughlin assessed RO's possibilities and problems. There, he attended to the themes of mastery, difference, and pluralism within RO's rhetorical strategy, themes we have detailed above with reference to RO's politics. Speaking of RO's genealogical strategies, Loughlin offered two ways of thinking about RO, which we delineate here:

A. RO's fondness for the Christian "master-narrative" which "positions the narratives of secular reason," and indeed all other narratives, through rhetorical subjection and/or absorption, betrays a proclivity toward mastery that forgets its own contingency and fragility as *narrative*. RO's rhetorical strategies—the "forms" in which the Christian story is articulated—exhibit modes of domination and colonization that betray the "content" of that story. RO is thus seen to offer a story which fails to acknowledge itself as such, a claim to mastery and finality cloaked in the attributes of narrativity while yet aspiring to totality.

B. "Rather than the monopoly of a master-narrative, which positions all other narratives," RO's story could be articulated as "an ever-extending tradition of narrative linkages, in which now some stories, now others, function as the synchronic animators of the rest, so that there is always a 'buzz' within the tradition, a movement of story against story, a never stable positioning and an always possible indeterminacy with regard to new linkages, new stories." Such a narrative practice acknowledges not only the contingency of its practice but also the provisionality and contestability of its claims. It thus aspires to dialogical encounter and receptive generosity to others.[71]

Our thought is that the most promising version of RO's political theology is something like Blue Labour read in terms of Loughlin's option B, where the spoken/made content of RO's gift-centered story of kenotic self-cancellation, what one might call a good form of mastery, can help RO resist mastery's deadly forms. Then we might arrive at what Loughlin describes as "a 'buzz' within the tradition" of RO, a "movement of story against story, a never stable positioning and an always possible indeterminacy with regard to new linkages, new stories." One might even name that buzz "democracy," the practice of forging political communities and discovering goods in common through negotiations that demand postures of receptivity to difference and change. Blue Labour's commitments to dialogical processes that prioritize pragmatic adaptation over aesthetic purity—"practice before theory," "people before programme" and "politics before procedure"—can put RO's "supernatural pragmatism" on the road to realizing the social hope at the center of its socialist politics.

Identifying commonalities and continuities between RO and Blue Labour comes to the question of imagination or what we earlier intimated as the ambition of political theory, "promises and warnings of what might be, investigations at the intersection of hope and despair." Political imagination begins with stepping into commonalities and continuities where they are to be found, along with acknowledging when and why they cannot be found, and motivating commonality and continuity when despair forces imagination underground. One can imagine the forms Blue Labour linked to Loughlin's RO "buzz" might take—everything from generating radical political agency out of rather than over against storied forms of place and community, to resisting neoliberal aggression by forging alliances that arise out of practices of scriptural reasoning between Muslim, Jewish, Christian, and other religious and non-religious readers of texts, to scenes of political repair occasioned when hierarchical self-canceling energizes re-memory of moral injury. Radical Orthodoxy and Blue Labour are both projects of political imagining. If they can respectively survive dismissal and reduction then they can begin to imagine together.

NOTES

1. Note the subtitle of Radical Orthodoxy's most developed treatment of politics: John Milbank and Adrian Pabst, *The Politics of Virtue: Post-Liberalism and the Human Future* (New York: Rowman & Littlefield, 2015).
2. John Milbank, *Beyond Secular Order: The Representation of Being and the Representation of the People* (Malden, MA: Wiley-Blackwell, 2013), 261.
3. For a discussion of RO, imperialism, and colonialism, see Romand Coles, "Storied Others and the Possibilities of *Caritas*: Milbank and Neo-Nietzschean Ethics," *Modern Theology* 8:4 (1992), 331–351; Graeme Smith, "Mission and Radical Orthodoxy," *Modern Believing* 44:1 (2003), 47–57; and the relevant essays in *The Poverty of Radical Orthodoxy*, ed. Lisa Isherwood and Marko Zlomislić (Eugene, OR: Wipf & Stock, 2012).
4. Milbank, *Beyond Secular Order*, 15. See, for example, the critique of Milbank in Kyle Gingerich Hiebert, *The Architectonics of Hope: Violence, Apocalyptic, and the Transformation of Political Theology* (Eugene, OR: Wipf & Stock, 2017), 94–95, 98–100. Gingerich Hiebert specifically draws attention to the way Milbank articulates this vision in such a way as to make impossible genuine self-criticism and to disable meaningful engagement with interlocutors.
5. Those interested in Red Toryism can consult Phillip Blond's *Red Tory: How the Left and Right Have Broken Britain and How We Can Fix It* (London: Faber and Faber, 2010), stemming from his February 28, 2008 *Prospect* essay, "Rise of the Red Tories."
6. See, for instance, Chapters 4, 6, and 10 of John Milbank, *Theology and Social Theory: Beyond Secular Reason*, 2nd ed. (Malden, MA: Blackwell, 2006).
7. Milbank, *Beyond Secular Order*, 42–49, 112–113. See also John Milbank, *The Word Made Strange: Theology, Language, Culture* (Malden, MA: Blackwell, 1997), 44–45.
8. "Preface to the Second Edition: Between Liberalism and Positivism," in Milbank, *Theology and Social Theory*, xiv.
9. Milbank contends that, lacking the necessary ontological foundations for a truly socialist politics, the political manifestation of postmodern differential ontologies can only be either liberalism or fascism—the former which rejects any notion of a common good and thus relegates difference to the sphere of private expression and self-cultivation; the latter which names politics as the site of agonistic struggle wherein the "fittest" survive and rule. See Milbank, *Theology and Social Theory*, 279, 323–325.

10. On the fundamental gift-structure of creation, see John Milbank, *Being Reconciled: Ontology and Pardon* (New York: Routledge, 2003), xi; John Milbank, "Liberality versus Liberalism," in *The Future of Love: Essays in Political Theology* (Eugene, OR: Wipf & Stock, 2009), 257–258; John Milbank, "Can a Gift Be Given? Prolegomena to a Future Trinitarian Metaphysics," *Modern Theology* 11 (1995), 116–161; and Milbank, *Beyond Secular Order*, 72–77, 107–108.

11. Milbank, *Theology and Social Theory*, 6.

12. Milbank delineates this account of difference in terms of the Trinity's "first" and "second" differences: "This is why (speculatively speaking), within the Godhead, there is held by Christianity to arise after the 'first difference' which is the Son, also the 'second difference' of the Holy Spirit, constituted as an equally pure relation to the Father, but 'through' the Son. The Spirit *is* this relation of the one and the many, this *ratio* of charity, but the relational character of this ratio is now truly affirmed, because the Son, and the differences contained within the Son, has now become a moment of *mediation* between Father and Spirit . . . Therefore difference, after first constituting unity (the Son causing 'backwards' the Father) becomes a *response* to unity that is more than unity, which unity itself cannot predict—since mediation exceeds unity just as it exceeds difference . . . The harmony of the Trinity is therefore not the harmony of a finished totality but a 'musical' harmony of infinity" (Milbank, *Theology and Social Theory*, 430–431). See also John Milbank, "The Second Difference," in *The Word Made Strange*, 171–193. See also John Milbank, *The Religious Dimension in the Thought of Giambattista Vico 1558–1774: Part I The Early Metaphysics* (Lampeter: The Edwin Mellen Press, 1991), 116–149.

13. For Milbank's most sophisticated account of gift-giving, see Milbank, "Grace: The Midwinter's Sacrifice," in *Being Reconciled*, 138–161 (see especially 154).

14. See Milbank, *Beyond Secular Order*, 53 fn82.

15. Milbank, "Can a Gift Be Given?" 125–152; and Milbank, *Being Reconciled*, 156–161.

16. Milbank, *Being Reconciled*, 53.

17. Milbank, *The Word Made Strange*, 280.

18. Milbank, *Being Reconciled*, 171.

19. Ibid., 199–200; and Milbank, *The Word Made Strange*, 84–113.

20. Milbank, *Theology and Social Theory*, 206–252 and *Beyond Secular Order*, 213–214. See also Milbank, *Beyond Secular Order*, 104–105, 195–198.

21. John Milbank, "The Transcendality of the Gift: A Summary," in *Future of Love*, 359–363. See also Milbank, *Beyond Secular Order*, 35–36, 267.

22. See also, for example, Milbank's account of forgiveness in Milbank, *Being Reconciled*, 46–47.

23. Milbank and Pabst, *Politics of Virtue*, 8.

24. Milbank, "Can a Gift Be Given?" 152.

25. Milbank, *Beyond Secular Order*, 228–236.

26. Milbank, *Theology and Social Theory*, 428.

27. Milbank relies much on Maurice Blondel's theory of action. See Maurice Blondel, *Action (1893): Essay on a Critique of Life and a Science of Practice*, trans. Oliva Blanchette (Notre Dame, IN: The University of Notre Dame Press, 2003).

28. Milbank, *Beyond Secular Order*, 233, 248.

29. See Milbank, *Being Reconciled*, 56–57, 148–149.

30. Milbank thus reads Nietzsche as not sufficiently different from the eighteenth- and nineteenth-century English political economists, in terms of how both imagine the condition

of primitive humanity as one of "*agon* or playful, competitive struggle" (Milbank, *Theology and Social Theory*, 283–284).
31. Ibid., xiv.
32. Ibid., xxi. Milbank notes similar critiques of postmodern thought from theorists on the secular left like Alain Badiou and Peter Hallward, who likewise see that "the philosophy of difference grounds only a social *agon* and therefore is complicit with capitalism."
33. Milbank, *Beyond Secular Order*, 262.
34. Milbank, "Can a Gift Be Given?" 124.
35. Milbank, *Beyond Secular Order*, 229. See also Milbank, *Being Reconciled*, 176–177.
36. For Milbank's delineation of this mixed arrangement, containing elements of democratic, aristocratic, and monarchical traditions, see Milbank, "Liberality versus Liberalism," 245–249; and Milbank and Pabst, *Politics of Virtue*, 205–244. On monarchical rule and the participation of all in "Christic kingship," see Milbank, *Beyond Secular Order*, 249.
37. Milbank, *Beyond Secular Order*, 263.
38. Milbank, *The Word Made Strange*, 285; Milbank, *Being Reconciled*, 183.
39. On the place of education in this political arrangement, see Milbank, *Being Reconciled*, 182–183; Milbank, "Liberality versus Liberalism," 249; and Milbank and Pabst, *Politics of Virtue*, 260–266, 286–294.
40. Milbank develops this notion of "complex" or "gothic" space in his essay "On Complex Space," in Milbank, *The Word Made Strange*, 268–292.
41. Milbank, *Being Reconciled*, 57.
42. Ibid., 107, 190. See also Milbank, *Beyond Secular Order*, 86–88; 158–159; and especially 210–211; and Milbank, *The Word Made Strange*, 276–277.
43. Milbank, *Theology and Social Theory*, 436–437.
44. Milbank, *The Word Made Strange*, 271.
45. Milbank, *Beyond Secular Order*, 161. See Milbank's distinction between hierarchy of this kind and that fixed within modern bureaucracies (176–177). See also 195–198, 210–213. See also Milbank, *Vico Part I*, 239.
46. See John Milbank, "Were the 'Christian Socialists' Socialists?" in *The Future of Love*, 63–74; and Milbank, *Being Reconciled*, 162–186.
47. Related to this is Milbank's argument that the "unity" of socially harmonious communities must be understood not as an entity or substance, but a *relation*. As he puts it, "Unity . . . ceases to be anything hypostatically real in contrast to difference, and becomes instead only the 'subjective' apprehension of a harmony displayed in the order of the differences" (Milbank, *Theology and Social Theory*, 435–436). For Milbank, this peaceful relation of difference is one of "analogical" relation, wherein there exists a commonness or "common measure" between differences that does not figure them with respect to a "third thing," some generic essence they share, to which various differences are ordered by univocal mediation. Rather various differences are ordered to one another in charity in generous attribution and truthful proportion, an "aesthetic relation."
48. Kenneth Surin argues such hierarchies are, in fact, intrinsic to the tradition of analogical thinking RO draws upon. In such a vision, charitable and peaceful relations of difference are only possible, Surin maintains, within an ontological "chain of being," that necessitates certain forms of subjection and mastery. See Kenneth Surin, "Rewriting the Ontological Script of Liberation: On the Question of Finding a New Kind of Political Subject," in *Theology and the Political: The New Debate*, ed. Creston Davis, et al. (Durham, NC: Duke University Press, 2005), 240–266.

49. Speaking of the church, Milbank writes, "[C]ontrary to all the assumptions of secular sovereignty, it is all the more democratic the more it is genuinely hierarchical. Moreover . . . this is the only possible real democracy, and the most extremely democratic" (Milbank, *Being Reconciled*, 108).

50. That is, in "the likelihood that a relatively well educated—morally trained and informed—populace will be better able to sift and refine proposals as to what is 'best' for them by genuinely 'aristocratic' thinkers and innovators at every level" (Milbank and Pabst, *Politics of Virtue*, 191).

51. Nowhere is this more evident than in Milbank's discussion of what he calls the "beast-angel," the human's ever-deepening into its own natural constitution, a desire-driven movement of creative ecstasy that expresses and draws deeper into God's love and creativity (Milbank, *Beyond Secular Order*, 209, 221–222).

52. On RO's extra-democratic justification of democracy, see Milbank, "Liberality versus Liberalism", 245; and Milbank and Pabst, *The Politics of Virtue*, 239–240.

53. Milbank and Pabst, *Politics of Virtue*, 137–171; and John Milbank, "The Real Third Way: For a New Metanarrative of Capital and the Associationist Alternative," in *The Crisis of Global Capitalism: Pope Benedict XVI's Social Encyclical and the Future of Political Economy* (Eugene, OR: Wipf & Stock, 2011), 27–70.

54. Milbank, *Beyond Secular Order,* 165. See also, Milbank, "Liberality versus Liberalism," 250–253.

55. Milbank, "Liberality versus Liberalism," 248.

56. Of central importance are the works of Luigino Bruni and Stefano Zamagni, as well as Pope Benedict XVI's encyclical *Caritas in Veritate*.

57. Milbank and Pabst, *Politics of Virtue*, 129–176. See also, Adrian Pabst, "'Civil Economy': Blue Labour's Alternative to Capitalism," in *Blue Labour: Forging a New Politics*, ed. Ian Geary and Adrian Pabst (London: I.B. Tauris, 2015), 97–119.

58. Milbank and Pabst, *Politics of Virtue*, 142–147.

59. See Milbank's discussion of contracts, much indebted to Edmund Burke, as a convention natural to the sociality of humanness in Milbank, *Beyond Secular Order*, 183. Regarding natural conventions, see Jonathan Tran, "Linguistic Theology: Completing Postliberalism's Linguistic Task," *Modern Theology* 33:1 (2017): 47–68.

60. Milbank and Pabst, *Politics of Virtue*, 143–145.

61. Milbank, "Liberality versus Liberalism," 263.

62. Milbank often turns to John Darwin's work, including *Unfinished Empire: The Global Expansion of Britain* (London: Penguin Books, 2012).

63. Milbank, *Beyond Secular Order*, 269.

64. For an overview of Blue Labour's political vision, see Adrian Pabst, "Introduction: Blue Labour and the Politics of the Common Good," in *Blue Labour*, 1–10.

65. To get a sense of the implications of Blue Labour's vision, see Jon Cruddas' April 23, 2018 *New Statesman* piece, "The Humanist Left Must Challenge the Rise of Cyber Socialism."

66. Particularly the work of London Citizens and the Industrial Areas Foundation. See chapter 2, "Faith and Citizenship in a World City," in Luke Bretherton, *Resurrecting Democracy: Faith, Citizenship, and the Politics of a Common Life* (Cambridge: Cambridge University Press, 2015), 57–75.

67. Luke Bretherton, "Vision, Virtue, and Vocation: Notes on Blue Labour as a Practice of Politics," in *Blue Labour*, 217–233. See also Bretherton, *Resurrecting Democracy*, 111–176.

68. Bretherton, "Vision, Virtue, and Vocation," 217.

69. We note, in this regard, how Milbank concludes his contribution to the edited volume *Blue Labour: Forging a New Politics*, for it betrays the way Milbank's project of Christendom stands at odds with the Blue Labour vision (John Milbank, "The Blue Labour Dream," in *Blue Labour*, 43–46). Milbank argues Blue Labour must recover a renewed appreciation of the British imperial legacy, which, he believes, better accommodates difference than homogeneous nation-states. A plain reading of the history of Britain's colonial enterprise seems, however, to suggest otherwise. Moreover, Glasman and Bretherton explicitly articulate Blue Labour as an *anti*-imperialist politics, wherein the turn to pluralist, participatory politics is precisely a rejection of politics as an imperial project.
70. Milbank, "The Blue Labour Dream", 43, 44, and 45.
71. Gerard Loughlin, "Christianity at the End of the Story or the Return of the Master-Narrative," *Modern Theology* 8:4 (1992), 365–384 (381).

SELECT BIBLIOGRAPHY

Bell, Daniel M., Jr. (2015), "Postliberalism and Radical Orthodoxy," *The Cambridge Companion to Christian Political Theology*, eds. Craig Hovey and Elizabeth Phillips, 110–132, Cambridge: Cambridge University Press.

Coles, Romand (1992), "Storied Others and the Possibilities of *Caritas*: Milbank and Neo-Nietzschean Ethics," *Modern Theology* 8:4: 331–351.

Cunningham, Conor (2005), *Genealogy of Nihilism: Philosophies of Nothing and the Difference of Theology*, New York: Routledge.

Davis, Creston, John Milbank, and Slavoj Žižek (2005), *Theology and the Political: The New Debate*, Durham, NC: Duke University Press.

Geary, Ian and Adrian Pabst, eds. (2015), *Blue Labour: Forging a New Politics*, London: I.B. Tauris.

Hankey, Wayne J. and Douglas Hedley, eds. (2016), *Deconstructing Radical Orthodoxy: Postmodern Theology, Rhetoric, and Truth*, New York: Routledge.

Loughlin, Gerard (1992), "Christianity at the End of the Story or the Return of the Master-Narrative," *Modern Theology* 8:4: 365–384.

Milbank, John (1997), *The Word Made Strange: Theology, Language, Culture*, Malden, MA: Blackwell, 1997.

Milbank, John (2003), *Being Reconciled: Ontology and Pardon*, New York: Routledge.

Milbank, John (2006), *Theology and Social Theory: Beyond Secular Reason,* 2nd ed., Malden, MA: Blackwell.

Milbank, John (2009), *The Future of Love: Essays in Political Theology*, Eugene, OR: Wipf & Stock.

Milbank, John (2013), *Beyond Secular Order: The Representation of Being and the Representation of the People*, Malden, MA: Wiley-Blackwell.

Milbank, John and Adrian Pabst (2015), *The Politics of Virtue: Post-Liberalism and the Human Future*, New York: Rowman & Littlefield.

Milbank, John, Catherine Pickstock, and Graham Ward, eds. (2002), *Radical Orthodoxy: A New Theology*, New York: Routledge.

Papanikolaou, Aristotle (2012), *The Mystical as Political: Democracy and Non-Radical Orthodoxy*, Notre Dame, IN: University of Notre Dame Press.

Ruether, Rosemary Radford, and Marion Grau, eds. (2006), *Interpreting the Postmodern: Responses to "Radical Orthodoxy,"* New York: T&T Clark.

Smith, James K. A. (2004), *Introducing Radical Orthodoxy: Mapping a Post-secular Theology*, Grand Rapids, MI: Baker Academic.

CHAPTER TWENTY-SEVEN

Liberating Barth?

From a Theological Critique of Idolatry to a Political Critique of Ideology

DEREK ALAN WOODARD-LEHMAN

INTRODUCTION

Karl Barth is commonly, though regrettably, understood as a conservative figure. Although, Barth famously remarks that the church must "starve the state religiously," many interpretations of Barth ironically tend to starve the Church politically.[1] Some read Barth as the progenitor of an evangelical scholasticism. They take him as a resource for modern trinitarian theology. Others read Barth as the pioneer of a postliberal traditionalism. They take him as the source of an antimodern ecclesiology. Absent from these readings, however, are the socialism of "the red pastor" of Safenwil and the anti-Nazism of the author of the Barmen Declaration. Silent is the connection between a theological critique of idolatry and a political critique of ideology. Just as Left Hegelians once sundered Hegel's radical method from his conservative politics, "Right Barthians" now sever Barth's confessional theology from his radical politics.

Attempts to retrieve or revive a radical Barth are nothing new. Political theologians like Friedrich Wilhelm Marquardt and Timothy Gorringe have long argued for the significance of socialism for Barth's theology.[2] Liberation theologians, like James Cone and J. Kameron Carter, have strongly argued for the prominence of liberation in Barth's theology.[3] Even so, these efforts remain somewhat on the margins of both interpretive and constructive study of Barth.

While many of Marquardt's specific arguments have been discredited, his general claim stands. From start to finish, Barth's theology is intrinsically political and characteristically socialist.[4] More specifically, it is social democratic. Barth both stands "against hegemony," as Gorringe puts it, and stands for social democracy. He does so as, and *because*, he sees such forms of political community as the secular analogy of the ecclesial community.[5]

Cone and Carter incorporate Barth's theology into their own, even as they indicate the limitations of his theology. They incorporate Barth's methodological focus on God's concrete historical action in Jesus Christ. They sharpen his material emphasis on the liberative dimensions of that divine action. Even so, Cone alleges, "[Barth] never really recovered from the early theme of God's transcendence and thus did not achieve the proper dialectical relationship between the historical Jesus and the Christ of faith."[6] He argues that, "Checks against ideology are not derived *abstractly* from the Word of God, because God's Word is not an abstract object, but is the liberating Subject in the lives of the oppressed struggling for freedom."[7] The material consequence of this methodological abstraction is that, "Barth did not set forth the social and political implications of the divine-human encounter with sufficient clarity."[8] These limitations make it all but impossible to give an account of the *theological* significance of black existence. Cone and Carter each move beyond Barth in order to do so. Cone draws on Tillich's theology of correlation to draw out the sociopolitical implications of Barth's emphasis on the Jewishness of Jesus. Carter further develops Cone's emphasis on the Jewishness of Jesus in relation to what he calls the "unlikely convergence" between Barth and W.E.B. Du Bois.[9]

My purposes here require neither an exhaustive assessment of their interpretations nor a comprehensive response to their objections. I will simply comment, in passing and without argument, that there are good reasons for Cone and Carter to read Barth this way. However, there also are good reasons to read Barth differently. For example, his account of subjective reception of revelation through the outpouring of the Holy Spirit makes room for historical and contextual interpretation of the Word of God within the witness of particular Christian communities. This, in turn, makes way for an account of the prophetic witness of black faith.[10] This is *not* to say that the validity or value of black faith depends on whether or not it "fits" into Barth's theology. Quite the opposite! Should Barth's theology have no place for the prophetic witness of the historic black church, it would count against the validity and value of his theology.

With that in mind, I pick up where Cone and Carter leave off; I pick up where they leave Barth behind; I pick up their challenge to confront what Cone calls "theology's greatest sin: silence in the face of white supremacy."[11] To do so, I begin with Cone, Carter, and their engagement with Barth. I then turn to Barth's long-neglected *Ethics* lectures in which he explicitly—if only momentarily—breaks this theological silence. There, in a few fleeting paragraphs, Barth reflects on personal responsibility for social conflict, the racial and colonial inflections of such conflict, as well as the direct and indirect violence it entails. By drawing on this forgotten text, I will draw out the political implications of his theological critique of anthropocentrism in terms of an ideological critique of Eurocentrism. I will redraw the lines that all too often divide "confessional theology" from "political theology" in order to show that aspirations for political liberation can be served by theological tradition, and that fidelity to tradition includes a duty to confront domination. And I will argue that there is more to Cone's early Barthian affinity and Carter's more recent Barthian inquiry; Barth not only indirectly converges with them, he directly concurs with their condemnation of white racism.

I do so, *not* to return Cone and Carter to the Barthian fold. I do so rather to turn "Barthians" toward Cone and Carter, and to fold them into theological projects of liberation. I am less interested in convincing liberation theologians of Barth's merits than I am in convicting Barthian theologians of the demerits of ignoring social justice, and conscripting them into ongoing struggles for liberation. If those who think nothing of Barth in relation to such projects—or, worse, think of him negatively—come to think of him more and more positively, all the better. It is not necessary for liberation theologians to draw on Barth. But it is possible. However, for those who think highly of Barth, who think of themselves as "Barthian," and yet think little or less about liberation, things are rather different. To be faithful to Barth's legacy, and to be worthy of the name "Barthian," it is necessary to draw on liberation theology; not only as academic discourse, but as theopolitical praxis.

BARTH IN BLACK AND WHITE

James Cone's early reliance on Barth and later reluctance about Barth are equally well known. Cone first engages Barth in his master's thesis and doctoral dissertation. In his first two books, Cone adopts Barth's theology even as he adapts it to his own purposes. Just as Barth once said, "Jesus *is* the movement for social justice,"[12] Cone has said, "Jesus is Black."[13] If, for Barth, God is a being-in-action, for Cone God is a being-in-liberation. As Cone puts it, quoting Barth, "'God always takes God's stand unconditionally and passionately on this side: against the lofty and on behalf of the lowly; against those who already enjoy right and privilege, and on behalf of those who are denied and deprived of it.'"[14] For Barth and Cone alike, the God of the Bible is the God of the oppressed.

Cone's journey with Barth starts from their shared recognition of the biblical and theological imperative for political engagement. For Cone, "Barth's theology may serve as an example of how to relate theology to life. The whole of his theology represents a constant attempt to engage the Church in life situations."[15] Like his teacher, William Hordern, and in contrast to most North American Barthians, Cone reads Barth as political theologian, and not just a confessional theologian. Indeed, for Hordern and Cone, Barth is a political theologian *because* he is a confessional theologian. As Hordern explains, "Almost every one of his interpretations of major doctrines led him to conclude that political involvement is necessary for Christians."[16] For this reason, Cone remarks, "I have always thought that Barth was closer to me than to them [i.e., American Barthians]."[17] Writing in the midst of the South African Church Struggle, and introducing the essays collected in *On Reading Karl Barth in South Africa*, Charles Villa-Vicencio echoes Cone's judgment. "This exercise has led people to rediscover that Karl Barth is closer to us than are many Barthians indifferent to the struggle for social justice."[18]

This is *not* to say that Barth is the first or final source of Cone's theology. He is not. Criticisms of Cone's initial reliance on white theologians notwithstanding, from *Black Theology and Black Power* (1969) to *The Cross and the Lynching Tree* (2011), the people and practices of the historic black church are the heart and soul of his theology. In this, we can say of Cone what Cornel West says of Martin Luther King, Jr. West writes, "[T]he black church's influence on King's views is the most *primordial* and *decisive* source of his thought.... King's response to the Euro-American Christian academic world was to select those viewpoints that gave philosophical and theological articulation to deeply held themes and beliefs he acquired in the black church."[19] At several points in his career, Cone says much the same about himself. In *For My People*: "The sources for [black] theology are not found in Barth, Tillich, and Pannenberg. They are found in the spirituals, blues, and sayings of our people."[20] In *My Soul Looks Back*: "At no point did a European theologian, not even Barth, control what I said about the gospel and the black struggle for freedom. It was the other way around. Jesus defined by the Black experience and the Bible decided how I used European theology."[21] From first to last, and whether used to greater or lesser extent, Barth is simply a vessel for Cone's theology.

Cone's journey away from Barth departs from his recognition of the disparity between Nazi Germany and Jim Crow America. Though Cone sees Barth as a comrade in the struggle against injustice, he knows their struggles are profoundly different. Just a few sentences after Cone remarks about the utility of Barth's theology, he reflects on its futility in the context of black struggle. This futility was particularly acute for Cone in his teaching. As early as 1963, Cone began to ask, "What could Karl Barth mean for black students who had come from the cotton fields of Arkansas, Louisiana, and Mississippi, seeking to change the structure of their lives in a society that had defined *black* as nonbeing?"[22] Just as Wilhelm Herrmann's theology didn't "preach" in Barth's pulpit, Barth's theology didn't "teach" from Cone's lectern. Cone's internal skepticism about Barth's theology was only compounded by external criticisms of his own "ready-made" Barthianism that followed the 1969 publication of *Black Theology and Black Power*.[23] Like new wine in old wineskins, Cone found that his black theology burst its Barthian vessel.

Although he turned away from Barth as he returned to the sources of the historic black church, as Raymond Carr observes, Cone never turned *against* Barth.[24] Cone found it necessary to coordinate Barth's theology of revelation with Tillich's theology of correlation. Yet, Tillich did not supplant Barth.[25] In Cone's own words, "My use of Barth diminished in later books, but I continued to use the work of European theologians when it suited my purposes."[26] As he explains, "I was angry not with Barth but only with European and North American Barthians who used him to justify doing nothing about the struggle for justice."[27] In other words, Cone's complaint is as much about the ideology of Barthians as it is about Barth's methodology. He charges that, "Barthians have confused God-talk with white talk, and thus have failed to see that there is no real speech about God except in relationship to the liberation of the oppressed."[28] In this, Cone's later work is, in J. Kameron Carter's words, "beyond-Barthian," yet without being anti-Barthian.[29]

Carter himself engages Barth in a trio of works. In the first, *Race: A Theological Account*, he does so only indirectly as he engages Cone. In the second and third—a pair essays that build on his 2010 Martin Luther King, Jr. Lecture at Princeton—Carter directly engages Barth in conversation with W.E.B. Du Bois. In *Race*, Carter reads Cone's later works as a "Barthianism beyond Barth." For Carter, Cone remains Barthian in two important respects. First, he retains Barth's focus on the concrete historical action of God in Christ. Second, he refines that focus with a further emphasis on the Jewishness of the historical Jesus, which, in turn, redefines God's historical action as liberation. It is this refinement that Carter finds most compelling about Cone's theology, and which he develops in his own theology.[30] Yet, despite this refinement, Carter remains dissatisfied with Cone's account of race, and disappointed in its inability to surmount racism.

As it is Barth, rather than Cone, that is our subject here, I will set aside Carter's criticism of Cone, and instead focus on his direct engagement with Barth himself. For my purposes, what is most important is that, for Carter, "Cone saw in Barth's fight against German nationalism a struggle against whiteness that Barth *found difficult to in fact isolate and name* in these terms."[31] In both, the lecture and essays, Carter "complements and supplements" Barth's theological insights into anthropocentrism with Du Bois' political insights into Eurocentrism in order to isolate and name the theopolitical problem as the struggle against whiteness. In so doing, Carter proposes what we might call a "Barthianism beyond Cone."

The 2010 King Lecture is entitled, "An Unlikely Convergence: W.E.B. Du Bois, Karl Barth, and the Problem of the Imperial God-Man." Carter published two versions of this lecture in 2012. An abridged version bearing the title, "Between W.E.B. Du Bois and Karl Barth: The Problem of Modern Political Theology," appeared in *Race and Political Theology*.[32] A revised, and significantly expanded, version of the lecture bearing its original title appeared in *The New Centennial Review*.[33] Although there are differences between the two essays, beyond their length, they are unanimous in substance.

Carter describes what he calls "an unlikely convergence" between Du Bois, the American founder of the NAACP, and Barth, a leader of the German Confessing Church.

This convergence is "unlikely," for several reasons. First, the two were unaware of each other. As far as anyone knows, they neither met in person nor read one another's work. Second, methodologically and materially, they focus on radically different subjects. Du Bois is a sociologist of race and racism. Barth is a theologian of revelation and redemption. Third, Du Bois and Barth are divided by the "colonial difference."[34] Du Bois writes from the "underside of modernity" as a colonial subject, while Barth writes from above as a metropolitan subject.[35] Despite all this, Carter reveals that Barth and Du Bois converge in their attention to what he calls "the problem of modern political theology."[36]

This problem emerges amidst the crisis of the First World War. For Barth and Du Bois, this sociopolitical moment is simultaneously the crisis of what Carter describes as the "theological architecture of secular modernity."[37] That architecture was constructed through the centuries-long interrelation and coarticulation of Western Civilization and European Christendom. As Carter explains at length in *Race*, this theopolitical project commences in the Patristic era with theological supersessionism by which Christianity severs itself from its Jewish roots. It consolidates itself around 1492 with the simultaneous *Reconquista* of the Iberian Peninsula and Columbian conquest of the West Indies, which, together, secure a Christian–European interior (metropole) over and against a pagan–barbarian exterior (colony). It culminates in the revolutions of the Enlightenment in which Christendom becomes secularized and racialized as Western Civilization.[38]

Carter argues that it is the initial theological *disidentification* of Israel as the bearer of God's purposes in history that paves the way for the eventual sociopolitical *misidentification* of other nations as the bearer of those purposes. Over time, this supersessionism, in turn, displaces the eschatological horizon of hope in the kingdom of God, and replaces it with an historical horizon of hope in the occidental-colonial civilization of the West. "As such," concludes Carter, "Western man is a new instance of what in classical Christian theology is called 'the Christological problem' in that the problem of Imperial Man is in fact the problem of the imperial God-Man. He carries out a 'soteriological' or 'missionizing' project of salvation—the civilizing mission of the West—aimed at ruling the world."[39] In the ashes and aftermath of the First World War, the plausibility and viability of this civilizational project was in crisis. It is this crisis to which Du Bois and Barth respond.

Barth confronts this crisis in his early theology leading up to the two editions of his *Romans* commentary (1919 and 1922). For him, the crisis is primarily theological and ecclesiological. He focuses on the complicity of bourgeois morality and Protestant religiosity in supporting the nationalism and militarism of the so-called religious war experience. The wider imperial-colonial context of the crisis remains peripheral. Even so, Carter notes that in several letters and lectures Barth makes remarks like this. "[T]*his* god is *not* God. This god is not righteous. This god cannot prevent their believers—all the excellent European and American people of culture and pilgrimage and progress, all the valiantly assiduous citizens and pious Christians—from falling upon one another with fire and sword to the amazement and derision of the poor heathens in India and Africa."[40] With observations like these, Carter says that Barth "unmask[s] how the West was functioning as an *eschaton* or a utopia," but only in the sense of a generic anthropocentric idolatry.[41] Barth stumbles into the racial and colonial dimensions of the crisis inadvertently, without consciously recognizing them for what they are, or explicitly reflecting on them as the Eurocentric ideology of whiteness.

Du Bois confronts the racial and colonial dimensions of the crisis self-consciously and explicitly. In his collection of essays *Darkwater*, Du Bois emphasizes the role of intra-European colonial competition in causing the war. Appearing between the first and second editions of Barth's *Romans*, Carter reads these essays as another "counternarrative of the origins of the war and the West" that "lodged the war within an imperial framework with Africa, not the North Atlantic world, at the center."[42] This additional counternarrative provides the larger context and longer history of the war that "complement and supplement Barth's analysis."[43] It also accents the role the colonial difference makes for their respective analyses of the crisis.

For Barth, the war contradicted the highest ideals of Protestant liberalism and religious socialism. He was especially shocked and dismayed by what he calls "that black day" in 1914 when ninety-three leading German intellectuals signed their names to a manifesto supporting the Kaiser's declaration of war.[44] Barth's biographer, Eberhard Busch, reports his remarks from a letter the following year. "'It was like the twilight of the gods when I saw the reaction of Harnack, Herrmann, Rade, Eucken, and company to the new situation,' and discovered how religion and scholarship could be changed completely 'into intellectual 42cm canons.'"[45] In other words, the war theology of his teachers revealed the hidden pagan foundations of Christendom.

For Du Bois, the war consummated the deepest logic of European imperialism and Western colonialism. He observes, "This is not Europe gone mad; this is not aberration or insanity; this *is* Europe; this seeming Terrible is the real soul of white culture."[46] Du Bois concurs with Barth that the war is a "terrible overturning of civilization."[47] However, for him, that fateful day in 1914 was not a black day, but a *white* day. Indeed, as Carter emphasizes, quoting Du Bois, "[T]he war manifests 'the utter failure of white religion.'"[48] For those marked by the colonial difference, the weaponization of Christianity was nothing new. As Carter says, it was all too consistent that "the darker peoples of the planet whose identities were once tied to slave ships are now tied to warships."[49]

Their differences notwithstanding, Carter argues that, "Du Bois and Barth converged in considering the modern condition and the contemporary problem of the human."[50] Both wrestle against the false religiosity and failed eschatology of Western civilization. Each, in their own way, gestures toward recovery of the Jewishness of Jesus as a solution to the problem of political theology, as does Cone. In this convergence, Carter recommends that we imagine Barth and Du Bois as engaging in an "analogical collaboration" that diagnoses the Promethean *libido dominandi* of whiteness.[51] More importantly, he commends that we ourselves reimagine theology as the praxis of the Judean *corpus Christi* of Christ's Jewish flesh. To these ends, Carter concludes *Race* with the exhortation to "reconceive theology beyond the racial imagination that has become its inner architecture . . ., [which] entails, as Barth said, 'beginning from the beginning,' that is, from the underside of modernity."[52]

Together, Cone and Carter paint a clear picture of Barth in black and white. As Carter demonstrates, Barth himself sees the world as a metropolitan European who was "caught inside nationalizing and imperial whiteness" and unable to "fully grasp the shape of this system."[53] As Cone illustrates, Barthians see Barth from within the anesthetizing objectivity of academic respectability. This means that the complaint against Barth is twofold. Carter wishes that Barth had said more. For him, "Barth has penetrated deeply into the order of things." Yet, "One wishes that he would have meditated longer on the problem of mastery and slavery—especially the slavery side of the problem."[54] For all his analysis and insight, Barth remained inarticulate about the theological problem of Eurocentric ideology. He failed to give an account of whiteness. He commits theology's greatest sin, if only as a sin of uncomprehending omission. Cone wishes that Barthians would do more. For him, "[T]he real test . . . is found in whether [they] are led to be involved on the same side in the historical struggles for freedom."[55] For all their talk about divine justification, Barthians—for the most part—do nothing about human injustice. They refuse to be held to account for white supremacy. They unrepentantly commit theology's greatest sin.

BARTH ON EMPIRE, CAPITAL, AND RACE

Carter is right to wish that Barth had said more. Yet, Barth does say something more or less identical to what Du Bois says. Reflecting on the causes of the First World War in his 1928 *Ethics* lectures, Barth observes:

> As the will of a people, the will to power means: we will . . . we will because we need, and we need because we will. And so, we will: coal and potash, ore and petroleum, as well as markets, trade agreements, lines of communication, *colonies*; and, in order to secure ourselves in the next war: such boundaries that are at the same time natural lines of defense; and, finally, as the crown and sum of it all: we need and will, will and need, prestige, world standing, and respect for our colors as a prerequisite for further future actualization of our will to power.[56]

Here, Barth and Du Bois not only analogically converge. They analytically concur. For Barth and Du Bois alike, the war was, in large part, a conflict over the resources and respect provided by colonies. The First World War between the great powers was a contest of the colonial will to power.

Barth makes this observation in Paragraph Seven, "The Command of Life," where he takes up questions of war and killing in the context of divine command and the doctrine of creation. As Creator, Barth says that God wills the life of the human creature. This means that God commands each creature's "will to life" and every creature's "reverence for [the] life" of others.[57] However, as humanity turns away from God, they turn against one another. Their will to life becomes the will to power. Most obviously, the will to power expresses itself in direct termination of life. Less obviously—and, for precisely that reason, all the more dangerously—the will to power also expresses itself in what Barth calls indirect "obstruction" of life.[58] Whether directly or indirectly, by destruction or obstruction, the natural *conatus* of the creature tends toward the diabolical *libido dominandi* of the master.

Barth is especially concerned about this less obvious, but more dangerous, obstruction of life. He depicts it as a race in which "we all are running for our lives."[59] We cannot live without running. Yet, we cannot run without competing with others. What's more, the course on which we compete is not level ground. Barth tells us that it is a "slippery slope" on which "our lives are at stake . . . our entire lives."[60] Whether directly or indirectly, intentionally or incidentally, he observes, "I cannot compete in the serious race of life without thereby obstructing the life of another, impairing them in their movement and forestalling them, and therefore not without placing myself on that slippery slope at whose lower edge humanity becomes the butcher of humanity."[61] In this, he laments, "As I live my life for myself, I necessarily live against others."[62] We can neither avoid the mortal competition of the will to life, nor evade the moral temptation of the will to power.

This lamentation is not permission for unbridled exercise of the will to power. Barth is not endorsing a "live and let die" attitude. He is enjoining greater responsibility for the fact that our lives are caught up with the deaths of others, whether or not we know or intend it. That other competitors live against us even as we live against them means that, like soldiers, we occupy positions of moral equality.[63] This does not mean that either of us occupies a position of moral impunity. That the lethal consequences of our will to life are not the primary end of our action, but only its secondary effects, in no way relieves their harm. Nor, for Barth, does it remove our responsibility for their wrong. He unflinchingly asserts, "If I beat a competitor in this contest . . . [s]omething has happened that is undeniably and fundamentally at the same level as if I were to kill him." Polemic and hyperbole aside, Barth unrelentingly insists, "It is not excluded, in any case, that my victorious competition at least approximates the killing of my competitor."[64] While not strictly equivalent, our responsibility for competitive obstruction of life approximates our responsibility for combative destruction of life.

The primary mode of competitive obstruction is appropriation. As an expression of the will to life, appropriation is activity to satisfy our creaturely needs, both natural and social. While there are some "natural limits" to our satiation and satisfaction, Barth recognizes that "this radius of my will to life can obviously be extreme in regard to what I lay aside for future use."[65] As appropriation surpasses what he describes as the "hand to mouth" subsistence of the daily bread included as a petition of the Lord's Prayer, it becomes surplus, reserve, and excess. Sometimes this is simply the prudent storing of a measure of the harvest for coming seasons. Other times it is the indulgent stockpiling of immeasurable wealth for coming generations. While Barth hesitates to specify just where prudence passes into indulgence, he does identify a distinction between appropriation based on need and that based on greed. "Since the pure will to power, which is not oriented to need, is also unquestionably a form of the will to life, and since it too operates in the form of appropriation (e.g., as capitalist imperialism), a natural limit cannot be drawn for this second possibility of appropriation."[66] The greedy will to power is itself an expression of the needy will to life.

Surplus appropriation may not have a natural limit. It does have moral limits. Barth identifies capitalist expropriation and imperialist exploitation as paradigmatic indications that the acquisitive will to life has devolved into the excessive and dominative will to power. This devolution is not simply a function of individual action. It is cumulative and collective. Barth explains, "The less my life resembles that of Robinson Crusoe, the more it takes place in coexistence with others, the more that coexistence itself turns out to be a whole system, or rather, chaos, of mutually overlapping circles with mutually intersecting, impeding, and infringing lines of action."[67] As Rowan Williams puts it, we are "willy-nilly involved in 'structural violence' in economic, political, religious, and private systems of relationship."[68] That we are entangled in this violence chaotically and systemically does not mean we are hapless victims of circumstance. It means we must diligently and vigilantly assess them.

Barth illustrates this with two socioeconomic examples: an inheritor and an investor. The inheritor asks, "As the legal heir of part of a family fortune, what do I have to do with the manner—it may be that I am the descendant of former robber-barons—in which this fortune came to be, perhaps in time immemorial?" They answer, "I do not actually take it from anyone; I have inherited only by law and right." The investor similarly asks, "Or, what do I, as a large or small pensioner, have to do with the manner in which the interest on which I am living is acquired, perhaps over there in America, or with enterprises into which my bank regards it as advantageous to invest my capital?" They too answer, "I merely take what belongs to me by God and by right." Like the inheritor and the investor, we all participate in "a whole series of delegated relationships" that constitute our society, and which give us the illusion, but only the illusion, that we "play the harmless role of the spectator."[69]

Barth rejects this illusion in no uncertain terms. He reminds us, "Again, the command of God does not ask about our nearer or more distant participation, but rather about our participation or non-participation in the activity." For Barth, the relative degree of directness or indirectness is, at most, a secondary consideration; so too our greater or lesser personal motivation for that participation. "Responsibility also does not diminish if my competing, perhaps, does not express my individual egoism but rather *collective* egoism." For Barth, "[The command] makes us responsible for our individual activity, not apart from, but intertwined with the activity of others in which it is in fact located." He concludes, "The activity of others through which we enjoy or take its fruits—as Adam ate the fruit that Eve had cut (Genesis 3:6)—becomes our own activity."[70] Whether we take part in a collective action, an action is undertaken on our behalf, or we partake of any benefits that result from an action, morally speaking it is *our* action.

Although Barth's rendering of action and intention lacks the systematic precision of Thomas Aquinas or Elizabeth Anscombe, his exemplification of the ends and effects of these actions aligns with theirs. Aquinas points out the fact that, "Nothing hinders one act from having two effects, only one of which is intended, while the other is beside the intention."[71] Anscombe points up the fact that, despite this possibility, "[A]n act does not merely have many descriptions, under some of which it is indeed not intentional: it has several under which it is intentional. So you cannot choose just one of these, and claim to have excluded the others by that."[72] Put more sharply, as she often does, the intention and effects of an action cannot be defined by "making a little speech to yourself: 'What I mean to be doing is. . . .'"[73] For Barth and Anscombe alike, the morally relevant sense of intention is not the internal mental state that motivates an action. It is the external state of affairs that eventuates from an action.

Like Anscombe, Barth denies that little speeches like those of the inheritor and investor can extricate our actions from those of their effects that, in Anscombe's words, are "an intrinsic certainty" and/or "a very great likelihood" given the nature of the case. Barth's heir says "lawful inheritance" rather than "ill-gotten gain." But their saying so doesn't make it so. Neither does ours. For this reason, Barth insists that the ethical question of reverence for life amidst the competition of the will to life and the domination of the will to power must be asked and answered "at every step."[74] This question is especially urgent when, "I do not at all think that my striving, my grasping and getting—conditioned by my will to life—imply any measure of strife, interference, or theft." Barth is all too aware that, "Our will to life surely is clever enough in ninety-nine out of one hundred cases that we do not first reflect about it, but rather allow ourselves to act joyfully, shamelessly, according to the inspiration of the moment and situation, since we do not know what we are doing."[75] Such action may be thoughtless. It is not blameless.

Ignorance is not innocence. Nor is it excuse. This is especially true when, as Barth says, "We suddenly are awakened by soft crying or loud protest from those around us who clearly seem to feel that they are the victim of our naive vitality."[76] He mocks the little speeches we offer in reply to such cries and protests. "'How is it possible?' we ask, and then we say, 'Dear God, it was not meant viciously,' as if it had fallen from the clouds." He chastises us for these replies. "God's command is not concerned with the distinction between conscious and unconscious, intentional or unintentional. . . . [I]f our action *has* the character of combative action, then it has it." Neither our confusion and consternation, nor God's justification and sanctification of us, can change this fact. Barth, thus, demands that, "Ethical reflection can mean nothing other than the destruction of naiveté."[77]

Yet, even this is not enough. Even when "we now *know* more or less clearly what we are doing," Barth warns, "we must still be on guard against a whole series of mystifications, deceptions, and manipulations by means of which we continually wish to rid ourselves of responsibility for the combative character of the pursuit of our will to life."[78] Although Barth does not explicitly mention the word "ideology" here, his discussion throughout this Paragraph does. If ideology (to use Althusser's definition) is, in part, "an imaginary relationship of individuals to the material conditions of their existence," then these mystifications, deceptions, and manipulations are ideological.[79] In order to take responsibility for the actual effects and consequences of our action, ethical reflection must make visible the real relationships in which we stand. In other words, ethical reflection requires ideology critique.

Within this train of thought about the will to life, and with these thoughts about the colonial will to power, Barth's concurrence with Du Bois becomes deeper still. At the center of Barth's reflections about our responsibility for the obstruction of life is this remarkable statement:

> When, as members of the white race, we all enjoy every possible intellectual and material advantage on the basis of the superiority of one race and, therefore, the subjection of many others, and on the use, that, for centuries, our race has made of both, I myself may not have bent a single hair of any Africans or Indians. Who knows? I may be quite friendly, perhaps, even missions-friendly. Yet, I am a member of the white race, who, as a whole, certainly have manipulated the possibility of appropriation against them quite radically. In whatever distance and indirectness that I participate in whatever sins may have been committed fifty or one hundred years ago in Africa and China, is it not the case that Europe would not be what it is, and, likewise, I would not be what I am, if this expansion had not taken place?[80]

Here, Barth links the three dimensions of colonial domination: capitalism, imperialism, and racism. He also links past collective action with present personal responsibility. Just as his hypothetical inheritor and investor cannot deny their ill-gotten monetary inheritance and interest, whites cannot deny the undue social and material advantages of expropriation and exploitation. Whether hypothetical or historical, the issue in cases like these is *neither* the directness nor indirectness of our agency, *nor* the temporal nearness or farness of these events. It is rather the material concreteness of their social, cultural, political, and financial advantages.

Barth agrees with liberation theologians that protestations like "I never owned any slaves!" or "I wasn't there when the conquistadors stole the land!" are wholly beside the point. Objections like Oliver O'Donovan's, that, "'Slavery' has existed, for most of the last millennium, *only on the fringes of civilisation*, as a colonial indulgence or as a sub-political pathology," are both blatant distortions of historical fact and flagrant derelictions of moral duty.[81] Slavery certainly was pathological. But, in the context of O'Donovan's own society, Great Britain, it just as certainly was neither peripheral nor non-political. Colonial expropriation and exploitation of nearly a quarter of the earth's land was at the heart of the Empire for three centuries. As Barth himself observes in his lectures on *Protestant Theology in the Nineteenth Century*, "Nothing is more characteristic of the extension of the European horizon and power than the fact that the attraction of overseas possessions, and, indeed, what made them possible, was primarily the slave trade and the possession of slaves. Moral scruples, let alone Christian ones, were so little in evidence that it was even possible to say of the flourishing town of Liverpool, without contradiction, that it was built on the skulls of negroes."[82] That "I wasn't there" or that "I didn't do that" is irrelevant to the fact that I inhabit a society and inherit an economy built on the backs of slaves and by the blood of indigenous peoples.

Barth's reflections not only concur with those of Du Bois, but with those of Cone as well. Throughout Cone's career, critics—especially, but not exclusively, *white* critics—have charged that he emphasizes liberation to the exclusion of reconciliation: that he lifts up justice, but leaves out love. These criticisms have been particularly acute on the question of revolutionary violence. Cone's response has been consistently astute in questioning the presuppositions of his critics. For example, in *God of the Oppressed*, he first remarks, "These are favorite *white* questions, and it is significant that they are almost always addressed to the oppressed and almost never to the oppressor."[83] Cone then reverses the question, and asks, "Why didn't we hear from so-called nonviolent Christians when black people were *violently* enslaved, *violently* lynched, and *violently* ghettoized in the name of freedom and democracy?"[84] He continues, "When whites ask me, 'Are you for violence?' my rejoinder is: '*Whose* violence? Richard Nixon or his victims? The Mississippi State Police or the students at Jackson State?'"[85] Like Cone, Barth refuses to excuse "white-collar violence" simply because it enjoys the good name of order and the good conscience of law.[86]

CONCLUSION

I will not make too much of this text. It is but one passage in Barth's massive corpus, and a brief one at that. It is an early passage that, sadly and surprisingly, is not repeated or reiterated in later works. Still, I will not make too little of it either. This text is a provocative moment of clarity about the connection between idolatry and ideology. It is indicative of wider ethical themes and deeper political resources in Barth's theology. It is a suggestive point of contact between postliberal confessional theology and postcolonial political theology. What we make of this text in the context of Barth's theology matters far less than what we make of it in the conduct of our own theology. The historical and hermeneutical task of getting Barth right is pointless apart from the further ethical and political task of setting the world right. As Marx said of philosophy, we must say of theology: its purpose is not simply to describe the world, but to change it. Or, as Barth often said, its purpose is to speak and act in analogical correspondence with the change that God in Christ has made in the world.

To that end, this essay, like Barth's text, is only a starting point, an interpretive point of departure for further constructive efforts. Those efforts must await another occasion. For now, I can only suggest a few additional texts in Barth's later *Dogmatics* that, as Carter puts it of Du Bois, complement and supplement this early text from the *Ethics*. Though incomplete at the time of his death, "The Doctrine of Reconciliation" includes several parallel reflections on structural injustice and personal responsibility. I will mention just two.

In Paragraph Seventy-Two, "The Service of the Community," Barth again implicates both the individual Christian and the Christian community in the disorders of their society. As they go about their service to the less fortunate, he says that they must recognize that poverty is caused by disordered social, economic, and political structures. They also must realize their complicity with these structures. Barth asks, "Do they not also belong to the human society in which those disorders came about? Have they not contributed to their creation, at least by their silence?" He challenges that relief of suffering is not enough.

They must not refrain from speaking this knowledge, communicating it to the community so that they raise their voice, calling upon the world with their proclamation of the Gospel to reflect on social injustice and its consequences, and to change those conditions and relations. The open *word* of Christian social criticism will have to intervene into this situation precisely for the sake of the Christian deed.[87]

Just as faith without works is dead, works of service without words of justice are a dead end.

Barth returns to these issues one last time in the final part of the *Dogmatics: The Christian Life*.[88] There, in Paragraph Seventy-Eight, "The Struggle for Human Righteousness," he again confronts "the demonism of politics [that] consists in the always and as such inhuman idea of *empire*."[89] He once more challenges "the close relative" of the imperial Leviathan, "Mammon."[90] And he calls into question ideology through which a "human ideal becomes an idol."[91] These, Barth tells us, are the lordless powers that revolt against God. We who pray the Lord's Prayer must revolt against their revolt. As we ask for the kingdom to come and the divine will to be done on earth as it is in heaven, we commit ourselves to act accordingly. For Barth, "[We] cannot pray this petition aright without in so doing being propelled into corresponding action of [our] own."[92] We act according to what we ask, not in spite of our human limitations, but in light of them. We act for the "little righteousness" that corresponds to God's "great righteousness," those "penultimate liberations" that anticipate the ultimate liberation of the heavenly kingdom, and that "little justice" that is an analogy to the great work of divine justification.[93]

While Cone is right to say that Barth doesn't always clarify the social and political implications of his theological positions, I have shown that, in these texts from the early *Ethics* and the late *Dogmatics*, he does identify concrete conclusions about capitalism, imperialism, and racism. On this basis, I have argued that interpretive and constructive work on Barth must take these conclusions into account and draw out their further implications. Although he himself does not say so, we may say that the generic anthropocentrism that is the object of *his* theological critique of idolatry is nothing other than the specific Eurocentrism that must be the object *our* political critique of ideology.

Whether or not Barth himself would embrace these recommendations, I cannot say for certain. I suspect he would. Of all those he met during his post-retirement lecture tour of the United States, he reported that Civil Rights activists William Stringfellow, Anna Hedgeman, and Martin Luther King, Jr. impressed him the most.[94] Toward the end of that tour, he remarked, "If I myself were an American citizen, and a Christian and a theologian, I would try to develop an American theology of freedom."[95] If the break from European liberal theology was the *terminus a quo* for Barth's theology, the breakthrough of postcolonial liberation theologies is the *terminus a quem* for twenty-first-century Barthian theologies.

NOTES

1. See, Karl Barth, *Der Römerbrief* (Bern: G.A. Bäschlin, 1919), 508. Cf. Karl Barth, *The Epistle to the Romans*, trans. Edwyn Clement Hoskyns (London: Oxford University Press, 1933), 483. Translations throughout are my own. When available, citations indicate English pagination followed by German.

2. See, Timothy Gorringe, *Karl Barth: Against Hegemony* (Oxford: Oxford University Press, 1999); Friedrich-Wilhelm. Marquardt, *Theologie Und Sozialismus: Das Beispiel Karl Barths* (München: Kaiser, 1972). Barth's commitment to democratic socialism and engagement with Marxism are the usual "point of contact" with liberation theologies. See, e.g., George

Hunsinger. "Karl Barth and Liberation Theology." *Journal of Religion* 63, no. 3 (1983): 247–263.

3. See, James H. Cone, *For My People: Black Theology and the Black Church* (Maryknoll, NY: Orbis Books, 1984); James H. Cone, *My Soul Looks Back* (Maryknoll, NY: Orbis Books, 1986); and J. Kameron Carter, *Race: A Theological Account* (Oxford University Press: Oxford, 2008), 157 Cone, James H. (1997), *Black Theology and Black Power*, Maryknoll, NY: Orbis Books 193; J. Kameron Carter, "An Unlikely Convergence: W.E.B. Du Bois, Karl Barth, and the Problem of the Imperial God-Man," *New Centennial Review* 11, no. 3 (2012), 167–224; J. Kameron Carter, "Between W.E.B. Du Bois and Karl Barth: The Problem of Modern Political Theology," in *Race and Political Theology*, ed. Vincent W. Lloyd, 83–11 (Stanford, CA: Stanford University Press, 2012).

4. For assessments and criticisms of Marquardt's arguments, see George Hunsinger ed., *Karl Barth and Radical Politics* (Philadelphia, PA: Westminster Press, 1976).

5. See, e.g., Karl Barth, "The Christian Community and the Civil Community," in *Community, State, and Church: Three Essays*, trans. E.M. Delacour (Eugene, OR: Wipf & Stock Publishers, 2004), 156/196–97, 169/112, and 184/130.

6. James Cone, *God of the Oppressed* (Mayknoll, NY: Orbis Books, 1997), 107.

7. Cone, *God of the Oppressed*, 93.

8. Cone, *God of the Oppressed*, 133.

9. See, Carter, "Unlikely Convergence" and "Between Du Bois and Barth."

10. See, *Church Dogmatics 1/2: The Doctrine of the Word of God*, trans. George Thomson and Harold Knight, Edinburgh: T&T Clark, 1956. Subsequent citations will be by volume, part-volume, paragraph, and section (e.g., CD I/2 §§20–24).

11. James Cone, "Theology's Greatest Sin: Silence in the Face of White Supremacy," *Union Seminary Quarterly Review* 55, no. 3–4 (2001), 1–14.

12. See, Karl Barth, "Jesus Christ and the Movement for Social Justice," in *Karl Barth: Theologian of Freedom*, ed. Clifford Green (Minneapolis, MN: Fortress Press, 1991), 99/386–387.

13. Cone, *God of the Oppressed*, 122.

14. James Cone, *Black Theology and Black Power* (Mayknoll, NY: Orbis Books, 1997), 45 quoting CD II/1 §30.2, 386/434. Cf. Karl Barth, "Poverty," in *Against the Stream: Shorter Post-War Writings 1946–1952*, ed. Ronald Gregor Smith, trans. E.M. Delacour (London: SCM Press, 1954), 245.

15. Cone, *Black Power*, 87.

16. William Hordern, "Barth as Political Thinker," *The Christian Century* March 26, 1969, 411.

17. Cone, *My Soul Looks Back*, 45.

18. Charles Villa-Vicencio, *On Reading Karl Barth in South Africa* (Grand Rapids, MI: Eerdmans Publishing, 1988), 12.

19. Cornel West, "Prophetic Christian as Organic Intellectual: Martin Luther King, Jr." in *The Cornel West Reader* (New York: Basic Civitas Books) 1999, 429.

20. Cone, *For My People*, 117–118.

21. Cone, *My Soul Looks Back*, 83.

22. Cone, *God of the Oppressed*, 5.

23. See, J. Deotis Roberts, *A Black Political Theology* (Louisville, KY: Westminster John Knox Press, 2005), 20. Cf. Cecil Cone, "The Identity Crisis in Black Theology: An Investigation of the Tensions Created By Efforts to Provide a Theological Interpretation of Black Religion in the Works of Joseph Washington, James Cone, and J. Deotis Roberts," PhD dissertation, Emory University, 1974), 49–96.

24. See Raymond Carr, "Barth and Cone in Dialogue on Revelatin and Freedom: An Analysis of James Cone's Critical Appropriation of Barthian Theology," PhD dissertation, Graduate Theological Union, 2011), 1–7, 29–39, and 307–311.
25. See Carr, "Barth and Cone," 53, 220–222, and especially 266–283.
26. Cone, *My Soul Looks Back*, 82.
27. Ibid., 45.
28. James Cone, *A Black Theology of Liberation* (Maryknoll, NY: Orbis Books, 1990), 83.
29. Carter, *Race*, 164.
30. See ibid., 160–164.
31. Carter, *Race*, 419 n10 emphasis added.
32. Carter, "Between Du Bois and Barth."
33. Carter, "Unlikely Convergence."
34. See, e.g., Walter Mignolo, "The Geopolitics of Knowledge and the Colonial Difference," *South Atlantic Quarterly* 101, no. 1 (2002), 57–96.
35. See, e.g., Linda Alcoff and Eduardo Mendieta ed., *Thinking from the Underside of History: Enrique Dussel's Philosophy of Liberation* (Norwich: Rowman & Littlefield Publishers, 2000).
36. Carter, "An Unlikely Convergence," 172.
37. Carter, "Between Du Bois and Barth," 83.
38. See, Carter, *Race*, 79–121.
39. Carter, "Between Du Bois and Barth," 84.
40. Karl Barth, "The Righteousness of God," in *The Word of God and Theology* trans. Amy Marga (London: T&T Clark, 2011), 11/240–241 quoted in Carter, "Between Du Bois and Barth," 91.
41. Carter, "Between Du Bois and Barth," 93.
42. Carter, "An Unlikely Convergence," 203.
43. Carter, "Between Du Bois and Barth," 98.
44. Karl Barth, "The Humanity of God," in *The Humanity of God*, trans. John Newton Thomas and Thomas Wieser (Richmond, VA: John Knox Press, 1960), 14/6.
45. Busch, 81 quoting Letter to W. Spoendlin 1/4/1915.
46. W.E.B. Du Bois, *Darkwater: Voices From Within the Veil* (New York: Oxford University Press, 2007), 39.
47. W.E.B. Du Bois, "The African Roots of War," *The Atlantic Monthly* May 1915, 707.
48. Carter, "Between Du Bois and Barth," 99, quoting Du Bois, *Darkwater*, 36.
49. Ibid., 98.
50. Ibid., 84.
51. Ibid., 84.
52. Carter, *Race*, 379.
53. Carter, "Between Du Bois and Barth," 86.
54. Ibid., 97.
55. Cone, *God of the Oppressed*, 93.
56. Karl Barth, *Ethics,* trans. Geoffrey W. Bromiley (New York: Seabury Press, 1981) §7.3, 159/266 (emphasis added).

57. Barth, *Ethics* §7.3, 117/193.
58. Barth, *Ethics* §7.3, 161/270.
59. Barth, *Ethics* §7.3, 161/271.
60. Barth, *Ethics* §7.3, 162/273.
61. Barth, *Ethics* §7.3, 162–163/273.
62. Barth, *Ethics* §7.3, 163/274.
63. See, Michael Walzer, *Just and Unjust Wars: A Moral Argument with Historical Illustrations* (New York: Basic Books, 2006), 34–37.
64. Barth, *Ethics* §7.3, 162/272.
65. Barth, *Ethics* §7.3, 163/273.
66. Barth, *Ethics* §7.3, 163/274.
67. Barth, *Ethics* §7.3, 163/274.
68. Rowan Williams, *Resurrection: Interpreting the Easter Gospel* (Cleveland: Pilgrim Press, 2004), 73.
69. Barth, *Ethics* §7.3, 165/277.
70. Barth, *Ethics* §7.3, 165/277–278.
71. Thomas Aquinas, *Summa Theologica* (Notre Dame, IN: Christian Classics, 1981), II.II.64.7.
72. G.E.M. Anscombe, "Action, Intention, and Double-Effect," in *Human Life, Action, and Ethics* (St Andrews: Imprint Academic, 2006), 223.
73. G.E.M. Anscombe, "War and Murder," in *Nuclear Weapons: A Catholic Response*, ed. Walter Stein (New York: Sheed and Ward, 1961).
74. Barth, *Ethics* §7.3, 163/275.
75. Barth, *Ethics* §7.3, 163/274–275.
76. Barth, *Ethics* §7.3, 163/275.
77. Barth, *Ethics* §7.3, 164/275.
78. Barth, *Ethics* §7.3, 164/276.
79. Louis Althusser, "Ideology and Ideological State Apparatuses," in *Lenin and Philosophy and Other Essays* trans. Ben Brewster (New York: Monthly Review Press, 2001), 109.
80. Barth, *Ethics* §7.3, 164–165/276–277.
81. Oliver O'Donovan. *The Desire of the Nations: Rediscovering the Roots of Political Theology* (Cambridge: Cambridge University Press, 1996), 184.
82. Karl Barth, *Protestant Theology in the Nineteenth Century: Its History and Prehistory* trans. Brian Cozens and John Bowden (Grand Rapids, MI: Eerdmans Publishing, 2002), 24/21.
83. Cone, *God of the Oppressed*, 179.
84. Ibid., 179–180.
85. Ibid., 180.
86. Ibid., 200.
87. Karl Barth, *Church Dogmatics IV/3.2: The Doctrine of Reconciliation,* trans. George Thomson and Harold Knight (Edinburgh: T&T Clark, 1962), 892/1023.
88. Karl Barth, *The Christian Life: Church Dogmatics Volume IV/4 Lecture Fragments,* trans. Geoffrey W. Bromiley (Edinburgh: T&T Clark, 1981).
89. Barth, CD IV/4 §78.2, 220/374.

90. Barth, CD IV/4 §78.2, 222/379.
91. Barth, CD IV/4 §78.2, 224/383.
92. Barth, CD IV/4 §78.1, 213/362.
93. Barth, CD IV/4 §78.4, 270/467–468.
94. Karl Barth, "Evangelical Theology in the Nineteenth Century," in *The Humanity of God* trans. John Newton Thomas and Thomas Wieser (Richmond, VA: John Knox Press, 1960), viii–ix.
95. Karl Barth, "Podium Discussion at Chicago," in *Gespräche 1959–1962* GA IV.25, ed. Eberhard Busch (1995), 489/279.

SELECT BIBLIOGRAPHY

Barth, Karl (1933), *The Epistle to the Romans*, trans. Edwyb Clement Hoskyns, London: Oxford University Press.
Barth, Karl (1954), *Against the Stream: Shorter Post-War Writings 1946–1952*, ed. Ronald Gregor Smith, trans. E.M. Delacour, London: SCM Press.
Barth, Karl (1956), *Church Dogmatics 1/2: The Doctrine of the Word of God*, trans. by George Thomson and Harold Knight, Edinburgh: T&T Clark.
Barth, Karl (1962), *Church Dogmatics IV/3.2: The Doctrine of Reconciliation*, trans. George Thomson and Harold Knight, Edinburgh: T&T Clark.
Barth, Karl (1981), *Church Dogmatics Volume IV/4: The Christian Life, Lecture Fragments*, trans. Geoffrey W. Bromiley, Edinburgh: T&T Clark.
Barth, Karl (1981), *Ethics*, trans. Geoffrey W. Bromiley, New York: Seabury Press.
Barth, Karl (2004), *Community, State, and Church: Three Essays*, trans. E.M. Delacour, Eugene, OR: Wipf & Stock Publishers.
Cone, James H. (1984), *For My People: Black Theology and the Black Church*, Maryknoll, NY: Orbis Books.
Cone, James H. (1986), *My Soul Looks Back*, Maryknoll, NY: Orbis Books.
Cone, James H. (1990), *A Black Theology of Liberation*, Maryknoll, NY: Orbis Books.
Cone, James H. (1997), *Black Theology and Black Power*, Maryknoll, NY: Orbis Books.
Cone, James H. (1997), *God of the Oppressed*, Maryknoll, NY: Orbis Books.
Du Bois, W.E.B. (2007), *Darkwater: Voices from Within the Veil*, New York: Oxford University Press.
Gorringe, Timothy (1999), *Karl Barth: Against Hegemony*, Oxford: Oxford University Press.
Hunsinger, George (1983), "Karl Barth and Liberation Theology," *Journal of Religion* 63, no. 3, 247–263.
Hunsinger, George, ed. (1976), *Karl Barth and Radical Politics*, Philadelphia: Westminter Press.
Karter, J. Cameron (2008), *Race: A Theological Account*, Oxford: Oxford University Press.

CHAPTER TWENTY-EIGHT

New Directions in Protestant Social Ethics

EMILY J. DUMLER-WINCKLER[1]

INTRODUCTION

Until recently, the sub-field of Protestant social ethics has not been sufficiently retrospective. The prospects for this tradition, I suggest, depend on a better grasp of the history of this particular form of Christian ethics.[2] That is, the way forward requires overcoming a selective memory and collective amnesia. Because certain forms of forgetfulness have plagued the field a number of basic questions remain underdeveloped. What exactly is "Protestant social ethics"? What narratives have been told about it and are they sufficient? Which figures have (or have not) shaped its legacy? Why these? Which significant figures have been forgotten along the way? What distinguishes Protestant social ethics from Protestant ethics broadly conceived? What is its relation to political and moral theology—specifically liberation, feminist, womanist, and black theologies—and to its surrogate discipline, social science? Given the rise of modern Catholic social thought, what, if anything, is distinctively Protestant about it? How does and how ought it relate to other faith, or non-faith traditions? What of this particular tradition is dead, living, or in need of resurrection for the church, academy, and society in our own time? These are some of the questions the next generation of Christian social ethicists, Protestant and Catholic alike, will need take up. The present chapter does not presume to sufficiently address each or any of these questions, but rather by considering the history of the field, to present a range of prospects—work already being done and work that remains. My main interest throughout is not so much the future of Protestant social ethics as a project, as it is those *doing* and *teaching* Protestant social ethics in some form. What this amounts to will, I hope, become clear in the end.

What is Protestant social ethics? Search any of the major recent introductions or works in Christian ethics and you will find "social ethics" but not "Protestant social ethics."[3] Even Gary Dorrien, in *Social Ethics in the Making*, only uses the latter phrase once.[4] Lest one assume that, absent "Catholic" as a modifier, social ethics simply *is* Protestant *in se*, Brian Matz in *Introducing Protestant Social Ethics* (2017) suggests otherwise. He depicts social ethics, as distinct from fundamental ethics, as the branch of ethics concerned with the social order.[5] According to this broad conception, this branch of ethics, by no means distinctively theological or modern, is characterized by shared principles: human dignity, common good, justice, solidarity, and subsidiarity. Protestant contributions to this ancient tradition of "Christian reflection on social ethics" are twofold: a biblically centered view of society and sustained reflection on the "two kingdoms" of church and state.[6] Protestant social ethics is impoverished, Matz cautions, insofar as it ignores the significant contributions of Catholic social ethics—from *Rerum novarum* (1891), Vatican II, and *Laudato Si* (2015) to liberation theologies and contemporary Catholic theologians.[7] Dorrien's intellectual histories of the field happily avoid this mistake.[8] Yet he, with other Christian ethicists, understands social ethics more narrowly, as a field or tradition that has a specific history.

On this view, what we have come to call social ethics is a distinctively Protestant invention, with distinctively modern roots, even as this tradition has been contested, expanded, refined, and enlivened by those who do as well as by those do not identify with it. As D. Stephen Long writes, "Although Protestant Christianity always had a concern for ethics, 'Protestant social ethics' identifies something narrower within this ongoing concern, a preoccupation with ethics that emerged within liberal Protestantism when subjectivity, moral experience, and historical mediation became central themes."[9] I will begin by considering this history—including prominent and lesser-known figures—before suggesting recent and new directions for the field.

LIBERAL PROTESTANTISM: SEEDBED FOR PROTESTANT SOCIAL ETHICS

Protestant social ethics has roots in the seedbed of eighteenth and nineteenth century German idealism, specifically of Kant and Hegel, and the soil of German, British, and American liberal Protestantism. As Dorrien notes, "The modern departure in religious thought begins with the unavoidable figure in modern philosophy, Immanuel Kant . . . Enlightenment rationalism had a critique of authority religion before Kant came along . . . But it had no theory of the creative power of subjectivity or the grounding of religion and freedom in moral experience."[10] Kant provided both. His insistence on the critical, spontaneous, self-legislating, autonomous nature of reason—"reason is occupied with nothing but itself"—constitutes a departure from earlier modern philosophers.[11]

Kant's notion of critique would come to define modernity as a crisis of legitimacy or authority, at once epistemological and ethical, and thereby social, political, and ecclesial. A particular paradox of Kant's formulation in the *Critique of Pure Reason* (1781/1787) would remain at the center of subsequent debates. Terry Pinkard describes the "quasi-paradoxical formulation of the authority of the moral law" as that which "seems to require a 'lawless' agent to give laws to himself on the basis of laws that from one point of view seem to be prior to the legislation and from another point of view seem to be derivative from the legislation itself."[12] Kant resolves this dilemma not through theoretical proofs but through his account of freedom and agency. This epistemological and ethical quandary is closely related to a theological and religious one.

While in *The Critique of Pure Reason,* Kant leveled arguments against the theoretical knowledge of God and against God's existence, *the Critique of Practical Reason* provided a moral proof for the existence of God. The arguments of the former were explicitly intended to make room for faith—"pure religious faith" and "saving faith"—and the arguments of the latter.[13] Kant would later explicitly make the point in a section of *Religion with the Limits of Reason Alone* (1793) entitled "The gradual transition of ecclesiastical faith to the exclusive sovereignty of pure religious faith is the coming of the Kingdom of God."[14] Kant anticipated the gradual replacement of historical or ecclesiastical faith in the dogma of the visible church, with the "saving," "living," "rational" or "pure religious faith" of the invisible church or kingdom of God (71). Kant's point is a reversal of conventional wisdom and Christian orthodoxy. As Pinkard puts it, "religion does not give rise to morality, so much as morality gives rise to religion."[15] The kingdom of God will be manifest on earth in the form of an ethical commonwealth, as distinct from a political commonwealth, insofar as individuals freely live according to the duties and ideals of the highest good, and insofar as this "(divine) ethical state on earth, has become general and has also gained somewhere a public foothold, even though the actual establishment of this state is still infinitely removed from us" (75). This constellation of themes—the kingdom of God, understood as a matter of individual moral and/or social salvation, as a regulative ideal or historical reality, and the relations among authority, religion, and morality—are the roots of later debates in Protestant social ethics. As Long notes, "If there is a continuous thread in 'Protestant Social Ethics' it is the Kingdom of God as its goal" (90).

G.W.F. Hegel endorses and extends several aspects of Kant's project while leaving others behind. He extends Kant's account of subjectivity and normativity by insisting on the intersubjective and socio-historical dimension of epistemology and ethics.[16] In the *Phenomenology of Spirit*, Hegel's solution to the Kantian paradox is to make these movements of Spirit, rather than self-legislation and universal law, central to the question of legitimate authority. He sought to overcome the subject/object, freedom/nature, mind/world divide that Kant bestowed, by using the Christian doctrine of the Trinity to develop an intersubjective account of Spirit that continually reconciles these antinomies. For Hegel, revealed religion (the highest form) grasps the truth of the Trinity. But it does so only in representational form insofar as it understands the Trinity as a historical event rather than as the ongoing incarnation of the divine in the social life of the religious community.[17] Philosophy grasps the latter. In this view, normative judgments—whether about interpretations of scripture, theological doctrines, legal codes, or scientific claims—are open to contestation from other self-conscious subjects. Moreover, their authority depends on what Robert Brandom calls a "social model of reciprocal recognition."[18] Through the give and take of reasons and the social practices of debate, contestation, sacrifice, confession, and reconciliation, subjects *take* certain norms to be authoritative. Whereas Kant's kingdom of God was merely ideal, lacking a substantive politic and embodied ethic, Hegel's Spirit reconciles freedom and nature through the mediation of social practices.

Hegel thus planted seeds that would continue to bear fruit in Protestant liberalism and Protestant social ethics in subsequent centuries. First, he holds that Protestantism is the highest expression of religious faith because it provides an intersubjective account of epistemology, freedom, and ethics. Second, by providing this intersubjective, socio-historical, and socio-practical account—one that sets *Sittlichkeit* (ethical life) against the insufficiencies of Kant's deontological *Moralität*—he cleared the way for an enduring focus on the mediation of ecclesial and social practices in the pursuit of the ideal or kingdom of God. Third, his Trinitarian, dialectical account of epistemology, ethics, and politics—wherein the master/slave dialectic is overcome in two confessing and thereby reconciled subjects, or in a self-conscious community of accountability—affirmed a legacy of resistance to domination, exploitation, and injustice, while suggesting an alliance between Protestant and democratic practices.

The seeds of this neo-Kantian philosophy and theology began to germinate among nineteenth-century liberal Protestant theologians in Germany, such as Friedrich Schleiermacher, Albrecht Ritchel, and Adolf von Harnack. At the same time, these ideas were transplanted to Britain, where they took root in the already fertile soil of Dissenters, Nonconformists, Christian socialists, and the evangelical "Low Church" element in the Church of England. Richard Price, Joseph Priestly, William Wilberforce, and Mary Wollstonecraft, among other eighteenth-century dissenters had tilled the soil with their theologically informed commitments to justice, equality, sociopolitical reforms, and support of the American and (at least, initially) French Revolutions. These ideas also found particularly fertile soil, often by way of Samuel Taylor Coleridge, in the theological landscape of New England in the early nineteenth century. William Ellery Channing, Ralph Waldo Emerson, Theodore Parker and the transcendentalists, David Walker, Henry Ward Beecher and Elizabeth Cady Stanton, as well as Theodore Munger and Washington Gladden cleared the way for the emergence of the field of Protestant social ethics and the Social Gospel at the close of the nineteenth century. This theologically diverse group of thinkers is united by their use of biblical hermeneutics, inspiration from the literature of British and German Romantics, attention to moral formation and social practices for the sake of sociopolitical reform, and a belief that personal and social transformation—most prominently, the abolition of slavery—are not only possible but central matters of Christian faith and practice. The accounts of the kingdom of God, as well as of social sin and salvation, central to social ethics and the Social Gospel, grew out of this soil.

THE BIRTH OF SOCIAL ETHICS: NINETEENTH CENTURY

In the twentieth and twenty-first centuries, so-called Christian social ethics would become a series of complex, more and less self-conscious debates about the legacy bequeathed by Kant and Hegel.[19] It arose in America in the 1880s as an academic response to the same social crises that gave rise to the Social Gospel. As Dorrien notes:

> It was not a coincidence that social ethics, the social gospel, Social Darwinism, and sociology all arose at the same time, also corporate capitalism and the trade unions. Social ethics was essentially a departmental subset of the social gospel; the social gospel was based on a doctrine of social salvation; social salvation was based on the sociological idea that there is such a thing as social structure; the rise of industrialism raised new social issues for the church; and the social gospelers had to figure out how to say yes to Darwinism as science while saying no to an ascending Social Darwinism.[20]

In the late nineteenth century, the emergence of Darwinian science and the academic discipline of sociology (influenced by Auguste Compte and Emile Durkheim) called into question the Scottish common-sense philosophy at the heart of the core curriculum course in moral philosophy standard at all American colleges. Social ethics was conceived as a successor that would combine Christian theology, biblical criticism, moral philosophy, and the inductive methods of social science. William Jewett Tucker, J.H.W. Stuckenberg, Graham Taylor, and most prominently Francis Greenwood Peabody, a professor and preacher of Harvard University and Divinity School from 1880 to 1914, founded the discipline.[21]

In 1900, Peabody reluctantly resigned as pastor of First Parish (Unitarian) church in Cambridge, Massachusetts, to become a lecturer at Harvard Divinity School. Perceiving the need to redesign the moral philosophy curriculum, he set out to create courses that would be more explicitly Christian and biblical by recovering the centrality of the kingdom of Jesus for modern Christianity. The titles of his lecture courses changed over the years until finally, at the suggestion of his colleague, William James, he landed on

"Social Ethics." By 1905, "Sociological Seminaries" were listed as "Social Ethics Seminaries" the titles of which included: "The Christian Doctrine of the Social Order," "The Ethics of Jesus Christ," "The Ethical Teaching of the New Testament," "Christian Ethics and Modern Life," and "The History of Social Ethics from Fichte to Tolstoy."[22] At a time when American education was undergoing a number of revolutions, one of Peabody's aims was to establish systematic Christian social ethics as a university discipline in *both* liberal and professional theological education. His book *Jesus Christ and the Social Question* (1900), coupled with Ernst Troeltsch's *The Social Teaching of the Christian Churches* (1911), was a watershed for the nascent field.

Social ethics, for Peabody, included at least three basic elements. First, it combined moral philosophy and social scientific studies of social movements and reforms. The aim was to pair the methods of social science (observation, generalization, and correlation or attention to the deeper unity of nature) with a historical approach to moral philosophy in order to develop "a method of ethics which would be constantly close to life, and which would gather up the real issues of conduct into their higher significance and tendency."[23] Yet alone, he thought, this method lacks two things: a distinctively Christian account of social reforms and of the ideals that fueled them. The second element, then, provided a Christian interpretation of the social upheaval and moral activism of the late nineteenth century meant to supplement scientific theories with the insights of Christianity. The Christian principle of *caritas*, rather than social science, can best account for the "power of ideals" and social reforms.[24] The third element is to formulate an ethics for Christian moral formation and social reform, based on biblical principles that Peabody derived from a hermeneutic approach to the teachings of Jesus. He wanted to demonstrate the practicability of discipleship and the timeless principles of Jesus' teaching for an industrial, urban, and scientific era. He rejected socialist and radical Social Gospel interpretations of the gospels that tended to ignore what he saw as the central religious and spiritual message. Jesus did not define a social ideal of the kingdom, but rather focused on the transformation of persons as the means to the kingdom: "first persons fit for the kingdom, then the better world,—that is the method of Jesus."[25]

From its inception, social ethics was meant to combine normative and descriptive methods, to overcome a rigid distinction between *is* and *ought*. It was also inherently interdisciplinary, drawing on history, philosophy, theology, biblical studies, politics, and social science. In order to become a new field in its own right, social ethics had to claim a distinct method. Yet, Dorrien notes the irony of this fact: "the field's greatest figures paid little attention to disciplinary or methodological concerns."[26] Of the three preeminent figures in the US tradition—Walter Rauschenbusch, Reinhold Niebuhr, and Martin Luther King, Jr.—only Niebuhr taught social ethics and he cared little for methodological issues.

The social gospel grew out of eighteenth-century Enlightenment humanitarianism, nineteenth-century liberal Protestant theology, and postmillennialist movements for social salvation that nurtured the evangelical anti-slavery movements. But it was primarily a response to the burgeoning labor movement of the Reconstruction era. Washington Gladden is considered the father of the Social Gospel, but Walter Rauschenbusch would become its most famous exponent. After his German American pietist upbringing and theological education, the most formative influences on Rauschenbusch were the eleven years of ministry he spent in the slums of New York City. There he encountered significant figures in the Social Gospel movement. During his time as professor of church history at Rochester Theological Seminary (1897–1918), his writings ushered the Social Gospel into the mainstream of American Protestant theology and church life. The issues of social justice, central to the kingdom of God, he argued, are not the recent invention of radical reformers, but are central to the Christian movement from its inception, from John the Baptist to the primitive church and beyond. His final book, *Theology for the Social Gospel* (1917), brought greater coherence to the movement's main theological themes: social sin and salvation, the personality and teachings of Jesus, the kingdom of God on earth as the end, the church as its mean, prophetic over priestly religion, systemic forms of good and evil, the will and power of God to redeem human society, and a focus on ethics rather than eschatology. He sought to articulate the contours of a Christian social order, especially in the economic sphere, aligning himself with the Christian socialist wing of the Social Gospel.

While the Social Gospel to some extent prophetically addressed economic issues, it generally failed to address other related social issues, most conspicuously the problems of race, racism, and the feminist movement. This fact is perhaps most evident in the "Social Creed" adopted by the General Conference of the Methodist Episcopal Church and by the Federal Council of Churches in 1908.[27] The creed does not even mention racial issues as the Jim Crow system tightened its stranglehold on the South, and as black leaders, including Ida B. Wells who was associated with the Black Social Gospel, began founding the NAACP. Neither does it mention war and peace six years prior to the catastrophic First World War; nor women's suffrage or equality, as the movement began its final push toward the goal of political enfranchisement. How could this be?

Dorrien has exposed the racism and white supremacy that infected the Social Gospel movement, diminishing its work for racial justice, and eclipsing rather than promoting the work of the black Social Gospel.[28] Several leaders in the South were, in Dorrien's words, "brutally racist without apology," while many in the North advocated for the assimilation of blacks to an Anglo-Saxon ideal, and only a minute group of less influential Social Gospelers defended the full dignity and rights of African Americans.[29] Even Gladden was a late convert to the justice perspective, finally swayed by W.E.B Dubois's *The Souls of Black Folk*. It was not until the last years of life (1912–1918) that Rauschenbusch broke his silence on the topic, confessing that "the problem of the two races in the South has seemed so tragic, so insoluble, that I have never ventured to discuss it in public."[30]

Of course, the black Social Gospelers—including Reverdy Ransom, Ida B. Wells, Henry McNeal Turner, Monroe Work, and Richard R. Wright, Jr.—did not have that perverse luxury. In 1933, Ransom lamented that, "Christ has not been able to break the color line. If Jesus wept over Jerusalem, he should have for America an ocean of tears."[31] Despite Du Bois's prediction that Ransom would be forever memorialized for his powerful speeches, and despite the work of Calvin S. Morris among others to ensure this, he and Ida B. Wells among the other black Social Gospelers have been nearly forgotten among Christian ethicists and theologians. The same could be said of many of the women in the abolitionist and feminist movements, from Lucretia Mott, Angelina and Sarah Grimke, Mary Dodge, Frances Willard, Francis P. Cobbe, and somewhat more famously Elizabeth Cady Stanton, Sojourner Truth, and later Jane Addams. The white Social Gospel movement, for all its prophetic tendencies with regard to labor, did not adequately imagine a kingdom of God that fully includes women and people of color.

TWENTIETH- AND TWENTY-FIRST-CENTURY DEBATES

The First World War effectively broke the momentum of the Social Gospel movement, even if its central themes would continue to resound—most prominently perhaps among liberation theologians in the second half of the twentieth century. The twentieth-century debates are generally more familiar to ethicists and moral theologians today. In the aftermath of the war, two prominent yet distinct criticisms of liberal theology and the Social Gospel would emerge. In the typical narrative, Karl Barth and Reinhold Niebuhr are pitted against one another, representing opposing responses to the theological crises triggered by the twentieth-century world wars.[32] Of course, there is some truth to that. But their similarities are just as striking. Both waged an intellectual war against the idealism of nineteenth-century liberal theology, its overly optimistic notion of human progress and its tendency to identify the kingdom of God with particular reform movements and social revolutions. Both understood the kingdom of God as a regulative ideal, which cannot be fully grasped or fulfilled on earth. Both became leaders of neo-orthodox theology in Europe and America. So too, they both revived a broadly Augustinian account of the radically sinful nature of humanity, society, and the world. Both had socialist leanings; neither was strictly pacifist.[33] Yet while Barth bestowed a thoroughly Christological "critical realism"—whereby dogmatics are ethics and vice versa, rendering ethics profoundly fraught because of the radical disparity between human and divine words and agency—Niebuhr became renowned for his realism—whereby Christians must imperfectly translate an ethic of love into practices and policies of justice.

In Barth's seminal essay "The Problem of Ethics Today," published in *The Word of God and the Word of Man*, he declares that *"mene mene tekel"* has been written over against humanity's confidence in itself, its supposed knowledge of what to do, and specifically against the ethics of the Ritschlian school and of Troeltsch.[34] The problem of ethics in this vein is that it presumed to know what to do—namely "to further this infinitely imperfect but infinitely perfectible culture."[35] Yet, the word of God or "the problem of the good calls in question all actual and possible forms of human conduct, all temporal happenings in the history both of the individual and of society."[36] In light of the resurrection of Christ, he concludes, "we must now fortify ourselves against expecting that our criticizing, protesting, reforming, organizing, democratizing, socializing, and revolutionizing—*however fundamental and thoroughgoing these may be*—will satisfy the ideal of the kingdom of God."[37] The kingdom of God, far from beginning with our movements of protest, is the ultimate revolution that calls all such efforts into question.

Despite Barth's privileging of theology over and often against philosophy, his work is deeply indebted to Kant and Hegel. In his more Kantian moments, which often characterize his epistemology and ethics, he ossifies the subject/object, man/God distinction. In his more Hegelian moments—through his Christology and embryonic pneumatology, coupled with his doctrine of creation and covenant—he provides a more substantive, participatory, and historical account of "the subject which is to be God's partner" in this covenantal history.[38]

As suggested above, Niebuhr was greatly influenced by Barth. His book *Kingdom of God in America* contains one of the most famous denouncements of liberal theology: "A God without wrath brought men without sin into a kingdom without judgment through the ministrations of a Christ without a cross."[39] But he denounced Barth's failure to provide substantive guidance for moral action, christening him the "apostle of the absolute."[40] Niebuhr's Christian realism takes Barth's insight that "we are men and not God" as the starting point for his account of human limitation, freedom, and responsible action. *Moral Man and Immoral Society* argues that individuals manifest a higher level of morality than social groups—an idea that King would recall in his "Letter from a Birmingham Jail." Because the sin of pride (individual and social) is pervasive laws are needed to ensure some measure of justice for the vulnerable. In the midst of two world wars, he provided a striking criticism of naïve pacifism, which regards living in perfect accordance with love in a world of sin to be a simple possibility. On the question of racial justice, Dorrien notes that Niebuhr was better than most white theologians of his time.[41] Even so, one irony of this public theologian of social and structural sin is that he did not grasp the depths of white supremacy or white privilege and so did not challenge his own institutions or government to grapple with these realities. Convinced by Edmund Burke of the glacial slowness of sustainable political reform, he refused King's request to sign an open letter to President Eisenhower requesting federal enforcement of school desegregation.

A pastor, preacher, scholar, and activist, King's primary source of inspiration was Jesus and the gospels, specifically the dual love command and the Sermon on the Mount. He managed to wed systematic, political, practical, historical, and moral theology, social ethics, preaching, political activism, and community organizing. He was influenced by Rauschenbusch and Niebuhr, but his commitment to nonviolence was shaped by Henry David Thoreau's "Civil Disobedience," Mahatma Gandhi, and American nonviolent activists such as Bayard Rustin. In his famous "Letter from a Birmingham Jail" he uses prominent themes of each of these figures to counter the white religious leaders' criticism of him for inciting violence and breaking civil law. The former two supplied an account of social sin. The whole structure of racial segregation is violent. King's nonviolent movement merely reveals this fact by bringing "to the surface the hidden tension that is already alive."[42] The others bolstered his distinction between just and unjust laws, and the nonviolent forms of resistance needed to overcome the latter. Nonviolence was compelling to King because it exposed the injustices of Jim Crow, and sought justice in a manner meant to reconcile oppressed and oppressor. In one of his last works, he defended his famous dream of a racially united community, of justice and love: "There is no salvation for the Negro through isolation."[43] We find echoes of Hegel in this profoundly interpersonal view of the kingdom of God understood as the "beloved community." His famous line, inspired by a Theodore Parker sermon, "The arc of the moral universe is long, but it bends toward justice," pairs a measure of realism with the idealism or hope of protestant liberal theology and social ethics.

Barth, Niebuhr, and King set the stage for subsequent twentieth- and twenty-first-century debates. Barth a was major influence on his student John Howard Yoder, whose significant defense of Christian pacifism in *The Politics of Jesus* set the course for Stanley Hauerwas. A theologian and Christian ethicist, Hauerwas has become renowned for his emphasis on narrative theology, virtue, the church, and pacifism or *The Peaceable Kingdom*. His enduring criticism of liberal theology and social ethics, simply put, is that "The church does not have a social ethic; the church is a social ethic," and "the first social ethical task of the church is [not to make the 'world' better or more just, but] to be the church."[44]

Ethicists and theologians from Jeffrey Stout and Robert Jenson, to Eric Gregory, James Logan, Gloria Albrecht, Christopher Beem, and Karen Guth have been critical of his sectarianism, his overly optimistic portrayal of the church, his excessive criticism of liberalism, his insufficient account of the tasks of the church, and his neglect of matters of race, class, and gender.[45] Responding to the quote above, Gregory notes that, "[Hauerwas] does not give an account of what a second, or third, social ethical task might be."[46] Guth adds that he "stops short of adequately developing his account of the first task" including "constitutive components of the church's witness of peace: resistance to the violence of sexism and racism."[47] Hauerwas has provisionally confessed as much, yet many have found his confessions dissatisfying. They worry that his justifications—namely, that the story of the black church is not *his* story to tell, or that he rejects liberalism, which he assumes undergirds feminist theologies—exacerbate the problems.[48] Of course, feminist and womanist theologians and ethicists, from Wollstonecraft to Emilie Townes, are sufficiently variegated to resist such a caricature. Moreover, the story of white supremacy that still infects the church in America is a story that someone must have the courage to tell, even if Hauerwas has not taken up this task.

The legacy of social ethics in Barth, Niebuhr, and King were taken in another direction by liberation theologians. Gustavo Gutierrez's *A Theology of Liberation* (1971), and James Cone's *A Black Theology of Liberation* (1970) and *God of the Oppressed* (1975) were groundbreaking. Both adopt Barth's Christological focus, while attending to the social structures of sin and salvation, and the kingdom of God this side of the eschaton. God acts in Israel, Jesus Christ, and today, they agree, decisively on behalf of the oppressed. Womanist and *mujerista* theologians and ethicists have extended their work by drawing attention to the specific forms of oppression and liberation of women, specifically women of color. At the same time, moral theologians and Christian ethicists—from Mary Daly, Rosemary Radford Reuther, Katie Cannon, and Emilie Townes, to Ada Maria Isasi-Diaz and Kwok Pui-Lan—have brought attention to women's experiences and narratives as a source of theological and ethical reflection that rejects all forms of patriarchy and domination.

Despite their shared concern for Christian faithfulness, ethicists in these streams of thought remain mostly at loggerheads to the extent that they engage one another at all. Their work suffers from the sort of "intellectual estrangement" that Cornel West has described between American pragmatist philosophers and liberation theologians. The former, for all of their philosophically nuanced historicism, suffer from "political insouciance."[49] The latter, despite their profound "moral vision, social analysis, and political engagement" suffer from "philosophical insularity."[50] Today, we might extend his claim that, "what is needed is a *rapprochement* between the philosophical historicism of [the former], the moral vision, social analysis, and political engagement of [the latter]," the attention to sociopolitical realities of Christian realists and liberation theologians, and the narrative theology and ecclesial focus of what Guth calls "witness theologians." Indeed, West's prophetic pragmatism, inspired by the prophetic traditions of the black church and Abrahamic faiths as well as American pragmatism, provides one example of a way forward.

Other examples of new directions in the field include, but are by no means limited to, the following. The Augustinianisms of Eric Gregory, Charles Mathewes, and Luke Bretherton provide a way beyond these impasses. In *Politics and the Order of Love*, Gregory provides an approach to Christian ethics and political theology that seeks to mediate between "*critics* of Augustine who *defend* liberal democracy" and "*fans* of Augustine who *attack* liberal democracy."[51] Like Jeffrey Stout, in *Democracy and Tradition* he moves the conversation beyond appeals to either tradition *or* critique, refusing to choose between the insights of the premodern and modern eras. In a similar vein, Jennifer Herdt in *Putting on Virtue*, examines certain continuities between a premodern and modern Augustinian legacy of the virtues. John Bowlin, in *Tolerance Among the Virtues*, provides a timely account of the timeless virtues of tolerance and forbearance. Newer voices such as Eboni Turman Marshall and Brian Bantum have made significant contributions by reinterpreting aspects of the premodern theological tradition to address matters of race, gender, ethics, and the church. So too, Keri Day in *Unfinished Business*, extends the legacy of King, by analyzing the gender and sexual politics of the Southern Christian Leadership Conference and the Poor People's Campaign Movement.

Stout and Bretherton point Christian ethicists to community organizing as a social practice that enables Christians to join other religious and non-religious citizens in taking responsibility for our common political life. After all, as Molly Farneth writes, "A Hegelian social ethics does not depend on a shared religious or philosophical standpoint—although it does presume that commitments about these and other matters are affirmed, contested, and transformed through ongoing social practices."[52] Far from precluding distinctively theological commitments, this social ethic treats them as a matter of ongoing debate mediated by the social practices of religious communities and society. Post-liberal Christian theologians—including Hans Frei, George Lindbeck, Bruce Marshall, and Sarah Haener Lancaster—as well as Kevin Hector, have drawn attention to the role of social practices and narratives in the formation and reformation of Christian commitments. All of these alternatives point toward a renewed emphasis on theology as one of many social practices of the church—reformed and ever reforming through practices, reflection, and the give and take of reasons—whereby it extends the narrative of faith in our time.

PROSPECTS: NEW DIRECTIONS IN PROTESTANT SOCIAL ETHICS

Having cast a backward glance at the amorphous field of Protestant social ethics, its philosophical and theological precursors and new directions, I close with prospects. My own hopes for the discipline are fourfold: that it be (1) robustly theological and philosophical, (2) somewhat de-clericized, (3) collaborative, ecumenical, and interdisciplinary, and (4) committed to the church's social witness.

Theological and *Philosophical*

The field of social ethics will move beyond some of the current impasses when we alleviate anxieties about legitimacy and authority bequeathed to us by Kant. A socio-historical account of continuing revelation, of God's spirit moving in the church visible and invisible, through communities of social practice, provides one panacea. It invites Christian social ethicists to be at once robustly theological, self-consciously philosophical, and open to the insights of liberal and democratic social movements within and beyond the church. If the Spirit of God indeed moves where it pleases, then Christians ethicists have good reason remain open to learning from those who do not (as well as those who do!) explicitly identify with this tradition.

De-clericalization

Peabody was intent to create a space in the core curriculum of *both* professional theological and liberal higher education for Christian social ethics. What has become of this hope? In traditionally Protestant institutions social ethics has been largely clericized or secularized. As for Peabody's institution, the new 2018 requirements of Harvard College mandate one course in the area of "Ethics and Civics." The only courses on offer in Christian ethics (2016–2018) are at the graduate level and taught by faculty in the Divinity school.[53] If this is a national trend (and some think it is), it means that liberal arts colleges, seminaries, and divinity schools alike have cast Christian social ethics (if taught as a sub-field at all) as an elective of graduate education, an optional bonus for those pursuing ordained ministry or advanced degrees in religious studies, or for the occasional undergraduate student.[54] Catholic institutions of higher education seem to have been more effective at creating and sustaining a space for Christian social ethics and moral theology as part of the core curriculum.

These trends are not particularly alarming. Their significance for the future size, direction, and identity of the field in the academy remains an open question. But for the church, it means that many (if not most) protestant laity receive no formal education in Christian, let alone social ethics. Prominent figures in the legacy outlined—from Channing and Emerson who lectured at the Boston Mechanic Apprentices Library Association, to King's work with the Southern Christian Leadership Conference—have found ways of integrating higher and public education, Christian ethics and activism, the church's social witness and the lived realities of laity. The next generation will need to think about the institutions, academic and otherwise, that might sustain these important conversations and practices.

Ecumenical, Collaborative, and Interdisciplinary

Paul Martens, in his response to the "2020 Society of Christian Ethics Committee Report," notes that an anxiety about what we mean when "we are talking about Christian ethics" haunts the report, and he predicts that "how we—collectively—address this anxiety will determine the future of the field."[55] Tracing this latent worry to the expansive size of the field and to increasing specialization and diversity, he concludes that Christian ethics must be a field in which expertise in foundational or theoretical and practical or social issues—to oversimplify, tradition and critique—mutually enrich one another. This is certainly in keeping with the history of Christian social ethics, which tends to be concerned with foundational matters insofar as they bear on social and ecclesial practices and issues. But this sort of work, he notes, will require reconceiving the ways that we—and our institutions— might promote interdisciplinary, collaborative, and ecumenical research and teaching. The questions raised at the beginning of this chapter can only be addressed collectively.

My sense is that anxieties about the nature or identity of "Christian ethics" as a field in the twenty-first century are related to the sorts of anxieties Peabody had about the authority and institutional status of Christian social ethics at the turn of the twentieth century, and these are related to the crisis of legitimacy named and thereby created by Kant. If this is right, then Hegel's socio-historical antidote may at least alleviate the anxiety about authority. Christian ethicists need not be anxious about defining in advance the center or periphery of the field, if the way forward depends on shared practices of mutual recognition; if ethics and epistemology are mediated by the social practices of the church, academy, and society; if the goal is to create a beloved community that strives to embody love and justice amidst differences and disagreements, rather than unanimity whether of method, foundational commitments, or sociopolitical views. This is related to my final point.

Church's Social Witness

The next generation of social ethicists will need to ask, as every generation must, which aspects of the inherited tradition are living, which of them dead, and which of them need to be resurrected, for the church's faithful social witness in this time and place, given the sociopolitical issues facing this historical moment—issues pertaining to gender, race, class, sexuality, the economy, labor, poverty, the environment, incarceration, immigration, refugee crises, imperialism, war, food, water, clothes, birth, death, and the list goes on. Intersectional theories reveal the inadequacy of considering some of the traditional foci of social ethics (labor, economics, war, and peace) apart from related matters of gender, sexuality, race, and class, among others. Of course, no one ethicist can sufficiently attend to *all* of these at once, but it is no longer adequate to address any one topic without some consideration of how they bear on others.

At its best, Protestant social ethics has always been confessional in at least a two-fold sense: distinctively Christian and repentant. Two prominent ethicists have begun to exemplify this dual confessional posture. Dorrien has confessed that most social ethicists—from Peabody and the Social Gospelers to Niebuhr—have paid insufficient attention to matters of racial justice or America's original sins of racism and white supremacy, and is actively seeking to remedy this failure. Hauerwas, however reticently, has begun to confess his own neglect of matters such as race, gender, and feminism, central to the life of the church, as well as his willful ignorance and neglect of John Howard Yoder's sexual harassment of women.[56] Much work remains to be done, in confessing the commitments that animate the social witness of the church, as well as the past sins of the field and church so that we may constructively move forward. Even if West doubts that the arc of the moral universe bends toward justice and love, we might agree with him, like Parker and King, that Christians are responsible for doing everything in our power to ensure that it does.[57]

NOTES

1. I am grateful to Davey Henreckson and Nathaniel Warne for their feedback on early drafts of this paper. It goes without saying that all of the blunders are my own.

2. Gary Dorrien's work, alongside a host of others to whom I will return, is a delightful exception to this trend and a significant contribution to the field. See especially: Gary J. Dorrien, *Social Ethics in the Making: Interpreting an American Tradition* (Chichester: Wiley-Blackwell, 2009); Gary Dorrien, *The New Abolition: W. E. B. Du Bois and the Black Social Gospel* (New Haven, CT: Yale University Press, 2015); Gary Dorrien, *Breaking White Supremacy: Martin Luther King Jr. and the Black Social Gospel* (New Haven, CT: Yale University Press, 2018); Gary Dorrien, *The Making of American Liberal Theology: Imagining Progressive Religion, 1805–1900*, 1st ed. (Louisville, KY: Westminster John Knox Press, 2001); Gary Dorrien, *The Making of American Liberal Theology: Idealism, Realism, and Modernity, 1900–1950*, 1st ed. (Louisville, KY: Westminster John Knox Press, 2003); Gary Dorrien, *The Making of American Liberal Theology: Crisis, Irony, and Postmodernity, 1950–2005* (Louisville, KY: Westminster John Knox Press, 2006).

3. J. Philip Wogaman, *Christian Ethics: A Historical Introduction*, 2nd ed. (Louisville, KY: Westminster John Knox Press, 2011); Harry J. Huebner, *An Introduction to Christian Ethics: History, Movements, People* (Waco, TX: Baylor University Press, 2011); Robin W. Lovin, *Christian Ethics: An Essential Guide*, 51103rd edition (Nashville, TN: Abingdon Press, 1999); Robin W. Lovin, *An Introduction to Christian Ethics: Goals, Duties, and Virtues* (Nashville, TN: Abingdon Press, 2011); Katie G Cannon, Emilie Maureen Townes, and Angela D Sims, *Womanist Theological Ethics: A Reader* (Louisville, KY: Westminster John Knox Press, 2011); Miguel A. De La Torre, *Doing Christian Ethics from the Margins: 2nd Edition Revised and Expanded* (Maryknoll, NY: Orbis Books, 2014); William Werpehowski, *American Protestant Ethics and the Legacy of H. Richard Niebuhr* (Washington, DC: Georgetown University Press, 2002); Paul Ramsey, *Basic Christian Ethics* (Louisville, KY: Westminster/John Knox Press, 1993); D. Stephen Long, *Christian Ethics: A Very Short Introduction*, 1st ed. (Oxford: Oxford University Press, 2010); Robin Gill, ed., *The Cambridge Companion to Christian Ethics*, 2nd ed. (Cambridge: Cambridge University Press, 2012); Stanley Hauerwas, *A Community of Character: Toward a Constructive Christian Social Ethic*, 1st ed. (Notre Dame, IN: University of Notre Dame

Press, 1991); Susan Frank Parsons, *Feminism and Christian Ethics*, first paperback edition (New York: Cambridge University Press, 1996).

4. Gary J. Dorrien, *Social Ethics in the Making: Interpreting an American Tradition* (Chichester: Wiley-Blackwell, 2009), 184.

5. Brian Matz, *Introducing Protestant Social Ethics: Foundations in Scripture, History, and Practice* (Grand Rapids, MI: Baker Academic, 2017), xiv.

6. Ibid., xvii.

7. Ibid., and Chapter 10.

8. See Dorrien, *Social Ethics in the Making*.

9. D. Stephen Long, "Protestant Social Ethics," in *The Cambridge Companion to Christian Political Theology*, eds. Craig Hovey and Elizabeth Phillips, Cambridge Companions to Religion (New York: Cambridge University Press, 2015).

10. Gary Dorrien, *Kantian Reason and Hegelian Spirit: The Idealistic Logic of Modern Theology*, 1st ed. (London: Wiley-Blackwell, 2015), 23.

11. Pippin, *Modernism as a Philosophical Problem*, xiv, 11, 54, 71. The citation is from Kant's *Critique of Pure Reason* (B708/A680).

12. Terry Pinkard, *German Philosophy 1760–1860: The Legacy of Idealism* (Cambridge: Cambridge University Press, 2002), 59.

13. Immanuel Kant, *Religion within the Limits of Reason Alone*, trans. Theodore M. Greene (United States: Digireads.com, 2011), 71–89.

14. Kant, *Religion within the Limits of Reason Alone*, 71. All page numbers in the text of this paragraph refer to this text.

15. Pinkard, *German Philosophy 1760–1860*, 61.

16. Molly Farneth, *Hegel's Social Ethics: Religion, Conflict, and Rituals of Reconciliation* (Princeton, NJ: Princeton University Press, 2017), 6–9. See Farneth's excellent description of these debates and the significance of Hegel's social ethics for Christian theology and ethics today.

17. Ibid., see Chapter 5, particularly 86–92.

18. Robert Brandom, *Reason in Philosophy: Animating Ideas* (President and Fellows of Harvard, 2009, 68, 72).

19. Long, "Protestant Social Ethics," 93. As Long writes, "Twentieth- and twenty-first century Protestant social ethics is an ongoing debate about the legacy Kant [and] Hegel . . . bequeathed us." Long is certainly right about the nature of these debates. Nonetheless, I do not think that the divergent poles that he presents—"those who would subordinate the church to the ethical common wealth" on the one hand, and "those who understand the church as an ethical commonwealth" on the others—even if understood on a spectrum, best capture the nuanced views of the prominent figures in these debates. By attempting to sketch, however provisionally, a more nuanced account of these figures, movements, and the theologies that animate them, I am suggesting that providing a richer account of the contributions of these thinkers and activists is precisely the sort of work needed to further the discipline and socio-ecclesial practices of Protestant social ethics in the twenty-first century.

20. Gary Dorrien, "Social Ethics in the Making: Method, History, White Supremacism, Social Salvation," *American Journal of Theology & Philosophy* 29, no. 2 (May 1, 2008): 126.

21. Grace Cumming Long, "The Ethics of Francis Greenwood Peabody: A Century of Christian Social Ethics (Focus: The Ethics of the Social Gospel)," *The Journal of Religious Ethics* 18, no. 1 (1990): 55. See Long's excellent article along with Dorrien's *Social Ethics in the Making* for more about Peabody's life and work.

22. Long, "The Ethics of Francis Greenwood Peabody," 56.
23. Ibid., 60.
24. Ibid., 61.
25. Francis Greenwood Peabody, *Jesus Christ and the Christian Character* (New York: Macmillan, 1905), 15.
26. Dorrien, "Social Ethics in the Making," 131.
27. Wogaman, *Christian Ethics*, 216.
28. Dorrien, "Social Ethics in the Making"; Dorrien, *Breaking White Supremacy*; Dorrien, *The New Abolition*. See also: Calvin S. Morris, *Reverdy C. Ransom: Black Advocate of the Social Gospel* (Lanham, MD: University Press of America, 1990); Terrell Dale Goddard, "The Black Social Gospel in Chicago, 1896–1906: The Ministries of Reverdy C. Ransom and Richard R. Wright, Jr.," *The Journal of Negro History* 84, no. 3 (n.d.): 227–246; Ralph E. Luker, *The Social Gospel in Black and White American Racial Reform, 1885–1912*, Studies in Religion (Chapel Hill, NC: University of North Carolina Press, 1991).
29. Dorrien, "Social Ethics in the Making," 135.
30. Ibid., 138. Original quote is from Rauschenbusch, "The Belated Races and the Social Problems," *Methodist Review* 40 (April 1914): 258.
31. Dorrien, "Social Ethics in the Making," 139. This quote in Dorrien is originally from Reverdy Ransom, *The Negro: The Hope or Despair of Christianity* (Boston: Ruth Hill, 1935).
32. For an excellent overview of these debates see Karen V. Guth, *Christian Ethics at the Boundary Feminism and Theologies of Public Life* (Baltimore, MD, Minneapolis, MN: Project Muse, Fortress Press, 2015).
33. Karl Barth, *Church Dogmatics* (Edinburgh: T&T Clark, 1936), III/4, 455. (Hereafter *CD*.)
34. Karl Barth, *The Word of God and the Word of Man*, trans. Douglass Horton (Gloucester, MA: Peter Smith Publisher, Inc., 1978), 149, 145.
35. Ibid., 145.
36. Ibid., 139. He reiterates this point in *CD*, II.2, 645.
37. Ibid., 320 (emphasis original).
38. Barth, *CD*, III/1, 97.
39. H. Richard Niebuhr, *The Kingdom of God in America* (Middletown, CT: Wesleyan University Press, 1988), 193.
40. Reinhold Niebuhr, *Essays in Applied Christianity*, Living Age Meridian Books LA26 (New York: Meridian Books, 1959), 141.
41. Dorrien, "Social Ethics in the Making," 140.
42. Martin Luther King, Jr., *A Testament of Hope: The Essential Writings and Speeches*, ed. James M. Washington, Reprint edition (San Francisco, CA: HarperOne, 2003), 295.
43. Martin Luther King, Jr., *Where Do We Go from Here: Chaos or Community?* (Boston: Beacon Press, 1968), 48.
44. Stanley Hauerwas, *The Peaceable Kingdom: A Primer in Christian Ethics*, 1st ed. (Notre Dame, IN: University of Notre Dame Press, 1983), 99. The insert is from a passage in Stanley Hauerwas, *A Community of Character: Toward a Constructive Christian Social Ethic*, 1 edition (Notre Dame, IN: University of Notre Dame Press, 1991), 10.
45. Jeffrey Stout, *Democracy and Tradition* (Princeton, NJ: Princeton University Press, 2004); Eric Gregory, *Politics and the Order of Love: An Augustinian Ethic of Democratic Citizenship* (Chicago: University of Chicago Press, 2008); Karen V. Guth, *Christian Ethics*

at the Boundary Feminism and Theologies of Public Life (Baltimore, MD, Minneapolis, MN: Project Muse, Fortress Press, 2015), http://proxy.library.nd.edu/login?url=https://muse.jhu.edu/books/9781451469752/; James Logan, "Liberalism, Race, and Stanley Hauerwas" *CrossCurrents* 55, no. 4 (2006): 522–533; Christopher Beem, "American Liberalism and the Christian Church: Stanley Hauerwas vs. Martin Luther King Jr.," *The Journal of Religious Ethics* 23, no. 1 (1995): 119–133; Stanley Hauerwas, "Remembering Martin Luther King Jr. Remembering: A Response to Christopher Beem," *The Journal of Religious Ethics* 23, no. 1 (1995): 135–48.

46. Gregory, *Politics and the Order of Love*, 132.
47. Guth, *Christian Ethics at the Boundary Feminism and Theologies of Public Life*, 42, 38.
48. Hauerwas, "Remembering Martin Luther King Jr. Remembering," 135–148; Stanley Hauerwas, "Failure of Communication or a Case of Uncomprehending Feminism," *Scottish Journal of Theology* 50, no. 2 (1997): 228–239.
49. Cornel West, *The Cornel West Reader*, 1st ed. (New York: Basic Civitas Books, 1999), 367.
50. Ibid, 367.
51. Gregory, *Politics and the Order of Love*, 2.
52. Molly Farneth, *Hegel's Social Ethics: Religion, Conflict, and Rituals of Reconciliation* (Prinnceto, NJ: Princeton University Press, 2017), 107.
53. Indeed, the fact that ethics is still listed as a core requirement may owe to Peabody's legacy. Neither Trinity College at Duke University, Yale College, nor Emory University's College of Arts and Science list "ethics" or "moral philosophy" as an aspect of the core curriculum.
54. See the 2020 Society of Christian Ethics Committee Report https://scethics.org/sites/default/files/SCE%202020%20Report%20Final_1.pdf.
55. Marten's address: https://scethics.org/about-sce/current-officers-and-committees/committees/2020-future-christian-ethics-committee.
56. Stanley Hauerwas, "In Defence of 'Our Respectable Culture': Trying to Make Sense of John Howard Yoder's Sexual Abuse," October 18, 2017, https://doi.org/http://www.abc.net.au/religion/articles/2017/10/18/4751367.htm.
57. See Cornel West's interview: https://opinionator.blogs.nytimes.com/2015/08/19/cornel-west-the-fire-of-a-new-generation/

SELECT BIBLIOGRAPHY

Barth, Karl (1936), *Church Dogmatics*, Edinburgh: T&T Clark.
Barth, Karl (1978), *The Word of God and the Word of Man*, trans. Douglass Horton, Gloucester, MA: Peter Smith Puslisher, Inc.
Brandom, Robert (2009), *Reason in Philosophy: Animating Ideas*, Cambridge, MA: Harvard University Press.
Cannon, Katie G., Emilie Maureen Townes, and Angela D. Sims (2011), *Womanist Theological Ethics: A Reader*, Louisville, KY: Westminster John Knox Press.
Dorrien, Gary (2008), "Social Ethics in the Making: Method, History, White Supremacism, Social Salvation," *American Journal of Theology & Philosophy* 29, no. 2: 123–145.
Dorrien, Gary (2009), *Social Ethics in the Making: Interpreting an American Tradition*, Malden, MA: Wiley-Blackwell.
Dorrien, Gary (2015), *Kantian Reason and Hegelian Spirit: The Idealistic Logic of Modern Theology*, 1st ed., London: Wiley-Blackwell.

Dorrien, Gary (2015), *The New Abolition: W. E. B. Du Bois and the Black Social Gospel*, New Haven, CT: Yale University Press.
Dorrien, Gary (2018), *Breaking White Supremacy: Martin Luther King Jr. and the Black Social Gospel*, New Haven, CT: Yale University Press.
Farneth, Molly (2017), *Hegel's Social Ethics: Religion, Conflict, and Rituals of Reconciliation*, Princeton, NJ: Princeton University Press.
Gregory, Eric (2008), *Politics and the Order of Love: An Augustinian Ethic of Democratic Citizenship*, Chicago: University of Chicago Press.
Guth, Karen V. (2015), *Christian Ethics at the Boundary Feminism and Theologies of Public Life*, Minneapolis, MN: Project Muse, Fortress Press. http://proxy.library.nd.edu/login?url=https://muse.jhu.edu/books/9781451469752/.
Hauerwas, Stanley (1991), *A Community of Character: Toward a Constructive Christian Social Ethic*, 1st ed., Notre Dame, IN: University of Notre Dame Press.
Hauerwas, Stanley (1991), *The Peaceable Kingdom: A Primer in Christian Ethics*, 1st ed., Notre Dame, IN: University of Notre Dame Press.
Kant, Immanuel (2011), *Religion within the Limits of Reason Alone*, trans. Theodore M. Greene. United States: Digireads.com.
King, Martin Luther, Jr. (1968), *Where Do We Go from Here: Chaos or Community?* Boston: Beacon Press.
Long, Grace Cumming (1990), "The Ethics of Francis Greenwood Peabody: A Century of Christian Social Ethics. (Focus: The Ethics of the Social Gospel)," *The Journal of Religious Ethics* 18, no. 1: 55–73.
Long, D. Stephen (2015), "Protestant Social Ethics," in *The Cambridge Companion to Christian Political Theology*, eds. Craig Hovey and Elizabeth Phillips, Cambridge Companions to Religion, New York: Cambridge University Press.
Lovin, Robin W. (1999), *Christian Ethics: An Essential Guide*, 3rd ed., Nashville, TN: Abingdon Press.
Matz, Brian (2017), *Introducing Protestant Social Ethics: Foundations in Scripture, History, and Practice*, Grand Rapids, MI: Baker Academic.
Niebuhr, H. Richard (1988), *The Kingdom of God in America*, Middletown, CT: Wesleyan University Press.
Peabody, Francis Greenwood (1905), *Jesus Christ and the Christian Character*, New York: Macmillan.
Pinkard, Terry (2002), *German Philosophy 1760–1860: The Legacy of Idealism*, Cambridge: Cambridge University Press.
Pippin, Robert B. (1999), *Modernism as a Philosophical Problem: On the Dissatisfactions of European High Culture*, 2nd ed., Malden, MA: Wiley-Blackwell.
Ransom, Reverdy (1935), *The Negro: The Hope or Despair of Christianity*, Boston: Ruth Hill.
West, Cornel (1999), *The Cornel West Reader*, 1st ed., New York: Basic Civitas Books.

CHAPTER TWENTY-NINE

Lex Naturae

A New Way into a Liturgical Political Theology

CLÁUDIO CARVALHAES

We know that the whole creation has been groaning in labor pains until now; and not only the creation, but we ourselves, who have the first fruits of the Spirit, groan inwardly while we wait for adoption, the redemption of our bodies. For in hope we were saved. Now hope that is seen is not hope. For who hopes for what is seen?

—Romans 8:22–24 (NRSV)

INTRODUCTION

The little Baptist Church of Santo Antonio in the Desert of Sonora in Mexico gathers to celebrate a feast of baptism. On the back of the church, there is a water reservoir. From that reservoir plants are watered, animals drink, and people boil water to drink and to cook. On baptismal day, the water reservoir becomes the baptismal font. All of those who are going to be baptized get dunked in the same reservoir while the congregation sings a hymn. The cleansing of life comes from the clean water of their community reservoir. After the worship ends, the water reservoir/baptismal font then becomes a pool party for the kids. For the rest of the day the children play in the pool and rejoice in the 110°F weather.

In the forgotten lands of São Feliz do Araguaia in the Mato Grosso state in Brazil, Don Pedro Casaldáliga chose to live and work with the forgotten people of the land, small farmers, and indigenous people. Casaldáliga was regarded as a "subversive and extremist," "impertinent and troublesome" bishop whose teaching "was dangerous because it was so much embedded in liberation theology."[1] With his life threatened by the agribusiness, he kept going, preaching and living a gospel fully enmeshed with the life of God in the honoring and the protection of the earth, of the poor, and in the memory of the martyrs who were made along the way. The prayers of the people, the sacraments, and corporate worship always gave sustenance and orientation to the people. Together, they survived. Now at ninety years old, and very debilitated, he still lives there among his own people. Surely Don Pedro Casaldaliga is a mixture of Saint Francis and Oscar Romero for of our times

Somewhere near East London in South Africa, a Christian community orients its life: worship, seeds, and animals in three circles united by a center. At the center of these tree circles there is a baptismal font. Earth, animals, and worship have equal standing in an equal community. They pray, they eat, they plant, they live their lives in a circle of mutuality that defies the Christian dualisms of immanence and transcendence, culture and nature, human and animals.

These three examples remind us that the most important political gesture the field of liturgy can offer to a Christian way of praying-believing-acting is to initiate, or rather continue in more radical ways to pray-believe-act under the orientation of Gaia.[2] The ways Western liturgical theology has evolved show us how Christians have become completely detached from the earth and its bio-ecological diversities and processes of relation. We have elevated the altar from the earth, we have turned sacraments into limited and exclusionary means of grace instead of ends of grace, we have separated earthly sources of faith into spiritual practices, we have denied matter for the spirit, and we have turned our attention from place to time. This essay is an attempt to recover the earth as central and fundamental to our lives as Christians from the perspective of liturgy. Liturgical spaces are indeed political spaces and a fundamental part of the environmental politics of bio power and interrelations between human/humus: people, animals, earth, plants, seeds, animals, societies, biomes, etc.

This investigation seeks to engage *Lex Naturae*, the orienting ground from which we can learn how to pray, to believe and to act, as one of the best gifts that liturgical rituals can give to the world, as a way of helping us pay attention to Gaia in the current Anthropocene[3] period. Humans have walked the earth for a mere 0.1 percent of earth's existence, what some people are calling the Anthropocene or the age of humans, or the geological age in which human intervention has devastated and depleted the earth.

Liturgical political theology, oriented by *lex naturae*, can engage public spaces, but not only that, it can help us pay attention to the millions of years of the earth's history prior to human existence, to recognize our limited time on the stage of history. *Lex Naturae* can orient us in renewing the earth by transforming our rituals, our religious vows, our sacred things, our beliefs, our symbols, our gestures, our actions, and our songs by decentering the human as the central, most significant agent in history.

Thus, I will start this essay by offering first, its reason and proposal by developing what I am calling *lex naturae*. Then I will connect the *lex naturae* to the other *leges* (plural of *lex*, "laws") of the Christian faith: *orandi-credendi-vivendi* (prayer-belief-way of life), assuming that every other *lex* has to be oriented by *lex naturae*. These connections organize an ethical dimension that presses ways of living that entails the fullness of life or, as the Andean people call it, *Sumak Kawsay*, the good living. Then, I will move to the problems that have brought us here by developing the relation between theology, liturgy, and ethics to time, place, and space. I will finish with some brief suggestions for how to read the liturgical calendar from a Gaia-centered perspective.

LEX NATURAE

In order for the Christian religion to reconnect us to God we need to *religare* (literally, "bind together") with the earth. In this way, religion is bound up with materiality and the world of nature. Celebrating the plurality of cultures is not enough to deal with our current ecological crisis, neither is the Marxist notion of class struggle without expanding to include plants, animals, and the full range of life affected by human consumption. In this way, the class struggles between different shades of humanity become way more complex as Viveiros de Castro points out, once we consider (with indigenous people) that animals are also forms of the human.[4]

The dominant Christian ontological, liturgical, and political notions of the sacred are a product of economies of desire that create mechanisms that end up neutralizing forms of connection with the earth and necessary transformation. This neutralization is not a total severing from nature since we are materially connected with the earth, but rather a pervasive ideology that does not consider, and is not grounded, on the earth and its needs and demands. Thus, when a sustained theological discussion is not organized around the main law of nature, our faith, prayers, and life continue under the grasp of anthropocentric patriarchal political economies that privilege human desires and consumerism where natural resources are objectified as simple a given, always already there to fulfill these needs.

Liturgical theologies, in order to respond to the current political moment, must engage the *lex naturae*, the law of nature that relates to *colōnus* and *colōnia*,[5] a place where culture, land, economy, and power are always intertwined. As Nancy Cardoso Pereira poignantly says:

> Three neighboring words clash here: economics, ecology, ecumenism. The three share the oikos: basic social unit (home, but also world). Simplifying: economy → oikos + nomos (law / norm); ecology → oikos + logos (understanding / study); ecumenismo → oikos + form of the passive participle feminine (inhabited / inhabitants). These are three ways of being in the world and of organizing life in the world. While the economy disposes, it regulates the way of production of life in relation to the world, ecology is concerned with understanding these relations their logics and implications and ecumenism asks about the (objective and subjective) forms of occupation / experience of the world.[6]

The liturgical space has, for its most part, forgotten its relation to the material realm. The matter that composes our life in fullness and all its power dynamics is often not addressed fully in worship. Fundamentally, the most important political turn in liturgical studies must be the creation and organization of a desperately needed *lex naturae*. This *lex* is not about the protection of religious traditions but mainly, and most importantly, the protection and restitution of the world itself. We are at a point where no book of common worship can continue without attention to the needs of the earth. No belief is more important than the preservation of the bio-diversity of the earth and the elevation of Gaia in the Anthropocene. In order to move towards a more ethically and morally sound relationship with creation we must attune our bodies, our communities, and our forms of worship to a deeper and more robust understanding of what it means to be responsible citizens in the Anthropocene.[7]

Since the Industrial Revolution, motivated and driven by the political desires of European nations, colonization has taken resources from the rest of the world to supply for its people in a continuous extractive process that rips the earth off of its life, creating environmental impacts that destroy the lives of those who live in these parts of the world. Not only has humanity committed genocide on a grand scale, its hegemonic goals have made countless numbers plant and animal species extinct. If we are to embrace the *lex naturae*, we must attend to the ways we have damaged, changed and destroyed earth's life, irreparably reduced the diversity of organic life, and altered long-established patterns of climate. Even liberation theologies that did not engage fully with the earth must re-write their precepts, proposals and analysis in relation to the patterns of destruction of the earth, so their liberative praxis would also include liberation with and for the earth.

Gaia, as Bruno Latour articulates, is "the occasion for a return to Earth that allows for a differentiated version of the respective qualities that can be required of sciences, politics, and religions, as these are finally reduced to more modest and more earthbound definitions of their former vocations."[8] Gaia, that indigenous people from the Andes call Pachamama, and the Kuna people Abya Yala, is the place of uncountable living organisms, including humanity in its diverse forms, which includes the animal kingdom as well, who live in interdependence with one another. Gaia is a site of constant struggle, survival, and flourishing of all that lives and occupies the earth. With Gaia, we must pay attention to the ways the earth changes and moves and how humans change and move the earth as well through their nation-state boundaries, territories, and geopolitical decisions.

Here we do well to recall Donna Haraway's, *Staying with the Trouble: Making Kin in the Chthulucene*. She calls into questions the ways in which our time is wrapped up in capital and proposes a new *Chthulucene*:

> The scandals of times called the Anthropocene and the Capitalocene are the latest and most dangerous of these exterminating forces. Living-with and dying-with each other potently in the Chthulucene can be a fierce reply to the dictates of both Anthropos and Capital . . . Chthulucene is a simple word. It is a compound of two Greek roots (khthôn and kainos) that together name a kind of timeplace for learning to stay with the trouble of living and dying in response-ability on a damaged earth. Kainos means now, a time of beginnings, a time for on- going, for freshness. Nothing in kainos must mean conventional pasts, presents, or futures. There is nothing in times of beginnings that insists on wiping out what has come before, or, indeed, wiping out what comes after. Kainos can be full of inheritances, of remembering, and full of comings, of nurturing what might still be. I hear kainos in the sense of thick, ongoing presence, with hyphae infusing all sorts of temporalities and materialities . . .[9]

Gaia in its Chthulucene time must be our ground, horizon, and orientation, delineating our speed, imposing our limits, and organizing our desires. Chthulucene in its current history, conditions, and demands must be the orienting rhizome axes from which we orient our prayers, our theologies beliefs, and our daily life, not only of individuals but as communities, the so-called nations, and all its production. Chthulucene is our call for our response-ability to nurture and change. Our main questions come from Larry L. Rasmussen:

> How, then, do we hymn the Earth differently? How do we write and sing a new song for a strange land, even though it be our own? How do we do it with our neighbors, all our neighbors—human and other-than-human—when Earth is "hot, flat and crowded" and borders and walls no longer protect? Where do we turn when we discover that the religion we have lived by since the industrial-technological era emerged— eternal and exponential economic growth— is an illusion, dogma masquerading as common sense and kept alive by willpower and little else?[10]

This set of questions about a necessary *lex naturae* poses serious challenges for all.

Lex naturae challenges the ways in which humankind inscribes the very notion of nature and how we understand nature. Since nature cannot speak and we do not know what nature is really like, any understanding of nature is a human idea, a self-inscribed notion of nature on nature, by the ways we see and know and engage the earth. Moreover, any look at nature is already an interpretation, a turning of nature into a subject of our objective lenses. This caution, however, does not prevent us from working with and from nature but challenges our very categories, such as supernaturalism, naïve realism, as well as the values we impose on nature, our own personal worldviews, i.e., beliefs (cosmology), prayers (ritual actions), and ethics (notions of good and bad). Thus every *lex naturae* is a construction that is not itself natural, and yet, cultural. The human reason or will to power must accede to the movements and demands of the earth so as to move from conflict against *natura* toward a conflict along with *natura*.

As an extension of this first challenge, the *lex naturae* also challenges our naïve or colonial view of nature, as if nature has only harmonious forms of living and sharing so long as they are at our service. In this way, *lex naturae* reminds us of the "species struggle" and how being human has produced many heteronomous patriarchal Christianities, white supremacist discourses, sexual prejudices, disembodied faith, fear of matter, and liturgies detached from the earth that are damaging for our future. With *lex naturae*, we seek to establish a circularity of life around humanity that encompasses animals, plants, and all forms of life—including human culture—that live on the earth.

As a way of overcoming this instrumental view of nature, earthly liturgies will have a preferential option for the poor and oppressed, broadened to include not only people, but also the whole of the natural order. Liturgies that deepen Christ's incarnation in our Adamic humus (organic soil), serve to remind us of what we have always already been: soil, matter, and water. As *Imago Dei* we are made of what God is made. In Christ, immanence and transcendence are undone and our notion of divinity leads to deeper forms of immanence and matter. Thus, the Christological liturgies are essentially liturgies of the land, reminding us not only of our origin and destiny but also that the soil we walk on—every private parcel to every nation-state—is stolen land. As Larry Rasmussen reminds us by citing Bonhoeffer: "the constructive work of faith and the experience of Jesus Christ will be this-worldy and earth-honoring. Transcendence, indeed God, is 'the beyond in the midst of life,' experienced as an ethic of responsibility for 'the whole of earthly life.'"[11] With *lex naturae*, our worship gains a much more expansive notion of life and death where soil, notions of class, race, sex, gender, and social conditions are all interrelated. With *lex naturae*, bodies will be considered in their many forms of vulnerability and resilience and with Sojourner Truth we will "speak upon the ashes," and also from the ashes.

Lex naturae thus challenges the exclusive use of the Bible in our communities, the limitations of our creeds, the sources of our revelation, the structures of our theologies, the power dynamics within our communities, the cosmologies of our denominations, the thinking of the sacraments, the limits of Christian holy things, and the insular juxtaposition of our liturgies. While challenging the Christian faith from the inside, the *lex orandi-credendi-vivendi* as oriented by the *lex naturae* will call attention to *res* ("matter"), which includes all natural things from rivers to oceans to phytoplankton, and from soil to seeds to flora, and all the bio-diversity of fauna from insect to birds to mammals, thereby revealing the conflict between the power dynamics of nature and the practices of capitalism and consumerism. This conceptual move creates and empowers our prophetic voices, it rings an end-of-the-world siren against the global mass production of products and exploitation of natural energies, the absurd forms of consumerism, even all forms of fallacy of sustainable development, racist environmental policies, the poisoning of the soil, the acidization of the oceans, the ongoing land grabbing from indigenous communities, and the ongoing destitution of established natural life cycles.

Given that we all belong to the same earth, the *lex naturae* fosters, in a new *natural key*, what Martin Luther King, Jr. said in his "Letter from a Birmingham Jail": "We are caught in an inescapable network of mutuality, tied in a single garment of destiny. Whatever affects one directly affects all indirectly."[12] This mutuality is also found in the voices and movements of the Spirit/spirits through the relationality of different forms of life to matter, moving in and through us, balancing our lives with a variety of energies in leaves, plants, soil. Our mutuality comes from the earth, from our shared beginning and end, our communitarian/cosmopolitan forms of living and our common mortality. From dust we come, and to dust we shall return. As Robin Kimmerer asks: "How can we begin to move toward ecological and cultural sustainability if we cannot even imagine what the path feels like? If we can't imagine the generosity of geese?"[13] *Lex naturae* has to turn our eyes to learn about the geese, the seeds, the turtles, and so on.

Pedro Casaldáliga, a prophetic voice in Latin America, calls us into this discernment: "This is our task: to discern the signs of places in which we do not yet belong but in which we will belong—'no places' that will become concrete utopias."[14] The concrete utopia to be thought now is somewhat illogical: If we are to "discern the signs of places in which we do not yet belong but in which we will belong," then we must think of the earth not only as the place we inhabit now but a place in part already gone, and soon to be fully gone and become a no place, at least for our kind of human existence. The earth has been made destitute of its basic forms of life through multiple acts of violence. The removal of mountaintops through strip mining is but one example of the unbalanced dynamics of power, threatening not only the earth but also the entirety of our common living. Other examples include over fishing and the disposal of plastic garbage into the oceans, showing no respect for the basic sources and structures of life, prioritizing consumption over the earth's natural cycles to set the tone and speed of our lives.

As liturgists and theologians, *lex naturae* helps us to debunk interpretations of the earth as God's gift—as an object given to us for the commodification of our desires—by proposing an alternative to the theological understanding that God makes an exclusive preference for humanity above other species. In this matter, the *lex naturae* challenges the interpretation of Genesis 1:26: "Then God said, 'Let us make humankind in our image, according to our likeness; and let them have dominion over the fish of the sea, and over the birds of the air, and over the cattle, and over all the wild animals of the earth, and over every creeping thing that creeps upon the earth.'"[15] *Lex naturae* pleads for an intertwined correlation of values and relationality where dominion is transcended in favor of a sharing of resources that will resist the unbalanced thinking that leads to the objectification and commodification of other forms of life. Moreover, God's promise to Noah must be reconsidered as water levels continue to rise and flood many parts of the earth. Bruno Latour calls our attention to those who deny climate change and consequent flooding through an appeal to Scriptures: "Some of them don't even hesitate to stand up in a political meeting and invoke the covenant in Genesis where God promises Noah that He will send no more floods: 'Never again will I curse the ground because of man, even though every inclination of his heart is evil from childhood, and never again will I destroy all living creatures, as I have done' (Gen. 8:21). With such solid assurance, it would be wrong indeed to worry!"[16] New theological frameworks must be proposed. The theological narrative of the *lex naturae* must join with other narratives, especially those indigenous cosmologies where the earth is the axis of life, where animals, spirits, and the whole biosphere live somewhat harmoniously. Thus, *lex naturae* opens itself to wonder and to the wonder-full ways of Gaia in all its varied existence. It orients people beyond the established, dominant scientific and theological narratives, and challenges them to cherish previously ignored or repressed conceptual worlds of wonder and awe.

In a more prescriptive move, the challenge of a liturgical political theology rooted in the practices of the *lex naturae* includes the foundational fallacy of "sustainable" development. The narratives of sustainable development still serve the modern, colonial mindset that continues to view the natural world as a commodity that exists only to serve human needs. A radical counternarrative ought to start with the Paris agreement and then further radicalize its political and economic possibilities. The *lex naturae* helps us pray and believe in ways that break existing forms of domination and oppression. For instance, it joins those who fight for extinguishing fossil fuel and coal energy, putting limits to global movement and local energy usage. We learn with Augustine that prayer orients human desire; Christian prayer can help people, especially in the developed world, to overcome their sense of entitlement and reject the narrative that everything exists to sate our immediate needs and wants. The ethics of *lex naturae* restructures the workers' market, reduces work hours, increases pay, and provides more time for leisure. The belief of *lex naturae* puts a halt on companies that pollute rivers, turns private lands into common lands, blocks transgenic products, abolishes pesticides, shuts down all of the agri-business companies, helps put limits to our consumption, adds resources for relations with the earth in curriculums in schools and helps us reorganize our whole life together. This is an exercise in thinking–doing *lex naturae*. *Lex naturae* can be a roadmap to our mutual transformation due to the extreme moments we are arriving. As Rosemary R. Ruether states, this work intends the "recovery of the Earth, the restoration of a healthy relationship between men and women, classes and nations, human beings and the Earth."[17]

Such a transformation does not occur without resistance and struggle, especially since *lex naturae* challenges any religiosity that sees humankind as detached and over against nature, or any ideology, including the Cartesian scientific ontological notion of nature, in which the earth is subjugated by human rationality. Instead what is called for is a new *fundamental* relationship to nature where humankind learns to listen to the earth and to the spirits, as we learn to listen to God. Nothing in our lives exists apart from the earth! We breathe, we drink, we eat, we shit, and we sleep because our bodies are part of the natural eco-systems that constitute life on earth. Consequently, the theological narrative of the *lex naturae* embodies the interreligious par excellence, and joins Pope Francis' Encyclical Letter *Laudato si'*, the Buddhist cosmologies of immanence, Buddha's relation with the earth, the Muslim prayers that honor the earth with people's foreheads, the earth festivities of Judaism, the balancing energies by Voduns and Orixas of the African religiosities, in thinking beyond solely Cartesian ways. As Amitav Ghosh said in a recent lecture at Union Theological Seminary, "In every culture of all time, there have been people who have been able to give voice to nature . . . If one does not allow for that we are trapped in the world of cognition—that what see and touch is all there is."[18] We need different forms of thinking and feeling and living and praying and believing! But we are all trapped by ossified political thinking, by otherworldly beliefs not connected to the earth, and by worldviews that reify the illusion of a spirit–body dualism.

With the construction of new theological narratives, we are thrown into realms of strangeness, disorientation, weirdness, loss, and potential disaster. Outmoded thought patterns prevent us from dealing with issues properly as we face contradictions armed with political solutions that do not allow the freedom to think in strange new ways. One mode of reasoning is not enough. We need a plurality of knowledges. The language of worship and its accompanying liturgies not only offer us an alternative rational discourse, but also a place for feelings and emotions to be engaged, expanded, and integrated. Visual arts, rituals, stories, songs all inhabit a place in our bodies that is not necessarily the objectivity of our minds, while providing ways to resist, and for new liturgical and life-giving imaginaries to develop. We need this *space to think, to feel*, to touch, to hear, to listen, to taste see, to perceive. Living and non-living actants together, creating new forms of assemblages and assemblies, solidarities and fluidarities,[19] composing and performing Gaia in new possible ways. We don't need another world as if we need another Gaia. What we need is to say: another kind of human being/being human is possible! In articulating a political liturgical theology, we must engage the full resources of human imagination and creativity. Under the immense responsibility to care for the earth, *lex natura* needs to be woven and engaged through new rituals for a new awareness with new companions: species, living and not living, for the new time called Anthropocene, for new relations and understandings with the spaces/places we live. This cannot be done by employing only Europeans forms of reasoning, old-religious rituals, or writing books and articles. We need other forms of imagining, of wonder, artistic, expansive forms of re-imagining the earth, with correlations and juxtapositions not yet known. It is time for us to pay attention to artists engaging *Gaia* through art.[20] Recently, Larry Rasmussen, one of the pioneers of eco-theology, visited my class on thinking about worship theologically, and spoke about the need for congregations to, "Lose themselves in wonder, telling and retelling of stories, do and create new rituals, resist and renew and sing a song, asking God and each other to 'give us the courage to enter the song.'"[21] Thus, the combination of all the leges: *orandi-credendi-vivendi*, now reorganized by *natura*, leads to a new liturgical political theology capable of reorganizing the whole *polis*, including the public, private, external, internal, objective, and subjective spaces of religion.

THE LITURGICAL LAWS, THE SACRED, AND THE EARTH

Liturgical space is fundamentally a political space. The term liturgy from the Greek civil notion of the public work of the people done on behalf of the people became the work of the church, thus constituting a different communal and political perspective. When the church started to define liturgy as ways of understanding faith and prayer, the church was defining its own space as public in relation to the larger public space. This is when the connection of two "laws," the *lex orandi* and *lex credendi* (law of prayer and law of belief), came to organize and define the form and content of both belief and prayer. These new forms of worship proved dangerous acts for the early Christians since their prayers and beliefs were performed under the shadow and threat of the Roman Empire. Hiding their worship places from public view, Christian prayers and liturgical actions focused on communion and baptism as community-defining practices, while also providing much-needed instruction on preparing oneself to die as martyrs if caught by the Empire. The ways the church prayed and believed and lived (*lex vivendi*) shaped their public witness.

As we see throughout the New Testament, the early Christian churches taught believers to care for each other in distinctive ways. The Book of Acts traces the early church's commitment to each other's needs, and the letters to the churches admonish congregations to help those in need (Ephesians 4:28), carry each other's burdens (Galatians 6:2), provide and share with others (Hebrews 13:16), give clothes and daily food to those in need (James 2:14–17), care for the interests of others (Philippians 2:4), welcome people (Romans 12:13), and care for the weak (Romans 15:1). Their *lex orandi-vivendi-credendi* was known widely and had both supporters and opponents, as evidence by the general disdain and hatred for the growing sect:

> The Christians are a gang ... of discredited and proscribed desperadoes who band themselves against the gods. Fellows who gather together illiterates from the dregs of the populace and credulous women with the instability natural to their sex, and so organize a rabble of profane conspirators, leagued together by meetings at night and ritual fasts and unnatural repasts ... a secret tribe that shuns the light, silent in the open, but talkative in hid corners ... Root and branch it must be exterminated and accursed. They (the Christians) recognize one another by secret signs and marks: They fall in love almost before they are acquainted, everywhere they introduce a kind of religion of lust, a promiscuous "brotherhood" and "sisterhood" by which ordinary fornication, under the cover of a hallowed name, is converted to incest.[22]

During the period of Roman persecution, the law of prayer and belief was fully connected with the *lex vivendi*, the distinctly Christian way of living and witnessing, but when the church was coopted by Constantine, the law of living came under the *lex* of the Empire, which determined new ways of praying and believing, including an attempt to homogenize Christian beliefs and prayers. The movement from the house churches to the basilicas sharply redefined what being a Christian was all about. For instance, the life of baptism summoning the three *leges* (*lex* in plural), prayer, faith and life—once the entry point into the Christian family—becomes a demand to submit to the Empire, with the pledge of faith to God now subsumed under the rule of the emperor.

If in the New Testament there are theological and liturgical gestures against the Empire, such as Paul calling God "father" to undermine the fatherhood of the Emperor (*pater patriae*), the new life of the churches under the Constantinian Empire now constituted a new political reality.[23] Since Constantine, the *leges* of Christianity have been used both for and against the Empire. Against empire, for instance, were those bishops who were friends of the poor, or in the Christian resistance to the Roman calendar, or in the critique of the blood sports that were so popular with the Romans. In favor of empire, when baptism became more a civilian code of "citizenship" in the Empire than the entry way into the Christian life. Liturgical changes became embroiled with political movements, shifting and moving the whole body of Christ in certain directions, orienting and reorienting a faith that more often than not moved away from the poor and closer to the seat of power. The grandiose liturgical spaces where prominent bishops with their pointy hats, golden rings, and fashionable dress coopted the church's hierarchy in service to the Empire, undermining the *orandi-credendi-vivendi* in order to maintain, support, and foster another *lex*: Caesar's *lex*.

Over time, the focal point of liturgical theologies became protecting the sacred (synonymous with those in power) at all costs, as in Carl Schmitt's understanding of "political theology." The who and the what of God is intrinsically related to the how of the sacred, or in other words, the way we liturgize God are the ways we organize our local communities and public spaces. Questions like "Who is God is and how is God known?" and "What are the means of salvation?" are often manipulated by certain political theologies in an effort to keep power and authority. The *lex ecclesia*, or the law of the church, subverted the other *leges*. Through the liturgical frames of content and forms, the church ostensibly provides the divine ruling of God, so the work of liturgists includes the role of watchdog protecting sanctioned ways of speaking about God. In this way, over time, the sacred was reduced to the sacraments by which the church controlled access to the means of grace.

Limiting access to God only to the officially recognized sacraments only contributed to the desacralization of the earth and alienation from nature, which allowed the natural order to become commodified for human consumption. If it is only at the altar that the sacred is to be celebrated and shared, the geographical spaces where the altars are located don't matter. The discontinuity of the sacraments from the earth is such that the materiality of its holy things and the economic aspects of the sacred transactions (bread and wine/ body and blood) are rarely expounded upon in liturgical practice. Rarely are the waters of baptism related to rivers and oceans, or grapes and wheat recognized as the labor of non-documented immigrants. In other words, the sacramental laws, *lex credendi-orandi*, have become detached from the *lex vivendi*, the law of living. Most Christian liturgical reforms only consider the aesthetic but rarely consider the ethical dimensions of worship. In order to do that, the sacred must be re-attached to the "natural world" as not only the location for God's revelation, but also as the means of God's salvation.

The presence of the three liturgical *leges*, even while acknowledging our complex relationship with space, matter, and time, are never fundamentally connected to the earth. Christian prayers, beliefs, and ethics all take for granted the existence of the earth, willing to acknowledge it as a *locus* of divine revelation, but never fully considering the earth as central to the church's most fundamental existence. Consequently, our prayers, beliefs, and ethics are never held accountable or called to task for the scandalous ecological destruction we have caused.

LITURGIES, TIME, AND SPACE

While growing up in a conservative church I often heard in worship that Jesus was coming and the world was going to end. I always thought that the world would end because, at some point, the time would come when God was going to put an end to the world, as Scripture (supposedly) promised. The end of times, I learned later, was related to the possibility of a millennium when Jesus would rule on earth. After that, I was taught that the earth was only a temporary receptacle bound to be destroyed, a necessary object of transition to the real (spiritual) life that was awaiting us. In my evangelistic zeal, I remember battling the Jehovah's Witnesses over their heresy that the earth would be a place for many of us to live in for eternity. I couldn't understand how they had this attachment to the earth when we ("Christians") were going to be in heaven.

This detachment from the earth is also shown by the absence of space/place in Christian theologies and liturgies, causing an abyss between faith and matter. The biblical war between flesh (*sarx*) and spirit (*pneuma*) as often interpreted in the apostle Paul's thinking created an aversion to matter, the body, earth, things, female sexuality, etc. Christian spirituality was thus fully organized around time and spirit, heaven and maleness. As Brazilian theologian Vitor Westhelle puts it so well in his superb book *Eschatology and Space: The Lost Dimension in Theology Past and Present*:

> The finitude of time and space is set in such radical opposition to eternity that transcendence is sequestered from the world we see and experience. Time is the only compass to guide us to the world to come. Space is at best a diversion, and at worst the very cause of our errings. Creation and consummation are absolute limits set by the span of time.[24]

In worship this is clear. Christian liturgies are ways of ordering life and faith through time. In many churches, life/faith is ordered through the liturgical calendar, which sets up theological emphases on life around *kronos* and *kairos*, through which God's plan of salvation is understood. Place, space and earth are to be considered under the notions of time. Throughout the calendar year we are eternally returning, not to the earth, but to the same event, always timely, but rarely spatial. Our sacraments are mostly a reification of time through matter. We learn that in Baptism we belong to God since time immemorial. In the Eucharist, we remember Jesus coming in the fullness of time, whose death is often detached from its political underpinnings. Both sacraments orient us toward an eschatological time, detached from an earthly space. *Kairos* without embodiment in space is an idea with dangerous consequences.

SPACE AND PLACE AND WORSHIP

As a consequence, the eschatological liturgies of Christianity too often resemble revolving doors forever spinning around their own narrow concerns and doctrines. The worship of the church turns in on itself, creating a provincial European God made universal through the repetition of the timeless notion of rituals. Worship happens in a rigidly controlled environment in which the institutional church limits and controls access to the presence of God, so that perpetuating its power becomes the church's only guiding value. We need to rethink and reclaim liturgical space.

Let us so briefly see how Yi-Fu Tuan and Edward Relph see space and place. Tuan says: "space is freedom, place is security,"[25] and Relph says "space and place are dialectically structured in human environmental experience, since our understanding of space is related to the places we inhabit, which in turn derive meaning from their spatial context."[26] Both authors note that space and place are often detached from economic practices. Liturgical spaces have the potential to change people's conceptions of how to relate to the material and natural world by welcoming people and comforting them through the security of its ritual offerings. We need to understand space differently in all its layers of complexity so that our sacred spaces come to include economic relationships and our interrelatedness to the natural material world. David Harvey's defines space:

> Space is neither absolute, relative or relational in itself, but it can become one or all simultaneously depending on the circumstances. The problem of the proper conceptualization of space is resolved through human practice with respect to it. In other words, there are no philosophical answers to philosophical questions that arise over the nature of space - the answers lie in human practice. The question "what is space?" is therefore replaced by the question "how is it that different human practices create and make use of different conceptualizations of space?" The property relationship, for example, creates absolute spaces within which monopoly control can operate. The movement of people, goods, services, and information takes place in a relative space because it takes money, time, energy, and the like to overcome the friction of distance. Parcels of land also capture benefits because they contain relationships with other parcels. . . . in the form of rent relational space comes into its own as an important aspect of human social practice.[27]

Within this understanding of space we can circulate objects, people, goods, structures, modes of production, economic developments and class struggle. We can count the history of colonial power and show that no space is value-free. Spaces are indeed places of official and contested meanings. That means that the whole structure of religious buildings is grounded in more than religious meaning, but is a product of the commodification and the economic relations that sustain private spaces. Churches have been fundamentally erected on portions of land stolen from indigenous communities, making every owner of private space carriers of injustice and oppression, re-inscribing violence, as they don't just carry markers of the injustice, but actively partake in the perpetuation of violence when this history is not brought to light or acknowledged. The question that lingers with us then is: how can holy liturgies speak of sacred things when the very space/ground they inhabit is marked by injustice?

The *place* of worship is also marked by those who inhabit that *space*, with boundaries and markers that show who is invited, or not, to that space. Let us not forget that during slavery in the US, Christian churches had the balcony reserved for black people, and pews closer to the altar/pulpit were bought and secured by rich families. Let us move even beyond that notion of space, towards native people's forms of thinking and relating to land and space. Winona LaDuke from the Dakota nation gives us an expansive notion of space:

> We have a word in our language which describes the practice of living in harmony with natural law: minocimaatisiiwin. This word describes how you behave as an individual in a relationship with other individuals and in relationship with the land and all things. We have tried to retain this way of living and this way of thinking in spite of all that has happened to us over the centuries. I believe we do retain most of these practices in our community, even if they are overshadowed at times by individualism ... Our traditional forms of land use and ownership are similar to those found in community land trusts being established today. The land is owned collectively, and each family has traditional areas where it fishes and hunts. We call our concept of land ownership Anishinaabeg akiing: "the land of the people," which doesn't imply that we own our land, but that we belong on it. Unfortunately, our definition doesn't stand up well in court because this country's legal system upholds the concept of private property.[28]

This expansive notion of space, land, living and believing, holds a circularity of relations that are based on natural law, not the natural law of Hobbes, Locke, and Rousseau, but that of the earth ruling and orienting our lives, our desires, and limiting our ways of living. Lakota people see space as more than a grid of abstract or independent notions, or independent meanings but rather, a place with a plethora of relations, a place of multi-naturalisms and human kinds, making the *ecos-oikos* a place where the worlds of fauna and flora co-exist in horizontal commonality and gnarly entanglement.

Unfortunately, at this moment, liturgical spaces fail to engage the earth as space in either of the ways conceived by Harvey or LaDuke. Instead, traditional liturgies quickly remind us that life is constituted by a spiritual relationship to a God who always seems above and beyond us. In a recent interreligious dialogue held in New York City, in which I participated, religious leaders were lamenting the lack of vertical connections with God, showing a clear detachment from the earth. The love of others, which is the other/same side of the love of God, often doesn't reach down to the land/earth and doesn't proliferate horizontally, like a grapevines or a rhizome. The ritual services of the Christian churches tend to keep us detached from the earth. Our spiritualities, springing from our ritual services, tend not to look to the lilies or the birds for comfort and security, as Jesus said, but rather, look to a higher spiritual space that we actually don't know exists.

In our worship services, we sing glory to a placeless One who is the same yesterday, today and forever. A placeless god who, by not being *rooted* in place, does not need to extend care for the place it inhabits since this God lives in eternity (*somewhen*), not *somewhere*, a physical place to be attached and accountable to, and in relationship with. Our sermons organize our lives through distinctions between the secular *chronos* and the sacred *kairos* overlooking the *topos* of the God of time. Our baptism is a testimony to a new time, where the old time is left behind and we become "new creatures" in a new time. Our Eucharist/Communion liturgies name God's salvific acts in history, moments in time when (without being fully "where") God has rescued God's people and manifested God's self in the fullness of time in Jesus Christ. The elements of the Eucharist are holders of this Kairos time when God is manifested fully in our midst and that is why many churches will call the sacraments the means of grace. Our offerings are to be expressions of the gratitude for the bounty of God in our lives. This bounty, which at first was related to the harvest of God's gifts, now contributes to our separation and alienation from the places of production. The charge and benediction announce that the Lord is coming in an eschatological promise in some future time. Through our liturgical actions and words, the church is called to be a witness in our time, announcing the now and not-yet presence of the Kingdom of God. And thus, detaching us from our response-ability[29] to respond to the urgencies of our common home (earth).

The political theology of our liturgies is condensed, expressed, and structured fundamentally around time. However, the very "ground" of liturgical theologies, time itself, is organized in a way that makes liturgies both timeless and placeless, which frees us from being accountable to the destruction of place, to the environmental racism, and other ecological injustices. There is a hope and a belief (and also illusion) that what we do in worship is and should be timeless just as God is not bound by time. Consequently, denominational worship books are full of expressions of this future-oriented eschatological theology and timeless liturgical orders. Worship books are celebrated as carriers of a timeless wisdom though they are actually written locally by a certain group of people at a particular time in history. The church's selective amnesia encourages us to forget the time and place, and by whom, the books of common worship were written, rendering the where of its ritual performance superfluous. By surreptitiously suppressing the locations and cultures where they were written, the magisterium of the church can hide behind the timeless faithfulness of eternal doctrine. Instead of being expressions of specific cultures, they have become placeless expressions of faith. The language of the Christian liturgies perpetuated in worship books elevates the eternal God, who is eternal and unchanging, thereby making the place where God is encountered unimportant. As Westhele says:

> Space indeed becomes illusory. What modernity then finally accomplished is a recombination of time and space in which space is no longer even linked to place. The words of Anthony Giddens, reading into utopian imagination the omens announcing the disappearance of real spaces, aptly states: The severance of time from space does not mean that these henceforth become mutually alien aspects of human social organization. On the contrary: it provides the very basis for the recombination in ways that coordinate social activities without necessary reference to particularities of place.[30]

Admittedly, since Vatican II the liturgical renewal movement has been marked by the concern with cultures and contexts.[31] The question of culture one of authenticity in relating individual cultures to the gospel, leading to the honoring of cultures and highly praising the cultural diversity of the liturgical *ordo* ("order"). However, this sensitivity to cultural context has done little to overcome the timelessness of the liturgy as above all cultures. Consequently, the liturgy serves as the standard of what is good or bad in each culture, such that new liturgies are little more than embellishments of the dominant, Eurocentric traditional forms of timeless liturgical order with some local "costume" added, such as Native American clothing or vestments, adorning the same old timeless liturgies while continuing to ignore power dynamics, real contexts, colonized spaces, and complex local experiences.

When we relate the liturgical *ordo*, which is the theological framing of the liturgical practice, to cultures, spaces and contextuality we need to talk about the material ways in which liturgies are to be enacted. For instance, when we talk about sacred spaces, most often we are talking about the architectural planning of manufactured spaces in churches that must be conducive to relating to a transcendent God through the performance of our timeless and unchanging liturgies. These traditional liturgies are intended to separate the believer from the world in order to focus only on God. Any material attachment or any "earthly" distraction has typically been excluded. However, liturgies are human actions originating in a particular time and space that must attend to the economic inequality, class struggle, racial conflicts, means of production, and its relation to the earth in which this space exists.

From this new awareness of the materiality of liturgical space, a liturgical political theology emerges designed to help the Christian community learn how to think, relate, act, and live in the material world. By challenging the timelessness of traditional liturgies, an embodied liturgy leads to new forms of organizing the church's moral and ethical life with a fundamentally new orientation for understanding what being human is all about. Thus, the politics of liturgical spaces and how we understand these spaces is central to how we live the Christian faith. Christian history shows that the political core of Christian liturgical theology has served to deny its spatial location and material embodiment in two ways: first, by developing a "placeless" theology that aims the message of Christ to the disembodied spirit while avoiding all the political structures that form the very spaces the community concretely inhabits; second, by evolving a contextual theology that, while dealing with some of the concrete situations of the church environment such as homelessness or the contributions of the artistic community, still manages to avoid the power dynamics of class and race. Both these theological forms of escapism avoid the material strictures of real life, leading Christian churches to perform political actions that either implement or uphold dominant political agendas under the guise of political neutrality. Thus, most churches continue to perpetuate the political status quo—with its crass consumerism and environmental blind spots—by electing the same candidates over and over, avoiding the conflicts arising from racial inequality, and supporting economic views that continue to benefit the few at the expense of the many.

CONCLUSION

The power of rituals in religious communities cannot be dismissed. The existence of rituals is political at its core and influences the politics of all communities, from small towns to entire nations. This investigation has tried to show how *lex naturae* must orient us to think, pray, relate, and live in concrete, material places. So conceived, worship can lead us to view the earth and Gaia as full incarnations of God in our midst. By way of conclusion, I offer some suggestions for discerning places and spaces within the liturgical calendar through which the church can celebrate the earth as central and fundamental to our lives as Christians.

All Saints Day—the earth is our main saint with Winona LaDuke, Wendel Berry, Cesar Chavez, and Dolores Huerta as the patron saints of the US. Through them we create movements of solidarity-fluidarity from the earth, bound to an ethics of response-ability and care, "taking stock," in Bonhoeffer's words, of Gaia today. *Christ the King*—Christ as king, transcendent, only exists sacramentally through service to the neighbor and her needs. As Bonhoeffer says: "The transcendent is not the infinite, unattainable tasks, but the neighbor within reach in any given situation. God in human form."[32] *Advent*—The preparation of the coming of Jesus is the preparation of the earth, announcing that the earth will be restored once again. *Christmastide*—Jesus is God's transcendence and immanence fully united in human existence with all its attending materiality, with new life springing from the earth in fulfillment of God's promises to build a new heaven and a new earth (Rev. 21). *Transfiguration*—Baptism carries a full circularity of life through water. We are water, becoming water and returning back to water. Grapes and wheat are soil, turning into the body of Christ, thus also carrying a circularity of life from humus to humus. We are soil, becoming Christ, humus, and returning to humus. *Lent*—We put our ears to the ground. We listen to the earth. We fast. We thank God for the bounty of life. We don't eat meat. We only eat what is in season. All of this designed to help us recognize and celebrate the earth all year long. *Eastertide*—We weep with the earth, we groan with the earth. We clean the rivers, the oceans. The resurrection of Jesus is the resurrection of the earth. We plant new trees and learn about biodiversity in celebration of new life springing. *Pentecost*—The celebration of the harvests everywhere. The spirit of life springing and showing us its renewal, renovation, and restoration. We feast on the bountiful gifts of the earth, on the generous givenness of the Spirit. With and through the Spirit, we correct injustices, we curb our lust and greed, reorient our desires, and we give back what we have taken beyond our measure. *Trinity Sunday*—The triune God is a society made of a quaternity: God the earth, God the water, God the air, God the fire. With this trinity, the *lex natura* counters the currently dominant trinity so vividly described by Eduardo Viveiros de Castro, "State the Father, Market the Son, and Reason/Science the Holy Spirit."[33] *Ordinary time*—We learn that the sacred is everywhere, heightened in some places but fully lived in the radical immanence of God in our lives. We rest, we work in our gardens, we share our harvest, we support local farmers, we develop house economies, we drink the water of our rivers, we pray the prayers of our communities and of communities across the world, celebrate our baptisms in the local rivers, and the Eucharist with the food harvested in our gardens.

Let the discerning of liturgical political places take place through an appreciation of *natura*. Amen.

NOTES

1. *Pedro Casaldáliga, 90 anos: bispo, poeta e defensor intransigente da dignidade humana,* Revista Ihu On-Line, 31 Janeiro 2018, http://www.ihu.unisinos.br/78-noticias/575711-pedro-casaldaliga-90-anos-bispo-poeta-e-defensor-intransigente-da-dignidade-humana

2. Gaia is the living and sacred earth. In Ecofeminism, Gaia has become a critical perspective and an orienting axis from which ecology and feminism work together to dismantle the structures of Western Christian culture. As Rosemary Ruether says "The purpose of this search is the recovery of the Earth, the restoration of a healthy relationship between men and women, classes and nations, human beings and the Earth. This recovery will only be possible if we recognize and modify the way in which, supported in part by Christianity, Western culture has justified domination." Rosemary Radford Ruether, *Gaia & God: An Ecofeminist Theology of Earth Healing* (New York: HarperCollins, 1992), 1; Ivone Gebara says that "Through ecofeminism, I have begun to see more clearly how much our bodies-my body, and the bodies of my neighbors-are affected, not just by unemployment and economic hardship, but also by the harmful effects the system of industrial exploitation imposes on them. I have begun to see more clearly how the exclusion of the poor is linked to the destruction of their lands, to the forces that leave them no choice but to move from

place to place in a ceaseless exile, to racism, and to the growing militarization of their countries." Ivone Gebara. *Longing for Running Water: Ecofeminism and Liberation* (Biblical Reflections on Ministry) (Kindle edition), 55–58.

3. Erle C. Ellis says: "Humans had so clearly reshaped Earth since the last ice age ended, the beginning of the Holocene Epoch. From this moment on, the proposal to rename Earth's current interval of geological time after us, the Anthropos . . . The Anthropocene demands an even greater adjustment of our perspectives. As geologists and others struggle for and against various proposals to formalize the Anthropocene, it should come as no surprise that their efforts have become entangled with both age-old worldviews and contemporary debates on the role of humans in nature and even what it means to be human." Erle C. Ellis, *Anthropocene: A Very Short Introduction* (Very Short Introductions) (Oxford: Oxford University Press, Kindle edition), 1, 2.

4. Eduardo Viveiros de Castro—A revolução faz o bom tempo, https://www.youtube.com/watch?v=CjbU1jO6rmE

5. Alfredo Bosi says that "Colonus is the one who cultivates the rural property instead of its owner; it is its administrator in the technical and legal sense of the word. It is mentioned in Titus Maccius Plautus and Cato the Elder, as colônia . . .; the inhabitant of colony, in Greek m. àpoikos, that comes from establish oneself in the place of *incolae*." In Alfredo Bosi, Silética da Colonização (São Paulo: Companhi das Letras, 1992), 11.

6. Nancy Cardoso Pereira, *V Congresso Latino-Americano De Gênero E Religião*, Faculdades EST, August 2017, http://eventos.est.edu.br/index.php/genero/Genero

7. See Leslie Head *Hope and Grief in the Anthropocene: Re-conceptualising Human–Nature Relations* (New York: Routledge, 2016).

8. Bruno Latour, *Facing Gaia: Eight Lectures on the New Climatic Regime*, Wiley. Kindle edition, 4.

9. Donna Haraway's, *Staying with the Trouble: Making Kin in the Chthulucene* (Durham, NC: Duke University Press, 2016), 2.

10. Larry Rasmussen, L. *Earth-honoring Faith: Religious Ethics in a New Key* (Oxford: Oxford University Press, Kindle edition), 5.

11. Dietrich Bonhoeffer in Larry Rasmussen, *Bonhoeffer and the Anthropocene*, NGTT DEEL 55, Supplementum 1, 2014, 947.

12. "Letter from Birmingham Jail," in James M. Washington, *A Testament of Hope: The Essential Writings of Martin Luther King, Jr.* (San Francisco, CA: Harper & Row, 1996), 190.

13. Robin Kimmerer, *Braiding Sweetgrass* (Minneapolis, MN: Milkweed Editions, 2013), 21.

14. Pedro Casaldáliga, Vitor W Esthelle, "Creation Motifs in the Search for a Vital Space: A Latin American Perspective," in Susan B. Thistlewaite and Mary P. Engel, eds., *Lift Every Voice: Constructing Christian Theologies from the Underside* (New York: Orbis, 1998), 148.

15. Genesis 1:26, *The Holy Bible*, NRSV.

16. Latour, *Facing Gaia: Eight Lectures on the New Climatic Regime*, 11.

17. Ruether, *Gaia & God*, 1.

18. Amitav Ghosh, *The Great Derangement: Climate Change and the Unthinkable*, https://www.youtube.com/watch?v=9eFT_eb_jRk&t=4390s

19. "Fluidarity is a process of being 'community-bound' without a clear arrival and with writing in 'fluidity' rather than assuming a solid space or identity from which to act. Fluidity is a practice and an analytics. . . . It is about trying to find a way to ethically articulate these relations: to articulate the sense of writing and speaking about (producing the book you hold in your hands), in the sense of paying attention to those orange and transformative connections that makes identities, and in the sense of constituting and being constituted by

those very connections." Diane M. Nelson, *A Finger in the Wound: Body Politics in Quincentennial Guatemala* (Berkeley, CA: University of California Press, 1999), 348–349.
20. Some environmental artists are Subhankar Banerjee, David Buckland, Basia Irland.
21. Marty Haugen, *Gather Us In* (Hymn) (Chicago: GIA Publications, Inc., 1982).
22. Octavius Minucious Feliz, 8.4;9.1–2 in Alan Kreider, *The Change of Conversion and the Origin of Christendom* (Eugene, OR: Wipf & Stock, 2006), 11.
23. For the work of Paul see Brigitte Kahl, *Galatians Re-Imagined: Reading with the Eyes of the Vanquished* (Minneapolis, MN: Fortress Press, 2010).
24. Vitor Westhelle, *Eschatology and Space. The Lost Dimension in Theology Past and Present* (New York: Palgrave Macmillan, 2012), 2.
25. Yi-Fu Tuan, *Space and Place: The Perspective of Experience* (Minneapolis, MN: University of Minnesota Press: 2001), 3.
26. Edward Relph's *Place and Placelessness*, quoted by David Seamon and Jacob Sowers, "Place and Placelessness, Edward Relph", in *Key Texts in Human Geography: A Reader Guide*, eds. Phil Hubbard, Rob Kitchin, and Gill Valentine, 2nd ed. (London: Sage, 2008), 44–45.
27. David Harvey, "Space as a Key Word," paper for Marx and Philosophy Conference, May 29, 2004, Institute of Education, London, http://frontdeskapparatus.com/files/harvey2004.pdf
28. Winona LaDuke, *Our Home on Earth*, excerpted and updated from "Voices from White Earth: Gaa-waabaabiganikaag," the Thirteenth Annual E.F. Schumacher Lecture, given at Yale University, October 1993. The lecture is sponsored by the New Economics Institute. This essay appears in OTC's book *All That We Share: A Field Guide to the Commons*. http://www.onthecommons.org/magazine/our-home-earth#sthash.HEifPfDt.kV1CNvWd.dpbs
29. The term "response-ability" intends to highlight both aspects of responsibility: response with ability. We are both responsible and able to provide the alternative answers to our world. We must respond and find the able ways to do so, this is responsibility. See Donna J. Haraway, *Staying with the Trouble: Making Kin in the Chthulucene* (Durham, NC: Duke University Press, 2016), 104–116.
30. Westhelle, *Eschatology and Space*, 13.
31. Anscar Chupungco was a Filipino Benedictine monk and the main name in the studies of these intersections. The Protestant response was the *Nairobi Statement on Worship and Culture*, *The Eucharistic Liturgy of Lima* and others. Recently, there has been an engaged conversation around all these issues, honoring Chupungco and expanding the Nairobi Lutheran declaration. See: Glaucia Vasconcelos Wilkey, *Worship and Culture: Foreign Country or Homeland?* (Grand Rapids, MI: Wm. B. Eerdmans Publishing Co., 2015).
32. Dietrich Bonhoeffer, "Outline for a Book," *Letters and Papers from Prison*, in Larry Rasmussen, *Dietrich Bonhoeffer: His Significance for North Americans* (Minneapolis, MN: Fortress Press, 1990), 186.
33. Eduardo Viveiros de Castro, *A revolução faz o bom tempo* https://www.youtube.com/watch?v=CjbU1jO6rmE

SELECT BIBLIOGRAPHY

Balasuriya, Tissa (2004), *The Eucharist and Human Liberation*, Eugene, OR: Wipf & Stock.
Banerjee, Subhankar (2012), *Arctic Voices: Resistance at the Tipping Point*, New York: Seven Stories Press.
Birch, Bruce C., Jacqueline E. Lapsley and Larry Rasmussen (2018), *Bible and Ethics in the Christian Life: A New Conversation*, Minneapolis, MN: Fortress Press.

Danowski, Déborah and Eduardo Viveiros de Castro (2016), *The Ends of the World*, Cambridge: Polity Books.

Haraway, Donna (2016), *Staying with the Trouble: Making Kin in the Chthulucene*, Durham, NC: Duke University Press.

Keller, Catherine (2017), *Entangled Worlds: Religion, Science, and New Materialisms*, New York: Fordham University Press.

Kimmerer, Robin Wall (2013), *Braiding Sweetgrass: Indigenous Wisdom, Scientific Knowledge and the Teachings of Plants*, Minneapolis, MN: Milkweed Editions.

LaDuke, Winona (2016), *Recovering the Sacred: The Power of Naming and Claiming*, Chicago: Haymarket Books.

Lathrop, Gordon W. (2009), *Holy Ground: A Liturgical Cosmology*, Minneapolis, MN: Fortress Press.

Latour, Bruno (2017), *Facing Gaia: Eight Lectures on the New Climatic Regime*, Cambridge: Polity Books (Kindle edition).

Mitchell, Nathan D. (2007), *Meeting Mystery: Liturgy, Worship, Sacraments*, Maryknoll, NY: Orbis Books.

Rasmussen, Larry L. (2015), *Earth-honoring Faith: Religious Ethics in a New Key*, Oxford: Oxford University Press.

Tsing, Anna Lowenhaupt (2015), *The Mushroom at the End of the World: On the Possibility of Life in Capitalist Ruins*, Princeton, NJ: Princeton University Press.

Viveiros de Castro, Eduardo (2016), *The Relative Native: Essays on Indigenous Conceptual Worlds*, London: Hau—Special Collections in Ethnographic Theory.

Westhelle, Vitor (2012), *Eschatology and Space: The Lost Dimension in Theology Past and Present*, New York: Palgrave Macmillan.

CHAPTER THIRTY

Slavoj Žižek

*Christianity, the Death of God, and
Enjoying Hopelessness*

SILAS MORGAN

INTRODUCTION

Few contemporary philosophers have figured more prominently in recent political theological literature than Slavoj Žižek. In large part this is because Žižek himself has been rather preoccupied with questions of religion, and of Christian theology in particular. What lies at the heart of Žižek's attention to theology is the way he frames Christianity *as* ideology critique; that it enacts on political thought a form of negative immanent critique that gives way to unfamiliar political options. Through a reading of the death of God theology, Žižek presents a negative politics of active refusal: "I prefer not to." While this negativity opens up material conditions of political possibility and clears the way for truly political acts, Žižek does not explain the relation between critique and praxis. It also does not clarify why theology—even the radical revolutionary impulse of "its perverse core"—is necessary to address social reality in a negative, and thus critical, way. To address these issues, this chapter explores first the general parameters of Žižek's political theology of critique and then takes up its implications for radical social and political activity, given Žižek's recent turn to hopelessness as a radical political posture.

ŽIŽEK'S THEORY OF IDEOLOGY CRITIQUE

The relation between theology and ideology in Žižek's critical theory is organized around three major ideas: his psychoanalytic critique of the big Other, his critique of cynicism through unbelief, and his political understanding of the Act. While Žižek's politics lack doctrines, he is motivated by a desire to provoke the authentic political Act and to explain its relation to the political subject.[1] Žižek is responding to what he sees as the primary ideological trap of liberalism, multiculturalism, toleration, and so on, all of which tries to convince subjects of the inevitable success of capitalism and the impossibility of radical social change. Ideology tells us that "the cadence of change" must be pragmatic and gradual—that large-scale shifts in the prevailing order are not necessary or desirable.[2] The whole point of Žižek's political theology is to shed light on the conditions of possibility for revolutionary subjectivity, over against the current coordinates of political life today that repress it. Thus, for Žižek, "ideology is always a field of struggle."[3]

Žižek's ideology critique is a "philosophy under the condition of the political," and so is an attempt to produce and establish the kind of subject necessary for this work; Žižek's theory of ideology is always a philosophy of the subject.⁴ And so, Žižek wants to reactivate the materialist aspects of modern subjectivity and to save the subject from the postmodernists and the left-liberal intelligentsia who are eager to announce its death.⁵ The prospect of critique starts and ends with the subject, since ideologies reside in how political subjects repetitively enact social reality. Ideology acts within and as the fundamental contradiction—the Gap—between *what* the subject believes and *how* the subject acts. The aim of critique is neither to resolve this antagonism nor to reveal its true nature, but to acknowledge its inescapability and to establish novel forms of collective life.

Žižek's aim in ideology critique is to identify the traumatic Gaps, the "non-All" in reality where its utmost, fundamental antagonisms reside, in order to clear an "empty" space, free from "any positively determined reality."⁶ It is only when these spaces are cleared, when the gaps are negated, that subjectivity is made possible again, and with it, authentic political acts with independent rationalities. Critique must hold open the space of the pre-ideological kernel, which, as the traumatic gap that engenders subjectivity, is nothing less than the "True Openness" of revolutionary politics. This calls for a kind of unstable, rupturing, apocalyptic thinking that Žižek finds in the structure of the Event.⁷ As it turns out, one of the foremost theorists of the Event, Alain Badiou, is fascinated with the political import of St. Paul's theology for rethinking revolutionary subjectivity.⁸ Žižek follows him there and in so doing, finds in Christianity, a "subversive kernel" of materialist theology at its "perverse core."⁹ For Žižek, "what is revealed in Christianity is not just the entire content, but more specifically that there is nothing—no secret—behind to be revealed . . . what God reveals is not His hidden power, only His impotence as such."¹⁰

Žižek's argument is that Christian theology is ideology critique at its best. He offers a political reading of the book of Job and the crucified Christ's "cry of dereliction," both of which express the single most important—and revolutionary—moment of theological truth: divine abandonment. "Insofar as we conceive of ideology as the imaginary mitigating of a traumatic Real", says Žižek, "the Book of Job provides what is perhaps the first exemplary case of the critique of ideology in human history, laying bare the basic discursive strategies of legitimizing suffering: Job's properly ethical dignity lies in the way he persistently rejects the notion that his suffering can have any meaning . . . and surprisingly, God takes his side at the end, claiming that every word that Job spoke was true."¹¹ This admission by God to God's own impotence against human suffering is the theological moment of ideology critique par excellence, leading Žižek to pursue its theoretical and political lessons. Christianity is politically necessary because it affords him the critical distance between theory and action that Žižek considers to be essential for any "really existing change": namely, it enacts *in thought* the authentic political Event proleptically announced in the theological figure of the crucified God.

Departing from "false consciousness" models of ideology critique, Žižek defines critique as that which "transverses the fantasy"; it lays bare the fundamental Lack within the symbolic order *without covering it up again*. Ideology critique frees the subject, not to see the way things really are, but to recognize that this desire—to see things as they are—this misses the point and is ideology itself. To critique ideology is to renounce all attempts to suture the void or reconcile the Lack; it admits that the Lack, which establishes the coordinates of desire and so is the origin, source, and condition of the subject, must remain empty. But this emptiness is not vacancy but ontological negation: it is "materialism without matter." The spirit of the "antimony of critic-ideological reason" protects the Voided empty place through a dialectical movement that offers no final closure, no hope of being explained or reconciled. The subject is left indigent, due to the unbearable pressure that comes with being unprotected by ideology from the contingency and unpredictability of existence without ontological guarantee.

The goal of ideology critique is to lay bare this empty place, this Nothing that undergirds subjectivity, and that renders reality incomplete, insubstantial, and truly open the possibility of the New. Critique itself is possible because of the primordial antagonism of social reality itself It is never "there" for the taking and so the critique of ideology is not about acquiring the truth about reality, but rather surfacing the fundamental antagonism that social reality itself represses in the socio-symbolic order. What the subject must do when faced with this antagonism is not to try to expose it, so that it can be erased, but rather to "over-identify" with it; like fantasy, when we "pretend to pretend to believe" in it, it disarms its effect on the subject.[12] What is left to do after the critique of ideology is *not* to return to that primordial kernel of the truth upon which we establish new norms or a more adequate political order. Rather we must actively resist any and all efforts to close the gap, to erase the Nothing, thereby objectifying this emptiness as the very act of exposure that gives birth to "this nothing itself, the nothing that is the subject."[13]

In the essay "St. Paul and the Truth-Event," Žižek turns to St. Paul in order to suggest that, when "short-circuited," Christianity presents truth as an Event that perverts the structure of being and so belongs to a wholly other register, "the pure Multiplicity of Nothing."[14] "A true Event emerges out of the 'Void' of the situation,"[15] and so its radically undecidable and spontaneous activity has neither an ontological guarantee nor a hidden content or agency.[16] It attaches itself to that localized Void inherent in the inconsistencies and transgressions of every situation, making a new Subject visible and intelligible *ex nihilo:* it ushers in the Subject from the empty Void. This "Void" is the ontological incompleteness of reality itself, says Žižek. It is not the nihilist "nothing that is still something," but rather the materialist "something that is nothing"; this is that terrifying and abyssal truth that is always already the site where subjectivity is borne. While Žižek links the Event to subjectivity itself,[17] the Event-structure of ideology critique is not good news for the Subject, for "the Event necessarily appears as standalone, as an undesirable, chaotic intrusion that has no place in the state of the situation."[18] It is here that Žižek clearly describes ideology critique and subject formation in the same terms: "the truth-Event is simply a radically new beginning: it designates the violent, traumatic and contingent, intrusion of another dimension not 'mediated' by the domain of terrestrial finitude and corruption."[19] The question is what role does theology have in instigating this "new beginning," that keeps the pure multiplicity of Void open?

To prefigure the argument to come, if Christianity houses the paradigmatic truth Event in its attestation to divine death and crucifixion,[20] then the Event of the death of God becomes truth "after the fact," "that is, when it leads to the constitution of the group of believers, of the engaged community held together by the fidelity to the Event: the traumatic encounter with the Real in Christ's death."[21] In other words, Christianity is true insofar as it is political in a specific way:

> Christian revelation is thus an example (although probably *the* example) of how we, human beings, are not constrained to the positivity of being; of how, from time to time, in a contingent and unpredictable way, a truth-Event can occur that opens up the possibility of participating in another life by remaining faithful to the truth-Event.[22]

Christianity dismisses the hold of the law on the subject, breaking the vicious cycle of law and transgression by instigating the death of the big Other, that quilting "nodal point" that anchors and so regulates the subject's life within the symbolic order.[23] This marks the new beginning of and for the subject who, in the absence of the deadlock of fantasy (rendered by Žižek as the ideological demands of the Ethical universal), is given the opportunity, in absolute freedom, to intervene into authentic political acts that generate Events, rather than Orders. The "death of God" theology as a political procedure clears the way for agents who are capable of acting outside the normal flow of things, or what Žižek called the "theologico-political suspension of the ethical."[24]

ŽIŽEK'S THEOLOGY AS IDEOLOGY CRITIQUE

The first principle of Žižek's theory of theology as ideology critique is that there is something unique about the "perverse core" of Christian materialism that is worth fighting for.[25] Žižek accounts for this through a Hegelian "death of God theology" that is tied to the theology of divine suffering and abandonment and so expressed in the crucified God's "cry of dereliction" at his death. This event results in the formation of the Spirit of love, the collective and democratized social bond that lives and acts in the radical absence of the big Other, finally disabused of and subtracted from the "forced choices" of currently available political options.[26] The Christian declaration of the death of God in the crucifixion of Jesus confronts the horrifying truth of the Lack at the center of subjectivity and gives way to the radical political freedom of the liminal "undead."[27] Žižek interprets the crucified Christ as the "vanishing mediator" between the law of the divine Father and the absolute freedom of the Holy Spirit, and so in doing, narrates "the passage" from Judaism to Christianity as one from "law to love."[28]

DEATH OF GOD THEOLOGY AND THE "NEGATION OF NEGATION"

Key to understanding how and why Žižek reconfigures political theology as ideology critique is his interpretation and use of the "negation of negation,"[29] a key element of his engagement with Hegelian dialectical materialism.[30] Hegelian dialectics is not a "vulgar evolutionism" whereby thought reconciles opposites through a totalizing process of synthesis and resolution. Instead, the negativity of this dialectic has a positive function of coming upon the truth, and so requires a series of errors—one must first make the wrong choice[31]—but this wrong choice is not merely discarded, but sublates the final truth, which not the same as a reconciliation with or grand synthesis of the prior error.[32]

The "negation of negation" is the core of dialectics. Dialectics is the critical act which shows that the negation (the first move, ". . . of the negation") is indeed still entangled in the master-signifier, the "big Other," and so it calls for a secondary move ("the negation . . .") that acts upon the first one. The effect of this procedure is the realization that nothing is beyond or outside the big Other and that as the master-signifier, the ideology of the big Other only serves to fill in the space of the "non-All" of social reality, so as to make the scripted life in social reality bearable. This "negation of negation," while being purely negative (in the sense that it shows the Void to be void without replacing it), nevertheless becomes the basis of all authentic political acts insofar as it is the "loss of loss": it is a "negation without a filling."[33] This negativity opens up the act itself so that it does not obey or submit itself to any pre-existing coordinates of social consensus or political options, but rather actively mocks the symbolic order by its self-enunciation as the "exception" to the big Other.

Žižek turns to Christian theology as a critical thought-form of negativity that clears the way for authentic political acts. He affirms the "direct lineage from Christianity to Marxism" in order to marshal its resources to combat "the onslaught of new spiritualisms": "the authentic Christian legacy is much too precious to be left to the fundamentalist freaks."[34] While he finds the "return of religion" to be "deplorable" (he is as critical of Derrida's "religion without religion" as he is of New Age spiritualisms),[35] Žižek nevertheless finds in Christianity a unique kernel of truth, a "perverse core" that incubates a political legacy and emancipatory logic that betrays its creedal repression.[36] This, he is convinced, is essential for revitalizing Hegelian dialectical critique, so much so that "this kernel is accessible only to a materialist approach—vice versa: to become a dialectical materialist, one should go through the Christian experience."[37]

While Žižek interprets Christian theology as ideology critique through the prism of a "death of God" theology, he does not draw on the actual tradition of the death of God in Christianity, whether in the 1960s "radical theology" or its more classic, patristic, or biblical roots. Žižek casts his theology as a part of the "new" reading of Hegel,[38] contributing to the place of Hegel in the reconsideration of radical and secular currents in constructive and political theology.[39] These theologies, which originate in Paul Tillich's theology of culture, gained some currency first in the 1960s "death of god" theology and then reemerged in the 1980s "postmodern" theology, but faded due to the success of narrative and post-liberal trends in the 1990s and 2000s. However, the sobering geopolitical events of the early 2000s and 2010s, as well as the return of religion in academic discourse more broadly in that period, has caused many to question the localist, ecclesiocentric, and sectarian aspects of those theologies. Radical theologies are well suited as alternative candidates because they are post-metaphysical and rely on social vocabularies and cultural categories. Žižek's atheistic theology is perhaps best characterized as a continuation and elaboration of this tradition, something that he himself has readily admitted, though Žižek has minimally engaged this work.[40]

Instead, Žižek turns to the kenotic elements of Protestant *theologia crucis*, where God empties Itself into the divine Son through a traumatic death that, in Žižek's reconstruction, represents the death of the Big Other, performed expertly by Christianity. This establishes a homological relationship between theology and ideology critique, between the Christian death of God and what Žižek stylizes as a Hegelian "negation of negation."[41] The death of God displays "the epochal political achievement" of Christianity itself, wherein the dialectics of the Incarnation, we discover the materialist immanence of theology "In itself": "God Himself is Man, 'one of us,'" meaning that, "there is no mystery, no hidden true content behind the mask (deceptive surface) of the other."[42] Žižek argues that "if, as Hegel emphasizes, what dies on the Christ is the God of beyond itself, the radical Other, then the identification with Christ ('life in Christ') means precisely the suspension of Otherness."[43]

Christianity testifies to the content of this experience in the crucified Christ's "cry of dereliction": "My god, my god, why have you forsaken me?" Here we find God admitting that God has abandoned God's self and as such, left humanity to itself—incapable of serving as its ontological guarantee, the ground of its acts.[44] By admitting to God's self-abandonment, and by virtue of the logic of the incarnation, the abandonment of humanity, Christianity "traverses the fantasy" and divulges itself *as* ideology critique by denouncing the big Other. This makes Christianity, says Žižek, the "first religion without the sacred"; it does not long for an external or transcendental limit and instigates the ruptural, practical stance that follows.[45] This is why Žižek insists that, "the longing for a new external/transcendent limit, for a divine agent who imposes such a limit, is profoundly non-

Christian."[46] Christianity, rather, possesses a kind of revolutionary courage, the courage of Christ's "empty sacrifice,"[47] wherein "it was God Himself who made a Pascalian wager: by dying on the Cross, He made a risky gesture with no guaranteed final outcome, that is, He provided us—humanity—with the empty S_1, Master-Signifier."[48] The incarnation is revelatory, but not in the sense that God shows himself to humanity as what God is to God's self, but that God shows God's self to God as what God is to humanity.[49]

And so, when Žižek says "what dies on the Cross is not God's earthly representative-incarnation, but God of beyond itself,"[50] it is clear that the incarnation cannot be unambiguously good news for humanity, especially since it ends with God's death.[51] Christ's death reveals God to God's self, and that revelation is traumatic for God as God finds God's self abandoned, alienated from itself, which mirrors the human experience of the same. To take the incarnation of God in Jesus Christ seriously is to know "Christ as the God who, in His act of Incarnation, freely identified Himself with His own shit."[52] And so, it is in the death of God that Christ is shown to be most human and where is shown to be most divine, whereby "the radical gap that separates God from man is transposed into God himself."[53] It is here that shows us that "we are one with God only when God is no longer one with himself, but abandons Himself, "internalizes" the radical distance which separates us from Him. Our radical experience of separation from God is the very feature which unites us with Him."[54]

Recalling the earlier discussion on belief as critique, this confession by God is God's own "fetishistic disavowal" of belief:[55] The critical structure of belief is tied directly to the "negation of negation," whereby we see that "the properly Hegelian negation of negation is not the return to direct belief, but the self-relating fake: 'I fake to fake to believe,' which means: 'I really believe without being aware of it.' Is, then, irony not the ultimate form of the critique of ideology today—[the] irony . . . of taking the statements more seriously than the subjects who utter them themselves?"[56]

In short, this illustrates how and why Christian theology of God (namely, of God's death) is indeed a critique of ideology. Christianity is at its critical best when it confesses, while talking about God, that, "I pretend to pretend to believe" (rather than "I do not believe"). Žižek explains theological structure of this ironic unbelief this way: "When Christ dies, what dies with him is the secret hope discernible in 'Father, why hast thou forsaken me?', the hope that there is a Father who abandoned me."[57] This is the moment of ultimate irony where God attests to God's own atheism, not by denying or negating claims to God's existence, but by calling out to God's self in the moment of God's non-identity.[58] This stunning admission is the political "calling card" of Christianity, and so becomes the key to thinking through the triangulation of theology, materialism, and ideology critique.[59]

ŽIŽEK AND POLITICAL THEOLOGY AFTER IDEOLOGY CRITIQUE

The political meaning of Christianity is not Jesus' benevolent ministry, the social vision in the synoptic gospels, solidarity with human suffering in death, or purported victory over death in resurrection, but rather is found in how Christian theology admits to the "negation of negation" that most clearly visible in the death of God in the crucified body of Jesus Christ. The theologic of the incarnation, which is then reinterpreted in the Event of divine death, shifts the perspective on the divine-human relationship. As such, Žižek's thesis is that Christian materialism betrays its "orthodoxy" by performing this negation as negation as ideology critique: namely, a critique of the ideology of big Other as the divine guarantee, the transcendental signifier that affords meaning, coherence, and sense to the world and human experience. Theology participates in "the same matrix of Hegelian paradoxical self-negating reversal" that is "also the fundamental procedure of Marxian critique of ideology"[60] that enacts "the radically negative break, rupture, with the old substantive order as the condition of a new universality."[61]

And so, for Žižek, Christianity is ideologico-critical because it is "far from boring, humdrum, or safe"; it is, indeed, "perilous," "daring," "subversive, even revolutionary,"[62] characteristics given to it by its most orthodox, but also "heretical" aspects, most notably the doctrine of the Incarnation.[63] For Žižek, "religion has two possible roles: *therapeutic* or *critical*. It either helps individuals to function better in the existing order, or it tries to assert itself as a critical agency articulating what is wrong with this order as such, a space for the voices of discontent—in this second case, religion *as such* tends toward assuming the role of a heresy."[64]

The practice of ideology critique teaches the political subject, not only about the failure that conditions our knowledge, but also about the Absolute freedom that comes from recognizing that the traumatic Gap gives rise to political subjectivity in the first place. If, as Žižek claims, this is the lesson of ideology critique, "does not exactly the same shift happen at the very core of the Christian experience?"[65] For Christianity, "it is the radical separation of man from God which unites us with God, since, in the figure of Christ, God is thoroughly separated from itself—the point is not to 'overcome' the gap that separates us from God, but to take note of how this gap is internal to God Himself."[66] This is accomplished in the person of Jesus Christ, in which the original negation ("the Fall") is shown via a subsequent negation ("the death of Christ") to be, in a startling reversal, "the emergence of freedom."[67] Ideology critique then is the "breaking out" whereby the shift in perspective activates the subject from the position of ultimate failure. Žižek puts it this way: "this is the key 'Hegelian' point of Christianity: the resurrection of the dead is not the 'real event' which will take place sometime in the future, but *something that is already here*."[68] That "something" is God's own fall into humanity, God's kenotic admission to impotence, performed by the crucified Christ.

As the crucified Jesus, God encounters God's own impotence, and confesses to it in the divine cry of dereliction recorded, most notably, in the gospel of Matthew: "My God, why have you forsaken me?" Žižek interprets this as a scandalous admission: "since we are dealing here not with the gap between man and God, but the split between God Himself, the solution cannot be for God to appear in all His majesty . . . it is rather like a child who, having believed in his father's powerfulness, discovers with horror that his father cannot help him."[69] This divine Fall is, at the very same time, our human redemption, not because of divine redemptive suffering, but because it shows that our world is of our own making— "there is no big Other"—and so it is our responsibility. It frees us from expecting a kind of apocalyptic divine intervention that will vindicate the righteous and punish the oppressors: "we, humans, are left with no higher Power watching over us, just with the terrible burden of freedom and responsibility for the face of divine creation, and thus of God himself."[70]

It is here that Christianity divulges its own heretical core as "the religion of atheism"[71] wherein the disclosure of divine powerlessness amounts to the death of God, the admission that "the Big Other does not exist."[72] What happens to God in Christ's death is that God is revealed to be "just one of us," is included in "the series of ordinary creatures,"[73] and so "traverses the fantasy," thereby linking the theological gesture of divine death to the political procedure of ideology critique. This incarnational logic disavows the ideological fantasy of the big Other through the Event of the cross, thereby opening up new space, not to be filled up again by some substitute, but with excessive negativity that refuses suturing up the central void of our desire. God admits to being human in Christ and to being impotent in the face of Christ's human suffering:

> it is quite logically the first and only religion radically to leave behind the split between the official and public text and its obscene initiatory supplement; *there is no hidden, untold story in it.* In this precise sense, Christianity is the religion of Revelation: everything is revealed in it, no obscene superego supplement accompanies its public message . . . what is revealed in Christianity is not just the entire content, but, more specifically, that *there is nothing—no secret—behind it to be revealed.*[74]

In their attestation to divine impotence, Christ teaches us how to ask, "do we need God?" in fresh political ways. It interjects into the political situation the properly Christian declaration that the big Other does not exist. This means "there is no one to turn to, to address, to bear witness to, no one to receive our plea, or lament."[75] This is Christianity's gospel, its "good news": "the miracle of faith is that it IS possible to traverse the fantasy, to undo the founding decision, to start one's life over again, from the zero-point . . ."[76] It is through Christ's death that God "falls into" materiality, subjects Itself to the incompleteness, the Truly Open character of the Real, and shows itself to be "one of us," rather than the grand Master-Signifier: the big Other.[77] And, while this is certainly a kind of atheism, Žižek maintains it is a distinctively *Christian* atheism, which is better named a "materialist theology."[78]

This unlocks Christianity's essential political truth: the perverse character of Christ's death. A "materialist theology," says Žižek "is a position that accepts the ultimate void of reality—the consequence of its central thesis on the primordial multiplicity is that there is no 'substantial reality,' that the only 'substance' of the multiplicity is void."[79] But for Christianity to realize this materialist core, "it has to sacrifice itself—like Christ who had to die so that Christianity could emerge."[80] For Žižek, "the 'death of God' theology marks the moment when the only way to keep its truth alive was through a materialist heresy split from its main corpse."[81]

Christianity is theologically instructive in how inaugurates the apocalyptic Event, expressed in a "double kenosis": God's self-alienation and the alienation of God from human persons overlaps at God's death, where "the distance of man from God is thus the distance of God from himself."[82] But what makes this kenotic self-emptying of God so politically important is that it clear the way for an authentic and revolutionary political subjectivity to take form:

> In order for (human) subjectivity to emerge out of the substantial personality of the human animal . . . as *the self-relating negativity of an empty singularity*, God himself, the universal Substance, has to "humiliate" himself, to fall into his own creation, "objectivize" himself, to appear as the singular miserable human individual, in all its abjection, i.e., abandoned by God.[83]

"THE SPIRIT": A THEOLOGY OF THE COLLECTIVE

How, then, is this "death of God" theology politically operationalized as a critique of ideology? The death of God does not inaugurate a political nihilism or a celebration of the Nothing, but rather "designates a rupture with the circular movement of death and rebirth, the passage to a wholly different dimension of the Holy Spirit."[84] In so doing, Christian attestation to God's death in Jesus Christ and *parousia* in the Spirit clears the way for a revolutionary kind of community that gains its revolutionary political character as "the community deprived of its support in the Big Other."[85] The political act of "God-becoming-human" brings forth a new political community whose unique founding moment—the death of God—promises to bring something altogether different to the political landscape.

Christianity's supposed renunciation of the big Other in the theological form of the death of God generates what Žižek has termed (borrowing from Kierkegaard) "the theologico-political suspension of the ethical,"[86] or, as Žižek is fond of saying himself, "if God does not exist, than everything is prohibited."[87] This opens up the political space for a new kind of collective, a new social bond, that relies not on some final guarantee, but is capable of matching the cruel world with an equally brutal realism, what he describes as "an ethics without morality," but what might better be called "a politics without ethics," made possible in the negation of negation of "transcendence" (which Žižek interprets as the "big Other") by the double kenosis of incarnation and crucifixion. Žižek describes the interplay between ideology critique and the sublating "negation of negation" as that which gives way to the revolutionary community of believers, whose kenotic acts of love, sacrifice, conversion, and, yes, even death, give rise to a new kind of subject, a new political community whose unique founding moment promises to bring something altogether different to the political landscape: "what is sublated in the move from the Son to the Holy Spirit is thus God Himself; after the Crucifixion, the death of God incarnate, the universal God returns as a Spirit of the community of believers."[88]

The political payoff of Žižek's negative dialectical use of the "death of God" theology is found in this collective social body: "with Christ's incarnation, the externalization/self-alienation of divinity, the passage from the transcendent God to finite/mortal individuals is *a fait accompli*, there is no way back, all there is, all that 'really exists,' from now on are individuals."[89] That the "finite existence of moral humans is the only site of the Spirit, the site where the Spirit achieves its actuality,"[90] is certified in Christ's own manifestation of itself as love "In-itself," the social bond present when "two or three are gathered in my name."[91] No longer stuck within "the force choice" of the particular coordinates of political possibility, "we catch a glimpse of Another Space which can no longer be dismissed as a fantastic supplement to social reality."[92] This is the Christian legacy of ideology critique that Žižek finds so important. In the Spirit is a thought-form, a critical rationality, a "short circuit" that promises to bring forth "the brief apparition of a future Utopian Otherness to which every authentic revolutionary stance should cling."[93]

CONCLUSION: THE END OF HOPE, OR "HOW TO ENJOY HOPELESSNESS"

As a Marxist, Žižek lives in constant awareness of the historical failures of revolutionary praxis: "the actual history that we live is itself a kind of realized alternative history, the reality we have to live in because, in the past, we failed to seize the moment and act."[94] Žižek is stubborn and so blames the anemic left whose "fetishistic" proclivity towards populism can only produce a truly ideological *passage á l'acte*, where people cry out with frustration, "This cannot go on! It must stop!" but it never ends. Nothing actually changes. All action ends up being nothing more than a "depoliticized pseudo-activity (new lifestyles, etc.), the very form of social passivity"[95] that puts on full display a reactive and impatient refusal to confront the complexity of the situation.

Reflecting on the political failures of the Left in Greece, the US, and elsewhere, Žižek has turned to "the courage of hopelessness" in order to discuss the ideology of hope and to offer contrarian perspectives on how to resist the social pathologies of our time. In calling on his readers to rehabilitate the critical power of hopelessness, Žižek repeats themes from his earlier work: what if the best way to critique ideology is not austerity, sobriety, and so on, but rather desire, excess, and *enjoyment*, precisely when both neoliberalism and multiculturalism cut the subject off from the surplus excess of self and the other? The compulsory imperative to act, fight, and struggle, to do something—anything!—are all responses to guilt and anxiety, new forms of submission, dependence, and domination, all of which regulate natural outbursts of desire and redirect them into market-structure economic choices.

Instead of casting about in despair and attempting to act our way out of this anxiety, Žižek seeks a darker alternative. He self-consciously quotes Lenin who, when it became clear that the European workers revolution had failed, wrote these words near the end of his life: "what if the complete hopelessness of the situation, by stimulating the efforts of the workers and peasants tenfold, offered us the opportunity to create the fundamental requisites of civilization in a different way . . . ?"[96] Žižek goes on:

> The true courage is not to imagine an alternative, but to accept the consequences of the fact that there is no clearly discernible alternative: the dream of an alternative is a sign of theoretical cowardice; it functions as a fetish that prevents us thinking through to the end of the deadlock of our predicament. In short, the true courage is to admit that the light at the end of the tunnel is most likely the headlights of another train approaching us from the opposite direction.[97]

This is classic Žižek: contrarian, over-the-top, and self-indulgent, but what if he is right? Žižek's position may be easily dismissed as fatalistic and disconnected from the material struggle of communities whose lives and wellbeing are on the line, but he is not alone in drawing out the possibility of this new, darker line of critique of hope and its politics.

After over half a century in which the "theology of hope" emerged as the starting place for late modern political theology—perhaps Žižek calls us to move in a darker direction. While it may be tempting to think of this as a product of political failure, this turn away from hope is rooted in descriptive articulations of long-standing social and political realities, originating far back into the history of Western settler colonialism, black enslavement in the US, and the systemic decimation of language, culture, and practices of indigenous communities at the global scale. In other words, this turn from hope is not a gloomy or melancholic fad; it is grounded in the catastrophic wreckage of history. There are few reasons to think it will get better.

Hope covers up the present. It obscures or otherwise distracts us from our state of affairs. For some, this is precisely what makes Christian hope so subversive. The role of hope in the liberated future promised in the repetition of Exodus throughout history continues to be essential to the survival and persistence of black communities of faith in times of oppression, slavery, and colonialism. It reminds the vulnerable that this, the present age, is not forever; it is not eternal, and that God's justice will come and it will vindicate them—that their cries, which often fall on deaf historical ears, will be heard at last. And yet, these same communities—particularly religious communities of color—have always curated a kind of hopelessness in their lived experience that is both defiant and militant in its unwillingness to see the present as an inevitable consequence of history, but nevertheless reads history not at progress but as a consequence of the world's powers.

Sociologist Tressie McMillan Cottom explains why the black experience of American whiteness and racism leads to a kind of hopelessness, one that refuses to give way to optimism, one "that doesn't absolve" the present. It is, as she notes, "tempered by a deep awareness of how thin is the veneer of white civility."

> My hopelessness is faith in things yet seen and works yet done. Hopelessness is necessary for the hard work of resisting tyranny and fascism. It is the precondition for sustained social movements because history isn't a straight line. It is a spinning top that eventually moves forward but also always goes round and round as it does. Those erasers applied post-mortem confuse us to this, blind us to the defeats that will come and ill prepare us for the reality that most of what we believe in will not come to pass in our lifetimes. A transactional hope is anathema to social progress.[98]

Latinx liberation ethicist Miguel De La Torre[99] takes issue with Christian theologies of hope and salvation-history theologies—both of which hold out the promise of a future restoration of justice to those who continue to endure systems of oppression. He names the myriad ways in which hope keeps systems of oppression in place rather than mobilizing resistance to them. Hoping for a better future does little for those struggling in the present; in fact, it often keeps those who have nothing more to lose from realizing truly how desperate their situation has become—and who did it to them. Liberating praxis comes only at the hands of those who know they have already lost—and have nothing in stake in what is. Hopelessness leads the political subject to take risks and employ tactics that rest far beyond the strategies set forth by hope. When there is no hope for justice, no expectation that things will get better, the only moral and political choice left for the oppressed is an "ethics that f*cks with."

For Žižek, this is the political goal of theology as ideology critique: to keep thinking openly about an altogether different world, one where the big Other is no longer present, and where the field of possibility for political action is interminably open and undetermined. The future of such a world is in the hands of "the Excluded" who presently suffer personal disrespect, social discrimination, and denial of rights that make the idea of equal and just participation in our global life hopeless. Žižek interprets the "death of God" Christianity as ideology critique because they both share a joint goal to keep open this "empty space," the traumatic gap that is continually sutured by the ideologies of the Symbolic, so that something like a "different collective organization" can emerge from within the Void as an unexpected alternative. It keeps open the Nothing of hopelessness, refusing to be sutured or seduced by parties, policies, or salvation-histories. This eschatological enjoyment of the genuinely New, promised in the Event, is best sustained by the theological vision of Christianity's "perverse core."

Žižek's alternative is a "subtractive politics" that expresses its negativity in the Bartlebyian phrase "I would prefer not to," rather than the ethical demand "I must."[100] The best course is a committed stance of aggressive passivity until the condition of possibilities shift, to refuse to allow one's acts to be co-opted by the parameters of currently existing options. The substantive point of this aggressive passivity is that while acts of commitment, resistance, protest, and action may seem to be interrupting, subversive, or emancipatory, they may well be protecting the grounding antagonisms of social reality that are the underneath our experiences of injustice, violence, and social inequality. These acts become the very sutures that ideology critique tears open. The only thing, given the established coordinates of political possibility, to do is to do nothing, to institute a politics of active refusal, with the hope this "short-circuits" the system and instigates an apocalyptic Event.

Might there be something here for political theology? Could we not use a bit of Žižek's contrarian spirit, his heterodox thinking, his willingness to slash through the "woke" culture of contemporary theology in order to interrogate whether the urgent calls to praxis are not themselves ideology, whether our desire to do something is not itself a sublation of transgressive desire? Žižek may help political theology leave behind hope-filled calls for a redemptive and productive future and opt instead for a critical iconoclasm that reclaims "terrifyingly empty spaces" as excessive sites of possibility for unpredictable and unconventional acting. Upon reading Žižek, we might realize that our options for engaging the world theologically expand far beyond the coordinates what seems politically feasible. Instead, Žižek might teach theologians how to fail and how to do so by becoming hopeless about our own ability to do anything more than interpret the world. Perhaps then we will learn how to be open to the unexpected agency of the Spirit yet again and so can be freed to act in truly revolutionary ways.

NOTES

1. Adrian Johnston, *Badiou, Žižek, and Political Transformations: The Cadence of Change* (Evanston, IL: Northwestern University Press, 2009), 85–126; Matthew Sharpe and Geoff Boucher, *Žižek and Politics A Critical Introduction* (Edinburgh: Edinburgh University Press, 2010), 60–86.
2. Johnston, *Badiou, Žižek, and Political Transformations*, 23.
3. Slavoj Žižek, *First as Tragedy, Then as Farce* (London: Verso, 2009), 37.
4. Razmig Keucheyan. *The Left Hemisphere: Mapping Critical Theory Today*, ed. Gregory Elliott (London: Verso, 2014), 183.
5. Slavoj Žižek, "Preface: Burning the Bridges," in *The Žižek Reader*, ed. Elizabeth Wright and Edmond Leo Wright (Oxford: Blackwell Publishers, 1999), vii–x.
6. Slavoj Žižek, "The Spectre of Ideology," in *Mapping Ideology*, ed. Slavoj Žižek (London: Verso, 1994), 17.
7. Slavoj Žižek, "Paul and the Truth Event," in *Paul's New Moment: Continental Philosophy and the Future of Christian Theology*, eds. Creston Davis, John Milbank, and Slavoj Žižek (Grand Rapids, MI: Brazos, 2010), 76–87, 90; Slavoj Žižek, *The Event: A Philosophical Journey through a Concept* (New York: Melville House, 2004), 159–169.
8. Alain Badiou, *Saint Paul: The Foundation of Universalism* (Stanford, CA: Stanford University Press, 2003). For more on the link between Badiou's and Žižek's theologies, see John Caputo and Linda Alcoff, ed., *St. Paul Among the Philosophers* (Bloomington, IN: Indiana University Press, 2009); Douglas Harink, ed., *Paul, Philosophy, and the Theopolitical Vision: Critical Engagements with Agamben, Badiou, Žižek, and Others* (Eugene, OR: Cascade Books, 2010).
9. Slavoj Žižek, *The Puppet and the Dwarf: The Perverse Core of Christianity* (Cambridge, MA: MIT Press, 2003).
10. Ibid., 127.
11. Ibid., 124–125.
12. Žižek, *Event*, 27–30.
13. Žižek, *Sublime Object of Ideology*, 195.

14. Žižek, "Paul and the Truth Event," 75.
15. Ibid., 87.
16. Ibid., 82–83.
17. Ibid., 38.
18. Ibid., 85.
19. Ibid., 93.
20. Ibid., 88.
21. Ibid., 87.
22. Ibid., 94.
23. Žižek, *Puppet and the Dwarf*, 120.
24. For vacations on this theme, especially as it pertains to ideology critique, see Žižek, *Less Than Nothing*, 963–1010; Slavoj Žižek, *Living in the End Times* (London: Verso, 2011), 80–135, especially 116–118; Slavoj Žižek, "For a Theologico-Political Suspension of the Ethical," in Slavoj Žižek and Boris Gunjević, *God in Pain: Inversions of Apocalypse* (New York: Seven Stories Press, 2012), 7, 27–102; Žižek, *The Parallax View*, 103–111; Žižek, *Absolute Recoil*, 129–130, 311–312.
25. Žižek's enthusiasm for religion and theology is not unbridled. *Pace* both fundamentalism and liberal toleration, we should not be "trying to redeem the pure ethical core of religion against its political instrumentalization, we should ruthlessly criticize this core—in *all* religions." What is required for this criticism is not secularism or atheism, but "a truly ascetic militant ethical stance", and as we shall see, it is, ironically, Christianity who provides this.
26. References to "the Spirit" as the dialectical "point" of Hegelian negativity (or theologically interpreted, the "uncoupling" accomplished in the "Fall" of God into humanity through Christ, "God's thorough desubstantialization") are scattered through Žižek's work. As the political community of love, the Spirit is describe as "uncoupled," "destitute," "collective," "outcasts," the "undead ghosts" who are "redeemed of all particular links," "a new subject no longer rooted in a particular substance." See Slavoj Žižek, *The Monstrosity of Christ: Paradox or Dialectic?* (Cambridge, MA: MIT Press, 2009), 29–33, 61, 74, 283–285, 289, 295; Žižek, *God in Pain*, 55; Žižek, *On Belief*, 83, 91; Žižek, *The Fragile Absolute*, 110–111, 115–120, 148–150; Žižek, *Puppet and the Dwarf*, 114–118, 130, 138–139, 171; Žižek, *The Parallax View*, 79–80.
27. Žižek, *Puppet and the Dwarf*, 93, 100; Žižek, *On Belief*, 104; Žižek frequently likens Christian "unbelief" to the "undead" existence of zombies, and it is frequently linked to the "negation of negation" involved in ideology critique. Zombies are "embodied apparitions of the spaces between life and death," and so they extend imaginings of the future as the "living dead." Zombies are from the "forbidden domain of the Thing." Insofar as they are reminders of the End, they underscore a partial future that is somewhere between hopeful and catastrophic. See Slavoj Žižek, "Neighbors and Other Monsters," in *The Neighbor: Three Inquiries into Political Theology*, ed. Slavoj Žižek, Eric Santer, and Kenneth Reinhard (Chicago: University of Chicago Press, 2005), 25.

    Theology and zombies are connected to Žižek's affinity for the politically apocalyptic (in the "revelatory" sense) wherein theology is the "zombie" figure in thought capable of resisting the form of "cultural criticism [that] shares the blindness of its object." See Theodor Adorno, "Cultural Criticism and Society" in *Prisms* (New York: Columbia University Press, 1967), 27. For a detailed description and analysis of this link, see Ola Sigurdson, "Slavoj Žižek, the Death Drive, and Zombies: A Theological Account," *Modern Theology* 19, no. 3 (2013): 361–380.

28. Whereas supersessionist Christianity has viewed the Jewish law as something to be escaped, to be overcome, whether by "gospel," *metanoia,* or love, for Žižek, the Jewish stance toward the law affords us a modality that is "unplugged" or "decoupled" from the ideological order. In this way, Christian love does not supersede Jewish "law" as much as it suspends it by exposing its "obscene superego supplement" (*Puppet and the Dwarf*, 127) and revealing God to be impotent, the horrifying secret kept so well by Jewish iconoclasm. See Žižek, *Puppet and the Dwarf*, 123–129, and Žižek, *On Belief*, 126–133, 137–151.

29. Žižek's use of Christianity as an exemplary form of this "downward-synthesis" is particularly of note here, as it demonstrates the "negation of negation" that serves as a focal point of Žižek's philosophy, and so his political theology. The self-reflexive character of Žižek's "materialist theology" is animated by "the Hegelian self-negation that is also the fundamental procedure of the Marxian critique of ideology." Žižek, *Puppet and the Dwarf*, 52, 87. For more on Žižek's reading of Hegelian "negation of negation" as the link between theology and ideology critique, see Žižek, *Sublime Object of Ideology*, 199; Slavoj Žižek, *For They Know Not What They Do: Enjoyment as a Political Factor* (London: Verso, 1991), 185–187, 266; Žižek *The Ticklish Subject*, 72–77; Žižek, *Puppet and the Dwarf*, 86–88, 100; Žižek, *The Monstrosity of Christ*, 70–73, 101; Žižek, *Less Than Nothing*, 292–305, 787–804; Žižek, *The Parallax View*, 9–12, 27–30, 346–354, 397n30; Žižek, *Absolute Recoil*, 330–349.

30. Žižek is often read as attempting to activate or rehabilitate Hegel in Lacanian terms, but what is often overlooked is that Žižek readily defends a reading of German Idealism *as a Marxist.* If the standard line is that Marx corrects or defends Hegel by upending his idealism in favor of materialism, Žižek negates this reversal by arguing that the only way to preserve the practical and liberative aspect of philosophy for emancipatory politics, that is, to generate a true materialism (Marx's goal), is through the idealism of (Hegel's) dialectical process. This, anyway, is the argument in his recent, and rather large work on Hegel. See Žižek, *Less Than Nothing*, 241–264, and Žižek, *Absolute Recoil*, 31–40, 192–193.

31. Žižek, *Puppet and the Dwarf*, 83–84; Žižek, *Less Than Nothing*, 69–70; Žižek, *The Parallax View*, 33ff.

32. Žižek, *Living in the End Times*, 27–29.

33. Žižek, *Less than Nothing*, 312–325.

34. Žižek, *The Fragile Absolute*, xxiv.

35. Žižek, *The Fragile Absolute*, xxix; Žižek, *Puppet and the Dwarf*, p. 139.

36. Žižek, *Puppet and the Dwarf*, 53, 169–170.

37. Ibid., 6.

38. While it has been called the "new" reading of Hegel, it is important to point out that it aims to correct what Žižek, Catherine Malabou, and others consider to be a distorted caricature of Hegel that was popularized by anti-modern and postmodern readers of Hegel, many of whom are eager to lay the blame of the "totalizing" gesture of modernity on Hegel's philosophy of history and ontology. For more on this, see Slavoj Žižek, Clayton Crockett, and Creston Davis, eds., *Hegel and the Infinite Religion, Politics, and Dialectic* (New York: Columbia University Press, 2011); Catherine Malabou, *The Future of Hegel: Plasticity, Temporality, and Dialectic* (New York: Routledge, 2005); Andrew Hass, *Hegel and the Art of Negation: Negativity, Creativity and Contemporary Thought* (London: I.B. Tauris, 2013).

39. Clayton Crockett, ed. *Secular Theology: American Radical Theological Thought* (London: Routledge, 2001); Noëlle Vahanian, *The Rebellious No: Variations on a Secular Theology of Language* (New York: Fordham University Press, 2014); F. LeRon Shults, *Theology After the Birth of God: Atheist Conceptions in Cognition and Culture* (New York: Palgrave

Macmillan, 2014); Clayton Crockett, and Jeffrey W. Robbins. *Religion, Politics, and the Earth: The New Materialism* (New York: Palgrave Macmillan, 2012).

40. Kotsko, *Žižek and Theology*, 152. In Žižek, *The Monstrosity of Christ*, 97, Žižek affirms the "death of God" theology because it "marks the moment when the only way to keep [Christianity's] truth alive was through a materialist heresy split from its main corpse." Žižek and the leading "death of God" theologian Thomas J.J. Altizer spoke together at the American Academy of Religion's annual meeting in Montreal on November 8, 2009. Altizer's paper was later published as Thomas J.J. Altizer, "The Self Annihilation of God," *International Journal of Žižek Studies* 4, no. 4 (2010), and Žižek's rejoinder, "'Whither the "Death of God': A Continuing Currency?" can be found here: http://vimeo.com/12744096. For contrastive readings of the link, see Cyril O' Regan, "Žižek and Milbank and the Hegelian Death of God," *Modern Theology* 26, no. 2 (2010): 278–286; and Katherine Sarah Moody, "Between Deconstruction and Speculation," in *The Future of the Continental Philosophy of Religion*, ed. Clayton Crockett, et al. (Bloomington, IN: Indiana University Press, 2104), 108–126.
41. Žižek, *Less Than Nothing*, 101: "The death of Christ is also the death/end of human mortality, the 'death of death', the negation of negation, the death of God is the rise of the undead drive."
42. Žižek, *Puppet and the Dwarf*, 138.
43. Ibid.
44. Ibid., 13–15.
45. Žižek, *God in Pain*, 68–69 and 47, respectively.
46. Ibid., 47.
47. Žižek, *On Belief*, 68–89; Žižek, *Puppet and the Dwarf*, 79–80; Žižek, *God in Pain*, 55–63.
48. Žižek, *Puppet and the Dwarf*, 136.
49. Žižek, *God in Pain*, 164–165.
50. Žižek, *The Monstrosity of Christ*, 29, 60.
51. Slavoj Žižek, *Did Somebody Say Totalitarianism?* (London: Verso, 2001), 56–57.
52. Žižek, *Living in the End Times*, 23.
53. Žižek, *The Parallax View*, 106. See Depoortere, *Christ in Postmodern Philosophy*, 115.
54. Žižek, *Puppet and the Dwarf*, 91.
55. Žižek, *The Parallax View*, 352–353.
56. Žižek, "'With or Without Passion': What's Wrong with Fundamentalism: Part 1," http://www.lacan.com/zizpassion.html
57. Žižek, *Puppet and the Dwarf*, 171.
58. Slavoj Žižek, "The Atheist Wager," *Political Theology* 11, no. 1 (2010): 136–140; Žižek, *The Monstrosity of Christ*, 48–50; Žižek, *Puppet and the Dwarf*, 14–15, 171.
59. Žižek, *The Parallax View*, 354.
60. Žižek, *Puppet and the Dwarf*, 53.
61. Ibid., 109.
62. Žižek, *Puppet and the Dwarf*, 35; Žižek, *The Monstrosity of Christ*, 12–14.
63. Heresy, for Žižek, is an internal transgression to "orthodoxy," inherent to its own failure to identify with itself; it is the parallax gap, the Void that resides within the symbolic order of "right belief," that shows itself to be the same with itself, only upon view of the "minimal difference," the shift in perspective that shows "Good and Evil" to be not obverse, but

symmetrical. There is nothing more heretical (and so, traditional) than the Christian declaration that, as Jesus Christ, God became human, and in so doing displayed the human being as divine. See Žižek, *The Monstrosity of Christ*, 96–98; Žižek, *On Belief*, 7–8.

64. Žižek, *Puppet and the Dwarf*, 3.
65. Ibid., 91.
66. Ibid., 78.
67. Ibid., 86.
68. Ibid., 89.
69. Ibid., 126.
70. Žižek, *The Monstrosity of Christ*, 26.
71. Žižek, *The Parallax View*, 352; Žižek, *Puppet and the Dwarf*, 14.
72. Žižek, *Puppet and the Dwarf*, 126.
73. Ibid., 136ff.
74. Ibid., 127.
75. Ibid., 168.
76. Žižek, *On Belief*, 148.
77. Žižek, *The Monstrosity of Christ*, 50.
78. Ibid., 101.
79. Žižek, *The Monstrosity of Christ*, 97; Žižek, "Paul and the Truth Event," 89f.
80. Žižek, *The Monstrosity of Christ*, 171.
81. Ibid., 97.
82. Ibid., 59.
83. Žižek, *God in Pain*, 169 (emphasis mine).
84. Žižek, *Fragile Absolute*, 110.
85. Žižek, *The Monstrosity of Christ*, 171.
86. Žižek, *God in Pain*, 36, 47ff.; Žižek, *Living in the End Times*, 116–118.
87. Žižek, *God in Pain*, 27–34.
88. Žižek, *The Monstrosity of Christ*, 61.
89. Ibid.
90. Žižek, *God in Pain*, 171.
91. Žižek, *Less Than Nothing*, 101.
92. Žižek, *The Monstrosity of Christ*, 149.
93. Ibid., 150.
94. Žižek, *Living in the End Times*, 87.
95. Žižek, *First as Tragedy*, 61.
96. Slavoj Žižek, *The Courage of Hopelessness: Chronicles of a Year of Acting Dangerously* (Brooklyn, NY: Melville House Publishing, 2018), xi.
97. Žižek, *The Courage of Hopelessness*, xi–xii.
98. Tressie McMillan Cottom, "Finding Hope in a Loveless Place." tressiemc. 27 November 2016. https://tressiemc.com /uncategorized/finding-hope-in-a-loveless-place/
99. Miguel De La Torre, *Embracing Hopelessness* (Minneapolis, MN: Fortress Press, 2017).
100. Žižek, *The Parallax View*, 381–385.

SELECT BIBLIOGRAPHY

Critchley, Simon (2012), *The Faith of the Faithless: Experiments in Political Theology*, London: Verso Books.
Davis, Creston, John Milbank, and Slavoj Žižek, eds. (2005), *Theology and the Political: The New Debate*, Durham, NC: Duke University Press.
Harink, Douglas Karel, ed. (2010) *Paul, Philosophy, and the Theopolitical Vision: Critical Engagements with Agamben, Badiou, Žižek, and Others,* Eugene, OR: Cascade Books.
Kotsko, Adam (2008), *Žižek and Theology,* New York: T&T Clark.
Milbank, John, and Slavoj Žižek (2005), *Theology and the Political: The New Debate*, ed. Creston Davis, Durham, NC: Duke University Press.
Milbank, John, and Slavoj Žižek (2010), *Paul's New Moment: Continental Philosophy and the Future of Christian Theology*, ed. Creston Davis, Grand Rapids, MI: Brazos Press.
Sigurdson, Ola (2012), *Theology and Marxism in Eagleton and Žižek: A Conspiracy of Hope*, New York: Palgrave Macmillan.
Žižek, Slavoj, and Boris Gunjević (2012), *God in Pain: Inversions of Apocalypse,* New York: Seven Stories Press.
Žižek, Slavoj, and John Milbank (2009), *The Monstrosity of Christ: Paradox or Dialectic?* ed. Creston Davis, Cambridge, MA: MIT Press.
Žižek, Slavoj (1989), *The Sublime Object of Ideology,* London: Verso.
Žižek, Slavoj (1991), *For They Know Not What They Do: Enjoyment as a Political Factor*, London: Verso.
Žižek, Slavoj (2000), *The Fragile Absolute, Or, Why Is the Christian Legacy Worth Fighting For?* London: Verso.
Žižek, Slavoj (2001), *On Belief,* London: Routledge.
Žižek, Slavoj (2003), *The Puppet and the Dwarf: The Perverse Core of Christianity,* Cambridge, MA: MIT Press.
Žižek, Slavoj (2010), *Living in the End Times,* London: Verso.
Žižek, Slavoj (2012), *Less than Nothing: Hegel and the Shadow of Dialectical Materialism*, London: Verso.

CHAPTER THIRTY-ONE

State(s) of Exception

The United States, the State of Israel, and the Legacy of Chosenness

ROBERT O. SMITH

INTRODUCTION

Exceptionalism has long provided a key for comprehending American self-understanding, including its forms of civil religion and nationalism. Although discussed less often in the same terms,[1] the State of Israel demonstrates similar self-understanding. Through a shared strategic alliance often described as a "special relationship," the United States and the State of Israel exercise their sovereignty by operating in a "state of exception" above and beyond legality. This essay seeks to provide a theological archaeology of American and Israeli exceptionalisms while exploring the contradictions and problems that arise from these secularized theological principles. What we find is that national identities based on religious foundations cannot fully escape the theological problems embedded within those theological systems. Political theology thus works in various directions to bolster and deconstruct exceptionalist claims.

THEOLOGIZING THE EXCEPTION

Carl Schmitt (1888–1985) and Giorgio Agamben (1942–) are the political theorists most closely associated with the "state of exception." Each reflects deeply on the theological foundations of the concept. Schmitt first theorized the state of exception in the early 1920s. Understood as the decision to suspend or transcend law, the exception was central to Schmitt's conception of sovereignty itself. The opening maxim of *Political Theology* (1922)—"Sovereign is he who decides on the exception"—is followed by the expanded reflection that "All significant concepts of the modern theory of the state are secularized theological concepts" and that "the exception in jurisprudence is analogous to the miracle in theology."[2]

Agamben's intensive engagement with Schmitt's concepts focuses as much on the material human effects of the "state of exception" as on the juridical theory through which the exception can be taken into account. Rejecting Schmitt's attempt to understand exception as a lawful expression of sovereign power (through the exercise of dictatorship), Agamben concludes that "the state of exception is . . . a space devoid of law, a zone of anomie in which all legal determinations . . . are deactivated." Since this state "seems to escape all legal definition," acts committed in this state "seem to be situated in an absolute non-place with respect to the law."³ The state's intentional construction of spaces devoid of law has deleterious effects on human life—illuminating the relationship between sovereign power and bare life explored in Agamben's *Homo Sacer*. Reflecting on "the camp" (exemplified by Nazi death camps) as "the space that is opened when the state of exception becomes the rule," Agamben concludes that "the fundamental activity of sovereign power is the production of bare life" and that, today, "it is not the city but rather the camp that is the fundamental biopolitical paradigm of the West."⁴

Agamben's revival of reflection on the "state of exception" provided important analytical tools for comprehending US policies concerning "enemy combatants" in the post-9/11 era. Slovenian philosopher Slavoj Žižek noted, for instance, that an official defense of detaining "enemy combatants" at the Guantánamo Bay Naval Base declared them to be "those who were missed by the bombs," thus putting "the prisoner almost literally into the position of living dead . . . so that they are now cases of what Giorgio Agamben calls *homo sacer*, the one who can be killed with impunity since, in the eyes of the law, his life no longer counts."⁵

Similarly, analysts have utilized Agamben's categories to describe Israeli policies toward Palestinians generally and especially toward the coastal enclave of the Gaza Strip, containing over 1.8 million Palestinians, the vast majority of them refugees. Israel's approach to its fifty-year military occupation of Palestinian territories, including Gaza, puts it at odds with the vast majority of interpretations of relevant international humanitarian law; in the longer term, the seemingly permanent refugee status of Palestinians displaced in Israel's founding war ties it to considerations of "the camp," not only through the reality of the Holocaust/Shoah but through the fifty-eight recognized Palestine refugee camps in Jordan, Lebanon, Syria, and the occupied Palestinian territories. Efforts to read Palestinian experience through Agamben's analysis have surfaced shortcomings in the Italian theorist's approach. David Lloyd, for instance, points out that the death camps of the Holocaust have their own genealogy in European colonial and settler-colonial practices while Nurhan Abujidi suggests that naming Palestinians as *homo sacer* in the face of totalizing Israeli power strips Palestinians of agency and, therefore, dignity.⁶

Through their "special relationship," the United States and the State of Israel assert the right to act uniquely to protect their perceived interests, both in the Middle East and globally. Neither country hesitates to violate the sovereignty of other states to achieve its objectives. As a permanent member of the UN Security Council, the United States has established a clear track record of vetoing interpretations of international law that would limit Israel's ability to prosecute its occupation of Palestinian territories in the manner it prefers. When taken together with the case of Guantánamo Bay detainees from both Afghanistan and Iraq and the extraordinary interpretations of international law through which Israel maintains its occupation of Palestinian territories, the United States, and the State of Israel exemplify projections of the "state of exception" into territories not within their undisputed sovereignty. This organization of global power acutely impacts Palestinians living within the State of Israel or in territory under Israeli military control.

The "state of exception" that constitutes Israeli control of Palestinian life and death, has another, less tangible element than the projection of raw power. Schmitt asserts that any state's capacity to declare or assert a "state of exception" is grounded, ultimately, in a theological claim. Schmitt views this reality positively; for him, it is a fact that must be acted upon if strong, centralized leadership is to properly guide the state. Agamben's rejection of any juridical legitimacy of the "state of exception" can therefore be read within the context of secularized reason. Although Agamben devotes a good deal of energy to analyzing the religious genealogy of contemporary political theory, this work does not imply legitimization of any one tradition. One can extrapolate from Agamben's critique of the "state of exception" a critique of any appeal to theological claims in the exercise of state power. In other words, one can combine Schmitt's positive assessment with Agamben's critique to conclude that theology, as an appeal beyond rationality in the realm of civil jurisprudential discourse, is the foundation of lawlessness. This lawlessness is enhanced when coupled with (1) state and imperial power, and (2) a robustly theological sense of exceptionalism, two characteristics shared by the United States and the State of Israel. It is to the religious sources of these exceptionalisms that we now turn.

Defining exceptionalism, in its American form, as "the idea that Americans are a people specially chosen by God and given a destiny to fulfill by him since colonial days," historian John Wilsey says, "Americans have always seen themselves as exceptional."[7] This combination of divine chosenness and mission was present even before there was such a thing as an "American." John Winthrop's speech, "A Modell of Christian Charity," delivered to settlers arriving to establish the Massachusetts Bay Colony, is often cited as a foundational expression of American civil religion.[8]

In these religious sources of American nationalism and exceptionalism, there is a profound emphasis on the "new," as symbolized in the motto of the Great Seal of the United States, *Novus ordo seclorum* ("A new order of the ages"). Stephen Prothero has suggested that in "this new place, the New World, the new Jerusalem, the new Israel, whatever you might call it . . . 'new' is the operative word." In this foundational period, "There was this idea that we are the new Adam and the new Eve" and that there is "some new kind of narrative, some new kind of story that we, as Americans, can tell that is going to be a story of us in relationship to God." It is, in effect, "the story of America's struggle from old religion to new."[9]

By contrast Zionism (the Jewish nationalism underlying the State of Israel) understood that it was creating something new, that a new thing was being accomplished in an old land. Thus, Israeli exceptionalism is grounded not in the newness of the state, but in the re-establishment of Jewish sovereignty over land ruled by Israelites millennia before. The practical necessity of Jewish immigration to Palestine was undergirded by an irredentist ideology bolstered by religious and even messianic claims; Israel's military victories are often described as "miraculous." This blend of secular commitments buoyed by theological sensibilities was apparent in Theodor Herzl who in 1904 said, "I once called Zionism an infinite ideal, and I believe that Zionism will not cease to be our ideal even after we come to settle in the land of our forefathers in Eretz Israel, for within the Zionist idea is contained the aspiration to moral and spiritual perfection."

Shaul Magid grounds "Jewish exceptionalism" in "Judaism's theology of election," while noting, "the secularization of the theology of election often yields an undertheorized notion of Jewish exceptionalism." Noting that "the idea of America as exceptional . . . has theological roots among radical Protestants who often viewed themselves as a 'New Israel,'" Magid suggests that "exceptionalism of one sort or another may be something America and Jews share and thus American Jews can find themselves as members of one exceptional people (the Jews) living in another exceptional country (America)."[10] In a less critical vein, contemporary American Christian Zionists extrapolate "Jewish exceptionalism" to include "Israeli exceptionalism" in a way that leads them to identify the United States and the State of Israel as "two nations under God."[11]

Both American and Israeli exceptionalism are grounded in a self-perception of "chosenness," the notion of being "elect" nations. Expanding analyses of the ways the

United States and the State of Israel impose biopolitical and necropolitical power on both domestic and international populations, Armenian Palestinian criminologist Nadera Shalhoub-Kevorkian has detailed how Israel cloaks its security policies within what she calls a "security theology": "Insofar as biblical claims of Jewish 'chosenness' and 'return' serve Israel's narrative as a legitimate and sovereign state, they also work to cast Israeli violence against Palestinians as a 'security necessity.' The discursive collapse of biblical and security claims works to exonerate racist structures; to mask state violence through the biblical/security prism that naturalizes the dispossession of Palestinians."[12] In an expanded analysis, Shalhoub-Kevorkian asserts that "it is this security theology, embedded in a political economy of sacralized violence, that, as criminologists would argue, neutralizes the offender's responsibility and distances the state from its criminality."[13] Given that theological claims of chosenness inform American as well as Israeli ideologies of exceptionalism, this critique can be analogously applied to the United States as well. Thus, the theological claim of chosenness informs both countries' willingness to create and act within non-legal states of exception.

Ideologies of exceptionalism are often critiqued for containing elements of presumed superiority or supremacy. In his analysis of American human rights policies in the post-9/11 era, Michael Ignatieff assailed both the George W. Bush and Barack Obama administrations for seeking to act outside the law. Ignatieff argued that "the first variant of exceptionalism is *exemptionalism*,"[14] the US insistence that it be exempt even from multinational treaties it helped negotiate. Such "exemptionalism" relates directly to Schmitt's notion of sovereignty. In a multilateral view of the world, one country's consistent desire to dictate or decide the exception (in this case, the exemption) means that country (in this case, the United States) is seeking, functionally, to act as the sovereign of the world.

CHOSENNESS AND TRIUMPH

The presumption of superiority inherent to American exceptionalism is linked inextricably to "the idea that Americans are a people specially chosen by God and given a destiny to fulfill."[15] As Conrad Cherry argued, "the belief in America as God's New Israel has come to support America's arrogant self-righteousness" even though "an attitude of international cooperation balks at any nation's assumption that it has a higher destiny than any other nation."[16] While for Cherry America's systemic failings of oppressed domestic populations—American Indians and black Americans among them—provided "threats to the mythology of American destiny," not all Americans are so sensitive to the plight of their neighbors, domestically and globally.[17] But does a sense of "chosenness" inevitably result in haughty supremacism?

As Magid points out, chosenness is a biblical category appropriated into American exceptionalist nationalism from Jewish foundations. That dynamic is confirmed in explicitly Christian notions of America as the "new Adam" or the "new Israel"—often with a specific reference to parts of America as "Zion" or the "New Jerusalem"[18]—as well as in distinctions between contemporary American and Israeli exceptionalisms. The distinctively Christian nature of American chosenness is further highlighted when Jews interpret the tradition of chosenness not as a triumphal claim but as a burden of special mission and purpose in a world where all communities have a relationship with God. Although, as Alan Kadish has written, "Textual references both to an Israelite elitism and a more universal mission are both present in scripture . . . The Jewish people's chosenness is meant to serve as a moral force for the world, by working to eliminate immorality." As

Rabbi Aharon Lichtenstein wrote in 1966, chosenness "resides in our covenantal relationship with God, rather than in any inherent superiority. We are both burdened and privileged to represent Hashem and Torah. . . . We do not boast of our prowess. We lay no claim to aboriginal merit."[19]

American exceptionalism, on the other hand, grounded in the Christian tradition of replacement theology (also known as supersessionism) exhibits a triumphalism that transmutes a Jewish tradition of "burden" into a claim of supremacy. British historian Clifford Longley, arguing that chosenness forms the foundational identity of both England and America, traces this triumphalist supremacy to theopolitical supersessionism. Suggesting that the "anti-Catholic elements in the English constitution . . . preserve England's unique status as the successor Chosen People of God to the Old Testament's Chosen People," Longley makes clear that "both the Roman Catholic claim and the Jewish claim to that title are set aside." Further, Longley demonstrates how, during the 1774 Continental Congress, "America formally introduced itself" into "Israel's shoes." From then on, "the Chosen People were to be not the Jews, not the Catholics, not the English, and not just the New Englanders, but all Americans." Longley identifies a chain of theopolitical supersession in which Catholics "stood, in relation to Protestants, as Jews had stood in relation to Catholics"; for Americans, "the English in turn proved unfaithful to their covenant, and so God made a new covenant with America."[20]

The triumphalism of American chosenness was galvanized during the country's continental expansion, accomplished largely in the nineteenth century. While envisioned by the "founding fathers" long before, this expansion began to be realized with the Louisiana Purchase and the Corps of Discovery expedition in 1803. The rapacious form of imperial acquisition that ensued systematically destroyed any community that stood in the way of civilizational progress; thus, American continental expansion was linked explicitly to white Anglo-Saxon Protestant (WASP) claims of racial superiority vis-à-vis Indigenous, immigrant, and arrivant inhabitants of the continent.[21] It is in this historical trajectory that the Jewish tradition of chosenness as a burden transmutes fully into an American Protestant claim of supremacy.

Longley's history of Christian theopolitical clamor for the status of "chosen" indicates what literary theorist Harold Bloom would call a weak misreading of the Jewish tradition. With his highly influential critical theory of "the anxiety of influence," Bloom asserted that, "poetic influence—when it involves two strong, authentic poets—always proceeds by a misreading of the prior poet, an act of creative correction that is actually and necessarily a misinterpretation."[22] Later in his career, Bloom leveled the charge against Christianity itself: "I think the Greek New Testament is the strongest and most successful misreading of a great prior text in the entire history of influence."[23] Ernest Renan offered a similar observation on the manufacture of nation identities: "To forget and—I will venture to say—to get one's history wrong, are essential factors in the making of a nation"; in the face of such historical misreadings, Renan continued, "the advance of historical studies is often a danger to nationality."[24]

CONCLUSIONS: EXCEPTIONALISM AND ITS EFFECTS

American and Israeli ideologies of exceptionalism are drawn from the same theological sources. Those sources, however, are interpreted through different lenses—one Jewish, the other Protestant Christian. Susannah Heschel has observed that Christianity, with its uniquely supersessionist drive, "colonized Judaism theologically, taking over its central theological concepts of the Messiah, eschatology, apocalypticism, election, and Israel, as well as its scriptures, its prophets, and even its God, and denying the continued validity of those ideas for Judaism." In this dynamic, "Judaism came to function in Christian theology as the other whose negation confirms and even constitutes Christianity."[25] Thus, chosenness and supersessionism (replacement theology), topics constituting the central problems facing Jewish–Christian relations in the post-Holocaust world, threaten to destabilize the "special relationship" between the United States and the State of Israel, perhaps the most potent military-industrial alliance in the world today. As Gil Hochberg has shown, even the political assemblage known as the "Judeo-Christian tradition" employed to cement the "special relationship" is susceptible to destabilization.[26]

While critical analysis does not immediately change the basis of American and Israeli self-perception and mutual strategic reinforcement, understanding the theological contradictions at the foundations of this strategic alliance provides resources for seeking liberation for those trapped within states of exception, those persons and communities reduced to the status of *homo sacer*. Through intentionally creating states of exception beyond the limits of legality, both the United States and the State of Israel engage in state crime; these states of exception are mystified, sustained, and protected by theologies of security related directly to theologically grounded ideologies of exceptionalism. Within the present organization of global power these states reinforce one another's operations within states of exception—globally, regionally, and domestically. Regionally, the State of Israel pursues its own interests while operating as a regional satrap supporting the broader imperial agenda of the United States. Domestically, both the United States and the State of Israel are best understood as settler-colonial states engaged in systematic human rights abuses against Indigenous nations and those communities, including migrant workers and those formerly enslaved, forced to live as permanent underclasses within their respective ethno-nationalist societies.

Internationally, the joint American–Israeli effort to maintain states of exception has the effect of eroding and delegitimizing international humanitarian law and human rights discourse. In the State of Israel, for instance, Jewish settlements in the West Bank, considered illegal by broadly accepted interpretations of the Geneva Conventions, are engaged in efforts to normalize their existence in order to retain Jewish Israeli control of the land.[27] At the same time, Israeli settlers and their supporters are active in shaping human rights discourse in ways that reinforce the security apparatus necessary for expropriating Palestinian land.[28] Israeli political discourse is filled with examples of racist sentiments based on notions of Jewish supremacy. The American investment in these Israeli policies is most apparent in the financial investment in Israel's "qualitative military edge"[29] and in US vetoes of United Nations Security Council resolutions critical of Israeli policies and practices.

While this essay has made the case that American exceptionalism is based on a conception of chosenness decidedly unlike traditional Jewish readings of the notion, it is also aware that many Jewish commentators balk at any sense that the State of Israel represents Judaism in any sense. As American Jewish theologian Marc Ellis has boldly argued, Judaism ≠ Israel.[30] Thus, it would be a mistake to assume that Israeli exceptionalism is somehow more authentically Jewish than American exceptionalism, that its will to a state of exception is necessarily distinct. Walter Mignolo, taking Ellis's observations as a starting point, suggests that the emergence of "political Zionism . . . in Europe during the nineteenth century is not a random event of universal history." It is, instead, "a logical consequence of the modern/colonial world. It was the unfolding of European history, self-fashioned as 'modernity,' that needed and invented the form nation-state."³¹ While Zionism originated as a liberation movement, Mignolo says further, "the State of Israel, once established, did not escape the logic of coloniality embedded in the form nation-state that has shaped and continues to shape the modern/colonial world since the end of the eighteenth century, an order that consolidated Western civilization's global designs."³² Thus, critiques of the State of Israel are not critiques of Zionism (Jewish nationalism) alone and certainly not of Judaism qua Judaism; they are, instead, critiques "leveled against the modern, European, and imperial form nation-state."³³ A central challenge for Jewish ethics in this era following the Holocaust, the founding, and the expansion of the State of Israel, is how to navigate the opportunity to exercise European (that is, Western Christian) forms of domination, including the opportunity to craft states of exception.

This essay has argued that the proclivity of the United States and the State of Israel to operate within states of exception is augmented by the ideologies of exceptionalism embedded within the self-understanding of each country. Both features—the state of exception and the attendant exceptionalism—are undergirded by theological claims. By mystifying the workings of state power—including activities without legal frameworks—such theology shields state crime from analysis and prosecution. This is especially deleterious for communities exploited within states of exception, made abject in the condition of *homo sacer*. Moreover, the specific theological traditions contained within the "special relationship" shared by the United States and the State of Israel indicates fundamental instability and anxiety. If the triumphal reading of chosenness at the core of American exceptionalism—a triumphalism shared by the modern State of Israel—is understood to be a weak Christian misreading of Jewish tradition, the resulting nationalism is necessarily derivative, a fragile foundation for national mission. Any "exemptionalist" reading of either American or Israeli exceptionalism is therefore suspect, with no real basis in theological sources or, to return to Agamben, non-transcendent civil juridical reason. To argue otherwise is to promote theology as the basis of lawlessness.

NOTES

1. For a notable exception, see M. Shahid Alam, *Israeli Exceptionalism: The Destabilizing Logic of Zionism* (New York: Palgrave Macmillan, 2010).
2. Carl Schmitt, *Political Theology: Four Chapters on the Concept of Sovereignty*, trans. George Schwab (Chicago: University of Chicago Press, 2006), 5, 36.
3. Giorgio Agamben, *State of Exception*, trans. Kevin Attell (Chicago: University of Chicago Press, 2005), 50, 51.
4. Giorgio Agamben, *Homo Sacer: Sovereign Power and Bare Life*, trans. Daniel Heller-Roazen (Stanford, CA: Stanford University Press, 1998), 168–169, 181.
5. Slavoj Žižek, "Biopolitics: Between Terri Schiavo and Guantanamo," *Artforum* (December 2005), available online at http://www.lacan.com/zizartforum1205.htm (accessed 28 June 2018). References to US policy through the lenses provided by Agamben are too many to mention individually.
6. See David Lloyd, "Settler Colonialism and the State of Exception: The Example of Palestine/Israel, Settler Colonial Studies," *Settler Colonial Studies* 2, no. 1 (2012): 59–80; and Nurhan Abujidi, "The Palestinian States of Exception and Agamben," *Contemporary Arab Affairs* 2, no. 2 (2009): 272–291.
7. John D. Wilsey, *American Exceptionalism and Civil Religion: Reassessing the History of an Idea* (Downers Grove, IL: InterVarsity Press, 2015), 16.

8. See Robert N. Bellah, *The Broken Covenant: American Civil Religion in Time of Trial*, 2nd ed. (Chicago: University of Chicago Press, 1992), esp. pp. 13–16.

9. *God in America*: "A New Adam." Directed and written by David Belton. Public Broadcasting System (PBS), October 2010. Transcript available at http://www.pbs.org/godinamerica/transcripts/hour-one.html.

10. Shaul Magid, "Where is the 'Jew' in the Judeo-Christian myth? Thoughts on Jewish and American Exceptionalism," *The Immanent Frame: Secularism, Religion, and the Public Sphere* (The Social Science Research Council); March 13, 2017, available at https://tif.ssrc.org/category/exchanges/american-exceptionalism/.

11. Tom Doyle, *Two Nations Under God: Why You Should Care about Israel* (Nashville, TN: B&H Publishing, 2008). For critical historical introductions to the topic of Christian Zionism, see Robert O. Smith, *More Desired than Our Owne Salvation: The Roots of Christian Zionism* (New York: Oxford, 2013), and Donald M. Lewis, *The Origins of Christian Zionism: Lord Shaftesbury and Evangelical Support for a Jewish Homeland* (Cambridge: Cambridge University Press, 2014).

12. Nadera Shalhoub-Kevorkian, *Security Theology, Surveillance and the Politics of Fear* (Cambridge: Cambridge University Press, 2015), 14–15.

13. Nadera Shalhoub-Kevorkian, Yossi David, and Sarah Ihmoud, "Theologizing State Crime," *State Crime* 5, no. 1 (Spring 2016), 140.

14. Michael Ignatieff, ed., *American Exceptionalism and Human Rights* (Princeton, NJ: Princeton University Press, 2009), 4.

15. Wilsey, *American Exceptionalism and Civil Religion*, 16.

16. Conrad Cherry, *God's New Israel: Religious Interpretations of American Destiny*, rev. ed. (Chapel Hill, NC: University of North Carolina Press, 1998), 21.

17. Ibid.

18. For some of the eighteenth- and nineteenth-century debates about the identity of America in relation to ideas of the "new Jerusalem," see Smith, *More Desired than Our Owne Salvation*, Chapter 6.

19. Alan Kadish, "Chosenness and Bias in the Jewish Community," *Lehrhaus* (April 24, 2017), available online at https://www.thelehrhaus.com/scholarship/chosenness-and-bias-in-the-jewish-community/.

20. Clifford Longley, *Chosen People: The Big Idea that Shapes England and America* (London: Hodder & Stoughton, 2002), 38, 67, 89.

21. See Reginald Horsman, *Race and Manifest Destiny: Origins of American Racial Anglo-Saxonism* (Cambridge, MA: Harvard University Press, 1981). For the use of "arrivant," see Chickasaw scholar Jodi Byrd's *The Transit of Empire: Indigenous Critiques of Colonialism* (Minneapolis, MN: University of Minnesota Press, 2011), who borrows the term from Kamau Brathwaite "to signify those people forced into the Americas through the violence of European and Anglo-American colonialism and imperialism around the globe" (xix).

22. Harold Bloom, *The Anxiety of Influence: A Theory of Poetry*, 2nd ed. (New York: Oxford University Press, 1997), xxiii, 30. Bloom expanded his methodology in *A Map of Misreading* (New York: Oxford University Press, 1980).

23. See Harvey Blume, "Divine (mis)Readings: Q&A with Harold Bloom," *The Boston Globe* (November 13, 2005), available online at http://archive.boston.com/ae/books/articles/2005/11/13/divine_misreadings/?page=1.

24. Ernest Renan, "What Is a Nation? (1882)" in *Modern Political Doctrines*, ed. Alfred Zimmern (London: Oxford University Press, 1939), 190.

25. Susannah Heschel, "Christ's Passion: Homoeroticism and the Origins of Christianity," in *Mel Gibson's Bible: Religion, Popular Culture, and The Passion of the Christ*, eds. Timothy K. Beal and Tod Linafelt (Chicago: University of Chicago Press, 2006), 100.
26. See Gil Z. Hochberg, "'Remembering Semitism' or 'on the prospect of re-membering the Semites,'" *ReOrient* 1, no. 2 (Spring 2016): 192–122.
27. See Ariel Handel, et al., eds., *Normalizing Occupation: The Politics of Everyday Life in the West Bank Settlements* (Bloomington, IN: Indiana University Press, 2017).
28. See Nicola Perugini and Neve Gordon, *The Human Right to Dominate* (New York: Oxford University Press, 2015).
29. See William Wunderle and Andre Briere, "Augmenting Israel's Qualitative Military Edge," Middle East Quarterly 15, no. 1 (Winter 2008), available online at https://www.meforum.org/articles/2008/augmenting-israel-s-qualitative-military-edge; and Peter Baker and Julie Hirschfeld Davis, "U.S. Finalizes Deal to Give Israel $38 Billion in Military Aid," *New York Times* (September 13, 2016), available online at https://www.nytimes.com/2016/09/14/world/middleeast/israel-benjamin-netanyahu-military-aid.html.
30. See Marc H. Ellis, *Judaism Does Not Equal Israel: The Rebirth of the Jewish Prophetic* (New York: New Press, 2009).
31. Walter Mignolo, "Decolonizing the Nation-State: Zionism in the Colonial Horizon of Modernity," in *Deconstructing Zionism: A Critique of Political Metaphysics*, eds. Gianni Vattimo and Michael Marder (New York: Bloomsbury, 2013), 65.
32. Ibid., 70.
33. Ibid.

SELECT BIBLIOGRAPHY

Agamben, Giorgio (1998), *Homo Sacer: Sovereign Power and Bare Life*, trans. Daniel Heller-Roazen, Stanford, CA: Stanford University Press.
Agamben, Giorgio (2005), *State of Exception*, trans. Kevin Attell, Chicago: University of Chicago Press.
Bellah, Robert N. (1992), *The Broken Covenant: American Civil Religion in Time of Trial*, 2nd ed., Chicago: University of Chicago Press.
Cherry, Conrad (1998), *God's New Israel: Religious Interpretations of American Destiny*, rev. ed., Chapel Hill, NC: University of North Carolina Press.
Fields, Gary (2017), *Enclosure: Palestinian Landscapes in a Historical Mirror*, Berkeley, CA: University of California Press.
Heschel, Susannah (1998), *Abraham Geiger and the Jewish Jesus*, Chicago: University of Chicago Press.
Ignatieff, Michael (2009), *American Exceptionalism and Human Rights*, Princeton, NJ: Princeton University Press.
Nirenberg, David (2013), *Anti-Judaism: The Western Tradition*, London: Head of Zeus.
Nirenberg, David (2014), "'Judaism' as Political Concept: Toward a Critique of Political Theology," *Representations* 128, no.1 (Fall): 1–29.
Ruether, Rosemary Radford (1979), "The *Adversus Judaeos* Tradition in the Church Fathers: The Exegesis of Christian Anti-Semitism," in *Aspects of Jewish Culture in the Middle Ages*, ed. Paul E. Szarmach, Albany, NY: State University of New York Press.
Ruether, Rosemary Radford (2014), *America, Amerikkka: Elect Nation and Imperial Violence*, reprint ed., New York: Routledge.

Schmitt, Carl (2006), *Political Theology: Four Chapters on the Concept of Sovereignty*, trans. George Schwab, Chicago: University of Chicago Press.

Shalhoub-Kevorkian, Nadera (2015), *Security Theology, Surveillance and the Politics of Fear*, Cambridge: Cambridge University Press.

Wilsey, John D. (2015), *American Exceptionalism and Civil Religion: Reassessing the History of an Idea*, Downers Grove, IL: InterVarsity Press.

CHAPTER THIRTY-TWO

Praying to the O/other

Rethinking Ecclesiology in the Context of Increasing Islamophobia

GYRID KRISTINE GUNNES

Freedom needs to be hospitable.[1]

—Nineteenth-century Norwegian Romantic poet
Henrik Wergeland in *Jøden* (*The Jew*), 1842

INTRODUCTION

The first Sunday of December 2009, I woke up to the sound of the bells from the majestic fourteenth-century cathedral of Nidaros, located in the historic city of Trondheim in Norway. The cathedral is regarded as the "national sanctuary" of Norway as the assumed burial place of the Olav Haraldson, the canonized Viking king who according to ecclesial celebrated legend and folklore brought Christianity to Norway by violently ridding the country of the Norse faith.[2] The sanctuary thus embodies the cultural and religious privileged position of the Lutheran denomination in the Scandinavian countries, the violent expulsion and suppression of other faiths and denominations, and the mutual legitimization of territorial politics and religious monopoly. With the arrival of the Reformation in 1537 to the kingdom of Denmark-Norway, the former Catholic Church in Norway was nationalized and the state confessionalized as a Lutheran state, outlawing all other denominations and banning the settlement of subjects who did not belong to the Lutheran faith.[3] In 2013, the Church of Norway seized to be a state-church[4] but is still in the 2012 amendments to the Constitution, the folk-church of Norway, publicly financed through taxes, a funding model which since 1981 also applies to other recognized faith communities or value-based communities.[5] In other words: although Norway today complies with the idea of freedom of religion stated in the Declaration of Human Rights, the Church of Norway has had a politically and legally sanctioned privileged position. With other countries of Europe, the Church of Norway shares a trajectory of legally sanctioned majority position that has made the majority-church deeply indigenized and intertwined with national culture and history.[6]

Working in 2009 as an ordinated Lutheran priest, it was my professional task to officiate services in the cathedral. This Sunday, however, something felt viscerally different. As a Lutheran priest, I was one of the living stones of the cathedral. Yet, the familiarity between the body of the cathedral and my own body felt ambivalent. What we shared, the cathedral and I, was not only that we were contemporary witnesses of the Christian faith. We also embody, in stones or flesh, the historically privileged position of the Lutheran denomination in Norway. And this Sunday, it was not the Jews[7] or Jesuits[8] who were the targets of alienating othering. This Sunday in December 2009 was the first Sunday after Switzerland held a general referendum against the architectural and auditory equivalent of the cathedral bells—the minaret—inside the borders of the Swiss state.[9] And even thougth the bells of Norwegian and Swiss cathedrals empirically share a similar religious function as minarets, Swiss and Norwegian cathedral bells will never be the subject of legally sanctioned prohibition fuelled by discourses of othering. Possessing a historical, cultural, and racial majority position protects church bells from being discursively targeted in discourses of ostracizing and alienation. The reason for this is that these religious artefacts belong to the religious tradition of the majority population.

Back in 2009, the full-blown violent potential of perceiving the Muslim and Islam as the *other* on European soil was unimaginable to most Norwegians. Two years later, Anders Behring Breivik carried out the deadliest massacre on Norwegian soil since the Second World War when, on July 11, 2011, bombing the government headquarters and shooting random participants at the summer camp of the Labour Party on the island of Utøya, killing seventy-seven adults and children and injuring more than two hundred. The reason for the killing was that Breivik identified the Latour Party as traitors to the white "ethnic population" by allowing "mass immigration" of Muslims. In Brevik's vision of Norway, articulated in his manifesto which was published on the internet simultaneously with the shooting, all Muslims will be deported so that "all traces of current and past Islamic influence in Europe will be removed."[10]

Although the Swiss referendum and Breivik's actions are vastly different in form, they share the notion that the physical presence of Islam and Muslims represent a threat to European culture, and thus should be obliviated, either by (unlawful) violence or by democratic law.

How do I as white, Norwegian-born clergy in the Christian majority tradition respond to such alienation of the religious other? What kind of ritual practices and ecclesiological reflections emerge from such responses? In this chapter I will present and discuss one ritual practice, *Prayers to Allah*,[11] which I performed at the national annual exhibition of modern art (Høstutstillingen) in 2014.[12] I will ask how this particular practice—committed yet ambivalent and unauthorized by the ecclesial governmental body—contribute to ecclesiological knowledge production.[13] Using Bruno Latour's and Judith Butler's work on religion as material and performative, I will argue that performative practices—in this case, *Prayers to Allah*—embody a creative appropriation of the material resources of a religious tradition. Such appropriations may transcend their concrete intentional purpose and hold the capacity to enlarge and reframe more traditional theological discourses, like the difference between invisible and visible church ecclesiology. Hence, ethical responses to social injustice (like Islamophobia) should be seen as occasions for destabilizing and blurring boundaries between the authorized ecclesial magisterium and non-conventional use of the ritual traditional to that very magisterium. Building on the ecclesiological reflections of queer theologian Linn Marie Tonstad, I will conclude by asking if such committed yet non-authorized uses may be perceived as examples of an ecclesiology of *ethical eccentricity*.

RESPONDING TO ISLAMOPHOBIA AS CLERGY: STRATEGIC DILEMMAS AND ECCLESIOLOGICAL POSSIBILITIES

The political othering and essentialization of Muslims condenses into *Islamophobia*, defined as "socially reproduced prejudice and aversions against Islam and Muslims, and actions and practices which attack, exclude and discriminate against people on account of these people being, or presumed to be Muslims and be associated with Islam."[14] Mattias Gardell points out that what Islamophobia shares with anti-Semitism is that images of "the Muslim" (or "the Jew") coming from the majority population take on a life of their own independent of the practices and lives of actual Muslims or Jews.[15] Islamophobia forecloses the Muslim as essentialized and "eternal" other and thus, within the internal logic of the Islamophobic, the *Muslim needs to be expulsed from the non-Muslim community* independently of what individual Muslims believe or do.[16] One example of this essentialization of the Muslim is found in the slogan of the Islamophobic blog, "Gates of Vienna," which reads: "At the siege of Vienna in 1683 Islam seemed poised to overrun Christian Europe. We are in a new phase of an old war."[17] Within the frames of an Islamophobic world-view, there is a direct political and ideological line from the war between the Central/Eastern European Ottoman and Austrian empires of the seventeenth century to current political discussions on hijabs, the presence of minarets, and European refugee politics.

There are, of course, numerous ecclesial practices which counter and respond to Islamophobia. Within the context of Norway, practices of religious dialogue have a long tradition.[18] Although such practices are highly laudable and important, it is important to recognize their potential shortcomings when faced with the internal logic of Islamophobia. As Gardell observes,[19] Islamophobic ideas cannot be easily (if at all) overcome by entering into relations with living Muslims, because, ironically, Islamophobia does not discursively allow the Muslim to be a living individual but construes the Muslim as an essentialized stereotype. Religious responses to Islamophobia cannot be combatted through the use of Muslims as token examples of the *good Muslim*. Thus, faced with the logic of Islamophobia, the goal of creating ethical responses to counter Islamophobia ought not to be "demonstrating" the civility of a westernized (and thus "good") Muslim, but to foster reflections within the majority population on questions of power, asymmetry and representation.

Thus, I will argue that in addition to traditional inter-religious dialogue, it is possible to imagine ecclesial responses to Islamophobia that redirect the problem of Islamophobia away from the individual Muslim and instead targets the collective imagination of the cultural majority. Within such a strategy, the goal is to interrupt the cultural-religious imaginations of the majority populations in order to expose, question, and de-naturalize images of the self and other as essentialized opposites. The ritual practices that make up the empirical basis for this chapter are an example of an ecclesial response to Islamophobia that thus *does not involve living Muslims*.[20] Such a strategy is of course vulnerable to critiques of paternalism and majority self-centeredness. Yet, the gain of submitting to this very real risk is to insist that it is the imaginations of the majority culture that is the problem of Islamophobia and (and in other cases: anti-Semitism), not the concrete presence of believers and practices of living people who are racialized as "Muslims" and "Jew." This implies creating an ecclesial response to Islamophobia which destabilizes and undoes imaginations of the majority population. A performative method of achieving such destabilization is to create and engage in practice ritual which undoes stable and normative identities as "Christian" and "church" and submit these identities to playful and creative investigation. In this chapter, I will call this *clerical self-iconoclasm*.

This strategy is especially valid in contexts which have historically and culturally been mono-religious denominations (like the Scandinavian countries) and where the organizational ecclesial political border and the nation-state overlap geographically. One may argue that this overlap creates an ecclesio-political union, where (in Norway until 2012) the state–church relationship formalized the link between political and ecclesial entities with the king as the head of both church and state. Given this historical church–state trajectory, the performative methodology of a politics of anti-Islamophobia and cultural inclusiveness needs to transgress and subvert ecclesiological insides and outsides and—in my opinion—the committed yet irreverent use of the cultural and religious prestigious material and immaterial religious tradition. Such irreverent and appropriated use of the material and ritual tradition may give rise to new ecclesiological reflections which transcend the concrete situation of Islamophobia.

JUDITH BUTLER AND BRUNO LATOUR: RELIGION AS PERFORMED MATERIALITY

In her millennium works, Butler questions humanism's claim that all human beings share equal worth. She argues that not only the experience of belonging to a gender, but also the ability to be perceived as a human being is socially produced. In order to become a human being, one needs to appear inside the frames of what is socially and culturally intelligible as a human being. Ontology is thus a social matter, because "we are not only constituted by our relations but dispossessed by them as well."[21] To be human is thus not to be in possession of an eternal dignity which cannot be broken. Such a position does not account for or theorize on the extremely unequal distribution of the recognition of this inherent dignity. Rather, to be human is to be dispossessed of dignity and to depend on the social context to render my life as intelligibly human or not. This framework unevenly distributes social reorganization geographically and politically.[22] It allows some to appear as living and, when death occurs, worthy of grief. To socially appear is thus the performative doing of others, not a result of my own being.

Butler's perspective is general and does not pay attention to religion in particular. Bruno Latour, on the other hand, has written extensively on religion.[23] In this context, the role and meaning of *mediators*[24] in religious practices surface is highly relevant. According to Latour, religion needs to be freed from its entrapment in the binary pair of either authenticity or artifice. Religion is not, as the atheist claims, false simply because it is constructed by humans. Nor does religion's claim to truth depend on, as believers traditionally believe, the experience of a transcendent essence that exists apart from humans and is thus not human-made. Religion works because humans fabricate it. Religion is lived and done through the use of sacred spaces, songs, artefacts, and religious holidays and because these are cultural and contextual. This, however, does not make religion false. What is false is the assumption that one has to choose between artifice and authenticity:

> Mediations are necessary everywhere. If you forbid them, you become mad, fanatic, but there is no way to obey the command and choose between the two-polar opposite: either it is made or it is real. There is a structural impossibility, an impasse . . . It is as

impossible as to request a Bunraku player to have to choose, from now on, either to show his puppet or to show himself on the stage.[25]

Thus, those who want to do away with religious images[26] have radically misunderstood their purpose. Religious images do not reveal a hidden truth somewhere else. Nor are they popular and degenerated popular versions of the true and pure religion, sometimes despised by the religious.[27] More than representations of a transcendent reality, religious images "allow one to move to another image, exactly as the fail and modest as the former one, but different."[28] Religion is a cascade of images, in the lived use of the mediators.

This understanding of religion stresses the importance of the institutions of religion. Religious institutions are not only the earthly and frail vessels of remembrance of an abstract truth beyond material expressions. They *are* religion. Institutions are, according to Latour "synonymous with innovation."[29] Innovation is not restricted to the authorized use of religious images, like sermons given by ordained clergy and liturgical reform introduced and sanctioned by ecclesial synods. Contested, conflictual, and even destructive use places itself in the cascade of religious images. Even the vandalization of religious images holds the capacity for pious and religious use. Faced with a broken pieta, Latour asks how the vandalizer has not obliviated the Pieta, but redirected its meaning: "What is the dead Christ if not another broken icon, the perfect image of God, desecrated, crucified, pierced, and ready to entomb? So the iconoclastic gesture has struck an image that had already been broken."[30] Even images which are unauthorized and unconventional harbor a hermeneutical surplus which allows the believer to move on to new images, some sanctioned by the ecclesial body, some expressions of private piety, some an amalgam of various images including impulses from other religious or spiritual traditions. Indeed, this process of creating and moving between different images—"a craving for carefully constructed mediators"—is civilization itself.[31]

THE POLITICAL POTENTIAL OF LITURGY: PRAYING TO ALLAH AS A CHRISTIAN PRIEST IN THE MIDST OF ISLAMOPHOBIA

Performance art is a notoriously contested genre.[32] Tracing its heritage from both Surrealism and the so-called Happening in New York in the 1960s, performance theorist Richard Schechner understands performance art as behavior that is *restored*. "Restored behaviour" is everyday behavior which is repeated deliberate and consciously as "twice-behaved behaviour."[33] In other words, performance art is a type of behavior that is self-reflexive in its execution of private mundane or professional practices. In the act of staging a performance, here is a reflexive distance between self and action. Even if the act done on stage is similar or identical to an action performed in everyday life, the actions are not the same. This first is simply "done," the other is consciously "performed."

The performance is very simple to visualize. One of the works consists of the following: On a section of one of the exhibition hall walls there is a shelf; on the shelf, there are sheets of paper with the two words "Dear Allah" and pens. Next to the sheets, a ceramic bowl and a laminated sheet with the following text in Norwegian:

> In most religions, people pray to a god. For a thousand years, the Christian god has been addressed in Norway, and according to the Constitution from 2014 Christianity is the state religion of Norway. Today people of different faiths live side by side in

Norway. One of the new gods is the god of Islam, in Arabic called "Allah." Right wing extremists want to give the impression that Islam is fundamentally different from Christianity and that the Christian god and the god of Islam have nothing in common. One of the ways to prove they are wrong is to do what they perceive to be impossible: to address in prayer one of the new gods in Norway. Do you want to pray to Allah? Write your prayer on a sheet of paper. Pray it yourself or glue it on the wall so that a priest will pray it for you the coming Sunday at twelve.

During the six weeks the national annual exhibition of modern art was open, I visited the space two times a week over a period of four weeks. On Friday afternoons I would collect the week's production of prayers on the wall and in the ceramic bowl. The wall and the gauge were full of sheets of papers with handwritten texts on them. I harvested the wall and gauge, brought the sheets back home, read them all, then selected between ten and twelve. I glued the selected prayers into my clergy copy of the Book of Common Prayers, which I used when leading services during my seven years as a Lutheran priest employed by the Church of Norway. On Sunday at one o'clock—the time when the Church of Norway Sunday services end—I returned to the exhibition hall wearing my full traditional vestments as an ordinated Lutheran priest (the white cassock and stole, the colors depending on the liturgical cycle). I positioned my body in the middle of the room, allowing visitors to gather around me. Next I do what I have been ordinated to do by the (then) state church, the Church of Norway, and what priests in the Church of Norway have done in an unbroken pattern since the sixteenth century Reformation: *To pray for and with people who belong to the racial, religious and cultural majority population of the nation-state.*

CLERICAL DESTABILIZATION OF THE PRIVILEGED MAJORITY TRADITION

In the light of Latour's work on the role of mediators in religious practice and Butler's social ontology, how does the performance *Prayers to Allah* embody the capacity of the majority Christian population to respond ethically in a context of Islamophobia? In the liturgical practices which I—and other clergy from majority traditions—are trained in, plan, rehearse and execute, the god who is evoked in the *kyrie* prayer, praised in the Gloria, remembered and interpreted in the Scriptural readings and sermon, eaten in the Eucharist, is discursively constructed as a distinctly Christian God.[34] In cultural and political contexts where Christianity is inherently tied to the majority culture through historical, cultural and legal bonds, this means that "God" may turn out to be a cultural artefact of the cultural and ethnic majority population.

Merging the question of ontology as social and performative (Butler) and religion as synonymous to its mediations (Latour), one may ask if the lack of performative presence of other gods in traditional liturgical practices *dispossess these other gods of being*. These gods are not performed into being. Thus, they are placed outside what constitutes common and social intelligibility. If social existence of gods depends on mediators, a lack of address and articulation of the possible existence of non-Christian gods in Christian services in mainline majority service, the only status renders possible for non-Christian gods is a social non-presence. Non-Christian gods are thus liturgically constructed as Agambian *homo sacers*.[35] The *homo sacer* is, according to Agamben, the one who is placed outside the frames of human intelligibility, included only by virtue of one's own exclusion.[36] The non-Christian god in the mainline Christian worship service is only present *as excluded*. Hence, the status of non-Christian gods in mainline churches of the cultural majority traditions is that of an *ethno-divine homo sacer*. In a context of decades of intertwinement between the state and a state-sanctioned Christian tradition that today enjoys a majority position, Islamophobia may be seen as the transformation of metaphysics into politics. Islamophobia merely turns metaphysical dispossession into a matter of territorial and material dispossession: like other gods that are ontologically illegitimate and socially unintelligible, human believers of these gods are dispossessed of a being which is legitimate and intelligible.

Prayers to Allah disturbs traditional prayer as a liturgical-ontological practice. It disrupts authenticity *as a condition for* imagining the relationship between the one who prays (the prayerer) and the divinity. It disrupts authenticity (direct contact between God and person) *as the result* of prayer. The reason for this disjunction is that non-Arab and non-Maltese speaking Christians do not address their divinity as "Allah." The person who prays in *Prayers to Allah* is a Norwegian-speaking Lutheran priest,[37] in other words, a person who believes in the reality of someone or something called "God." Yet, the disjunction of language ruptures the relation as self-evident and non-reflexive. Clearly, in *Prayers to Allah*, the human-made dimension of prayer is not merely a decorative wrapping (candles, rosaries) that facilitates and cushions the immaterial and pure relationship between the believer and divinity. Religion itself *as human made*—practice of making and imagining my own deity and the deities of the religions and cultural others—is at the very center of the act of engaging in a religious practice as a believer. We pray and meta-pray simultaneously.

What is the result of this simultaneity, as persons who embody the ethnic, cultural, religious majority tradition in a context of increasing alienating discourses like Islamophobia? One interpretation may look like this: Naming my god as Allah as a white Norwegian clergy in a cultural and political context where Allah is associated with Islam, my co-prayers and I undergo an *ethno-liturgical transubstantiation*. Performatively, we are transformed from being Christians/atheists/agnostics into Muslims. Such an ethno-liturgical transubstantiation may fall short of metaphysical claims compared to the transubstantiation of the Eucharist. But it does not fall short of political impact claimed by the transformation. Like the human being who *is brought into being* by appearing as socially intelligible as a human being, the ethno-liturgical transubstantiation performatively "does" Allah into existence. Like the bread and wine in the Eucharist, the participants/spectators and I at the performance are performatively transformed into Muslims. We become Muslims because we relate to the word Allah with all the variations of sentiment that are available in the relation between the prayer and her divinities, from gratitude to rage. Performatively, Norwegians are thus given a conceptual space to relate to Allah as a divinity. Performatively, Norwegians are given a space to see other white Norwegians relate to Allah with the same sentiment the believer has towards her deity, from gratuity to rage. We experience—and we let others see that we experience—a mutual and deliberate redirecting of our imaginations of Islam as an ideological component in media-driven images of wars in order to resist normalizing discourses that use the challenges and costs for Norwegian-born tax payers of integrating refugees into Norwegian society to negatively impact Norwegian foreign policy or government policy on refugees. This discursive displacement of the term "Allah" de-naturalizes it and *performatively* redirects imaginations of Islam into a category of existential meaning. It is not a retreat to religious essentialism, by claiming that Islam is essentially "good." What we were doing was simply to *religiously* and *performatively* enact into existence a spiritual entity that is called "Allah" within the boundaries of the nation state of Norway in a context where this entity and those who believe in it are the targets of alienation.[38]

... AND, OF COURSE, *WE DON'T BECOME MUSLIMS*

And, of course, this is not the only interpretation. Even more valid is the following reading of the performance: *Prayers to Allah* does not transform my co-prayerers and myself into Muslims. We do not become Muslims because we are spatially placed in a gallery, not a sanctuary. I am a priest-turned-performance artist, the co-prayers are visitors to an art exhibition. We are not converts. Nor are we pretending to be converts, as the customary manner to become Muslims is to articulate the Creed. Indeed, the performance makes no use of artefacts, official recognized clerics, formulas, Scriptural quotations, liturgical gestures, or vestments that are deliberately associated with Islam *save the word "Allah."*

Neither do we become Muslims in a relational and political sense of the term: the social and economic condition of those who call their god "Allah" in their sanctuary space cannot be grasped performatively. Performance is not lived life. Economic and political realties are not altered through the practice of a ritual, even an ethically motivated one. The emotional, psychological, and intellectual burden of belonging to a racialized and religious minority (racial profiling, the pervasive identification between Islam and "terror" by the non-Muslim) can never be reduced to a "knowable fact"[39] accessible to the majority population: epistemologies of suffering are always local and embodied.

Yet, in spite of this second interpretation, can one still hold that something of ethical and existential value is at stake in the performance? I will argue that what does happen in *Prayers to Allah* is the production of an *imaginative friction*. This friction occurs by embodying two incompatible identities. The friction occurs when a behavior is both behaved as "twice behaved" (as performance art in a gallery), and simultaneously "once" behaved, as a religious practice performed by one who is trained and authorized to do so; I am not a trained actor or a merited artist. The *only* credential of the performer that allows her a place at the exhibition is that she is an ordained priest. As an ordained priest, I affirm—personally and professionally—belief in a divine Other, and that this divine Other in my tradition is represented as the triune God. I am a member of the clergy doing what has been the job of clergy in the state church (until 2012) of the Lutheran church in Norway for an unbroken line of a thousand years: to evoke God on behalf of the majority population. The words and instructions of the Common Book of Prayers that the prayers are glued into is physically the same book I used every Sunday when working as a parish priest. And yet, the deity who is addressed in the prayers belongs to a different historical, liturgical, dogmatic, and architectural trajectory than the religious that has enabled and authorized me to occupy the professional position I am now exercising.

The participation of the co-prayers is equally multi-layered: on the one hand, the visitors have travelled to a location to see the national annual exhibition of modern art. They have paid to get in. They have looked at contemporary art produced by Norwegian artists or non-Norwegian artists living in Norway. On the other hand, they have been asked to write prayers and they have done so; a person who is and remains an ordained priest dressed in her liturgical garments has publicly prayed their prayers.

Prayers to Allah is thus not traditional liturgical prayer, but it is also not not-prayer. If I did not believe in a divine Other, Høstutstillingen would take no interest in an artist posing as a Lutheran priest. Yet, if I were not ethically and intellectually motivated to performatively create an imaginative friction, I would have remained a traditional parish priest. *Prayers to Allah* is neither religion posing as unmediated experience of transcendence, nor merely a human constructed practice of art.[40] In this double negation, the binary of religion as either "authentic" or "socially constructed" is broken. *Prayers to Allah* is religious behavior that resides outside the binary pair of "real" or "human made." It is a kind of prayer which is simultaneously "once" and "twice behaved" thus becoming a cascade of images, moving on from my own divinity to the precarity of presence and vulnerable wellbeing of the divinity (and thus also the body) of the religiously and cultural other.

The political stakes of breaking the binary are, as a religious leader—especially within a monotheistic religion—high. Engaging as a religious leader in simultaneously "once" and "twice" behaved behavior is *clerical self-iconoclasm*, because my "doing" of religion is broken by a breach of the rules—by myself. I am undone as clergy, because I pray to a different divinity than the God who has authorized the very professional role that authorizes me to the position that enabled me to address this non-Christian divinity. As a Lutheran authorized through ordination by the majority religion, I am undone by the act which preconditions the very act of becoming and remaining a religious leader authorized through ordination by the majority religion. Indeed, I should be—as Vedbjørn Selbekk, the Norwegian publisher of the Mohammed caricatures argued in the editorial in his newspaper *Dagen*—defrocked.[41] His anger is understandable: I performatively revealed to the public what the atheists have claimed to be the case with religion all along: prayer may not be an authentic relationship between the believer and divinity. The human made artefacts of prayer are not limited to candles, prayer books, pews, and rosaries. The artefacts of prayer also include the productions of images of self, my own divinities, and the divinities of the religious other. To a conservative like Selbekk, this is epistemological infidelity.

Yet, Selbekk's call for defrockment misses that clerical auto-iconoclasm and professional suicide are two very different things. The latter means to transgress professional codes of ethical conduct. The former means to undo the binary of the relation between the believer and the divinity as either real ("religion") or human made (atheism). Like an ecclesial version of Michael Duchamp's urinal on the art gallery pedestal, clerical auto-iconoclasm dethrones the role of clergy as a professional guarantor of religious truth of a given essentialized ontology ("Is God true?" Answer: "Yes," and "Which divinity is real, Islam or Christianity?" Answer: Either "Islam" or "Christianity"). Instead, negations on the *condition and ethical and political outcome of* religious mediators ("What kind of images do I have of my own divinity and the divinity of the other?") are placed at the core of clerical performance. Professional auto-iconoclasm is thus not clerical machoism but a performative, embodied and public articulation of the Latourian insight: in order to "welcome, to gather, to recollect truth and sanctity,"[42] believers need to fabricate images of self, their own god, others and the god of the others. The human made stitches of religion are thus made visible by engaging in a religious practice that is both "once"- and "twice"-behaved. It reveals and performs to the public the insight that the religious relationship to the divine is a human made product, which (along with endless other practices and images) constitutes the common world we share.

To interrupt Christian prayer (by addressing as a Christian Norwegian speaking my divinity as "Allah") the prayer (and the onlookers) de facto celebrate a *sacrament of epistemological reflection:* one is partaking *in and as* a religious practice the refusal to understand the relationship to divinity as unmediated. Celebrating the sacrament of epistemological reflection is to perform that prayer—like any other kind of liturgical endeavor—has a *civilizational dimension*, because, according to Latour, civilization is nothing but the extraordinary fragile process of creating images and objects.[43] We "do" (or perform) civilization when *we pray to prayer*, by performatively enacting a reflection on the responsibility our fabrication and construction of images of self and others and their gods installs on us. Using the vocabulary of German scholar Ulrich Schmiedel,[44] *Prayers to Allah* may thus be an example of a *performative political theology*.

ECCLESIOLOGICAL RECONFIGURATIONS IN THE WAKE OF ISLAMOPHOBIA

Liturgical prayer by clergy is a liturgical practice that derives from the official *ecclesia* of the cultural and religious majority Christian population of Europe. It is in this context that such practices have been formed and performed for centuries as "once behaved" practices. It is the cultural and historical weight of tradition that gives liturgical prayer performed by clergy a social credibility, also among citizens who do not participate in church activities on a weekly basis. Thus, the capacity for hermeneutical transformation (which I have called ethno-religious transubstantiation) is dependent on a status and position as traditional ecclesial practices: Without a reverent use, there is nothing to use irreverently.[45]

What happens when practices like *Prayers to Allah* are submitted to ecclesiological knowledge production? Doing this epistemologically honors its current status as "twice-behaved" behavior and does not reduce it to a prodigal liturgical practice which has been led astray by free-spirited clergy and long to be welcomed back home as "once"-behaved, "real" prayer by forgiving ecclesial mother–father authorities. Contrary to Selbekk's wish, the impurity and simultaneity of the practice needs to be preserved and treasured. Hence, to articulate such practices as *ecclesiology* means firstly to theorize on the friction between the official ecclesial institution and the displaced use of the practices of this institution. Secondly, it means to place that *friction at the very core of ecclesiological knowledge production*.[46]

Undertaking such an analysis means to recognize that these practices perform into being a space between, on the one hand, the official and authorized use of liturgical practices and, on the other hand, non-religious secularity. In this in-between space, figments of official and authorized liturgical practices are used, but the way they are used is wrong. *Prayers to Allah* cannot be recognized as an example of the *empirical church* because the governing bodies within the concrete church do not authorize it. Indeed, it generated calls for defrockment. In the four years that have passed, I have not once been asked to write or speak about it or the material that it created in official ecclesial contexts, or by agencies that work with inter-religious dialogue. Yet, *Prayers to Allah* cannot be categorized as *invisible church*. Asserting the reality of an invisible church hermeneutically asserts that any practice may potentially be a manifestation of the church because Creation belongs to God and only She knows the true church. In contrast, *Prayers to Allah* is accessible to ecclesiological research not as a hermeneutical perspective on general Creation, but is accessible to ecclesiological discernment by using the same criteria as the ecclesiologist uses for making the empirical church appear intelligible: *through* and *in* the use of the material and immaterial artefacts and practices of the organization and tradition called "church." In the particular case discussed in this essay, the material and immaterial artefacts at stake are the practice of prayer by a person ordained as priest using the vestments of clergy.

Hence, *Prayers to Allah* is neither the visible church nor invisible church. To make this in-between space ecclesiologically intelligible, the scholar needs to conceptually dismantle the bifurcate of ecclesiology in categories of "visible church" and "invisible church," and ask if, in fact, visibility/invisibility is a spurious question. It recognizes that the question of the invisible church/visible church makes visibility a hostage of what is ecclesially authorized. This renders practices that are empirical, yet ecclesially unauthorized (like *Prayers to Allah*), ecclesiologically unintelligible. Thus, the question becomes, if the ecclesiologist can imagine an alternative ontological basis for ecclesiology that rests on the creative and ethical use of the material and immaterial dimensions of the majority religious traditions, *independently of their compliance with or submission to governing ecclesial bodies*. This means to recognize as valid and relevant to the ecclesiological discourse any practice that is materially constituted by the artefacts of the religious majority traditions, but where these artefacts are used in a manner not authorized by ecclesial governmental bodies. *It is empirical, but not ecclesially authorized.* Articulating this as an ecclesiological model one may call this church as *ethical eccentricity*. Eccentricity is not the opposite of the normal.[47] Eccentricity is the non-authorized and non-compliant doing of the materiality and immaterial fabrics of normality. Church as *ethical eccentricity* is an ecclesiological imagination that describes *as church* the irreverent use of the culturally recognized ecclesial practices of the majority population as a means of responding to the marginalization of the vulnerable other. In this chapter, the context is the presence of growing Islamophobia. In other contexts, the threats of othering stem from different ideological discourses, like misogyny. In this case, an example of church as ethical eccentricity would the punk prayer of Pussy Riot, performed in the Cathedral of Our Saviour in Moscow in 2012. In the punk prayer, the liturgical music and space of authorized Orthodox Russian Church is used in an irreverent manner in order to address the misogyny and abuse of ecclesial power of Patriarch Kirill, head of the Russian Orthodox Church.

The ecclesiological reflections of Norwegian-American queer theologian Linn Marie Tonstad is of great importance to an idea of church as ethical eccentricity. Tonstad argues that the Ascension, not Pentecost, is the theological founding moment of the *ecclesia* and its fundamental epistemological device. Pentecost as a foundational ecclesiological text is susceptible to serve as a biblical legitimatizing for ontologizing ecclesial hierarchies as lines of authorization from Christ to ecclesial clerical sons (and, in recent years, ecclesial daughters) through dogmas like apostolic succession or practice like ordination of clergy. In contrast, Ascension suggests a state of divine presence-in-absence which opens for superseding invisibility/visibility as the ontological bases of ecclesiology. Ascension recognizes non-knowledge as primary ecclesiological *res*: church occurs outside the spaces, practices and persons who appear as intelligible as "church," yet it does not cease being empirical. Tonstad writes:

> Christ's body went away. It never belonged to the church in the first place. The church lost the body of Christ or never had it for itself, and the church exists in the anticipation of a redirection of its own action as its primary mode of being . . . It anticipates the arrival of a word that it cannot straight forwardly speak to itself . . . Instead of asserting that the body of the Christ has been handed over to the church, it recognizes that the body of Christ, elsewhere and outside itself, is its only hope.[48]

If this is the case, the relationship between the visible church and church as ethical eccentricity is not one of temporal succession. Rather, church as ethical eccentricity feeds on the empirical church. As noted earlier: without a reverent use, there is no irreverent use. Nor is the relationship concentric, as if the church as ethical eccentricity exists inside the larger and unknown formation of the invisible church. The relationship is one of imaginary expansion, as if the Common Book of Prayer is hemorrhaging, diluting, and scandalizing itself by not knowing where its border is. In church as ethical eccentricity, reverence, and irreverence thus feed on each other. The reverent, traditional use provides performative scrips, spaces, and artefactual material that are recognized and honored by the majority population and a sensitivity to the situation of the marginalized call for an irreverent use in order to address this marginality. However, irreverence and brokenness of ritual is not only the *other* of authorized ecclesial practices. Upon seeing the vandalized Pieta, Latour notes that iconoclasm and blasphemy in Christianity is never the *other* of pious truth, because by crucifying the crucifix, one is only deepening and materializing the scandal which God herself set in motion: To be fully God, and fully scandalized by Empire and dispossessed of hope. Incarnation is thus a theological device of centripetal force, where God is—to paraphrase Althaus-Reid—both the system and the alien.[49] One may argue that irreverence—the breaking and destruction of ecclesial practice—performatively embodies a movement for which the incarnation itself is its genesis. This simultaneity of reinforcement and subversion transforms question like "Who or where is God?" (and "Where is liturgy?" "Where is church?") into questions that can never be fully settled or claimed. In other words, these practices reconceptualize theological reflection as unsettled, open-ended, and always in need of revision in light of human experience.

Prayers to Allah may be said to be an example of church as ethical eccentricity if it succeeds in redirecting the theological motive of transubstantiation from being de-racialized and uncritical to renegotiating the majority imaginations of who the other and her gods are. In other words, through an eccentric use of the cultural and religious majority tradition, the cultural and political entitlement of that very same tradition is performatively questioned, as *clergy orchestrated auto-iconoclasm*. The protective shield of the privileged majority of Swiss and Norwegian cathedral bells is removed when the bells are vulnerable to a kind of use which summons the majority to attentiveness and spatial presence, not primarily to come to church to take part in ecclesial rituals, but to encounter and participate in the vulnerability of the cultural and religious other. This irreverent use calls into question the ontology of liturgical practices, and artefacts like church bells, as given and stable in order to open them to ontological negation. This ontology of vulnerability should, of course, never be mistaken for the politically caused ontological vulnerability of the cultural and religious other. Yet, submerging and submitting indigenous forms of Christianity from a position of cultural and religious privilege to a position of vulnerability means—if only for a moment—to de-essentialize the difference between the traditional and the other. This is a hermeneutical perspective open to seeing both cathedral bells and minarets as mediators in a contested, plural and changing religious practice. This perspective is the opposite of an Islamophobic imagining of the other as the eternal and totalized other.

NOTES

1. The Norwegian text goes: *"Friheten må gjestfri være."*
2. Thus, in ecclesial parlance, Olav Haraldson is titled "the holy." A grand vigil and service is celebrated every year in the cathedral of Nidaros, to commemorate the day of his death.

The cathedral is the seat of the leading bishop of the bishops' conference of the Church of Norway.

3. With the merger of state and church, civil and ecclesial rights and duties came to be seen as interchangeable. The establishment of the ecclesial practice of confirmation in 1736 prohibited entering into marriage, attending military service, and seeking employment without being confirmed in the Lutheran church (Hallgeir Elstad, *Illustrert Norsk kirkehistorie* (Oslo: Fagbokforlaget, 2002)). In the rather liberal constitution of the independent Norwegian state from 1814, Jews and Jesuits were barred from entering the kingdom of Norway. Only in 1851 were Jews allowed to settle. Since 1845 Norwegian citizens have been allowed to resign as members of the Church of Norway and establish certain recognized new churches (Ingvill Plesner "State and Religion in Norway," *European Journal of Church and State* 8 (2002): 317–327). In 1964 all citizens were granted freedom of religion. This implies that when Norway ratified the Declaration of Human Rights in 1951, Norway was the only European country which was not able to sign unconditionally. *Norges offentlig utredninger: Det livvsynsåpne—en helhetlig tros-og livssynspolitikk* (Oslo: 2013), 41. In 2017, 70.6 percent of the population of Norway were members of the Church of Norway, 57 percent of all fourteen-year-olds were confirmed in the Church of Norway, and as many as 88.2 percent of all funerals were officiated by clergy in the Church of Norway. Statistics Norway, https://www.ssb.no/kultur-og-fritid/statistikker/kirke_kostra/aar/2018-06-04?fane=tabell&sort=nummer&tabell=351319 (accessed July 30, 2018).

4. Sunniva Holberg, og Ånund Brottveit, *Tilstandsrapport for Den norske kirke* (Oslo: KIFO, 2014).

5. An example of a value-based society receiving public funding according to the same legislation as faith communities is the Society of Humanists, Human-etisk Forbund.

6. For a sociological review of the particular church–state relationship and its consequences for contemporary culture, see Grace Davie, *Religion in Modern Europe: A Memory Mutates* (Oxford: Oxford University Press, 2000). For the Scandinavian countries as case studies, see Trygve E. Wyller, Rosemarie Van Den Breemer, and Jose Casanova, eds., *Secular and Sacred? The Scandinavian Case of Religion in Human Rights, Law and Public Space* (Göningen: Vandenhoeck & Ruprecht, 2014).

7. See note 2.

8. See note 2.

9. The referendum was held on November 29, 2009.

10. For a discussion on the ideological basis of the terrorist attacks, see Sindre Bangstad and Øystein Sørensen, "Bare en gal manns verk?" in *Motgift: Akademisk respons på den nye høyreekstremismen*, eds. Wergeland Indregard and Wold Bendik (Oslo: Flamme forlag, 2012) and Sindre Bangstad, *Anders Breivik and the Rise of Islamophobia* (London: Zed books, 2014).

11. This chapter thus documents and discusses my own intention and reflection on the performance. This auto-ethnographic epistemological starting point is both a limit and a resource to this chapter. The chapter does not contain a discussion on the actual material produced. As the performance was not initially planned nor executed for research purposes, I have not obtained permission from the Norwegian Centre for Data Research to use the material created by the participants for research purposes. It would thus be unethical to do so. The performance has been described earlier in research literature in the article "The Social Production of Sacred Space in Urban Oslo" by Swedish researcher Daniel Enstedt (*Stellenboch Theological Journal* 1, no. 2 (2015), 15–41). The empirical basis for Enstad's article is the media attention the performance attracted, as Enstedt has not been in contact with me nor has he had access to the prayers produced by the performance.

12. The national annual exhibition of modern art is an artist-run event financed by the Norwegian state. Participation is open to all who reside in Norway and all Norwegians living abroad. The selection process is anonymous and artistic training or credentials is not required. The exhibition has a reputation for choosing controversial works, and the selected works are often debated in national media beyond circles of art critique. One of the controversies in the 2014 exhibition was the opening ceremony, where an invited professional man's choir performed the Soviet National anthem. This outraged the speaker of parliament who attended the opening as the representative of the government on behalf of the Conservative Party (Høyre). https://www.aftenposten.no/kultur/i/WL1ba/Stortingspresidenten-reagerte-sterkt-pa-apningen-av-Hostutstillingen (accessed June 18, 2018).

13. I am and remain an ordained priest in the Lutheran church of Norway. I worked six years as a parish priest in rural and Arctic parts of Norway and as a university chaplain before re-entering the academy in 2013 to do a fully funded PhD in the intersection between ecclesiology and social justice (*diakonia*) at VID specialized university, an ecclesial university college (and one of the three theological institutions in Norway which awards a Master of Divinity). The empirical starting point of my PhD is the non-conventional use of a concrete Lutheran sacred space in response to experiences of marginality like drug abuse and migrant labour. Before and after *Prayers to Allah* (2014) I have created ritual practices in the intersection between authorized liturgy and performance art, like *Homage à Pussy Riot* https://www.youtube.com/watch?v=Evx5oxPsJrw) and the upcoming theological performative response to the Me Too movement, *Herre du har skapt meg/livet mitt jeg gir deg/bruk meg/mee too (Lord you have created me/I give my life to you/use me/me too)*. Although some of the performances have attracted public outcry, I am committed to my tradition yet insisting that when it comes to both concrete ecclesial practices and ecclesiology, *the positive and the possible are not identical entities*. In advance of all the performances, ecclesial authorities have been informed, but they have not been asked to condone or authorize the practice. Altogether neither this chapter nor *Prayers to Allah* are part of my PhD; both are part of a cumulative process of developing ecclesiology via diverse platforms, from traditional liturgy, performance and academic writing. In light of this, *Prayers to Allah* should be seen as an empirical example of performative and academic explorations of how non-conventional use of my majority tradition and practices open for new experiences of potential social justice and ecclesiological/theological reflections.

14. Mattias Gardell, *Islamofobi* (Oslo: Spartacus, 2011), 12; translated into English by Bangstad in Sindre Bangstad, *Anders Breivik and the rise of Islamophobia*, 18. Islamophobia is a debated and contested term. For a discussion, see Bangstad, *Anders Breivik*, 18.

15. Gardell, *Islamofobi*, 15.

16. Indeed, in Brevik's vision for Norway, all Muslims will be deported so that "all traces of current and past Islamic influence in Europe will be removed." Anders Behring Breivik, *2083: A European Declaration of Independence*, 3.137, cited by Øystein Sørensen, "En gal manns verk?" 47.

17. https://gatesofvienna.net/ (accessed June 27, 2018). Brevik's main ideological inspiration, Norwegian Peder Nøstvold Jensen ("Fjordman"), has published a great number of articles on blog, and even posted on July 22, 2011; his texts can be found on the blog as "the Fjordman Archives."

18. Empirically speaking, the Lutheran church in Norway has over the past decades engaged in efforts to counter stereotypes of the cultural and religious other in practices like inter religious dialogue. For a description and reflection on these practices, see Anne Hege Grung and Lena Larsen, *Dialog med og uten slør* (Oslo: Pax forlag 2000), Oddbjørn Leirvik, *Religionsdialog på norsk* (Oslo: Universitetsforlaget 2001), and Beate Fagerli, Anne Hege Grung, Sven Thore Kloster, and Line Onsrud, eds., *Dialogteologi på norsk* (Oslo:

Verbum Akademisk 2011). Back in 2009, I was no newcomer to such practices: I had taken part in such practices as a theological student and I had initiated such practices as a university chaplain. However, when it comes to religious performance and liturgy, the tone is different. In the document *The Meeting of Religions in Liturgical Practices—A Guide from The Bishops' Conference* (2016), the bishops of the church of Norway warn against co-prayer between Christians of other faiths as "deeply problematic" because this kind of prayer violates the first commandment (13)."Cultic" actions of other religions, like the recitation of the Qur'an may not take place in a Christian service (18) and ritual practice from a non-Christian religion cannot take place in a Christian church (18). The most striking feature of the document is that it discursively locates inter-religious work within a discourse of syncretism, and not within a context of asymmetrical power balance between the minority and the majority population. The document is thus blind to the privileged position it originates from and thus perpetuates. *Religionsmøtet ved Kirkelig handlinger—en veiledning fra bispemøtet* accessible at https://kirken.no/globalassets/kirken.no/aktuelt/filer-2016/bispemoetet_februar_2016_religionsmoetet_kirkelige_handlinger.pdf (accessed July 30, 2016).

19. Gardell, Mattias *Islamofobi*, 12.
20. However, Norwegian Muslims were involved in the preparations. In advance, the performance was discussed via email with a number of Muslims intellectuals of both genders and one male imam. This was of extreme importance, given that the violence and deaths in Europe and the Middle East in the aftermath of the publications of the Mohammed caricatures in Denmark in 2005, and 2006 in Norway, by the Christian conservative newspaper *Magazinet* under the auspices of the then editor Vedbjørn Selbekk. In addition, scholars of inter-religious dialogue and comparative religion were consulted. I informed the Norwegian Islamic Council and Lutheran bishop of Oslo in writing about the performance in advance so that both would be prepared for media attention. The performance attracted no negative reaction from Muslims and negative reactions (emails and SMS messaging with condemnations of various sorts, threats of demonstrations, etc.) all originated from conservative Christians. The demonstrations never materialized, but the organizers still chose to hire security officers during the first Sunday.
21. Judith Butler, *Precarious Life: The Power of Mourning and Violence* (London: Verso, 2004), 26.
22. Judith Butler, *Frames of War: When Is Life Grievable?* (London, Verso, 2010).
23. The use of Latour in this chapter does not do justice to the multiple and innovative writings of Latour on religion. For an overview on Latour's engagement with religion, see Andreas Melson Gregersen and Søren Riis, "The Living-dead and the Existence of God," *Danish Yearbook of Philosophy* 47, 2012.
24. Latour understands mediations as "inscriptions, objects, icons, idols, images, picture and sign"; Bruno Latour, *On the Modern Cult on the Factish Gods* (Raleigh, NC: Duke University Press, 2010), 79.
25. Latour, *On the Modern Cult*, 81.
26. Latour has an inclusive way of understanding religious images. It refers not only to religious visual effects, but to "any sign, work of art, inscription or picture that acts as a mediation to access something else" (*On the Modern Cult*, 69). Elsewhere in the same text, he describes mediations as "inscriptions, objects, icons, idols, images, picture and sign" (79).
27. "If you start to break the idols . . . with what mediations will you welcome, collect, access, assemble and gather your divinities?" (*On the Modern Cult*, 81).
28. Ibid., 91.
29. Latour, *Rejoicing—or the Torments of Religious Speech* (Cambridge: Polity Press), 163.
30. Latour, *On the Modern Cult*, 2.

31. Ibid., 97.
32. Marvin Carlson, *What Is Performance Art? A Critical Introduction* (London: Routledge, 2004), 1.
33. Richard Schechner, *Performed Imaginations* (London: Routledge, 2015), 160.
34. Of course, clergy members might privately and or professionally adhere to a theological understanding of salvation as inclusive to all religions. However, even though one may cognitively believe that belief in other gods leads to salvation, and such views may be voiced in the sermon, this is usually not reflected in the authorized liturgical practices of mainline churches.
35. Giorgio Agamben, *Homo sacre—den suverne makten og det nakne livet* (Rakkestad: Valdisholm forlag, 2010).
36. This argument does, of course, not mean that monotheism, either as a dogma or as liturgical practice is inherently Islamophobic. Rather, what it means is that in the contextual situation of a historic Christian, and increasingly xenophobic, majority position, a conventional and unruptured usage of prayer in the Sunday service will easily reproduce a religious discourse where the Christian God is the only and true God, a cultural-religious claim sustained by (and sustaining) the cultural, ethnic, and historical position of the Lutheran denomination as state church with a legacy of half a Millennium. In other word: the cultural and political context of islamophobia makes religious monotheism—and its liturgical counterparts—politically ambivalent.
37. In fact, the one prayer among the estimated seven hundred prayers written which was written in Arabic, was barred from being publicly performed, because I am not Arabic speaking.
38. A different, yet related, example is the funeral of one of the victims of the July 22 massacre, Bano Rashid, who was eighteen years at the time of her murder. During the funeral service, the local female Lutheran priest, Anne Marit Tronvik, and the male imam Senaid Kobilica, both officiated as clergy in traditional liturgical attire. The press photo of Tronvik and Kobilica walking side by side in the funeral procession became in the Norwegian media an iconic performative resistance to the political motivation of the massacre. Breivik killed in the name of an ideology, which sees Islam and Christianity as eternal and essential opposites. Through the cooperation between Tronvik and Kobilica, the funeral of the Rashid became a performance of the ontological bankruptcy of his claim and thus an occasion of not only mourning but also healing (Jon Michelet, "Om Bano, presten og imamen: Og om Ali på Utøya og en fakkel fra Larkollen," in *Respons 22 Juli*, ed. Gunnstein Bakke (Oslo: Oktober 2011), 99). The photo is accessible at https://www.vg.no/nyheter/innenriks/i/02xAG/imam-om-koranlesing-i-kirken-helt-uproblematisk (accessed July 30, 2018).
39. Alison Kafer *Feminist, Queer, Crip* (Bloomington, IN: Indiana University Press, 2013), 4.
40. Of course, this point has been made long ago by feminist theologians when they spoke to the politics of the gendered nature of liturgical language and how a liturgically gendered asymmetry perpetuates a patriarchal ontological asymmetry between human woman and asymmetry perpetuates an asymmetry between human woman and men (Rutherford Ruther, *Sexism and God Talk* (Boston: Beacon Press, 1993)). Hence, insisting on the human involvement (and ethical responsibility) when engaging in god-talk is not a new claim. Latour and Butler add to the feminist discourse on religious language a theorization of the ontological stakes not only of verbal language but of materiality and performativity.
41. Newspaper Dagen, editorial, http://www.dagen.no/Meninger/20/09/2014/Performance-presten-116099 (accessed June 19, 2018).
42. Latour *On the Modern Cult*.

43. Ibid., 97.
44. Schmiedel Ulrich, "Mourning the Un-Mournable: Political Theology between Refugees and Religion," *Journal of Political Theology*, 18, 2017. https://doi.org/10.1080/1462317X.2017.1291399.
45. Postcolonial and queer theologian Marcella-Althaus Reid articulates this agonistic tension when she writes: "Queer theologians do not disregard church traditions. However, the process of queering may turn them upside down, or submit them to collage style processes of adding and highlighting from them precisely those elements which did not fit well in the constructions of the church tradition and thus where excluded or ignored" (Marcella Althaus Reid, *The Queer God* (London: Routledge, 2003), 8).
46. After the performance was over, I applied for and received a $17,000 grant from the Foundation of Free Speech (Fritt ord) and The Norwegian Non-Fiction Writers and Translators Association to produce a manuscript where I reflect theologically and existentially on the performance. The manuscript is written, but five publishing houses in Norway have turned down the text. For the secular publishing houses, the performance is too religious to be of interest. For the two major Christian publishing houses, a publication of the prayers was perceived to be either too risky economically or, as the then editor of Verbum phrased it in an email December 20, 2015, "too demanding and narrow to be prioritized."
47. The eccentric person is the person who behaves in a way that is strange or unsettling through a displaced used of social conventions like gender roles or economic resources. Eccentricity is not a manner of mental illness, but rather a choice not to live within the social confinements of one's social context.
48. Linn Marie Tonstad, *God and Difference* (London: Routledge, 2016), 272–223.
49. Althaus-Reid, *The Queer God*, 30.

SELECT BIBLIOGRAPHY

Agamben, Giorgio (2010), *Homo sacre—den suverne makten og det nakne livet*, Rakkestad: Valdisholm forlag.
Althaus Reid, Marcella (2003), *The Queer God*, London: Routledge.
Bangstad, Sindre (2014), *Anders Breivik and the Rise of Islamophobia*, London: Zed Books.
Bangstad, Sindre and Øystein Sørensen (2012), "Bare en gal manns verk?" in *Motgift: Akademisk respons på den nye høyreekstremismen*, eds. Wergeland Indregard and Wold Bendik, Oslo: Flamme forlag.
Butler, Judith (2004), *Precarious Life: The Power of Mourning and Violence*, London: Verso.
Butler, Judith (2010), *Frames of War: When Is Life Grievable?* London: Verso.
Carlson, Marvin (2004), *What Is Performance Art? A Critical Introduction*, London: Routledge.
Davies, Grace (2000), *Is Europe and Exceptional Case and Religion in Modern Europe: A Memory Mutates*, Oxford: Oxford University Press.
Elstad, Hallgeir (2002), *Illustrert norsk kristendomshistorie*, Bergen: Fagbokforlaget.
Enstedt, Daniel (2015), "The Social Production of Sacred Space in Urban Oslo," *Stellenboch Theological Journal* 1, no. 2, 15–41.
Fagerli, Beate, Anne Hege Grung, Svenn Thore Kloster and Lene Onsrud, eds. (2011), *Dialogteologi på norsk*, Oslo: Verbum Akademisk.
Gardell, Mattias (2011), *Islamofobi*, Oslo: Spatacus forlag.
Gregersen Andreas Melson and Søren Riis (2012), "The Living-dead and the Existence of God," *Danish Yearbook of Philosophy* 47.

Grung, Anne Hege and Lena Larsen (2000), *Dialog med og uten slør*, Oslo: Pax forlag.
Holberg, Sunniva og Ånund Brotttveit (2014), *Tilstandsrapport for Den norske kirke*, Oslo: KIFO.
Kafer, Alison (2013), *Feminist, Queer, Crip*, Bloomington, IN: Indiana University Press.
Latour, Bruno (2010), *On the Modern Cult on the Factish Gods*, Raleigh, NC: Duke University Press.
Latour, Bruno (2013), *Rejoicing—or the Torments of Religious Speech*, Cambridge: Polity Press.
Leirvik, Oddbjørn (2001), *Religionsdialog på norsk*, Oslo: Universitetsforlage.
Michelet, Jon (2011), "Om Bano, presten og imamen: Og om Ali på Utøya og en fakkel fra Larkollen," in *Respons 22 Juli*, ed. Bakke, Oslo: Oktober.
Norges offentlig utredninger (2013), *Det livvsynsåpne—en helhetlig tros-og livssynspolitikk*, Oslo: Den norske regjering.
Plesner, Ingvil (2002), "State and Religion in Norway," *European Journal of Church and State* 8: 31–327.
Rutherford Ruther, Rosemary (1993), *God Talk and Sexism*, Boston: Beacon Press.
Schechner, Richard (2015), *Performed Imaginations*, London: Routledge.
Schmiedel, Ulrich (2017), "Mourning the Un-Mourable: Political Theology between Refugees and Religion," *Journal of political theology* 18, https://doi.org/10.1080/146231 7X.2017.1291399
Tonstad, Linn Marie Tonstad (2016), *God and Difference*, London: Routledge.
Wyller, Trygve, Rosmaerie Van Den Brecmer, and Jose Casanova, eds. (2014), *Secular and Sacred? The Scandinavian Case of Religion in Human Rights, Law and Public Space*, Göningen: Vandenhoeck & Ruprecht.

INTERNET SOURCES

http://www.dagen.no/Meninger/20/09/2014/Performance-presten-116099 (accessed June 19, 2018).
https://www.vg.no/nyheter/innenriks/i/02xAG/imam-om-koranlesing-i-kirken-helt-uproblematisk (accessed July 30, 2018).
https://www.aftenposten.no/kultur/i/WL1ba/Stortingspresidenten-reagerte-sterkt-pa-apningen-av-Hostutstillingen (accessed June 18, 2018).
https://www.ssb.no/kultur-og-fritid/statistikker/kirke_kostra/aar/2018-06-04?fane=tabell&sort=nummer&tabell=351319 (accessed July 30, 2018).
https://www.youtube.com/watch?v=Evx5oxPsJrw
https://www.youtube.com/watch?v=Evx5oxPsJrw (August 29, 2018).
https://gatesofvienna.net/ (accessed June 27, 2018).
https://kirken.no/globalassets/kirken.no/aktuelt/filer-2016/bispemoetet_februar_2016_religionsmoetet_kirkelige_handlinger.pdf (accessed July 30, 2016).

CHAPTER THIRTY-THREE

Social Trinitarianism through Iconic Participation

JESSICA WAI-FONG WONG

INTRODUCTION

We are a divided people. Whether along the lines of race, religion, class, politics, education, economics, or sexuality—the modern Western body politic is becoming increasingly fractured. Broken up into smaller, more homogeneous pockets of people, this growing segregation seems to coincide with a newfound interest in social trinitarianism among Western Christian theology in the late twentieth century. From Jürgen Moltmann and Miroslav Volf to Catherine Mowry LaCugna, a number of prominent scholars have taken up the heretofore largely Eastern tradition of reading the Trinity through a social lens. Tenets of social trinitarianism are certainly not new. The basis for these claims about the Trinity can be traced back to the Cappadocian Fathers, who argue for an understanding of the immanent Trinity through the framework of relationship. The import being that God's ontological reality is essentially relational; God is constituted by relationship, which is to say, through communion.[1]

With the West's more recent foray into social trinitarianism a number of prescriptive social claims emerged. The sheer diversity of these claims, however, suggest a potential problem, namely, that of human projection.[2] Theological projects that begin with the immanent Trinity are particularly at risk of reflecting the author's pre-established convictions rather than any fundamental theological truth.[3] Such interpretations and anthropological findings risk being skewed by differing human desires, preferences, and predispositions.

At the heart of the matter is ontology. God is God and humans are not. What is true about God is not necessarily true about human beings.[4] Taking up this issue, Kathryn Tanner argues that, given the ontological distinction between God and humanity, there are two ways that humans are able to participate in the reality of the Trinity. The first is through the weak participation of analogy. The second is through strong participation by means of the person of Jesus Christ. It is within this latter approach that Karl Rahner's basic axiom proves fundamental: "The 'economic' Trinity is the 'immanent' Trinity and the 'immanent' Trinity is the 'economic' Trinity."[5] This essential claim acknowledges the real connection that exists between the reality of God in and of God's self and the reality of God in the world. Moreover, when considered within the larger scope of Christian theology, it suggests that the tie between the immanent and economic Trinity is most profoundly realized in the person of Jesus. Instead of beginning with the immanent Trinity and extrapolating an understanding of what human sociality should look like from there, it is sounder to begin with Jesus, who is not only fully God, but also fully human.[6]

As the Son, Jesus participates in the reality of the immanent Trinity. And, as a human, he models what this trinitarian reality is to look like within the context of humanity.[7] With kindness, love, and compassion that disregards established social barriers, Jesus engages others in authentic community. Moreover, by drawing those who follow him into his body through the power of the Spirit, otherwise diverse peoples are unified. Existing in Christ and manifesting distinct gifts endowed by the Spirit for the good of the body, Christians live out a form of the divine diversity of the triune God.[8] Just as the Son relates to the Father and the Spirit as he lives out a life of joyful service toward others, so, through participating in the divine reality of God in Christ, humans are transformed to do the same.[9] Instead of modeling human relationships upon an analysis of the ontologically transcendent and, therefore, ultimately ungraspable immanent Trinity, human sociality should be grounded in the person of Jesus.

However, even when beginning with Jesus, there are various lenses through which He can be viewed, each interpretation leading to a slightly different picture of ideal human social engagement. This chapter considers the way in which viewing Jesus through the lens of icon theology provides a unique understanding of the relationality to which humanity is called. An iconic reading of Jesus reveals not only how the social nature of the immanent Trinity is found in Him and how it functions to transform human beings, enabling those limited by the boundaries of creaturely existence to embody the ontologically foreign social character of God's triune reality, but it provides a particular sense of ideal human sociality.

Jesus, the Holy Icon of God

At the most basic level to describe Jesus as a natural icon points to the material manifestation of the divine, most fully realized in the incarnation. In fact, John of Damascus, who advocates for the artificial icon's use during the iconoclastic controversy of the eighth century, identifies the incarnation of Jesus as proof of the fundamental legitimacy of icon veneration. While his iconoclastic contemporaries argue that the use of icons is illegitimate insofar as it attempts to circumscribe God, who is, by nature, beyond circumscription, Damascene insists that representation is not circumscription. In fact, God paves the way for this kind of representation in the person of Jesus.[10] Like an icon, Jesus is the material representation of the divine. He is divinity communicated in the stuff of flesh and blood, bone and sinew. The existence of Jesus as the Son incarnate is not the containment of God, but the revelation of the divine within the material world in a manner that does not preclude God's continued existence beyond it. Damascene insists that the same is true of the holy icon. The communication of God's presence through the icon does not limit God to the space of the wooden plank upon which the artificial icon is written. God might communicate God's self through this material medium, but is not limited by it.

Beyond the important role that the incarnation plays in Damascene's argument, scriptural accounts of Jesus's life further support an iconic reading. Orthodox understandings of the artificial icon recognize that an encounter with the icon is not just an encounter with the material form, but a threshold to the divine. Icons never point to themselves. They always point beyond themselves to another, to the prototype that they represent. The same can be said of the person of Jesus. Like the artificial icon, he images a prototype. However, in the case of the incarnation, Jesus does not represent himself as the second person of the Trinity so much as he represents the Father. The Apostle Paul recognizes that, in the incarnation, the Son kenotically empties himself.[11] He releases all claims to his own glory and, instead, opens himself up as a vessel to communicate the reality of God the Father. At a fundamental level, Jesus reveals the image not simply of himself, but of the Father. "Anyone who has seen me has seen the Father," Jesus tells his disciples, "I am in the Father and the Father is in me."[12] Echoes of this position emerge in letters to the Colossians and the Hebrews. "The Son is the image (*eikon*) of the invisible God," the author of Colossians writes. He "is the radiance of God's glory and the exact representation of His nature."[13] Jesus is the natural icon of God the Father and, therefore, reveals the Father to those who turn toward him. He is the divine threshold; He is the way to the Father.[14]

The iconic referentiality that exists between the Father and Jesus is present in the latter's response to Philip's request that he show them the Father.[15] "Have I been with you all this time, Philip, and you still do not know me?" Jesus asks. "Whoever has seen me has seen the Father. How can you say, 'Show us the Father'? Do you not believe that I am in the Father and the Father is in me? The words that I say to you I do not speak on my own; but the Father who dwells in me does his works."[16] In short, God the Father, who is absolutely other than creation, is known through Jesus, God incarnate. To encounter the Son is to encounter the Father. To know the Son is to know the Father. This intimate connection indicates not only the perichoretic relationality of the immanent Trinity (as the Father is in the Son, the Son is in the Spirit, and so forth), but also Jesus' role as the natural icon of the Father. Jesus reflects the Father. His will is not his own, but that of the Father. His words are not his own, but the words of the Father. His works are not his own, instead, he is about the Father's business. In each of these ways, Jesus acts as an iconic reflection of the Father, communicating the unseen God to those with ears to hear and eyes to see.

THE DIVINE ECONOMY OF THE TRIUNE GOD

What connects Jesus with the Father is not a shared personhood, as though the Father and Son are one *hypostasis*. Instead, what links the two is the sharing of and participation in the same divine ordering. Jesus' ability to represent the Father iconically is rooted in their common economy, which constitutes both the divine nature and the divine manner of existence. At the heart of this economy is the sociality of the Trinity, which is often explained within social trinitarianism as a natural byproduct of God's triune identity as three *hypostases* in one *ousia*. While the three persons of the Trinity are not the same, they are nonetheless in, within, and for one another as they participate in the divine dance.[17] While never collapsing other into self (e.g., the Son is not the Father, the Father is not the Spirit), each *hypostasis* of the Trinity is intimately present in the movement of the others. This intertwining interpenetration not only characterizes their unity and colors their relationality, but also determines their identity. Far from being constituted in purely individual terms, each *hypostasis* is given meaning through loving relationship (e.g., the Father is only Father in relation to the Son, a relationship bound together through the love of the Spirit). And, yet, no *hypostasis* is subsumed or collapsed. One and yet three, this diversity in unity is central to the social character and essential identity of God.

More than the essential truth of who God is in and of God's self, this divine ordering determines how God engages creation, a creation that is absolutely other than its Creator.

God chooses to enter into relationship with creation, while, at the same time, respecting the integrity of its distinctiveness. Thus, the very ordering that is essential to the fundamental character of the triune God also colors God's salvific work in the world. Who God is and what God does are always consistent. This shared ordering is most clearly manifest in the person of Jesus Christ. Insofar as Jesus is the Son, who images the Father, and is central to the divine work of salvation, he necessarily exhibits God's holy order. Through him, God's character is most clearly displayed.

Jesus reveals the divine order both in his teachings and his life. Directing his followers toward a form of sociality and socially constituted identity that coincides with that of the Trinity, he calls his disciples to a radical love in shared community and a deep compassion for the other, even for one's enemy. In this way, he encourages a manner of being in relationship that coincides with God's character.[18] Acknowledging those who have otherwise been rendered invisible and relegated to the margins of society, Jesus engages the socially, economically, and ethnically disenfranchised. Instead of living according to the societal expectations that produce division, he moves toward others in a way that fosters reconciliation and, in doing so, points toward the possibility of an alternative social existence. Paul advocates for this same form of relational ordering when he encourages the Philippians to "be of the same mind, having the same love, being in full accord and of one mind . . . . Let each of you look not to your own interests, but to the interests of others. Let the same mind be in you that was in Christ Jesus."[19] A selfless love that fosters unity among otherwise disparate peoples, even between Jews and Gentiles, Paul calls all Christians to live out a human iteration of the perichoretic unity essential to God's self. By loving one another, the disciples are set apart as followers of Christ, for they embody the alternative social reality that Jesus not only teaches, but enacts in his own life.[20]

The divine relationality that organizes and constitutes the immanent Trinity, however, is not simply a part of Jesus' character. This holy order comprises his very existence, that is, the space of his physical body into which he calls his disciples. Jesus embodies the divine economy both figuratively and literally. He carries the divine order with him insofar as it determines the nature of his flesh. It is here, around the idea of Jesus' embodiment of the divine economy, that the iconic lens offers a particularly powerful means of understanding the social implications of participating in the body of Christ.

An icon's most powerful aspect is not the image itself, but the ordering economy that the image communicates. An icon has the capability to speak to the devotee, conveying its internal state to him.[21] This iconic address engages the faithful on an emotional level.[22] Through the visceral pull of God's holy order, it draws the devotee into communion with the divine, equipping him with the ability to see through the lens of God's alternative sociality.[23] This reorientation shifts how he comes to understand the world. What a person worships determines what he recognizes as meaningful or valuable.[24] It determines what he judges to be good, true, and beautiful. It influences what he accepts and what he rejects.[25] Thus, participating in God's alternative order has the power to alter a person at a fundamental level. And the more deeply he enters into this sensibility, the more significant the transformation.

A number of Christian hagiographies provide rich examples of the transformative power of the divine economy insofar as they relate accounts of not only the way in which the faithful exist outside of the normal rhythms of the world, but also the physical changes that can attend spiritual reordering. From stigmata and divine radiance to no longer needing the basic sustenance of food and the closing off of orifices, the saint's profound participation in the divine economy of God is at times born out in the body.[26] In such cases, the saint's flesh reveals the truth of her existence within another realm, one governed by an entirely different logic from that of the world. Beyond her own transformation, the saint communicates this very sacred reality to those around her. Her very presence, while alive, and her relics, after death, convey the holy order that has come to define her.[27] She becomes a living icon, both revealing this order in her own life and drawing others into it.[28]

As the natural icon of God, Jesus actualizes the same form of contagious transformation. He, too, acts as a threshold to the divine, turning his followers back toward God. He draws the disciples into the divine economy that constitutes and defines him. Through the sacrament of baptism, he draws his disciples into the divine economy of his body. Through the power of the Spirit, they are brought into right relationship with the Father. Likewise, Eucharistic practices entail sharing in the body of Christ perichoretically, in a way that, given the nature of human ontology, would otherwise be impossible. Through their consumption of the body and blood of Christ, Jesus comes to dwell within the disciples just as they reside within him. This mutual indwelling not only parallels the relationship between Jesus and the Father, but actually draws the disciples into the divine relational dynamic that characterizes God's holy order. "I am in my Father, and you in me, and I in you," Jesus tells his disciples, for all participate in God's alternative ordering.[29] In this way, they enter into communion with not only the Son, but, through the Son, with the Father and the Spirit.[30] And in right relationship with God, they are reconciled with other creatures, both human and non-human.[31]

SIGHT: FALLEN AND REDEEMED

The restoration enacted by Jesus takes place, in no small part, through a redirection of the venerating gaze. Using the language of sight and image, Athanasius of Alexandria describes the restoration that Christ enables. Though created with his eyes fixed upon God as the *telos* of his love and worship, the Fall shifts the human's contemplation elsewhere. *Incurvatus in se*—an inward turning occurs. Shifting his eyes downward, toward himself and the things of this world, the human creature no longer properly contemplates God in worship. Consequently, Athanasius writes that the human falls "into lust of [himself], preferring what was [his] own to the contemplation of what belonged to God."[32] No longer recognizing God rightly, as the absolute other and, therefore, as the one in relation to whom meaning and value are established, the human becomes his own center, the *telos* of his own devotion and love.

In his lectures on the first three chapters of Genesis, Dietrich Bonhoeffer identifies the human's turn away from God and toward self, as a way of repositioning himself at the center, reinterpreting God as a reflection of himself and, in turn, the creaturely other as a hated reminder of the limitations that he desires to overcome on his journey toward god-likeness. The human projects his image upon God and, in this way, begins to identify himself with God. Slowly, he comes to imagine his characteristics, culture, and concepts as divine. Insofar as the human creature becomes the center of his own devotion and, in turn, like God through his own efforts, he also begins to desire God's limitlessness. His newly expected divinity means that he should no longer be restricted by the boundaries that naturally attend human interaction.[33] The distortion that takes root in how he sees God warps all of his relationships. Division and isolation corrupt what was previously marked by divine diversity unified in love. Creator and creature, man and woman, human and non-human—the perversion of the venerating gaze produces a deterioration of each relationship, changing it from one of identity constituted through otherness to one of identity constituted over-against the other.[34] Existing within a corrupt economy, characterized by broken relationships and self-constitution, the image of God within the human creature degenerates.

For Athanasius, the turning of humanity's vision away from God prevents the human being from being able to restore the image of God on her own. Her eyes are no longer focused upon the original, the one after whom God's image is modeled. Only Jesus, who is the holy icon of God, can reorient humanity's contemplative gaze and, thereby, restore the *imago dei*.[35] In much the same way that an artificial icon redirects the gaze of a devotee toward its holy prototype, the act of focusing upon Jesus in devotion ushers her into God's holy order and, thereby, turns her contemplation away from herself and toward the Father. The redirection of her venerating gaze through Jesus changes how she comes to see herself, her fellow humans, and the rest of creation. Participating in the divine economy that is the body of Christ, the disciple is brought back into a unified relational existence, which is marked by the oneness of spirit that characterizes the divine economy constituting God's very self. Praying to the Father, Jesus articulates the oneness this defines this divine relationality.

> I pray . . . that all of them may be one, Father, just as you are in me and I am in you. May they also be in us so that the world may believe that you have sent me. I have given them the glory that you gave me, that they may be one as we are one—I in them and you in me—so that they may be brought to complete unity.[36]

Drawing those around him into his body and, therefore, into the salvific economy of God, those who follow Christ are redeemed as they are made into his image.

And, like Jesus, his followers come to communicate God's holy order within their own teaching and lives. They, too, invite others into the same economy.[37] Through the act of iconically engaging Jesus or, alternatively, iconically engaging those who have been transformed through their encounter with Jesus, the Christian embarks upon the journey of reflecting Christ, of becoming His living icon. Christian discipleship is fundamentally iconic. Paul describes the icon-like, mimetic nature of discipleship when he directs the Christian community in Corinth to imitate him as he imitates Christ: "Be imitators of me, as I am of Christ."[38] Insofar as Paul conforms to the image of Christ, imitation of the Apostle produces the same results as imitating Jesus directly. Whether emulating Paul or Jesus, the iconicity of discipleship results in *imitatio Christi*. Those who are living icons, that is, those who clearly reflect their prototype, Jesus Christ, communicate the divine economy that defines Jesus in such a way that they, too, produce living icons. They, too, make disciples. Manifesting the divine economy of God, which is the fundamental character of Jesus, the saints draw others into God's alternative order. And, as one might expect, this cycle of iconic reproduction continues, producing more and more disciples who iconically bear the image of Christ, embody His economy, and invite those around them to do the same.

THE MYSTERY OF OTHERNESS

This iconically mimetic expansion of God's holy reality, what one might call the Kingdom of God on earth, champions a particular sociality. While, as previously recognized, this economy is marked by diversity bound together in unity, Jesus's act of iconically drawing people into right relationship with the Father, who remains mysterious even in His revelation, communicates something unique about the social reality into which God invites humanity. While the Father is known through Jesus, this knowledge is not totalizing.[39] There is an aspect of God that remains mysterious and hidden from view. Even in self-disclosure through the Son, there is a simultaneous veiling that corresponds with the unfathomable nature of God.[40] As wholly other than creation, the God made known through Jesus is beyond humanity's full grasp. The Father remains unseen even as he is seen in Jesus. He remains unknown even as he is being made known. Such is the nature of the relationship between the creature and his Creator. God's self-disclosure is always accompanied by hiddenness. Looking iconically to Jesus, entering into his body, and participating in the divine economy, humanity is able to know God and, yet, being human, this knowledge is always partial. In this way, God as the quintessential other to creation reveals the fundamentally ungraspable nature at the heart of all otherness.

Jesus's iconicity opens up the possibility of a redeemed venerative gaze and, with it, a healed and healing way of seeing others. According to God's alternative order, the other is beyond direct or complete knowledge. Rightly recognizing God as God through the iconic mediation of Christ, the human creature accepts the natural limitations of her humanity. Whether divine, human, or non-human, the other can never be fully known, fully grasped, or fully contained. The social order offered through Jesus acknowledges the persistent mystery of otherness as a gift to be celebrated instead of an obstacle to be overcome. This relational dynamic stands in stark contrast with the totalizing knowledge central to both unconscious biases and stereotypes, which undergird much of modernity's sociopolitical division. Jesus offers a way of knowing others that is always mediated.[41] It is a knowledge that does not require mastery. Instead, recognizing the mystery of the other serves as its own kind of knowledge.[42] It is the knowledge that arises at the point where the limitations of human existence meet the mystery of self-disclosure. Thus, Jesus invites humanity into a way of seeing and being in the world that subverts the problematic relationality at the heart of a divided body politic, that is, the way of understanding and relating to others that is built upon objectifying assumptions.

In sharp contrast with the proliferating divisions that characterize the modern World, God invites humanity into an alternative relationality. More than modeling the immanent Trinity's transcendent social existence for humanity to emulate, the iconic flesh of Jesus Christ invites humanity into the alternative reality grounded in God's self. Just as an artificial icon draws spectators into the divine economy, people are brought into God's holy order through Jesus, and, in him, are reoriented, reordered, and transformed. They are made into living icons, people who embody the alternative social economy of God and, thereby, reflect Jesus, who is their iconic prototype. This relational ordering toward God is the intended posture for all Christian disciples and, as such, it is the intended sociality of the body of Christ, the Church. For, by moving further into this relational reality, the Christian presses even deeper into Jesus and, thereby, into the reality of the triune God. More than simply living out God's alternative social economy through the weak participation of analogy, an iconic reading of Jesus suggests that his followers are fully subsumed within God's holy order, so much so, that their very sense of self and, in turn, how they act in the world are determined by the rhythm of its reality. Jesus's body becomes the fundamental truth of their lives, defining every aspect of who they are and, in turn, what they do. Discipleship entails iconic embodiment. Entry into the divine economy of God is not a distant imitation of the immanent Trinity, it is full participation in God's holy order, an order that transforms everything that it touches.

In this way, the Kingdom of God spreads iconically, shifting the fundamental paradigm of how one sees and engages in the world, thereby rendering what was once profane into something holy.

NOTES

1. For an insightful overview of Cappadocian trinitarianism, see John Zizioulas, "The Doctrine of the Holy Trinity: The Significance of the Cappadocian Contribution," in *Trinitarian Theology Today: Essays on Divine Being and Act*, ed. Christoph Schwöbel (Edinburgh: T&T Clark, 1995).
2. Kathryn Tanner, *Christ the Key*, Current Issues in Theology (Cambridge: Cambridge University Press, 2010), 222.
3. Ibid., 223.
4. Ibid., 220–21. Belief in the possibility that humans can actualize the relationality of the immanent Trinity is, at least in part, rooted in the terminology applied to the Triune God. Translating *hypostasis* as "person" leads to a sense that God is the same as three human people in relationship. This primary assumption is part of what makes possible a secondary assumption, namely, that humans are able to replicate the relational reality of God.
5. Karl Rahner, *The Trinity*, trans. J. Donceel (Bloomsbury Publishing, 2001), 22. Rahner originally italicized this sentence.
6. See Moltmann, *Trinity and the Kingdom* and LaCugna, *God For Us*.
7. Tanner, *Christ the Key*, 236–237.
8. Ibid., 238.
9. Ibid., 240–241.
10. John of Damascus argues that humans are able to honor matter because it is through the material reality of the incarnation that our salvation was achieved. (John of Damascus, *On the Divine Images: Three Apologies against Those Who Attack the Divine Images* (Crestwood, NY: St. Vladimir's Seminary Press, 1980), I.14.) He writes that, previously, "God, who is without form or body, could never be depicted. But now when God is seen in the flesh conversing with men, I make an image of the God whom I see. I do not worship matter; I worship the Creator of matter who became matter for my sake, who willed to take His abode in matter; who worked out my salvation through matter. Never will I cease honoring the matter which wrought my salvation! I honor it, but not as God" (ibid., I.16.)
11. Philippians 2:5–11.
12. John 14:9, 11.
13. Col. 1:15; Hebrews 1:3.
14. John 14:6.
15. John 14:8.
16. John 14:9–10.
17. John Zizioulas' *Communion and Otherness* provides an excellent treatment of the Cappadocian understanding of the Trinity and its social implications.
18. Tanner notes that the way in which Jesus lives out the divine economy in relation to other humans or other persons of the Trinity might not be identical to the way in which the Son participates in the triune relationship. What is possible for God is not necessarily possible for human beings (Tanner, *Christ the Key*, 244–245.) The idea of shared economy or order, however, leaves ample room for diverse manifestations of the divine relationality. If imaging God is less identical replication and more orientation, as the concept of economy

suggests, then becoming properly oriented by living into the divine economy means that human relationality does not have to be identical to that of God; it only has to be consistently ordered. Even if divine relationality manifests differently from one context to the next, all instances reveal the same fundamental order.

19. Philippians 2:2–5.

20. John 13:34–35.

21. The icon's "inner state" or alternative economy is visually represented in the particular aesthetic of iconic representation. Léonide Ouspensky, *Theology of the Icon*, ed. Léonide Ouspensky (Crestwood, NY: St. Vladimir's Seminary Press, 1992), 97.

22. Marie-José Mondzain describes the emotional power of the icon. "The eye and the ear are thus only the 'meatuses,' orifices that open the visceral body to discourse," she writes, "speech and the image must speak to the gut" (Marie-José Mondzain, *Image, Icon, Economy: The Byzantine Origins of the Contemporary Imaginary*, Cultural Memory in the Present (Stanford, CA: Stanford University Press, 2005), 59).

23. Leonid Ouspensky argues that sight of the truth conveyed through the icon is a byproduct of the Holy Spirit, which grants the ability to see the profound spiritual reality or, one might say, the economy being transmitted through Christ, the saints, and the image (Ouspensky, *Theology of the Icon*, 198).

24. James K.A. Smith provides a clear and accessible treatment of the power of desire in *Desiring the Kingdom*.

25. Mondzain, *Image, Icon, Economy*, 59.

26. In certain cases, living into the divine economy is manifest through the body as transformation into the likeness of an artificial icon. Daniel the Stylite, for instance, is said to have lived so thoroughly into the divine reality of God that, upon his death, he takes on a two-dimensional, parchment-like quality. Becoming flat, he is then nailed to a board and paraded around so that the faithful might venerate him. "Like an icon," the account states, "the holy man was displayed to all on every side; and for many hours the people all looked at him and also with cries and tears besought him to be an advocate with God on behalf of them all" (*Three Byzantine Saints: Contemporary Biographies*, ed. Elizabeth A.S. Dawes and Norman Hepburn Baynes (Crestwood, NY: St. Vladimir's Seminary Press, 1996), 69).

27. John of Damascus attributes this ability to communicate the divine economy, which is the grace of God, in both life and death (John of Damascus, *On the Divine Images: Three Apologies against Those Who Attack the Divine Images*, I.19).

28. Iconicity is contagious. The way that its order so easily spreads is the icon's fundamental power. The icon not only changes those who engage it directly, but can also those who engage people who have already been changed by it. For more on the contagious nature of the iconic economy, see Mondzain, Image, Icon, Economy, 160–162.

29. John 14:18–19.

30. Athanasius of Alexandria makes the same argument for unity with the Father through Jesus in his exegesis of John 17. "Christ's unity with the Father is what ensures our unity with the Father, in that our relationship with the Father comes by way of him" (Athanasius, "Four Discourses," Discourse 3, chapter 25, section 21, 238). Athanasius goes on to argue that the way in which Jesus participates in the Father is different than how humans participate in God (ibid., section 24, 407). The former is an issue of nature, while the latter is one of grace. This is correct if nature refers not to shared substance, but to shared economy. The divine economy is essential to the nature of the Trinity. Humans only come to participate in it by God's grace, through the person of Jesus Christ.

31. Dietrich Bonhoeffer understands proper human relationship with God as one of dependence. The human's creaturely existence means that she is inevitably limited and finite.

And, yet, such a condition is not an evil that must be overcome, but a good that is rendered as such by a good Creator. The creature's limitations and her natural dependence upon God maintain her proper relationship with God insofar as these attributes help her to recognize that God is God and she is not. Likewise, the other human being and God's good creation are understood as gifts insofar as the limits they pose, help to remind her of who she is as a creature and, in turn, who God is. This prelapsarian sense of identity and its accompanying social dynamic change with the Fall (Dietrich Bonhoeffer, *Creation and Fall: A Theological Exposition of Genesis 1–3* (Fortress Press, 2004), 60–64; original paginations).

32. Athanasius of Alexandria, *On the Incarnation of the Word*, ed. Philip Schaff and Henry Wace, St. Athanasius: Select Works and Letters (Grand Rapids, MI: Eerdmans Publishing Company, 1987), 3.2.
33. Bonhoeffer, *Creation and Fall*, 107; original pagination.
34. Ibid., 116; original pagination.
35. "For as, when the likeness painted on a panel has been effaced by stains from without, he whose likeness it is must needs come once more to enable the portrait to be renewed on the same wood . . . the outline is renewed upon it; in the same way also the most holy Son of the Father, being the Image of the Father, came to our region to renew man once made in His likeness" (Athanasius of Alexandria, *On the Incarnation*, 14.1-3).
36. John 17:20–23.
37. Jesus gestures toward the iconic nature of discipleship when he prays to the Father that those who come to believe in him through the message of his followers will also enter into the unity of the divine economy, "that all of them may be one, Father, just as you are in me and I am in you" (John 17:20). Relational unity through participation within the divine economy not only occurs through the teachings, life, and work of Jesus, but also through that of his disciples.
38. 1 Corinthians 11:1.
39. John 14:9–10.
40. Elizabeth Johnson describes God's mystery as being beyond human comprehension. "This sense of an unfathomable depth of mystery, of a vastness of God's glory too great for the human mind to grasp, undergirds the religious significance of speech about God; such speech never definitively possesses its subject but leads us ever more profoundly into attitudes of awe and adoration" (Elizabeth A. Johnson, "The Incomprehensibility of God and the Image of God Male and Female," *Theological Studies* 45, no. 3 (1984): 441). According to Johnson, worship and mystery go hand-in-hand. The depth of God's vastness produces awe and worship. And, perhaps, it is fair to say that, insofar as proper worship of God that is made possible through Jesus brings us into a deeper knowledge of God, worship itself drives us further into God's mystery. Knowledge and mystery are not mutually exclusive. Instead, both are profoundly experienced through the act of right worship.
41. Unconscious bias and stereotypes project commonly held images, ideas, and myths housed within the social imaginary upon the bodies of others in a way that silences them. This assumed totalizing knowledge of others forecloses self-articulation. For more on the relationship between visuality and power, see Nicholas Mirzoeff, *The Right to Look: A Counterhistory of Visuality* (Durham, NC: Duke University Press, 2011). For a treatment of the psychological toll of preconceived notions of race that renders people both silent and invisible see Anne Anlin Cheng, *The Melancholy of Race* (Oxford: Oxford University Press, 2001).
42. Kallistos Ware describes mystery as revelation that is not exhaustively understood in light of the unfathomable nature of God (Kallistos Ware, *The Orthodox Way* (London: Mowbrays, 1979), 15).

SELECT BIBLIOGRAPHY

Athanasius of Alexandria (1987), *On the Incarnation of the Word*. St. Athanasius: Select Works and Letters, ed. by Philip Schaff and Henry Wace, Grand Rapids, MI: Eerdmans Publishing Company.

Bonhoeffer, Dietrich (2004), *Creation and Fall: A Theological Exposition of Genesis 1–3*, Minneapolis, MN: Fortress Press, 2004.

Cheng, Anne Anlin (2001), *The Melancholy of Race*, Oxford: Oxford University Press.

John of Damascus (1980), *On the Divine Images: Three Apologies against Those Who Attack the Divine Images*, Crestwood, NY: St. Vladimir's Seminary Press.

Johnson, Elizabeth A. (1984), "The Incomprehensibility of God and the Image of God Male and Female," in *Theological Studies* 45, no. 3: 441–465.

Mirzoeff, Nicholas (2011), *The Right to Look: A Counterhistory of Visuality*, Durham, NC: Duke University Press.

Mondzain, Marie-José (2005), *Image, Icon, Economy: The Byzantine Origins of the Contemporary Imaginary*, Cultural Memory in the Present, Stanford, CA: Stanford University Press.

Ouspensky, Léonide (1992), *Theology of the* Icon, ed. by Léonide Ouspensky, Crestwood, NY: St. Vladimir's Seminary Press.

Rahner, Karl (2001), *The Trinity*, trans. by J. Donceel, New York: Continuum.

Tanner, Kathryn (2010), *Christ the Key*, Current Issues in Theology, Cambridge: Cambridge University Press.

Three Byzantine Saints: Contemporary Biographies, ed. Elizabeth A.S. Dawes and Norman Hepburn Baynes, Crestwood, NY: St. Vladimir's Seminary Press.

Ware, Kallistos (1979), *The Orthodox Way*, London: Mowbrays.

Zizioulas, John (1995), "The Doctrine of the Holy Trinity: The Significance of the Cappadocian Contribution," in *Trinitarian Theology Today: Essays on Divine Being and Act*, ed. by Christoph Schwöbel, Edinburgh: T&T Clark, 44–60.

PART FIVE

The Future of Political Theologies

CHAPTER THIRTY-FOUR

Toward an Islamic Theology of World Religions

From Polemics to a Critical Theology of Self and Other

VINCENT J. CORNELL

People who shut their eyes to reality simply invite their own destrction, and anyone who insists on remaining in a state of innocence long after that innocence is dead turns himself into a monster.

—James Baldwin, *Notes of a Native Son*[1]

THE POLEMICAL LEGACY OF THE PAST: NO EXIT?

A remarkable theological manuscript can be found in the library of El Escorial Monastery outside the Spanish capital of Madrid. Written in Arabic in the year 1361 CE, it contains a *fatwā* or juridical opinion by the Imam, preacher, and Mufti (chief jurisconsult) of Granada, Abū Saʿīd Faraj ibn Lubb (d. 1381 CE), on the subjects of destiny (*qaḍā*) and fate (*qadar*), from the standpoint of Ashʿarite theology.[2] What makes this *fatwā* noteworthy is that it responds to questions from a Jewish petitioner, who complains about being caught in a theological double bind. He asks: if Ashʿarite theology is correct that God predetermines all human actions, how can a Jew be blamed for not converting to Islam? Far from being considered a subject of reproach, shouldn't he be accepted as a loyal servant of God because he follows the divine will and thus remains a Jew? The petitioner voices his complaint in a poem, which is written in a sophisticated style that shows the author to have been a person of considerable erudition.

> Oh scholars of religion, a *dhimmī* of your religion[3]
> Is perplexed. So guide him with the clearest proof.
> If my Lord has decreed, in your opinion, my unbelief
> And then does not accept it of me, what is my recourse?
> He decrees my misguidance and says, "Be satisfied with your fate."
> But how can I be satisfied with the cause of my complaint?
> He curses me and shuts the door against me. Is there any
> Way out at all for me? Show me the outcome!
> For if, oh people, I were to be satisfied with my current fate,
> Then my Lord would not be pleased with my evil calamity.

How am I to be satisfied with what does not please my Master?
Thus, I am perplexed. So guide me to the solution of my perplexity.
If my Lord wills my unbelief as a matter of destiny,
How can I be disobedient in following his will?
Do I even have the choice of going against his ruling?
So by God, cure my malady with clear arguments!

In his response to this petition, Ibn Lubb criticizes the Jew (f. 151r) for willfully misrepresenting the Islamic theological doctrines of predestination and moral choice or limited free will. Specifically, he refutes the questions posed by the Jew according to the Mālikī legal doctrine of personal responsibility (*taklīf*) and the Ash'arite theological doctrine of acquired moral responsibility (*kasb*). He dismisses the Jew's key complaint, "Do I even have the choice of going against [God's] ruling?" as pure sophistry. He explains that according to Ash'arite theology, moral responsibility is a combination of divine will and personal choice. Since the will of God and the choice of the human being are both brought into being at the same time, the Jew cannot claim that he is a helpless puppet in the hands of God. In theological terms, he has "earned" God's reproach by choosing to remain a Jew (f. 152v). In other words, when it comes to the choice of one's religious identity, what the human being proposes and what God disposes are the very same thing.

Although the complaint of the Jew and Ibn Lubb's response to it may at first seem to be a medieval example of interreligious dialogue, it is not an interreligious dialogue in the way that this concept is understood today. Rather, it is better described as a dialogue of the deaf. On neither side is there any real desire to understand the other's position. The Jew poses his theological question about destiny and fate not as a problem that demands a serious answer, but as a rhetorical challenge that is meant to highlight the absurdity of Islamic theology. In this sense the Mufti of Granada was right to dismiss the petition out of hand; the key theological question posed in the poem is indeed sophistical. By criticizing the tenets of Ash'arism (the dominant form of Sunni Islamic theology) as radically predestinarian, the Jew implies that Islamic theology in general is absurd. Although Ibn Lubb attempts to deal with this criticism seriously, he is responding to an intentional misrepresentation of Islam that goes back to some of the earliest encounters between Muslims and Christians and Jews. As early as the eighth century CE, the Christian polemicist St. John of Damascus (d. 754 CE) composed a famous (albeit fictitious) debate between a Christian and a Saracen in which the Saracen was similarly portrayed as a predestinarian and the Christian—like the Jewish author of the poem—was portrayed as a believer in free will.[4]

The polemical tactic of accusing Islam of predestinarian theology and/or fatalism has continued down to the present day. Sometimes this polemic is so absurd that it borders on the ridiculous. In 1984, the French philosopher and born-again Protestant polemicist Jacques Ellul blamed the influence of fatalism caused by tolerance of Islam and Muslims for the mystical proclivities of the Roman Catholic Church.[5] A century earlier, in 1884—but still more than 500 years after the *fatwā* penned by Ibn Lubb—the Egyptian jurist and reformist theologian Muḥammad 'Abduh (1849–1905) was forced to make many of the same arguments (this time against Western academic critiques of Islam) in an article on the Islamic theology of destiny and fate in the journal *al-'Urwa al-Wuthqa* (The Unbreakable Bond):

[All Muslims believe] that there is an element of choice (*juz' ikhtiyārī*) in their actions (which is called *kasb*), and that this [concept of moral desert] is responsible for their reward or punishment. They further believe that the element of choice makes them accountable for what God has bestowed on them. In a like manner they are asked to follow the divine commands and prohibitions that call to every good and guide to every success, and that the element of choice is [also] the basis of the legal responsibility (*al-taklīf al-shar'ī*) through which [God's] wisdom and justice are made complete.[6]

I must confess that I have never understood why some Christian, Muslim, and Jewish scholars of religion have chosen to build their academic careers around the study of religious polemics. Although from a historical point of view polemics is an important genre of theological literature, it is a poor pathway to knowledge of the Spirit. Like the "Poem of the Jew" and Ibn Lubb's response to it discussed above, it is not a meaningful form of interreligious dialogue. Nor is it a valid form of "Scriptural Reasoning." Rather, it is an example of what the French aptly term *huis clos*—an internal dialogue of the deaf that takes place entirely "behind closed doors." To use a well-known Southern metaphor, the polemicist "preaches to his own choir" instead of the "choir" of the opponent. His real purpose is not to convince the opponent of the error of her ways but to prevent his own coreligionists from ever taking the opponent's ideas seriously.

In 1944 the French existentialist philosopher Jean-Paul Sartre (1905–1980) published a one-act play called *Huis Clos*, which was translated into English as "No Exit."[7] In this play, three sinners are condemned in the afterlife to coexist eternally in a closed room. They continually torment each other with morally bereft and circular arguments and self-justifications until, finding themselves exhausted, they run out of things to say. However, after some time has passed, one of the characters sighs and says, *Eh bien, continuons . . .* ("Oh well, let's continue"), and the eternal round of apologetics and recriminations starts all over again. Sartre's play *No Exit* serves as an excellent metaphor for the current state of Abrahamic interreligious polemics (note that this tiresome religious drama also has three characters); this dialogue of the deaf has been carried on with two or more of the main characters participating for at least two millennia without resolution.

THE PROBLEM OF TOLERANCE: AVOIDING THE THEOLOGICAL QUESTIONS

Religious polemics can be described as a *huis clos* situation because the official premise of polemics is false; a polemical debate is neither a true religious dialogue nor a debate. As such, it creates a "No Exit" situation that condemns the participants to argue eternally in a closed room. Despite the purported goal of refuting the doctrinal mistakes of the other, polemics in reality constitutes a quarrel rather than a true argument. For the sake of the quarrel, critical theology is bartered away at a cheap price. Seldom, if ever, does either side describe the doctrines of the opponent as the opponent herself would describe them. Consequently, polemical arguments are not convincing for the other side. In more than thirty years as a theologian and scholar of Islam I have never met anyone who was converted by means of polemics. The reason for this is easy to see. In reality, polemics are not designed to convince the other but to convince one's own side of the other's folly. The real goal is not to convince the other of the error of her ways but to prevent one's own coreligionists from engaging seriously with the other's doctrines and beliefs. This is why polemicists often employ doctrinal caricatures instead of serious theological arguments.

In Islam as well as in Christianity and Judaism, dialectical theology (*'ilm al-kalām*) has been the bedfellow of both polemics and apologetics since the Middle Ages. In Islam, this has not only hindered the development of interreligious understanding but it has also contributed to a lack of interest in both critical and constructive forms of theology. Although it is unfair to accuse Islamic theology of fatalism, traditionalism has become a serious problem since the early modern period. Partly as a result of this, in contemporary Sunni Islam, theological reasoning has been largely replaced by legal reasoning. Although dialectical theology is still studied in Shiite seminaries, the trend in Iran since the revolution of 1979 has also been in a legal direction.

In Islamist ideology, such as the political theology espoused by the Muslim Brotherhood activist Sayyid Quṭb (1906–1966), the dominance of the legal paradigm has led to what I have called "Sharī'a Fundamentalism."[8] Sharī'a Fundamentalism is a holistic reification of the concept of Natural Law in which an idealized notion of the Sharī'a (divorced from the logic and practice of Islamic jurisprudence) is posited as a trans-historical expression of the divine will and the sole locus of truth for humanity. For Quṭb, the Sharī'a as revealed to the Prophet Muḥammad in the Qur'ān and elaborated in the Hadith is literally "a chip off the block" of the Law by which God governs the universe. In his 1964 manifesto *Milestones* (*Ma'ālim fī al-ṭarīq*), Quṭb states, "[The Sharī'a] goes back to its most comprehensive origin in its decisive role in all of existence, not just in human existence alone, and in its application to all of existence, not in its application to human life alone."[9] He also states, "The human being is part of this cosmic existence; thus, the specific laws (*qawānīn*) that govern his natural instincts (*fiṭra*) are not to be separated from the cosmic law (*nāmūs*) that governs existence as a whole."[10]

The response to polemics and apologetic theologies by most modern proponents of interreligious dialogue has been to promote tolerance. However, this is also not a sufficient basis for interreligious understanding. The philosopher T.M. Scanlon has observed that tolerance is a problematical attitude because it occupies an intermediate position between acceptance and opposition. Although tolerance is usually seen as a better alternative than intolerance, it falls short as a solution to the problem of religious difference because it avoids most of the key theological issues. Establishing a theological basis for tolerance is an important first step toward creating a theology of world religions. As Scanlon explains, the indeterminacy of tolerance as it is normally practiced limits its effectiveness: too often it can be dismissed as merely a second-best alternative, "a way of dealing with attitudes that we would be better off without but that are, unfortunately, ineliminable."[11]

As we have seen in the above example of Ibn Lubb and the Jew, this pessimistic view of tolerance corresponds closely to the way that tolerance has traditionally been practiced in Islam. The mere fact that people of different religions can manage to live together for long periods of time does not mean that they will understand or even like each other. The Indian psychiatrist Sudhir Kakar has argued that a major factor leading to the incitement of communal violence in his country has been the inability of Muslims and Hindus to develop more than instrumental relationships with each other, despite the fact that they have lived next to each other for centuries. Even today, different religious communities in India continue to live in what Kakar calls "zones of indifference" with respect to each other.[12] This unfortunate fact suggests that previous attempts to create theologies of religious difference are not likely to be found in the writings of mainstream theologians. Instead, they are more likely to be found in liminal zones of interaction or on the margins of majoritarian systems of belief.

In the medieval Islamic world, in the rare cases where meaningful inter-communal or interconfessional relations existed between believers of different religions, comparative discussions of theological issues tended to take place in contexts that allowed believers to engage in discourse on a higher level than was normally available to the majority. For example, what allowed the Muslim Peripatetic philosopher Abū Naṣr al-Fārābī (d. 950 CE) to take wisdom from his Christian teacher, the Nestorian monk Yuḥannā ibn Ḥaylān (d. 910 CE) was not exoteric Islam but the Alexandria school of philosophy, which could be traced back to the (pagan) Hellenistic philosophers of late antiquity. For most of his Muslim contemporaries, Fārābī was suspected of divided loyalties. Were it not for his elite genealogy (his father was a Central Asian Turkish military commander) and the protection of powerful patrons, he would not have been able to gain the exalted reputation of "Second Teacher" in the field of Islamic philosophy after Aristotle. In his time just as today, exoteric monotheism was a zero-sum game: Fārābī's respect for Alexandrian philosophy meant for most people that he disrespected Islam. His loyalty to Nestorian Christian teachers of philosophy such as Ibn Ḥaylān and Mattā ibn Yūnus of Baghdad (d. 940 CE) only exacerbated this predicament.

"EPISTEMIC MODESTY" AND THE PROBLEM OF HETERODOXY

It has often been observed that if the quest for interreligious understanding is to progress beyond the level of theological "show-and-tell," it requires what the scholar of religion Adam B. Seligman has called "epistemic modesty." Epistemic modesty is a form of epistemological relativism that leads the religious practitioner to restrain her desire to use moral and theological judgments as grounds for coercion.[13] This more meaningful type of religious tolerance was in very short supply in the medieval Muslim world. Nor was it common in medieval Christian and Jewish exoteric circles either. Partisans of all three religions firmly believed in the superiority of their faith and it was rare if not impossible to find major religious figures that gave even partial validity to the worldviews of other religions. In most cases, the best that could be hoped for from an exoteric Muslim scholar was the belief that useful knowledge might accidentally be found among non-believers. The historian, litterateur, and Qur'ān commentator Abū Muḥammad Ibn Qutayba (d. 889 CE) expresses just such a sentiment in his masterpiece of Islamic civilizational history, 'Uyūn al-akhbār (The Wellsprings of Knowledge):

> Knowledge is the stray camel of the believer; it benefits one regardless from where one takes it. It will not lessen the truth if you hear it from pagans, nor can those who harbor hatred derive any advice from it. Shabby clothes do no injustice to a beautiful woman, nor do shells to pearls, nor does gold's origin from dust. Whoever neglects to take the good from the place where it is found misses an opportunity, and opportunities are as fleeting as the clouds ... ['Abdullāh] Ibn 'Abbās [the cousin of the Prophet Muḥammad] said: "Take wisdom from whomever you hear it, for a fool may utter a wise saying and a target may be hit by a beginner."[14]

This observation, which at first glance seems open-minded, is actually more an expression of political and cultural triumphalism than of true epistemological modesty. For Ibn Qutayba, who lived in Baghdad at the apogee of the Abbasid Empire, Islamic civilization was the crown of human cultural achievement. For this reason, he had no fear in appropriating cultural products from other civilizations, which he saw as foreshadowing Islam in a quasi-evolutionary manner. The fact that useful knowledge could sometimes be obtained from non-Muslims did not mean that their civilizations were equal to that of

Islam or that their religious beliefs had much of value in and of themselves. This is the kind of tolerance that T.M. Scanlon criticizes—a smug and ultimately self-centered acceptance of difference that merely allows one to enjoy the extraneous benefits of what normally would be unacceptable. Most importantly from a theological perspective, the thought never seems to cross Ibn Qutayba's mind that the world's cultural and religious diversity is a manifestation of the will of God. In *Rights of Man*, Thomas Paine (1737–1809) ridiculed the tolerance of triumphalism as a type of theological hypocrisy: "Who then, art thou, vain dust and ashes . . . that obtruded thine insignificance between the soul of man and its Maker? Mind thine own concerns. If he believes not as thou believest, it is a proof that thou believest not as he believeth, and there is no earthly power that can determine between you."[15]

According to Adam Seligman, "Tolerance is a virtue that has everything to do with boundaries and with margins."[16] This is an astute observation. However, for this very reason, the kind of religious tolerance that most closely resembled a theology of world religions could only exist in the past on the margins of a religious community's identity. To borrow a phrase from the Islamic historian Richard Bulliet, such a theological perspective represented a "view from the edge" and thus could often be dismissed as heterodox.[17] In premodern religious communities, theological worldviews were closely bound up with group loyalties. In medieval Islam, believers were not seen as individual actors but as members of corporate religious communities, in which "religion" was defined primarily in terms of religious law. In premodern Islamic states, the concept of "religion" was subsumed under the concept of the *milla* (Ottoman *millet*). This was a legally demarcated and semi-autonomous community of believers that existed concurrently with but in structural separation from other *milal* of the same type.[18] Islam was a *milla* too; the main difference was that it was the politically dominant *milla*. As such, it was defined legally as a community in which all members formally submitted to God's authority under the Sharī'a. Doctrines and traditions that came from outside the Islamic *milla* lacked authenticity because they were not Sharī'a-based. Instead, they were based on the whims of individual human opinion (*ahwā* or *ẓann*) rather than on the commands of God.

Because of this legacy, even today it is difficult for many Muslims not to see themselves as part of an Islamic *milla*. In the modern West, Muslim advocates of religious pluralism who wish to maintain the legal authority the Sharī'a tend to conceive of Islam's place in democratic societies in terms of what Kwame Anthony Appiah has called "Millet Multiculturalism."[19] Millet Multiculturalism is a corollary of the politics of identity, in which pluralism is defined in legal terms as the equal standing of culturally or religiously defined interest groups.[20] For advocates of this approach, defining Islam as a *milla* has the advantage of establishing the legal right of Muslims to follow the Sharī'a in matters such as personal conduct, marriage, and inheritance. However, a communalistic definition of religious pluralism such as this also has the disadvantage of potentially limiting the Muslim dissenter's right to freedom of conscience, which Thomas Paine considered an inalienable "right of the mind."[21] In practice, most Muslims in Western democracies would likely agree with Paine's perspective, regardless of their professed attitude toward the Sharī'a.

Because of the prevailing pattern of *milla*-based communalism in premodern Muslim societies, advocates of epistemic modesty tended to be far removed intellectually and spiritually from their co-religionists. Most of those whose works have come down to us today were social and intellectual elites. Their status allowed them to experiment theologically, an indulgence that was not available to the lower classes. As stated earlier, the partisans of this perspective attempted to appeal upward to a higher truth, to a higher standard of authority than the revealed Sharīʿa of the Prophet Muḥammad, for only by means of such a transcendent epistemology could the boundaries of creedal identity be crossed. For some of these elites, a popular recourse was to appeal to the Neo-Platonic and Neo-Aristotelian philosophies of late antique Hellenism, such as the Peripatetic philosophy of the Alexandria school, described previously for Abū Naṣr al-Fārābī.

Another, more daring approach was to follow the esoteric path of Hermetism. Although the doctrines of Muslim Hermetists tended to differ somewhat from each other, the followers of this movement all believed in the revelation of a transcendent or higher form of wisdom and a "perennial philosophy" (*ḥikma qadīma*), whose historical representatives included—along with the Qurʾānic and biblical prophets—the legendary Egyptian sage Hermes Trismegistos (*Hirmis al-Harāmisa*) and Pre-Socratic mystical philosophers such as Pythagoras (d. c. 495 BCE) and Empedocles (d. c. 430 BCE).[22] Most importantly for the present discussion, they also believed in a form of theological relativism in which spiritual practices could be shared across confessional boundaries with like-minded Christians and Jews.[23] For example, in a manuscript found in the Staatsbibliothek of Berlin, the Iberian Muslim Hermetist ʿAbd al-Ḥaqq Ibn Sabʿīn of Ricote (d. 1270 CE) calls on the spiritual powers (*rūḥāniyyāt*) of Jewish Throne Angels such as Metatron and Yahoel to defend him against his enemies.[24] In a lengthy essay on the invocation of God (*dhikr Allāh*), Ibn Sabʿīn also cites the spiritual practices of several different cultures and religions, including an alleged initiatory prayer made at the installation of a new Pope in Rome: "The Franks do not confirm a Pope in his position until he invokes his Lord and [God's] divinity (*lāhūt*) by the tongue (*bi-lisānihi*). He invokes by the tongue until he goes into an altered state (*ḥatta yaghība*) and he invokes [God's] divinity until he enters a state that seems like madness (*shibh al-junūn*). He invokes God through the Hypostases (*al-uqnūmīyya*), which is the attribute of [the divine] Essence, and these are many."[25]

Ibn Sabʾīn based his pluralistic epistemology on a theology of radical monism (most often described as *al-waḥda al-maḥḍa* or "absolute oneness"), which conceived of the Creator as immanent in all realms of existence, from the spiritual to the material. In the essay on invocation, he sums up this doctrine in a short verse:

In everything He has left a sign,
Pointing to the fact that He is One.
Wa fī kulli shay'in lahu āyatun,
Tadullu ʿalā annahu wāḥidun.[26]

Both modern scholars and medieval critics have observed that Ibn Sabʿīn's theology of "absolute oneness" is reminiscent of the more famous Sufi doctrine of "oneness of existence" (*waḥdat al-wujūd*) ascribed to his countryman and predecessor Muḥyiddīn ibn al-ʿArabī of Murcia (d. 1240 CE). However, Ibn Sabʿīn's notion of divine oneness was more literal and all encompassing than that of Ibn ʿArabī, who focused more on divine manifestation (*tajallī*) than on the oneness of being per se. In some cases Ibn Sabʿīn's monism even verged on pantheism, as can be seen in the following passage from his longest and most important work, *Budd al-ʿārif* (The Idol of the Gnostic):

What I wish to counsel you is this: that you firmly believe that the universal and the particular and the material and the spiritual are all one. Do not differentiate between them in your mind from the standpoint of whether or not they were brought into existence at the "first creation" (*al-khalq al-awwal*) and do not believe that the primordial order of existence (*al-niẓām al-qadīm*) is internally differentiated . . . Do not let the monotheism (*tawḥīd*) that you hear others profess betray you. For the knower, knowledge, and the known are all one. Know that all that is necessary is existence (*wujūd*) itself, and that nothing comes forth from it but the One.[27]

In the contemporary world, the place of the Muslim scholar of religion in the secular university is analogous in many ways to that of the philosopher or Hermetist in the medieval Islamic world. The more one knows about other religions in detail, the harder it is to adhere to a simplistic form of creedal monotheism. Furthermore, the phenomenological concept of *epoché* (epistemological detachment), which is central to the comparative study of religion, puts the scholar of religion on the fence with respect to theological truth-claims. In fact, the very idea of a theology of world religions is problematical from a soteriological point of view. As Mohammad Hassan Khalil has demonstrated in his book *Islam and the Fate of Others*, despite the fact that few major authorities of the past were exclusivists who damned all non-Muslims to perdition, it was virtually impossible to find true soteriological pluralists, who believed that different religions could be equally effective in terms of salvation.[28] In addition, none of the spiritual giants of the Islamic past had to face today's neoliberal "free market of ideas" or a global cosmopolitanism of multiple competing "world religions." No prominent Muslim scholar before the modern period was aware of Lutheran or Calvinist theology, much less of Hindu fundamentalism or nationalistic Buddhism.

Paradoxically therefore, although the epistemological contexts of the medieval and modern periods are very different, the threat of alienation faced by modern scholars of Islam and their premodern predecessors is much the same. Whatever position one takes on the question of religious difference, the answer is inherently political. This is in part due to the influence of creedalism, which has been used politically throughout the history of monotheism to harden the boundaries of orthodoxy. In the past—much like today— cosmopolitan Islamic scholars who transgressed the accepted limits of orthodoxy were often compelled to live in a state of intellectual exile, in alternate universes of belief that few of their coreligionists shared. The universalistic form of Islam that they followed was not the Islam that other Muslims knew; more often than not, it was an artificial construct— an elite "religion after religion," to use a term coined by the scholar of Judaism Steven Wasserstrom—in which similarly inspired unbelievers were more one's co-religionists than ordinary Muslims.[29] Thus, it is not for nothing that the Imam of a mosque in Durham, North Carolina recently felt moved to warn his congregation, "Beware of academic Islam!"

As the Imam understood, the academic study of religion tends to view theological and/ or soteriological pluralism as a normal state of affairs. The key problem in creating a doctrinally acceptable theology of world religions, as Seyyed Hossein Nasr has observed, "is how to preserve religious truth, traditional orthodoxy, the dogmatic theological structures of one's own tradition, and yet gain knowledge of other traditions and accept them as spiritually valid ways and roads to God."[30] Can this be done without trampling over one's own creedal boundaries or trivializing one's core beliefs? How is one to find resources for a constructive theology of world religions without falling into the trap of uncritically embracing the relativism of secular modernity?

Nasr's admonition reminds us that despite its apparently humble premise, the "epistemic modesty" that Adam B. Seligman advocates as the starting point for a pluralistic approach to religion is in fact a radical concept. Especially for exclusivistic missionary religions such as Christianity and Islam, Seligman's "modest proposal" is not modest at all. The unfortunate historical record of Islamic philosophy and Hermetism—which never succeeded in gaining widespread acceptance as authentic Islamic theologies—serve as important reminders against straying too far in the direction of epistemic relativism or, to paraphrase Jeffrey Stout, "Theological Esperanto."[31] Although Islamic philosophy is still kept alive in Shiite seminaries, many Sunni Muslim scholars would argue that it became a dead letter in the late Middle Ages because it created an "Epistemological Esperanto" by trying to reconcile incompatible Aristotelian and Qur'ānic worldviews. From the standpoint of Sunni orthodoxy, Islamic philosophy and Hermetism were elite and marginal sects—premodern "religions after religion"—that merely succeeded in bringing together free-thinking intellectuals who were dissatisfied with the status quo. Centered primarily in Iraq, Greater Iran (which included Central Asia), and Islamic Spain, the most culturally diverse regions of the premodern Muslim world, these intellectual movements were unable to gain traction in environments that were more mono-cultural or mono-doctrinal. The Iberian philosopher Abū al-Walīd Ibn Rushd (Averroes, d. 1198 CE) ended his days as an exile in his own country. The theosophical mystic Shihāb al-Dīn al-Suhrawardī (d. 1191 CE) was executed for heresy in Syria. The Hermetist Ibn Sabʿīn was accused of suicide by exoteric polemicists such as Ibn Taymiyya (d. 1328 CE) but most likely was poisoned in Mecca by agents of the Mamluk ruler of Egypt.[32]

FINDING "INVESTMENT BANKS" OF THEOLOGICAL RESOURCES

However, in at least two respects these unsuccessful experiments in epistemological pluralism provide some hope that creating an Islamic theology of world religions may be a more fruitful endeavor now than in the past. First, the adherents of the Islamic philosophical and Hermetic traditions viewed "the divine religion" (*al-dīn al-ilāhī*) of the Qur'ān as a universalistic world religion that transcended its Middle Eastern origins. They saw the theological simplicity of Qur'ānic Islam as expressing more clearly than Christianity or Judaism the "primordial" or "perennial" spiritual truths that lay behind religion in general. This universalistic outlook allowed them to draw from the "cutting-edge" epistemologies of their day in the way advocated by Ibn Qutayba for more secular subjects. Second, the fact that these pluralistic traditions of Islam were based in imperial metropoles and centers of international trade highlights the cosmopolitan nature of their origins. Despite the recent turn to political nativism in many parts of the world, cosmopolitanism remains today a global fact of life. Whereas in the past a theology of world religions was relevant only to a small and highly educated elite, today such a project is arguably relevant for everyone—including Muslims—wherever in the world they may live. In the modern contexts of postcoloniality, mass migration, and globalism, the fact of religious plurality has been forced upon Muslims in a way that can no longer be ignored. The creation of such new realities calls for new theological responses. Under such circumstances it is hard to imagine how some premodern orthodoxies can rationally be sustained.

For example, most Sunni Muslims still consider themselves adherents of Ashʿarite theology, even though they have no idea what Ashʿarite doctrine actually entails. I have seen this numerous times among Muslim students in my Islamic theology classes. Central tenets of classical Ash'arite theology include the concepts of atomism and occasionalism. According to Ash'arite atomism, the universe is divided into tiny particles of matter, qualities, space, and time. However, these particles have no discernible mass and cannot be measured, as in modern particle physics. Ash'arite occasionalism asserts that every action or event can be broken down into a series of separate and unconnected moments, which are completely independent of each other. Such moments are joined together solely through the action of the divine will. No logical continuity or order connects them together. For medieval Ash'arite theologians, the act of hitting a nail with a hammer was not perceived as a single motion. Instead, bringing down the hammer and striking the nail were conceptualized as a series of discrete events, in which the hammer is brought down closer and closer to the nail, until it strikes it. This view of action is analogous to a movie film, in which what appears to be a single moving picture is in reality a series of still pictures of different events, which only seem to be continuous because of the speed at which they are run through the projector. Although a human agent strikes the nail with the hammer, he only does so through the will of God. Similarly, objects, actions, and events in general exist only for a single moment. They continue to exist only by being created again and again by God in a series of successive creations (*khalq fī kull waqt*), whose continuity is purely illusory. Although there have been attempts to relate these concepts to modern subatomic theory and quantum mechanics, the classical Ash'arite view of reality clearly contradicts the logic of cause-and-effect that is fundamental to modern science. Equally important is the rejection of any idea of "nature" or even of a natural order. The early modern Western notion of a clockwork universe could not exist in the Ash'arite worldview. Instead, God is the agent for everything and everything is possible for God, who can and often does change reality at will. No limitation on divine power is allowed to exist.

Clearly, it is possible to make the argument that classical Ash'arite theology should be replaced by a theology that better reflects the empirical realities of modern science. However, despite such incongruities, it is equally important to address the problem of authenticity that condemned earlier pluralistic epistemologies of Islam to irrelevancy. While finding a solution to this problem is a long-term project that will take many years to complete, an important first step is to collect and make use of the spiritual and intellectual resources of the Islamic past that allow us to build conceptual bridges between the spiritual perspective of the Qur'ān and modern worldviews.

I would argue that despite the epistemological challenges mentioned above, the best institutional site for marshaling such resources is the modern secular university and that scholars of Islam in these universities are best prepared to lead such a project. The German philosopher Peter Sloterdijk has argued that cultures and civilizations create depositories or "collection points of affect" that can be drawn upon for investment purposes in the way that one draws funds from a bank. Universities serve as such depositories in the modern "knowledge economy." Once one gets over the idea that a "bank" exclusively deals with monetary resources, it becomes possible to see that "the function of a bank consists in covering a much broader domain of phenomena. Analogous processes are present whenever cultural and psychopolitical entities such as scientific theories, acts of faith, works of art, political acts of protest, and so on are accumulated."[33] One may also add theological resources to this list of cultural and psycho-political entities. Functioning analogously to financial institutions, these "banks" of cultural and intellectual resources can "enable the investment of cultural capital in new forms of constructive politics."[34] Through libraries, research institutes, and graduate and undergraduate faculties, modern universities function as "investment banks" of civilizational resources and cultural capital. Because of this—both within and outside of the Islamic world—faculties of religious studies, Islamic Studies, and Middle East Studies in modern secular universities are well placed to provide the intellectual resources for creating an Islamic theology of world religions.

What makes Sloterdijk's banking analogy particularly relevant for the present discussion is that he uses a religious institution—the Roman Catholic Church—as the prime example of a globally operative "bank of affect," whose archive of spiritual and intellectual resources extends from the distant past into the present. The concept of banking originally grew out of the agrarian habitus of storing surplus harvests for later use, which in turn led to the creation of the operational models of savings, resource management, and redistribution according to need.[35] Eventually people realized that "[a]ll forms of treasure can be stockpiled as supplies. In the beginning this happened to weapons and jewelry and extended to include the treasures of healing, the arts, law, and knowledge. With these resources a culture secures its symbolic survival."[36]

A similar process occurred in the world of Islam, where the economic concepts of resource accumulation, savings, redistribution, and investment developed along similar lines as in the West. During the period of the first Islamic conquests in the seventh century CE, military cities (*miṣr*, pl. *amṣār*) were built as advance bases. Such cities included Kairouan in Tunisia, al-Fusṭāṭ (Old Cairo) in Egypt, and Basra and Kufa in Iraq. In these cities the first institution to be created after the mosque and the command center was the *bayt al-māl* ("treasury," literally, "house of wealth"), which stored booty from conquest and taxes in kind for future distribution in case of emergency. The creation of a permanent market followed close behind the establishment of the *bayt al-māl*. In addition, rural weekly markets were created at key distribution points in the regions conquered by the Muslim armies. These developments facilitated the circulation of wealth that provided the basis for the unparalleled economic growth of the early Abbasid Empire.[37] Also in the Islamic world, the concept of economy (*iqtiṣād*) and related terminologies migrated into the domain of religion, such as can be seen in the title *al-Iqtiṣād fī'l-iʿtiqād* (The Economy of Belief), a well-known theological treatise by Abū Ḥāmid al-Ghazālī (d. 1111 CE).

However, a storehouse is not the same as a bank. A storehouse keeps goods in their original state for later use. A bank transforms goods into capital and invests them for transformative purposes. Similarly, in the knowledge economy, "storehouses of knowledge" such as museums, archives, and libraries have a different function from research institutes and universities, which make productive use of their contents. Without engaging in such transformative processes, storehouses of knowledge can do little more than preserve the artifacts of tradition, thus fostering an ethos of traditionalism. "By holding on to the ancient ... archetype of an accumulated supply or treasure," says Sloterdijk, "the [traditionalist] thinker refused to accept the modernization of the production of knowledge through research. He sensed a fatal disfiguration of the 'organically grown,' pretechnical mode of the being of things through this modernization."[38]

In previous publications I have argued that since the turn of the twentieth century the "crisis of the holy" in Islam has been, more than anything else, an epistemological crisis.[39] The term "epistemological crisis" was coined by the philosopher Alasdair MacIntyre to describe what happens when a tradition of inquiry fails to adapt to changing conditions according to previous standards of rationality. In an epistemological crisis, former methods of inquiry become sterile, "conflicts over rival answers to key questions can no longer be settled rationally," and forms of argumentation that have worked in the past "have the effect of increasingly disclosing new inadequacies, hitherto unrecognized incoherencies, and new problems for the solution of which there seem to be insufficient or no resources within the established fabric of belief."[40] Using Sloterdijk's terminology, one could say that during epistemological crises, ideas and concepts that are not "organically grown" (i.e., traditionally authentic) are rejected and traditions of the past are fetishized and kept in a "museum of tradition" instead of being reinvested productively in the cultural economy.

In the modern Muslim world as in the West, the main institution of knowledge production is no longer the *madrasa* or seminary, but the secular university. The only partial exception is in Shiite Islam, where the scholarly institution of the seminary or *ḥawza ʿilmīyya* is kept alive through religious taxation. As Sloterdijk explains, the epistemological importance of universities as "investment banks" for the modern knowledge economy cannot be overstated:

> Contemporary research is . . . surprisingly analogous to the unfolding of the banking industry in the more recent financial economy. Scientific academies and modern universities play the role of authentic knowledge banks. Traditional banks cooperate as partners and observers of corporations. In the cognitive [i.e., intellectual] domain the managerial function is taken over by research institutions. Once the treasury form of knowledge . . . passes over into the form of capital, it may no longer be accumulated as an inactive supply. The educative rule "earn it in order to own it" is suspended for the kind of knowledge that is made dynamic for the purpose of research. It is no longer an acquired possession but serves as the base material for its extended reproduction, like modern money, which, instead of being stored in chests under the mattress, returns to the sphere of circulation in order to become productive on higher levels.[41]

In the modern university, "research corresponds to investing within the monetary sphere. Research implies the controlled risking of what has already been earned for the chance of future gains."[42] This commodification of knowledge, however, does not occur without the risk of side effects, which may include epistemological crises. When these occur, the most economically rational response is often analogous to what economists call "creative destruction." Fear of the "creative destruction" of traditional or functionally inefficient forms of knowledge is a major cause of the reactionary political and cultural response to paradigm shifts in the knowledge economy:

> It is admittedly the case that knowledge capital, just as monetary capital, experiences specific crises in which its future productivity is called into question. The solution for such crises usually consists in what recent sociologists of knowledge refer to as a "paradigm change." In the course of development of such paradigm changes, older cognitive values are destroyed, while business continues more intensively than ever before, albeit with different basic conceptual parameters.[43]

However, paradigm change does not always have to result in "creative destruction." In the knowledge economy, paradigm change may also be effected through "creative re-use." This recently occurred with respect to religion in Turkey, where reformist theologians working in secular universities used premodern theologies in creative ways to open up new possibilities for bridging the conceptual divide between the religious and the secular. In one prominent example, a group of Islamic scholars trained at the Faculty of Divinity of Ankara University attempted to formulate a theology of Islamic Humanism by creatively drawing on the empirical epistemology of the Central Asian theologian Abū Manṣūr al-Māturīdī (d. 944 CE), and combining his theology with hermeneutical methods drawn from Ḥanafī jurisprudence, functionalist theories of sociology, and Western historical research on Islamic civilizations. The goal of this project was the creation of a contemporary version of "Turkish Islam" that was pragmatic, amenable to scientific epistemologies, and able to respond creatively to changing social conditions.[44]

PREPARING THE WAY FORWARD[45]

Today many Muslim scholars are attempting similar projects in secular universities throughout the Islamic world and the West. For example, Emory University's PhD programs in Religion and Islamic Civilizations Studies have drawn promising graduate students not only from top American universities but also from Bilkent and Bogaziçi Universities in Turkey, Ain Shams University in Egypt, and Lahore University of Management Sciences in Pakistan. What ties all of these students and programs together is the common desire to transcend cultural, intellectual, and epistemological boundaries. In an article that has been republished several times, I argued—drawing in part from Sufi theology—that the Qur'ān posits life, dignity, and freedom of choice as fundamental and inalienable human rights.[46] As such, it is the individual responsibility of each Muslim to uphold these rights for all people according to the divine mandates of mercy and justice, which are also expressed in the Qur'ān. The Qur'ānic conception of rights and duties constitutes an important but overlooked theological basis for religious tolerance in Islam. However, to grant an unbeliever the right to practice her religion under conditions of mutual respect does not necessarily imply, in line with Sayyid Hossein Nasr's admonition given above, that one must also accept the unbeliever's theology as a fully valid understanding of God. On the contrary, it is sufficient under the rules of tolerance merely to accord others the right to practice their beliefs without overt restrictions, while at the same time disagreeing about the tenets and foundations of their beliefs.

On the other hand, if the adherents of different religions are to live together in peace as more than just rivals competing over the same territory, our understanding of the theologies of world religions must go further. As T.M. Scanlon makes clear, a more robust form of tolerance requires the recognition of common membership in global society that goes deeper than our exoteric differences, "a recognition of others as being just as entitled as we are to contribute to the definition of our society."[47] Achieving this goal is one of the most important tasks of an Islamic theology of world religions.

However, before such a theology can be formulated, certain preconditions or ground rules must first be established. Such preconditions would necessarily entail the rejection of ideologies and approaches to religion that are inherently incompatible with a theology of world religions. For an Islamic theology of world religions, the first such demand would be the rejection of political Islamism and other forms of Sharā'a Fundamentalism. If Muslims are to allow others the God-given rights of life, dignity, and freedom of religious choice, it is necessary to reject such doctrines as Sayyid Quṭb's totalitarian view of the Sharī'a as a positive divine law governing the entire universe. Such a view denies validity to all forms of religious diversity, including diversity within Islam. An Islamic theology of world religions needs to express and help bring back to light the historical traditions and theologies of Islam that accepted diversity among different sects and religions. It should hardly need to be said that an Islamic theology of world religions could not exist without acknowledging the fact of diversity, both among religions and within Islam itself.

Another precondition or ground rule for the development of an Islamic theology of world religions is a more inclusive notion of religious identity that is better able to transcend confessional boundaries. That is to say, the concept of "believer" should include more than just Muslims, at least at the macro level. One of the problems of the *milla* system in Islam was that it sharpened confessional boundaries through legal means and highlighted the importance of secondary differences in customs and practices as a means of establishing group identity. As a result, different religious communities lost sight of their commonalities, and the legal concept of a modus vivendi was established at the cost of theological understanding. Also as noted previously, the concept of a Sharī'a-based identity—in the sense of the Sharī'a as a code of law or an "Islamic constitution"—has had a distorting effect both on how Islam views others and on how Islam is viewed by others. Because of the historical dominance of this paradigm over the last 100 years, it is necessary to give more attention theologically to Qur'ānic verses that seem to promote a more universalistic vision of religious differences. For example, when the Qur'ān states: "As for those who believe, and the Jews, and the Christians, and the Sabaeans: Whoever believes in God and the Last Day and works righteousness, their reward is with their Lord; no fear shall come upon them, nor shall they grieve (Q 2:62)," it is important to ask whether this verse speaks only of Muslims, Jews, Christians, and Sabaeans (a sect that has not been clearly identified), or is it possible to give a wider meaning to the phrase, "those who believe?"

The late modern economic context of globalization teaches us that the economic health of the world depends on interdependence. The related concept of globalism has extended this notion of interdependence into the cultural sphere. Such facts remind us that political, cultural, and religious communities no longer have the luxury of remaining isolated and ignorant of each other. In theological terms, the reality of globalism creates a new imperative for rereading and reinterpreting traditional texts and sacred scriptures. In other words, contemporary Muslims in the global community are faced with a hermeneutical challenge. Thus, the third precondition for the development of an Islamic theology of world religions must include the development of new hermeneutical strategies and a critical theology of self and other.

Although the concept of an Islamic theology of world religions is based on the conviction that the Qur'ān and the Sunna are open (at least in part) to more inclusivist understandings, the very same resources are being used every day to promote exclusivist understandings and policies. For this reason, the development of a critical theology of self and other is necessary for political as well as hermeneutical reasons. Whoever seeks to articulate a more inclusive understanding of Islam and its scriptures must also address critically the hermeneutics of exclusivist understandings. For example, what does rational faith entail in light of traditional Islamic concepts of God's sovereignty? Do premodern sources exist that promote the kind of rational pluralism implied by an Islamic theology of world religions?[48] What implications might this have for the policies of Muslim states with respect to non-Muslim minorities?

Questions such as these remind us that in preparing the hermeneutical ground for an Islamic theology of world religions we need to come up with new hermeneutical strategies, a project that in Arabic would be called *adab al-ta'wīl*.[49] In premodern Islam, an important but currently overlooked way of approaching scriptural hermeneutics was through the concept of *adab*, a term that variously connoted personal behavior, etiquette, and choosing the appropriate response for different interpretive situations. The concept of *adab* was not a simplistic "one size fits all" notion but a nuanced approach for understanding what is appropriate for each context. Because of the relevance of *adab* to moral theology, some of the earliest figures associated with the Sufi tradition of Islam were masters of this discipline.[50]

Because of its importance as a hermeneutical strategy, the Sufi Muḥyīddīn ibn al-ʿArabī discussed the hermeneutics of *adab al-taʾwīl* at some length in his major treatise, *al-Futūḥāt al-Makīyya* (The Meccan Revelations). He opens his discussion by stating that the Sufi practitioner of *adab* "[must comport] himself with each spiritual station according to that station; with each state, according to that state; and in the same way with [respect to] each virtue and goal. He unites in himself the Noble Virtues (*makārim al-akhlāq*); he knows the ignoble ones without qualifying himself by them." Most importantly, "He embraces all degrees of praiseworthy and blameworthy knowledge, for there is nothing to which ignorance is preferable to knowledge for any man endowed with intelligence."[51]

With respect to the Qurʾān, Ibn ʿArabī argues that the practice of hermeneutics involves four separate contexts of scriptural interpretation, each of which requires a different mode of knowledge and action. These contexts are as follows:

1. The *Adab* of the Law: Ibn ʿArabī calls this, the "divine *adab*" (*al-adab al-ilahī*), which God undertakes to teach to humanity through revelation and inspiration. Hermeneutically, it requires the most universalistic reading of the Qurʾān because in this context the concept of Law implies universality of revelation.

2. The *Adab* of Service: This form of *adab* is based on the concept of etiquette. It obliges Muslims to follow the Sharīʿa and the other requirements of their religion. However, following common precedent, it is considered specific to Muslims only and is not to be imposed on non-Muslims.

3. The *Adab* of Right: This form of *adab* proceeds from the Qurʾānic notion of *ḥaqq*, which may mean "right," "duty," "justice," or "truth." It is confirmed by the Qurʾānic verse, "We have created the heavens and the earth only through *ḥaqq*" (Q 15:85 and Q 46:3). It confers on each person— regardless of religion— a degree of right and truth, which Muslims must respect and understand. Hence, this form of *adab* can be used as a basis for interreligious understanding.

4. The *Adab* of Reality: This form of *adab* is a corollary of the *Adab* of Right, which is applied to God Himself in respect to the uniqueness of His being. It can be used as a basis for an Islamic theology of world religions because it obliges Muslims to affirm the present reality of the world as God created it.

The foregoing discussion of *adab al-taʾwīl* also brings to mind the following two verses of the Qurʾān, which remind Muslims to affirm the reality of the world, just as God created it. These verses are well known to proponents of interreligious dialogue, Scriptural Reasoning, and religious pluralism:

For each one of you we have made a Law (*shirʿa*) and a way of life (*manhaj*). If God had wished, He would have made you into a single community. Instead, He has done this so that He may try you with what He has given you. So strive against each other in good works, for to God is the return for all of you and He will inform you about that wherein you differ.

—Q 5:48

If your Lord had willed it, everyone on earth would have believed. Would you then force people to become believers?

—Q 10:99

In order to emphasize the theological ramifications of these verses, one could also add another, which states, "God does whatever He wants" (Q 2:253). Reflecting on these verses in light of the concept of *adab al-ta'wīl* brings up the final and theologically most important precondition for creating an Islamic theology of world religions: This is the full recognition in theological terms that the diversity of world religions—like all other forms of diversity—is the will of God. Since diversity is an ontological fact, each Muslim has the obligation to recognize this fact and try to understand what it means. In particular, the triumphalists and exclusivists among the Muslim *umma* need to ask themselves: "If Islam hasn't prevailed over all other religions in more than 1400 years—and even more, if there are still more Christians than Muslims—what does this imply for Islam and Islamic history in future generations?" So far the response to this question has mainly been political: Islam has not prevailed because Muslims have not followed the Sharī'a sufficiently; thus, Muslims must create Sharī'a states so that God will approve of them and grant them the final victory.

Although the Muslim world has not yet given up the project of political Islamism (witness recent developments in Turkey, where many liberal academic theologians in secular universities have been dismissed from their teaching positions), I would argue that Islamism has failed to produce its intended results. The historical wave of Islamism has crashed on the shore, leaving only flotsam and jetsam in its wake. Ironically, a major reason for this failure is soteriological. In the ideology of Islamism, the concept of spirituality and essential Islamic virtues such as *adab* have been ignored to such an extent that even the political victory of the Islamist state cannot ensure that anyone will get to heaven. Over the past decades, the example of Shiite vs. Salafī sectarianism and extremist groups such as al-Qaeda and ISIS have proven the maxim once cited to me by the French Islamic scholar Gilles Kepel: "When one becomes an Islamist, three things are lost: The first is mercy, the second is hygiene, and the third is *adab*."[52]

The message of the Qur'ān is clear that God's revelation is universal and that different revelations have come down to different peoples at different times. As Muslims we have an obligation to take this fact seriously as an essential part of the word of God. But even more, as theologians, we need to ask, "What does 'universality of revelation' mean for the modern world?" Because we live in a technologically advanced and globalized era that is fundamentally different from the Muslim experience of any other age, we need to reimagine the *Umma Muslima* not just as a collection of nations under the Sharī'a, but as a global community of God's servants. We also need to accept that it is God's will for us to come face to face with alternative views of divinity and ultimate reality. If God indeed wants things to be this way, we must learn to appreciate the value of other religions and share their wisdom as much as we can, while still maintaining our identity as Muslims. This challenge to identity calls for discernment regarding the key problems with which Muslims around the world must grapple. Drawing a clear distinction between the challenges and questions that arise from purely theological and religious concerns and those arising from other aspects of Muslim life, culture, or nationhood will be one of the key tasks of an Islamic theology of world religions.

NOTES

1. James Baldwin, *Notes of a Native Son: Collected Essays*, ed. Toni Morrison (New York: The Library of America, 1998), 129.
2. Biblioteca de El Escorial, Spain (No. 1810ff. 147–155v). The translation is mine. I am indebted to Professor Hayat Kara of Université Mohammed V, Rabat, Morocco, for sharing this text with me. For a biography of Ibn Lubb see Aḥmad Bābā al-Timbuktī (d. 1627 CE), *Nayl al-ibtihāj bi-taṭrīz al-Dibāj*, edited by 'Abd al-Majīd al-Ḥarama (Tripoli, Libya: 1989), 357–360.

3. The term *dhimmī* connotes the protected status of Christian and Jewish minorities in Muslim societies. However, the use of this term in the poem is an Arabic pun. The verb *dhamma*, the root of *dhimmī*, means "to blame." Thus, the Arabic phrase in the poem, *dhimmīyu dīnikum*, may mean either "a non-Muslim whom your religion protects" (the juridical definition of *dhimmī*) or "one whom your religion blames."
4. W. Montgomery Watt, *The Formative Period of Islamic Thought* (Edinburgh: Edinburgh University Press, 1973), 97.
5. Jacques Ellul, *The Subversion of Christianity* (Grand Rapids, MI: William B. Eerdmans Publishing Company, 1986), 105–109.
6. Muḥammad 'Abduh and Jamāl al-Dīn al-Afghānī, "Destiny and Fate" (*al-Qaḍā wa al-qadar*), *al-'Urwa al-Wuthqa*, No. 7, 1884 (Beirut: Dār al-Kitāb al-'Arabī, 1980), 89–98; my translation.
7. Jean-Paul Sartre, *No Exit and Three Other Plays*, trans. Stuart Gilbert (New York: Vintage Books, 1989).
8. See Vincent J. Cornell, "Reasons Public and Divine: Shari'a Fundamentalism, Liberal Democracy, and the Epistemological Crisis of Islam," in *Rethinking Islamic Studies: From Orientalism to Cosmopolitanism*, eds. Carl W. Ernst and Richard C. Martin (Columbia, SC: University of South Carolina Press, 2010), 23–51.
9. Sayyid Quṭb, *Ma'ālim fī al-ṭarīq* (Beirut: Dār al-Sharq, 2000), 110; my translation.
10. Ibid.
11. T.M. Scanlon, "The Difficulty of Tolerance," Rajeev Bhargava, Ed., *Secularism and Its Critics* (New Delhi: Oxford University Press, 1998), 54–55.
12. Sudhir Kakar, *The Colors of Violence: Cultural Identities, Religion, and Conflict* (Chicago: University of Chicago Press, 1996), 150.
13. Adam B. Seligman, *Modest Claims: Dialogues and Essays on Tolerance and Tradition* (Notre Dame, IN: Notre Dame University Press, 2004), 20 and 140. Instead of epistemological relativism Seligman uses the term "epistemological humility."
14. Vincent J. Cornell, "Religion and Philosophy," in *World Eras, Volume 2: The Rise and Spread of Islam, 622–1500*, ed. Susan L. Douglass (Farmington Hills, MI: Gale Publications, 2002), 368.
15. Thomas Paine, *Rights of Man*, in *Thomas Paine: Selected Writings* (New York: The Library of America, 1995), 482–483. The ending of this statement is reminiscent of *Sūrat al-Kāfirūn* of the Qur'an (Q 109): "Say: Oh unbelievers! I do not worship what you worship; and you do not worship what I worship. I shall not worship what you worship and you will not worship what I worship. To you your religion and to me mine."
16. Seligman, *Modest Claims*, 155.
17. See Richard Bulliet, *Islam: The View from the Edge* (New York: Columbia University Press, 1995). Note, however, that for Bulliet, "the edge" is defined in cultural rather than theological terms.
18. The communal separation found by Sudhir Kakar between Muslims and Hindus in India is in part a legacy of the *milla* system imposed by the Moghul Empire. In the colonial period the British maintained this system largely for pragmatic reasons based on medieval works of Islamic law. The scriptural justification for the *milla* system is Qur'ān 12:37–38, where the Prophet Joseph states, "I have forsaken the *milla* of a people who do not believe in Allah and reject the Hereafter. Instead, I follow the *milla* of my fathers Abraham, Isaac, and Jacob. Never was it our practice to associate partners with God."
19. Kwame Anthony Appiah, *The Ethics of Identity* (Princeton, NJ: Princeton University Press, 2005), 71–79.

20. I have critiqued Millet Multiculturalism as incompatible with both Rawlsian notions of liberal democracy and social contract forms of constitutionalism. See Cornell, "Reasons Public and Divine." Recent Muslim advocates of Millet Multiculturalism in the US include Imam Feisal Abdul Rauf and Sherman Jackson. See Imam Feisal Abdul Rauf, *What's Right with Islam: A New Vision for Muslims and the West* (San Francisco, CA: Harper San Francisco, 2004); and Sherman A. Jackson, *Islam and the Blackamerican: Looking Toward the Third Resurrection* (New York: Oxford University Press, 2005).

21. Paine, *Rights of Man*, 464.

22. John Walbridge, *The Wisdom of the Mystic East: Suhrawardī and Platonic Orientalism* (Albany, NY: State University of New York Press, 2001), 42–50.

23. Vincent J. Cornell, "The All-Comprehensive Circle (*al-Iḥāṭa*): Soul, Intellect, and the Oneness of Existence in the Doctrine of Ibn Sab'īn," in *Sufism and Theology*, ed. Ayman Shihadeh (Edinburgh: Edinburgh University Press, 2007), 32.

24. 'Abd al-Ḥaqq ibn Sab'īn, *Da'wat li-ḥarf al-qāf*, Staatsbibliothek zu Berlin, Wetzstein II, 1769 fols. 117a–119b.

25. 'Abd al-Ḥaqq ibn Sab'īn al-Ghāfiqī, *Risālat al-naṣīḥa aw Risālat al-nūriyya*, 'Abd al-Rahman Badawi, ed., *Revista del Instituto Egipcio de Estudios Islámicos de Madrid*, 4 (1), 1957, 151–189; my translation.

26. Ibid; p. 4 of the Arabic text.

27. 'Abd al-Ḥaqq ibn Sab'īn, *Budd al-'ārif* (The Idol of the Gnostic), ed. Georges Kattoura (Beirut: Dār al-Andalus/Dār al-Kindī, 1978), 196; my translation.

28. Mohammad Hassan Khalil, *Islam and the Fate of Others: The Salvation Question* (New York: Oxford University Press, 2012), 7.

29. See Steven M. Wasserstrom, *Religion after Religion: Gershom Scholem, Mircea Eliade, and Henry Corbin* (Princeton, NJ: Princeton University Press, 1999).

30. Seyyed Hossein Nasr, "Islam and the Encounter of Religions," *Sufi Essays* (New York: Shocken Books, 1972), 127.

31. Stout's original term is "Moral Esperanto." Following his definition, I use this concept to include any "artificial . . . language invented in the (unrealistic) hope that everyone will want to speak it." Jeffrey Stout, *Ethics after Babel: the Languages of Morals and Their Discontents* (Princeton, NJ: Princeton University Press, 2001), 294.

32. Vincent J. Cornell, "The Way of the Axial Intellect: The Islamic Hermetism of Ibn Sab'īn," *Journal of the Muhyiddin Ibn 'Arabi Society* 23, 1997: 48.

33. Peter Sloterdijk, *Rage and Time: A Psychopolitical Investigation*, trans. Mario Wenning (New York: Columbia University Press, 2012), 137.

34. Ibid.

35. Ibid., 139.

36. Ibid.

37. On the development of the exchange economy in the early Islamic period, see Mahmood Ibrahim, *Merchant Capital and Islam* (Austin, TX: University of Texas Press, 1990). See also Maurice Lombard, *The Golden Age of Islam* (London: Markus Wiener Publishers, 2009) and Jacob Lassner, *The Shaping of Abbasid Rule* (Princeton, NJ: Princeton University Press, 1980).

38. Sloterdijk, *Rage and Time*, 140.

39. See Vincent J. Cornell, "Islam," in *The Crisis of the Holy: Challenges and Transformations in World Religions*, ed. Alon Goshen-Gottstein (Lanham, MD: Lexington Books, 2014), 125–150; Vincent J. Cornell, "Islam: Epistemological Crisis, Theological Hostility, and the

Problem of Difference," in *The Religious Other: Hostility, Hospitality, and the Hope of Human Flourishing*, ed. Alon Goshen-Gottstein (Lanham, MD: Lexington Books, 2014), 69–98; Idem, "Die Kriese des Heiligen: Islam," in Maria Reis Habito and Alon Goshen-Gottstein Eds., *Die Krise des Heiligen* (St. Ottilien, Germany: EOS Verlag, 2008), 175–212.

40. Alasdair MacIntyre, *Whose Justice? Which Rationality?* (Notre Dame, IN: University of Notre Dame Press, 1988), 361–362.
41. Sloterdijk, *Rage and Time*, 140.
42. Ibid.
43. Ibid., 140–141.
44. See Philip Dorroll, "'The Turkish Understanding of Religion': Rethinking Tradition and Modernity in Contemporary Turkish Islamic Thought," *Journal of the American Academy of Religion*, 82 (4), December 2014, 1033–1067.
45. Some of the material in this section is derived from the unpublished notes of the conference "Toward a Muslim Theology of World Religions," held at Al-Akhawayn University, Ifrane, Morocco, May 27–31, 2007. The conference was funded by the Rockefeller Brothers Fund under the auspices of the Elijah Interfaith Institute of Jerusalem and its Director, Alon Goshen-Gottstein, with the participation of the Al Khoei Foundation of London. As Project Director, I was responsible for laying out the overall theme of the conference and presenting papers on the subjects of "Law and Rights" and "Sovereignty and Loyalty." Alon Goshen-Gottstein worked closely with me as the Facilitator of the project and took most of the notes.
46. Vincent J. Cornell, "Practical Sufism: An Akbarian Foundation for a Liberal Theology of Difference," *Journal of the Muhyiddin Ibn 'Arabi Society*, Volume XXXVI, 2004, 59–84.
47. Scanlon, "The Difficulty of Tolerance," 61.
48. For a well-reasoned investigation of this issue, see Ahmed Abdel Meguid, "Reversing Schmitt: The Sovereign as a Guardian of Rational Pluralism and the Peculiarity of the Islamic State of Exception in al-Juwaynī's Dialectical Theology," *European Journal of Political Theory*, Sept. 12, 2017, 1–27. https://doi.org/10.1177/1474885117730672
49. *Adab al-ta'wīl* is my term, although it corresponds to a well-established premodern intellectual discipline in Islam. It is taken from the phrase *Qānūn al-Ta'wīl* (The Rules of Hermeneutics), the title of a treatise by the Mālikī jurist Abū Bakr ibn al-'Arabī of Córdoba (d. 1148).
50. See, for example, the chapter "Rabi'a the Teacher," in Rkia E. Cornell, *Rabi'a from Narrative to Myth: The Many Faces of Islam's Most Famous Woman Saint, Rabi'a al-'Adawiyya (ca. 717–801 CE)* (London: Oneworld Academic, 2019).
51. This quotation and what follows are taken from Denis Gril, "*Adab* and Revelation as One of the Foundations of the Hermeneutics of Ibn 'Arabī," *Muhyiddin Ibn 'Arabi, A Commemoration Volume*, eds. S. Hirtenstein and M. Tiernan (Shaftesbury: Element Books, 1993), 228–263.
52. This statement was conveyed personally to me over dinner during a visit by Gilles Kepel to Duke University in the late 1990s.

SELECT BIBLIOGRAPHY

'Abduh, Muḥammad (1897/1966), *The Theology of Unity*, trans. Isḥāq Musa'ad and Kenneth Cragg, London: George Allen & Unwin, Ltd.

Ali, Souad T. (2009), *A Religion, Not A State: Ali 'Abd al-Raziq's Islamic Justification of Political Secularism*, Salt Lake City, UT: University of Utah Press.

Appiah, Kwame Anthony (2006), *Cosmopolitanism: Ethics in a World of Strangers*, New York: W.W. Norton & Company Inc.
Goshen-Gottstein, Alon, ed. (2014), *The Crisis of the Holy: Challenges and Transformations in World Religions*, Lanham, MD: Lexington Books.
Goshen-Gottstein, Alon, ed. (2014), *The Religious Other: Hostility, Hospitality, and the Hope of Human Flourishing*, Lanham, MD: Lexington Books.
Juergensmeyer, Mark, ed. (2005), *Religion in Global Civil Society*, Oxford: Oxford University Press.
Kymlicka, Will (2007), *Multicultural Odysseys: Navigating the New International Politics of Diversity*, Oxford: Oxford University Press.
Lee, Robert D. (1997), *Overcoming Tradition and Modernity: The Search for Islamic Authenticity*, Boulder, CO: Westview Press.
Marshall, David, ed. (2013), *Tradition and Modernity: Christian and Muslim Perspectives*, Washington, DC: Georgetown University Press.
Mirsepassi, Ali and Fernée, Tadd Graham (2014), *Islam, Democracy and Cosmopolitanism: At Home and in the World*, New York: Cambridge University Press.
Mohammadi, Ali, ed. (2002), *Islam Encountering Globalization*, London: Routledge Curzon.
Neusner, Jacob and Chilton, Bruce, eds. (2008), *Religious Tolerance in World Religions*, West Conshohocken, PA: Templeton Foundation Press.
Ramadan, Tariq (2009), *Radical Reform: Islamic Ethics and Liberation*, Oxford: Oxford University Press.

CHAPTER THIRTY-FIVE

Political Theologies in a Post-Christian World

HILLE HAKER

WHAT IS POLITICAL THEOLOGY AND WHY DOES IT MATTER TODAY?

Over the last decades, the question of political theology has reemerged as a lens to interpret and understand the current global order, structures of governance, the moral question of normativity, and theology's or religion's role in the public sphere. Several contributors to the debate presuppose an understanding of God or the Divine that many theologians would consider uncritical, if not ideological. In the current discourse, the Divine serves as the "ultimate" authority regarding normative claims, legitimacy of (political or biopolitical) power,[1] and divine power over history.

Modern political theology has grappled with the distinction between the "religious" and the "secular" order as defining concepts of modernity or postmodernity. The *discourse* on political theology can therefore be regarded as the self-reflection of modern political and moral theory and theology itself regarding its normative sources. Because I am interested in an *ethical* analysis of this discourse, I will address three dimensions: the problem of moral justification, political legitimization, and theology's own grappling with its political dimension. Just like political theology claims that secularism cannot deal with legitimization of political power without framing it in a theological paradigm, many claim that ethics, too, cannot justify its normative claims without the turn to God. Both versions of the idea of divine authority conclude that obedience and duty are anchored in "the old idea of God the law-giver," as Margalit has stated.[2] The question is whether this image of God must—and can—be critiqued from within theology.

Christian theology—the perspective from which I write—has contributed to the discussion of political theology on all three levels, the political, the moral, and the underlying attributes to the divine. Over its whole history, political theology has distinguished between the human and the divine realm. But since Augustine who introduced the concept into theology, Christian theology also claimed that human history rests upon God's *providence*. With this, not just the "human person" or "nature" but *history* is seen in light of God's omniscience and omnipotence. But even in this imagery, God is not *only* the "old lawgiver"— God relates to the world as a lover relates to the beloved; hence, God's attributes are divine benevolence, caritas, justice, and mercy.[3]

Political theology engages in the reflection on the institutional dimension of faith as *ecclesia*. Already the early faith communities required an institutional structure—the letters of Paul to the different communities, among other biblical and non-biblical sources of Early Christianity—offer the historical trace of the effort to allow for differences while sustaining the unity of the faith. But in the Western "Holy Roman Empire" that lasted for more than a millennium and certainly shaped the understanding of Christianity in the West, Christian theology accommodated to its political role within the empire, shaping both the *empire's* understanding of worldly authority and the *church's* role in the world. Christian theology throughout its history agreed that any theology is, somehow, political theology, but the different groups within Christianity make different claims on how theology should interact with political power—differing in the political spheres of power, and differing depending on what point in history one examines. And, of course, it matters even within Christianity, not to speak of Judaism or Islam, Buddhism, Hinduism, or any of the world religions, whether one speaks from a Roman Catholic, Protestant, Orthodox Christian, or any other denominational perspective, and it matters whether one speaks from the Western political perspective or from another cultural perspective. *Any* political theology, that is, must reflect on the history that is inscribed into the concepts of political theology: political theology in the singular disguises one's particular context and perspective and is therefore prone to absolutizing a specific reading.

Today, the "old" Western political theology that is centered on the question of authority, legitimacy, and political power is often identified with the name of Carl Schmitt who wrote from the particular context of German legal philosophy in the early and mid-twentieth century. He argued for a theology that is like the dwarf in Walter Benjamin's chess machine, hiding under the chess table and secretly steering the moves the visible puppet seems to make.[4] But what does the historical context tell us about this particular notion of political theology, and how does this context inform the concept? When the monarchy collapsed in Germany after a short and failed revolution in 1918/19, at the end of the First World War, Schmitt joined the opponents of democratic governance. With the establishment of the Weimar Republic in 1919, Germany was transformed into a parliamentary democracy. The transition from monarchy to democracy through a revolution was anything but smooth. Many Catholic leaders were sympathetic to the underlying thought of Carl Schmitt's *Political Theology*, because his views mirrored their own political-theological views, secured in the explicitly anti-modern, authoritarian political theology that had been cemented at the First Vatican Council in 1871–1875.[5] Schmitt reinterpreted his political theology—and his views on the National Socialists—after the Second World War, but he certainly never changed his critique of modern liberal democracies.

Over the last few decades Schmitt's critique has, surprisingly, reemerged. Political theology that grapples with Western societies, political systems, and the dominant Christian religion is a term that is used to either *analyze* the legitimization crisis of democracy in Schmitt's vein, to *describe* the anti-liberal groups who turn to religion as the foundation of their value systems, or to *embrace* the theological foundation of modernity. This particular Western discourse on political theology therefore signals both the unresolved relation between religion and modernity in the "West," and it points to two conflicting visions for the role of religion in the public sphere—the one is serving as a moral foundation of the political and moral normative order, and the other is post-Christian. Today, the discourse seems to shift once again. Western democracies are currently witnessing a wave of nationalist populist movements that embrace an authoritarian political governance structure, while left-wing movements advocate for more rather than less democracy. Both movements in Europe and the US coincide in their critique of the "establishment"—i.e., the current governance structure of Western (liberal) democracies—so interruption of the liberal or neoliberal political order is a goal shared by both movements. Even though the Right and the Left differ in their assessment of the concept of *sovereignty and authority*, they both agree in their *critique of modernity* and the *critique of liberal democracy* as a political theory. Right-leaning populists often invoke the Christian political-theological narrative of a state that should be politically and morally guided by God. Insofar as Christian groups promote the political theology in question, the "revolutionary" and "interruptive" understanding of political theology overlaps with the question of how civic/public (moral) discourses are translated into political deliberations and institutional decisions. What is sometimes called a new "culture war" between the two worldviews reflects the political polarization of public discourses, spilling over into the political systems of the US and some European countries.

In the next section, I will explore the question of moral normativity and political legitimacy more closely, narrowing this essay to the Western perspective that grapples with Christianity.[6]

WESTERN MODERNITY AND THE CHALLENGE OF NORMATIVITY AND LEGITIMACY

Moral Justification and the Divine Law

The discourse on political legitimization is part of a shift in modernity that began in the seventeenth century but took another turn in the late eighteenth century. This is often associated with the Kantian Copernican Turn in epistemology and moral thinking. Modern philosophy since Kant assumes that it is impossible to justify normative claims substantively; justification becomes agent-dependent or subject-centered, even though for Kant this does *not* mean that the principles of action are "subjective," i.e., *merely* based on personal convictions. With the concept of autonomy, Kant established a moral principle (the categorical imperative) that every agent must accept qua being an agent, and as an agent among other agents.[7] In the post-Kantian development of modern moral philosophy, moral justification strategies become subject to critiques and deconstruction. Today, postmodern and poststructural theories, for example, hold that the justification of norms is either infinitely *deferred* (Derrida) or contingent on the truth regimes or "norms of intelligibility" that we cannot escape as discursive constraints (Foucault). When moral philosophy invokes human rights or any universal claims, an unjustifiable metaphysics or theology always seems to loom in the background, especially in the form of a normative claim of human nature.[8] Modernity's reference to "inalienable" rights, human dignity, or equality and justice reveals a paradox, postmodern critique implies: it cannot secure "moral truths"—but it cannot turn away from them either. Its blind spot is the invisible, secret, unspoken relation between the human moral "natural law" and a "divine law" that cannot be invoked on rational grounds; rather, this construct is embedded in the metaphysical worldview of the middle ages. Political theology can therefore be understood as a postmodern critical concept that exposes modernity's debt to a metaphysical truth theory without accounting for it. In this premodern worldview the imagery of the Divine reveals an omnipotent, omniscient, and self-sufficient ruler of the world. Within Catholic theology (my own tradition), this view was upheld by the nineteenth- and early-twentieth-century neo-scholastic (political) theology that dominated Catholic moral theology and dogmatic theology until the Second Vatican Council. Though changed considerably since then, it continues to be the theological paradigm of some explicitly anti-modern Catholic groups; and though it has different roots, it is also dominant in a certain strand of US evangelicalism. E. Schuessler-Fiorenza calls this the "kyriarchial theology" within Christianity, alluding to the ecclesial structure of domination and patriarchy that has provoked—among others—the thorough critique of feminist theology.[9]

But the claim of political theology concerning a hidden theological authority may be too quickly accepted in postmodern thinking. Hans Blumenberg, who wrote a seminal study on the "legitimization of modernity," for example, explicitly rejected Carl Schmitt's claim of a secret theological foundation of secularism in the 1960s.[10] He laid out how modernity developed its own *reflective* strategies of justification and legitimization. In a more specifically ethical vein, other German philosophers such as Jürgen Habermas, Karl-Otto Apel, and more recently Rainer Forst have claimed that the justification of normative claims is the *core element* of modern moral philosophy and the backbone of an otherwise arbitrary legitimization of political power.[11] The modern truth theory does not rest upon the "correspondence" between *res* (the objects of knowledge) and *intellectum* (reason), which informed the medieval and early modern natural law theology. Rather, modern truth theory is reflective, *transcendental*, and, in Apel's version, for example, *pragmatic* (Apel calls his justification theory a transcendental pragmatic theory of truth): speakers cannot but make normative claims to each other, which they can only give up at the price of a breakdown of any communication. I will return below to the crucial distinction that Blumenberg, Apel, and Habermas all make, though their theories may differ in other ways: with the recourse to *language*—its possibilities to name "things" metaphorically (Blumenberg), its function, namely communication (Habermas), or its underlying transcendental structure (Apel), the question of normativity and legitimization can be addressed adequately and non-metaphysically. And since language is pivotal for theology, emphasizing hermeneutics and communication, it may also pave the way for a new understanding of political theology. For ethics, this critique of the critique, namely of postmodern relativism, is of utmost importance for a theological-ethical renewal of political theology that I will develop further below. Here, I just wanted to point to the fact that a modern truth theory is possible without reference to foundational metaphysical claims. That there is almost no engagement with these opposing analyses within political theology may well point to its own blind spot, namely the imagery of divine authority.

The Authority of the Sovereign God/Führer in Political Theology

In an essay on the "authority of God" from 2005, which he revised in 2013 (the revisions concerned Islamic political theology that is beyond the scope of this essay), Avishai Margalit states the following: "In my account, authority and sovereignty have contents which are independent of a religious theological frame, yet these notions are in the grip of a theological picture of the world. To be in the grip of a picture is to confuse a model of reality with reality without being aware of it."[12] Margalit is interested in the images at play in political theology, and he offers a genealogy that is, at least in part, interesting for my perspective, because it further contextualizes the early-twentieth-century debate between anarchists and authoritarians, to which Schmitt's political theology belongs. The debate on the justification of coercion and violence—either as state violence against certain groups within the citizenry or as the violence of revolutionary groups—had accompanied modern political theory since the French Revolution but became virulent again in view of the Russian Revolution of 1917 and after the German November

Revolution of 1919 and the subsequent Weimar Republic.[13] Bakunin stood for the anarchist view, Schmitt for the authoritarian one. In both versions, Margalit argues, God appears as "father," "king," or "sovereign," even though the conception of this sovereign power differs strikingly in each political approach, revealing a "fascist picture of God." Beyond the need of any justification, political deliberation, or expertise, "God" is conceived as the supreme leader and the "supreme decision maker." His (sic!) authority is based on his omniscience, omnipotence, and supreme benevolence; hence he commands, and he demands obedience. Schmitt's political theology does not critique but *evokes* a God whose authority rests on his absolute will that is "beyond good and evil," beyond the "laws of nature," and unconstrained by any reasoning. The relationship to him is one of "fear and love." Margalit demonstrates how the imagery of political power and the divine reinforce each other until they blend into the one imagery of the sovereign *Führer*: "The secular counterpart to the principle of the authority of the big decider is terribly grim. It is the Führerprinzip that establishes the absolute authority of the leader, due to his charismatic power as a resolute decider" (90). A renewed political theology has therefore three options regarding the justification of normative claims: first, it may embrace the critique of "secular" legitimacy and justification and opt for a political-theological *decisionism* regarding political legitimacy as well as moral justifications—but if it does so, it must be clear about the "grim" implications concerning the model of authority it uses. Second, it may adopt the postmodern radical critique of normativity and focus its work on the critical deconstruction of truth claims, or on genealogies of concepts that contribute to the different truth regimes.[14] This option is taken up by many philosophers today—but it must also be aware of the fact that in the practical and political realm, this may result in the same decisionism that the postmodernists criticize as the political ramifications of Schmitt's position. Third, a renewed political theology may embrace more fully the "modern" non-metaphysical theory of truth that rests upon the subject or agent and the freedom that is necessarily presupposed in any action. I think it is indeed possible for theology to embrace this theory of moral justification, whether in a Neo-Kantian or transcendental-pragmatic fashion.

Freedom and Security in Twenty-First-Century Political Theory

The question of legitimacy has accompanied modern political theory from the beginning. In Hobbes' influential theory, the social contract requires a "trade-off" between the individual's need for security and their (natural) desire for freedom. In this version, political power, personified in the sovereign, accommodates both needs and is legitimized as enforcing the will of all. In spite of political theology's claim that we still live in the Hobbesian paradigm, the concept of security has changed considerably since the seventeenth century, and our understanding of freedom and individual rights, too, has been further developed, for example, as social, economic, and cultural rights, most prominently represented in the UN human rights framework after the Second World War. At the end of the twentieth century, the UN proposed a *Human Security Paradigm* as a response to the insufficient perspective of "national security." The 1994 *Human Development Report*, for example, articulated a particularly modern understanding of the function of security as tied to all human rights, not just the security against violence but also poverty, education, healthcare, etc.[15] But since the 9/11 terror attacks, the paradigm of security has changed again, returning to the Hobbesian version of "trading" one's liberty as a price for security.[16] Following the political-theological script of a distinction between friend and foe, and the Western metaphor of a "crusade" against international terrorism,[17] the US Bush Administration re-framed the threat to security in the lines of a war on terrorism; this "war" is a de-localized, de-contextualized, global conflict, rendering new ways of warfare necessary and legitimate under the virtual concept of "homeland security."[18]

Sovereign authority becomes virulent in declared states of exceptions that endanger the fragile equilibrium of security and freedom. One explanation for the return of the discourse on political theology may therefore be the tension between the United Nations human security paradigm and the "homeland security" paradigm promoted by the US and NATO, while other powers, such as China or Russia, emphasize the previous paradigm of national security. The "homeland" is not merely the physical space of the nation state but rather the virtual space of political influence. The close interaction of private and political surveillance blurs several spheres previously separated; it can be observed when the military contracts more and more with private military and security companies, which not only act in the shadow of public oversight but, also have a high motivation to sell their technologies.[19] Furthermore, military and police collaborate more and more closely, blurring the lines between these two political authorities, too. Finally, commercial data mining and state surveillance programs are no longer separable.[20] *Together*, they transcend any separation of the public and the private sphere that the Hobbesian political theory presupposed, subjecting *all* dimensions of the lives of citizens to surveillance. This means "security" does not necessarily serve the freedom of citizens but becomes an end in itself. The total surveillance even dwarfs Bentham's nineteenth-century panopticon, which Bentham had imagined as a space of surveillance for inmates of prisons. The trade-off between liberty and security envisioned by Hobbes is lost in the totalizing data-mining, whether for commodification or political surveillance. To quote Margalit again: "Security philosophers put a premium on securing *life* rather than securing a *good life*. Security is the only goal worth pursuing in politics. Any power that can secure life is thereby authoritative."[21] Any political theory must attend, however, to the new contexts and constellations of our societies of security and surveillance, and it must factor in its economic dimension.

Liberalism versus Libertarianism

The security paradigm demonstrates how interwoven state authority and economic interests are, but it also reveals a deep conflict between two distinct modern visions, namely political liberalism that builds upon the freedom rights of citizens and individuals that are to be secured by political institutions, and libertarianism, which is an "anarchical" model of freedom that eschews state governance as much as possible.[22] The way the economy operates at the beginning of the twenty-first century has shifted the political parameters towards the libertarian political-economic model: governments continue to withdraw more and more from regulation, especially of the financial market economy since the 1970s,[23] and have thereby followed the libertarian model of political economy rather than liberalism. As a result, politics becomes more and more economy's handmaiden; as their premodern counterparts, governments legitimize property rights, free trade, and economic growth; but the side effect of the libertarian paradigm, critics hold, is a new form of global economic imperialism and economic colonialism.

If political theology is used as an analytical tool to describe the lack of legitimacy, it must adjust to these realities and integrate the intersection of political and economic power concerning the so-called trade-off of liberty for security. The imagery of divine authority may turn out to be far too simplistic, if not even a false imagery to describe the new forms of political and economic power. In the next section I will show how theology must go beyond the justification of normative claims and the debate on political legitimization to offer a more explicitly *critical* theory as political theology and ethics. The first step toward such a critical theology and ethics was made by the so-called "New Political Theology."

A NEW POLITICAL THEOLOGY FOR THE TWENTY-FIRST CENTURY?

The philosophical discourse on political theology raises the question whether theology itself can escape the authoritarian model that rests upon the metaphysics of divine authority and divine law, or, in other words, whether it is possible to envision the *theological* dimension in the concept of political theology differently. This will be my question in the remainder of the chapter, and fortunately I can build upon the works within Christian, and more particularly Catholic, theology developed since the second half of the twentieth century.

Liberation from Injustice and Political Theology as Critique of Modern Ideologies

Seen from a philosophical perspective, the so-called New Political Theology that emerged in the 1970s may be easily tied to revolutionary efforts to overcome the current political order of capitalism and neoliberalism, because it called for the "interruption" of an unjust order. But the New Political Theology started first and foremost as a *theology* that had to grapple with the history of German fascism and the Shoah—and Christianity's complicity within this historical "eclipse of reason" (Horkheimer). The New Political Theology, as the counterpart to Schmittian political theology of the early twentieth century, consequently emerged in the very particular context of post-Second World War Germany. From here, it evolved further both as a political and as a theological approach, with many overlaps between non-Christian and Christian actors and scholars who are engaging in the struggle against injustice, oppression, or domination.[24]

In the following, I will narrow my perspective again to my own denomination, Catholicism, although I claim that the concept of the "theological" speaks for Christian theology as such. In its own self-understanding, the Roman Catholic Church is organized as *community* of all Christian believers (the Greek term *katholikos* means universal), although its nineteenth-century ecclesial model followed the paradigm of the "*societas perfecta*," promoted, among others, by the ultramontane theologians at the First Vatican Council, and highly influenced by German theologians.[25] In spite of the changes of its self-identity as a sacramental Church at the Second Vatican Council (1961–1965), the internal *governance* structure of the Catholic Church still reflects a pre-democratic, premodern, and hierarchical political theory. The pontiff's power was affirmed under Pope John Paul II and Pope Benedict XVI,[26] although under the papacy of Pope Francis it has begun a new reform process that is more episcopal than papal. Today, the political status of the Vatican at the United Nations is interesting: Neither "merely" a nongovernmental organization nor a state proper, the Catholic Church has a special status as a "permanent observer." With this, it can use its authority to influence initiatives even though it has no voting right.

It is not necessary here to rehearse the history of the New Political Theology; rather, I want to point to some of its elements that I find still relevant today. As a *theological* concept it spoke "ad intra" rather than "ad extra," aiming at reflecting theology's role in its own time. As a *political* concept, it unmasked the privatization of theology as cutting itself off from the political affairs that must be a concern for theology, namely the suffering and harm of people, and the oppression and structural sins against peoples or groups. As a *public political theology*, the New Political Theology unmasked the partiality of liberalism and its involvement and/or complicity with structural injustice from its own partial perspective, namely the solidarity with the suffering. The new movement departed strikingly both from the political-theological decisionism *and* a hermeneutic theology that erases theology's political dimension. Instead, it offered a radical reinterpretation of the "authority of God," embodied in the suffering individual or suffering people. It refocused Christian theology's emphasis on dogmas to the *orthopraxis* of liberation and the struggle for justice. Finally, it offered theology a method, namely critical theory, that it adapted from the German Frankfurt School, especially the "Critical Theory" of Max Horkheimer, further developed by Theodor W. Adorno. Horkheimer had claimed as early as 1937 that "critical theory," in contrast to "traditional theory," reflects its *situatedness* within societal contexts and its function within the capitalist context of modernity.[27] Critical theory is *self-critique* of the modern subject and *social critique* of the capitalist order that transforms any good into a commodity. Critical theory is *partial*, because it has an emancipatory (or liberationist) *interest* in changing the practices that reify and commodify human nature as much as the non-human nature, and human practices in general.

After the Second World War, critical theory intensified its critique of modern subjectivity; what had been envisioned by the liberal modern theory as the "autonomous, sovereign subject" had turned out to be the "bureaucratic murderous subject," later exemplified in the German National Socialist Adolf Eichmann.[28] Adorno and Horkheimer responded to the "eclipse of reason" with a "negative critique," i.e., the critique of injustice, violence, oppression, and human evil as the only vision sustainable after the Shoah.[29] Others later argued for a communitarian philosophy, in order to counter the "atomism" and individualism of modern morality.[30] Metz agreed with critical theory's central focus on the "suffering subject," turning the utopian vision of modernity into a negative universalism, i.e., the imperative to "negate" and overcome moral harm, structural oppression, and, ultimately, any form of injustice, instead of depicting another ideal or "perfect society." Metz's political theology could embrace, with a greater persuasion than ever before, the *eschatological proviso* that had accompanied political theology since Augustine, without having to give up on theology's hope of the "rupture" in and of history.[31] Metz famously claimed that anthropology without the turn to history loses its critical edge; as theology, however, it must see history in "the eschatological horizon of hope."[32] With a view to this *critical, historical*-hermeneutical horizon, theology became a critical political theology.

In Metz's theology in particular, Christianity's Jewishness turns out to be its own forgotten "other side." The Shoah is the abyss that separates the two religions, and yet the *recognition* of Auschwitz is the presupposition for any Christian theology from this point in time onwards. Theological reasoning cannot, Metz holds, evade theodicy as long as human suffering and evil exists, but theodicy is exactly what has become impossible after Auschwitz. Theology, therefore, is first and foremost a question to God, and a questioning of the image of God as sovereign, omniscient, and omnipotent ruler of history. Put differently: when theology speaks *of* God (*theo-logein*), it must not render invisible or inaudible the question addressed *to* God that initiated theology's reflection in the first place, and this is the question how the hope in God can be justified in a world of evil.

Political theology was (and is) therefore a theology and *ethics* of the suffering human person and the oppressed people—and not a theology of the "polis" as state, or a theology of political sovereignty. Schmitt's political theology was the secularized "theology" of the emperors; the *new* political theology was the theology of the forgotten people, the "wretched of the earth" (Fanon). For twentieth-century Christian theology, these were not abstract alternatives of theological or political systems; they were the alternatives between standing with Hitler or the Confessional Church and Catholic resisters, with Pinochet or the dissidents in Chile, with the South African white apartheid regime or the prisoner Nelson Mandela. And within the Catholic Church, it was the alternative between standing with the Vatican pontiff or the women, the victims of sexual abuse, the homosexuals, and all the other forgotten and overlooked victims of modern church history—they all were now declared the *subjects of theo-logy*, no longer the obedient recipients of the supreme pontiff's commands. The New Political Theology that I explored from my own particular context in Germany was a diverse global theological movement, urging Christianity to let the "subaltern" speak (Spivak), listen, and stand with them. Liberation theology, postcolonial theology, contextual theology—and finally, the many faces of feminist, womanist, or *mujerista* theology are all part of this new, multifaceted, contextual political theology. They all rest at least on three premises: first, personal freedom cannot be conceived without social, economic, and political liberation; second, political institutions must be constantly scrutinized for structures of oppression and injustice; and third, theology is necessarily critical of Christianity's own political structures and institutions.

Political Theology in the Public-Political Moral Discourse

Theology's contribution to the discourse on political theology was twofold: on the one hand, it insisted on the difference between the political and the theological, while remapping the political engagement of the Church and theology; on the other hand, it upheld the hope that human freedom *together* with social, economic, and political justice is possible. As *theology*, it was more than a theological hermeneutics of the plural contexts;[33] at its core, it entailed a Christian *ethics*: it defined its core task to *remember* what—and who—would otherwise be forgotten; to stand in *solidarity* with and to *advocate* for those who are the victims of modernity's progress. Political theology vowed to make the undignified, suffering people not the recipient and object of theology but its acting subject.

Political theology stands for the relation of the public political and moral discourse and theology's own *ethical* reflection on four intersecting levels. First, it reflects on the person's values, commitments, and goods; second, on these values as socially mediated, expressed in habits or dispositions; third, it reflects on the normative principles of action; and fourth, on the structures of justice.[34] As a political-theological ethics, it confronts the relationship of the institutionalized political deliberations and decision-making procedures in democracies as well as the Church's governance structures with the social-ethical principles of moral judgment: among these principles, developed in the history of Catholic social teaching, are the principle of *solidarity* and *justice* and/or the common good, the principle of the *priority* of those who are most dependent on assistance and institutional support, and the principle of *subsidiarity* and *participation* in the enforcement of action plans. The emphasis on agency, agents' necessary participation in social actions, and the contribution to political decisions all point to the public sphere as the forum for a peaceful, yet agonistic competition of ideas, visions, and ways to transform injustice into more justice. It obviously raises the question of representation and the ways the plurality of values and voices are mirrored in the democratic decisions. In this discourse, Christian theology insists on the fundamental moral principles of *freedom and dignity*, and their connection with social, economic, and political justice. As a political theology, it does not confront these principles from a "disinterested," impartial perspective; rather, it advocates for them in the public competition of political ideas, visions, and ways to transform the present injustice into justice. It is partial, because it speaks from the perspective of those whose stakes in the current order are a question of survival, namely the victims who may not have a voice in the public discourses. As *theology*, its recourse to God is not the emperor-king or sovereign as a secret power above and beyond history—quite to the contrary, its recourse (and authority) is the *crucified God* (Moltmann), encountered *in* history and *in* the world, in any suffering individual or group. Theology's deck in the public political and moral discourse therefore entails no trump card. All it has is its faith as *conviction and commitment* that to claim respect of human freedom and dignity, to care for all creatures, and to insist on justice as the foundation of the global social contract *is* the human way to encounter God in the world.

But here an abyss opens between the New Political Theology, liberation theology, and my own approach. Whereas the New Political Theology is in the most part (still) indebted to a theory of freedom that is rooted in the tradition of natural law (though reinterpreted in line with human rights), it is *also* indebted to a teleological theology of history, be it in the name of a salvation history or God's providence, eschatology or apocalypticism as the "interruption" of time. I do not think that this is a possible path for a theology informed by postcolonialism, and it has ramifications both for theology's own theory of truth regarding moral justifications and political legitimizations, and for its relation to history.

Political Theology and the Question of Normativity

A theological justification of moral claims does not require a metaphysical foundation of truth; as ethics, it can follow modern philosophy's non-metaphysical, *reflective* justification of normativity. This means, however, that political theology must *itself* reject a metaphysical principle of morality or any theological legitimization of politics, because both would necessarily result in the authoritarian model of the "old lawgiver." This has multiple ramifications for a renewal of Christian ethics as one element of political theology.

First, a renewed Christian political ethics will take up the correction of liberation theology that modifies and corrects the philosophical theory of freedom; over against the transcendental and ahistorical freedom of eighteenth and early nineteenth centuries moral philosophy, liberation reflects the dynamic, historical, and social dimension of freedom. Liberation, we can take from this, is a *task* while freedom is a transcendental condition of agency; and it requires to practically transform the lack or loss of rights into the agential freedom and capability to act, to wit, in concrete historical, cultural, and political contexts.

Second, Christian theology can explain through its own sources why morality is not blind obedience to a "divine law" but, to the contrary, it enables human freedom. Taking the agency of an agent seriously, morality turns the self into a responsible subject who must not only respond to the other and others, but who must also justify her actions to others (and herself). The conviction and commitment to faith gives a person's responsive and responsible action a direction, namely to seek God in others, while these "others" are those who are disregarded and misrecognized in the different contexts of social norms and values.

Third, regarding our present political context in the West, political theology must continue to be a *critical theology*; for example, it must not only confront the current security paradigm as contrary to the broader paradigm of human security that is linked to human rights and responsibilities; it must also critique the individualized concept of liberal *and* libertarian freedom, emphasizing instead the necessary connection of individual and social freedom as a way to provide a fuller picture of human security.

Fourth, as a critical *public* and, hence, political-ethical voice, political theology must therefore advocate for the memory and visibility, i.e., for the *recognition* of those who are forgotten or "thrown away" in the uninterrupted grand narrative of freedom and self-determination.

Fifth, as a *constructive political theology*, it must make its faith publicly intelligible; it will promote its faith in the God of love and compassion, and of liberation and justice, who may give meaning to human existence, experientially and existentially. It takes the divine not as an abstract concept but as a God who addresses the world and humans and responds to them, notwithstanding that *She Who Is* is, ultimately, a mystery.[35] This God can (and must) be addressed in the performative forms of human language that we call dialogue, conversation, or prayer. In contrast to the authoritarian political theology in which the "sovereign" calls for obedience and submission, political theology's models are Abraham, Moses, and the prophets, whom God calls, seeking the conversation, even negotiation, who in turn may not only respond devotedly, but also with questions and questioning. After all, as Margalit says at the end of his essay, "Human understanding is a constraint on the way God understands Himself, even when God is trying to be a decisionist God who is not constrained by morality."[36]

A POLITICAL-HISTORICAL HERMENEUTICS

Theo-logy itself is indeed bound to and bound by its own *language*. Therefore, theology is necessarily hermeneutics, the theory of understanding, interpretation, and translation. Political theology claims that God has made herself intelligible throughout history: seeking freedom and peace, standing with the human beings despite all their evil acts. All the metaphors we may use for God—the sovereign, the ruler, the king—ultimately point back to us. A renewed political theology will, however, help us to unlearn the empire imageries of God and learn to replace them with the images of the caring and loving parent, the passionate and suffering brother, and the anamnetic spirit of remembrance who reminds us not to forget our commitment and our hope. Hermeneutics is necessarily historical, contextual, and partial. It will be in part critical (of normative orders who disguise their origin and entanglement with the finite history of injustice), political, and "deconstructive," but it will also be constructive. For Walter Benjamin, understanding requires contemplation as attention to the other, be it a text or another person, but it is also a *sudden moment* of insight that brings the other and the self—or the past and the present—into a constellation that flashes up as if they were meant for each other. The image of the past that appears in a sudden constellation is deeply *historical*. Its contours are dependent on the moment in which the constellation occurs, the present moment or *Jetztzeit*, as Benjamin called it. Working on a new philosophy of history, Benjamin inserts an image (sic!) of this encounter between past and present, namely the constellations of stars; despite their "givenness" (in this case: their positions) they are never exactly the same over time, and they depend on the perspective of the observer. His hermeneutics is therefore akin to phenomenology's premise of intentionality, without, however, transforming the act of knowledge into an a-historical and a-political theory of experience, as Husserl did. Gadamer's later developed theory of understanding as "blending of horizons" also differs from this concept of the constellation, because it still rests on a metaphysical ontology of truth that manifests in history. Following Benjamin, understanding reveals a *historical* rather than an ontological truth—but it is the truth of negative universalism: "history" is dangerous for its victims at any given moment, and the danger of the victims of the past is that they will be forgotten. The historian's task is to fan "the spark of hope in the past": "Only that historian will have the gift of fanning the spark of hope in the past who is firmly convinced that *even the dead* will not be safe from the enemy if he wins. And this enemy has not ceased to be victorious."[37] Benjamin wrote this in 1940, in the midst of the Nazi terror that had stripped him of his citizenship, forced him to emigrate, with little hope for his own future. Likewise, James Carroll reminds us of the task of memory today: "Memory is a political act. Forgetfulness is the handmaiden of tyranny."[38] The political theologian's task, however, goes beyond the historian's task since political theology insists that hope exists at any moment; it exists in the "back" of action, not in its front, which means that a theology focused on the transformative actions and practices must not forget that its task is to fan the spark of hope in the here and now.

CONCLUSION

In the seventeenth century, a popular image showed "Lady World" who in the front was beautiful and fashionable, while rotting in ugliness at her back, being eaten away by worms and death. The (Protestant) religion-inspired dramas of the time responded to the devastation of the Thirty Years War (1628–1648), which destroyed much of Europe, with a political theology that urged the submission to God, the sovereign of history, as salvation from the hubris that had led to the downfall of empire after empire. Another history of early modern and modern Protestant Christian political theology would need to start here, with the blending of this sovereign God with the Anglo-Saxon myth of the "white man's" supremacy in the nineteenth and twentieth centuries.[39] In the narrative of modern political theology, modernity's visible public face seems to have a hidden side of destruction similar to depictions of "Lady World" in the seventeenth century.

When the more recent discourse on political theology emerged, it pointed to the blending of the premodern image of the omniscient, omnipotent, and sovereign God above law and beyond history with the political powers in Western liberal democracies. But the history of the "Empire" is not the *only* story of modernity: like the European world responded to the Thirty Years War with the Westphalian Order, the "United Nations" responded to the atrocities of Hitler's Nazism, the war, and the atom bombs dropped on Hiroshima and Nagasaki with a new moral framework, one that is grounded in universal individual human rights, moral and political responsibilities, and democratic procedures.

These human rights entail both the right to personal, social, and political freedom, and the right to "human security" as defined in its personal, social, cultural, and economic dimensions by the UN. For this "alternative" paradigm to freedom, formerly understood as liberty of citizens, and political power as national sovereignty, the philosophical theory of freedom is indispensable and must be embraced by theology too. Theology does not need to skirt modernity's turn to subjectivity in favor of a metaphysical concept of nature;

rather, it must take the vulnerable, yet responsible self as the starting point and center of its ethics.[40] It can neither follow Thomas Aquinas' concept of theo-nomy (natural law resting on the divine law) nor can it fully embrace Kant's concept of auto-nomy (the self-imposed universal law, as respect of dignity); rather, it will follow an understanding of human freedom that rests upon the dialectic of the self's fundamental heteronomous origin or *givenness* and its *affectability* by others and *effectiveness* on others through its own actions. Hence, just like philosophy, theology insists that reason *and* faith require the self-reflective process of discernment and justification. At the beginning of the twenty-first century, we are still only beginning to see how this concept of the self or human subjectivity translates into a new political theology and a new ethics of Christian theology.[41] Seen from theology's view, faith does not take away but *requires* the commitment to freedom, understood as the responsibility for liberation from injustice, and this points to the space of political debates. This is the alternative story of modernity that needs not fear theology but may be inspired by it: obedience to God is not the blind submission to a sovereign power but commitment to the engagement for freedom and justice.

Throughout human history, freedom and justice have always been fragile and always at risk of being pushed aside in the name of a higher purpose that *sacrifices* (sic!) the individual. It is for this reason that political theology must be *critical*. Being one voice among others in the critique of injustice and repression and oppression of freedom, and speaking from the inside (or underside) rather than from a view "above and beyond" the world, Christian political theology will strive to bring the present into a constellation with its own tradition, trusting that the theo-political remembrance of God's call to a metanoia (as *change* of actions and practices, due to the insight in injustice, harm, or evil) may indeed motivate political actions that transform oppression into freedom, and injustice into justice.

Any Christian theology, and political theology in particular, must justify its faith that is based on this hope: "Always be prepared to give an answer to everyone who asks you to give the reason for the hope that you have" (1 Pet 3:15). I have argued that political theology's hope is not bound to a providential theology of history. Rather, it is conceived from the space of human suffering and is prompted by those without hope: "Only for the sake of the hopeless ones have we been given hope."[42] A renewed critical political theology claims that the God who became human is still *among us*—and not doing well. Hidden in the "dark side" of modernity, she is invisible and forgotten. She does not dwell among the "presidents." She is not safe and sovereign but *crucified*, again and again. God, Christian theology insists, dwells among the "undignified" of our time, among the starving, suffering, raped, and tortured children, women, and men, and among the killed bodies that are piling up in history.

In the back of modern life, several non-places mirror the u-topias of modernity, yet as their negative; they are the literal and virtual spaces where nobody can live, or live a good life, such as landfills, porn studios, refugee camps, maquiladoras, war zones, but also homes that do not offer protection against domestic violence, etc. Doing theo-logy from the *perspective* of these *non-spaces*, political theology will speak to humans about God, and to God about humans. It will speak of suffering, despair, injustice, anger—and hope, and, maybe even of the hope of *interruption*—not as the "end of the law," as so many anti-Judaistic theologies have done, but as the end of the passion of all suffering people. Political theology reminds God and humans of the cries that God hears and the pain that God feels as her own pain. Speaking about its own history, political theology will remember Christianity's own sins against humanity. It will listen and speak to the victims and to the perpetrators in the ever-changing contexts of history; but at the same time, political theology will not cease to trans-late, i.e. to bring forth the human stories to God, in the hope that she will reciprocate not as a judge but as a lover who responds, again and again, to the beloved.

NOTES

1. With Foucault, I distinguish between the "sovereign" power that dominates until early modernity, and biopower that governs through self-disciplinary and managerial regimes. Since the end of the nineteenth century, this "regime" of biopower has been further developed as a system of surveillance. At the end of the twentieth century, however, we see the effort to complement biopower with the sovereign power of the state through new surveillance technologies that Foucault could not foresee; this changes the analysis of the "self-governance" yet again. Cf. Foucault: sexuality and truth; governmentality.
2. Avishai Margalit, "Revisiting God's Authority," *Social Research* 80, no. 1 (2013): 84.
3. The juxtaposition of the Jewish Law and Christian Love has often been used as an anti-Judaistic trope within Christianity.
4. 'Walter Benjamin, "On the Concept of History," in *Selected Writings: 4: 1938–1940* (Cambridge, MA: Harvard University Press, 2006), 389–400; Slavoj Žižek, *The Puppet and the Dwarf: The Perverse Core of Christianity* (Cambridge, MA: MIT Press, 2003).
5. Cf. Brian Fox, "Schmitt and Political Catholicism: Friend or Foe?" (CUNY, 2015).
6. I acknowledge this explicitly as one perspective among many.
7. There are several versions of a Kantian ethics in contemporary ethics, among others offered by Onora O'Neill, Alan Gewirth, or Christine Korsgaard.
8. And insofar as modernity's normative ideal of "human nature" mirrored the white European male, it rendered everyone else to be "deviant," "not yet" at the same stage, or simply the "other," e.g. the "other sex," as Simone Beauvoir famously held. Feminist, postcolonial, and postmodern thinkers alike point to this "blind spot" in the moral edifice of modern moral thought that had disastrous ramifications for global colonial and patriarchal politics.
9. Elisabeth Schüssler Fiorenza, *Discipleship of Equals: A Critical Feminist EkkleēSia-Logy of Liberation* (New York: Crossroad, 1993); *The Power of the Word: Scripture and the Rhetoric of Empire* (Minneapolis, MN: Fortress Press, 2007). John Paul II and Pope Benedict also claimed that moral truths are *divine* truths that are as unchangeable as the laws of nature.
10. Pini Ifergan, "Cutting to the Chase: Carl Schmitt and Hans Blumenberg on Political Theology and Secularization," *New German Critique* 111, no. Fall (2010). Blumenberg and Schmitt corresponded extensively about this dispute, and it is surprising how little attention Blumenberg's critique has received in the current discourse.
11. Habermas and Apel take up the insights of the Pragmatist tradition, especially the philosophy of C.S. Peirce. For a very insightful summary of the arguments cf. Karl-Otto Apel, "Pragmatism as Sense-Critical Realism Based on a Regulative Idea of Truth: In Defense of a Peircean Theory of Reality and Truth," *Transactions of the Charles S. Peirce Society: A Quarterly Journal in American Philosophy* 37, no. 4 (2001). For Habermas' and Forst's works cf. Jürgen Habermas, *Justification and Application: Remarks on Discourse Ethics* (Cambridge, MA: MIT Press, 1994); Rainer Forst, *Das Recht Auf Rechtfertigung. Elemente Einer Konstruktivistischen Theorie Der Gerechtigkeit* (Frankfurt: suhrkamp, 2007).
12. Margalit, "Revisiting God's Authority," 84.

13. Walter Benjamin's essay "On the Critique of Violence", which offers a stark critique of decisionism on both sides. For a more thorough analysis Cf. Hille Haker, "Walter Benjamin and Christian Critical Ethics—a Comment," in *Walter Benjamin and Theology*, ed. Colby Dickinson and Stephane Symons (New York: Fordham University Press, 2016).

14. Derrida has offered multiple works that concretize deconstruction, e.g., of forgiveness, of justice, or universalism more general; Foucault has offered major works on truth regimes, e.g., concerning sexuality, madness, punishment, of policing. Both "paths" are indispensable for any ethical or political analysis and must therefore be taken up by a Christian ethics. They certainly offer a methodology that is akin to Adorno's "negative critique" that the "New Political Theology" embraced. However, Derrida and Foucault never clarified the relation between critical analyses and normative claims they must nevertheless make, rendering their own strategies of justification arbitrary and at times immune to critique.

15. Cf. Hille Haker, "The Future of Security and Surveillance," *Journal of Political Science and Public Affairs* 3, no. 1 (2015), 1–6.

16. Conor Gearty, *Liberty and Security* (Cambridge: Polity Press, 2013).

17. Cf. the still valuable article in the Atlantic on the "crusade" metaphor from 2004. James Carrol summarizes Bush's political theology as a cosmic war: "Bush's war openly remains a cosmic battle between nothing less than the transcendent forces of good and evil. Such a battle is necessarily unlimited and open-ended, and so justifies radical actions—the abandonment, for example, of established notions of civic justice at home and of traditional alliances abroad." https://www.thenation.com/article/bush-crusade/

18. Cf. President Bush's speech in the wake of the 9/11 attacks, declaring the war on terror, https://www.theguardian.com/world/2001/sep/21/september11.usa13

19. James Pattison, *The Morality of Private War: The Challenge of Private Military and Security Companies* (Oxford: Oxford University Press, 2014).

20. Susan Landau, *Surveillance or Security? The Risks Posed by New Wiretapping Technologies* (Cambridge, MA: MIT Press, 2011).

21. Margalit, "Revisiting God's Authority," 91.

22. Cf. Robert Nozick, *Anarchy, State, and Utopia* (New York: Basic Books, 1974).

23. Wolfgang Streeck, *Buying Time: The Delayed Crisis of Democratic Capitalism* (New York: Verso, 2014).

24. Cf. for a good overview of the multiple approaches, for example, Craig Hovey and Phillips, Elisabeth, eds., *The Cambridge Companion to Christian Political Theology* (Cambridge MA: Cambridge University Press, 2015).

25. Cf. for a comparison between the First and Second Vatican Council Patrick Granfield, "The Church as Societas Perfecta in the Schemata of Vatican I," *Church History* 48, no. 4 (1979), 434–435. Granfield summarizes the relation in this way: "Emphasis has shifted dramatically from the sociological to the biblical; from the jurisdictional to the sacramental; from the sectarian to the ecumenical; from the papal to the episcopal; from the hierarchical to the collegial" (446).

26. The "Fundamental Law of the Vatican City State", introduced by Pope John Paull II in 2000 and replacing the former Law from 1929 in its entirety, reinforces the pope's sovereign power.

    https://www.google.com/url?sa=t&rct=j&q=&esrc=s&source=web&cd=1&ved=0ahUKEwjBhMys3drXAhWs6YMKHULkBwAQFggoMAA&url=http%3A%2F%2Fwww.vaticanstate.va%2Fcontent%2Fdam%2Fvaticanstate%2Fdocumenti%2Fleggi-e-decreti%2FNormative-Penali-e-Amministrative%2FFundamentalLaw1.pdf&usg=AOvVaw0zbhMJq0chL9sW7Vnc4zk0

27. Max Horkheimer, *Critical Theory: Selected Essays* (New York: Herder and Herder, 1972).
28. Hannah Arendt, *Eichmann in Jerusalem: A Report on the Banality of Evil*, Rev. and enl. ed. (New York: Penguin Books, 1976).
29. Max Horkheimer, *Eclipse of Reason* (New York: Seabury Press, 1974). Theodor Adorno and Max Horkheimer, *Dialectic of Enlightenment* ([S.l.]: Verso Books, 2016). Theodor W. Adorno, *Negative Dialectics* (New York: Continuum, 1983). The latter is a response to the Hegelian and Marxian progressivist philosophy of history. Likewise, the *Dialectic of Enlightenment* provides a critique of modern reason, especially instrumental reason. The philosophy of progress was, however, already questioned at the turn to the twentieth century, when Nietzsche declared the "death of God" and a new philosophy of history that dared to break with teleology as eschatology, to replace the "end" of history with the perfection of history in the "highest exemplars" (Nietzsche). Cf. for the current discussion Amy Allen, *The End of Progress* (New York: Columbia University Press, 2016). She opens a debate that—finally—confronts critical theory with the different perspective on modernity, offered by postcolonial theories.
30. Cf. Charles Taylor, *Sources of the Self: The Making of the Modern Identity* (Cambridge, MA: Harvard University Press, 1989); *Modern Social Imaginaries* (Durham, NC: Duke University Press, 2008); Michael Walzer, *Thick and Thin: Moral Argument at Home and Abroad* (Notre Dame, IN: University of Notre Dame Press, 1994); Alasdair MacIntyre, *Dependent Rational Animals: Why Human Beings Need the Virtues* (Chicago: Open Court Publishing, 1999).
31. The works by Metz, Moltmann, and Sölle are well known and will not be listed here; cf., however, for a discussion among the scholars who shaped political theology: Michael Welker, Francis Schüssler Fiorenza, and Klaus Tanner, eds., *Political Theology: Contemporary Challenges and Future Directions* (Louisville, KY: Westminster John Knox Press, 2013). Cf. for a recent interpretation though with a different emphasis than my own: Lieven Bouve, *God Interrupts History: Theology in a Time of Upheaval* (New York: Continuum, 2007). For my own works on Metz, cf. Hille Haker, "'Compassion Als Weltprogramm Des Christentums'—Eine Ethische Auseinandersetzung Mit Johann Baptist Metz," *Concilium* 37, no. 4 (2001), 436–450; "Walter Benjamin and Christian Critical Ethics—a Comment." Both offer a more thorough analysis of Metz's works.
32. Metz, *Theology of the World*, cit. in Welker, et al., *Political Theology*, 1.
33. David Tracy, *Plurality and Ambiguity: Hermeneutics, Religion, Hope* (San Francisco, CA: Harper & Row, 1987).
34. For a thorough argument of these four spheres of ethics cf. Hille Haker, *Ethik Der Genetischen Frühdiagnostik. Sozialethische Reflexionen Zur Verantwortung Am Menschlichen Lebensbeginn* (Paderborn: mentis, 2002), Chapter 1.
35. Elizabeth A. Johnson, *She Who Is: The Mystery of God in Feminist Theological Discourse* (New York: Crossroad, 1992).
36. Margalit, "Revisiting God's Authority," 98.
37. Benjamin, "On the Concept of History," 391.
38. James Carroll, "The Bush Crusade," in *The Nation* (Sept. 2, 2004). https://www.thenation.com/article/bush-crusade/
39. Eric P. Kaufmann, *The Rise and Fall of Anglo-America* (Cambridge, MA: Harvard University Press, 2004). For an actual account in light of the current racism in the US, cf. Kelly Brown Douglas, *Stand Your Ground: Black Bodies and the Justice of God* (Maryknoll, NY: Orbis Books, 2015).
40. Even though this human rights approach has been criticized, too, by Hannah Arendt or more recently by Christoph Menke, for its shortcomings to secure the "right to have

rights" (Arendt) I have defended it, pointing to Paul Ricœur's concept of capability as responsibility and accountability. Cf. Hille Haker, "No Space. Nowhere. Refugees and the Problem of Human Rights in Arendt and Ricoeur," *Ricoeur Studies* 8, no. 2 (forthcoming).

41. A promising approach has been recently proposed by Linda Zerilli who explores a theory of political judgment that is not based on shared values but on the plural voices within the one "shared world," building upon Arendt's theory of judgment, arguing for the "polis" as the space for disputes and actions: Linda M.G. Zerilli, *A Democratic Theory of Judgment* (Chicago: University of Chicago Press, 2016). This approach is close to Elisabeth Schuessler Fiorenza's understanding of the "katholikos" or a non-kyriarchial ecclesia. Cf.

42. Benjamin, *Selected Writings*, Vol. 1, 356.

SELECT BIBLIOGRAPHY

Arendt, Hannah (1976), *Eichmann in Jerusalem: A Report on the Banality of Evil*, rev. ed., New York: Penguin Books.

Habermas, Jürgen (1994), *Justification and Application: Remarks on Discourse Ethics*, Cambridge, MA: MIT Press.

Horkheimer, Max (1972), *Critical Theory: Selected Essays*, New York: Herder and Herder.

Hovey, Craig, Elisabeth Phillips, eds. (2015), *The Cambridge Companion to Christian Political Theology*, Cambridge: Cambridge University Press.

Johnson, Elizabeth A. (1992), *She Who Is: The Mystery of God in Feminist Theological Discourse*, New York: Crossroad.

Nozick, Robert (1974), *Anarchy, State, and Utopia*, New York: Basic Books.

Schüssler Fiorenza, Elisabeth (1993), *Discipleship of Equals: A Critical Feminist Ekklēsia-Logy of Liberation*, New York: Crossroad.

Schüssler Fiorenza, Elisabeth (2007), *The Power of the Word: Scripture and the Rhetoric of Empire*, Minneapolis, MN: Fortress Press.

Taylor, Charles (1989), *Sources of the Self: The Making of the Modern Identity*, Cambridge, MA: Harvard University Press.

Tracy, David (1987), *Plurality and Ambiguity: Hermeneutics, Religion, Hope*, San Francisco, CA: Harper & Row.

Welker, Michael, Francis Schüssler Fiorenza, and Klaus Tanner, eds. (2013), *Political Theology: Contemporary Challenges and Future Directions*, Louisville, KY: Westminster John Knox Press.

Žižek, Slavoj (2003), *The Puppet and the Dwarf: The Perverse Core of Christianity*, Cambridge, MA: MIT Press.

CHAPTER THIRTY-SIX

Everybody Hates the Prophet

Failure and the Good Society in Jewish Political Theology

LAURIE ZOLOTH

INTRODUCTION: A POLITICAL THEOLOGY OF THE BREACH

58:1 Cry aloud, spare not, lift up your voice like a trumpet, and show my people their transgression, and the house of Jacob their sins.

58:2 Yet they seek me daily, and delight to know my ways, as a nation that did righteousness, and forsook not the ordinance of their God: they ask of me the ordinances of justice; they take delight in approaching God.

58:3 Why have we fasted, say they, and you see not? Why have we afflicted our soul, and you take no knowledge? Behold, in the day of your fast you find pleasure, and perform all your ordinary work.

58:4 Behold, you fast for strife and debate, and to smite with the fist of wickedness: you shall not fast as you do this day, to make your voice to be heard on high.

58:5 Is it such a fast that I have chosen? a day for a man to afflict his soul? Is it to bow down his head as a bulrush, and to spread sackcloth and ashes under him? will you call this a fast, and an acceptable day to the Lord?

58:6 Is not this the fast that I have chosen? To loosen the bands of wickedness, to undo the heavy burdens, and to let the oppressed go free, and that you break every yoke?

58:7 Is it not to deal your bread to the hungry, and that you must bring in the poor that are cast out to your house? When thou see the naked, that you must cover him; and that you should hide yourself not from your own flesh?

58:8 Then shall your light break forth as the morning, and your health shall spring forth speedily: and your righteousness shall go before you; the glory of the Lord shall be your reward.

58:9 Then shall you call, and the Lord shall answer; you shall cry, and He shall say, Here I am. If you take away from the midst of you the yoke, the putting forth of the finger, and speaking vanity;

58:10 And if you draw out your soul to the hungry, and satisfy the afflicted soul; then shall your light rise in darkness, and your darkness be as the noon day:

58:11 And the Lord shall guide you continually, and satisfy your soul in drought, and make fat your bones: and you shall be like a watered garden, and like a spring of water, whose waters fail not.[1]

What can we say about this text?

Isaiah is angry with the anger of the prophet. He is complaining, as Jewish prophets are wont to do, to God, and turning, after three verses, to the failing people of Israel, the choreograph of his position just under the words, as his imprecations become the trumpet he has asked God to sound. The alchemy of the verses transforms first the prophet into a divine instrument of rebuke, and finally, if the people can manage to reorder their society and economy, the people will become another divine instrument: "your light shall rise in darkness." This is no ordinary text: in the Jewish liturgical cycle, it occupies a central place, read each year during the fast of Yom Kippur, the Day of Atonement, when Jews for the last thousand years are the most likely to be listening to a formalized reading: ritual is meaningless, the text insists, unless the economy is just. Religion cannot stand apart from politics, from hungry people, from your vulnerable human flesh, from the homeless one, naked in the autumn, slanted, sun outside your synagogue. It is quite a claim on a day at the end of a season of complex rituals wherein, for example, palm branches and willows are shaken while medieval chants are sung, where the priestly ritual of the Second Temple is read aloud and enacted by a crowd of worried Jews in the synagogue. But Isaiah is there to mock you, and to turn you toward the door, where the political world of power and loss is where one must live. The world is broken, in his time and in ours, and this broken, chaotic, unlawful quality of the world is our fault entirely, an error of greed, and a theological error as well. The God of Israel has written the care of the poor into the Law, and a just world is the entire task, it is all that dispels darkness.

This essay will turn to the critique of Israel's failure, and argue that Jewish political theology is largely, though not, of course, entirely, a rebuke. Humans, the People Israel, who are to live within a covenantal relation with a Divine lawgiver, fail over and over again, managing only in teleological time to imagine a consistent return to a well-ordered, divinely righteous theo-political economy. Jewish political theology cannot escape the repeated construction of a negation, an absence, a breech. This breech, this absence, is the first response, of course, to God's intense presentness at Sinai.

THE ORGANIZATION OF JUSTICE

The organization of the system of economic justice is based on two core concepts in Jewish political theology. First, that the seminal moral experience of the Jewish people is the liberation by God from Egyptian genocidal slavery, a slavery so totalizing and a liberation so astonishing that it has shaped the rationale for behavior, the capacity for solidarity with other oppressed people, and, as analyzed by Michael Walzer,[2] allowed a unifying story of liberation to be continuously associated with religious faith. Second, the act of giving the law as a public event (and an event that is repeated three times in the rabbinic imagination) means that each person[3] is capable of participation in the covenant, capable of enacting the law, and responsible to do so. This is radical equality, based on the possession of equal plots of land, in a holy, Promised Land that is imagined in the first five books of Jewish Scripture. It is intended to be an egalitarian theory of justice, based on the concept, so difficult to maintain, as Emmanuel Kant understood, that every individual is a kingdom of ends. This ipseity, this dignity, this authority and capacity make it possible to own and to choose and to give, the basis of politics itself.

Moreover, woven into the theo-political is the economic reality, which is detailed along with the promises of equality. An agricultural society is by nature unfair: crops fail, drought sweeps across regions, there are locusts, and crazy oxen who gore and must be killed. The children can die, one by one, in a day of the plague. People lose their minds, sometime they are a bit lazy. One can lose everything, one can sell their land by pieces and end up with nothing. You can arrive at the gate of your neighbor wearing only one shirt, one pair of pants, over your nakedness.

This failure is inevitable, a feature of labor in an unredeemed world. God, moreover, is not physically present to offer assistance, not to actually provide manna and columns of fire, and salvation from locusts. But the theo-political rests on two realities: the extraordinary abundance of God's creation, and the infinite possibility of generosity between persons. Thus we see in this section of Leviticus, in the midst of the giving of complex ritual laws for priests, this admonition—you are the one responsible for justice.

> Leviticus 25:35 If your brother grows poor and his hand falters with you, you shall support him, as though he is a resident alien, so that he shall live with you.
> 36 Do not take interest and profit, but fear your God, that your brother may live with you.
> 37 You shall not give him money for interest nor shall you give him your food for profit.
> 38 I, am your God, and I brought you out of the land of Egypt to give to you the land of Canaan to be your God.
> 39 And if your brother grows poor with you and sells himself to you, do not work him in the work of a worker.
> 40 As a hired hand and as a resident alien he shall be with you; until the year of the jubilee he shall serve with you.
> 41 And then he will go away from being with you; he and his children with him. He will return to his family; he will return to the holding of his fathers.
> 42 Because they are my servants, the ones that I brought forth from the land of Egypt. They shall not be sold for sale as slaves.
> 43 You shall not have dominion over him with harshness, but you shall fear your God.

In the biblical imaginary, the world is abundant and fecund in antiquity. The harvest is usually overwhelming, there is enough food growing wild for a sabbatical year to be sustainable. If food is not hoarded, or people do not descend into gluttony, there is enough to share: that is the order of the world created by God, a theological claim. This extra, the corners of the field, the harvest left over for gleaning, for you cannot even gather it all, is not yours. It is not because you are so clever. It is the possession of the poor, left to them by God—this is the argument of the texts. This is to be a world in which every single festival meal is to be shared by the people that are working for you, the poor a part of the festival, intrinsic to its proper celebration.

Of concern in the biblical texts, and continuing throughout the rabbinic period, is the problem of debt and forgiveness. In Jewish texts, this means literal, monetary debt and debt forgiveness, not metaphysical or existential debt. Interest between Jews—making money off of money—cannot be charged. What this attention to debt means is the surfacing of assumed "takings." In our own period, this has particular resonance, of course, for we live in a world made possible only by the invisible labor of others, but in antiquity this was equally the case, however rich the theological possibility that one loan could right the individual and restore him and his family to their land. Intuitions like the sabbatical year, which was intended to cancel all debt, and the jubilee year, which was intended to restore the original biblical allotment system, were part of the radical promise of a new life in a new land.

Dignity and ipseity continue to exist after the Roman occupation and subsequent laws that prohibited owning land. As Jews moved into urban centers, rabbinic adaptations were made to reinterpret the Scriptural laws. But the larger, stable premises remained: Jews were freed slaves where each person was capable of liberatory choices, given a Law that if followed would create a well-ordered and just world.

For Abraham Joshua Heschel, the call of God to the People Israel continues to exist in the relationship between religious law, halacha, and the ethical obligations one continues to carry toward the other, despite one's own conditions. One has an obligation toward liberation: "The glory of a free society lies not only in the consciousness of my right to be free, and my capacity to be free, but also in the realization of my fellow man's right to be free, and his capacity to be free." The other-directedness of this theology—not only my freedom, but also yours—allows the Jew to always imagine that she lives within a polity of inescapable concern, under God's gaze, and human enactment, whenever she lives within the binding of the Law.

SO WHY IS IT SO HARD TO BE GOOD?

In short, in a theo-political economy much of the problem is, well, politics. Power is seductive, even in the short term, even if the stakes are low. The temptation for power over the other, especially the vulnerable other, to take what is his and turn away in haste, even the temptation just to shut the door is powerful, and sin crouches by that door.

Here is the paradox: a freedom giving God gives the Jewish people, as a people, as a collective in which as Levinas notes, everyone watches the Other receive the law, and thus everyone is responsible for her keeping of the divine Law. Everyone knows, everyone can read the very straightforward instructions. From the early ritual period, a section of Scripture was incorporated into daily prayer, the contingency clearly delineated . . . but only "if you will."

"If you will . . ." Thus begins the Sh'ma, the prayer Jews are liturgically commanded to call out two times a day, every morning and every evening. This is a daily prophecy, and it could not be clearer:

> if you will listen constantly and diligently to My commandments that I command you this day, to love HaShem, your God, and to serve God with all your heart and with all your soul, then I will give the rain of your land in its right season, the early rains and the late rains, so that you may gather in your grain, and your wine, and your oil. And I will give grass in your fields for your cattle, and you shall eat and be satisfied. Watch yourselves, beware, because your heart can be deceived and seduced, and you will turn away astray, and serve other gods, and bow down them;
>
> Then the anger of God be blaze against you! And He will shut up the heavens, so that there shall be no rain, and the ground shall not yield her fruit; and you will quickly be banished, starving, from off the good land which God gives you.
>
> —Deuteronomy 11:13–17

The stakes are high. How you enact God's law, how you treat the poor, is critical, and your life depends on it. It could not be clearer or more forthright: justice, the Sabbath, the care of the stranger, the ordering law and the narrative of exile. It is this covenant that keeps the world a good world. Yet it is so hard not to desire, not to collect, not to want more things. The economics of the market are powerful measures of our worth and the competition is strong. The world we live in has so many people, so many of them sitting on the street in their one, last coat, and it is so easy to forget their capacity for legislative power. The logic of scripture: there is abundance, and you are generous, allows logic and reason to every stranger, but there is growing scarcity, and the world less generous, or we would not walk to classes and pass every beggar with our head down, or worse.

Let me return to the rabbinic idea that revelation happens several times, that the Torah is given not only on Mt. Sinai, but again when Moses, under the advice of his father in law, Jethro, sets up a system of courts and judges, and again when the leaders of the tribes of Israel go into the Land, at Mt. Gerazim, between one chorus of praise and one chorus of imprecations. This section of the Torah is read, typically, shortly prior to Rosh Hashanah, for the curses, read in an undertone when the section "Ki Tavo," is vocalized during services, are so devastating. It is far more difficult for the literate listener, for the curses are those repeated by the Prophets—but this time as factual events. Thus, the biblical curses are read and understood as a foreshadowing of failure. There will be generations of failure, and thus, the world stands, unperfected, the Messiah hanging around waiting with the lepers, according to rabbinic midrash, wrapping and unwrapping and wrapping his bandages again.

It is hard to be good because we often fail to believe that there is enough, we turn from abundance into fearfulness, and the stranger provides not a romanticized philosophical encounter, for he is dirty and wild-eyed, and wants your money, for he knows it is his, the gleanings of the field. You need to get to work, there is an important meeting, the child, your child, needs to be picked up from school, you are too late to stop and engage as if he is important.[4] Why is he not? Largely because in a libertarian system of justice, the one under which we all, consciously or not operate, he does not mix his labor with natural resources to create wealth. Thus he has no power and no social claim on us. There would be only the theological one, Isaiah's scorn: why did you not bring the poor into your home? Under conditions of libertarian capitalism, it seems absurd: what good would it do if as an individual I took the poor smelly, slightly threatening guy into my house? And of course, it would not be "worth it," it would not make a change you could see, and of course, you cannot see that his smelly flesh is your smelly flesh.

Isaiah does not want your piety, but is after something else. Annoyingly enough, his goal is to change you, to make you an actor for God, and it is hard to be good in this way every day. It is hard to be good because modernity prizes anonymity, privacy, and autonomy. In the modern world, I can turn from the beggar because, really, no one will know. The non-encounter, the breach, will be unobserved, and it will look ordinary, the way of the world—I am alone in my failure.

NO MORAL ACTION IS TAKEN ALONE

Hannah Arendt resists this aspect of modernity, this anonymity of the modern condition. In her work, she both allows each person to be responsible for herself in full dignity, but she also insists that each is responsible for "the world." How ought we to judge action?

> The question is never whether an individual is good but whether his conduct is good for the world he lives in. In the center of interest is the world and not the self . . . no moral, individual and personal stands of conduct will ever be able to excuse us from collective responsibility. This vicarious responsibility for things we have not done, this taking upon ourselves the consequences for things we are entirely innocent of, is the price we pay for the fact that we live our lives not by ourselves but among our fellow men, and that the faculty of action which, after all, is the political faculty par excellence, can be actualized only in one of the many and manifold forms of human community.[5]

We are not alone, not in a theological sense, but not in a political one, either. This, for Arendt, is the great gift that is granted to you if you live with others. For the faculty of action and not just talk, the possibility that one can make beliefs real, ideas for which one can fight for become legitimate, become policy, are in fact legitimated by the community that surrounds us. We are allowed this arena of the public, but of course, the price is that we are then beholden to everyone, and to every moral action taken in the name of our publics. We are responsible for the responsibility of others, we are witness to one another's arguments, and that then creates a public square worthy of collective action. But she is both political and bears the responsibility of the prophet. In her prophetic stance, Arendt refuses to avoid judgment. She remind us that individuals who make these choices bear the guilt alone, for while responsibility is collective, guilt is always individual.

For Arendt, the danger and power of the political is the great temptations of power. We create positive law based on a core idea of Western thought, that just as there is "a starry sky above us" in the argument of Kant, there is an "internal law within us." For generations, since Greek notions of the *polis* and the *demos*, the human law derived its power from the gods, or in Jewish terms, from God as law-giver, prophet as first interpreter. However, when modernity begins to erode this source of power, the warrant is uncertain: without a prophet to rebuke you, why be good? Without God as the justification for law, the space of justification is too easily filled by the words of a tyrant.

Arendt, too, associated the political with freedom:

> One cannot speak about politics without also speaking about freedom; and one cannot speak about freedom without speaking about politics. Where men live together but do not form a body politic—as, for example, in primitive tribal societies or in the privacy of the household—the factor ruling their activities is not freedom but the necessities of life and concern for its preservation. Moreover, wherever the man-made world does not become the scene for political action—as in despotically ruled communities that banish their subjects to the narrowness of the home and to private concerns—Freedom has no worldly reality. Without a politically guaranteed public realm, freedom lacks the worldly space to make its appearance.[6]

For Arendt, it is the "love of the world" that draws one into the public "space of appearance." It is here that one's actions are taken, fully seen, and then judged. The prophetic voice is always a judgment in public. Who are the bystanders? Who allows the despot? Did the leaders always defend the poor? Who brought the poor into their home? When did the choice for evil become so ordinary?

For this judgment, of course, many people hated her words. Everyone hates the prophet.

THE INTRINSIC STRUCTURE OF FAILURE

For the prophet sees . . . This means he sees not only the terrible future, but he sees the vivid, failed present. The prophet is furious because he must see, in advance, the ravaged city, the burned scrolls, the starved children and the foxes, nosing the courtyard, and he must also see the petty, tribal power, the little, mean lies, the greed for goodies, more and more, the gossip and the hand on the scale. He knows where this is going, he has, unlike the people he admonishes, a sense of the limits, he is upset about everything, and he is annoying, a goody-goody. This "seeing" is a key idea in the political theology of Jewish thought, for just as Arendt reminds us that nothing happens, in a sense, unless it happens in public, the theological corollary in that everything that happens, happens in the full view of God, every gesture a moral gesture, the small act of cruelty, the way one walks by the beggar, it is all seen, witnessed by God.

The Prophet is harsh, to be sure, but perhaps, the very repetition of the failure of the people, the foreshadowing of the failure in the text of the Law even as it is given, means that the strictures of the Law are too difficult. For Arendt, law is the limit on power, and perhaps also the limit on desire.

To live within this theological claim is to not only to be concerned for your own desire, but to have mortal concern that your neighbor, your brother, your Other, in Emmanuel Levinas's terms, may be unable to flourish: "Justice means we are responsible beyond our commitments . . . You are not free, you are also bound to others beyond your freedom, you are responsible for all. Your liberty is also fraternity."[7] For Hanoch Ben Pazi, this responsibility takes the shape of witnessing and testifying.[8] Testimony signals one's participation in the life of the world—your bearing the narrative of the other in the bearing of his flesh—exactly what Isaiah is calling for: "Glory is but the other face of the passivity of the subject. Substituting itself for the other, a responsibility ordered to the first one on the scene, a responsibility for the neighbor, inspired by the other, I, the same, am torn up from my beginning in myself. The glory of the Infinite, is glorified in this responsibility."[9] In this sense, Israel is always a failure, always imperfect, always subject to imprecation and curse, right along with election and blessing. Again, and again, it proves impossible to be "responsible for all." On the journey from the land of slavery to the land of promised liberation, even then, there are rebellions and despair, even with columns of smoke and a rain of manna, it is written that is was hard to be good—thus forty years, exile on exile. It is not only liberation that seems insufficient, revelation's power lasts only briefly until the people lose heart, and want dancing and a big gold idol. The text, that is read aloud every year, recounts the failures and the shame. The prophets themselves are no models of behavior: abandoning families, killing children when they mock one's baldness; they, too, are angry impatient men, their clarity about failure their only real use.

NOT YET: THEOLOGICAL HOPEFULNESS

The prophetic texts are traditionally read out of historical order, but in the order of the ritual passage of time during the liturgical year. Selected by rabbinic authorities in the first and second centuries to accompany the public reading of the Torah, the practice was likely codified in the Masoretic period (600 CE–900 CE). In each case the readings relate to a theme in the weekly Torah portion, which is one of fifty-four sections that are read, one a week, and on holidays (there is some repetition). Most Jewish congregations, then, read from a section of admonition, which, if it ends on a dismal note, has an appended, hopeful or redemptive excerpt to end the reading. This is, of course, central to the theological structure of the prayer service.

Thus, the political theology in which the inevitability of failure so defines the order of the world also has another aspect: one of redemptive hope, which cannot occur without repentance and return to the Law.

Isaiah is, in addition to the Great Rebuker, the Great Comforter—"Comfort ye, comfort ye," begins a section of his call that is read in synagogue on the first Sabbath of communal *repentance*. For Hermann Cohen, the act of forgiveness of sin and repentance is the entire point of the Torah. The falling and rising of the People Israel remind us both of the reality of evil, and of the possibility of overcoming it. Here, as understood by Jacques Derrida:

> Hermann Cohen does not dissociate forgiveness from repentance. With this 'forgiveness,' which is, he says, explicitly designed as the objective of Torah, he then associate, as if it were one a d the same thing, teshuva which he recalls, designate repentance and means 'return,' 'change,' return to the good, return unto oneself. The instigator of sacrificial worship is also the herald of repentance that figures as a major act in any "ethics and the core of any divine worship." "Even God cannot redeem me," Cohen dares to say, "without my own moral effort and repentance."[10]

CONCLUSION: TESTIMONY

Is it too bold to suggest that a political theology implies both the inevitability and the glory of return? This implies a frank and frontal confrontation with the reality of human limits, fragility and brokenness, and policies that allow for the possibility of regret and return, more than second chance, but an abundance of chances to return from evil. It is a political theology for a world that, in Rosenzweig's terms, is "not yet" complete.

Political theology has an eschatology—a world in which the fundamental realization that one bears the very flesh of the stranger as your own flesh. This is the prophetic necessity, and it assumes that this is both terrible and possible. It is a call for more than justice, and this may render it always at a distance, at the margin, in the next breath, in the world to come. But Jewish political theology insists on hearing about this word, this rebuke now in this actual economy, in your actual home, on your actual street, so that if you witness, and if you testify, then that glory, then God will be witness to you.

> Isaiah 58:9 Then shall you call, and the Lord shall answer; you shall cry, and He shall say, Here I am.

NOTES

1. Isaiah 58 1–9, *TANAKH: The Holy Scriptures*, reprint (Philadelphia: Jewish Publication Society, 1985). All scripture citations are from this translation unless otherwise noted.
2. See Michael Walzer, *Exodus and Revolution* (New York: Basic Books, 1995).
3. "Person" means at times men, and it clearly seems to only men in many contexts in classic biblical and rabbinic literature. However, there are inconsistencies, and at some point, "All of Israel" seems to be women, slaves and children, the three normally excluded categories. This is, of course, also the case in much of the literature of antiquity, and it is by now hardly a feminist insight to note it; however, it is important in an essay about equality and justice to be clear about this historical reality. See Judith Plaskow, *Standing Again at Sinai:*

Judaism from a Feminist Perspective, New York: HarperCollins, for a full treatment of the exclusion of women in the polity.

4. A common riposte for my students about beggars and their excuses: if it was George Clooney standing there, asking to talk, of course you would, for you think he is worthy, so thus, the problem is not really time, it is your sense that the beggar is not worthy, is not worth as much as a Hollywood actor. Thus, the American gods also have a theo-political economy, revealed always to be a system of justice.
5. Hannah Arendt, *Responsibility and Judgement*, ed. Jerome Kohn (New York: Schocken Books, 1968).
6. Hannah Arendt, "Freedom and Politics, A Lecture," in *Thinking Without a Banister: Essays in Understanding, 1953–1975*, ed. Jerome Kohn (New York: Schocken Books, 2018).
7. Emmanuel Levinas, "The Pact," in *Modern Jewish Ethics*, ed. Norman Fox (Columbus, OH: Ohio State University Press, 1975).
8. Hanoch Ben Pazi, "Ethical Dwelling and The Glory of Bearing Witness," in *Levinas Studies* 10 (2014), 221–248.
9. Emmanuel Levinas, *Otherwise than Being or Beyond Essence*, trans. Alphonso Lingis (Berlin: Springer Science and Business Media, 2013).
10. Jacques Derrida, "Avowing—the Impossible: 'Returns,' Repentance, and Reconciliation, a Lesson," in *Modern French Jewish Thought: Writings on Religion and Politics*, edited by Sarah Hammerschlag (Boston: Brandeis University Press, 2018).

SELECT BIBLIOGRAPHY

Arendt, Hannah (1968), *Responsibility and Judgement*, ed. Jerome Kohn, New York: Schocken Books.
Arendt, Hannah (2018), "Freedom and Politics, A Lecture" in *Thinking Without a Banister: Essays in Understanding, 1953–1975*, ed. Jerome Kohn, New York: Schocken Books.
Derrida, Jacques (2018), "Avowing—the Impossible: 'Returns,' Repentance, and Reconciliation, a Lesson," in *Modern French Jewish Thought: Writings on Religion and Politics*, ed. Sarah Hammerschlag, Boston: Brandeis University Press, 214–244.
Levinas, Emmanuel (1975), "The Pact," in *Modern Jewish Ethics*, ed. Norman Fox, Columbus, OH: Ohio State University Press.
Levinas, Emmanuel (2013), *Otherwise than Being or Beyond Essence*, trans. Alphonso Lingis, Berlin: Springer Science and Business Media.
Plaskow, Judith (1991), *Standing Again at Sinai: Judaism from a Feminist Perspective*, New York: HarperCollins.
Rosenzweig, Franz (1985), *The Star of Redemption*, trans. William W. Hallo, South Bend, IN: Notre Dame University Press.
Walzer, Michael (1995), *Exodus and Revolution*, New York: Basic Books.

INDEX

Abraham 304, 543, 557
Abrahamic religions xx, xxii, 289–290, 377, 441, 529
Agamben, Giorgio 66, 485–487, 491, 500
Anabaptism 145, 151–152, 357
anthropology (theological) 162, 164, 170, 255, 261, 272, 317, 343, 374, 380, 554
anti-Semitism 4–6, 67, 212, 223, 291, 497
Anzaldúa, Gloria 286–287, 384
apartheid 3, 13, 26, 62, 555
apocalypticism 131, 140, 164–165, 168, 217, 356, 468, 473–474, 478, 490, 556
apophatic theology 216, 337, 376
Arendt, Hannah 8, 92, 107, 563–563, 569, 573
Aristotle 100, 137, 531
Asad, Talal 390, 392, 394
asceticism 122, 152, 337
atheism 161, 164, 167–168, 170, 172, 215–216, 218, 338, 472–474, 503
Augustine of Hippo xx, xxii, 68, 89–103, 167, 225, 230, 232, 242–243, 275, 320, 346, 355, 404, 441, 455, 547, 554
Augustinian republicanism 100–102 (*see also* republicanism)
autocracy 339–340, 344–345

Badiou, Alain 66, 414, 468
baptism 89, 146, 149–152, 266, 361, 449, 456–460, 463, 517
Barmen Declaration 23, 177–189, 417
Barth, Karl 23, 31, 164, 177–189, 201, 215, 255, 257, 263, 265, 383–384, 417–428, 439–441
Bartolomé de las Casas 31, 131–139, 386
black liberation theology 29, 40, 205, 235–237, 255–267, 272, 286, 288, 380, 418–420, 422, 427, 433, 438, 441, 476–477
black power 258–267, 379–380, 419–420
Bloch, Ernst 19, 23, 213–216, 219, 221
Bonhoeffer, Dietrich 19, 181, 193–205, 517, 521–522

Bulgakov, Sergei 341–342, 345–346, 348
Bultmann, Rudolph 20, 25–26, 64, 67, 255, 265

Calvin, John xx, 91, 94–95, 145–147, 154–156
Calvinism 145, 154–156
capital punishment 55, 79, 329, 344
capitalism 24, 30, 61, 63–64, 66, 166, 185, 200, 205, 220, 226–228, 230, 233, 277, 312, 317, 327, 404, 406, 408, 426, 428, 436, 453, 467, 553, 569
Catholic social teaching 38, 276, 317–330, 433, 555
Christendom 147, 161, 244–245, 251, 252, 364, 401–402, 404–405, 409–411, 421–422
Christology 35, 188, 198, 200–201, 250, 287, 355, 362, 364, 439
City of God, The (*De civitates Dei*) 68, 90–91, 93–95, 97–98, 355, 404–405
civil rights 19, 155–156, 236, 257–259, 261, 322, 345, 428, 507 (*see also* human rights)
climate change 61, 319, 324–325, 329, 333, 373, 382, 451, 454
Cold War 67, 225, 233–235, 324
colonialism xxi, 63, 68, 205, 235, 272, 324–325, 364, 371, 378, 390, 392, 394, 396–397, 401, 406, 409, 422, 476, 552, 556
common good 100–102, 237, 318, 321–323, 325–327, 379–380, 382–383, 405–406, 408–412, 433, 435
communism 67, 93, 178, 232–236, 317, 319, 338
Cone, James H. xx, 29, 251, 255–267, 417–428, 441
Confessing Church 177–188, 420
Constantinianism 99–100, 359–360, 457
consumerism 324, 451, 453, 462
covenant 6, 33, 40, 49–53, 64, 154, 187–188, 248, 303, 310–312, 375, 377, 439, 454, 489, 566, 569

decolonialism xxi, 205, 355–356, 360, 363–367
De La Torre, Miguel 355, 359–365, 367–368, 477
democracy 4, 21, 25, 37, 112, 155, 166, 212, 228, 231–237, 306–308, 312, 320, 338–346, 347, 395–396, 402, 407–411, 415, 417, 427, 441, 544, 548–549
Derrida, Jacques 83, 168, 402, 406, 471, 549, 561, 572
Du Bois, W.E.B. 418, 420–423, 426–427, 438

ecclesiology 32, 97–99, 202, 244–245, 286, 338, 344, 365, 417, 495–506
Elshtain, Jean Bethke 92, 94, 97, 110
enlightenment 30, 32, 219, 243, 250, 306, 402, 421, 434, 437
eschatology 65, 98, 165, 217, 341, 382, 422, 438, 458, 490, 556, 562, 572
ethnic cleansing 7, 14–15 (*see also* genocide)
Eucharist 32, 219, 337, 343–344, 382, 402–404, 459, 461, 463, 500–501, 517
Evangelii Gaudium 328
Exodus 38, 40, 49, 171, 215, 220–221, 249–250, 264–265, 301–313, 321, 476

Fanon, Frantz 258, 365, 555
fascism 94, 225, 232–233, 236, 319, 383, 412, 477, 553
feminist theology 97, 185, 231, 235, 271–280, 285–293, 304, 308–309, 433, 438, 441, 550, 555
Florovsky, Georges 337, 371–372
Foucault, Michel 406, 549, 560–561
Frankfurt School 23, 214, 216, 250, 554
freedom 8, 36, 38–39, 67, 101, 119, 126, 131, 134, 137, 146–149, 152, 156, 161, 164, 177, 179, 181–183, 185, 187, 189, 197, 199, 203–204, 212, 215, 217–219, 230, 232, 237, 247, 256–266, 304, 317, 321, 323, 327, 340–345, 349, 378, 395, 402, 418–419, 423, 427–428, 434–435, 439, 455, 459, 470, 473, 495, 532, 539, 551–552, 555–559, 568, 570–571

Gaudium et spes 37–38, 246–247
gender xx–xxi, 55–56, 61, 66, 281–282, 286–290, 292, 318, 328, 368, 381, 390, 394–395, 397, 440–441, 443–444, 453, 498, 511
genocide 18, 56, 155, 170, 355, 364, 376, 401, 451 (*see also* ethnic cleansing)

Greenberg, Irving 4–5, 7, 9, 338
Gutiérrez, Gustavo xx, 30, 32, 97, 195, 241–251, 364, 441

Hauerwas, Stanley 99–100, 362, 440–441, 444
Hegel, G.W.F. 164, 168–169, 231, 378–379, 383, 402, 417, 434–436, 439–440, 442–443, 470–473, 562
Heschel, Abraham Joshua 24, 568
Hobbes, Thomas 94, 212, 225, 231, 344, 375, 460, 551–552
Holocaust xix, xxii, 3–14, 17, 19–21, 24, 26, 94, 184–185, 214, 285, 288, 486, 490–491 (*see also* Shoah)
Homo sacer 82, 486, 490–491, 500–501
human rights 8, 25–26, 30, 36–39, 48, 54–56, 134, 137, 155–156, 171, 183, 195, 213, 218–219, 236, 247, 259, 261, 285, 290, 308, 319, 321–326, 333, 338, 340–345, 373, 378–379, 385, 428, 438, 488, 490, 495, 507, 532, 539, 549, 551–552, 556–558 (*see also* Civil Rights)

imago dei 286, 364–365, 453, 518
immigration xix, 55, 81, 278, 319, 322, 391, 443, 487, 496
imperialism 25, 66, 185, 232–233, 236, 292–293, 371, 396, 401, 410, 412, 422, 424, 426, 428, 443, 552
industrialization 47, 243, 436–437, 451
interreligious dialogue xxii, 460, 528–530, 541
Isasi-Diaz, Ada María 272, 286, 360, 384, 441
Islam xx, 75–84, 233, 288–289, 378, 389–397, 496–498, 500–503, 527–542, 548, 550
Islamic holocaust 389
Islamist 81, 84, 530, 542 (*see also* Jihadism)
Islamophobia 495–506
Israel, ancient/biblical 24, 40, 48–57, 63, 121, 133, 187–188, 264–265, 301–313, 381, 421, 441, 566, 568–569, 571–572
Israel, modern state 3–14, 26, 235, 302–303, 305–313, 485–491

Jesus 6, 23–24, 31, 35, 64–65, 67–69, 109–110, 119, 132, 162, 164–165, 168–169, 171–172, 177–183, 185–188, 200, 202, 211, 216–217, 219, 221–222, 229–230, 248, 251, 256, 259–266, 321, 327, 356–364, 367, 375, 381, 417–420,

422, 436–438, 440–441, 453, 458–461, 463, 470, 472–473, 475, 513–520
Jewish Constantinianism 13–14
Jihadism 76 (*see also* Islamist)
Jim Crow 256, 260, 267, 419, 438, 440
Judaism xx, 3, 7, 13, 75, 78, 187–188, 215, 288–289, 292, 302, 375, 378, 455, 470, 487, 489–491, 529, 534–535, 548
justice 5, 8–10, 12, 18, 23, 29–33, 36–37, 40, 65–66, 82, 92, 94, 96–97, 102, 118, 120, 122, 124, 132, 137, 148, 168, 172, 177, 183–185, 188–189, 195, 200, 204, 215–219, 229–232, 236–237, 245, 247–251, 256–261, 263, 272–276, 278, 285, 288, 293, 305, 309, 318, 322, 325–326, 328, 340, 342, 345, 361, 365, 377, 379, 382, 405, 418–420, 427–428, 433, 435–436, 436, 438–440, 443–444, 459–461, 476–477, 529, 539, 541, 547, 549, 553–559, 565, 566–569, 571–572

Kant, Immanuel 378–379, 383, 402, 434–436, 439, 442–443, 549, 559, 567, 570
kenosis 167, 169, 406, 474, 475
King, Martin Luther Jr. 19, 97, 236, 259, 261, 419–420, 428, 437, 444, 453
Kingdom of God 39, 64, 95, 214–215, 217–222, 231, 266, 339–341, 361, 421, 428, 434–441, 461, 518
kingship 48, 51–52, 66, 118, 414

Laudato Si' 329, 434, 455
Levinas, Emmanuel 168, 309, 568, 571
liberation theology xx–xxi, 3, 11–14, 25, 29–40, 49, 61, 64, 185, 193–205, 211, 218–220, 222, 235, 241–251, 255–267, 274, 285–286, 303, 306–307, 310, 312, 326, 328, 340–341, 345, 355, 359, 362, 366, 374, 382, 417–420, 426–428, 433–434, 438, 441, 449, 477, 490–491, 553–557, 559, 566, 568, 571
liberalism (political) 92, 94–102, 105, 198, 228, 236, 261, 304, 312, 338, 340–343, 345–346, 440–441, 467, 552–554
liberalism (Protestant) 23, 31, 422, 435
Locke, John 154, 231, 460
Luther, Martin 91, 94–95, 145, 147–150, 152, 154–156, 164, 177–178, 190, 216, 225, 230–231, 355
Lutheranism 145, 148–150, 152, 154, 177–178, 180–184, 231, 236, 495–496, 500–503, 534

MacIntyre, Alasdair xx, 92, 98–99, 537
Mahatma Gandhi 229–230, 440
martyrdom 34–36, 40, 138, 151, 249
Marx, Karl 64, 162, 168, 225, 228, 230, 232, 378–379, 427
Marxism 25–26, 197, 242, 249–50, 342, 348, 471
Medellín Conference 29, 31–32, 34, 41–42, 69, 326, 334
Metz, Johann Baptist xix, 18–22, 24–26, 30, 213, 242, 250–251, 285, 340, 554
Milbank, John 98–100, 219, 346–347, 402–410
misogyny 61, 291, 505
Mohammed xxii, 76–84, 503, 509
Moltmann, Jürgen xix, 17–22, 24–26, 30, 211–223, 285, 340, 513, 556
Moses 49, 82, 121, 148, 301, 303–306, 309–310, 312–313, 557, 569
mujerista theology 205, 271–280, 286, 332, 441, 555
mysticism 19, 36, 64, 165, 242, 249, 250–251, 337–341, 406, 528, 533, 535

nationalism 64, 186, 205, 233–234, 246, 259, 261, 289, 305, 340, 380, 384, 420–421, 485, 487–488, 491
natural law 154–156, 378–379, 385–386, 406, 424, 451, 457–460, 488, 530, 549–551, 556, 559
Nazis (National Socialist German Workers' Party) xix, 3–4, 9, 17–18, 20, 25, 67, 94, 177–184, 186–187, 189, 193, 198–199, 211–212, 230–232, 417, 419, 486, 558
neoconservative 235, 304
neoliberalism 61–62, 66, 166, 317, 323, 327, 384, 404–409, 412, 476, 534, 549, 553
Niebuhr, Reinhold 19, 92–93, 225–237, 368–369, 437, 439
Nietzsche, Friedrich 161–164, 166–168, 171–172, 406, 562
nonviolence 36–37, 259–260, 305, 324, 440
nouvelle théologie 30, 243–244
nuclear proliferation 26, 234, 319, 324

Orientalism 380, 390

pacifism 225, 228–229, 236, 440
Palestine/Palestinian 5–14, 235, 307–308, 486–488, 490

Patriarch Kirill 341, 505
patriarchy 56, 61, 289, 291, 390, 401, 441, 550
Peace of Westphalia 145, 149, 378, 558
Plaskow, Judith 285, 288, 309
pneumatology 355, 365, 439
preferential option for the poor 32–34, 40, 242, 248, 318, 321, 325–326, 453
prophetic 9–10, 13–14, 32, 36–40, 48–50, 52, 55, 76–77, 79–80, 83–84, 131–132, 139, 184–185, 193, 195, 198, 206, 222, 246, 249–251, 285, 288, 290, 340, 356, 358–359, 361, 363, 392, 403, 418, 438, 441, 453–454, 570–572
Pope Benedict XVI 329, 330, 553, 560
Pope Francis 35, 276–277, 282, 318–319, 324–325, 327–328, 455, 553
Pope John XXIII 29, 331, 333
Pope John Paul II 34, 317, 330, 333, 553, 560–561
Pope Paul VI 29, 38, 331–333
poverty 29, 32–35, 40, 62, 139, 177, 189, 198, 219, 222, 241, 246–248, 251, 259, 266, 287–288, 318–319, 342, 364–365, 427, 443, 551
praxis 25, 134, 172, 195, 218, 242, 244–245, 248–249, 251, 290–291, 327, 330, 355, 358, 362–363, 363, 366, 410, 418, 422, 451, 467, 475, 477–478, 554
public theology xix, 6, 12–13, 18–20, 24, 33, 62, 92, 96–100, 102, 193, 198, 211–212, 221–222, 237, 272, 275, 280, 286, 317–319, 394, 396, 435, 440, 443, 450, 456–457, 548–549, 552, 554–555

Qur'an 75–84, 261, 289, 509, 530, 539, 541–542

racism 14, 61, 94, 177–181, 184–188, 222, 236, 251, 255–259, 262–263, 265, 269, 286, 288, 291, 334, 378, 390, 394, 418, 420–421, 426, 428, 438, 440, 444, 461, 477
Radical Orthodoxy 100, 401–412
Rahner, Karl 20–21, 25, 245, 250, 513
Rauschenbusch, Walter 228, 437–438, 440
Rawls, John 92, 96–97, 101, 544
realism 92–94, 96, 102, 110, 225, 230–237, 356, 359, 368, 371, 404, 439–440, 452, 475
republicanism 92, 100–102 (*see also* Augustinian republicanism)

Rerum Novarum 317, 319, 321–322, 325, 434
revelation (divine) 32, 77–78, 80–81, 83, 92, 164, 167, 171–172, 177, 183, 186–187, 199, 248, 262–265, 270, 306, 360, 381, 418, 420–421, 442, 453, 458, 469, 472, 474, 514, 519, 533, 541–542, 569, 571
Romero, Archbishop Óscar 30–40, 200, 449
Rousseau, Jean-Jacques 91, 106, 231, 460
Ruether, Rosemary Radford 286, 291–292, 455, 463

sacraments/sacramentality 31–32, 125, 133, 137, 139, 147, 149–152, 183, 219, 242, 403, 449–450, 453, 457–459, 461–462, 503–504, 517, 553
Said, Edward 380, 390
Schüssler Fiorenza, Elisabeth 286, 291, 550
Schmitt, Carl xix–xx, 21–24, 30, 47, 53–54, 57, 211–213, 225, 391, 457, 485–488, 548, 550–551, 553
Second World War xix, 17, 67, 197, 211, 213, 231, 246, 324, 356, 391, 496, 548, 551, 553–554
secularization 22, 147, 167, 170, 197, 201, 338, 343, 487
segregation 259–260, 262, 293, 440, 513
separation of church and state 151–152, 154, 183, 213, 341, 345, 359
sexuality 56, 177, 274, 279, 288, 443–444, 458, 513, 560–561
Shklar, Judith 92, 94, 96
Shoah 486, 553–554 (*see also* Holocaust)
slavery xix, 40, 61, 66, 68, 94, 101, 135, 137, 139, 142, 197, 215, 232, 262, 288, 292, 301, 309–310, 323, 378, 384, 392, 401, 422, 426, 436–437, 460, 476, 566, 571
Sobrino, Jon 35, 38, 200, 232
social gospel 225, 227–230, 237, 436–440, 444
socialism 66, 215, 225–230, 232, 236, 312, 403–404, 406–409, 411, 417, 422
solidarity 25, 32, 37, 172, 177, 180–181, 184, 188, 198, 216, 219, 222–223, 247–248, 250, 271, 276, 278, 290, 321–323, 325–326, 329–330, 362, 404, 406, 433, 462, 472, 554–555, 566
Sölle, Dorothee xix, 17–22, 24–26, 30, 285
Soloviev, Vladimir 339, 341–342, 345–346
sovereignty 21–22, 30, 48, 51, 53–54, 68, 75–77, 80–81, 83–84, 99, 118, 137, 161,

166, 168, 212, 301, 308, 312, 324, 332, 339, 407, 434, 485–488, 549–550, 555, 558
Spanish Inquisition 146, 391–393
state of exception 75, 79, 212, 485–491, 552
Stout, Jeffrey xxii, 102, 440, 535, 544
subsidiarity 323, 326, 433, 555
supersessionism 67, 421, 489–490
symphonia 339–340, 342, 344–345

Taylor, Charles 105, 394
theosis 338, 342–343, 347
Thomas Aquinas 21, 91, 154, 243, 425, 559
Thomas Becket 117–127
Tillich, Paul 255, 257, 263, 418–420, 471
Torah 52–57, 82–83, 288–289, 304, 489, 569, 571–572
totalitarianism 166, 177, 188
Trinity 22, 164, 216, 227, 242, 337, 343, 367, 403, 413, 435, 463, 513–516, 519, 521
Troeltsch, Ernst 355, 437, 439
two kingdoms theology 91, 95, 148, 150, 183, 434

Vatican II 29, 32, 37, 246–247, 326, 434, 461, 553
Vietnam War 17, 19, 26, 64, 215, 225, 234–236
violence 17, 26, 29, 33, 36–40, 61–62, 81, 84, 94, 99, 102, 117, 133, 136, 147, 150–151, 164, 166–167, 170–172, 178, 212, 218–219, 229–230, 241, 259–261, 266–267, 277–278, 285–288, 291–293, 301, 303–305, 324, 327–329, 358–359, 362, 394, 403, 406, 418, 424, 427, 440, 454, 460, 477, 488, 496, 530, 550–551, 554, 559

West, Cornel 235, 419, 441
Wiesel, Elie 3–5, 7, 11, 13, 24
womanist theology xxii, 185, 205, 255, 286, 288, 433, 441, 451, 555

Yoder, John Howard 355–364, 440, 444

Zionism 8–9, 305, 308, 312–313, 487, 490–491
Žižek, Slavoj 66, 168–170, 467–478, 486
Zizioulas, John 342–343, 520

www.ingramcontent.com/pod-product-compliance
Lightning Source LLC
Chambersburg PA
CBHW080528300426
44111CB00017B/2649